# Botanica's

# ROSES

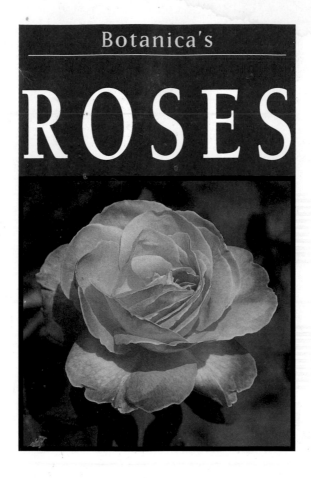

# Botanica's

# ROSES

**Over 1,000 pages & over 2,000 plants listed**

**Foreword by William A. Grant**

LAUREL
GLEN

First Published in the United States by
Laurel Glen Publishing
An imprint of the Advantage Publishers Group
5880 Oberlin Drive
San Diego, CA 92121-4794
www.advantagebooksonline.com

ISBN 1-57145-661-9
Library of Congress Cataloging-in-Publication Data available
upon request.

Printed in Hong Kong.

3  4  5  02  03  04

*Chief Consultant:* **William A. Grant**
*Consultants and Contributors:* **David Austin, Peter Beales, Dr Gerlinde
von Berg, Geoff Bryant, Dr Tommy Cairns, Walter Duncan, Gwen
Fagan, Ken Grapes, Peter Harkness, Kevin Hughes, John Mattock,
David Ruston, Barbara Segall, Elwyn Swane**
*Publisher:* **Penny Martin**
*Managing Editor:* **Susan Page**
*Senior Editor:* **Ken Tate**
*Editorial Assistant:* **Dee Rogers**
*Cover Design:* **Bob Mitchell, James Mills-Hicks**
*Photolibrarian:* **Antony Page**
*Assembly:* **Joy Eckermann**
*Typesetting:* **Dee Rogers**
*Index:* **Ken Tate**
*Production Manager:* **Linda Watchorn**
*Printed by* **Sing Cheong Printing Co. Ltd, Hong Kong**
*Film separation:* **Pica Colour Separation, Singapore**

PHOTOGRAPHS,
PRELIMINARY PAGES
AND CHAPTER OPENINGS

*Photographic Acknowledgments:*
Rob Blakers, Geoff Bryant, Claver Carroll, Leigh Clapp,
Ed Gabriel, William A. Grant, Denise Greig, Gil Hanly,
Ivy Hansen, Ray Joyce, Gary Lewis, Stirling Macoboy,
Eberhard Morell, Maggie Oster, Suzanne de Pelsenaire,
Dick Roberts, Italo Vardaro, Brent Wilson and
James Young

# Contents

# Foreword

What luck to have a rose book you can read in bed, carry
to a nursery, use in the garden! Whether you are planning
a new garden or adding roses to an established one, you need
to know what choices are available. The size of the plant,
the amount of care that is needed, the frequency of bloom,
and even the appearance of the plant when there are no
flowers—all these must be considered before purchase.
Spending several evenings reading the entries in this book
will help make those choices.

When visiting a nursery, where there are scores of roses
offered to the public, the gardener can use this book to choose
what is appropriate. Whether a rose requires full sun or part
shade; if it can grow well in poor soil; whether it is disease-
resistant; if it has attractive autumn foliage and hips—the
information is right here in this pocket edition. And such
detail is rarely available on labels.

The cultivation section of this volume will be invaluable,
especially for the beginner. Not only does it describe how
to judge a plant before buying it, but also how to plant, to
prune, and to take care of the rose in different circumstances.
Hardiness zones are listed after every entry. Many roses are
sold under different names in different countries and you
will find the alternative names listed. If you are interested
in the date of the introduction, the name of the person who
hybridized the rose, if it has won any gold medals, the parents
of the rose—all that information is here.

No other plant has so many enthusiastic growers. No
other flower matches the rose in annual sales. Rose societies
everywhere require proper identification when people
participate in competitions and shows. A book like this will
be welcomed to help identify the unlabeled or unknown roses.

An easy-to-use reference table, an index and hardiness
zone maps complete the rich contents of *Botanica's Pocket Roses.*

WILLIAM A. GRANT

# Introduction

**P**alaeontologists claim roses date back to the Tertiary period, 70 million years ago. Fossil plants in a slate deposit in Colorado indicate that roses existed 40 million years ago in North America. Other important fossil findings in the Northern Hemisphere have confirmed that roses grow as far north as Alaska and Norway and as far south as Mexico. No Wild Roses have been found to grow below the equator.

There is evidence in ancient writings that roses were known as far back as 2350 BC, but scholars may only have assumed that these descriptions referred to roses. King Sargon of Sumer is reputed to have returned from a campaign in about 2200 BC bearing 'vines, figs and roses to his country'. In 500 BC, Confucius wrote about the roses growing in the Imperial Rose Garden of the Chinese Emperor, who also had an extensive library of rose books. Manuscripts, inscriptions and drawings show that the rose was known and cultivated around 400 BC.

In the Palace of Knossos (built 2000–1700 BC) a fresco depicts roses but many historians believe it was painted much later. An Egyptian tomb of 1500 BC displays a painting of roses. It was not until the Greek philosopher Theophrastus (382–287 BC) wrote about the cultivation of the rose, as well as describing pruning in winter, that any real light was shed on its history.

We know from Pliny the Elder (AD 23–79) that the Romans cultivated roses widely. We know also that they used roses as garlands of victory, and tombs were festooned with rose petals. The main groups of cultivated roses were named by the Romans.

The title 'Queen of flowers' was first bestowed, it is believed, by the Greek rhetorician, Achilleus Tatios, around the end of the second century AD.

Roses were possibly introduced to England and France by the Romans and some species were later used in heraldry. Henry VII united 'White Rose of York' and 'Red Rose of Lancaster' in the stylized Tudor Rose. It was also an emblem of quality in silver and pewter craftsmanship. Paintings and drawings decorated manuscripts and surfaces of wood and stone.

'Leander' *(left)*

'The Fairy' *(right)*

Some paintings in Persian manuscripts of the sixth century attest to their presence in Persia and Palestine, and Indian artworks for the Moghul emperors of the sixteenth century also feature roses. European plant hunters in the late eighteenth century showed that roses had been cultivated in China for centuries and the repeat-flowering species discovered in western China during the nineteenth century make that the birthplace of the Modern Garden Rose.

France became the major commercial center as early as the Middle Ages. An industry was devoted to their herbal and medicinal qualities. In the sixteenth century, exciting new Wild Roses appeared from North America. With the current blend of Wild, Old and Modern hybrids, it is hard to think they were grown for anything less than their beauty and fragrance, but in medieval Europe they were grown as medicinal plants; 'rose juice' was used as a cure-all. The hips of several Wild Roses are the world's richest and cheapest source of Vitamin C. The hips of *Rosa rugosa* can contain sixty times as much as oranges or apples of the same weight.

## Scented Air

Food-gatherers lived, in a literal sense, from hand to mouth. After they had learned to farm and settle on the land, the daily struggle to exist was eased, and as communities grew wealthy, luxuries were sought. The heartland of Western culture is thought to lie in what today we call Iraq. Here we find the first written evidence of the rose on a clay tablet in Sumerian script, which seems to be a receipt for rosewater. Life then was doubtless 'nasty, brutish and short', but rose petals, rosewater, rose oil and rose essence could at least alleviate some of the nastiness.

Over the next few centuries the rulers—if they were rich enough—did not stint their use of it. Stories tell of Cleopatra wooing Antony with thousands of rose petals, of Nero burying his guests in them, of 30 000 bottles of rosewater ordered by the Caliph of Baghdad and 500 camel loads used by Saladin to purify a mosque.

Rosarian Graham Thomas is surely right with the answer to his own question:

*'What has the rose to offer that other flowers lack?*
*I have no doubt that it owes its perennial popularity to its scent; it was for this priceless quality that it was originally cultivated.'*

Some roses are scent-laden, some have little or none and a few are unpleasant. The roses whose fragrance could be harnessed were intensely cultivated, and their products became big business. Damask and Alba Roses were best for rose oil or attar. The techniques probably originated in Persia. The 'Apothecary's Rose' was valuable for its scent of a more enduring character, for the petals seem to yield more of it when dried than they do when on the plant.

## Buying a Rose

The new gardener has come to expect a container-grown, fairly well-developed plant that is usually in full flower, but with roses grown as a field crop, and dug when dormant in winter, the resulting product is the complete opposite. The plant is entirely leafless with the root system exposed. Both stems and roots will also have been pruned to

'Peace' *(left)*

reduce size and bulk for packaging and delivery.

New introductions and novelty roses will always sell quickly, especially if a variety is particularly stunning whether in color or in form. At first release, however, plants are scarce because it takes time to build a stock from a limited number of 'bud eyes', 'grafted' or 'budded' to rootstock.

## Growing Roses Through the Year

Most rose books include a calendar, but the seasonal weather will vary between districts. One way to ensure an area is good for roses is to walk within a 1 mile (1.6 km) radius and note where roses grow really well. If none are to be seen, the area is likely to be unsuitable. But when roses are seen to be growing in almost every garden, it will be obvious that the district is good for rose cultivation.

'Sunsprite' (foreground) and 'Playboy' (*above*)

### AUTUMN

Autumn is the time to plan and prepare for a rose garden. To ensure plentiful blooms, the rose bed should have at least five hours of full sunlight every day. Improve and enrich poor soils with plenty of organic matter, such as good garden compost or manure, and work it well into the soil. Allow a couple of months for manures to rot down well before the roses are planted; this will prevent damage to new root systems as they develop. It is an advantage to test the pH of the soil.

It is always a good idea to visit a rose garden to see roses in their 'true' colors; even the best publications cannot replicate colors exactly.

### WINTER

Winter is the ideal time to plant bare-rooted roses as there is very little transplant shock due to water loss from the foliage. However, even though it is winter and the plant is dormant, the plant will require water for survival. Roses grown in containers, often available in full leaf and flower, may be planted out at any time without disturbing the soil in the container. In cold districts, planting of dormant, bare-rooted rose stock can be held over until the danger of frost has passed. Where frost is extreme, it may be necessary to construct a frost-protection barrier.

In established rose gardens, winter is pruning time. Old plants should have all unproductive wood removed, and the rest of the growth pruned by approximately one-third. Cut stems to outward facing, plump buds, and open up the bush in the center to allow better light penetration and good air circulation. All diseased prunings should be removed and disposed of: never place them in the compost bin. The bushes and surrounding ground can also be sprayed with a lime-sulfur chemical to prevent fungal spores from 'overwintering'. In the absence of good rainfall, continue to water plants in winter, but less often than in spring or summer.

## SPRING

Spring should see the garden heavily abloom and heady with fragrance. It brings an abundance of new life, both in plant growth and insect populations as well as the early symptoms of fungal disease in humid areas. Regular spraying with either low-toxic organic or chemical controls, should be maintained. Use either a complete (or balanced) chemical plant food or an organic fertilizer such as animal manure or pelletized poultry product at regular six-weekly intervals. Periodic soakings at least twice a week will also be necessary.

Many Old or Wild Roses will only flower once in the season, unlike the repeat-blooming Modern Roses. Even so, it is still necessary to maintain good plant vigor by regular feeding and watering. Deadheading of the spring blooms of modern hybrid roses is the best pruning as it will help stimulate another flowering within about six weeks in sunny or fine weather. However, low light can discourage good blooming, and heavy spring rainfall can spoil flowers.

'Phyllis Bide' *(left)*

'Bantry Bay' (on wall); 'Gertrude Jekyl' and 'Mary Rose' (foreground) *(right)*

## SUMMER

In areas of high humidity, summer can be the most difficult time to grow roses. In recent years, hybridists have concentrated on disease-resistant varieties rather than exotic new colorings or larger blooms. Breeders, as well as consumers, have become ever more conscious of the excessive use of chemicals.

Most Modern Garden Roses will repeat-flower during summer provided they are fertilized and soaked regularly. A recommended summer pruning to produce blooms six to eight weeks later requires the removal of about one-third of the bush.

## Queen of Flowers

In this book the reader should discover many interesting facts. There are more than 40 000 roses on the International Rose Register, which includes roses of historical and botanical importance and all Modern Garden Roses. This book describes a selection of roses but has done so with discretion, presenting mainly those that continue to have significance.

Many rose species and varieties are either hard to find or are lost, but roses are great horticultural survivors; despite their beauty and their fame, they have proved to be extremely hardy and ever-popular. Most other flowers can only be traced through several centuries; none has been more inspirational nor more widely loved than the rose.

## Plant Hardiness Zones

The system of Plant Hardiness Zones developed by the US Department of Agriculture for North America has been extended to other parts of the world. The coldest is Zone 1, corresponding to a subarctic climate such as central Canada or Siberia; the warmest is Zone 12, which covers much of the equatorial tropics. Each zone covers a range of 10 Fahrenheit degrees (5.5 Celsius degrees), as shown in the table accompanying the map. (The Celsius value is rounded to the nearest degree.) The lowest zone that is mostly frost-free is Zone 10.

For each plant listed, both a minimum and maximum zone are indicated. A listing of Zones 6–11, for example, means that the plant will survive the average winter frosts expected in at least the warmer parts of Zone 6, in which temperatures fall below 0°F (−16°C), but it will also grow reasonably well in zones up to at least the cooler parts of Zone 11, where winter minimums are above 40°F (4°C). The indication of a maximum zone goes beyond the original intent of the Plant Hardiness Zones, but it serves a useful purpose in that most non-tropical plants have definite limits to how warm a climate they will tolerate—in many cases they will survive in warmer zones but fail to flower or fruit, or prove very short lived.

These zones indicate only one part of a plant's climatic requirements. There are many plants, for example, that are extremely frost hardy but will only grow well in climates with hot, humid summers; other plants require climates with cool wet winters and very dry summers.

## The Rose Heritage

The rose is known as 'the world's favorite flower'. It has been estimated that 150 million plants are purchased by gardeners worldwide every year, dominating the cut-flower market. The rose has been and still is depicted in many national and business emblems.

### THE ORIGINS OF CULTIVATED ROSES

Rose species have a natural distribution throughout the Northern Hemisphere.

*Europe and the Middle East—The Dawn of Rose Breeding*

Well before the Christian Era, the transportation of useful plants had played an essential part in the expansion of civilization. The dog rose *(Rosa canina)*, for example, was long thought to be a native of Britain, but was taken there by the Romans. By about AD 1200 the first five groups had already begun to evolve in cultivation: Albas, Centifolias, Damasks, Gallicas and Scots Roses.

*The Far East—The Birthplace of the Modern Garden Rose*

It was not until the end of the eighteenth century, with the discovery of R. *chinensis* in China, that a major step forward was achieved. 'Parson's Pink China', 'Slater's Crimson China', 'Hume's Blush Tea-scented China' and 'Parks' Yellow Tea-scented China'—the first cultivated varieties—opened up a new vista of roses with a modern classical shape, a true crimson color with a very pale hint of the early yellows, and a repeat-flowering performance.

*East Meets West*

For centuries, new forms of once-blooming roses appeared until the list was long: Gallicas, Albas, Centifolias, Damasks, etc. The search was always on for repeat-flowering plants. Early hybridizing was a haphazard affair as nature did most of the work. English cattle breeder Henry Bennett, demonstrated in the nineteenth century that careful choice of parents could produce a rose of a desired color and form. French nurserymen perfected a hybridizing system that produced repeat-blooming roses. Although 'La France' (1887) is frequently given as the first Hybrid Tea, there were many others that came earlier.

### The Last 100 Years

Between the two World Wars, the Hybrid Tea was the most popular rose. The era came to a close in 1945 with the introduction of 'Peace'. Since that time, ground cover roses, a wide variety of polyanthas, floribundas, patio roses, climbers and ramblers, David Austin roses, and miniatures have joined the hybrid teas in a wide assortment for the gardening public.

### THE ROSE IN THE ECONOMY

It is as a cut flower that the rose excels as an economic plant. Roses can be cut, graded and packaged in Kenya and be on sale in the UK within 24 hours. The world's principal cut-rose nurseries are in The Netherlands, Denmark, Israel, Kenya, Zimbabwe, California and Colombia.

## How Roses Are Classified

The rose family, Rosaceae, comprises many genera. The group

'Maigold' *(right)*

of true roses is known as the genus *Rosa* with about 140 species: 95 of Asian origin, 18 North American and the remainder from Europe and northwest Africa. No rose species have ever been found in the Southern Hemisphere.

## CLASSIFICATION SYSTEMS

Several attempts have been made to classify the available rose varieties. Three principal institutions that have attempted this exercise have had varying degrees of success.

**The World Federation of Rose Societies** has produced the most comprehensive, descriptive list, but it has very little practical use for nurseries.

**The American Rose Society** has compiled a classification system that is closely allied to the requirements of exhibitors. The American Rose Society, the official international registrar, produces from time to time *Modern Roses*, a book giving descriptions of most roses.

**The British Association Representing Breeders** has published a list that is very relevant to hybridists. It is probably the most succinct, but it is in need of revision.

Most rose gardeners simply want to grow good plants, and have little use for the complex botanical classification. To this end, a simplified version of the World Federation of Rose Societies' system has been used in this book.

## TYPES OF WILD ROSE

The true species roses are known as Wild Roses. Botanically,

they are classified into four subgenera.

### Hulthemia

This very small subgenus from Western Asia contains *Hulthemia persica* and *H. hardii*.

### Hesperhodes

This interesting group of only two species is native to southwestern USA. They are repeat-flowering and the hips show a remarkable affinity to gooseberry fruit.

### Platyrhodon

Originating in southeastern China, this group contains *R. roxburghii*, which is more often called the chestnut rose.

### Eurosa

Most rose species belong to this subgenus, which has ten groups.

## TYPES OF OLD GARDEN ROSE

Grown in the gardens of Europe and Asia for many hundreds of years, Old Garden Roses were originally derived from Wild Roses. Further changes came about with hybridization.

### Gallica Roses

The main member of this predominantly European and western Asian group is *R. gallica*, which has single red flowers. Gallica Roses have become known as the finest of the Old Garden Roses, and they flower once in summer.

### Damask Roses

The Summer Damasks, which flower once only in summer, are derived from crosses between the

Gallica Roses and *R. phoenicea*. Hybridization of Gallica Roses with *R. moschata* produced the very similar Autumn Damasks.

### Centifolia (or Provence) Roses

These 'one hundred-petalled roses' were raised in the seventeenth century by Dutch hybridists. They flower for just a brief period in summer.

### Moss Roses

These are really aberrant Centifolia Roses, which appeared in the mid-seventeenth century. They have a moss-like growth on the sepals. They are only once-flowering.

## Botanica's Pocket Roses
### *Rose Classes*

| | | |
|---|---|---|
| **Roses** | **Modern Garden Roses** | |
| | Bush Roses | Large-flowered/Hybrid Tea |
| | | Cluster-flowered/Floribunda |
| | | Patio/Dwarf Cluster-flowered |
| | | Polyantha |
| | Shrub Roses | Modern Shrub |
| | | Hybrid Rugosa |
| | | Ground Cover |
| | Climbing Roses | Rambler |
| | | Large-flowered Climber |
| | | Cluster-flowered Climber |
| | Miniature | Climbing Miniature |
| | | Miniature |
| | **Old Garden Roses** | |
| | Non-climbing | Gallica |
| | | Damask |
| | | Centifolia (or Provence) |
| | | Moss |
| | | Alba |
| | | China |
| | | Tea |
| | | Portland |
| | | Bourbon |
| | | Hybrid Perpetual |
| | | Scots |
| | | Sweet Briar |
| | | Miscellaneous |
| | Climbing | Ayrshire |
| | | Climbing China |
| | | Laevigata |
| | | Sempervirens |
| | | Noisette |
| | | Boursalt |
| | | Climbing Tea |
| | | Climbing Bourbon |
| | **Wild Roses** | |

# American Rose Society
## Rose Classes

| | | | | | | |
|---|---|---|---|---|---|---|
| 1 | Alba | 19 | Floribunda | 38 | Hybrid Rugosa |
| 2 | Ayrshire | 20 | Gallica | 39 | Hybrid Sempervirens |
| 3 | Bourbon | 21 | Grandiflora | 40 | Hybrid Setigera |
| 4 | Boursault | 22 | Hybrid Alba | 41 | Hybrid Spinosissima |
| 5 | Centifolia | 23 | Hybrid Bracteata | 42 | Hybrid Suffulta |
| 6 | China | 24 | Hybrid Blanda | 43 | Hybrid Tea |
| 7 | Climbing Bourbon | 25 | Hybrid Bourbon | 44 | Kordesii |
| 8 | Climbing China | 26 | Hybrid China | 45 | Large-flowered Climber |
| 9 | Climbing Floribunda | 27 | Hybrid Foetida | 46 | Moss |
| 10 | Climbing Grandiflora | 28 | Hybrid Hugonis | 47 | Miniature |
| | | 29 | Hybrid Laevigata | 48 | Miscellaneous Old Garden Rose |
| 11 | Climbing Hybrid Perpetual | 30 | Hybrid Macounii | | |
| 12 | Climbing Hybrid Tea | 31 | Hybrid Macrantha | 49 | Noisette |
| 13 | Climbing Moss | 32 | Hybrid Moyesii | 50 | Portland |
| 14 | Climbing Miniature | 33 | Hybrid Musk | 51 | Polyantha |
| 15 | Climbing Polyantha | 34 | Hybrid Multiflora | 52 | Rambler |
| 16 | Climbing Tea | 35 | Hybrid Nitida | 53 | Shrub |
| 17 | Damask | 36 | Hybrid Nutkana | 54 | Species |
| 18 | Eglanteria | 37 | Hybrid Perpetual | 55 | Tea |

# World Federation of Rose Societies
## Rose Classes

MODERN GARDEN ROSES
1  Modern Shrub Recurrent Large-flowered
2  Modern Shrub Recurrent Cluster-flowered
3  Ground-cover Recurrent Large-flowered
4  Large-flowered
5  Cluster-flowered
6  Dwarf Cluster-flowered
7  Polyantha
8  Miniature
9  Modern Shrub Non-Recurrent Large-flowered
10  Modern Shrub Non-recurrent Cluster-flowered
11  Ground-cover Non-recurrent
12  Rambler Recurrent
13  Large-flowered Climber Recurrent
14  Cluster-flowered Climber Recurrent
15  Climbing Miniature Recurrent
16  Rambler Non-recurrent
17  Large-flowered Climber Non-recurrent

18  Cluster-flowered Climber Non-recurrent
19  Climbing Miniature Non-recurrent

OLD GARDEN ROSES
20  Alba
21  Bourbon
22  Boursault
23  China
24  Damask
25  Gallica
26  Hybrid Perpetual
27  Moss
28  Portland
29  Provence (Centifolia)
30  Sweet Briar
31  Tea
32  Ayrshire
33  Climbing Bourbon
34  Climbing Boursalt
35  Climbing Tea
36  Noisette
37  Sempervirens

WILD ROSES
38  Wild Roses Non-climbing
39  Wild Roses Climbing

# British Association representing Breeders
## Rose Classes

1  Species and Groups
2  China
3  Noisette
4  Tea
5  Hybrid Tea
6  Floribunda
7  Florishrub
8  Miniature
9  Patio
10  Climbing Hybrid Tea
11  Climbing Floribunda
12  Climbing Miniature
13  Polyantha
14  Climbing Polyantha
15  Hybrid Musk
16  Wichurana Rambler
17  Wichurana Carpet
18  Wichurana Shrub
19  Gallica
20  Damask
21  Centifolia
22  Moss
23  Portland
24  Bourbon
25  Hybrid Perpetual
26  English
27  Scotch
28  Alba
29  Sweet Briar
30  Rugosa

## Alba Roses

Also known as 'white roses', the Albas make noble, once-flowering shrubs. The leaves have a characteristic blue-green appearance.

## China Roses

In China and east Asia, an extremely significant group of roses had developed in isolation: they flowered repeatedly throughout summer and autumn. They culminated in the creation of the Modern Garden Roses.

## Tea Roses

Developed from two tea-scented Chinas, a whole new repeat-flowering race called Tea Roses was introduced with beautiful and graceful blooms.

## Portland Roses

This repeat-flowering group is the result of a Gallica, Damask, Centifolia and China cross.

## Bourbon Roses

These were the first repeat-flowering roses to be created from the Chinas.

## Hybrid Perpetual Roses

This repeat-flowering group was the result of intense hybridization and selection, mainly in open-field cultivation.

## Scots Roses

These hardy hybrids of *R. pimpinellifolia* originated in northern Europe. They had a brief spell of popularity in the eighteenth century as bedding roses, flowering once only in summer.

'Silver Jubilee' *(above)*

## Sweet Briar Roses

Developed from *R. eglanteria*, these non-repeat-flowering roses are valued for their small, apple-scented leaflets.

## Ayrshire Roses

This group of rambling roses is apparently descended from *R. arvensis*, a trailing species of European hedgerows.

## Laevigata Roses

The one species in this class is a native of China. It is grown extensively in southern USA. Two offspring, 'Ramona' and 'Anemone', have the same characteristics as their parent, dark green leaves and large, hooked prickles.

## Sempervirens Roses

This small group of once-flowering ramblers are descendants of *R. sempervirens*, commonly known as the evergreen rose.

### Noisette Roses

These repeat-flowering climbers were developed by Philippe Noisette of Charleston, South Carolina.

### Boursault Roses

This small group of rambling roses was once thought to be derived from *R. pendulina* and *R. chinensis*, but because their stems are almost without prickles, and their bloom non-repeating, some experts place them as derivatives of *R. blanda*.

## TYPES OF MODERN GARDEN ROSE

The bush roses are the most significant of the Modern Garden Roses, and are the ones people are most likely to grow.

### Large-flowered (or Hybrid Tea) Roses

For over a hundred years, these roses have been popular around the world because of their reblooming character. Nearly all have large flowers, frequently pointed buds, with large leaves and strong canes. Not all of them have fragrance, and many are subject to black spot and mildew.

### Cluster-flowered (or Floribunda) Roses

As a consequence of crossing Large-flowered Roses with *R. multiflora*, a species characterized by large flower clusters, a very free-flowering bush rose was produced.

As many crosses have been made between Large-flowered and Cluster-flowered Roses, it has become more and more difficult to distinguish between them. In the USA, these in-between roses are often classified as Grandifloras.

### Patio (or Dwarf Cluster-flowered) Roses

Patio Roses freely produce bunches of well-formed flowers. They are also easy to train as standards.

Standard roses at Isola Bella, Lake Maggiore, Italy *(left)*

## Polyantha Roses

Polyantha Roses is a group of compact bushes with small flowers. They are extremely heavy bloomers throughout the season. Most are winter hardy.

## Modern Shrub Roses

Roses that are perhaps a little bigger, more vigorous and spreading than bush roses, defy attempts to classify them simply and are called Modern Shrubs. They have a range of color and fragrance, and because they are easy to grow, are popular with both beginners and experienced rosarians.

Modern Shrub Roses are often further divided into more specific categories: Hybrid Musks and English Roses.

## Hybrid Rugosa Roses

These attractive and large shrub roses are related to *R. rugosa*, an oriental species noted for its wrinkled, or rugose foliage. Hybrid Rugosas are hardy and disease resistant.

## Ground Cover Roses

This group enhances the environment, whether in large public plantings or giving color to parts of the garden once considered inhospitable. The majority are repeat-flowering.

## Miniature Roses

Dwarf China roses had been grown for many years before a Colonel Roulet found a miniature rose in a pot on the window-sill of a farmhouse in Switzerland in 1917, which was later used in the propagation of these roses in modern times. Ralph Moore of California is the most

'Texas' *(above)*

famous hybridizer of miniatures today, and a number of his creations are in this book.

## Rambler Roses

With the introduction of *R. wichurana* and *R. multiflora* from Asia, this type of plant quickly became popular and appealed to the Victorian sense of being big, sensuous and brash.

## Climber Roses

These roses are classified as either Large-flowered Climbers or Cluster-flowered Climbers. They are usually bred from bush roses, which have the tendency to throw climbing mutations. They are only summer flowering. Their vigor, however, is prodigious and the quality of the flowers is very high.

# Genetics and Rose Breeding

Breeders are now able to be much more specific and innovative in the development of new varieties. Occasionally, a cultivar will spontaneously produce a different color or form of growth. These are generally called sports, and are caused by mutation. Climbing mutations are rare, a phenomenon to be valued. If this occurs, the stem must be propagated vegetatively, usually by budding. Climbing sports tend to be summer-flowering only.

# The Form and Fragrance of Roses

## PLANT FORMS

Many aspects of the growth of roses are determined by climate. Catalogues can be quite variable, often only relevant to a particular country (or state).

Roses range in size from just a few inches to giant climbers and ramblers with the potential to grow up to 50 ft (15 m). They have upright, arching, scrambling or occasionally trailing stems. The usually deciduous leaves are alternately arranged, composed of an odd number of leaflets, and are borne on generally prickly stems. Blooms are carried either singly or in corymbs of up to 100; each flower has many stamens, styles and petals (most Wild Roses have single flowers with 5 petals). After flowering, the receptacle becomes fleshy to form a hip, which encloses a few to many seeds.

### Prickles

Usually a consistent characteristic among roses, prickles may be absent. Roses with *R. pimpinellifolia* and *R. rugosa* ancestry tend to have very small, needle-shaped bristles, and Large- and Cluster-flowered varieties have wing-shaped prickles that can be very large.

### Leaves

Rose leaves mostly have five leaflets, as in Large- and Cluster-flowered Roses. Seven leaflets are typical of lines with *R. wichurana* and *R. multiflora* in their ancestry, and many Asiatic species can have as many as fifteen leaflets and appear almost fernlike.

### Flower Shape and Size

Flowers are borne either singly or in clusters. There is a tremendous variety of flower shapes and sizes.

### Hips

Rose hips have a variety of shapes and sizes, but are more easily classified into three types: subglobose, the hips so typical of roses with *R. rugosa* ancestry; globose, the small round hips usually associated with the majority of bush roses; and the dramatic flask-shaped hips so splendidly borne by descendants of *R. moyesii*.

## FRAGRANCE

Appreciation of scent is subjective. In short, no two human beings have the same reaction to fragrance. With roses, what one person may describe as sweet, another may pass off as fetid.

### Breeding for Fragrance

Fragrance is a recessive factor that is easily lost through cross-

## ROSE FLOWER SHAPES

*Flat Single, semi-double and occasionally double flowers that are fully open and almost flat.*

*Cupped Open, single to double flowers with petals that curve out from the center.*

*High-centered Semi- to very double flowers with high, pointed centers that are tightly closed.*

*Rosette Very double flowers with many slightly overlapping petals of different sizes.*

*Quartered-rosette Very double flowers with many overlapping petals packed into quarters.*

*Pompon Small and rounded, very double flowers filled with masses of tiny petals.*

breeding. Recent successes by Sam McGredy suggest that this problem has been partially resolved, but not without a diminution of the color range. The Bourbons are the prime example of a class that collectively has much fragrance.

### Attar of Roses
The essential oil of rose petals—attar of roses—is a precious commodity. In the Kazanlik Valley in Bulgaria, some 10 000 acres (4050 hectares) of land are cultivated with *R. damascena trigintipetala* (see 'Kazanlik').

### Potpourri
Rose petals also make a very good base for potpourri. Damask and Gallica Roses are very popular.

# The Future of the Rose
So how will the rose develop in the new millennium? Although the last one hundred years have seen incredible development, it is not too hard to predict the next few years, provided the objectives of rose breeders remain the same and there are no unexpected discoveries.

The development of a large shrub rose that freely bears high-quality blooms will probably be the first goal. In fact many hybridists are well on the way to success.

Fragrance and color are both a matter of fashion and will only be determined by the vagaries of change. The perfect rose, according to public demand, is a Large-flowered Rose with classically shaped, red, yellow, pink or white, fragrant flowers that are also weatherproof and repeat-flowering. This has still to be achieved.

The greatest priority must go to the ultimate goal: freedom from disease.

There is a definite need to develop new types of rootstock. Unfortunately the search for a new rootstock has not proved fruitful.

Only a fraction of the total number of rose species are used by hybridists. There must be around 140 species of Wild Roses, yet only about twenty have ever contributed to the development of the Modern Garden Rose.

## Cultivation of Roses

Despite the misconceptions in the extensive literature, roses are easy to grow. However, it is prudent to

*A good bare-root rose should have strong branches, a thick rootstock and abundant roots.*

see a summer through before finally deciding on garden design.

Roses have an astonishing variety of shapes and sizes, allowing great versatility in the garden. The main factor affecting planning is sunlight. They do best in full sun, but four hours can be adequate. Climbers can be planted in shade if they reach up to flower in sunlight. Avoid cold drafty sites.

They root deeply and do not need heavy watering, but an irrigation system will repay its investment. Roses like a soil deep enough for the roots to hold the plant firmly in place. It should be rich in organic matter. Good roses can be grown in clay soil because it retains moisture and nutrients but they grow well in other soils if rich in organic matter. They will grow well in acid or alkaline conditions if not extreme. It is best to aim for a pH of 6 to 6.5.

A garden plan needs to take into account the timing of flower display as well as color and fragrance. Formality or informality, and inclusion of companion plants, need to be considered. Even rose foliage and variations in rose hips can be design features.

### HOW TO CHOOSE AND BUY ROSES

The best selection of varieties is to be found at specialist rose nurseries. The plant should look fresh and healthy. There should be several thick and fibrous roots, and the rootstock or stem should be at least as thick as the average thumb.

A healthy rose has top growth of two or three good stout branches.

Container plants should be actively growing and have healthy, well-spread branches. Carefully remove the plant from its pot and check that the compost is not loose, and that the roots are not pot-bound.

## HOW TO PLANT ROSES

Bare-root and pre-packed roses should be planted so that the bud union (where the first branches arise) is under the ground by about 2 in (5 cm). When the soil settles, the bud union will be at the correct level.

First reduce any exceptionally long roots to the general length. Cut off any broken roots or branches just before the damage and snip off any leaves, buds or hips. Then, dig a hole large and deep enough to accommodate the roots *at the correct depth*.

Do not spread the roots by force. If the roots run in one direction, place the plant by the edge of the hole, and allow the roots to run across it. Fill in the hole with a planting mixture. When the hole is full, firm down *gently* and top up with the originally excavated soil, or the soil from the next planting hole. Then soak the plant in well with about 1 gallon (5 L) of water. Finally, prune the branches hard so that they are about 4–6 in (10–15 cm) in length; this will allow the plant to direct its

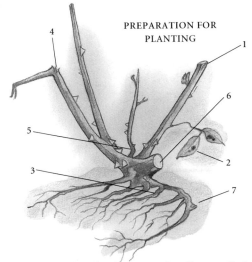

PREPARATION FOR PLANTING

*Before planting a rose, trim off any or all of the following pieces of stem that will die back to the eye (1), diseased or damaged leaves, roots or stems (2,3,4), shoots too thin to keep (5), rootstock 'snags' (6), and developing suckers (7).*

PLANTING A BARE-ROOT ROSE

*Round hole for roots that spread out in all directions.*

*Fan-shaped hole for roots that run in one direction only.*

energy to making new roots without having to maintain a lot of top growth.

Climber and Rambler Roses should be planted in exactly the same way as bare-root and pre-packed roses. Climbers should not be pruned after planting.

Standard roses are planted as for bare-root and pre-packed roses, with the addition of a stout hardwood stake. The branches should then be pruned to about 6 in (15 cm) from the junction with the stem.

For container-grown roses, a hole should be dug about 3 in (7 cm) deeper than the container. Next, place a 2 in (5 cm) layer of planting mixture in the bottom of the hole and position the rootball carefully. Fill around the rootball with some more planting mixture, finally covering it with soil, then gently firm it down.

All mulches are valuable. They help retain moisture, deter weeds and in some cases add nutrients. A good mulch will be about 4 in (10 cm) deep.

## PRUNING AND TRAINING ROSES

Very hard pruning necessitates heavy feeding to help the rose grow again. Trials conducted over eight years have proved conclusively that the more foliage a rose carries, the better its performance. Gardeners are therefore advised not to remove the twiggy (non-flowering) growths when pruning.

Garden roses are pruned for two reasons: to keep them within bounds and to make them flower. It is usually worth while to reduce the height of tall bushes and shrubs by about a third in late autumn to avoid wind rock.

Shrub, Old Garden and Wild Roses can be left for three to five years with little or no pruning other than deadheading. Occasionally an old stem can be removed at the base. This minimal pruning results in large and attractive plants. Alternatively, they can be pruned every year as though they were large bushes.

For Bush and Miniature Roses first remove all dead, diseased and damaged branches. Disease usually shows as a discoloration in the pith in the branch. Each year, the oldest branch should be removed at its base, which promotes regeneration of the plant. Next, reduce the remaining branches by about half, but leave any thin, twiggy stems that will help the plant to make a good start in the next year.

On a well-trained climbing rose, first, remove all dead, diseased and damaged wood, then reduce all side shoots, no matter how long, to stubs 2–3 in (5–8 cm) long. The main shoots are not pruned at all unless they end in flowers. In this case, they should be cut back to the first side shoot, which then takes over as leader. When the main shoot has filled its allotted space, the tip should be removed.

Every one or two years, or when there are sufficient shoots (more than three), remove the oldest at the base of the rose. This will cause the production of new shoots from the base.

Ground Cover Roses need little or no pruning.

Standard roses are simply roses that grow on top of a long stem. They need only moderate pruning to reduce the branches by no more than one-third, with the aim of creating a nice circular head. If the plant is a weeping standard, old flowered shoots should be shortened by half or removed entirely if there is plenty of new growth.

## ROUTINE CARE OF ROSES

Roses need to be fed, mulched and deadheaded and any suckers that may be produced from the rootstocks or the standard stem need to be removed. Like many other garden plants, roses can be attacked by fungal diseases.

Roses must be properly fed. The simplest way is to give them a good dressing of a proprietary rose fertilizer twice a year; once in the spring and once in the summer. Foliar feeds involve much effort and give very little apparent benefit.

## THE CHIEF FUNGAL DISEASES OF ROSES

With regular applications of fertilizer there should be no nutrition problem, but the principal deficiencies and remedies are listed below.

Fertilizer should be applied on top of the mulch. The rain will usually wash it through to the soil beneath, but during a very dry spell

| SYMPTOM | DIAGNOSIS | REMEDY |
|---|---|---|
| Young leaves are pale green | lack of nitrogen | Apply $1\frac{1}{2}$ oz/yd$^2$ (60 g/m$^2$) of hoof and horn, urea or blood and bone or $\frac{3}{4}$ oz/yd$^2$ (30 g/m$^2$) of sulfate of ammonia where the soil is not very acid |
| Small leaves with purplish undersides | lack of phosphorus | Apply $\frac{3}{4}$ oz/yd$^2$ (30 g/m$^2$) of superphosphate of $1\frac{1}{2}$ oz/yd$^2$ (60g/m$^2$) of bone meal |
| Purple or brown edges to leaves, and young leaves unnaturally red | lack of potassium | Apply $\frac{3}{4}$ oz/yd$^2$ (30 g/m$^2$) of sulfate of potash |
| Brown spots near the edges of leaves | lack of calcium | Apply $\frac{3}{4}$ oz/yd$^2$ (30 g/m$^2$) of gypsum |
| Pale patches towards centers of leaves and areas of dead tissue near main vein | lack of magnesium | Apply $\frac{3}{4}$ oz/yd$^2$ (30 g/m$^2$) Epsom salts |
| Yellowish leaves | lack of iron | Apply iron chelates |

it can always be watered through. If there are any nutrient deficiencies, the application of the appropriate remedy on top of the mulch will eventually work.

Roses are deep rooted and, after new plants have become established, will seldom need any water. In a prolonged dry spell, it is better to water using a drip-feed or 'leaky pipe' system, thoroughly soaking the roots. Garden plants given small quantities of water will be encouraged to develop surface roots, which are more prone to drought damage. Roses in containers, window boxes and hanging baskets will need water at least once a day.

After the flowers fade, the rose will set seed and cease to produce new flowering shoots. It is necessary, therefore, to remove these spent blooms, an activity called deadheading, to fool the plant into producing more flowers. Recent trials have clearly established that the more foliage a rose plant bears, the better its performance. It is now recommended that dead flower-heads be snapped off at the abcission layer. This principle of retaining the maximum foliage should also be observed when deadheading Cluster-flowered Roses.

Roses that are healthy and well cultivated will be better equipped to resist pests and diseases. As with every other plant, some varieties of roses are simply not worth growing, because of their poor health. The three main fungal diseases are black spot, mildew and rust. They are all quite simple to deal with, but the best tactic by far is prevention.

Use a good rose fungicide. Always use chemicals as instructed, and remember to shake or stir the spray container at regular intervals while

Black spot, a common disease of roses, is easily dealt with by preventive spraying with a fungicide. (above)

Powdery mildew can be treated with a good rose fungicide. (above)

The color of a rose may vary with its position, the soil, the climate and
. the age of the bloom.

spraying. Roses should be sprayed early in the spring.

If the fungus appears during the growing season because spraying has been overlooked, the rose should be sprayed as soon as possible with two repeats at two-week intervals. Most fungicide instructions permit the use of the spray at double strength in these cases.

## COMMON ROSE PESTS

The main insect pests of the rose garden, and the best means of eliminating them, are listed below:

**Aphids** (or greenfly) are best squashed by finger and thumb. Otherwise, spray with a pesticide that does not harm beneficial insects.

**Thrips** may prevent blooms from opening; blooms that partially open have brown or black spots. As flowers must be inspected very carefully to find them, their effect is often underestimated. They can be controlled by spraying buds and blooms.

**Leaf-rolling sawfly** is worst where roses are growing in shade under trees. It is not really worth spraying because affected, rolled up leaves can be picked off, and plants should be given an extra dose of fertilizer.

**Caterpillars** (sometimes called rose slugworms) usually eat the surface of the leaves to create a skeleton effect. They are easily controlled either by picking off the caterpillars and affected leaves, or by spraying with an insecticide.

'Veilchenblau'  *(above)*

**Spider mites** are worst in hot, dry conditions and cause a bronze discoloration on the uppersides of the leaves. The simplest remedy is to put an irrigation spray at ground level and thoroughly wet the undersides of the leaves.

**'Cuckoo Spit'** (the common froghopper) is not serious. Wash it off with a squirt from a hose.

### SAFETY WITH CHEMICALS
Always read the label and follow instructions when using chemicals, and avoid skin contact, especially when they are undiluted. Remember to shake or stir the diluted chemical so that it is thoroughly mixed.

### SUCKERS AND BLIND SHOOTS
Suckers are unwanted growths from the rootstocks of budded plants. They should be removed. Suckers usually have leaves that are of different color and shape from the rest of the rose because the budded rootstock comes from a different type of rose. Standard roses sometimes also produce suckers from the stem below the bud union. Stem suckers are best rubbed off when small.

In blind shoots, the embryo flowers have been damaged in some way that prevents their development. The modern procedure is to remove only the tips of the blind shoot, or simply to leave it untouched.

## How to Propagate Roses
### CUTTINGS
Roses can most easily be propagated by cuttings in autumn. First, take pieces of stem about 8 in (20 cm) in length from well-ripened branches that have grown during the previous five or six months. The cuttings should have all but the top leaf snipped off (to show which is the right way up). Then, make a slit in the ground by levering a spade to and fro to create a wedge-shaped hole about 6 in (15 cm) deep. It will help if a little sharp sand is placed in the bottom of the hole. Next, place the cuttings in the hole about 4 in (10 cm) apart and firm the soil around the hole. The cuttings should then be labeled and marked by a stick with a scrap of bright plastic or similar attached, to prevent the area being accidentally disturbed. Cuttings that 'take' will eventually produce new shoots and can be transplanted one year later into a 'holding' bed.

## LAYERING

Most roses with lax stems can be 'layered' into the soil to produce new plants. This is best done after summer flowering.

## SEED

Hybrid roses will not come true from seed, but Wild Roses will. In autumn, the ripe hips, which contain the seed, should be placed in a refrigerator for a month or so. It will then germinate when planted one seed to a pot. The pots should be kept in a cold frame or sheltered spot outdoors and, after germination, potted on.

## HYBRIDIZING

This is quite a simple operation that involves the transfer of pollen from one rose (the pollen parent) to the stigma of another (the seed parent). This is normally done in insect-free conditions so that the breeder can guarantee the identity of both parents. When the rose hip swells and matures, its seeds are sown.

## BUDDING

Most commercially grown roses are propagated by budding. Individual new rose seedlings can be increased in number by the insertion of a bud or 'eye' taken from the new rose into a T-shaped slit made in the stem of a Wild Rose rootstock. When the new bud or 'scion' takes and grows, the top growth of the original rootstock plant is cut off.

A red standard rose is the focus of attention in this cottage garden. *(below)*

# Suggested Roses for Special Purposes

**FOR DISEASE RESISTANCE**
'Alba Semi-plena'
'Aloha'
'Great Maiden's Blush'
'Jens Munk'
'Lavender Lassie'
'Mme Plantier'
'Perle d'Or'
'Prosperity'
'Scabrosa'
'White Meidiland'

**FOR CUT FLOWERS**
'Anne Harkness'
'Belle Story'
'Blue Moon'
'Cardinal de Richelieu'
'Just Joey'
'Kazanlik'
'Mary Rose'
'Mme Hardy'
'Peace'
'Silver Jubilee'

**FOR REPEAT-FLOWERING**
'Cécile Brünner'
'Cornelia'
'Crépuscule'
'Felicia'
'Graham Thomas'
'Iceberg'
'Just Joey'
'Mutabilis'
'Rosy Cushion'
'The Fairy'

**FOR CLIMBING/RAMBLING**
'Albéric Barbier'
'Albertine'
'American Pillar'
'Dublin Bay'
'Francis E. Lester'
'Kiftsgate'
'Mme Alfred Carrière'
'Mme Caroline Testout'
'Veilchenblau'
'Zéphirine Drouhin'

**FOR FRAGRANCE**
'Apricot Nectar'
'Autumn Damask'
'Belle Amour'
'Charles de Mills'
'Double Delight'
'Fragrant Cloud'
'Mary Rose'
'Mme Isaac Pereire'
'Prospero'
'Velvet Fragrance'

**FOR HARDINESS**
'Blanc Double de Coubert'
'Fru Dagmar Hastrup'
'Hansa'
'John Cabot'
'John David'
*Rosa fedtschenkoana*
*Rosa moyesii*
*Rosa mulliganii*
*Rosa rugosa*
'Stanwell Perpetual'

**FOR LANDSCAPING**
'Avon'
'Bassino'
'Cambridgeshire'
'Immensee'
'Magic Carpet'
'Pink Bells'
'Ralph's Creeper'
'Rosy Cushion'
'Sea Foam'
'Snow Carpet'

'Graham Thomas' *(above)*

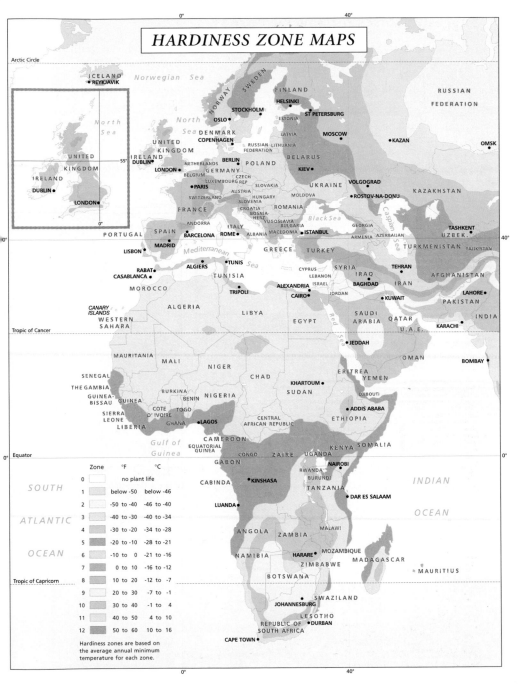

# HARDINESS ZONE MAPS

**Arctic Circle**

ICELAND
• REYKJAVIK

*Norwegian Sea*

*North Sea*

ICELAND
• REYKJAVIK

*North Sea*

NORWAY
SWEDEN
FINLAND

STOCKHOLM
OSLO •
• HELSINKI
• ST PETERSBURG

ESTONIA
LATVIA

RUSSIAN FEDERATION

• MOSCOW
• KAZAN
OMSK •

DENMARK
COPENHAGEN •
RUSSIAN LITHUANIA
FEDERATION

UNITED
KINGDOM

IRELAND
DUBLIN •
LONDON •

55°

UNITED
KINGDOM

IRELAND

DUBLIN •

LONDON •

0°

BELARUS

NETHERLANDS BERLIN
BELGIUM GERMANY
LUXEMBOURG CZECH
REP
SLOVAKIA
AUSTRIA
SWITZERLAND HUNGARY
SLOVENIA
CROATIA
BOSNIA-
HERZ.
YUGOSLAVIA
BULGARIA

• PARIS

FRANCE

ANDORRA
ITALY

POLAND

KIEV •

UKRAINE

MOLDOVA

ROMANIA

VOLGOGRAD •

• ROSTOV-NA-DONU

KAZAKHSTAN

PORTUGAL    SPAIN
LISBON •    • MADRID
BARCELONA •  ROME •
MACEDONIA • ISTANBUL
ALBANIA

*Black Sea*

GEORGIA
ARMENIA AZERBAIJAN

*Caspian Sea*

TASHKENT •
UZBEK.

40°

*Mediterranean Sea*

RABAT •
CASABLANCA •

ALGIERS •
• TUNIS

TUNISIA

GREECE    TURKEY

CYPRUS
LEBANON

SYRIA
IRAQ
• TEHRAN

TURKMENISTAN TAJIKISTAN

AFGHANISTAN

MOROCCO

TRIPOLI •

ALEXANDRIA •
CAIRO •

ISRAEL
JORDAN

BAGHDAD •

IRAN

• KUWAIT

LAHORE •
PAKISTAN

CANARY
ISLANDS
WESTERN
SAHARA

ALGERIA

LIBYA

EGYPT

SAUDI
ARABIA    QATAR
U.A.E.

KARACHI •

INDIA

**Tropic of Cancer**

MAURITANIA
MALI

NIGER

CHAD

• JEDDAH

*Red Sea*

OMAN

BOMBAY •

SENEGAL
THE GAMBIA
GUINEA-
BISSAU GUINEA
SIERRA
LEONE
LIBERIA

BURKINA
BENIN
COTE TOGO
D'IVOIRE
GHANA • LAGOS

NIGERIA

KHARTOUM •

SUDAN

ERITREA
YEMEN

DJIBOUTI

• ADDIS ABABA

ETHIOPIA

CAMEROON

*Gulf of Guinea*

EQUATORIAL
GUINEA

CENTRAL
AFRICAN REPUBLIC

SOMALIA

KENYA

UGANDA

**0°  Equator**

GABON
CONGO
ZAIRE

RWANDA
BURUNDI

NAIROBI •

0°

*INDIAN*

*SOUTH*

CABINDA

• KINSHASA

TANZANIA

• DAR ES SALAAM

*OCEAN*

*ATLANTIC*

LUANDA •

MALAWI

*OCEAN*

ANGOLA    ZAMBIA

MOZAMBIQUE

*OCEAN*

NAMIBIA    HARARE •
ZIMBABWE

MADAGASCAR

* MAURITIUS

**Tropic of Capricorn**

BOTSWANA

SWAZILAND

JOHANNESBURG •

LESOTHO
REPUBLIC OF • DURBAN
SOUTH AFRICA

CAPE TOWN •

| Zone | °F | °C |
|------|-----|-----|
| 0 | no plant life | |
| 1 | below -50 | below -46 |
| 2 | -50 to -40 | -46 to -40 |
| 3 | -40 to -30 | -40 to -34 |
| 4 | -30 to -20 | -34 to -28 |
| 5 | -20 to -10 | -28 to -21 |
| 6 | -10 to 0 | -21 to -16 |
| 7 | 0 to 10 | -16 to -12 |
| 8 | 10 to 20 | -12 to -7 |
| 9 | 20 to 30 | -7 to -1 |
| 10 | 30 to 40 | -1 to 4 |
| 11 | 40 to 50 | 4 to 10 |
| 12 | 50 to 60 | 10 to 16 |

Hardiness zones are based on
the average annual minimum
temperature for each zone.

0°    40°

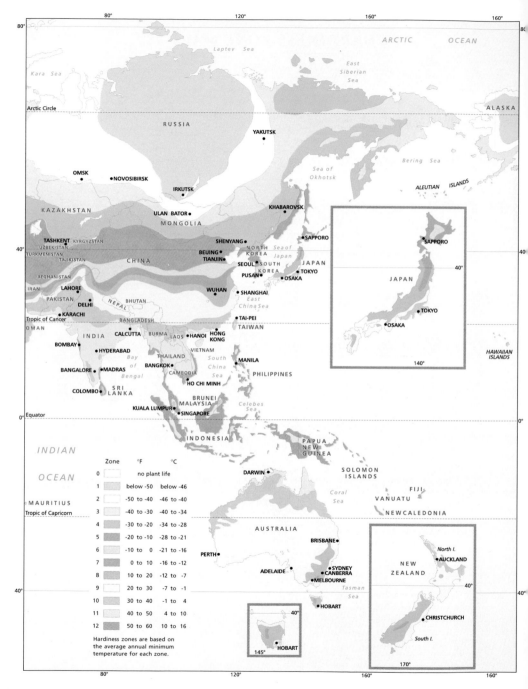

Zone | °F | °C
0 | no plant life |
1 | below -50 | below -46
2 | -50 to -40 | -46 to -40
3 | -40 to -30 | -40 to -34
4 | -30 to -20 | -34 to -28
5 | -20 to -10 | -28 to -21
6 | -10 to 0 | -21 to -16
7 | 0 to 10 | -16 to -12
8 | 10 to 20 | -12 to -7
9 | 20 to 30 | -7 to -1
10 | 30 to 40 | -1 to 4
11 | 40 to 50 | 4 to 10
12 | 50 to 60 | 10 to 16

Hardiness zones are based on the average annual minimum temperature for each zone.

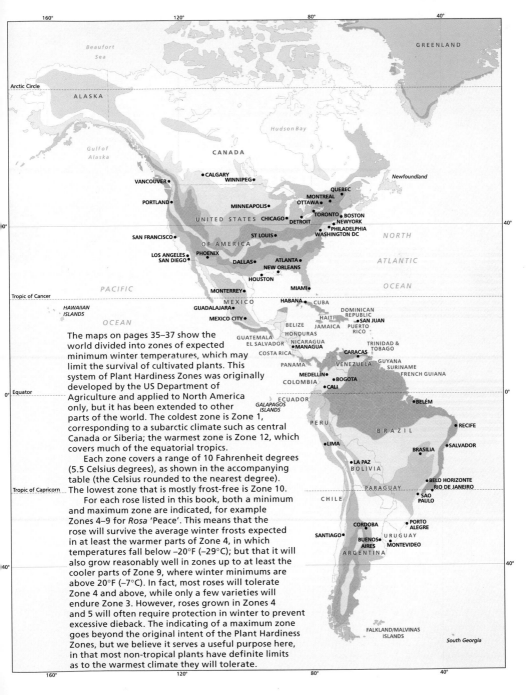

The maps on pages 35–37 show the world divided into zones of expected minimum winter temperatures, which may limit the survival of cultivated plants. This system of Plant Hardiness Zones was originally developed by the US Department of Agriculture and applied to North America only, but it has been extended to other parts of the world. The coldest zone is Zone 1, corresponding to a subarctic climate such as central Canada or Siberia; the warmest zone is Zone 12, which covers much of the equatorial tropics.

Each zone covers a range of 10 Fahrenheit degrees (5.5 Celsius degrees), as shown in the accompanying table (the Celsius rounded to the nearest degree). The lowest zone that is mostly frost-free is Zone 10.

For each rose listed in this book, both a minimum and maximum zone are indicated, for example Zones 4–9 for *Rosa* 'Peace'. This means that the rose will survive the average winter frosts expected in at least the warmer parts of Zone 4, in which temperatures fall below –20°F (–29°C); but that it will also grow reasonably well in zones up to at least the cooler parts of Zone 9, where winter minimums are above 20°F (–7°C). In fact, most roses will tolerate Zone 4 and above, while only a few varieties will endure Zone 3. However, roses grown in Zones 4 and 5 will often require protection in winter to prevent excessive dieback. The indicating of a maximum zone goes beyond the original intent of the Plant Hardiness Zones, but we believe it serves a useful purpose here, in that most non-tropical plants have definite limits as to the warmest climate they will tolerate.

# Wild
# Roses

### Rosa acicularis nipponensis *(below)*
DEEP PINK

This small, dense shrub to 3 ft (1 m) is armed with tiny prickles, although some of its older, dark green shoots may bear relatively few. The leaves are made up of matt green, elliptical, serrated leaflets, and the small, deep pink

flowers, which are produced singly, appear in late spring. The ripe red hips are pear-shaped and red when ripe. This is a hardy species, which, as a garden plant, is superior in many ways to the North American and European *Rosa acicularis*. ZONES 4–11.

JAPAN, 1894

### Rosa arkansana *(below)*
syns 'Arkansas Rose', *Rosa suffulta*
MEDIUM PINK

A short shrub with greenish stems up to 2 ft (60 cm) *Rosa arkansana* bears many stems with thin prickles. These stems often die off each year and are replaced by new suckers. The leaves are made of seven to eleven broadly elliptical, bright green, heavily serrated leaflets. Small flowers, about 1 in (2.5 cm) across, are produced in corymbs in early summer. The fruit are small, dark red and globular. This is an interesting species, but is of little garden value. ZONES 4–11.

NORTH AMERICA, 1896

*Rosa arvensis* *(above)*
syn. 'The Field Rose'

WHITE

A native of Europe, except for the cold north and the warmer Mediterranean regions, *Rosa arvensis* is commonly found in neglected hedgerows where it grows as a shade-tolerant and disease-free, relaxed scrambler or creeper up to 10 ft (3 m). Its flowers are creamy white, 1½ in (3 cm) across, with pronounced yellow stamens, and are produced singly or in small corymbs during early summer. Despite some descriptions to the contrary, this rose is slightly scented. The oval hips are red when ripe, and appear amid the serrated, deep green foliage mostly made up of seven leaflets. Numerous hooked thorns cover the slender, dark green and flexible stems. This is a useful species for the natural garden; it was crossed with various Old Garden Roses in the early nineteenth century, which gave rise to a small group of ramblers known as the Ayrshires. The best known of these is 'Splendens', which is described in the main section of this book, and bears lovely double, silvery pink blooms. **ZONES 4–10.**

EUROPE, 1750

### Rosa banksiae normalis *(above)*

WHITE

Of the four forms of *Rosa banksiae* now in cultivation, this is considered to be the wild form. It is vigorous—up to 30 ft (9 m)—in warm temperate climates or under glass. The scented flowers are white, single, small and borne in corymbs amid the light green broadly elongated leaves, which are composed of about five leaflets. All four varieties of *R. banksiae* are normally thornless and evergreen. *R. banksiae banksiae* (syns 'Banksiae Alba', 'Lady Banksia Snowflake', *R. banksiae alba plena*, 'White Lady Banks') was introduced in 1807. It is a cultivated form of the wild species, and its behavior is similar in all respects, except for its loosely double, white flowers. *R. banksiae lutea* (syn. 'Yellow Lady Banks'; Royal Horticultural Society Award of Garden Merit) is the best known and most widely grown form. Its corymbs of small, fully double, bright yellow flowers are produced in late spring in great profusion. They cover this vigorous and healthy, densely growing thornless Rambler, which grows up to 30 ft (9 m). *R. banksiae lutescens*, introduced in 1870, is a slightly less vigorous form with single, sulfur yellow flowers. It has a stronger perfume than any of the others.

*R. × fortuniana* (syn. *R. banksiae × R. laevigata*) is often used as a rootstock in warm climates. It has larger, double white flowers than the wild species, and unlike the purer forms of *R. banksiae normalis*, this rose is well armed with thorns. *Rosa cymosa* was introduced in 1904 and has many similarities to *R. banksiae normalis*. It is a rare rose, and has interesting, single white flowers. **ZONES 4–10.**

CHINA, CIRCA 1877

## *Rosa blanda*   *(rose hip, right)*
syns 'Hudson's Bay Rose', 'Labrador Rose', *Rosa fraxinifolia*
MEDIUM PINK

This spring-blooming shrub grows to a height of 5 ft (1.5 m). Its stems are usually without thorns and prickles. The single, pink flowers are 2–2½ in (4–6 cm) wide and are usually borne several to a stem amid the foliage. Globular, sometimes elongated hips follow. **ZONES 4–11.**

NORTHERN NORTH AMERICA, 1773

## *Rosa bracteata*   *(below)*
syns 'Chicksaw Rose', 'Macartney Rose'
WHITE

A dense shrub or wall plant to 10 ft (3 m), *Rosa bracteata* has long, grayish brown stems that are well armed with hooked thorns, often arranged in pairs. There is a plentiful covering of dark green, roundish and glossy leaves that have tomentose undersides. There are nine leaflets. The white flowers, with pronounced stamens, sometimes have a hint of cream showing through. They are borne singly on the end of stubby laterals throughout summer, and are followed by plumply rounded, orange hips. Although it is not suitable for cold climates, it makes an excellent shrub in temperate zones; it has, in fact become naturalized in the southern states of the USA. This is a superb wall plant, as it is evergreen and easy going. 'Mermaid', which is described in the main A–Z section of this book, is a famous offspring of this species and is much hardier. **ZONES 4–11.**

CHINA, 1793

### *Rosa brunonii*
*(right)*
syn. 'The Himalayan Musk'

WHITE

This very vigorous scrambler with brownish green unyielding wood and vicious hooked thorns can reach 40 ft (12 m) in height. The drooping leaves are long, narrowly oval and grayish green. Large corymbs of small, white flowers appear in mid-summer, followed by oval hips that quickly change from red to brown in maturity. This rose is not totally hardy, and it has been widely distributed erroneously as *Rosa moschata* for many years. 'La Mortola' is a superior garden form that has longer, grayer leaves and bigger flowers; it is described in the main A–Z section of this book. *Rosa moschata nepalensis* is a distinct form that is often incorrectly classed as a synonym of *R. brunonii*. **ZONES 3–10.**

HIMALAYAS, CIRCA 1823

*Rosa brunonii*
(rose hips) *(right)*

## Rosa californica
*(right)*
syn. 'California
Wild Rose'

**LIGHT PINK**

This vigorous shrub
grows up to 10 ft (3 m)
and produces many
young branches each
year; like the older
wood, these are well
endowed with slender,
hooked prickles. The
soft dull green leaves
have five to seven
broadly elongated leaf-
lets, and are a backdrop
to the small corymbs
of blooms that are
produced over a fairly
long period from early
summer; the color is
mid-pink with little or
no scent. Plumply oval
hips, which are red
when ripe, follow in
autumn. *Rosa califor-
nica* is a useful shrub
for wild gardens that
appears to be hardy
in all but the coldest
areas. *R. californica*
'Plena', a semi-double
form, is a much more
useful and decorative
garden shrub. It freely
produces lilac-pink
flowers and orange-red
fruit. **ZONES 3–10**.

NORTH AMERICA, CIRCA 1878

*Rosa californica*
'Plena' *(right)*

### Rosa canina *(right)*
syns 'Briar Bush',
'Dog Rose'
**LIGHT PINK**

The common rose of
hedgerows in central
and western Europe,
*Rosa canina* is a stoutly
branching shrub that
varies in height from
6 to 12 ft (2–4 m). The
thorny stems are
adorned with mid-
green leaves that have
five to seven broadly
elongated and serrated
leaflets. The small,
scented flowers are
borne singly or in
threes, and the color
varies from blush white
to pink. Oval, bright
red hips follow; they
are very conspicuous
*en masse*, are a valuable
source of vitamin C
and can be used to
make superb syrup
or jelly. It is not an
auspicious garden
shrub, perhaps, but
makes an excellent
ornamental hedge. For
many years, this species
was used in Europe as
the main rootstock in
commercial rose pro-
duction. **ZONES 3–10.**
EUROPE, PRE-1730

### Rosa carolina
*(right)*
syns 'Caroline Rose',
'Pasture Rose'
**MEDIUM PINK**

Stout to medium in
size, this rose is a dense,
free-suckering shrub.
Its young shoots are
bristly, although the

older stems only occa-
sionally bear prickles,
and are covered by
leaves made up of
five mostly elongated,
elliptical and serrated,
lightly glossy dark
green leaflets. The
pink flowers are borne
in profusion in mid-
summer. Like the
flowers, the globular,
bright red hips are pro-
duced one to a stem.

*Rosa carolina
glandulosa* was intro-
duced in 1902. It is
similar to *R. carolina*
but with glandular leaf
stalks. *R. carolina
grandiflora* has both
larger flowers and
leaves, often with seven
leaflets. *R. carolina*
'**Plena**' is a double
form that is slightly
shorter in growth.
*R. carolina alba*, as
the name indicates,
has white flowers. All
of these make good
dense, spreading
shrubs for group
planting and low
hedges. They tolerate
even the poorest soils.
**ZONES 4–11.**
NORTH AMERICA, 1826

### Rosa chinensis *(top)*
syns 'Bengal Rose', 'China Rose', *Rosa chinensis indica*
MEDIUM PINK/DARK RED

This rose was lost to cultivation for many years, and has only recently come back into circulation. Although it is not a true species, it is an important rose for its genes; in the eighteenth century, some of its early hybrids were crossed with European roses, such as the Damasks and Gallicas, which brought forth almost all the repeat-flowering now taken for granted in Modern Garden Roses. The growth is upright, to about 4–8 ft (1.2–2.5 m), and is irregularly armed with sizeable thorns. They are covered with mid- to dark green leaves made up of three to five leaf-lets that are reddish when young. The flowers are produced either singly or in large, well-spaced clusters and vary in color from pale pink to deep red. They usually deepen with age and there is little or no scent. Small, dull red hips follow the blooms. *Rosa chinensis* probably gave rise to R. × *odorata*, which is also variously known as R. *indica odorata* and R. *indica fragrans*. R. *indica* 'Major' is

now regarded as another offspring, and is used as a rootstock in warm climates. Each of these hybrids is probably the result of natural or even deliberate cross-ing with R. *gigantea*. Both are double and soft pink, and make useful repeat-flowering shrubs. 'Mutabilis', described in the main A–Z section of this book, is closely related.
ZONES 5–11.
CHINA, CIRCA 1759

### Rosa cinnamomea *(below)*
syns 'Cinnamon Rose', *Rosa majalis*
MAUVE

This medium to tall shrub reaches 6 ft (1.8 m) in good soil. Its slim brownish stems are only partially armed with squat thorns. The leaves are matt dark green, gray beneath, and made up of five to seven leaflets. The sin-gle flowers are pinkish mauve, have no scent, and are produced singly or in small groups in late spring. The hips are small globular, smooth and dark red.
*Rosa cinnamomea*

*plena,* (syns 'Rose de Mai', 'Rose de Plaquer', 'Rose du Saint-Sacrement') is a rarely seen double form. Graham Stuart Thomas tells us that it is one of the oldest of recorded roses. **R.** *cinnamomea foecundissima* is another double form with paler flowers.
ZONES 4–11.
EUROPE, CIRCA 1600

### *Rosa davidii* (right)
syn. 'Father David's Rose'

**LIGHT PINK**

This tall, stoutly arching shrub of firm stature grows up to 10 ft (3 m) or more in good soil. The stems are armed with long, sharp but broadly based thorns, and the leaves are broadly elongated, heavily veined with mid-green, smooth above, hairy beneath and have seven to nine leaflets. The flowers appear along the branches in small corymbs and are produced in mid-summer. They are mid-pink, scented and up to 1¼ in (5 cm) across with soft yellow stamens. Pendulous hips are borne in small clusters; although not large, each scarlet hip is an attractive, plump flagon shape with persistent long calyces. This species makes a superb shrub and will fit into most gardens. *Rosa davidii elongata* has fewer flowers, but both the leaves and fruit are larger. **ZONES 4–10.**

TIBET, 1908

### *Rosa ecae* (above)
**DEEP YELLOW**

A small, densely branching shrub up to 3 ft (1 m) tall in good soil, *R. ecae* has chocolate brown stems that are thickly populated with short and stubby, reddish, sharp thorns. The dark green leaves are made up of five to nine small, broadly oval, smooth leaflets. The single flowers, produced in late spring, are about ¼ in (6 mm) across and bright buttercup yellow; there is no scent. The hips are small, round and bright red. This species needs a good soil and full sun to give of its best, although it is apparently quite hardy. It is best when only lightly pruned to keep it in shape, and seems to do well when grown in pots, tubs or urns. When *Rosa ecae* was crossed with 'Canary Bird' by A. E. Allen in the UK in 1963, it gave rise to the excellent shrub rose 'Golden Chersonese', which appears in the main A–Z section of this book. **ZONES 4–11.**

AFGHANISTAN, 1880

## *Rosa eglanteria*
(right)
syns *Rosa rubiginosa*,
'Sweet Briar'
LIGHT PINK

This vigorous and tall shrub up to 10 ft (3 m) has densely prickly, fawny-green stems covered by strong and sharply hooked thorns. The dark green foliage smells strongly of apples, especially when crushed, and each leaf has five to seven leaflets. The single flowers, 1½ in (4 cm) in diameter, are soft clear pink, scented and very beautiful, followed by oval, slightly bristly and rich red hips. This species has many uses in the garden as a flowering shrub, not least as a dense hedge, when it can be kept in shape by regular clipping; although this practice tends to reduce the yield of flowers, it encourages many new young aromatic shoots which waft their scent into the surrounding air, especially on warm, early summer evenings after rain. ZONES 4–10.

EUROPE, CIRCA 1594

ROYAL HORTICULTURAL SOCIETY
AWARD OF GARDEN MERIT

## *Rosa elegantula*
'Persetosa' *(above)*
syns *Rosa farreri persetosa*, 'The Threepenny Bit Rose'
MEDIUM PINK

This broad and arching shrub grows to 5 ft (1.5 m). The young stems are densely covered in soft reddish brown bristles, yet the older stems are only sparsely prickled. The small and furry leaves are composed of seven to nine little leaflets, which are dark green, burnished bronze and serrated; there is an excellent autumn coloring. Each flower is less than 1 in (3 cm) across, star-like in form and pinkish. They are not over-conspicuous, even *en masse*. The fruit does not always set, but when it does it is small, drooping and broadly elliptical, and orange when ripe. This shrub needs plenty of space to develop into its most graceful form. It is particularly attractive when covered with hoar-frost in mid-winter. *Rosa elegantula* 'Persetosa' is still commonly listed in catalogues by its old name, *R. farreri persetosa*. ZONES 4–10.

CHINA, 1900

## Rosa fedtschenkoana *(bottom)*

WHITE

This broadly upright, dense shrub to 6 ft (1.8 m) tall has reddish green stems that are moderately armed with long sharp spines. It is freely suckering, grows on its own roots and bears dense foliage that is soft to touch, oblong and made up of leaves with up to nine to fifteen, grayish green leaflets. The white flowers with golden stamens are borne either singly or in small clusters continuously, if spasmodically, throughout summer and autumn. The scent is almost repellent. The small and slender, elliptical, drooping, orange and bristly fruit look attractive together with the flowers in early autumn. The agreeable nature of this shrub, together with the repeat-flowering ability make this a most useful garden plant.

It is good as a broad and informal hedge. ZONES 4–11.

CENTRAL ASIA, CIRCA 1876

## Rosa filipes *(left)*

WHITE

In its wild form this species is seldom seen in gardens. However, *Rosa filipes* 'Kiftsgate', which appears in the main A–Z sequence, has become very popular since it was introduced in 1938; the original plant still thrives as a giant among roses at Kiftsgate Court, Gloucestershire in the UK. ZONES 4–11.

CHINA, 1908

*Rosa foetida* *(top left)*
syns 'Austrian Briar',
'Austrian Yellow'
MEDIUM YELLOW

This upright shrub is capable of attaining 5 ft (1.5 m) in height. It bears rich dark green stems that are heavily overlaid with mahogany-brown and have many large, light-green thorns, becoming brown with age. The foliage is bright deep green—lighter beneath—smooth and downy with five to nine leaflets. The single flowers are produced generously on short stalks in early summer. They have an unpleasant scent, which gives the rose its name. *Rosa foetida bicolor* (syn. 'Austrian Copper') is a popular sport of this species and is similar in all respects except for color, which is bright almost luminous orange-red. It was introduced in 1596. *R. foetida persiana* (syn. 'Persian Yellow') is a double yellow form that appeared in 1835. All of these roses are very susceptible to black spot, which is partly responsible for many Modern Roses being subject to this disease; it was *R. f. persiana* that was used as a pollen parent by French breeder Pernet-Ducher in the late nineteenth century to breed the first yellow and orange Large-flowered Rose called 'Soleil d' Or'. That was a significant event, which sadly had its downside because black spot is an inherent affliction of many of its progeny even to this day. **ZONES 4–11.**

ASIA MINOR, PRE-1596 OR
EARLIER

*Rosa foetida persiana* *(above)*

*Rosa foliolosa*
**(rose hips)** *(top right)*

## Rosa foliolosa
MEDIUM PINK

This low growing shrub to about 4 ft (1.2 m) seems to prefer light, almost impoverished soils. Best grown on its own roots, it is almost impossible to propagate vegetatively in any other way than from cuttings. The semi-glossy, dark green foliage is produced all along the wiry, greenish purple, thornless canes, and has 7–9 oblong leaflets that are soft and furry. Deep cerise-pink blooms are mostly borne singly on short pedicels with long sepals about 2 in (5 cm) across. They are produced later in the summer than many species. Small, rounded red hips develop from the early flowers only. It is an interesting rose, but of little garden value. There is also a white form. **ZONES 4–10.**

USA, 1880

## Rosa forrestiana
*(left)*

**DEEP PINK**

This shrub rose has long arching canes, about 6 ft (2 m), covered with oval leaflets. Rose-pink, cup shaped blooms contain a halo of dark yellow stamens. Clusters of up to 5 flowers are produced over a long period in spring, and in autumn small round hips are covered in bristles. It is an attractive, hardy, landscaping plant. **ZONES 4–10.**

WESTERN CHINA, 1918

## Rosa gallica   *(left)*
syn. 'French Rose'

**DEEP PINK**

Growing to 3 ft (1 m), this free-suckering rose is most certainly much older than indicated. Its dark green stems are almost thornless. The light green foliage is small to medium in size, and somewhat rounded. Each leaf is made up of just five leaflets. Lightly scented single blooms, $2\frac{1}{2}$ in (6 cm) in diameter, are borne in early summer and are clear mid-pink with pronounced yellow stamens. The hips are dull reddish when ripe, held upright and urn shaped. This plant is ideal in a mixed border or with herbs. *Rosa gallica* was important in the development of the cultivated rose. **ZONES 5–11.**

PRE-1759

## Rosa gentiliana
*(right)*
syn. *Rosa polyantha grandiflora*

WHITE

This vigorous climbing rose is capable of attaining heights of 20–30 ft (6–9 m). The thick and firm stems are dark green, mottled with reddish purple and moderately armed with large thorns. The leaves are large, shiny deep green, reddish when young and are made up of seven to nine broadly oblong leaflets. The flowers, which emerge from small creamy yellow buds in mid-summer, are pure white and single, and each is conspicuously endowed with deep yellow stamens and arranged in large clusters. They have a distinct smell of citrus. The orange-red hips are oval. The species is a first-class climber of distinction, and could have arisen as a chance hybrid. ZONES 4–11.

CHINA, CIRCA 1907

*Rosa gigantea*
(rose hip) *(above)*

## Rosa gigantea *(above)*
syn. *Rosa* × *odorata gigantea*

WHITE

A medium to tall climber up to 20 ft (6 m), taller in its natural habitat, *Rosa gigantea* has long, arching branches of purplish-green, randomly armed with hooked thorns. The leaves are made up of seven prominently veined, long and narrow leaflets. The flowers are white, very large—up to 4 in (10 cm) in diameter at their best—sweetly scented and are produced in early summer. Yellowy orange, pear-shaped hips about 1 in (2.5 cm) long appear after the blooms. This tender species is unsuitable for cold climates. It is an ancestor of the early Tea Roses. ZONES 4–11.

BURMA AND CHINA, 1889

### Rosa giraldii *(top)*

MEDIUM PINK

A shrub to a height of some 6 ft (1.8 m) in good soil, *Rosa giraldii* bears long and arching shoots armed with sharp, slender prickles that are mostly arranged in pairs. The broadly oval, mid-green leaves are made up of seven to nine leaflets. Borne singly or a few together in small groups, the flowers are single, soft mid-pink and produced in mid-summer. The small, bright red, roundly oval hips follow. It is not the most conspicuous of Wild Roses, but it is an easygoing plant and worthy of space in any collection. ZONES 4–10.

CHINA, 1897

formation and soft lilac-pink with soft creamy yellow stamens. They appear in early summer, and have no scent. The hips are at first red, then turn to burnished coppery purple in autumn. The species makes an excellent shrub that can be kept in bounds by regular pruning; this practice also encourages many colorful young shoots for the flower arranger, with whom this rose is very popular. It is also good as an informal hedge. ZONES 4–10.

PRE-1820

ROYAL HORTICULTURAL SOCIETY AWARD OF GARDEN MERIT

### Rosa glauca *(right)*
syn. *Rosa rubrifolia*
MEDIUM PINK

This rose is probably much older than the given date. It is a very useful garden species, making an open dense shrub of around 6 ft (1.8 m) tall. The arching, reddish purple, thornless shoots are well furnished with broadly oval, heavily serrated, grayish purple leaves that are made up of five to nine leaflets. Borne in small clusters, the flowers are little more than 1 in (2.5 cm) wide, single, star-like in

## Rosa helenae *(above)*

WHITE

Ever since the species was discovered by
E. H. Wilson in Central China in 1907 and named
for his wife, *Rosa helenae* has been one of the
most popular of the Wild Roses for the garden.
A large scrambler for climbing up into the
branches of trees and covering large expanses of
wall, *R. helenae* attains a height of some 20 ft
(6 m) in fertile soils. The thick, grayish green
stems are heavily mottled brown and have
numerous strong, hooked thorns. The bark of
the older stems is inclined to flake. Dark grayish
green leaves with seven to nine leaflets that are
red when young give good autumn color. The
flowers are single, fragrant and white, and they
appear in large corymbs in early to mid-summer.
These are followed by drooping, oval and bright

orange-red hips. Said to be tender, the species
tolerates all but the most severe frosts. It is one
of the most attractive tree scramblers, and is good
in most soils. *R. helenae* seedlings (hybrids) are
often sold as the original, so problems with
identification have arisen. All of the hybrids are
characterized by long, slender canes covered with
corymbs of fragrant blossoms, 1–2 in (2.5–5 cm)
across, which are white with pronounced yellow
stamens. In autumn there is a spectacular display
of red, oval hips. All forms of this rose are easy
to train as climbers, and look especially good in
trees. They do well on poor soil or in shade. If
they are damaged by frost and need to be cut
down, they will readily produce new growth in
spring. **ZONES 4–11.**

CHINA, 1907

### Rosa holodonta *(rose hips, left)*
syn. *Rosa moyesii rosea*
**LIGHT PINK**

This close relative of *Rosa moyesii* bears small clusters of pretty, light pink, single blooms. After the flowering season has ended, they develop into pear-shaped, glossy orange-red hips. The drooping fruits have persistent calyces, which give the appearance of short tentacles. **ZONES 4–10.**
WESTERN CHINA, 1908

### Rosa hugonis
*(left & below)*
syns 'Father Hugo's Rose', 'Golden Rose of China'
**MEDIUM YELLOW**

John Mattock believes that this rose is much older than the given date. It is a tallish and upright, branching shrub to 7 ft (2.2 m) tall, and made up of brown stems with many sharp, flattish thorns. The fern-like leaves are composed of seven to thirteen leaflets. The flowers are single, bright yellow and borne singly all along the young, wiry lateral branches in late spring and early summer; their texture is silky and sometimes they appear slightly crumpled. Approximately 2 in (5 cm) across, they are followed by small, purple hips later in late summer and autumn. This species has much to commend it; it is more refined than most of the other single yellow roses. It does not seem to mind impoverished soil and is quite hardy in most climates. **ZONES 4–10.**
CIRCA 1899

ROYAL HORTICULTURAL SOCIETY
AWARD OF GARDEN MERIT

*Rosa laevigata* *(top)*
syn. 'The Cherokee
Rose'
WHITE

This evergreen climber
grows up to 15 ft (5 m)
tall in warm climates.
It needs protection
or a sheltered warm
position in cold areas.
The mid-green stems
have well-spaced,
broad-hooked, reddish
thorns and glossy dark
green leaves that are
made up of just three
leaflets. The scented
flowers, which appear
in late spring for a
short season only, are
large, single, creamy
white and have promi-
nent yellow stamens.
Very bristly, oval to
pear-shaped, orange
hips follow the flowers,
but quickly change to
brown with age. This
species has naturalized
in several southern
states of the USA.
*Rosa anemonoides*
'Anemone' and its
sport 'Ramona' are
both related to this
species, as is the lovely,
if shy blooming, 'Silver
Moon'. They are
described in the main
A–Z section of this
book. ZONES 4–10.
CHINA, 1759

## *Rosa longicuspis*
*(right)*
WHITE

A vigorous, almost
evergreen climber to
20 ft (6 m) tall, *Rosa
longiscuspis* has reddish

wood with many
sharply hooked thorns.
The leaves are large,
dark green and glossy,
made up of five to
seven broadly oblong,
serrated leaflets that are
tinted red until they
mature. The flowers,
which appear in mid-
summer, are up to 2 in
(5 cm) across; they are
produced in tightly
packed corymbs, which
are white and waxy with
a scent reminiscent of
bananas. The small
hips are orange-red
and oval in shape.
Until recently,
especially in the UK,
*R. mulliganii* has been
distributed under this
name; it is a similar,
but much hardier
species. ZONES 4–11.
CHINA, 1915

## *Rosa* × *macrantha* 'Macrantha' *(right)*
**LIGHT PINK/WHITE**

This relaxed shrub has arching, dark green stems up to 4 ft (1.2 m) in height and almost twice as broad. The thorns are hooked and numerous, and the matt, dark green leaves are oval and long. Relatively large, scented, single flowers are produced freely in small clusters in early summer; at first they are blush pink, then they fade to off-white, showing many creamy yellow stamens. The hips are dark red and round. Clearly not a true species, this rose is probably closely related to *Rosa gallica*. It makes a useful semi-procumbent shrub, although in some situations it is susceptible to mildew. Despite this affliction, the plant always seems to grow well no matter what the soil. **ZONES 4–11.**

FOUND NEAR LA FLÈCHE, FRANCE, 1923

## *Rosa moschata* *(bottom)*
**syn. 'The Musk Rose'**
**WHITE**

A tall shrub or small climber to 10 ft (3 m) tall with firm, grayish green wood, *Rosa moschata* is sparsely populated with brown, hooked thorns. The gray-green leaves are soft to touch, downy on the undersides, especially on its prominent veins, inclined to droop and made up of five to seven leaflets. The flowers are fragrant and creamy white, with well-spaced single petals; on hot days they reflex backward. Each flower is about 1½ in (4 cm) across and loosely arranged in large corymbs that first appear in late summer, and repeat well into autumn. *R. moschata* is an ancestor of many Modern Garden Roses. Until it was rediscovered by Graham Stuart Thomas in 1963, the species was thought to be lost to cultivation. Prior to then, *R. brunonii* had been erroneously distributed through nurseries as *R. moschata*, a confusion that is still prevalent in some parts of the world. It is an excellent small climber or shrub. *R. moschata* '**Plena**' is a seldom-seen, double form. **ZONES 4–10.**

MEDITERRANEAN EUROPE, 1614

## Rosa moyesii  (right)
MEDIUM RED

A sturdy and angular shrub to 10 ft (3 m) tall, this species has strong, reddish brown stems with numerous sharp, stout thorns often arranged in pairs. Each leaf has seven to eleven, mid-green to grayish green, serrated and oval leaflets. The flowers, which appear in early summer, are arranged in small groups and are dark glowing red and have very prominent golden stamens; the petals are often dusted with their profuse pollen. The hips appear in late summer and are drooping, flagon-shaped and bright orange-red. These are probably of more garden value than its flowers. *Rosa moyesii* has brought forth several good Modern Shrubs over the years, including 'Eos', 'Geranium', 'Highdownensis' and 'Sealing Wax', which can be found in the main A–Z section of this book. *R. moyesii fargesii* is a pink-flowered form that is similar to the species in all respects, except that it is not as tall.
ZONES 4–10.

CHINA, CIRCA 1890

## Rosa mulliganii (right)
WHITE

This vigorous scrambler of distinction produces long, dark green branches with broad strong thorns. It grows up to 20 ft (6 m) tall. The glossy dark green leaves are reddish purple when young, and are made up of five to seven large, elliptical leaflets. Fragrant flowers are borne in broad panicles in early summer; they are large for this type of climber, attaining a size of up to 2½ in (6 cm) in good soil and an agreeable climate. The smooth and broadly oval hips have persistent sepals, and are orange-red. This species is quite hardy, and is said to occasionally give a modest repeat-bloom in favorably warm conditions. It is an excellent garden-worthy species that has, until recently, been wrongly and widely distributed as *Rosa longicuspis*.
ZONES 4–11.

CHINA, 1917

### Rosa multiflora
**(right)**

WHITE

This small climber, rambler or relaxed arching shrub is dense in habit with wiry, greenish brown branches that are only partially armed with darkish thorns. The leaves are made up of seven to nine leaflets, which are soft but leathery, mid-green and oblong. Small single flowers with a distinctly fruity scent are produced in great profusion in mid-summer in upright conical clusters. The flowers are usually creamy white, but some are pink-edged. They are followed by small and rounded, inconspicuous orange hips each autumn. This species propagates easily from seeds or cuttings, so has been used widely as a hedging plant. It also makes a good rootstock; it is still commonly used for this purpose in commercial rose production, especially in warm climates. In some areas, especially in the USA, it has become so naturalized that it is considered a despised weed. It is an important ancestor of many good summer-flowering Ramblers. *Rosa multiflora carnea*, introduced in 1804, is a

stronger-growing, double, light pink form. **R. multiflora cathayensis**, which first appeared in 1902, is similar in most respects to the species except for its color, a shade of soft blush pink. **R. multiflora watsoniana** (syn. 'Bamboo Rose') is treated as a novelty because of its creamy variegated leaves. It was introduced in 1870. 'De la Grifferaie' and 'Seven Sisters' are also descendants of *R. multiflora*, and the latter appears in the main A–Z section of this book. **ZONES 4–11.**

KOREA AND JAPAN, 1862

### Rosa nitida   (bottom)
MEDIUM PINK

This well-foliated, dense and short-growing shrub has many spines and prickles. It grows up to 3 ft (1 m) in good soils and is particularly good on its own roots

as a free-suckering ground cover. The leaves are composed of seven to nine small, serrated, narrowly oblong leaflets, which are glossy dark green and dull and downy on the undersides; they change to brownish red in autumn. Single blooms—up to 2 in (5 cm) across—are borne in mid-summer. They are bright mid-pink, silky in texture and are followed in late summer and autumn

by small, globular and slightly hairy bright red hips. This species grows readily from seed and is consequently used extensively for large-scale ground cover work. **'Corylus'** *(Rosa nitida × R. rugosa)* is a useful off-spring that performs in much the same way as its parent, except that it grows a little taller and has more intense autumn coloring. **ZONES 4–11.**

NORTH AMERICA, CIRCA 1807

## Rosa nutkana
syn. 'Nutka Rose'
MEDIUM PINK

This medium-sized shrub to 5 ft (1.5 m) tall is upright in habit with slender purplish brown stems. The thorns, which are generally found on older wood only, are straight and sharp. The young shoots are bristly, and the leaves are made up of five to nine smooth, broadly elliptical, dark green, serrated leaflets that have downy undersides. Produced singly, the flowers are single, lavender-purple with pronounced creamy yellow stamens. They are up to $2\frac{1}{2}$ in (6 cm) across and appear in mid-summer. Very conspicuous, plumply oval, bright red hips follow. *Rosa nutkana* 'Cantab', introduced in 1927, is the best-known hybrid, being deep pink and flowering late in summer. It is slightly taller than the species. 'Schoener's Nutkana', another garden-worthy hybrid, appears in the main A–Z section of this book. ZONES 4–11.

NORTH AMERICA, CIRCA 1876

## Rosa pendulina
*(top)*
syns 'Alpine Rose',
*Rosa alpina*
DEEP PINK/MAUVE

This upright, medium to tall shrub is about 6 ft (1.8 m) tall and has reddish purple, almost thornless stems. The leaves are composed of seven to nine slightly serrated, oblong leaflets which are dark green with purple undertones. The blooms are produced singly or in small groups of up to five, and are deep mauve-pink with prominent creamy yellow stamens. They are produced in late spring and early summer. The slim and flask-shaped hips are bright orange-red. *Rosa pendulina* is a good shrub where a thornless rose is wanted, giving excellent, richly colored autumn foliage that combines well with the fruit. ZONES 4–10.

EUROPE, 1789

## Rosa pimpinellifolia
*(bottom)*
syns *Rosa spinosissima*,
'Altaica', 'Burnet Rose',
'Scots Rose'
WHITE

This short-growing, dense and prickly shrub suckers freely when grown on its own roots. The branches are upright or only slightly arching and greenish brown, thickly populated with both sharp thorns and bristles. There are five to eleven heavily serrated and broadly oval leaflets per leaf, which look almost fern-like *en masse*. They are darkish green, changing to russet-brown in autumn. The flowers are borne in great profusion in late spring to early summer, and they are creamy white, single and quite beautiful with golden brown stamens. The globular hips are mahogany to black when ripe. *Rosa pimpinellifolia altaica*, (syn. *R. p.* 'Grandiflora'), introduced from western Asia in 1820, is a taller grower with larger, soft primrose flowers. It is a superior plant to the species, but both are worthwhile in any type of garden. In Victorian times, *R. pimpinellifolia* was extensively used as a parent, giving rise to many double and single, short-growing shrub roses in a variety of colors. They include such varieties as 'Mary Queen of Scots' and 'William III'. In the 1950s some excellent shrub roses were raised in Germany from this species, such as 'Frühlingsgold'. These can be found in the main A–Z section of this book. ZONES 3–11.

EUROPE, VERY ANCIENT

*Rosa roxburghii plena* *(above)*

### Rosa pisocarpa
*(top left)*
MEDIUM PINK

This summer flowering shrub bears small pink flowers, about 1 in (2.5 cm) in diameter. They are carried on very short stalks in many clusters, and are followed by globular hips. ZONES 4–10.
WESTERN NORTH AMERICA, CIRCA 1882

### Rosa pomifera
syns *Rosa villosa*, 'Apple Rose'
MEDIUM PINK

This dense shrub to 6 ft (1.8 m) carries grayish green wood, sometimes slightly mottled with purple, that is randomly armed with straight sharp prickles. The young wood is reddish. The plentiful foliage made up of five to nine broadly oblong and generously serrated leaflets is dull grayish green and downy to touch. In mid-summer, usually in clusters of three, but sometimes only singly, clear pink, slightly fragrant flowers, some 2 in (5 cm) across, are borne. The hips are very bristly, globular to oval, medium sized, and deep red when fully ripe. 'Duplex', a semi-double form, which is more free-flowering, appears in the main A–Z section of this book. ZONES 4–11.
EUROPE AND ASIA

### Rosa primula
*(top right)*
syn. 'Incense Rose'
LIGHT YELLOW

The main characteristic of this rose is its fabulously incense-scented foliage that adorns a medium-sized shrub 2–4 ft (60–120 cm) tall. The leaves are small, and the thin, flexible stems are covered with many red prickles. In very early spring, *Rosa primula* carries a flush of yellowish white blooms. In North America, it was wrongly cultivated for a long time as *R. ecae*, which is a different species. ZONES 4–11.
TURKESTAN TO NORTHERN CHINA, 1910

ROYAL HORTICULTURAL SOCIETY AWARD OF GARDEN MERIT

### Rosa roxburghii
syns 'Burr Rose', 'Chestnut Rose'
MEDIUM PINK

This is an interesting and somewhat un-rose-like shrub to 8 ft (2.5 m). It is angular and stiff in habit and the bark of the buffy brown stems flakes and peels with age; it is well armed with stout thorns that protrude from just below its leaves in pairs. The leaves are composed of seven to fifteen mid-to dark green, small, oblong leaflets, each distinctly hairy. In early summer, reasonably large, bright pink, satiny flowers are produced with prominent bosses of soft creamy yellow stamens. The fruit is very distinctive, like small chestnuts in their husks, turning from green to russet brown as they age. *Rosa roxburghii normalis* is similar in all respects, except that it has blush pink to white flowers. *R. roxburghii plena*, introduced in 1814, is an excellent double, deep pink form that was known long before the species. Its beautiful flowers are often hidden by the foliage. ZONES 4–11.
CHINA AND JAPAN, 1908

*Rosa rugosa* (right)
syns 'Hedgehog Rose',
'The Japanese Rose'

**MAUVE**

This rose makes a
dense, free-branching
shrub to a height of
8 ft (2.5 m). Its fawny
brown stems are
heavily endowed with
sharp, similar colored
thorns. The leaves
usually have seven to
nine leaflets that are
dark green and semi-
glossy, broadly oval
and serrated, often
appearing wrinkled.
They change to shades
of rich yellow in the
autumn. The single,
scented flowers, pro-
duced singly or several
together, open to 2½ in
(6.5 cm) across and are
bright deep pink with
soft yellow stamens.
They continue to
appear from early
summer through to
autumn. The hips are
large, globose, bright
red, and held on short
stalks, and are a major
ornamental feature of
this species and of its
many forms and hybrids.
*Rosa rugosa alba* is
a white form that is
particularly good with
larger flowers up to
3 in (8 cm) across.
Its fruits are more
conspicuous in both
size and color. *R. rugosa
rubra* is a reddish
purple form. *R. rugosa
kamtchatica,* intro-
duced in 1770, is
probably the result of

a chance cross with
*R. rugosa* and another
species. It is less coarse
than *R. rugosa* with
greenish wood and
fewer prickles, and its
foliage is less wrinkly
and brighter green.
It has bright pink,
single flowers. *R. rugosa*
has been extensively
hybridized over the
years, resulting in a
wide selection of
healthy and hardy
cultivars. 'Roseraie de
l'Haÿ', 'Blanc Double
de Coubert' and 'Fru
Dagmar Hastrup' are
just three of its better-
known offspring, which
can be found in the
main A–Z section of
this book. ZONES 3–10.

CHINA AND JAPAN, PRE-1854

## *Rosa sempervirens*
(bottom)

**WHITE**

This vigorous climbing,
evergreen species up to

20 ft (6 m) has flexible,
long and trailing,
dark green stems
armed with moderate
numbers of reddish
prickles. The leaves
are made up of five to
seven long and pointed,
oval and glossy leaflets.
The single flowers are
produced in corymbs,
and are up to 1½ in
(4 cm) in diameter,
white, fragrant and
appear in mid-summer.
The oval hips are bright
red. *Rosa sempervirens*

is important as the
progenitor of several
good Rambler Roses
known collectively as
'The Evergreens'.
The species is also
significant in playing
a part in the early
development of the
Ayrshires. It is not fully
hardy, although its
offspring appear to
tolerate much lower
temperatures.
ZONES 4–11.

MEDITERRANEAN AND
NORTHERN AFRICA, 1629

## *Rosa sericea pteracantha*  *(above left)*
syns *Rosa omeiensis pteracantha,*
'Wingthorn Rose'
WHITE

This tall, angular shrub becomes stiff and rugged with age. Its older wood is brown with numerous fawny vicious thorns, and will reach a height of 10 ft (3 m) if left unpruned; however, the shrub is better kept to much lower proportions, for by so doing, its most ornamental features, which are displayed in the new growth each year, will be encouraged. The young shoots are purplish and armed with many large, translucent cherry red, wing-like thorns all along their length. The leaves are small, dark green and fern-like, and made up of seven to eleven small leaflets, hairy on their undersides. Composed of only four white petals, the flowers are about 1½ in (4 cm) across and appear in late spring. The fruit is small, plump and yellow-orange, and of little significance overall. *Rosa sericea chrysocarpa* has yellow fruits.
**ZONES 4–10.**

CHINA, 1890

## *Rosa setipoda*  *(above right)*
LIGHT PINK

This sturdy shrub up to 12 ft (4 m) unpruned has brownish older wood. It is very branching in habit, with sparsely arranged stout and pointed thorns. The leaves are composed of seven to nine, dark green, broadly oval and deeply serrated leaflets. The flowers, which appear in early summer, are about 2 in (5 cm) across, clear pink, paler in the centers, and have large bosses of creamy yellow stamens with profuse pollen. The petals are sometimes notched on the outer edges. These blooms are arranged in clusters and are scented. It is the hips, though, that make this rose so valuable as a garden plant; these can be up to 2½ in (6.5 cm) long and are plumply flagon shaped, whiskery, and bright orange-red.
**ZONES 4–10.**

CHINA, 1895

## *Rosa soulieana*
WHITE

This tall shrub is capable of growing up to 15 ft (5 m) in good conditions. Its relaxed habit also provides it with a very broad girth. The long, grayish green stems are covered with an armature of long and slender, sharp yellowish prickles, and the leaves, plentiful and soft grayish green, are made up of seven to nine leaflets, which are broadly elliptical, sharply serrated and slightly downy to touch. The flowers, about 1½ in (4 cm) across are single, white and fragrant and borne in tightly packed corymbs along the arching branches in mid-summer. They are quite a sight when a mature plant is in full flush. A great abundance of small round orange hips follow. *Rosa soulieana* is probably best in climates where severe frosts are not a regular occurrence. **ZONES 4–10.**

CHINA, 1896

ROYAL HORTICULTURAL SOCIETY AWARD OF GARDEN MERIT

## Rosa stellata mirifica
syns 'The Gooseberry Rose', 'The Sacramento Rose'
**MAUVE**

This unusual little shrub to 3 ft (1 m) is in many ways more like a gooseberry bush than a rose. It is dense and free branching, very prickly with slender pointed light green spines and many bristles. The leaves are made up of three to five grayish green, broadly oval and serrated leaflets. Single flowers are produced; they are lilac-pink with orange-yellow stamens and 1½ in (4 cm) across. Globular to urn-shaped, bristly, inconspicuous red hips follow. It is quite a hardy rose, but is better grown in warm climates. *Rosa stellata*, introduced from southern USA in 1829, is shorter with deep purple flowers. **ZONES 4–10.**

SOUTHWESTERN NORTH AMERICA, 1916

## Rosa sweginzowii
*(top)*
**MEDIUM PINK**

This upright and sturdy shrub up to 15 ft (5 m) carries thick, brownish green wood with many bristles and large, flat, sharp thorns. The leaves are made up of seven to eleven oval

to oblong, bright green, serrated leaflets, which have smooth uppersides and downy undersides with a prickly central rib. The flowers are 1½ in (4 cm) in diameter, and are produced singly or in threes together; they are bright pink with creamy yellow stamens, and appear in early summer. The hips are flagon shaped, slightly hairy and bright red. If space permits, this is a very showy shrub, for it is best left unpruned and allowed to develop its natural stature. *Rosa sweginzowii macrocarpa* is a superior form that came later from Germany. It has larger flowers and hips, and the color is much deeper. **ZONES 3–10.**

CHINA, 1909

## Rosa tomentosa
*(above)*
syn. *Rosa cuspidata*
**LIGHT PINK**

Of upright and sturdy stature, this medium to tall shrub, 7 ft (2.2 m) tall, has greenish gray stems, that have stout, strong and sharp thorns. The leaves have five to seven leaflets that are broadly elliptical, dull grayish green, serrated and slightly furry to touch. The flowers are approximately 1½ in (4 cm) wide, single and light pink. Small and oval red hips follow. *Rosa tomentosa* is of little importance as a garden plant and is perhaps best grown as a hedge. **ZONES 4–10.**

EUROPE AND ASIA MINOR, 1820

in early summer. Medium-sized, flask-shaped, bright scarlet and polished hips follow. This is a very ornamental species that tolerates all types of soil and climate. **ZONES 4–11.**

HIMALAYAS AND TURKEY, 1879

### Rosa wichurana
*(bottom)*
syns 'Memorial Rose', *Rosa luciliae*
WHITE

This semi-evergreen Rambler or prostrate trailing rose up to 20 ft (6 m) tall is especially good in fertile soil. Its long and pliable, dark green stems are sparsely armed with hooked thorns. The plant is well foliated with glossy dark green leaves, each with seven to nine rounded leaflets. Conical clusters of single white, fragrant flowers—$1\frac{1}{2}$ in (4 cm) wide—appear in mid- to late summer. Small, oval to round, dark red hips follow. This really is a first-class garden plant in its own right, especially when allowed to expand as a ground cover, since it makes an impenetrable mound. It is also good when scrambling up into the branches of trees. *R. wichurana poteriifolia* is a compact form of the species. **ZONES 3–11.**

CHINA AND JAPAN, 1843

serious rose lover should be without; it makes an excellent hedge. *Rosa virginiana* 'Alba' is a white form. Although it performs in much the same way as the pink species, it is less showy in most respects. **ZONES 3–11.**

NORTH AMERICA, PRE-1807

ROYAL HORTICULTURAL SOCIETY AWARD OF GARDEN MERIT

### Rosa webbiana
*(top right)*
MEDIUM PINK

This graceful shrub attains a height and width of 5 ft (1.5 m). Its flexible stems are reddish purple, especially when young, later turning brownish; they develop long and sharp, straight, creamy yellow thorns as they age. The leaves are very small and broadly elliptical, bluish dark green, and made up of five to nine leaflets. The flowers are borne singly or in threes together, are lilac-pink, $1\frac{1}{2}$ in (4 cm) in diameter and produced

### Rosa virginiana
*(rose hips, top left)*
syns *Rosa lucida*, 'Virginia Rose'
MEDIUM PINK

This upright-growing, small and free-suckering shrub to 5 ft (1.5 m) produces many reddish brown stems each with a few hooked brown thorns; the younger wood is often bristly. The leaves are made up of between seven and nine leaflets, which are glossy bright green at first, then turn

to rich russet-red and yellow in autumn, broadly elliptical and generously serrated. Slightly scented, bright pink flowers, which are sometimes mottled slightly deeper, and up to $2\frac{1}{2}$ in (6.5 cm) across with many long yellow stamens, are produced either singly or in small groups over a long period during summer. The rounded hips are a shiny orange-red. This is an excellent garden shrub which no

## Rosa willmottiae
*(above)*

MAUVE

Wider than tall, this shrub will attain a height of about 10 ft (3 m) in good soil. It produces long thin shoots that are purplish red and often covered in grayish bloom that is armed with tiny bristles and sharp prickles. The leaves are made up of three to nine, small and grayish, heavily serrated, oval leaflets. The flowers, which are borne all along the branches, are single, purplish pink and slightly scented, first appearing in early summer. Small, orange-red, pear-shaped hips follow. All these distinctive features make a charming, graceful shrub that is worthy of space in any garden. **ZONES 3–11.**

CHINA, 1904

## Rosa woodsii
*(above right)*
syn. 'Mountain Rose'

MEDIUM PINK

This shrub grows to 6 ft (1.8 m) in most situations, but it is not of great garden value. *Rosa woodsii fendleri,* introduced from North America in 1888, is superior to *R. woodsii* and more commonly grown. It is an upright shrub that freely produces stems of purplish gray with an abundance of slender prickles, although the slim and arching, flowering branches have fewer prickles. The leaflets are five to seven per leaf and are widely oval, serrated and grayish dark green. In mid-summer, flowers are produced singly or in twos and threes; they are lilac-pink and about 1½ in (4 cm) across. The fruit is about the size and shape of a cherry and bright red, their weight often causing the strong branches to arch over in an attractive way. It is a good shrub for hedging or for a wild garden. **ZONES 3–11.**

NORTH AMERICA, 1820

## Rosa xanthina
*(above)*
syn. 'Manchu Rose'

MEDIUM YELLOW

This is an upright, branching shrub to 6 ft (1.8 m) tall, with smooth mahogany brown stems and many thorns. The leaves are made up of seven to fifteen dark green leaflets. The flowers are bright yellow, single or occasionally semi-double, and they have golden brown stamens. They are borne in abundance in late spring, but there is only a small crop of oval, brownish red hips. *Rosa xanthina lindleyii* is a consistently semi-double form. *R. xanthina spontanea* is often confused with 'Canary Bird' (probably *R. hugonis × R. xanthina*), which is by far the best known of this group. It appears in the main A–Z section of this book. **ZONES 3–11.**

CHINA AND KOREA, 1906

A

### 'Aalsmeer Gold'
*(above)*
syn. 'Bekola'

MODERN, LARGE-FLOWERED/
HYBRID TEA, DEEP YELLOW,
REPEAT-FLOWERING

'Aalsmeer Gold' has
been a cut-flower rose
for growing under glass
for 20 years. It is also
an excellent garden
rose, bearing its deep
yellow 25-petalled
flowers both singly and
in small clusters. The
buds are tinged with
red on the outer petals
when grown outdoors.
The medium-sized,
very well-formed
blooms have high
centers and hold well,
both on the bush and
when picked. The
foliage is glossy dark
green and abundant
and the plant has a
very bushy growth
habit and a quick
repeat. There are no
disease problems.
ZONES 4–9.

KORDES, GERMANY, 1978

'BEROLINA' × SEEDLING

### 'Abbaye de Cluny'   MEIbrinpay

MODERN, LARGE-FLOWERED/HYBRID TEA, APRICOT BLEND,
REPEAT-FLOWERING

This very free-blooming rose has fragrant flowers
of an apricot blend that hold their form rather
well. They are repeat-flowering. A bushy, healthy
grower with dark green foliage, it is suitable as a
bedding rose or as a standard. Propagation is by
budding. This variety, which has a remarkable
track record for awards in European trials, is
curiously not as widely grown as it deserves to be.
ZONES 4–9.

MEILLAND, FRANCE, 1996

'JUST JOEY' × (MEIRESIF × MEINAN)

MONZA GOLD MEDAL 1993, LYON GOLD MEDAL 1994, PLUS BELLE DE
FRANCE 1994, BELFAST GOLD MEDAL 1995

### 'Abbeyfield Rose'

COCbrose   *(below left)*

MODERN, LARGE-FLOWERED/
HYBRID TEA, DEEP PINK,
REPEAT-FLOWERING

'Abbeyfield Rose' has
deep pink to rose red,
very double and large,
well-formed flowers
consisting of 35 petals;
they have a slight
fragrance and are
repeat-flowering. Mid-
green, semi-glossy foli-
age appears on a bushy
plant of medium height,
which makes for a
good bedding plant or
a well-proportioned
standard. It is hardy
and moderately resist-
ant to disease and
should be propagated
by budding. It was
named to raise the pro-
file of a charitable trust.
ZONES 4–9.

COCKER, UK, 1985

'NATIONAL TRUST' × 'SILVER
JUBILEE'

GLASGOW GOLDEN PRIZE 1990,
ROYAL HORTICULTURAL SOCIETY
AWARD OF GARDEN MERIT 1993

### 'Abbotswood'

MODERN, MODERN SHRUB,
MEDIUM PINK

'Abbotswood' has pink
double flowers that are
slightly fragrant and
which appear right
throughout summer.
With its tall and
spreading habit it is
perhaps better suited to
the wild garden. It is a
healthy, vigorous var-
iety that is generally
propagated from
cuttings. **ZONES 3–9.**

HILLING, UK, 1954

A CHANCE HYBRID OF *ROSA
CANINA* × AN UNKNOWN
GARDEN VARIETY

### 'Abraham Darby'

AUScot   *(below)*

syns 'Abraham',
'Country Darby'

MODERN, MODERN SHRUB,
ORANGE-PINK,
REPEAT-FLOWERING

The cup-formed, very
large flowers of this rose
appear in small clusters;
they are a peachy pink/
apricot blend and have
a strong fragrance.
The variety has dark
green foliage and bushy
growth that spreads
slightly but is well
shaped and tall. It
enjoys moderate resist-
ance to disease but can
be susceptible to rust.
Popular in a shrub
border, it is repeat-
flowering and was
named after one of
the founders of the
Industrial Revolution.
**ZONES 4–9.**

AUSTIN, UK, 1985

'ALOHA' × 'YELLOW CUSHION'

### 'Acapulco'   DICblender   *(right)*

MODERN, LARGE-FLOWERED/HYBRID TEA, RED BLEND,
REPEAT-FLOWERING

The beautifully shaped long ivory yellow buds
with scarlet tips on 'Acapulco' merge into
classically shaped double flowers. The blooms,
which are produced singly or in small clusters,
are moderately fragrant. It is an upright grower
with handsome dark green foliage and is
reasonably disease resistant. Originally tested
and launched as a cut-flower variety, it is gaining popularity as a very good garden plant.
**ZONES 4–9.**

DICKSON, UK, 1997

PARENTAGE UNKNOWN

A

## 'Acey Deucy'

SAVathree *(above)*

MODERN, MINIATURE, MEDIUM
RED, REPEAT-FLOWERING

The vibrant electric red blooms contain approximately 20 petals, with a high-centered Large-flowered form suitable for exhibition. A black overlay on the reverse of the petals gives additional depth to the color. The bush may be slow to establish in cooler climates but the growth habit, 12–24 in (30–60 cm) tall, is quite compact and is complemented by small, mid-green, semi-glossy foliage. In warmer climates the florets are usually borne singly and have a light fragrance. It naturally grows one bloom per stem exclusively and can last 3–5 days. 'Acey Deucy' is one of many great Miniatures developed during the late 1970s and early 1980s from experimenting with 'Sheri Anne' as pollen parent.
ZONES 5–11.

SAVILLE, USA, 1982

('YELLOW JEWEL' × 'TAMANGO')
× 'SHERI ANNE'

## 'Adair Roche'

*(below)*

MODERN, LARGE-FLOWERED/
HYBRID TEA, PINK BLEND,
REPEAT-FLOWERING

The large pink double flowers of 'Adair Roche', which are composed of 30 petals, have a silver reverse. They are well formed and slightly fragrant. The mid-green, glossy foliage is borne on a vigorous bush that is resistant to disease. Used as a bedding plant or as a standard, it is repeat-flowering. It was named for the architect who designed McGredy's house.
ZONES 4–9.

MCGREDY, NEW ZEALAND, 1968

'PADDY MCGREDY' × SEEDLING
OF 'FEMINA'

BELFAST GOLD MEDAL 1971

## 'Adam' *(right)*

OLD, TEA, MEDIUM PINK, REPEAT-FLOWERING

'Adam' helped to establish the reputation of the new class of Tea Roses. It was popular throughout the nineteenth century, having been raised by Monsieur Adam in his garden at Rheims, France. Semi-double, copper-pink, large globular blooms appear in clusters on short canes with hooked, purple prickles. The buds are very attractive. Its only weakness is a slight tendency to mildew in wet weather. 'Adam', a Tea Rose that really smells like tea, is easy to grow and is stronger than most of its kin as it will survive in cooler climates.

**ZONES 5–10.**

ADAM, FRANCE, 1838

POSSIBLY 'HUME'S BLUSH' × 'ROSE EDOUARD'

## 'Adam Messerich' *(above)*

OLD, BOURBON, MEDIUM RED, REPEAT-FLOWERING

This is one of the more popular Bourbons because of its disease resistance and abundant rebloom. The rose red blossoms are medium sized, semi-double and cupped and fade in strong sunlight. The growth is upright and vigorous, and the bush will reach 5 ft by 4 ft (1.5 m by 1.2 m) at maturity. There is a slight raspberry fragrance.

It is frequently seen in bouquets because of its erect stems and flowers. When the rose opens, the lovely stamens vie for attention. This was very popular in Victorian England, and Bourbon Roses frequently appear in paintings of the time.

**ZONES 5–10.**

LAMBERT, GERMANY, 1920

'FRAU OBERHOFGARTNER SINGER' × (SEEDLING OF 'LOUISE ODIER' × 'LOUIS PHILIPPE')

A

## 'Adélaïde d'Orléans' *(above)*
syn. 'Léopoldine d'Orléans'
OLD, SEMPERVIRENS, WHITE

The small buds of this gracious rambling rose are
rosy pink before opening into pale white flowers
that enfold striking yellow stamens. The clusters
of loosely double blooms offer a delicate primrose
scent. Sempervirens Roses are a result of the
work of Monsieur Jacques, gardener to the Duc
d'Orléans at the Chateau de Neuilly; the duke
later became King Louis Philippe, after whom
several roses were named. *Rosa sempervirens*
blood gives them a strong constitution. In mid-
summer, the long, slender canes with red prickles
are covered with blooms. It looks wonderful on
arches or pergolas—an attractive addition to any
garden. **ZONES 5–11.**

JACQUES, FRANCE, 1826

PARENTAGE UNKNOWN

ROYAL HORTICULTURAL SOCIETY AWARD OF GARDEN MERIT 1993

## 'Admiral Rodney'
*(below)*

MODERN, LARGE-FLOWERED/
HYBRID TEA, PINK BLEND,
REPEAT-FLOWERING

This Large-flowered
variety is grown for its
potential and for its
appeal, and almost ex-
clusively for exhibition
purposes. A robust
grower, it has large,
glossy dark green
foliage. A bushy plant
with classically shaped,
fragrant blooms of rose
pink and a deeper re-
verse, composed of 45
petals, it is a respected
favorite on the show
bench. **ZONES 4–9.**

TREW, UK, 1973

PARENTAGE UNKNOWN

## 'Adolf Horstmann'
*(right)*
syn. 'Adolph Horstmann'

MODERN, LARGE-FLOWERED/
HYBRID TEA, YELLOW BLEND,
REPEAT-FLOWERING

This has rich yellow-orange, medium-sized, double flowers with a classic Large-flowered form. They are slightly fragrant. With its glossy foliage, vigorous upright form and repeat-flowering capacity it is a good subject for bedding or for growing as a standard. Reasonably healthy and free flowering, it was named after the principal of a well-known nursery in northern Germany. **ZONES 4–9.**

KORDES, GERMANY, 1971
'COLOR WONDER' × 'DR A. J. VERHAGE'

## 'Agatha Christie'
KORmeita *(right)*
syn. 'Ramira'

MODERN, LARGE-FLOWERED
CLIMBER, PINK,
REPEAT-FLOWERING

This rose bears large, fragrant, glowing pink blooms. The foliage is dark green and glossy on a reasonably healthy plant. It is a great rose for walls or pillars, and it also makes an attractive large shrub. It was named for the British mystery writer, who died in 1976. **ZONES 4–9.**

KORDES, GERMANY, 1990
PARENTAGE UNKNOWN

A

## 'Agathe Incarnata' *(above)*

OLD, GALLICA, MEDIUM PINK

Though the blossoms look fragile, this beautiful rose is a member of one of the hardiest groups of roses. The pale, soft pink blooms are very freely produced in sizeable clusters, each bloom about $1\frac{1}{2}$ in (4 cm) across, perhaps slightly bigger in good fertile soil, which it prefers. The fragrant blooms, which appear in early summer, are composed of many narrow petals to form flat, often quartered flowers with a pronounced button eye in the center. The very thin petals are not happy in wet weather. This is a fairly prickly shrub of tidy habit to some 4 ft (1.2 m) in height. The foliage is grayish green and soft in texture. This Gallica has remained popular ever since its introduction. **ZONES 3–9.**

PRE-1811

UNKNOWN GALLICA × UNKNOWN DAMASK

## 'Aglaia'

syn. 'Yellow Rambler'

MODERN, RAMBLER, LIGHT YELLOW

Although not popular with the critics, this is one of the most dependable Ramblers; it also has the distinction of being the first yellow-flowered one. It is known that *Rosa multiflora*, when used in crosses with yellow roses, reverts to its white origin, so the yellow in 'Aglaia' fades rather quickly during its long blooming period. But the healthy foliage and profuse blooms, wedded to a strong fragrance, are reasons enough to add it to a collection. *Aglaia* is one of the Three Graces in Greek mythology; the remaining two, *Euphrosyne* and *Thalia*, were used by the breeder to name other creations. 'Aglaia' is thought to be a parent of 'Trier', a very important breeding rose. **ZONES 5–10.**

SCHMITT, FRANCE, 1896

*ROSA MULTIFLORA* × 'RÊVE D'OR'

### 'Agnes' *(right)*

MODERN, HYBRID RUGOSA, LIGHT YELLOW

Yellow Rugosas are few and far between and not
particularly distinguished at present, although
this one is more successful. The large double
blooms are a pale amber with a deeper center,
are fragrant and produced in small clusters. The
foliage is typically rugose, that is, light, glossy and
wrinkled. It is a vigorous healthy bush that is
listed as summer flowering, although in warm
autumns there will be a second crop of color.
It is propagated from cuttings or by budding.
ZONES 3–9.

SAUNDERS, CANADA, 1900

*ROSA RUGOSA* × *R. FOETIDA PERSIANA*

### 'Agnes Bernauer' KORnauer
*(left)*

MODERN, LARGE-FLOWERED/HYBRID TEA, LIGHT PINK,
REPEAT-FLOWERING

'Agnes Bernauer' has light pink flowers with
a slight fragrance. Very free flowering, it has
a bushy, healthy growth habit and is an ideal
plant for bedding and for growing as a standard.
It has good repeat-flowering capabilities and is
propagated by budding. ZONES 4–9.

KORDES, GERMANY, 1989

PARENTAGE UNKNOWN

### 'Aïcha' *(left)*

OLD, SCOTS, DEEP YELLOW

The special virtue of the Scots
Roses is their hardiness and
many hybrids have been bred
from them for cool conditions,
notably by Kordes in Germany.
'Aïcha' has probably been pre-
empted by a look-alike from
Kordes, 'Frühlingsgold', which
is better known. There are two
main types of Scots Roses, the
low-growing ones and the taller
Asian types. This variety has
deep yellow flowers that are
large and very fragrant. It is a
bushy, vigorous grower with
light green foliage. ZONES 4–9.

PETERSEN, DENMARK, 1966

'SOUVENIR DE JACQUES VERSCHUREN' ×
'GULDTOP'

A

## 'Aimable Rouge'
### syn. 'Le Triomphe'

OLD, GALLICA, DEEP PINK, REPEAT-FLOWERING

There is an interesting rendering of this rose
in a drawing by the French artist Redouté
(1759–1840). The purple-pink blooms with some
veining of deeper pink have a strong perfume.
They are almost serrated, rounded and well
formed. The bush can reach 5 ft (1.5 m) and
the flowers repeat well. It was very popular in
Europe in the 1820s. **ZONES 4–10.**

VIBERT, FRANCE, 1819

PARENTAGE UNKNOWN

## 'Aimée Vibert' *(top left)*
### syns 'Bouquet de la Mariée', 'Nivea'

OLD, NOISETTE, WHITE, REPEAT-FLOWERING

The buds and blooms together offer an enchanting scene, with the brilliant foliage adding to this
charming rose. The outer petals are concave and
the inner ones are small and tousled. The flowers
are medium sized in umbel-like clusters, and the
buds have a red flush. The strong musk scent
helped this rose to become the most popular of
the early Noisettes. Vibert raised the plant at his
test grounds at Longjumeau near Paris, and he
named it after his devoted daughter. 'Aimée
Vibert' may take 3 years before it blooms as it
expends its early energy in producing canes and
bountiful foliage. It is at its best in autumn.
**ZONES 5–10.**

VIBERT, FRANCE, 1828

'CHAMPNEYS' PINK CLUSTER' × HYBRID OF *ROSA SEMPERVIRENS*

## 'Alain' *(bottom left)*

MODERN, CLUSTER-FLOWERED/FLORIBUNDA, MEDIUM RED,
REPEAT-FLOWERING

This variety was the first of a notable collection of
Cluster-flowered Roses bred by Francis Meilland,
the distinguished breeder of 'Peace'. A very free-
flowering plant growing to medium height, it has
semi-double, large bright carmine red blooms
that are slightly fragrant, and each has 28 petals.
Repeat-flowering, it has dark glossy foliage and is
disease resistant; it makes a good bedding subject.
Budding is the principal method of propagation.
This rose was named after the son of Francis
Meilland. **'Climbing Alain'** was raised from
a sport by Delforge of Belgium in 1957. It is
particularly popular in France. **ZONES 4–9.**

MEILLAND, FRANCE, 1948

('GUINEÉ' × 'SKYROCKET') × 'ORANGE TRIUMPH'

GENEVA GOLD MEDAL 1948

### 'Alain Blanchard'
*(above)*

OLD, GALLICA, MAUVE

This is a wide-growing shrub that in good soil can attain a height of 5 ft (1.5 m). The stems are a burnished, dark green and have several thorns. The foliage is mid-green and well serrated. The fragrant flowers are up to 3 in (8 cm) across when fully open, rather more than single in make-up and usually arranged in clusters. The first blooms appear in early summer, from when it goes on flowering spasmodically for about another month; they are deep crimson, mottled with blotches of purple and deep pink. A feature of this rose is the prominent display of brilliant golden stamens, which set off the flowers to beautiful effect. This is an easy to grow shrub but is never one to give a mass display. ZONES 5–10.

VIBERT, FRANCE, 1839

*ROSA CENTIFOLIA* × *R. GALLICA*

### 'Alba Maxima'
*(above right)*

syns *Rosa alba maxima*, 'Great Double White', 'Maxima', 'The Jacobite Rose', 'Cheshire Rose'

OLD, ALBA, WHITE

This rose suffers from too many names, only a few of them listed above. Everyone wants to claim it and for good reason, as this is the creamiest of all the Albas. A popular rose for centuries, it grows to a large bush, reaching 8 ft (2.4 m) tall with a sparse habit. The flowers are 3–4 in (8–10 cm) in diameter, opening flat with a faint buff edge and a lovely fragrance. Pale, gray-green foliage covers the canes, which have a few large prickles. 'Alba Maxima' flowers in summer, is disease re-sistant and needs little pruning. ZONES 3–9.

PRE-1500

POSSIBLY *ROSA CANINA* × *R. GALLICA*

ROYAL HORTICULTURAL SOCIETY AWARD OF GARDEN MERIT 1993

### 'Alba Meidiland'   MEIflopan  *(above)*
syns 'Alba Meillandécor', 'Alba Sunblaze', 'Meidiland Alba'

MODERN, MODERN SHRUB, WHITE, REPEAT-FLOWERING

'Alba Meidiland' is a very pretty ground-cover shrub that has large clusters of small, very double blooms with over 40 petals each; unfortunately they have little scent. Small, glossy, medium green foliage appears on a plant that will spread effectively to give color throughout summer and autumn. It is useful on banks and borders, makes a good subject for pots and window boxes and is very effective as a short weeping standard. It propagates very easily from cuttings and by budding. ZONES 4–9.

MEILLAND, FRANCE, 1987

*ROSA SEMPERVIRENS* × 'MARTHA CARRON'

FRANKFURT GOLD MEDAL 1989

A

## 'Alba Semi-plena'
*(right)*

syns *Rosa × alba nivea,*
*R. × alba suaveolens*

OLD, ALBA, WHITE

The origin of the Albas is lost, but there are many conjectures as to their parentage. With nearly single blooms with significant anthers, the largest of the Albas has a sweet scent and pure white flowers. The attractive gray-green leaves and autumn hips extend the season. Sometimes offered as 'Semi-plena', rosarians are divided over its worthiness. Some feel it is underrated and others feel that other Albas far outshine it. Michael Gibson, an English rosarian, puts it on his list of favorite roses. It was introduced into the UK by invading Roman armies and shares the honor with the simple white Alba as the White Rose of York. ZONES 3–4.

PRE-1600

POSSIBLE SPORT OF 'ALBA MAXIMA'

ROYAL HORTICULTURAL SOCIETY AWARD OF GARDEN MERIT 1993

## 'Alba Suaveolens'
syn. 'Suaveolens'

OLD, ALBA, WHITE

Graham Thomas and Peter Beales claim this is the same rose as 'Alba Semi-plena', while historian Roy Shepherd and Gerry Krueger, who has the largest collection of Albas in the USA, say there is a difference. Photographs rarely help in these disputes. Krueger states that the inner petals do not have the anthers found in 'Alba Semi-plena'; Trevor Griffiths concurs. All agree that it is sweetly scented. Very little work with the Albas has been done in the twentieth century, save for the German hybridizer Rolf Sievers, creator of the Blush series. They are bred with a mixture of old-fashioned and Kordesii roses. ZONES 3–9.

PRE-1750

PARENTAGE UNKNOWN

## 'Albéric Barbier'
*(above right)*

MODERN, RAMBLER, WHITE

This very popular once-blooming Rambler has many uses—as a climber, as a tree and even as a ground cover. It has been used effectively as a weeping standard. Its creamy white flowers, rather large for a Rambler, have a yellow center, and the pliable, glossy branches are dotted with flower clusters outlined against the dark foliage. The vigorous, thin canes can be easily trained, while no real pruning is needed. The apple fragrance in early summer is strong, and blooms appear on lateral shoots as well as new ones. 'Albéric Barbier' does well in the shade and can grow to 20 ft (6 m) in a year. The Barbier nursery in Orléans produced the most popular Ramblers of the century. These include 'Albertine', 'Alexandre Girault' and 'François Juranville'. Barbier's created 23 Climbers and Ramblers. ZONES 4–10.

BARBIER, FRANCE, 1900

*ROSA WICHURANA* × 'SHIRLEY HIBBERD'

ROYAL HORTICULTURAL SOCIETY AWARD OF GARDEN MERIT 1993

A

### 'Albertine' *(above)*

MODERN, LARGE-FLOWERED CLIMBER, ORANGE-PINK

'Albertine' has been popular for some 75 years.
A very vigorous plant with striking deep green,
almost purple stems and foliage, it has semi-lax
stems that require continuous securing as the
plant grows. It does well on pergolas, while a
position on a wall in full sun can encourage
a magnificent plant; in some gardens it is grown
as a weeping standard. The heavily scented
flowers are deep pink to salmon with hints of
copper, but sadly they flower for only about
3 weeks in mid-summer. The cupped blooms are
medium sized and appear in clusters. The foliage
is prone to mildew but not to its detriment.
**ZONES 4–9.**

BARBIER, FRANCE, 1921

*ROSA WICHURANA* × 'MRS ARTHUR ROBERT WADDELL'

ROYAL HORTICULTURAL SOCIETY AWARD OF GARDEN MERIT 1993

### 'Alchymist' *(above)*
syns 'Alchemist', 'Alchymiste'

MODERN, MODERN SHRUB, APRICOT BLEND

'Alchymist' is an extremely vigorous, upright
shrub with glossy bronze foliage that is very
healthy. Its round buds produce very large,
cupped flowers that are extremely fragrant; they
are a yellow shaded orange color that is officially
described as an apricot blend. It makes a good
shrub or a short climber. **ZONES 3–9.**

KORDES, GERMANY, 1956

'GOLDEN GLOW' × *ROSA EGLANTERIA* HYBRID

A

## 'Alec's Red' COred *(above)*

MODERN, LARGE-FLOWERED/HYBRID TEA, MEDIUM RED,
REPEAT-FLOWERING

Most catalogues would describe the flowers on
this rose as turkey red, although they can easily
discolor to a dirty red as they age. The large size
(each flower has some 45 petals) and fantastic
scent has enabled this variety to retain its popularity. It is a vigorous, bushy plant with dark
green foliage and is repeat-flowering, coming into
flower very early in the season. It was named after
a well-known Scottish rose grower who started
breeding late in life, this being his first big success;
it is now grown worldwide. It was named at a
time when roses did not have code names, and
every judge just knew it as 'Alec's Red'. A good
bedding plant and also useful as a standard, it is
propagated by budding. **'Climbing Alec's Red'**
(Harkness, UK, 1975) is a very vigorous, climbing
form that is identical to its parent in most other
respects; like many sports, it is only summer
flowering. **ZONES 4–9.**

COCKER, UK, 1970

'FRAGRANT CLOUD' × 'DAME DE COEUR'

EDLAND FRAGRANCE MEDAL 1969, ROYAL NATIONAL ROSE SOCIETY
PRESIDENT'S INTERNATIONAL TROPHY 1970, BELFAST FRAGRANCE
PRIZE 1972, ANERKANNTE DEUTSCHE ROSE 1973

## 'Alexander' HARlex *(above)*
syn. 'Alexandra'

MODERN, LARGE-FLOWERED/HYBRID TEA, ORANGE-RED,
REPEAT-FLOWERING

This extremely vigorous rose astonished every
rose lover with its luminosity. Growing with the
vigor of a Modern Shrub and having healthy foliage that is glossy and bright green, it certainly has
the potential to be a match for 'Queen Elizabeth'.
The brilliant, bright vermilion large double
flowers with 25 petals are produced in profusion
on long stems in small clusters. Rather big for a
bed, it is better grown as a specimen shrub. The
breeder, Jack Harkness, named this after his
World War II commanding officer in northern
Africa. It is propagated by budding. **ZONES 4–9.**

HARKNESS, UK, 1972

'TROPICANA' × ('ANN ELIZABETH' × 'ALLGOLD')

HAMBURG GOLD MEDAL 1973, BELFAST GOLD MEDAL 1974,
ANERKANNTE DEUTSCHE ROSE 1974, ROYAL NATIONAL ROSE SOCIETY
JAMES MASON MEDAL 1987, ROYAL HORTICULTURAL SOCIETY AWARD
OF GARDEN MERIT 1993

### 'Alexandre Girault'
*(right)*

MODERN, LARGE-FLOWERED CLIMBER,
PINK BLEND

Those who have visited the great garden outside Paris, Roseraie de l'Haÿ, will remember the impressive display of this rose—800 plants spread on an enormous steel fence. The pink-carmine blend of the flowers in a mass demonstration is the largest of its kind in the world. The large, double blooms on pliable canes are ideal for training on pergolas and trellises. They have a strong apple scent. Although it blooms only once in mid-summer, this rose helped to establish the reputation of its breeder, Barbier, throughout Europe; it is not as popular elsewhere. It is very tolerant of shade and poor soil, and likes plenty of room. **ZONES 5–10.**

BARBIER, FRANCE, 1909

*ROSA LUCIAE* × 'PAPA GONTIER'

### 'Alfred Colomb' *(above)*

OLD, HYBRID PERPETUAL, PINK BLEND,
REPEAT-FLOWERING

Some call this a 'vulgar' rose, but it has stayed in the trade ever since its introduction. The strawberry red, reflexed crimson blooms are large, full and symmetrical, much like the Centifolias. It ranges from medium to vigorous in its growth and has a handsome, bushy appearance with large dark leaves. The wood is green and full of prickles. This rose blooms later than other Hybrid Perpetuals, even well into autumn. Many say it does best in heavy soils, it doesn't mind rain and it has good disease resistance. It reached the peak of its popularity around the 1880s when 800 of this breed were advertised in William Paul & Sons' catalogue. Lacharmé also produced such popular roses as 'Boule de Neige', 'Mme Lombard' and 'Salet'. **ZONES 5–10.**

LACHARMÉ, FRANCE, 1865

SEEDLING OF 'GÉNÉRAL JACQUEMINOT'

### 'Alfred de Dalmas'
*(above)*

syn. 'Mousseline'

OLD, MOSS, LIGHT PINK,
REPEAT-FLOWERING

This very popular rose is a short-growing, densely branching tidy shrub to about 3 ft (1 m). It sends up strong thornless shoots that are completely clothed in gingery brown, tightly packed soft bristles. These shoots are well foliated with roundish mid-green leaves, which are bright green when young. The ample moss, which surrounds the receptacles and the calyx, is at first light green, turning brownish green as the buds open. The fragrant flowers are creamy white, heavily overlaid with silvery pink, and can reach a diameter of up to 4 in (10 cm) in good soil; they first appear in early summer and continue almost without a break well into autumn. It repeats well. Being little more than semi-double, they show off rich golden anthers to advantage when fully open. This is a trouble-free old variety, useful for group planting or growing in containers. It tolerates shade. ZONES 4–10.

LAFFAY, FRANCE, 1855
PARENTAGE UNKNOWN

### 'Alida Lovett'
*(above right)*

MODERN, LARGE-FLOWERED
CLIMBER, LIGHT PINK

'Alida Lovett' is a very vigorous Climber that produces huge clusters of shell pink flowers with a sulfur-shaded base. The blooms have a slight fragrance, while the foliage is glossy and disease resistant. Summer flowering, it is useful for fences and pergolas and is very tolerant of semi-shade. Although bred by a famous American hybridist, it was introduced by J. T. Lovett, a nurseryman in Little Silver, New Jersey and named after his wife. Propagation is by budding. ZONES 4–9.

VAN FLEET, USA, 1905

'SOUVENIR DU PRESIDENT
CARNOT' × ROSA WICHURANA

### 'Alister Clark'
*(above)*

MODERN, POLYANTHA, LIGHT
PINK, REPEAT-FLOWERING

This lovely little rose occurred as a sport on a bush of 'Marjory Palmer' in Victoria, Australia. 'Marjory Palmer' had the Rambler 'Jersey Beauty' as a parent, and it is from this that 'Alister Clark' gets its large, glossy, abundant foliage. The bush has a short and spreading growth habit and the flowers are large for a Polyantha Rose. They come in clusters and have widely flaring outer petals. Flowering is continuous and there are no disease problems. Laurie Newman asked the descendants of Alister Clark for permission to name the rose, which was introduced in 1990, after him. It is a fitting tribute to Australia's greatest rose breeder. ZONES 4–10.

NEWMAN, AUSTRALIA, 1990

SPORT OF 'MARJORY PALMER'

### 'Alister Stella Gray' *(right)*
syn. 'Golden Rambler'
OLD, NOISETTE, LIGHT YELLOW,
REPEAT-FLOWERING

Long, pointed buds on this variety open to light yellow blooms with a dark yellow center. The beautiful, blowsy, quartered flowers change color as they age. Thin canes hold few prickles, and the foliage is a healthy, dark green. It needs time to establish itself but will grow into a vigorous shrub, sometimes as high as 10 ft (3 m). Many who grow it say there is no other rose that will bloom so continuously, displaying cascades of beautifully formed blossoms in full sun. This Noisette should be deadheaded regularly. **ZONES 5–10.**

GRAY, UK, 1894

PARENTAGE UNKNOWN

ROYAL HORTICULTURAL SOCIETY AWARD OF
GARDEN MERIT 1994

### 'Alleluia'   DELatur
syn. 'Hallelujah'
MODERN, LARGE-FLOWERED/HYBRID TEA,
RED BLEND, REPEAT-FLOWERING

'Alleluia' produces large, heavy blooms with 30 petals that are velvety red with a silver reverse, which makes them a good subject for exhibition. They have little fragrance. A strong, robust, bushy plant with deep green glossy foliage, it is suitable for bedding. It is propagated by budding. **ZONES 4–9.**

DELBARD, FRANCE, 1980

(['IMPECCABLE' × 'PAPA MEILLAND'] ×
['GLOIRE DE ROMA' × 'IMPECCABLE']) ×
'CORRIDA'

### 'Allen Chandler'
*(bottom right)*
MODERN, LARGE-FLOWERED CLIMBER,
MEDIUM RED, REPEAT-FLOWERING

Brilliant crimson, semi-double, large flowers in clusters of 3–4

and with pointed buds are produced on this variety. Slightly fragrant, they are open and repeat their blooming from summer to autumn. It is a moderate grower with dark, leathery, glossy foliage that is suitable as a large shrub or to train up a pillar; it grows successfully on north walls. Historically it was one of the first of the repeat-flowering climbers. Although very healthy and tough, it has dropped out of popularity because it is such a reluctant bloomer. Propagation is by budding. **ZONES 4–9.**

CHANDLER, UK, 1923

'HUGH DICKSON' × SEEDLING

NATIONAL ROSE SOCIETY GOLD MEDAL 1923

### 'Allgold' *(right)*
syn. 'All Gold'

MODERN, CLUSTER-FLOWERED/FLORIBUNDA, MEDIUM YELLOW,
REPEAT-FLOWERING

The deep, unfading, pure buttercup yellow,
slightly fragrant, medium-sized blooms with
15–20 petals on this variety are borne singly or
in large trusses. They are a striking color; in fact
'Allgold' was the first Cluster-flowered Rose to
possess an unfading yellow. A bushy plant with
medium, pale green, glossy foliage, it is a nice
bedding variety that makes a good subject as a
standard. Its chief claim to fame is its ability to
produce healthy progeny, although as a nursery
plant it is disappointing because of the small
proportion of saleable plants it actually produces.
Propagation is by budding. The blooms of the
climbing variant, **'Climbing Allgold '** (syns
'Grimpant Allgold', 'Grimpant All Gold'; Gandy,
UK, 1961), are superior to its parent, although
they only appear in summer and are very sparse.
**ZONES 4–9.**

LEGRICE, UK, 1956

'GOLDILOCKS' × 'ELLINOR LEGRICE'

NATIONAL ROSE SOCIETY GOLD MEDAL 1956

### 'Allotria' TANal
*(left)*

MODERN, CLUSTER-FLOWERED/
FLORIBUNDA, ORANGE-RED,
REPEAT-FLOWERING

Medium-sized flowers
of brilliant orange-
scarlet appear on
'Allotria' in large clus-
ters. They are slightly
fragrant and repeat
their blooming from
summer to autumn. It
is a vigorous, healthy
bush with dark glossy
foliage that is suitable
for bedding purposes,
and is one of many
Cluster-flowered Roses
of this color that were
bred at the same time.
Propagation is by bud-
ding. **ZONES 4–9.**

TANTAU, GERMANY, 1958

'FANAL' × SEEDLING OF
'CINNABAR'

## 'Aloha' *(right)*

MODERN, LARGE-FLOWERED
CLIMBER, MEDIUM PINK,
REPEAT-FLOWERING

This widely grown
variety is suitable as
a short climber or as a
free-flowering shrub.
Its large, round buds
develop into big multi-
petalled blooms that
are rose pink with a
deeper reverse and have
58 petals. The flowers
have a pronounced
fragrance of apple
blossom and are very
hardy. Although slow
to establish, 'Aloha'
makes a fantastic shrub
that is particularly good
in sunless situations
and is repeat-flowering.
**ZONES 3–9.**

BOERNER, USA, 1949

'MERCEDES GALLART' ×
'NEW DAWN'

## 'Alpine Sunset' *(right)*

MODERN, LARGE-FLOWERED/HYBRID TEA, APRICOT BLEND,
REPEAT-FLOWERING

This delightful rose is a restful combination of
peaches, pinks, apricots, creams and yellows. The
blooms, which are sweetly scented, very large and
globular in form, are borne on firm stems close
to the foliage on a neat compact plant. The leaves
are light green and shiny and are large enough to
furnish the bush well. Although repeat-flowering,
there is usually a pause between summer flowering and the next flush because the plant needs
time to recover after producing its large blooms
in quantity. New stems are not made freely;
dieback will affect it in severe winters. **ZONES 5–9.**

CANT, UK, 1974

'DR A. J. VERHAGE' × 'GRANDPA DICKSON'

ROYAL NATIONAL ROSE SOCIETY TRIAL GROUND CERTIFICATE 1974,
BELFAST CERTIFICATE OF MERIT 1976, THE HAGUE FRAGRANCE
AWARD 1976

A

### 'Altissimo' DELmur
*(above)*

syns 'Altus',
'Sublimely Single'

MODERN, LARGE-FLOWERED
CLIMBER, MEDIUM RED,
REPEAT-FLOWERING

This is an excellent climbing rose for walls and fences and to train up a pillar or on a pergola. The saucer-shaped, lightly scented blooms are fairly large, with about 7 petals, and open wide to show yellow stamens. A rich and bright deep scarlet, becoming crimson, they repeat-flower throughout summer and autumn against a background of large dark leaves. The plant grows vigorously with stiff branching stems to the average height one expects of a climber, though it is apt to flower high unless trained horizontally. The flowers, which may appear one to a stem, are more often borne several together in wide clusters, which explains why this variety can be described by the Royal National Rose Society as a Cluster-flowered Climber, and by the American Rose Society as a Large-flowered Climber. *Altissimo*, Italian for 'in the highest', is an appropriate name for this rose.
ZONES 4–9.

DELBARD-CHABERT, FRANCE, 1966

'TENOR' × SEEDLING

ROYAL HORTICULTURAL SOCIETY
AWARD OF GARDEN MERIT 1993

### 'Amadis'   *(below)*
syns 'Crimson
Boursault', 'Elegans'

OLD, BOURSAULT, DARK RED

Of the 50 Boursaults listed 200 years ago, there are only a few left. However, 'Amadis' has survived, surely because of its elegant, upright posture and large, cupped, semi-double flowers. They are deep crimson and purple and are borne in large, long-lasting clusters. The young wood is whitish green; the old wood is red-brown, and there are no prickles. Although it has neither perfume nor fruits, its deeply serrated leaves of brilliant green add to its winning traits. It blooms early in the season on old growth, and partial shade brings out the subtle colors. This rose is frequently found in old cemeteries as it was once used as an understock, and it was named for an amateur horticulturist.
ZONES 5–10.

LAFFAY, FRANCE, 1829

*ROSA PENDULINA* × UNKNOWN

### 'Amalia' MEIcauf
(above)
syn. 'Fiord'

MODERN, LARGE-FLOWERED/
HYBRID TEA, DARK RED/
LIGHT RED

This light to medium
red Large-flowered
Rose is very elegant—
urn-shaped as the buds
begin to swell and
keeping well-propor-
tioned, high-centered
flowers as they open.
It carries its blooms
singly on long stems,
making it good as a cut
rose for decoration or
exhibition as they last
well. It is best grown
in a part of the garden
reserved for cut flowers
because the habit is too
tall to make it suitable
for bedding. The flower
production through
summer and autumn is
good, but there is little
fragrance, always re-
grettable in a red rose.
The leaves are large and
furnish the lower part of
the plant well. 'Amalia'
is at its best in a sunny
climate. ZONES 5–9.

MEILLAND, FRANCE, 1986
PARENTAGE UNKNOWN

### 'Amatsu-Otome'
(above right)

MODERN, LARGE-FLOWERED/
HYBRID TEA, YELLOW BLEND,
REPEAT-FLOWERING

This variety is very
popular in Japan, and
has found favor abroad
despite the long name.
At its best it is a beauty,
bearing large, high-
centered blooms of
yellow with a hint of
orange at the margins;
however, these flowers
are most likely to be
seen in the exhibitors'
classes at shows where
they often win prizes,
because they are con-
structed with wide firm
petals that keep the
blooms in good shape
until judging time is
well past. There is a
slight fragrance. As a
garden rose, 'Amatsu-
Otome' is not nearly
as popular, being tall
and somewhat leggy
and with mid-green,
slightly glossy foliage
that may need protec-
tion against black spot.
The number of blooms
produced in summer
and autumn is respect-
able in view of their
size, but it is as an
exhibitor's rose, not
a gardener's rose that
most people plant it
today. ZONES 5–9.

TERANISHI, JAPAN, 1960

'CHRYSLER IMPERIAL' ×
'DOREEN'

### 'Ambassador'
MEInuzeten (above)

MODERN, LARGE-FLOWERED/
HYBRID TEA, ORANGE BLEND,
REPEAT-FLOWERING

The color of this var-
iety appears two-toned,
because the outside of
the petals is creamy
yellow and the inside a
strong shade of apricot.
As the large conical
buds open into moder-
ately full, cupped
blooms, the contrast
shows to good effect
until the color deepens
and reddish apricot
takes over. There is a
nice light fragrance.
'Ambassador' is a
long-stemmed variety
bearing flowers
through summer and
autumn and is excel-
lent for cutting and for
exhibition, but would
not be among the top
choices as a bedding
rose. The plant grows
vigorously with dark
foliage, which may on
occasion need spraying
against mildew. It does
best in a warm climate.
ZONES 5–9.

MEILLAND, FRANCE, 1979

SEEDLING × 'WHISKY MAC'

A

### 'Amber Queen' HARroony *(below)*
syn. 'Prinz Eugen von Savoyen'

MODERN, CLUSTER-FLOWERED/FLORIBUNDA, APRICOT BLEND,
REPEAT-FLOWERING

From its many awards it is clear there are special qualities that endear it to the judges. Its value as a garden item comes from the pure amber color, its ability to produce clusters of quite large well-formed blooms freely throughout summer and autumn, its neat bedding habit, generally robust

health and sweet fragrance. There is in addition an appealing quality about 'Amber Queen', derived from the refreshing effect of the bright clean flowers against the dark leathery leaves. The growth habit is cushiony, and it normally grows to medium height. As a bedding rose it is splendid, it makes a fine standard, and it is also seen in exhibition classes. 'Rosemary Harkness' was the name originally intended for this variety, but when it won Britain's Rose of the Year competition a change was made on grounds of commercial acceptability. The synonym comes from an Austrian national hero. **ZONES 4–9.**

HARKNESS, UK, 1984

'SOUTHAMPTON' × 'TYPHOON'

ROYAL NATIONAL ROSE SOCIETY CERTIFICATE OF MERIT 1983, LYONS ROSE DU SIECLE 1984, UK ROSE OF THE YEAR 1984, BELFAST BEST FLORIBUNDA 1986, GENOA ROSA EUROFLORA 1986, ORLÉANS ROSE D'OR 1987, ALL-AMERICA ROSE SELECTION 1988, NEW ZEALAND GOLD STAR 1988, ORLÉANS GRAND PRIX D'EXCELLENCE 1989, THE HAGUE GOLDEN ROSE AND SILVER MEDAL FOR FRAGRANCE 1991, ROYAL NATIONAL ROSE SOCIETY JAMES MASON GOLD MEDAL 1993, ROYAL HORTICULTURAL SOCIETY AWARD OF GARDEN MERIT 1993

### 'Amélia' *(left)*
OLD, ALBA, MEDIUM PINK

'Amélia' is quite a short-growing rose for an Alba. The foliage is gray-green and plentiful, and although there are numerous thorns at least they are small. The flowers are up to 3 in (8 cm) across, semi-double to double and bright pink, and display golden stamens to stunning effect when fully open. They are highly scented and borne in small clusters in mid-summer. It is hardy in difficult situations. Planted as an impenetrable hedge or in a woodland situation, it improves with the cutting back of old wood after flowering. This rose is really quite rare and could easily be classified as a Damask. **ZONES 4–10.**

PRE-1823

PARENTAGE UNKNOWN

## 'America' JACclam *(right)*
MODERN, LARGE-FLOWERED CLIMBER, ORANGE-PINK,
REPEAT-FLOWERING

Few climbing roses have achieved the All-America
Rose Selection award, and by its long commercial
life, this variety has shown that the judges were
right. It flowers very freely in summer, with a
reasonably good repeat bloom. The medium to
large-sized blooms are full and prettily formed
with overlapping petals, opening cupped from
high-centered buds, and well scented. They appear in open clusters in a warm shade of coral-
salmon, and pale as they age. The growth is
vigorous and free branching, while the leaves are
of medium size, semi-glossy and reasonably
healthy. It makes an excellent climber of lower
than average height, so is suitable for walls, fences
and pillars, and it does not resent being pruned to
form a big shrub. The name 'America' is significant because the rose was introduced in the
bicentennial year of the USA. ZONES 4–9.

WARRINER, USA, 1976

'FRAGRANT CLOUD' × 'TRADITION'

ALL-AMERICA ROSE SELECTION 1976

## 'American Beauty'
syn. 'Mme Ferdinand Jamin'
OLD, HYBRID PERPETUAL, DEEP PINK

In spite of its name, this is a French rose that
became famous in the USA as a greenhouse variety that caused a revolution in the cut-flower
industry. The buds are globular and develop into
large, pink-carmine flowers. These blooms are
composed of 50 petals to give a cup shape. The
strong perfume and the long, stiff stems were
the main reason for its commercial success.
Sometimes it repeats its flowers in late summer
and autumn. It is no longer grown for cut flowers
as others have replaced it. Its transition to the outdoors was successful in warm climates, although
it is subject to rust and black spot. There is a
climbing form but it is rarely grown. ZONES 5–10.

LÉDÉCHAUX, FRANCE, 1875

PARENTAGE UNKNOWN

## 'American Heritage' LAMlam *(above)*
MODERN, LARGE-FLOWERED/HYBRID TEA, YELLOW BLEND,
REPEAT-FLOWERING

There are many shapes and colors to be seen in
this pretty rose, and it is delightful at every stage.
Long pointed buds of cream and ivory open into
large full-petalled blooms, producing a melange
of ivory, salmon, pink and yellow shades in the
broad petals. They open out wide to reveal an
expanse of light yellow with pink tinges. This is a
pleasing item for the garden and good to cut, the
flowers being carried on long stems and appearing through summer and autumn. There is a light
scent. The plant growth is upright and vigorous
and it is well furnished with dark leathery leaves
that should be checked for mildew. ZONES 4–9.

LAMMERTS, USA, 1965

'QUEEN ELIZABETH' × 'YELLOW PERFECTION'

ALL-AMERICA ROSE SELECTION 1966

A

### 'American Home' *(above)*

MODERN, LARGE-FLOWERED/HYBRID TEA, DARK RED, REPEAT-FLOWERING

This variety is appreciated especially for its perfume, which is rich and sweet and reminiscent of the Old Garden Roses. The plump pointed buds open into large, dark red blooms of cupped form, moderately full of petals. They are carried on long stiff stems, which makes them very suitable as cut flowers. 'American Home' makes a good garden rose as it is a steady performer, bearing flowers on a vigorous, upright plant of average height through summer and autumn. The leaves are tough, mid-green and leathery, and it has a generally good health record. **ZONES 4–9.**

MOREY, USA, 1960

'CHRYSLER IMPERIAL' × 'NEW YORKER'

### 'American Pillar' *(above & bottom)*

MODERN, RAMBLER, PINK BLEND

Its parentage makes this rose a candidate for pergolas, pillars and for climbing into trees. The carmine-pink blooms have a white eye and golden stamens. They are 3 in (8 cm) in diameter, and are frequently borne in large clusters. The thick canes are vigorous, reaching 20 ft (6 m) in a season, and are easily trained. The foliage is leathery, glossy, and subject to mildew. It blooms on old wood later than other ramblers and hates hot, dry weather, but will tolerate partial shade. Although the single blossoms are uninteresting, collectively they are stunning. The rose is now enjoying a comeback—possibly because public gardens are using it again to great effect. **ZONES 5–10.**

VAN FLEET, USA, 1902

*(ROSA WICHURANA* × *R. SETIGERA)* × UNNAMED RED HYBRID PERPETUAL

### 'Améthyste'

MODERN, RAMBLER, MAUVE

Trusses of intensely packed, double, crimson-violet blooms are arranged on long arching canes on this rose. The healthy foliage is glossy. Blooming only once, it is best as a tree climber or in the wild garden, and usually reaches 12 ft (3.5 m). Early critics called 'Améthyste' coarse and unmanageable as the flowers sometimes appear to be steel-blue with purplish undertones. It tolerates some shade. **ZONES 5–10.**

NONIN, FRANCE, 1911

SPORT OF 'NON-PLUS ULTRA'

## 'Amy Johnson'

*(right & bottom)*

MODERN, LARGE-FLOWERED
CLIMBER, MEDIUM PINK,
REPEAT-FLOWERING

This is a very vigorous climber that produces an abundance of very fragrant, rosy pink blooms on long stems; they are scarce in summer, although a good flush is produced in the cool of autumn. They open out from plump buds into large, full-petalled, double, cupped flowers. The leaves are wrinkled. Amy Johnson was a pioneer aviator who, in 1930, achieved the feat of flying solo to Australia. It makes a good pillar rose, or can be grown over an arch or fence. **ZONES 5–11.**

CLARK, AUSTRALIA, 1931
'SOUVENIR DE GUSTAV PRAT' ×
UNKNOWN

## 'Amy Robsart'

OLD, SWEET BRIAR, DEEP PINK

During a short period between 1890 and 1895, Lord Penzance produced a group of roses that are still popular. Although he was not the first to experiment with these hybrids he marketed them well, as they did not have an enthusiastic audience at first but gained a popularity they have not lost. An attractive, tall shrub, 'Amy Robsart' has large, semi-double, deep rose blooms that are lovely when fully opened, the stamens adding to their beauty. In spite of its parentage the healthy foliage is not fragrant, although the rose is. Best in the background as its form is sprawling and rough, it tolerates shade. Red fruit adds to its usefulness as a hedge. It should be pruned lightly. **ZONES 4–10.**

PENZANCE, UK, 1894

*ROSA EGLANTERIA* × HYBRID
PERPETUAL OR BOURBON

## 'Anabell' KORbell
*(above)*
syns 'Annabelle',
'Kordes' Rose Anabel'
MODERN, CLUSTER-FLOWERED/
FLORIBUNDA, ORANGE BLEND,
REPEAT-FLOWERING

This variety sometimes bears open clusters of blooms, with each flower on a short but distinct stem, and sometimes tight clusters with the flowers close together. The color is a warm shade of salmon-orange, deepening towards the petal edges. The blooms are large with a score of petals and open cupped, with a light fragrance. 'Anabell' is a good bedding rose as it bears flowers freely through summer and autumn. It grows upright, to average height for a bush rose, with attractive glossy foliage, coppery when young then becoming mid-green. ZONES 4–9.

KORDES, GERMANY, 1972

'ZORINA' × 'COLOR WONDER'

ROYAL NATIONAL ROSE SOCIETY
TRIAL GROUND CERTIFICATE 1971

## 'Anaïs Ségalas'
*(right)*
OLD, GALLICA, PINK BLEND

This is a branching shrub up to about 3 ft (1 m) in height with prickly gray-green stems, denoting some Centifolia influence. The foliage is light green, rounded and tidily presented all over the plant. The flowers, about 1½ in (4 cm) across and beautifully formed, are arranged in clusters, and every petal seems to be groomed into place to create a flattish cushion with a central green eye. They are a deep mauve-pink, paling towards the edges. This is a free-flowering, healthy rose with a strong fragrance and it does well in poor soil. It is a good candidate for potting. ZONES 4–10.

VIBERT, FRANCE, OR
PARMENTIER, BELGIUM, 1837

POSSIBLY UNKNOWN GALLICA ×
UNKNOWN CENTIFOLIA

## 'Anastasia'

MODERN, LARGE-FLOWERED/HYBRID TEA, WHITE,
REPEAT-FLOWERING

There is a striking contrast between the dark,
rugged-looking foliage of this rose and the excellent white flowers. They are carried, usually one
to a stem, on a strong, vigorous, leafy plant that
grows to average height or more. Plump, pointed
buds open into large rounded blooms made up of
about 30 wide petals, appearing through summer
and autumn. There is little fragrance, however,
the flowers of 'Anastasia' last well so they are good
for flower arrangements and exhibition. This is a
rose for drier climates, as the white flowers will
mottle in damp conditions. **ZONES 5–9.**

GREFF, USA, 1980

JOHN F. KENNEDY' × 'PASCALI'

## 'Andalusien' KORdalu *(above)*

MODERN, CLUSTER-FLOWERED/FLORIBUNDA, MEDIUM RED,
REPEAT-FLOWERING

For a short bedding rose, this is a good performer
that blooms throughout summer and autumn on
a neat, short, bushy plant. The flowers are set close
together in sprays that stand just above the foliage,
and open from long slender buds into loosely
formed, double flowers of medium size in a clear
scarlet-crimson. When the blooms are fully open,
the petals are often folded into each other. They
carry no fragrance. Small, bright green leaves
clothe this vigorous plant. It is exceptionally frost
hardy. **ZONES 3–9.**

KORDES, GERMANY, 1977

SEEDLING × 'ZORINA'

ANERKANNTE DEUTSCHE ROSE 1976

**A**

### 'Anemone' *(right)*

syns *Rosa × anemonoides*,
'Anemone Rose', 'Pink
Cherokee', *R. laevigata*
'Anemone'

MODERN, MODERN SHRUB, LIGHT PINK,
REPEAT-FLOWERING

This is a most unusual-looking
rose, with mauvish pink flowers
that have been described as both
silky and papery, qualities not
usually ascribed to roses. They
are made up of 5 large heart-
shaped petals of uniform size,
which form a setting for the
attractive golden stamens in
the center; the effect resembles
a clematis rather than an
anemone. 'Anemone' is lightly
fragrant, and in warmer climates
there is likely to be some repeat-
flowering. This is one of the
earliest garden roses to come
into bloom, and can be very
early indeed if treated as a
climber and sited against a
warm wall; it will also tolerate
shadier walls. When grown as a
shrub, it makes a stiff, branching grower of medium to large
size with dark, rather sparse,
shiny foliage and brownish
stems. **ZONES 5–9.**

SCHMIDT, GERMANY, 1896

POSSIBLY *ROSA LAEVIGATA* × UNKNOWN
TEA ROSE

### 'Angel Darling' *(right)*

MODERN, MINIATURE, MAUVE,
REPEAT-FLOWERING

This variety is probably one of
the first lavender Miniatures developed in the twentieth century
by the master of hybridizing
Miniatures. The charm of this
variety is gauged by the ador-
able single form containing 10
petals, although some growers
regard the size of the blooms,
about 1½ in (35 mm), too large
for the surrounding foliage. The
contrasting yellow stamens on a
fresh bloom are very beautiful,
but that beauty is fleeting, lasting only a few days at best. This
striking variety is a popular
Miniature for garden display
and exhibition. This vigorous
plant is very productive and
has leathery disease-resistant
foliage. **ZONES 4–11.**

MOORE, USA, 1976

'LITTLE CHIEF' × 'ANGEL FACE'

## 'Angel Face' *(above)*

MODERN, CLUSTER-FLOWERED/FLORIBUNDA, MAUVE,
REPEAT-FLOWERING

This rose, highly popular in the USA for 30 years, has deep mauve-lavender flowers that darken with ruby flushes towards the edges and are formed of up to 40 ruffled petals. They open with high centers, and become cup shaped as the firm petals reflex to show yellow stamens. There is a lemony fragrance and good continuity of bloom through summer and autumn. Sometimes the blooms are carried singly, sometimes in clusters of a few flowers. The growth habit is low and rounded, and the leaves are dark green, leathery and semi-glossy. Good for bedding and for cutting, it is better suited to warmer climates, perhaps because plenty of sunshine is needed to bring out the beauty of the color tones. ZONES 5–9.

SWIM, USA, 1968

('CIRCUS' × 'LAVENDER PINOCCHIO') × 'STERLING SILVER'

ALL-AMERICA ROSE SELECTION 1969, AMERICAN ROSE SOCIETY JOHN COOK MEDAL 1971

## 'Angela'  KORday
(above)
syn. 'Angelica'

MODERN, MODERN SHRUB,
DEEP PINK, REPEAT-FLOWERING

This variety covers itself with heavy sprays of medium-sized, cupped flowers. They are predominantly deep rose pink with highlights of light pink, especially in the center. The blooms are carried on short stems close to the dark green foliage, and their combined weight causes the stems to bow, creating a pleasingly lax habit. There is a slight perfume and good repeat bloom. The plant has bright foliage, lots of vigor and a neat, robust habit. It is bushy, grows up to average height, and is very suitable to plant in a mixed flower border or to make a hedge or bed. ZONES 4–9.

KORDES, GERMANY, 1984
'YESTERDAY' × 'PETER FRANKENFELD'
ANERKANNTE DEUTSCHE ROSE 1982

## 'Angela Rippon'
OcaRU  (above right)
syn. 'Ocarina'

MODERN, MINIATURE, MEDIUM PINK, REPEAT-FLOWERING

The distinctive salmon-pink blooms of this variety are preceded by very attractive urn-shaped buds usually borne in large clusters. Some growers have labeled this variety more of a Patio Rose than a Miniature because of the large, very double blooms. These have a frilly effect when fully open. The compact bush grows as a vigorous plant in nearly all climatic zones and is adaptable enough to be grown in containers, or even for edging pathways. However, the repeat cycle is slow. This variety is a sister seedling to 'Amorette', gaining its genealogy from the orange-red Cluster-flowered Rose, 'Zorina', developed by Boerner in 1963. The variety was named for a famous British television personality. ZONES 4–11.

DE RUITER, THE NETHERLANDS, 1977
'ROSY JEWEL' × 'ZORINA'

A

## 'Ann Endt' *(right)*

MODERN, HYBRID RUGOSA,
DARK RED, REPEAT-FLOWERING

The flowers of 'Ann Endt' are single and show a tuft of cream stamens that light up the flowers. The long, sepaled buds are an inheritance from *Rosa foliolosa*. There is a strong cinnamon scent. The foliage is small, soft and abundant and the plant has a good repeat cycle. It forms a very attractive small shrub that can be used as a hedge or border or combined with perennial plants. Ann Endt was a gardener, for many years, to Nancy Steen, author of *Charm of Old Roses*. Ann then created a wonderful garden of her own where she was one of the pioneers of mass planting of roses with bulbs, perennials and shrubs. She lived in New Zealand.
**ZONES 3–9.**

NOBBS, NEW ZEALAND, 1978

*ROSA RUGOSA* × *R. FOLIOLOSA*

## 'Anna de Diesbach' *(right)*

syns 'Anna von Diesbach', 'Gloire de Paris'

OLD, HYBRID PERPETUAL, DEEP
PINK, REPEAT-FLOWERING

Although in the late nineteenth century the popularity of the Hybrid Perpetuals was overshadowed by the new Large-flowered Roses (Hybrid Teas), they still exist, and one of the most popular is 'Anna de Diesbach'. It has long, pointed, Large-flowered-like buds that open to double, cupped pink blooms with a darker pink center. The vigorous, tall shrub is covered with blooms from summer to autumn. They can be 4 in (10 cm) across with long sepals that may be pointed or foliated. The leaves are glaucous green, the prickles small, and the canes large. The hybridizer dedicated the rose to the daughter of Countess Diesbach of Fribourg, Switzerland.
**ZONES 5–10.**

LACHARMÉ, FRANCE, 1858

'LA REINE' × SEEDLING

### 'Anna Ford' HARpiccolo *(right)*

MODERN, PATIO/DWARF CLUSTER-FLOWERED,
ORANGE BLEND, REPEAT-FLOWERING

The semi-double flowers of this plant are deep orange with a yellow eye, an attractive combination. This variety was one of the first to be referred to as a Patio or Dwarf Cluster-flowered Rose, resembling the Cluster-flowered Roses but with flowers, leaves and stems neatly scaled down. The pointed buds open to cup-shaped blooms borne several to a stem with 10 petals and narrow, reddish brown thorns. There is a slight fragrance. It has bushy growth and repeats well; it is nearly always in bloom throughout the year. It was named for a British writer and television star. **ZONES 4–11.**

HARKNESS, UK, 1980

'SOUTHAMPTON' × 'DARLING FLAME'

ROYAL NATIONAL ROSE SOCIETY PRESIDENT'S
INTERNATIONAL TROPHY 1981, GENOA GOLD
MEDAL 1987, GLASGOW GOLD MEDAL 1989

### 'Anna Livia' KORmetter *(right)*
syns 'Sandton Smile', 'Trier 2000'

MODERN, CLUSTER-FLOWERED/FLORIBUNDA,
ORANGE-PINK, REPEAT-FLOWERING

There is not much orange in 'Anna Livia', despite the official color description. It is basically a clear and restful shade of rose pink, bearing sprays of full-petalled, high-centered blooms in good succession through summer and autumn. They are fairly large, rounded in form, and the placement of each bloom in the spray is particularly pleasing. There is a light refreshing scent. The habit is excellent, being bushy and spreading, to average height, and with plentiful leathery mid-green foliage. It is also useful for exhibition. Anna Livia is the main character of James Joyce's novel *Finnegans Wake,* set on the River Liffey in Dublin, and the rose was named to commemorate the Irish capital's millennium in 1998. **ZONES 4–9.**

KORDES, GERMANY, 1985

(SEEDLING × 'TORNADO') × SEEDLING

BELFAST CERTIFICATE OF MERIT 1987,
ORLÉANS GOLD MEDAL 1987, GLASGOW
GOLD MEDAL 1991, ROYAL HORTICULTURAL
SOCIETY AWARD OF GARDEN MERIT 1994

## 'Anna Olivier'
*(right)*

OLD, TEA, PINK BLEND,
REPEAT-FLOWERING

This fine old favorite
has ruffled petals that
are pink blended with
a yellowish flesh color
and changing to a
shaded salmon with
a rose-colored reverse.
The blooms are well
formed, full, large, and
high centered with
frequent rebloom. The
blooms, which hang
down on a vigorous,
branching bush, exude
a delicate Tea scent and
make good cut flowers.
It has light green,
pointed leaves and
should be moderately
pruned. **ZONES 5–10.**

DUCHER, FRANCE, 1872

PARENTAGE UNKNOWN

## 'Anna Pavlova' *(right)*

MODERN, LARGE-FLOWERED/HYBRID TEA, LIGHT PINK,
REPEAT-FLOWERING

The beauty of this rose lies in its wonderfully constructed flowers. They have many broad petals of
the most subtle light pink shade, making up huge
high-centered flowers of rounded form. The rose
is also exceptionally sweet scented. Unfortunately,
the plant is not always worthy of the treasure it
produces, as it has upright, rather spindly growth
and large nondescript leaves. It is perhaps best
kept in a part of the garden where it can be visited
and admired, or cut to bring indoors, so that its
beauty and fragrance can be enjoyed during the
summer to autumn flowering season. It may need
preventive spraying against black spot, and in
poorer soils is best left unpruned. **ZONES 4–9.**

BEALES, UK, 1981

PARENTAGE UNKNOWN

### 'Anne Cocker'
*(below)*

MODERN, CLUSTER-FLOWERED/
FLORIBUNDA, ORANGE-PINK,
REPEAT-FLOWERING

The color has neither true orange nor pink in it, so the official coding is misleading. It is an eye-catching scarlet, rich and bright. The small to medium-sized flowers are carried in wide sprays, each individual bloom being neat in all respects—in its roundelay form, the arrangement of its petals, and its placement relative to the other flowers. There is little fragrance. The flower stems are thick and strong and are covered with fine prickles. It is ideal for indoor display or for shows; exhibitors have found it useful because it comes into flower a little later than most roses. The blooming period then extends through to autumn. The growth habit is upright, rather stiff and narrow, and the leaves are plentiful and dark green. It was named for the raiser's wife, who has bred many fine varieties. ZONES 4–9.

COCKER, UK, 1970

'HIGHLIGHT' × 'COLOR WONDER'

ROYAL NATIONAL ROSE SOCIETY
CERTIFICATE OF MERIT 1969

### 'Anne de Bretagne'
MEIturaphar   *(bottom)*
syns 'Décor Rose',
'Meilland Décor Rose'

MODERN, MODERN SHRUB, DEEP
PINK, REPEAT-FLOWERING

This vigorous shrub rose is well suited to modern parks and landscaping use. The flowers, carried in well-filled sprays on firm stems, are fairly full of petals, and open from cone-shaped buds into neatly formed blooms with high centers, in a rich shade of deep salmon-pink. As they open out they form loose cups and the color lightens. There is not much fragrance. There is good continuity of bloom through summer and autumn. The variety grows vigorously with an upright habit, and is well furnished with semi-glossy light green leaves. Anne of Brittany was the sole heiress of that duchy.
ZONES 4–10.

MEILLAND, FRANCE, 1979

('MALCAIR' × 'DANSE DES
SYLPHES') × (['ZAMBRA' ×
'ZAMBRA'] × CENTENAIRE DE
LOURDES)

### 'Anne Diamond' LANdia *(above)*

MODERN, LARGE-FLOWERED/HYBRID TEA, APRICOT BLEND, REPEAT-FLOWERING

This is a rose that would be well served by the American term 'Grandiflora', because it bears fully double flowers of Large-flowered quality with the profusion one expects of a Cluster-flowered Rose. The urn-shaped buds show pink as the sepals part, but on the inside the petals are apricot, and this color predominates as the blooms expand. They fade off buff yellow in the fully open flowers, which are well scented. They are usually carried in sprays of 3 or 4, appearing through summer and autumn on stems long enough to cut for flower arrangement. The plant grows to above average height but is apt to branch awkwardly, so it is not ideal for bedding. The foliage is dark green. Anne Diamond is well known in England as a television presenter. **ZONES 4–9.**

SEALAND, UK, 1988

'MILDRED REYNOLDS' × 'ARTHUR BELL'

ROYAL NATIONAL ROSE SOCIETY TRIAL GROUND CERTIFICATE 1987

### 'Anne Harkness' HARkaramel *(above)*

MODERN, CLUSTER-FLOWERED/FLORIBUNDA, APRICOT BLEND,
REPEAT-FLOWERING

This is a remarkable rose because of its spectacular flower sprays, in which each perfect flower
is evenly spaced to create a natural floral bouquet.
They open cupped, with wavy petal edges filling
the bloom, and hold their regular form for a long
time, before dropping cleanly. The double,
medium-sized flowers are apricot, tinged with
apricot pink as they age. There is little scent. The
plant requires much energy to produce such large
sprays and so the first flowering is distinctly later
than that of other Cluster-flowered Roses though,
once started, they flower on into autumn with
hardly a pause. It grows tall and upright, with
adequate mid-green foliage, and is suitable to
group among other plants or to grow as a hedge.
The rose was named for the raiser's niece to mark
her 21st birthday. ZONES 4–9.

HARKNESS, UK, 1980

'BOBBY DAZZLER' × SEEDLING

ROYAL NATIONAL ROSE SOCIETY TRIAL GROUND CERT IFICATE 1978,
BRITISH ASSOCIATION OF ROSE BREEDERS SELECTION 1980

### 'Anne-Marie de Montravel' *(above)*
syn. 'Anna-Maria de Montravel'

MODERN, POLYANTHA, WHITE, REPEAT-FLOWERING

This is a very early survivor of the innovative
breeding work done with dwarf forms of *Rosa
multiflora* around Lyon in nineteenth-century
France, and as such it would be worth growing as
a curiosity. It is a most charming rose, making a
dense, rather sprawling shrublet full of twiggy
growth and graced with pointed dark green leaflets. The pure white flowers are small, and quite
full of rather ragged petals that open out to reveal
the stamens. Their scent is reminiscent of lily-
of-the-valley, and they are borne profusely in big
clusters in summer and more sparingly through
to autumn. The raiser, a widow, was the mother-
in-law of Francois Dubreuil, who himself raised
many roses from the 1880s onwards. **ZONES 4–9.**

RAMBAUX, FRANCE, 1879

DWARF STRAIN OF *ROSA MULTIFLORA* × 'MME DE TARTAS'

### 'Annie Vibert' *(above right)*
OLD, NOISETTE, WHITE BLEND, REPEAT-FLOWERING

After the double, pink, medium-sized blooms
on this variety open they change to white. The
flowers continue from summer until autumn and
have a pleasant perfume; the long, arching canes
reach up to 12 ft (3.5 m). Noisettes were crosses
between *Rosa chinensis* and an *R. moschata* variety. The hybridizer, John Champneys of South
Carolina, gave his neighbor, Philippe Noisette,
seedlings of this rose, which the latter sent to his
brother in Paris; many think it is a French rose,
which it is not. All Noisettes require a warm
climate. **ZONES 5–10.**

VIBERT, FRANCE, 1828

PARENTAGE UNKNOWN

### 'Another Chance' *(above)*

**MODERN, LARGE-FLOWERED/HYBRID TEA, WHITE, REPEAT-FLOWERING**

The large, pointed buds of 'Another Chance' are
pure white and open to creamy, very full flowers
of exhibition form. Flower production is good,
the flowers lasting well on the bush, and the petals
are tough and do not mark easily. There is a mild
perfume. This variety grows to medium height
and has bushy, matt, dark green foliage that is
resistant to disease. The breeder gave this rose
'another chance', as it improves so much after its
initial flowering in the seed bed; it deserves to be
grown more widely than it is. **ZONES 4–10.**

HEYES, AUSTRALIA, 1994

'MOUNT SHASTA' × 'SAFFRON'

### 'Anthony Meilland' MEItalbaz, MEIbaltaz

*(above)*

MODERN, CLUSTER-FLOWERED/FLORIBUNDA, MEDIUM YELLOW,
REPEAT-FLOWERING

This variety bears fully petalled flowers in a bright
and cheerful shade of yellow. They are often
produced in clusters of a few blooms, but they are
so unusually large for a Cluster-flowered Rose
that, when the blooms open, the heads may be
crowded together. It certainly makes for a showy
display, and the petals have attractive folds and
scalloped edges. There is a pleasing fragrance, and
the repeat-flowering through summer to autumn
is good. This therefore makes a very suitable rose
for a bed, and the bushy growth habit at or a little
under average height is in its favor. The leaves of
this variety are large, mid-green, and somewhat
glossy. The rose was named after a member of the
raiser's family. **ZONES 5–11.**

MEILLAND, FRANCE, 1990

'SUNBLEST' × MEILENANGAL

**A**

### 'Antike 89' KORdalen
*(below)*
syns 'Antique',
'Antique 89'

MODERN, LARGE-FLOWERED
CLIMBER, PINK BLEND,
REPEAT-FLOWERING

The flowers of this
climber are full pet-
alled, rounded in form,
and open with con-
fused centers, the petals
enfolded against each
other in all directions.
The background color
of the petals is blush,
heavily overlaid with
rose red, especially
towards the petal
margins. The flowers,
which have only a
modest fragrance,
appear from summer
to autumn on stiffly
branching stems. This
plant is useful for
pillars, fences and
pergolas. The growth is
vigorous, and there is a
good coverage of tough
leathery dark green
foliage. **ZONES 4–9.**

KORDES, GERMANY, 1988
PARENTAGE UNKNOWN

### 'Antique Rose' MORcara, MORcana *(above)*
MODERN, MINIATURE, MEDIUM PINK, REPEAT-FLOWERING

Pointed buds reveal old-fashioned-looking rose
pink blooms on a vigorous, tall, upright-growing
bush. The blooms are naturally produced one
to a stem and have a high center and a slight
fragrance. They tend to lose their brilliance of
color and substance rather fast, especially in dry
climates. The foliage is dark green with brown
prickles. This rose is well named as it has good
color and form and resembles an Old Garden
Rose. **ZONES 4–11.**

MOORE, USA, 1980
'BACCARA' × 'LITTLE CHIEF'

## 'Antique Silk' KORampa *(above)*

syn. 'Champagner'

MODERN, LARGE-FLOWERED/HYBRID TEA, WHITE,
REPEAT-FLOWERING

This is an exception to the rule that florists' roses lack scent, because it does have a pleasant almond fragrance. The buds as they open are tightly coiled. They expand to create star-shaped blooms with several layers of petals, pointed at the tips and with high centers. The petals are very firm, ensuring the flowers will last well whether they are cut for arrangement or left to develop on the plant. The whiteness of the blooms is touched with cream and ivory, which imparts a silky sheen. 'Antique Silk' produces a good succession of flowers through summer and autumn, carried on firm upright stems, which are pleasant to handle as there are few thorns. As well as being a good cut-flower variety, this performs well as a garden rose in warmer climates. Growth is upright and bushy, and the leaves medium green.
**ZONES 4–9.**

KORDES, GERMANY, 1982

SEEDLING OF 'ANABELL' × SEEDLING

### 'Antoine Rivoire'
*(below)*

MODERN, LARGE-FLOWERED/
HYBRID TEA, LIGHT PINK,
REPEAT-FLOWERING

For many years this Large-flowered Rose was a standby for cutting, both in the garden and commercially. The color is a pretty blend of pale creamy yellow with flushes of rosy pink, and the flat blooms caused it to be likened to a camellia. Its numerous petals are substantial enough to hold the centers of the blooms in shape for several days, even in a warm climate, though they yield only a light fragrance. The growth is strong and upright, though not many stems are produced, and flower production is limited between the summer and autumn flushes. The foliage is bronzy green, large and leathery, and needs watching for black spot. Antoine Rivoire was the president of the Lyon Horticulturalists' Association. ZONES 4–7.

PERNET-DUCHER, FRANCE, 1895

'DR GRILL' × 'LADY MARY FITZWILLIAM'

### 'Antonia Ridge'
MEIparadon *(bottom)*

MODERN, LARGE-FLOWERED/
HYBRID TEA, MEDIUM RED,
REPEAT-FLOWERING

This variety bears its blooms sometimes singly and sometimes several together. They are large, full petalled, carried upright on long stems, and open with high centers to display the rich deep red color. There is only a light fragrance which is disappointing in a red rose, but for garden display it is attractive, continuing in bloom through summer and autumn. The plant grows upright and bushy to average height, with sizeable mid-green leaves. Antonia Ridge wrote *For Love of a Rose*, which tells the fascinating story of the Meilland nursery and became a best seller. The raiser, professionally known as Marie-Louise Paolino, is Mme Marie-Louise Meilland. ZONES 4–9.

PAOLINO, FRANCE, 1976

('CHRYSLER IMPERIAL' × 'KARL HERBST') × SEEDLING

A

## 'Anusheh' PAYable (above)
syn. 'Anushcar'
MODERN, CLUSTER-FLOWERED/FLORIBUNDA, RED BLEND,
REPEAT-FLOWERING

This Modern Garden Rose bears large clusters of
flowers in rather crowded heads that open into
full-petalled medium-sized rosettes. The petals
are strawberry red on the inside and light yellow
on the back, creating a pretty color combination
as the young flowers unfold; the tones alter as
the flowers age, but still manage to do so without
clashing unacceptably. There is a modest fragrance,
and flowering is maintained through summer and
autumn. The plant grows bushy and upright to
average height, with glossy mid-green leaves, and
is useful for bedding and to cut for small arrangements. Archie Payne, who died in December
1997, was a keen amateur raiser with a discerning
eye. ZONES 4–9.

PAYNE, UK, 1993

'LEN TURNER' × SEEDLING

ROYAL NATIONAL ROSE SOCIETY TRIAL GROUND CERTIFICATE 1990

## 'Apart'
MODERN, HYBRID RUGOSA, MAUVE BLEND, REPEAT-FLOWERING

There have been many excellent Hybrid Rugosas
in recent years, and this one displays the rugged
qualities that make them especially valuable for
colder zones. 'Apart' bears medium-sized, loosely
double flowers with ruffled petals in a mauvish
shade of pink over a long period through summer
into autumn. The flowers are very fragrant.
In autumn there is an outstanding display of
tomato-shaped hips. The plant grows to average
height or more with the rounded shrubby habit
typical of many Rugosas, and is healthy and
hardy. ZONES 3–7.

UHL, GERMANY, 1981

PARENTAGE UNKNOWN

'Apollo' ARMolo *(above)*

MODERN, LARGE-FLOWERED/HYBRID TEA, MEDIUM YELLOW,
REPEAT-FLOWERING

The flowers of this variety are a light and cheerful
shade of yellow, opening from long tapered buds
into fully double blooms. They have a pleasant
fragrance and last well when cut. The plant grows
bushy and upright, with dark leathery foliage,
which needs watching for black spot. Although
this rose achieved a prestigious award, its record
as a garden rose has proved disappointing and it
achieved a poor 4.8 out of 10 in the American
Rose Society's National Rose Ratings. **ZONES 4–9.**

ARMSTRONG, USA, 1971

'HIGH TIME' × 'IMPERIAL GOLD'

ALL-AMERICA ROSE SELECTION 1972

A

## 'Apothecary's Rose' *(right)*
syns *Rosa gallica officinalis*, 'Rose of Provins',
'Red Rose of Lancaster'

OLD, GALLICA, DEEP PINK

This is possibly the oldest rose to be cultivated in
Europe. It has been used for medicinal purposes
ever since its birth, and it is also part of the story
of the War of the Roses. The semi-double blooms
with 4 rows of petals change from bright crimson
to near purple, and are crowned with prominent
stamens. The branching canes hold few prickles,
and the dark green foliage is most attractive. It
blooms later than its offspring and is highly disease resistant. The hips produce abundant seeds,
ideal for naturalizing. It suckers readily when on
its own roots and has an intense fragrance, the
petals being ideal for potpourri. It serves well as
erosion control on steep sites. **ZONES 4–10.**

PRE-1600

PARENTAGE UNKNOWN

## 'Apple Blossom' *(above)*
MODERN, RAMBLER, LIGHT PINK

Luther Burbank was a famed hybridizer of fruits,
trees and plants, and this rose is his rose memorial.
'Apple Blossom' is the only one of his hybrids
still in catalogues around the world. The vigorous
canes support huge trusses of pink-white flowers
with crinkled petals throughout summer. It is
ideal for training up trees and on pergolas. The
pliable stems are covered with dark green, healthy
foliage and few prickles. **ZONES 5–10.**

BURBANK, USA, 1932

'DAWSON' × *ROSA MULTIFLORA*

## 'Apricot Gem'
*(below)*

MODERN, CLUSTER-FLOWERED/
FLORIBUNDA, APRICOT BLEND,
REPEAT-FLOWERING

This small-growing rose was not registered when it was first released and has only been grown in limited quantities since. The strong, double, apricot flowers are borne in clusters that cover the bush, creating quite a charming effect. Its height at maturity is low, so it is ideal as a bush for a patio or at the edge of a bed. It has poor resistance to disease and needs care and attention throughout the season to keep it flowering and growing well. The plant does best in warm, dry conditions. It is not strong in cold, damp climates, although it is in these conditions that the most intense color is to be found. **ZONES 5–9.**

DELBARD AND CHABERT,
FRANCE, 1978

PARENTAGE UNKNOWN

## 'Apricot Nectar'
*(bottom)*

MODERN, CLUSTER-FLOWERED/
FLORIBUNDA, APRICOT BLEND,
REPEAT-FLOWERING

This has been a firm favorite since it first appeared on the market over 30 years ago. The attraction is provided by a beautiful shade of golden apricot with just a hint of pink, the pretty cupped formation of the blooms, and their value for floral arrangement, because if cut at a young stage they will open slowly and give pleasure for many days. Flowers are full petalled, quite large, and especially in warmer climates, they can become crowded in the cluster and require disbudding. There is a pleasant fruity scent and a good succession of blooms through summer and autumn. Growth is bushy and reasonably vigorous, and the plant is well covered in mid-green leaves. This is generally good as a garden rose but is not happy in dull cool conditions.
**ZONES 4–9.**

BOERNER, USA, 1965

SEEDLING × 'SPARTAN'

ROYAL NATIONAL ROSE SOCIETY
CERTIFICATE OF MERIT 1965,
ALL-AMERICA ROSE SELECTION
1966

### 'Apricot Silk' *(right)*

MODERN, LARGE-FLOWERED/
HYBRID TEA, APRICOT BLEND,
REPEAT-FLOWERING

The beauty of this rose is found in the color, a fusion of orange and orange-red shades in the high-centered flowers. The long buds open to full-petalled blooms that do indeed have a silky look, but they do not last long either on the plant or when cut, nor do they have much scent. The bush grows upright to average height or less, and its covering of dark glossy leaves is hardly adequate, therefore giving the plant a spindly look. This is accentuated if black spot causes leaf loss, which is likely, and this in turn will affect the plant's repeat-flowering capabilities. Old-time catalogues used to give their customers a coded warning about roses of this nature with the words 'rewards good cultivation'. ZONES 4–9.

GREGORY, UK, 1965

SEEDLING × 'SOUVENIR DE JACQUES VERSCHUREN'

### 'April Hamer'
*(above)*

MODERN, LARGE-FLOWERED/
HYBRID TEA, PINK BLEND,
REPEAT-FLOWERING

This variety is an excellent garden and show rose that is magnificent for cutting and for the show bench. Consisting of 40 petals and with moderate fragrance, the flowers are very pale pink, flushed much deeper pink at the petal edges. It is one of the best of all Australian-raised roses. The plentiful dark green foliage acts as a foil to the pale flowers. It is a strong, healthy, upright grower, free from disease and can produce high-quality flowers throughout the year. ZONES 6–11.

BELL, AUSTRALIA, 1983

'MOUNT SHASTA' × 'PRIMA BALLERINA'

**'Aquarius'** ARMaq *(above)*
MODERN, LARGE-FLOWERED/HYBRID TEA, PINK BLEND,
REPEAT-FLOWERING

Also known as a Grandiflora Rose, this variety has
high-centered flowers of medium size filled with
quite broad petals, and carried singly or in sprays
of several together. The color is a blend of reddish
pink and cream, paling as the flowers open. They
are good to cut as they last well; for this objective,
the flower sprays should be thinned by removing
some of the buds when they are very small. They
do not carry much scent, but flower production
is good through summer and autumn. The plant
grows tall and vigorous, with tough leathery
leaves. **ZONES 4–9.**

ARMSTRONG, USA, 1971

('CHARLOTTE ARMSTRONG' × 'CONTRAST') × ('FANDANGO' ×
['WORLD'S END' × 'FLORADORA'])

GENEVA GOLD MEDAL 1970, ALL-AMERICA ROSE SELECTION 1971

## 'Archduke Charles' *(right)*
syn. 'Archiduc Charles'

OLD, CHINA, RED BLEND, REPEAT-FLOWERING

The blossoms on this rose change color. Thomas
Rivers remarked that it is a chameleon: the crimson outer petals with pink centers later deepen to
solid crimson, and in full, hot sun, everything
turns red. The full, lasting blooms, with banana
fragrance, are cupped with large 'guard' petals
enclosing small petals of pale pink to white.
Growing up to 6 ft (1.8 m), it has a neat, upright
appearance and few prickles. Frequent pruning is
recommended to shape the lanky bush. For many
years in Bermuda this was thought to be 'Seven
Sisters'. ZONES 5–10.

LIFFAY, FRANCE, PRE-1837

SEEDLING OF *ROSA CHINENSIS* 'PARSON'S PINK'

## 'Archiduc Joseph'
*(above)*

OLD, TEA, PINK BLEND,
REPEAT-FLOWERING

There has been much
controversy over this
rose as it has been in-
correctly labeled as
'Monsieur Tillier' and
vice versa—the two are
close in appearance.

The buds of 'Archiduc
Joseph' are dark pink,
opening lighter and
then turning copper,
with strong pink over-
tones. Thin canes with
glossy foliage are some-
times not strong enough
to hold the quartered
blooms upright. Colors
vary depending on the

weather and the
location: the petals
become purple-orange
in humid climates but
rose and pink in dry,
hot weather. The canes
are brownish red with
dark, ashy green leaves.
ZONES 7–8.

NABONNAND, FRANCE, 1892

SEEDLING OF 'MME LOMBARD'

A

### 'Archiduchesse Elizabeth d'Autriche' *(right)*

OLD, HYBRID PERPETUAL,
MEDIUM PINK,
REPEAT-FLOWERING

The double, rose pink, very large, full blooms of this variety open flat. The petals resemble satin, and are medium pink with a lighter reverse. Vigorous and nearly thornless, this rose reaches 3 ft (1 m) and is quite floriferous in mid-summer. Hard pruning helps to shape its appearance. The archduchess was the daughter of Emperor Franz-Josef of the Austro-Hungarian Empire. Jack Harkness states that this rose is repeat-flowering, but it does not bloom continuously. **ZONES 5–10.**

MOREAU ET ROBERT, FRANCE,
1881

PARENTAGE UNKNOWN

### 'Ardoisée de Lyon' *(above)*

OLD, HYBRID PERPETUAL,
MAUVE, REPEAT-FLOWERING

Opening bright red and turning to a violet finish, the full, large and quartered blooms of this rose are rather muddled. In full sunlight they appear a rich cerise but the color is often criticized because of a blue reflection that detracts from the overall effect. The flowers have strong necks on a shrub that is 4 ft (1.2 m) high and 3 ft (1 m) wide. It has a sweet, rich fragrance, and the long hips that appear later in the season add to its great charm. The foliage is dark, gray-green and rather coarse with brown prickles. Like so many Hybrid Perpetuals, it is subject to mildew and rust. **ZONES 5–10.**

DAMAIZIN, FRANCE, 1858

PARENTAGE UNKNOWN

### 'Ards Rover' *(right)*

OLD, HYBRID PERPETUAL, DARK RED

'Ards Rover' has large, crimson-velvet, globular blossoms with stiff petals that develop into a muddled form. The sparse and straggly, climbing growth does not detract from its value because red climbers have always been scarce and there is a strong fragrance. It shares many characteristics of a Large-flowered Rose, and its flowers are good for cutting. It is slow to establish itself but, once established, the vigorous and rapid growth of the rigid canes needs little pruning except for the dead wood. It does not like hot sun and does well in shady situations, flowering throughout summer. The Ards Peninsula is in Ireland, where the Dickson nursery was established well over 100 years ago. **ZONES 4–10.**

DICKSON, UK, 1898

PARENTAGE UNKNOWN

### 'Arethusa' *(right)*

OLD, CHINA, YELLOW BLEND,
REPEAT-FLOWERING

Clusters of clear yellow, blowsy blooms cover this short shrub from summer until autumn. Although it is gawky in appearance, it is a valuable plant in the border if it is surrounded by perennials. The foliage is healthy, shiny and sparse. William Paul and Sons of England produced scores of roses, including 'Hébé's Lip' and 'Magna Charta'. Arethusa was a famous spring in Syracuse, Sicily, in ancient times and, according to legend, a naiad of the same name made it her home. **ZONES 5–10.**

PAUL, UK, 1903

PARENTAGE UNKNOWN

A

### 'Arianna' MEIdali *(above)*

MODERN, LARGE-FLOWERED/HYBRID TEA, PINK BLEND,
REPEAT-FLOWERING

This is a rose for warmer climates, where its large, high-centered flowers can be used to great effect as a hedge or large bed, because it is a very free-flowering variety. The blooms are double with about 36 petals, and are basically rose pink with a suffusion of coral-salmon, a soft and unusual tone. They have a light fragrance and, being long stemmed, are suitable as cut flowers. The continuity of bloom through summer and autumn is good, the autumn flowers being particularly fine. The growth is vigorous, to above average height and with an open, spreading habit, and a profusion of dark leathery leaves. **ZONES 5–9.**

MEILLAND, FRANCE, 1968

'CHARLOTTE ARMSTRONG' × ('PEACE' × 'MICHÈLE MEILLAND')

BAGATELLE GOLD MEDAL 1965, ROME GOLD MEDAL 1965,
THE HAGUE GOLD MEDAL 1965

## 'Arielle Dombasle'
*(right)*
syn. 'Arielle Dombasie'
MODERN, LARGE-FLOWERED
CLIMBER, ORANGE BLEND,
REPEAT-FLOWERING

Although unremarkable, this makes a very effective and well-behaved climbing rose for all the usual purposes—wall, fence, pillar—for which a plant of average extent is required. The official color code is perhaps misleading, because this rose is very much on the scarlet side of orange. Flowers are medium-sized, double, and borne in clusters of several together, and the petals open wide to display the bright warm color to good effect. As the flowers age they admit some reddish pink, but the tones of both old and new flowers go together well. There is a slight fragrance, and flowering continues through summer and autumn. The leaves are plentiful, rugged and dark green. **ZONES 4–9.**

MEILLAND, FRANCE, 1991
PARENTAGE UNKNOWN

## 'Arizona' WErina
*(above right)*
syn. 'Tocade'
MODERN, LARGE-FLOWERED/
HYBRID TEA, ORANGE BLEND,
REPEAT-FLOWERING

Like many roses with orange-salmon tones, this rose's color varies according to location. The base color is coppery orange, with salmon-red towards the petal edges and yellow in the petal depths; the tones are richer in cool climates. The flowers are of medium size, with sufficient petals to form shapely high-centered blooms of Large-flowered Rose character, opening from urn-shaped buds. In the USA it is regarded as a Grandiflora, presumably because it is tall and bears flowers on long stems with good continuity through summer and autumn. The blooms have a sweet fragrance. The plant is a vigorous, upright grower with crisp dark green foliage. It is sometimes affected by fungus troubles. **ZONES 4–9.**

WEEKS, USA, 1975

(['FRED HOWARD' × 'GOLDEN
SCEPTER'] × 'GOLDEN RAPTURE')
× (['FRED HOWARD' × 'GOLDEN
SCEPTER'] × 'GOLDEN RAPTURE')

ALL-AMERICA ROSE SELECTION
1975

### 'Armada' HARuseful *(left)*
### syn. 'Trinity Fair'

MODERN, MODERN SHRUB, MEDIUM PINK, REPEAT-FLOWERING

'Armada' makes a modest-sized shrub, ideal for mixed borders or to plant as a small group or as a hedge. The flowers are a rich deep pink, of medium size with about 18 petals, cupped in form and appearing in big clusters on strong stems with good repeat-flowering. They have a pleasing scent. The plant is vigorous and free branching, with glossy green foliage, healthy and very hardy. The rose was named for a National Trust appeal in aid of Buckland Abbey, once the home of Sir Francis Drake, on the quatercentenary of the Spanish Armada's attempted invasion of Britain. **ZONES 3–9.**

HARKNESS, UK, 1988

'NEW DAWN' × 'SILVER JUBILEE'

COPENHAGEN DIPLOMA 1988, COURTRAI SILVER MEDAL 1988, THE HAGUE GOLD MEDAL 1994

### 'Arthur Bell' *(bottom)*

MODERN, CLUSTER-FLOWERED/FLORIBUNDA, MEDIUM YELLOW, REPEAT-FLOWERING

This most satisfying garden rose has flowers that are clear yellow, bright in bud, opening paler and finishing almost primrose and transforming from pointed buds to pretty cups along the way. The 20 or so petals are firm and well able to withstand wet weather, which must have been needful on the Ulster breeder's nursery. The flower clusters are held above the foliage on upright, stiff stems, and the vigorous bush is handsomely clothed with shiny bright green leaves. The sweetly scented flowers repeat their bloom through summer and autumn, making this an excellent choice for a bed or group. They are also used for cutting and ex-hibition, as they last well. **'Climbing Arthur Bell'** (Pearce, UK, 1978) freely bears flowers just as lovely as the bush form, in summer and with some later bloom. The plant grows vigorously, putting out stiff stems that are best suited to being trained against a sizeable wall, where stems and shoots can be attached laterally or fanwise to a solid background. **ZONES 4–9.**

MCGREDY, UK, 1965

'CLÄRE GRAMMERSTORF' × 'PICCADILLY'

ROYAL NATIONAL ROSE SOCIETY CERTIFICATE OF MERIT 1964, BELFAST FRAGRANCE PRIZE 1967, ROYAL HORTICULTURAL SOCIETY AWARD OF GARDEN MERIT 1993

A

## 'Arthur de Sansal'
*(right)*

**OLD, PORTLAND, MAUVE, REPEAT-FLOWERING**

This is a short, almost spindly shrub that grows to a maximum height of 3 ft (1 m) and has dark, fairly thorny wood and very dark green foliage. The flowers are produced in large tightly packed clusters, starting in mid-summer and going on through to autumn. Each flower is some 2 in (5 cm) across and full of small layered petals, which creates a very flat effect when fully open. These richly perfumed flowers are deep maroon-red in color, ageing to a rather muddy purple. Time does not seem to have dealt any favors to this rose for it is now rather prone to both rust and mildew, but it can be most rewarding if these afflictions can be controlled or over-looked. **ZONES 4–10.**

COCHET, FRANCE, 1855
SEEDLING OF 'GÉANT DES BATAILLES'

## 'Arthur Hillier'
*(above)*

**MODERN, MODERN SHRUB, DEEP PINK, REPEAT-FLOWERING**

Arthur Hillier was the creator of the Hillier Arboretum at Win-chester in England, one of the most famous collections of plants in the world. This rose named after him is a cross between two Himalayan species with single flowers of 5 rich rosy crimson petals. They are 2½ in (6 cm) across, and are borne in clusters on long arching canes with attractive ferny foliage. Lightly perfumed, there is some repeat-bloom. This is a large shrub suitable for planting in parks and wild gardens. **ZONES 3–9.**

HILLIER, UK, 1961

*ROSA MACROPHYLLA* × *R. MOYESII*

**A**

## 'Artistry' JACirst *(right)*
MODERN, LARGE-FLOWERED/HYBRID TEA,
ORANGE BLEND, REPEAT-FLOWERING

The plump buds of this rose
open into fairly large blooms of
reddish coral-orange, which are
usually borne singly but sometimes in clusters. Each flower
has about 30 petals that hold a
neat center, which becomes
cupped as the outer petals reflex. They hold their shape
for a long time. There is a light
fragrance, which makes this a
fine variety for cutting as well
as for beds and borders. A succession of bloom is well maintained through summer and
autumn. The plant is vigorous,
with an upright, well-branched
habit, and grows to average
height or more with mid-green,
healthy foliage. ZONES 4–9.

ZARY, USA, 1996

PARENTAGE UNKNOWN

ALL-AMERICA ROSE SELECTION 1997

## 'Aspen' POUlurt *(below)*
syns 'Gold Magic Carpet',
'Gwent', 'Sun Cover'
MODERN, MODERN SHRUB, MEDIUM YELLOW,
REPEAT-FLOWERING

This is often sold as a Ground
Cover Rose and it will spread
about twice as wide as it grows
high, the dimensions both
ways being modest; it is even
recommended for a large hanging basket, and if care is taken
not to let it dry out and a small
rooted plant is chosen (one
grown on its own roots, for
example) then it will suit the
purpose. The flowers are semi-
double, cupped, of small to
medium size and in a pleasing
shade of yellow. They are carried in pretty clusters fairly
close to the dark glossy foliage
through summer and autumn,
and have a light scent. Growth
is vigorous, with many shoots
appearing. It will benefit from
preventive spraying where black
spot is prevalent. ZONES 4–9.

OLESEN, DENMARK, 1992

PARENTAGE UNKNOWN

A

### 'Assemblage des Beautés' *(right)*
syns 'Assemblage de Beauté', 'Rouge Eblouissante'
OLD, GALLICA, DARK RED

This is an upright, tidy shrub to 4 ft (1.2 m) with darkish green, burnished wood, few prickles, and luxuriant light green foliage. It produces abundant blooms on dense, rich gray-green canes. The buds expand into medium-sized double blooms with a button eye, ranging in color from crimson-scarlet to purple. The very fragrant flowers are composed of many petals, with the inner ones curving toward a small green pip at the center. The full bloom resembles a cushion, $2^{1}/_{2}$ in (6.5 cm) in diameter. It is an outstanding cut flower and does well in the shade or in mixed borders. This is perhaps the brightest colored of all the Gallicas. ZONES 5–10.

DELANGE, FRANCE, 1823
PARENTAGE UNKNOWN

### 'Asso di Cuori'   KORred
syns 'Ace of Hearts', 'Toque Rouge'
MODERN, LARGE-FLOWERED/HYBRID TEA, DARK RED, REPEAT-FLOWERING

This variety is splendid for flower arrangers because its firm petals keep the blooms in shape for many days and because the blooms are carried on long stems that are ideal for cutting, and rarely have more than one flower to a stem. The large dark crimson buds open slowly into full-petalled flowers of classic Large-flowered shape, high centered, with symmetry of form and a rounded outline to the flowers. The open blooms are rich velvety crimson-scarlet, and often grace the show bench. They are produced with good succession through summer and autumn on an upstanding, vigorous bush, well covered with dark green, glossy leaves. There is one imperfection, and that is the lack of a good fragrance, which in a red rose is greatly missed. ZONES 4–9.

KORDES, GERMANY, 1981
PARENTAGE UNKNOWN

### 'Asta von Parpat'   *(above)*
OLD, RAMBLER, MAUVE

This rose produces clusters of purple, medium-sized blooms that change to mauve-carmine in direct sun and which form on long branches during the summer flowering. The ruffled blooms are double and sit erect on their stems. This vigorous shrub has dark, blue-green foliage and is one of a series of roses hybridized by Rudolf Geschwind in Hungary, where he used Wild Roses in his crosses. All of them carry the strong, disease-resistant genes of Wild Roses. He also created some still-popular shrubs, such as 'Gruss an Teplitz' and 'Gipsy Boy'. ZONES 5–10.

GESCHWIND, HUNGARY, 1909
HYBRID OF *ROSA MULTIFLORA*

### 'Astrée' (below)

MODERN, LARGE-FLOWERED/
HYBRID TEA, PINK BLEND,
REPEAT-FLOWERING

The legacy of 'Peace' has been logged by Dr Tommy Cairns of California, and up to 1995 he found that as a seed parent it had spawned 192 commercialized varieties. 'Astrée' is a fine rose in its own right, bearing large blooms of classic form. The buds are deep salmon-orange and open into fully double flowers, showing orange and salmon-pink as the petals expand. There is a satisfying fragrance, and the plant continues to bloom repeatedly through summer and autumn. It is fairly compact and well foliaged, making this a fine variety for a bed, and the flowers last well when cut. Following in the footsteps of its famous parent, 'Astrée' has produced a climbing form. 'Climbing Astrée' is a vigorous grower that flowers well over a long season. **ZONES 4–9.**

CROIX, FRANCE, 1956

'PEACE' × 'BLANCHE MALLERIN'

PLUS BELLE ROSE DE FRANCE
1956

### 'Athena' RühKOR (bottom)

MODERN, LARGE-FLOWERED/
HYBRID TEA, WHITE BLEND,
REPEAT-FLOWERING

In many ways this fulfils the requirements of a good cut-flower rose: it bears a lot of flowering stems, and a high proportion carry just one plump bud. The buds open into shapely, high-centered blooms consisting of over 30 petals that are gleaming white in color with just a faint pink edge to the petals to make it interesting. The plant grows bushily to average height with a plentiful supply of mid-green leaves. As a bonus, there is a whiff of scent. In warmer climates this can be grown as a garden rose, but it is primarily a commercial item for the greenhouse. **ZONES 4–9.**

KORDES, GERMANY, 1984

SEEDLING × 'HELMUT SCHMIDT'

### 'Auckland Metro' MACbucpal  *(right)*
syns 'Métro', 'Precious Michelle'

MODERN, LARGE-FLOWERED/HYBRID TEA, WHITE BLEND,
REPEAT-FLOWERING

The flowers of this variety are made up of many
overlapping petals, giving them a camellia-like
appearance. They are creamy blush to white, well
scented, and often produced in large trusses with
the individual stems long enough to cut, a purpose for which the rose is well suited because the
flowers are at their most beautiful when fully
open. It is repeat-flowering, though after a prolific first flush there is often a pause before the
next cycle of growth and bloom. The plant is
sturdy and bushy, below average height and well
furnished with glossy dark leaves, and good for
bedding. It does best in warmer climates and is
popular in New Zealand, and also in Australia
where it is called 'Precious Michelle' in memory
of a young lady named Michelle Joy Cowley.
**ZONES 5–9.**

MCGREDY, NEW ZEALAND, 1988

'SEXY REXY' × (SEEDLING × 'FERRY PORSCHE')

### 'Auguste Gervais'
*(right)*

MODERN, LARGE-FLOWERED
CLIMBER, APRICOT BLEND

This vigorous grower
is more of a Rambler
than a Climber, be-
cause it produces long,
flexible stems and is
easy to train over per-
golas and open fences,
and to grow as a weep-
ing standard. The
blooms are moderately
full of petals, which
open out randomly to
create large, informal-
looking flowers. They
have good scent, and
change color from cop-
pery yellow and salmon
in the bud stage to
almost white by the
time the petals fall. The
summer flowering is
prolific but it does not
repeat its bloom. The
leaves are small, plenti-
ful and shiny, though
seasonal mildew may
affect them. **ZONES 4–9.**

BARBIER, FRANCE, 1918

*ROSA WICHURANA* ×
'LE PROGRÉS'

## 'Auguste Renoir'  MEItoifar

MODERN, LARGE-FLOWERED/HYBRID TEA, MEDIUM PINK,
REPEAT-FLOWERING

This new rose with an old-fashioned look has big
flowers full of petals, opening with substantial
quartered blooms to resemble a Hybrid Perpetual.
They are a warm shade of rosy pink, very fragrant,
usually carried one bloom per stem, and flower
on through summer and autumn. The plant
grows to average height with a bushy habit, and
is well clothed with slightly shiny leaves. One
justification for naming a rose after Auguste
Renoir (1841–1919) is that he is said to have used
petals of his favorite roses as a skin tone guide
when his models were away. **ZONES 4–9.**

MEILLAND, FRANCE, 1993

('VERSAILLES' × 'PIERRE DE RONSARD') × 'KIMONO'

## 'Augustine Guinoisseau'  *(below)*

syns 'Mademoiselle Augustine Guinoisseau',
'White La France'

MODERN, LARGE-FLOWERED/HYBRID TEA, WHITE BLEND,
REPEAT-FLOWERING

'La France' was recognized in 1867 as a landmark
in roses, and became retrospectively the first
Large-flowered Rose. It was so famous that any
sport of it was assured of public interest. It resembles the parent except in color, which is
not absolutely white but has blush tints, and
in substance, being not quite so fully petalled.
In other respects—scent, general habit and the
ability to repeat the cycle of growth and flower—
the two roses are similar. **ZONES 4–9.**

GUINOISSEAU, FRANCE, 1889

SPORT OF 'LA FRANCE'

## 'Australia Felix'
*(bottom)*

MODERN, LARGE-FLOWERED/
HYBRID TEA, MEDIUM RED,
REPEAT-FLOWERING

The flowers of this var-
iety open from small,
rounded buds into
moderately full blooms
of cupped form. They
are silvery pink with
tints of lavender, have
a pleasing fragrance,
and appear through
summer and autumn.
The growth is average
for a Large-flowered
Rose, and it is reason-
ably vigorous, with a
bushy habit and glossy
foliage. **ZONES 4–9.**

CLARK, AUSTRALIA, 1919

'JERSEY BEAUTY' × 'LA FRANCE'

A

## 'Australia's Olympic Gold Rose' WEKblagab

MODERN, CLUSTER-FLOWERED/
FLORIBUNDA, DEEP YELLOW,
REPEAT-FLOWERING

This rose is named for the Sydney 2000 Olympics. A mild fruity fragrance accompanies clusters of long-lasting, deep golden yellow flowers, which are carried on long strong stems above dark green foliage. The bush is upright, standing 4–5 ft (1.2–1.5 m) tall. It is a vigorous grower and the flowers repeat quickly through the season. ZONES 5–9.

## 'Autumn Damask' *(above)*

syns 'Quatre Saisons', 'Four Seasons Rose',
'Rose of Castile', *Rosa damascena semperflorens*

OLD, DAMASK, MEDIUM PINK, REPEAT-FLOWERING

The shapely pink buds open to a crumpled bed of blowsy petals, darker pink in the center. The yellowish green serrated leaves cover a sparse and open plant. If it is happy, the rose will be covered with strongly perfumed blooms. It flowers in early summer and again in autumn and does not like any shade. This rose makes an attractive container plant and contributes a good share of fragrance to potpourri. ZONES 4–10.

POSSIBLY FROM MIDDLE EAST TO ITALY, PRE-1633

POSSIBLY *ROSA GALLICA* × *R. MOSCHATA* OR *R. ABYSSINICA*

A

### 'Autumn Delight'
*(below)*

MODERN, MODERN SHRUB,
WHITE, REPEAT-FLOWERING

The buds of 'Autumn Delight' are pointed and apricot yellow, opening to near single flowers of very soft creamy yellow with beautiful stamens. The flowers fade quickly to white in hot weather, but are particularly beautiful in autumn when huge heads of 30–50 blooms appear on strong shoots. These are long-lasting and retain their color well. It forms a large shrub with leathery, dark green, disease-resistant foliage and few thorns and is useful for beds, borders, hedges and for planting in groups among perennials. It has a huge spring flush, rather sparse bloom in summer and then puts on a wonderful autumn display. **ZONES 3–9.**

BENTALL, UK, 1933

PARENTAGE UNKNOWN

### 'Autumn Sunlight'
*(bottom)*

MODERN, LARGE-FLOWERED
CLIMBER, ORANGE-RED,
REPEAT-FLOWERING

The flowers of this variety are of medium size and rounded form, full of petals, and are carried in large clusters on strong stems with good continuity through summer and autumn. They are pale vermilion and look dull until sunlight catches the petals and brings out a beautiful luminous orange tone. There is a pleasant fragrance. The plant grows to average size for a climber and, being vigorous and free branching, it is easy to train on fences, walls, pillars and pergolas. The leaves are plentiful, glossy and bright green. **ZONES 4–9.**

GREGORY, UK, 1965

'DANSE DU FEU' × 'CLIMBING GOLDILOCKS'

## 'Autumn Sunset'
*(right)*

MODERN, MODERN SHRUB,
APRICOT BLEND,
REPEAT-FLOWERING

The difference between
this rose and its parent
lies in the color, which
in 'Autumn Sunset' is
apricot with touches
of orange and deep
yellow, whereas
'Westerland' is deeper
orange with reddish
flushes. This rose has
loose, rather shaggy-
looking cupped flowers
of middling size,
fragrant and borne
in clusters on strong
stems. It can make a
hefty upright shrub,
or be pruned to form a
thick hedge. The bloom-
ing period extends
through summer and
autumn, and the leaves
are large, abundant and
usually very healthy.
**ZONES 4–9.**

LOWE, USA, 1986

SPORT OF 'WESTERLAND'

## 'Ave Maria' KORav
*(above)*
syn. 'Sunburnt
Country'

MODERN, LARGE-FLOWERED/
HYBRID TEA, ORANGE-PINK,
REPEAT-FLOWERING

This is a rose for color
impact. The elegant
buds are a rich salmon-
orange, and open into
broad-petalled flowers
of lovely high-centered
form with tints of
salmon-orange flushed
salmon-red. It is agree-
ably fragrant and is a
good rose to cut, as the
flowers usually come
singly on long stems
and the firmness of the
petals improves their
holding qualities. The
flowers repeat their
bloom in autumn and
stand wet weather
well. The bush grows
vigorously with an up-
right habit and ample
dark green foliage.
**ZONES 4–9.**

KORDES, GERMANY, 1981

'UWE SEELER' × 'SONIA'

A

### 'Aviateur Blériot' *(above)*

OLD, RAMBLER, YELLOW BLEND

A popular rose, this Rambler has coppery orange
buds that reveal large flowers of saffron and gold
that fade to white. Large trusses of strongly
fragrant blooms crowd the vigorous canes. It has
bright green, glossy foliage with bronze overtones.
This is a handsome plant, especially when used as
a weeping standard. Louis Blériot was the first
aviator to cross the English Channel. **ZONES 4–10.**

FAUQUE, FRANCE, 1910

*ROSA WICHURANA* × 'WILLIAM ALLEN RICHARDSON'

## 'Avon' *(above)*

MODERN, LARGE-FLOWERED/
HYBRID TEA, DARK RED,
REPEAT-FLOWERING

This dark red rose has the virtue of holding its color tone, which has made it very popular in warmer countries, where reds so often turn purplish. The flowers open on long stems to show elegant high-centered young flowers; they are good to cut at this stage. On the bush they develop into large, rather loosely formed flowers that give out a wonderful fragrance, flowering continuing through summer and autumn. The variety has an upright habit to above average height, so is suitable for a hedge or sizeable bed, and it is well furnished with leathery mid-green foliage. It seems happiest in warm dry climates, as in cool conditions it may mildew.
ZONES 5–9.

MOREY, USA, 1961

'NOCTURNE' × 'CHRYSLER IMPERIAL'

## 'Awakening' *(right)*
syn. 'Probuzini'

MODERN, LARGE-FLOWERED,
CLIMBER, LIGHT PINK,
REPEAT-FLOWERING

In 1988, Mr D. Balfour, former President of the Royal National Rose Society, paid a visit to Czechoslovakia where he noticed a rose similar to the Rambler 'New Dawn', the only difference being that the bloom had double the usual number of petals. He brought back some wood for propagation by Peter Beales' nursery, and the rose was re-introduced in 1990 under the name 'Awakening'. With its muddled, petal-packed centers, it is a charmer, with the good points of its parent: sweet fragrance, long flowering period, hardiness, excellent foliage and adaptability to being trained on or over almost anything one can think of.
ZONES 3–9.

BLATNA, CZECHOSLOVAKIA, 1935

SPORT OF 'NEW DAWN'

**B**

### 'Baby Alberic' *(left)*

MODERN, POLYANTHA, LIGHT YELLOW, REPEAT-FLOWERING

The color of this rose is yellow in the pointed
buds, fading to almost creamy white as the small
ruffled petals unfold. They have a pleasant light
fragrance and maintain a good succession of
bloom through summer and autumn, the earlier
flowering being particularly good. The plant
grows vigorously with a low, spreading habit.
Like the *Rosa wichurana* Rambler from which it
derives, 'Baby Alberic' has a good health record
and is long lived. It appeared in Britain at a time
when shrubby dwarf roses were going out of
favor, and has never won recognition there.
Today it is grown mostly in Australia. **ZONES 4–9.**

CHAPLIN, UK, 1932

SEEDLING OF 'ALBÉRIC BARBIER'

### 'Baby Bio' *(left)*

MODERN, PATIO/DWARF
CLUSTER-FLOWERED, DEEP
YELLOW, REPEAT-FLOWERING

Because they are large
in proportion to the
plant, the cheerful
bright yellow flowers,
carried close to the
foliage in big sprays,
create a bold effect.
They are full of petals,
rounded in form,
lightly scented, and
keep flowering through
summer and autumn.
This variety is good
in a bed or group, or
as a neat hedge, where
a short-growing rose
is wanted. It has a vig-
orous, bushy habit and
an ample coverage of
dark shiny leaves; it is
named for a plant food.
**ZONES 5–9.**

SMITH, UK, 1977

'GOLDEN TREASURE' × SEEDLING

ROYAL NATIONAL ROSE SOCIETY
CERTIFICATE OF MERIT 1976,
ROME GOLD MEDAL 1976

### 'Baby Darling' *(right)*
MODERN, MINIATURE, APRICOT BLEND,
REPEAT-FLOWERING

Elegant well-shaped apricot-pink buds yield beautiful double (20 petals) flowers with Large-flowered form. The florets have good color and substance and are suitable for exhibition. The bush is considered dwarf (12 in [30 cm] high) in most climates. 'Baby Darling' is yet another fine example of the classic Miniature Roses that were developed in the early 1960s to capture the attention of the rose-growing public to this evolutionary step in the history of the rose. The extensive use by Moore of the yellow blend Cluster-flowered Rose, 'Little Darling' as seed parent resulted in dozens of award-winning Miniatures. Still grown and shown today, it has remained a popular variety for garden display. **'Climbing Baby Darling'** (Trauger, USA, 1972) sends out canes about 6 ft (1.8 m) long and the blooms occur in small clusters at almost every leaf axil on the horizontal plane. The bush is spreading and without cultivated annual pruning it will become somewhat unruly. **ZONES 4–11.**

MOORE, USA, 1964

'LITTLE DARLING' × 'MAGIC WAND'

B

### 'Baby Faurax' *(above)*
MODERN, POLYANTHA, MAUVE,
REPEAT-FLOWERING

This is said by some to be the nearest there is to a blue rose, the color having been described as amethyst and violet. The rosette-type blooms are small and packed together in dense clusters, which look large because the plant is short and stumpy, like a Miniature Rose. A little fragrance may be detectable on a warm day. It continues in bloom through summer and autumn. It is suspected of having *Rosa multiflora* ancestry because the petite dull green leaflets look to be of that type, and there are a number of purple-lilac Ramblers in that family. This is a curious rose, good for small spaces, and has proved useful in breeding. **ZONES 4–9.**

LILLE, FRANCE, 1924

PARENTAGE UNKNOWN

### 'Baby Gold Star'  *(left)*
syn. 'Estrellita de Oro'

MODERN, MINIATURE, DEEP YELLOW,
REPEAT-FLOWERING

This variety is a good example
of the pioneering work done in
the hybridizing of Miniature
Roses by Pedro Dot. By crossing
the progenitor of most modern
Miniatures, 'Rouletii', with
'Eduardo Toda', he developed
a Miniature with only 14 golden
yellow petals. This marked a
giant step forward in the early
development of Miniature
Roses and proved that miniature genes could be passed
on to a Large-flowered Rose.
Many of Dot's achievements
in hybridizing Miniature Roses
were fundamental to the future
successes of other hybridizers.
The flowers are semi-double
and are borne on a small
compact bush. **ZONES 5–11.**

DOT, SPAIN, 1940

'EDUARDO TODA' × 'ROULETII'

### 'Baby Katie'  *(above)*

MODERN, MINIATURE, PINK BLEND,
REPEAT-FLOWERING

Ovoid pointed buds on a
compact, vigorous, bushy
plant flower into lovely pastel
cream and pink small florets
(28 petals) with magnificent
Large-flowered form. The
blooms are show quality. This is
a rose for everyone, as it has the
basic charming features that
epitomize the Miniature Rose.
However, wide variation in
color has been detected relative
to climate zone. The foliage is
matt green, complementing the
blooms perfectly. 'Baby Katie'
is just one of many successful
seedlings that Harm Saville
hybridized using 'Sheri Anne'
as the seed parent. **ZONES 4–11.**

SAVILLE, USA, 1978

'SHERI ANNE' × 'WATERCOLOR'

### 'Baby Love' SCRIvluv *(above)*
MODERN, PATIO/DWARF CLUSTER-FLOWERED, DEEP YELLOW, REPEAT-FLOWERING

This is a splendid dwarf shrublet, bearing with great freedom and continuity, saucer-shaped, buttercup yellow flowers. They are small, with 5 petals and borne one to a stem, close to the foliage at all levels on a low, rounded plant. They have a slight fragrance. The small, mid-green, semi-glossy foliage is an ideal complement to the blooms. ZONES 4–11.

SCRIVENS, UK, 1992

'SWEET MAGIC' × SEEDLING

ROYAL NATIONAL ROSE SOCIETY AND TORRIDGE AWARD 1993

### 'Baby Masquerade' TANba; TANbakede *(right)*
syns 'Baby Carnaval', 'Baby Carnival', 'Baby Maskarade', 'Baby Mascarade', 'Baby Maskerade'
MODERN, MINIATURE, RED BLEND, REPEAT-FLOWERING

This is a classic variety from the 1950s. The flowers open to golden yellow and age to a luminous but dull attractive red. The floret size is generally small—with about 23 petals. In modern rose shows it qualifies as a micro-Miniature. Leathery foliage surrounds the slight blooms, which have a fruity fragrance, to give a compact low-growing bush about 8 in (20 cm) tall. The use of the classic 'Tom Thumb', hybridized by de Vink of Holland in 1936, as seed parent for this rose recognizes the evolutionary importance of such early varieties. ZONES 4–11.

TANTAU, GERMANY, 1956

'TOM THUMB' × 'MASQUERADE'

**B**

### 'Baccará' MEger *(right)*
### syn. 'Jaqueline'

MODERN, LARGE-FLOWERED/HYBRID TEA, ORANGE-RED, REPEAT-FLOWERING

The quoted parentage is a surprise as both the varieties named are poor performers, whereas 'Baccará' makes a vigorous, rangy plant. For years it was renowned as a foremost rose for florists, thanks to its long stems and the lasting qualities of the very full-petalled flowers. These open slowly and rather flat, showing a vivid deep vermilion color, with blackish shadings on the outer petals, and continue to flower well through summer and autumn. There is no fragrance. The dark leathery leaves are reddish when young, and clothe the plant reasonably well. This rose is best in a warm climate as rain spoils the flowers. ZONES 5–9.

MEILLAND, FRANCE, 1954

'HAPPINESS' × 'INDEPENDENCE'

### 'Ballerina' *(below)*

MODERN, MODERN SHRUB, MEDIUM PINK, REPEAT-FLOWERING

One of summer's treats is to see hundreds of small single, shallow-cupped light pink flowers cramming themselves all over 'Ballerina' like so many hydrangea heads. There is no scent to speak of, but in other respects it is hard to fault this rose. There is a pause after the first marathon blooming, and then a good second crop follows in autumn. This is a real enthusiast's rose, with a graceful rounded habit and abundant mid-green foliage, growing to average height. It can be planted on its own (in either shrub or standard form) where something special is wanted, or will make a splendid group or hedge. It does not mind being pruned to reduce the height. The parents are unknown, but the flowers remind one of the climbing rose 'Blush Rambler'. ZONES 4–9.

BENTALL, UK, 1937

PARENTAGE UNKNOWN

ROYAL HORTICULTURAL SOCIETY AWARD OF GARDEN MERIT 1993

### 'Bantry Bay' *(above)*

MODERN, LARGE-FLOWERED CLIMBER, MEDIUM PINK,
REPEAT-FLOWERING

Through summer and autumn this variety always
seems to have something to show. The loosely
double cupped flowers are deepish rose pink, a
warm and kindly shade, showing their stamens
as they open; they have a light fragrance. They
are borne in clusters and appear at different levels
on the plant, which clothes itself effectively in
dark green foliage. This vigorous, free-branching
rose is an excellent garden performer of restrained
growth, with a good health record and suitable
for all purposes. One of the best varieties to withstand wet weather, it is named after a scenic inlet
in Ireland's County Cork. **ZONES 4–9.**

MCGREDY, UK, 1967

'NEW DAWN' × 'KORONA'

ROYAL NATIONAL ROSE SOCIETY CERTIFICATE OF MERIT 1967,
BELFAST CERTIFICATE OF MERIT 1970

### 'Banzai '83' MEIzalitaf
*(right)*

syn. 'Spectra'

MODERN, LARGE-FLOWERED
CLIMBER, YELLOW BEND,
REPEAT-FLOWERING

Although not widely grown, this is a most eye-catching climber. The high-centered young flowers are yellow with a rosy flush, and open to reveal pretty tints of orange-gold and pale crimson in the large, loosely double blooms, the balance of colors altering as the petals age. The flowers continue through summer and autumn, but there is not much scent. Of rather rigid upright habit, this looks well when trained against fences and walls or up a pillar. It grows to average height, with glossy, deep green foliage, and is likely to be giving of its best in a warm climate.
**ZONES 4–9.**

MEILLAND, FRANCE, 1983

PARENTAGE UNKNOWN

### 'Baron de Bonstetten'

OLD, HYBRID PERPETUAL,
DARK RED

This is one of the most elegant roses of its class; a robust, compact bush, it has velvety maroon, flat blooms that appear in summer on strong stems. The glossy flowers, tightly packed with 80 petals, turn from crimson to very dark purple, sun or shade determining the depth of color. The canes are armed with numerous prickles, and the foliage is rough. It has a strong fragrance. This rose is not suited to hot weather, as the petals will crisp. The Baron was a wealthy Swiss estate owner and rose fancier.
**ZONES 5–10.**

LIABAUD, FRANCE, 1871

'GÉNÉRAL JACQUEMINOT' ×
'GÉANT DES BATAILLES'

### 'Baron de Wassenaer'
*(above right)*

OLD, MOSS, DEEP PINK

This is one of the few Mosses that can be used as a climber. It is a largely vigorous shrub to 7 ft (2.2 m) tall with dark prickly stems and equally dark green, coarse leaves. The flowers emerge from rounded, moderately mossed buds in mid-summer. The moss, like the foliage, is dark green, bordering on brown. When fully open the flowers attain a diameter of some 3 in (8 cm). They are each packed with many petals, at first bright red but quickly changing to a glowing crimson, slightly cupped until fully open and borne in clusters. Always a popular Moss, it requires little pruning and does well in poor soil. It occasionally repeats with an odd autumn bloom. There were three Verdiers— Charles, Victor and Eugene (who bred this rose). **ZONES 5–10.**

VERDIER, FRANCE, 1854

PARENTAGE UNKNOWN

## 'Baron Girod de l'Ain'
*(right)*
syns 'Baron Giraud de l'Ain',
'Princesse Christine von Salm'
OLD, HYBRID PERPETUAL, RED BLEND,
REPEAT-FLOWERING

This is something of a novelty
rose, looking as though some-
one has cut the edge of the
petals with pinking shears. It
has cupped, red blooms with a
scalloped edge of white, which
makes it a dramatic cut flower.
The compact blooms are true
crimson surrounded by broad,
round, leathery leaves. The stiff,
healthy green wood bears some
prickles. It blooms all summer
and may develop black spot in
hot weather. The perfume is
sweet. ZONES 5–10.

REVERCHON, FRANCE, 1897

SPORT OF 'EUGENE FÜRST'

## 'Baron J. B. 'Gonella'
syns 'Baron G. B. Gonella',
'Baron J. G. Gonella'
OLD, BOURBON, PINK BLEND,
REPEAT-FLOWERING

The rounded and cupped
blooms of this rose are very
double, about 3 in (8 cm)
across, and are bright pink
with compact, ruffled centers.
Lilac shading appears on the
large petals, which are smooth
and thick. A rare Bourbon, it is
vigorous and tall and has strong
canes. It has a light fragrance,
and blooms in summer only. The
smooth, green bark is covered
with red prickles. Guillot Père
produced 80 varieties.
ZONES 5–6.

GUILLOT PÈRE, FRANCE, 1859

SEEDLING OF 'LOUISE ODIER'

## 'Baronne Adolphe de Rothschild' *(above)*
syn. 'Baroness Rothschild'
OLD, HYBRID PERPETUAL, LIGHT PINK,
REPEAT-FLOWERING

This marvellous cut flower
looks as regal as its namesake;
the very large buds open flesh
pink with silver-edged petals.
A full, cupped flower usually
appears on a single cane. The
vigorous bush is erect and
hardy, with light green prickly
canes; it blooms early and again
in autumn. The gray-green foliage is most attractive. It should
be pruned like a Large-flowered
Rose. The only attribute this
rose lacks is a strong fragrance.
Pernet and partners produced
many successful roses from
1854 to 1931 that are still
popular. ZONES 5–10.

PERNET, FRANCE, 1868

SPORT OF 'SOUVENIR DE LA REINE
D'ANGLETERRE'

B

### 'Baronne Henriette de Snoy'
*(below)*
syn. 'Baroness Henrietta Snoy'
OLD, TEA, PINK BLEND

Brent Dickerson characterizes this rose thus: 'Distressing at its worst, beautiful at its best, trial is merited.' In the right place in full sun the Baronne can be quite charming. The peach, globular, very large blooms with a deeper pink reverse and a green eye are high centered. The foliage is bronze-green. Like so many Tea Roses, the bush is gawky and needs to be placed where its blooms show, and not its feet. **ZONES 7–11.**

BERNAIX, FRANCE, 1897

'GLOIRE DE DIJON' × 'MME LOMBARD'

### 'Baronne Edmond de Rothschild'    MEIgriso
*(above)*
syns 'Baroness E. de Rothschild',
'Baronne de Rothschild'
MODERN, LARGE-FLOWERED/HYBRID TEA, RED BLEND,
REPEAT-FLOWERING

Many bicolor roses are garish, but this one has subtler tones. It has broad petals, and they reflex to reveal an expanse of ruby red verging on deep mauvish pink as the flowers age; this contrasts with a petal reverse that is basically white with reddish tints. The flowers are very large, double and high centered, and appear sporadically through summer and autumn, sometimes in wide clusters. They have a pleasing fragrance. Growth is taller than average, and the vigorous bush has an adequate cover of bronze green, leathery foliage. This is a good rose for the garden and to cut, and is especially suited to warmer climates, but a watch needs to be kept for black spot. **ZONES 4–9.**

MEILLAND, FRANCE, 1969

('BACCARÁ' × 'CRIMSON KING') × 'PEACE'

LYON GOLD MEDAL 1968, MONZA FRAGRANCE PRIZE 1968,
ROME GOLD MEDAL 1968, BELFAST FRAGRANCE PRIZE 1991

### 'Baronne Prévost'
(*right*)
OLD, HYBRID PERPETUAL, MEDIUM
PINK, REPEAT-FLOWERING

Extremely popular for many years, this early Hybrid Perpetual retains the shape of the Old Rose form. Large, globular buds open to full, flat, quartered, pink blooms that fade with age and make most attractive cut flowers. The stiff, stout canes are covered with attractive foliage and short red prickles. This tough, compact shrub blooms in summer with an occasional autumn repeat, and is best placed at the back of the border. It likes sun and rich soil. Desprez sold the ownership of the rose to Cochet senior for 100 francs; it is the oldest variety of its class still sold. **ZONES 5–10.**

DESPREZ, FRANCE, 1842

PARENTAGE UNKNOWN

ROYAL HORTICULTURAL SOCIETY
AWARD OF GARDEN MERIT 1993

### 'Bassino' KORmixal
(*right*)

syn. 'Suffolk'
MODERN, GROUND COVER,
MEDIUM RED,
REPEAT-FLOWERING

This makes a prostrate growing plant, with a spreading though not very extensive habit, more of a ground covering rose than a shrub. The single flowers are bright red when they open, their cupped deep scarlet petals making a vivid contrast with the yellow stamens. They are carried in wide clusters of many small blooms, and nestle close to the dark shiny leaflets, so the overall effect is spectacular. The color fades somewhat but keeps its scarlet tone. Flowering continues through summer and autumn, though it can be greatly affected in a bad black spot year. There is very little fragrance. In Britain it is sold as 'Suffolk'. **ZONES 4–9.**

KORDES, GERMANY, 1988

('SEA FOAM' × 'RED MAX GRAF')
× SEEDLING

ROYAL NATIONAL ROSE SOCIETY
TRIAL GROUND CERTIFICATE 1990

B

### 'Beauté' *(below)*

MODERN, LARGE-FLOWERED/
HYBRID TEA, APRICOT BLEND,
REPEAT-FLOWERING

Although not so widely grown today, for years after World War II many people considered this variety their first choice for its color, a lovely shade of apricot-yellow with some deeper flushes. The buds are long and open into high-centered flowers of elegant form. They are moderately full of petals, which soon reflex to give a cupped rose with a rounded outline, effectively displaying the pretty color. Flowering continues through summer and autumn, the blooms carried singly or 3 to a stem, and there is a light fragrance. The growth is lower than average, and it spreads rather unevenly. The leaves are large and rich green but not plentiful; it becomes an open, rather bare-looking bush after a few years and seems reluctant to put out new stems. ZONES 5–9.

MALLERIN, FRANCE, 1953

'MADAME JOSEPH PERRAUD' ×
SEEDLING

ROYAL NATIONAL ROSE SOCIETY
CERTIFICATE OF MERIT 1954

### 'Beautiful Britain'   DICfire   *(above)*

MODERN, CLUSTER-FLOWERED/FLORIBUNDA, ORANGE-RED,
REPEAT-FLOWERING

The flowers of this variety are borne in rather uneven clusters, and open from neat rounded buds into cupped blooms of medium size, fairly well filled with petals that fall cleanly as they age. They are the color of not quite ripe tomatoes. This rose stands wet weather well, and continues to flower freely through summer and autumn. There is a light scent. The growth is upright, to a little below average height, with mid-green, rather sparse foliage that detracts from its value as a bedding rose. For planting in a group and as a source for buttonholes, it is a good performer. It is widely grown for sale in the UK, where it was named in connection with the Keep Britain Tidy Group. ZONES 4–9.

DICKSON, UK, 1983

'RED PLANET' × 'EUROROSE'

UK ROSE OF THE YEAR 1983, BELFAST CERTIFICATE OF MERIT 1985

## 'Beauty of Rosemawr' *(top right)*

OLD, TEA, PINK BLEND, REPEAT-FLOWERING

Upright, large, full flowers with overlapping
petals and a raised center, veined with carmine-
crimson and white markings, are the hallmarks
of this rose. It is believed to be half-China and
half-Tea. The twiggy, upright, dense foliage
supports loosely formed, fragrant blooms. There
is little foliage on this 4 ft x 2 ft (120 cm x 60 cm)
shrub. It blooms continuously through summer,
does well in poor soil and enjoys the sun. It makes
a good subject for a container or for hiding
among perennials. ZONES 7–10.

VAN FLEET, USA, 1903

PARENTAGE UNKNOWN

## 'Beauty Secret' *(top left)*

MODERN, MINIATURE, MEDIUM RED, REPEAT-FLOWERING

'Beauty Secret' is considered the classic Miniature
Rose of the mid-1960s. The cardinal red flowers
are high-centered with a characteristic point to
the terminal edge of the petals. Grown on a vigorous bushy plant, the florets are mainly grouped
in clusters of 4–10 blooms on strong straight stems.
The color is fast and the blooms last a reasonably
long time on the bush without serious fading. So
attractive and well liked was this variety that when
the American Rose Society award program started
off in 1975, it was given the honor without hesi-
tation. ZONES 4–11.

MOORE, USA, 1965

'LITTLE DARLING' × 'MAGIC WAND'

AMERICAN ROSE SOCIETY AWARD OF EXCELLENCE 1975

## 'Bel Ange' *(above)*
syns 'Bella Epoca', 'Belle Ange', 'Belle Epoque',
'Rosa Stern'

MODERN, LARGE-FLOWERED/HYBRID TEA, MEDIUM PINK,
REPEAT-FLOWERING

This makes a vigorous upright plant, rather stiff
in growth, but well endowed with handsome dark
green foliage. The foliage acts as a good foil to the
flowers, which open from dark red buds to show
two color tones, the petals being rosy salmon on
the inside with a deeper carmine-pink reverse.
The blooms are full and open slowly, revealing
classic exhibition form with high centers, and
there is good fragrance. The flowers are borne
freely through summer and autumn on a plant
of average height or above, making this a good
dual purpose rose for garden display in a bed and
to cut for rose shows. ZONES 4–9.

LENS, BELGIUM, 1962

('INDEPENDENCE' × 'PAPILLON ROSE') × ('CHARLOTTE ARMSTRONG'
× 'FLORADORA')

COURTRAI GOLD MEDAL 1965

### 'Belle Amour' *(bottom left)*

OLD, ALBA, LIGHT PINK

This is a medium-sized bushy shrub to 5 ft (1.5 m) with thorny stems. The foliage is mid- to dark green, serrated and coarse to touch. The fully double flowers are cushion shaped when fully open and arranged in small clusters, appearing in great profusion in early summer. The color is bright pink approaching salmon with an occasional paler petal. The spicy and pungent fragrance is reminiscent of myrrh. In autumn the thorny canes are decorated with oval, orange hips. This shrub rose, easy to grow even in the most impoverished of soils, was discovered by Englishwoman Nancy Lindsay in 1940 at a convent in Elboeuf, Normandy. Peter Beales considers it to be a Damask. **ZONES 4–10.**

ROSA ALBA × R. DAMASCENA

### 'Bella Rosa' KORwonder *(top)*
syn. 'Toynbee Hall'

MODERN, CLUSTER-FLOWERED/FLORIBUNDA, MEDIUM PINK, REPEAT-FLOWERING

This makes a splendid bedding rose where a neat short grower is required. The flowers are a warm rose pink, a very pure and even shade, and they are carried close to the foliage on short stems in very full clusters. The round buds open to disclose about 36 overlapping petals, which eventually part to frame the stamens. They flower with good continuity through summer and autumn, and have what the raiser described as a 'wild rose scent', which in this instance means light. The plant has a low, spreading habit, and is well clothed in small polished leaves. In England this rose is called 'Toynbee Hall', which refers to a social center in London that celebrated its centenary in 1984. **ZONES 4–9.**

KORDES, GERMANY, 1982

SEEDLING × 'TRAUMEREI'

COPENHAGEN GOLD MEDAL 1982, BADEN-BADEN GOLD MEDAL 1983

### 'Belle Blonde' MEnap
*(above)*

MODERN, LARGE-FLOWERED/
HYBRID TEA, MEDIUM YELLOW,
REPEAT-FLOWERING

The name of this rose was a happy choice, for the flower is wonderful, fashioned from 24 big petals in bright, unfading golden yellow, revealing deeper golden yellow in the heart of the flower as the petals reflex. There is good fragrance, and flowering continues through summer and autumn. More often than not the plant beneath belies the promise of the flower; liability to black spot is the most serious problem, but even in a fungus-free summer the plant is a slow mover, below average height and with only adequate leaf cover. Growing it could be justified on sentimental or historic grounds, with the understanding that if it looks a poor thing today, then that is a measure of how roses have improved since the middle of the twentieth century. **ZONES 5–9.**

MEILLAND, FRANCE, 1955

'PEACE' × 'LORRAINE'

### 'Belle de Crécy'
*(top right)*
syn. 'Le Météore'

OLD, GALLICA, MAUVE

This rose produces large cerise and purple blooms that turn to lavender-gray or violet in hot weather. The full, flat flowers have a button eye that is surrounded by incurved center petals. A profuse bloomer and quite fragrant, it is a relaxed, slightly flimsy shrub with flexible green mottled brown stems that bear few thorns. The leaves are darkish green overlaid bluish gray, and a little coarse in texture. It is said that it came from Madame de Pompadour's chateau at Crécy, but is probably named after Crécy-en-Brie, where Roeser had his nursery. **ZONES 4–10.**

ROESER, FRANCE, PRE-1836

PARENTAGE UNKNOWN

ROYAL HORTICULTURAL SOCIETY
AWARD OF GARDEN MERIT 1993

### 'Belle des Jardins'
*(above)*

OLD, GALLICA, MAUVE BLEND

This is a complex, variegated bloom of purplish violet-red with stripes of white. The double, velvety flowers are strongly scented and are produced in mid-summer. The dark leaves are prickly, and strong canes cover the 5 ft (1.5 m) bush. Other Guillot hybrids still popular are 'Etoile de Lyon' and 'Comtesse du Cayla'; the Guillot firm is one of the few old Lyon rose nurseries still in business. This rose is frequently sold under other names and has been the subject of some dispute for a long time. **ZONES 4–10.**

GUILLOT, FRANCE, 1872

'VILLAGE MAID' × SEEDLING

**'Belle Epoque'**   FRYaboo   *(top)*

MODERN, LARGE-FLOWERED/HYBRID TEA, ORANGE BLEND,
REPEAT-FLOWERING

A beautiful feature of this large rose is the two-toned effect within the flower. The inside of the petals is a pretty golden-bronze, while the outside surface is deeper—the raiser calls it 'nectarine-bronze'. The colors make a delightful contrast as the flowers expand. They have long buds, big petals and the high-centered form of the classic Large-flowered Rose. The fragrant flowers continue to appear through summer and autumn on vigorous plants a little taller than average height, with ample dark green foliage and a good health record. This is suitable as a bedding variety, as a standard and for cutting. *La belle époque,* meaning 'fine period', refers to the period of comfortable living in France before World War I. ZONES 4–9.

FRYER, UK, 1994

'REMEMBER ME' × 'SIMBA'

ROYAL NATIONAL ROSE SOCIETY TRIAL GROUND CERTIFICATE 1995

**'Belle Isis'**   *(center)*

OLD, GALLICA, LIGHT PINK

This is a tidy 4 ft (1.2 m) shrub with clear, gray-green, toothed foliage. It has fat buds streaked with deep crimson and the double, quartered blossoms have reflexed outer petals, which slowly unfold to expose a white base. There is a strong myrrh perfume. This rose, which is ideal for the small garden, is frequently used in arrangements as the petals, arranged in tiers, are a photographer's delight. It is disease resistant and has prickles. Its outstanding character is reflected in an offspring, 'Constance Spry', one of the most popular of all David Austin's creations.
ZONES 4–10.

PARMENTIER, BELGIUM, 1845

PROBABLY A HYBRID OF *ROSA GALLICA* × *R.* × *CENTIFOLIA*

**'Belle Poitevine'**   *(left)*

syn. *Rosa rugosa* 'Belle Poitevine'

MODERN, MODERN SHRUB, MEDIUM PINK, REPEAT-FLOWERING

While the parentage is not known, from the general appearance of its flowers, growth and foliage, it seems clear this is a *Rosa rugosa* hybrid. Long pointed buds open out into almost flat, quite large flowers with loosely crinkled petals. They are a cool shade of pale magenta pink, showing creamy stamens, and fragrant, and are produced over a long period in summer and autumn. The plant grows large and shrubby, with a more angular outline than that of wild Rugosas, and also with coarser foliage. Large dark red hips are sometimes produced. It is a good subject for a big hedge or shrubbery. The name translates as 'Beauty of Poitou', the region where the French raiser had his nursery. ZONES 3–9.

BRUANT, FRANCE, 1894

PARENTAGE UNKNOWN

ROYAL HORTICULTURAL SOCIETY AWARD OF GARDEN MERIT 1993

B

## 'Belle Portugaise'

*(right)*

syn. 'Belle of Portugal'

MODERN, LARGE-FLOWERED
CLIMBER, LIGHT PINK

This very vigorous rose
has become almost
naturalized in parts of
California. In other
parts of North America
it will not grow at all,
as it is not frost hardy
on account of the *Rosa
gigantea* parentage.
It is often considered
a Climbing Tea, and
the large flowers have
the elegant pointed
buds, silky petal texture
and delicate fragrance
associated with that
group. A mixture of
light salmon, pink,
peachy and creamy
shades, they open wide
and rather loosely with
reflexed petal rims and
hang down on pen-
dulous stems. The olive
green leaves droop
elegantly but are
subject to seasonal
mildew at times when
the enormous amount
of growth being made
outstrips the food re-
sources available. There
is only one flowering,
but in climates that suit
it the sight of hundreds
of blooms on a high
wall or fence is one of
summer's horticultural
treats. ZONES 6–10.

CAYEUX, PORTUGAL, 1903

ROSA GIGANTEA × 'REINE MARIE
HENRIETTE'

## 'Belle sans Flatterie'

*(above)*

OLD, GALLICA, MAUVE BLEND,
REPEAT-FLOWERING

This was a very popular
rose in France in the
1800s, and it is still
not well known outside
Europe. The double,
quartered, mid-sized
blooms appear in
clusters. The lilac-pink
petals at the edge are
complemented with a
rich pink at the center,
while the outer petals
are reflexed. There is
some rebloom in late
summer but little
scent. The plant grows
to a 4 ft (1.2 m) shrub
and has dark green
foliage. This rose was
grown in the garden
of Empress Josephine
at Malmaison.
ZONES 5–10.

GODEFROY, THE NETHERLANDS,
PRE-1806

PARENTAGE UNKNOWN

**B**

### 'Belle Story' AUSelle, AUSspry
*(left)*
syn. 'Bienenweide'
MODERN, MODERN SHRUB, LIGHT PINK

The large flowers on this variety, borne in sprays, open to resemble peonies, with petals incurving towards the center and reflexing round the outer edges of the flower, revealing the red-gold stamens within. They are rose pink, the shade lightening towards the petal tips, full-petalled, fragrant and bloom in summer. Growth is bushy and vigorous, to average height. The dark semi-glossy foliage is rather small and does not adequately clothe the plant, which needs well-drained, fertile soil to thrive. The name honors one of the first nursing sisters to join Britain's Royal Navy in 1864. It is also classified as an English Rose. **ZONES 4–9.**
AUSTIN, UK, 1984

('CHAUCER' × 'PARADE') × ('THE PRIORESS' × 'ICEBERG')

### 'Bengale Rouge' *(left)*
OLD, CHINA, MEDIUM RED, REPEAT-FLOWERING

A prolific bloomer over a long period, this China is one of the most recent creations in that family. The ovoid buds of bright carmine open to double, large, red blooms of 35 petals. The abundant foliage is large and dark green on a plant that is taller than most Chinas. There are several roses with Bengale in their names; all of them require a warm position and all are strongly resistant to diseases. **ZONES 7–10.**
GAUJARD, FRANCE, 1955

'GRÜSS AN TEPLITZ' × SEEDLING

B

## 'Bengali' KORal
*(right)*

MODERN, CLUSTER-FLOWERED/
FLORIBUNDA, ORANGE-RED,
REPEAT-FLOWERING

As the plump buds unfold, the petals show a pretty shade of golden orange, richly veined with orange-red. The flowers are of medium size, well filled with petals, and are borne in small, rather open clusters on firm stems. They open with high centers, and are excellent for button-holes and small flower arrangements. There is light fragrance, and they appear with good continuity through summer and autumn, making this a good rose for bedding. The plant grows vigorously with a well-branched spreading habit to below average height, furnished with leaves that are reddish when young, then becoming bright green and shiny.
**ZONES 4–9.**

KORDES, GERMANY, 1969

'DACAPO' × SEEDLING

## 'Benita' DICquarrel
*(above right)*

MODERN, CLUSTER-FLOWERED/
FLORIBUNDA, DEEP YELLOW,
REPEAT-FLOWERING

The pretty golden yellow blooms of this variety have a frilled edge to the petals. They open from urn-shaped buds into full-petalled, fairly large-cupped flowers, borne on firm stems in big, widely spaced sprays like a candelabra, which may include up to 12 blooms. A few plants of 'Benita' will prove a useful source for small flower arrangements and for buttonholes. There is a light perfume, and flowering continues through summer and autumn. The growth habit is uneven but overall it reaches average height and is furnished with mid-green leaves. By arrangement with the raiser it was named by Mrs Barbel Abela in memory of her mother.
**ZONES 4–9.**

DICKSON, UK, 1995

('KORRESIA' × 'BRIGHT SMILE') ×
SEEDLING

ROYAL NATIONAL ROSE SOCIETY
TRIAL GROUND CERTIFICATE 1990,
DUBLIN GOLD MEDAL 1992, UK
BREEDERS' CHOICE 1995

B

### 'Bennett's Seedling' *(left)*
syn. 'Thoresbyana'

OLD, AYRSHIRE, WHITE

This rose was discovered growing in a hedge by the gardener of Earl Manvers at Thoresby in Nottinghamshire in 1835. Looking very much like a double form of *Rosa arvensis*, the pure white blooms have a faint perfume and continue over a long period in summer. It can reach 20 ft (6 m) and can be used as a climber or ground cover. It is happy in sun or shade. ZONES 5–11.

BENNETT, UK, CIRCA 1840

BELIEVED TO BE A SEEDLING OF *ROSA ARVENSIS*

### 'Benson and Hedges Gold' MACgem *(left)*

MODERN, LARGE-FLOWERED/HYBRID TEA, YELLOW BLEND, REPEAT-FLOWERING

This is a satisfying bedding rose, bearing full-petalled flowers of high-centered form and good size, though the centers are not held for long and the petals dissolve into a pleasant muddle. The blooms of deep yellow with flushes of red have an enjoyable fragrance, and give an excellent succession of blooms through summer and autumn. The plant usually grows vigorously with a bushy habit, to below average height, with rugged leaves. It is happier in cooler climates, because the color fades in hot sun. The dedication of this rose to a brand of cigarettes almost certainly harmed its commercial prospects; history has come a long way since tobacco was described by Robert Burton in the seventeenth century as 'a sovereign remedy to all diseases'! ZONES 5–9.

MCGREDY, NEW ZEALAND, 1978

'YELLOW PAGES' × ('ARTHUR BELL' × 'CYNTHIA BROOKE')

ROYAL NATIONAL ROSE SOCIETY TRIAL GROUND CERTIFICATE 1976, NEW ZEALAND GOLD STAR OF THE SOUTH PACIFIC 1978

B

## 'Benvenuto' MEIelpa *(right)*

MODERN, LARGE-FLOWERED
CLIMBER, MEDIUM RED,
REPEAT-FLOWERING

This cheerful garden rose bears well-filled clusters of deep cherry red buds that open to show light centers where the yellowish petal bases surround the yellow stamens. The color deepens to a crimson tone as the petals unfold, and the shapely semi-double flowers open out rather flat. They are medium sized and lightly scented, and the trusses are produced spasmodically through summer and autumn. It makes vigorous, thorny growth, with an upright free-branching habit and ample deep green, shiny foliage, but it is of modest size as climbers go and is best suited where a restrained grower is needed for screening walls and fences or to train up a pillar.
ZONES 4–9.

MEILLAND, FRANCE, 1967

('ALAIN' × 'GUINEE') ×
'COCKTAIL'

## 'Berlin' *(right)*

MODERN, MODERN SHRUB,
ORANGE BLEND,
REPEAT-FLOWERING

Wilhelm Kordes raised a series of shrub roses suitable for parks, naming them after German cities. As befits a park rose, this is a vigorous, trouble-free grower, tall, upright and shrubby with thick leathery leaves and well armed with prickles. The saucer-shaped flowers appear very bright when their few petals first open, being vivid orange-scarlet with yellow at the base. As the petals expand they become waved at the edges, lose their brilliance of tone and turn cherry red. The color impact is considerable because the trusses are large and contain many blooms, and flowering continues through summer and autumn. There is little scent. Sometimes this has been called a Hybrid Musk Rose, although it more closely resembles a tough, overgrown Cluster-flowered Rose.
ZONES 4–9.

KORDES, GERMANY, 1949

'EVA' × 'PEACE'

ROYAL NATIONAL ROSE SOCIETY
TRIAL GROUND CERTIFICATE 1950

B

### 'Bernstein-Rose'

TANeitbar *(right)*

syn. 'Amaroela'

MODERN, CLUSTER-FLOWERED/
FLORIBUNDA, DEEP YELLOW,
REPEAT-FLOWERING

This is a Modern Garden Rose with an old-style flower. Its plump buds at first show red flushes, but when the flowers are open they are a pure and even shade of amber yellow. They are of medium size and full of petals, which are enfolded tightly against each other as the blooms open wide, the inner petals incurving and the outer ones reflexing in the manner of an Old Garden Rose. They continue in flower through summer and autumn, and stand up well to bad weather.

The fragrance is light. For a bedding rose this is a useful and robust variety. A compact, vigorous plant, it grows to below average height and is furnished with dark green, narrow leaves. Bernstein is the German word for amber. **ZONES 4–9.**

TANTAU, GERMANY, 1987

PARENTAGE UNKNOWN

### 'Berries 'n' Cream'

POUlclimb *(top)*

syn. 'Calypso'

MODERN, LARGE-FLOWERED
CLIMBER, PINK BLEND,
REPEAT-FLOWERING

At first sight, 'Berries 'n' Cream' looks very much like 'Rosa Mundi', the old Gallica, which has pale pink blooms splashed with crimson. The modern version is best described as old-rose pink and cream, semi-double, medium in size and ruffled. The blooms on both old and new wood appear in bouquet-like clusters on strong stems. The canes are practically free of prickles, which makes the training of the climber on a wall or pergola easy. Light green foliage covers the long branches.

The flowers repeat several times during the season, and they have a light fragrance. Because of its strong colors, placement of the climber, which can reach 10 ft (3 m), in an isolated spot is often the best choice for showing off its spectacular first flush in spring. **ZONES 4–9.**

POULSEN, DENMARK, 1997

B

### 'Betty Harkness' HARette *(right)*

MODERN, CLUSTER-FLOWERED/FLORIBUNDA, ORANGE BLEND,
REPEAT-FLOWERING

The flowers are on the large size for a Cluster-
flowered Rose, and are well spaced in the cluster.
They make a good color impact, therefore, as
they open in big, upright trusses of saucer-
shaped, full-petalled flowers. The color is a pretty
blend of coral-orange and copper, and there is
a sweet fragrance, which is unusual for varieties
in this spectrum. After a plentiful first blooming,
flowers appear with good continuity through
summer and autumn. For a bed or a group in a
border, or as a hedge rose, this is a suitable choice
as the plants grow vigorously to average height,
attaining a bushy habit and an ample provision
of shiny, dark green leaves. The late Jack Harkness
loved the combination of beauty, scent and good
health in this rose, and named it for his wife.
**ZONES 4–9.**

HARKNESS, UK, 1998

PARENTAGE UNKNOWN

COURTRAI GOLD MEDAL 1997, PARIS SILVER MEDAL 1997

### 'Betty Prior' *(left)*

MODERN, CLUSTER-FLOWERED/FLORIBUNDA, MEDIUM PINK,
REPEAT-FLOWERING

This is a remarkable survivor of the forerunners
of the Cluster-flowered Roses, which were termed
Hybrid Polyanthas. It produces large clusters
of modest-sized 5-petalled blooms, which open
out like so many saucers. The effect is cheerful,
because the flowers are a pretty shade of pink,
lighter on the inside of the petal, and with a
whitish base to give them pale hearts. They are
produced in continual cycles of growth and
bloom through summer and autumn on upright
plants of average height or more, with ample
healthy matt green foliage. This is a dependable
garden and parks rose, being long lived and hardy
and, despite a lack of fragrance, these good qualities have enabled it to survive as a widely grown
rose where most of its contemporaries have long
since disappeared. Betty Prior was a member of
the raiser's family at their nursery near Colchester
in Essex. **ZONES 4–9.**

PRIOR, UK, 1935

'KIRSTEN POULSEN' × SEEDLING

NATIONAL ROSE SOCIETY GOLD MEDAL 1933

B

### 'Betty Uprichard'
*(above)*

MODERN, LARGE-FLOWERED/HYBRID TEA,
APRICOT BLEND, REPEAT-FLOWERING

'Apricot blend', the official description, reflects the novelty of this variety's coloring in the 1920s: 'a luminous glow, unequalled since' as an old nurseryman put it. Today it would surely be considered a 'pink blend', being salmon-pink with a copper flush on the inside of the petals with a carmine flush on the outside. The effect is a delightful two-toned flower, which opens its slender buds to display high centers while the outer petals slowly reflex. There are only 20 or so broad petals, and it is wonderful to see how they contrive to create so elegant, if fleeting, a bloom. The bush is quick to repeat its fragrant flowers through summer and autumn on vigorous upright plants that grow above average height and are clothed

with leathery mid-green leaves. It was named after a friend of the Dickson family in County Down, Northern Ireland, who was known as a keen huntswoman. **ZONES 4–9.**

DICKSON, UK, 1922

PARENTAGE UNKNOWN

NATIONAL ROSE SOCIETY GOLD MEDAL 1921

### 'Bewitched' *(below)*

MODERN, LARGE-FLOWERED/HYBRID TEA,
MEDIUM PINK, REPEAT-FLOWERING

This child of 'Queen Elizabeth' remains, after over 30 years, a popular choice in warm climates. The flowers are large, with fairly full-petalled flowers of an even shade of phlox pink and they hold their color even in hot weather. They open with high centers and take on a pleasing rounded outline as the petals reflex, yielding a sweet Damask fragrance. Long stems make this an excellent rose for cutting as well as for general garden use, and it will provide a succession of blooms through summer and autumn. The plant is vigorous and grows upright to above average height, and is clothed with large apple-green leaves. It is at its best in warmer climates, as the soft petals are easily marked in cool wet conditions. **ZONES 4–9.**

LAMMERTS, USA, 1967

'QUEEN ELIZABETH' × 'TAWNY GOLD'

ALL-AMERICA ROSE SELECTION 1967,
PORTLAND GOLD MEDAL 1967

## 'Bing Crosby'   *(top)*

MODERN, LARGE-FLOWERED/HYBRID TEA, ORANGE BLEND,
REPEAT-FLOWERING

This rose is a powerful dark orange or lively red, its appearance to the eye depending on the season and the light. The flowers are usually produced individually, are full of wide petals, and open from plump buds into large blooms of high-centered form that become cupped as the petals reflex. They last well, so are useful for cutting, and have a light spicy scent. The cycle of growth and flower is repeated through summer and autumn, and the later displays are often found to give better blooms. 'Bing Crosby' makes a good bedding rose, growing tall and upright with a slowly spreading habit and a covering of leathery leaves, which when they first grow are wrinkled, with reddish tints, before turning olive green. The famous singer died in 1977 so did not live to see the rose achieve its high All-America Rose Selection award, nor the wiles of the catalogue writers, who aver that it will 'croon a sweet tune in the garden'. It is at its best in warm climates. **ZONES 4–9.**

WEEKS, USA, 1981

SEEDLING × 'FIRST PRIZE'

ALL-AMERICA ROSE SELECTION 1981

## 'Bischofsstadt Paderborn'
### syns 'Fire Pillar', 'Paderborn'

MODERN, MODERN SHRUB, ORANGE-RED, REPEAT-FLOWERING

The synonym 'Fire Pillar' summarizes this variety well, as its flowers are quite large in a fiery shade of orange-scarlet with whitish yellow petal bases. They do not have many petals so the golden stamens are quickly revealed, adding extra flamboyance to the heart of the saucer-shaped flowers. These are long lasting, and appear through summer and autumn with good continuity on a robust shrub of average height. For parks display and for hedges, this rose is a good choice as it grows vigorously with a free-branching habit and is well furnished with deep green glossy leaves. Against a pillar it can be trained to make a short climber. Paderborn is an historic Hanseatic market town and the seat of an ancient bishopric. **ZONES 4–9.**

KORDES, GERMANY, 1964

'KORONA' × 'SPARTAN'

ANERKANNTE DEUTSCHE ROSE 1968

## 'Bishop Darlington'   *(bottom)*

MODERN, MODERN SHRUB, APRICOT BLEND, REPEAT-FLOWERING

Out of some 40 named roses raised by Captain George C. Thomas, this is one of the most widely grown. The long, pointed buds are a pretty shade of coral-pink, and open in a blend of peach and cream with yellow bases to the flowers, which have a pleasing scent. They are semi-double and soon reveal prominent stamens, often half-obscured by a stray curled petal. The flowers make an effective display even when seen from a distance, and their repeat-flowering increases their value as a background shrub for mixed borders. It can also be grown with support as a climber. It is a substantial plant, larger than average for a shrub rose, with an upright habit and a good complement of bronze green foliage. **ZONES 4–9.**

THOMAS, USA, 1926

'AVIATEUR BLÉRIOT' × 'MOONLIGHT'

## 'Bit o' Sunshine'
*(right)*
syn. 'Little Bit o'
Sunshine'

MODERN, MINIATURE, DEEP
YELLOW, REPEAT-FLOWERING

'Bit o' Sunshine' is an-
other classic Miniature
of the 1950s from
Ralph Moore. The
flowers are bright
buttercup yellow and
have 18–20 petals. They
grow on an upright, low,
bushy plant 12–14 in
(30–35 cm) high. Even
the buds are attractive
before they open up.
The plant is strong and
healthy. However, it is
prone to mildew if not
sprayed for protection.
It is a great rose, but
has lost popularity in
its color class mainly
due to the explosion
of other yellow Min-
iatures onto the
market. ZONES 4–11.

MOORE, USA, 1956

'COPPER GLOW' × 'ZEE'

## 'Black Beauty'
*(right)*

MODERN, LARGE-FLOWERED/
HYBRID TEA, DARK RED,
REPEAT-FLOWERING

More than 24 roses
have been described
as black, although none
is truly so, for as far as
is known black is not
a pigment that exists
in the rose family. This
one appears black to
the eye in the bud stage
and opens to a rich
crimson-scarlet with
the reverse of the petals
dark velvety blackish
red. The flowers are full
of petals that are on
the short side, open
cupped with rather
muddled centers, and
have disappointingly
little fragrance. They
keep blooming well
through summer and
autumn unless mildew
strikes. The plant is
an uneven grower,
bearing the flowers
aloft on long stems,
and has adequate mid-
green foliage. Although
it is not a great garden
rose in cool conditions,
it is useful to have
for cutting because
the color is so superb
when good blooms
come along.
ZONES 5–9.

DELBARD, FRANCE, 1973

('GLOIRE DE ROME' ×
'IMPECCABLE') × 'PAPA MEILLAND'

## 'Black Boy' *(right)*
syn. 'Blackboy'
MODERN, LARGE-FLOWERED CLIMBER, DARK RED

This is a popular climber in Australia where it has been passed around through cuttings for many years. It is not as dark as the name implies, being a rich deep crimson, paler on the petal reverse, and lightening in color as the flowers age. They are carried in clusters that bow under the weight when several open together. They are large and fairly full, sweetly fragrant, and when they open, there is an appealing informality about the arrangement of the petals. Since many blooms appear together, this is a very effective climbing plant for the garden, best used in places where the vigorous canes can be accommodated, such as a pergola or large fence. After the main burst of summer flowering, there is not usually any significant later bloom. The foliage is light olive green. ZONES 5–9.

CLARK, AUSTRALIA, 1919

'ETOILE DE FRANCE' × 'BARDOU JOB' (OR VICE VERSA)

## 'Black Ice' *(right)*
MODERN, CLUSTER-FLOWERED/FLORIBUNDA, DARK RED, REPEAT-FLOWERING

The buds on this variety are indeed very blackish, and on opening reveal clusters of the darkest scarlet flowers, which carry only very slight fragrance. They are full petalled and fairly large for a Cluster-flowered Rose, with many blooms in the truss; the flowers continue through summer and autumn. The growth is below average height, compact and sturdy, with glossy deep green foliage. The name is not intentionally meteorological, but was inspired by the fact that 'Iceberg' is in the parentage. In practice, the dark flowers and dark leaves give the plant a somewhat funereal aspect, especially when touched by mildew, and it is grown more for its curiosity value than for horticultural excellence. ZONES 4–9.

GANDY, UK, 1971

('ICEBERG' × 'EUROPEANA') × 'MEGIDDO'

B

### 'Black Jade' BENblack

*(top)*

MODERN, MINIATURE, DARK
RED, REPEAT-FLOWERING

This rose is very close in color to black. The vigorous, upright plant supports clusters of 5–10 blooms on very strong, straight stems. The florets have good exhibition form. When the bloom is fully open, it sports very attractive bright golden yellow stamens, which contrast with the dark red petal color. As a garden variety it has a fairly rapid repeat bloom cycle. So dark is the bloom that some show judges have taken to using a flashlight to shine into the bloom center to properly observe the actual form. The very glossy foliage provides a natural barrier to mildew and other diseases.

**ZONES 4–11.**

BENARDELLA, USA, 1985

'SHERI ANNE' × 'LAGUNA'

AMERICAN ROSE SOCIETY
AWARD OF EXCELLENCE 1985

### 'Black Velvet'

*(bottom)*

MODERN, LARGE-FLOWERED/
HYBRID TEA, DARK RED,
REPEAT-FLOWERING

Although it originated in the USA, the only country in which this rose currently appears to be offered is Australia, where conditions evidently suit it best. The color is a deep burgundy red with a dark overlay that, when it reflects the light, gives the velvety effect described by the name. It normally bears its flowers one to a stem, and the plump oval buds open into large semi-double blooms that have a pleasing fragrance. They are high centered at first but soon become cupped in form, and repeat their flowering through summer and autumn. The plant grows with reasonable vigor, has an upright habit to average height and is well furnished with leathery, dark green foliage.

**ZONES 5–9.**

MOREY, USA, 1960

'NEW YORKER' × 'HAPPINESS'

B

## 'Blairii No. 2' *(above)*

OLD, HYBRID CHINA, LIGHT PINK

The 2 levels of pink in this flower are dramatic and elegant. The large, flat, globe-shaped blooms, which are pink at the edge and darker in the center, are cupped and full of petals. The luxuriant canes are mahogany in color when young and have a branching habit. The lax growth can reach 15 ft (4.5 m) but it is easily trained on walls, fences or pergolas. There are horrid prickles. It blooms in early summer but rarely repeats, and requires little pruning. There is probably no rose that has received such universal praise.
**ZONES 5–10.**

BLAIR, 1845

*ROSA CHINENSIS* × A BOURBON ROSE

ROYAL HORTICULTURAL SOCIETY AWARD OF GARDEN MERIT 1993

## 'Blanc de Vibert'

syn. 'Blanche de Vibert'

OLD, PORTLAND, WHITE, REPEAT-FLOWERING

This rose would be more popular if its qualities were better known. Large, very full, flat blooms open lemon-yellow at first, quickly fading to milky white. The medium-sized, cupped, upright flowers are crested at the center, on strong canes. The downy, light green foliage appears to have a Gallica background. Happier in the shade in rich soil, its 3 ft by 3 ft (1 m by 1 m) size makes it ideal for a container. It hates wet weather to the point where the flowers ball and can rot off, before opening. **ZONES 4–10.**

VIBERT, FRANCE, 1847

PARENTAGE UNKNOWN

B

## 'Blanc Double de Coubert' (above)

MODERN, HYBRID RUGOSA, WHITE, REPEAT-FLOWERING

This shrub has such close affinity to *Rosa rugosa*
from the appearance of its foliage, inflorescence
and fine prickles that the raiser's claim that
'Sombreuil' was the pollen parent has been doubted,
though the plant has a more open aspect than
the wild *R. rugosa*. It bears clusters of large flowers
with crumpled petals, the flowers being as white
as one can imagine—unless spoiled by rain, for
their texture is soft and they mark easily. The
semi-double blooms open out flat at different
levels on the plant, and diffuse a pervasive
fragrance, detectable even at night. Flowering
continues through summer and autumn, and
though hips are not normally produced, if they
do appear they are orange-scarlet. The foliage is
dark, leathery and wrinkled, and the plant grows,
usually quite vigorously, to about average height.
'Coubert' in the name refers to the raiser's home
village. ZONES 3–9.

COCHET–COCHET, FRANCE, 1892

POSSIBLY *ROSA RUGOSA* × 'SOMBREUIL' OR *R. RUGOSA ALBA* ×
*R. RUGOSA ALBA*

ROYAL HORTICULTURAL SOCIETY AWARD OF GARDEN MERIT 1993

## 'Blanche Moreau'

OLD, MOSS, WHITE

Although sired by a Damask rose, little of its
influence shows through in the growth habit of
this rose. Lovely in bud and surrounded by dark,
heavy moss, it is the best white member of the
Moss family. The very double, fragrant blooms
are pure white with a pink center, and are
arranged in clusters. The blooms are surrounded
by a sea of dark green leaves, and the canes are
bristly on a medium-sized shrub to about 5 ft
(1.5 m). It flowers in mid-summer. It hates rain,
but needs plenty of water in a warm summer.
Unfortunately, when conditions dictate, it can
suffer from bouts of mildew. ZONES 5–10.

MOREAU-ROBERT, FRANCE, 1880

'COMTESSE DE MURINAIS' × 'PERPETUAL WHITE MOSS'

B

### 'Blanchefleur'
*(right)*

OLD, CENTIFOLIA, WHITE

This rose, which is probably related to the Gallicas, is a vigorous shrub of semi-relaxed habit that grows to some 5 ft (1.5 m) high and wide. The arching shoots are thorny but well foliated, with light grayish green leaves. The flowers are grouped in small clusters and open from reddish tinted buds to soft milky white with a distinct but soft blush in the center. Fragrant, fully double and often quartered, the outer petals fold backwards when the flower is fully open to form a sort of ball effect that is most attractive. It flowers in early summer and looks wonderful in a rose border or mixed shrubbery. **ZONES 4–10.**

VIBERT, FRANCE, 1835

PARENTAGE UNKNOWN

### 'Blaze' *(right)*

MODERN, LARGE-FLOWERED CLIMBER, MEDIUM RED, REPEAT-FLOWERING

'Blaze' is extremely popular in the USA, where its scarlet blooms form sheets of color in summer. They are carried in large clusters on strong stems, and open to fairly full-petalled blooms of neatly cupped form. There are often so many blooms that even though they are not large they become rather crowded and the stems may bow under the weight. There is a pleasant light scent. It is an easy plant to grow where an extensive, pliable, all-purpose climber is required, for it makes vigorous climbing shoots and covers itself with plentiful medium green leaves, which are generally very healthy, though when introduced into Britain they proved susceptible to mildew. Some say 'Blaze' repeats its bloom in the autumn, but it may be that it has been confused with a selected form introduced a few years later. **ZONES 4–9.**

KALLAY, USA, 1932

'PAUL'S SCARLET CLIMBER' × 'GRÜSS AN TEPLITZ'

B

### 'Blessings'  *(above)*

MODERN, LARGE-FLOWERED/HYBRID TEA, ORANGE-PINK, REPEAT-FLOWERING

This rose bears urn-shaped rosy salmon buds, usually several together, on tall upright stems. They open cupped into quite large blooms of rosy pink, well filled with petals, so that they are able to display the color well. Because so many flowers come out together, 'Blessings' makes a fine bedding rose; it is splendid to cut, though disbudding would be necessary if it were grown for that purpose alone. It is hardly ever troubled by wet weather, and flowering continues through summer and autumn. There is a pleasant though not pronounced fragrance. The plant grows taller than average and with an upright habit, and is well clothed in large dark leaves. **ZONES 4–9.**

GREGORY, UK, 1968

'QUEEN ELIZABETH' × SEEDLING

ROYAL NATIONAL ROSE SOCIETY CERTIFICATE OF MERIT 1968, BADEN-BADEN GOLD MEDAL 1971, ROYAL HORTICULTURAL SOCIETY AWARD OF GARDEN MERIT 1993

### 'Bleu Magenta'

OLD, RAMBLER, MAUVE

Graham Stuart Thomas received this rose from Roseraie de l'Haÿ, the famous garden outside Paris, but has been unable to trace its origin. The blooms, which begin as violet-cerise, fading to light violet, are double and occasionally have white streaks, but, depending on its placement in sun or shade, the colors may range from deep red, crimson, and violet to cerise. The yellow stamens

add a touch of drama to this, the largest flower of any purple Rambler. The dainty blooms are held aloft on thin canes. The foliage is dark and shiny. There are no prickles. **ZONES 6–10.**

CIRCA 1900

PARENTAGE UNKNOWN

ROYAL HORTICULTURAL SOCIETY AWARD OF GARDEN MERIT 1994

### 'Bloomfield Abundance'  *(above)*
syn. 'Spray Cécile Brünner'

MODERN, POLYANTHA, LIGHT PINK, REPEAT-FLOWERING

The unmistakable features of this rose are the long, whiskery calyx lobes that hang down beneath the small light pink blooms. Apart from the sepals, the flowers resemble 'Cécile Brünner', having tiny urn-shaped buds that open into double pink rosettes. They are produced through summer and autumn and have a light scent. The plant grows upright, tall and arching, with thin brownish stems and small, shiny, sparse foliage that gives it a rather spindly aspect. With this rose no one is sure whether it is correctly named or whether another rose, 'Spray Cécile Brünner' from 1941 (which was a sport of 'Cécile Brünner') has usurped its place. **'White Bloomfield Abundance'** is a white sport. **ZONES 4–9.**

THOMAS, USA, 1920

'SYLVIA' × 'DOROTHY PAGE-ROBERTS' OR SPORT OF 'CÉCILE BRÜNNER'

**B**

## 'Bloomfield Courage' *(right)*

OLD, RAMBLER, RED BLEND

Of the 41 Bloomfield roses that were created by Captain George C. Thomas, this is one of three still popular with gardeners. He named them after his estate in Bloomfield, Pennsylvania. Small, single, dark velvety-red blooms with white centers and prominent stamens completely hide the foliage. The open clusters hold 20 or more blooms at one time, but the color is rather hard and does not mix easily with others. The canes are easy to train and hold only a few prickles. It needs lots of room. There is some re-flowering in autumn, and scarlet hips extend its season. It can climb a tree or cover an arch, and blooms on old wood. ZONES 5–11.

THOMAS, USA, 1925

*ROSA WICHURANA* × 'CRIMSON RAMBLER'

## 'Bloomfield Dainty' *(right)*

MODERN, MODERN SHRUB, MEDIUM YELLOW

Pointed orange buds on 'Bloomfield Dainty' open into pretty 5-petalled, saucer-shaped flowers of a fairly bright yellow, which soon turn light yellow and admit flushes of pink towards the petal tips as they age. There is a pleasant musky fragrance, and some repetition of bloom through summer and autumn. The variety is well named, since its flowers are indeed dainty, but they seem rather incongruous perched on the rugged canes that support them because the habit of the plant is to grow wide and tall, making a large, rather untidy shrub. It is well furnished with deep green glossy leaves and can, thanks to its flexible arching stems, be trained as a climber on a short fence or pillar. It seems happiest in a warm climate. ZONES 5–9.

THOMAS, USA, 1924

'DANAË' × 'MADAME EDOUARD HERRIOT'

**B**

continuity through summer and autumn. This rose can be grown short or tall depending on what is required. It can be trained as a pillar rose, grown to the average dimensions of a climbing rose or allowed to go higher and wider. In other words it is adaptable, and will respond to whatever pruning and training it receives and always provide a satisfactory background of glossy, bronze green leaves. **ZONES 4–9.**

O'NEAL, USA, 1951

'NEW DAWN' × SEEDLING

## 'Blossomtime'
*(above)*

MODERN, LARGE-FLOWERED CLIMBER, MEDIUM PINK, REPEAT-FLOWERING

The flowers of this rose are a little over medium size and very full of petals, and they combine two shades of china pink. The pretty oval buds are deep pink, and as they open they reveal the paler pink of the inner petal surfaces. They are high centered and fragrant, and are produced in well-spaced clusters of flowers with good

## 'Blue Bajou'

KORkultop *(below)*

syns 'Blue Bayou', 'Blue-Bijou'

MODERN, CLUSTER-FLOWERED/ FLORIBUNDA, MAUVE BLEND, REPEAT-FLOWERING

There have been many roses incorporating the word 'blue' but so far no truly blue one has been developed, though geneticists are hoping to introduce delphinidin—the necessary pigment— into a rose from another flower, perhaps a petunia. Meanwhile, the rose world must make the best of the mauves and lilacs that come nearest to blue, some of which, in warm climates or under glass, can look close to the real thing. The Kordes firm has produced several, including this recent scented Cluster-flowered Rose, which produces very full silvery lilac flowers of rounded form. The petals are short, and as the outer ones reflex, those in the middle hold a tight center for some time before opening cupped. The pretty color contrasts beautifully with the glossy, dark green leaves, and the variety is very good for bedding and cutting and to grow in a container. 'Blue Bajou' continues to bear flowers, sometimes singly, sometimes in a spray, throughout summer and autumn on a neat, vigorous plant of below average height. **ZONES 4–9.**

KORDES, GERMANY, 1993

PARENTAGE UNKNOWN

B

### 'Blue Moon' TANnacht *(right)*
syns 'Mainzer Fastnacht', 'Blue Monday', 'Sissi'
MODERN, LARGE-FLOWERED/HYBRID TEA, MAUVE, REPEAT-FLOWERING

This is deservedly the most commercially success-ful of the 'blue' roses, being very close to the blue side of lavender. The flowers are large and full-petalled, with high centers and good symmetry of form, and they last well, finally opening cupped to show the stamens. Usually there is one flower on the long stems, which makes them excellent for cutting. They are sweetly fragrant, and are produced through summer and autumn. The plant grows vigorously but it is somewhat splayed and reluctant to make new wood, and has a rather sparse cover of deep green foliage. Generally the plant is healthy and can overcome occasional mildew and black spot, but is liable to die-back in hard winters. 'Mainzer Fastnacht' is the Shrove Tuesday festival in Mainz. Herr Tantau changed the name to 'Sissi' as it was easier for non-Germans to pronounce, but 'sissy' means a weakling, so a third alternative had to be found. **'Climbing Blue Moon'** (syn. 'Climbing Sissi'; Mungia, USA, 1981) grows strongly to above average height. The most suitable site is against a sheltered high wall or fence. It also needs plenty of sunshine for good flower production; a warm climate suits it best. **ZONES 4–9.**

TANTAU, GERMANY, 1965

SEEDLING × 'STERLING SILVER'

ANERKANNTE DEUTSCHE ROSE 1964, ROME GOLD MEDAL 1964, NATIONAL ROSE SOCIETY CERTIFICATE OF MERIT 1964

### 'Blue Nile' DELnible *(bottom right)*
syn. 'Nil Bleu'
MODERN, LARGE-FLOWERED/HYBRID TEA, MAUVE, REPEAT-FLOWERING

This is a substantial flower, thanks to its large broad petals. The pointed buds are usually pro-duced singly, sometimes 2 or 3 together, and open on long stems into full-petalled blooms that can be good enough for exhibition. A faint magenta flush with delicate veining enlivens the lavender blue color. The fragrant flowers are good for cutting, and there is good repeat. It is vigorous with an upright, spreading habit, grows to above average height and is well furnished with large olive green leaves. It prefers warmer climates. **ZONES 4–9.**

DELBARD, FRANCE, 1976

('HOLSTEIN' × 'BAYADÈRE') × ('PRELUDE' × 'SAINT-EXUPERY')

BAGATELLE GOLD MEDAL

### 'Blue Parfum' TANfifum, TANfifume, TANtifum
syns 'Blue Perfume', 'Violette Parfum'
MODERN, LARGE-FLOWERED/HYBRID TEA, MAUVE, REPEAT-FLOWERING

The parentage of this rose is not disclosed, as is usual with Tantau Roses, but it doubtless follows the line he used to obtain 'Blue Moon'. This is shorter and more compact in growth, leafier and not as vigorous. The flowers are quite large, full petalled and beautifully formed, in a color that varies subtly through the season, encompassing lilac, mauve, pale violet and blush. It is among the earliest of the Large-flowered Roses to come into bloom, and after a good initial display, more blooms are produced through summer and autumn. They have an excellent fragrance and are good to cut. The plant grows to below average height with a neat, bushy upright habit and glossy dark green foliage. **ZONES 4–9.**

TANTAU, GERMANY, 1978

PARENTAGE UNKNOWN

B

**'Blue Peter'** RUlblun *(left)*
syns 'Azulabria', 'Bluenette'
MODERN, MINIATURE, MAUVE BLEND,
REPEAT-FLOWERING

Deep lilac-purple blooms with
contrasting yellow stamens
make this rose a real talking
point in the garden, as it is the
bluest Miniature Rose yet. The
flowers have about 20 petals
and last for weeks on the bush.
It is treasured by floral arrangers
who love the color combination
and the light green, semi-glossy
foliage. The bush is compact and
grows to 12–20 in (30–50 cm)
high. ZONES 5–11.

DE RUITER, THE NETHERLANDS, 1983

'LITTLE FLIRT' × SEEDLING

**'Blue River'** KORsicht
*(left)*
MODERN, LARGE-FLOWERED/HYBRID TEA,
MAUVE BLEND, REPEAT-FLOWERING

This is one of those varieties
that appear uncertain whether
to behave as Large-flowered or
Cluster-flowered Roses, for the
stems often carry several blooms.
The rounded buds open to lilac
flowers randomly splashed with
deep magenta-pink, especially
towards the edges of the petals,
providing an unusually strong
color effect. The blooms are
fragrant, full of petals and
last well when cut, and if the
flowering shoots are disbudded
early enough, they can produce
quality exhibition blooms.
They continue through summer
to autumn on a vigorous and
upright plant of average size
and with dense dark green foliage. 'Blue River' does best in
warmer climates. ZONES 5–9.

KORDES, GERMANY, 1984

'BLUE MOON' × 'ZORINA'

BADEN-BADEN GOLD MEDAL

B

### 'Blueberry Hill'
**WEKcryplag** *(right)*
MODERN, CLUSTER-FLOWERED/
FLORIBUNDA, MAUVE

It is not just the color that will steal your heart—this lovely lilac rose also has a sweet apple fragrance. The blooms are large and semi-double and they smother the clean glossy foliage, much like an azalea bush in spring. 'Blueberry Hill' makes a medium sized rounded bush that stands 4 ft (1.2 m).
**ZONES 5–9.**

CARRUTH, USA, 1997

'CRYSTALLINE' × 'PLAYGIRL'

### 'Blush Damask'
*(right)*
syn. 'Blush Gallica'
OLD, DAMASK, LIGHT PINK

This is a dense broad twiggy shrub to 6 ft (1.8 m) that clearly has a Gallica influence. The stems are grayish green and moderately armed with short thorns; the foliage is dark green and plentiful. The flowers, which are produced in great numbers all over the bush in early summer, are fragrant and full and cushion-like, and when fully open attain a size of about 2 in (5 cm) across. The center of each bloom is mauve-pink and the outer petals are milky white, creating a very pretty effect. 'Blush Damask' is an easy-to-grow shrub that needs space to develop, but it will tolerate even the most dry and impoverished soil.
**ZONES 5–11.**

PARENTAGE UNKNOWN

### 'Blush Hip'
OLD, ALBA, LIGHT PINK

For many rosarians, this is the best of the Alba class. Classic in form and highly fragrant, 'Blush Hip' looks a great deal like 'Maiden's Blush' but it is taller. The bright red buds open to double blooms of soft pink with a button center and a green eye. This variety flowers early and there is no rebloom. The foliage is coarse with toothed leaves. **ZONES 5–11.**

PRE-1846

PARENTAGE UNKNOWN

**B**

### 'Blush Noisette'
*(right)*
OLD, NOISETTE, WHITE, REPEAT-FLOWERING

This was the first Noisette to be sold to the public and it is still highly regarded by rose gardeners; one of the American Noisettes, it started its life in South Carolina. Loosely double, perfectly formed blush-pink blooms open from dark pink buds. The dainty petals are supported on glossy, green foliage and have a perfume that many declare is strongly clove-like. It is often seen on pillars or as a hedge. The rose, which is vigorous and healthy and continues to bloom into autumn, grows well in light shade. Redouté has portrayed it as *Rosa noisettiana*. **ZONES 7–10.**

NOISETTE, USA, CIRCA 1814

SEEDLING OF 'CHAMPNEY'S PINK CLUSTER'

### 'Blush Rambler'
*(right)*
MODERN, RAMBLER, LIGHT PINK

This vigorous Rambler is often found in old cottage gardens. It is an almost thornless bush with light green leaves. The small cupped light pink flowers are borne in clusters. They have a light scent, a trait inherited from 'The Garland', an early Musk/Multiflora cross. The other parent, nicknamed 'The Engineer' from the occupation of Albert Smith, who found it in Japan and sent it to Turner of Edinburgh (the introducer), was very famous and set the trend for ramblers at the close of the nineteenth century. Unfortunately it suffered from mildew and was overtaken by many other rambling varieties. **ZONES 4–9.**

CANT, UK, 1903

'CRIMSON RAMBLER' × 'THE GARLAND'

## 'Bobbie James'  *(right)*

MODERN, RAMBLER, WHITE

This rose has semi-double, small, slightly cupped blooms with creamy white petals and brilliant yellow stamens. The large clusters are borne on long, thin, attractive canes with troublesome prickles and full of glossy leaves with coppery edges. Because of its rampant growth, this rose needs plenty of room and a strong support, such as a tree. Although it blooms only in summer, it is a memorable event when the large clusters open and the extremely fragrant perfume permeates the garden. 'Bobbie James' was introduced by Graham Stuart Thomas who named it in honor of a renowned Yorkshire horticulturist, 'one of the grand old men of gardening'. Its popularity has not flagged since its introduction. **ZONES 5–10.**

SUNNINGDALE NURSERIES, UK, 1960

PARENTAGE UNKNOWN

ROYAL HORTICULTURAL SOCIETY AWARD OF GARDEN MERIT 1993

## 'Bobby Charlton'
*(right)*

MODERN, LARGE-FLOWERED/
HYBRID TEA, PINK BLEND,
REPEAT-FLOWERING

This is among the best roses for exhibition, thanks to its very large full-petalled flowers which are borne singly on long stems. They open deep pink and have a silvery reverse to the petal but rain can spoil them, and exhibitors in damp climates have learnt to protect their potential prize-winners. In warmer climates this should make a more acceptable garden rose, but because so much effort goes into producing each flower, blooms in late summer and autumn are not plentiful. There is a spicy fragrance. The plant grows to above average height, making an upright, rather leggy bush with dark leathery foliage. It is named for the soccer maestro who was capped for England 106 times. **ZONES 4–9.**

FRYER, UK, 1974

'ROYAL HIGHNESS' × 'PRIMA BALLERINA'

BADEN-BADEN GOLD MEDAL 1976, PORTLAND GOLD MEDAL 1980

**B**

### 'Bon Silène' *(below)*

OLD, TEA, DEEP PINK,
REPEAT-FLOWERING

This elegant rose has well-formed buds and deep rose, double blooms that are carmine-pink on the reverse of the petals. A cup shape is main- tained by the stiff, upright petals. A strong tea-fruit perfume and elongated, leathery leaves complement this rampant grower. Its hardy growth will reach 5 ft (1.5 m). It has a few prickles and large hips, while the cut flowers are long lasting. Slow to establish itself and much underrated, 'Bon Silène' likes a sunny, warm position and has been found in many cemeteries in southern USA , disease free and surviving neglect for over 100 years. The breeder, Alexandre Hardy, was the chief horticulturalist of the Luxembourg Palace in Paris. ZONES 5–10.

HARDY, FRANCE, PRE-1837

PARENTAGE UNKNOWN

### 'Bonfire Night'
*(below left)*
syn. 'Bonfire'

MODERN, CLUSTER-FLOWERED/
FLORIBUNDA, RED BLEND,
REPEAT-FLOWERING

A bed of this rose at the height of summer provides a wonderful sight with the large semi- double flowers opening cupped to reveal a vivid blend of yellow with scarlet overlays. They are produced in well- spaced clusters that display the colors to great effect, especially against a background of abundant dark foli- age. There is a pleasant light fragrance, and the flowers reliably appear through summer and autumn. The plant is vigorous and upright, growing fairly evenly to average height. Friends questioned associating a rose with a bonfire, but the connection comes from the Bonfire Night celebrations in the UK on 5 November, the day King and Parliament were saved from being blown up in 1605. ZONES 4–9.

MCGREDY, UK, 1971

'TIKI' × 'VARIETY CLUB'

ROYAL NATIONAL ROSE SOCIETY
TRIAL GROUND CERTIFICATE 1969

## 'Bonica' MEIdomonac
(right)

syns 'Bonica 82',
'Demon', 'Bonica
Meidiland'

MODERN, MODERN SHRUB,
MEDIUM PINK,
REPEAT-FLOWERING

Every garden should
have this delightful
rose. It bears sprays of
clear rose pink flowers
at different levels on a
neat, spreading plant
of modest size, covered
in abundant rich green
foliage that is attractive
even before flowering
starts. Once it does
start, there is hardly
any time when the plant
is out of bloom until
the winter frosts. The
flowers are full of small
petals and are cupped
in form, and have a
light fragrance. For
a specimen plant or a
group, or to form a low
mounded hedge, 'Bonica'
is a lovely rose to have
and a good one to
recommend to people
who say they 'can't
grow roses', for its
constitution and health
are excellent. The name
'Bonica 82' is given to
distinguish it from an
earlier 'Bonica' from the
same raiser. ZONES 4–9.

MEILLAND, FRANCE, 1981

POSSIBLY (ROSA SEMPERVIRENS ×
'MLLE MARTHE CARRON') ×
'PICASSO'

ANERKANNTE DEUTSCHE ROSE
1983, BELFAST CERTIFICATE OF
MERIT 1983, ALL-AMERICA
ROSE SELECTION 1987, ROYAL
HORTICULTURAL SOCIETY AWARD
OF GARDEN MERIT 1993

## 'Bonn' (above)

MODERN, MODERN SHRUB,
ORANGE-RED,
REPEAT-FLOWERING

The vigor, freedom of
flower and health of
'Bonn' explain why it
is so valuable for use
in parks, although
gardeners may feel
these qualities do not
compensate for its lack
of charm. It has light
to moderate scent and
orange-scarlet flowers
of good size, in clusters
of up to 10, held aloft
on strong stems. The
flowers are semi-double,
loosely formed and age
to a pinky magenta. In
growth the plant ex-
tends taller and wider
than an average shrub
rose, with light green
glossy foliage. It is
repeat-flowering, and
when it was introduced
half a century ago it was
welcomed for this and
its other good points.
Choice has widened
immensely since those
days, and tastes in
roses have changed.
One rosarian summed
up 'Bonn' by saying
'Rather crude for my
taste, but at least you
can see it.' It was named
for the administrative
capital of the German
Federal Republic.
ZONES 4–9.

KORDES, GERMANY, 1950

'HAMBURG' × 'INDEPENDENCE'

ROYAL NATIONAL ROSE SOCIETY
CERTIFICATE OF MERIT 1950

B

## 'Borderer' *(below)*

MODERN, POLYANTHA, PINK BLEND, REPEAT-FLOWERING

This was one of Alister Clark's earliest releases. The lightly formed flowers are cupped, and open to reveal attractive stamens among the mid-pink petals. The blooms continue throughout the season and it is rarely without flowers. The growth is small and thin, creating a tightly growing bush that makes a good hedge plant. It is also ideal for informal edging of a rose bed. Clark's aim when breeding was to produce plants that were healthy and strong and flowered continuously throughout the year in warmer climates. 'Borderer' was a pioneer in this style. **ZONES 5–9.**

CLARK, AUSTRALIA, 1918

'JERSEY BEAUTY' × SEEDLING

## 'Botanica' TOMboy *(above)*

MODERN, CLUSTER-FLOWERED/FLORIBUNDA, LIGHT PINK, REPEAT-FLOWERING

'Botanica' has beautiful pink flowers with just a touch of lilac. These are borne in large clusters and have a delicious fruity perfume. What sets this glorious rose apart from the other Cluster-flowered Roses is its ability to produce blooms in profusion. The foliage is healthy, matt and medium green on an extremely vigorous, disease-resistant bush with a slightly spreading habit. It can grow to 3–4 ft (1–1.2 m) tall and about 3 ft (1 m) in width. The breeder, George Thomson of Mount Barker in South Australia, had long felt that the flower size of many modern Cluster-flowered Roses is too big, and he attempted various crosses to reduce the size of the blooms. With this cross his dreams were realized, and 'Botanica' was born. It was named for the successful plant book *Botanica.* **ZONES 5–9.**

THOMSON, AUSTRALIA

'AVANDEL' × 'MADAM PRESIDENT'

## 'Botzaris'

OLD, DAMASK, NEAR WHITE

This rose is not given the attention it deserves, despite being a reliable, versatile grower and is glorious at its best. The creamy white, double, flat, quartered blooms emerge from pinkish buds with long foliated sepals; these are usually arranged in clusters and are richly perfumed. The muddled petals surround a button eye. It blooms only in summer; its foliage is dark green and it has prickles. A short, compact shrub to about 4 ft (1.2 m), it makes an effective hedge or an ornament in the wild garden. This is a rose that rewards a little extra loving care with much satisfaction, especially in fine weather. Its only flaw is that like many white double roses 'Botzaris' dislikes too much rain.
ZONES 5–10.
INTRODUCED BY ROBERT, 1856
PARENTAGE UNKNOWN

## 'Bougainville'

(top right)
OLD, NOISETTE, PINK BLEND

Like so many Noisettes, this vigorous rose looks best on structures in open ground. The red buds open to reveal pink flowers tinged with lilac at the edge, and turning pale with age. The very double, cupped blooms are medium in size, while the narrow foliage is shiny with a lacy appearance. It was named after Admiral Louis Antoine de Bougainville (1729–1811), as is the popular, tropical vine *Bougainvillea*, and several locations including the island in the Solomons.
ZONES 7–11.
COCHET, FRANCE, 1822
PARENTAGE UNKNOWN

## 'Boule de Neige'

(bottom right)
syn. 'Snowball'
OLD, BOURBON, WHITE, REPEAT-FLOWERING

The opening buds of this rose are striped with pink, and illustrate why

old roses have been the subject of so many paintings. The pure white blooms are full and compact; the small clusters of densely packed petals reflex quickly into a ball. The dark, glossy foliage has a leathery finish and there are some prickles. This is a good candidate for borders or to use as a hedge, and it should be pruned carefully. It has been successful as a container plant and is tolerant of shade. ZONES 5–10.
LACHARMÉ, FRANCE, 1867
'MLLE BLANCHE LAFITTE' × 'SAPPHO'

B

### 'Bouquet d'Or' *(above)*

OLD, NOISETTE, YELLOW BLEND, REPEAT-FLOWERING

On the vigorous branches throughout summer and into autumn, buff-yellow, coppery salmon blooms crowd the stout canes. The flowers are perfectly shaped, double and quartered and have a strong scent. Many claim that this rose is an improvement on its parent, 'Gloire de Dijon'. The half-open flower shows this rose at its best. The foliage is dark green. It likes a sunny spot in a large garden and is highly disease resistant. **ZONES 7–11.**

DUCHER, FRANCE, 1872

'GLOIRE DE DIJON' × SEEDLING

### 'Bourgogne'

MODERN, MODERN SHRUB, MEDIUM RED

*Rosa pendulina* is a purplish pink species that has been little used by hybridizers. This variety is an interesting derivative, bearing medium to large-sized single pink blooms that open cupped and are borne freely in summer. They are followed in autumn by magnificent long scarlet hips, which appear in pendulous clusters at different levels on the plant and give off brilliant gleams of color when caught by the sun. The growth of the plant is interesting, being wide and bushy, and there are many slender stems that rise in an arch and then bow towards the ground under the weight of the hips and the leaves; the leaves are rather dark and narrow and are composed of 7 leaflets. **ZONES 4–9.**

ILSINK, THE NETHERLANDS, 1983

DERIVED FROM *ROSA PENDULINA*

**B**

### 'Bow Bells' AUSbells *(right)*

MODERN, MODERN SHRUB, DEEP PINK,
REPEAT-FLOWERING

This rose, also classified as an English
Rose, bears large clusters of deep pink
blooms. The medium-sized flowers
have up to 24 petals that give the young
blooms the shape of an artichoke before
opening out into a cupped form. They
are fragrant and are borne through summer and autumn. It is useful for a mixed
border, growing to average height and
width with an upright bushy habit; it
has medium green, semi-glossy leaves.
The raiser named it because of a fancied
resemblance of the flowers to bells and
with reference to the church at Bow,
in London's East End. ZONES 4–9.

AUSTIN, UK, 1991

SEEDLING × 'GRAHAM THOMAS'

### 'Boys' Brigade' COCdinkum *(right)*

MODERN, PATIO/DWARF CLUSTER-FLOWERED,
MEDIUM RED, REPEAT-FLOWERING

Bright red 5-petalled florets (carmine
and crimson) literally cover this plant.
The blooms have a lighter eye with dull
yellow stamens. Usually borne in large
clusters on strong straight stems, the
blooms last for several weeks before
falling off naturally and repeating the
bloom cycle. This rose was named for
the centenary of the UK Boys' Brigade.
ZONES 4–11.

COCKER, UK, 1983

('DARLING FLAME' × 'SAINT ALBAN') × ('LITTLE FLIRT' ×
'MARLENA')

ROYAL NATIONAL ROSE SOCIETY TRIAL GROUND
CERTIFICATE 1983

B

### 'Brandy' AROcad
*(right)*

MODERN, LARGE-FLOWERED/
HYBRID TEA, APRICOT BLEND,
REPEAT-FLOWERING

'The richest apricot color yet in roses', say the catalogues. When 'Brandy' received its high award in the USA, the color certainly caught the judges' eyes, and the form of the young blooms is very elegant with 20 or more petals forming neat-looking high centers. As the petals open, the large flowers become loose and informal in shape, and the bright golden stamens are soon revealed. There is a strong fruity fragrance and flowering continues through summer and autumn, so despite the fleeting nature of the blooms it is a suitable rose for a bed or hedge. It may prove vulnerable to black spot and, while it prefers cooler weather, it is not dependably frost hardy. The growth is taller than average, with an upright habit and plentiful medium green glossy leaves of good size. ZONES 5–9.

SWIM AND CHRISTENSEN, USA, 1981

'FIRST PRIZE' × 'DR A. J. VERHAGE'

ALL-AMERICA ROSE SELECTION 1982

### 'Brass Ring' DICgrow
*(right)*
syn. 'Peek-a-Boo'

MODERN, DWARF CLUSTER-
FLOWERED/PATIO, ORANGE
BLEND, REPEAT-FLOWERING

Masses of coppery orange flowers on a rounded bush are the hallmark of this rose. After opening, the orange blooms fade to a wonderful rose pink, creating a masterpiece of color combination in the garden. The blooms have only 21 petals and are at their best when fully open. The bush carries many short stems that tend to arch so that it forms a leafy hummock. The plant is inclined to arch upward, gaining considerable height over the traditional compact Miniature bush. It is an excellent specimen for growing in containers. ZONES 5–11.

DICKSON, UK, 1981

'MEMENTO' × 'NOZOMI'

ROYAL NATIONAL ROSE SOCIETY
CERTIFICATE OF MERIT 1981,
BELFAST CERTIFICATE OF MERIT
1983

B

### 'Breath of Life'
HARquanne *(right)*

MODERN, LARGE-FLOWERED
CLIMBER, APRICOT BLEND,
REPEAT-FLOWERING

'Breath of Life' has the unusual color of apricot skin, becoming apricot-pink as the flowers age. The medium to large-sized flowers are full petalled and develop like Cluster-flowered Roses, with high centers in the young flowers, becoming cupped with waved petals as they age. It is a very good rose for flower arrangements as the blooms are long lasting and hold their color when cut; old flowers on the plant are best deadheaded. Flowering continues through summer and autumn, and there is a pleasing fragrance. The growth is stiff and upright, to average size, and if it is to be trained sideways, this needs to be done early while the long stems are still pliable. It has medium green leaves. Britain's Royal College of Midwives chose the name, which signifies both the Creator Spirit in Genesis and everybody's first vital act on coming into the world. ZONES 4–9.

HARKNESS, UK, 1982

'RED DANDY' × 'ALEXANDER'

JAPAN CERTIFICATE OF MERIT
1983, NEW ZEALAND CERTIFICATE
OF MERIT 1985

### 'Breathless' JACchry
*(right)*

MODERN, LARGE-FLOWERED/
HYBRID TEA, DEEP PINK,
REPEAT-FLOWERING

This recently introduced variety has elegant urn-shaped buds that open into fairly full flowers of excellent form, high centered in the early stages, then becoming rounded in form as the petals expand. They are deep pink, paler on the outside of the petals, of good size and are borne usually one to a stem, which means they are useful for cutting as well as for garden display. There is a pleasing light scent, and flowering continues through summer and autumn. The plant grows to above average height with an upright habit, and is furnished with large medium green leaves that are purplish red when young. ZONES 4–9.

WARRINER, USA, 1994

SEEDLING × 'CHRYSLER
IMPERIAL'

B

## 'Bredon' AUSbred *(left)*

MODERN, MODERN SHRUB, APRICOT BLEND, REPEAT-FLOWERING

The young flowers of 'Bredon' are a delicate creamy pink with gentle apricot shades in the depths of the petals; as they open the apricot tones predominate, growing paler as the blooms expand. They are medium sized and beautifully formed, with many petals infolding against one another and creating muddled centers. Flowering continues through summer and autumn and there is a fruity scent. It grows like a shrubby Cluster-flowered Rose and is suitable for a border, preferably with shorter plants in front, because the stems tend to be leggy and arching. In winter they need to be pruned to keep the plant tidy. The mid-green leaves are large. Bredon is a scenic area in the west of England. 'Bredon' is also classified as an English Rose. ZONES 4–9.

AUSTIN, UK, 1984

'WIFE OF BATH' × 'LILIAN AUSTIN'

## 'Breeze Hill' *(right)*

MODERN, LARGE-FLOWERED CLIMBER, APRICOT BLEND

This interesting rose is like a rambler because it produces many flexible stems, yet like a climber in the fairly large size of its flowers and the dull, rounded character of its leaves. The quoted parentage has been queried and descent from 'Dr Van Fleet' suggested instead. The flowers, usually borne in clusters of 3 or more, are packed to the center with petals and open rather flat, showing creamy blush and apricot shades that pale to creamy buff. Tolerating bad weather well, they appear freely in summer with an occasional flower later and have a light apple scent. Though a slow starter, the plant can extend beyond the average for a climbing rose, or it may be trimmed and grown as a big arching shrub. It is well covered with rather small leaves and has a good health record. 'Breeze Hill' was named after the home of eminent rosarian Dr J. H. McFarland in Harrisburg, Pennsylvania. ZONES 4–9.

VAN FLEET, USA, 1926

*ROSA WICHURANA* × 'BEAUTÉ DE LYON'

B

## 'Brenda' *(right)*

OLD, SWEET BRIAR, LIGHT PINK

Peach blossom to pink, single blooms appear in spring on vigorous canes on this rose. It does best in shade for bloom color. The vigorous, attractive, tall shrub is covered with hips in autumn. Lord Penzance, an English judge, raised several hybrids using *Rosa eglanteria* as seed parent for fragrance and habit, crossed with pollen from Hybrid Perpetuals and Bourbons to add color and size. His aim was to raise repeat-flowering roses with fragrance, but 'Brenda' never achieved the widespread popularity of his other hybrids. **ZONES 5–11.**

PENZANCE, UK, 1894

PARENTAGE UNKNOWN

## 'Brennus'

syns 'Brutus', 'Queen Victoria', 'St Brennus'

OLD, HYBRID CHINA, DARK RED

Not well known except in warm climates, this hybrid is either a Bourbon or a China, depending on whom you trust. The fully flat, brilliant crimson, globular blooms are dark red, shaded violet. Very large in size, they are cupped with wavy petals. Although it blooms only once, it does so over a long period, and its excellent foliage and flowers make it a good subject for a pillar. Brennus was a Gallic leader whose forces captured Rome around 329 BC, although historians state that his existence is probably a legend. **ZONES 7–11.**

LAFFAY, FRANCE, 1830

PARENTAGE UNKNOWN

## 'Bridal Pink' JACbri

*(above right)*

MODERN, CLUSTER-FLOWERED/
FLORIBUNDA, MEDIUM PINK,
REPEAT-FLOWERING

The name indicates one purpose that this rose has served for 30 years, for the flower clusters are suitable for wedding bouquets. They open from elegant pointed buds into full-petalled, high-centered blooms of good size and perfection of form, and last well. The color is light pink with creamy tones and they have an appreciable fragrance. In warm climates it is rewarding in a sunny position, both as a pleasing border and to cut for small flower arrangements. The blooms are produced through summer and autumn, though wet or cool weather will spoil their beauty. It grows to average height with an upright habit and has leathery dark green foliage. **ZONES 5–9.**

BOERNER, USA, 1967

SEEDLING OF 'SUMMERTIME' ×
SEEDLING OF 'SPARTAN'

B

### 'Bride's Dream' ROYroyness *(above)*
### syns 'Fairy Tale Queen', 'Marchenkonigin'
MODERN, LARGE-FLOWERED/HYBRID TEA, LIGHT PINK, REPEAT-FLOWERING

This is one of the best of pale pink roses. Bred from 'Royal Highness', it is the same soft pink color, but the buds are much longer, growth is much taller, and it does not suffer from mildew. The particularly long elegant buds open to large, double flowers with 30 high-centered petals. There is slight fragrance. Flower production is very high and its very long stems make this an excellent rose for picking. The foliage is dark green and very profuse. The bush grows too tall for bedding, but it is a wonderful rose at the back of the border. **ZONES 4–9.**

KORDES, GERMANY, 1985
'ROYAL HIGHNESS' × SEEDLING

### 'Brigadoon' JACpal
MODERN, LARGE-FLOWERED/HYBRID TEA, PINK BLEND, REPEAT-FLOWERING

This rose is popular because of the color of the flowers; these are a delightful blend of pink, cream and strawberry red, the deeper shades beautifully marked towards the petal tips. As the buds open, they reveal some 40 petals forming a tight coil in the heart of the flower. The petals slowly reflex to show a spiral center that slowly subsides as the blooms gradually open out. There is a spicy fragrance, and the flowers appear from summer to autumn. It is an attractive rose and can prove useful for exhibition too, although the stems are too often on the short side to make it dependable for cutting. It grows tall and bushy and has a good coverage of large deep green glossy leaves, but it may die back in a hard winter. **ZONES 5–9.**

WARRINER, USA, 1991
SEEDLING × 'PRISTINE'
ALL-AMERICA ROSE SELECTION 1992

B

## 'Bright Smile' DICdance *(right)*

MODERN, CLUSTER-FLOWERED/FLORIBUNDA, MEDIUM YELLOW,
REPEAT-FLOWERING

This is well named, for its cheerful blooms
always seem to give a welcome. Slender buds
open out wide into fairly large semi-double
flowers, effectively showing off the bright
yellow petals and prominent stamens. There
is a pleasing scent, and the plant always
seems to have flowers showing on it somewhere throughout summer and autumn.
The growth is neat, bushy and spreading to
below average height and it has plenty of
shiny foliage, so it maintains an attractive
appearance even before the first flowers
appear. Occasionally the young shoots are
touched by seasonal mildew. **ZONES 4–9.**

DICKSON, UK, 1981

'EUROROSE' × SEEDLING

BRITISH ASSOCIATION OF ROSE
BREEDERS SELECTION 1980,
BELFAST PRIZE 1982, GLASGOW
SILVER MEDAL 1989

## 'Broadway' BURway *(right)*

MODERN, LARGE-FLOWERED/
HYBRID TEA, YELLOW BLEND,
REPEAT-FLOWERING

The color of 'Broadway'
is delightful—'orange
suffused with gold' is
how the catalogues
describe it. There is a
good deal of reddish
pink towards the
margins of the petals,
the coloring deepening
and extending in very
sunny weather. The
blooms are fully double
and quite large, open-
ing with high centers
and holding a pretty,
regular shape as the
petals reflex. The
flowers have a strong,
spicy fragrance, and
continue to bloom
through summer and
autumn, though the
mid-season ones are
of lesser quality. The
plant grows to average
height with an upright,
bushy habit and is fur-
nished with shiny dark
green leaves. It makes a
pleasing bedding rose,
and gives flowers suit-
able for cutting which,
by reason of their color
changes, are delightful
to see as they open in
a vase. There is a risk
of die-back in severe
winters. **ZONES 5–9.**

ANTHONY PERRY, USA, 1985

('FIRST PRIZE' × 'GOLD GLOW')
× 'SUTTER'S GOLD'

ALL-AMERICA ROSE SELECTION
1986

### 'Bronze Masterpiece' (right)

syn. 'Bronce Masterpiece'

MODERN, LARGE-FLOWERED/
HYBRID TEA, APRICOT BLEND,
REPEAT-FLOWERING

The best flowers on this rose come early in the flowering season, when the bronzy orange tones are at their deepest. The brownish amber buds open into high-centered, full-petalled flowers that become more orange-yellow in tone as the petals reflex. They hold their form for a long time in cooler weather, when they can give exhibition blooms. They have a rich fruity fragrance and continue through summer and autumn, provided there are no fungus troubles. The plant grows to average height with an upright habit and has leathery, glossy dark green foliage. 'Bronze Masterpiece' is little grown today except in warm climates. ZONES 5–9.

BOERNER, USA, 1960

'GOLDEN MASTERPIECE' ×
'KATE SMITH'

GENEVA GOLD MEDAL 1958

### 'Brother Cadfael'

AUSglobe (bottom right)

MODERN, MODERN SHRUB,
MEDIUM PINK,
REPEAT-FLOWERING

A special attraction of this rose is the shape of the flowers, deeply cupped with an old-fashioned style like peonies. They are fully double and have substantial thick petals. The color is a rich shade of rose pink and there is good fragrance. It makes a sturdy upright bush of average height and has large dark leaves. It was named after a monastic sleuth created by Edith Pargeter, who wrote under the name Ellis Peters. It is also classified as an English Rose. ZONES 4–9.

AUSTIN, UK, 1990

'CHARLES AUSTIN' × SEEDLING

B

### 'Brown Velvet' MACcultra *(right)*
### syn. 'Colorbreak'
MODERN, CLUSTER-FLOWERED/FLORIBUNDA, RUSSET, REPEAT-FLOWERING

Sam McGredy has constantly surprised the rose world with his roses of extraordinary coloring; this one is a blend of orange-red and brown. In cooler climates the brownish tones predominate; in sunnier climes the brown becomes overlaid with orange. Crowded clusters of round buds open into double flowers with quartered petals, which soon reflex to allow golden stamens to peep through. The medium-sized, lightly fragrant flowers continue blooming through summer and autumn. It makes an upright bush of average height with glossy dark green leaves. **ZONES 4–9.**

MCGREDY, NEW ZEALAND, 1982

'MARY SUMNER' × 'KAPAI'

GOLD STAR OF THE SOUTH PACIFIC, NEW ZEALAND 1979

### 'Brownie' *(right)*
MODERN, CLUSTER-FLOWERED/ FLORIBUNDA, RUSSET, REPEAT-FLOWERING

The work of Gene Boerner produced some extraordinary roses in the post-war years, including 'Lavender Pinocchio' whose parent was 'Grey Pearl'. When these two were crossed with one another, 'Brownie' was the result. It has tan-colored buds that open into cupped flowers of chocolate brown, with gold shading at the base and pinky red at the petal edges. Copper and creamy shades

appear as the full-petalled flowers open out almost flat. Blooms appear sporadically through summer and autumn and are pro-

duced in well-spaced clusters, on upright plants that grow below average height, with leathery leaves. It is not constitutionally

vigorous or healthy and needs good conditions to thrive. **ZONES 4–9.**

BOERNER, USA, 1959

SEEDLING OF 'LAVENDER PINOCCHIO' × 'GREY PEARL'

B

### 'Buccaneer' *(below)*

MODERN, LARGE-FLOWERED/HYBRID TEA, MEDIUM YELLOW,
REPEAT-FLOWERING

In the USA this is called a Grandiflora, indicating
a plant built on a more generous scale than most
bushes; it fits that concept well, producing long
urn-shaped buds in open clusters that open into
cupped, rather loose blooms of bright yellow,
carried boldly on stiff stems and with a pleasant
fragrance. The flowers have about 24 petals and
make a bold and noticeable splash of color in the
garden. 'Buccaneer' flowers through summer and
autumn; it withstands bad weather well. This rose
can be difficult to site, because its habit is considerably taller than average. It can make a splendid
pillar or semi-climber if trained on a stout pole
or fence and lightly pruned. The plant is vigorous
and usually very healthy, with an upright, free-
branching habit and abundant deep bright green
foliage. ZONES 4–9.

SWIM, USA, 1952

'GEHEIMRAT DUISBERG' × ('MAX KRAUSE' × 'CAPTAIN THOMAS')

GENEVA GOLD MEDAL 1952, ROYAL NATIONAL ROSE SOCIETY TRIAL
GROUND CERTIFICATE 1955

### 'Buff Beauty'
*(above)*

MODERN, MODERN SHRUB,
APRICOT BLEND,
REPEAT-FLOWERING

This is a rose for the
enthusiast, a desirable
garden item even when
not in bloom, thanks to
its gracefully rounded
plant habit and ample
covering of handsome
dark shiny leaves. In
summer and again
in autumn it produces
trusses of pale apricot
blooms that show up
tellingly against this
dark background. The
flowers have many
petals that open out
in the shape of powder
puffs, showing charm-
ing muddled centers.
They carry hints of
buff yellow as well as
apricot, have a pleasing
fragrance and with-
stand bad weather well.
This variety grows to
average height or more,
is excellent in borders
or to plant against a
low wall, and has a
good health record.
ZONES 4–9.

BENTALL, UK, 1939

'WILLIAM ALLEN RICHARDSON' ×
UNKNOWN

ROYAL HORTICULTURAL SOCIETY
AWARD OF GARDEN MERIT 1993

B

### 'Bullata' *(right)*
**syns 'Lettuce-leafed Rose', *Rosa × centifolia bullata*, 'Rose à Feuilles de Laitue'**

OLD, CENTIFOLIA, MEDIUM PINK

This is a lax shrub, to 5 ft (1.5 m) and almost as broad. The stems are long, arching, dark green and well populated with reddish thorns. The leaves of this rose make it interesting: each leaf is a clear rich green, large and very crinkled, like that of a lettuce. Very fragrant flowers emerge in mid-summer from tight round buds, arranged in small clusters. The fully opened flowers are a rich deep glowing pink and are made up of many tightly packed petals. They dislike rain, sometimes rotting off before opening in prolonged wet spells of weather, but this should not put anyone off this fascinating rose. It is almost identical to 'Centifolia', from which it probably sported or self-seeded in the distant past. **ZONES 5–10.**

PRE-1815

PARENTAGE UNKNOWN

### 'Bulls Red' MACrero
*(right)*

MODERN, LARGE-FLOWERED/
HYBRID TEA, MEDIUM RED,
REPEAT-FLOWERING

This rose is appreciated for its keeping qualities, which have made it very useful as a cut flower variety. It bears its flowers usually one to a stem, opening out from plump buds into large broad-petalled blooms. They are double, with high centers, and in color are on the darker side of medium red; however, they lack the rich fragrance one expects from a red rose. The plant flowers freely and maintains a good succession of bloom on long stems through summer and autumn. It is an upright grower, vigorous and taller than average, and has dark leaves. **ZONES 4–9.**

MCGREDY, NEW ZEALAND, 1977

'SYMPATHIE' × 'IRISH ROVER'

## 'Burgundian Rose'
*(right)*
syns 'Pompon de Burgogne', 'Burgundy Rose', *Rosa burgundica, R. centifolia parvifolia*
OLD, CENTIFOLIA, PINK BLEND

This rose has a long but not very clear history; it requires a patient reader to find it in most books as it goes under a number of names. The small, deep pink blossoms suffused with purple, with a paler center, the dark, gray-green foliage and the few prickles make it a charming plant for a dense, low shrub or a pot. There is some fragrance. **ZONES 4–10.**

BURGUNDY, FRANCE, CIRCA 1664

PARENTAGE UNKNOWN

## 'Burnaby' *(right)*
syns 'Gold Heart', 'Golden Heart'
MODERN, LARGE-FLOWERED/ HYBRID TEA, LIGHT YELLOW, REPEAT-FLOWERING

The parents of this rose do not carry very large flowers, so the raiser must have been surprised to conjure out of them a flower like 'Burnaby'. With over 50 big petals it makes a wonderful cabbage of a rose with high-centered form, opening majestically to show a rounded outline. Only a tendency to produce split blooms denies it a place among top-class roses for exhibition, but it is sufficiently vigorous and free flowering for the garden, maintaining a sporadic succession of lightly fragrant blooms through summer and autumn in a clear primrose yellow color, paling to cream. The plant grows to average height with a bushy habit and has rather sparse dark glossy foliage that needs watching for black spot. **ZONES 4–9.**

EDDIE, CANADA, 1954

'PHYLLIS GOLD' × 'PRESIDENT HERBERT HOOVER'

NATIONAL ROSE SOCIETY GOLD MEDAL 1954, PORTLAND GOLD MEDAL 1957

## 'Buttons 'n' Bows' *(right)*

syns 'Felicity II', 'Teeney-Weeny'

MODERN, MINIATURE, DEEP PINK, REPEAT-FLOWERING

Double flowers in shades of pink adorn this compact upright bush. They are usually borne singly or in small sprays and have a fruity perfume. The form is high-centered and cupped, reflexing at full maturity. It is popular throughout the world, providing a fast repeat-bloom cycle in most climates. ZONES 4–11.

POULSEN, DENMARK, 1981

'MINI-POUL' × 'HARRIET POULSEN'

## 'By Appointment'

HARvolute *(right)*

MODERN, CLUSTER-FLOWERED/
FLORIBUNDA, APRICOT BLEND,
REPEAT-FLOWERING

This rose is a creamy apricot color, very pale when the slim urn-shaped buds first open, then deepening to show the subtle buff shades found in some Old Tea Roses. The double flowers are carried in rather crowded heads on upright stems, and at their best give wonderful sprays to cut and show because of the breathtaking effect of so many perfect tightly coiled young flowers seen together. Flowering starts late, and flowers appearing through the end of summer and into autumn are somewhat sparsely produced and rarely match the quality of the earlier ones. The plant grows upright and narrow to average height and has very dark leaves, which may be touched by mildew late in the season. It was named to commemorate the 150th anniversary of The Royal Warrant Holders' Association. ZONES 4–9.

HARKNESS, UK, 1990

'ANNE HARKNESS' ×
'LETCHWORTH GARDEN CITY'

C

### 'Café' (above)

MODERN, CLUSTER-FLOWERED/
FLORIBUNDA, RUSSET,
REPEAT-FLOWERING

Comment was sharply divided when this novel rose came on the market: 'We should hope never to be served coffee of this color' said one, while for another it was 'the precise color of café-au-lait'. Like many strangely colored roses, this one is affected by climate and season; if conditions are cool, the coffee-with-cream is pleasing, but where it is hot and dry, the flowers become an unattractive fawnish brown. The slightly fragrant flowers are double, borne in clusters and fairly large, tending to hang their heads. They open saucer shaped, with the petals rather loosely disposed, but if cut young they will last well in flower arrangements. Despite the vigor evident from the seed parent line, the plant makes low growth and needs good cultivation

to be worth keeping for its curiosity value. 'Café' has a sturdy and bushy habit and olive green foliage. **ZONES 4–9.**

KORDES, GERMANY, 1956

('GOLDEN GLOW' × *ROSA KORDESII*) × 'LAVENDER PINOCCHIO'

### 'Calocarpa' (bottom)

MODERN, HYBRID RUGOSA,
MEDIUM PINK,
REPEAT-FLOWERING

This rose bears clusters of sizeable fragrant single flowers with crumpled petals and prominent golden stamens. They appear through summer and autumn and have a color that appears to vary from bright red to rich rose pink to lilac-crimson, according to reports from different countries, which suggests that either a mutating Chinese gene has been at work or that more than one variety is involved. The growth is average for a shrub rose; it has slender, bristly stems and is clothed with leaves that are large, coarse, mid-green and slightly wrinkled. 'Calocarpa' makes a useful hedge, but its true attractions are the bunches of round scarlet hips that hang from it in autumn. **ZONES 4–9.**

BRUANT, FRANCE, PRE-1891

POSSIBLY *ROSA RUGOSA* × UNKNOWN CHINA

### 'Cabbage Rose'
*(top left)*
syns 'Centifolia',
'Provence Rose',
*Rosa × centifolia*

OLD, CENTIFOLIA, MEDIUM PINK

'The Rose of Painters' is the French name for this beautifully scented rose, which is seen in many Dutch still-life pictures and in Redouté's art as well. 'Cabbage Rose' is an unfortunate name because a bloom in its full glory is a sight to behold. Medium pink, very double blooms with overlapping petals appear singly or in clusters in summer.

The flowers tend to nod as there are so many petals, but not always 100 as some catalogues claim. It has coarse gray-green leaves and prickles and performs best in full sun. It reaches 6 ft (1.8 m) in maturity and is not particular about soil, but does not like wet weather. It needs pruning in late winter and some support if planted alone. **ZONES 4–9.**

THE NETHERLANDS, CIRCA 1596

PARENTAGE UNKNOWN

## 'Camaieux' *(right)*

OLD, GALLICA, MAUVE

'Camaieux' has sweetly scented, loosely double flowers that appear in mid-summer and have a magenta-pink background ageing to soft lavender or even soft purple; each petal is heavily splashed with white to give a very pleasing overall bicolor effect. Although its 3 ft (1 m) growth is short for a Gallica, it is vigorous and makes a fine pot plant or hedge, and is especially good for a small garden. On its own roots it can become invasive. It has attractive gray-green leaves and only a few prickles. **ZONES 4–9.**

VIBERT, FRANCE, 1830

PARENTAGE UNKNOWN

## 'Camaieux Fimbriata' *(right)*

OLD, GALLICA, MAUVE

This sport is one of the most attractive of all Gallicas and was found growing in a row of 'Camaieux' at Bell's Roses in Auckland, New Zealand. The color is the same, but instead of the blooms being striped and semi-double, they are marbled with purple and are very double. The many small petals are massed together to enclose a button eye, and the marbled effect is very attractive. Like all Gallicas, it only flowers once. The growth is dwarf and covered with a profusion of matt dark green foliage; there may be a little mildew late in the season. If planted with the bud union below ground level, the plant will form a thicket on its own roots. 'Camaieux Fimbriata' was imported into Australia, where it has become more popular

than it is in New Zealand. 'Camaieux' is probably the only Gallica to have ever produced a sport in the Southern Hemisphere; the sport is practically unknown in Europe or America. **ZONES 5–9.**

BELL'S ROSES, NEW ZEALAND, 1980

SPORT OF 'CAMAIEUX'

## 'Cambridgeshire' KORhaugen
## syn. 'Carpet of Color'

MODERN, MODERN SHRUB/GROUND COVER, RED BLEND, REPEAT-FLOWERING

This variety is claimed to be the first multi-colored ground-cover rose. 'Cambridgeshire' bears clusters of many pointed buds that open out into small semi-double blooms. As the petals reflex they disclose a mix-

ture of colors, with gold, cerise, pink and scarlet all present in the small cupped flowers. As the flowers are crowded together and the clusters are borne with freedom all over the plant, the effect is startling rather than restful. Flowering continues through summer and autumn, with quiet intervals while the plant gathers its strength. There is little in the way of scent. The growth habit is spreading but fairly compact, so this is a Ground-Cover Rose suitable for a comparatively small space. The leaves are dark and shiny and furnish the plant well. **ZONES 4–9.**

KORDES, GERMANY, 1994

PARENTAGE UNKNOWN

C

## 'Camélia Rose'
*(top left)*
syn. 'Camellia Rose'
OLD, CHINA, LIGHT PINK,
REPEAT-FLOWERING

Because it looks like a camellia, this China Rose makes an attractive plant at the back of the border; some writers list it as a Noisette. The bright, rosy pink, double, cupped flowers are of medium size, and tend to nod above the glossy leaves. There are occasional white streaks on the petals. It does well in a shady spot but must be warm. There are four other roses with the same name. ZONES 7–10.

PRÉVOST, CIRCA 1830

PARENTAGE UNKNOWN

## 'Camelot' *(top right)*
MODERN, LARGE-FLOWERED/
HYBRID TEA, ORANGE-PINK,
REPEAT-FLOWERING

Regarded as a Grandiflora in the USA, this variety bears its flowers both one to a stem and in clusters. They are that shade often described as coral-pink or reddish salmon, and it is seen as a deep and rather hard tone on the young petals, but lightens and softens as the flowers age. They are very full petalled, of medium to large size and open with high centers before becoming cupped as the petals unfold. There is a spicy scent, and blooms continue to appear through summer and autumn. This long-stemmed rose is suitable for cutting, as well as for general garden display. The plant is taller than average and has dark leathery foliage. ZONES 4–9.

SWIM AND WEEKS, USA, 1964
'CIRCUS' × 'QUEEN ELIZABETH'
ALL-AMERICA ROSE SELECTION
1965

## 'Cameo' *(bottom)*
MODERN, POLYANTHA, ORANGE-
PINK, REPEAT-FLOWERING

This variety, one of many Polyantha sports that became popular between the two World Wars, bears crowded clusters of small, rosette-shaped semi-double blooms, which last well on the plant and give good color impact. The flowers are 'a peculiar mixture of salmon, coral and orange', all of those colors being present at some stage of the season, the petals perhaps responding to different light intensities as summer turns to autumn. There is little fragrance and a susceptibility to mildew, which is one of the reasons why the Polyanthas faded away in favor of the healthier and bigger Cluster-flowered Roses from the 1940s onward. The growth of 'Cameo' is bushy and upright but short and very compact, and it has petite, light gray-green leaves. ZONES 4–9.

DE RUITER, THE NETHERLANDS,
1932

SPORT OF 'ORLÉANS ROSE'

C

## 'Canary Bird'
*(top)*
syn. *Rosa xanthina*
'Canary Bird'
MODERN, MODERN SHRUB,
DEEP YELLOW

This is a spectacular
rose in the right place,
where it has room to
spread its arching gar-
lands of single bright
yellow flowers in late
spring. The blooms are
small, are borne close
to the brownish red
stems and nestle
among light green,
ferny leaflets. They
open saucer-shaped
and have a pleasing
scent. A few blooms
may appear towards
the end of the growing
season. The plant can
become very large,
so giving it space is
important because
pruning will not only
spoil its natural grace
but also is often re-
sented, resulting in die-
back; the only pruning
needed is the removal
of crossing shoots and
time-expired stems.
'Canary Bird' is one of
the healthiest roses but
a site exposed to cold
winds can cause injury
to tender buds in
spring. Its parentage
must involve Chinese
species, perhaps *Rosa
hugonis* crossed with
*R. xanthina*. ZONES 4–9.

FOUND IN ENGLAND, POST-1907

PROBABLY *ROSA HUGONSIS* ×
*R. XANTHINA*

ROYAL HORTICULTURAL SOCIETY
AWARD OF GARDEN MERIT 1993

## 'Candelabra'
JACcingo
MODERN, GRANDIFLORA, ORANGE
BLEND, REPEAT-FLOWERING

Although available
mainly in the USA, its
immediate popularity
there has made this
rose a top candidate
for other parts of the
world. The coral-
orange blooms are
double, medium in
size, and occur in small
clusters. The petals
have the same coral-
orange on the reverse.
'Candelabra', a 4–5 ft
(1.2–1.5 m) shrub, dis-
plays glossy, dark green
foliage; there are some
prickles. The blooms
produce a slight but
delightful fragrance.
Used as a hedge or bed-
ding plant, it flowers
on and off throughout
the season. ZONES 4–9.

ZARY, USA, 1999

'TOURNAMENT OF ROSES' ×
SEEDLING

## 'Candella'  MACspeego
*(bottom)*
syn. 'Eternally Yours'
MODERN, LARGE-FLOWERED/
HYBRID TEA, RED BLEND,
REPEAT-FLOWERING

The flowers of this var-
iety are a rich maroon-
crimson with silvery
white on the reverse
of the petals and are
produced in candelabra
style, that is, in wide
clusters, each bloom
having a fairly long
supporting stem. The
pointed buds open into
loosely formed blooms
of medium size with
about 20 petals, some-
times nodding on their
stems. There is a light
fragrance, and they
repeat reasonably well
through summer and
autumn. This variety
makes a satisfactory
garden rose for beds
and borders, the
growth being vigorous,
if somewhat spindly. It
grows to average height
or above. 'Candella'
is hardy and healthy
except for occasional
trouble with mildew,
and has large, glossy
dark green leaves.
ZONES 4–9.

MCGREDY, NEW ZEALAND, 1990

'HOWARD MORRISON' ×
'ESMERALDA'

C

## 'Candy Rose'

MEIranovi  *(right)*

MODERN, MODERN SHRUB, RED
BLEND, REPEAT-FLOWERING

This sturdy plant pro-
duces big clusters of
rather small pink
blooms that have white
eyes and are reddish
pink on the petal re-
verse. They have about
10 petals and open out
like saucers, giving a
little fragrance. They
are borne with great
freedom in summer
and there is good re-
peat flowering through
to autumn. The plant
grows to average height
but wider than average
with overhanging
shoots. For use in
the landscape as, for
example, a large bed or
hedge in a public park,
this is an excellent rose.
It makes a good speci-
men or mixed border
plant. The spreading
plant is well covered
with shining medium
green leaves that are
reddish when young.
ZONES 4–9.

MEILLAND, FRANCE, 1983

(ROSA SEMPERVIRENS × 'MLLE
MARTHE CARRON') × (['LILLI
MARLEEN' × 'EVELYN FISON'] ×
['ORANGE SWEETHEART' ×
'FRÜHLINGSMORGEN'])

## 'Candy Stripe'
*(top right)*

MODERN, LARGE-FLOWERED/
HYBRID TEA, PINK BLEND,
REPEAT-FLOWERING

This variety can give
beautiful roses for cut-
ting. Its plump buds
open into very large,
headily fragrant flowers
of 60 petals, among the
largest in the rose world.
They are a dusty, rather
hard shade of pink,
streaked or striped with
blush and open to a
cupped form that is
held for a long time.
The plant blooms
through summer and
autumn, growing vig-
orously with a dense
habit to average height
or more. It is well
clothed with large,
leathery dark green
leaves. ZONES 4–9.

MCCUMMINGS, USA, 1963

SPORT OF 'PINK PEACE'

## 'Cannes Festival'
*(above)*

MODERN, LARGE-FLOWERED/
HYBRID TEA, YELLOW BLEND,
REPEAT-FLOWERING

The flowers of this
cultivar are yellow and
amber. The young
blooms are long and
slender, made up of
about 35 petals, which
slowly reveal their
centers and become
cupped as they open
out. There is a slight
fragrance, and the
flowering is maintained
through summer and
autumn. Although not
currently in commerce,
'Cannes Festival' was
for some years a useful
garden rose for beds
and borders, more suc-
cessful in drier climates,
because wet weather
can mark the petals. The
plant grows vigorously
to average height with
an upright, branching
habit and deep green
foliage. Meilland also
produced another
Large-flowered Rose
called 'Cannes Festival'
(MEIlicafal) in 1983,
which is an apricot
blend. ZONES 5–9.

MEILLAND, FRANCE, 1951

'PEACE' × 'PRINSES BEATRIX'

NATIONAL ROSE SOCIETY
CERTIFICATE OF MERIT 1951

C

### 'Cantabrigiensis' *(right)*
syn. 'The Cambridge Rose'
MODERN, MODERN SHRUB, LIGHT YELLOW

On a well-established plant, hundreds of pale yellow flowers decorate the branches of this rose. They are single, borne close to the small ferny leaflets on short stems, open cupped and have a pleasing scent. There is not normally any later flower, but in autumn small round orange-red hips appear; they can hardly be called decorative because they are not easy to see against the extensive growth the plant makes. Its main stems grow erect and bristly, then become bowed under the weight of side shoots and their foliage, by which time it is well above the average height for a shrub rose. The best place for 'Cantabrigiensis' is a naturalized garden where it can have plenty of space. The name means 'of Cambridge'. ZONES 4–9.

CAMBRIDGE BOTANIC GARDEN, UK, 1931

PROBABLY *ROSA HUGONIS* × *R. SERICEA HOOKERI*

ROYAL HORTICULTURAL SOCIETY CORY CUP 1931, ROYAL HORTICULTURAL SOCIETY AWARD OF GARDEN MERIT 1994

### 'Canterbury' AUSbury *(right)*
MODERN, MODERN SHRUB, MEDIUM PINK, REPEAT-FLOWERING

The large flowers of this rose may be considered single, having only about 8 petals, but they make the most of what they have by opening wide and reveal-ing golden stamens set in an expanse of warm rose pink. The petals have a silky quality and yield a pleasant fragrance. Flowering continues sporadically through summer and autumn. The plant is not a strong grower, being con-siderably below average height, and it has a spreading habit of growth with dark green leaves. It is likely to thrive best in an open sunny location in fertile ground or in a warm climate such as that of Australia. ZONES 4–9.

AUSTIN, UK, 1969

('MONIQUE' × 'CONSTANCE SPRY') × SEEDLING

C

### 'Capitaine John Ingram'  *(above)*
OLD, MOSS, MAUVE

This rose has one of the richest colors in good
weather. The pine-scented buds are well covered
with reddish, sticky, dark greeny brown moss.
The pompon blooms change color from dark
purple to velvety crimson to reddish purple.
There may be recurring bloom in late summer.
The recurving blooms have a button eye. Attaining about 5 ft (1.5 m) in good soils, this is a vigorous, dense shrub with many small prickles on
its stems and lots of dark brownish red bristles.
With its numerous dark green leaves of medium
size, it makes an effective hedge. ZONES 4–9.

LAFFAY, FRANCE, 1854

PARENTAGE UNKNOWN

### 'Capitaine Basroger'  *(above)*
OLD, MOSS, RED BLEND

Although lacking much moss on the big, tight
buds, this rose is an attractive red blend with full,
double blooms. The flowers, borne in sizeable
clusters, are up to 3 in (8 cm) in diameter and
have a strong fragrance. The apex flower of each
cluster often opens well ahead of those surrounding it, nestling among the buds in an attractive
fashion. The petals reflex, and the carmine may
change to shades of purple, depending on the
weather and exposure to the sun. There are fearsome prickles. It reaches a height of 8 ft (2.4 m)
and can be trained as a climber, looking very
effective on a pillar; in any case it does need a
support. ZONES 4–9.

MOREAU-ROBERT, FRANCE, 1890

PARENTAGE UNKNOWN

### 'Cappa Magna'  DELsap
MODERN, CLUSTER-FLOWERED/FLORIBUNDA, MEDIUM RED,
REPEAT-FLOWERING

Delbard-Chabert is the same nursery that created
the very popular 'Altissimo', and this rose looks
like a close relative. The medium-red blooms
are cupped with wavy petals. The strong, yellow
stamens are centered in the large, open blooms,
which appear in clusters of 20–30. The upright
growth is marked with dark, glossy green foliage.
It is an attractive bedding plant, especially when
placed in groups of 3 or more. Blooming constantly from spring until the first frost, the rose
is excellent for cutting. ZONES 4–9.

DELBARD-CHABERT, FRANCE, 1965

'TENOR' SEEDLING

### 'Captain Christy'  *(right)*

MODERN, LARGE-FLOWERED/HYBRID TEA, LIGHT PINK,
REPEAT-FLOWERING

One of the earliest Large-flowered Roses still in
cultivation, this variety is loved for the beauty of
the flowers, its repeat-flowering ability and its
vigor. The large blooms are light rose pink, very
full of petals and open out cupped and eventually
rather flat, displaying charming muddled centers.
In the depths of the petals the color is deeper, and
in warmer conditions the flowers improve—they
can be spoilt by rain, which may cause them to
ball and refuse to open. Scent is present but is
not strong. The height is average or above and
the foliage is robust, reasonably plentiful and
frequently likened to that of mahonias. For an
historical garden this would be a good example
of a successful early Large-flowered Rose, being
easy to grow and giving a summer display followed
by a dependable autumn show, with a few
blooms in between. The raiser named it to honor
a Londoner who was a keen amateur rosarian.
'Climbing Captain Christy' (Ducher, France, 1881)
has the same flower characteristics as its parent,
and it also gives a certain amount of repeat
bloom. In the climbing form the informality
of the petal arrangement is very appealing, and
the attractive veining on the petals is also easier
to appreciate. The plant grows strongly to average
height or more for a climber, and has a good
covering of foliage. It benefits from being sited
in a sunny aspect, preferably against a wall where
the vigorous growth can be spread out and well
supported, because the blooms it carries are often
on long heavy flower stems. ZONES 4–9.

LACHARMÉ, FRANCE, 1873

'VICTOR VERDIER' × 'SAFRANO'

### 'Cardinal de Richelieu'  *(right)*
syns 'Cardinal Richelieu', 'Rose van Sian'

OLD, GALLICA, MAUVE

This is one of the most floriferous of the
Gallicas, and its reputation and popularity are
well merited. The long-lasting flowers, borne in
small clusters, open from globular buds to a rich
dark red that quickly changes to royal purple,
ageing to slate-gray. The central petals fold inwards to show off a lighter color on the reverse.
'Cardinal de Richelieu' is a medium-growing
shrub to 4 ft (1.2 m), of tidy habit, and needs to
be pruned well. The stems are burnished dark
green with few or no thorns of consequence,
and the leaves are a lush dark green, bordering
on glossy. Cardinal Richelieu (1585–1642) was
minister to Louis XIII. ZONES 4–9.

PARMENTIER, BELGIUM, PRE-1847

PARENTAGE UNKNOWN

ROYAL HORTICULTURAL SOCIETY AWARD OF GARDEN MERIT 1993

C

## 'Carefree Beauty'

BUCbi  *(left)*

syn. 'Audace'

MODERN, MODERN SHRUB,
MEDIUM PINK,
REPEAT-FLOWERING

This popular shrub produces small clusters of pointed buds that open to a rich rose pink, but it rarely carries more than 4 flowers per stem. Each big and blowsy flower, to 4½ in (11 cm) wide, has 10–20 petals and gives a good fragrance. The blooms appear freely on their first flush, with repeat-flowering later in the season. The foliage is smooth and olive green and wonderfully resistant to disease. It is an upright plant that spreads readily, which makes it good for a low-maintenance hedge, but it is also fine on its own as a specimen plant. The orange-red hips that develop after the flowers add interest in winter. The growth is relatively winter hardy and it can be propagated by budding. ZONES 4–9.

BUCK, USA, 1977

SEEDLING × 'PRAIRIE PRINCESS'

## 'Cardinal Song'

MEImouslin  *(above left)*

syn. 'Jacques Prévert'

MODERN, LARGE-FLOWERED/
HYBRID TEA, MEDIUM RED,
REPEAT-FLOWERING

Although in the USA this rose is called a Grandiflora (a classification not recognized by the World Federation of Rose Societies), the large size of the flowers qualifies it to be considered a Large-flowered rather than a Cluster-flowered Rose. The blooms average over 40 petals, and are borne singly, or sometimes in clusters. They open flattish and carry a light fragrance, blooming through summer and autumn. This is a useful rose for beds and borders and it lasts well when cut. The plant grows to average height with a bushy, fairly upright habit, and is well furnished with large, glossy dark green leaves. ZONES 5–9.

MEILLAND, FRANCE, 1992

'OLYMPIAD' × ('MICHEL LIS LE JARDINIER' × 'RED LADY')

LYON GOLD MEDAL 1993

## 'Cardinal Hume'

HARregale  *(above)*

MODERN, MODERN
SHRUB, MAUVE BLEND,
REPEAT-FLOWERING

This popular and widely grown Modern Shrub bears large clusters of magnificent medium-sized maroon-purple cupped blooms. They are produced throughout summer and autumn with excellent continuity, and have a strong fragrance of musk. The dark foliage in association with the color of the flowers makes this variety a very desirable plant, although it is a little prone to black spot. It has moderate, slightly spreading growth and is useful as a specimen

plant in borders, where its distinct color adds a different spectrum. 'Cardinal Hume' has a complicated pedigree and, like 'International Herald Tribune', was the start of a new type of rose bred from *Rosa californica*. The name was given to honor G. Basil Hume, the leading Roman Catholic cleric in England in the 1970s. It is easily propagated by budding or from cuttings. ZONES 4–9.

HARKNESS, UK, 1984

([SEEDLING × {'ORANGE SENSATION' × 'ALLGOLD'}] × *ROSA CALIFORNICA PLENA*) × 'FRANK NAYLOR'

ROYAL NATIONAL ROSE SOCIETY CERTIFICATE OF MERIT 1984, COURTRAI CERTIFICATE OF MERIT 1986

## 'Carefree Wonder'

MEIpitac *(bottom)*
syns 'Dynastie',
'Carefully Wonder'

MODERN, MODERN SHRUB, PINK
BLEND, REPEAT-FLOWERING

This repeat-flowering shrub rose bears a profusion of small clusters of double blooms that cover the plant well with a display of rich pink. The flowers have 26 petals and are of medium size, have a pale reverse and a slight fragrance. The dense foliage is bright green and has great resistance to disease. This variety is a pretty, bushy growing, relatively compact shrub with reddish prickles and a good harvest of hips in autumn. It is useful for specimen planting or as a hedge rose; it is especially spectacular when planted in groups.
ZONES 3–9.

MEILLAND, FRANCE, 1978

('PRAIRIE PRINCESS' ×
'NIRVANA') × ('EYEPAINT' ×
'RUSTICA')

ALL-AMERICA ROSE SELECTION
1991

## 'Carina' MEIchim
*(top left)*

MODERN, LARGE-FLOWERED/
HYBRID TEA, MEDIUM PINK,
REPEAT-FLOWERING

The large, double blooms of this rose each have about 40 petals that form a beautiful flower with a high center and a good form. They are medium pink and fragrant, and are borne through summer and autumn. The disease-resistant foliage is deep green and leathery, and is produced on an upright plant of medium height. This variety is useful as a bedding plant and as a show rose. It can be propagated by budding.
ZONES 4–9.

MEILLAND, FRANCE, 1963

'WHITE KNIGHT' × ('HAPPINESS'
× 'INDEPENDENCE')

ANERKANNTE DEUTSCHE ROSE
1966

## 'Carla' *(top right)*

MODERN, LARGE-FLOWERED/
HYBRID TEA, ORANGE-PINK,
REPEAT-FLOWERING

This variety makes an excellent show rose; the very large flowers are soft salmon-pink, each with over 24 petals. There is also a pleasing fragrance that persists as the blooms continue to appear throughout summer and autumn. The foliage is dark green, which makes a good foil to the colorful roses. The plant gives vigorous growth that is resistant to disease, and can be propagated by budding.
ZONES 4–9.

DE RUITER, THE NETHERLANDS,
1963

'QUEEN ELIZABETH' ×
'THE OPTIMIST'

C

### 'Carmen'

MODERN, HYBRID RUGOSA,
MEDIUM RED

For a position where a disease-resistant hedge rose is needed, 'Carmen' is a useful variety. It produces large and single crimson flowers with yellow stamens that give a modest scent. The dark green, wrinkled leaves are borne on vigorous growth that occasionally produces a few flowers in autumn. It can be propagated from cuttings or by budding. ZONES 4–9.

LAMBERT, GERMANY, 1907

ROSA RUGOSA ROSEA ×
'PRINCESSE DE BÉARN'

### 'Carmenetta'

*(above)*

syn. *Rosa rubrifolia*
'Carmenetta'

MODERN, HYBRID GLAUCA,
LIGHT PINK

Looking very much like one of its parents, this rugged, healthy, spreading plant produces scores of single, light pink flowers during the heart of the summer. The clusters of blooms have some fragrance. The slick, red foliage covers the many small prickles that dot the canes. Reaching 10 ft (3 m) in 2 years, it is a strong candidate for hedging or the wild garden.

An additional feature is the attractive autumn foliage. ZONES 3–9.

CENTRAL EXPERIMENTAL FARM,
CANADA, 1923

ROSA GLAUCA × R. RUGOSA

### 'Carol'

MODERN, LARGE-FLOWERED/
HYBRID TEA, PINK BLEND,
REPEAT-FLOWERING

The flowers of this variety are an attractive cyclamen rose with an apricot center. They are well formed blooms, each composed of about 45 petals, with a slight fragrance. Throughout summer and into autumn, 'Carol' can be relied upon to produce its

flowers in colorful clusters on a moderate-sized bush. The stems are almost thornless, and it has good disease resistance. This rose is a suitable bedding variety, and can be grown under glass for its cut flowers. ZONES 4–9.

HERHOLDT, SOUTH AFRICA, 1964

'QUEEN ELIZABETH' ×
'CONFIDENCE'

### 'Caroline de Monaco'  MElpierar

syn. 'Cameo Cream'

MODERN, LARGE-FLOWERED/
HYBRID TEA, CREAMY WHITE,
REPEAT-FLOWERING

This is one of a series of roses named for the Monaco royal family, the Grimaldis, by the Meilland firm. With a slight darkening of the color to yellow, the rose would look very much like 'Peace', also from the same nursery. Rich, dark green, glossy leaves cover the medium-sized bush, which is covered with creamy white blooms throughout the summer. The strong, bushy growth makes this rose an ideal landscaping plant. As a cut flower it matches its close relative with its large, loose petals. ZONES 4–9.

MEILLAND, 1988

PARENTAGE UNKNOWN

C

### 'Carrot Top'  POUltop
*(right)*

MODERN, MINIATURE, ORANGE
BLEND, REPEAT-FLOWERING

The fire engine orange
color certainly makes
this rose stand out in
the garden crowd! The
very shapely buds hold
their brilliance from
beginning to end on an
attractive rounded
bush surrounded with
dark green foliage. The
plant itself is clean,
easy to maintain and
not too susceptible to
disease. The flowers
have a high center and
although there are not
many petals (20–25),
they hold their form
well for exhibition.
An excellent repeat-
bloomer, the plant is
almost always in
flower. The blooms
have a slight fragrance.
ZONES 4–11.

OLESEN, DENMARK, 1994

CLUSTER-FLOWERED SEEDLING ×
MINIATURE SEEDLING

### 'Carrousel'
*(top right)*

MODERN, LARGE-FLOWERED/
HYBRID TEA, MEDIUM RED,
REPEAT-FLOWERING

This vigorous plant
makes a good variety
for garden beds. It
can be propagated by
budding. It produces
double flowers that
each have about 20
medium red petals,
blooming is continuous
through summer and
autumn. There is a
pleasant fragrance.

'Carrousel' has a bushy,
upright-growing habit
and glossy, dark green,
leathery foliage.
ZONES 4–9.

DUEHRSEN, USA, 1950

SEEDLING × 'MARGY'

PORTLAND GOLD MEDAL 1955,
AMERICAN ROSE SOCIETY GOLD
MEDAL 1956

### 'Casino'  MACca
*(bottom left)*
syn. 'Gerbe d'Or'

MODERN, LARGE-FLOWERED
CLIMBER, LIGHT YELLOW,
REPEAT-FLOWERING

This really is one of the
best yellow-flowered
climbing roses around;
it is good to grow on
a warm wall and is
quite remarkably
floriferous. The soft
yellow, double, quar-
tered blooms of 'Casino'

are well formed, very
full and fragrant; they
hold their large, old-
fashioned shape well
and usually repeat
superbly, up to 5 times
per year. The hips, if
deadheading is not
completed, are large,
round and attractive.
This also makes a
good cut flower. The
foliage is dark green
and healthy. Growers
in regions with hard
winters may be dis-
couraged from growing
this rose because it
likes warm climates.
It has not received the
attention it deserves.
ZONES 5–9.

MCGREDY, NEW ZEALAND, 1963

'CORAL DAWN' × 'BUCCANEER'

NATIONAL ROSE SOCIETY GOLD
MEDAL 1963

### 'Cassandre'  MEldenji
*(bottom right)*

MODERN, LARGE-FLOWERED
CLIMBER, MEDIUM RED,
REPEAT-FLOWERING

This variety is grown
mostly in warm cli-
mates. The flowers are
of medium size, carried
in clusters, with about
24 petals, and open
cupped with a rounded
outline, showing light
yellow stamens. They
are light red, ageing to
rich carmine pink, with
appreciable fragrance.
Blooms appear through
summer and autumn
against a background
of glossy dark green
leaves. The plant grows
vigorously to average
height. ZONES 5–9.

MEILLAND, FRANCE, 1989

PARENTAGE UNKNOWN

C

abundance of matt mid-green foliage that is very disease resistant. The buds are produced mainly singly and are long, pointed, and open fairly quickly to deep coral pink blooms of 20 petals. They are fragrant, have excellent substance and last well without fading; flower production is high and there is quick repeat. It is an excellent rose for bedding, borders and for use as a standard rose. **ZONES 5–9.**

MEILLAND, FRANCE, 1981

PARENTAGE UNKNOWN

ROME GOLD MEDAL 1979

### 'Catherine Guillot'
*(bottom right)*
syn. 'Michel Bonnet'
OLD, BOURBON, DEEP PINK, REPEAT-FLOWERING

The carmine-rose blooms of 'Catherine Guillot' are quartered, full and very large, the smooth purple-pink petals making a perfect cup. This is a vigorous bush reaching 6 ft (1.8 m) and even higher, and when used as a small climber it flowers freely through-out summer. The leaves are attractive, purple and long. It is an excellent cut flower with a strong fragrance. **ZONES 5–9.**

GUILLOT, FRANCE, 1860

SEEDLING OF 'LOUISE ODIER'

### 'Caterpillar' POUlcat
*(top left)*
syns 'Charming Bells', 'Kiki Rose', 'Pink Drift'
MODERN, MINIATURE, LIGHT PINK

This is a low-growing, healthy Miniature Rose that spreads consider-ably, which makes it ideal as a ground cover. In summer it produces small, double, light pink blooms in medium to large clusters. There is only a little scent. The leaves are small, dark green and glossy, and the variety is easily propagated from cut-tings or by budding. 'Caterpillar' is a devel-opment of the Bells varieties, and has a more sophisticated

plant structure. How-ever, it was quickly superseded by repeat-flowering forms. **ZONES 4–9.**

OLESEN, DENMARK, 1985

'TEMPLE BELLS' × SEEDLING

### 'Cathedral'
*(top right)*
syns 'Coventry Cathedral', 'Houston'
MODERN, CLUSTER-FLOWERED/ FLORIBUNDA, APRICOT BLEND, REPEAT-FLOWERING

This is a free-flowering Cluster-flowered Rose with reddish apricot-shaded, salmon blooms. The large, slightly fragrant flowers are borne on a bushy plant with glossy olive green foliage in small clus-ters. Disease resistant

and hardy, one of its names celebrates the rebuilding and re-dedication of Coventry Cathedral, which was devastated during World War II. It can be propagated by budding. **ZONES 4–9.**

MCGREDY, NEW ZEALAND, 1975

'LITTLE DARLING' × ('GOLDILOCKS' × 'IRISH MIST')

NEW ZEALAND GOLD MEDAL 1974, PORTLAND GOLD MEDAL 1974, ALL-AMERICA ROSE SELECTION 1976

### 'Catherine Deneuve' MEIpraserpi
*(bottom left)*
MODERN, LARGE-FLOWERED/ HYBRID TEA, ORANGE-PINK, REPEAT-FLOWERING

'Catherine Deneuve' grows into a strong, spreading bush with an

## 'Cécile Brünner'
*(above)*

syns 'Mme Cécile Brünner', 'Mlle Cécile Brünner', 'Mignon', 'Sweetheart Rose', 'Maltese Rose'

MODERN, POLYANTHA, LIGHT PINK, REPEAT-FLOWERING

This long-lived variety, which is classed as an Old Garden Rose, China, by some authorities, clearly has its origins in Asia, although authorities are divided between *Rosa multiflora* and *R. chinensis*. Almost thornless, it repeatedly produces large clusters of very small, perfectly shaped pink blooms. The long, pointed buds open to pale, silvery pink blooms. The perfectly formed, miniature blooms are double and rise above light red peduncles. The scent is sweet and slightly spicy. It is a small bush with sparse, dull green foliage of 3–5 leaflets, but it is very healthy. The shrub is low growing, which makes it ideal for small gardens or small beds. The continuous blooming is one reason why it has been so popular since its introduction. It was named for the daughter of Ulrich Brünner, renowned rose grower at Lausanne, Switzerland. It can be propagated by budding or from cuttings. '**Climbing Cécile Brünner**' (syns 'Climbing Mme Cécile Brünner', 'Climbing Mlle Cécile Brünner', 'Climbing Mignon', 'Climbing Sweetheart Rose,'; Hosp, USA, 1894) is a very vigorous climber. Stronger growing than 'Cécile Brünner', it will grow to great heights. It produces large clusters of very small, perfectly shaped pink blooms, reminiscent of those sometimes seen on China Roses. The scent is sweet and slightly spicy. Although technically a summer flower, it is a good plant on a warm wall and will flower spasmodically well into autumn. This is a long-lived variety with almost thornless stems. Although the dull green foliage is quite sparse, it is very healthy. The variety is occasionally misnamed 'Bloomfield Abundance', which is understandable because the blooms are almost identical. It is also very difficult to propagate because of the scarcity of budding eyes, although micropropagation may solve this problem.
ZONES 4–9.

DUCHER, FRANCE, 1881

PARENTAGE DISPUTED

ROYAL HORTICULTURAL SOCIETY AWARD OF GARDEN MERIT 1994

## 'Céleste' *(above right)*
syn. 'Celestial'

OLD, ALBA, LIGHT PINK

The buds of 'Céleste' are described as 'fabulous' and artists have painted it many times, especially Redouté and Alfred Parsons, illustrator of *The Genus Rosa*. The flowers are beautiful, especially in the furled bud stage; when open they are loosely semi-double and bright soft silvery pink, blending beautifully with the leaden gray foliage of early summer. There are 5 rows of petals, which emit a strong fragrance during its summer season. This Old Garden Rose will do well in almost any situation in the garden, even in partial shade and impoverished soils. The dense, erect bush grows to 6 ft (1.8 m) and should not be pruned too much. There are three roses with this name.
ZONES 5–9.

PRE-1848

PARENTAGE UNKNOWN

ROYAL HORTICULTURAL SOCIETY AWARD OF GARDEN MERIT 1993

C

summer, the large flowers need a happy, warm spot to show off well. The canes are spiny, reaching 6 ft (1.8 m), and the foliage is dark green and glossy. There are prickles. **ZONES 7–10.**

TROUILLARD, FRANCE, 1842

NOISETTE × *ROSA ODORATA*

ROYAL HORTICULTURAL SOCIETY AWARD OF GARDEN MERIT 1993

## 'Celsiana'
*(top right)*

OLD, DAMASK, LIGHT PINK

'Celsiana' has pale pink, semi-double, large blooms that occur in clusters on typically Damask-style short stalks in early summer. The nodding blooms prefer semi-shade and have a strong musk fragrance. Impervious to weather, they are a delight to the eye, especially just before the fluted, crinkled petals fade to a delicate soft blush color. This plant performs well in any type of soil or climate, growing to 4 ft (1.2 m) and is fairly dense in structure for a Damask. The gray-green foliage is smooth; sharp little prickles line the canes. It is mislabeled in Redouté's book as 'Incarnata Maxima'. The Dutch painter Jan Van Huysum often featured this rose. **ZONES 4–9.**

PRE-1750

PARENTAGE UNKNOWN

## 'Céline Delbard'   DELceli, DELcélit, DELcet   *(above)*

MODERN, CLUSTER-FLOWERED/FLORIBUNDA, ORANGE BLEND, REPEAT-FLOWERING

This variety carries large, cupped flowers in small clusters. They each have about 24 salmon-colored petals with silver undersides. There is no fragrance, but there are repeat-blooms through summer. The foliage is dark green, and the plant is a healthy moderate grower. **ZONES 4–9.**

DELBARD-CHABERT, FRANCE, 1986

SEEDLING × ('MILROSE' × 'LEGION D'HONNEUR')

MONZA GOLD MEDAL

## 'Céline Forestier'
*(top left)*
syns 'Liesis', 'Lusiades'

OLD, NOISETTE, LIGHT YELLOW, REPEAT-FLOWERING

This rose has pale yellow blooms, darkening at the center, that open from attractive buds. The quartered blooms have a green, button eye, and the clusters have a spicy fragrance. Exquisite at maturity and repeating all

## 'Centenaire de Lourdes' DELge

syns 'Centennaire de Lourdes', 'Mrs Jones'

MODERN, CLUSTER-FLOWERED/ FLORIBUNDA, MEDIUM PINK, REPEAT-FLOWERING

Bred in France, 'Centenaire de Lourdes' is an exceptional variety that is very popular throughout Europe. It was voted one of the world's top ten roses at the World Rose Convention in 1994. It is an extremely vigorous and floriferous Cluster-flowered Rose that has never been as popular as it deserves. It bears large, old-fashioned flowers comprising 15 soft rose petals in clusters that appear in huge numbers throughout summer, although there is little scent. The variety has a bushy habit and is clothed with healthy, large mid-green foliage. It makes a fine bedding rose but is also suitable to grow as a standard. The beautiful crop of pear-shaped, orange hips that first appear in autumn are a bonus, and they last well into winter. **'Centenaire de Lourdes Rouge'** (DELflora) is a red-flowered mutation. ZONES 4–9.

DELBARD-CHABERT, FRANCE, 1958

('FRAU DRUSCHKI' × SEEDLING) × SEEDLING

## 'Centifolia' *(right)*

syn. *Rosa* × *centifolia*

OLD, CENTIFOLIA, MEDIUM PINK

'Centifolia' is frequently listed as a species rose but this is not so; according to Cambridge botanist C. C. Hurst, it is probably a complex hybrid with genealogy comprising such diverse species as *Rosa rubra, R. phoenicia, R. moschata* and *R. canina.* This shrub rose can attain a height of some 6 ft (1.8 m) in good soil, producing long strong shoots with numerous reddish thorns and prickles. Its leaves are coarse, both in appearance and to touch, and are grayish green. The flowers, which appear in early to mid-summer, are arranged in small clusters and emerge from tight feathery buds. They are flattish, very double and very fragrant, and are a deep glowing pink. ZONES 4–9.

PRE-1596

PARENTAGE UNKNOWN

## 'Centifolia Muscosa'

syn. *Rosa* × *centifolia muscosa*

OLD, MOSS, MEDIUM PINK

This lax shrub grows to 6 ft (1.8 m). It has many reddish colored thorns and smallish prickles, the latter like finely textured moss. The coarse foliage is grayish light green. The

fragrant flowers are deep pink, and appear in mid-summer. They are very double, sometimes quartered and open flat from mossy buds. ZONES 4–9.

PRE-1696

POSSIBLY A SPORT OF 'CENTIFOLIA'

## 'Century Two'
*(above)*

MODERN, LARGE-FLOWERED/ HYBRID TEA, MEDIUM PINK, REPEAT-FLOWERING

The long, pointed buds of this bushy rose develop into quite large, cupped, double flowers. The color is medium pink, and there is a considerable fragrance. This is a medium-sized rose bush with mid-green, leathery foliage. It makes a good bedding rose that can be propagated by budding. ZONES 4–9.

ARMSTRONG, USA, 1971

'CHARLOTTE ARMSTRONG' × 'DUET'

C

C

### 'Cerise Bouquet'
*(above)*

MODERN, MODERN SHRUB,
DEEP PINK

This free-flowering shrub produces an outstanding display of medium-sized, eye-catching blooms on strong, slightly arching branches in summer. The flowers are bright cerise with a light fragrance. Growth is vigorous and it is clothed with dull green foliage. 'Cerise Bouquet' is a perfect subject for tall hedges and as a specimen plant. Propagate by budding or from cuttings. ZONES 4–9.

TANTAU, GERMANY, 1958

*ROSA MULTIBRACTEATA* ×
'CRIMSON GLORY'

ROYAL HORTICULTURAL SOCIETY
AWARD OF GARDEN MERIT 1993

### 'Champagne'
*(bottom left)*

MODERN, LARGE-FLOWERED/
HYBRID TEA, YELLOW BLEND,
REPEAT-FLOWERING

'Champagne' has buff yellow flowers with an apricot shade. The pointed buds develop into large, oval flowers

with 28 petals that form a high center. There is a good fragrance and the blooms continue to appear after the initial flush. The foliage is dark green, leathery and disease resistant, and the habit is upright and bushy. This is a good variety both for bedding and exhibition. ZONES 4–9.

LINDQUIST, USA, 1961

'CHARLOTTE ARMSTRONG' ×
'DUQUESA DE PEÑARANDA'

### 'Champagne Cocktail' HORflash
*(bottom right)*

MODERN, CLUSTER-FLOWERED/
FLORIBUNDA, YELLOW BLEND,
REPEAT-FLOWERING

'Champagne Cocktail' has everything: shapely blooms, a gorgeous fragrance and a low susceptibility to disease. The pale yellow, medium-sized double flowers, strongly flecked and splashed with pink, have 20 petals with yellow undersides. There is a reliable repetition of bloom after the first flush. It has a bushy habit and glossy mid-green foliage, and is suitable for bedding, or can be grown as a standard. ZONES 4–9.

HORNER, UK, 1983

'OLD MASTER' × 'SOUTHAMPTON'

ROYAL NATIONAL ROSE SOCIETY
TORRIDGE AWARD AND TRIAL
GROUND CERTIFICATE 1982,
BELFAST CERTIFICATE OF MERIT
1985, GLASGOW GOLD MEDAL
1990

### 'Champion'
*(top right)*

MODERN, LARGE-FLOWERED/
HYBRID TEA, YELLOW BLEND,
REPEAT-FLOWERING

Packed with up to 55 petals per flower, 'Champion' is a rose particularly suited to exhibition. It has very large, high-centered double blooms. They are yellow-cream, flushed with red and pink. The blooms are very fragrant, and give repeat displays through summer. It has large, pale green leaves. ZONES 4–9.

FRYER, UK, 1976

'IRISH GOLD' × 'WHISKY MAC'

### 'Champion of the World' *(above)*
syns 'Mrs DeGraw', 'Mrs de Graw'

OLD, HYBRID PERPETUAL, MEDIUM PINK, REPEAT-FLOWERING

This rose, which needs plenty of time to establish
itself, is a vigorous shrub that likes to sprawl. The
rose pink blooms are double, large and fragrant.
The light green foliage is small, and the prickles
are light brown. It grows to 4 ft (1.2 m) and
makes a good pot plant. ZONES 5–9.

WOODHOUSE, UK, 1894

'HERMOSA' × 'MAGNA CHARTA'

### 'Champlain' *(top right)*

MODERN, MODERN SHRUB, DARK RED, REPEAT-FLOWERING

This repeat-flowering shrub gives moderately
vigorous, bushy growth that is very healthy. It
was bred to exist in the hard climate of North
America, so tolerates extremely cold winters. It
carries dark red, double flowers, each holding up
to 30 petals, that are large, slightly fragrant and
are borne in profusion on this compact plant. The
leaves are small and dark yellow-green. Budding
or cuttings are the best methods of propagation.
ZONES 3–9.

SVELDA, CANADA, 1982

(ROSA KORDESII × SEEDLING) × ('RED DAWN' × 'SUZANNE')

### 'Champneys' Pink Cluster' *(above)*
syns 'Champneys' Rose', 'Champneyana'

OLD, NOISETTE, LIGHT PINK, REPEAT-FLOWERING

The lovely, dark pink buds of this rose open to
small, double blooms that are gathered in clusters
on purple canes. Highly fragrant, the blooms repeat from spring until autumn. The foliage is light
green. Many claim that this is the first Noisette,
having originated in South Carolina. Like all of
its clan it does best with lots of sun and good air
circulation, and when used as a pillar, it can reach
10 ft (3 m). In 1986 it was unofficially renamed
'The Charleston Rose' in honor of its birthplace.
ZONES 7–10.

CHAMPNEYS, USA, CIRCA 1811

POSSIBLY 'OLD BLUSH' × ROSA MOSCHATA

C

with glossy dark green foliage. This is a healthy and vigorous plant. **ZONES 4–9.**

MCGREDY, NEW ZEALAND, 1959

'MA PERKINS' × ('FASHION' × 'MRS WILLIAM SPROTT')

NATIONAL ROSE SOCIETY CERTIFICATE OF MERIT 1958, MADRID GOLD MEDAL 1959

### 'Charles Albanel'

MODERN, HYBRID RUGOSA, MEDIUM RED, REPEAT-FLOWERING

'Charles Albanel' was developed for hardiness by its Canadian breeder. The wrinkled foliage, grassy green and leathery, is also very disease resistant. The blooms are medium red and double, with 20 petals per rose. They are fragrant and give repeat displays after the first bloom. This variety makes a good ground cover, and it has been widely planted in environmental landscaping. Even when not in flower, it is admired for its handsome foliage. **ZONES 3–9.**

SVEJDA, CANADA, 1982

'SOUVENIR DE PHILEMON COCHET' × SEEDLING

(MEIcarlsar; 1969) has similar characteristics, although it is now more difficult to find. It was bred in France in 1969. **ZONES 4–9.**

MEILLAND, FRANCE, 1957

'MONIQUE' × 'HAPPINESS'

MADRID GOLD MEDAL 1957

### 'Chanelle' *(top)*

MODERN, CLUSTER-FLOWERED/ FLORIBUNDA, ORANGE-PINK, REPEAT-FLOWERING

The large, peachy pink or pale pink flowers of this rose were named to commemorate the famous fashion house of Chanel. They are large, loose and double, and also have a shade of rose pink. Each flower has about 20 petals that hold a good form. They are carried in fragrant clusters that flower freely and repeatedly. This variety is a medium-sized bush

### 'Champs-Elysées'

MEIcarl, MEIcari *(above)*

MODERN, LARGE-FLOWERED/ HYBRID TEA, DARK RED, REPEAT-FLOWERING

This rose has lovely red-crimson, double flowers with their 35 petals arranged to form a cup shape. They are slightly fragrant and continue to appear after the initial bloom. This is a vigorous plant that gives bushy and compact growth, clothed with dark green foliage. 'Champs-Elysées' has good resistance to disease and can be propagated by budding. The variety looks good in beds and borders and is also suitable trained as a standard. The climbing sport, '**Climbing Champs-Elysées**'

**'Charles Austin'**

AUSles, AUSfather

*(bottom right)*

MODERN, MODERN SHRUB,
APRICOT BLEND

Named for the breeder's father, this rose bears large, double blooms packed with up to 70 apricot, pink-tinged petals that pale with age. Although it is not repeat-flowering, an occasional bloom may be produced in autumn. Its flowers are carried singly or in clusters of up to 7 and the arrangement of petals gives a pinwheel effect; there is a strong fruity fragrance. It is best suited for planting in groups in borders or for use as a pillar rose when supported and lightly pruned. It grows vigorously to form an upright plant, which the raiser suggests should be cut by half early in spring. It is also classified as an English Rose. **Yellow Charles Austin'** (1981) is a yellow-flowered sport that has similar characteristics. **ZONES 4–9.**

AUSTIN, UK, 1973

'ALOHA' × 'CHAUCER'

**'Charles de Gaulle'**

MEIlanein *(top left)*

syn. 'Katherine Mansfield'

MODERN, LARGE-FLOWERED/
HYBRID TEA, MAUVE BLEND,
REPEAT-FLOWERING

This strong-growing, medium-sized rose has large, double flowers with a good form and a unique warm lilac color. They are very fragrant, as is the case with many of the 'blue' roses, and are mostly borne singly. Each flower has about 38 petals per bloom to form a globular or cupped shape. It is considered by many to be the finest of the mauve Large-flowered Roses, but it does not like damp or humid conditions. The variety is useful in beds or borders and is propagated by budding. 'Charles de Gaulle' was named after the great French statesman, but in New Zealand it is better known as 'Katherine Mansfield', one of their great writers. **ZONES 4–9.**

MEILLAND, FRANCE, 1974

('SISSI' × 'PRELUDE') ×
('KORDES' SONDERMELDUNG' ×
'CAPRICE')

BELFAST FRAGRANCE PRIZE 1978

**'Charles de Mills'** *(top right)*
syns 'Charles Mills', 'Charles Wills',
**'Bizarre Triomphant'**

OLD, GALLICA, MAUVE

Often seen in photographs as the 'perfect Old Garden Rose,' this Gallica is the largest of its family. The flowers, which are made up of a multitude of petals, are quite large, and at their best often exceed 3 in (8 cm) in diameter. They emerge in mid-summer from flat-topped buds, at first cupped and then flatly saucer shaped; their color is rich glowing purple with subtle crimson highlights. The petals, which have the feel of textured velvet, are only slightly scented. The arching canes reach 6 ft (1.8 m) on an erect bush with very few prickles and dark green leaves. It is sometimes found in the wild. All Gallicas sucker freely. **ZONES 4–9.**

THE NETHERLANDS, PRE-1700

PARENTAGE UNKNOWN

ROYAL HORTICULTURAL SOCIETY AWARD OF GARDEN MERIT 1993

C

### 'Charles Lawson'
*(bottom left)*

OLD, BOURBON, DEEP PINK

During its short blooming season in mid-summer, this vigorous shrub produces fragrant, deep pink blooms, which are veined and deeper in tone on the back of the petals. Used as a climber, it can reach 8 ft (2.4 m). The handsome foliage is large, and the prickles are hooked. It needs the support of a pillar or fence. **ZONES 5–9.**

LAWSON, UK, 1853
PARENTAGE UNKNOWN

### 'Charles Lefèbvre'
*(below)*

syns 'Paul Jamain', 'Marguerite Brassac'

OLD, HYBRID PERPETUAL, DARK RED, REPEAT-FLOWERING

This rose has bright crimson blooms with purple centers. They are cupped, large and high centered; the full blooms have as many as 70 petals and sit erect on strong necks. It was very popular at the time of its introduction; Graham Thomas called this rose a landmark for its bright crimson color. It is vigorous and tall, has smooth bark and some prickles, and it tolerates rain. Moderate pruning is recommended. **ZONES 5–9.**

LACHARMÉ, FRANCE, 1861

'GÉNÉRAL JACQUEMINOT' × 'VICTOR VERDIER'

### 'Charles Mallerin'
*(bottom right)*

MODERN, LARGE-FLOWERED/ HYBRID TEA, DARK RED, REPEAT-FLOWERING

When first introduced, this rose was described as the darkest red ever launched. The vigorous growth is sparse and erratic, with disease-prone dark green, leathery foliage; its scent, however, is still memorable. The long and pointed, elegant buds develop into large, flat, double blooms with 38 velvety, dark crimson petals. Its unique coloring established this variety as a good seller and it was named to honor Francis Meilland's teacher, a retired railway engineer, who bred many beautiful roses himself. 'Charles Mallerin' has been a valuable parent, giving us 'Papa Meilland', 'Mister Lincoln' and 'Oklahama'. **ZONES 4–9.**

MEILLAND, FRANCE, 1951

('ROME GLORY' × 'CONGO') × 'TASSIN'

## 'Charles Rennie Mackintosh' AUSren
*(right)*
syns 'Glücksburg', 'Rosarium Glücksburg'

MODERN, MODERN SHRUB, PINK BLEND, REPEAT-FLOWERING

The deep dusky lilac-purple, cupped flowers of this rose turn to pure lilac and open wider as they age. They have an old-fashioned style, a frilly appearance and are fragrant, flowering repeatedly throughout summer. It is reminiscent of many incurved and cupped Bourbon Roses with intriguing inner petals that twist, which is typical of some Gallicas. 'Charles Rennie Mackintosh' forms a shrub of many thin, wiry yet tough stems and spiky thorns. It has a good covering of small, dark green leaves and is excellent for mixing with other colors in floral arrangements. The variety was named after the famous designer and architect, and is very popular. Budding is the best method of propagation. It is also classified as an English Rose. ZONES 4–9.

AUSTIN, UK, 1988

('CHAUCER' × 'CONRAD F. MEYER') × 'MARY ROSE'

## 'Charlotte' AUSpoly
*(top right)*
syn. 'Elgin Festival'

MODERN, MODERN SHRUB, LIGHT YELLOW, REPEAT-FLOWERING

The parentage of 'Graham Thomas' is evident in this variety, although the fragrant flowers are a softer yellow, rather more cupped and becoming incurved in late summer. It makes a bushy and healthy, freely branching shrub that produces a flush of bloom in mid-summer, followed by intermittent color throughout autumn. It is suitable as a specimen shrub, and a few nurseries are developing this variety as a standard. It should be propagated by budding. In South Africa the variety is known as 'Elgin Festival', named after a town near Cape Town, that is home to a successful rose festival. It is also classified as an English Rose. ZONES 4–9.

AUSTIN, UK, 1993

SEEDLING × 'GRAHAM THOMAS'

## 'Charlotte Armstrong' *(above)*

MODERN, LARGE-FLOWERED/HYBRID TEA, DEEP PINK, REPEAT-FLOWERING

This highly acclaimed rose was one of the parents of 'Queen Elizabeth'. The large, pointed buds develop into deep pink, double flowers with 35 petals. They are fragrant and well formed. The foliage is dark green and leathery on a vigorous yet compact plant. ZONES 4–9.

LAMMERTS, USA, 1940

'SOEUR THÉRÈSE' × 'CRIMSON GLORY'

ALL-AMERICA ROSE SELECTION 1941, AMERICAN ROSE SOCIETY DAVID FUERSTENBERG PRIZE 1941, ARS JOHN COOK MEDAL 1941, PORTLAND GOLD MEDAL 1941, ARS GERTRUDE M. HUBBARD GOLD MEDAL 1945, NATIONAL ROSE SOCIETY GOLD MEDAL 1950

C

C

### 'Château de Clos Vougeot' *(left)*

MODERN, LARGE-FLOWERED/
HYBRID TEA, DARK RED,
REPEAT-FLOWERING

The dark, velvety red flowers of 'Château de Clos Vougeot' have a powerful Damask perfume. They are large, packed with as many as 75 petals per bloom. These are borne on a slightly lax, sprawling bush against dark green and leathery foliage. The variety is an old favorite and is still grown by connoisseurs. It was named after the splendid home of the finest French clarets. Budding is the easiest method of propagation. 'Climbing Château de Clos Vougeot' (Morse, UK, 1920) is a climbing form of the famous bush variety; a mutation that arose spontaneously in 1920. It is still widely grown and many plants are found in old gardens around the world. For maximum effect, this variety is best grown against a warm wall. ZONES 4–9.

PERNET-DUCHER, FRANCE, 1908

PARENTAGE UNKNOWN

### 'Charmian'   AUSmian
*(above left)*

MODERN, MODERN SHRUB,
MEDIUM PINK,
REPEAT-FLOWERING

This is a free-flowering shrub rose with an arching habit; it bears large, rosette-shaped, medium pink, very fragrant flowers that open flat, then curve in slightly as they mature. The mid-green foliage is semi-glossy and disease resistant. Because of its lax or spreading, rather floppy growth, 'Charmian' lends itself to growing in clumps in a border, or as a semi-climber on low fences and walls; its heavy flowers often weigh the branches down so that they touch the ground. The best method of propagation is by budding. It is also classified as an English Rose. ZONES 4–9.

AUSTIN, UK, 1982

SEEDLING × 'LILIAN AUSTIN'

### 'Charlotte Rampling'   MEIhirvin
*(above)*
syn. 'Thomas Barton'

MODERN, LARGE-FLOWERED/
HYBRID TEA, MEDIUM RED,
REPEAT-FLOWERING

The large flowers of this variety are a unique and striking color of wine red, and produce a very good scent. They are carried on an upright bush against dark green foliage, and are repeat-flowering. The unusual color of this variety makes it both a good bedding plant and standard. It is propagated by budding. ZONES 4–9.

MEILLAND, FRANCE, 1988

PARENTAGE UNKNOWN

MONZA GOLD MEDAL 1987,
GLASGOW FRAGRANCE AWARD
1995

C

### 'Chaucer' AUScer, AUScon *(above)*

MODERN, MODERN SHRUB, MEDIUM PINK, REPEAT-FLOWERING

This is an early Austin introduction, which the raiser now considers to be *passé*. However, it fits well in a small garden and bears small clusters of deeply cupped, light pink blooms that pale towards the edges and show some stamens at the center. They give off a considerable myrrh-like scent that is delicious to some, but is not appreciated by all noses. Its repeat-flowering performance is somewhat surprising, given that 'Constance Spry' does not; the assumption is that one of the parents has a repeat-flowering ancestor. The foliage is matt mid-green, and the stems are covered in red thorns similar to those found on Gallica Roses. It has a bushy, upright, medium-sized habit, but is prone to mildew. 'Chaucer' is always suitable for the rose border or as a specimen plant, and can be propagated by budding; it has featured in the breeding of many good roses after 1970. It is also classified as an English Rose. **ZONES 4–9.**

AUSTIN, UK, 1970

SEEDLING × 'CONSTANCE SPRY'

### 'Cherish' JACsal *(top right)*

MODERN, CLUSTER-FLOWERED/ FLORIBUNDA, ORANGE-PINK, REPEAT-FLOWERING

One of a series of compact, slightly spreading roses, 'Cherish' bears short, flat buds that develop into flowers of coral pink, each with 28 petals. There is a slight fragrance. This is a good rose for the cutting garden: the flowers last well in a vase. The foliage is dark green and healthy, and it clothes a compact yet slightly spreading plant that can be propagated by budding. 'Love' and 'Honor' were also raised by Warriner, and they too won awards. **ZONES 4–9.**

WARRINER, USA, 1980

'BRIDAL PINK' × 'MATADOR'

ALL-AMERICA ROSE SELECTION 1980

### 'Cherry Brandy '85' TANryrandy *(above)*

MODERN, LARGE-FLOWERED/ HYBRID TEA, ORANGE BLEND, REPEAT-FLOWERING

The large, double, fragrant flowers on this variety are borne singly or in clusters of 3–7, with a good high-centered form; the 30 petals are a delightful shade of orange. Throughout summer and autumn there is good continuity of bloom against the glossy dark green, leathery foliage, which provides the necessary contrast to the flowers. 'Cherry Brandy '85' is a vigorous plant, with spreading but upright growth, that is good for bedding schemes. The variety maintains good health, and is easily propagated by budding. **ZONES 4–9.**

TANTAU, GERMANY, 1985

PARENTAGE UNKNOWN

ROYAL NATIONAL ROSE SOCIETY TRIAL GROUND CERTIFICATE 1986, BELFAST GOLD MEDAL 1989

C

### 'Cherry Meillandecor'  MEIrumour  *(bottom left)*
syn. 'Cherry Meidiland'

MODERN, MODERN SHRUB, RED BLEND, REPEAT-FLOWERING

A colorful addition to any garden, 'Cherry Meillandecor' bears single, bright red blooms that have bold white centers with golden yellow stamens. The petals are gently ruffled at the margins. It is a large, spreading shrub rose that has a good covering of shiny, dark green foliage, topped by continuous blooms through summer. In the garden, this rose is tolerant of poor soil and is extremely resistant to disease—most growers say it will never need spraying—and is ideal planted either in groups to form a hedge or simply on its own as a specimen. If the flowers are not deadheaded, they will develop into attractive rosehips that will continue to give interest into winter. **ZONES 5–9.**

MEILLAND, FRANCE, 1994

PARENTAGE UNKNOWN

GENEVA GOLD MEDAL 1994

### 'Cheshire Life'
*(top)*

MODERN, LARGE-FLOWERED/
HYBRID TEA, ORANGE-RED,
REPEAT-FLOWERING

The large, double, vermilion-colored flowers of 'Cheshire Life' are urn-shaped and composed of 36 petals per rose. Some blooms may grow to as much as 5 in (13 cm) across. There is a slight fragrance but it is barely noticeable, and the foliage is dark green, leathery and resistant to disease. In the garden it is a useful rose for bedding, and is valued for its summer blooms that repeat into autumn. **ZONES 4–9.**

FRYER, UK, 1972

'PRIMA BALLERINA' ×
'PRINCESS MICHIKO'

### 'Chianti'
**(bottom right)**

MODERN, MODERN SHRUB,
MAUVE BLEND

One of the first of David Austin's English Roses, 'Chianti' is a cross between a Modern Cluster-flowered Rose and an Old Garden Gallica Rose. The result has large, purplish maroon, semi-double, rosette-type flowers. They have a powerful Old Rose fragrance and are borne in small, rounded clusters, but sadly they are only summer flowering. It is a vigorous, very healthy grower with dark green, glossy foliage, and is suitable for shrub borders where there is plenty of room for it to develop. **ZONES 4–9.**

AUSTIN, UK, 1967

'DUSKY MAIDEN' × 'TUSCANY'

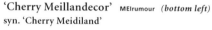

## 'Chicago Peace'
JOHnago *(bottom)*

MODERN, LARGE-FLOWERED/
HYBRID TEA, PINK BLEND,
REPEAT-FLOWERING

This sport of the famous 'Peace' bears phlox pink, lightly perfumed, well-formed flowers that have a base of canary yellow. There is a good display in summer, with a reliable repeat performance in autumn. The growth is identical in many ways to the original parent cultivar, although the blooms are more intense. Like its parent, it needs protection from black spot; it should be propagated by budding. This is one of several mutations of 'Peace' which all appeared at about the same time. This particular form was discovered by a breeder in Chicago, hence the name. A climbing form, **'Climbing Chicago Peace'**, is extremely reluctant to flower. **ZONES 4–9.**

JOHNSTON, USA, 1962
SPORT OF 'PEACE'
PORTLAND GOLD MEDAL 1962

## 'China Doll'
*(top left)*

MODERN, POLYANTHA, MEDIUM
PINK, REPEAT-FLOWERING

This once popular, almost thornless variety still has its admirers. It is a compact and short, very free-flowering, upright bush rose that bears large trusses of small, cupped, slightly fragrant flowers with 24 petals of rose with a base of mimosa yellow. The foliage is leathery with mostly 5 leaflets. It is a good, repeat-flowering subject for low-growing borders or as a short standard. 'China Doll' is quite healthy, and can be propagated by either budding or from cuttings. It produces a constant display of flowers. **'Climbing China Doll'** (syn. 'Weeping China Doll'; Weeks, USA, 1977) is a climbing mutation. It is a very free-growing sport, but its repeat-flowering performance is open to doubt. It is a good rose for pergolas and as a lax-growing standard. **ZONES 4–9.**

LAMMERTS, USA, 1946
'MRS DUDLEY FULTON' ×
'TOM THUMB'

## 'Chinatown'
*(top right)*
syn. 'Ville de Chine'

MODERN, CLUSTER-FLOWERED/
FLORIBUNDA, DEEP YELLOW,
REPEAT-FLOWERING

'Chinatown' is a vigorous and outstanding plant that would properly be described as a shrub rose, although is mostly catalogued as a Cluster-flowered bush rose; it grows bigger if supported. The long, strong stems are clothed in luxuriant, mid-green foliage and bear big clusters of large, yellow blooms that are edged with pink. This is a fragrant rose with a heavy peach scent, and gives a continuous bloom of both single flowers and clusters through summer and into autumn. It should be pruned lightly to produce a balanced plant, and can be propagated by budding. 'Chinatown' is a wonderful rose in every way, as it is resistant to disease, easy to grow, and makes a fine hedge. **ZONES 3–9.**

POULSEN, DENMARK, 1963
'COLUMBINE' × 'CLÄRE
GRAMMERSTORF'
ROYAL NATIONAL ROSE SOCIETY
GOLD MEDAL 1962, ROYAL
HORTICULTURAL SOCIETY AWARD
OF GARDEN MERIT 1993

C

### 'Chivalry' MACpow *(left)*
syn. 'Rittertum'

MODERN, LARGE-FLOWERED/HYBRID TEA, RED BLEND,
REPEAT-FLOWERING

The large double blooms of this rose are made
up of 35 slightly incurved petals; they are red
with yellowish undersides. There is only a little
fragrance. This is a reasonable variety for beds or
borders, and the foliage is dark green and glossy.
The vigorous growth is disease resistant but
sparse, and can be propagated by budding.
**ZONES 4–9.**

MCGREDY, NEW ZEALAND, 1977

'PEER GYNT' × 'BRASILIA'

### 'Chloris' *(left)*
syn. 'Rosée du Matin'

OLD, ALBA, LIGHT PINK, REPEAT-FLOWERING

This vigorous rose is known poetically as 'Dew
of the Morning'. It is very ancient, and grows to
6 ft (2 m) tall with very dark green leaves and
few thorns. The flowers are similar to those of
'Celeste': double, with many reflexed petals that
form a quartered arrangement with a button eye.
They are gentle pink and look most attractive
against the dark foliage. **ZONES 5–9.**

PRE-1848

PARENTAGE UNKNOWN

### 'Chorus' MEIjulito, MEIjalita *(left)*

MODERN, CLUSTER-FLOWERED/FLORIBUNDA, ORANGE-RED

This extremely free-flowering variety deserves the
highest recognition. It has healthy, glossy dark
green foliage covered with medium-sized clusters
of bright vermilion, double flowers. Each bloom
consists of 35 petals and there is a slight fragrance
of fruit. 'Chorus' certainly makes a brilliant splash
of color in the garden and an even greater impact
when planted *en masse*. It makes a good choice for
a rose bed, or can be trained as a standard. This
plant is not susceptible to pests or diseases and
is propagated by budding. **'Climbing Chorus'**
(MEIjulitasar; Meilland, France, 1986) is a
mutation of this variety that is suitable for walls
and pergolas. **ZONES 4–9.**

PAOLINO, FRANCE, 1977

'TAMANGO' × ('SARABANDE' × 'ZAMBRA')

ANERKANNTE DEUTSCHE ROSE 1977

## 'Christian Dior'
MEllie *(right)*

MODERN, LARGE-FLOWERED/
HYBRID TEA, MEDIUM RED,
REPEAT-FLOWERING

Named for the Parisian fashion designer, the large, well-formed, bright crimson, double blooms of this rose have a lighter underside and a high-centered and pointed shape, although some open out into a cupped form. The exhibition standard flowers are packed with 55 petals each, and give a subtle fragrance. 'Christian Dior' flowers with great freedom, and these displays are repeated through the warmer months. It makes a bushy plant with glossy green, leathery foliage that is useful as a standard rose or in beds or borders. The long-stemmed blooms are good for cutting. When protected from powdery mildew, the growth is really healthy and can be propagated by budding. **'Climbing Christian Dior'** (Chang, 1966) is a popular form of this Large-flowered Rose. **ZONES 4–9.**

MEILLAND, FRANCE, 1958

('INDEPENDENCE' × 'HAPPINESS')
× ('PEACE' × 'HAPPINESS')

GENEVA GOLD MEDAL 1958, ALL-
AMERICA ROSE SELECTION 1962

## 'Christopher Columbus' *(right)*
MEInronsse, MEIronsse

syns 'Christoph Colomb', 'Christoph Columbus', 'Columbas', 'Cristobal Colon', 'Cristoforo Colombo', 'Flamboyance'

MODERN, LARGE-FLOWERED/
HYBRID TEA, ORANGE BLEND,
REPEAT-FLOWERING

The large, copper blooms of this rose are well formed and full, with between 26 and 40 petals. Each flower is borne singly, and there are repeat flushes that give a light fragrance throughout summer and autumn. Dark green, semi-glossy foliage covers a plant that is otherwise very thorny. 'Christopher Columbus' has an upright growth habit so is ideal for rose beds or borders. It should be propagated by budding and is resistant to disease. **ZONES 4–9.**

MEILLAND, FRANCE, 1991

MEIGURANI × ('AMBASSADOR' ×
MEINAREGI)

## 'Chrysler Imperial'
*(top right)*

MODERN, LARGE-FLOWERED/
HYBRID TEA, DARK RED,
REPEAT-FLOWERING

This rose was very popular when it was first introduced. 'Chrysler Imperial' is a compact, vigorous grower with dark green, semi-glossy leaves. It bears long, pointed buds, developing into large, double, well-formed flowers with 45 velvety, rich crimson petals that turn bluish as they age. The blooms have a good fragrance. This is a very good bedding variety that is also quite popular as a standard, but it does suffer from die-back after a few years and mildew in cold weather. It should be propagated by budding. There was some dispute raised by the car company over the name, as it was originally intended to be named 'Chrysler'. **'Climbing Chrysler Imperial'** (syn. 'Grimpant Chrysler Imperial'; Begonia, USA, 1957) is a striking mutation that bears high-quality blooms, but only in summer. **ZONES 4–9.**

LAMMERTS, USA, 1952

'CHARLOTTE ARMSTRONG' ×
'MIRANDY'

PORTLAND GOLD MEDAL 1951,
ALL-AMERICA ROSE SELECTION
1953, GAMBLE FRAGRANCE
AWARD 1965

C

### 'Cider Cup'  DIClalida

MODERN, MINIATURE, ORANGE
BLEND, REPEAT-FLOWERING

This plant boasts deep apricot blend blooms that have a glowing quality to them. Often described as one of the most attractive Miniatures in this color class, the plant is a prolific bloomer, providing weatherproof blooms all season long. The flowers are borne singly or in small sprays on a bushy, well-groomed plant. Because of the size of the blooms, some rose growers consider this a Patio Rose. This has not reduced its popularity in England, where it is a favorite exhibition rose. It made its debut as a show winner in 1990 in Ohio, USA, where it was declared 'King of Show'. **ZONES 4–11.**

DICKSON, UK, 1987

'MEMENTO' × ('LIVERPOOL
ECHO' × 'WOMAN'S OWN')

### 'Cinderella'
*(top left)*

MODERN, MINIATURE, WHITE,
REPEAT-FLOWERING

Satiny white, tinged with a pale flesh tone is the best description of the blooms of 'Cinderella'. The very small blooms with 55 petals, complemented by dainty, small foliage, definitely classify this classic rose as a micro-Miniature. The plant always seems to be covered with blooms, mostly borne in large clusters. Introduced in 1953 by the Dutch pioneer of Miniature Roses, Jan de Vink, it is still very popular with arrangers. Cooler climates tend to enhance the fresh tone of the blooms. It is regarded by Nola Simpson, a New Zealand rosarian, as the standard by which she judges Miniatures. **ZONES 4–11.**

DE VINK, THE NETHERLANDS, 1953

'CÉCILE BRÜNNER' × 'TOM THUMB'

### 'Circus'  *(top right)*

MODERN, CLUSTER-FLOWERED/
FLORIBUNDA, YELLOW BLEND,
REPEAT-FLOWERING

This free-flowering rose has yellow flowers flecked with pink, salmon and scarlet. The large, very full, double, high-centered blooms that develop from urn-shaped buds consist of about 50 petals, and are borne in large clusters on a vigorous, medium-sized bush. It has a spicy Tea fragrance and the foliage is semi-glossy and leathery. 'Circus' is moderately disease free. This variety was a favorite for many years and still retains its popularity. It makes a good bedding variety that can be propagated by budding. 'Climbing Circus' (House, USA, 1961) is a vigorous summer-flowering sport of 'Circus' that occasionally produces a few blooms in autumn. It is suitable for walls or pillars. **ZONES 4–9.**

SWIM, USA, 1956

'FANDANGO' × 'PINOCCHIO'

GENEVA GOLD MEDAL 1955,
ROYAL NATIONAL ROSE SOCIETY
GOLD MEDAL 1955, ALL-
AMERICA ROSE SELECTION 1956

### 'City of Auckland'

MACtane  *(bottom)*

MODERN, LARGE-FLOWERED/
HYBRID TEA, ORANGE BLEND,
REPEAT-FLOWERING

This free-flowering cultivar is noted for its strong fragrance. The mid-green, semi-glossy foliage is covered by large, double flowers in shades of orange that bloom repeatedly after the first flush. The growth is bushy and disease resistant and can be propagated by budding. **ZONES 4–9.**

MCGREDY, NEW ZEALAND, 1981

'BENSON AND HEDGES GOLD' ×
'WHISKY MAC'

C

### 'City of Belfast' MACci *(above)*

MODERN, CLUSTER-FLOWERED/FLORIBUNDA, ORANGE-RED,
REPEAT-FLOWERING

This outstanding Cluster-flowered Rose has large
clusters of brilliant orange to blood red or scarlet
blooms. These have only a little scent, but are
truly repeat-flowering. The bush itself has a
slightly spreading habit and is covered with glossy
green, disease-resistant foliage; it is a favorite variety for bedding and as a standard. ZONES 4–9.

MCGREDY, UK, 1968

'EVELYN FISON' × ('CIRCUS' × 'KORONA')

NEW ZEALAND GOLD MEDAL 1967, ROYAL NATIONAL ROSE SOCIETY
PRESIDENT'S INTERNATIONAL TROPHY 1967, BELFAST GOLD MEDAL
1970, THE HAGUE GOLD MEDAL 1976

### 'City of Leeds' *(top right)*

MODERN, CLUSTER-FLOWERED/FLORIBUNDA, ORANGE-PINK,
REPEAT-FLOWERING

Named for the city's Flower Show, this variety
has deep salmon-pink, medium-sized to large,
cupped to flat, double flowers that are borne in
clusters repeatedly through summer and autumn.
The well-formed blooms are slightly fragrant and
are made up of almost 20 petals. The dark green,
healthy foliage is an excellent foil to the abundance of blooms that appear in summer. This
very good bedding variety also excels as a standard and is good for cut flowers. ZONES 4–9.

MCGREDY, UK, 1966

'EVELYN FISON' × ('SPARTAN' × 'RED FAVORITE')

ROYAL NATIONAL ROSE SOCIETY GOLD MEDAL 1965, BELFAST
CERTIFICATE OF MERIT 1968

### 'City of London' HARukfore *(above)*

MODERN, CLUSTER-FLOWERED/FLORIBUNDA, LIGHT PINK,
REPEAT-FLOWERING

Named for the 800th anniversary of the city's
charter, 'City of London' is a soft pink rose that
fades to blush. The cupped, double flowers are
large, becoming flat with age. The small clusters
of blooms repeat continuously, and are noted for
their good fragrance during this time. The glossy
green foliage clothes sparsely prickled stems. This
vigorous, healthy, well-rounded bush rose grows
bigger on a support and can be trained as a short
climber. ZONES 4–9.

HARKNESS, UK, 1988

'NEW DAWN' × 'RADOX BOUQUET'

LEROEULX GOLD MEDAL 1985, BELFAST GOLD MEDAL 1990, NEW
ZEALAND FRAGRANCE AWARD 1992, THE HAGUE GOLD MEDAL 1993,
ROYAL HORTICULTURAL SOCIETY AWARD OF GARDEN MERIT 1993

C

### 'City of York'
*(top left)*
syn. 'Direktör Benschop'
MODERN, LARGE-FLOWERED
CLIMBER, WHITE

This extremely vigorous plant is better suited to covering pergolas and fences rather than walls, because its growth habit is more similar to a Rambler than a Climber. The plant has leathery, glossy green foliage. It displays large clusters of up to 15 fragrant, creamy white flowers, but only in early summer. The blooms are large and slightly cupped, and are made up of 15 petals with the stamens exposed. Budding is the best method of propagation. It was named for the city in Pennsylvania.
ZONES 4–9.

TANTAU, GERMANY, 1945

'PROFESSOR GNAU' × 'DOROTHY PERKINS'

AMERICAN ROSE SOCIETY NATIONAL GOLD MEDAL CERTIFICATE 1950

### 'Clair Matin'
MEImont  *(top right)*
syn. 'Grimpant Clair Matin'
MODERN, LARGE-FLOWERED CLIMBER, MEDIUM PINK, REPEAT-FLOWERING

The pretty pink flowers of this rose have a very sweet fragrance. They are medium sized and semi-double, with 15 petals arranged in a flattened cup shape. The flowers unfurl from their pointed buds to reveal attractive gold stamens. The leathery dark green foliage is adorned with huge, rounded clusters of up to 40 of these flowers. Very few hips are produced, which leads to almost continuous flowering from summer into autumn; 'Clair Matin' is one of the most free-blooming of all roses. The growth is vigorous and well branched, with cocoa-colored stems—ideal for walls and pergolas, because it grows taller when supported and is easily propagated by budding. The huge panicles of flowers make excellent floral arrangements, and in 1960 this rose thoroughly deserved the Gold Medal it was awarded at Bagatelle in Paris. Translated into English, the French name means 'morning light'. ZONES 4–9.

MEILLAND, FRANCE, 1960

'FASHION' × (['INDEPENDENCE' × 'ORANGE TRIUMPH'] × 'PHYLLIS BIDE')

BAGATELLE GOLD MEDAL 1960

### 'Claire Jacquier'
*(bottom)*
syn. 'Mlle Claire Jacquier'
OLD, NOISETTE, LIGHT YELLOW

The semi-double, numerous blooms, which appear at branch endings, are buff yellow but fade in the sun. This rampant but delicate rose does not like to be tied down and prefers to roam on structures or into trees; it flowers once in early summer. The pliable canes are covered with large, pointed, dark green leaves. A robust, healthy plant, 'Claire Jacquier' tolerates shade and is sweetly scented. ZONES 7–9.

BERNAIX, FRANCE, 1888

POSSIBLY *ROSA MULTIFLORA* × TEA ROSE

C

## 'Claire Rose' AUSlight
*(right)*

**MODERN, MODERN SHRUB,
MEDIUM PINK,
REPEAT-FLOWERING**

This is one of the most exquisitely beautiful of the Modern Shrub Roses; it is also classified as an English Rose. The long-lasting sprays of flowers are large and repeat-flowering and of perfect old-fashioned form, in a delicate blush pink shade that fades attractively to almost white as they age. They are cupped at first, opening to flat, many-petalled, slightly incurved rosettes with a lovely perfume on a strong, reasonably big, upright plant. The branches spread a little and are covered with an abundance of pale green leaves. This is a variety that enjoys a hot, dry climate and can become marked by rain, but this is a small fault and it makes an excellent companion plant in a border; it is sometimes a little ungainly on its own, like its parent 'Charles Austin'. It can be propagated by budding. The superb flowers on long stems are ideal for cutting. David Austin named this rose for his daughter, Claire Calvert. **ZONES 4–9.**

AUSTIN, UK, 1990

'CHARLES AUSTIN' × (SEEDLING × 'ICEBERG')

## 'Clarita' MEIbyster
*(top right)*
syn. 'Atoll'

**MODERN, LARGE-FLOWERED/
HYBRID TEA, ORANGE-RED,
REPEAT-FLOWERING**

This cultivar has large, vermilion flowers that carry a light fragrance. The blooms are double and high centered, each filled with up to 35 petals; they adorn the matt, dark green foliage repeatedly through summer. A good choice for rose beds or mixed borders, 'Clarita' is a very vigorous, upright bush rose that is reliably resistant to disease. The best method of propagation is by budding. **ZONES 4–9.**

MEILLAND, FRANCE, 1971

'TROPICANA' × ('ZAMBRA' × 'ROMANTICA')

LYON GOLD MEDAL 1971, GENEVA GOLD MEDAL 1971

## 'Class Act' JACare
*(above)*
syns 'First Class', 'White Magic'

**MODERN, CLUSTER-FLOWERED/
FLORIBUNDA, WHITE,
REPEAT-FLOWERING**

Borne in sprays of 3–6, the creamy flowers of this rose have a slight fragrance of fruit. They are medium-sized and semi-double, and have 25 flatly arranged, loose petals. In summer the dark green, semi-glossy, bushy foliage adds a good color contrast, which serves to highlight the flowers. This upright plant grows to medium height and has long prickles on its stems. It is a useful and popular variety for beds and borders or as a standard. Propagate by budding. **ZONES 4–9.**

WARRINER, USA, 1988

'SUN FLARE' × SEEDLING

ALL-AMERICA ROSE SELECTION 1989, PORTLAND GOLD MEDAL 1989, NEW ZEALAND GOLD MEDAL 1990

C

### 'Classic Sunblaze'   MEIpinjid
syns 'Duc Meillandina', 'Duke Meillandina'

MODERN, MINIATURE, MEDIUM PINK, REPEAT-FLOWERING

This compact, fast-blooming Miniature rose was
the first of the 'Sunblaze' series released by the
House of Meilland. The blooms are medium pink
and are borne singly or in small clusters. As with
all the roses in the series, 'Classic Sunblaze' is easy
to cultivate. It is long-lasting as a cut flower but
has only a slight fragrance. **ZONES 4–11.**

MEILLAND, FRANCE, 1985

SPORT OF 'PINK MEILLANDINA'

### 'Cleopatra'   KORverpea   *(above left)*
syns 'Kleopatra', 'New Cleopatra',
'Peace of Vereeniging'

MODERN, LARGE-FLOWERED/HYBRID TEA, RED BLEND,
REPEAT-FLOWERING

This variety produces fairly large double blooms
that open with high centers, becoming rounded as
the petals reflex. Their colors make a striking contrast as the uppersides of the petals are rich scarlet
and the undersides golden yellow. The lightly
scented flowers appear freely in summer, and they
continue to bloom through to autumn, which
makes this a very suitable garden rose for beds,
borders and hedges. It grows to average height
with a vigorous upright habit, and is well furnished with dark shiny leaves that are reddish
when young. There was a similarly colored
'Kleopatra' from the same raiser in 1955.
**ZONES 4–9.**

KORDES, GERMANY, 1992

PARENTAGE UNKNOWN

### 'Clio'

OLD, HYBRID PERPETUAL, LIGHT PINK, REPEAT-FLOWERING

The flowers of this rose are flesh colored, very
double, globular and bloom in clusters. A silver-
pink overtone and sweet fragrance add to its
charm. The graceful arching canes reach 4 ft
(1.2 m) and are covered with rich green, leathery
foliage and prickles. It flowers during a long
period in summer, it hates the rain, and will ball
quickly in such weather. It should be pruned
lightly. In Greek mythology *Clio* is the muse of
history. **ZONES 5–9.**

WILLIAM PAUL AND SON, UK, 1894

PARENTAGE UNKNOWN

### 'Clos Fleuri Blanc'   DELblan   *(above right)*
syn. 'Snowy Summit'

MODERN, CLUSTER-FLOWERED/FLORIBUNDA, WHITE,
REPEAT-FLOWERING

This plant is sufficiently vigorous for some catalogues to describe it as being a semi-climber; it is
suitable either as a pillar rose or in a shrub border. 'Clos Fleuri Blanc' bears large white double
flowers, each packed with up to 40 petals, and
delicately fragranced. They bloom repeatedly
throughout the summer months, which can be
further encouraged by regular deadheading.
The foliage is bright green. **ZONES 4–9.**

DELBARD AND CHABERT, FRANCE, 1988

('MILROSE' × 'LEGION D'HONNEUR') × 'CANDEUR'

C

### 'Clos Vougeot'

DELific (*bottom*)

syns 'Red Prolific',
'Rouge Prolific'

MODERN, CLUSTER-FLOWERED/
FLORIBUNDA, MEDIUM RED,
REPEAT-FLOWERING

This free-flowering
plant bears clusters of
medium-sized, double
red flowers, each filled
with over 24 petals.
It has a bushy growth
habit and bright green
foliage, and is suitable
for a rose bed; it
blooms repeatedly
through the warmer
months. There is no
discernible fragrance.
'Clos Vougeot' should
not be confused with
'Chateau de Clos
Vougeot', a fragrant
Large-flowered Rose
bred in 1908 that is
still in commerce.
ZONES 4–9.

DELBARD-CHABERT, FRANCE, 1983

('ALAIN' × 'CHARLES MALLERIN')
× ('LAFAYETTE' × 'WALKO')

foliage. The rose has a
spreading habit that
shows its best as a
specimen plant, partic-
ularly when planted in
groups. Budding is the
best method of propa-
gation. 'Clytemnestra'
is typical of the roses
bred by Pemberton.
ZONES 4–9.

PEMBERTON, UK, 1915

'TRIER' × 'LIBERTY'

NATIONAL ROSE SOCIETY GOLD
MEDAL 1914

### 'Clytemnestra'

MODERN, MODERN SHRUB,
ORANGE-PINK,
REPEAT-FLOWERING

The copper buds of this
rose develop into small
flowers with an inter-
esting color. They are
deep salmon-copper
and gradually fade to
chamois with age; the
petals have a ruffled
or crinkled appearance.
Throughout summer,
the blooms appear in
fragrant clusters amid
the leathery, dark green

### 'Cocktail' MEImick

(*top*)

MODERN, MODERN SHRUB,
RED BLEND, REPEAT-FLOWERING

'Cocktail' is one of the
brightest roses avail-
able. Although its
parents either have
double or semi-double
flowers, this variety
bears brilliant single
flowers with just 5
petals. Borne in large
clusters continually
through summer and
autumn, they emerge
from pointed buds and

are geranium red with
a glowing, primrose
yellow eye. There is a
delicate, spicy fragrance.
This is a vigorous,
strong-growing rose
clothed with glossy,
leathery foliage, that is
generally treated as a
semi-climber; however,
it is suitable for use as a
standard or in a shrub
border, as well as a
short climber or pillar

rose. The variety is
spectacular because of
the unusual intense
color of the flowers,
perfect if a plant is
needed to liven up a
garden. It can be
propagated by bud-
ding, and is said to
tolerate poor soils.
ZONES 4–9.

MEILLAND, FRANCE, 1957

('INDEPENDENCE' × 'ORANGE
TRIUMPH') × 'PHYLLIS BIDE'

dark, shiny foliage. The canes are covered with many small prickles. **ZONES 4–9.**

MEILLAND, 1994

('FIONA' × 'FRIESA') × 'PRAIRIE PRINCESS'

### 'Colibri' MEImal
*(bottom right)*
syn. 'Colibre'

MODERN, MINIATURE, ORANGE BLEND, REPEAT-FLOWERING

This is a Miniature Rose from the same magic hands that hybridized the famous Large-flowered Rose 'Peace', which changed the perception of Large-flowered form forever. The ovoid buds open to reveal orange-yellow double flowers that are color-fast in most climates. The blooms are characteris-tically small and occur in small clusters. They have a light fragrance. The glossy foliage com-plements the brightly colored blooms. While no longer grown exten-sively, it must go down in history as one of the classic Miniatures of the twentieth century. **ZONES 4–11.**

MEILLAND, FRANCE, 1958

'GOLDILOCKS' × 'PERLA DE MONTSERRAT'

THE HAGUE GOLDEN ROSE 1962

### 'Cocorico' MEllano
*(top)*

MODERN, CLUSTER-FLOWERED/ FLORIBUNDA, ORANGE-RED, REPEAT-FLOWERING

'Cocorico' was one of the earliest red Cluster-flowered Roses suitable for bedding displays in large parks and gardens. The buds are pointed, geranium red and open to large, almost single flowers of 8 petals that are borne in small and large clusters. The bush is vigorous and upright and bloom production is very high. Repeat-bloom is very rapid if spent flowers are re-moved. As with most single roses, hips are produced in abun-dance if trimming is not carried out regu-larly. The semi-glossy foliage is bright green and abundant. *Cocorico* is colloquial French for 'something to crow about'. After nearly 50 years in commerce, it is still a good bedding rose. **ZONES 5–9.**

MEILLAND, FRANCE, 1951

'ALAIN' × 'ORANGE TRIUMPH'

GENEVA GOLD MEDAL 1951, NATIONAL ROSE SOCIETY GOLD MEDAL 1951

### 'Colette' MEIroupis
*(bottom left)*
syn. 'John Keats'

MODERN, LARGE-FLOWERED/ HYBRID TEA, LIGHT PINK, REPEAT-FLOWERING

Two world-famous authors share the name of this rose, although 'Colette' has become more famous in the garden. The light ocher-pink, full, medium-sized blooms are borne in small clusters. They are very fragrant and recur throughout the summer. The spreading 6 ft (1.8 m) shrub is covered with small,

C

### 'Colorama' MEIrigalu
*(above)*
syns 'Colourama',
'Dr R. Magg'
MODERN, LARGE-FLOWERED/
HYBRID TEA, RED BLEND,
REPEAT-FLOWERING

This rose bears fragrant flowers continuously through summer on a plant that is vigorous, bushy and upright. The large, double, cup-shaped blooms are red and yellow and emerge from oval buds. It has very glossy green leaves and is a good bedding variety for rose beds or mixed borders. It can be propagated by budding. **ZONES 4–9.**

MEILLAND, FRANCE, 1968

'SUSPENSE' × 'CONFIDENCE'

### 'Colour Wonder'
KORbico *(below right)*
syns 'Königin der
Rosen', 'Queen of
Roses', 'Reine des Roses'
MODERN, LARGE-FLOWERED/
HYBRID TEA, ORANGE BLEND,
REPEAT-FLOWERING

The large, coral-orange double blooms of this rose have cream undersides and are packed with up to 50 petals. They emerge from oval buds in early summer and continue to flower for as long as the weather remains warm. There is a nice light fragrance. Also quite curious is the glossy bronze foliage that covers this vigorous, upright bush rose. 'Colour Wonder' can boast a lineage of two of the most widely grown roses in the twentieth century as its parents; it, too, has become a parent of many new varieties. **ZONES 4–9.**

KORDES, GERMANY, 1964

'KORDES' PERFECTA' ×
'TROPICANA'

ANERKANNTE DEUTSCHE ROSE
1964, BELFAST GOLD MEDAL 1966

### 'Commandant Beaurepaire'
*(top right)*
syn. 'Panachée
d'Angers'
OLD, BOURBON, PINK BLEND

This elegant plant is often proclaimed the best of the striped roses. The rose pink blooms are streaked with purple-violet and marble white. They are cupped and upright and offer a strong fragrance. The foliage is light green with long, pointed leaves and the plant has prickly canes that need to be thinned after blooming has finished. 'Commandant Beaurepaire' does well in cool weather in the shade where it can reach 5 ft (1.5 m) high, which makes it a good candidate for a hedge. **ZONES 5–9.**

MOREAU-ROBERT, FRANCE, 1879

SEEDLING OF AN UNNAMED
HYBRID PERPETUAL

C

## 'Compassion' *(top left)*
syn. 'Belle de Londres'

MODERN, LARGE-FLOWERED CLIMBER, ORANGE-PINK,
REPEAT-FLOWERING

This is one of the all-time greats in rose breeding,
and has deservedly won many awards. Its combination of high-quality blooms and wonderfully
sweet fragrance on a plant that grows to the size
of a big shrub makes it a perfect subject for a
garden, equally at home on a fence, pergola or wall.
It is the most popular climbing rose in England.
Throughout summer and autumn, 'Compassion'
is completely repeat-flowering. It bears large
salmon-pink, apricot-shaded blooms that are
filled with about 36 petals. They are borne either
singly or in clusters of 3 amid the large, dark
green, leathery foliage. The plant itself is an extremely healthy variety with reasonably vigorous
growth and a bushy, branching habit. It can be
propagated by budding. ZONES 4–9.

HARKNESS, UK, 1973

'WHITE COCKADE' × 'PRIMA BALLERINA'

BADEN-BADEN GOLD MEDAL 1975, GENEVA GOLD MEDAL 1975,
ORLÉANS GOLD MEDAL 1979, ROYAL NATIONAL ROSE SOCIETY
FRAGRANCE MEDAL 1973, ANERKANNTE DEUTSCHE ROSE 1976, ROYAL
HORTICULTURAL SOCIETY AWARD OF GARDEN MERIT 1993

## 'Complicata' *(left)*
syn. 'Ariana d'Algier'

OLD, GALLICA, PINK BLEND

This is a broad, dense,
vigorous shrub attain-
ing a height of 6 ft
(1.8 m) or even more
if given something to
scramble on or into,
such as a small tree.
It has strong, gray-
green, partially thorned
stems that are abun-
dantly clothed in large,
durable foliage. The
flowers appear in early
summer only and are
up to 4 in (10 cm) in
diameter at their best.
Very bright, clear pink
and single, they are
moderately fragrant
and are considerably
enhanced by a lovely
boss of bright creamy
yellow stamens. Apart
from making a superb
specimen shrub, this
rose will also do well
as an informal hedge.
It is very healthy, tolerant of impoverished
soils and very hardy.
ZONES 5–9.

PARENTAGE MAY INVOLVE *ROSA
CANINA* OR *R. MACRANTHA*

## 'Comte Boula de Nanteuil' *(left)*
syns 'Boule de Nanteuil', 'Comte de Nanteuil'

OLD, GALLICA, MAUVE

The large, crimson-
purple blooms of this
rose have silver over-
tones and crimson
centers. They are
filled with many petals,
compact, flat and
quartered, and are
admirably set off by
prominent stamens.
Its manageable size and
Damask-like fragrance
make it an ideal can-
didate for a pot plant.
It can also be used as
a low hedge and is
quite tolerant of shade.
Some confusion exists
between this rose and
one sold as 'Comte de
Nanteuil'; both are
popular cut flowers.
ZONES 4–9.

ROESER, FRANCE, 1834

PARENTAGE UNKNOWN

C

### 'Comte de Chambord' *(right)*

OLD, PORTLAND, PINK BLEND, REPEAT-FLOWERING

This is a sturdy shrub to 4 ft (1.2 m) with strong, grayish green stems well populated with reddish prickles and thorns. The light gray-green foliage is serrated and slightly downy. The flowers are borne in small clusters or singly, and in great profusion from early summer to autumn. In the late stage of bud they are beautifully high centered and scrolled, then later densely packed with petals; they go through a cupped stage to become fully flat, often quartered and up to 3 in (8 cm) across when fully open. These powerfully perfumed flowers are dense rich pink, with hints of lilac and lavender. 'Comte de Chambord' is ideal for group planting; it also makes a good hedge and is excellent as a container plant. Some think this rose is actually 'Mme Boll' (Boll, France, 1859). ZONES 5–9.

ROBERT AND MOREAU, FRANCE, 1863

PERHAPS 'BARONNE PRÉVOST' × 'DUCHESS OF PORTLAND'

ROYAL HORTICULTURAL SOCIETY AWARD OF GARDEN MERIT 1993

### 'Comtesse Cécile de Chabrillant' *(above)*

OLD, HYBRID PERPETUAL, PINK BLEND, REPEAT-FLOWERING

This rare rose bears fragrant, satiny rose pink flowers with silver undersides over a long period. They are full, globular and of medium size with petals shaped like shells. The tall canes have leathery, dark green foliage and tiny prickles. ZONES 5–9.

MAREST, FRANCE, 1858

SEEDLING OF 'JULES MARGOTTIN'

### 'Comtesse de Murinais' *(top right)*

OLD, MOSS, WHITE

This tall shrub grows well as a small climber; it is equally good as a shrub. The leaves are bright green and slightly crinkled. The buds have finely textured moss and tightly packed, small prickles, and the fragrant flowers are pure white with a hint of blush. ZONES 5–9.

VIBERT, FRANCE, 1843

PARENTAGE UNKNOWN

C

The growth habit is upright and bushy. **ZONES 4–9.**

MEILLAND, FRANCE, 1953

'ALAIN' × 'FLORADORA'

NATIONAL ROSE SOCIETY PRESIDENT'S INTERNATIONAL TROPHY 1953

### 'Conditorum' *(left)*
syns 'Hungarian Rose', *Rosa gallica conditorum*, 'Tidbit Rose'

OLD, GALLICA, DARK RED

With a bushy and reasonably dense habit, this rose grows to about 3 ft (1 m) high. It has dark green stems, which are moderately thorny, and the plentiful foliage is gray-green and a little coarse. The very fragrant flowers are held upright in sizeable clusters and at their best are up to 3 in (8 cm) across when fully open. Appearing in early summer, they are slightly more than semi-double and somewhat disorderly in structure. They are cerise-crimson with strong magenta tints showing through; the display of bright yellow stamens is an added attraction. 'Conditorum' has many similarities to 'Officinalis'. **ZONES 5–9.**
1629

PARENTAGE UNKNOWN

### 'Comtesse du Caÿla' *(above)*
OLD, CHINA, ORANGE BLEND, REPEAT-FLOWERING

For many, this is the best of all the Chinas. Purple, nodding stems carry large, loosely cupped, flat blooms of carmine tinted orange with yellow undersides. The highly scented blooms are reminiscent of sweet peas and tea. The flowering season lasts as long as the warm summer weather permits. 'Comtesse du Caÿla' does best in full sun, looking rather straggly in the shade.

The thin canes and glossy bronze-green foliage form a compact bush to 3 ft (1 m) tall. This is an excellent rose to plant among perennials because of its handsome appearance and constant bloom. The cut flowers, especially if taken when in bud, last a long time indoors. The countess, for whom this rose was named, was a mistress of Louis XVI of France. **ZONES 7–11.**

GUILLOT, FRANCE, 1902

(SEEDLING OF 'RIVAL DE PAESTUM' × 'MME FALCOT') × 'MME FALCOT'

### 'Concerto' *(top left)*
MODERN, CLUSTER-FLOWERED/ FLORIBUNDA, MEDIUM RED, REPEAT-FLOWERING

Brilliant, medium red flowers emerge from pointed, oval buds on this variety to form loosely cup-shaped, semi-double blooms with 12–15 petals. There is a light perfume. In summer, sizeable clusters of blooms that hold their color well cover the dark green foliage. 'Concerto' makes a good bedding rose that can be propagated by budding.

### 'Confidence' *(right)*

MODERN, LARGE-FLOWERED/
HYBRID TEA, PINK BLEND,
REPEAT-FLOWERING

C

The large, double blooms of this variety are a pearly light pink with a hint of yellow at the base. The 38 petals unfurl from oval buds to form flowers with high centers and good fragrance. Throughout summer, this upright and bushy Large-flowered Rose carries these blooms amid the dark green, leathery foliage. 'Confidence' is a relatively healthy rose that should be propagated by budding. It was the first successful variety to be bred from the enormously popular 'Peace', although it performs better in hot, dry climates, appreciating neither wet weather nor hard pruning. ZONES 4–9.

MEILLAND, FRANCE, 1951

'PEACE' × 'MICHÈLE MEILLAND'

BAGATELLE GOLD MEDAL 1951

### 'Congratulations'

KORlift *(bottom)*
syns 'Kordes' Rose Sylvia', 'Sylvia'

MODERN, LARGE-FLOWERED/
HYBRID TEA, ORANGE-PINK,
REPEAT-FLOWERING

'Congratulations' is a valuable addition to any collection of Modern Roses. It freely bears perfectly formed, medium pink blooms either singly or in small clusters on a bushy plant with large, dark green, healthy foliage. Each flower develops from a long, pointed bud and is filled with about 42 petals to form a double urn shape with a high center. It has a nice fragrance and is a very good variety for grouping in a border. The long, upright flower stems are ideal for cutting; disbudding causes the plant to produce even larger blooms. Propagation is best achieved by budding. ZONES 4–9.

KORDES, GERMANY, 1979

'CARINA' × SEEDLING

ANERKANNTE DEUTSCHE ROSE 1977, BRITISH ASSOCIATION OF ROSE BREEDERS SELECTION 1977

### 'Conrad Ferdinand Meyer' *(top right)*

MODERN, HYBRID RUGOSA, LIGHT PINK, REPEAT-FLOWERING

This widely grown cultivar can almost be classed as a semi-climber. It is a rampant, haggard, arching rose with its stems clothed with a plethora of thorns; it makes a good pillar rose or tall shrub. The freely borne flowers are double and very fragrant with soft silvery pink, cupped petals. The quality of the flowers improves each time they repeat through summer, although autumn blooms are unreliable. It should be propagated by budding or from cuttings, and the coarse, leathery foliage can be prone to rust. ZONES 4–9.

MÜLLER, GERMANY, 1899

('GLOIRE DE DIJON' × 'DUC DE ROHAN') × *ROSA RUGOSA* 'GERMANICA'

C

### 'Conservation'

COCdimple *(above)*

MODERN, MINIATURE, PINK
BLEND, REPEAT-FLOWERING

Although its official
color is listed as a pink
blend, the florets are
more of a salmon-
red to orange. The
blooms contain only
18 petals, but their
staying power is re-
markable. Usually borne
in clusters, the sprays
appear as mounds of
color against the glossy
green foliage. There
is a light fragrance on
the opening day of the
blooms but it dissipates
quickly. The plant has
a dense bushy habit
and is disease resistant.
This rose was named
to celebrate the 50th
anniversary of the
World Wildlife Fund.

The city of Aberdeen
in Scotland has mass
public plantings of
this home-grown
Miniature. ZONES 4–11.

JAMES COCKER & SONS, UK,
1986

(['SABINE' × 'CIRCUS'] × 'MAXI')
× 'DARLING FLAME'

DUBLIN GOLD MEDAL 1986,
GLASGOW CERTIFICATE OF MERIT
1990

### 'Constance Spry'

*(above)*

syn. 'Constanze Spry'

MODERN, MODERN SHRUB,
LIGHT PINK

This variety was the
very first of its kind—
the ancestor of all those
Modern Shrubs that
some breeders classify
as English Roses (the
reds excluded, being
mainly derived from
the 'Chianti'/'Tuscany'
line). It has proved
to be enormously
popular. For anyone
who wishes to grow
roses, 'Constance Spry'
would be a premier
choice for every garden
that has the room for
this exceptional, lax-
growing, rampant
plant with large, soft
luminous pink, cup-
shaped, double flowers.
Being a cross between
a Modern Cluster-
flowered Rose and an
Old Garden Gallica
Rose, it is not repeat-
flowering, but this is
not really a drawback

because the single
summer blooms are
long lasting, spectac-
ular and have a delicious
fragrance of myrrh,
a feature that has been
passed on to many of
its progeny. The growth
is covered with large,
dark green foliage that
is very winter hardy
and has a good health
record. It is useful in
groups at the back of
a mixed border, but
because it can be quite
sprawling it is better
trained as a climber on
walls to attain its best.
This graceful rose was
named after the famous
pioneer of flower
arranging of the 1950s
and 1960s. ZONES 4–9.

AUSTIN, UK, 1961

'BELLE ISIS' × 'DAINTY MAID'

ROYAL HORTICULTURAL SOCIETY
AWARD OF GARDEN MERIT 1993

C

## 'Cooper's Burmese'

syns 'Gigantea Cooperi', *Rosa* × *cooperi*

OLD, LAEVIGATA, WHITE

This beautiful rose is best appreciated in a warm climate, where it bears large, saucer-shaped, single, creamy white flowers with prominent yellow stamens, and diffuses a pleasing fragrance. They appear quite freely in summer but are not dependably repeat flowering. The delicacy of the blooms is in contrast with the character of the plant, for it produces prickly branching stems and can extend three times as far as the average climbing rose. The leaves are large and green and make a handsome foil to the pale, silky looking flowers. The use of this variety is limited in cooler climates owing to its tenderness; for it to succeed, it needs a large wall that can give shelter from frost and cold winds. The original plant was grown by Roland Cooper, curator of the Royal Botanic Garden in Edinburgh, Scotland, who collected the seed in Burma. ZONES 6–9.

COOPER, UK, 1927

POSSIBLY *ROSA LAEVIGATA* × *R. GIGANTEA*

## 'Copenhagen'
*(right)*

syn. 'Kobenhavn'

MODERN, LARGE-FLOWERED CLIMBER, MEDIUM RED, REPEAT-FLOWERING

This repeat-flowering climbing rose bears large, crimson-scarlet, semi-double, well-formed blooms that each have about 20 petals. They are produced in small clusters and there is a reasonable fragrance. Although the growth is sometimes vigorous, it could be termed a low-growing climber, ideal for pillars or small walls. The foliage is dark green with a coppery tinge and healthy. This was one of the first Modern Climbing Roses to be repeat-flowering, but it has now been superseded by more vigorous varieties that sadly do not have the same quality bloom. It can be propagated by budding. ZONES 4–9.

POULSEN, DENMARK, 1964

SEEDLING × 'ENA HARKNESS'

NATIONAL ROSE SOCIETY CERTIFICATE OF MERIT 1963

## 'Coppélia' *(above)*

MODERN, CLUSTER-FLOWERED/FLORIBUNDA, ORANGE BLEND, REPEAT-FLOWERING

'Coppélia was originally introduced as a Large-flowered Rose, although it is correctly classed as a Cluster-flowered Rose. The blooms are medium sized, cupped and double, made up of 25 petals of good substance. They are a luminous rosy pink color with a hint of orange in the pink, and there is a slight fragrance. The foliage is mid-green and semi-glossy, and the bush is tall, spreading and extremely free flowering over a long period. 'Coppélia' is good as a bedding rose, and can also be planted as an informal hedge. ZONES 5–9.

MEILLAND, FRANCE, 1952

'PEACE' × 'EUROPA'

C

### 'Coral Cluster'
*(top left)*

MODERN, POLYANTHA, ORANGE-PINK, REPEAT-FLOWERING

'Coral Cluster' is a typical example of the pompon-type repeat-flowering Polyanthas that were popular before the introduction of Cluster-flowered Roses. They were prone to mutation, producing flowers in a variety of colors ranging from pale pink through to crimson. This rose bears small, coral pink, double blooms throughout summer amid the pale green foliage. It is a hardy cultivar, although subject to mildew from mid-summer. Propagate from cuttings or by budding. **ZONES 4–9.**

MURRELL, UK, 1920

SPORT OF 'ORLÉANS ROSE'

NATIONAL ROSE SOCIETY GOLD MEDAL 1921

### 'Coral Satin'
*(bottom)*

MODERN, LARGE-FLOWERED CLIMBER, ORANGE-PINK, REPEAT-FLOWERING

The large, double, coral flowers of 'Coral Satin' emerge from oval buds and it reliably repeat-flowers throughout summer. Blooms have a very good form, each having about 25 petals arranged to form a high center. This is a moderate-growing climbing rose that is fragrant, healthy and well furnished with large, leathery foliage. It is a suitable subject for pillars and walls. Budding is the most reliable method of propagation. **ZONES 4–9.**

ZOMBORY, USA, 1960

'NEW DAWN' × 'FASHION'

### 'Coralin'
syns 'Carolin', 'Carolyn', 'Karolyn'

MODERN, MINIATURE, ORANGE-RED, REPEAT-FLOWERING

This classic Miniature Rose was developed in the 1950s. It boasts coral-red florets with 40 petals on a low-growing, compact plant. The pollen parent had been successfully used by Francis Meilland in the development of the prize-winning 'Colibri'. This rose was one of the first modern Miniatures but is no longer commercially available. It is, however, still grown in many countries via exchange of cuttings, and so continues to survive extinction. **ZONES 5–11.**

DOT, SPAIN, 1955

'MÉPHISTO' × 'PERLA DE ALCAÑADA'

### 'Cordula'   KORtri
*(top right)*

MODERN, CLUSTER-FLOWERED/FLORIBUNDA, ORANGE-RED, REPEAT-FLOWERING

The large clusters of orange-red, medium-sized, double blooms of this rose develop from globular buds and yield a light fragrance. They bloom repeatedly through summer and contrast well with the bronze-tinged, dark green, leathery foliage. The plant is a Dwarf, with bushy growth that can be propagated by budding. 'Cordula' is suitable for a rose bed and makes a good standard. **ZONES 4–9.**

KORDES, GERMANY, 1972

'EUROPEANA' × 'MARLENA'

C

## 'Cornelia' *(right)*

MODERN, MODERN SHRUB, PINK
BLEND, REPEAT-FLOWERING

Raised by the Reverend
Joseph Pemberton of
Essex, possibly from
a seedling of 'Aglaia',
'Cornelia' has been
popular ever since its
release in 1925. The
flowers range in color
from pale apricot-
copper to salmon-pink
or strawberry flushed
yellow; the base is
usually orange. They
are small, very double,
rosette shaped and are
borne in large, arching
trusses. The fragrance
is distinctly musky.
'Cornelia' is a superb,
strong-growing shrub
rose that blooms
continually well into
autumn. It has immense
beauty and can look
very effective cascading
down a low wall or
veranda, or trained
around a pillar. There
are no thorns, the
foliage is dark green,
bronze tinged and
glossy and it prefers a
sunny spot out of the
wind. To propagate it,
take cuttings or retrieve
the buds. **ZONES 4–9.**

PEMBERTON, UK, 1925

PARENTAGE UNKNOWN

ROYAL HORTICULTURAL SOCIETY
AWARD OF GARDEN MERIT 1993

## 'Coronado'

MODERN, LARGE-FLOWERED/
HYBRID TEA, RED BLEND,
REPEAT-FLOWERING

This bicolored rose
produces large red

blooms with yellow
undersides from long,
pointed buds. Each is
filled with about 40
petals that form a high
center and is reasonably
fragrant. 'Coronado'
is a vigorous, repeat-
flowering rose with
dark green, glossy
foliage on an upright
plant. It makes a good
bedding variety and
can be propagated by
budding. **ZONES 4–9.**

ABRAMS, USA, 1961

('MULTNOMAH' × 'PEACE') ×
('MULTNOMAH' × 'PEACE')

## 'Corso' *(top right)*

MODERN, LARGE-FLOWERED/
HYBRID TEA, ORANGE BLEND,
REPEAT-FLOWERING

This vigorous, upright
variety had the poten-
tial to be a popular
subject for cut flowers,
but was never success-
ful on the international
market owing to its
susceptibility to mildew.
In the garden, however,
'Corso' produces lovely
coppery orange, double
blooms that are borne
on long stems and
have a good, classic
form. The flowers are

composed of 33 petals
and are large, to 4½ in
(11 cm) across. They
are repeat-flowering
and have a light per-
fume. The foliage is
dark green and glossy
and budding is the
recommended method
of propagation.
**ZONES 4–9.**

COCKER, UK, 1976

'ANNE COCKER' × 'DR A. J.
VERHAGE'

## 'Cottage Rose'

AUSglisten *(above)*

**syn. 'The Cottage Rose'**

MODERN, MODERN SHRUB,
MEDIUM PINK,
REPEAT-FLOWERING

Also classified as an
English Rose, this is a
good shrub rose for
a small garden. It bears

shallowly cupped,
quartered-rosette,
warm glowing pink
flowers during summer
and autumn. Soon
after the first flush
appears, the next is in
bud and ready to burst
into bloom. This is a
charming, small, bushy
plant useful for small
beds or in a container,
although it has little
scent. It can be propa-
gated by budding or
from cuttings. For
any gardener looking
for a Modern Rose
with the character of
an Old Garden Rose,
'Cottage Rose' is with-
out comparison.
**ZONES 4–9.**

AUSTIN, UK, 1991

'WIFE OF BATH' × 'MARY ROSE'

C

## 'Country Dancer'

*(above)*

MODERN, MODERN SHRUB,
DEEP PINK, REPEAT-FLOWERING

This is an upright, dwarf shrub rose that produces large, rose red, double blooms repeatedly through the warmer months. The foliage is big, dark green and glossy. It is a useful plant for the front of a mixed border or in pots and has a reasonable fragrance. The growth habit is vigorous. ZONES 4–9.

BUCK, USA, 1973

'PRAIRIE PRINCESS' × 'JOHANNES BOETTNER'

## 'Country Lady'

HARtsam

MODERN, LARGE-FLOWERED/
HYBRID TEA, ORANGE BLEND,
REPEAT-FLOWERING

The medium-sized blooms of this tall, vigorous plant have a burnt look: reddish salmon-pink with undersides suffused pale scarlet, fading to orange-salmon, then pink. They are borne with good continuity through summer and into autumn, usually singly or in small clusters. Each flower is urn shaped to pointed with about 24 loosely arranged petals. There is a spicy fragrance. If the flowers are not deadheaded, attractive oval fruits appear in autumn. 'Country Lady' was named for the Country Gentlemen's Association and is furnished with mid-green, healthy foliage and reddish, downward curving prickles. It can be propagated by budding. ZONES 4–9.

HARKNESS, UK, 1987

'ALEXANDER' × 'BRIGHT SMILE'

GENEVA CERTIFICATE OF MERIT 1985, ROYAL NATIONAL ROSE SOCIETY TRIAL GROUND CERTIFICATE 1986

## 'Country Living'

AUScountry *(above)*

MODERN, MODERN SHRUB,
LIGHT PINK, REPEAT-FLOWERING

Also classified as an English Rose, 'Country Living' is a must for any gardener who collects this sort of rose. The breeder claims that it is 'more old rose than old rose', yet it is a Modern Garden Rose that repeatedly produces perfectly shaped, medium-sized, delicate blooms freely through summer and into autumn. At times, each of these rosette-type flowers has a green eye at its confused center, although they are mostly blush to flesh pink, fading to palest pink. There is a pleasing scent. 'Country Living' is a small-leafed variety with a twiggy, bushy character, probably better described as a bush rose rather than a shrub rose; it is good at the front of a rose bed or in containers in a small garden. Some shoots do not appear to be winter hardy because they sometimes die back, but this is not a problem since the plant quickly recovers with new shoots at the base. Budding is the best method of propagation; take care of the small thorns. It was named for the magazine *Country Living*. ZONES 4–9.

AUSTIN, UK, 1991

'WIFE OF BATH' × 'GRAHAM THOMAS'

C

### 'Coupe d'Hébé'

OLD, BOURBON, DEEP PINK

With a name like this, one would be right to assume that the rose has cupped flowers. They are deep pink, very double and have waxy textured petals with wavy, crumpled edges. There is a strong, heady fragrance. This is a free-flowering rose but only in the first part of the season, and the blooms are heavy and hang down in an attractive manner. They last well when cut. Looking best in shade, the bush is vigorous and upright and can be used for a pillar if left unpruned. It does well even in poor soil. The foliage is glossy and light green but is subject to mildew. **ZONES 5–10.**

LAFFAY, FRANCE, 1840

BOURBON HYBRID × CHINA HYBRID

### 'Courtoisie' DELcourt
*(above)*

MODERN, CLUSTER-FLOWERED/ FLORIBUNDA, ORANGE BLEND, REPEAT-FLOWERING

The large, double, orange blooms of 'Courtoise' have undersides that are blended with yellow. They appear repeatedly in small clusters throughout the warmer months and have a pleasing scent. It is a medium-sized, bushy bedding rose with mid-green foliage. **ZONES 5–9.**

DELBARD-CHABERT, FRANCE, 1984

'AVALANCHE ROSE' × SEEDLING OF 'FASHION'

### 'Courvoisier' MACsee
*(above)*

MODERN, CLUSTER-FLOWERED/ FLORIBUNDA, DEEP YELLOW, REPEAT-FLOWERING

The deep yellow double blooms of this Cluster-flowered Rose have a shape that is more characteristic of a Large-flowered Rose. They are large, filled with up to 50 petals, very fragrant and appear in attractive trusses throughout summer. This is an upright rose, with glossy dark green foliage, that makes a fine bedding plant. **ZONES 5–9.**

MCGREDY, NEW ZEALAND, 1970

'ELIZABETH OF GLAMIS' × 'CASANOVA'

ROYAL NATIONAL ROSE SOCIETY TRIAL GROUND CERTIFICATE 1969

### 'Cramoisi Picoté'

OLD, GALLICA, RED BLEND

This stiffly upright, medium-sized Gallica grows up to 4 ft (1.2 m) high and has cane-like, dark green stems and few thorns. The small foliage is dark green and coarse to touch, and the flowers are arranged in tight clusters. These are pompon shaped, deep pink and have reddish touches to the edges of the petals. This rose, which is bright and cheerful rather than just beautiful, is moderately fragrant and very useful in mixed borders or even in pots. **ZONES 5–9.**

VIBERT, FRANCE, 1834

PARENTAGE UNKNOWN

C

wall. If properly culti-
vated the variety can
produce two flushes
of flowers in a season.
**ZONES 4–9.**

AUSTIN, UK, 1983

'RUGOSA CONRAD F. MEYER' ×
'CHAUCER'

## 'Crested Moss'
*(bottom)*
syns 'Chapeau de
Napoléon', 'Cristata',
*Rosa* × *centifolia*
'Cristata'

OLD, MOSS, MEDIUM PINK

This is not perhaps a
true Moss Rose as there
is little or no moss
anywhere on the plant,
except on that part
which takes the shape
of a cocked hat on the
calyxes of the flowers;
this gives the rose its
name. It is an angular,
rather sparsely foliated,
open shrub that grows
to 5 ft (1.5 m) high
and almost as wide.
The stem is moderately
populated with sharply
pointed spines, and
the gray-green leaves
are heavily serrated.
The flowers are similar
to those of a Centifolia,
both in form and
size, but of a slightly
brighter pink color.
This very healthy and
easygoing shrub rose
is often found listed by
its other popular name
'Cristata'. **ZONES 4–9.**

FRIBOURG, SWITZERLAND,
PRE-1820

PROBABLY SEEDLING OF *ROSA* ×
*CENTIFOLIA*

ROYAL HORTICULTURAL SOCIETY
AWARD OF GARDEN MERIT 1993

## 'Crépuscule'
*(top right)*
OLD, NOISETTE, APRICOT BLEND,
REPEAT-FLOWERING

For warmer climates,
perhaps no rose enjoys
more acclaim as a
climber than this one.
It blooms from early
spring until the first
frost, and has become
popular simply because
it is hardy, floriferous
and quite beautiful.
The apricot-yellow
blooms develop from
perfect buds into clus-
ters of silky petals. The
young leaves are tinged
with bronze, ageing to
light green and the
plant has few prickles.
It apparently does as
well in shade as it does
in the sun. The sweet
fragrance adds another
dimension to its worth,
and it is especially
suited to pergolas or
as a floral blanket on
a fence. **ZONES 6–11.**

DUBREUIL, FRANCE, 1904

PARENTAGE UNKNOWN

## 'Cressida'  AUScress
*(top left)*
MODERN, MODERN SHRUB,
APRICOT BLEND,
REPEAT-FLOWERING

One of the tallest roses
in the Austin range and
also classified as an
English Rose, this
variety makes strong,
upright growth and
is covered with big,
rough-textured, light
green leaves. It carries
small clusters of very
large, full, cupped
flowers that have a
strong scent of myrrh.
They are apricot-pink
in the center, gradu-
ating to pale pink to-
wards the margins and
apricot on the under-
sides; these colors
mingle together well.
'Cressida' requires
plenty of room to grow,
for example in a shrub
border or against a

C

## 'Cricket' AROket
*(right)*

MODERN, MINIATURE, ORANGE
BLEND, REPEAT-FLOWERING

'Cricket' has tangerine buds that open to light orange florets, decorating a healthy, compact, disease-resistant bush. This rose is a winner for bloom production and ease of maintenance. Since the pollen parent is a deep yellow Cluster-flowered Rose, one might expect some transmission of color and yet there is none. Instead, the pollen parent transmitted its great form and substance. Although the flowers contain only 25 petals and the form is globular, 'Cricket' managed to win 'Queen of Show' at a popular All-Miniature show in Southern California in 1989. It has leathery foliage. **ZONES 4–11.**

CHRISTENSEN, USA, 1978

'ANYTIME' × 'KATHERINE LOKER'

## 'Crimson Globe'
syn. 'Dr Rocques'

OLD, MOSS, DARK RED

This once-popular Moss Rose displays enormous buds that open to large, globular, deep crimson blooms; during early summer they produce a lovely fragrance. It is a vigorous bush that can reach a height of 4 ft (1.2 m) and is suitable for bedding displays. Unfortunately the leaves are subject to mildew and in wet weather the blooms ball. It needs only moderate pruning. **ZONES 5–11.**

PAUL, UK, 1890

PARENTAGE UNKNOWN

## 'Crimson Glory'
*(top left)*

MODERN, LARGE-FLOWERED/
HYBRID TEA, DARK RED,
REPEAT-FLOWERING

For many years 'Crimson Glory' was the most reliable dark red Large-flowered Rose available. It bears large, deep velvety crimson blooms that emerge from long, pointed buds and is truly repeat-flowering right through summer and into autumn. There is an exceptionally pronounced damask fragrance. The double flowers each consist of 30 petals arranged to form a rounded cup. It is a bushy variety with vigorous, slightly spreading growth and dark green, leathery leaves, making a good bedding rose that will also flourish as a standard. It can be propagated by budding, but is prickly, so wear gloves when handling the stems. Many hybridists have attempted to use 'Crimson Glory' as a parent; the most famous and successful result is 'Ena Harkness'. **'Climbing Crimson Glory'** was discovered by Millar of South Africa in 1941. It is similar to the parent, but is only summer flowering and has stiff, branching growth that is best trained on a cool wall where it will not burn. Both forms of this variety are fairly vulnerable to mildew. **ZONES 4–9.**

KORDES, GERMANY, 1935

'CATHRINE KORDES' SEEDLING ×
'W. E. CHAPLIN'

NATIONAL ROSE SOCIETY GOLD
MEDAL 1936, JAMES ALEXANDER
GAMBLE ROSE FRAGRANCE
AWARD 1961

C

### 'Crimson Shower'
*(top)*

MODERN, RAMBLER,
MEDIUM RED

The flowers produced on this rose are carried in large, dense clusters on a very vigorous but lax plant. The small, scarlet-crimson, double blooms are made up of 20 petals to form a rosette shape and are slightly fragrant. Although the variety is not repeat-flowering, the first flush begins late after mid-summer to early autumn, which can give the wrong impression. The trailing stems of this rose make it a very suitable subject for pergolas and pillars, but it really excels as a weeping standard or 'umbrella rose'. It is remarkably free of disease for this type of plant, which can be propagated either by budding or from cuttings. The light green foliage is made up of many small leaflets. **ZONES 4–9.**

NORMAN, UK, 1951

SEEDLING OF 'EXCELSA'

NATIONAL ROSE SOCIETY TRIAL
GROUND CERTIFICATE 1951,
ROYAL HORTICULTURAL SOCIETY
AWARD OF GARDEN MERIT 1993

### 'Criterion'

MODERN, LARGE-FLOWERED/
HYBRID TEA, DEEP PINK,
REPEAT-FLOWERING

This bedding variety bears large, double, rose red flowers that are very fragrant. They have good form and are repeat-flowering. It is a vigorous and tall plant with dark green foliage, easily propagated by budding. **ZONES 4–9.**

DE RUITER, THE NETHERLANDS,
1966

('INDEPENDENCE' × 'SIGNAL
RED') × 'PEACE'

### 'Crystal Palace'
POUlrek *(bottom)*
syn. 'Cristel Palace'

MODERN, PATIO/DWARF CLUS-
TER-FLOWERED, APRICOT BLEND,
REPEAT-FLOWERING

Valued for its light peachy cream, double blooms that repeat through summer and autumn, 'Crystal Palace' is a compact plant that grows to about 24 in (60 cm) tall. The shiny, mid-green leaves make a perfect backdrop to the lovely cup-shaped, medium-sized flowers. There is a light scent. **ZONES 5–9.**

OLESEN, DENMARK, 1995

PARENTAGE UNKNOWN

C

### 'Crystalline' ARObipy *(right)*

MODERN, LARGE-FLOWERED/HYBRID TEA, WHITE, REPEAT-FLOWERING

A variety that excels as an exhibition rose, 'Crystalline' bears large white blooms filled with 35 petals tightly arranged to give a high center. There is a spicy fragrance. Usually borne singly on strong, upright stems, the flowers repeat through the warmer months. If the old blooms are not deadheaded, they develop into large, globular orange hips that decorate this tall, bushy plant through autumn and into winter. The foliage is medium sized and semi-glossy. When handling it, be careful of the light green-tan prickles. ZONES 4–9.

CHRISTENSEN AND CARRUTH, USA, 1987

'BRIDAL PINK' × ('BLUE NILE' × ['IVORY TOWER' × 'ANGEL FACE'])

### 'Cuddles' *(top)*

MODERN, MINIATURE, ORANGE-PINK, REPEAT-FLOWERING

Ovoid buds, opening to deep coral-pink flowers that contain in excess of 55 petals, make 'Cuddles' a natural for hot climates. The slightly fragrant florets have Large-flowered form. Repeat bloom is fast with good production of both single blooms and small sprays. It is one of the few Miniatures with a Cluster-flowered Rose as its seed parent. The hybridizer died the year before this rose was honored by the American Rose Society. ZONES 4–11.

SCHWARTZ, USA, 1978

'ZORINA' × SEEDLING

AMERICAN ROSE SOCIETY AWARD OF EXCELLENCE 1979

C

## 'Cuisse de Nymphe Emué'

syns 'Belle Therese', 'Incarnata', 'La Royale',
'La Séduisante', 'La Virginale', 'Maiden's Blush'

OLD, ALBA, MEDIUM PINK

This is one of the oldest of the popular roses in
England and France, and its history is crowded
with names. The earliest forms may date from the
fifteenth century. The name is translated from
French as the 'thigh of a passionate nymph',
which prompted the Victorians to give it a new
set of labels. It bears distinctive, fat, rich pink
blooms that are beautiful as they open, becoming
reflexed with age and paling at the edges. There is
a strong but refined fragrance. The strong, arching canes are covered with blue-gray leaves.
ZONES 4–10.

PARENTAGE UNKNOWN

## 'Cupcake' SPIcup (*above*)

MODERN, MINIATURE, MEDIUM PINK, REPEAT-FLOWERING

This lovely rose is still one of the best-selling
varieties in the USA. The clear pink blooms containing about 60 petals have the traditional high
center characteristic of modern Large-flowered
Roses, and this accounts for the success of this
rose on the show tables. The florets are produced
in small clusters of 1–5 blooms and have no
fragrance. The foliage is a glossy dark green,
indicating a high degree of resistance to diseases.
It is one of the few Miniature Roses bred by an
amateur hybridizer to win the American Rose
Society Award of Excellence. ZONES 4–11.

SPIES, USA, 1981

'GENE BOERNER' × ('GAY PRINCESS' × 'YELLOW JEWEL')

AMERICAN ROSE SOCIETY AWARD OF EXCELLENCE 1983

## 'Cupid' *(right)*

MODERN, LARGE-FLOWERED
CLIMBER, LIGHT PINK

Although only summer flowering, the very large, cupped flowers on this variety glow with color. The blooms are pale pink, tinted with peach, and display golden stamens. The blooms are borne singly on stiff, branching stems amid large leaves, and if left uncut, will develop into large, decorative hips that provide autumn and winter color. Vigorous and upright, it is suitable for pillars.
**ZONES 4–9.**

CANT, UK, 1915

PARENTAGE UNKNOWN

## 'Cuthbert Grant'

MODERN, MODERN SHRUB, DARK
RED, REPEAT-FLOWERING

This bushy grower gives an intermittent display of deep purplish red, semi-double, large, cupped blooms through the summer season. They emerge from oval buds and give a slight fragrance. The plant is vigorous and upright, and is decorated with glossy green foliage. It is propagated by either budding or from cuttings. **ZONES 4–9.**

MARSHALL, CANADA, 1967

('CRIMSON GLORY' ×
'ASSINIBOINE') × 'ASSINIBOINE'

## 'Cymbaline' AUSlean *(right)*

syns 'Cymbelene', 'Cymbeline'

MODERN, MODERN SHRUB,
LIGHT PINK, REPEAT-FLOWERING

Although the flowers of this shrub rose may not please all tastes because of their unusual color, they can be used to beautiful effect in most color schemes. The breeder describes them as 'gray-pink', although they can be almost ashy. They are large and double and are filled with about 35 petals. There is a pronounced fragrance of myrrh, and the variety is truly repeat-flowering. This is an elegant rose with arching growth that spreads to ground level, showing its flowers to full effect. It can be propagated by budding. Unfortunately, it is a little prone to black spot. **ZONES 4–9.**

AUSTIN, UK, 1982

SEEDLING × 'LILIAN AUSTIN'

**D**

**D**

## 'D'Aguesseau' *(above)*

OLD, GALLICA, MEDIUM RED

Upright and vigorous with strong stems and few thorns, this fine rose can reach 5 ft (1.5 m) high and has plentiful foliage, which is a luscious dark green. The nicely scented flowers are borne in tight clusters from fat, dark red buds. They are very full of vibrant cerise petals with paler undersides, and form full, flat flowers that are quartered in form with tight buttons in the center. The color neither fades nor deepens with age. It is well scented and flowers in mid-summer. Vibert, the giant of French rose hybridizing, grew up in Paris during the Revolution and served as a soldier in Napoleon's army. Shortly before he died, aged 89, he told his young grandson, 'I have loved only Napoleon and roses.' ZONES 4–10.

VIBERT, FRANCE, 1837

PARENTAGE UNKNOWN

## 'Daily Mail Scented Rose' *(top right)*

MODERN, LARGE-FLOWERED/HYBRID TEA, RED BLEND, REPEAT-FLOWERING

Pronounced the best scented rose when it was introduced in 1927, this variety has crimson flowers that are shaded maroon and vermilion and have dark crimson undersides. The blooms are very fragrant and appear through summer and autumn. A vigorous plant with dark green foliage, it is propagated by budding. ZONES 4–9.

ARCHER, UK, 1927

'CHÂTEAU DE CLOS VOUGEOT' × 'KITCHENER OF KHARTOUM'

## 'Dainty Bess' *(above)*

MODERN, LARGE-FLOWERED/HYBRID TEA, LIGHT PINK, REPEAT-FLOWERING

'Dainty Bess' has been described as one of the loveliest roses ever bred. It has large single blooms that are a soft rose pink with very distinct maroon stamens which give an added beauty. The fragrant flowers continue to bloom through summer and autumn on a plant that has vigorous, upright growth and deep green leathery foliage. It is propagated by budding. **'Climbing Dainty Bess'** (van Barneveld, USA, 1935) is summer flowering, and a good variety to grow on a wall. ZONES 4–9.

ARCHER, UK, 1925

'OPHELIA' × 'KITCHENER OF KHARTOUM'

### 'Dairy Maid' *(right)*

MODERN, CLUSTER-FLOWERED/FLORIBUNDA, LIGHT YELLOW,
REPEAT-FLOWERING

The buds on this rose are yellow, splashed carmine,
opening into flowers that are yellow, fading to
white. Large and single, they are produced in big
clusters from summer to autumn. It is an upright
grower with glossy foliage. ZONES 4–9.

LEGRICE, UK, 1957

('POULSEN'S PINK' × 'ELLINOR LEGRICE') × 'MRS PIERRE S. DUPONT'

NATIONAL ROSE SOCIETY CERTIFICATE OF MERIT 1957

**D**

### 'Dame de Coeur'
*(right)*
syns 'Dama di Cuori',
'Herz-Dame', 'Queen
of Hearts'

MODERN, LARGE-FLOWERED/
HYBRID TEA, MEDIUM RED,
REPEAT-FLOWERING

This variety has large,
cherry red, double
blooms with consider-
able fragrance that
appear through
summer and autumn
with good continuity.
The growth is vigorous
and upright, and it
has glossy dark green
foliage. An important
variety in the history
and development of the
rose, it is a reliable bedding plant. ZONES 4–9.

LENS, BELGIUM, 1958

'PEACE' × 'D'AGUESSEAU' ×
'INDEPENDENCE'

NATIONAL ROSE SOCIETY TRIAL
GROUND CERTIFICATE 1958

they are borne continu-
ously from summer
to autumn on long,
strong stems. A suitable
plant for bedding, it
has vigorous bushy
growth and leathery
foliage. ZONES 4–9.

DICKSON, UK, 1926

PARENTAGE UNKNOWN

NATIONAL ROSE SOCIETY GOLD
MEDAL 1926

### 'Dame Edith Helen'

MODERN, LARGE-FLOWERED/
HYBRID TEA, MEDIUM PINK,
REPEAT-FLOWERING

The very large, glowing
pink double blooms
of 'Dame Edith Helen'
have a strong perfume.
Although not very
free in appearance,

### 'Dame Prudence'
*(above right)*

MODERN, MODERN SHRUB,
LIGHT PINK

Also classified as an
English Rose, 'Dame
Prudence' was devel-
oped in the 1960s and

has since been dis-
carded by the breeder,
yet it is still widely
grown. The double
flowers are soft pink
with lighter undersides,
and have 65 petals with
a good fragrance. It has

loose, floppy growth
that is slightly subject
to disease; it is best
planted as a specimen.
ZONES 4–9.

AUSTIN, UK, 1969

'IVORY FASHION' × ('CONSTANCE
SPRY' × 'MA PERKINS')

**D**

### 'Dame Wendy' CANson *(left)*

MODERN, CLUSTER-FLOWERED/FLORIBUNDA,
MEDIUM PINK, REPEAT-FLOWERING

The medium-sized, double flowers of 'Dame Wendy' are clear pink and mildly scented. They are borne from summer to autumn on a moderately growing, slightly spreading plant. A good subject for bedding or as a standard, it has glossy dark green, healthy foliage. ZONES 4–9.

CANTS, UK, 1991

'ENGLISH MISS' × 'MEMENTO'

ROYAL NATIONAL ROSE SOCIETY TRIAL GROUND
CERTIFICATE 1990

### 'Danaë' *(right)*

MODERN, MODERN SHRUB,
LIGHT YELLOW,
REPEAT-FLOWERING

The clusters of medium-sized double blooms on this variety are deep yolk yellow, fading white as they age. They have very little scent, and they continue to appear through summer and autumn. 'Danaë' is a healthy medium-sized shrub with rich green shining foliage; a good subject for a shrub border when planted in groups. ZONES 4–9.

PEMBERTON, UK, 1913

'TRIER' × 'GLOIRE DE CHÉDANE-
GUINOISEAU'

### 'Danse des Sylphes' MALcair *(left)*

syn. 'Grimpant Danse de Sylphes'

MODERN, LARGE-FLOWERED CLIMBER,
ORANGE-RED, REPEAT-FLOWERING

This vigorous Climber has flowers that are rich red suffused with geranium red. Globular and medium sized, they appear in large clusters and have little scent. A good healthy plant for walls and pillars, it has glossy deep green foliage on upright stems. ZONES 4–9.

MALLERIN, FRANCE, 1959

'SPECTACULAR' ('DANCE DU FEU') × ('PEACE' ×
'INDEPENDENCE')

D

### 'Dapple Dawn'
AUSapple *(above)*

syn. 'English Dawn'

MODERN, MODERN SHRUB,
LIGHT PINK, REPEAT-FLOWERING

Probably one of the most floriferous of the English Roses, 'Dapple Dawn' has large single blooms that are a delicate shade of pink. They have little scent, but the flowers appear in big clusters that are produced in profusion throughout summer and autumn. It is a good subject for borders and as a specimen plant and is propagated by budding. ZONES 4–9.

AUSTIN, UK, 1983

SPORT OF 'RED COAT'

### 'Darling Flame'
MEliucca *(top right)*

syns 'Minuette', 'Minuetto'

MODERN, MINIATURE, ORANGE-RED, REPEAT-FLOWERING

The blooms on this rose are mandarin-red to vermilion with yellow anthers. They are double with 25 petals, globular, small and have a slight fragrance. The foliage is glossy dark green on a vigorous plant. 'Darling Flame' has been used extensively in borders and in containers for patios. The bloom cycle is fairly rapid during the growing season. This is one of the few Miniatures used as a tree, as it usually blooms in clusters that cover the entire bush. Jack Harkness used it in his hybridizing program for new Miniature Roses. ZONES 5–11.

MEILLAND, FRANCE, 1971

('RIMOSA' × 'JOSEPHINE WHEATCROFT') × 'ZAMBRA'

### 'Dawn Chorus'
DICquaser *(above)*

MODERN, LARGE-FLOWERED/HYBRID TEA, ORANGE BLEND, REPEAT-FLOWERING

Medium-sized, classically shaped blooms of deep orange appear very freely on short stems on this bushy variety. There is a continuity of bloom through summer and autumn, the flowers having a light scent. It has reddish leaves and is a suitable subject for bedding or as a well-furnished standard. ZONES 4–9.

DICKSON, UK, 1993

'WISHING' × 'PEER GYNT'

DUBLIN GOLD MEDAL 1993, ROSE OF THE YEAR 1993, GLASGOW CERTIFICATE OF MERIT 1995

D

### 'Day Light' INTerlight
### (above)
#### syn. 'Daylight'

MODERN, CLUSTER-FLOWERED/
FLORIBUNDA, APRICOT BLEND,
REPEAT-FLOWERING

The large clusters of big apricot-yellow, double flowers of this bush rose make a delightful display in summer. The plant would be especially suited to either a mixed shrub border or massed planting. The foliage is quite a deep green. It is reasonably healthy and can be propagated by budding. **ZONES 4–9.**

ILSINK, THE NETHERLANDS, 1991

PARENTAGE UNKNOWN

BELFAST GOLD MEDAL 1992

### 'Daybreak'
#### syn. 'Day Break'

MODERN, MODERN SHRUB, MEDIUM YELLOW, REPEAT-FLOWERING

'Daybreak' has clusters of golden yellow flowers that turn light yellow and have dark golden stamens. They are just semi-double (almost single), have a rich musk fragrance and appear through summer and autumn. It is a tidy shrub with very dark chocolate brown foliage that turns dark green with age, and is a good subject to plant as a specimen shrub. Propagation is by budding or from cuttings. **ZONES 4–9.**

PEMBERTON, UK, 1918

'TRIER' × 'LIBERTY'

### 'Daydream' (left)

MODERN, CLUSTER-FLOWERED
CLIMBER, LIGHT PINK

This climbing variety has large, semi-double flowers. The blooms are a very pale pink to almost white, and have a slight scent. 'Daydream' has medium green glossy foliage. Free flowering, it is suitable for growing on a trellis or as a pillar rose. From the famous Australian breeder Alister Clark, it is now only available from Australian nurseries. **ZONES 5–10.**

CLARK, AUSTRALIA, 1925

PROBABLY SEEDLING ×
'ROSY MORN'

**‘De la Maître-École’**
*(right)*
syn. ‘Rose du Maître
d’École’

OLD, GALLICA, MAUVE

This rose was named
after a village near
Angers in France and
for many years was
wrongly named ‘Rose
du Maître d’École’.
It is a relaxed, dense
shrub up to about 3 ft
(1 m) high and wide.
The stems are arching,
dark grayish to green
and practically thornless,
and the foliage is dark
green and profuse. The
highly scented flowers
are very large, 4 in
(10 cm) in diameter,
and even larger in good
soils. They are very
double and almost
always quartered, with
a little green pip in the
center surrounded by
a button of infolding
petals. The color is
difficult to describe—
it is basically deep pink
with silvery highlights
and shadings of mauve
and soft purple. For
a few weeks in mid-
summer it is a sheer
delight. ZONES 5–11.

COQUEREAU, FRANCE, 1831

PARENTAGE UNKNOWN

ROYAL HORTICULTURAL SOCIETY
AWARD OF GARDEN MERIT 1993

**‘De Meaux’** *(above)*

OLD, CENTIFOLIA, MEDIUM PINK

This is one of the
smallest of the
Centifolia Roses, both
in stature and size of
flower. It seldom grows
above 3 ft (1 m) high,
sending up many
gray-green shoots with
numerous prickles.
The light greenish gray
foliage is small, firm
and rugged. The small,
full, scented flowers are
rather like frilly pom-
pons; they are arranged
in sizeable bright pink
clusters and are at their
best quality early in
summer. This rose
makes a useful short
dividing hedge and is
excellent for group
planting. It is also a
good container plant.
There is a white form
available, generally
listed as ‘White de
Meaux’. ZONES 5–11.

SWEET, UK, PRE-1789

PARENTAGE UNKNOWN

**'Deb's Delight'**  LEGsweet
*(below left)*

MODERN, CLUSTER-FLOWERED/FLORIBUNDA,
PINK BLEND, REPEAT-FLOWERING

This low-growing, bushy variety is
a good subject for small borders and
pots and to grow as a short standard.
Its silvery salmon-pink, double
flowers appear very freely through
summer and autumn; they each
have 35 petals and they are fragrant.
'Deb's Delight' has mid-green, semi-
glossy foliage and is propagated
from cuttings or by budding.
**ZONES 4–9.**

LEGRICE, UK, 1983

'TIP TOP' × SEEDLING

ROYAL NATIONAL ROSE SOCIETY TRIAL GROUND
CERTIFICATE 1978

**'Dearest'** *(above)*
MODERN, CLUSTER-FLOWERED/
FLORIBUNDA, PINK BLEND,
REPEAT-FLOWERING

A very popular variety,
'Dearest' has rosy
salmon-pink double
flowers with golden
stamens. Appearing
through summer and
autumn, they are well
shaped and fragrant.
The growth habit is
bushy and to medium
size; it has dark glossy
foliage and prefers a
position in full sun,
and is suitable for
bedding or to grow
as a standard. **'Climbing
Dearest'** (Ruston,
Australia, 1970) is
vigorous and mostly
summer flowering,
although some blooms
appear intermittently
in autumn. **ZONES 4–9.**

DICKSON, UK, 1960

SEEDLING × 'SPARTAN'

NATIONAL ROSE SOCIETY GOLD
MEDAL 1961

**'Debutante'**  *(above right)*
MODERN, RAMBLER, LIGHT PINK

Those who have seen this rose
paired with 'Bleu Magenta' at
Mottisfont will understand why
Graham Thomas holds such a high
opinion of this *Rosa wichurana*
hybrid; rose pink blossoms on short
stems adorn the long canes, and
the clusters fade quickly in the sun.
It has a delicious apple fragrance.
The healthy, dark green glossy foli-

age is not subject to mildew, which
makes it a stronger rose than its
more famous relative 'Dorothy
Perkins'; in fact, New Zealand rose
author Sally Allison says it is 'more
beautiful and refined'. It has been
submerged in the fame of the older
rose. It is easy to grow and can reach
15 ft (4.5 m). **ZONES 4–11.**

WALSH, USA, 1902

'BARONNE ADOLPHE DE ROTHSCHILD' ×
*ROSA WICHURANA*

### 'Deep Secret'  *(right)*
syn. 'Mildred Scheel'

**MODERN, LARGE-FLOWERED/HYBRID TEA, DARK RED, REPEAT-FLOWERING**

The very deep crimson flowers of this variety are double with 40 petals, large and very fragrant; they appear continuously throughout summer and autumn. It has upright growth to medium height and glossy dark green foliage, and is a good subject for a bedding scheme. **ZONES 4–9.**

TANTAU, GERMANY, 1977

PARENTAGE UNKNOWN

ANERKANNTE DEUTSCHE ROSE 1978

### 'Delambre'  *(below)*
**OLD, PORTLAND, DEEP PINK, REPEAT-FLOWERING**

Portland Roses have always been praised for their brilliant scarlet flowers, and 'Delambre' is no exception—the carmine, deeply reddish pink blooms fade to lilac-pink and are fully double and quartered. The many clusters are packed with petals. The blooms are produced freely through summer and autumn, and are very fragrant. The upright, compact shrub bears healthy foliage and a few prickles and is particularly attractive when covered in autumn foliage and hips. This rose, which will repeat its display of flowers if given rich soil and frequent feeding, is a good subject for a container. The firm of Moreau & Robert of Angers, France, produced many outstanding roses, some of which have been in the catalogues since their creation. **ZONES 4–11.**

MOREAU & ROBERT, FRANCE, 1863

PARENTAGE UNKNOWN

### 'Delicata'  *(below)*
**MODERN, HYBRID RUGOSA, LIGHT PINK, REPEAT-FLOWERING**

'Delicata' has lilac-pink, semi-double flowers with a light scent. It has 10 petals, and flowering continues through summer and autumn. One of the shorter-growing Hybrid Rugosas, it has deep green wrinkled foliage. In the past this variety has proved notoriously difficult to propagate, although modern methods may have circumvented this problem. **ZONES 4–9.**

COOLING, UK, 1898

PARENTAGE UNKNOWN

**D**

### 'Demokracie' *(left)*
syns 'Blaze Superior', 'Blaze Improved', 'New Blaze'

MODERN, LARGE-FLOWERED CLIMBER, DARK RED, REPEAT-FLOWERING

'Demokracie' produces large clusters of intense red flowers with a good form, appearing in procession through summer and autumn on lateral growth. They are semi-double but have virtually no scent. This is a vigorous plant for walls, pergolas and pillars. ZONES 4–9.

BÖHM, CZECHOSLOVAKIA, 1935

PARENTAGE UNKNOWN

### 'Denise Grey'  MEIxetal  *(left)*
syns 'Caprice', 'Make-Up'

MODERN, MODERN SHRUB, LIGHT PINK

A winner of two prestigious awards, 'Denise Grey' is a very floriferous shrub valued for its large bunches of medium-sized, gentle pink flowers. They are semi-double, flat to cupped in shape and show off a mass of dark stamens at the center. This is a medium-growing, healthy rose that is well furnished with reasonably large, glossy green foliage. For a mixed border, it makes a beautiful, summer-flowering shrub. It is disease resistant. ZONES 5–9.

MEILLAND, FRANCE, 1988

PARENTAGE UNKNOWN

BAGATELLE GOLD MEDAL 1992, FRANKFURT GOLD MEDAL 1992

### 'Dentelle de Bruxelles'  *(left)*

MODERN, MODERN SHRUB, LIGHT PINK, REPEAT-FLOWERING

'Dentelle de Bruxelles' grows into a large shrub, often wider than it is tall. It grows with great freedom in the spring, covering itself in pale pink blooms in small and large clusters. There is some repeat bloom. The mid-green foliage is abundant and right down to ground level. This variety is an excellent choice for planting in large gardens and parks where its pale-colored flowers show up very well from a distance. It also makes a good, tall informal hedge. There are no disease problems. So far it is not well known outside Europe. ZONES 4–11.

LENS, BELGIUM, 1988

PARENTAGE UNKNOWN

D

## 'Dentelle de Malines' *(above)*
syn. 'Lens Pink'

**MODERN, MODERN SHRUB, MEDIUM PINK**

This shrub with its pretty pink flowers is reminiscent of a Hybrid Musk but it is only summer
flowering and the blooms have a light scent. It is
a medium to tall grower with dark green foliage
that looks its best when planted in groups in a big
border. **ZONES 4–9.**

LENS, BELGIUM, 1986

PARENTAGE UNKNOWN

## 'Desprez à Fleur Jaune' *(above right)*
syns 'Jaune Desprez', 'Jean Desprez',
'Noisette Desprez'

**OLD, NOISETTE, YELLOW BLEND, REPEAT-FLOWERING**

The pink buds of this rose open to reveal pale
yellow blooms overshot with pink. Silky, fragrant
petals smelling of bananas form large, cupped
blooms. It can produce a range of colors, depending on soil, weather, shade or sun. The flowers
appear on short stems with the inner petals
muddled. There is a long blooming season and
some late repeat-flowering. It can reach 20 ft
(6 m) in a few seasons, has few prickles, does well
in poor soil and is best used on a wall or trellis
or climbing a tree; it likes shade in hot weather.
It has been said that the creator was handed this
rose just before he died. **ZONES 4–9.**

DESPREZ, FRANCE, 1830

'BLUSH NOISETTE' × 'PARKS' YELLOW TEA-SCENTED CHINA'

ROYAL HORTICULTURAL SOCIETY AWARD OF GARDEN MERIT 1993

## 'Deuil de Paul Fontaine' *(above)*
syn. 'Paul de Fontaine'

**OLD, MOSS, MAUVE, REPEAT-FLOWERING**

This rose is subject to mildew, but if this is controlled it will give some of the most sumptuous
blooms of any Moss Rose. Reaching only about
3 ft (1 m), the shrub is bushy and fairly tidy in
habit although it is quite thorny. The leaves are
red at first, ageing to dark green, and are relatively
smooth for a Moss Rose. The buds are well endowed with finely textured, dark green moss. The
fragrant flowers, which are very dark red to purple
with unusual chocolate-colored shadings, are
cupped until fully open when the blooms become
flat and cushion-like. There is some repeat-
flowering in late summer. If it is deadheaded
regularly, it will bloom until autumn. **ZONES 4–11.**

FONTAINE, FRANCE, 1873

PARENTAGE UNKNOWN

D

### 'Devoniensis'
*(right)*
syns 'Magnolia Rose',
'Victoria'

OLD, TEA, WHITE,
REPEAT-FLOWERING

This shrub rose would
be extinct now if a
climbing sport had not
shown up; '**Climbing
Devoniensis**' is now
more popular than
the shrub. Both bloom
early and profusely
and have buds that are
tinged red and open
to very large, white
blooms with yellow
centers. The inner
petals are curled and
there is a strong Tea
or lemon fragrance.
As the first Tea Rose
to be bred in England
it has not found a
warm home there,
but it has been extra-
ordinarily popular in
mild climates. Brilliant
dark green foliage
covers the long canes,
which have few prickles.
It repeats from spring
until autumn and has
been one of the parents
of some important
roses, such as 'Lady
Mary Fitzwilliam'.
ZONES 6–11.

FOSTER, UK, 1838

'SMITH'S YELLOW CHINA' ×
'PARKS' YELLOW TEA-SCENTED
CHINA'

### 'Diablotin'  DELpo *(above)*
syn. 'Little Devil'

MODERN, CLUSTER-FLOWERED/FLORIBUNDA, MEDIUM RED,
REPEAT-FLOWERING

This variety has brilliant medium red, semi-
double flowers with 17 petals that are produced
in small clusters and have a slight fragrance. They
appear freely throughout summer and autumn
on a compact-growing plant. 'Diablotin' deserves
to be more widely acknowledged but is now unfortunately only available in France. ZONES 4–9.

DELBARD-CHABERT, FRANCE, 1961

'ORLÉANS ROSE' × 'FASHION'

### 'Diadem'  TANmeda
syn. 'Diadeem'

MODERN, CLUSTER-FLOWERED/
FLORIBUNDA, MEDIUM PINK,
REPEAT-FLOWERING

This relatively small-
growing bush rose
bears long-stemmed
clusters of rounded,
clear pink blooms.
There is a light scent
and the foliage is dark
green. 'Diadem' would
be a suitable choice
near the front of a bed
or border, where it will
repeat-flower through
summer and autumn.
The relatively healthy
growth can be propa-
gated by budding.
ZONES 4–9.

TANTAU, GERMANY, 1986

PARENTAGE UNKNOWN

DURBANVILLE GOLD MEDAL 1990
BELFAST CERTIFICATE OF MERIT
1994, GLASGOW CERTIFICATE OF
MERIT 1995

### 'Diamond Jubilee' *(right)*

MODERN, LARGE-FLOWERED/HYBRID TEA, LIGHT YELLOW, REPEAT-FLOWERING

This variety has buff yellow, double, cupped flowers with 28 petals. They are strongly fragrant and continue to appear through summer and autumn. Suitable as a bedding subject, 'Diamond Jubilee' has an upright, compact growth habit and leathery foliage. **ZONES 4–9.**

BOERNER, USA, 1947

'MARÉCHAL NIEL' × 'FEU PERNET-DUCHER'

ALL-AMERICA ROSE SELECTION 1948, ROYAL NATIONAL ROSE SOCIETY TRIAL GROUND CERTIFICATE 1952

**D**

### 'Dick Koster'

MODERN, POLYANTHA, DEEP PINK, REPEAT-FLOWERING

This variety, one of a whole host of the Koster family of roses, bears profuse clusters of cup-shaped, deep pink blooms. It is short and compact in stature and is used extensively as a subject for the pot-rose trade; it is very apt to produce color sports. The foliage is typical for a Polyantha: light green and suscep-tible to mildew in autumn. Propagation is by budding or from cuttings. **ZONES 5–9.**

KOSTER, THE NETHERLANDS, 1929

SPORT OF 'ANNEKE KOSTER'

### 'Dicky' DICkimono *(above)*

syns 'Anisley Dickson', 'Münchner Kindl'

MODERN, CLUSTER-FLOWERED/FLORIBUNDA, ORANGE-PINK, REPEAT-FLOWERING

This very free-flowering Cluster-flowered Rose has long, pointed buds that develop into reddish salmon-pink flowers with a lighter reverse. Slightly fragrant and double with 35 petals, blooms are produced in clusters of 5–10 on gold stems. 'Dicky' is a bushy variety that grows to medium height and has glossy green foliage. **ZONES 4–9.**

DICKSON, UK, 1983

'CATHEDRAL' × 'MEMENTO'

ROYAL NATIONAL ROSE SOCIETY PRESIDENT'S INTERNATIONAL TROPHY 1984, BELFAST CERTIFICATE OF MERIT 1985, ROYAL HORTICULTURAL SOCIETY AWARD OF GARDEN MERIT 1993

D

### 'Die Welt' DIEkor
*(above)*
syn. 'The World'

MODERN, LARGE-FLOWERED/
HYBRID TEA, ORANGE BLEND,
REPEAT-FLOWERING

Large, perfectly formed flowers that are slightly fragrant and are a blend of orange, red and yellow appear through summer and autumn on this variety. They are double, with 25 petals, and high centered, which makes 'Die Welt' a very popular exhibition rose. It is a very tall plant with glossy foliage that can sometimes be subject to mildew in autumn.
**ZONES 4–9.**

KORDES, GERMANY, 1976

SEEDLING × 'PEER GYNT'

### 'Diorama'
*(above right)*

MODERN, LARGE-FLOWERED/
HYBRID TEA, YELLOW BLEND,
REPEAT-FLOWERING

Appearing with good continuity through summer and autumn, the large flowers of this variety are high-centered and apricot-yellow. They open loose and flat and are very fragrant. 'Diorama' is a healthy, large-growing plant with big, mid-green, semi-glossy foliage. It is good for bedding schemes.
**ZONES 4–9.**

DERUITER, THE NETHERLANDS,
1965

'PEACE' × 'BEAUTÉ'

ROYAL NATIONAL ROSE SOCIETY
TRIAL GROUND CERTIFICATE 1965

### 'Dirigent' *(above)*
syn. 'The Conductor'

MODERN, MODERN SHRUB, MEDIUM RED, REPEAT-FLOWERING

This shrub has blood red semi-double blooms that have a slight fragrance. They appear in clusters made up of as many as 28 blooms. 'Dirigent' is a vigorous plant with very healthy, leathery foliage that is good for borders or as a specimen shrub. **ZONES 4–9.**

TANTAU, GERMANY, 1956

'FANAL' × 'KARL WEINHAÜSEN'

ANERKANNTE DEUTSCHE ROSE 1958

## 'Disco Dancer' DICinfra *(right)*

MODERN, CLUSTER-FLOWERED/FLORIBUNDA, ORANGE-RED,
REPEAT-FLOWERING

This bush bears sprays of orange-scarlet, cupped, double flowers from spring through to autumn. They appear on a dense, rounded plant that produces a mass of glossy green foliage. This variety is suitable for bedding and as a standard. There is a slight fragrance. **ZONES 4–9.**

DICKSON, UK, 1984

'CATHEDRAL' × 'MEMENTO'

THE HAGUE GOLD MEDAL 1982, ROYAL NATIONAL ROSE
SOCIETY TRIAL GROUND CERTIFICATE 1982, BELFAST
CERTIFICATE OF MERIT 1985

**D**

## 'Dr A. J. Verhage' *(right)*
syn. 'Golden Wave'

MODERN, LARGE-FLOWERED/HYBRID TEA, DEEP YELLOW,
REPEAT-FLOWERING

This variety, which set the standard for greenhouse roses when it appeared in 1963, was bred from the poor-growing but brilliantly colored 'Tawny Gold' and the slow-opening greenhouse variety 'Baccará'; it gained its gorgeous old-gold coloring from the former and its strength from the latter. The short-growing bush produces great quantities of lovely buds that open to show amber stamens, and strongly fragrant flowers with 22–30 nicely waved petals. 'Dr A. J. Verhage' is still a lovely rose for cutting, although it does not travel as well to overseas markets as more recent yellows. The dark foliage is subject to mildew.
**ZONES 5–11.**

VERBEEK, THE NETHERLANDS, 1963.

'TAWNY GOLD' × ('BACCARÁ' × SEEDLING)

ROYAL NATIONAL ROSE SOCIETY TRIAL GROUND
CERTIFICATE 1960

## 'Dr Eckener'

MODERN, HYBRID RUGOSA, PINK BLEND, REPEAT-FLOWERING

'Dr Eckener' forms a tall, vigorous shrub with huge, coarse, *Rosa rugosa*-like leaves and huge thorns. The flowers are yellow, tinged with coppery rose, fading to soft pink, their unique color probably being the reason for this variety's continued use in gardens. The large, fragrant blooms are cupped and semi-double and appear on the plant from summer through to autumn.
**ZONES 4–11.**

BERGER, GERMANY, 1930

'GOLDEN EMBLEM' × UNKNOWN HYBRID RUGOSA

**D**

### 'Dr Huey' *(right)*
syn. 'Shafter'

MODERN, LARGE-FLOWERED
CLIMBER, DARK RED

An extremely strong grower, 'Dr Huey' covers itself early in the season with masses of small, 2 in (5 cm), semi-double blooms with 10–15 petals. The flowers appear only once, but they have some fragrance and are a grand spectacle for a short period. 'Dr Huey', much used in Australia and elsewhere as an understock, and growing strongly in many old gardens, is handy when a strong-growing, dark-colored Climber with flexible canes is required. It looks superb growing into and cascading from an old tree. **ZONES 4–11.**

THOMAS, USA, 1920

'ETHEL' × 'GRÜSS AN TEPLITZ'

AMERICAN ROSE SOCIETY GOLD
MEDAL, GERTRUDE M. HUBBARD
GOLD MEDAL 1924

### 'Dr Jackson'
AUStdoctor *(top right)*

MODERN, MODERN SHRUB,
MEDIUM RED,
REPEAT-FLOWERING

Also classified as an English Rose, 'Dr Jackson' has 5-petalled scarlet flowers with a central boss of golden stamens; they are borne singly and in small clusters and have no fragrance, but they do repeat-flower. With its mid-green foliage, few thorns and medium-

sized, spreading growth, it makes a good shrub for landscaping, especially if pruned lightly. It has no disease problems. **ZONES 4–11.**

AUSTIN, UK, 1987

PARENTAGE UNKNOWN

### 'Dr W. Van Fleet' *(center)*

MODERN, LARGE-FLOWERED
CLIMBER, LIGHT PINK

This historically important rose, which sported the repeat-flowering 'New Dawn', has pointed buds that open to large, double, crisp blooms with stamens. The flowers are a soft pink, ageing to flesh white, and are fragrant. It is a vigorous climber to over 20 ft (6 m) with good dark green glossy foliage. Spectacular in full bloom, it looks very effective when cascading from a tree, or covering a shed. **ZONES 4–11.**

VAN FLEET, USA, 1910

(ROSA WICHURANA ×
'SAFRANO') × 'SOUVENIR DU
PRÉSIDENT CARNOT'

### 'Dolly Parton' *(above)*

MODERN, LARGE-FLOWERED/HYBRID TEA,
ORANGE-RED, REPEAT-FLOWERING

This rose produces large, luminous orange-red, double blooms with good continuity from summer to autumn. They each have 35 petals and are very fragrant. A medium-height, upright grower, it has semi-glossy green foliage. **ZONES 4–9.**

WINCHEL, USA, 1984

'FRAGRANT CLOUD' × 'OKLAHOMA'

## 'Don Juan'

*(above)*

MODERN, LARGE-FLOWERED
CLIMBER, DARK RED,
REPEAT-FLOWERING

The large, double
blooms of this Climber
are dark velvety red, and
appear in succession
throughout summer
and autumn. They are
particularly fragrant
and have 35 petals.
'Don Juan' reaches a
moderate height and
is furnished with glossy
dark green, leathery
foliage. It is a good
subject for growing
on walls and up pillars.
ZONES 4–9.

MALANDRONE, USA, 1958

'NEW DAWN' SEEDLING ×
'NEW YORKER'

## 'Donau' *(top right)*

MODERN, LARGE-FLOWERED
CLIMBER, MAUVE

The mauve flowers of
this beautiful climbing
variety are borne
in small clusters in
summer. They are
semi-double and open
flat; the very centers
are almost white where
there is also a tiny
clump of stamens.
This is a lovely Large-
flowered Climber for
walls and pillars, covered
with delicate, glossy
green foliage that is
often admired when
the plant is not in
flower. ZONES 4–9.

PRASKAC, CZECHOSLOVAKIA,
1913

PARENTAGE UNKNOWN

## 'Doris Tysterman'

*(above right)*

syn. 'Doris Tijsterman'

MODERN, LARGE-FLOWERED/
HYBRID TEA, ORANGE BLEND,
REPEAT-FLOWERING

This bush bears large,
double, tangerine and
gold blooms with 28
petals through summer
and autumn. They
have a light fragrance.
A good bedding var-
iety, it has an upright
growth habit and
disease-resistant, glossy
foliage. ZONES 4–9.

WISBECH PLANT CO, UK, 1975

'PEER GYNT' × SEEDLING

## 'Dornröschen'

HACicularis

syn. 'Sleeping Beauty'

MODERN, MODERN SHRUB,
PINK BLEND, REPEAT-FLOWERING

Well-shaped blooms
of salmon to deep pink
with a reverse of yellow
are produced on this
variety from summer
to autumn. They are
double and fragrant
and appear in large
clusters. It is a good
subject for growing as
a specimen or in small
groups in borders.
ZONES 4–9.

KORDES, GERMANY, 1960

'PIKES PEAK' × 'BALLET'

D

### 'Dorola' MACshana
*(right)*
syns 'Benson & Hedges Special', 'Parkay'

MODERN, MINIATURE, DEEP YELLOW, REPEAT-FLOWERING

Deep yellow flowers, each with 26 petals, cover this vigorous bush. It grows like a small Cluster-flowered Rose, with blooms that do not fade with age, even in strong sunlight. The flowers have a strong fragrance when they first open. The foliage is a semi-glossy mid-green. Growing this rose is rewarding as it provides a con-stant supply of blooms throughout the season. 'Dorola' needs min-imum maintenance and is disease resistant. ZONES 4–11.

MCGREDY, NEW ZEALAND, 1982

'DARLING FLAME' × 'NEW DAY'

ROYAL NATIONAL ROSE SOCIETY CERTIFICATE OF MERIT 1980

### 'Dorothy Perkins'
*(top right)*

MODERN, RAMBLER, LIGHT PINK

This rose was very popular from the start, in part because it did well in a wide range of climates. 'Dorothy Perkins' is full of rose pink blooms for one month in summer. Its small flowers with fragrant, quilled petals appear in huge clusters, supported by glossy dark green foliage. The flexible canes with hooked prickles are easy to train, but when left to itself, the plant can ramble over barns, banks and buildings; it can reach up to 20 ft (6 m) in a single grow-ing season. The rose was named for the granddaughter of the founder of the nursery firm of Jackson & Perkins, and it became an overnight success. It has a strong tendency to mildew, but the German hybridizer Hetzel developed a mildew-free cultivar called 'Super Dorothy'. ZONES 4–11.

MILLER, USA, 1901

'MADAME GABRIEL LUIZET' × ROSA WICHURANA

### 'Dortmund' *(above)*

MODERN, LARGE-FLOWERED CLIMBER, MEDIUM RED, REPEAT-FLOWERING

The large open flowers, with 5–10 petals, are scarlet-red with a white eye. They have a light scent and are borne in clusters from spring to autumn on a vigorous plant with dark green glossy foliage. The growth habit is upright, although it may be pruned to make a shrub; it may also be grown as a pillar rose or on a north wall. It needs regular and heavy deadheading. ZONES 4–9.

KORDES, GERMANY, 1955

SEEDLING × ROSA KORDESII

ANERKANNTE DEUTSCHE ROSE 1954, PORTLAND GOLD MEDAL 1971

### 'Double Delight'
ANDeli *(right)*

MODERN, LARGE-FLOWERED/
HYBRID TEA, RED BLEND,
REPEAT-FLOWERING

This very bushy rose has large and double, high-centered blooms that are unique and immensely popular. They are creamy white, turning to strawberry red, have a considerable spicy scent and appear from spring to autumn. It is a fine bedding rose, although its disease resistance is suspect. It has an upright and spreading growth habit. **'Climbing Double Delight'** (AROclidd; syn. 'Grimpant Double Delight'; Christensen, USA, 1982) has precisely the same coloring. Summer flowering, it grows well on walls. ZONES 4–9.

SWIM AND ELLIS, USA, 1977

'GRANADA' × 'GARDEN PARTY'

BADEN-BADEN GOLD MEDAL 1976, ROME GOLD MEDAL 1976, ALL-AMERICA ROSE SELECTION 1977, BELFAST FRAGRANCE PRIZE 1980, JAMES ALEXANDER GAMBLE ROSE FRAGRANCE MEDAL 1986

### 'Douceur Normande' MEIpopul
*(top right)*
syns 'Coral Meidiland', 'Goose Fair', 'Sandton City', 'Stadt Hildescheim'

MODERN, MODERN SHRUB,
MEDIUM PINK,
REPEAT-FLOWERING

This landscape rose, bred for hardiness and for growing in difficult areas, grows strongly to 6 ft x 13 ft (2 m x 4 m) and forms a dense prickly barrier, which makes it good for planting along median strips and difficult steep banks. The single flowers are coral-pink and bloom in both large and small clusters. Hips form but the plant will continue to flower for a long period. It is very colorful in spring and keeps flowering well into autumn. If it grows too big it can be hard pruned in winter and still produce good spring blooms. It is immune to disease. ZONES 4–9.

MEILLAND, FRANCE, 1993

HYBRID OF *ROSA WICHURANA*

### 'Dove' AUSdove
*(above)*
syn. 'Dovedale'

MODERN, MODERN SHRUB,
LIGHT PINK, REPEAT-FLOWERING

'Dove' is a delightful little rose of the palest pink on a small, stocky bush. The lightly scented flowers are most attractive in the bud at all stages and open to a 40-petalled bloom 4 in (10 cm) across. Flower production is high and it repeat-flowers rapidly. The spreading growth makes it ideal as a standard or for bedding, while the thin wiry stems make the blooms ideal for posies. The disease-free foliage is small, dark green and semi-glossy, acting as a foil for the delicacy of the flowers and appearing on a plant that performs very well in extremely high heat. It is also classified as an English Rose. ZONES 4–10.

AUSTIN, UK, 1984

'WIFE OF BATH' × SEEDLING OF 'ICEBERG'

D

### 'Dream' *(right)*

MODERN, LARGE-FLOWERED/
HYBRID TEA, LIGHT PINK,
REPEAT-FLOWERING

This variety from
Kordes is grown world-
wide under glass for
the cut-flower trade.
The buds open very
slowly to show tints of
the palest pink flushed
pale apricot and salmon.
The medium-sized
blooms, which have
many petals and keep
extremely well when cut,
are produced profusely.
The glossy dark green
foliage has excellent
disease resistance.
'Dream' has produced
several very good
sports. **ZONES 5–11.**

KORDES, GERMANY, 1979
PARENTAGE UNKNOWN

### 'Dream Time'
*(top right)*
syn. 'Dreamtime'

MODERN, LARGE-FLOWERED/
HYBRID TEA, MEDIUM PINK,
REPEAT-FLOWERING

'Dream Time' has
large, to 5 in (13 cm),
double, high-centered,
pink flowers with
38 petals and a strong
scent. It lacks the
magnificent dark green
foliage and the strong
growth of 'Prima
Ballerina', being only
a moderately vigorous
plant with light green
foliage. It is a suitable
subject for bedding.
**ZONES 5–11.**

BEES, UK, 1977

'KORDES' PERFECTA' × 'PRIMA
BALLERINA'

### 'Dreaming Spires'
*(above)*

MODERN, LARGE-FLOWERED
CLIMBER, DEEP YELLOW,
REPEAT-FLOWERING

With two rich yellow
parents, the former
so strong as to be very
nearly a climbing rose,
it is not surprising to
find that 'Dreaming
Spires' is a deep
yellow Large-flowered
Climber. The richly
fragrant flowers are
well formed, double
with two dozen petals
and of medium size
to 3 in (8 cm) in
diameter. The repeat-
flowering performance
is excellent. 'Dreaming
Spires' was named by
John Mattock after
the university city of
Oxford, which is close
to where he lives. The
rose has dark green
foliage that sets the
flowers off to good
advantage. Unfortu-
nately it has been
largely overlooked, in
spite of winning a gold
medal in Northern
Ireland in 1977.
**ZONES 4–11.**

MATTOCK, UK, 1973

'BUCCANEER' × 'ARTHUR BELL'

BELFAST GOLD MEDAL 1977

## 'Dresden Doll'
### (right)

MODERN, MINIATURE, LIGHT
PINK, REPEAT-FLOWERING

The flowers of this rose
are a soft but delicate
dusty pink. The cupped
blooms are small,
with 18 petals, and are
moderately fragrant.
When fully open they
display another attrac-
tive feature—golden
stamens, which add to
the quality and appear-
ance of the florets. The
bush is compact and
throws many large
clusters that are archi-
tecturally attractive, but
large for a Miniature.
The plant seems to
want to grow outward
rather than upward. It
has won many awards
in the fully opened
bloom class. It is a
second generation of
repeat-flowering Moss
Miniatures born from
'Fairy Moss'. Moore
struggled for almost
25 years to introduce
the Moss Rose charac-
teristics of the once-
blooming Old Garden
Roses into repeat-
flowering Miniature
Roses. ZONES 4–11.

MOORE, USA, 1975

'FAIRY MOSS' × SEEDLING OF
UNKNOWN MOSS

## 'Drummer Boy'

HARvacity  (top right)

MODERN, CLUSTER-FLOWERED/
FLORIBUNDA, DARK RED,
REPEAT-FLOWERING

With three small
growers in its pedigree,

it is not surprising
that 'Drummer Boy'
is a spreading, low-
growing bush. The
semi-double, cup-
shaped flowers with
15 petals are a vivid
scarlet; they form small
sprays and have a spicy
fragrance. If spent
flowers are not dead-
headed, small, oval
greenish hips will form,
contrasting well with
the later flowers. It is
a good choice where
low color is required,
especially when planted
en masse for maximum
effect. The variety
has mid-green, semi-

glossy foliage and
purplish red thorns.
ZONES 5–11.

HARKNESS, UK, 1987

('WEE MAN' × ['SOUTHAMPTON'
× 'DARLING FLAME']) × 'RED
SPRITE'

DUBLIN CERTIFICATE OF MERIT
1986, ROYAL NATIONAL ROSE
SOCIETY TRIAL GROUND
CERTIFICATE 1987, BADEN-BADEN
ÖRP 1990, GLASGOW SILVER
MEDAL 1990

## 'Dublin Bay'    MACdub
### (above)

MODERN, LARGE-FLOWERED
CLIMBER, MEDIUM RED,
REPEAT-FLOWERING

One of the best red
Climbers available
today, 'Dublin Bay' has

oval buds and well-
shaped, bright red,
fragrant flowers, pro-
duced singly and in
clusters. The repeat-
flowering is outstand-
ing: no sooner has one
crop of flowers finished
than another is on the
way. It has dark green
glossy foliage and good
disease resistance. It
is one of the most pop-
ular Climbers in New
Zealand, also gaining
great acclaim in
Australia. ZONES 4–11.

MCGREDY, NEW ZEALAND, 1975

'BANTRY BAY' × 'ALTISSIMO'

ROYAL HORTICULTURAL SOCIETY
AWARD OF GARDEN MERIT 1993

D

### 'Duc de Cambridge'
*(top left)*

syn. 'Duchesse de Cambridge'

OLD, DAMASK, MAUVE

Although the prickly canes of this rose look ominous, when it blooms all bad thoughts are discarded as the flowers are impressive. This Damask has deep, purple-rose petals forming double, full, large blooms. It is probably the darkest of all Damask flowers. The bush has a sprawling growth habit and can reach 6 ft (1.8 m) without pruning, but if it is pruned after the summer flush it will respond better the next year. The foliage is dark and reddish when young. ZONES 4–11.

PRE-1848

PARENTAGE UNKNOWN

### 'Duc de Fitzjames'
*(top right)*

OLD, GALLICA, DARK RED/
DEEP PINK

'Duc de Fitzjames' is sometimes classified as a Centifolia. It is a dense, vigorous, thorny and upright shrub that can reach 6 ft (1.8 m) high, covered with large and lush gray-green foliage. The highly fragrant blooms, borne in sizeable clusters in mid-summer, are very large and full, up to 4 in (10 cm) across. They develop from round buds through a high-centered stage to become quartered and cupped in form when fully open. The color is a consistent deep glowing pink with paler undersides. It was named for Duc Edouard de Fitzjames (1776–1836), a supporter of the Bourbon kings. ZONES 4–11.

PRE-1837

PARENTAGE UNKNOWN

### 'Duc de Guiche'
*(bottom left)*

syns 'Senat Romain', 'Senateur Romain'

OLD, GALLICA, MAUVE

This is a dense, rather sprawling shrub to about 4 ft (1.2 m) with moderately armed darkish green stems. The clear rich green foliage is plentiful, roundly oval and almost glossy. The flowers, which emerge from small clusters of feathery buds, are about 3 in (8 cm) across, very double when open and flatly cushion-shaped around a prominent green central eye. The color is reddish magenta, sometimes overlaid with violet. The outer petals reflex as they age, and the center ones change to a deep purple in hot weather. They are very fragrant. Many of the de Guiche family served as diplomats and as politicians in France, especially during the nineteenth century. ZONES 4–11.

FRANCE, PRE-1810

PARENTAGE UNKNOWN

## 'Duchess of Portland' *(right)*

syns 'Portlandica', 'Duchesse de Portland', 'Portland Rose', *Rosa paestana, R. portlandica,* 'Scarlet Four Seasons'

OLD, PORTLAND, MEDIUM RED, REPEAT-FLOWERING

This rose inaugurated the Portland class of roses, also known as Damask Perpetuals. The fragrant blooms appear from mid-summer to late autumn. The large, semi-double, cupped flowers of deep rose and sometimes bright scarlet have yellow stamens with conspicuous anthers. Occasional white streaks on the petals indicate a China background. It is a low, compact shrub and is good as a bedding plant, hedge, or in a container. The oval-shaped foliage is light green; there are hooked prickles. Deadheading keeps the plant attractive. Jack Harkness said 'the Portlands were the first hint of what the China rose was about to do', which implies that reblooming roses were on the horizon. **ZONES 4–10.**

PRE-1800

POSSIBLY UNKNOWN RED CHINA × 'AUTUMN DAMASK'

## 'Duchesse d'Angoulême' *(top right)*

syns 'Duc d'Angoulême', 'Wax Rose'

OLD, GALLICA, LIGHT PINK

This is a small, arching shrub that grows to 3 ft (1 m). The shoots are very green and almost unarmed, and the light to mid-green foliage is superb. The pointed buds are arranged in small clusters. The flowers, which appear in mid-summer, are rather more than semi-double and are held on quite weak necks. Each flower is about 3½ in (9 cm) across, rich in fragrance and made up of sizeable petals, and remains consistently bright blush-pink shaded slightly deeper. At times they seem translucent and so are very beautiful. This is a rewarding and healthy shrub for any situation; few of its kind are so refined. **ZONES 5–10.**

VIBERT, FRANCE, 1821

PARENTAGE UNKNOWN

## 'Duchesse d'Auerstädt' *(above)*

syn. 'Madame la Duchesse d'Auerstädt'

OLD, NOISETTE, YELLOW, REPEAT-FLOWERING

Blooming in the spring and autumn, this Noisette starts with round, pointed, yellow buds which open into globular, full blooms 5 in (12 cm) across. The golden yellow petals are quartered; the center ones have a hint of apricot. The blooms appear on strong stalks either singly or in threes. It is a disease-free mature plant which can reach 20 ft (6 m) high and is happiest in full sun. The vigorous, branching stems hold a few hooked prickles and beautiful, dark, serrated, leathery leaves. The flowers do not like rain. The Duchess was the wife of the Duc d'Auerstädt, Prince of Eckmuehl, Maréchal de France, whose strategic talents and high morality made him Napoleon's best officer. **ZONES 7–11.**

BERNAIX, FRANCE, 1887

SPORT OF 'RÊVE D'OR'

D

D

Like most Gallicas, it tolerates poor soil. It should be placed where its colors match the other flowers in the garden. **ZONES 4–10.**

VIBERT, FRANCE, 1837

PARENTAGE UNKNOWN

### 'Duchesse de Montebello'  *(left)*
OLD, GALLICA, PINK

This beautiful Gallica has always been a popular cut flower, although it needs some extra care. The coral-rose or shell pink blooms are double, quartered, medium-sized, and often look like pink saucers with white centers. They have a light, sweet scent. The flowers fade to flesh pink in the sun; the inner petals are reflexed around a green eye. It blooms in summer, and is a compact, erect bush with gray-green foliage and long sprays on its 5 ft (1.5 m) form. It is attractive at the back of a border or as a hedge. It tolerates poor soil, and should be given room to relax. Pruning improves its shape. **ZONES 4–10.**

LAFFAY, FRANCE, 1824–25

UNKNOWN GALLICA ×
UNKNOWN CHINA

### 'Duchesse de Brabant'  *(top left)*
syns 'Comtesse de Labarthe', 'Comtesse Ouwaroff', 'Countess Bertha', 'The Shell Rose'
OLD, TEA, LIGHT PINK, REPEAT-FLOWERING

This vigorous, spreading bush produces free-flowering blooms from late spring until autumn. The large, soft pink, very double, cupped blooms are shaped like tulips. The lovely buds open to 45 upright petals that have a salmon-pink flush. It is a slow-growing bush with light green, pointed leaves, which are subject to mildew in the spring. It grows to 4 ft (1.2 m) and looks best when 3 or 4 are planted together. President Theodore Roosevelt helped to widen its fame by wearing the buds in his buttonhole. It is also a good cut flower. '**Climbing Duchesse de Brabant**' has all the characteristics of its parent but needs a warm spot to do its best. **ZONES 5–11.**

BERNÈDE, FRANCE, 1857

PARENTAGE UNKNOWN

### 'Duchesse de Buccleugh'
*(top right)*
OLD, GALLICA, RED BLEND

This late, and prolific-blooming Gallica has full, cupped, large blooms that range in color from pink to lavender to strong crimson, depending on the weather, soil and light. The color of the blooms is quite unusual. The dark edges fade, and the flattened, quartered blooms have a green eye. The vigorous bush has gray-green foliage and hardly any prickles.

## 'Duet' *(bottom left)*

MODERN, LARGE-FLOWERED/
HYBRID TEA, MEDIUM PINK,
REPEAT-FLOWERING

One of the twentieth century's greatest roses for sheer exuberance, health and continuity of flowers, 'Duet' has few equals. It produces oval, well-formed buds that open into high-centered, large—to 4 in (10 cm)—double flowers, light pink on the uppersides and deep pink on the undersides. The blooms, with 30 petals, are in clusters of 3–5 and are slightly fragrant; they appear all over the bush, with sometimes six flushes per year in warm countries. The growth habit is vigorous and upright, the foliage is leathery, and it has superb resistance to disease. Extremely popular in warm climates, this variety is a great bedding rose. **ZONES 5–11.**

SWIM, USA, 1960

'FANDANGO' × 'ROUNDELAY'

BADEN-BADEN GOLD MEDAL 1959, NATIONAL ROSE SOCIETY TRIAL GROUND CERTIFICATE 1960, ALL-AMERICA ROSE SELECTION 1961

## 'Duftrausch'

TANschaubud *(top left)*
syns 'Olde Fragrance',
'Senteur Royale'
MODERN, LARGE-FLOWERED/
HYBRID TEA, MEDIUM PINK,
REPEAT-FLOWERING

This bush bears magnificent, deep mauve-pink double flowers with over 40 petals, which are neatly arranged and open flat. It has disease-resistant and upright growth with semi-glossy green foliage. There is a superb Damask perfume. **ZONES 5–11.**

TANTAU, GERMANY, 1986

PARENTAGE UNKNOWN

## 'Duke of Edinburgh' *(top right)*

OLD, HYBRID PERPETUAL, DARK RED, REPEAT-FLOWERING

This rose needs a lot of cosseting to show its best, and it dislikes wet weather. The deep crimson, full, large blooms are veined with dark red. They are semi-double, well-formed and fragrant and look their best in semi-shade. The upright shrub is 2 ft (60 cm) tall and wide with large leaves. It prefers a rich soil. **ZONES 5–11.**

PAUL, UK, 1868

'GÉNÉRAL JACQUEMINOT' × SEEDLING

## 'Duke of Windsor' *(bottom right)*

syn. 'Herzog von Windsor'

MODERN, LARGE-FLOWERED/
HYBRID TEA, ORANGE BLEND,
REPEAT-FLOWERING

'Duke of Windsor' produces brilliant fluo-rescent orange flowers on an upright-growing, vigorous, very thorny plant with magnificent large, glossy dark green leaves. Strangely enough, the thorns and canes, but not the foliage, are susceptible to mildew. Flower production is poor but their fragrance is very strong, which is unusual in a rose of this color. The blooms are well formed and double, with 27 petals. **ZONES 4–9.**

TANTAU, GERMANY, 1969

PARENTAGE UNKNOWN

EDLAND FRAGRANCE AWARD 1968, ANERKANNTE DEUTSCHE ROSE 1970

D

## 'Dupontii'

*(bottom left)*

syns 'Dupont Rose',
*Rosa × dupontii*,
'Snow-Bush Rose'

OLD, MISCELLANEOUS, WHITE,
REPEAT-FLOWERING

This vigorously healthy shrub is attractive as a hedge or a tree climber, or as a screen on fences. The blooms appear in clusters on arching canes in early summer. The pink buds unfold to blushed snow-white blooms. Overlapping petals surround the showy, golden stamens. The fragrance is rich; for some the scent of bananas. The long-lasting blooms are excellent when cut for indoors. Gray-green leaves line the arching canes, and there are orange hips in the autumn. It prefers full sun. Dupont was the founder of the Luxembourg Gardens in Paris, and Empress Josephine commissioned him to aid her in creating the Malmaison rose collection. Susan Verrier lists this rose as a Gallica; a late-flowering cross between *Rosa gallica* and *R. moschata*. ZONES 4–11.

PRE-1817

PARENTAGE UNKNOWN

## 'Dundee Rambler'

*(top left)*

OLD, AYRSHIRE, WHITE

This hardy and robust rose with a rambling habit can reach 20 ft (6 m) high. The double, milky white blooms appear in large clusters. A pink flush covers the small, fragrant flowers, which have many tightly packed petals. Its dense growth makes it a good woodland plant. There are large prickles. Careful pruning when trained on an arch, pillar or pergola increases its attraction in summer. ZONES 5–10.

MARTIN, UK, 1837

*ROSA ARVENSIS* × UNKNOWN
NOISETTE

## 'Dunwich Rose'

syn. 'Dunwichiensis'

MODERN, MODERN SHRUB,
WHITE

The origin of this beautiful rose is not known except that it was found on the sand dunes in Dunwich, Suffolk, England in 1956. The flowers comprise 5 heart-shaped white petals surrounding prominent yellow stamens. It has the typical *pimpinelli-folia* foliage and tiny prickles. The low-growing shrub is covered with blooms in the summer and with small hips in the autumn. It is used extensively by land-scapers because of its low growth. It likes a warm, sunny position. ZONES 4–9.

ENGLAND, 1956

PARENTAGE UNKNOWN

## 'Duplex'   *(top right)*

syns 'Apple Rose',
*Rosa pomifera duplex*,
*R. villosa duplex*,
'Wolley-Dod's Rose'

OLD, MISCELLANEOUS,
MEDIUM PINK

This rose, which was discovered in the garden of the Reverend Wolley-Dod in Cheshire in 1900, is a double-flowered form of *Rosa pomifera* known for its gray leaves and very large apple-shaped hips which are covered in bristles and turn red in autumn. The flowers are clear pink and semi-double and the foliage is downy and gray-green. Strong and gaunt growth to 10 ft (3 m) tall and 6 ft (2 m) wide makes this a good shrub for the back of a border. ZONES 4–11.

VIBERT, FRANCE, PRE-1838

*ROSA POMIFERA* × UNKNOWN
GARDEN ROSE

### 'Dupuy Jamain'
*(right)*

OLD, HYBRID PERPETUAL,
MEDIUM RED,
REPEAT-FLOWERING

This once popular
rose lays claim to a
very strange blend of
colors—from red to
cherry to cerise. The
large and double, well-
formed blooms flower
freely from summer
to autumn; they are at
their best if the autumn
is a cool season. They
contain about 30
petals, which can easily
burn under a hot sun.
The vigorous, stiff and
stout canes reach 5 ft
(1.5 m) high and dis-
play a few prickles
and gray-green foliage.
This rose does well in
poor soil and needs
to be pruned to keep
its shape. Monsieur
Dupuy Jamain, who
died in 1888 in Paris,
was regarded as a
distinguished nursery-
man. **ZONES 5–11.**

JAMAIN, FRANCE, 1868
PARENTAGE UNKNOWN

### 'Düsterlohe'
*(bottom)*

MODERN, RAMBLER, DEEP PINK

When this rose is in full
bloom in mid-summer,
no other plant will
outshine its beauty.
Semi-double, rose pink
blooms flower freely
on the sprawling canes.
The fragrant, globular
blooms flatten and
turn lilac-pink as they
age; the center petals
curve inwards around
the attractive yellow
stamens. A vigorous
bush to 8 ft (2.4 m)
high, it can be trained
as a climber. The
canes are prickly, and
in autumn, plump,
pear-shaped, orange
hips appear, decorating
the bush throughout
winter. Raised by
Wilhelm Kordes II
(1891–1976), head of
the famous nursery,
it is but one of his
many roses that have
achieved worldwide
fame. Dr A. S. Thomas
of Australia said of
Kordes that he was
'possibly the greatest
rose man of all time'.
**ZONES 6–11.**

KORDES, GERMANY, 1931
'DANCE OF JOY' × 'DAISY HILL'

### 'Dutch Gold'
*(top right)*

MODERN, LARGE-FLOWERED/
HYBRID TEA, MEDIUM YELLOW,
REPEAT-FLOWERING

This rose, which
was bred in England
from two well-known
parents, has double
flowers with 30–35 rich
golden yellow petals.
They are large, to 5 in
(15 cm), and have a
good fragrance. The
growth is strong and
healthy and flower
production fair, the
blooms surviving bad
weather and keeping
their color well both on
the bush and when cut.
The foliage is glossy
dark green. **ZONES 5–11.**

WISBECH PLANT COMPANY,
UK, 1978

'PEER GYNT' × 'WHISKY MAC'

THE HAGUE GOLD MEDAL

E

E

purple-foliaged trees and also looks good on arbors and arches, the canes being very pliable and easy to train. **ZONES 4–9.**

EASLEA, UK, 1932

PARENTAGE UNKNOWN

NATIONAL ROSE SOCIETY GOLD MEDAL 1932

### 'Easter Morning'
*(top right)*
syn. 'Easter Morn'
MODERN, MINIATURE, NEAR WHITE, REPEAT-FLOWERING

The flowers of 'Easter Morning' are ivory white and have 60–70 petals. The foliage is a leathery, glossy dark green. It is an excellent compact bush that tends to spread, in most climates being a vigorous grower with a haunting fragrance that is not always noticeable at first breath. Because of the high petal count, the florets last a long time on the bush. This is an excellent choice of plant for a border or a window box. After 40 years in commerce this rose is still popular worldwide. **ZONES 5–11.**
MOORE, USA, 1960

'GOLDEN GLOW' × 'ZEE'

### 'Earthquake'
MORquake *(above)*
MODERN, MINIATURE, RED BLEND, REPEAT-FLOWERING

Brilliant bright striped red and yellow flowers with a yellow reverse literally cover this plant. The blooms are small and have about 40 petals and there is no fragrance. This rose loves the heat but it does better in part shade, where the magnificent blooms keep their color. There is no doubt that the striped effect is more pro-nounced if it is given shade rather than full sun—it is a real eye catcher in the garden. The plant is winter tender and may need protection to survive. This rose was named after an earthquake hit the small town of Coalinga in Central California near Moore's home base, Sequoia Nursery in Visalia. 'Climbing Earthquake' (MORshook) was introduced by Moore in 1990. It produces long arching canes, with each leaf axil throwing up small clusters of 3–5 florets. The elevated splash of bloom color that the plant creates against a wall or fence in the first spring flush is spectacular; later in the season, however, bloom production on the climbing version is somewhat reduced. **ZONES 6–11.**

MOORE, USA, 1983

'GOLDEN ANGEL' × SEEDLING

### 'Easlea's Golden Rambler' *(top left)*
syn. 'Golden Rambler'
MODERN, LARGE-FLOWERED CLIMBER, YELLOW BLEND/ MEDIUM YELLOW

'Easlea's Golden Rambler' was a latecomer to the list of rambling roses, most of which were bred early in the twentieth century. It has rich yellow flowers, sometimes marked with red, that are 4 in (10 cm) across and bloom in clusters. They are double with 35 petals, and strongly fragrant, but the yellow color fades quickly in hot climates and there is no repeat-bloom after the copious early flush. The vigorous climbing growth to 10–13 ft (3–4 m) supports leathery, rich olive green foliage. This variety looks mag-nificent growing into

## 'Echo' *(right)*
syn. 'Baby Tausendschön'

**OLD, CHINA, PINK BLEND, REPEAT-FLOWERING**

This offspring of a very popular rose does best in partial shade. It has prolific, large, semi-double blooms that are cupped, and change from white to deep pink. The outer curved petals shape the rose like a bowl. The large trusses of blooms cover the strong, erect stems, which can reach 3 ft (1 m) on a compact bush with glossy foliage. It is subject to mildew where there is no air circulation. There are no prickles. The shrub needs deadheading during its flowering from summer until autumn. It is an ideal subject for a container or border, and it also makes a long-lasting cut flower. China Roses are ancestors of the modern Cluster-flowered Roses. **ZONES 4–9.**

LAMBERT, GERMANY, 1914
SPORT OF 'TAUSENDSCHÖN'

## 'Éclair' *(bottom left)*
syn. 'Gärtendirektor Lauche'

**OLD, HYBRID PERPETUAL, DARK RED, REPEAT-FLOWERING**

This outstanding member of the Hybrid Perpetual family has folded outer petals like rich velvet that surround the quartered center, and a strong perfume. The well-shaped, dark red blooms are shaded black and open to form a large, flat circle of color. It is a tall, vigorous bush that produces flowers from summer to autumn and has little foliage but many prickles. This is a rose that needs to be given plenty of water and fertilized regularly; it will repay this care accordingly. It is a lovely cut flower. Lacharmé of Lyon, France, produced many roses; among the most notable are 'Salet' and 'Victor Verdier'. **ZONES 4–9.**

LACHARMÉ, FRANCE, 1883

'GÉNÉRAL JACQUEMINOT' × SEEDLING

## 'Eclipse'
*(bottom right)*

**MODERN, LARGE-FLOWERED/ HYBRID TEA, LIGHT YELLOW, REPEAT-FLOWERING**

The medals indicate that 'Eclipse' set a high standard for yellow roses in the 1930s; it has long, elegant, pointed buds of cadmium yellow shading to old gold, with interesting long narrow sepals that took the florist world by storm. The double blooms have 28 petals, open to a rather loose shape and are very fragrant. The growth habit is strong and bushy, making it an excellent bedding plant, and the foliage is dark and leathery. **ZONES 5–9.**

NICOLAS, USA, 1935

'JOANNA HILL' × 'FEDERICO CASAS'

PORTLAND GOLD MEDAL 1936, ROME GOLD MEDAL 1935, BAGATELLE GOLD MEDAL 1936, AMERICAN ROSE SOCIETY DAVID FUERSTENBERG PRIZE 1938

E

Rose' has a vigorous, upright growth habit and reasonably disease-resistant glossy dark green foliage. **ZONES 4–9.**

MEILLAND, FRANCE, 1950

'PEACE' × 'SIGNORA'

NATIONAL ROSE SOCIETY GOLD MEDAL 1950

### 'Edith Clark'
*(top right)*

MODERN, LARGE-FLOWERED/
HYBRID TEA, MEDIUM RED,
REPEAT-FLOWERING

Named after the breeder's wife and one of the few of Alister Clark's Large-flowered Roses that is a dwarf grower in habit. This variety has double, globular, crimson red flowers that are slightly fragrant and are produced continuously. It has rich green foliage. **ZONES 5–9.**

CLARK, AUSTRALIA, 1928

'MME ABEL CHATENAY' ×
SEEDLING

### 'Eddie's Jewel'
*(top left)*

MODERN, MODERN SHRUB,
MEDIUM RED,
REPEAT-FLOWERING

'Eddie's Jewel' has fiery red flowers and red thorns; it looks quite dramatic when in full bloom against a blue sky. It grows vigorously to 8 ft (2.5 m) and is repeat-flowering, although hips are not freely produced. It suffers from sun scald in hot climates. **ZONES 4–9.**

EDDIE, CANADA, 1962

'DONALD PRIOR' × ROSA
MOYESII HYBRID

### 'Eden Rose'  *(above)*

MODERN, LARGE-FLOWERED/
HYBRID TEA, DEEP PINK,
REPEAT-FLOWERING

This variety should not to be confused with the climbing rose 'Pierre de Ronsard' also bred by Meilland, which is known as 'Eden Rose' in the UK. The plant described here has ovoid buds that open to deep tyrian rose flowers with 60 petals. They are cupped, 4 in (10 cm) wide and fragrant and hold their color and shape extremely well. 'Eden

### 'Edith Holden'
CHEwlegacy *(right)*

syns 'Edwardian Lady',
'The Edwardian Lady'

MODERN, CLUSTER-FLOWERED/
FLORIBUNDA, RUSSET,
REPEAT-FLOWERING

This upright grower is unique in color; in cool weather the young flowers are a russet golden brown with a yellow center while the reverse of the petals is pale; they age to gray and fawn. Semi-double with 15 petals and urn shaped, the slightly fragrant flowers are borne in long sprays of 10–20, appearing both profusely and continuously. This unique rose is lovely for flower arranging. In warm climates it grows to 10 ft (3 m) in height and is ideal for pillars or tripods, but it is also sturdy enough to be used without support as a free-standing shrub rose. The mid-green glossy foliage is large and plentiful and disease free. **ZONES 4–9.**

WARNER, UK, 1988

'BELINDA' × ('ELIZABETH OF GLAMIS' × ['GALWAY BAY' × 'SUTTER'S GOLD'])

### 'Editor Stewart'
*(bottom)*

MODERN, LARGE-FLOWERED/
HYBRID TEA, MEDIUM RED,
REPEAT-FLOWERING

This short-growing climber has deep cherry red, semi-double, large flowers that open to reveal gold stamens. After a prolific spring blooming, flowering continues in summer and autumn, rare in red climbing roses. The foliage is bronze in the early stages, then turns to dark green as it matures. 'Editor Stewart' is a good rose for a tripod or pillar, or it can be used as a large, free-standing shrub; it is one of the best roses bred in Australia. **ZONES 5–9.**

CLARK, AUSTRALIA, 1939

PARENTAGE UNKNOWN

### 'Eglantyne' AUSmak
*(top right)*

syn. 'Eglantyne Jebb'

MODERN, MODERN SHRUB,
LIGHT PINK, REPEAT-FLOWERING

One of the best of David Austin's newer roses, 'Eglantyne' is moderately tall and extremely bushy with excellent disease resistance and a continuous display of large, very cup-shaped blooms, composed of many petals. They are the palest pink and have beautiful form, showing up well against the most attractive green foliage, and they are strongly scented. The flowers last very well on the bush, and their vase life is exceedingly long. This variety is well suited to being planted in groups. It is also classified as an English Rose. **ZONES 4–9.**

AUSTIN, UK, 1994

PARENTAGE UNKNOWN

E

### 'Elégance' *(left)*

MODERN, LARGE-FLOWERED/
HYBRID TEA, PINK BLEND

With large, fragrant, rose-copper flowers that emerge from globular buds, 'Elégance' is a beautiful bush rose for a bedding scheme. The dark green, leathery foliage makes a good backdrop to the bright, double blooms. The moderate growth can be propagated by budding. **ZONES 5–9.**

BUYL, BELGIUM, 1955

PARENTAGE UNKNOWN

### 'Elegance'

MODERN, LARGE-FLOWERED
CLIMBER, MEDIUM YELLOW,
REPEAT-FLOWERING

'Elegance' is a good climbing rose with dark green glossy foliage and large mid-yellow blooms that fade to white at the edges. The flowers are double with 40–50 petals and are large for a climbing rose, and there is not much repeat-bloom. This variety, which does best in cooler climates because the yellow color of the blooms bleaches out in hot conditions, is excellent for pillars, tripods, arbors and fences where a disease-free, well-foliaged rose is needed. It has a vigorous growth habit. **ZONES 4–9.**

BROWNELL, USA, 1937

'GLENN DALE' × ('MARY WALLACE' × 'MISS LOLITA ARMOUR')

### 'Elegant Beauty'

KORgatum *(bottom)*
syns 'Delicia', 'Kordes' Rose Delicia'

MODERN, LARGE-FLOWERED/
HYBRID TEA, LIGHT YELLOW,
REPEAT-FLOWERING

'Elegant Beauty' produces lovely long buds on long stems, hence the name. The flowers are a very soft yellow flushed with pink and have only 20 petals. They make good cut flowers as the buds open slowly in spite of there being few petals. The large foliage is dark matt green on a plant with an upright, bushy growth habit. This variety is not well known in Australia or New Zealand, although it is a rose of great refinement. **ZONES 5–9.**

KORDES, GERMANY, 1982

'NEW DAY' × SEEDLING

### 'Eiffel Tower'
*(top left)*
syns 'Eiffelturm', 'Tour Eiffel'

MODERN, LARGE-FLOWERED/
HYBRID TEA, MEDIUM PINK,
REPEAT-FLOWERING

'Eiffel Tower', a magnificent rose in warm, dry climates, has extremely long, urn-shaped buds that open into mid-pink, high-centered double flowers with 35 petals. The blooms are large, to 3–5 in (8–13 cm) wide and are very fragrant; crops of them appear profusely in quick succession. This variety resents rain and cold and does not perform so well in cold climates, although in warmer areas it is one of the best roses. The growth habit is extremely strong and upright, and the foliage is semi-glossy and leathery; new growth can burn in heatwave conditions. **ZONES 4–9.**

ARMSTRONG, USA, 1963

'FIRST LOVE' × SEEDLING

GENEVA GOLD MEDAL 1963,
ROME GOLD MEDAL 1963

**E**

**'Elina'** DICjana *(right)*
syn. 'Peaudouce'
MODERN, LARGE-FLOWERED/
HYBRID TEA, LIGHT YELLOW,
REPEAT-FLOWERING

This variety is a strong, vigorous bush with excellent dense, glossy dark green, disease-resistant foliage that acts as a foil to the huge, magnificently formed deep cream blooms. The flowers, which are often 6 in (15 cm) across and have 35 petals, last particularly well when picked, and are beautiful at all stages of development from bud to full bloom, forming perfect exhibition subjects. The first flush is a little later than for most other varieties, a bonus that extends the spring flowering season, and flower production is excellent. The flowers have a slight fragrance.
ZONES 4–9.

DICKSON, UK, 1983

'NANA MOUSKOURI' × 'LOLITA'

ANERKANNTE DEUTSCHE
ROSE 1987, NEW ZEALAND
(GOLD STAR) GOLD MEDAL 1987,
GLASGOW SILVER MEDAL 1991,
ROYAL HORTICULTURAL SOCIETY
AWARD OF GARDEN MERIT
1993, JAMES MASON GOLD
MEDAL 1994

**'Elizabeth Harkness'** *(top right)*
MODERN, LARGE-FLOWERED/
HYBRID TEA, LIGHT YELLOW,
REPEAT-FLOWERING

This most refined rose with some of the form and delicacy of 'Ophelia' and 'Michèle Meilland'

has 30 petals of lovely form that open to off white to buff, often with yellow and pink tones. In color it is distinct from other roses and can be variable according to the season and weather, but it is always beautiful. Flowering is profuse and the fragrance strong on an upright, bushy plant with dark, plentiful foliage. It was named after Jack and Betty Harkness' only daughter to mark her 21st birthday; and she carried the rose in her wedding bouquet.
ZONES 4–9.

HARKNESS, UK, 1969

'RED DANDY' × 'PICCADILLY'

ROYAL NATIONAL ROSE SOCIETY
CERTIFICATE OF MERIT 1969

**'Elizabeth of Glamis'** MACel *(bottom)*
syns 'Elisabeth', 'Irish Beauty'
MODERN, CLUSTER-FLOWERED/
FLORIBUNDA, ORANGE-PINK,
REPEAT-FLOWERING

'Elizabeth of Glamis' was named after Queen Elizabeth the Queen

Mother, whose ancestral home was Glamis Castle in Scotland. It is an excellent Cluster-flowered Rose with lush dark green plentiful foliage on a bushy, medium-sized plant that is very quick to repeat-flower. The buds are well shaped and open to show stamens and 35 petals that are a luminous salmon-orange. This is an excellent bedding

rose as the flowers and foliage appear from ground level and completely cover the bush. In some climates it can be difficult to transplant. ZONES 5–9.

MCGREDY, UK, 1964

'SPARTAN' × 'HIGHLIGHT'

NATIONAL ROSE SOCIETY
PRESIDENT'S INTERNATIONAL
TROPHY 1963

E

*The Genus Rosa* and for her gardens at Warley Place and the south of France; she once employed 65 gardeners. The flowers are soft pink tinted yellow with pronounced claret-colored stamens. The strong, healthy bush has good dark green, leathery foliage. **ZONES 4–9.**

ARCHER, UK, 1936

'DAINTY BESS' × 'LADY HILLINGDON'

### 'Elmshorn'   *(left)*
MODERN, MODERN SHRUB,
DEEP PINK, REPEAT-FLOWERING

This variety, one of the strongest growing and most free flowering of all shrub roses, has small, cupped, double, well-formed flowers borne in huge well-spaced trusses. They have a slight scent, and the autumn display on huge arching shoots is deeper in color than in spring. Disease resistance is high, and the foliage is glossy light green, profuse and wrinkled. 'Elmshorn' can be used most effectively either singly, or in groups for continuous color; it is repeat-flowering and deserves to be more widely grown. **ZONES 4–9.**

KORDES, GERMANY, 1951

'HAMBURG' × 'VERDUN'

ANERKANNTE DEUTSCHE ROSE 1950, NATIONAL ROSE SOCIETY CERTIFICATE OF MERIT 1950

### 'Ellen'   AUScup
*(top left)*
MODERN, MODERN SHRUB,
APRICOT BLEND,
REPEAT-FLOWERING

This variety (also classified as English Rose), has rich but soft apricot flowers tinged with brown. They are beautifully cupped in the bud stage and open to a loose quartered formation. Strongly scented, they have short stems and about 40 petals in cool weather but fewer in summer heat. After an excellent performance in spring, flowering is continuous but sparse in summer and then more profuse in autumn. The leaves are large and rather coarse and there are many thorns. The growth is bushy but rather ungainly, with long shoots towering above shorter growth. **ZONES 4–9.**

AUSTIN, UK, 1984

'CHARLES AUSTIN' × SEEDLING

### 'Ellen Poulsen'
*(top right)*
MODERN, POLYANTHA, MEDIUM
PINK, REPEAT-FLOWERING

'Ellen Poulsen' is a bushy plant of low to medium height with dense glossy foliage, the leaves packed very close together on the stems. The double, fragrant, bright cherry pink flowers appear in tight trusses continuously; they are large, have good form and hold their shape well. This variety, which is resistant to mildew, can be pruned hard or lightly to form a small shrub; it makes a good border or small hedge because of the dense foliage cover. **ZONES 4–9.**

POULSEN, DENMARK, 1911

'MME NORBERT LEVAVASSEUR' × 'DOROTHY PERKINS'

### 'Ellen Willmott'
*(bottom left)*
MODERN, LARGE-FLOWERED/
HYBRID TEA, YELLOW BLEND,
REPEAT-FLOWERING

W. E. B. Archer produced some excellent single Large-flowered Roses in the 1930s, and this was one of the best. It was named after Miss Willmott of Essex, famous for her book

## 'Elveshörn' KORbotaf
### *(right)*
MODERN, MODERN SHRUB,
MEDIUM PINK,
REPEAT-FLOWERING

This wonderful small
shrub rose has a
moderate and spread-
ing growth habit and
healthy dark green,
semi-glossy foliage.
The flowers, which
come in well-spaced,
elongated panicles,
have 35 petals. They
retain their cherry pink
color very well and have
excellent substance.
Flowering is extremely
profuse in spring
and continuous in
summer and autumn.
'Elveshörn' makes a
very colorful low hedge
or border, or can be
used in groups among
herbaceous plants.
**ZONES 4–9.**

KORDES, GERMANY, 1985

'THE FAIRY' × SEEDLING

## 'Elysium' KORumelst
### *(top right)*
MODERN, CLUSTER-FLOWERED/
FLORIBUNDA, MEDIUM PINK,
REPEAT-FLOWERING

This variety has long,
pointed buds that open
to double, salmon-pink
flowers with a boss of
stamens. The buds are
attractive at all stages
of development and the
fragrant flowers look
good when arranged
under artificial light.
They have 35 petals.
The foliage is glossy
and disease free on a
profusely blooming,
vigorous, tall plant.
'Elysium' makes an
excellent bedding rose.
**ZONES 5–9.**

KORDES, GERMANY, 1961

PARENTAGE UNKNOWN

NATIONAL ROSE SOCIETY
CERTIFICATE OF MERIT 1961

## 'Emanuel' AUSuel
### *(bottom)*
### syn. 'Emmanuelle'
MODERN, MODERN SHRUB,
APRICOT BLEND,
REPEAT-FLOWERING

This variety has very
full flowers of 100 or
more petals that open
to form a flat rosette
and are borne in small
clusters. Like many
Austin roses it can vary
greatly in color: in
cool weather it is quite
apricot whereas in
summer heat it is quite
pink with apricot tones
at the base of the petals.
However, it is attractive
at all times. The blooms
are large and fragrant.
'Emanuel' is a medium,
bushy, spreading plant
with small, mid-green,
semi-glossy, extremely
dense foliage. It looks
attractive in groups
in perennial borders
with other plants and
is an excellent choice
in both large and small
gardens; it is also ideal
for growing as a stand-
ard. 'Emanuel', which
is also classified as an
English Rose, was
named after the dress
designers responsible
for the late Princess
Diana's wedding gown.
**ZONES 4–9.**

AUSTIN, UK, 1985

('CHAUCER' × 'PARADE') ×
(SEEDLING × 'ICEBERG')

E

variety is best suited to warm, dry climates. **ZONES 5–9.**

GAUJARD, FRANCE, 1962

'PEACE' × ('VIOLA' × SEEDLING)

### 'Empereur du Maroc'

syn. 'Emperor of Morocco'

OLD, HYBRID PERPETUAL, RED, REPEAT-FLOWERING

This rose, which has never lost its popularity, has double, crimson-tinged purple blooms containing 40 petals that are borne in large clusters of 5–10. The intensely fragrant flowers are small, compact and muddled, and turn almost black with age. This low, compact bush needs rich cultivation to do its best. The foliage is sparse but there are strong prickles; hard pruning will strengthen its performance. This rose is ideal for a small garden or a border because of its color and fragrance but it is subject to mildew, and the flowers can easily burn in the sun. **ZONES 4–9.**

GUINOISSEAU, FRANCE, 1858

'GÉANT DES BATAILLES' SEEDLING

### 'Emily'  AUSburton
*(top left)*

MODERN, MODERN SHRUB, LIGHT PINK, REPEAT-FLOWERING

'Emily', a most refined little rose, has soft pink flowers that are at first cup-shaped, then become a rosette shape. They open to show a core of small petals that are paler on the outside, then become deeper in color in the center. There is a very strong fragrance. The small, upright bush produces many blooms, their unique shape making them ideal for cutting for use in arrangements.

It is a good rose for small gardens but needs extra treatment to perform well. It is also classified as an English Rose. **ZONES 4–9.**

AUSTIN, UK, 1992

'THE PRIORESS' × 'MARY ROSE'

### 'Emily Gray'
*(top right)*

MODERN, LARGE-FLOWERED CLIMBER, DEEP YELLOW

This lovely yellow rambler has deep gold flowers infused with buff shades and with yellow stamens. They have 25 petals and are borne in clusters; there is little repeat-bloom.

One of the healthiest of all yellow climbing roses, it has glossy, dark, bronze foliage on an extremely vigorous plant with pliable canes. 'Emily Gray' is a good rose for pergolas and arches and for growing into trees. **ZONES 4–9.**

WILLIAMS, UK, 1918

'JERSEY BEAUTY' × 'COMTESSE DU CAYLA'

NATIONAL ROSE SOCIETY GOLD MEDAL 1916

### 'Éminence'  GAXence
*(bottom)*

MODERN, LARGE-FLOWERED/ HYBRID TEA, MAUVE, REPEAT-FLOWERING

This is a sturdy, moderately vigorous bush with light green, leathery foliage. The large, double flowers with 40 petals are dark lavender. At their best the strongly scented flowers are well formed and attractive, but in cold wet weather they can ball and open to a dirty gray mauve color; however, they do last very well on the bush and when cut. This

## 'Empress Joséphine'

*(bottom left)*

syns 'Francofurtana', 'Souvenir de l'Impératrice Josephine', 'The Frankfurt Rose'

OLD, GALLICA, MEDIUM PINK

The origin of 'Empress Joséphine' is so shrouded in mystery that it has acquired many names. It is an improved form honoring Napoleon's first wife, who was really the patroness of Old Roses. The rich pink, veined, semi-double, loosely shaped blooms are large, and appear during summer; the wavy, textured petals appear translucent. Although it has little scent, its fame rests on its beauty as a cut flower. The sprawling, well-branched 5 ft (1.5 m) shrub has coarse, deeply veined grayish leaves, some prickles and large hips. It prefers shade in warm areas and may need support. ZONES 3–9.

DESCEMET, FRANCE, PRE-1815

*ROSA CINNAMOMEA ×
R. GALLICA*

ROYAL HORTICULTURAL SOCIETY
AWARD OF GARDEN MERIT 1993

## 'Empress Michiko'

DICnifty *(bottom right)*

MODERN, LARGE-FLOWERED/
HYBRID TEA, LIGHT PINK,
REPEAT-FLOWERING

'Empress Michiko', named after the Empress of Japan, has lovely colorings of pastel pink, cream and even pale apricot. The buds are high centered and the outer petals attractively pointed. The buds hold well and open to flowers of excellent substance. Flower production is good. Growth is moderate, and the dark green foliage is resistant to disease. ZONES 4–9.

DICKSON, UK, 1992

'SILVER JUBILEE' × ('BRIGHT
SMILE' × 'PEER GYNT')

ROYAL NATIONAL ROSE SOCIETY
TRIAL GROUND CERTIFICATE
1987, GLASGOW CERTIFICATE OF
MERIT 1994

## 'Ena Harkness'

*(right)*

MODERN, LARGE-FLOWERED/
HYBRID TEA, MEDIUM RED,
REPEAT-FLOWERING

'Ena Harkness' was bred by an amateur hybridist, A. Norman, and introduced by the Harkness firm; it was named after a prominent flower arranger. This variety was bred for cool climates where blooms can be of the highest exhibition quality. Of the purest unfading crimson and with the true Damask perfume of its parent 'Crimson Glory', it was grown in most rose gardens of the world in the 1950s. The rather weak leaf stalks and sparse leathery foliage led to a loss of popularity, but it is still grown in Tasmania, Australia. The growth habit is moderately strong and upright and it is disease resistant. 'Climbing

Ena Harkness' (1954) is a powerfully scented climbing sport that is wonderful for a high trellis or for growing up the walls of houses. It flowers reasonably continuously after an abundant spring flush. ZONES 4–9.

NORMAN, UK, 1946

'CRIMSON GLORY' ×
'SOUTHPORT'

NATIONAL ROSE SOCIETY GOLD
MEDAL 1945, NATIONAL ROSE
SOCIETY CLAY CUP FOR
FRAGRANCE 1945, PORTLAND
GOLD MEDAL 1955

**E**

E

### 'Enfant de France'

OLD, HYBRID PERPETUAL,
LIGHT PINK, REPEAT-FLOWERING

Produced on the eve of
the birth of the Large-
flowered or Hybrid
Tea class of roses, this
repeat-blooming var-
iety has proved its worth
over a long period. The
blowsy, pink-white,
fragrant blooms are
double and sometimes
quartered and there
is a silvery pink cast to
them. A velvet texture
adds to the charm of
the petals. The upright,
strong bush does well
in poor soil and has
abundant leaves.
ZONES 4–9.

LARTAY, FRANCE, 1860

PARENTAGE UNKNOWN

### 'English Elegance'

AUSleaf (above)

MODERN, MODERN SHRUB,
PINK BLEND, REPEAT-FLOWERING

This variety, also classified as an English Rose,
has flowers that are an
unusual combination
of pink, copper and
salmon. The large
blooms have loosely
arranged inner petals
of a deeper color, dis-
played within a ring
of large outer petals of
a lighter tint, but there
is not much fragrance.
Flowering is profuse
and the repeat-bloom
is good, particularly
in cooler autumn
weather, when the
color combination is
more pronounced. The
large, spreading plant
lends itself to espalier
work; it is strong
enough in habit to
form a wide, arching
shrub without support,
or it can be trained as
a small climber. The
foliage is light green
and disease free and
the nodes are very close
together. ZONES 4–9.

AUSTIN, UK, 1986

PARENTAGE UNKNOWN

### 'English Garden'

AUSbuff (bottom left)
syn. 'Schloss
Glücksburg'

MODERN, MODERN SHRUB,
APRICOT BLEND,
REPEAT-FLOWERING

This small, upright
plant is more like a
Large-flowered Rose
in growth than a shrub
rose and has plentiful
pale green foliage. The
flowers are variable in
color and deepen in
hot weather, changing
from soft yellow to
buff to pale apricot.
The blooms are flat
with many small petals
and often a quartered
center; they are wonder-
ful as cut flowers and
last well when picked.
'English Garden',
which is also classified
as an English Rose,
blends happily with
most other flowers in
the bed. It is proving to
be popular in gardens
throughout the world.
ZONES 4–9.

AUSTIN, UK, 1986

('LILIAN AUSTIN' × SEEDLING) ×
('ICEBERG' × 'WIFE OF BATH')

E

### 'English Miss' *(bottom right)*

MODERN, CLUSTER-FLOWERED/
FLORIBUNDA, LIGHT PINK,
REPEAT-FLOWERING

With two excellent pink Cluster-flowered Roses as parents, it is not surprising that 'English Miss' has soft, clear pale pink flowers. They are extremely double, with up to 60 petals, open from exquisite buds to large, flat, full blooms, and are borne in well-spaced clusters. There is a strong fragrance. The very dark green to purple foliage acts as a nice background to the flowers. This popular, compact-growing bush has no disease problems.
**ZONES 4–9.**

CANT, UK, 1978

'DEAREST' × 'SWEET REPOSE'

ROYAL NATIONAL ROSE SOCIETY
TRIAL GROUND CERTIFICATE
1977, BRITISH ASSOCIATION OF
ROSE BREEDERS SELECTION 1978

### 'Eos' *(top left)*

MODERN, MODERN SHRUB,
RED BLEND

This tall, gaunt shrub to 6 ft (2 m) in height has small, ferny foliage. Its ovoid buds open to semi-double, cupped, medium blooms that are sunset red with white centers and are borne several together on a stem. There is a slight fragrance but no repeat-bloom. 'Eos' appears to set fruit only in cold climates, which is a pity as the chief beauty of forms of *Rosa moyesii* are the long, flagon-shaped hips.
**ZONES 4–9.**

RUYS, THE NETHERLANDS, 1950

*ROSA MOYESII* × 'MAGNIFICA'

### 'Erfurt' *(top right)*

MODERN, MODERN SHRUB,
PINK BLEND, REPEAT-FLOWERING

'Erfurt' has a trailing, bushy growth habit and leathery, wrinkled, rich bronze-tinted disease-free foliage. Flowering is continuous, despite a large crop of medium-sized round hips that turn from green to orange-red and are produced after the first flush of flowers. The blooms are pink and develop from attractively scrolled buds that open to reveal cream to yellow towards the base of the petals and prominent stamens. The open flowers are attractive, particularly when the hips appear among them to add to the effect; the hips are very effective for indoor decoration, lasting a number of months on the bush. **ZONES 4–9.**

KORDES, GERMANY, 1939

'EVA' × 'RÉVEIL DIJONNAIS'

E

because of its color,
perfume and reliability.
**ZONES 4–9.**

KORDES, GERMANY, 1964

PARENTAGE UNKNOWN

ROYAL NATIONAL ROSE SOCIETY
GOLD MEDAL 1965

### 'Erotika' *(top right)*
syns 'Eroica', 'Eroika',
'Erotica'

MODERN, LARGE-FLOWERED/
HYBRID TEA, DARK RED,
REPEAT-FLOWERING

'Erotika' is a dark red
rose with a very strong
fragrance. The well-
shaped buds develop
into large blooms that
contain 35 firm-textured
petals with a velvety
sheen. The disease-free
foliage is glossy dark
green on a tallish, vig-
orous, upright plant. It
is popular in Germany
where its color, strength,
vigor and continuity
of bloom earned it an
award. Although grown
worldwide it deserves to
be more popular.
**ZONES 4–9.**

TANTAU, GERMANY, 1968

PARENTAGE UNKNOWN

ANERKANNTE DEUTSCHE
ROSE 1969

### 'Erinnerung an Brod' *(above)*
syn. 'Souvenir de Brod'

OLD, HYBRID PERPETUAL, RED
BLEND, REPEAT-FLOWERING

This rose was named
for a town in Bosnia.
Its dark crimson,
flat blooms are very
double, very full and
heavy with scent and
are best seen in partial
shade where the colors
remain constant. A long,
floriferous blooming
occurs in mid-summer.
This is one of the most
stunning cut flowers,
especially just after
the buds open. It is a
healthy shrub that will
reach 6–7 ft (1.8–2.1 m)
and is winter hardy. It
is popular in Germany.
**ZONES 4–10.**

GESCHWIND, HUNGARY, 1886

*ROSA SETIGERA* × SEEDLING OF
'CHÂTEAUBRIAND'

### 'Ernest H. Morse' *(top left)*

MODERN, LARGE-FLOWERED/
HYBRID TEA, MEDIUM RED,
REPEAT-FLOWERING

'Ernest H. Morse'
was bred in Germany
and named after the
nurseryman in England
who introduced it.
The flowers are bright
Turkey red, well formed
with 30 petals and large,
to 4 in (10 cm) across.
They are extremely
fragrant, retain their
color well in the full
blooms, and appear
continuously. The plant
is of medium height
and has good leathery,
disease-resistant foli-
age. It is still being
sold by nurseries after
30 years in commerce

### 'Escapade' HARpade
### (center)

MODERN, CLUSTER-FLOWERED/
FLORIBUNDA, MAUVE,
REPEAT-FLOWERING

There are not many roses that can be identified from a distance but 'Escapade' is one of them. Breeder Jack Harkness said that its flowers were so full of nectar that there was usually a bee in almost every bloom. The soft mauve-pink semi-double flowers, which have 12 petals, a central boss of yellow stamens and a white eye, come in large clusters and look lovely against the glossy pale green, dense foliage. Flowering is prolific, although the flowers fade rather quickly in hot climates. With its shrubby growth habit, this plant is perfect for a hedge, and its lovely simple flowers also blend happily with herbaceous borders. ZONES 4–9.

HARKNESS, UK, 1967

'PINK PARFAIT' × 'BABY FAURAX'

BADEN-BADEN GOLD MEDAL 1968,
BELFAST GOLD MEDAL 1968,
COPENHAGEN FIRST PRIZE 1970,
ANERKANNTE DEUTSCHE ROSE
1973, ROYAL HORTICULTURAL
SOCIETY AWARD OF GARDEN
MERIT 1994

### 'Especially For You'

FRYworthy (top)

MODERN, LARGE-FLOWERED/
HYBRID TEA, MEDIUM YELLOW,
REPEAT-FLOWERING

'Especially For You' is a newish rose with a very strong fragrance.

The bright mimosa-yellow, double flowers have 25 petals; they are large and well formed, and are borne both singly and in clusters. The foliage is dark green and disease free and flower production is high, with very good repeat-bloom. It is suitable for bedding and for borders. ZONES 4–9.

FRYER, UK, 1996

SEEDLING × 'JOHNNIE WALKER'

### 'Essex' POUlnoz
### (right)
### syns 'Aquitaine',
### 'Pink Cover'

MODERN, GROUND COVER,
MEDIUM PINK,
REPEAT-FLOWERING

'Essex' is one of the County Series of Ground Cover Roses bred by Poulsen of Denmark and Kordes of Germany and introduced by Mattock of England; there are nearly 20 of these short-growing roses named after English counties.

This variety grows about 2 ft (60 cm) high and 5 ft (1.5 m) across, and its dark green foliage is covered with small, single blooms of a rich deep pink. Flowering is continuous, especially if deadheaded, and there are no disease problems. If the plant is left for a number of years without pruning and becomes too woody, a hard cut-back in winter will not affect the next spring display. ZONES 4–9.

POULSEN, DENMARK, 1988

PARENTAGE UNKNOWN

ROYAL NATIONAL ROSE SOCIETY
CERTIFICATE OF MERIT 1987,
GOLD MEDAL DUBLIN 1987,
GLASGOW CERTIFICATE OF
MERIT 1995

E

E

## 'Etain'  *(above)*

MODERN, RAMBLER, ORANGE-PINK

This is a very useful rose for climbing smaller trees or stretching over arches. It bears salmon-pink trusses that offer some fragrance during the summer flush. The glossy foliage is truly evergreen in milder climates, making it an attractive plant all year round; it looks wonderful as a backdrop to a perennial border. Its thin, pliable canes make it an easy rose to train, but be careful of the prickles. It requires little maintenance and is never touched by disease. Offered by the English nursery firm of Cants in 1953, it deserves to be more popular. **ZONES 4–9.**

CANTS, UK, 1953

PARENTAGE UNKNOWN

## 'Ethel'

MODERN, RAMBLER, LIGHT PINK

A catalogue of 1912 describes this as 'a delightful shade of flesh pink with semi-double flowers', yet a 1998 catalogue calls it mauve-pink with double flowers—this makes one wonder if the variety now in commerce is the correct rose. Turner's creation flowered in profusion in large trusses, and was noted for its light green foliage and vigorous habit. That rose, and its present-day counterpart, are suitable for scrambling up and over pergolas, fences and substantial arches; it grows to twice the average extent for a climbing rose, and forms an excellent weeping standard. It flowers in summer only. **ZONES 4–9.**

TURNER, UK, 1912

SEEDLING OF 'DOROTHY PERKINS'

## 'Étoile de Hollande'  *(above)*

MODERN, LARGE-FLOWERED/HYBRID TEA, MEDIUM RED, REPEAT-FLOWERING

'Étoile de Hollande' has been a popular rose for nearly 80 years, and is still widely grown. The flowers are bright red and fairly double, with 30–35 petals that are cupped at first and later open to large, full blooms. There is a very strong, true Damask fragrance. The foliage is rather soft, mid-green and not over-abundant on a moderately growing open plant. Many new red roses have been introduced with a fanfare of trumpets and then disappeared from commerce, but this one is still seen in most large rose collections; its color, velvety texture and perfume are its great attributes. **'Climbing Étoile de Hollande'** (1931; Royal Horticultural Society Award of Garden Merit, 1993) is a vigorous climbing sport that is excellent for pillars, tripods or arbors or for growing against the walls of houses, where its fragrance can be appreciated. **ZONES 4–9.**

VERSCHUREN, THE NETHERLANDS, 1919

'GENERAL MACARTHUR' × 'HADLEY'

## 'Étoile de Lyon'
*(right)*

OLD, TEA, MEDIUM YELLOW, REPEAT-FLOWERING

No rose works harder all year than this one, which produces blooms from early spring through to winter. It has a strong Tea fragrance and is very healthy. Although the outer petals sometimes look poor, when the bud opens the saffron yellow petals cover any flaws. The globular, full, open blooms are quite heavy, and they may droop on the thin canes. At first glance the buds indicate a Large-flowered Rose because of their long, pointed shape. Easy to establish, especially on its own roots, the vigorous bush will grow in shade or sun, hot or cold weather. One of the many roses named after the famous French center of rose breeding in the nineteenth century, it is quite resistant to all diseases and requires little care. ZONES 6–9.

GUILLOT, FRANCE, 1881

SEEDLING OF 'MADAME CHARLES'

## 'Eugène Fürst'
*(bottom)*
syn. 'General Korolkow'

OLD, HYBRID PERPETUAL, DEEP RED, REPEAT-FLOWERING

Grown around the world for its glowing

color and healthy habit, this upright, tall, vigorous shrub produces flowers from spring until autumn, the autumn flush often being better than the spring flowering. The lovely fragrant crimson-purple blooms are full, globular and large, and, when viewed from the side, they appear to be goblets. The 5 ft (1.5 m) bush has handsome leaves that are subject to mildew. 'Eugène Fürst' is a parent of 'Reveil Dijonnais' and 'Baron Girod de l'Ain'. ZONES 4–9.

SOUPERT AND NOTTING, FRANCE, 1875

'BARON DE BONSTETTEN' × SEEDLING

## 'Eugénie Guinoiseau'
*(top right)*
syn. 'Eugénie de Guinoisseau'

OLD, MOSS, MEDIUM RED

Although a Moss Rose usually stays close to the ground, this one can be used as a climber. Growing to over 6 ft (2 m), the vigorous, upright plant needs support. The cherry red to violet-purple blooms are full, large and flat and streaked with white. The mossy buds are fat, and the petals change from dark to light if planted in the sun. The bristly stems are covered with attractive leaves, and are serrated and dark. Long, narrow hips add charm in autumn, the end of its blooming period. ZONES 4–9.

GUINOISSEAU, FRANCE, 1864

PARENTAGE UNKNOWN

E

### 'Europeana' *(left)*

MODERN, CLUSTER-FLOWERED/
FLORIBUNDA, DARK RED,
REPEAT-FLOWERING

For many years
'Europeana' has set the
standard for judging
red Cluster-flowered
Roses. The flowers are
dark crimson, double
with a rosette shape,
large to 3 in (8 cm)
across, and borne in
big clusters of up to
30 blooms. They have
some fragrance, flower
production is excellent
and the well-spaced
heads are lovely for
exhibition purposes.
The plant is vigorous
and has large, plentiful,
bronze-green foliage
after maturing from
plum purple new
growth. There can be
some mildew at times
and the heavy, large
trusses are inclined
to blow over in windy
weather. 'Europeana'
well deserved its awards
and is still popular after
more than 30 years in
commerce. **ZONES 4–9.**

DERUITER, THE NETHERLANDS,
1963

'RUTH LEUWERIK' × 'ROSEMARY
ROSE'

THE HAGUE GOLD MEDAL 1962,
ALL-AMERICA ROSE SELECTION
1968, PORTLAND GOLD MEDAL
1970

### 'Euphrosyne' *(left)*
syn. 'Pink Rambler'

MODERN, RAMBLER, MEDIUM
PINK

This variety likes a
shady spot best. Its
bright carmine buds
appear in clusters and
open to pure dark pink,
full, small blooms.
The flat flowers change
from a rich pink to
pink to pale pink. The
Tea fragrance is strong.
A vigorous climber, it
looks best on an arch
or a pillar and has
pale green foliage that
covers the pliable
canes, which should
be pruned lightly. It
requires at least 3 years
to establish itself, and
was favored by Gertrude
Jekyll in her garden
designs. *Euphrosyne* is
one of the three Graces
of Greek mythology;
*Aglaia* and *Thalia*,
the other two, are also
offered as Ramblers by
Schmitt, and all are still
grown. **ZONES 4–9.**

SCHMITT, FRANCE, 1895

*ROSA MULTIFLORA* ×
'MIGNONETTE'

### 'Euphrates'

HARunique  *(top left)*

MODERN, MODERN SHRUB,
PINK BLEND

This unique rose has
single, slightly fragrant
pale salmon-pink
flowers with a deep
pink eye that last well
in water and are always
a talking point. They
have 5 petals and appear
in clusters along the
branches of the previous
season's growth, flower-
ing only in spring.
When in bloom the
plant looks more like
a flowering *Cistus* than
a rose. Not a strong
grower, this variety
performs best in hot,
dry climates and lighter
soils. It has small, long,
narrow pale green
foliage. **ZONES 4–9.**

HARKNESS, UK, 1986

*ROSA PERSICA* × SEEDLING

## 'Eurostar' POUlreb
### *(right)*
MODERN, CLUSTER-FLOWERED/
FLORIBUNDA, MEDIUM YELLOW,
REPEAT-FLOWERING

'Eurostar' produces
large, golden yellow
flowers both singly
and in clusters on an
upright plant with dark
green, glossy foliage.
There is a deeper
color in the center of
the blooms, which are
many petalled and
open to globular,
cupped, old-fashioned
type flowers. They are
fragrant, look attractive
both close up and at a
distance and last well.
Disease resistance is
good and the repeat-
bloom is quick. It is an
excellent bedding rose
and is also good for
borders. **ZONES 4–9.**
OLESEN, DENMARK, 1994
PARENTAGE UNKNOWN

E

## 'Eutin' *(right)*
### syn. 'Hoosier Glory'
MODERN, CLUSTER-FLOWERED/FLORIBUNDA, DARK RED,
REPEAT-FLOWERING

'Eutin' is an early Cluster-flowered Rose
well known for its enormous heads of
lightly fragrant, small, dark carmine-red
double flowers. The buds are globular
and pointed, and the trusses can have 50
or more blooms in the spring flush. The
growth is vigorous and the bush is covered
by glossy, dark, leathery, disease-resistant
foliage. The repeat-bloom is good. This
variety makes an ideal hedge, is excellent
for bedding and can also be used in the
perennial border. Its huge flower clusters
come from its parent 'Eva'. **ZONES 4–9.**
KORDES, GERMANY, 1940
'EVA' × 'SOLARIUM'

E

### 'Eva' *(top)*

MODERN, MODERN SHRUB, RED
BLEND, REPEAT-FLOWERING

This great shrub rose, which is used extensively in landscape planting, bears huge panicles of 75 or more flowers. They are semi-double and carmine-red with a white center that lights up the flower. Flowering is continuous if spent blooms are removed, but if they are left on the bush a wonderful crop of unusually colored pinkish red hips is produced in large clusters; these are ideal for flower arranging. 'Eva' has large, lush, disease-free foliage on a vigorous bush. It is excellent for use among flowering shrubs or as a background to perennials and bulbs.
ZONES 4–9.

KORDES, GERMANY, 1933

'ROBIN HOOD' ×
'J. C. THORNTON'

### 'Evangeline'
*(bottom)*

MODERN, RAMBLER, PINK BLEND

*Evangeline*, the long narrative poem by American poet Henry Wadsworth Longfellow, was a very popular work in the nineteenth century. This variety has rose-white single blooms that are veined pink. They appear as clusters on long stems, much like pyramids of apple blossoms. The large yellow anthers high-light the 2 in (5 cm) blooms, which are sweetly scented. It is a vigorous Rambler that will reach 15 ft (4.5 m) and has dark, leathery foliage. There are hooked prickles and plenty of attractive hips. It likes to climb trees, but if it is to be used on a pergola, intelligent, regular pruning is necessary. This rose does well in the shade. Walsh produced a series of successful Ramblers from his home in Woods Hole, Massachusetts, between 1901 and 1920. **ZONES 4–9.**

WALSH, USA, 1906

*ROSA WICHURANA* × 'CRIMSON
RAMBLER'

## 'Evelyn' AUSsaucer
*(right)*

MODERN, MODERN SHRUB,
APRICOT BLEND,
REPEAT-FLOWERING

'Evelyn', which is also classified as an English Rose, gets its color from 'Tamora' and its vigor from 'Graham Thomas'. The huge, very full blooms with over 40 petals open from a very broad shallow cup to a rosette form at maturity and have a most delicious perfume. They are usually rich apricot with a yellow base but can be much more pink in hot weather, a color change inherited from 'Gloire de Dijon'. It is a strong, upright-growing, medium-sized shrub that flowers continuously and profusely. The firm Crabtree and Evelyn chose it to advertise their perfume company. ZONES 4–9.

AUSTIN, UK, 1992

'GRAHAM THOMAS' × 'TAMORA'

## 'Evening Star'

JACven

MODERN, CLUSTER-FLOWERED/
FLORIBUNDA, WHITE,
REPEAT-FLOWERING

This nice little rose was bred from the lovely cream-tipped 'Saratoga', and has white blooms with pale yellow at the base of the petals. They are double with a beautiful form, large and high centered. The foliage is plentiful, dark green and leathery on an upright, vigorous bush with very good repeat-bloom. There are no disease problems and the flowers have a slight fragrance. ZONES 6–9.

WARRINER, USA, 1974

'WHITE MASTERPIECE' ×
'SARATOGA'

BELFAST GOLD MEDAL AND
FRAGRANCE PRIZE 1977,
PORTLAND GOLD MEDAL 1977

## 'Everest Double Fragrance'
*(above right)*

MODERN, CLUSTER-FLOWERED/
FLORIBUNDA, LIGHT PINK,
REPEAT-FLOWERING

This rose has heavily veined foliage that is dark green and sets off the pale pink flowers, which are borne in clusters of 3–7 blooms. The buds are long and pointed, and the full blooms have good substance and attractive stamens. They are very fragrant. This is a good rose for bedding, and as a hedge or border. It is particularly disease free and flowers continuously. ZONES 4–9.

BEALES, UK, 1980

'DEAREST' × 'ELIZABETH
OF GLAMIS'

E

when this Rambler is seen tumbling down a wall or structure it is easy to see why it earned its gold medal. The vigorous, climbing canes are covered with prickles. Often found in old cemeteries, where it has natural-ized, it is used in Europe as a weeping standard. If pruned severely, this rose makes an effective hedge. To prevent mildew, ensure good air circu-lation. An improved form of the rose, 'Super Excelsa', is also popular. ZONES 6–9.

WALSH, USA, 1909

AMERICAN ROSE SOCIETY GOLD MEDAL 1914

### 'Exciting'
syns 'Roter Stern', 'Queen of Bermuda'
MODERN, LARGE-FLOWERED/ HYBRID TEA, MEDIUM RED, REPEAT-FLOWERING

This is a popular rose for the cut-flower trade, mainly because of its strikingly narrow and pointed red buds that are borne on long sturdy stems. They open to medium-sized, semi-double flowers of a dullish red. These have no scent, but they last well. 'Exciting' is a tall, vigorous and healthy shrub that is covered with flowers for most of the year. ZONES 4–10.

MEILLAND, FRANCE, 1958

'HAPPINESS' × 'INDEPENDENCE'

that are produced in autumn. This rose is late to come into flower in spring, but flowering is continuous until early winter. It is ideal where a large shrub is required and can be used in groups or as a tall hedge. ZONES 4–9.

LAMBERT, GERMANY, 1909

'MME NORBERT LEVAVASSEUR' × 'FRAU KARL DRUSCHKI'

### 'Excelsa' *(left)*
syn. 'Red Dorothy Perkins'
MODERN, RAMBLER, MEDIUM RED

'Excelsa' has bright red, double, cupped blooms with a white center that appear in irregular, large clusters. These clusters are often pendent. The color is variable depending on place-ment in sun or shade. Pliable stems make it possible to train the plant on pergolas, and

### 'Excellenz von Schubert' *(top)*
MODERN, POLYANTHA, DEEP PINK, REPEAT-FLOWERING

'Excellenz von Schubert' has carmine-rose flowers that are shaded lilac, and borne in enormous clusters on long, arching canes. The blooms are double and are set amid dark green foliage on a vigorous bush. Small round hips are produced in large clusters if spent blooms are not removed, the hips looking most attractive among the huge sprays of flowers

### 'Exploit' MEllider *(right)*
### syns 'All In One', 'Grimpant Exploit'

MODERN, LARGE-FLOWERED CLIMBER, DEEP PINK/MEDIUM RED

'Exploit' is an eye-catching rose in spring when
its deep pink to red double flowers with 20 petals
completely cover the vigorous growth. Flowering
is sparse after the spring flush. The small, mid-
green foliage is disease-free on a plant that is good
for pillars and fences. **ZONES 4–9.**

MEILLAND, FRANCE, 1985

'FUGUE' × 'SPARKLING SCARLET'

E

### 'Eyeopener' INTerop *(center)*
### syns 'Erica', 'Eye Opener', 'Tapis Rouge'

MODERN, MODERN SHRUB, MEDIUM RED, REPEAT-FLOWERING

As both parents have a distinctive white eye to
each flower, it is no surprise that the single, vivid
red flowers of 'Eyeopener' have a white eye and
gold stamens. They come in large and small
clusters on a big, arching plant, broader than it is
tall. Late in the season, large shoots bear hundreds
of blooms on long stems with many lateral shoots
also bearing blooms. The foliage is small, dark
and plentiful. Disease resistance is good except
for black spot in moist climates. **ZONES 4–9.**

ILSINK, THE NETHERLANDS, 1987

(SEEDLING × 'EYEPAINT') × (SEEDLING × 'DORTMUND')

ROYAL NATIONAL ROSE SOCIETY CERTIFICATE OF MERIT 1986,
BELFAST PRIZE 1989

### 'Eyepaint' MACeye *(bottom)*
### syns 'Eye Paint', 'Tapis Persan'

MODERN, CLUSTER-FLOWERED/FLORIBUNDA, RED BLEND,
REPEAT-FLOWERING

'Eyepaint' can be classed as hand painted since
the bright red, single flowers with 5–6 petals and
a white eye and golden stamens have streaks of
white through them. The medium-sized flowers
are borne in large and small clusters. Strong in
growth and with disease-free, plentiful glossy
foliage, it makes a good border or hedge, can be
used in group plantings, and even as a short pillar
rose. **ZONES 4–9.**

MCGREDY, NEW ZEALAND, 1975

SEEDLING × 'PICASSO'

ROYAL NATIONAL ROSE SOCIETY TRIAL GROUND CERTIFICATE 1973,
BADEN-BADEN GOLD MEDAL 1974, BELFAST GOLD MEDAL 1978

F

It has lovely, medium-sized flowers that are flat and quartered, forming full rosettes. They appear in clusters, are very double with 60 or more petals, and have a variable color, being quite pink in the center of the bloom in hot weather, and buff in autumn. There is a strong myrrh fragrance, and flowering is continuous. An average-sized upright plant, it looks charming with perennial plants and bulbs in borders. Clumps of 3, 5 or 7 plants look far more pleasing than single specimens. **ZONES 4–9.**
AUSTIN, UK, 1982
DESCENDED FROM 'BELLE ISIS'

Flowering is continuous and no hips are produced. This rose, together with 'Pink Grootendoorst' and 'Grootendoorst Supreme', are sometimes known as the carnation roses; all make impenetrable hedges that are quite good for security purposes. **ZONES 3–9.**
DE GOEY, GERMANY, 1918
*ROSA RUGOSA RUBRA* × POSSIBLY 'MME NORBERT LEVAVASSEUR'

### 'Fair Bianca'   AUSca
*(bottom)*
MODERN, MODERN SHRUB, WHITE, REPEAT-FLOWERING

'Fair Bianca', the first of David Austin's white roses, is also classified as an English Rose.

### 'Fair Play'   INTerfair
MODERN, MODERN SHRUB, MAUVE, REPEAT-FLOWERING

'Fair Play' has some of the color of the Harkness shrub rose 'Yesterday' but is much more prostrate in growth. The flowers are mauve, semi-double with 18 petals and are borne in large clusters. They have some fragrance. The foliage is smallish and dark green on a plant that blooms from summer through to autumn. It can be grown as a tall-growing ground cover and will cover quite a lot of space. **ZONES 4–9.**
ILSINK, THE NETHERLANDS, 1977
'YESTERDAY' × SEEDLING

### 'F. J. Grootendorst'
*(top)*
syns 'Grootendorst', 'Grootendorst Red', 'Nelkenrose'
MODERN, HYBRID RUGOSA, MEDIUM RED, REPEAT-FLOWERING

This is a good thorny shrub with largish wrinkled leaves and a tall spreading habit. The small, bright crimson flowers, which have serrated edges like a carnation, are very double, are borne in clusters of up to 20 in a head, and have a slight fragrance.

### 'Fairy Damsel' HARneatly

**MODERN, POLYANTHA, DARK RED, REPEAT-FLOWERING**

From the same crossing as 'Fairy Changeling', this variety has double, dark red flowers composed of 24 petals on a low, spreading bush. The foliage is plentiful and disease-free and flowering is continuous. This rose is suitable for use as a low hedge or as an edging to taller-growing varieties. **ZONES 4–9.**

HARKNESS, UK, 1981

'THE FAIRY' × 'YESTERDAY'

MUNICH IGA SILVER MEDAL 1983

### 'Fairy Dancers' *(right)*

**MODERN, LARGE-FLOWERED/HYBRID TEA, APRICOT BLEND, REPEAT-FLOWERING**

Although classed as a Large-flowered Rose, 'Fairy Dancers' could just as easily be a Cluster-flowered Rose in spite of having two tall-growing Large-flowered Roses as parents. It is a low, spreading bush with quite large thorns, rather sparse foliage and medium-sized flowers produced singly and in small clusters. The fragrant blooms are a beautiful buff apricot and of excellent form, opening slowly to a nicely formed full shape. Repeat bloom is a little slow, but disease resistance is fair. This is a good rose for cutting, the soft color showing up well under artificial light. **ZONES 5–9.**

COCKER & SONS, UK, 1969

'WENDY CUSSONS' × 'DIAMOND JUBILEE'

### 'Fairyland' HARlayalong
*(bottom)*

**MODERN, POLYANTHA, LIGHT PINK, REPEAT-FLOWERING**

'Fairyland' is probably the best known of the little Polyantha Roses. It is the one most like 'The Fairy' in color and growth habit, which is shrub-like and spreading, growing wider than it does tall with many slender stems. However, it is not so vigorous. Fat little buds open to light pink flowers that are double, with 24 petals, and cupped. The fragrance is strong and the repeat-flowering is good. It has disease-free, glossy foliage. **ZONES 4–9.**

HARKNESS, UK, 1980

'THE FAIRY' × 'YESTERDAY'

ROYAL NATIONAL ROSE SOCIETY TRIAL GROUND CERTIFICATE 1978, BADEN-BADEN SILVER MEDAL 1980, NEW ZEALAND SILVER MEDAL 1982

F

### 'Falkland' *(bottom)*
OLD, SCOTS, WHITE

Scots Roses, as these species hybrids are known, are tough plants. This one has pale pink petals fading to white. The double, fragrant blooms gather in clusters on low canes. The late spring flush lasts for several weeks. The 3 ft by 3 ft (1 m by 1 m) prickly shrub has upright stems and small gray leaves. In autumn a good crop of maroon hips adds interest to this rose, which is excellent for a hedge or container. Extremely healthy and suckering readily, it was possibly named for Viscount Lucius Falkland (1610–43), an English statesman. ZONES 4–9.

HYBRID OF *ROSA PIMPINELLIFOLIA*

### 'Fame!' JACzor
MODERN, CLUSTER-FLOWERED/ FLORIBUNDA, DEEP PINK, REPEAT-FLOWERING

There is no doubt of the identity of this rose when placed on the show table; the shocking pink gives it its name. But the classic flower form lowers the color temperature. Thirty petals form tight blooms that sit high on the straight canes and the bushy, upright plant. From the start of the season until the first frost, it produces a continuous series of blooms. The mild fragrance and dark green leaves provide a perfect foil for the flowers. ZONES 4–9.

ZARY, USA, 1998

'TOURNAMENT OF ROSES' × 'ZORINA'

### 'Fandango' *(top)*
MODERN, LARGE-FLOWERED/ HYBRID TEA, ORANGE-RED, REPEAT-FLOWERING

The chief virtue of 'Fandango' is its color, which is a brilliant flame orange-red with coral tones. The lovely color fades quickly in hot climates, so it is a better rose under cooler conditions. It has pretty buds that open very quickly in warm climates to loose, fragrant flowers of 20 petals. The foliage is glossy, leathery and plentiful on a bush that is vigorous and upright in growth habit. There is some repeat bloom after a prolific flowering in spring. ZONES 4–9.

SWIM, USA, 1950

'CHARLOTTE ARMSTRONG' × SEEDLING

NATIONAL ROSE SOCIETY TRIAL GROUND CERTIFICATE 1952

### 'Fantin-Latour' *(right)*

OLD, CENTIFOLIA, LIGHT PINK

The sumptuous powdery pink blooms of this rose appear in mid-summer, and can be 3 in (8 cm) across when fully open. At first they are cupped; later the outer petals reflex to expose a central button of tightly packed smaller petals. The scent is intoxicating and there are few prickles. The shrub usually reaches about 4 ft (1.2 m); if not pruned it can climb to 10 ft (3 m). Pruning after flowering increases the number of blooms for the following year. It is not bothered by hot, dry weather but doesn't grow as big as it does when cooler, and it is subject to some mildew. Henri Fantin-Latour (1836–1904) was a famous French painter renowned for still lifes and flowers, many of them Old Garden Roses. **ZONES 4–9.**

PARENTAGE UNKNOWN

ROYAL HORTICULTURAL SOCIETY AWARD OF GARDEN MERIT 1993

### 'Fascination' JACoyel *(below)*

MODERN, LARGE-FLOWERED/HYBRID TEA, ORANGE-PINK, REPEAT-FLOWERING

'Fascination' is a very full rose of 60 petals, a blend of orange and rosy pink. The globular buds open to large, high-centered flowers borne singly on upright stems. It has very little fragrance. The large, semi-glossy foliage is huge and the prickles are large and hooked. This rose won a gold medal in New Zealand, its size, unusual color and abundant foliage being its chief attributes. **ZONES 4–9.**

WARRINER, USA, 1982

SEEDLING × 'SPELLBINDER'

NEW ZEALAND GOLD MEDAL 1976

F

### 'Felicia' *(bottom)*

MODERN, MODERN SHRUB, PINK
BLEND, REPEAT-FLOWERING

'Felicia' has strongly fragrant flowers that are the delicate soft pink and cream color of 'Ophelia', fading to almost white. Flowering is most profuse in spring and rather sparse in summer, followed in autumn by huge panicles bearing the most highly colored and longest lasting flowers of the year. If spent blooms are not removed, large round hips are produced; these stay green for a long time before slowly turning to red, and look most attractive among the autumn flowers. This strong-growing plant is disease-resistant, with plentiful foliage and close-jointed stems. It is a good free-standing shrub if pruned lightly; if trimmed hard in winter, it produces a medium-sized spreading bush. **ZONES 4–9.**

PEMBERTON, UK, 1928

'TRIER' × 'OPHELIA'

NATIONAL ROSE SOCIETY
CERTIFICATE OF MERIT 1927,
ROYAL HORTICULTURAL SOCIETY
AWARD OF GARDEN MERIT 1993

### 'Fashion' *(top)*

MODERN, CLUSTER-FLOWERED/
FLORIBUNDA, PINK BLEND,
REPEAT-FLOWERING

With all its awards, it is clear that 'Fashion' was a unique Cluster-flowered Rose; an entirely new color bred by Eugene Boerner. Boerner is recognized as one of the best breeders of that particular class of rose of all time. Its buds are a deep peachy coral color, opening to flowers of 23 petals that are a glowing coral-peach. The fragrance is very strong. The flowers are borne in clusters on a bushy plant, with foliage that is slightly prone to mildew and very prone to rust. 'Fashion' was much used for bedding and for borders in the 1950s and 1960s and is still sold in most countries; there is a free-flowering climbing form. The unique color and free-flowering capacity of this variety led to an upsurge in demand for Cluster-flowered Roses throughout the world. **ZONES 4–9.**

BOERNER, USA, 1949

'PINOCCHIO' × 'CRIMSON GLORY'

NATIONAL ROSE SOCIETY GOLD
MEDAL 1948, BAGATELLE GOLD
MEDAL 1949, PORTLAND GOLD
MEDAL 1949, ALL-AMERICA ROSE
SELECTION 1950, DAVID
FUERSTENBERG PRIZE 1950,
AMERICAN ROSE SOCIETY GOLD
MEDAL 1954

## 'Félicité Parmentier' *(right)*
**OLD, ALBA, LIGHT PINK**

The fat buds of this rose have a trace of yellow before opening to reveal soft, flesh pink blooms that are white at the edges, fading to almost white in hot climates. A magnificent cut flower, the petals appear to swirl in circles. After opening flat, the double, sweetly scented blooms reflex during the late spring–early summer flowering. A compact, sturdy if slightly sprawling rose, it grows to 4 ft (1.2 m) with stout, moderately thorny stems and profuse light grayish green foliage. It is ideal for a small garden or to grow in containers, and is happiest in partial shade; it will do well in poor soil. The strong fragrance and its disease resistance make it a great landscaping plant. **ZONES 4–9.**

PRE-1834

PARENTAGE UNKNOWN

ROYAL HORTICULTURAL SOCIETY AWARD OF GARDEN MERIT 1993

## 'Félicité-Perpétue' *(bottom)*
syn. 'Félicité et Perpétue'
**OLD, HYBRID SEMPERVIRENS, WHITE**

The breeder named 'Félicité-Perpétue' for his new-born twin daughters, their names

commemorating Christians martyred together in AD 203. It is one of the most popular Ramblers, because of its vigor and disease resistance. The flowers have a delicate primrose scent. The pale pink blooms, which quickly turn white during the summer flush, are very double and flat and are borne in clusters that cover the bright green canes. These are armed with slender red prickles. When used as a ground cover it will form pyramid mounds; it is happy in any weather and it resents pruning. It was found recently on Alcatraz, the prison island, years after it was planted. **ZONES 4–9.**

JACQUES, FRANCE, 1828

*ROSA SEMPERVIRENS* × NOISETTE

ROYAL HORTICULTURAL SOCIETY AWARD OF GARDEN MERIT 1993

## 'Fellenberg'
syns 'Fellemberg', 'La Belle Marseillaise'
**OLD, NOISETTE, MEDIUM RED, REPEAT-FLOWERING**

In this variety, dramatic color changes occur during the long summer to autumn blooming period; the bright crimson may sometimes change to cerise. The double, cupped, fragrant flowers have 36 petals and appear as trusses on vigorous canes. There are usually 3–4 blooms in a corymb at the ends of new shoots. Easy to grow from cuttings, it has a spreading habit and can easily reach 7 ft (2.1 m) on a rich site. Small red prickles and dark foliage make it an ideal candidate to grow around a pillar. There is a lovely drawing of this rose by Alfred Parsons in *The Genus Rosa*, the famous book produced by Ellen Willmott in the Edwardian years. **ZONES 4–9.**

FELLEMBERG, FRANCE, 1835

PARENTAGE UNKNOWN

## 'Ferdinand Pichard' *(right)*

OLD, HYBRID PERPETUAL, RED BLEND, REPEAT-FLOWERING

One of the last Hybrid Perpetuals put on the market, this striped, cupped rose has stayed on the bestseller list since its birth. The 25 scarlet, streaked, clear pink petals change to a blush purple as they age. The tight clusters are cupped and may reach 4 in (10 cm) across. It likes sun, but very hot weather may crisp the blooms. It is a vigorous, tall, upright bush that is suitable for a small garden; however, if it is pegged down it will produce twice the amount of blooms. The foliage is smooth and light green. This rose makes an effective hedge provided it is deadheaded and fed well. **ZONES 4–9.**

TANNE, FRANCE, 1921

PARENTAGE UNKNOWN

ROYAL HORTICULTURAL SOCIETY AWARD OF GARDEN MERIT 1993

## 'Ferdy' KEItoli *(right)*
syn. 'Ferdi'

MODERN, MODERN SHRUB, DEEP PINK

This variety was one of the first ground-cover roses of very spreading habit. The foliage, which is mid-green and is closely packed on very long arching stems, has excellent disease resistance. The blooms are produced on small laterals along the canes of the previous season's growth; because of this the plant should not be pruned in winter. The double flowers are deep pink, have 20 petals, are small and are borne in clusters, the effect in spring being that of a mass of blooms completely covering the bush. Unfortunately, the flowers fade to a dirty color and remain on the bush for too long and there is very little repeat bloom. It is sufficiently cascading in growth to make a superb weeping rose when grafted onto a tall standard stock, where after a few years it will cascade down to ground level and provide a wonderful sight in spring. **ZONES 4–9.**

SUZUKI, JAPAN, 1984

CLIMBING SEEDLING × 'PETITE FOLIE' SEEDLING

'Festival' KORdialo

MODERN, PATIO/DWARF
CLUSTER-FLOWERED, RED BLEND,
REPEAT-FLOWERING

'Festival' produces
large clusters of semi-
double blooms of
glowing crimson with a
silvery white reverse
that cover a disease-
resistant compact bush
with luxurious foli-
age—a hallmark of
Kordes. The bloom
cycle on this rose is
fairly fast, producing
a rich abundance of
florets that start off a
rich crimson-scarlet
and then age with a
gold and silver center.
The plant is a low-
growing bush in the
tradition of Kordes.
It is rounded, compact
and dense and has great
foliage. **ZONES 4–11.**

KORDES, GERMANY, 1993

'REGENSBERG' × SEEDLING

ROYAL NATIONAL ROSE SOCIETY
TRIAL GROUND CERTIFICATE 1994,
UK ROSE OF THE YEAR 1994,
RNRS ROSE DAY AWARD 1998

F

'Feuerwerk' *(above)*
syns 'Feu d'Artifice', 'Fireworks', 'Magneet'
MODERN, MODERN SHRUB, ORANGE BLEND

This lovely shrub rose bears clusters of bright
orange-red, medium-sized blooms. They are
semi-double and open from pointed buds in
summer to form flat flowers centered with a mass
of golden yellow stamens. It is upright and bushy
in habit, covered with glossy green leaves. Some
sources incorrectly describe this rose as extinct.
**ZONES 5–9.**

TANTAU, GERMANY, 1962

PARENTAGE UNKNOWN

F

### 'Figurine' BENfig
*(bottom)*

MODERN, MINIATURE, WHITE,
REPEAT-FLOWERING

This aptly named rose has flowers that are ivory white, tinged with pink, on a medium, upright, dense plant. In tropical climates the blooms are light pink all over. 'Figurine' truly has elegant buds and a classic bloom form. The florets have only 15–25 petals, yet the form is stunning— a classic Miniature Rose in all respects. The blooms are normally borne one to a stem. There is no doubt that these stems were made for cutting—it is grown in South Africa in greenhouses, and the cut flowers are shipped worldwide. The long stems are the hallmark of this rose, and represent Benardella's achievement in producing a Miniature strictly hybridized for the cut-flower trade. 'Figurine' made a stunning appearance at the Royal National Rose Society All Miniature Show, winning the basket class. **ZONES 4–11.**

BENARDELLA, USA, 1991

'RISE 'N' SHINE' × 'LAGUNA'

AMERICAN ROSE SOCIETY
AWARD OF EXCELLENCE 1992

### 'Fidélio' MEIchest
*(top right)*

MODERN, CLUSTER-FLOWERED/
FLORIBUNDA, ORANGE-RED,
REPEAT-FLOWERING

This excellent Cluster-flowered Rose has bright red flowers with dark shading on the outer petals, which has been inherited from 'Fire King'. The buds are very shapely and open very slowly, being exquisite at the half-open stage, to brilliantly colored full blooms with 35 petals of wonderful substance. The bush is strong and spreading and has bronze-green young foliage that turns green at maturity. The flowers completely cover the bush from ground level upward, which makes 'Fidélio' unsurpassed as a bedding or border rose; it is also an excellent standard. **ZONES 4–9.**

MEILLAND, FRANCE, 1964

('RADAR' × 'CAPRICE') ×
'FIRE KING'

### 'Feuerzauber'
KORfeu *(top left)*
syns 'Fire Magic',
'Magic de Feu'

MODERN, LARGE-FLOWERED/
HYBRID TEA, ORANGE-RED,
REPEAT-FLOWERING

'Feuerzauber' has large, bright orange-red flowers with a lighter reverse to the petals. They are double, containing 30 petals, and are high centered and of good form. The buds open quickly to well-formed, long-lasting blooms that retain their color well. The dark, glossy foliage is disease resistant, and flower production is continuous. Strangely enough, for offspring of the highly scented 'Fragrant Cloud' there is not much scent; however, this variety with its vigorous upright growth habit is an excellent rose for bedding or for borders where a strong color is desired. **ZONES 4–9.**

KORDES, GERMANY, 1973

'FRAGRANT CLOUD' × SEEDLING

F

### 'Fimbriata' *(right)*
syns 'Diantheflora',
'Dianthiflora',
'Phoebe's Frilled Pink'

MODERN, MODERN SHRUB,
LIGHT PINK, REPEAT-FLOWERING

This unusual little rose
has pale pink blooms
from 'Mme Alfred
Carrière' and large
rugose leaves from
*Rosa rugosa*. The flowers
are small and fringed
like a carnation, very
fragrant, and blooming
is continuous. Strong
enough to use in the
shrub or perennial
border, it has good
disease resistance.
**ZONES 4–9.**

MORLET, FRANCE, 1891

*ROSA RUGOSA* × 'MME ALFRED
CARRIÈRE'

### 'Finale' KORam
syn. 'Ami des Jardins'

MODERN, CLUSTER-FLOWERED/
FLORIBUNDA, ORANGE BLEND,
REPEAT-FLOWERING

'Finale', one of the
earliest, low-growing
Cluster-flowered Roses,
has clusters of salmon-
orange, double, large
flowers to 3½ in (9 cm)
across. The blooms,
which have 20 petals,
are rather large com-
pared to the bush.
For maximum effect
this variety should be
planted at no less than
18 in (45 cm) intervals.
With its light green
foliage it can provide a
colorful low border or
small hedge. **ZONES 4–9.**

KORDES, GERMANY, 1964

'NORDLICHT' × 'METEOR'

### 'Financial Times Centenary' AUSfin
*(right)*

MODERN, MODERN SHRUB,
DEEP PINK

Commemorating
the centenary of the
*Financial Times*, this
rose has a rich Old
Garden Rose fragrance.
The flowers are large
and of great depth,
globular, and resemble
an old Centifolia Rose.
The petals curve in-
ward, enclosing the
center of the blooms.
The plant is upright and
of moderate vigor but
many rose enthusiasts
have been disappointed
in its growth and
flower production in
warmer climates. It can
suffer from die-back,
and appears to grow
much more strongly in
cooler areas. 'Financial
Times Centenary' is also
classified as an English
Rose. **ZONES 4–9.**

AUSTIN, UK, 1989

SEEDLING × SEEDLING

F

### 'First Edition' DELtep
*(left)*
syn. 'Arnaud Delbard'

MODERN, CLUSTER-FLOWERED/
FLORIBUNDA, ORANGE-PINK,
REPEAT-FLOWERING

Considering that
there are four Cluster-
flowered Roses and a
Polyantha Rose in this
variety's breeding, it
is not surprising that
'First Edition' is a
brightly colored rose,
the flowers being a
luminous coral with
orange shading. They
are double with 28
petals and of medium
size, to 2½ in (6 cm)
across. The flowers
open from buds that
are well shaped and
pointed and are most
attractive. The foliage
is glossy light green
and acts as a foil to
the brightly colored
blooms. This plant has
good disease resistance,
is upright and pro-
duces its flowers in
abundance. 'First
Edition' is still a popu-
lar rose in the USA,
well deserving its
prestigious award.
**ZONES 5–9.**

DELBARD, FRANCE, 1976

('ZAMBRA' × ['ORLÉANS ROSE' ×
'GOLDILOCKS']) × ('ORANGE
TRIUMPH' SEEDLING ×
'FLORADORA')

ALL-AMERICA ROSE SELECTION
1977

### 'Fiona' MEIbeluxen
*(above)*

MODERN, MODERN SHRUB,
DARK RED, REPEAT-FLOWERING

'Fiona', a rose for
all seasons, has dark
rose red flowers that
are double, smallish
and are produced
continuously in
well-spaced clusters.
They have 20 petals
and some fragrance.
The foliage is small,
dark, semi-glossy
and extremely free of
disease, on a plant with
a spreading growth
habit. If spent flowers
are not removed, an
amazing display of
large, round, extremely
long-lasting hips are
produced that persist
until late winter if they
are not picked for in-
door decoration, where
they can last for several
months. In autumn,
flowers and fruit can
cover the bush at the
same time and look
most effective. This
variety is a good little
rose that grows wider
than tall. **ZONES 4–9.**

MEILLAND, FRANCE, 1979

'SEA FOAM' × 'PICASSO'

F

### 'First Lady' *(right)*

MODERN, LARGE-FLOWERED/
HYBRID TEA, DEEP PINK,
REPEAT-FLOWERING

'First Lady' was named in 1961 in honor of Jacqueline Kennedy, the wife of US President John F. Kennedy. It is a short-growing, healthy bush that produces semi-double flowers with 20 petals that are rose to clear soft pink, although its 'official' color is deep pink. The flowers are large and well formed, 3–4½ in (8–11.5 cm) across and they open to very attractive full blooms with a slight fragrance. The foliage is leathery, dark and disease free on a medium-sized plant with an upright growth habit. The blooms, produced continuously, are excellent for cutting as they show up well in artificial light. The breeder, American Herbert Swim, was a dominant figure in rose breeding in the 1950s and 1960s. **ZONES 4–9.**

SWIM, USA, 1961

'FIRST LOVE' × 'ROUNDELAY'

### 'First Light'   DEVrudi *(top)*

MODERN, MODERN SHRUB,
LIGHT PINK, REPEAT-FLOWERING

This variety is an attractive shrub rose with bright pink single flowers. Each has 5 large petals and shows off a center that is massed with stamens and anthers. 'First Light' has healthy, mid-green foliage and should be propagated by budding. **ZONES 5–9.**

MARCIEL, USA, 1998

'BONICA' × 'BALLERINE'

ALL-AMERICA ROSE SELECTION 1998

**'First Love'** *(bottom)*
syn. **'Premier Amour'**
MODERN, LARGE-FLOWERED/
HYBRID TEA, LIGHT PINK,
REPEAT-FLOWERING

'First Love' is a much loved rose, admired by all for its small, beautifully formed pale pink buds, shaded with a deeper tone. The long, pointed buds open to semi-double, slightly fragrant blooms with 20–30 petals. The foliage is small, leathery and light green. It is one of the first roses to flower each spring and repeats quickly, giving up to 6 flushes of flowers per year in warmer districts. The blooms are borne in enormous quantities and completely cover the bush. Unfortunately, older plants do not produce basal breaks and old trunks can become very gnarled and woody, but this does not seem to affect flower production. The plant, which seems to grow more strongly in cooler areas than it does in warmer areas, has set a standard of refinement in the bud stage. It has very few thorns. **ZONES 4–9.**

SWIM, USA, 1951

'CHARLOTTE ARMSTRONG' ×
'SHOW GIRL'

NATIONAL ROSE SOCIETY
CERTIFICATE OF MERIT 1952

**'First Prize'**
*(left)*

MODERN, LARGE-FLOWERED/
HYBRID TEA, PINK BLEND,
REPEAT-FLOWERING

'First Prize' is quite distinct from 'First Love'; the latter is refined, while the former is very large with huge, fat buds that develop to large, double, high-centered flowers of rose pink, shading towards ivory at the center. The flower color tends to bleach quickly, particularly on hot days that follow dewy nights, but there is a good fragrance. In keeping with the size of the flowers, the dark and leathery foliage is very large, with good disease resistance, apart from some mildew in autumn. The growth habit is vigorous and upright and the heavy stems are covered with huge thorns. **ZONES 5–9.**

BOERNER, USA, 1970

SEEDLING OF 'ENCHANTMENT' ×
SEEDLING OF 'GOLDEN
MASTERPIECE'

ALL-AMERICA ROSE SELECTION
1970, AMERICAN ROSE SOCIETY
GERTRUDE M. HUBBARD GOLD
MEDAL 1971

**F**

### 'Fisher and Holmes' *(right)*
syn. 'Fisher & Holmes'
OLD, HYBRID PERPETUAL, DARK
RED, REPEAT-FLOWERING

This was one of the most popular roses during the Victorian period, and still has its admirers. The long, pointed buds open to reveal reddish scarlet blooms, shaded deep velvety crimson. The double blooms contain 30 petals; they are large and cupped, and are supported by long, strong stems. The 3 ft (1 m) bush is upright and vigorous; pegging it down will increase the number of blooms during the long flowering season. The autumn flush is even better than the summer one, although it is subject to mildew and rust. 'Fisher and Holmes' has been used as an effective container plant. ZONES 4–9.
VERDIER, FRANCE, 1865

SEEDLING OF 'MAURICE
BERNARDIN'

### 'Fisherman's Friend' AUSchild *(right)*
syn. 'Fisherman'
MODERN, MODERN SHRUB,
DARK RED, REPEAT-FLOWERING

'Fisherman's Friend', named after a brand of throat lozenge, on behalf of children in need, is also classified as an English Rose. It is a huge, tall-growing variety with enormous prickles and thick canes but it produces one of the most beautifully formed and largest of all the roses of this class. The buds are large, cupped at first and later open to a rosette shape. The blooms, filled with 60 or more petals, open to a confused center and are deep garnet-crimson,

becoming more purple with age; in cold weather they can be 6–7 in (15–18 cm) across and are extremely beautiful. They have a heavy damask fragrance. 'Fisherman's Friend' is somewhat prone to mildew and black spot, but in spite of this, it is worth a place in the garden. It flowers very well in spring if the long canes are trained horizontally on a fence or support, and probably does best in warmer, drier areas. ZONES 4–9.
AUSTIN, UK, 1987

'LILIAN AUSTIN' × 'THE SQUIRE'

F

## 'Flamingo' KORflÿg
(below)

syns 'Margaret Thatcher', 'Porcelain', 'Veronica', 'Veronika'

MODERN, LARGE-FLOWERED/
HYBRID TEA, LIGHT PINK,
REPEAT-FLOWERING

'Flamingo', a great greenhouse and garden rose, has large, long, pointed buds that open slowly to well-formed double blooms with 25 thick petals. The high-centered blooms are borne mainly singly on thick, very thorny stems, are moderately fragrant and last well when cut. The foliage is matt mid-green, the growth habit vigorous and upright, and the plant repeat blooms very quickly. There can be mildew in autumn, but the main fault is the numerous thorns. **ZONES 4–9.**

KORDES, GERMANY, 1979
SEEDLING × 'LADY LIKE'

## 'Flaming Peace'
MACbo (above)
syn. 'Kronenbourg'

MODERN, LARGE-FLOWERED/
HYBRID TEA, RED BLEND,
REPEAT-FLOWERING

'Flaming Peace' has all the fine qualities of its parent 'Peace', except that the color is a dull red, shaded purple; however, the reverse is yellow and this helps to give life to the flowers. The blooms are well formed and beautiful at the full bloom stage, where the petals of great substance are arranged very evenly. The plant has a tall growth habit, magnificent glossy foliage, good disease resistance and fair continuity of bloom. Its unique color will assure it a place in the gardens of the future—there is no other rose quite like it. **ZONES 4–9.**

MCGREDY, UK, 1966
SPORT OF 'PEACE'

## 'Flammentanz' KORflata
### syn. 'Flame Dance'
MODERN, LARGE-FLOWERED CLIMBER, MEDIUM RED

This variety has very large, double, high-centered crimson flowers that are borne in clusters and have good fragrance. The foliage is dark and leathery on an extremely vigorous plant that does not repeat bloom. 'Flammentanz' is very hardy in cold climates and is most attractive in full bloom, especially where there is sufficient space for it to grow to its full size. ZONES 4–9.

KORDES, GERMANY, 1955

*ROSA EGLANTERIA* HYBRID × *R KORDESII*

ANERKANNTE DEUTSCHE ROSE 1952

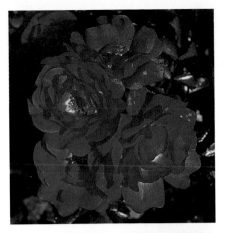

F

## 'Flower Carpet' NOAtraum *(top right)*
### syns 'Heidetraum', 'Emera', 'Blooming Carpet', 'Emera Pavement', 'Pink Flower Carpet'
MODERN, MODERN SHRUB, DEEP PINK, REPEAT-FLOWERING

'Flower Carpet' was launched in most countries with great publicity, with the claim that it flowers continuously for 10 months of the year; it completely covers the soil and smothers all weeds. This is a highly exaggerated claim. Because of its Rambler blood, the variety flowers later than most roses and has long periods without flowers between flushes. Also, it does not flower well into winter as was claimed. However, it is a very good ground-cover rose bearing deep pink globular flowers with 15 petals of good substance, borne in sprays of 10–25 blooms. There is a slight scent. The globular fruit are small and do not seem to inhibit any flowering if spent blooms are not removed, while the spring flowering is particularly profuse, making 'Flower Carpet' a most attractive ground cover rose. If it gets too woody, a hard winter prune every few years will bring back vigor without much loss of flower production. Black spot can occur in moist climates. ZONES 4–9.

NOACK, GERMANY, 1989

'IMMENSEE' × 'AMANDA'

GLASGOW GOLD MEDAL 1993, ROYAL HORTICULTURAL SOCIETY AWARD OF GARDEN MERIT 1993

## 'Flower Power' KORpon *(above)*
### syns 'Blühwunder', 'Ponderosa'
MODERN, CLUSTER-FLOWERED/FLORIBUNDA, ORANGE-RED, REPEAT-FLOWERING

'Flower Power', which inherits its small bush size from 'Marlena', has globular buds and orange-red, double, cupped flowers of medium size on very short but sturdy growth. There are many thorns. The foliage is leathery and abundant, with particularly short nodes, and it contrasts well with the flowers. It makes a very good low-growing hedge, or is suitable as an edging to taller roses where a strong color is desired, especially when planted close together. ZONES 4–9.

KORDES, GERMANY, 1970

SEEDLING × 'MARLENA'

ANERKANNTE DEUTSCHE ROSE 1971

### 'Flutterbye'

**WEKplasol**

MODERN, MODERN SHRUB,
YELLOW BLEND

This rose is fascinating.
The large, single blooms
are a deep yellow,
changing to pinks and
golds as they open.
There is a red zone in
the center of the flower
and the effect of all
these colors together
on the plant is unique.
The color changes
are more pronounced
than in *Rosa chinensis
mutabilis.* The foliage
is rich green and plenti-
ful, as is its parent
'Playboy', and the
leaves on both varieties
are extremely glossy.
Tall in growth habit,
'Flutterbye' can be
used as a free-standing
shrub, or trained onto
a pillar or tripod as
a small climber.

Becoming popular in
America, 'Flutterbye'
will be much in demand
when it becomes better
known. **ZONES 5–9.**

CARRUTH, USA, 1996

'PLAYBOY' × *ROSA SOULIEANA*
SEEDLING

### 'Folklore'   **KORlore**
*(below left)*

MODERN, LARGE-FLOWERED/
HYBRID TEA, ORANGE BLEND,
REPEAT-FLOWERING

'Folklore' is a great
rose with extremely
strong growth, almost
reaching climbing pro-
portions with stems up
to 3 ft (1 m) in length.
The fragrant flowers
are large and particu-
larly well formed, with
45–50 thick petals each,
making it an excellent
variety for exhibition.
The blooms, which
hold their shape re-
markably well, are a

beautiful glowing
salmon-orange; they
are excellent for cutting
and have a good vase
life. The foliage is very
large, disease-free and
glossy. Because of its
height, it should be
planted at the back of
the border or bed. It
has produced a soft
creamy biscuit sport
called 'Delores'.
**ZONES 4–9.**

KORDES, GERMANY, 1977

'FRAGRANT CLOUD' × SEEDLING

### 'Fortune's Double Yellow'   *(below)*

**syns 'Beauty of
Glazenwood', 'Gold of
Ophir',** *Rosa × odorata
pseudindica,* **'San
Rafael Rose'**

OLD, MISCELLANEOUS, YELLOW
BLEND, REPEAT-FLOWERING

An extremely popular,
easy-to-grow rose in
warm climates, this
variety was discovered
by plant hunter Robert
Fortune (1812–80) in
the Chinese garden of a

wealthy mandarin.
The short, fat, round
buds are followed by
apricot-yellow, semi-
double blooms on
short stems; as they
age, the outer petals
reflex. There is a slight
flush of red on the
outside petals. The
fragrant blooms last
well when cut, and
the long, pliable canes
are easily trained on
pergolas or up trees.
Brown, hooked prickles
and serrated leaves line
the stems. It can be
used as a ground cover,
tumbling down a bank
or wall, but its most
spectacular role is as a
tree climber. In warm
climates it blooms early
and profusely with
some intermittent
flowers until late
autumn. **ZONES 5–9.**

FORTUNE, UK, 1845

PARENTAGE UNKNOWN

### 'Fortuniana'
syns 'Double Cherokee', 'Fortuneana',
*Rosa* × *fortuniana*
OLD, MISCELLANEOUS, WHITE

Often seen covering a small barn or arch, this variety is probably one of the healthiest roses available. The small, double, creamy white blooms have a violet scent and are usually solitary on short, bristly pedicules. The canes are gawky and need support. Glossy, attractive foliage with few prickles makes it a handsome plant even when not in bloom. It has been used as understock in humid areas, and in early summer, in the right spot and even in poor soil, this healthy rose will produce hundreds of blooms on well-established plants. It was introduced into England by Robert Fortune in 1845 and is quite similar to *Rosa banksiae* except that all its parts are larger. ZONES 6–7.

FORTUNE, UK, 1845

ROSA BANKSIAE × R. LAEVIGATA

### 'Fountain'
syns 'Fontaine', 'Red Prince'
MODERN, LARGE-FLOWERED/HYBRID TEA, MEDIUM RED,
REPEAT-FLOWERING

'Fountain' gained two premier awards in the one year but does not seem to have lived up to its early promise. Although not now available in many countries, it is a good rose with a shrubby habit that freely produces large, cupped, double flowers with 35 petals. The fragrance is very strong. The dark green foliage is glossy and disease resistant on a plant that is a good bedding rose. ZONES 4–9.

TANTAU, GERMANY, 1970

PARENTAGE UNKNOWN

ANERKANNTE DEUTSCHE ROSE 1971, ROYAL NATIONAL ROSE SOCIETY
PRESIDENT'S INTERNATIONAL TROPHY 1971

### 'Fourth of July'  WEKroalt  *(below)*
syn. 'Crazy For You'
MODERN, LARGE-FLOWERED CLIMBER, RED BLEND, REPEAT-FLOWERING

As the first climber to be awarded an All-American Rose Selection award in 22 years, this colorful climber has also gained awards abroad: for example, the Breeder's Choice in the UK. One of the few striped climbers in history, 'Fourth of July' celebrates American Independence. It is understandable that the rose is known in England by its synonym. Large, semi-double, velvety blooms of scarlet-red, striped white cover every part of the vigorous climber. Large sprays fill the air with their sweet fragrance. Reaching 12 ft (3.6 m) in maturity, the rose is often trained on fences for a spectacular effect. Deep green foliage acts as a dramatic background for the long blooming season. In cool climates it is grown as a shrub. ZONES 4–9.

CARRUTH, USA, 1999

'ROLLER COASTER' × 'ALTISSIMO'

ALL-AMERICA ROSE SELECTION 1999

## 'Fragrant Cloud'
TANellis *(right)*

syns 'Duftwolke',
'Nuage Parfumé'

MODERN, LARGE-FLOWERED/
HYBRID TEA, ORANGE-RED,
REPEAT-FLOWERING

'Fragrant Cloud', one of the best loved roses of the twentieth century, has extremely fragrant blooms as one would expect from a rose bred from 'Prima Ballerina'. The flowers are an unusual coral-red to geranium red, double with 30 petals, and very well formed; it has a particularly clear color and there is very little fading. The large foliage is a rich, glossy dark green on a vigorous bush that is very quick to repeat bloom. Mildew can be a problem in autumn, black spot can occur in damp weather, and die-back can occur in some strains. This variety is an excellent rose for bedding and for borders. **'Climbing Fragrant Cloud'** was propagated by Collin & Sons in England in 1973. The same coral-red blooms appear on the long canes, covered with dark, reddish-green foliage. Rising to 12 ft (3.6 m), this rose produces very fragrant blooms during the summer only.
ZONES 4–9.

TANTAU, GERMANY, 1967

SEEDLING × 'PRIMA BALLERINA'

NATIONAL ROSE SOCIETY PRESIDENT'S INTERNATIONAL TROPHY 1964, PORTLAND GOLD MEDAL 1966, JAMES ALEXANDER GAMBLE ROSE FRAGRANCE AWARD 1970, WORLD'S FAVORITE ROSE 1981

## 'Fragrant Delight'
*(left)*

MODERN, CLUSTER-FLOWERED/
FLORIBUNDA, ORANGE-PINK,
REPEAT-FLOWERING

'Fragrant Delight' is an excellent Cluster-flowered Rose in cold climates where its light orange-salmon pink double flowers with 22 petals retain their color well. The flowers fade very quickly in hot climates in summer, but do quite well in spring and autumn in these areas. It is extremely fragrant, an inheritance from 'Whisky Mac', and is extremely popular in the UK, where it won the James Mason Gold Medal. The foliage is glossy, healthy apart from some seasonal mildew, and red tinted in the early stages.
ZONES 4–9.

WISBECH PLANT COMPANY, UK, 1978

'CHANELLE' × 'WHISKY MAC'

EDLAND FRAGRANCE AWARD 1976, JAMES MASON GOLD MEDAL 1988

F

### 'Fragrant Dream'

DICodour *(above)*

MODERN, LARGE-FLOWERED/
HYBRID TEA, APRICOT BLEND,
REPEAT-FLOWERING

The parents of this variety are all in apricot-orange tones, as is the case with 'Fragrant Dream'; it is a most attractive color. The blooms are double with 20 petals and are very fragrant. The foliage is large and mid-green on an upright, bushy plant that blooms continuously and has good disease resistance.
ZONES 4–9.

DICKSON, UK, 1989

('EUROROSE' × 'TYPHOON') ×
'BONFIRE'

BELFAST FRAGRANCE PRIZE 1991

### 'Fragrant Hour'

*(top right)*

MODERN, LARGE-FLOWERED/
HYBRID TEA, ORANGE-PINK,
REPEAT-FLOWERING

'Fragrant Hour' has double, 35-petalled flowers which are an unusual shade of peachy apricot-pink. They open quickly to full blooms of good substance on long stems and have a very strong scent. The foliage is light green and abundant and disease resistance is good, but repeat bloom is a little slow. This variety is good for bedding.
ZONES 4–9.

MCGREDY, NEW ZEALAND, 1973

'ARTHUR BELL' × ('SPARTAN' ×
'GRAND GALA')

BELFAST GOLD MEDAL AND
FRAGRANCE PRIZE 1975

### 'Fragrant Plum'

AROplumi *(right)*

MODERN, LARGE-FLOWERED/
HYBRID TEA, MAUVE,
REPEAT-FLOWERING

'Fragrant Plum' forms an upright, very strong-growing bush that produces large candelabra-like heads of flowers where the side arms have long enough stems for

cutting. The sweet-scented flowers are very double, high centered and last well, with little fading of color either in the vase or on the bush. Bloom production is high. Lush new growth can burn on very hot days in hot climates, which applies to other roses such as 'Paradise', 'First Love', 'Josephine Bruce' and 'Thäis'.
ZONES 5–9.

CHRISTENSEN, USA, 1990

'SHOCKING BLUE' × ('BLUE NILE'
× 'IVORY TOWER')

F

### 'Frances Phoebe'
*(left)*
**syn. 'Francis Phoebe'**

MODERN, LARGE-FLOWERED/
HYBRID TEA, WHITE,
REPEAT-FLOWERING

'Frances Phoebe' was sent by Edward LeGrice to Treloar Roses in Australia for testing; Ted Treloar was very impressed with the very full, white, beautifully formed flowers and asked for permission to name the rose after his mother. The buds are long and develop slowly into 50-petal flowers of the highest exhibition quality that appear on short to moderate length stems. Flower production is very high on a disease-resistant bush with a reasonably tall growth habit. **ZONES 4–9.**

LEGRICE, UK, 1979

PARENTAGE UNKNOWN

### 'Francesca'
*(bottom)*

MODERN, MODERN SHRUB,
APRICOT BLEND,
REPEAT-FLOWERING

'Francesca' gets its buff apricot color from the early Large-flowered Rose 'Sunburst' and its spreading habit of growth from the shrub 'Danaë'. The lightly fragrant, almost single flowers are borne on long sprays on a tall, spreading bush with healthy, soft green foliage. Flower production is excellent in spring; the plant then blooms continuously from summer until autumn. An excellent shrub rose, 'Francesca' combines well with bulbs and perennials of similar coloring in a mixed border; in warmer areas it retains its foliage in winter in the manner of the Noisette Roses.
**ZONES 4–9.**

PEMBERTON, UK, 1922

'DANAË' × 'SUNBURST'

F

## 'Francine Austin'

AUSram *(right)*

MODERN, MODERN SHRUB,
WHITE, REPEAT-FLOWERING

'Francine Austin', which was named after the breeder's daughter, is a small, spreading, heavily foliaged shrub that grows much wider than tall. The slightly fragrant flowers are white, very double pompons on extremely tall, arching canes. The leaves are pale green and the leaflets long, narrow and widely spaced. This variety seems to become more compact and bushy in the UK than it does in warmer climates such as Australia, where the horizontal canes can suffer from sunburn in hot areas. It is good for picking and is excellent for cascading downward in church pedestal arrangements. **ZONES 4–9.**

AUSTIN, UK, 1988

'ALISTER STELLA GRAY' ×
'BALLERINA'

GLASGOW CERTIFICATE 1990

## 'Francis Dubreuil'

*(right)*
syn. 'François
Dubreuil'

OLD, TEA, DARK RED,
REPEAT-FLOWERING

One of the darkest blooms in the rose world, this handsome rose needs part-shade to prevent its delicate, blood-red petals from scorching. The long, pointed buds open to reveal large, full, cupped flowers looking very much as if they were cut from velvet. The thick petals are peony-like and are quite destroyed in wet weather. The 3 ft (1 m), upright, somewhat lanky shrub is an ideal container plant, although it does have some prickles. It should be placed where its lovely scent can be enjoyed during its long blooming period. Dubreuil was a tailor in Lyon, France, before he took up rose hybridizing; he was the grandfather of Francis Meilland. **ZONES 4–9.**

DUBREUIL, FRANCE, 1894

PARENTAGE UNKNOWN

F

### 'Francis E. Lester'
*(above)*

MODERN, MODERN SHRUB, WHITE

'Francis E. Lester' is a very vigorous climbing rose, growing to 13–16 ft (4–5 m) that has thorny stems and pliable canes. The blooms, which appear rather late in spring in large panicles of up to 60 blooms, are white flushed with pale pink, single, 2 in (5 cm) across and look like huge heads of apple blossom. The huge hips that follow the flowers also appear in big clusters and last right through winter as birds do not seem to like them. Some growers get repeat bloom, but this is not common. In Odile Masquelie's garden, La Bon Maison in Lyon, a repeat-flowering seedling has occurred under 'Francis E. Lester' that is an excellent rose, flowering through summer and autumn and remaining shrub-like. 'Francis E. Lester' itself is a superb rose for growing into trees, where it can cascade downwards and show its huge sprays of flowers and hips to perfection. **ZONES 4–9.**

LESTER ROSE GARDENS, USA, 1946

'KATHLEEN' × SEEDLING

### 'François Juranville' *(bottom)*

MODERN, RAMBLER, ORANGE-PINK

The late Jack Harkness praised this rose as the most beautiful of all the *wichurana* hybrids. The bright

salmon-pink blooms appear as clusters over a long flowering period in summer. They are flat and a deeper pink in the center with a yellow base. The petals are quilled and quartered, and the fragrance is reminiscent of apples. Reaching almost 25 ft (8 m) at maturity, it has upright, very vigorous canes with shiny dark leaves, which are bronze-green at the edges, and a few prickles. It seems happiest climbing a tree, although it is often used as a ground cover. **ZONES 4–9.**

BARBIER, FRANCE, 1906

*ROSA WICHURANA* × 'MME LAURETTE MESSIMY'

ROYAL HORTICULTURAL SOCIETY AWARD OF GARDEN MERIT 1993

### 'Frau Astrid Späth'

syns 'Astrid Späth', 'Direktör Rikala'

MODERN, CLUSTER-FLOWERED/ FLORIBUNDA, DEEP PINK, REPEAT-FLOWERING

Both this rose and 'Lafayette' are shortish roses with good foliage and heads of flowers in clusters. The foliage is dark and glossy and there are plenty of blooms in a clear carmine rose color. This variety was used for low borders and bedding for many years in Europe and is still seen in many large parks and country gardens today. Disease resistance is excellent and the plant is particularly hardy to winter cold, which is probably the reason why 'Frau Astrid Späth' is still grown in abundance.

ZONES 4–9.

SPÄTH, GERMANY, 1930

SPORT OF 'LAFAYETTE'

### 'Frau Karl Druschki' *(top right)*

syns 'F. K. Druschki', 'Reine des Neiges', 'Schneekoenigen', 'Snow Queen', 'White American Beauty'

OLD, HYBRID PERPETUAL, WHITE, REPEAT-FLOWERING

For many this is the best of all the white roses, both as a bloom in the garden and as an elegant cut flower. The solitary snow-white blooms, which have 35 petals, are cupped with prominent stamens and appear in summer with a strong repeat-bloom in early autumn. The blooms do not like wet weather. The 6 ft (1.8 m) robust shrub is covered with handsome foliage and brutal prickles and there are many round, red hips. It needs careful pruning and is a good subject for pegging down. The husband of Frau Druschki was president of the German Rose Society. 'Climbing Frau Karl Druschki' is identical to its parent, except that the flowers are smaller; it will reach 15 ft (4.5 m) and needs to be pruned of dead wood annually.

ZONES 4–9.

LAMBERT, GERMANY, 1901

'MERVEILLE DE LYON' × 'MME CAROLINE TESTOUT'

### 'Fred Loads'

*(above)*

MODERN, CLUSTER-FLOWERED/ FLORIBUNDA, ORANGE-RED, REPEAT-FLOWERING

'Fred Loads' gets is vigor from its parent, 'Dorothy Wheatcroft'. It produces enormous clusters of single 3 in (8 cm) blooms at the top of extremely long canes with abundant, glossy foliage. If it is pruned hard to reduce its ungainly height in winter, it then produces enormous heads of flowers that can often win prizes in shows; the only other contender for such huge trusses is 'Sally Holmes'. It can make an impenetrable tall hedge and is also suitable for bright color at the back of a mixed border, combined with such flowers as kniphofias, golden rod and sunflowers.

ZONES 4–9.

LOADS, UK, 1967

'DOROTHY WHEATCROFT' × 'ORANGE SENSATION'

NATIONAL ROSE SOCIETY GOLD MEDAL 1967, ROYAL HORTICULTURAL SOCIETY AWARD OF GARDEN MERIT 1993

F

Budding is the recommended method of propagation. **ZONES 5–9.**

MEILLAND, FRANCE, 1996

('PERFUME DELIGHT' × 'PRIMA BALLERINA') × MEIZELI

BADEN-BADEN FRAGRANCE AWARD 1993, LEROEUIX FRAGRANCE AWARD 1994, MONZA FRAGRANCE AWARD 1994, BELFAST FRAGRANCE AWARD 1996

## 'Freedom' DICjem
### (bottom)
**MODERN, LARGE-FLOWERED/ HYBRID TEA, DEEP YELLOW, REPEAT-FLOWERING**

'Freedom' has well formed, fragrant, large blooms with 35 petals. The color is a rich chrome yellow, probably inherited from its parent, 'Bright Smile'. The foliage is mid-green and glossy on a medium bush. Flower production is excellent and there is a quick repeat blooming between flushes. This superb rose for bedding or for hedges is very popular in the UK and its gold medal award was well deserved. **ZONES 4–9.**

DICKSON, UK, 1984

('EUROROSE' × 'TYPHOON') × 'BRIGHT SMILE'

ROYAL NATIONAL ROSE SOCIETY GOLD MEDAL 1983, GLASGOW CERTIFICATE OF MERIT 1989, ROYAL HORTICULTURAL SOCIETY AWARD OF GARDEN MERIT 1993, JAMES MASON AWARD 1977

## 'Frederic Mistral'
**MEItebros** *(above)*

### syn. 'The Children's Rose'
**MODERN, LARGE-FLOWERED/ HYBRID TEA, LIGHT PINK, REPEAT-FLOWERING**

As a winner of so many awards for its fragrance, gardeners can expect much from this rose. As well as their fragrance, the flowers have excellent shape; fully double, filled with many petals to form an urn shape with a tight center. 'Frederic Mistral' is covered with mid-green foliage and makes a good bedding variety.

## 'Freisinger Morgenröte'

KORmarter *(right)*

syns 'Morgenröte', 'Sunrise'

MODERN, LARGE-FLOWERED CLIMBER, ORANGE BLEND, REPEAT-FLOWERING

The flowers of this rose are red, blended with orange. They have 25 petals, and are borne profusely in spring on a tall plant. The foliage is small and dark and the growth quite free. There is some repeat bloom. **ZONES 4–9.**

KORDES, GERMANY, 1988

SEEDLING × 'LICHTKÖNIGEN LUCIA'

## 'French Lace' JAClace *(left)*

MODERN, CLUSTER-FLOWERED/FLORIBUNDA, WHITE, REPEAT-FLOWERING

'French Lace', which is as beautifully formed as its parents, is a lovely little rose with the most delicate coloring of tints of ivory, buff and palest apricot. The flowers have 30 petals and are borne usually singly or in clusters of up to 5 blooms. There is, unfortunately, very little scent, which is surprising as 'Dr A. J. Verhage' is very well scented. The foliage is small and dark on a very bushy plant of low to medium height. This rose makes a lovely border or low hedge and is an excellent low bedding rose. In spite of the short growth, flower production is excellent and regrowth is rapid. It is very popular in Australia, New Zealand and the USA. It is an excellent rose for indoor decoration when a small arrangement of delicate coloring is required. **ZONES 4–9.**

WARRINER, USA, 1980

'DR A. J. VERHAGE' × 'BRIDAL PINK'

ALL-AMERICA ROSE SELECTION 1982, PORTLAND GOLD MEDAL 1984

F

### 'Frensham' *(above)*

MODERN, CLUSTER-FLOWERED/FLORIBUNDA, DARK RED,
REPEAT-FLOWERING

This rose set the standard of excellence for red
Cluster-flowered Roses for over 30 years. The
medium-sized flowers are deep scarlet red, semi-
double with 15 petals and are borne in large
clusters. The growth is vigorous and spreading.
There is only a little fragrance, which is strange
for a rose with 'Crimson Glory' as a parent.
'Frensham' is a good rose for bedding and for
hedges, but lost favor because of mildew problems on young growth, and its thorns, of which
it has its fair share, but over the years it seems to
have come back into favor. One of the great roses
of the late 1940s and 1950s, it was probably the
first really popular red Cluster-flowered Rose.
**ZONES 4–9.**

NORMAN, UK, 1946

PROBABLY 'MISS EDITH CAVELL' × 'EDGAR ANDREW'

NATIONAL ROSE SOCIETY GOLD MEDAL 1949

## 'Frenzy' MEIhigor
*(right)*

syn. 'Prince Igor'

MODERN, CLUSTER-FLOWERED/
FLORIBUNDA, RED BLEND,
REPEAT-FLOWERING

This rose gets its stunning color from a combination of colors from all its parents. It is a short-growing rose with blooms of a particularly brilliant nasturtium red, with a vivid apricot-yellow reverse. Borne singly and in small clusters, they are well formed in the bud, opening to semi-double blooms of 25 petals that are 2 in (5 cm) across. The fragrance is fruity and the foliage is matt, dark green and acts as a good background for the flowers. It makes an excellent low border or hedge, and also looks good arranged with rosehips and autumn foliage for display in the home. The long-flowering 'Climbing Frenzy' produces the same sweet fragrance as its parent. Because it is so brilliant, it looks best when planted alone. ZONES 4–9.

MEILLAND, FRANCE, 1970

('SARABANDE' × 'DANY ROBIN)'
× 'ZAMBRA'

F

## 'Fresh Pink'

MODERN, MINIATURE, LIGHT PINK, REPEAT-FLOWERING

This rose has delicate ovoid buds that open to reveal light pink florets tipped with salmon. The florets are double with 25 petals, cupped and usually occur in very floriferous clusters (in excess of 20 blooms per stem). They have a light fragrance and are nicely complemented by leathery, glossy foliage. The bush thrives on neglect—it tends to clean itself and restart the bloom cycle. As the name suggests, the florets are a quite refreshing pink and look lovely in the garden. It is certainly a decorative rose. The seed parent is the key seedling developed by Moore to carry the ease of propagation into Miniature Roses. ZONES 4–11.

MOORE, USA, 1964

(ROSA WICHURANA × 'FLORADORA') × 'LITTLE BUCKAROO'

F

### 'Freude' DeKORat
*(below)*
syn. 'Decorat'

MODERN, LARGE-FLOWERED/
HYBRID TEA, ORANGE-RED,
REPEAT-FLOWERING

'Freude' is an extremely strong-growing rose with fragrant, vermilion flushed gold blooms with a gold reverse to the petals. They are of very good form, opening slowly to exhibition-type flowers. Growth is free, and flower production is good, although flushes are a fair way apart. It is good for cutting and for use where a strong color is desired. Too tall for bedding but suitable for the back row of a rose bed, this variety deserved its award. **ZONES 4–9.**

KORDES, GERMANY, 1975

'FRAGRANT CLOUD' ×
'PEER GYNT'

ANERKANNTE DEUTSCHE ROSE
1975

### 'Friendship' LINrick
*(below)*

MODERN, LARGE-FLOWERED/
HYBRID TEA, DEEP PINK,
REPEAT-FLOWERING

This rose makes a strong bush with an upright growth habit and large, leathery, dark green, profuse foliage. The flowers on long stems are an unusual color—deep pink flushes with coral pink. They are double with 28 petals and open slowly to large, flat, well-formed blooms that are very fragrant. Flower production is good and continuous, and the flowers last well both on the bush and indoors, where their color is enhanced by artificial light. It has excellent disease resistance. **ZONES 4–9.**

LINDQUIST, USA, 1978

'FRAGRANT CLOUD' ×
'MARIA CALLAS'

F

## 'Fritz Nobis'
**(bottom)**

MODERN, MODERN SHRUB,
PINK BLEND

This is one of the most aesthetically satisfying roses ever raised, seeming to have every leaf, petal and flower in the right place. It produces arching branches and covers them with an abundance of leathery grayish green leaves, and then produces a show of flowers in summer that creates as lovely a shrub as you could find in any species. The blooms are like small-scale Large-flowered Roses in the young flower, then open cupped. They are double, of medium size, borne in clusters of up to 20, and are chiefly light rose and salmon-pink, though cream and yellow tints are also present. There is a pleasing fragrance, but, unfortunately, no extension of the flowering period beyond the first flush. For a shrubbery or mixed border, this is a splendid rose to grow. It needs room, being about twice the size of an average shrub rose, and is remarkably healthy and hardy. **ZONES 4–9.**

KORDES, GERMANY, 1940

'JOANNA HILL' × 'MAGNIFICA'

ROYAL HORTICULTURAL SOCIETY
AWARD OF GARDEN MERIT 1993

## 'Fru Dagmar Hastrup' *(above)*
syn. 'Frau Dagmar Hartopp'

MODERN, MODERN SHRUB,
MEDIUM PINK,
REPEAT-FLOWERING

There is much controversy as to the correct spelling of the name of this rose, but be that as it may, it is an excellent shrub that produces large single flowers of a very clear silvery pink, continuously from spring until winter, that show up very well against the healthy rich green wrinkled foliage. A short, stocky grower, it produces a large crop of bright red, round hips, the first lot ripening for Christmas and able to be used for Christmas decorations in lieu of holly, which of course is not in fruit in summer in the Southern Hemisphere. 'Fru Dagmar Hastrup' suckers and forms a small thicket if the bud union is planted below ground level. It makes a lovely low hedge when the flowers and fruit are on the bush at the one time, and it can also be planted in the woodland or a shrub border as a foreground to large-growing species roses. This variety is a simple yet sophisticated rose of a beautiful color and is very popular in all countries. **ZONES 3–9.**

HASTRUP, DENMARK, 1914

PARENTAGE UNKNOWN

ROYAL HORTICULTURAL SOCIETY
AWARD OF GARDEN MERIT 1993

F

### 'Frühlingsanfang'
*(below)*
syn. 'Spring's Beginning'
MODERN, MODERN SHRUB, WHITE

This variety produces large, white, single flowers that open out like shallow saucers to reveal prominent creamy yellow stamens. The blooms appear in spring when the arching branches are laden with flowers, and with their scent, but they do not give a repeat performance, although by autumn there are maroon hips. The growth habit is very large, and it is such a dominating plant that it needs a position with plenty of room where it can be allowed to grow naturally. The leaves are dark green and healthy and attractive when they change color in autumn. ZONES 4–9.

KORDES, GERMANY, 1950

'JOANNA HILL' × ROSA PIMPINELLIFOLIA ALTAICA

### 'Frühlingsduft'
*(right)*
syn. 'Spring Fragrance'
MODERN, MODERN SHRUB, PINK BLEND

Wilhelm Kordes' crossing of the Large-flowered 'Joanna Hill' with a tough rose from the Altai mountain region in central Asia produced a remarkably large and vigorous plant. It bears fully double Large-flowered-type blooms that are light yellow to cream with some pink tints. They are freely produced in clusters of up to 5 fairly large blooms and open out loosely cupped, with muddled centers. The synonym indicates that this variety is strongly scented, but the show of bloom occurs only in spring. Growth is very vigorous, to 2 or 3 times that of the average shrub rose, and the plant is well furnished with large, leathery leaves. ZONES 4–9.

KORDES, GERMANY, 1949

'JOANNA HILL' × ROSA PIMPINELLIFOLIA ALTAICA

## 'Frühlingsgold'  *(right)*
syn. 'Spring Gold'

MODERN, MODERN SHRUB, MEDIUM YELLOW

This variety is easily recognized in parks and gardens by its open, tree-like growth, decorated lavishly along the arching branches with big pale yellow semi-double flowers that open like saucers and have prominent sulfur yellow stamens. They are among the earliest roses to bloom in springtime, and have a pleasing refreshing scent. There is scarcely any later bloom, but it is an excellent rose where space is available for it. Spent and crossing stems should be pruned out but otherwise it is best left alone, because blooms are produced along side shoots made in previous years, and pruning will mean loss of potential flowers. The young basal shoots have a downy fuzz of red-gold prickles, a magical sight when they are caught by the sun. The plant grows about double the size of an average shrub rose and has light green, rather wrinkled leaves and, in autumn, round purplish black hips, which are interesting but not particularly decorative.

**ZONES 4–9.**

KORDES, GERMANY, 1937

'JOANNA HILL' × *ROSA PIMPINELLIFOLIA HISPIDA*

ROYAL HORTICULTURAL SOCIETY AWARD OF GARDEN MERIT 1993

## 'Frühlingsmorgen'  *(bottom)*
syn. 'Spring Morning'

MODERN, MODERN SHRUB, PINK BLEND

'Frühlingsmorgen' is not as dominating a grower as most members of the 'Frühlings' group, and perhaps for that reason it is more often seen in gardens. The flowers are large, single and strikingly beautiful, being pale primrose in the center, rimmed with cherry pink. Particularly fine are the maroon stamens, which are well displayed as the petals open wide. The flowers have quite a pleasant scent, and after the main flush in spring a few appear sporadically during summer and autumn. The plant makes a rather open, freely branching shrub with ample, dark grayish green foliage, growing up to twice the dimensions of an average shrub rose. The hips are maroon and fairly large.

**ZONES 4–9.**

KORDES, GERMANY, 1941

('E. G. HILL' × 'CATHRINE KORDES') × *ROSA PIMPINELLIFOLIA ALTAICA*

F

## 'Frühlingszauber'
*(top)*

MODERN, MODERN SHRUB, MEDIUM PINK

This rose is similar to 'Frühlingsmorgen', which is not surprising since they have the same parentage; the differences lie in the number of petals and the habit of growth. 'Frühlingszauber' has semi-double, eye-catching blooms that open to show rich cerise petal margins with prominent whitish yellow centers. They appear freely in spring in clusters of up to 10 blooms and carry a moderate fragrance, but do not repeat their bloom. The plant is upright, growing to about twice average size, but is open in habit to the extent of appearing spindly; it has a good covering of mid-green leaves. The name means 'spring magic', but its popularity has not equalled that of others in this group. ZONES 4–9.

KORDES, GERMANY, 1942

('E. G. HILL' × 'CATHRINE KORDES') × *ROSA PIMPINELLIFOLIA ALTAICA*

## 'Fruité'   MElfructoz
*(bottom)*

syn. 'Fruitee'

MODERN, CLUSTER-FLOWERED/ FLORIBUNDA, ORANGE BLEND, REPEAT-FLOWERING

'Fruité' makes a wonderful bedding rose, laden as it is with clusters of flowers. They are semi-double and open cupped to reveal a blend of apricot-yellow, salmon and orange-red in a cheerful melange of colors. They are lightly fragrant, are borne very freely on the first flowering, and continue to provide cycles of growth and bloom through summer and autumn. As well as its usefulness for bedding, this variety is a pleasing rose to cut for the home or to show, withstanding bad weather well. The growth habit is neat and fairly even to average height, the plant is well clothed in glossy green leaves, and it has a good health record. Only the superb abundance of good roses can explain why it is not more widely known and grown. ZONES 4–9.

MEILLAND, FRANCE, 1985

PARENTAGE UNKNOWN

BELFAST GOLD MEDAL 1987

### 'Fuchsia Meidiland'

MEIpelta *(right)*
syns 'Cyclamen
Meillandécor', 'Fuchsia
Meillandécor'

MODERN, MODERN SHRUB,
DEEP PINK, REPEAT-FLOWERING

The Meilland rose-
breeding station has
developed many var-
ieties with park use
in mind, and this rose
answers that purpose
well. It is very free
blooming, bearing
flowers of 12 or so
petals in large clusters.
They are medium sized
in a deep pink shade,
open cupped, and
repeat their bloom
satisfactorily through
summer and autumn,
though they do not
have much fragrance.
The growth is low and
spreading so it is some-
times considered a
ground cover rose, but
it is hardly procumbent
enough to fit happily
in that group. The
leaves are light green
and glossy, of medium
size and plentiful.
ZONES 4–9.

MEILLAND, FRANCE, 1991

'BORDURELLA' × 'CLAIR MATIN'

### 'Fulgurante'

*(bottom)*

MODERN, LARGE-FLOWERED/
HYBRID TEA, MEDIUM RED

Although very little
is known about
'Fulgurante', it is
valued for its superbly
urn-shaped, double,
velvety red flowers.
It is a good bedding

variety, which can be
propagated by bud-
ding. ZONES 5–9.

PARENTAGE UNKNOWN

### 'Fulton MacKay'

COCdana
syns 'Maribel',
'Senteur des Iles'

MODERN, LARGE-FLOWERED/
HYBRID TEA, YELLOW BLEND,
REPEAT-FLOWERING

The beauty of this rose
lies in the outstanding
quality of the flowers,
which open from long
buds to classically
shaped Large-flowered
blooms with high
centers, surrounded by
broad reflexing petals.
They are a rich apricot-
yellow with pink veining,
with reddish salmon
tints on the outer
petals. It has a pleasing

spicy scent, and after a
prolific first flush of
bloom, more flowers
appear through sum-
mer and autumn. This
rose is good for cutting
and for a bed or group.
It is not immune to
black spot in a bad
year but its vigor over-
comes it. The plant has

a bushy, upright habit
and plentiful glossy
mid-green foliage. It
was named for a distin-
guished Scottish actor.
ZONES 4–9.

COCKER & SON, UK, 1989

'SILVER JUBILEE' × 'JANA'

ROYAL NATIONAL ROSE SOCIETY
TRIAL GROUND CERTIFICATE
1984, GLASGOW GOLD MEDAL
1992

F

G

G

### 'Gabriel Noyelle'
*(below)*
syn. 'Gabrielle Noyelle'
OLD, MOSS, APRICOT BLEND,
REPEAT-FLOWERING

When the small, shapely, oval buds of this variety open fully, they reveal double orange-salmon blooms with a yellow base; the color fades with age. The cupped blooms have a strong scent. The foliage is dark green and leathery on an upright, bushy plant that grows to a height of 4 ft (1.2 m). This popular Moss Rose

blooms later than most and sometimes repeats in autumn. The firm of Buatois also created the climbing Large-flowered Rose 'Reveil Dijonnais'. ZONES 4–9.
BUATOIS, FRANCE, 1933
'SALET' × 'SOUVENIR DE MME KREUGER'

### 'Gabriella'    BERgme
*(below)*
syn. 'Gabrielle'
MODERN, CLUSTER-FLOWERED/
FLORIBUNDA, MEDIUM RED,
REPEAT-FLOWERING

This is grown by the thousands for the cut flower industry, having been discovered by a Swedish grower as a sport on a plant of another celebrated florists' rose, 'Mercedes'. It is medium red, and through summer and autumn it provides a good supply of flowers on short, wiry, almost thornless stems and needing little disbudding to obtain them. The flowers open in roundelay fashion, with overlapping petals, and last for ages. They have little scent. There is little point in growing 'Gabriella' in the garden except in very warm climates, but in a greenhouse it is rewarding. The bush grows to medium height or above and has olive green, leathery leaves. ZONES 5–9.
BERGGREN, SWEDEN, 1977
SPORT OF 'MERCEDES'

## 'Galaxy' MORgal
*(below right)*

MODERN, MINIATURE, DARK
RED, REPEAT-FLOWERING

The long, pointed buds of this rose develop into deep velvety red, double flowers made up of 23 petals. The small, non-fragrant blooms have typical Large-flowered form and occur either singly or in small clusters of 5–10 blooms. There is a nice color contrast between the vivid red petals and the heavy yellow stamens at the fully open stage—a stunning combination, which can be disappointingly muddy in cool weather. It really takes the heat to bring out the sparkle. This ever-blooming bush can be planted as a hedge to give constant color throughout the growing season; it is also covered with small leaves and slightly downward-curving prickles. The plant has vigorous growth and is upright in habit. ZONES 4–11.

MOORE, USA, 1980

'FAIRY MOSS' × 'FAIRY
PRINCESS'

## 'Galway Bay' MACba
*(below)*

MODERN, LARGE-FLOWERED
CLIMBER, ORANGE-PINK,
REPEAT-FLOWERING

The given color classi-fication of this variety is misleading because it is a rich deep cerise-pink; it holds its color through the life of the flower, with little obvious hint of orange about it. It is a vigorous climber that bears clus-ters of several blooms in summer, continuing to flower through late summer and autumn. The flowers are of medium size, fairly full of petals and open cupped, the petals overlapping in an at-tractive way. There is a pleasant light scent. The growth is stiff and branching to average height, and it is best trained against a wall, fence or pillar. The foliage is dark green, oval, plentiful and usually very healthy. Galway Bay is off the windswept and beautiful west coast of Ireland. ZONES 4–9.

MCGREDY, UK, 1966

'HEIDELBERG' × 'QUEEN
ELIZABETH'

G

G

## 'Garden Party'
*(above)*

MODERN, LARGE-FLOWERED/
HYBRID TEA, WHITE,
REPEAT-FLOWERING

Both parents of this
rose have rewarded
breeders with some ex-
cellent offspring, and
'Garden Party' is a fine
example. The blooms
are beautifully con-
structed, opening from
urn-shaped buds into
large, full flowers of
delicate and graceful
appearance. They are
double, with long
petals that form a high
center, and become
prettily waved as they
reflex to form a wide
bowl-shaped flower.
The color is basically
ivory merging into
creamy yellow, with
flushes of pink; these
cool shades look sooth-
ing among brighter-
hued roses whether
the variety is cut for the
house or used for
bedding in the garden.

The first flush of bloom
is very free for so large
a rose, and flowering
continues through
summer and autumn.
There is a pleasant light
fragrance. The plant
grows bushily to average
height or more and
is well clothed in dark
foliage. ZONES 4–9.

SWIM, USA, 1959

'CHARLOTTE ARMSTRONG' ×
'PEACE'

BAGATELLE GOLD MEDAL 1959,
ALL-AMERICA ROSE SELECTION
1960

## 'Gardenia'

MODERN, RAMBLER, WHITE

This Rambler has
recently regained its
popularity as one of the
best white roses in its
class. The pointed yel-
low buds develop into
creamy white flowers
with a yellow center.
The large, full, cupped
blooms appear in
small sprays on short,
strong stems during a
prolonged blooming

period; muddled and
fragrant, the flowers
will stay yellow if
planted in the shade.
The foliage is small,
dark and glossy. It makes
a stunning display on
an arch or pergola or
climbing up a tree,
reaching 20 ft (6 m).
The same nursery pro-
duced 'Jersey Beauty'.
ZONES 7–10.

MANDA, USA, 1899

*ROSA WICHURANA* × 'PERLE
DES JARDINS'

## 'Garnette'
*(above right)*
syns 'Garnet',
'Garnette Red', 'Red
Garnette'

MODERN, CLUSTER-FLOWERED/
FLORIBUNDA, DARK RED,
REPEAT-FLOWERING

'Leave it to the florists'
is the advice of one
expert regarding this
rose. Although it has
been immensely popu-
lar as a cut rose in all
parts of the world, it
defies attempts to

replicate the dainty
well-spaced sprays of
garnet red flowers out
of doors. There the
sprays arrange them-
selves less obligingly,
the stems failing to grow
to the required length,
and mildew is likely
to ruin the whole en-
semble. When it is
grown for the florist,
the sprays open slowly
to show cupped flowers
of regular form, with
each row of firm petals
neatly lapping its
neighbor and main-
taining perfect shape
and color tone for
many days. Flowering
continues through
summer and autumn,
but there is very little
scent. Under glass it
grows to above average
height, but it is shorter
in the open garden.
The leaves are purplish
when young, becoming
deep green. ZONES 4–9.

TANTAU, GERMANY, 1951

('ROSENELFE' × 'EVA') × 'HEROS'

## 'Gartendirektor Otto Linne'

MODERN, MODERN SHRUB, DEEP PINK, REPEAT-FLOWERING

Except in one important respect, this is a rose with all the virtues. It is vigorous, healthy and easy to grow, is handsomely foliaged, flowers very freely and has the sort of habit that pleases fastidious gardeners who look to the outline and appearance of the whole plant. Where it falls down is in lack of scent, which is a considerable drawback for a rose with its appearance of old-fashioned charm. The modest-sized blooms are deep pink with a little yellow at the base, shaped like pompons with many small petals, and appear in big clusters of up to 30 flowers. They continue, with intervening rest periods, through summer and autumn. It will give good value as a garden plant, growing to about average height, with many light green leaves. ZONES 4–9.

LAMBERT, GERMANY, 1934

'ROBIN HOOD' × 'RUDOLPH KLUIS'

## 'Gavnø' POUlgav
*(below)*
syn. 'Bucks Fizz'

MODERN, CLUSTER-FLOWERED/ FLORIBUNDA, ORANGE BLEND, REPEAT-FLOWERING

This is grown by a number of British nurseries under its synonym, which in this case refers to a pop group rather than the popular drink. The roses are a cheerful and rather gentle shade of orange, borne in clusters of several together and shaped like small-scale Large-flowered blooms. They are of middling size and have about 20 broad petals, sufficient to create a high center as the petals begin to unfold and later become cupped. There is little scent and the flowers continue to appear through summer and autumn. Despite its Scandinavian origin, the variety seems liable to frost damage in a severe winter, and therefore a site protected from cold spring winds is advisable. The plant grows upright to average height or a little less, and has dark foliage that is reddish when young. ZONES 5–9.

OLESEN, DENMARK, 1988

SEEDLING × 'MARY SUMNER'

ROYAL NATIONAL ROSE SOCIETY TRIAL GROUND CERTIFICATE 1987

## 'Géant des Batailles' *(below)*
syn. 'Giant of Battles'

OLD, HYBRID PERPETUAL, MEDIUM RED

This rose was extra-ordinarily popular in the late 1800s, and it retains its place as a fine cut flower. The round, fat buds open to full (85 petals), flat, deep crimson blooms

that turn maroon with age. The inner petals fold upon themselves. Groups of blooms appear at the ends of branches, supported by sturdy pedicels. It is a moderately vigorous, erect but low-growing bush with robust stalks, dark green, serrated leaves, and prickles that line the canes. It is susceptible to mildew and rust. ZONES 5–9.

NÉRARD, FRANCE, 1846

HYBRID OF 'GLOIRE DES ROSOMANES'

## 'Geisha' *(bottom)*
syn. 'Pink Elizabeth Arden'

MODERN, CLUSTER-FLOWERED/ FLORIBUNDA, MEDIUM PINK, REPEAT-FLOWERING

There is a bed of this variety in the Gardens of the Rose in St Albans in England, which has looked splendid ever since it was planted decades ago. In spite of that it has never become well known in the UK, perhaps be-cause other good roses of similar color such as 'Dearest' and 'Vera Dalton' were already on the market. 'Geisha' produces many clusters of up to 20 pointed buds that open into quite large semi-double blooms of a very pure rose pink shade, set off by dark stamens. They are lightly scented, and repeat-flowering is excellent through summer and autumn, opening cleanly in all weathers. The plant grows evenly and bushily to average height and is well endowed with deep green glossy leaves. The raiser wanted to call it 'Elizabeth Arden', but there was a white rose of that name already and, as 'Pink Elizabeth Arden' is such a mouthful, it is more often sold as 'Geisha'. ZONES 4–9.

TANTAU, GERMANY, 1964

PARENTAGE UNKNOWN

G

## 'Gene Boerner'

MODERN, CLUSTER-FLOWERED/FLORIBUNDA, MEDIUM PINK, REPEAT-FLOWERING

'Gene Boerner' has pink flowers of exceptional size and quality for a Cluster-flowered Rose. They open from plump buds into double, deep pink roses with centers of beautiful symmetry, which hold their form while the outer petals slowly reflex. In the depths of the flower, deeper pink tones are seen. This is a good variety for cutting and bedding, though the old flowers are liable to be blemished as they age. It continues to give a display through summer and autumn. The plant grows vigorously with an upright, slender habit to above average height and has a good complement of mid-green, glossy and healthy foliage. Eugene Boerner (1893–1966), known affectionately as 'Papa Floribunda' for his major contributions to this group of roses, was in charge of hybridizing for the Jackson & Perkins nursery. **ZONES 4–9.**

BOERNER, USA, 1968

'GINGER' × ('MA PERKINS' × 'GARNETTE SUPREME')

ALL-AMERICA ROSE SELECTION 1969

## 'Général Galliéni'  *(above)*

OLD, TEA, RED BLEND

The fresh Tea fragrance of this rose becomes obvious on a warm day as the blowsy, coppery red blooms open. The cupped flowers change color, depending on the weather and whether it is placed in sun or shade. The color range during the long blooming season includes apricot, pink, yellow, blood red and maroon. It is a fine cut flower. The vigorous shrub displays dark green foliage and hooked red prickles, and does best in a warm position. It was named for the Governor-General of Madagascar, then part of the French empire. **ZONES 7–9.**

NABONNAND, FRANCE, 1899

'SOUVENIR DE THÉRÈSE LEVET' × 'REINE EMMA DES PAYS-BAS'

G

### 'Général Jacqueminot' *(above left)*
syns 'General Jack', 'Jack Rose', 'La Brilliante', 'Mrs Cleveland Richard Smith', 'Triomphe d'Amiens'

OLD, HYBRID PERPETUAL, RED BLEND, REPEAT-FLOWERING

There are at least 500 seedlings and up to 60 sports of this honored Hybrid Perpetual on the books, and most of today's red roses can trace their ancestry to it. Scarlet-crimson buds open to immense, dark red flowers that rest on long, strong stems and the fragrant, velvety, double blooms have 27 petals. The large outer petals are closely packed, with occasional white streaks. It flowers freely from summer until autumn, but the blooms do not like hot sun. The foliage is tinged with red on a bushy plant, and prickles line the stout stems. Mildew and rust may be a problem. Amateur breeder Roussel of Meudon, France named this rose for a French general of the early nineteenth century. ZONES 5–9.

ROUSSEL, FRANCE, 1853

SEEDLING OF 'GLOIRE DES ROSOMANES'

FIRST PRIZE VERSAILLES EXHIBITION 1854

### 'Général Kléber' *(above)*

OLD, MOSS, MEDIUM PINK

This Moss Rose, which is outstanding in all respects, has flowers that appear only once in early to mid-summer and are full, shapely and large, up to 4 in (10 cm) across. They are arranged in small clusters and are a soft silvery pink but, despite this pale coloring, the blooms stand up well to wet weather. There is a most delicious fragrance. It grows up to 5 ft (1.5 m) in good soils. Both the bright green leaves and numerous buds and flower stalks are generously covered with bright green, soft-to-touch moss; the stems are also amply mossed but have few thorns. Général Kléber was in charge of Napoleon's army during the Egypt campaign. ZONES 4–9.

ROBERT, FRANCE, 1856

PARENTAGE UNKNOWN

### 'Général Schablikine' *(bottom)*

OLD, TEA, ORANGE-PINK, REPEAT-FLOWERING

This rose has fat buds of strong purple-pink that open to coppery pink, fragrant blooms that are double, flat and quartered. The outer petals curl away from the paler, inner ones. Only occasionally nodding, the blooms sit on firm stems and love the sun. The 3 ft (1 m) bush has plum-colored shoots with medium-sized, blue-green leaves; there are tiny prickles under the leaf stalks. It requires little pruning and can be groomed with constant deadheading, and makes a fine bedding plant as it is strongly disease resistant. The Nabonnand family created a dynasty of roses at their Riviera nursery from 1872 to 1924. Schablikine was a Crimean war hero. ZONES 6–9.

NABONNAND, FRANCE, 1878

PARENTAGE UNKNOWN

## 'Gentle Touch'

DIClulu  *(right)*

MODERN, PATIO/DWARF
CLUSTER-FLOWERED, LIGHT PINK,
REPEAT-FLOWERING

The light pink, double
flowers have about
20 petals, and are
small, urn-shaped and
neatly formed. The
blooms are produced
in clusters as long as
the weather remains
warm, which makes it
an ideal candidate for
a small garden. It is
particularly attractive
in a container. There
is a slight fragrance.
The foliage is small
compared with the
blooms, and is mid-
green and semi-glossy.
**ZONES 4–11.**

DICKSON, UK, 1986

('LIVERPOOL ECHO' × 'WOMAN'S
OWN') × 'MEMENTO'

UK ROSE OF THE YEAR 1986,
ROYAL HORTICULTURAL SOCIETY
AWARD OF GARDEN MERIT 1993

## 'Georg Arends'
*(right)*
syns 'Fortuné Besson',
'George Arends',
'Rose Besson'

OLD, HYBRID PERPETUAL,
MEDIUM PINK,
REPEAT-FLOWERING

This variety has large
buds that open to very
big and blowsy, high-
centered, pink and
lilac blooms that
appear singly on erect
stems from mid-summer
to autumn. The petals
roll back, creating a
cabbage-rose effect.
The blooms do best
in cool weather or in
the shade, and they
make excellent cut
flowers. This 5 ft (1.5 m)
bush has large, gray-
green foliage and few
prickles. 'Georg
Arends' does well in
poor soil and ranks
highly as a hedge rose,
although it is subject
to mildew. Hinner
changed the original
name, which was
'Fortuné Besson', and
he also produced
'Gruss an Aachen'.
**ZONES 6–9.**

HINNER, GERMANY, 1910

'FRAU KARL DRUSCHKI' ×
'LA FRANCE'

G

## 'George Dickson'

MODERN, LARGE-FLOWERED/HYBRID TEA, MEDIUM RED,
REPEAT-FLOWERING

Named after the founder of a still-flourishing
nursery, 'George Dickson' enjoyed great popularity when it was first released. The large, perfectly
formed, fragrant flowers, which are 5 in (12 cm)
across, are medium red, with dark red veining
on the undersides. The foliage is dull green.
Although this variety has been criticized by some
as 'a large bloom on a weak stem', it won a valued
medal at its inaugural showing and stayed on top
of the English exhibition rose list for 20 years.
ZONES 5–9.

DICKSON, UK, 1912

PARENTAGE UNKNOWN

NATIONAL ROSE SOCIETY GOLD MEDAL 1911

## 'Georges Vibert'
*(top)*

OLD, GALLICA, RED BLEND

This striped rose is
elegant both in the
garden and in a vase.
The small, compact,
crimson buds reveal
fragrant, loosely double
blooms that are striped
pale pink. When the
petals recurve, they
surround a center of
gold stamens. The
quilled and quartered
flowers change color
according to the weather
and light availability;
sometimes they revert
to light purple. The 4 ft
(1.2 m) bush is com-
pact and upright, and
has dark green foliage,
numerous small leaves
and prickly canes. It
is an ideal plant for a
small garden or for a
hedge, and was named
for the grandson of one
of the most renowned
rose hybridizers.
ZONES 4–9.

ROBERT, FRANCE, 1853

PARENTAGE UNKNOWN

## 'Geraldine'   PEAhaze
*(bottom)*

MODERN, CLUSTER-FLOWERED/
FLORIBUNDA, ORANGE BLEND,
REPEAT-FLOWERING

The flowers of this va-
riety are orange, of an
unusually clear tone,
although in strong sun
they are liable to fade.
Clusters of plump
buds open into double
flowers of medium size,
the petals in the center
being tightly coiled
and holding this form
for some time before
reflexing to form a cup.
When taken young
they are useful for
small flower arrange-
ments, and the variety
is also suitable for a
bed or border. The
flowers have a light
scent and maintain
a good continuity
of bloom through
summer and autumn.
The growth habit is
upright, with some
splayed shoots, to
average height or less,
and the plant has light
green, semi-glossy
leaves. Raiser Colin
Pearce of Devon
named it for his wife.
ZONES 4–9.

PEARCE, UK, 1984

SEEDLING × SEEDLING

G

'Geranium' *(above)*
syn. *Rosa moyesii* 'Geranium'

MODERN, MODERN SHRUB, MEDIUM RED

There are many forms of *Rosa moyesii* and this
is one of the best for gardens, being slightly more
compact in habit than the species. The small
to medium-sized, single flowers are a brilliant
geranium red, with creamy stamens, opening
freely along the branches in summer. They do
not repeat-flower and there is very little scent. In
autumn there is a striking display of bright hips,
slightly larger and smoother than in the wild form
and deep orange-red. This rose will go well in a
mixed border or where plants can be allowed to
grow naturally, reaching nearly twice the height
of an average shrub rose with arching stems. It
has dainty, rather light green leaves. The variety
was selected at the Royal Horticultural Society
garden at Wisley 'some time before 1937' and
introduced in 1938. **ZONES 4–9.**

ROYAL HORTICULTURAL SOCIETY, UK, 1938

VARIETY OF *ROSA MOYESII*

ROYAL HORTICULTURAL SOCIETY AWARD OF GARDEN MERIT 1993

G

### 'Gerbe Rose' *(top)*

MODERN, LARGE-FLOWERED
CLIMBER, LIGHT PINK,
REPEAT-FLOWERING

This is a charming variety, bearing up to 10 rose pink blooms per cluster. They are fully double, of medium to large size, and open cupped with ruffled, crinkled petals, allowing a glimpse of yellow stamens in the depths of the flower. They have a fragrance like peonies, especially noticeable in the evening. The main flush of flower is in early summer, and it continues to provide a few blooms later in the season. As this makes a less vigorous plant than most ramblers, it is well suited to be grown up a pillar, on a wall (although not in full sun), or even trimmed and made into a specimen bush. It has smooth, reddish wood, and the leaves are dark green, glossy and are generally healthy. **ZONES 4–9.**

FAUQUE, FRANCE, 1904

*ROSA WICHURANA* × 'BARONNE
ADOLPHE DE ROTHSCHILD'

### 'Gertrude Jekyll'

AUSbord   *(left)*

MODERN, MODERN SHRUB,
MEDIUM PINK,
REPEAT-FLOWERING

The large full-petalled flowers of 'Gertrude Jekyll' open in the random fashion associated with Old Garden Roses, and the comparison is enhanced by their sweet scent and rich deep pink color. The flowering period extends right through summer and autumn. Raiser David Austin used the old Portland Rose 'Comte de Chambord' to achieve this, one of his best creations, which is splendid in a mixed bed or border; it looks especially effective grown with 'Jacqueline du Pré'. In cool climates the plant grows vigorously to average height with a somewhat uneven and lanky habit, but in warm conditions it makes much taller growth and is best treated as a climber. It has abundant grayish green leaves. The rose was named after Miss Jekyll (1843–1932), whose writings and practical example did much to influence garden design, especially in the grouping of plants for color effect. **ZONES 4–9.**

AUSTIN, UK, 1986

'WIFE OF BATH' × 'COMTE
DE CHAMBORD'

ROYAL HORTICULTURAL SOCIETY
AWARD OF GARDEN MERIT 1994

G

## 'Ghislaine de Féligonde'

MODERN, RAMBLER, LIGHT YELLOW, REPEAT-FLOWERING

This pretty rose has small, bright yellow, fragrant flowers tinged with orange that age to yellow-white tinted flesh. They are borne in clusters of 10–20. The flowers may also change from yellow to pink, orange, salmon and red. It is a moderately vigorous shrub growing to 8 ft (2.4 m) with few prickles and an attractive crop of red hips. If treated as a shrub or climber, it will do equally well in rich or poor soil and in sun or shade. G. A. Stevens wrote that it is the 'loveliest of all the Multiflora Ramblers', and anyone who has seen it tumbling down an embankment or over a wall would agree. It produces blooms profusely in early summer and occasional clusters in autumn. **ZONES 6–9.**

TURBAT, FRANCE, 1916
'GOLDFINCH' × SEEDLING

## 'Gilbert Becaud' MEIridorio *(above)*

MODERN, LARGE-FLOWERED/HYBRID TEA, YELLOW BLEND, REPEAT-FLOWERING

Fat conical buds on this variety give promise of a yellow flower to come, because yellow is the color of the outside of the petals. When the blooms open and reflex to reveal the inner surfaces, a beautiful mix of orange and copper is seen in addition to the yellow, together with delicate pale red veining on the petals. The large double flowers are high centered and neatly formed, and are suitable for cutting if taken young. They have a slight fragrance. 'Gilbert Becaud' has an upright bushy habit of growth, making it suitable for bedding, with attractive matt foliage that is bronzy when young, then becomes medium green. **ZONES 5–9.**

MEILLAND, FRANCE, 1979
('PEACE' × 'MRS JOHN LAING') × 'BETTINA'

G

### 'Gilda' *(above)*

MODERN, RAMBLER, DARK RED/MAUVE

This rose has very double, medium-sized striped blooms that are a combination of red and violet as they age, and finally change to gray-mauve. Direct sunlight bleaches the red as the blooms open. It is a large and rambling shrub with an upright form, and the long canes support a floriferous production of blooms in mid-summer. There is no scent. This is one of Geschwind's many winter-hardy creations. **ZONES 4–9.**

GESCHWIND, HUNGARY, 1887

PARENTAGE UNKNOWN

### 'Gina Lollobrigida' MEllivar *(above)*
### syns 'Children's Rose', 'The Children's Rose'

MODERN, LARGE-FLOWERED/HYBRID TEA, DEEP YELLOW, REPEAT-FLOWERING

The flowers of this rose, like huge golden orbs, seem much better suited to the film star than to their association with children, though it has to be added that sales have benefited The Children's Hospital in Britain. The blooms are a deep and unfading golden yellow, and very double with broad thick petals. They open into the shape of cabbages, making a bold show of bright color in the garden and lasting well when cut for the house. The petals may stick in wet weather. The variety is better in a border than a bed because it grows taller than average, holding the flowers aloft on long stiff stems like so many lollipops; this ungainly habit can be masked by using shorter plants in front. There is a light fragrance, and flowering is well maintained through summer and autumn, considering the size of the flower. The leaves are large and a rich deep green. **ZONES 4–9.**

MEILLAND, FRANCE, 1990

MEIDRAGELAC × MEIKINOSI

G

## 'Gingernut' COCcrazy

MODERN, PATIO/DWARF CLUSTER-FLOWERED, RUSSET,
REPEAT-FLOWERING

The colors in this rose are unusual, being deep
reddish orange on the outside of the petals and
bronzy orange with pinky orange tints towards
the petal tips on the inside. The flowers, though
fairly small, have more than 40 petals, which
lie back row upon row in neat array, disclosing
all these pretty shades to view. They are carried
in well-spaced clusters of many blooms, which
appear with good continuity through summer
and autumn. They withstand bad weather well,
and there is a light spicy fragrance. 'Gingernut'
is an interesting rose to grow for any small space
or in a container. The plant is compact, free
branching and very short, with small mid-green
glossy leaflets. **ZONES 4–9.**

COCKER, UK, 1989

('SABINE' × 'CIRCUS') × 'DARLING FLAME'

## 'Gingersnap' *(above)*

syns 'Apricot Prince', 'Prince Abricot'

MODERN, CLUSTER-FLOWERED/FLORIBUNDA, ORANGE BLEND,
REPEAT-FLOWERING

The shape of the open flowers on this rose is
appealing. Long urn-shaped buds develop into
large, fully double blooms with broad petals,
which overlap one another and become very
ruffled as they open out. The color is a lively
shade of deep tangerine, with orange-red shading
towards the petal rims. The roses have a fruity
fragrance, and the continuity of flower is well
maintained through summer and autumn. It is
useful for beds and borders, and as the flowers
are borne on long stems, they give scope for cutting. The plant grows upright with a bushy habit
to average height or even more, and has ample
deep green glossy foliage. Seeming to do best in
warm climates, it does not appear to be grown
commercially outside the USA. **ZONES 4–9.**

DELBARD-CHABERT, FRANCE, 1978

('ZAMBRA' × ['ORANGE TRIUMPH' × 'FLORADORA']) ×
('JEAN DE LA LUNE' × ['SPARTAN' × 'MANDRINA'])

G

## 'Gipsy'
syns 'Kiboh', 'Gipsy Carnival', 'Kibō', 'Lovita'

MODERN, CLUSTER-FLOWERED/FLORIBUNDA, ORANGE-RED,
REPEAT-FLOWERING

'Gipsy' is considered a Hybrid Tea by some growers. Clusters of large blooms cover the upright,
vigorous bush. The orange-red flowers with a
yellow reverse are cupped, double, and have
a slight fragrance. The foliage is dark green and
semi-glossy, with prickles slanted downward.
It well deserves its two gold medals. ZONES 4–9.

SUZUKI, JAPAN, 1986

'LIBERTY BELL' × 'KAGAYAKI'

MONZA TRIAL GOLD MEDAL 1985, THE HAGUE GOLD MEDAL 1985

## 'Gipsy Boy'  *(above)*
syn. 'Zigeunerknabe'

OLD, BOURBON, DARK RED

This Bourbon Rose has stayed at the top of the
list of favorite shrubs for nearly a century. Some
classify it as a China and others as a Tea, because
it combines the qualities of both. The reflexing,
violet-purple blooms are semi-double, flat and
medium-sized with golden stamens at the center,
crowned with lemon anthers. There is also a slight
scent. The wrinkled foliage covers this arching,
graceful plant that can be treated as either a shrub
or a climber. This variety also makes an attractive
and useful boundary hedge since it has prickly
stems and orange-red hips. New canes are always
appearing from the base. It is strongly disease
resistant, and with 'Gruss an Teplitz' makes up
the outstanding creations of its Bohemian
hybridizer. ZONES 4–9.

GESCHWIND, HUNGARY, 1909

HYBRID OF 'RUSSELLIANA'

### 'Gitte' KORita *(right)*
### syn. 'Peach Melba'

MODERN, LARGE-FLOWERED/
HYBRID TEA, APRICOT BLEND,
REPEAT-FLOWERING

This rose seems to enjoy warmer climates, where its long pointed buds open into cheerful copper-apricot flowers, deepening to orange-red at the petal tips and blending into light yellow and pink towards the center. The flowers are quite large with about 30 firm petals, enough to maintain a symmetrical high center while the petals unfold, curling prettily at the tips. They are carried on firm stems, have good fragrance, and are very suitable for cutting and for bedding, as flowers continue through summer and autumn. The plant grows to average height on bushy, free-branching stems, and has dark semi-glossy leaves.
**ZONES 4–9.**

KORDES, GERMANY, 1978

('FRAGRANT CLOUD' × 'PEER GYNT') × (['DR A.J. VERHAGE' × 'COLOR WONDER'] × 'ZORINA')

### 'Givenchy' AROdousna *(right)*
### syn. 'Paris Pink'

MODERN, LARGE-FLOWERED/
HYBRID TEA, RED BLEND,
REPEAT-FLOWERING

The coloring of this rose varies considerably, depending on the amount of sunlight the plant receives. It is usually cyclamen pink in garden conditions, with paler pink on the petal reverse, but blendings of orange, yellow and red can also be seen, as well as the 'raspberry juice' rimming of the petals found in its pollen parent, 'Double Delight'. The flowers have around 30 petals but they are substantial enough for this high-centered rose to be used for exhibition. Disbudding is necessary for this purpose because the blooms often come more than one to a stem. There is excellent scent, as one would expect of a rose named for a Parisian parfumier, and flowering continues through summer and autumn, making this a very rewarding variety for the garden. The plant grows to average height with a bushy habit and is clothed in dark green foliage. **ZONES 4–9.**

CHRISTENSEN, USA, 1986

'GINGERSNAP' × 'DOUBLE DELIGHT'

## 'Glad Tidings'

TANtide *(right)*

syns 'Lübecker Rotspon', 'Peter Wessel'

MODERN, CLUSTER-FLOWERED/ FLORIBUNDA, DARK RED, REPEAT-FLOWERING

This variety bears showy clusters of deep velvety crimson blooms on firm upright stems. The flowers are of medium size, with about 20 crisp petals, and open into neatly cupped rosettes that show the attractive stamens. There is little scent, but the continuity of flower through summer and autumn is good, and they withstand wet weather exceedingly well. This variety is useful for exhibition and cutting because the blooms last well, and it can make a splendid bed, although protective spraying against black spot is advisable. The plant is upright, with a bushy habit and grows to a little below average height; it has glossy dark green leaves. **ZONES 4–9.**

TANTAU, GERMANY, 1989

SEEDLING × SEEDLING

ROYAL NATIONAL ROSE SOCIETY TRIAL GROUND CERTIFICATE 1988, UK ROSE OF THE YEAR 1989, DURBANVILLE GOLD MEDAL 1991

## 'Gladsome' *(left)*

MODERN, RAMBLER, MEDIUM PINK

This lovely Rambler bears clusters of bright pink, single blooms that look very attractive against the abundant, mid-green foliage. Each bloom has a central boss of golden yellow stamens, and the petals are almost white at their bases. 'Gladsome' is a useful variety for disguising unattractive walls or fences; alternatively it can be trained as a pillar rose. **ZONES 5–9.**

CLARK, AUSTRALIA, 1937

PARENTAGE UNKNOWN

## 'Glamis Castle'

AUSlevel *(right)*

MODERN, MODERN SHRUB,
WHITE, REPEAT-FLOWERING

The flowers on 'Glamis Castle' are carried in small clusters, and individually are quite large with around 40 petals. They open out into wide shallow cups, showing the pointed petal edges to endearing effect. The color is creamy white, with buff tints in the heart of the blooms. The flowers, which have a sharp myrrh scent, are not spoilt by wet weather, and the plant continues to produce them through summer and autumn—all qualities that make this rose suitable for a mixed border. The plant grows to average height, making a twiggy but productive shrub. The leaves are semi-glossy and mid-green, and are rather prone to seasonal mildew. The rose was named for the Scots seat of the Bowes-Lyon family, where Queen Elizabeth the Queen Mother spent some of her childhood and where Princess Margaret was born. The breeder regards this as his best white rose, and it is also classified as an English Rose. **ZONES 4–9.**

AUSTIN, UK, 1992

'GRAHAM THOMAS' ×
'MARY ROSE'

## 'Glastonbury'

*(above)*

MODERN, MODERN SHRUB,
RED BLEND, REPEAT-FLOWERING

Although a comparatively recent rose, this is available from only a few nurseries and is not offered by its originator, having been superseded by later introductions. It produces globular buds, sometimes one to a stem, sometimes up to 5 in a cluster, that open into double dark crimson to deep purple flowers. There can be over 50 petals, making for a heavy flower that can be adversely affected if rain causes it to ball and fail to open, or the stem to bow under the extra weight of moisture. There is a pungent fragrance and flowering continues during summer and autumn. It grows with an open, spreading habit to average height or less, with sparse mid-green foliage. It is also classified as an English Rose. **ZONES 4–9.**

AUSTIN, UK, 1981

'THE KNIGHT' × SEEDLING

G

### 'Glenfiddich' *(right)*

MODERN, CLUSTER-FLOWERED/FLORIBUNDA, DEEP YELLOW, REPEAT-FLOWERING

Despite the official color coding, the true color is a light amber yellow, a clear and soothing tone, acceptably close to that of the raiser's favorite malt whisky for which the rose was named. The flowers have about 24 large petals and open loosely double, with sizeable flowers for a Cluster-flowered Rose. They are carried on firm straight stems either singly or several together in open sprays, and contrast well with the glossy dark green leaves. The continuity of bloom is very good, though in quality the blooms seem larger and finer in cooler areas; hot sun turns them pale yellow. There is a pleasing sweet fragrance, and for a hedge or bed or group, this is a satisfactory rose, giving flowers for cutting also. It grows vigorously to average height with an upright habit. **ZONES 4–9.**

COCKER, UK, 1976

'ARTHUR BELL' × ('SABINE' × 'CIRCUS')

### 'Gloire de Chédane-Guinoisseau' *(left)*

OLD, HYBRID PERPETUAL, MEDIUM RED

The flowers of this rose are crimson-red, double and give an occasional repeat display. They are cupped and very large, filled with about 40 petals. The bush is strong, upright, tall and thorny with dark green leaves and strong flower stems. It was originally recommended for pot culture and for exhibition. It is still available to gardeners, although not as freely as its parent, 'Gloire de Ducher'. **ZONES 5–9.**

CHÉDANE-PAJOTIN, FRANCE, 1907

'GLOIRE DE DUCHER' × SEEDLING

### 'Gloire de Dijon'
*(right)*
syn. 'Old Glory'
OLD, CLIMBING TEA, ORANGE-PINK, REPEAT-FLOWERING

So many have praised this beautiful Climbing Tea over the past 140 years that it still stands with the most favored roses in the world. Fat, squat buds open to reveal large, rich buff pink blooms that are large, full, globular, quartered and quilled. The center petals are apricot and the outer petals fade quickly in the sun. There is a pleasant scent. The vigorous, climbing growth is best on a wall or a pillar, and it is wise to bend the stalks down to develop laterals and more blooms. The reddish canes have hooked prickles. It blooms from summer until the first frost; the flowers do not like wet weather and it is prone to mildew and black spot. ZONES 5–9.

JACOTOT, FRANCE, 1853

'SOUVENIR DE LA MALMAISON' × 'DESPREZ À FLEUR JAUNES'

FIRST PRIZE DIJON HORTICULTURAL FAIR 1852, PARIS GOLD MEDAL 1853, ROYAL HORTICULTURAL SOCIETY AWARD OF GARDEN MERIT 1993

### 'Gloire de Ducher'
*(right)*
syn. 'Germania'
OLD, HYBRID PERPETUAL, DARK RED, REPEAT-FLOWERING

David Austin, creator of the English Roses, praises this one for the splendor of its flowers. The abundant, 4 in (10 cm) blooms are dark red, full and large, and have maroon centers. The quilled petals are folded around a button eye. Flowers appear in summer, although the best crops are seen if flowering extends into autumn. The arching canes reach 7 ft (2.1 m), and the strong branches have light, reddish bark and hooked prickles. Its lanky growth is best on a wall or pillar; pegging down produces more blooms. It is subject to mildew. ZONES 5–9.

DUCHER, FRANCE, 1865

PARENTAGE UNKNOWN

### 'Gloire de France' *(right)*
syn. 'Glory of France'

OLD, GALLICA, LIGHT PINK

Changing its colors in shade or sun, this Gallica appears to be a Centifolia hybrid. The double, informally quartered, pink blooms have cerise centers, and the pink edges fade to light purple. The vigorous, well-formed canes create a spreading and arching thicket that becomes covered with flowers in early summer. It has soft, gray-green foliage. Recent research indicates that this rose was bred by an amateur who was a Court official at Angers, and that it is not synonymous with 'Fanny Bias' as once thought. **ZONES 4–9.**

BIZARD, FRANCE, 1828

PARENTAGE UNKNOWN

### 'Gloire de Guilan'
*(right)*

OLD, DAMASK, LIGHT PINK

This rose was discovered in the Middle East by Nancy Lindsay. The medium-sized, fragrant flowers, which are at first cupped, open flat and quartered and appear in mid-summer. They are rich clear pink with softer highlights, created by the many reflexing petals. It is a tallish but relaxed shrub that can, in good conditions and when left unpruned, attain a height of 6 ft (1.8 m) and a similar width. It has many small, hooked thorns and mid- to bright green, finely textured leaves. This very floriferous variety needs space to develop; it is tolerant of poor soils. **ZONES 5–9.**

INTRODUCED BY HILLING, UK, 1949

PARENTAGE UNKNOWN

### 'Gloire des Mousseux' *(right)*
syns 'Gloire des Mousseuses', 'Madame Alboni'

OLD, MOSS, MEDIUM PINK

The flower buds and calyces of this rose are heavily covered with light green moss. The flowers are large—4 in (10 cm) across—and very full of pink petals that give a cushion effect when fully open. They pale to almost blush as the flowers mature. It is a tall shrub to 6 ft (1.8 m) and is sturdy in habit, with plentiful light to mid-green foliage. This is an excellent shrub with much to recommend it, not least a healthy disposition.
ZONES 4–9.

LAFFAY, FRANCE, 1852

PARENTAGE UNKNOWN

### 'Gloire des Rosomanes' *(right)*
syns 'Jupiter's Lightning', 'Ragged Robin', 'Red Robin'

OLD, CHINA, MEDIUM RED, REPEAT-FLOWERING

One of the hardiest roses ever created, this China is placed in the Bourbon class by some rosarians. Blooming from spring until autumn, the fragrant rose begins with dainty, pointed buds that develop into sparkling maroon or glowing crimson flowers with white streaks. The semi-double, very large, widely cupped blooms appear in clusters and turn purple in hot weather. This rose has been the parent of many other varieties and is often used as an understock. 'Gloire des Rosomanes' is a vigorous, upright bush to 5 ft (1.5 m) covered with prickles on its long branches. It does well on poor soil and produces many orange hips.
ZONES 7–9.

VIBERT, FRANCE, 1825

PARENTAGE UNKNOWN

G

### 'Gloire Lyonnaise'
*(above)*

OLD, HYBRID PERPETUAL, WHITE,
REPEAT-FLOWERING

There are many roses with reference to Lyon in their names, which is not surprising as Lyon was the center of rose breeding in the nineteenth century. This is a cupped, creamy white, very double rose with 84 thin petals. The very large, fragrant blooms are somewhat flat and of medium size, and in the shade are chrome yellow. It is a floriferous shrub with dark green, leathery foliage, some prickles and good disease resistance. It should be pruned moderately. The 4 ft (1.2 m) canes make it an ideal shrub for the back of the border. ZONES 5–9.

GUILLOT, FRANCE, 1885

'BARONNE ADOLPHE DE
ROTHSCHILD' × 'MME FALCOT'

### 'Gloria Mundi'

MODERN, POLYANTHA, ORANGE-
RED, REPEAT-FLOWERING

Before World War II this rose was offered by nurseries as an orange variety, and it is a measure of the progress made by breeders that such a description now seems utterly misleading. Today it would be considered a scarlet-red, but at the time the label 'orange' or 'orange-red' certainly helped sell the roses. It was an important color break, due to a chemical change whereby pelargonidin, common in pelargoniums, entered the kingdom of the rose, and even though 'Gloria Mundi' was not the rose destined to carry that innovation forward, it became amazingly popular. Its small double rosettes are borne in clusters of many blooms, and it continues in flower throughout summer and autumn. It was formerly used for hedges and beds in parks and gardens everywhere. Some shoots tended to revert to a parent form, showing an ugly clash of scarlet and magenta, one of the reasons why Polyanthas were ousted in favor of the healthier and color-fast Cluster-flowered Roses. ZONES 4–9.

DE RUITER, THE NETHERLANDS,
1929

SPORT OF 'SUPERB'

## 'Gloriana 97'  CHEwpope  *(below)*

MODERN, CLIMBING MINIATURE, MAUVE, REPEAT-FLOWERING

The double, medium-sized blooms of this rose each bear 15–25 mauve-pink petals with dark lilac undersides. The flowers are usually borne in small clusters amid the semi-glossy, mid-green foliage,

and give a slight fragrance. 'Gloriana 97' is a tall Climbing Miniature that is one of the latest varieties to come from the winning hybridizing program of Chris Warner in England.
**ZONES 5–11.**

WARNER, UK, 1997

PARENTAGE UNKNOWN

## 'Glory of Edsell'  *(below)*
syn. 'Glory of Edzell'

OLD, SCOTS, LIGHT PINK

This is one of the first roses to bloom in spring. It offers clear pink, single blooms with white centers that open flat and display large, attractive stamens. It is a 6 ft (1.8 m) tall shrub that does well in the shade. Small, dense, ferny foliage covers the upright, spiny canes; its growth habit makes it a good plant either for the woodland garden or as a hedge. Like other Scots Roses, it blooms only in spring. **ZONES 5–9.**

PRE-1900

PARENTAGE UNKNOWN

G

### 'Goethe'
(*right*)

OLD, MOSS, MAUVE BLEND

This is a tall, very vigorous bush as befits a hybrid of such unusual parentage. *Rosa multiflora* was normally used to produce Ramblers, and this may have been Lambert's original intention since he admired them. It is very prickly and there is much brownish moss on the buds. The deep magenta-pink flowers with yellow stamens are single, or almost so, and only bloom once in early summer. There are not many single Mosses available now, so this may be worth growing as a curiosity, although Graham Thomas disparages it. **ZONES 5–9.**

LAMBERT, GERMANY, 1911

*ROSA MULTIFLORA* × UNIDENTIFIED MOSS ROSE

### 'Gold Badge'  MEIgronuri
(*right*)

syns 'Rimosa 79', 'Gold Bunny'

MODERN, CLUSTER-FLOWERED/FLORIBUNDA, MEDIUM YELLOW, REPEAT-FLOWERING

This is a very popular yellow rose in warmer climates, praised for its clear unfading color, pleasant scent, freedom of flowering and ability to maintain a good succession of bloom. It opens from conical buds into lemon yellow flowers full of petals that undulate into each other, which explains the use of the Latin word *rimosa* as one of the names, indicating the many chinks and crevices glimpsed between them. The flowers have the classic Large-flowered form, and when fully expanded are almost as big. They last well, so are useful to cut, as well as for a bed or hedge in the garden. In cooler climates, although the blooms withstand bad weather well, they seem to lose color and become subject to black spot and rust. The plant grows vigorously to less than average height and is amply provided with dark green glossy leaves. '**Climbing Gold Badge**' (MEIgro-nurisar; syns 'Climbing Gold Bunny', 'Climbing Rimosa'; Meilland, France, 1991) is a sport of 'Gold Badge'. It won the Baden-Baden Gold Medal and the Saverne Gold Medal in 1991. **ZONES 4–9.**

PAOLINO, FRANCE, 1978

'POPPY FLASH' × ('CHARLESTON' × 'ALLGOLD')

## 'Gold Glow' *(right)*

MODERN, LARGE-FLOWERED/
HYBRID TEA, DEEP YELLOW,
REPEAT-FLOWERING

This rose was credited to H. A. Conklin in the 1960 *American Rose Annual*, and to Anthony Perry in editions of *Modern Roses* since then. It has up to an incredible 120 petals in its bright yellow flowers, which open up like double dahlias with ruffled petal edges and may fade in hot weather. The medium to large-sized blooms are borne singly and last well. There is a modest fragrance. The plant grows vigorously with an upright habit and has a covering of dark and glossy leathery leaves. **ZONES 5–9.**

PERRY/CONKLIN, USA, 1959

'FRED HOWARD' × 'SUTTER'S GOLD'

## 'Gold Medal'

AROyqueli *(right)*
syn. 'Golden Medal'

MODERN, LARGE-FLOWERED/
HYBRID TEA, MEDIUM YELLOW,
REPEAT-FLOWERING

This is a fine yellow rose for warmer countries. In the USA it is called a Grandiflora, but the flower size qualifies it to be accepted as a Large-flowered Rose elsewhere. The blooms are carried usually in open trusses, sometimes singly, and open from plump pointed buds into flowers of classic Large-flowered shape, with high centers that are maintained for some time while the outer petals reflex. The color is a shining deep yellow, sometimes streaked with orange and light red, and there is a pleasing fruity fragrance. For a bed or group or hedge where a large growing rose is wanted, and one that will keep blooming through summer and autumn, this is an excellent choice, and it gives splendid flowers for cutting. The plant grows tall and vigorously to above average height and is well furnished with deep green foliage. **ZONES 5–9.**

CHRISTENSEN, USA, 1982

'YELLOW PAGES' ×
'SHIRLEY LANGHORN'

NEW ZEALAND GOLD STAR OF
THE SOUTH PACIFIC 1983

G

G

### 'Goldbusch' *(right)*

MODERN, MODERN SHRUB, MEDIUM YELLOW, REPEAT-FLOWERING

This is an interesting shrub to grow where there is plenty of space. It produces clusters of up to 20 pinkish buds, which develop into medium to large-sized semi-double flowers in a pretty shade of pale gold. The blooms are loosely formed, and open cupped with ruffled petals, half concealing the attractive gold stamens. They have a pleasant light fragrance, and are carried on arching stems freely in summer and sporadically later. For a garden where plants can be allowed to grow naturally, this is a useful item, reaching double the size of an average shrub rose with an arching, sprawling habit. In warmer climates the growth is extensive enough to make it suitable for training as a climbing or pillar rose. The foliage is light green and leathery and has barely a hint of the scent the raiser no doubt hoped for through his use of *Rosa eglanteria*, the wild sweet briar. **ZONES 4–9.**

KORDES, GERMANY, 1954

'GOLDEN GLOW' × *ROSA EGLANTERIA* HYBRID

### 'Golden Celebration'

AUSgold *(right)*

MODERN, MODERN SHRUB, DEEP YELLOW, REPEAT-FLOWERING

The round buds of this rose open into large flowers of cupped form, recessed in the center. They are fully double and intricately formed, with the larger petals forming a ring and overlapping each other round the outside, while the base of the cup is filled with smaller petals, creased and folded. The deep yellow color is more golden than most roses that lay such a claim in their title. There is a strong fragrance and the variety continues to bloom through summer and autumn, though in wet weather the arching stems may be bowed down by the heavy flowers. It is very suitable for a border, making a rounded shrub of average height with dark glossy leaves. 'Golden Celebration' is also classified as an English Rose. **ZONES 4–9.**

AUSTIN, UK, 1992

'CHARLES AUSTIN' × 'ABRAHAM DARBY'

G

### 'Golden Chersonese' HILgold
*(above)*

MODERN, MODERN SHRUB,
MEDIUM YELLOW

This is an interesting cross between *Rosa ecae*, a species not easy to establish in cooler countries, and 'Canary Bird', a species hybrid that is more vigorous. The offspring combines the bright yellow of the first with the vigor of the second. The flowers are like brilliant buttercups, borne close to the branches on tall arching stems and are pleasantly fragrant. They appear in spring; this is one of the first roses to bloom. The wood is reddish and the small light green leaflets have a dainty ferny shape. The plant is best grown where it does not need pruning, except to remove dead wood. It makes an upright, narrow, arching plant up to about twice the average height for a shrub rose. It should be grown where it is not exposed to the risk of die-back caused by frost-bearing winds in early spring. The name is an ancient one referring to the Malay Peninsula. ZONES 5–9.

ALLEN, UK, 1969

*ROSA ECAE* × 'CANARY BIRD'

### 'Golden Delight'
*(above right)*

MODERN, CLUSTER-FLOWERED/
FLORIBUNDA, MEDIUM YELLOW,
REPEAT-FLOWERING

'Golden Delight' has a compact habit with shorter than average growth. The flowers have a substantial number of petals, nearly 60 in all. The cheerful yellow blooms are carried in crowded clusters, and when fully open are cupped, with the petals infolded against each other and the stamens peeping through. They have a sweet fragrance, and more flowers appear through summer and autumn. Given a fertile soil and good cultivation, it makes a fine bedding rose, as it has a neat habit and attractive glossy dark green foliage. ZONES 4–9.

LEGRICE, UK, 1956

'GOLDLOCKS' ×
'ELLINOR LEGRICE'

G

### 'Golden Holstein' KORtikel *(above)*
### syn. 'Surprise'

MODERN, CLUSTER-FLOWERED/FLORIBUNDA, DEEP YELLOW,
REPEAT-FLOWERING

This is a lovely and unusual rose, bearing bright golden yellow flowers that look almost single, having only 12 or so rather small wavy petals. From pointed buds they open out like little saucers, and they are perched close together in clusters at the top of the stem with their attractive stamens exposed to view. They have a light scent, maintain an excellent succession of bloom, and withstand bad weather, though they fade in hot sun. For a group in a mixed border, this rose is very suitable, though a watch needs to be kept for mildew. It grows strongly with a vigorous, upright habit to average height and has dark green shiny leaves. **ZONES 4–9.**

KORDES, GERMANY, 1989

PARENTAGE UNKNOWN

### 'Golden Jubilee' COCagold

MODERN, LARGE-FLOWERED/HYBRID TEA, MEDIUM YELLOW,
REPEAT-FLOWERING

This is a fine rose, handsome in its proportions, being fully double with about 30 firm petals. It carries its blooms upright on stiff stems, usually singly but sometimes in threes, the flowers opening with high centers and developing into large flowers of symmetrical form as the petals reflex. The color is a medium shade of yellow, with touches of pink. For cutting, as a bedding rose, or for a group in a border, this is very suitable. The flowers have a light fragrance, and blooming continues through summer and autumn, though usually with an interval after the first generous flush while the plant regathers its strength. It grows vigorously with an upright, lanky habit and has large mid-green leaves that may show seasonal mildew. **ZONES 4–9.**

COCKER, UK, 1981

'PEER GYNT' × 'GAY GORDONS'

### 'Golden Masterpiece' *(right)*

MODERN, LARGE-FLOWERED/
HYBRID TEA, MEDIUM YELLOW,
REPEAT-FLOWERING

The petals of this lemon yellow rose are long and broad; they open well in good weather but can ball up and spoil in the rain. Even when the sun shines, there can be split centers and color fading, but when it is behaving well its 30 petals form elegant high centers as the young flowers emerge from long pointed buds. They have some fragrance. In its heyday it was a successful rose for a bed or border. It is an upright, vigorous grower but is prone to black spot. **ZONES 4–9.**

BOERNER, USA, 1954

'MANDALAY' × 'SPEK'S YELLOW'

NATIONAL ROSE SOCIETY
CERTIFICATE OF MERIT 1954

### 'Golden Scepter'
syn. 'Spek's Yellow'
*(bottom right)*

MODERN, LARGE-FLOWERED/
HYBRID TEA, DEEP YELLOW,
REPEAT-FLOWERING

The brilliance of the rich golden yellow color, and its unfading quality even in the hottest weather, tended to blind rosarians to the faults of this early postwar rose. The growth habit is ungainly, and the blooms, each containing 36 petals, are produced in wide

sprays on stems not quite firm enough for so many roses. In spite of this, due to its freedom of bloom, general good health and, above all, its incomparable yellowness, it became one of the most popular roses of the 1950s, used for beds, borders and cutting. There is a little scent, flowering is well maintained through summer and autumn, and it grows vigorously, if gawkily, to above average height, with glossy leathery leaves.

'**Climbing Golden Scepter**' (syn. 'Climbing Spek's Yellow'; Walters, USA, 1956) is a sport of 'Golden Scepter'. The disadvantages of the bush form of this rose are less of a problem in the climber because, when they are elevated, the flowers bowing on their long sprays are brought conveniently

into the gardener's view. This vigorous plant is difficult to control, for it is capable of growing twice the size of the average climber. Also, the growth becomes very stiff after the first season, so training needs to be done early while the wood is still pliable. A high wall is the best and perhaps the only sensible site for this rose, because it can provide a firm support and many points of attachment.

Shoots need to be trained laterally or slantwise, otherwise the base will quickly become bare. Both the flowers and foliage are identical to those of the bush, but after the main summer flush the climbing form does not normally produce further flowers. **ZONES 4–9.**

VERSCHUREN-PECHTOLD, THE
NETHERLANDS, 1950

'GEHEIMRAT DUISBERG' ×
SEEDLING

NATIONAL ROSE SOCIETY TRIAL
GROUND CERTIFICATE 1947

G

### 'Golden Showers'
*(below)*

MODERN, LARGE-FLOWERED
CLIMBER, MEDIUM YELLOW,
REPEAT-FLOWERING

The virtues of 'Golden Showers' are its cheer-ful blooms, elegant in the young bud; the sweet scent of its wide opening semi-double flowers and the way they drop cleanly when they are done; its continuity of bloom almost without pause from summer to late autumn; its pleasing glossy foliage; its compliance in growing as far as gardeners wish it to, and not sulking however badly it is pruned; and its comparative smoothness, which makes it an easy rose to handle. Against the assets must be weighed the disadvantages—the fleeting nature of the flowers, their loss of color as they age, and a tinge of seasonal mildew. On balance, and lacking serious competition, this all-purpose climber must be considered still a front-rank rose. **ZONES 4–9.**

LAMMERTS, USA, 1956

'CHARLOTTE ARMSTRONG' ×
'CAPTAIN THOMAS'

ALL-AMERICA ROSE SELECTION
1957, PORTLAND GOLD MEDAL
1957, ROYAL HORTICULTURAL
SOCIETY AWARD OF GARDEN
MERIT 1993

### 'Golden Wedding'
AROkris *(bottom)*

MODERN, CLUSTER-FLOWERED/
FLORIBUNDA, DEEP YELLOW,
REPEAT-FLOWERING

This well-behaved rose produces its lightly scented flowers usually in small clusters, but sometimes singly, on firm upright stems. They are a cheerful shade of yellow, full petalled and of excellent form, holding their centers while the outer petals reflex to form a bloom of classic symmetry. Although a Cluster-flowered Rose, some of the blooms are as big as on many Large-flowered Roses. It flowers through summer and autumn, and for cutting, bedding and group planting this is a rose that will give great pleasure. The mid-green foliage is shiny and plentiful, and the plant grows compactly and with a vigorous habit to average height. **ZONES 4–9.**

CHRISTENSEN, USA, 1992

'SOUVENIR DE H. A.
VERSCHUREN' × SEEDLING

### 'Golden Wings'
*(top)*

MODERN, MODERN SHRUB,
LIGHT YELLOW,
REPEAT-FLOWERING

Roy Shepherd was an
eminent rose historian
who died in 1962,
and it is fitting that his
inspiration lives on in
this remarkable variety.
It produces large, pale
yellow flowers with only
a few petals that open
like saucers, showing
dark stamens. They look
frail but in fact with-
stand wind and rain
very well. Deadheading
will help bring on more
blooms. There is a light
and pleasing scent, and
for a mixed border this
is an excellent healthy
garden plant. The bush
is vigorous and prickly,
with many twiggy
stems and light green
leaves, and it grows to
average height or more.
**ZONES 4–9.**

SHEPHERD, USA, 1956

'SOEUR THERESE' × (*ROSA
PIMPINELLIFOLIA ALTAICA* ×
'ORMISTON ROY')

AMERICAN ROSE SOCIETY
GOLD MEDAL 1958, ROYAL
HORTICULTURAL SOCIETY AWARD
OF GARDEN MERIT 1993

### 'Golden Years'
HARween  *(below)*

MODERN, CLUSTER-FLOWERED/
FLORIBUNDA, MEDIUM YELLOW,
REPEAT-FLOWERING

The flowers on 'Golden
Years' open with tight
centers, but as the pet-
als expand they take on
an old-fashioned ap-
pearance with over 40
crowding one another
in the cupped blooms.
They are carried in
small clusters and
present a lovely show
of color, a rich golden
yellow tinted bronze.
There is a fruity scent,
and it flowers freely; it
withstands bad weather
well, although mildew
can be a problem. This
rose grows vigorously
to just below average
height with a neat
upright habit and dark
green pointed leaves.
It was named for the
centenary of the Girls'
Grammar School in the
raiser's home town of
Hitchin. **ZONES 4–9.**

HARKNESS, UK, 1990

'SUNBLEST' × 'AMBER QUEEN'

HRADEC GOLDEN ROSE 1989,
ORLÉANS GOLD MEDAL 1990

G

**G**

### 'Goldener Olymp'
**KORschnuppe** *(below)*

syn. 'Olympic Gold'

MODERN, LARGE-FLOWERED
CLIMBER, DEEP YELLOW,
REPEAT-FLOWERING

This rose gives a generous first flush of bloom, bearing several flowers together on arching stems. A deep yellow when they first open, the petals then turn bronzy yellow and become paler as they reflex to form large shallow-cupped blooms. There is a light fragrance. More flowers appear through summer and autumn, but not in generous numbers. It is best treated as a short climber or pillar rose, suitable for a fence or stout post. It grows with a stiff and upright habit, and has large dark green semi-glossy leaves. **ZONES 4–9.**

KORDES, GERMANY, 1984

SEEDLING × 'GOLDSTERN'

### 'Goldfinch' *(below)*
MODERN, RAMBLER, LIGHT
YELLOW

The brief mid-summer flowering has not stopped this rose from becoming extremely popular, its demure color being part of its charm. Small, oval, fat buds of deep yellow open to small, semi-double blooms that are borne in clusters. The blowsy petals surround many stamens and there is a slight fruity fragrance of oranges or bananas. The flowers fade fast in the sun, so planting it in light shade is recommended. It is easy to train the vigorous, angular growth onto a pillar or pergola, yet it can simply be left as a sprawling bush in a wild setting. There are glossy, pointed leaves and a few hooked prickles. **ZONES 7–9.**

PAUL, UK, 1907

'HÉLÈNE' × SEEDLING

G

## 'Goldilocks' *(above)*
syn. 'Goldie Locks'

MODERN, CLUSTER-FLOWERED/FLORIBUNDA, MEDIUM YELLOW, REPEAT-FLOWERING

When this rose was introduced, it had no obvious rival among Cluster-flowered Roses due to its novel features. The most important of these were its color, deep yellow in the round buds, paling when fully open, combined with its blooms, very full petalled and shaped like small-scale Large-flowered Roses. It also scored well for freedom of bloom in its first flush, for flowering on through summer and autumn, for having some fragrance, and for its neat low habit of growth, with the flowers nestling close against the foliage. For beds and the front of borders 'Goldilocks' was a favorite for several years until supplanted by its own descendants such as 'Allgold' and 'Golden Delight'. It has small glossy leaves, which may be affected by black spot. **ZONES 4–9.**

BOERNER, USA, 1945

SEEDLING × 'DOUBLOONS'

AMERICAN ROSE SOCIETY JOHN COOK MEDAL 1947, NATIONAL ROSE SOCIETY CERTIFICATE OF MERIT 1948

## 'Goldstern' TANtern
syn. 'Gold Star', 'Goldstar'

MODERN, MODERN SHRUB, MEDIUM YELLOW, REPEAT-FLOWERING

The young flowers of this shrub rose are rounded in form and develop into large, full-petalled blooms of clear deep golden yellow that become flat as they expand. They are often borne in clusters, sometimes singly, have a modest scent and continue to show color through summer and autumn. The plant makes a useful addition to the border—it grows larger than the average shrub rose—and it can also be made to serve as a climber for walls, fences and pillars. The growth is vigorous with a plentiful cover of glossy, leathery, dark green leaves. **ZONES 4–9.**

TANTAU, GERMANY, 1966

PARENTAGE UNKNOWN

G

### 'Goldtopas' KORgo, KORtossgo (below)

syns 'Gold Topaz', 'Goldtopaz'

MODERN, CLUSTER-FLOWERED/ FLORIBUNDA, MEDIUM YELLOW, REPEAT-FLOWERING

This rose has an attractive and unusual color, a pleasing blend of amber, tan and yellow that is not evident at first, as the long young buds are apricot. The buds open into sizeable double flowers of cupped form, sometimes borne singly and sometimes in a cluster. There can be as many as 10 blooms to a stem which, when it happens, makes for ungainly, overcrowded flowerheads. The petals show wavy edges as they reflex, and there is a sharp fragrance. It is suitable for beds and borders where a shorter than average grower is needed. The habit is bushy, and the ample foliage is dark green and very glossy.
ZONES 4–9.

KORDES, GERMANY, 1963

'DOCTOR FAUST' × 'CIRCUS'

ANERKANNTE DEUTSCHE ROSE 1963

### 'Good As Gold'

CHEwsunbeam (bottom)

MODERN, CLIMBING MINIATURE, DEEP YELLOW, REPEAT-FLOWERING

The deep yellow flowers of this rose are moderately full with about 24 petals per bloom. Like many of the offspring of the pollen parent 'Laura Ford', the florets are large and borne in small clusters. The blooms have a deeper golden yellow center and a sweet fragrance. The foliage is a fine semi-glossy, light green but there are some prickles. It takes a few years to establish. The plant is well suited to a pillar or narrow wall space. It has good disease resistance.
ZONES 5–11.

WARNER, UK, 1994

'ANNE HARKNESS' × 'LAURA FORD'

ROYAL NATIONAL ROSE SOCIETY TRIAL GROUND CERTIFICATE 1993, BRITISH ASSOCIATION OF ROSE BREEDERS SELECTION 1995, ROYAL NATIONAL ROSE SOCIETY ROSE DAY AWARD 1998

### 'Gourmet Pheasant'
*(right)*

MODERN, GROUND COVER,
MEDIUM RED,
REPEAT-FLOWERING

This rose was listed in the 1995 catalogue of Heirloom Old Garden Roses in Oregon, USA but without a disclosure of its origin. It is claimed to be a ground cover rose of the procumbent type, spreading about 7 times as far sideways as its height above the ground. The blooms are in that color range where rich red meets deep cherry pink, and open semi-double to show golden stamens. They are borne in massive clusters on arching shoots that lie along the ground under the weight of the blooms and foliage. There is little scent, but a good succession of bloom through summer and autumn. It suits banks, the tops of walls and anywhere that a fast-growing ground cover is required. The leaves are bright green and glossy. ZONES 4–9.

USA, 1995

PARENTAGE UNKNOWN

### 'Gourmet Popcorn'

WEOpop

syn. 'Summer Snow'

MODERN, MINIATURE, WHITE,
REPEAT-FLOWERING

This floriferous, semi-double Miniature Rose has been consistently voted by USA growers as one of their favorites. The bush is vigorous, compact and cushion-like, covered by massive cascading clusters of 30–60 short-stemmed, pure white flowers with contrasting golden yellow stamens. The flowering season lasts through summer and autumn, and the fragrance is like rose honey. It is complemented by deep green, disease-resistant foliage. This dainty garden rose is ideal for mass plantings and is easily grown in containers, hanging baskets or in any small space. ZONES 4–9.

DESAMERO, USA, 1986

SPORT OF 'POPCORN'

ROYAL NATIONAL ROSE SOCIETY
TRIAL GROUND CERTIFICATE 1995

### 'Grace Darling'  *(above)*

OLD, TEA, NEAR WHITE

Grace Darling (1815–42) became an international celebrity in 1838 when she and her father risked their lives to rescue the crew of a ship wrecked off the English coast. This compact bush is covered with large, creamy white shaded pink blooms in late spring, and there is some autumn flowering. The fragrant, cupped, globular blooms have peach-pink petals. The shrub is covered with gray-green leaves. ZONES 6–9.

BENNETT, UK, 1884

PARENTAGE UNKNOWN

G

### 'Grace de Monaco'
**MEImit** *(right)*

MODERN, LARGE-FLOWERED/
HYBRID TEA, LIGHT PINK,
REPEAT-FLOWERING

This rose is little grown today but a generation ago it was widely available, reflecting the popularity of Grace Kelly as she ceased to be a film star and became a royal. She was a lover of roses, and 'Grace de Monaco' was a wedding gift from the breeder. It has splendid flowers, large, full petalled, rounded in form and very fragrant. The color is a clear rose pink, a kindly, warm and even shade, though because the big petals are soft they are liable to be marked and spoilt by rain. They are borne freely and continue to give a show through summer and autumn, making this a good garden rose for drier climates and for cutting. It grows strongly to average height or more and has tall, branching stems that sometimes bow under the weight of a heavy load of blooms. It is well supplied with large leathery leaves.
**ZONES 4–9.**

MEILLAND, FRANCE, 1956

'PEACE' × 'MICHÈLE MEILLAND'

### 'Graham Thomas'
**AUSmas** *(right)*
syns 'English Yellow', 'Graham Stuart Thomas'

MODERN, MODERN SHRUB, DEEP
YELLOW, REPEAT-FLOWERING

When this rose was introduced it was a novelty because it was the first real yellow rose to resemble, in form and petal arrangement, the hardy Old Garden Roses of the previous century whose color range had been limited to reds, purples, pinks and pale shades. 'Graham Thomas' is a clear yellow, deeper in the heart of its cupped blooms, which are borne with remarkable freedom considering their size and fullness. They are carried on long arching stems, which often bow under their weight. There is a pleasant fragrance, and flowering continues through summer and autumn, making this a good shrub for a border; it can also make a fine standard. In cool climates it grows to average height, but in warmer countries it extends much further and can be treated as a climber on a wall, fence or tall pillar. The rose was named to honor one of England's foremost rosarians, and is also classified as an English Rose.
**ZONES 4–9.**

AUSTIN, UK, 1983

'CHARLES AUSTIN' × ('ICEBERG'
× SEEDLING)

ROYAL HORTICULTURAL SOCIETY
AWARD OF GARDEN MERIT 1993

## 'Granada' *(right)*

syn. 'Donatella'

MODERN, LARGE-FLOWERED/
HYBRID TEA, RED BLEND,
REPEAT-FLOWERING

The blooms on this rose are sometimes borne singly but often appear several together in a wide cluster, so although called a Large-flowered Rose, it resembles an over-sized Cluster-flowered Rose. The flowers have about 24 petals that form a neat high center, then reflex so that the old blooms are loosely cupped. They are a colorful blend of pink, orange red and light yellow. After the initial generous flush, flowers continue to appear through summer and autumn; they have a spicy scent. 'Granada' is not reliably winter hardy. Its dark green leaves have a crinkled, leathery appearance and can be subject to powdery mildew.

**ZONES 5–9.**

LINDQUIST, USA, 1963

'TIFFANY' × 'CAVALCADE'

ALL-AMERICA ROSE SELECTION
1964, GAMBLE FRAGRANCE
AWARD 1968

## 'Grand Hotel'

MACtel *(right)*

syn. 'Grandhotel'

MODERN, LARGE-FLOWERED
CLIMBER, MEDIUM RED,
REPEAT-FLOWERING

A feature of many older climbers was the excessive growth they made in relation to their short period of flowering. 'Grand Hotel' is a fine example of how a modern climber sacrifices some of the growth but more than makes up for that by continuing to bear flowers after the main flush, right through summer and autumn. The sizeable blooms are fairly full, borne in clusters, and open loosely cupped. They withstand bad weather well, but have only a light fragrance. The growth is stiff and branching, making it easy to train on a wall or fence; it needs a good circulation of air if mildew and black spot are to be avoided, so a well-supported trellis is the best option of all. It grows to average height and can be kept shorter by pruning with no ill effects. The plant has a good covering of dark leaves.

**ZONES 4–9.**

MCGREDY, UK, 1972

'BRILLIANT' × 'HEIDELBERG'

ANERKANNTE DEUTSCHE ROSE
1977

### 'Grand Nord'

DELgrord *(right)*

syns 'Great Nord',
'Great North'

MODERN, LARGE-FLOWERED/
HYBRID TEA, WHITE,
REPEAT-FLOWERING

When does a bush
become a shrub? It has
been said of this variety
that 'the great north
implies mountains and
that is also the appear-
ance of this rose.' This
comment is based on
its performance in
South Africa, and
the writer adds that a
mature plant in that
climate can be 10 ft
(3 m) high and wide
and covered with over
100 blooms suitable
for cutting. In cooler
climates it outstrips
other Large-flowered
Roses, but by a less
dramatic margin,

reaching twice the
average height for a
bush rose. Elegant
pointed buds open into
high-centered, double
white blooms with a
noticeable scent. They
open slowly, preserving
good symmetry of
form. On established
plants, flowers continue
through summer and
autumn. As a garden
rose 'Grand Nord' is
suitable for the back of
a border; it is vigorous,
producing many short
flowering branches to
give a fairly dense,
dark-leafed effect.
ZONES 4–9.

DELBARD-CHABERT, FRANCE, 1975

(['QUEEN ELIZABETH' ×
'PROVENCE'] × ['VIRGO' ×
'CARINA']) × (['VOEUX DE
BONHEUR' × 'VIRGO'] ×
['VIRGO' × 'PEACE'])

PARIS GOLD MEDAL 1970, ROME
GOLD MEDAL 1973

### 'Grand Siècle'

DELegran *(below)*

syn. 'Great Century'

MODERN, LARGE-FLOWERED/
HYBRID TEA, PINK BLEND,
REPEAT-FLOWERING

'Feminine, elegant,
beautiful' says the
raiser of this, one of
his favorite roses. The
large flowers are made
up of over 30 wide
petals in the classic
Large-flowered Rose

tradition, forming
blooms of grace and
symmetry as they
slowly expand. They
are a gentle blend of
cream and pink, with
rose pink showing in
the depths of the
flower as the petals
open wide. There is a
refreshing scent, in
which hints of rasp-
berry, apple and rose
are to be found. This
is a good rose for
cutting as well as for
garden display, bear-
ing its flowers singly
or in wide sprays
through summer and
autumn and growing
to average height or
a little more. It is
vigorous and free
branching and is
furnished with large,
mid- to dark green
leaves. ZONES 4–9.

DELBARD-CHABERT, FRANCE,
1987

(['QUEEN ELIZABETH' ×
'PROVENCE'] × ['MICHÈLE
MEILLAND' × 'BAYADÈRE']) ×
(['VOEUX DE BONHEUR' ×
MEIMET] ×
['PEACE' × 'DR DÉBAT'])

BAGATELLE GOLD MEDAL

## 'Grand'mère Jenny'

*(right)*

syn. 'Grem'

MODERN, LARGE-FLOWERED/
HYBRID TEA, YELLOW BLEND,
REPEAT-FLOWERING

This offspring of 'Peace' has a beautiful flower made up of subtle shades, basically light yellow with tinges of pink on the outer petals and peach-yellow towards the middle. The blooms appear singly or several to a stem, and open from pointed buds into fully double flowers with long petals that create a well-formed cone at the center before reflexing fairly soon and dropping cleanly. The variety is free flowering and quick to repeat the cycle of growth. There is a sweet fragrance, and the blooms withstand bad weather very well. Its susceptibility to black spot has, however, caused it to fall out of favor. It is a moderately vigorous plant with an upright habit and handsome dark leaves. François Meilland named this rose for Jeanne Meilland, his grandmother, who helped and encouraged him in his work during good and bad times, and died in 1943, aged 87. 'Climbing Grand'mère Jenny' (syn. 'Gremsar', 1958) is a sport of

'Grand'mère Jenny'. It repeat-flowers only sporadically, but in growth it is strong and vigorous. It is therefore best suited to a high wall or big fence or a pergola, where the branches have plenty of space to be trained.
ZONES 5–9.

MEILLAND, FRANCE, 1950

'PEACE' × 'SIGNORA'

NATIONAL ROSE SOCIETY GOLD
MEDAL 1950, ROME GOLD
MEDAL 1955

## 'Great Maiden's Blush' *(right)*

OLD, ALBA, LIGHT PINK

The lovely blush pink flowers of this large, arching shrub have fine fragrance, the color aptly described in the name. The foliage is grayish in the Alba

fashion. There is also a 'Small Maiden's Blush', which was recorded and perhaps raised at Kew Gardens in 1797. These roses are inclined to sport variations, and there is a deeper-flowered version named 'Cuisse de Nymphe Emué'. Thrips and wet weather can damage this rose considerably.
ZONES 5–9.

CIRCA 1400

PARENTAGE UNKNOWN

### 'Great News' *(right)*

MODERN, CLUSTER-FLOWERED/
FLORIBUNDA, MAUVE,
REPEAT-FLOWERING

The flowers of this variety are so sizeable and sufficiently full, having nearly 36 petals, that the raiser considered it a Large-flowered Rose. They are deep plum-purple, with silvery tones on the outside of the petals, which become delightfully waved and ruffled as they open wide to give a good display of this warm and unusual color. There is good fragrance, and the blooms appear through summer and autumn. The variety is suitable for lovers of curious roses, in either a bed or a border. It is a reasonably vigorous plant, but its uneven growth makes the height variable. The leaves are large and olive green. **ZONES 4–9.**

LEGRICE, UK, 1973

'ROSE GAUJARD' ×
'CITY OF HEREFORD'

### 'Great Western' *(above)*

OLD, BOURBON, MAUVE

This fragrant rose starts with round, fat buds; there are so many of them that thinning is recommended to help them open. The double, globular, rounded blooms are by turns deep red, magenta-crimson or purple-maroon. They appear in early summer in clusters of 10–15 and look their best in the shade. It is a vigorous shrub that grows to 6 ft (1.8 m) high, and has branching stalks and canes that are covered with prickles. It does well on poor soil. **ZONES 5–9.**

LAFFAY, FRANCE, 1840

PARENTAGE UNKNOWN

## 'Green Ice' *(right)*

MODERN, MINIATURE, WHITE, REPEAT-FLOWERING

White pointed buds open to white to soft green flowers. These small, double blooms are complemented by equally small, attractive, glossy foliage. The flower form is decorative with the fully open blooms reminiscent of Old Garden Roses. Large trusses of flowers start off white with a hint of pink and as the blooms mature, they gradually acquire an attractive light green hue. The plant has a sprawling and spreading habit, which makes it an excellent choice for a hanging basket. **ZONES 5–11.**

MOORE, USA, 1971

(*ROSA WICHURANA* × 'FLORADORA') × 'JET TRAIL'

G

## 'Green Rose' *(above)*

syns *Rosa chinensis viridiflora*, 'Rosa Monstrosa', *R. viridiflora*

OLD, CHINA, GREEN, REPEAT-FLOWERING

This curious rose sports green sepals instead of petals, and has long been a favorite with flower arrangers. The small oval buds of blue-green open to double, leaf-like sepals that are bronze at the tips. It is free flowering over a long period. 'Green Rose' is an upright, 4 ft (1.2 m) bush that is easy to grow and does well in poor soil. It is suitable for containers and is disease resistant. **ZONES 7–9.**

PRE-1833

PERHAPS A SPORT OF 'OLD BLUSH'

G

### 'Griseldis' *(above)*
OLD, BOURBON, MEDIUM PINK

This is one of the so-called 'northern' roses produced by a Bohemian hybridizer to withstand severe winter frosts. The large, full, flat pink blooms appear in clusters on long canes and have no scent. It makes a 9 ft (3 m) shrub covered in healthy, bright green foliage and prickles. Abundant bloom production more than makes up for any perceived drawbacks.
ZONES 3–9.

GESCHWIND, HUNGARY, 1895

HYBRID OF *ROSA CANINA*

### 'Grootendorst Supreme' *(above)*
MODERN, HYBRID RUGOSA, DARK RED, REPEAT-FLOWERING

This variety carries clusters of many small, garnet red roses. They are fully double, with attractively serrated petals, and there is very little scent. It is best used in a border, where a tough and easy plant is wanted. Alternatively, it can be sited in a cutting garden, because the dainty flowers are useful in small arrangements and will last many days. The variety makes a gaunt and prickly shrub that grows to or above average height for a shrub rose. It has a good complement of small leathery leaves, although they are not sufficient to clothe its twiggy, spiky appearance. It has an exemplary record of good health.
ZONES 4–9.

GROOTENDORST, THE NETHERLANDS, 1936

SPORT OF 'F. J. GROOTENDORST'

G

## 'Gros Choux d'Hollande' *(above)*

OLD, BOURBON, LIGHT PINK

The name of this rose means literally 'big cabbage of Holland', yet the flowers are neither big nor cabbage-like: they are fragrant, full, cupped and soft pink, and there do not seem to be many repeats. The bush is extremely vigorous and covers a lot of ground, growing up to 6 ft (2 m) high.
ZONES 5–9.

PARENTAGE UNKNOWN

## 'Gros Provins Panaché' *(right)*

OLD, GALLICA, MAUVE

This 5 ft (1.5 m) shrub blooms once in early spring and bears large, double, highly fragrant flowers. The purple-rose petals are blotched with white, making it one of the best-looking 'striped' roses. It is disease-resistant and suits a mixed border or a woodland setting.
ZONES 4–9.

FONTAINE, FRANCE, PRE-1855

PROBABLY A GALLICA × CHINA HYBRID

## 'Gruss an Aachen'
*(right)*

syn. 'Salut d'Aix la Chapelle'

MODERN, CLUSTER-FLOWERED/ FLORIBUNDA, LIGHT PINK, REPEAT-FLOWERING

This rose bears large clusters of medium-sized blooms, which are pale orange-red with yellow in the bud stage, and open to a soothing blend of pearly blush and cream. Before becoming cupped, they display well-formed centers, with many petals folding in upon one another in a charming random fashion. There is a pleasing scent. It is normally short, making it useful to edge a border, or for a small bed or group. The leathery foliage is a rich dark green. The name means 'greetings to Aachen', which was the raiser's home city.
ZONES 4–9.

GEDULDIG, GERMANY, 1909

'FRAU KARL DRUSCHKI' × 'FRANZ DEEGEN'

## 'Gruss an Teplitz'
*(above)*

syn. 'Virginia R. Coxe'

OLD, BOURBON, MEDIUM RED, REPEAT-FLOWERING

This rose has been on the most popular rose list for over 100 years for its long blooming season and lovely fragrance. Pointed buds open to shiny red, double blooms that darken with age and have prominent stamens. The cupped flowers hang in loose clusters which change color in bright sun. Used as a climber or a shrub, it is easy to grow or train. The young purple foliage matures to green.
ZONES 5–9.

GESCHWIND, HUNGARY, 1897

(['SIR JOSEPH PAXTON' × 'FELLENBERG'] × 'PAPA GONTIER') × 'GLOIRE DES ROSOMANES'

### 'Gruss an Zabern' (right)

MODERN, RAMBLER, WHITE

The white, fragrant, double blooms of this variety appear only once in early summer. They are medium-sized and are gathered together in flat clusters. This rose can be trained easily as a climber, as the canes are thin and pliable; it looks wonderful on a pergola or an arch. It is healthy and disease resistant and is covered with small prickles. ZONES 7–9.

LAMBERT, FRANCE, 1904

'EUPHROSINE' × 'MADAME OCKER FERENCZ'

G

### 'Guinée' (right)

MODERN, LARGE-FLOWERED CLIMBER, DARK RED, REPEAT-FLOWERING

This is perhaps the best of the blackish red climbing roses, combining great beauty with ease of cultivation. The intensely dark flowers have a velvety sheen on the young petals, which open into fairly large, full-petalled, cupped to flat blooms, with golden stamens half-revealed as they open wide. There is a good fragrance on warm days, but it becomes hard to detect in windy or cool weather. It is best grown on a fairly sunny wall or strong fence where there is room to train the main stems sideways and slantwise. This will produce the maximum yield of flowers, which normally appear in summer with a few token blooms later on. The plant is vigorous and stiffly branching, with leathery, dark green foliage that may form mildew if the roots do not get enough moisture. ZONES 4–9.

MALLEXRIN, FRANCE, 1938

'SOUVENIR DE CLAUDIUS DENOYEL' × 'AMI QUINARD'

G

### 'Guitare' GAegui
*(above)*

MODERN, CLUSTER-FLOWERED/
FLORIBUNDA, ORANGE BLEND,
REPEAT-FLOWERING

This is a bright and cheerful rose, and it bears clusters of plump buds that open to show full-petalled flowers of rounded form. They are of medium size, and display a colorful mixture of gold and orange, with coral-red shading towards the petal margins, and orange on the petal undersides. They have a good scent. It is well suited for bedding and planting in a border, and owing to its firm petals, the flowers last well when cut. The plant grows vigorously with a bushy habit to reach an average height with leathery, light green leaves.
ZONES 4–9.

GAUJARD, FRANCE, 1963
'VENDÔME' × 'GOLDEN SLIPPERS'
BAGATELLE GOLD MEDAL 1966

### 'Guy de Maupassant'
MEIsocrat *(right)*

MODERN, CLUSTER-FLOWERED/
FLORIBUNDA, MEDIUM PINK,
REPEAT-FLOWERING

Although this is classified as a Cluster-flowered Rose, it is marketed by the raiser as a 'Romantica Rose', one of several offered that combine the confused, quartered shape of some Old Garden Roses with the upright habit and repeat-flowering of many modern ones. The flowers of this rose open from globe-shaped buds into very full blooms that are packed with 100 or so infolded petals. They are light carmine-pink in both bud and open flower, and have a tart and spicy apple scent. Individual flowers in the cluster are suitable to cut for small arrangements. The plants will give color through summer and autumn in a bed or border behind shorter growing roses; they grow tall, up to twice the average height of a Modern bush rose, with a vigorous bushy, leafy habit.
ZONES 4–9.

MEILLAND, FRANCE, 1994
PARENTAGE UNKNOWN

### 'Gwen Nash'
*(right)*

MODERN, LARGE-FLOWERED
CLIMBER, PINK BLEND,
REPEAT-FLOWERING

This variety bears long, pointed buds that open to rather silky-looking blooms of a gentle rose pink, with yellowish white towards the base of the petals, and prominent golden stamens. The flowers are large, with 12 or more big, waved petals, and eventually develop a cupped form. The raiser said that he believed this rose to be 'the most beautiful thing in decorative pinks I can hope to produce'. There is a light fragrance. It needs a warm climate to thrive, and is best suited to a pergola or trellis where it is not limited for space. The plant grows vigorously with clambering stems, and large wrinkled leaves that are grayish green.
**ZONES 6–10.**

CLARK, AUSTRALIA, 1920
'ROSY MORN' × SEEDLING

### 'Gypsy Moth'
*(above)*

MODERN, CLUSTER-FLOWERED/
FLORIBUNDA, ORANGE-PINK,
REPEAT-FLOWERING

The flowers are a very pure and delicate shade of light salmon-pink with a light scent. They are carried on firm stems, sometimes singly but usually in clusters, and open from long buds into high-centered flowers of medium size. The blooms hold a classic Large-flowered Rose shape, with the outer petals slowly reflexing to finally become open cupped. 'Gypsy Moth' is suitable for bedding and to cut for small arrangements. It grows vigorously to an average height with a bushy habit, and has long, glossy mid-green foliage.
**ZONES 4–9.**

TANTAU, GERMANY, 1968
PARENTAGE UNKNOWN

H

### 'Hakuun' *(above)*
syn. 'White Cloud'

**MODERN, PATIO/DWARF CLUSTER-FLOWERED, WHITE, REPEAT-FLOWERING**

This low grower bears masses of rounded, semi-double blooms in closely packed, short-stemmed sprays. They are of medium size and open from long pointed buds into neatly formed young flowers, which become cupped. The color in the early stages is buff-orange, paling to white, sometimes with pink flecks as the petals expand. There is a light scent, and after the first flush, when the stems and leaves are almost lost to sight by the amount of bloom, flowers continue through summer and autumn. To edge a border or for any small space, this is an excellent garden rose, especially useful where a cool color is required. It grows very short with a bushy, slightly spreading habit, and has light green leaves. The name is Japanese, and 'White Cloud' is a direct translation. **ZONES 4–9.**

POULSEN, DENMARK, 1962

SEEDLING × ('PINOCCHIO' × 'PINOCCHIO')

### 'Hamburg'

**MODERN, MODERN SHRUB, DARK RED, REPEAT-FLOWERING**

Although now listed as a Shrub Rose, the Kordes nursery labeled it a climber when it was first released. The large buds are long, pointed and glowing crimson. They open as semi-double blooms on long, strong stems. The foliage is abundant, large, leathery, and glossy. A vigorous rose, it can be used either as a climber or as a bush. It produces many blooms all season. It received a certificate of merit in the German Trial-grounds. **ZONES 4–9.**

KORDES, GERMANY, 1935

'EVA' × 'DAILY MAIL SCENTED ROSE'

H

## 'Hamburger Phoenix'

MODERN, MODERN SHRUB, MEDIUM RED, REPEAT-FLOWERING

This rose can also be described as a Climber, since it can be trained up a tall pillar or a wall or fence, as well as making a strong specimen shrub of above average size. It is a rose to plant for overall color impact rather than for the individual beauty of the semi-double blooms. They are large and dark crimson and are carried in big clusters, opening cupped to show a glimpse of whitish yellow around the stamens in the heart of the flowers. There is a light fragrance, and blooms constantly appear through summer and autumn. The plant grows freely with arching stems, has a fine health record and appears dense in character thanks to its ample covering of large, shiny leaves. **ZONES 4–9.**

KORDES, GERMANY, 1954

*ROSA KORDESII* × SEEDLING

NATIONAL ROSE SOCIETY TRIAL GROUND CERTIFICATE 1950

## 'Hampshire' KORhamp *(above)*

MODERN, GROUND COVER, MEDIUM RED, REPEAT-FLOWERING

For a position where a ground-cover rose of modest size is wanted, this is a useful variety. The flowers are borne in well-filled clusters, and their bright color catches the eye as the single, scarlet flowers unfold, especially when the petals open out flat to reveal golden yellow stamens. There is excellent continuity of bloom through summer and autumn, and attractive orange hips will follow if the spent trusses are not removed. There is only a light scent. The plant forms a low, spreading mound, two-and-a-half times as wide as it is high, and has glossy, mid-green leaves. The name was given by the English introducers to celebrate the centenary of Hampshire County Council. **ZONES 4–9.**

KORDES, GERMANY, 1989

PARENTAGE UNKNOWN

H

### 'Handel' MACha *(above)*
syns 'Haendel', 'Händel'

MODERN, LARGE-FLOWERED CLIMBER, RED BLEND, REPEAT-FLOWERING

This rose bears many blush flowers rimmed with pinky red, in wide clusters on upright stems. The slender buds open into loosely double blooms of small to medium size. Neatly formed with high centers in the young flower, they open cupped, and look their very best in cooler weather. There is little scent, and the continuity of bloom through summer and autumn is excellent, though mid-season blooms are often ragged. Apart from its value as a good climber with a moderate extent, 'Handel' is one of the best varieties to grow as a source of buttonholes. The well-spaced clusters of flowers are also valued by exhibitors. The plant is stiff and branching, so it needs to be planted on a wall, fence or trellis where it can spread out, or it can be grown up a pillar like an extra-tall bush. It has glossy mid-green leaves, which can be affected by black spot. ZONES 4–9.

MCGREDY, NEW ZEALAND, 1965

'COLUMBINE' × 'HEIDELBERG'

ROYAL NATIONAL ROSE SOCIETY TRIAL GROUND CERTIFICATE 1965, PORTLAND GOLD MEDAL 1975, ROYAL HORTICULTURAL SOCIETY AWARD OF GARDEN MERIT 1993

### 'Hansa'
syn. 'Hansen's'

MODERN, HYBRID RUGOSA, MEDIUM RED, REPEAT-FLOWERING

The sizeable double blooms of this rose are reddish violet with mauve highlights, a striking and unusual color, and have attractively crinkled petals. They are heavy enough to cause the short necks to bow. The flowers have a strong clove-like scent, and are produced freely in summer with good continuity through to autumn, by which time the hips will have become large and red. This decorative variety is suitable for a shrubbery or mixed border where it will grow to above the average height for a shrub rose. It is very hardy. In milder climates it can become leggy and lose color. Its close relationship to *Rosa rugosa* is manifest in the general growth habit and strong, leathery leaves, which are veined and wrinkled. ZONES 3–9.

SCHAUM AND VAN TOL, THE NETHERLANDS, 1905

PARENTAGE UNKNOWN

### 'Hansa-Park'
KORfischer *(right)*
syn. 'Hanza Park'

MODERN, MODERN SHRUB,
MAUVE, REPEAT-FLOWERING

This rose is soft pink, deeper on the outside of the petals. The flowers are of middling size, very full petalled and carried in well-spaced clusters. They have a light fragrance and are good for cutting, since the high-centered blooms open slowly to develop a symmetrical, rounded form that displays the warm color to good effect as the petals re-flex. Flowering is well maintained through summer and autumn, and the plant grows vigorously with an up-right habit to above average height with an ample covering of large, semi-glossy leaves.
**ZONES 4–9.**

KORDES, GERMANY, 1994

PARENTAGE UNKNOWN

### 'Happy' *(right)*
syn. 'Alberich'

MODERN, POLYANTHA, MEDIUM
RED, REPEAT-FLOWERING

The flowers of this var-iety have been variously described as crimson and currant red. They appear as a sheet of color, because the clusters have scores of buds that open into small rosettes packed close together. The blooms are fairly double, with stiff petals, and will outlast their beauty if the heads are not removed once they start to fade. The first flowering is lavish, after which there is a pause while the plant regains strength to produce more blooms in late summer and autumn. Before the advent of Ground Cover and Patio Roses, 'Happy' and its associ-ated 'Compacta' roses were recommended for rockeries and small spaces, but they are little grown today. The plant is cushion-like in habit, very low and spreading, with small, dark, glossy leaves. **ZONES 4–9.**

DE RUITER, THE NETHERLANDS, 1954

'ROBIN HOOD' × 'KATHARINA ZEIMET' SEEDLING

H

### 'Happy Child' AUScomp *(above)*

**MODERN, MODERN SHRUB, MEDIUM YELLOW, REPEAT-FLOWERING**

This variety from David Austin is also classified as
an English Rose. It has quite large flowers that are
bright yellow in the center and pale towards the
petal margins. They open from plump buds into
wide-cupped blooms full of petals, most of them
infolded against each other to create attractively
confused centers, which are held for a long time
while a few of the outer petals reflex to give a
rounded outline to the flowers. There is a pleasing
scent, and blooming continues through summer
and autumn. The variety is suitable for a mixed
border, being of average size for a shrub rose with
a bushy habit and shiny, camellia-like mid-green
leaves. It was named to help raise funds for the
charity Population Concern. **ZONES 4–9.**

AUSTIN, UK, 1993

(SEEDLING × 'ICEBERG') × 'HERO'

H

### 'Happy Wanderer' *(above)*

MODERN, CLUSTER-FLOWERED/FLORIBUNDA, MEDIUM RED,
REPEAT-FLOWERING

Although it has never become popular, this short-growing rose attracts many favorable comments. It produces short-stemmed sprays, so they bloom close to the plant. Cone-shaped buds open into neatly formed flowers in a warm and even shade of crimson-scarlet. They are of medium size, with about 30 petals, and in warm climates they open fast enough to show a contrast with the golden stamens. There is a light scent, and after a very free first blooming, more flowers appear during summer and autumn. For a small space, or a bed where a really short plant is wanted, this is a good choice. The bush is compact, vigorous and bushy, with slightly glossy, small leaves. **ZONES 4–9.**

MCGREDY, NEW ZEALAND, 1974

SEEDLING × 'MARLENE'

ANERKANNTE DEUTSCHE ROSE 1975

### 'Harison's Yellow' *(above right)*

syns *Rosa × harisonii* 'Harison's Yellow',
'Harisonii', 'Pioneer Rose', *Rosa × harisonii*,
'Yellow Rose of Texas'

OLD, MISCELLANEOUS, DARK YELLOW

The small, semi-double blooms of bright yellow on this variety produce a brief but spectacular spring show, and they have a fruity fragrance. The long canes create a bushy, open shrub with many prickles. This rose is one of the hardiest in the family and spreads quickly by suckers; in fact, the best way to propagate it is by planting the runners. There are black, bristly oval hips. Reaching 10 ft by 12 ft (3 m by 3.5 m) in two seasons, it produces more blooms when in dry, cool positions. After it appeared in the garden of attorney and amateur hybridist George F. Harison in 1830 in what is today downtown Manhattan, it was carried by many pioneers on their journey west. **ZONES 4–9.**

HARISON, USA, CIRCA 1830

PERHAPS *ROSA PIMPINELLIFOLIA* × *R. FOETIDA*

ROYAL HORTICULTURAL SOCIETY AWARD OF GARDEN MERIT 1993

### 'Harlekin' KORlupo

syns 'Arlequin', 'Harlequin', 'Kiss of Desire'

MODERN, LARGE-FLOWERED CLIMBER, PINK BLEND,
REPEAT-FLOWERING

This Climber bears clusters of large flowers that have creamy white bases and are generously margined with rose red. The flowers are very full petalled and have neatly formed centers at the young stage, to become cupped as the petals open wide. The stems bow under the weight of the blooms. There is a Wild Rose scent, and after the main flush, more flowers appear sporadically through summer and autumn. For a wall, fence or pillar, this is a suitable rose that will grow to average extent. The plant is well furnished with dark green, shiny foliage. **ZONES 4–9.**

KORDES, GERMANY, 1986

PARENTAGE UNKNOWN

H

### 'Harmonie' KORtember2 (left)
MODERN, LARGE-FLOWERED/HYBRID TEA, ORANGE-PINK, REPEAT-FLOWERING

This variety has long, pointed buds that are borne both in clusters and singly, and open into elegantly formed flowers with high centers and good scent. There are only about 20 petals but they are so broad and firm that the flowers hold their shape, which makes them useful for cutting as well as in beds and borders. The color is basically a glowing salmon-pink, a tone that holds well through the life of the bloom. A good succession of flowers is maintained through summer and autumn, the later blooms being particularly good. The plant grows vigorously to above average height and has an upright, bushy habit, well endowed with leaves that are large, leathery and semi-glossy. ZONES 4–9.

KORDES, GERMANY, 1981

'FRAGRANT CLOUD' × 'UWE SEELER'

BADEN-BADEN GOLD MEDAL 1981

### 'Harry Wheatcroft' (left)
syns 'Caribia', 'Harry'
MODERN, LARGE-FLOWERED/HYBRID TEA, YELLOW BLEND, REPEAT-FLOWERING

The blooms on this variety are similar to those of 'Piccadilly', which is yellow on the undersides of the petals and orange-red on the uppersides, except that the orange-red surfaces appear to be rather bizarrely striped and streaked. A freak of nature has caused the color pigment to be missing in these areas, to show the natural blush of the petal given a yellowish tone by the color on the undersides. For lovers of the unusual this is a pretty rose to grow; it is also lightly scented and free flowering, continuing to bloom through summer and autumn. It grows to a little less than average height with a bushy habit and handsome, glossy, dark green leaves. It bears the name of one of Britain's most successful nurserymen, who lived from 1898 to 1977, and whose extrovert behavior cloaked a shrewd head and kind heart. ZONES 5–9.

WHEATCROFT & SONS, UK, 1972

SPORT OF 'PICCADILLY'

'Harvest Fayre' DICnorth *(above)*

MODERN, CLUSTER-FLOWERED/FLORIBUNDA, ORANGE BLEND,
REPEAT-FLOWERING

This variety produces flowers of yellowish apricot,
a luminous shade that makes them stand out
well in the garden from a considerable distance,
especially as the clusters are evenly spaced so each
bloom stands a little apart from the rest. They are
of medium size with about 20 firm petals, and open
from long, pointed buds to show pretty conical
centers before they become rounded in outline,
with the petals randomly arranged. There is a
light fragrance, and flowering continues through
summer and autumn. This rose will add sparkle
to either a border or a bed. The plant grows
sturdily but rather unevenly, so some flowers
are lost to sight among overgrowing shoots. The
height of the plant is a little below average, and it
has shiny, light green leaves. **ZONES 4–9.**

DICKSON, UK, 1990

SEEDLING × 'BRIGHT SMILE'

UK ROSE OF THE YEAR 1990

'Hawkeye Belle' *(above)*

MODERN, MODERN SHRUB, WHITE, REPEAT-FLOWERING

The flowers of this rose are large and beautiful in
their construction, and are borne in clusters on
strong stems. The plump, pointed buds open to
show high centers at first, then, as they expand,
the many petals resemble a coiled spring at the
heart of the bloom. The petals gradually part to
create overlapping layers, which give a charming
effect at the fully open stage. The color is ivory
white, lightly suffused with azalea pink as the
flowers open. There is a sweet scent and flowering
continues through summer and autumn, which
makes this a good subject for mixed borders
where a vigorous shrub of average growth is
required. The plant grows as wide as it does
tall, with an abundance of healthy, dark green,
leathery foliage. **ZONES 4–9.**

BUCK, USA, 1975

('QUEEN ELIZABETH' × 'PIZZICATO') × 'PRAIRIE PRINCESS'

H

### 'Headliner' JACtu *(above)*

MODERN, LARGE-FLOWERED/HYBRID TEA, PINK BLEND,
REPEAT-FLOWERING

This rose is a confection of blush white and cherry
red, the red suffusing most of the petal surface
towards the rims. The big flowers have all the
elegant form of a classic Large-flowered Rose,
holding their high centers while the outer petals
reflex to create the symmetrical, balanced effect
that will win prizes at the shows. In the garden the
spiral patterns of color displayed as the blooms
open will attract the eye, but it is a variety for
warmer climates as it will spoil in rain. Flowering
continues through summer and autumn, and
there is a slight fragrance. The plant grows
strongly with an upright habit to above average
height, and has large, shiny leaves. ZONES 5–9.

WARRINER, USA, 1985

'LOVE' × 'COLOR MAGIC'

### 'Heart of Gold' MACyelkil *(above)*

MODERN, LARGE-FLOWERED/HYBRID TEA, YELLOW BLEND/DEEP
YELLOW, REPEAT-FLOWERING

This well-formed, double rose bears beautiful
yellow flowers throughout summer and autumn.
The color is also enhanced by the backdrop of
glossy dark green foliage, which makes this rose
an ideal candidate for brightening up uninspiring
parts of the garden. ZONES 5–9.

MCGREDY, NEW ZEALAND, 1995

'SOLITAIRE' × 'REMEMBER ME'

H

### 'Hébé's Lip' *(above)*

syns 'Reine Blanche',
'Rubrotincta'

OLD, SWEET BRIAR, WHITE

The scented flowers
of this rose are borne
singly or in small clus-
ters. They are cupped,
shapely and tidy semi-
double blooms with
the golden stamens
shown off superbly
by the creamy white
petals that are brushed
crimson at the outer
edges. Flowering in
early to mid-summer,
each flower can attain
a diameter of up to
3 in (8 cm) in good
soil. This is a tidy,
compact shrub that
grows to 4 ft (1.2 m).
The leaves are fresh
mid-green, coarse to
touch and well serrated.
It is thought to be a
cross between a Damask
and *Rosa eglanteria*, but
there is no detectable
scent from its foliage
which one might expect
from such parentage.
It is very healthy.
**ZONES 4–9.**

LEE, UK, PRE-1846; REINTRO-
DUCED BY PAUL, UK, 1912

*ROSA EGLANTERIA* × A DAMASK
ROSE

### 'Heidekönigin'

KORdapt *(above right)*
syns 'Palissade Rose',
'Pheasant'

MODERN, GROUND COVER, LIGHT
PINK, REPEAT-FLOWERING

The lightly fragrant
flowers of this variety
are large, light pink and
double, each with 35
petals. The foliage is
semi-glossy and mid-
green. The disease-
resistant plant has a
spreading habit, making
it suitable as a ground
cover or for training on
a pillar. It is interesting
to note that the work
by Moore using *Rosa
wichurana* to pass on
its vigor and rambler
habit to its progeny has
also been employed by
Kordes in producing
this lovely Miniature
Rose. **ZONES 5–11.**

KORDES, GERMANY, 1985

'ZWERGKÖNIG '78' × SEEDLING
OF *ROSA WICHURANA*

ROYAL NATIONAL ROSE SOCIETY
CERTIFICATE OF MERIT 1986

H

## 'Heidelberg' KORbe
*(above)*
syn. 'Gruss an
Heidelberg'

MODERN, MODERN SHRUB,
MEDIUM RED,
REPEAT-FLOWERING

The flowers on this variety are carried on strong stems in clusters of up to 10, and they are quite large and full of petals, opening cupped to flat. The color is deep crimson as the buds begin to part, then open to a rich shade of crimson, finally paling with age. The scent is light and pleasant and, after a prolific first flush of bloom, there is a sporadic repeat-bloom through summer and autumn. For a shrubbery or to train on a pillar or against a wall not facing the full heat of the sun, this is a vigorous and upright rose with moderate lateral spread to above average height. There is an ample covering of large, leathery, semi-glossy leaves. **ZONES 4–9.**

KORDES, GERMANY, 1959

'WORLD'S FAIR' × 'FLORADORA'

ROYAL NATIONAL ROSE SOCIETY
CERTIFICATE OF MERIT 1958

## 'Heideröslein'
*(right)*

MODERN, CLUSTER-FLOWERED
CLIMBER, YELLOW BLEND,
REPEAT-FLOWERING

The pointed, pinky red buds of this variety develop into flowers of delicate rosy pink, with sulfur yellow at the base of the petals. They are of medium size, with 5 crinkled petals, and are borne in great clusters of up to as many as 60 blooms that open out flat to show attractive golden stamens. There is a good scent. This repeat-flowering rose can be kept pruned and grown as a shrub, or trained against a wall, fence or pillar. Round hips ripen in autumn to orange-red, and persist right through winter. The plant grows wide and bushy, with dark green leaves. **ZONES 4–9.**

LAMBERT, GERMANY, 1932

'CHAMISSO' × 'AMALIE DE
GREIFF'

H

## 'Heideschnee' KORconta *(right)*
syns 'Moon River', 'Snow on the Heather'

MODERN, GROUND COVER, WHITE, REPEAT-FLOWERING

This is a prolific ground-covering variety that bears long, ground-hugging stems. It produces great numbers of medium-sized, pure white flowers in summer, borne close to the stems in large clusters. The blooms have 5 petals and become like little stars as they mature, with their tips furling into narrow points. After the first flush, more flowers appear through summer and autumn, and they withstand bad weather well. There is a light fragrance. The variety is useful on banks, where the long canes will readily root themselves. It is also particularly effective in weeping standard form. The plant has a low, spreading habit and attractive shiny, dark green leaves. **ZONES 4–9.**

KORDES, GERMANY, 1990

PARENTAGE UNKNOWN

## 'Heidesommer'
KORlirus *(right)*
syns 'Cevennes',
'Heidi Sommer'

MODERN, CLUSTER-FLOWERED/
FLORIBUNDA, WHITE,
REPEAT-FLOWERING

The classification of this variety is a problem because it is not extensive enough to be called a Ground Cover Rose yet it is more spreading than most Cluster-flowered Roses. It is useful to plant in a group at the front of a border, to cover a fairly small area or to grow in a container. The plant has small, semi-double, creamy white flowers borne with great freedom in dense sprays, and they open flat to show golden stamens. The blooms contrast well against a background of small, dark, shiny leaves. They continue to appear through summer and autumn, and have a pleasant scent that becomes sweet and pervasive in warm settled weather and is attractive to bees. Perhaps they are led astray by the name label, for *Heidesommer* means 'summer in the heather'. **ZONES 4–9.**

KORDES, GERMANY, 1985

'THE FAIRY' × SEEDLING

H

## 'Heidi' NOAheid *(above)*

MODERN, MODERN SHRUB, MEDIUM PINK, REPEAT-FLOWERING

In bud this is deep pink, and becomes clear pink as it opens out. The small to medium-sized flowers are borne in immense heads, each with up to 100 blooms that are carried on rigid stems above the foliage. They open with just a few petals to reveal prominent golden stamens. This is a suitable rose for garden display in beds and borders, and flowering continues through summer and autumn. There is little scent. The plant grows below the average height for a shrub rose with a vigorous, spreading habit, and is well furnished with semi-glossy, bright green leaves that become darker as they mature. Black spot may be a problem in a season when conditions favor the fungus. ZONES 4–9.

NOACK, GERMANY, 1987

'FAIRY MOSS' × 'ICEBERG'

FREILAND GOLD MEDAL 1987

## 'Heinrich Münch'

syn. 'Pink Frau Karl Druschki'

OLD, HYBRID PERPETUAL, MEDIUM PINK, REPEAT-FLOWERING

The round, pointed buds of this rose become large, double, soft pink blooms suffused with silvery pink. The full, fragrant blooms, which contain 50 petals and are slow to open, appear singly on long, upright canes. When fully open they look like cabbage roses, and they are fine cut flowers. The 6 ft (1.8 m) shrub, covered with soft green foliage, is vigorous, and pegging down the canes will produce a better crop of flowers. There may be some autumn rebloom. It was named after its discoverer, who gave it to Hinner. ZONES 4–9.

INTRODUCED BY HINNER, GERMANY, 1911

'FRAU KARL DRUSCHKI' × ('MME CAROLINE TESTOUT' × 'MRS W. J. GRANT')

## 'Helen Traubel'
*(top)*

MODERN, LARGE-FLOWERED/
HYBRID TEA, PINK BLEND,
REPEAT-FLOWERING

The flowers on this variety are a fetching combination of warm peach-pink with flushes of yellow at the base, fading slightly as they age. Borne sometimes singly but quite often in threes, they open from long buds into elegant flowers made up of 24 petals, and sustain high centers for a short period before they become cupped. They have a sweet scent, and appear with good continuity through summer and autumn. Weak flower stems often cause the blooms to nod, particularly in windy conditions, which detracts from its value as a bedding rose on its own, but in a border among other plants it fits in well. The plant grows vigorously to average height with a bushy, branching habit and dark green, semi-glossy foliage. **ZONES 4–9.**

SWIM, USA, 1951

'CHARLOTTE ARMSTRONG' ×
'GLOWING SUNSET'

ROME GOLD MEDAL 1951, ALL-
AMERICA ROSE SELECTION 1952,
NATIONAL ROSE SOCIETY TRIAL
GROUND CERTIFICATE 1953

## 'Helmut Schmidt'

KORbelma *(bottom)*
syns 'Goldsmith',
'Simba'

MODERN, LARGE-FLOWERED/
HYBRID TEA, MEDIUM YELLOW,
REPEAT-FLOWERING

The large, pointed buds of this variety give promise of big flowers to come, and they are beauties. The urn-shaped, young blooms develop high centers around which the outer petals are arranged with wonderful symmetry. They usually appear one per strong, upright stem, which makes the variety an excellent cutting rose, especially as the blooms hold their shape and last well. It is a good rose for general garden use, flowering on through summer and autumn, though tending to produce a flush of bloom followed by a pause. The plant grows neat and upright to below average height, with matt green foliage. In Germany this was introduced to honor a former chancellor; in the USA it is called 'Goldsmith', and the British name commemorates a dog— a golden labrador owned by the raiser's agent, Mark Mattock— called Simba (the Swahili word for lion) because of the color of its coat. **ZONES 4–9.**

KORDES, GERMANY, 1979

'NEW DAY' × SEEDLING

COURTRAI GOLD MEDAL 1979,
GENEVA GOLD MEDAL 1979,
ROYAL NATIONAL ROSE SOCIETY
TRIAL GROUND CERTIFICATE 1979

H

## 'Henri Martin'
*(right)*

syn. 'Red Moss'

OLD, MOSS, MEDIUM RED

The double flowers of this rose, which are loosely arranged in large clusters, open flat and are up to 3 in (8 cm) across. They are claret red to crimson and pale slightly to a softer red. They are very fragrant. It is a vigorous, wide-growing shrub to 6 ft (1.8 m) with few thorns but many soft bristles on gracefully arching stems. The foliage is rich green, as is the moss on the flower buds and calyces; the moss is aromatic and smells like balsam. It has very attractive hips in autumn. 'Henri Martin' does not mind poor soil, but needs space to develop as it can get quite broad. It needs support, such as a tripod or trellis, to give its best. ZONES 4–9.

LAFFAY, FRANCE, 1863

PARENTAGE UNKNOWN

ROYAL HORTICULTURAL SOCIETY
AWARD OF GARDEN MERIT 1993

## 'Henry Hudson'
*(bottom)*

MODERN, HYBRID RUGOSA,
WHITE, REPEAT-FLOWERING

Dr Felicitas Svejda and the Canadian Department of Agriculture have worked for many years to introduce roses hardy enough to withstand severe winter conditions, and this is one of the most successful. It is a low, suckering plant, bearing pink-tipped buds that open into double white flowers. These become cupped as the petals expand to display golden stamens. They are of medium size with a good scent and, after the first generous flush, more blooms appear through summer and autumn. The old flowers do not fall readily and should be removed. This hardy, healthy plant is suitable for bedding, and has an abundance of tough, deep green foliage. The rose commemorates the explorer who died vainly seeking the Northwest Passage, and whose name lives on in a bay, straits and river, none of which were actually discovered by him. ZONES 3–9.

SVEJDA, CANADA, 1976

SEEDLING OF 'SCHNEEZWERG'

H

H

### 'Henry Kelsey' *(above)*

MODERN, MODERN SHRUB, MEDIUM RED, REPEAT-FLOWERING

This is an exceptionally hardy rose for cold climates. The flowers are borne in heavy clusters of up to 18 medium to large-sized flowers. They are full petalled and are a warm, bright shade of red. As the petals reflex, the blooms become cupped to reveal prominent golden stamens. There is a sharp, spicy scent. The flowers age to rose red before dropping their petals cleanly, and they repeat-bloom through summer and autumn. This can be planted in a border to make an arching, pendulous shrub of lower than average height, but spreading in habit, with trailing stems. It can be more easily controlled if trained on a trellis, arch or fence as a modest-sized climber. It has glossy foliage that withstands mildew. ZONES 3–9.

SVEJDA, CANADA, 1984

HYBRID OF *ROSA KORDESII* × SEEDLING

### 'Henry Nevard' *(above)*

OLD, HYBRID PERPETUAL, DARK RED, REPEAT-FLOWERING

One of the last Hybrid Perpetuals introduced to the trade, this vigorous bush is covered with large round buds that open to dark red, double blooms with 30 petals during summer. The large, cupped, highly fragrant flowers hold together well in warm weather. The bush has dark, leathery green foliage, and should be pruned lightly. ZONES 4–9.

CANT, UK, 1924

PARENTAGE UNKNOWN

H

## 'Heritage' AUSblush *(above)*
### syn. 'Roberta'

MODERN, MODERN SHRUB, LIGHT PINK, REPEAT-FLOWERING

The plump buds of this rose open into big, cupped flowers that are full of petals that crowd the center of the blooms, randomly folding in upon one another in the style of an Old Garden Rose. They display a variety of light pink shades, from palest blush to warm rose pink deep in the center of the blooms. There is a good lemon fragrance, and after the first flush of flowers, the plant continues to show color through summer and autumn. This is a good rose for a border, bed or as a hedge. It grows vigorously and fairly compactly on its bowing branches, to average height for a shrub rose, with a good covering of dark green, semi-glossy leaves. 'Heritage' is also classified as an English Rose. **ZONES 4–9.**

AUSTIN, UK, 1984

SEEDLING × ('WIFE OF BATH' × 'ICEBERG')

## 'Hermosa'
### syns 'Armosa', 'Mme Neumann', 'Mélanie Lemaire'

OLD, CHINA, LIGHT PINK, REPEAT-FLOWERING

This is a rose without any critics; it is healthy and vigorous, and fine as a bedding plant as well as by itself. 'Hermosa' has flourished in cultivation ever since its introduction. The pointed, attractive buds open to reveal light pink, highly centered, small blooms containing 35 petals. The cupped, globular flowers are nearly white at the base, and the outer petals reflex as the blooms age. The bushy growth is covered with blue-green, smooth leaves and a few prickles. This variety produces fragrant flowers, and it should be planted in groups of 3 or more. **ZONES 5–9.**

MARCHESSEAU, FRANCE, PRE-1837

PROBABLY CHINA × BOURBON

### 'Hertfordshire'
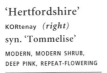
KORtenay *(right)*
syn. 'Tommelise'
MODERN, MODERN SHRUB,
DEEP PINK, REPEAT-FLOWERING

During several years of trials for disease resistance at The Gardens of the Rose in England, conducted without spray protection, this rose emerged with an unblemished record for good health. The flowers are small and single, and are produced in great abundance in short-stemmed clusters. They soon open out into flat, carmine-pink flowers with pale centers, displaying attractive stamens, to resemble scores of cheerful yellow eyes nestling against small, bright, shiny leaves. After the main flush it is rare for the plant to be without some flowers through summer and autumn. The habit of growth is low, undulating and some-what spiky, which adds to the unusual character of this rose. In the garden, 'Hertfordshire' is suitable to be grown near the front of a border or to cover small spaces. This plant is so densely foliaged that a group can serve as ground-cover plants, suppressing weeds during the growing season. It is prickly, however, so weeding, when necessary, can be painful. **ZONES 4–9.**

KORDES, GERMANY, 1991
PARENTAGE UNKNOWN

### 'Hiawatha'
MODERN, RAMBLER, RED BLEND

Named for the Indian hero of Longfellow's narrative poem, this Rambler has retained its popularity even after other, superior forms have been introduced. The tiny, round buds appear in mid-summer and are followed by deep crimson, single, cupped blooms in large trusses that feature white centers and golden anthers. Bright yellow stamens crown the flowers. This plant grows well in shade or sun, and the vigorous, lanky canes can sometimes reach 20 ft (6 m) in height. They are lined with leathery, rich green, glossy leaves. 'Hiawatha' does well on poor soil and looks best when climbing trees. M. H. Walsh of Woods Hole, Massachusetts, produced 40 Ramblers between 1901 and 1920. **ZONES 4–9.**

WALSH, USA, 1904
'CRIMSON RAMBLER' × 'PAUL'S CARMINE PILLAR'

H

## 'Hidalgo' MEItulandi
(right)
syn. 'Michel Hidalgo'

MODERN, LARGE-FLOWERED/
HYBRID TEA, MEDIUM RED,
REPEAT-FLOWERING

The cone-shaped buds
of this variety open
to reveal currant red
flowers of about 30
petals, which open into
very large, cupped
blooms carried on long
stems. The fragrance
is excellent and the
flowers last well. Con-
tinuity of bloom is
maintained through
summer and autumn.
When planted in a
group as a source of
flowers for cutting,
'Hidalgo' can be a use-
ful rose. Ornamentally
it is less merited, tend-
ing to have an untidy,
straggling, albeit vig-
orous habit, with a
ration of crooked flower
stems and weak necks.
The bush is well
furnished with large,
leathery, bronzy green
foliage and has a good
health record. Miguel
Hidalgo was a Mexican
revolutionary hero who
lived from 1753 to
1811. **ZONES 4–9.**

MEILLAND, FRANCE, 1979

(['QUEEN ELIZABETH' × 'KARL
HERBST'] × ['LADY' ×
'PHARAON']) × (MEICESAR ×
'PAPA MEILLAND')

BADEN-BADEN FRAGRANCE
AWARD 1978

## 'High Hopes' HARyup

MODERN, LARGE-FLOWERED CLIMBER, MEDIUM PINK,
REPEAT-FLOWERING

The light rose pink flowers of this variety are
double and provide a fine display all through
spring and autumn. They are moderately sweetly
scented and adorn this strong, vigorous plant,
which has smaller stems than most Climbers but
without any thick heaviness. The foliage is strong
and healthy although it tends to suffer mildly
from black spot. 'High Hopes' is excellent for
growing on all arches, pergolas and frames of
average height that need a special rose over them;
it is a most rewarding specimen to grow and sure
to bring delight. **ZONES 5–9.**

HARKNESS, UK, 1992

'COMPASSION' × 'CONGRATULATIONS'

THE HAGUE FIRST CLASS CERTIFICATE 1992, TOKYO GOLD MEDAL
1992, AUCKLAND BEST CLIMBER 1996

## 'Highdownensis' *(right)*
syn. *Rosa highdownensis* 'Hillier'

**MODERN, MODERN SHRUB, MEDIUM RED**

This variety is a hybrid seedling from *Rosa moyesii*. 'Highdownensis' has single, oriental red flowers, purpling with age, with contrasting lighter fresh red, golden-tipped stamens. The orange rose hips are a magnificent bottle shape and hang on the branches from the end of their early flowering season until mid-winter, when they rot and fall. It is a vigorous, tall, upright-growing plant that is best grown as a shrub, with small, neat foliage. It is hard to propagate by budding in the nursery, but once it has established itself in the garden it is extremely hardy and is best left unpruned. **ZONES 5–9.**

STERN, UK, 1928

SEEDLING OF *ROSA MOYESII*

ROYAL HORTICULTURAL SOCIETY AWARD OF GARDEN MERIT 1994

**H**

## 'Hilda Murrell'
**AUSmurr** *(right)*

**MODERN, MODERN SHRUB, MEDIUM PINK**

Also classified as an English Rose, this beautiful variety has deep glowing pink flowers that may dull with age. The blooms have a flat, symmetrical, rosette formation and are strongly fragranced. 'Hilda Murrell' is a moderately disease-resistant, thorny, strong bush that reaches average height and has large, leathery foliage. The rose was named for Miss Hilda Murrell, one of the pioneers of the reintroduction of Old Garden Roses after World War II. **ZONES 5–9.**

AUSTIN, UK, 1984

SEEDLING × ('PARADE' × 'CHAUCER')

H

### 'Himmelsauge'
*(above)*
syn. 'Francesco Dona'

MODERN, RAMBLER, MAUVE

One of the darkest
and hardiest of the
Ramblers, this 'eye
of heaven' is a late
bloomer. The large,
dark purple, fragrant
flowers do best in
shade or partial shade
as the sun can be harsh
on the petals. Easy to
train on a fence or over
an arch, an autumn
display of hips adds to
its charm. ZONES 4–9.

GESCHWIND, AUSTRIA, 1894

ROSA SETIGERA × R. RUGOSA

### 'Hippolyte' *(right)*
syn. 'Souvenir de Kean'

OLD, GALLICA, MAUVE

The fat buds of this
rose open to vivid,
carmine-shaded violet
blossoms. Globular at
first, the flowers reflex
and change color to a
deep wine red. Tiers
of petals cascade down
the arching canes, and
the deep fragrance adds
another dimension to
its charms. Varying
in its form from other
Gallicas, this compact
bush reaches to 5 ft
(1.5 m) high and has
neat, small leaves and
no prickles. It is an
ideal choice for a small
garden or as a hedge.
Hippolyte was the
Amazon queen in
Greek mythology.
ZONES 4–9.

PRE-1842

PROBABLY GALLICA × CHINA

### 'Holy Toledo' ARObri
*(above)*

MODERN, MINIATURE, APRICOT
BLEND, REPEAT-FLOWERING

'Holy Toledo' has ovoid buds that open to flowers that are apricot-orange with a yellow-orange reverse. The florets are double with 28 petals, overlap and are suitably complemented by small, dark green, disease-resistant foliage. It is a vigorous and bushy plant. This Miniature Rose is a much admired variety, mainly for its wonderful color range, pretty flower shape, growth habit and clean foliage. The unique color combination is striking and needs to be seen to be believed. The blooms can come in large trusses on strong stems that are resistant to damage from wind or rain. This award-winning rose has maintained its popularity worldwide for two decades. **ZONES 5–11.**

CHRISTENSEN, USA, 1978

'GINGERSNAP' × 'MAGIC CARROUSEL'

AMERICAN ROSE SOCIETY AWARD OF EXCELLENCE 1980

### 'Homère' *(right)*

OLD, TEA, PINK BLEND, REPEAT-FLOWERING

The lovely buds of this variety open to pale pink, cupped, full blooms with a white center; the crinkled petals are flecked with lilac. The erect stems make this rose a fine cut flower. 'Homère' is a bushy plant that doesn't mind the rain and has sturdy branches with finely serrated leaves and red, curved prickles. It should be pruned lightly and is an ideal plant for the border or a container. It has a pleasant Tea fragrance, and is quite popular as a buttonhole flower. This rose was named in honor of the great Greek epic poet. **ZONES 7–9.**

ROBERT AND MOREAU, FRANCE, 1858

POSSIBLY SEEDLING OF 'DAVID PRADEL'

H

### 'Honeyflow' *(above)*
MODERN, CLUSTER-FLOWERED/FLORIBUNDA, PINK BLEND, REPEAT-FLOWERING

This small, low-growing but spreading plant is well worth growing in a larger garden where there is enough space to make a worthwhile planting. It should be planted in long rows on either side of a formal path. The wood is thin and masses of shoots are produced from the base, each one carrying a large head of small, single, off-white flowers with the palest touch of pink. The foliage is pale green. Free flowering and hardy, it is very disease resistant and shows only some mildew. **ZONES 5–9.**

RIETHMULLER, AUSTRALIA, 1957

'SPRING SONG' × 'GARTENDIREKTOR OTTO LINNE'

### 'Honor'  JAColite
syns 'Honour', 'Michèle Torr'
MODERN, LARGE-FLOWERED/HYBRID TEA, WHITE, REPEAT-FLOWERING

The graceful, long, pointed buds of 'Honor' open to reveal delicate soft white flowers with golden stamens in the full-blown stage. The blooms are large, carrying 25–30 petals, are borne on long stems and are lightly fragrant. 'Honor' was released in 1980 to complete a series that also contained 'Love' and 'Cherish', and was easily the best; its awards are testament to its excellence. A repeat-flowering, vigorous, tall and upright-growing plant, it has a high level of disease resistance to both black spot and mildew. It is an excellent plant in the garden, and the flowers are good for cutting as they last well in arrangements and stand out on the show bench. **ZONES 5–9.**

WARRINER, USA, 1980

PARENTAGE UNKNOWN

PORTLAND GOLD MEDAL 1978, ALL-AMERICA ROSE SELECTION 1980

H

### 'Honorable Lady Lindsay' *(above)*
syn. 'Honorine Lady Lindsay'

**MODERN, MODERN SHRUB, PINK BLEND, REPEAT-FLOWERING**

This variety is not very strong growing and has probably only been persisted with in cultivation because of its flowers. An early pre-war hybrid, the full, double flowers are pink with darker undersides. It is repeat-flowering and there is a slight fragrance, although it tends to flower better in hot conditions than it does in cooler climates. 'Honorable Lady Lindsay' is a bushy plant that grows as tall as it does wide. **ZONES 5–9.**

HANSEN, USA, 1939

'NEW DAWN' × 'REVEREND F. PAGE-ROBERTS'

### 'Honoré de Balzac' MEIparnin

**MODERN, LARGE-FLOWERED/HYBRID TEA, PINK BLEND, REPEAT-FLOWERING**

The plump buds of 'Honoré de Balzac' open into big blooms of rounded form. These are filled with many wide petals that, having a somewhat soft texture, tend to ball in wet weather. This variety is therefore best suited for drier climates. The color is a cool shade of light pink in the center of the flowers, fading to blush white on the outer petals. There is a pleasant light peach fragrance, and blooms are produced through summer and autumn. The plant grows strongly, with an uneven habit, to above average height with dark shiny leaves. In the garden, the variety is useful in beds and mixed borders. The name commemorates the celebrated French novelist who lived from 1799 to 1850. **ZONES 4–9.**

MEILLAND, FRANCE, 1993

PARENTAGE UNKNOWN

H

## 'Honorine de Brabant' *(below)*

OLD, BOURBON, PINK BLEND, REPEAT-FLOWERING

Regal and temperamental, this rose bears blush pink, fragrant flowers that are spotted and striped; in the shade they may change to mauve and crimson. Not as brash as other striped roses, the large, loosely cupped blooms have many petals in a quartered arrangement. The mid-summer blooms are the best and there is some autumn flowering. Lush, leathery foliage covers the vigorous, compact bush and, under the leaves there are some prickles. 'Honorine de Brabant' does well on poor soil and is ideal at the back of the border or on a fence. It is one of the most popular roses in the world. ZONES 4–9.

SPORT OF 'COMMANDANT BEAUREPAIRE'

## 'Hot Chocolate' SIMcho *(above)*

MODERN, CLUSTER-FLOWERED/FLORIBUNDA, RUSSET, REPEAT-FLOWERING

Bred by an amateur breeder from New Zealand, this variety created a sensation when released because it was a brand new color—a deep rich orange, so dark that as the flowers age it could be described as a soft brown. This color, like many unusual informal flowers, requires cool weather to fully intensify; hot weather does not allow sufficient time for the full browning effect since the blooms open and fall too quickly. 'Hot Chocolate' is a hardy, disease-resistant, medium-sized plant that looks best when planted in a bed of its own to avoid color clashes. ZONES 5–9.

SIMPSON, NEW ZEALAND, 1986

'PRINCESS' × ('TANA' × 'MARY SUMNER')

NEW ZEALAND GOLD MEDAL 1986

### 'Hot Tamale' JACpoy
*(right)*
syn. 'Sunbird'

MODERN, MINIATURE, YELLOW
BLEND, REPEAT-FLOWERING

The flowers of this
variety are an eye-
catching yellow-orange
blend that age dramat-
ically to yellow-pink
providing almost an
electric glow to the
blooms. This attractive
color combination lasts
for a long time, even
in the midday sun of
southern California.
The florets have con-
sistent Large-flowered
form, making 'Hot
Tamale' a frequent
winner on the show
tables. Blooms are
borne mostly singly
but small clusters
can develop in cooler
climates. They have a
light scent. The foliage
is a highly comple-
mentary semi-glossy,
dark green which is
disease resistant on a
compact, tall-growing
plant. This rose was
a hit at the Royal
National Rose Society
National Miniature
show in St Albans,
England in 1997 where
a basket of over 100
blooms caught every-
one's attention. What
a pity it cannot trace
back its characteristics
to its parents.
**ZONES 5–11.**

ZARY, USA, 1993

PARENTAGE UNKNOWN

AMERICAN ROSE SOCIETY
AWARD OF EXCELLENCE 1994

### 'Hugh Dickson'
*(right)*

OLD, HYBRID PERPETUAL,
MEDIUM RED,
REPEAT-FLOWERING

Jack Harkness hated
it, but Graham Thomas
loves it: 'Hugh Dickson'
has been popular for
nearly 100 years, espe-
cially as a cut flower
and a bedding plant.
The thick, round buds
open to show dark red,
double, high-centered
blooms containing
38 petals. These enor-
mous, fragrant blooms
are carried erect on long
stems and the large,
rounded petals open to
reveal an exposed
center. It likes sun or
shade and produces a
lovely harvest of autumn
blooms. The thick
canes are covered with
foliage that is red when
young; they look best
trained horizontally on
a wall, or pegged down
to create a hedge. It
should be deadheaded
regularly. **ZONES 5–9.**

DICKSON, UK, 1905

'LORD BACON' × 'GRUSS AN
TEPLITZ'

H

H

### 'Hula Girl' *(right)*

MODERN, MINIATURE, ORANGE
BLEND, REPEAT-FLOWERING

The long pointed buds
on this variety open to
double, deep orange or
salmon-pink flowers
with a touch of yellow
at the base of the 45
petals. The blooms
have a fruity fragrance.
The foliage is small,
dark green and glossy
and the plant has a
vigorous, tall growth
habit. Bloom produc-
tion is profuse in all
climates and there is a
good repeat cycle time.
This award-winning
rose was bred from two
unusual parents rarely
used for hybridizing
by other breeders.
**ZONES 5–11.**

WILLIAMS, USA, 1975

'MISS HILLCREST' × 'MABEL DOT'

AMERICAN ROSE SOCIETY
AWARD OF EXCELLENCE 1976

### 'Hume's Blush Tea-scented China'

*(above)*

syns 'Odorata', 'Spice'

OLD, TEA, LIGHT PINK,
REPEAT-FLOWERING

As the first Tea Rose
introduced to the West
from China, 'Hume's
Blush Tea-scented
China' has been the
center of much specu-
lation in recent years.
It was thought to be
lost entirely, but plants
growing in Bermuda,
which had been named
'Spice', have since been
recognized as the real
thing. The pale, creamy,
flesh pink, full, flat
blossoms are large and
double, and they line
the long branches. In
the sun, the very fragrant
flowers turn to white.
It can be grown as a
shrub or trained as a
climber. It has attrac-
tive, glossy, evergreen
foliage. **ZONES 7–9.**

HUME, UK, PRE-1809

*ROSA × ODORATA* VARIETY

**H**

**'Hunter'** *(above)*
syn. 'The Hunter'
MODERN, HYBRID RUGOSA,
MEDIUM RED,
REPEAT-FLOWERING

This rose bears clusters
of faintly scented,
crimson flowers with
the main flush in spring,
but with continuous
repetition in a lesser
way until autumn. It is
a tall, vigorous, bushy
shrub with dark green
foliage; the wrinkled
veining so typical of
these roses has been
overshadowed by the
influence of the pollen
parent, 'Independence';
the leaves, while rough,
bear a close resem-
blance to this parent.
**ZONES 5–9.**

MATTOCK, UK, 1961

*ROSA RUGOSA RUBRA* ×
'INDEPENDENCE'

**'Hurdy Gurdy'**
MACpluto *(above)*
syn. 'Pluto'
MODERN, MINIATURE, RED
BLEND, REPEAT-FLOWERING

The white stripes on
the dark red flowers of

this variety make it
unusually appealing.
They are small and
double blooms and
have a slight fragrance.
'Hurdy Gurdy' is a
Miniature Rose with

an upright habit and
glossy green leaves
that have a medium
resistance to disease.
**ZONES 5–9.**

MCGREDY, NEW ZEALAND, 1986

'MATANGI' × 'STARS 'N' STRIPES

**'Iceberg'** KORbin *(above)*
syns 'Fée des Neiges', 'Schneewittchen'
MODERN, CLUSTER-FLOWERED/FLORIBUNDA, WHITE,
REPEAT-FLOWERING

It is hard to believe that 40 years have elapsed since 'Iceberg' was first introduced by Reimer Kordes. It is a unique variety that is head and shoulders above its peers and counterparts, a most shapely, dainty bloom that is rain resistant and long lasting, both as a cut flower and on the bush. The flowers are semi-double and well formed, pure white with occasional pinkish flushes in the bud stage, especially in early spring and autumn when the nights are cold and damp. Some pink spotting may occur on the petals at this time, caused by rain or dewdrops remaining on the petals overnight and then being color activated by the morning sunshine. The blooms are produced in clusters of up to 15 per spray and they have a moderate but not overpowering rose fragrance. This variety can be used as a bedding plant for massed display; it is almost entirely resistant to mildew and suffers only mildly from black spot. All in all it is one of the best roses produced during the twentieth century. **'Climbing Iceberg'** (syn. 'Climbing Fée des Neiges'; Cant, UK, 1968), which is never without bloom, is a disease-resistant, healthy, robust plant, although

*'Climbing Iceberg'* *(above)*

it sometimes fails to climb, a fault of the propagation technique when the incorrect buds or eyes have been chosen for propagation. It is not too rampant and can be used to cover small fences or garden outbuildings, being particularly suitable for use on feature poles in the garden or on veranda posts. **ZONES 4–9.**

KORDES, GERMANY, 1958

'ROBIN HOOD' × 'VIRGO'

NATIONAL ROSE SOCIETY GOLD MEDAL 1958, BADEN-BADEN GOLD MEDAL 1958, WORLD'S FAVORITE ROSE 1983, ROYAL HORTICULTURAL SOCIETY AWARD OF GARDEN MERIT 1993

### 'Iced Ginger'
*(right)*

MODERN, CLUSTER-FLOWERED/
FLORIBUNDA, ORANGE BLEND,
REPEAT-FLOWERING

Pat Dickson created a winner when he bred 'Iced Ginger', an enchanting variety with its blends of pink and copper and delicate fragrance. The flowers, which are produced in small, even clusters on strong, short growth, can be picked and used as cut flowers, the coppery pink tones mixing well in most arrangements. A short-growing bush that needs careful pruning to correct its awkward growth habit, it is probably best suited for use in massed bedding or as an edging plant. The foliage is healthy and dark green and reasonably resistant to mildew, although it does succumb to black spot especially in wet areas. ZONES 5–9.

DICKSON, UK, 1971

'ANNE WATKINS' × SEEDLING

### 'Iced Parfait' *(right)*

MODERN, CLUSTER-FLOWERED/
FLORIBUNDA, LIGHT PINK,
REPEAT-FLOWERING

Sister Mary Xavier of Launceston, Tasmania, crossed 'Pink Parfait' and 'Iceberg' in 1972 to produce this ever-charming rose. The blooms are a blend of the palest pink and are produced during a flowering period that stretches from early spring until the coldest part of winter, and they have a sweet scent. 'Iced Parfait' is a reliable plant that grows to medium height and has pale green foliage and strong disease tolerance. It can be used as a bedding plant. ZONES 5–9.

XAVIER, AUSTRALIA, 1972

'PINK PARFAIT' × 'ICEBERG'

### 'Ilse Krohn Superior'

MODERN, MODERN SHRUB,
WHITE

This very sprawling, vigorous plant has some useful applications. The flowers, which are only abundant in spring as it spends the rest of its time growing, are double and white, lovely as buds, and have a mild scent. It has healthy, glossy dark green leaves and a rampant, long, spreading habit that makes it ideal to grow over walls or even to climb a tree. It is hardy and resistant to black spot, all of which make it worth a try in a large garden that needs a tough plant. ZONES 4–9.

KORDES, GERMANY, 1964

SPORT OF 'ILSE KROHN'

### 'Immensee' KORimro *(right)*
syns 'Grouse', 'Lac Rose', 'Kordes' Rose
Immensee'

MODERN, MODERN SHRUB/GROUND COVER, LIGHT PINK

This charming rose was one of the first roses bred
specifically as a ground cover; others of course
have followed, but with this rose a new trend appeared. 'Immensee' covers the soil densely and is
suitable to cover and stabilize sloping earth banks
when planted in pockets created especially to retain water. It spreads rapidly. Early in the season
it covers itself along the entire length of the newer
shoots with single, bright pink buds that open to
light pink, slightly scented flowers that fade more
to white as they age. The foliage is dark and glossy
and mostly disease resistant. **ZONES 4–9.**

KORDES, GERMANY, 1983

'THE FAIRY' × SEEDLING OF *ROSA WICHURANA*

ROYAL NATIONAL ROSE SOCIETY GOLD MEDAL 1984

### 'Impératrice Farah'
DELivour *(right)*

MODERN, LARGE-FLOWERED/
HYBRID TEA, WHITE BLEND/PINK
BLEND, REPEAT-FLOWERING

In warm climates, the
unfolding creamy
white petals of this var-
iety become coral red
at their tips and edges
where they are exposed
to the heat of the sun,
giving a beautiful effect.
The blooms are large,
of neat, regular form
with many crisp petals,
and good for cutting,
as they last well. There
is a slight fragrance,
and flowering is main-
tained through sum-
mer and autumn. In
the garden, this rose
needs careful placement
as it grows considerably
above average height.
It is useful towards the
back of a bed or mixed
border, and for screen-
ing walls and fences

where climbing roses
are not appropriate.
The growth is upright
and vigorous, with
a covering of large
leathery leaves. The
raiser's father met

Queen Farah of Iran in
1974 when he named
the rose 'Vivre' for a
children's charity of
which she was the
President, and this led to
an ongoing friendship.

The Delbard family
dedicated it to her.
**ZONES 4–9.**

DELBARD, FRANCE, 1992

PARENTAGE UNKNOWN

GENEVA GOLD MEDAL 1992,
ROME GOLD MEDAL 1992

### 'Improved Cécile Brünner' *(left)*
syn. 'Rosy Morn'

MODERN, CLUSTER-FLOWERED/FLORIBUNDA, ORANGE-PINK,
REPEAT-FLOWERING

As can be seen by its parentage, this rose has no
real relationship to the famous 'Cécile Brünner'.
It bears clusters of salmon-pink to pink, double
flowers made up of about 30 petals and which
develop from long, pointed buds. There is a light
fragrance. The growth is very vigorous and
upright, and is covered by leathery, dull green
foliage. ZONES 5–9.

DUEHRSEN, USA, 1948

'DAINTY BESS' × ROSA GIGANTEA

### 'Ingrid Bergman' POUlman *(above)*

MODERN, LARGE-FLOWERED/HYBRID TEA, DARK RED,
REPEAT-FLOWERING

This wonderful rose has been acclaimed in
rose trials all over the world, which gives a good
indication of its performance. The high-quality
flowers are velvet red, fully double and very
fragrant. The color holds well, and new flowering
shoots appear freely after each flush of bloom.
It has vigorous, upright growth and dark green
leathery leaves. 'Ingrid Bergman' is a strong plant,
almost entirely disease resistant and worth a place
in any rose garden as it gives so much pleasure.
ZONES 4–9.

POULSEN, DENMARK, 1985

SEEDLING × SEEDLING

ROYAL NATIONAL ROSE SOCIETY TRIAL GROUND CERTIFICATE 1983,
BELFAST GOLD MEDAL 1985, MADRID GOLD MEDAL 1986, GOLDEN
ROSE OF THE HAGUE 1987, ROYAL HORTICULTURAL AWARD OF
GARDEN MERIT 1993

I

I

not have much scent, but 'Inner Wheel' has been well received as a decorative garden rose. It is a low, bushy plant with good dark green foliage and reasonable disease resistance, and it is suitable for many climates. It was introduced to honor the Association of Rotarian Ladies in the UK.
**ZONES 4–9.**

FRYER'S NURSERY, UK, 1984

'PINK PARFAIT' × 'PICASSO'

### 'International Herald Tribune'

HARquantum    *(left)*
syns 'Margaret Isobel Hayes', 'Violetta', 'Viorita'

MODERN, CLUSTER-FLOWERED/
FLORIBUNDA, MAUVE BLEND,
REPEAT-FLOWERING

The unusual varieties Jack Harkness used to develop 'International Herald Tribune'

resulted in a deep violet, cupped, medium-sized bloom—a novelty in a Modern Garden Rose, especially one with such a gentle scent. It flowers constantly all summer and is rarely without blooms. It was introduced in 1985 to honor the famous newspaper. The semi-glossy dark green foliage covers a vigorous low-growing bush that does not develop much height, so it is good for the edge of the garden or a bed where the view over the top is not to be hindered.
**ZONES 4–9.**

HARKNESS, UK, 1984

SEEDLING × (['ORANGE
SENSATION' × 'ALLGOLD'] ×
*ROSA CALIFORNICA*)

GENEVA ROSE D'OR, GENEVA
GOLD MEDAL 1983, MONZA
GOLD MEDAL 1984, TOKYO
GOLD MEDAL 1983, BELFAST
CERTIFICATE OF MERIT 1986

### 'Inner Wheel'

FRYjasso    *(top)*

MODERN, CLUSTER-FLOWERED/
FLORIBUNDA, PINK BLEND,
REPEAT-FLOWERING

A mass planting of this variety produces a wonderful effect, for as the flowers age, an interesting range of color is produced. They begin bright salmon-pink on the outer edge of the flowers with ivory in the center; then, as the blooms fade, they become a delicate pink that endures. They do

## 'Intervilles' (right)

MODERN, LARGE-FLOWERED
CLIMBER, MEDIUM RED,
REPEAT-FLOWERING

Although popular in France at the time of its release, 'Intervilles' is not now widely grown. A moderately vigorous scarlet-flowered climbing rose, it produces masses of color all through the season, from spring to autumn. The blooms grow in clusters of 6–7 on a stem and are of medium size and, while the strong texture of the petals enhances their lasting qualities, it is best used as a garden plant rather than a cut flower as the blooms lack delicacy and sharpness of form. It is not a vigorous Climber, probably best described as a pillar rose, and is well suited to small spaces or a pole or on the veranda post of a house. It is healthy, tolerant of black spot and mildew, and covers itself with glossy green leaves. ZONES 5–9.

ROBICHON, FRANCE, 1968

'ÉTENDARD' × SEEDLING

## 'Intrigue' JACum (right)

MODERN, CLUSTER-FLOWERED/
FLORIBUNDA, MAUVE,
REPEAT-FLOWERING

'Intrigue' has lemon-scented, well-formed blooms like small-scale Large-flowered Roses, made up of some 20 petals. The rich reddish purple makes it reminiscent of a nineteenth-century rose. The bush grows to average height with an upright habit. The flowers are good for cutting, and it blooms through summer and autumn. It is well furnished with glossy dark green leaves. The warm coloring of this rose goes well with many other garden flowers, so it is good to plant in mixed borders as well as in beds of one variety. ZONES 4–9.

WARRINER, USA, 1984

'WHITE MASTERPIECE' × 'HEIRLOOM'

ALL-AMERICA ROSE SELECTION 1984

'Invincible'  RUnatru
*(right)*

syn. 'Fennica'

**MODERN, CLUSTER-FLOWERED/
FLORIBUNDA, DARK RED,
REPEAT-FLOWERING**

This rose is popular
in Europe, but it is
not widely grown in
other countries. Dark
crimson in color, the
large blooms are
symmetrical but have
a muddled center that
covers golden stamens.
The flowers hold their
shape well and are
good for cutting, last-
ing for a long time
when picked. The bush
is tall and compact and
the disease-resistant
foliage is glossy dark
green. It is a pity that
this variety is not more
widely grown as it is
worth its place in the
garden. **ZONES 4–9.**

DE RUITER, THE NETHERLANDS,
1983

'RUBELLA' × 'NATIONAL TRUST'

'Ipsilanté'  *(left)*
syn. 'Ypsilante'
**OLD, GALLICA, MAUVE**

A popular Gallica, this rose offers a strong, rich
perfume in addition to its attractive mauve-pink
flowers. Round, fat buds open in mid-summer to
large, cupped, double blooms with crinkled petals
that twist in different directions. The outer petals
fade with age. This sprawling, vigorous shrub will
reach 5 ft (1.5 m) and has dense, rough, dark
green foliage and red prickles. It does well on
poor soil and is disease resistant. This variety was
named for the Greek patriot and general Prince
Alexandr Ypsilante (1792–1828). **ZONES 4–9.**

VIBERT, FRANCE, 1821

PARENTAGE UNKNOWN

## 'Irene of Denmark' *(right)*

syns 'Irene au Danmark', 'Irène de Danemark',
'Irene von Dänemark',

MODERN, CLUSTER-FLOWERED/FLORIBUNDA, WHITE,
REPEAT-FLOWERING

The white flowers of this variety are borne in
clusters, and often show traces of soft pink, either
as spots on the petals or as a pink infusion in cool,
damp weather. It is a delicate plant that is useful
for edging rose beds as it is low and compact in
growth. The wood is light in color but hard in
texture, while the leaves are a pale, shiny glossy
green and are mildew resistant. Black spot may
present problems when conditions are favorable.
**ZONES 4–9.**

POULSEN, DENMARK, 1948

'ORLÉANS ROSE' × ('MME PLANTIER' × 'EDINA')

NATIONAL ROSE SOCIETY CERTIFICATE OF MERIT 1952

## 'Irène Watts' *(right)*

OLD, CHINA, LIGHT PINK/WHITE, REPEAT-FLOWERING

This rose, which is hardier than many Chinas, has
long apricot buds that reveal pale pink, double
blooms with large petals and a button eye. When
fully open, the flowers resemble large carnations.
Small, dark green leaves cover a bushy, short, low-
growing shrub that usually reaches 2 ft (60 cm).
This is an excellent plant for the container or in
the border, and is also effective as a low hedge.
It blooms from spring until autumn. **ZONES 5–9.**

GUILLOT, FRANCE, 1896

SEEDLING OF 'MME LAURETTE MESSIMY'

ROYAL HORTICULTURAL SOCIETY AWARD OF GARDEN MERIT 1993

## 'Irish Elegance' *(right)*

MODERN, LARGE-FLOWERED/HYBRID TEA, ORANGE BLEND/APRICOT
BLEND, REPEAT-FLOWERING

The survival of this variety has probably been
guaranteed by its uniqueness—it has long buds
that open to wide, flat, yellow-bronze flowers that
are gently smudged with pale pink. The blooms
are scented and are produced prolifically. A tall,
vigorous grower, 'Irish Elegance' has semi-glossy
green leaves and is remarkably disease resistant,
especially as it was bred over 90 years ago. The
best results have been gained by growing it as a
small shrub, as this removes coarseness from the
flowers. **ZONES 4–9.**

DICKSON, UK, 1905

PARENTAGE UNKNOWN

## 'Irish Gold' *(right)*
### syn. 'Grandpa Dickson'

MODERN, LARGE-FLOWERED/
HYBRID TEA, MEDIUM YELLOW,
REPEAT-FLOWERING

This popular Large-flowered Rose has certainly stood up well against newer roses. Its fully double blooms are well formed from the bud all the way through to opening; they have been widely used on the rose show bench for exhibition purposes and have won many prizes for their crispness of style. The blooms are a pleasing yellow, without any harshness of tone, while the outer petals sometimes carry some tinges of pink and the open flowers can often be seen with an edged overlay of pink. A good bush for any garden, it is not always a strong grower and the wood is covered with many thorns. The mid-green leaves are extremely glossy on growth that is strong and stout. Like all yellow roses, it sometimes reacts badly to black spot, and should be sprayed regularly in spring. **ZONES 5–9.**

DICKSON, UK, 1966

('KORDES' PERFECTA' ×
'GOVERNADOR BRAGA DA CRUZ')
× 'PICCADILLY'

ROYAL NATIONAL ROSE SOCIETY
PRESIDENT'S INTERNATIONAL
TROPHY 1965, GOLDEN ROSE OF
THE HAGUE 1966, BELFAST GOLD
MEDAL 1968, PORTLAND GOLD
MEDAL 1970

## 'Irish Rich Marbled' *(above)*

OLD, SCOTS, RED BLEND

This rose has soft, rounded, pink buds that are followed by deep pink flowers with a lilac-pink reverse. Three rows of petals outline a yellow center around the stamens, and the outer petals reflex. As they age, the blooms fade towards the center. There is a musky scent. It is a very prickly shrub to 3 ft (1 m) high with small, dark, ferny leaves and round, black hips. It suckers freely and should be planted either in a container or where it will not interfere with other plants. Scots Roses were popular between 1790 and 1830 when there were several hundred in commerce. **ZONES 4–9.**

PARENTAGE UNKNOWN

**'Ispahan'** *(right)*
syns 'Pompon des
Princes', 'Rose
d'Isfahan'

OLD, DAMASK, MEDIUM PINK

The flowers of this rose
appear in clusters in
early summer and
continue through to
late summer. They are
full and almost modern
looking, at first being
high centered and
shapely, and later be-
coming loosely double
and muddled when
fully open, but always
with the most delicate
texture. The fragrant
blooms are up to 2½ in
(6.5 cm) across and
are consistently bright
clear pink. The bush
can reach about 5 ft
(1.5 m) with an erect
and fairly dense habit.
The stems are grayish
green and there are
few thorns. The foliage
is smooth, semi-glossy
and mid-green with
hints of gray. It is
seldom afflicted by
any disease other than
an occasional touch of
mildew. **ZONES 4–9.**

PRE-1832

PARENTAGE UNKNOWN

ROYAL HORTICULTURAL SOCIETY
AWARD OF GARDEN MERIT 1993

**'Ivory Fashion'**
*(above)*

MODERN, CLUSTER-FLOWERED/
FLORIBUNDA, NEAR WHITE,
REPEAT-FLOWERING

The ivory white buds
on this variety change
to a more creamy white
as the blooms open.

They are high pointed,
shapely and appear in
clusters; when they open
they cover the bush well.
The semi-double blooms
have a slight spice scent
in the early stages that
diminishes quickly,
and they have attractive

red stamens. It is ideal
as a standard or patio
standard. **ZONES 5–9.**

BOERNER, USA, 1958

'SONATA' × 'FASHION'

NATIONAL ROSE SOCIETY
CERTIFICATE OF MERIT 1957,
ALL-AMERICA ROSE SELECTION
1959

JK

### 'Jacaranda' JacaKOR *(right)*
syn. 'Jackaranda'

**MODERN, LARGE-FLOWERED/HYBRID TEA, MEDIUM PINK,
REPEAT-FLOWERING**

Probably better known to cut-flower growers, this
useful tall rose is a good example of the direction
that breeding is taking for the mass cut-flower
market. Its strong scent and rapid repeat-flowering
make it a good greenhouse proposition. The
flowers are held on very long, strong stems and
are medium pink, the color remaining constant
even as the flowers age. A strong and healthy
plant with large, mid-green leaves, it has good
disease resistance and little susceptibility
to mildew. **ZONES 5–10.**

KORDES, GERMANY, 1985

('MERCEDES' × 'EMILY POST') × SEEDLING

### 'Jack Frost' *(above)*
**MODERN, CLUSTER-FLOWERED/
FLORIBUNDA, WHITE,
REPEAT-FLOWERING**

With its long stems
and wonderful scent,
this is still a popular
cut-flower rose under
glass. The flowers are full
and double with very
pointed and attractive
buds. The bush is vig-
orous and upright, the
leaves are dark green,
and it has a fair resist-
ance to mildew and
black spot. 'Jack Frost'
is most popular in the
Americas; it has not
always been widely
grown around the
world. **ZONES 5–10.**

JELLY, USA, 1962

'GARNETTE' × SEEDLING

### 'Jackie' *(left)*

**MODERN, MINIATURE, LIGHT YELLOW, REPEAT-FLOWERING**

This rose has beautifully shaped buds that open to straw yellow flowers, which change to white on full maturity. The flowers are very double with more than 60 petals, have Large-flowered form and a delicate fragrance. The lovely, soft yellow blooms are shown to advantage against the glossy dark green foliage on a vigorous, dwarf spreading plant. The bloom cycle is quite fast so the plant is nearly always in bloom throughout the year. It is an excellent choice for growing indoors or in shade, as flowers tend to fade to white very quickly in full sun. It is disease-resistant and self-cleaning. Sadly, being an older variety, it is not as popular as it once was. **'Climbing Jackie'** is a sister seedling from the same cross, and bears generous floriferous clusters of soft yellow to creamy white 60-petalled blooms. It has very sharp thorns for a Miniature. 'Climbing Jackie' can grow to 10 ft (3 m) in warm zones. Like 'Jackie' and all light yellow flowers, it needs a little shade during the day to preserve its color. **ZONES 6–11.**

MOORE, CALIFORNIA, 1955

'GOLDEN GLOW' × 'ZEE'

**J**

### 'Jacqueline Nebout' MEIchoiju
*(right)*
syns 'City of Adelaide',
'Sanlam-Roos'

**MODERN, CLUSTER-FLOWERED/FLORIBUNDA,
MEDIUM PINK, REPEAT-FLOWERING**

The full, double, mid-pink flowers of this variety have an abundance of color and style. Opening quite well but not fully, they have long stems and good lasting ability as cut flowers and appear exceptionally freely in late autumn, when the full richness of the color develops. It is a healthy, medium-sized bush, with thick, glossy dark green leaves, that is suitable for border planting or as a standard. The synonym 'City of Adelaide' was used to celebrate the first Rose Festival in Adelaide, South Australia. **ZONES 5–10.**

MEILLAND, FRANCE, 1989

PARENTAGE UNKNOWN

DUBLIN GOLD MEDAL 1988

### 'James Mason'

OLD, GALLICA, MEDIUM RED

This lovely Gallica Rose was named to honor the famous actor (1909–1984). It has a tremendous fragrance, but like all Gallicas is not repeat-flowering. The large bright blood-red flowers are striking and bear only 2 rows of petals, while the yellow stamens show out clearly on the flat, open blooms. The medium-sized bush is upright in habit, spreading only a little; it enjoys good health and makes an ideal plant for growing in a spot that receives little attention through the year. The new growth is fresh and quick to shoot both after and during flowering on a plant that will always provide a good late spring show. **ZONES 5–11.**

BEALES, UK, 1982

'SCHARLACHGLUT' × 'TUSCANY SUPERB'

### 'James Mitchell'
*(left)*

OLD, MOSS, DEEP PINK

The flowers of 'James Mitchell' are produced freely in mid-summer and are seldom more than 2 in (5 cm) across. They emerge from small and rounded, heavily mossed buds, and they are bright glowing pink, fading slightly with age. Each highly scented bloom is full of small petals, which creates a pom-pon effect. It is a wide, dense shrub growing to a height of some 5 ft (1.5 m) and has stems that are densely covered with tiny soft spines; these are a darkish green to brown color. The plentiful, well-serrated foliage is a grayish dark green. This is an exceptionally healthy rose for any situation. **ZONES 4–10.**

VERDIER, FRANCE, 1861

PARENTAGE UNKNOWN

### 'James Veitch'
*(bottom)*

OLD, MOSS, MAUVE, REPEAT-FLOWERING

This rose is good for the front of a border, since it has a low-growing, reasonably vigorous habit to 3 ft (1 m) tall. The stems are very thorny, covered with bristly moss and carry full, dark magenta, double blooms. It is very free flowering and is one of the 'per-petual' forms, which display throughout the season provided that deadheading is carried out. It is important, though, to feed this rose well if a good second flowering is to be expected. The rose is named either after James Veitch the son (1792–1863) or James Veitch the grandson (1815–1869) (or both), of the founder of the famous Veitch nursery in England, which was responsible for many plant hunting expeditions—most notably those of Wilson and Lobb. **ZONES 5–9.**

VERDIER, FRANCE, 1865

PARENTAGE UNKNOWN

## 'Janet Morrison'
*(right)*

MODERN, LARGE-FLOWERED
CLIMBER, DEEP PINK

Alister Clark raised this
Climber, which bears
deep pink, medium-
sized flowers on long
stems. They are semi-
double and have a
good scent. The growth
is rampant, and it will
grow quite large if
left unpruned. The
disease resistance is
fair, although it is sub-
ject to some mildew in
cooler weather.
**ZONES 6–11.**

CLARK, AUSTRALIA, 1936

'BLACK BOY' × SEEDLING

## 'Janina' TANija
*(right)*

MODERN, LARGE-FLOWERED/
HYBRID TEA, ORANGE BLEND,
REPEAT-FLOWERING

The deep salmon-rose
pink flowers of 'Janina'
have deeper maize
yellow undersides to
the petals giving an
overall effect of apricot.
The buds are short and
firm. This rose has an
upright growth habit,
very few thorns and
fair disease resistance;
it only needs attention
in early spring to
ensure the health of
the glossy mid-green
leaves. **ZONES 5–10.**

TANTAU, GERMANY, 1974

PARENTAGE UNKNOWN

J

J

**'Jaquenetta'** AUSjac
*(above)*
syn. 'Jacquenetta'

MODERN, MODERN SHRUB,
APRICOT BLEND

Also classified as
an English Rose,
'Jaquenetta' is unreliable
in its repeat-bloom,
and for this reason it
has been withdrawn
from some Austin
lists. However, it is an
attractive shrub with
Old Garden Rose style,
healthy in leaf and
stem. **ZONES 5–10.**

AUSTIN, UK, 1983

PARENTAGE UNKNOWN

**'Jardins de
Bagatelle'** MEImafris
*(right)*
syns 'Drottning Silvia',
'Gardin de Bagatelle',
'Karl Heinz Hanisch',
'Queen Silvia', 'Sarah'

MODERN, LARGE-FLOWERED/
HYBRID TEA, WHITE,
REPEAT-FLOWERING

The beautiful pale
cream-white flowers
of this variety have a
pale pink flush in cool
weather. They are fully
double, have a sweet
scent and are good for
picking. It is a strong-
growing, medium-
sized upright plant
with large, glossy green
leaves and good disease
resistance; it is easy to

prune and maintain.
Named after famous
gardens in France, this
rose is ideal for any
gardener who wants
either a single or mass
planting, as it is quite
hardy and tolerates a

range of different con-
ditions. **ZONES 6–11.**

MEILLAND, FRANCE, 1986

('QUEEN ELIZABETH' × 'ELEG') ×
MEIDRAGELAC

BAGATELLE FRAGRANCE AWARD
1984, GENEVA GOLD MEDAL
1984, POITIERS GOLD MEDAL
1986, GENOA GOLD MEDAL 1987

J

## 'Jazz' *(above)*

MODERN, CLUSTER-FLOWERED/FLORIBUNDA, ORANGE BLEND,
REPEAT-FLOWERING

This Cluster-flowered Rose has double, medium-sized, orange-yellow flowers with a pink-crimson blushing over the whole bloom. They have a slight rose fragrance and give repeat displays throughout summer. The variety has glossy dark green foliage that is moderately resistant to disease. 'Jazz' has an openness that can be a problem, as it tends to expose the center of the plant; this can be overcome with careful pruning and tidying up during the year. The rose is vigorous and healthy. **ZONES 5–11.**

DE RUITER, THE NETHERLANDS, 1960

'MASQUERADE' × SEEDLING

## 'Jean Bach Sisley' *(bottom)*

OLD, CHINA, PINK BLEND, REPEAT-FLOWERING

The long buds of this variety open to upright pink blooms whose outer petals are salmon-rose. They are veined carmine. The bicolor blooms have a Tea fragrance and are happiest in cool weather. It blooms from late spring until autumn and is a moderately sized, sturdy, sprawling shrub with new leaves that are purple before turning dark green. 'Jean Bach Sisley' should only be pruned occasionally, and is an excellent bedding plant. **ZONES 5–10.**

DUBREUIL, FRANCE, 1889

PARENTAGE UNKNOWN

## 'Jean Ducher' *(above)*
syns 'Comte de Sembui', 'Ruby Gold'

OLD, TEA, ORANGE-PINK, REPEAT-FLOWERING

As a cut flower or in full bloom, this Tea Rose is one of the hardiest of its kind. The globular blooms are full and large and range in color from salmon to peach to pink, a factor that depends on the weather. The fragrant, blowsy blooms have red centers and hate wet weather. It is quite vigorous for a Tea, reaching 4 ft (1.2 m) high and as much across. It should be pruned only lightly. 'Jean Ducher' makes an effective container plant as it is highly disease resistant. ZONES 5–11.

DUCHER, FRANCE, 1874

PARENTAGE UNKNOWN

## 'Jean Giono'  MEIrokoi

MODERN, LARGE-FLOWERED/HYBRID TEA, YELLOW BLEND, REPEAT-FLOWERING

This is one of the raiser's 'Romantica' roses, which combines Old-style flower form with freedom of bloom over a long period through summer and autumn. The flowers are a vibrant blend of golden yellow with a suffusion of tangerine orange. They are of medium size, opening from round buds into rather shaggy, low-centered blooms of uneven shape, crowded with petals (about 120 in an average flower). The center petals are often quilled. The growth is vigorous, to average height or a little below, and the habit bushy, with lush and plentiful dark green foliage. There is a light spicy scent and the plants are suitable for beds and borders. ZONES 4–9.

MEILLAND, FRANCE, 1994

PARENTAGE UNKNOWN

## 'Jean Kenneally'

TINeally *(above)*

MODERN, MINIATURE, APRICOT
BLEND, REPEAT-FLOWERING

'Jean Kenneally' is
a true star among
Miniature Roses. In
every respect it is as
close to perfection as
anyone can hope for—
it has vigor, form, color,
size and profusion, and
is a must for serious
exhibitors. The small,
double flowers are pale
to medium apricot and
have very high quality
Large-flowered form.
The bloom can have a
light fragrance. In cold
climates a slight pink
tinge may develop on
the petals. The foliage
is a semi-glossy mid-
green, and the plant
has a very upright habit,
with large clusters of
10–12 blooms and
the occasional single
bloom being normal.
It is one of the many
sister seedlings derived
from the same cross
that ended up being
award winners—
'Futura' was a great
seed parent for

Bennett. This rose is
a consistent winner
on the show tables with
perhaps its greatest
achievement, the
International Ralph
Moore Trophy at the
Royal National Rose
Society National
Miniature Show in
1997 for a basket of
125 blooms. **ZONES 5–11.**

BENNETT, USA, 1984

'FUTURA' × 'PARTY GIRL'

AMERICAN ROSE SOCIETY
AWARD OF EXCELLENCE 1986,
INTERNATIONAL RALPH MOORE
TROPHY, ROYAL NATIONAL ROSE
SOCIETY NATIONAL MINIATURE
SHOW 1997

## 'Jean Mermoz'
*(top right)*
syn. 'Jean Marmoz'

MODERN, POLYANTHA, MEDIUM
PINK, REPEAT-FLOWERING

This lovely, free-
flowering Polyantha is
a delight in any garden.
The large clusters of
mid-pink, cupped
blooms are well placed
away from the bush
and have a slight sweet
fragrance. Ideal for
mass plantings or a
border along a path or
drive, 'Jean Mermoz'

flowers well through
most of the season. It
is a small, low-growing
bush with glossy dark
green leaves on a
stout, vigorous frame.
Disease resistance is
good and it needs little
care, but it needs to be
watched for mildew as
the cool of autumn
overtakes the summer
days. **ZONES 5–11.**

CHENAULT, FRANCE, 1937

*ROSA WICHURANA* × SEEDLING

## 'Jeanne D'Arc'
*(above)*

OLD, ALBA, WHITE

This tall and sprawling
shrub bears flowers that
are rather muddled in
the center and fade
quickly from cream to
white in the sun. The
characteristic blue-gray
look in the older leaves
may have been inher-
ited from *Rosa canina*.
It can best be described
as a smaller version of
the Jacobite rose, 'Alba
Maxima'. **ZONES 4–9.**

VIBERT, FRANCE, 1818

PARENTAGE UNKNOWN

J

J

## 'Jeanne de Montfort'

OLD, MOSS, MEDIUM PINK, REPEAT-FLOWERING

The fragrant flowers of this rose are arranged in large clusters, each opening to slightly less than fully double blooms of clear pink, with bright golden yellow stamens showing through the petals when fully open. It is a tall shrub or even a small climber, and reaches a height of some 8 ft (2.5 m), especially if allowed to grow unpruned. The long stout stems are covered in purplish, stubble-like moss, as are the flower buds. The profuse foliage is slightly glossy and mid-green. Given plenty of space, it is an excellent rose that will sometimes oblige with a repeat-flowering in autumn. ZONES 4–10.

ROBERT, FRANCE, 1851

PARENTAGE UNKNOWN

## 'Jeanne LaJoie'
(below)

MODERN, CLIMBING MINIATURE, MEDIUM PINK, REPEAT-FLOWERING

This popular rose has long pointed buds that open to medium pink, exhibition type blooms. The flowers are double with 40 or more petals, and have just a hint of fragrance. The foliage is small, glossy, dark green and embossed. The tall canes can be easily trained to assume the lateral horizontal position to optimize bloom production along the cane. Trained on a fence or trellis, bloom production is staggering. The non-fading florets have good form and substance, making it one of the best climbers available. It has a vigorous nature and is an excellent choice when a huge display of color against a wall is desired. ZONES 5–11.

SIMA, USA, 1975

'CASA BLANCA' × 'INDEPENDENCE'

AMERICAN ROSE SOCIETY AWARD OF EXCELLENCE 1977

### 'Jennifer' BENjen
*(right)*

MODERN, MINIATURE, PINK
BLEND, REPEAT-FLOWERING

The small double
florets (35 petals or
fewer) have classic form
at all stages of bloom.
The flowers are light
pink to light mauve
with a white reverse.
Great form and color
are the hallmarks of this
rose but in some climates
the blooms open very
quickly. However, the
porcelain-like flowers
win everyone over and
the color does not fade
in the hot midday sun.
They usually occur in
small clusters and have
a light fragrance. The
foliage is medium, semi-
glossy and dark green.
This is a great exhibition
rose whether shown as
one bloom per stem or
in sprays. The stems
are straight and strong.
This rose brought ama-
teur hybridizer, Frank
Benardella, his first
Award of Excellence.
**ZONES 5–11.**

BENARDELLA, USA, 1985

'PARTY GIRL' × 'LAGUNA'

AMERICAN ROSE SOCIETY
AWARD OF EXCELLENCE 1985

### 'Jenny Duval'
*(above right)*
syn. 'Jenny'

OLD, GALLICA, MAUVE

Color changes occur so
frequently in this rose,
probably caused by
variations in weather,
soil and temperature,
that it has often been
confused with 'Président
de Sèze', but Gallica
authorities Suzanne
Verrier and François
Joyaux state that the
two are entirely differ-
ent roses. Colors range
from rose, pink, violet
and smoky lavender to
mauve. This rose has
large, loosely double
blooms with undulating
petals and deep centers
of yellow stamens. The
fragrant flowers appear
on bending canes. The
5 ft (1.5 m) shrub,
which is erect with
gray-green leaves and
stalwart prickles, does
well in poor soil and is
an effective hedge.
Verrier believes it is a
Gallica–China cross.
**ZONES 5–10.**

PRE-1842

PARENTAGE UNKNOWN

## 'Jens Munk'
### (right)

MODERN, HYBRID RUGOSA,
MEDIUM PINK,
REPEAT-FLOWERING

Released from Canada,
the hardiness of this
rose is obvious, with
good cold weather
bringing out the best
it has to offer. Its semi-
double flowers are a
soft pink with a tone
of lilac thrown over the
blooms. The stamens
are yellow and add a
good definition to the
flower's depth, while
the fragrance is slight.
'Jens Munk' is a vig-
orous, medium-height
plant that can be
sprawling and unshapely
when young but, as the
bush matures, it makes
a good disease-resistant
shrub for the garden or
parks. ZONES 3–9.

SVEJDA, CANADA, 1974

'SCHNEEZWERG' ×
'FRU DAGMAR HASTRUP'

## 'Jersey Beauty'
### (right)

MODERN, RAMBLER, LIGHT
YELLOW

Jack Harkness rated
this a two-star rose,
which is a rare accolade
from the late, great
rosarian. Prominent
yellow stamens radiate
to the creamy, pale
yellow petals that form
large, very fragrant,
single blooms, which
appear in clusters. The
flowers fade to white
in the sun and there
is no rebloom. The
variety is a rampant
Rambler reaching
15 ft (4.5 m) when
established, and it loves
a warm spot in the
garden, doing well on
structures as well as on
banks. The glossy,
handsome leaves are
evergreen in milder
climates. The famous
Australian hybridizer,
Alister Clark, used this
rose several times in his
crosses. ZONES 4–10.

MANDA, USA, 1899

*ROSA WICHURANA* ×
'PERLE DES JARDINS'

## 'Joanna Hill' *(right)*

MODERN, LARGE-FLOWERED/
HYBRID TEA, LIGHT YELLOW,
REPEAT-FLOWERING

This rose has a
wonderful scent that
is rich and full, and
no doubt caused quite
a following when it was
released in 1928. The
flowers are delicate
cream-yellow with a
base flushed orange
and are found in
singles or very small
groups on the bush.
It is a vigorous, small-
growing bush with
sometimes poor health
and it will need much
attention and care to
ensure that the best
blooms are produced.
The foliage is leathery.
For all that, though, the
fragrance will certainly
please everyone and it
is worth trying, if only
for that reason.
**ZONES 5–10.**

J. H. HILL CO., USA, 1928

'MME BUTTERFLY' ×
'MISS AMELIA GUDE'

## 'Joasine Hanet'
*(above)*

OLD, PORTLAND, MAUVE,
REPEAT-FLOWERING

This early blooming
rose, rare today, is one
of the survivors in a
class that briefly held
the center of attention.
The deep rose blooms
are tinged with violet,
turning almost purple-
red, depending on its
site in the garden. The
heavy, full, quartered
blooms, which are 3 in
(8 cm) across and
appear in clusters, are
strongly scented. This
vigorous shrub is quite
hardy and disease
resistant. Some would
classify it as a Damask–
Perpetual, a term that
has become increas-
ingly popular, because
of its repeat-flowering
quality. **ZONES 5–10.**

VIBERT, FRANCE, 1847

PARENTAGE UNKNOWN

J

J

### 'Johann Strauss' MEIoffic *(above)*
### syns 'Forever Friends', 'Sweet Sonata'
MODERN, CLUSTER-FLOWERED/FLORIBUNDA, PINK BLEND, REPEAT-FLOWERING

'Johann Strauss' produces fully double blooms with 40 or more petals that are well scented and slightly globular. A soft salmon-pink, they appear singly or in small clusters on moderate length stems from early spring and are quick to repeat their bloom. Glossy bright green leaves produce a thick covering canopy on a medium-height bush that is mildew tolerant and only slightly troubled by black spot. This variety is a good all-round performer both for picking and for garden display, growing well as a bush and as a full standard. ZONES 4–10.

MEILLAND, FRANCE, 1994

(MEITURAPHAR × 'MRS JOHN LAING') × 'EGESKOV'

### 'John Cabot'
MODERN, MODERN SHRUB, MEDIUM RED, REPEAT-FLOWERING

A free-flowering shrub with a multitude of uses, this variety can be grown in tough conditions and will require little maintenance. The semi-double, medium red flowers fade as they age and show their stamens well. These blooms are found in clusters, and they are not at all fragrant. 'John Cabot' is very tolerant of disease and is suitable for use as a hedge or for any place where little attention will be paid to it. It has plentiful, dense leaf coverage and will grow quite tall in warm climates, almost enough to be classified as a small climber. ZONES 3–9.

SVEJDA, CANADA, 1978

*ROSA KORDESII* × SEEDLING

### 'John Clare' AUScent
**(right)**

MODERN, MODERN SHRUB,
DEEP PINK, REPEAT-FLOWERING

This David Austin rose, which is also classified as an English Rose, has the most free-flowering habit of all the Austin roses released to date. The cupped, light crimson flowers are not for the purist rose form lover as they are a little informal and can be very loose. They fade a little as they open and develop to the full-blown stage, and the petals fall cleanly. 'John Clare' is not a tall grower and has a low-growing, spreading habit that is suited to its flower. It was named after the poet, John Clare, for The John Clare Society in the UK. **ZONES 5–10.**

AUSTIN, UK, 1994

'WIFE OF BATH' ×
'GIANT MEYER'

### 'John Davis' *(below)*

MODERN, MODERN SHRUB,
MEDIUM PINK,
REPEAT-FLOWERING

This rose produces large heads of mid-pink flowers with cream to yellow at the base of the petals. They are double, with around 40 petals, and have a strong spicy fragrance. It has a strong, healthy growth habit, tough leaves and long canes that flow well and tend to run or trail along the ground. Disease resistance is good and it needs little care in most normal circumstances, with some attention being paid to mildew and black spot in areas that suffer from heavy infestation. **ZONES 3–9.**

SVEJDA, CANADA, 1986

(*ROSA KORDESII* × SEEDLING) ×
SEEDLING

**J**

J

### 'John F. Kennedy' (left)
**syns 'JFK', 'President John F. Kennedy'**
MODERN, LARGE-FLOWERED/HYBRID TEA, WHITE, REPEAT-FLOWERING

This variety bears tall, elegant buds that open into pure white flowers with some slight green tinges in the early bud stage. They are ideal as cut flowers and are produced quite freely on a strong, upright bush with good disease resistance. The leaves are thick and tough, although in cool climates they can sometimes suffer a little from mildew. Obviously named after the former American president John F. Kennedy, this rose did not win any awards when released, although it still stands up well against newer white introductions. ZONES 5–11.

BOERNER, USA, 1965

SEEDLING × 'WHITE QUEEN'

### 'John Hopper' (left)
OLD, HYBRID PERPETUAL, PINK BLEND, REPEAT-FLOWERING

A compact Hybrid Perpetual, this variety has bright rose blooms edged in lilac. The large, cupped, double flowers have 70 petals each with a carmine center; the outer petals fade with age. They appear on short stems, are very fragrant and cover the shrub in summer; there is some autumn repeat. The 4 ft (1.2 m) canes create an erect and bushy plant, and are covered with large leaves and light red, hooked prickles. It should be deadheaded to encourage the autumn blossoms. 'John Hopper' makes an effective hedge. ZONES 5–10.

WARD, UK, 1862

'JULES MARGOTTIN' × 'MADAME VIDOT'

### 'John S. Armstrong'
*(top)*

MODERN, LARGE-FLOWERED/
HYBRID TEA, DARK RED,
REPEAT-FLOWERING

Also classified as a
Grandiflora Rose,
'John S. Armstrong' is
a fine, free-flowering
bush rose that bears
very deep red blooms.
They have high centers
made up of about 48
petals that are arranged
with precise symmetry.
While not true exhi-
bition style, the variety
makes an excellent
cutting rose for general
use. The scented blooms
keep well when picked,
and they are produced
on long stems. The
bush is tall and strong
in growth, and it is
well covered with
shiny dark green leaves.
There is minimal
trouble with fungus
disease. 'John S.
Armstrong' is well
suited to hot conditions.
**ZONES 5–10.**

SWIM, USA, 1961

'CHARLOTTE ARMSTRONG' ×
SEEDLING

NATIONAL ROSE SOCIETY TRIAL
GROUND CERTIFICATE 1961, ALL-
AMERICA ROSE SELECTION 1962

### 'John Waterer'
*(bottom)*

MODERN, LARGE-FLOWERED/
HYBRID TEA, DARK RED,
REPEAT-FLOWERING

This variety is a very
good dark red that has

a good production of
flowers and quickly
and freely reproduces
each crop of blooms.
It has many top points:
the fragrance is good
without being strong,

it has classic form and,
with above-average-
sized blooms, it has a
presence rarely found
in a rose. The flowering
shoots tend to be weak
and the flowers too
heavy for this new
growth, but they last
well when picked. It
suffers a little from
mildew, although the
growth is otherwise
strong. It is still being
grown in large num-
bers, even though it
was released in 1970.
**ZONES 5–10.**

MCGREDY, UK, 1970

'KING OF HEARTS' × 'HANNE'

ROYAL NATIONAL ROSE SOCIETY
CERTIFICATE OF MERIT

**J**

### 'Joie de Vivre'  *(left)*

MODERN, LARGE-FLOWERED/HYBRID TEA, PINK BLEND, REPEAT-FLOWERING

This bush has large, well-shaped flowers, which are both fragrant and colorful. Classic in form, they are found alone or in small groups and are pink with some gold at the bases. Although not large, this variety is strong and vigorous and moderately resistant to disease, although the younger bronze-green growth suffers some mildew late in the season. **ZONES 5–10.**

GAUJARD, FRANCE, 1949

PARENTAGE UNKNOWN

NATIONAL ROSE SOCIETY CERTIFICATE OF MERIT 1950

**J**

### 'Josephine Baker'

MEImaur *(above)*
syn. 'Velvet Flame'

MODERN, LARGE-FLOWERED/ HYBRID TEA, DARK RED, REPEAT-FLOWERING

This is an excellent disease-resistant, dark red rose that has been overlooked, never really becoming popular. The long, pointed buds open to double flowers containing 25 petals of very good substance. Flower production is excellent and the repeat cycle is reliable. It has a strong and upright growth. 'Josephine Baker' was named after the flamboyant American entertainer who made her home in France in the 1930s. **ZONES 5–10.**

MEILLAND, FRANCE, 1973

'TROPICANA' × 'PAPA MEILLAND'

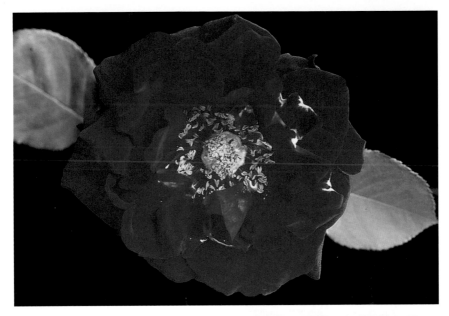

J

### 'Josephine Bruce' *(above)*

MODERN, LARGE-FLOWERED/HYBRID TEA, DARK RED,
REPEAT-FLOWERING

This lovely dark red variety repeat-flowers very
well, being both free and abundant. The blooms
are very strongly fragrant. Its low growth is wide
and sprawling, and it needs special care to keep it
healthy and safe from mildew. Special pruning is
also required, cutting to an inward-pointing eye
to try to rectify the spreading growth habit.
**'Climbing Josephine Bruce'**, a sport discovered
by the same breeder in 1954, is superior to the
bush. Although not every garden has room for a
Climber of this size, it is well worth finding some
space for it to grow. The flowers are similar to
those of the parent. **ZONES 5–10.**

BEES, UK, 1949

'CRIMSON GLORY' × 'MADGE WHIPP'

NATIONAL ROSE SOCIETY TRIAL GROUND CERTIFICATE 1953

### 'Joseph's Coat' *(above)*

MODERN, LARGE-FLOWERED CLIMBER, RED BLEND, REPEAT-FLOWERING

Best described as a yellow and red blend, this rose
is a good example of a small, multi-colored
Climber. 'Joseph's Coat' grows upright, and it is
best suited to being layered out for the maximum
amount of bloom, which is best in spring. The
average-sized flowers are double and open almost
flat to show the stamens clearly. **ZONES 4–10.**

ARMSTRONG AND SWIM, USA, 1964

'BUCCANEER' × 'CIRCUS'

NATIONAL ROSE SOCIETY TRIAL GROUND CERTIFICATE 1963,
BAGATELLE GOLD MEDAL 1964

## 'Joy of Health'

HARxever *(right)*

MODERN, CLUSTER-FLOWERED/
FLORIBUNDA, MEDIUM PINK,
REPEAT-FLOWERING

The flowers of this variety, which are full and double, are found in clusters. They are a soft salmon-pink with peach tones and old-fashioned in shape, being cupped and opening slowly without exposing the center entirely, keeping that form until falling. For smaller gardens, this healthy, vigorous bush is ideal. It has dark green matt leaves and was named and released in Australia in 1996 to benefit the Australian Rotary Health Research Fund. **ZONES 5–10.**

HARKNESS, UK, 1996

SEEDLING × 'AMBER QUEEN'

## 'Judy Fischer'
*(right)*

MODERN, MINIATURE, MEDIUM
PINK, REPEAT-FLOWERING

Pointed high centered pink buds open slowly to small, double, deep rose pink flowers, which hold their color well. In hot weather, the deep rose pink petals may be a shade lighter. The florets are complemented by small, dark green, leathery foliage. The bush is a vigorous, low growing compact plant that is easy to establish. Often described as an all-weather variety, the bloom cycle is fast whatever the climate—sun, rain or high water. It is easy to maintain as it is completely disease resistant. What's more, its quality blooms are always available for a rose show. **ZONES 5–11.**

MOORE, USA, 1968

'LITTLE DARLING' ×
'MAGIC WAND'

AMERICAN ROSE SOCIETY
AWARD OF EXCELLENCE 1975

### 'Jules Margottin'
*(top)*

OLD, HYBRID PERPETUAL, MEDIUM PINK, REPEAT-FLOWERING

The blooms of this rose can vary from semi-double to very full, with up to 90 petals, although a lesser number is more common. The large, pink flowers are like swirls of color, and appear on long stems. It is a vigorous and robust bush with light green, oval, pointed leaves and dark red prickles. It grows to 6 ft (1.8 m) tall, but can be pruned to half that height. There is a good crop of autumn blooms. It is subject to mildew in wet weather. Jacques Margottin (1817–92), the creator of the famous 'Louise Odier', named this rose for his eldest son; there is also a climbing form. ZONES 5–10.

MARGOTTIN, FRANCE, 1853

SEEDLING OF 'LA REINE'

### 'Julia Mannering'
*(below)*

OLD, SWEET BRIAR, LIGHT PINK

One of the 16 *Rosa eglanteria* hybrids that Lord Penzance created in 5 years, 'Julia Mannering' has pearly, flesh pink, single to semi-double blooms veined with deeper pink; the colors are stronger in the shade. They are borne on long canes and both the dark green foliage and the blooms are redolent with an apple fragrance. This once-blooming shrub is vigorous and needs plenty of space. It does well in poor soil and makes a strong hedge with bristly canes, or an attractive shrub in a woodland setting. The rose was named after a character in Sir Walter Scott's novel *Guy Mannering*. ZONES 5–11.

PENZANCE, UK, 1895

PARENTAGE UNKNOWN

J

### 'Julia's Rose'
*(below)*

MODERN, LARGE-FLOWERED/
HYBRID TEA, RUSSET,
REPEAT-FLOWERING

This is a most popular plant simply for its color—the flowers are various shades of copper, parchment and brown, all mixed into a handsome tone that intensifies dramatically in cool to cold cond-

itions. 'Julia's Rose' has a place in every collection, even though it is not a strong bush and needs to be looked after; the rewards are there for those who take the challenge, as it flowers well for most of the season and provides a unique color for floral arrangements. The growth is upright, and the foliage is reddish. It is recommended only for gardeners who are willing to take the time to control disease, as it is not a strong grower. **ZONES 5–10.**

WISBECH PLANT CO., UK, 1976

'BLUE MOON' ×
'DR A. J. VERHAGE'

BADEN-BADEN GOLD MEDAL
1983

### 'Julie de Mersan'
syn. 'Julie de Mersent'
OLD, MOSS, MEDIUM PINK

This rose bears medium-sized flowers that are double and striped with pink and white. 'Julie de Mersan' would be difficult to find nowadays; it seems to be available only on the continent of Europe, mainly in France. **ZONES 4–9.**

THOMAS, FRANCE, 1854

PARENTAGE UNKNOWN

### 'Julischka'   TANjuka
*(bottom)*
syn. 'Juleschke'

MODERN, CLUSTER-FLOWERED/
FLORIBUNDA, MEDIUM RED,
REPEAT-FLOWERING

This unusual but excellent rose produces good-quality Cluster-flowered heads. The bush has medium red flowers that are semi-double with about 20 petals. The fragrance is pleasing. It is not widely grown, except by specialist rose nurs-eries for the collectors who appreciate a unique rose. It is a clean, healthy, disease-free bush with fresh new glossy bronze growth. **ZONES 5–11.**

TANTAU, GERMANY, 1974

PARENTAGE UNKNOWN

NEW ZEALAND GOLD MEDAL 1976,
THE HAGUE GOLDEN ROSE 1982

J

## 'Juno'

OLD, CHINA, LIGHT PINK

This rose is non-repeating, and was perhaps accidentally created when Laffay was seeking a Hybrid Perpetual. The globular buds open to fine, flat, 3 in (8 cm) blush pink flowers, each with a central button eye. It is a beautiful rose and has a delicious fragrance. Its growth is lax and arching with large dark green foliage, smoother than most others of its type except 'Fantin-Latour' and with only a few thorns. Given space towards the front of a border, it can make a gracefully sturdy, very rewarding shrub. **ZONES 5–10.**

LAFFAY, FRANCE, 1847

PARENTAGE UNKNOWN

## 'Just Joey' *(above)*

MODERN, LARGE-FLOWERED/HYBRID TEA, ORANGE BLEND, REPEAT-FLOWERING

Looking at the two parents of this variety, it gives little indication of the offspring, and what a rose it is; an ever-popular variety that will still be so for many years to come. It has big, loose, double flowers that are an orange blend, and they are usually found in small clusters. They are well recommended for both cutting and garden display. The bush is sprawling and grows to medium height, while the leaves are dark green. It is hard to compare 'Just Joey' with other Large-flowered Roses, as the richness of the flower and the loose-ness of the form make it so exciting and unusual. **ZONES 5–10.**

CANT, UK, 1972

'FRAGRANT CLOUD' × 'DR A. J. VERHAGE'

ROYAL NATIONAL ROSE SOCIETY JAMES MASON GOLD MEDAL 1986, ROYAL HORTICULTURAL SOCIETY AWARD OF GARDEN MERIT 1993, WORLD'S FAVORITE ROSE 1994

K

### 'Kabuki' MEIgold
*(above)*
syn. 'Golden Prince'
MODERN, LARGE-FLOWERED/
HYBRID TEA, DEEP YELLOW,
REPEAT-FLOWERING

'Kabuki' has rich deep
yellow flowers that
show a darker pink
tinge in cool weather.
They are fully double
and open well, falling
freely as they age. An
upright grower of me-
dium height, the bush
is strong and has large
leaves with stout
frameworks. It can be
susceptible to some
die-back after pruning
and needs light cutting
to help it overcome this
problem. ZONES 5–10.

MEILLAND, FRANCE, 1968

('MONTE CARLO' × 'BETTINA') ×
('PEACE' × 'SORAYA')

### 'Kaikoura' MACwalla
*(right)*
MODERN, MINIATURE, ORANGE
BLEND, REPEAT-FLOWERING

The large, bright
orange-red flowers of
this rose are outstand-
ing. The florets are
double with about
27 petals and can be a
little larger than the
traditional Miniature
Rose. This rose is
popular in New Zealand
where it wins consist-
ently at rose shows.
The blooms open to
beautiful, flat, neon
orange florets that
hold their color for a
long time, whatever
the climate. The foliage
is an attractive, glossy,
dark green. This is a
vigorous, compact
bush with good disease
resistance. 'Kaikoura' is
a masterpiece from the
hybridizing program of
Sam McGredy where
he has taken two of
his other masterpieces
and successfully trans-
mitted both their
desirable characteristics.
It is named after a town
in New Zealand.
ZONES 5–11.

MCGREDY, NEW ZEALAND, 1978

'ANYTIME' × 'MATANGI'

K

### 'Kardinal' KORlingo
*(right)*

MODERN, LARGE-FLOWERED/
HYBRID TEA, MEDIUM RED,
REPEAT-FLOWERING

Most people will
have seen this rose on
display at their local
florist's but would not
be aware of its name.
The flowers are rich
cardinal red and are
lightly scented. They
usually appear singly
on long stems and can
be easily arranged. In
the greenhouse and
in the open, 'Kardinal'
grows to a medium-tall
bush and has a good
resistance to mildew
and black spot. The
repeat-flowering
intervals are short
but it is a wonderful
rose for all purposes.
**ZONES 5–10.**

KORDES, GERMANY, 1986
SEEDLING × 'FLAMINGO'

### 'Karen Julie' *(top)*

MODERN, LARGE-FLOWERED/
HYBRID TEA, ORANGE/RED,
REPEAT-FLOWERING

This rose, which is
excellent for exhibition,
has well-shaped
blooms that are deep
orange and contain
45 petals. There is a
salmon-orange reverse

to the petals. The
flowers keep their form
and color well on a
medium-sized, bushy
plant with matt mid-
green foliage, and the
flowering is quite good
for an exhibition-type
rose. There are no
disease problems. It is
a fine rose for picking.
**ZONES 5–10.**

ALLENDER, AUSTRALIA, 1979
'ALEXANDER' ×
'VIENNA WOODS'

### 'Karl Herbst'

(*above*)

syn. 'Red Peace'

MODERN, LARGE-FLOWERED/
HYBRID TEA, MEDIUM RED,
REPEAT-FLOWERING

The enormous flowers of a well-grown specimen of this rose have graced many a show, for with 60 broad petals it combines size and symmetry of form to a rare degree. The high-centered blooms open slowly, revealing a rather dull deep red color, darker on the inside of the petal. Blooming is well maintained through summer and autumn, although the flowers are impatient of rain and tend to ball. There is a light fragrance, and for a mixed bed or border, this is a sturdy and reliable rose, still fairly widely grown after nearly half a century. The plant grows vigorously with a branching habit to above average height, and is well furnished with large, leathery leaves that are semi-glossy and dark green. Karl Herbst was a life-long friend of Wilhelm Kordes, both of them having been interned as enemy aliens by the British in World War I. As 'Peace' is one of its parents, '**Climbing Karl Herbst**' has all the beauty of its ancestor. Its quartered blooms and fragrance are happiest in cooler weather and in the autumn. **ZONES 4–9.**

KORDES, GERMANY, 1950

'INDEPENDENCE' × 'PEACE'

NATIONAL ROSE SOCIETY GOLD MEDAL 1950

### 'Karlsruhe'

MODERN, CLUSTER-FLOWERED
CLIMBER, DEEP PINK,
REPEAT-FLOWERING

The flowers of 'Karlsruhe' are large, carried in clusters of up to 10, full-petalled and globular at first, becoming cupped as they open out. They are rose pink and have a slight scent. Following a prolific early flush, the blooms are produced intermittently through summer and autumn on a well-branched plant. The variety grows with a spreading, climbing habit to average extent and is best suited for growing up pillars and on walls where the situation is not too dry. The leaves are plentiful and glossy. Karlsruhe is a city near the French border in southwest Germany, the name meaning 'Charles's Peace' with reference to Charlemagne. **ZONES 4–9.**

KORDES, GERMANY, 1957

*ROSA KORDESII* ×
'GOLDEN GLOW'

### 'Kassel'   (*top right*)

MODERN, LARGE-FLOWERED
CLIMBER, ORANGE-RED,
REPEAT-FLOWERING

There seems to be disagreement on the parentage of this variety. The blooms are scarlet red, fairly large, and are borne in clusters of up to 10 semi-double flowers. The young blooms are neatly formed with high centers, becoming wide and loosely cupped as they open. They have an appreciable fragrance and appear freely in summer, with sporadic later blooming through summer and autumn. This rose has a vigorous, arching habit and can be grown as a shrub or trained on a light support such as a short pillar or low fence, since it extends more than the average expected of a shrub, and less than that of a climber. The leathery leaves are large, matt and reddish when young. This is one of many Kordes' roses named for a German city. **ZONES 4–9.**

KORDES, GERMANY, 1957

'HAMBURG' × 'SCARLET ELSE'

NATIONAL ROSE SOCIETY
CERTIFICATE OF MERIT 1957

## 'Katharina Zeimet'
### syn. 'White Baby Rambler'

MODERN, POLYANTHA, WHITE, REPEAT-FLOWERING

This dainty rose bears double white flowers in airy sprays of up to 50 blooms, making a very free display on the first flush of bloom with a good continuation of bloom throughout summer and autumn. There is a delicate fragrance, and the flowers are remarkably tolerant of bad weather. 'Katharina Zeimet' is suitable to group in beds or near the front of a border, beside a path, to make a low dense hedge, and in a container. The plant is normally dwarf and compact but can become sizeable if not pruned. It grows vigorously with many twiggy shoots to average height or above for a Polyantha, and is well provided with many small, rich dark green leaflets. ZONES 4–9.

LAMBERT, GERMANY, 1901

'ÉTOILE DE MAI' × 'MARIE PAVIÉ'

## 'Kathleen' *(right)*

MODERN, MODERN SHRUB, LIGHT PINK, REPEAT-FLOWERING

The pale color of this variety was modestly described by the raiser as 'pink blush, after the shade of *Rosa canina*'. The flowers are small and single, each with a charming arrangement of 5 separated petals and showing yellow stamens. They are carried in big clusters so that the overall effect is of apple blossom, and from them wafts a light fragrance, sweet and musky. The blooms appear very freely during the first flush, and more flowers are produced intermittently through summer and in autumn, when the blooms can be accompanied by sprays of orange hips. 'Kathleen' makes an excellent addition to a shrub border, having a somewhat sprawling habit and growing larger than the average shrub rose, while in milder climates it grows big enough to make a useful climber. The leaves are long, drooping and dark green. ZONES 4–9.

PEMBERTON, UK, 1922

'DAPHNE' × 'PERLE DES JARDINS'

K

## 'Kathleen Ferrier'

MODERN, CLUSTER-FLOWERED/FLORIBUNDA, ORANGE-PINK, REPEAT-FLOWERING

The semi-double flowers on 'Kathleen Ferrier' are a picture of simplicity and charm as they open like saucers to show prominent yellow stamens. These blooms are light salmon-pink with white towards the bases of the petals, have a pleasing scent and are carried in well-filled sprays on long stems throughout summer and autumn. This bush rose reaches shrub proportions in mild climates; it is also excellent as a hedge. 'Kathleen Ferrier' is vigorous and bushy to above average height, and is well supplied with shiny dark green leaves. The variety commemorates the popular British contralto who lived 1912–53 and inspired many through her glorious voice, warm personality and faith in times of adversity. ZONES 4–9.

BUISMAN, THE NETHERLANDS, 1952

'GARTENSTOLZ' × 'SHOT SILK'

NATIONAL ROSE SOCIETY TRIAL GROUND CERTIFICATE 1955

### 'Kathleen Harrop' *(right)*

OLD, BOURBON, LIGHT PINK, REPEAT-FLOWERING

Retaining all the good points of its parent, this popular rose is one of the last Bourbon Roses introduced. The large buds open to soft, shell pink blooms that are semi-double and are marked with transparent veins; the petals are dark on the undersides, although the color fades in direct sunlight. Some blooms appear in clusters. It reaches 10 ft (3 m) high as a climber, or half that as a shrub, has no prickles, and is covered by gray-green, pointed leaves. The plant is not bothered by wet weather, but during its mid-summer to autumn flowering it needs good air circulation to prevent mildew. **ZONES 4–10.**

DICKSON, UK, 1919

SPORT OF 'ZÉPHIRINE DROUHIN'

K

### 'Kathryn Morley'

AUSclub, AUSvariety  *(right)*

MODERN, MODERN SHRUB,
LIGHT PINK, REPEAT-FLOWERING

The flowers of 'Kathryn Morley' are of medium to large size and very full, with over 40 petals. They are borne singly or in small clusters and open into pale pink flowers of charming old-fashioned appearance; the outer petals reflex while the remainder are enfolded and slightly incurved, giving what has been described as a 'cup and saucer' effect. There is a pleasant scent, and flowering continues through summer and autumn. The plant makes a somewhat uneven, rangy grower with long canes, as well as shorter stems; it is best grown in a border where the beauty and scent of the flowers can be appreciated, but with lower growing plants in front. It grows vigorously and is furnished with large, mid- to dark green leaves. The rose was named in memory of the 17-year-old daughter of Mr and Mrs Eric Morley. It is from David Austin and is also classified as an English Rose. **ZONES 4–9.**

AUSTIN, UK, 1990

'MARY ROSE' × 'CHAUCER'

### 'Keepsake' KORmalda *(top)*
syns 'Esmeralda',
'Kordes' Rose
Esmeralda'

MODERN, LARGE-FLOWERED/
HYBRID TEA, PINK BLEND,
REPEAT-FLOWERING

The flowers of this
variety are large and
full with 40 petals, and
open with high centers.
They are deep pink,
with hints of light
carmine and blush.
There is a light fragrance,
and flowering is well
maintained through
summer and autumn,
the blooms being
borne singly and some-
times in clusters of 3.
The stems are medium
in length and occasion-
ally have crooked
pedicels. 'Keepsake' is
often used for bedding
and is suitable to group
in a border and to grow
for showing as the
flowers last well, hold-
ing their form to a late
stage and withstanding
bad weather. The plant
grows to average height
or less with a bushy,
rather untidy habit and
has mid- to dark green,
glossy and robust
foliage. ZONES 4–9.

KORDES, GERMANY, 1981

SEEDLING × 'RED PLANET'

ROYAL NATIONAL ROSE SOCIETY
TRIAL GROUND CERTIFICATE 1980,
PORTLAND GOLD MEDAL 1987

### 'Kazanlik' *(bottom)*
syns *Rosa damascena*
*trigintipetala*,
'Trigintipetala'

OLD, DAMASK, DEEP PINK

This plant is extensively
grown in Kazanlik,
Bulgaria, because it
is one of the varieties
used to make the
famous 'attar of roses'.
The flowers, which
are arranged in loose
clusters on short thin
stalks and appear in
early to mid-summer,
are soft pink and a bit
more than semi-double
when fully open; each
is about 2 in (5 cm)
across and exposes
many creamy colored
stamens. They are
deliciously fragrant.
'Kazanlik' is an angular
shrub to some 6 ft
(1.8 m) high and almost
as wide, with a twiggy
growth habit and
moderately thorny,
brownish green wood.
The light gray-green,
serrated leaves are soft
to touch. ZONES 5–11.

PRE-1700

PARENTAGE UNKNOWN

K

## 'Kent' POUlcov
### syns 'Pyrenees', 'Sparkler', 'White Cover'
MODERN, GROUND COVER, WHITE, REPEAT-FLOWERING

This is a spreading dwarf shrub with a low, rounded outline, rather than a true Ground Cover Rose, but in a limited space it is most useful either as a specimen plant, in a small group, or near the front of a shrub border. The plant produces large trusses of small semi-double white flowers that open cupped, then become flat. They are borne close to the plant, effectively providing a cushion of white at the height of the flowering season and maintaining a good succession of blooms through the rest of summer and autumn. There is a light fragrance, and the flowers look fresh and clean whatever the weather. It is as wide as an average shrub rose but half the height, and is well covered with small, shiny dark green leaves. **ZONES 4–9.**

POULSEN, DENMARK, 1988

PARENTAGE UNKNOWN

BADEN-BADEN GOLD MEDAL 1990, ROYAL NATIONAL ROSE SOCIETY PRESIDENT'S INTERNATIONAL TROPHY 1990, GLASGOW CERTIFICATE OF MERIT 1992, ROYAL NATIONAL ROSE SOCIETY BRITISH ROSE AWARD 1998

## 'Kerryman' *(top)*
MODERN, CLUSTER-FLOWERED/FLORIBUNDA, PINK BLEND, REPEAT-FLOWERING

The flowers of this variety are a pretty shade of salmon-pink in the center, paling to rosy salmon towards the margins. They are large for a Cluster-flowered Rose and are made up of 24 broad petals, so the combined weight of the blooms in their clusters tends to bow the stems, giving the plant a pleasing rounded effect. This works in its favor, especially when it is required for bedding. 'Kerryman' is a good rose for a border and also a low hedge, though it is likely to be troubled by black spot in seasons when that fungus is prevalent. Flowering through summer and autumn is well maintained, and there is a light scent. The plant grows to average height or below, and has a well-spread, bushy habit and semi-glossy leaves. The raiser named the rose to reflect his love of Kerry in Ireland. **ZONES 4–9.**

MCGREDY, UK, 1971

'PADDY MCGREDY' × ('MME LÉON CUNY' × 'COLUMBINE')

ROYAL NATIONAL ROSE SOCIETY CERTIFICATE OF MERIT 1971

## 'Kew Rambler' *(above)*
MODERN, RAMBLER, MEDIUM PINK

The pointed, bright pink buds of this rampant Rambler open to reveal pink-white, single blooms with paler centers. They bloom later than most in the class and appear in trusses on the long, pliable canes. The large, moderately fragrant clusters are highlighted by the gold stamens. The attractive, gray-green foliage covers both the prickles and the orange-red hips. This summer-blooming rose can be used as a large shrub in the wild garden or trained on a pergola or high fence. It reaches 18 ft (5 m) in two years. **ZONES 4–11.**

KEW GARDENS, UK, 1913

*ROSA SOULIEANA* × 'HIAWATHA'

### 'Kiese' *(right)*
MODERN, MODERN SHRUB,
MEDIUM RED

'Not a rose for the fainthearted' warns Britain's Keith Jones, one of the few nurserymen to offer this undisciplined vigorous shrub. It produces heads of semi-double or almost single, medium-sized blooms on strong prickly stems; they are a bright shade of cherry red, fading with age, with a yellowy white eye, large golden stamens and slight scent. It flowers in summer only, but bears large, round red hips in autumn. It is especially suited to areas where plants are allowed to become naturalized and look after themselves for it needs no maintenance apart from trimming to keep it in bounds. Of an arching, free-branching habit, this rose will make a thicket up to twice as large as the average shrub rose, and could be trained to create a pillar. The leaves are dark green, bright and glossy. The raiser's original intention was to create a rootstock, and as a standard stem it is excellent and long lived, though quite prickly. **ZONES 4–9.**

KIESE, GERMANY, 1910

'GÉNÉRAL JACQUEMINOT' ×
*ROSA CANINA*

### 'Kiftsgate' *(right)*
syn. 'Filipes Kiftsgate',
*Rosa filipes* 'Kiftsgate'
MODERN, LARGE-FLOWERED
CLIMBER, WHITE

Among rose enthusiasts in the USA 'rose rustling' has become a popular pastime, and one of the most successful varieties acquired in this way came from Murrell's nursery, who obtained 'Kiftsgate' from a well-established plant growing in the Gloucestershire garden whose name it bears. It has spectacular clusters of many single, creamy white flowers on vigorous arching canes, and a pleasing scent that wafts around on still days. The best place for this variety is where it can grow naturally,

and it is often planted to clamber into a large tree. It can be grown on big walls, but since one English specimen on a tithe barn has extended to over 148 ft (45 m), caution is needed in siting it. The blooms appear *en masse* in mid-summer only, succeeded by small round hips. The leaves are large and shiny, and the canes carry large prickles that can make pruning an uncomfortable task; apart from the removal of dead branches, it is best to leave this rose to nature. **ZONES 4–9.**

MURRELL, UK, 1954

SEEDLING OF *ROSA FILIPES*

ROYAL HORTICULTURAL SOCIETY
AWARD OF GARDEN MERIT

K

## 'Kimono' *(right)*

MODERN, CLUSTER-FLOWERED/
FLORIBUNDA, PINK BLEND,
REPEAT-FLOWERING

The flowers of this rose are rounded in outline and of medium size and are carried in broad clusters. They are fully double, with over 40 small petals, and open out flat when fully expanded. The color is a kindly shade of salmon-pink, there is a pleasing fragrance, and flowers continue to appear through summer and autumn. This is an effective and dependable all-round performer for beds, borders and hedges, and it is still widely available after nearly 40 years in commerce. The plant grows vigorously, maintaining a uniform habit of growth to average height, and it is plentifully supplied with medium green foliage that is coppery when young. ZONES 4–9.

DE RUITER, THE NETHERLANDS, 1961

'COCORICO' ×
'FRAU ANNY BEAUFAYS'

ROYAL NATIONAL ROSE SOCIETY
TRIAL GROUND CERTIFICATE 1961

## 'King's Ransom' *(above right)*

MODERN, LARGE-FLOWERED/
HYBRID TEA, DEEP YELLOW,
REPEAT-FLOWERING

This rose has been a standby for gardeners and nurseries for many years and remains popular. Its strengths are the quality of the large double blooms, which open from urn-shaped buds into high-centered blooms before becoming cupped and falling cleanly; the clear color, which shows little variation in its bright and cheerful yellow tone from start to finish; the neat habit, upright and bushy, making it suitable for beds, hedges, borders and as a standard; its additional value for cutting and showing; its long flowering period through summer and autumn and tolerance of bad weather; and its foliage, dark green, glossy and reasonably plentiful. There is some scent, and the plant grows to average height or a little more. ZONES 4–9.

MOREY, USA, 1961

'GOLDEN MASTERPIECE' ×
'LYDIA'

ALL-AMERICA ROSE SELECTION 1962

### 'Kiss' KORikis, KORokis
*(top)*

MODERN, CLUSTER-FLOWERED/
FLORIBUNDA, ORANGE-PINK,
REPEAT-FLOWERING

'Kiss' has pale salmon-pink, full-petalled flowers that are carried on long wiry stems either singly, or in a cluster so open that each flower develops with a stem long enough to cut. They have the high-centered form of a Large-flowered Rose and last for ages. It performs well in warm climates, being vigorous and easy to grow, and continues to produce lightly fragrant blooms over a long period through summer and autumn. The plant grows to above average height and has dark green leaves. **ZONES 4–9.**

KORDES, GERMANY, 1988

SEEDLING × SEEDLING

### 'Kitty Kininmonth'
*(below)*

MODERN, LARGE-FLOWERED
CLIMBER, DEEP PINK,
REPEAT-FLOWERING

The semi-double flowers of this variety are very large and open cupped, showing golden stamens in the heart of the deep pink blooms. They have a slight scent, and there are likely to be sporadic flowers after the generous main flush. This is another of Alister Clark's beautiful roses. It needs a warm climate and frost-free conditions to thrive, so in cooler countries it should be grown against a large, sheltered wall. It has wrinkled, dark green foliage. **ZONES 5–9.**

CLARK, AUSTRALIA, 1922

PARENTAGE UNKNOWN

K

### 'Königin von Dänemark' *(right)*
syn. 'Queen of Denmark'

OLD, ALBA, MEDIUM PINK

The flowers of this rose open from tight, stubby buds to flattish flowers packed full of bright deep pink petals. These can be up to 3 in (8 cm) across and provide an exquisite fragrance. The blooms appear in mid-summer in heavy clusters, sometimes so heavy that they bend the branches over in an arching fashion so that they almost touch the ground. It is a very thorny shrub to about 4 ft (1.2 m), covered with deep bluish green leaves—an attraction in themselves. While comparisons may be odious, this has to be one of the best of the Albas; it is an easygoing rose that always exceeds expectations—except in very wet seasons when it does not fully open—even in the poorest soils. **ZONES 4–10.**

BOOTH, DENMARK, 1826

*ROSA ALBA* × HYBRID OF UNKNOWN DAMASK

ROYAL HORTICULTURAL SOCIETY AWARD OF GARDEN MERIT 1993

### 'Konrad Adenauer' *(right)*
syn. 'Konrad Adenauer Rose'

MODERN, LARGE-FLOWERED/ HYBRID TEA, DARK RED, REPEAT-FLOWERING

Roses named for statesmen do not always measure up to expectations, and in one respect this variety falls literally short, for Adenauer was a big man and his namesake is a low grower. In other respects it is a pleasing rose, giving a good succession of well-formed deep blood-red blooms through summer and autumn. They are of medium to large size, borne singly or in small open clusters and open cupped, and they have a strong fragrance. In a bed or border and for cutting, this is a useful variety, and it is also capable of providing exhibition blooms. It grows sturdily to below average height with an upright habit and has a covering of glossy light green foliage. From 1949 to 1963 Konrad Adenauer served as the first Chancellor of the West German Republic. **ZONES 4–9.**

TANTAU, GERMANY, 1955

'CRIMSON GLORY' × 'HENS VERSCHUREN'

K

### 'Konrad Henkel' KORjet *(above)*
syn. 'Avenue's Red'
MODERN, LARGE-FLOWERED/HYBRID TEA, MEDIUM RED,
REPEAT-FLOWERING

When the sun catches them there is a beautiful velvety sheen on the deep red petals of this variety, which form large, full-petalled roses borne sometimes singly and often in small open clusters on strong stems. The flowers have a pleasant light fragrance and continue to bloom freely through summer and autumn, being suitable for cutting as well as for use in beds and borders and as hedges. The plant grows vigorously with a stiff upright habit to average height and has dark green, semi-glossy leaves. The rose was named to mark the 75th birthday of one of the main architects of the German post-war economic revival. **ZONES 4–9.**

KORDES, GERMANY, 1983

SEEDLING × 'RED PLANET'

### 'Kordes' Brillant' KORbisch
syn. 'Kordes' Brilliant'
MODERN, MODERN SHRUB, ORANGE BLEND, REPEAT-FLOWERING

The fully double flowers of 'Kordes' Brillant' are borne in big sprays and are quite large, neatly formed and of a most vibrant orange-red hue. They open cupped and, having stiff petals, hold their shape for a long time. There is a slight fragrance. The first flush of bloom is very prolific, and flowers continue to appear through summer and autumn. This gives good value in the garden where a hot color tone is required; it also looks well in mixed borders and makes an effective screening plant. The plant grows strong and bushily to average height or more and has attractive bright green shiny leaves. **ZONES 4–9.**

KORDES, GERMANY, 1983

SEEDLING OF 'SYMPATHIE' × SEEDLING

### 'Korona' KORnita
*(right)*
syn. 'Orange Korona'

MODERN, CLUSTER-FLOWERED/
FLORIBUNDA, ORANGE-RED,
REPEAT-FLOWERING

This rose's orange-scarlet blooms brought a bright and cheerful color to many gardens in the 1950s, and it was notable at the time because as they aged to salmon-pink, they still toned in with the younger flowers. Up to that time the bright reds nearly all turned purple, creating a dreadful color clash. The lightly scented cupped blooms are fairly double, of medium to large size, and are carried boldly in trusses. They appear freely in summer and continue to repeat their flowering through to autumn, performing well whatever the weather and giving excellent garden value as hedges and in beds and borders. The plant grows upright with a bushy habit to average height or more and is well furnished with olive green, semi-glossy leaves. **ZONES 4–9.**

KORDES, GERMANY, 1955

'OBERGÄRTNER WIEBICKE' ×
'INDEPENDENCE'

NATIONAL ROSE SOCIETY GOLD
MEDAL 1954

### 'Ko's Yellow'
MACkosyel *(above)*

MODERN, MINIATURE, YELLOW
BLEND, REPEAT-FLOWERING

The flowers of this rose are yellow, edged with red or deep pink, fading to cream. The double florets with 39 petals have classic form. In warm weather the large blooms have a lovely fragrance that even the dullest of senses can detect. The large foliage is glossy mid- to dark green on a well-rounded, compact bush. Parentage of this rose is a complex combination of unusual breeding lines experimented with by Sam McGredy during the 1970s. It was named for Ko Schuurman, the wife of a close colleague and friend of the hybridizer. **ZONES 5–11.**

MCGREDY, NEW ZEALAND, 1978

('NEW PENNY' × 'BANBRIDGE') ×
('BORDER FLAME' ×
'MANX QUEEN')

## 'Kristin' BENmagic
### (right)
MODERN, MINIATURE, RED
BLEND, REPEAT-FLOWERING

'Kristin' has white
flowers with a dramatic
broad red edging on
each and every petal.
They are double
(27–30 petals) and have
excellent, consistent
Large-flowered form.
Blooms are usually
borne one to a stem,
or in small clusters on
strong, straight stems.
The foliage is semi-
glossy and dark green,
and is a little large for
the bloom size. This
rose requires warm
weather for the blooms
to open fully and the
color is more intense
in hot climates, with
the edging extending
deeper into each petal.
The color combination
is striking with the edg-
ing giving definition
to the classic shape of
the blooms. In cooler
climates only the outer
petals seem to move,
which gives a cup-
and-saucer shape to
the florets. 'Kristin'
made its international
exhibition debut in
St Albans, England
at the Royal National
Rose Society National
Miniature Show in
1995. It received
several key awards.
**ZONES 5–11.**

BENARDELLA, USA, 1992

DICMICKEY × 'TINSELTOWN'

AMERICAN ROSE SOCIETY
AWARD OF EXCELLENCE 1993

## 'Kronprincessin
## Viktoria' (above)
syn. 'Kronprincessin
Viktoria von Pruessen'
OLD, BOURBON, WHITE,
REPEAT-FLOWERING

This rose has pure white,
oval buds that are
followed by milk white,
large blooms with a
light yellow center.
During the flowering
period from summer
until autumn there are
abundant blooms with
a strong Alba scent.
They are cupped and
ruffled and 4 in (10 cm)
across, and remain open
for a long time. As with
its parent, the flowers
ball easily in wet
weather. It is a vigor-
ous, erect bush with
short branches and
light green leaves, and
is an excellent choice
for a small garden as
it only reaches 3–4 ft
(1–1.2 m). **ZONES 4–10.**

VOLVERT, GERMANY, 1887

SPORT OF 'SOUVENIR DE LA
MALMAISON'

K

## 'La Belle Distinguée'
syns 'La Petite Duchesse', 'Lee's Duchess',
'Scarlet Sweet Brier'
OLD, SWEET BRIAR, MEDIUM RED

A truly distinguished and popular rose, 'La Belle Distinguée' has fully double, small, flat, bright crimson blooms. Although there is no rebloom, the slightly fragrant rose makes up for it by providing a spectacular display in early summer. Reaching 5 ft (1.5 m), the compact, upright shrub displays dainty foliage that does not have much of the typical scent of this family. There are a few prickles and some small hips. It is a good candidate for a hedge or a woodland garden. **ZONES 4–10.**

PRE-1837

PARENTAGE UNKNOWN

## 'La Belle Sultane' *(top right)*
syns 'Belle Sultane', 'Gallica Maheca', 'Violacea'
OLD, GALLICA, DARK RED

The haunting color of this rose has helped to make its reputation. The spectrum of change includes mauve, purple, crimson, maroon and reddish violet, and the flowers pale to white at the base. After the round buds open, flat, almost single blooms with heart-shaped petals form around a crown of golden stamens. At times the fragrant petals appear to swirl. It is a tall shrub with an arching form and long canes covered with red bristles. 'La Belle Sultane' is an outstanding plant for the mixed border or for use as a hedge. A crop of round, red hips appears after the summer flowering. **ZONES 4–10.**

PROBABLY FROM THE NETHERLANDS, 1700s, INTRODUCED IN FRANCE BY DUPONT PRE-1811

PARENTAGE UNKNOWN

## 'L. D. Braithwaite' AUScrim *(above)*
syns 'Braithwaite', 'Leonard Dudley Braithwaite'
MODERN, MODERN SHRUB, DARK RED, REPEAT-FLOWERING

The flowers of this variety are attractively formed. They are fairly large, have 40 or more petals, and open to show a rounded form, with many petals infolded one against another in the center. The color is a rich even tone of dark crimson, and it holds well through the whole life of the flowers, which are borne singly and in wide-spaced clusters on firm, upright stems. They have a pleasing fragrance. The blooms continue to appear through summer and autumn and they withstand wet weather well. 'L. D. Braithwaite' makes a good rose to group in a border, the flower color according particularly well with that of older roses. Unfortunately the plant grows unevenly, so some flowers become lost amid the younger growth, but generally this is a worthwhile variety that grows sturdily to below average height and has gray-green leaves. **ZONES 4–9.**

AUSTIN, UK, 1988

'THE SQUIRE' × 'MARY ROSE'

## 'La France' (top)

MODERN, LARGE-FLOWERED/
HYBRID TEA, LIGHT PINK,
REPEAT-FLOWERING

This variety has long pointed buds that open into full-petalled light pink flowers with flushes of deeper pink on the petal reverse. They are high centered, have a fragrance that many praise and others find elusive, and continue in bloom through summer and autumn. The shape and texture of the flower, as well as the general refinement of the growth, sufficiently impressed 50 rosarians for it to be chosen out of 1000 candidates to bear their country's name, and it later came to be considered the first Large-flowered Rose. The plant grows vigorously to average height or below and has mid-green, semi-glossy foliage. Queries have been raised about the true identity of the rose offered by some growers; the variety sold by Ralph Moore of the USA was grown by his grandmother and has been known to him as 'La France' for over 80 years. **'Climbing La France'** was discovered in 1893 by Henderson in the USA. Since the full-petalled flowers of 'La France' tend to nod on their stems, it is quite an advantage to plant the climber so that they can be viewed from below. ZONES 4–9.

GUILLOT, FRANCE, 1867

PERHAPS 'MME VICTOR VERDIER' × 'MME BRAVY'; OR A SEEDLING OF 'MME FALCOT'

## 'La Marne' (bottom)

MODERN, POLYANTHA, PINK
BLEND, REPEAT-FLOWERING

Many Polyantha Roses have disappeared, but

this example has survived, thanks to its vigor and general charm. The semi-double flowers, borne freely in well-filled clusters, are reminiscent of apple blossom, being rosy blush with bright salmon-rose towards the edges of the petals. They continue in bloom through summer and autumn but do not have much fragrance. This variety is particularly useful for borders and as a specimen plant in a container, and it is well worth including as a fine example of its type in a garden of rose history. The plant is vigorous, growing evenly to above average height, and it has a shrubby habit. It is almost thornless, with dark green shiny leaves that are held on the plant to a late stage in winter. ZONES 4–9.

BARBIER, FRANCE, 1915

'MME NORBERT LEVAVASSEUR' × 'COMTESSE DU CAYLA'

**L**

L

### 'La Marseillaise' DELgeot *(above)*
syn. 'Isobel Champion'

MODERN, LARGE-FLOWERED/HYBRID TEA, DARK RED,
REPEAT-FLOWERING

The plump buds of this variety correctly indicate
that a big flower is on the way. The blooms have
about 40 petals and are well formed, opening with
high centers and maintaining a good symmetry of
form as the petals expand. They are velvety deep
scarlet and have a pleasing fragrance. After the
first flush, blooming is well maintained through
summer and autumn, making this suitable for
beds and borders and also to grow for cutting. It
seems to do particularly well in warmer climates,
making a handsome vigorous bush of average
height or more with light green foliage.
**ZONES 4–9.**

DELBARD-CHABERT, FRANCE, 1976

(['GLORY OF ROME' × 'IMPECCABLE'] × ['ROUGE MEILLAND' ×
'SORAYA']) × (MEISAR × 'WALKO')

### 'La Mortola'
syn. *Rosa brunonii* 'La Mortola'

MODERN, LARGE-FLOWERED CLIMBER, WHITE

This is an extra fine form of *Rosa brunonii*, with
clusters of small silky petalled white flowers that
open wide to display yellow stamens. There is a
good musky fragrance. The summer blooming
is spectacular, but it does not repeat-flower.
This variety should be grown where there is
ample space, for its vigor is such that it can extend
4 times as far as the average climbing rose,
producing very long arching growths that will
bush out over trees, walls and hedgerows. It is
not tolerant of frost and therefore needs careful
placement, since the right conditions for so large
a plant are hard to provide. The leaves are long,
limp, gray-green and downy. **ZONES 5–9.**

HANBURY, UK, 1954

FORM OF *ROSA MOSCHATA NEPALENSIS*

## 'La Noblesse'

OLD, CENTIFOLIA, LIGHT PINK

This rose, which deserves to be better known, has flowers that are at first rather high centered but open flat and fairly full to about 3 in (8 cm) across. They are bright deep pink, paling with age to softer shades, and when fully open, expose brownish stamens. The petals are of a silky texture, which adds considerably to their charm, and are superbly scented. A broad, upright shrub that grows to about 5 ft (1.5 m) high, it has plentiful dark green, rather coarse foliage in the typical Centifolia mold. Little is known about this rose and it may have been introduced under a different name, but whatever its provenance it is well worth space in any garden. ZONES 5–10.

CIRCA 1856

PARENTAGE UNKNOWN

## 'La Paloma 85'

TANamola

syn. 'The Dove'

MODERN, CLUSTER-FLOWERED/
FLORIBUNDA, WHITE,
REPEAT-FLOWERING

'La Paloma 85' has brilliant creamy white flowers that reveal glimpses of gold in the depths of the petals as they open. The first flowers are often borne singly, but later ones frequently appear in close clusters of up to 12 blooms. They are full petalled, not very fragrant, and stand up well to wet weather; they continue to appear through summer and autumn. This is a useful rose for beds, borders, and to grow for cutting. It grows vigorously with an upright, bushy habit to below average height, and is furnished with leathery, shiny and robust leaves. The name means, as the synonym reveals, 'The Dove'. ZONES 4–9.

TANTAU, GERMANY, 1985

PARENTAGE UNKNOWN

## 'La Reine' *(below)*

syns 'Reine des Français', 'Rose de la Reine'

OLD, HYBRID PERPETUAL,
MEDIUM PINK,
REPEAT-FLOWERING

'La Reine' has indeed reigned ever since its introduction in France over a century and a half ago; its outstanding quality as a cut flower during a long blooming season may account for this popularity. After the fat, high-centered buds open, glossy rose pink blooms appear that are tinged with lilac. The large globular flowers with 78 petals have inner petals that fold back upon themselves. The plant reaches 4 ft (1.2 m), and needs support when young. The pale green leaves have wavy edges, and there are some prickles on the smooth bark. It thrives best in rich soil, and deadheading will help increase the autumn flowering. Laffay produced many lovely roses, including 'Cardinal de Richelieu' and 'La Vésuve'. ZONES 5–10.

LAFFAY, FRANCE, 1842

POSSIBLY A SEEDLING OF
'WILLIAM JESSE'

L

L

### 'La Sévillana'

**MEIgekanu** *(above)*
syn. 'Sévillana'

MODERN, CLUSTER-FLOWERED/
FLORIBUNDA, ORANGE-RED,
REPEAT-FLOWERING

This rose produces lightly scented deep bright vermilion flowers in clusters of up to 5 on long flexible stems. They are of medium size, are formed with neat centers, and become cupped as they open. The first flush of flower is very colorful and showy, and more blooms are produced with good continuity through summer and autumn. The growth is dense, leafy and shrubby, making this a good variety for hedges, as well as beds and borders. It grows somewhat taller and wider than the average Cluster-flowered Rose. The leaves are dark green and glossy. ZONES 4–9.

MEILLAND, FRANCE, 1978

([MEIBRIM × 'JOLIE MADAME'] ×
['ZAMBRA' × 'ZAMBRA']) ×
(['TROPICANA' × 'TROPICANA'] ×
['POPPY FLASH' × 'RUSTICANA'])

ANERKANNTE DEUTSCHE ROSE
1979, BELFAST CERTIFICATE OF
MERIT 1984

### 'La Ville de Bruxelles'
*(above right)*

OLD, DAMASK, DEEP PINK

This variety has large flowers, up to 3 in (8 cm) wide when fully open. The blooms are arranged in well-spaced clusters and appear in mid-summer. They are

clear bright pink and fragrant. Each bloom is full of reflexing petals and usually has a tight button eye in the center. This upright though dense shrub grows to some 5 ft (1.5 m) high with dark green, fairly thorny stems. The substantial foliage is a rich mid-green. It is not too happy in wet weather, but the little extra care required is well worth it. ZONES 5–10.

VIBERT, FRANCE, 1849

PARENTAGE UNKNOWN

ROYAL HORTICULTURAL SOCIETY
AWARD OF GARDEN MERIT 1993

## 'L'Abondance'
*(top)*

OLD, NOISETTE, WHITE/
LIGHT PINK

'L'Abondance' is one of the lesser-known Noisettes, producing flesh pink, double blooms that are borne in well-spaced clusters of 50–100 flowers. There is some fragrance. The plant is a vigorous rambler, reaching 10 ft (3 m) in 2 years, that can be used as a climber on pillars or pergolas; it does well in poor soil. The foliage is shiny and light green. The firm of Moreau & Robert has produced other famous roses including 'Marbrée' and 'Homère'. ZONES 5–10.

MOREAU & ROBERT, FRANCE,
1877

PARENTAGE UNKNOWN

## 'Lady Curzon'
*(bottom)*

MODERN, HYBRID RUGOSA,
MEDIUM PINK,
REPEAT-FLOWERING

The large rose pink blooms of this variety open their 5 crinkled petals like shallow saucers, displaying handsome golden stamens. Their refinement and delicacy is at odds with the character of the plant, which is vigorous, producing prickly, arching stems that are capable of clambering through bushes and low trees and can be trained up as a climber on a strong support. It needs plenty of space, and is suitable for a border among big plants, for it is twice as high and 3 times as wide as the average shrub rose. The flowers are produced freely in summer and have a light scent. The foliage is rough, robust and mid- to dark green. This prickly, tangly, coarse-looking shrub can hardly be termed lady-like, and one wonders what Lady Curzon, the wife of the Viceroy of India, really thought of it. ZONES 4–9.

TURNER, UK, 1901

ROSA MACRANTHA × R. RUGOSA
RUBRA

L

## 'Lady Diana'

syn. 'Lady Di'

MODERN, LARGE-FLOWERED/
HYBRID TEA, LIGHT PINK,
REPEAT-FLOWERING

'Lady Diana' is grown
mainly for the cut-
flower trade. The
blooms, of a delicate
light pink shade, are
borne singly or in small
sprays. When young
they are long and
slender, and as their
30 or so petals expand
they create a fairly large
flower of classic Large-
flowered form. There
is a slight fragrance,
and the continuity of
bloom through summer
and autumn is good. In
warmer climates this
can be cultivated out-
of-doors. The plant
growth is tall and
upright, and it has
matt mid-green leaves.
ZONES 5–9.

HOY, USA, 1986

'SONIA' × 'CARESS'

## 'Lady Hillingdon'

(top)

OLD, TEA, YELLOW BLEND,
REPEAT-FLOWERING

Popular around the
world, this Tea Rose
offers a wide range
of colors during its
extended blooming
period. The long,
pointed buds open
to flat, deep apricot-
yellow blooms that
fade in the sun. The
large, thin petals are
semi-double and hang
down in a blowsy

'Climbing Lady Hillingdon'  (above)

fashion. There are
attractive stamens,
a few prickles and a
strong Tea fragrance.
Red-bronze when
young, the somewhat
sparse, attractive
foliage lines the thin
canes. It is one of the
healthiest of roses and
is a lovely cut flower.
**'Climbing Lady
Hillingdon'**, (Hicks,
USA, 1917) blooms
from late spring until
the approach of winter.
Although easy to train
on a structure, it takes
time to establish itself.
ZONES 5–10.

LOWE AND SHAWYER, UK, 1910

'PAPA GONTIER' × 'MME HOSTE'

### 'Lady Huntingfield'  *(right)*

MODERN, LARGE-FLOWERED/HYBRID TEA, MEDIUM YELLOW,
REPEAT-FLOWERING

The flowers of this rose are yellow with a touch
of golden apricot, paler on the reverse. They are
rounded in form and are well filled with spoon-
shaped, rather soft-textured petals that jostle for
space in the open blooms, creating a pleasingly
informal, muddled center. It has an appreciable
fragrance, and continuity of bloom is well maintained through summer and autumn. This variety
is currently offered only in Australia, where there
has been a revival of interest in the varieties raised
by Alister Clark. The warmer climate suits its
use for general garden purposes. The plant grows
vigorously with a bushy habit to average height
and has glossy olive green leaves. **ZONES 5–9.**

CLARK, AUSTRALIA, 1937

'BUSYBODY' × 'ASPIRANT MARCEL ROUYER'

### 'Lady Like'  TANekily

MODERN, LARGE-FLOWERED/HYBRID TEA, PINK BLEND,
REPEAT-FLOWERING

'Lady Like' has pointed buds that open into somewhat low-centered flowers that are made up of
over 30 petals. They are a rich shade of deep pink,
and have a touch of yellow at their base. The
petals open wide, which creates a colorful effect
on the free-flowering bushes during the main
season's flush, after which a satisfactory continuity of bloom is maintained through summer and
autumn. The flowers have a moderate fragrance
and are able to withstand bad weather well. 'Lady
Like' is a dependable rose to use in beds and
borders and it is good to cut, thanks to its long
flower stems. The plant has a bushy and fairly
even growth habit to about average height and
has a good covering of glossy deep green, leathery
leaves. **ZONES 4–9.**

TANTAU, GERMANY, 1989

PARENTAGE UNKNOWN

### 'Lady Mary Fitzwilliam'  *(bottom)*

MODERN, LARGE-FLOWERED/HYBRID TEA, LIGHT PINK,
REPEAT-FLOWERING

This is one of the best known names in the history
of the modern rose, but the impressions it made
at the time of its introduction were mixed. It
tends to put much strength into forming perfect
flowers at the expense of growth, and therefore
it delighted rose exhibitors. The Secretary of
Britain's National Rose Society gave his opinion
of its worth as a garden plant by saying that it
would be difficult to find a weaker and more un-
satisfactory grower than 'Lady Mary Fitzwilliam'.
Thus it is surprising first that it should have
become one of the most influential pollen parents
of the modern roses, and second that it could
survive for more than a century and still be found
in nursery lists, though it is hard to be certain if
the variety offered is the right one. It has pale flesh
pink blooms of regular form that are globular,
full, long lasting and scented. They are repeat-
flowering and are borne on short branches on a
plant of below average height that has matt green
foliage. **ZONES 5–9.**

BENNETT, UK, 1882

'DEVONIENSIS' × 'VICTOR VERDIER'

L

## 'Lady Meilland'

MEIalzonite *(above)*

MODERN, LARGE-FLOWERED/
HYBRID TEA, ORANGE-PINK,
REPEAT-FLOWERING

The flowers on this rose are a gentle shade of salmon with hints of vermilion-orange. The urn-shaped blooms are of medium size for a Large-flowered Rose and are well filled with large petals that open to show high centers and symmetrical form. They are borne on long stems and last well, so are excellent to cut, as well as being useful in the garden, where the vigor of the plant makes it good in borders and bedding schemes. The continuity of flowering is well maintained through summer and autumn, though the blooms can be spoilt in wet weather. This variety grows sturdily with a spreading, free-branching habit, usually to above average height, and has ample dark green shiny foliage that sometimes proves susceptible to rust. **ZONES 4–9.**

MEILLAND, FRANCE, 1986

PARENTAGE UNKNOWN

NEW ZEALAND GOLD MEDAL 1982

## 'Lady of the Dawn'

INTerlada *(above right)*

MODERN, CLUSTER-FLOWERED/
FLORIBUNDA, LIGHT PINK,
REPEAT-FLOWERING

This rose is variously described as a Cluster-flowered Rose and as a Modern Shrub. It produces long stiff shoots that become bowed under the weight of the blooms, which can easily number 20 or more in the cluster. The lightly scented flowers are creamy blush and rimmed pink around the petal edges. They are fairly large, semi-double and open like saucers to reveal red and gold stamens. Blooming continues through summer and autumn. This is very suitable for making a hedge, including in a border, or planting in a bed where a sizeable grower is required, for it is capable of growing to the dimensions of an average shrub rose. It grows vigorously with an upright, arching habit and has dark green leathery leaves. **ZONES 4–9.**

ILSINK, THE NETHERLANDS, 1984

INTERDRESS × 'STADT DEN HELDER'

## 'Lady Penzance'

OLD, SWEET BRIAR,
ORANGE-PINK

Looking quite elegant, 'Lady Penzance' is the best of the large crop of Sweet Briar hybrids created by Lord Penzance at the end of the nineteenth century. The cupped, single, salmon-pink blooms are flushed with a coppery pink and grow yellow towards the edges, and they are studded with yellow stamens. There is little evidence of the apple scent associated with these hybrids, except in the foliage. The 6 ft (1.8 m) shrub has an arching form with dark, dense foliage and bright red hips. It is subject to black spot during the summer flowering, but is nevertheless a vigorous bush that is ideal for a tall hedge or in a woodland garden. **ZONES 5–10.**

PENZANCE, UK, 1894

*ROSA EGLANTERIA* × *R. FOETIDA BICOLOR*

## 'Lady Roberts' *(right)*

OLD, TEA, APRICOT BLEND, REPEAT-FLOWERING

This rose loves a warm spot in the garden, and will repay any cultivation effort with abundant blooms from late spring until autumn. The long, pointed buds open to reveal rich, reddish apricot blooms with a coppery base. Sometimes the petals appear orange at the edge, the colors varying, depending on their placement in sun or shade. The big, blowsy blooms have a strong tea fragrance and nod on the bushy plant, the olive green leaves being an attractive background to them. Its usual size is 4 ft (1.2 m), but if left unpruned it can be trained as a small climber. It also does well as a container plant. This rose does not mind wet weather. **ZONES 5–10.**

CANT, UK, 1902

BUD SPORT OF 'ANNA OLIVIER'

## 'Lady Rose' KORlady *(right)*

MODERN, LARGE-FLOWERED/ HYBRID TEA, ORANGE-PINK, REPEAT-FLOWERING

This variety produces long pointed buds, borne singly or several together, that open into large high-centered blooms. They consist of over 30 petals, which reflex so that the flowers become cupped as they open out. They are salmon-red with an orange cast, a warm and bright color, appear with remarkable freedom through summer and autumn, and have a pleasant fragrance. They are also good to cut for floral arrangements. It is an excellent garden plant for hedges, beds and borders and is especially well suited to growing in standard form. It makes a vigorous plant with an upright habit, growing to above average height, and is well furnished with dark green, semi-glossy leaves. **ZONES 4–9.**

KORDES, GERMANY, 1979

SEEDLING × 'TRAUMEREI'

BELFAST GOLD MEDAL 1981

L

## 'Lady Sunblaze'

MEIllarco  *(right)*

syns 'Lady
Meillandina',
'Peace Meillandina',
'Peace Sunblaze'

MODERN, MINIATURE, LIGHT
PINK, REPEAT-FLOWERING

This rose, raised by
Marie-Louisette
Meilland, has pale
orient pink to light
coral pink, fully double
flowers with 40 petals
which have no
fragrance. The delicate
blooms are usually
borne on short stems
and the repeat cycle is
fast. The color is excel-
lent on first opening
but unfortunately fades
all too quickly. The
foliage is an attractive
glossy dark green on a
plant with a compact,
bushy, yet upright
growth habit. All in all,
'Lady Sunblaze' makes
a great garden display
because of its ability
to resist most rose
diseases, its quick
repeat cycle and the
fact that it is nearly
always in bloom. It is
an ideal choice for
growing in a container.
ZONES 5–11.

MEILLAND; FRANCE, 1985

('FASHION' × 'ZAMBRA') ×
'BELLE MEILLANDINA'

## 'Lady Sylvia'  *(right)*

MODERN, LARGE-FLOWERED/
HYBRID TEA, LIGHT PINK,
REPEAT-FLOWERING

The creamy rose pink
flowers of this sweet-
scented rose are among
the loveliest one could
wish to see. The young
petal tips part to reveal
deeper tints of pink
and a hint of gold at
the heart of the bloom
which, although it
opens rather fast,
maintains a pleasing
rounded outline until
the petals fall. This is
a rose much grown
formerly by florists,
and many brides have
carried it in their
bouquets. It is worth
its place in the border
as a historic rose and
is a great resource for
buttonholes and as
a cut flower. The
plant blooms through-
out summer and
autumn and grows
quite vigorously, with
a branching habit, to
average height or more.
'Lady Sylvia' is long
lived and sometimes
survives in old gardens
where other roses
have disappeared. The
foliage is dark green
and by modern stand-
ards rather sparse.
**'Climbing Lady Sylvia'**
(1933) is a marketable,
vigorous, low-growing
climbing sport with
pink-blended flowers.
ZONES 4–9.

STEVENS, UK, 1926

SPORT OF 'MME BUTTERFLY'

## 'Lady Waterlow' *(right)*
MODERN, LARGE-FLOWERED CLIMBER, PINK BLEND

This old climber bears pleasantly scented, light salmon-pink blooms, singly or in small clusters, that open loosely cupped. They are semi-double with petals of a rather silky texture, and are quite large when fully open. They appear freely in summer, with sometimes a few blooms later in the year. This variety is useful for most purposes appropriate to a climber, such as on walls, fences, arches, pillars and pergolas. The growth habit is stiff and branching and, although it is not a rapid grower, the plant is capable of extending slightly farther than the average climbing rose. It is reasonably well furnished with large, pointed, mid-green leaves. **ZONES 4–9.**

NABONNAND, FRANCE, 1903

'LA FRANCE DE '89' × 'MME MARIE LAVALLEY'

## 'Lady X'   MEIfigu
*(right)*
MODERN, LARGE-FLOWERED/
HYBRID TEA, MAUVE,
REPEAT-FLOWERING

The mauve coloring on the flowers of this variety is not very pronounced, for this is on the pink side of it, a light and even shade that looks attractive early in the life of the flower but becomes rather pallid by the time the petals fall. The blooms are fairly large, full petalled and prettily formed with high centers. Most of them are produced one to a stem, they have a light sweet scent, and there is a good succession of flowers through summer and autumn. This rose is suitable for the middle or back of a border since it is a taller than average grower. It has an upright, free-branching habit and vigorous growth, and its prickly stems carry rather sparse, leathery, semi-glossy leaves. **ZONES 4–9.**

MEILLAND, FRANCE, 1965

SEEDLING × 'SIMONE'

PORTLAND GOLD MEDAL 1968

### 'Lafayette'
**syns 'August Kordes',
'Joseph Guy'**

MODERN, CLUSTER-FLOWERED/
FLORIBUNDA, DEEP PINK,
REPEAT-FLOWERING

Currently this rose
appears to be listed by
only one nursery, in
California; it had a role
as a parent of some
early Cluster-flowered
sports when that class
of rose was in its
infancy. The large
semi-double blooms
in a rich deep shade of
cherry red are carried
in immense clusters of
up to 40 blooms and
open like saucers,
displaying the bold
color well. They have
a light scent and main-
tain a good succession
of bloom through
summer and autumn.
For a historic collection,
this is an interesting
rose to have, deserving
a place near the front
of a border where its
colorful sprays can be
enjoyed. The plant
grows vigorously with
a bushy, compact habit
to less than average
height and is supplied
with glossy rich green
leaves. The Marquis
de Lafayette played a
role in French politics
and the American War
of Independence.
**ZONES 4–9.**
NONIN, FRANCE, 1924

'RÖDHÄTTE' × 'RICHMOND'

### 'Lagerfeld'  AROlaqueli  *(above)*
**syn. 'Starlight'**

MODERN, LARGE-FLOWERED/HYBRID TEA, MAUVE, REPEAT-FLOWERING

'Lagerfeld' has flowers that are a strange shade of
grayish lavender, are made up of some 30 petals
and open with high centers, becoming rounded in
outline as they develop, and maintaining good
symmetry of form. Because they are fairly large
and are carried in candelabra-style sprays of
5–15 blooms, they tend to nod on the flower
stems under their own weight, creating an untidy
effect. There is good fragrance, especially on
warm days, and blooming continues through
summer and autumn. This rose, called a
Grandiflora in the USA, is an interesting subject
to include in a mixed border or bed but is best
grown in a cutting garden where the growth
defects will matter less and the blooms can be
taken for arrangements, a purpose for which they
are very well suited. The plant grows vigorously
with a bushy, uneven habit to average height and
has large, mid-green leaves. It was named for a
Parisian couturier. **ZONES 4–9.**
CHRISTENSEN, USA, 1986

'BLUE NILE' × ('IVORY TOWER' × 'ANGEL FACE')

## 'L'Aimant' HARzola
*(below)*
**syn. 'Doux Parfum'**
MODERN, CLUSTER-FLOWERED/
FLORIBUNDA, MEDIUM PINK,
REPEAT-FLOWERING

The flowers of 'L'Aimant' are a warm shade of salmon-pink, fading to rose pink, and are carried sometimes singly but usually in clusters of several blooms, which open like small-scale Large-flowered Roses, with 30 or so petals forming neat centers. The blooms become cupped as the petals reflex, yielding an excellent fragrance; in warmer countries the quality of bloom and fragrance is considerably enhanced. It flowers with good continuity through summer and autumn, standing bad weather well, is splendid for cutting and is a useful garden plant in beds and borders. The growth is vigorous, though somewhat uneven and with many branching shoots, to average height or more, while the leaves are leathery, olive green and shiny. The variety is named after the Coty perfume. ZONES 4–9.

HARKNESS, UK, 1994

'SOUTHAMPTON' × ('RADOX
BOUQUET' × 'MARGARET
MERRIL')

BAGATELLE FRAGRANCE PRIZE
1991, ROYAL NATIONAL ROSE
SOCIETY EDLAND MEDAI FOR
FRAGRANCE 1992, ROYAL
NATIONAL ROSE SOCIETY BRITISH
ROSE FRAGRANCE AWARD 1998

## 'Lamarque'
*(bottom)*
**syns 'General Lamarque', 'The Marshal'**
OLD, NOISETTE, WHITE,
REPEAT-FLOWERING

An amateur hybridizer raised this valuable Noisette in a window box in Angers, France, little knowing that it would become one of the most popular ramblers in rose history. The high-centered buds are followed by pure white, double blooms with a lemon-yellow center. The large, full, loose flowers have muddled centers and are pendulous. The violet fragrance is very strong, especially in the sun. Once established, this hardy climber will grow 20 ft (6 m) in a single season. The long, trailing canes are covered with smooth, gray-green foliage and there are small, hooked, red prickles. It is quite lovely on a trellis or large arch and was named in honor of a French general. ZONES 4–10.

MARÉCHAL, FRANCE, 1830

'BLUSH NOISETTE' × 'PARKS'
YELLOW TEA-SCENTED CHINA'

L

### 'Lancôme' DELboip
*(bottom)*

MODERN, LARGE-FLOWERED/
HYBRID TEA, DEEP PINK,
REPEAT-FLOWERING

This is primarily a greenhouse rose grown for the cut-flower trade, but in warmer climates it can give good results in the garden. The buds are long and elegant and open into large, full-petalled blooms of a rich and clear deep pink, which even in hot sunshine maintain their depth of color with little sign of fading. The hard petal texture, which makes the flowers marketable to florists, unfortunately prevents the scent glands from operating, which is especially disappointing in a rose of this color. Flower arrangers will none-theless accept it for the value it gives them in beauty of form, long-lasting quality and length of stem. It flowers freely through summer and autumn, grows sturdily to above average height, and has glossy deep green leaves. It was named for a leading French cosmetic company.
**ZONES 4–9.**

DELBARD-CHABERT, FRANCE, 1973

('DR ALBERT SCHWEITZER' ×
['MICHÈLE MEILLAND' ×
'BAYADÈRE']) × (MEIMET ×
'PRÉSENT FILIAL)

### 'Las Vegas' KORgane
*(top)*

MODERN, LARGE-FLOWERED/
HYBRID TEA, ORANGE BLEND,
REPEAT-FLOWERING

This rose is an attrac-tive confection of orange and yellow, the inside of the petals being orange-vermilion and the reverse chrome yellow with red vein-ing, so both colors are seen together as the flowers unfold. The effect is gaudy but fortunately more re-strained than the lights of the city whose name it bears. The blooms are of medium to large size and fairly full with about 24 broad petals. They open loosely with low centers, the rows of petals overlapping one another and maintain-ing a neat attractive form throughout the life of the flower, although the weight of the blooms sometimes causes them to nod. There is a light fragrance, good continuity of bloom is maintained through summer and autumn and they are suitable for cutting. This is a rewarding performer in beds and borders and as a hedge, for the growth is vigorous and upright, with plenty of basal growth to produce a well-filled, rounded plant. It grows to average height or a little more and has ample provision of dark green, semi-glossy foliage. **ZONES 4–9.**

KORDES, GERMANY, 1981

'LUDWIGSHAFEN AM RHEIN' ×
'FEUERZAUBER'

GENEVA GOLD MEDAL 1985,
PORTLAND GOLD MEDAL 1988

## 'Laughter Lines'

DICkerry *(right)*

MODERN, CLUSTER-FLOWERED/
FLORIBUNDA, PINK BLEND,
REPEAT-FLOWERING

There are many colors in the medium to large-sized flowers on this variety, which open from clusters of pointed buds into semi-double cupped blooms of red, gold and white on a rosy pink background, the golden stamens showing up noticeably in the center. The lightly scented blooms continue through summer and autumn. 'Laughter Lines' gives a colorful garden display as a bedding, border or hedge rose and is delightful to cut for inclusion in small arrangements. It grows vigorously with a bushy, leafy habit to average height or less and has attractive dark green, shiny foliage. ZONES 4–9.

DICKSON, UK, 1987

('PYE COLOUR' × 'SUNDAY TIMES') × 'EYEPAINT'

ROYAL NATIONAL ROSE SOCIETY GOLD MEDAL 1984, BELFAST CERTIFICATE OF MERIT 1989

## 'Laura'   MEIdragelac

*(right)*

syns 'Laura 81', 'Natilda'

MODERN, LARGE-FLOWERED/
HYBRID TEA, ORANGE BLEND,
REPEAT-FLOWERING

The flowers on this variety are a pastel shade of salmon pink with an orange tinge, paler on the petal reverse. The blooms are double with about 30 petals and are carried on firm stems, often several together in open sprays. They open with high centers before becoming loosely cupped as the petals reflex. There is a light fragrance and, after the initial generous flush, flowers continue through summer and autumn. This rose is useful for cutting and for use in beds and borders and to form a hedge. It grows vigorously with an upright habit to average height and has fresh green semi-glossy leaves. ZONES 4–9.

MEILLAND, FRANCE, 1981

('PHARAOH' × 'COLOR WONDER') . × (['SUSPENSE' × 'SUSPENSE'] × 'KING'S RANSOM')

JAPAN GOLD MEDAL 1981

### 'Laura Ashley'

CHEWharla *(bottom)*

MODERN, MODERN SHRUB, MAUVE, REPEAT-FLOWERING

When the pointed buds of this rose open, lilac-mauve to pink flowers with a pink reverse and lots of golden yellow stamens are revealed. The flowers, mostly 5-petalled, occur as massive sprays of 10–30 blooms. They have a fruity fragrance. The foliage is semi-glossy and mid-green, with hooked prickles on a plant with a spreading, low growth habit. What is wonderful about this rose is that the large trusses, when in peak bloom, literally cover the plant from head to toe! In some cooler climates the blooms are more of a rosy violet color with a white base to each petal. Although sometimes mistakenly classified as a Climbing Miniature, 'Laura Ashley' makes an ideal ground cover and is better there than against a trellis. It was named in memory of the celebrated clothes and fabric designer. ZONES 5–11.

WARNER, UK, 1989

'MARJORIE FAIR' × 'NOZOMI'

### 'Laura Ford'

CHEWarvel *(top)*

syn. 'Normandie'

MODERN, CLIMBING MINIATURE, MEDIUM YELLOW, REPEAT-FLOWERING

On this variety, pointed buds open up to medium yellow flowers with a lighter yellow reverse, with ageing bringing on a pink flush to the petals. The florets are double with 22 petals, have good Large-flowered form and are normally borne in small, neatly formed clusters of 5–10 florets with a definite fruity scent. The foliage is light green. This plant is a vigorous, upright, tall bush and a great choice as a climber against a wall, fence or trellis where it will provide an eye-catching display all year round. 'Laura Ford' is weatherproof, providing an abundance of blooms throughout the year on an easy to maintain and disease-resistant plant. ZONES 5–11.

WARNER, UK, 1989

('ANNA FORD' × ('ELIZABETH OF GLAMIS' × ['GALWAY BAY' × 'SUTTER'S GOLD']))

ROYAL NATIONAL ROSE SOCIETY CERTIFICATE OF MERIT 1988, ROYAL HORTICULTURAL SOCIETY AWARD OF GARDEN MERIT 1993

## 'Lauré Davoust'
*(right)*
syns 'Abondonnata',
'Marjorie W. Lester'
MODERN, MISCELLANEOUS,
LIGHT PINK

Spectacular as a weeping standard or as a tree climber, 'Lauré Davoust' has frequently been given other names. The well-formed, double, pink blooms have a flesh tint. The pompon flowers turn lavender with age and appear in clusters on the thin canes. This variety is quite floriferous during its summer bloom. The 15 ft (4.5 m) stalks can easily be trained and have very few prickles. **ZONES 4–10.**

LAFFAY, FRANCE, 1834

PARENTAGE UNKNOWN

## 'Lavaglut' KORlech
*(right)*
syns 'Intrigue',
'Lavaglow'
MODERN, CLUSTER-FLOWERED/
FLORIBUNDA, DARK RED,
REPEAT-FLOWERING

The velvety textured petals of this deep red Cluster-flowered Rose are a beautiful sight when lit up by the sun. There are about 24 of them to each medium-sized flower, and many flowers make up the freely produced, evenly spaced clusters. The overall color impact is therefore considerable. The blooms are shaped like camellias and hold this form to a late stage. They have little scent. Flowering is well maintained through summer and autumn, the blooms withstanding the effects of hot sun and rain much better than other dark reds. As a rose for bedding it is outstanding, thanks to its even growth habit, and it is also excellent in a border and as a hedge. It has, however, proved to be vulnerable to black spot in some areas. The plant grows strongly with a bushy, spreading habit to a little below average height and has ample glossy purplish green glossy foliage. This variety, widely planted under its English name, should not be confused with the reddish purple 'Intrigue' raised by Warriner of the USA in 1984. **ZONES 4–9.**

KORDES, GERMANY, 1978

'GRUSS AN BAYERN' × SEEDLING

ROYAL NATIONAL ROSE SOCIETY
TRIAL GROUND CERTIFICATE 1980

L

### 'Lavender Dream'
INTerlav *(right)*
MODERN, MODERN SHRUB,
MAUVE, REPEAT-FLOWERING

This is a beautiful shrub rose that covers itself in big close clusters of small, deep lilac-pink blooms, showing golden stamens. They are semi-double with about 16 petals, and after a very free initial blooming they continue to produce flowering shoots through the rest of summer and autumn. There is little fragrance. This is a fine variety for a specimen plant, to mix with others in a border, or to use for a bed of one variety. The plant grows vigorously making many shoots, spreading out wide and building up to the shape of a low mound. In height it grows to about half the average height for a shrub rose. The foliage, which is matt and light green, is sometimes touched by seasonal mildew. **ZONES 4–9.**

ILSINK, THE NETHERLANDS, 1984
'YESTERDAY' × 'NASTARANA'
ANERKANNTE DEUTSCHE ROSE 1987

### 'Lavender Jewel'
*(below left)*
MODERN, MINIATURE, MAUVE, REPEAT-FLOWERING

As the name suggests, the flowers of this variety are a wonderful clear lavender-mauve. They are double with 38 petals and can have Large-flowered form in certain warm climates. When the soft lavender buds open they usually have an attractive magenta marking on the edge of the petals. The dark green foliage is disease free. This plant has a low, compact, bushy growth habit that may tend to sprawl but it responds well to discipline, continuing to be vigorous. It loves climates with high humidity where the vigor is more marked than usual. **ZONES 5–11.**

MOORE, USA, 1978
'LITTLE CHIEF' × 'ANGEL FACE'

### 'Lavender Lace'
*(right)*
MODERN, MINIATURE, MAUVE, REPEAT-FLOWERING

The clear lavender flowers tend to open too fast on this plant and so lose form and substance. However, the color can be improved by growing in partial shade. The flowers are double, have Large-flowered form and are fragrant. The foliage is small and glossy dark green. Borne in trusses with high centers at first, the blooms quickly open to flat, fully open florets with yellow stamens. While the blooms are attractive, the quality is unpredictable. It has a dwarf, vigorous growth habit and tends to sulk in cold climates. Winter protection is required if the plant is to survive frost or snow. **ZONES 5–11.**

MOORE, USA, 1968

'ELLEN POULSEN' × 'DEBBIE'

### 'Lavender Lassie'
*(below)*
MODERN, MODERN SHRUB, MAUVE, REPEAT-FLOWERING

'Lavender Lassie' produces long stems that arch under the weight of big clusters of 60-petalled blooms. They are of medium size, open cupped and become flat with muddled centers as the petals reflex, finally resembling oversized rosettes. The color is a pleasing shade of pink with a hint of lavender, though in some seasons it loses much of the lavender tone and appears to be rose pink. It has good fragrance, and it blooms through summer and autumn. This variety is ideal in a shrub border. The plant is strong, freely branching and rather open in habit, giving the effect of an overgrown Cluster-flowered Rose and achieving the average height of a shrub rose. In warm climates the long canes can be trained on a pillar, fence or wall, thus converting it into a climber. The foliage is rather sparse, semi-glossy and mid-green. **ZONES 4–9.**

KORDES, GERMANY, 1960

'HAMBURG' × 'MME NORBERT LEVAVASSEUR'

ROYAL HURTICULTURAL SOCIETY AWARD OF GARDEN MERIT 1993

**L**

**L**

### 'Lavender Pinocchio' *(above)*

MODERN, CLUSTER-FLOWERED/
FLORIBUNDA, MAUVE,
REPEAT-FLOWERING

The raiser's use of unusually colored parents for this rose was rewarded, for it has buds of light chocolate brown that open in a shade of deep lavender with brownish centers, tinged with yellow at the base. As the flowers mature they take on mauve tints, finally fading to grayish pink before the ruffled petals fall. They are full-petalled, fairly large, loosely formed and change from cupped to almost flat form as they age. There is a pleasing fragrance, and flowers continue to appear through summer and autumn. This variety remains widely available after 50 years in commerce, which speaks as well of its plant qualities as of its endearing character. The plant is compact, growing below average height, and has leathery mid-green leaves. **ZONES 4–9.**

BOERNER, USA, 1948

'PINOCCHIO' × 'GREY PEARL'

### 'Lawinia'  TANklawi, TANklevi, TANklewi *(below)*
syn. 'Lavinia'

MODERN, LARGE-FLOWERED CLIMBER, MEDIUM PINK,
REPEAT-FLOWERING

This is an attractive climber, bearing 20-petalled blooms of loosely cupped, rounded form. They are fairly large, an even shade of pink, and appear singly or sometimes in clusters of a few or many flowers. There is a pleasant fragrance, and blooming continues through summer and autumn. This is an all-purpose variety for walls, fences, arches, pergolas and especially pillars, and it can be expected to grow to the average extent of a climbing rose. The plant is vigorous with stiff, upright, branching stems that are well furnished with mid-green leaves. **ZONES 4–9.**

TANTAU, GERMANY, 1980

PARENTAGE UNKNOWN

ROYAL HORTICULTURAL SOCIETY AWARD OF GARDEN MERIT 1995

L

### 'Le Havre' (above)
OLD, HYBRID PERPETUAL,
MEDIUM RED,
REPEAT-FLOWERING

This variety, which was named for a seaport in northern France, has large, overlapping vermilion, double blooms paling to purplish. It is quite floriferous during a long flowering period and displays attractive, leathery foliage and only a few prickles. Its bushy 6 ft (1.8 m) form makes it a good candidate for the back of the border.
**ZONES 5–10.**

EUDES, FRANCE, 1870

PARENTAGE UNKNOWN

### 'Lawrence Johnston' (right)
syn. 'Hidcote Yellow'
MODERN, LARGE-FLOWERED
CLIMBER, MEDIUM YELLOW

This climber bears a lavish crop of strongly scented flowers in an eye-catching bright clear yellow, that open loosely cupped. They are semi-double with about 15 petals, quite large and are borne in clusters. Usually the flowering is restricted to summertime, but occasionally a few later blooms appear. As the plant is very vigorous it requires plenty of space, where the long arching stems can spread over a roof, or a very high wall. It is likely to extend 2 or 3 times as much as an average climber. The leaves are light green and glossy and are subject to black spot, due doubtless to *Rosa foetida* genes in the pollen parent.
**ZONES 4–9.**

PERNET-DUCHER, FRANCE, 1923

'MME EUGÈNE VERDIER' ×
'PERSIAN YELLOW'

## 'Le Rêve'

MODERN, LARGE-FLOWERED CLIMBER, LIGHT YELLOW

Clusters of pointed yellow buds on this variety open into light canary yellow, loosely formed, single or semi-double blooms of medium to large size. They open wide like saucers, and the petals pale to primrose yellow before they fall. The blooms are pleasantly scented and are usually borne rather early in summertime, giving a prolific display but not repeating their bloom. The plant is strong stemmed and vigorous, and suitable for pergolas, fences and arches; it can extend twice as far as the average climber. It is well furnished with rich green glossy foliage. Pernet-Ducher introduced this, his 'dream' rose, in preference to 'Lawrence Johnston', which he derived from the same parents, and it does have an altogether better health record. **ZONES 4–9.**

PERNET-DUCHER, FRANCE, 1923

'MME EUGÈNE VERDIER' × 'PERSIAN YELLOW'

## 'Le Rouge et Le Noir' DELcart *(below)*

MODERN, LARGE-FLOWERED/HYBRID TEA, DARK RED,
REPEAT-FLOWERING

Clearly the petals of this variety are not actually black, but when the sun strikes their surface when the flowers are young they reflect what to the eye appears as a blackish sheen. The blooms are rich deep red and are made up of numerous rather short petals, which reflex so that each ring overlays the one below, giving the effect of an outsize glowing red rosette, relieved by a glimpse of yellow stamens in the center. They have a light scent. This rose is suitable for beds and borders, though its distribution appears to be limited to France. It grows strongly with an upright habit to average height and has dark green leaves that are reddish when young. **ZONES 4–9.**

DELBARD, FRANCE, 1973

PARENTAGE UNKNOWN

L

## 'Le Vésuve' *(right)*
### syn. 'Lemesle'
OLD, CHINA, PINK BLEND,
REPEAT-FLOWERING

'La Vésuve' has shapely, pointed buds that open to loose blooms of carmine to pink and sometimes to fiery red. They are very large, full flowers and are delicately veined. The blowsy flowers, with a wide center, will change color depending on whether it is planted in the sun or shade. Thriving best in a warm position, 'Le Vésuve' is a vigorous, small shrub of 4–5 ft (1.2–1.5 m) with an angular growth pattern. The foliage changes from coppery to shiny green as it ages. The mounded shape makes it an ideal bedding plant, and it is also good as a container plant. Large red prickles and a delicate Tea scent add to its charm. **ZONES 6–10.**

LAFFAY, FRANCE, 1825

PARENTAGE UNKNOWN

## 'Leander' AUSlea
*(right)*
MODERN, MODERN SHRUB,
APRICOT BLEND

Also classified as an English Rose, 'Leander' has pink to apricot flowers, more intense in the center depths. They are darker in bud. The blooms open flat and are closely packed with petals all enfolded together as they seek to expand into the space available, for this is a plant with rather small flowers. In terms of growth it is very large, especially in warm climates, where it can reach half as tall again as an average shrub rose or be supported and grown as a sizeable climber on a wall, fence or pillar. It therefore needs careful placement so that it has enough room. The blooms are scented, borne in wide sprays on slim stems and give of their best in summer, for the production of later flowers is limited. It has a somewhat open growth habit and smooth, mid-green foliage. **ZONES 4–9.**

AUSTIN, UK, 1982

'CHARLES AUSTIN' × SEEDLING

L

## 'Leaping Salmon' PEAmight
### syn. 'Emmanuelle'

MODERN, LARGE-FLOWERED CLIMBER, ORANGE-PINK, REPEAT-FLOWERING

This variety bears large double salmon-pink flowers of classic Large-flowered quality, having high centers, opening with graceful symmetry and lasting well either on the plant or when cut for floral arrangement. There is a pleasing fragrance, and following the main flush there is a steady succession of later blooms through summer and autumn, sometimes borne singly, sometimes in clusters. This rose is suitable for most purposes appropriate to a climber of average extent, especially on walls and fences, where its stiff branches can be spread out and given firm support, and on a pillar. It is well furnished with large, semi-glossy leaves. ZONES 4–9.

PEARCE, UK, 1983

(['VESPER' × 'ALOHA'] × ['PADDY MCGREDY' × 'MAIGOLD']) × 'PRIMA BALLERINA'

## 'Léda' *(below left)*
### syn. 'Painted Damask'

OLD, DAMASK, WHITE BLEND

Still a popular rose after 170 years, 'Léda' has red-brown buds that open to reveal a button eye, with the inner petals reflexing into a ball. The milky white petals finish with a crimson edge. Although it sprawls, it can be kept as a compact plant. The foliage is dark green, downy and semi-glossy on a shrub of about 3 ft (1 m) in height. If pruned of old wood after flowering, this hardy, disease-resistant rose will produce highly fragrant flowers during late spring with some repeat-flowering in autumn. Some say it is not a Damask but should rather be in the Portland class. It was named for the mythological queen who was seduced by Zeus when he appeared in the form of a swan. There is also a pink form known as 'Pink Léda'. ZONES 4–10.

PRE-1827

PARENTAGE UNKNOWN

## 'Legend' JACtop *(below right)*
### syn. 'Top Star'

MODERN, LARGE-FLOWERED/HYBRID TEA, MEDIUM RED, REPEAT-FLOWERING

'Legend' has pointed, plump buds that open to reveal large flowers composed of about 30 broad petals. The young blooms are high centered but become rounded in outline as they mature, with the petals symmetrically arranged. The flowers are bright red and are usually borne singly. Their lasting quality and long stems make them good for cutting, as well as serving the usual garden purposes in beds, borders and as hedges. There is some scent, and blooms continue to appear through summer and autumn. The plant grows vigorously with a stately, upright, bushy habit to above average height and has matt dark green leaves. ZONES 4–9.

WARRINER, USA, 1992

'GRAND MASTERPIECE' × SEEDLING

### 'Lemon Blush'

SIElemon *(above)*

MODERN, MODERN SHRUB,
LIGHT YELLOW

This variety was raised in northern Germany as one of a series of hardy roses, the stated breeding line including Albas and roses developed from *Rosa kordesii*. The blooms are pale yellow, shading to cream and open rather flat, with dozens of small petals enfolded together. The petals are soft textured and fragrant, and there is a prolific summer blooming but no repeat bloom later in the year. The plant grows with a strong shrubby habit, producing vigorous upright shoots that then begin to arch over under the weight of the stems and the leaves. It does well in a border among substantial plants, for the growth is appreciably larger and wider than that of an average shrub rose, and it has robust mid-green foliage. ZONES 4–9.

SIEVERS, GERMANY, 1988
PARENTAGE UNKNOWN

### 'Lemon Delight'

*(above right)*

MODERN, MINIATURE, MEDIUM
YELLOW, REPEAT-FLOWERING

Long, pointed, mossy buds on this rose open to reveal 10-petalled small blooms that are a bright butter yellow. The lovely florets have a strong lemon scent. This hardy plant is free blooming, vigorous, bushy and upright. The color is generally fast in most climates and the mossing adds extra charm. 'Lemon Delight' is another outstanding achievement by Moore—the successful introduction of mossing into Miniature Roses with retention of the repeat-blooming characteristics. ZONES 5–11.

MOORE, USA, 1978
'FAIRY MOSS' × 'GOLDMOSS'

### 'Lemon Sherbet'

*(above)*

MODERN, LARGE-FLOWERED/
HYBRID TEA, LIGHT YELLOW,
REPEAT-FLOWERING

This variety sported from a white rose and it has a lot of white in it, the yellow coloring being confined to the center of the bloom. The flowers open from plump buds and are large with about 36 petals. They are high centered and are borne on upright stems of cuttable length. Since the flowers last well, they are suitable for floral arrangement and also for showing. They can give satisfactory value in the garden, for blooms appear with good continuity through summer and autumn. There is a light fragrance. The plant grows vigorously with an upright habit to average height and has large leathery leaves. ZONES 4–9.

KERN, USA, 1973
SPORT OF 'FLORENCE'

L

## 'Lemon Spice'  *(above)*

MODERN, LARGE-FLOWERED/HYBRID TEA, LIGHT YELLOW,
REPEAT-FLOWERING

The name of this rose has reference to the fruity, spicy scent, described as 'heavy, unusual but likeable', which seems to be the chief reason for growing it. The elegant pointed buds develop into large full-petalled blooms with high centers, which become rounded as the petals expand. A pale yellow color, the flowers are attractively formed but often prove too heavy for the slim stems and bow down, which detracts from its value as a garden plant and for use for cutting. The initial flowering is prolific, and more blooms are produced intermittently through summer and autumn. The plant grows with a spreading habit to average height and has dark, leathery textured leaves. **ZONES 4–9.**

ARMSTRONG & SWIM, USA, 1966

'HELEN TRAUBEL' × SEEDLING

## 'Léonardo de Vinci'  MEIdeauri

syns 'Léonard de Vinci', 'Leonardo da Vinci'

MODERN, CLUSTER-FLOWERED/FLORIBUNDA, LIGHT PINK,
REPEAT-FLOWERING

This variety is one of a group of roses marketed by Meilland and named after artists and poets to meet a perceived need for roses 'that are characteristically old fashioned in style while imbued with modern day qualities of disease resistance and repeat flowering'. The lightly scented blooms of 'Léonardo de Vinci' are large and well filled and have over 40 petals, those in the center enfolded against one another as the flowers open. They are borne in clusters on firm stems and continue to flower through summer and autumn. This rose, which is useful for borders as well as for hedges and beds, grows vigorously with a bushy habit to average height or more and is furnished with dark green glossy leaves. **ZONES 4–9.**

MEILLAND, FRANCE, 1994

'SOMMERWIND' × (MEIROSE × 'ROSAMUNDE')

MONZA GOLD MEDAL 1993

### 'Léonie Lamesch'
(*right*)

MODERN, POLYANTHA, ORANGE
BLEND, REPEAT-FLOWERING

'Léonie Lamesch' seems surprisingly flamboyant for a nineteenth-century rose. The American introducers informed their customers that 'ten distinctly colored flowers are frequently shown on the bush at one time, varying from cochineal red in the bud to glowing coppery red tinged with orange when the flower opens'. The spicy scented blooms are loosely double, are carried on long springy stems either singly or in clusters of up to 24 and open wide to display their brilliance. They continue flowering through summer and autumn. This rose is worth growing for its beauty and history in any small space where a somewhat stalky habit is acceptable. The bush is vigorous and grows upright to above average height for a Polyantha; it has rich green foliage that is reddish when young. It is long lived, which is why this old variety has endured. ZONES 5–9.

LAMBERT, GERMANY, 1899

'AGLAIA' × 'KLEINER ALFRED'

### 'Léontine Gervais'
(*right*)

MODERN, LARGE-FLOWERED
CLIMBER, APRICOT BLEND

The coppery red buds of this rose open to cupped blooms that develop into semi-double flowers of salmon and yellow that fade with age. The dramatic trusses gather in clusters of 3–10, and the mixture of colors in the large, fragrant blooms is most attractive. The young growth is bronzy, maturing to dark glossy foliage. Easily reaching 20 ft (6 m) in 3 or 4 years, it is ideal for pergolas, walls and trees and will tolerate some shade. In warm areas it will rebloom. This rose was one of 30 varieties created by Barbier and Compaigne of Orléans, France, during the first quarter of the twentieth century. ZONES 4–10.

BARBIER, FRANCE, 1903

*ROSA WICHURANA* × 'SOUVENIR
DE CATHERINE GUILLOT'

## 'Les Amoureux de Peynet' MEItobla (right)

syns 'Efekto 21',
'Simply Magic'

MODERN, CLUSTER-FLOWERED/
FLORIBUNDA, DEEP PINK,
REPEAT-FLOWERING

This variety has a low
and spreading habit,
and could almost be
described as a scaled-
down Ground Cover
Rose. It is very suitable
for small gardens and
patio areas, where the
maximum of color is
required and space
is limited, and can also
be used to advantage
in more extensive
plantings. The semi-
double flowers are a
warm shade of pinky
red, which is deeper on
the undersides of the
petals, so as the blooms
expand there is an
overall bicolor effect.
They are cupped with
slightly ruffled petal tips,
of small to medium
size with a pleasant
light scent, and are
produced in large
clusters through sum-
mer and autumn. The
plant grows vigorously
to below average height
and is covered with
glossy bright green
leaves. ZONES 5–9.

MEILLAND, FRANCE, 1992

PARENTAGE UNKNOWN

BAGATELLE GOLD MEDAL 1991,
LYON ROSE OF THE CENTURY
1992

## 'Leverkusen' (right)

MODERN, CLUSTER-FLOWERED
CLIMBER, LIGHT YELLOW,
REPEAT-FLOWERING

The medium-sized
flowers of this variety
are semi-double and
appear in well-filled
clusters, opening out
into rosettes of light
yellow. The main sum-
mer flush on a well-
grown 'Leverkusen' is
one of summer's treats,
for the gentle pale color
of the flowers contrasts
beautifully with the
bright, shiny, light
green foliage. There is
a pleasant light scent,
and a few sporadic
blooms are likely to
appear in late summer
and autumn. This
climber lends itself
to being trained on
arches, pillars, fences
and walls, producing
many slender arching
stems that can readily
be tied in place. It
extends to the average
dimensions expected of
a climber, around 8 ft
(2.4 m), and can also be
grown without support
and allowed to make
a sprawling, tangled
shrub of greater width
than height. It is one
of several of Kordes'
roses named for a
German town.
ZONES 4–9.

KORDES, GERMANY, 1954

ROSA KORDESII × 'GOLDEN
GLOW'

L

## 'Leveson Gower'
*(right)*
syns 'Leverson Gower',
'Leweson Gower',
'Souvenir de la
Malmaison Rose'

OLD, BOURBON, ORANGE-PINK,
REPEAT-FLOWERING

This rose from Lyon,
France, is often con-
fused with the red form
of 'Souvenir de la
Malmaison', which
might explain why it is
sometimes seen under
that name. It looks a
lot like a Modern
Large-flowered Rose,
with pointed buds that
open to full, cupped,
very large blooms with
red shaded salmon
petals. The fragrant
flowers are held above
smooth, light green
foliage. It is a robust
bush, growing to 6 ft
(1.8 m), and although
it has a tendency to
mildew in wet weather,
it has few prickles;
a large crop of hips
appears in autumn.
G. G. Leveson-Gower
(1773–1846), first Earl
Granville, was the
English ambassador to
France. ZONES 5–10.

BÉLUZE, FRANCE, 1845

PARENTAGE UNKNOWN

## 'Lichtkönigin
Lucia' KORlilub
syns 'Lucia', 'Reine
Lucia'

MODERN, MODERN SHRUB,
MEDIUM YELLOW,
REPEAT-FLOWERING

'Probably the most
underrated yellow
shrub that has ever been
raised' is the verdict of
one authority about
this rose. The blooms,
borne in clusters of
several together on
strong stems, are an
intense shade of lemon
yellow. They are of
medium to large size
with about 18 petals
and open like shallow
saucers, with pretty red
stamens half-hidden
in the centers. There is
a pleasing fragrance
and, after a prolific
first flush, continuity
of flowering is well
maintained through
summer and autumn.
This is an excellent
subject for a mixed
border, and in milder
climates it can be
grown on a pillar or as
a short climbing rose.
The plant grows tall
with an upright, free-
branching habit to
the average height
expected of a shrub
rose. The stems are
prickly and the leaves
large, wrinkled and
rather glossy. The
name means 'Lucia,
Queen of Light'.
ZONES 4–9.

KORDES, GERMANY, 1966

'ZITRONENFALTER' × 'CLÄRE
GRAMMERSTORF'

ANERKANNTE DEUTSCHE ROSE
1968

L

## 'Liebeszauber' KORmiach *(above)*
### syn. 'Crimson Spire'

**MODERN, LARGE-FLOWERED/HYBRID TEA, MEDIUM RED, REPEAT-FLOWERING**

On this variety the flowers are fairly large and a rich blood red, and they are freely produced and normally carried one to a stem. After opening with high centers, they become loosely cupped with wavy, infolded petals in the middle of the bloom, looking attractive at each stage. The petals fall cleanly when they are spent. There is a noticeable fragrance, and after the first flowering is finished the succession of bloom through summer and autumn is well maintained. The plant grows very vigorously, making many shoots, with a stiff, upright habit to taller than average height. In South Africa the variety is termed a 'Spire' rose, one of several roses recommended on account of their vigor and flower freedom for growing on as extra tall bushes. The leaves, reddish when young, become dark green as they mature. The name means 'love's magic', for which of course a red rose has to be first choice. **ZONES 4–9.**

KORDES, GERMANY, 1990

SEEDLING × 'PINK PANTHER'

## 'Lilac Charm'

**MODERN, CLUSTER-FLOWERED/FLORIBUNDA, MAUVE, REPEAT-FLOWERING**

The flowers of 'Lilac Charm' are a pretty shade of pale lilac-mauve, showing prominent red stamens. Composed of 5–7 large petals, they are saucer-shaped open blooms that appear big for a Cluster-flowered Rose. They have a pleasing fragrance, and flower with good continuity through summer and autumn. Despite the lapse of over 30 years since its introduction, this variety is still widely available, especially in warmer countries where cold and rain cannot so easily wash out the lilac tones within the flowers, and it makes an unusual and beautiful addition to a bed or border. It is also good to cut if taken young, when the mauvish color is at its best. The very spreading plant grows with moderate vigor to less than average height and has matt dark green leaves. **ZONES 4–9.**

LEGRICE, UK, 1962

SEEDLING OF 'LAVENDER PINOCCHIO'

ROYAL NATIONAL ROSE SOCIETY GOLD MEDAL 1961

### 'Lilac Rose' AUSlilac *(right)*
syn. 'Old Lilac'

**MODERN, MODERN SHRUB, PINK BLEND, REPEAT-FLOWERING**

This variety bears large flowers of lilac-pink, with over 40 petals. The blooms are borne in small clusters and open out wide like big rosettes, though they may ball and fail to open in wet conditions. There is a strong fragrance, and blooms appear through summer and autumn. It can add interest towards the front of a shrub border, the color according well with Old Garden Roses and many other garden plants. 'Lilac Rose' grows with a bushy, upright habit to a little below average size and has olive green semi-glossy leaves. It is also classified as an English Rose. **ZONES 4–9.**

AUSTIN, UK, 1990

SEEDLING × 'HERO'

### 'Lilian Austin' AUSli
*(right)*

**MODERN, MODERN SHRUB, ORANGE-PINK, REPEAT-FLOWERING**

The blooms of this variety are large and full, with 30 or so ruffled petals in a warm shade of rosy salmon pink, revealing a glimpse of stamens as well as a good expanse of color as they open out wide. They are sometimes borne singly, sometimes with up to 5 per cluster, and they have a pleasing fragrance. After the initial flush, more flowers appear during the rest of summer and autumn. This variety sits well in borders among other plants, being of spreading but fairly compact habit and of average size for a shrub rose. In warm climates the stems grow longer with an arching habit, and can be trained on a fence to form a low climber. The plant is amply furnished with dark semi-glossy foliage. The raiser, David Austin, thought highly enough of this rose to name it for his mother. It is also classified as an English Rose. **ZONES 4–9.**

AUSTIN, UK, 1973

'ALOHA' × 'THE YEOMAN'

### 'Lilli Marleen'

KORlima *(right)*

syns 'Lili Marléne', 'Lilli Marlene'

MODERN, CLUSTER-FLOWERED/
FLORIBUNDA, MEDIUM RED,
REPEAT-FLOWERING

'Lilli Marleen' is a good rose for a continuous display of low color. The ovoid buds open to fragrant, double flowers with 25 petals; at 3 in (8 cm) across they are large for a Cluster-flowered Rose. The rich red flowers, which completely smother the bush in spring, have a velvety sheen and stand up very well to both hot and cold conditions. They occur in small clusters of 10–15 blooms and last very well on the bush. The foliage is leathery and dark green on a rather thick and stocky plant that is still a very popular rose after nearly 40 years in commerce. **'Climbing Lilli Marleen'** (PEKlimasar; syns 'Grimpant Lilli Marleen', 'Climbing Lili Marlene', 'Climbing Lilli Marlene'; Pekmez, France 1983) is a shortish, stocky climber that completely covers itself in shapely, long-lasting red flowers.
**ZONES 5–10.**

KORDES, GERMANY, 1959

('OUR PRINCESS' ×
'RUDOLPH TIMM') × 'AMA'

ROYAL NATIONAL ROSE SOCIETY
CERTIFICATE OF MERIT 1959,
ANERKANNTE DEUTSCHE ROSE
1960, GOLDEN ROSE OF THE
HAGUE 1966

### 'Limelight'　KORikon

*(bottom)*

syn. 'Golden Medaillon'

MODERN, LARGE-FLOWERED/
HYBRID TEA, LIGHT YELLOW,
REPEAT-FLOWERING

This well-named rose has light yellow flowers that can be tinged with soft green. At the half-open stage, 'Limelight' has the formal elegance of a double camellia with petals of great substance in a very symmetrical arrangement. The double, high-centered blooms have 35 petals and are very fragrant. The foliage is dark green and semi-glossy on an upright, medium-sized bush. This variety is excellent to pick for indoor decoration as the green in the flower retains its color very well. **ZONES 5–10.**

KORDES, GERMANY, 1984

'PEACH MELBA' × SEEDLING

## 'Lincoln Cathedral'

GLAnlin *(right)*

syn. 'Sarong'

MODERN, LARGE-FLOWERED/
HYBRID TEA, ORANGE BLEND,
REPEAT-FLOWERING

One of several roses such as 'Winchester Cathedral' and 'Coventry Cathedral' named after English cathedrals, 'Lincoln Cathedral' has double flowers of 28 petals that are large and very well formed. The outer petals are pink, the inner ones orange with a yellow reverse— the mixture of colors giving the rose its synonym. The foliage is dark green and glossy and there are many red prickles on the bushy plant. This excellent garden rose is suitable for bedding, the combination of color in the flowers always attracting attention. In spite of its gold medal it is not often seen in gardens.
ZONES 5–11.

LANGDALE, UK, 1985

'SILVER JUBILEE' × 'ROYAL DANE'

ROYAL NATIONAL ROSE SOCIETY
GOLD MEDAL 1985

## 'Linda Campbell'

MORten *(right)*

syn. 'Tall Poppy'

MODERN, HYBRID RUGOSA,
MEDIUM RED,
REPEAT-FLOWERING

This rose was named after a former editor of the *American Rose Annual*, who died of cancer at a young age. The offspring of a Hybrid Rugosa crossed with a Miniature, it is a rose of very dense Rugosa-like growth that bears medium-sized flowers that repeat very quickly. The buds are pointed, and are medium red, ageing to a paler shade. They are cupped, have 25 petals, and occur in dense sprays of 5–20 blooms. There is no fragrance. The foliage is dark green and abundant. It is extremely hardy in very cold areas where temperatures fall well below zero. A bush of 'Linda Campbell' in full bloom is indeed a very colorful sight.
ZONES 4–11.

MOORE, USA, 1990

'ANYTIME' × 'RUGOSA
MAGNIFICA'

L

## 'Little Artist'
MACmanly *(above)*
syn. 'Top Gear'

MODERN, MINIATURE, RED
BLEND, REPEAT-FLOWERING

The flowers of this
'hand-painted'
masterpiece have
bold splashes of red
with random white
markings. The florets
are semi-double with
14–21 petals and quite
large for a Miniature
Rose. The low, spread-
ing, disease-resistant
plant blooms all year
long, providing a
canopy of glorious
blooms, each with
different markings.
As the blooms age, the
color markings disappear
to give an attractive,
solid, medium red
coloration to the petals.
The bush is well-
rounded with mostly
upright growth that
looks wonderful
as a container-grown
plant on the patio
or in the backyard.
ZONES 5–11.

MCGREDY, NEW ZEALAND, 1982

'EYEPAINT' × 'KO'S YELLOW'

## 'Little Darling'
MODERN, CLUSTER-FLOWERED/FLORIBUNDA, YELLOW BLEND,
REPEAT-FLOWERING

'Little Darling' is considered one of the best introductions of the 1950s. This vigorous, spreading
plant has glossy dark green, disease-resistant
foliage. It produces large elongated sprays of
20–30 flowers that are a soft salmon-pink blend
with yellow at the base of the petals. The medium-
sized, double blooms are well formed, have 25
petals, and are spicily fragrant. The long panicles
are good for cutting as the soft color shows up
well indoors. ZONES 5–10.

DUEHRSEN, USA, 1956

'CAPTAIN THOMAS' × ('BABY CHÂTEAU' × 'FASHION')

PORTLAND GOLD MEDAL 1958, ALL-AMERICA ROSE SOCIETY
DAVID FUERSTENBERG PRIZE 1964

## 'Little Flirt'  *(above)*
MODERN, MINIATURE, RED
BLEND, REPEAT-FLOWERING

The fragrant double
flowers of 'Little Flirt'
have 42 petals and are
orange-red with a dis-
tinctive yellow reverse
and a gold base. This is
a very attractive color
combination for
garden display. The
flowers do, however,
have a sort of loose
form. The plant has a
vigorous, upright habit
with light green foliage
that is susceptible to
mildew. This rose is
now all but forgotten
among the many new
color combinations.
ZONES 5–11.

MOORE, USA, 1961

(*ROSE WICHURANA* ×
'FLORADORA') × ('GOLDEN
GLOW' × 'ZEE')

### 'Little Gem' *(right)*
syn. 'Valide'

OLD, MOSS, DEEP PINK, REPEAT-FLOWERING

The buds of this rose are only slightly mossed, and are arranged either singly on short stalks or a few together in small clusters. The fragrant, many-petalled flowers open full to form a flat cushion, and are consistently reddish pink. Each flower is about 3 in (8 cm) in diameter, and they regularly repeat their bloom each autumn. The foliage is relatively small, darkish green and prolific on a dense, free-flowering shrub that attains a height of some 4 ft (1.2 m) in good soils. The almost thornless stems are liberally covered with mossy stubble. This shrub rose is of considerable garden merit and also makes a great container plant. It should not be confused with the Schuurman-bred Miniature of the same name. ZONES 4–10.

PAUL, UK, 1880

PARENTAGE UNKNOWN

### 'Little Girl' *(right)*

MODERN, CLIMBING MINIATURE, ORANGE-PINK, REPEAT-FLOWERING

'Little Girl' has long pointed buds that reveal shapely coral to salmon-pink blooms on a plant with a climbing habit. The double florets have excellent form and substance, and are borne in profusion, mostly in small clusters. The foliage is glossy mid-green. This rose grows more like a traditional pillar rose than a spreading climber. Its hallmarks are vigor, the profusion of bloom, color fastness, ease of maintenance and the fact that it is almost thornless. This rose is still one of the most popular climbing Miniatures in the USA. ZONES 5–11.

MOORE, USA, 1973

'LITTLE DARLING' × 'WESTMONT'

L

## 'Little Opal' SUNpat
*(below)*

MODERN, MINIATURE, LIGHT PINK, REPEAT-FLOWERING

The small flowers of 'Little Opal' are pale pink and fairly full, with 15–25 petals. They open rather quickly and there is a slight fragrance. Repeat-flowering occurs fairly quickly. The foliage is small, mid-green and glossy. The growth habit is upright and bushy, and the plant has good disease resistance. ZONES 5–10.

SCHUURMAN, NEW ZEALAND, 1992

'WHITE DREAM' × 'DICKY BIRD'

L

## 'Little Jackie' SAVor *(above)*

MODERN, MINIATURE, ORANGE BLEND, REPEAT-FLOWERING

The flowers on this award-winning rose are a light orange-red with a yellow reverse. The florets are double, with more than 20 petals, and have outstanding exhibition-style Large-flowered form. Bloom cycle repeat times are generally fast in most climates. The foliage is semi-glossy, mid-green and can develop mildew if not protected. The plant has a vigorous, upright growth habit with remarkable foliage density. 'Little Jackie' created quite a sensation at the first Royal National Rose Society National Miniature Show in St Albans, England in 1991, when it captured the newly created International Ralph Moore Trophy with a basket entry containing over 100 blooms. ZONES 5–11.

SAVILLE, USA, 1982

('PROMINENT' × 'SHERI ANNE') × 'GLENFIDDICH'

AMERICAN ROSE SOCIETY AWARD OF EXCELLENCE 1984

## 'Liverpool Echo'
*(right)*

syn. 'Liverpool'

MODERN, CLUSTER-FLOWERED/
FLORIBUNDA, ORANGE-PINK,
REPEAT-FLOWERING

'Liverpool Echo' gets its very large elongated panicles of flowers from its parent 'Little Darling'. They are salmon-pink, double with 25 petals, have good Large-flowered form, are up to 4 in (10 cm) across and the petals have extremely good substance. The plant is very tall and bushy and can be used as a shrub rose. The foliage is large, light green, extremely plentiful and comes up to flower level in the manner of the Portland Roses. Spring blooming is abundant and continuity good. ZONES 5–10.

MCGREDY, UK, 1971

('LITTLE DARLING' ×
'GOLDILOCKS') × 'MÜNCHEN'

PORTLAND GOLD MEDAL 1979

## 'Liverpool Remembers' FRYstar

syn. 'Beauty Star'

MODERN, LARGE-FLOWERED/
HYBRID TEA, ORANGE-RED,
REPEAT-FLOWERING

This rose bears very large flowers of 40 petals each that are a glowing vermilion color, and borne mostly singly on very long stems. The foliage is mid-green and glossy on a plant that is extremely tall and upright, with an almost climbing habit. There are many prickles. This is a good rose for the back of the border, blending well with such roses as 'Freude' and 'Folklore'. It is great for cutting, as the long stems add extra charm to the bright color scheme. ZONES 5–10.

FRYER, UK, 1990

'CORSO' × SEEDLING

BELFAST CERTIFICATE OF MERIT 1992

## 'Living Fire'
*(bottom)*

MODERN, CLUSTER-FLOWERED/
FLORIBUNDA, ORANGE BLEND,
REPEAT-FLOWERING

This is a well-named rose as the flowers are orange suffused with orange-red. They are double with 33 petals, have rosette form and are of medium size. The flowers, which are fragrant (which is unusual in a rose of this color), come singly and in small clusters on a moderate sized bush with dark green foliage that nicely complements the flowers. Flower production is continuous and the plant has good disease resistance. 'Living Fire' is a good rose to use where a luminous color is required. ZONES 5–11.

GREGORY, UK, 1973

'TROPICANA' × SEEDLING

ROYAL NATIONAL ROSE SOCIETY CERTIFICATE OF MERIT 1973

### 'Lolita' KORlita, LITakor
*(right)*

MODERN, LARGE-FLOWERED/
HYBRID TEA, APRICOT BLEND,
REPEAT-FLOWERING

The soft apricot-bronze color of this rose is unique. The very large, double flowers with 28 petals open to large blooms with quartered centers, much like a peony. The buds are large and ovoid on long stems with large bronze-green foliage in the early stages, maturing to mid-green. There is a strong fragrance. With its long stems and lovely flowers, 'Lolita' is a superb rose for cutting, and lasts well indoors. It grows a little tall for use as a bedding rose but is excellent as a tall hedge or for planting at the back of a rose bed. It can be affected in climates with very cold winters, but there are no disease problems. **ZONES 5–10.**

KORDES, GERMANY, 1972
'COLOUR WONDER' × SEEDLING
ANERKANNTE DEUTSCHE ROSE
1973

### 'Long John Silver'
*(right)*

MODERN, LARGE-FLOWERED
CLIMBER, WHITE

This fine once-blooming climbing rose bred from the cold-hardy, disease-free *Rosa setigera* has large, white, cupped, long-lasting fragrant flowers. They come in clusters and are very double with muddled centers like an old Centifolia Rose. The growth is vigorous and the plant has large leathery leaves. After an enormous spring flowering, an occasional bloom may be produced in summer and autumn. This is a good rose to grow into trees, where its strong stems soon hook onto a support. With the extremely late-flowering *R. setigera* in its breeding, the rose season is extended. **ZONES 4–10.**

HORVATH, USA, 1934
SEEDLING OF *ROSA SETIGERA* ×
'SUNBURST'

L

L

### 'Lord Gold' DELgold
*(above)*

MODERN, LARGE-FLOWERED/
HYBRID TEA, DEEP YELLOW,
REPEAT-FLOWERING

'Lord Gold' produces a
continuous supply of
large, shapely, clear
yellow, double flowers
with 25–30 petals.
Opening from well-
formed buds, the lightly
scented flowers are
produced both singly
and several together.
The foliage is a healthy
dark green on a strong,
medium to tall bush.
This makes a good bed-
ding rose. **ZONES 5–10.**

DELBARD, FRANCE, 1980

PARENTAGE UNKNOWN

### 'Lord Penzance'
*(right)*

OLD, SWEET BRIAR,
YELLOW BLEND

The hybridizer of
many Sweet Briar
Roses is remembered
in this attractive,
summer-blooming
shrub. Dainty, single
petals of soft, rosy
yellow surround attrac-
tive yellow stamens.
Both the flowers and
the small dark leaves
are fragrant, and bright
red hips appear in

autumn. It is a vig-
orous bush that does
well in poor soil, and is
a good choice for a
woodland garden or
a hedge. It has a ten-
dency to develop black
spot. Lord Penzance

began his breeding
program in 1890;
he was nearly 80 when
his hybrids were intro-
duced. **ZONES 5–10.**

PENZANCE, UK, 1894

*ROSA EGLANTERIA* × 'HARISON'S
YELLOW'

## 'Lordly Oberon'

AUSron **(below)**

MODERN, MODERN SHRUB,
LIGHT PINK, REPEAT-FLOWERING

The flowers of this rose are very double, cupped, large and extremely fragrant. They are similar in color and shape to its parent 'Chaucer', but there the similarity ends; 'Chaucer' is a shortish, stocky grower while 'Lordly Oberon' is very tall and has an almost climbing habit. The flowers are pro-

duced on tall, arching canes rather later in spring than most shrub roses. The foliage is large, matt, mid-green and very profuse on an upright plant with good disease resistance. It makes a suitable pillar rose in warm climates, or it can be used on a tripod. 'Lordly Oberon' repeat-blooms but because of its long stems takes a long time to do so; the flowers are excellent for picking, especially when long-stemmed pale pinks are required. It is also classified as an English Rose.
**ZONES 4–10.**

AUSTIN, UK, 1982

'CHAUCER' × SEEDLING

## 'L'Oréal Trophy'

HARlexis **(bottom)**

syn. 'Alexis'

MODERN, LARGE-FLOWERED/
HYBRID TEA, ORANGE BLEND,
REPEAT-FLOWERING

This sport of 'Alexander' shares the characteristics of that rose except color, which is a luminous shade of reddish salmon overlaid with orange. Medium sized and double, the blooms have a pleasant light scent and are at their best in cool weather, when they open with neatly formed high centers on long stems; they also last well. In hot conditions they fly open and develop scalloped petals. The flowers are freely produced through summer and autumn, and they are good for cutting, provided they are taken young, just as the sepals are parting. This plant makes a suitable subject for a tall hedge or bed, and it looks good in a border. It is a vigorous, easy grower with an upright, free-branching habit, to above average height, and has a good complement of dark green shiny leaves.
**ZONES 4–9.**

HARKNESS, UK, 1982

SPORT OF 'ALEXANDER'

BAGATELLE GOLD MEDAL
1982, ROYAL NATIONAL ROSE
SOCIETY CERTIFICATE OF MERIT
1982, BELFAST GOLD MEDAL
1984, COURTRAI GOLDEN
ROSE 1986

## 'Lorraine Lee'
*(right)*
OLD, TEA, PINK BLEND,
REPEAT-FLOWERING

One of the most famous of all Australian-bred roses, 'Lorraine Lee' is a second generation *Rosa gigantea* hybrid. Clark spent years producing roses suited to the warm Australian climate zones. The pointed buds open to double, cupped, rosy, apricot-pink blooms. It is fragrant and will bloom from early spring until the first frost. The rich green foliage has a leathery, glossy finish. A vigorous shrub, it can reach 6 ft (2 m) in 2 years; it can also be grown as a hedge. Australian rosarian Susan Irvine says that Clark created roses for the garden and not for the show table; however, he won the highest award for rose lovers—the Dean Hole Medal of the Royal National Rose Society. **'Climbing Lorraine Lee'** (McKay, 1932) is identical in all respects to the parent except that it reaches 18 ft (5 m) in 3 seasons. **ZONES 5–10.**

CLARK, AUSTRALIA, 1924

'JESSIE CLARK' × 'CAPITAINE MILLET'

## 'L'Ouche' *(right)*
OLD, CHINA, PINK BLEND/LIGHT PINK, REPEAT-FLOWERING

This rose has double, perfectly cupped flowers that emerge from large, full, conical buds. The blooms are rose, sometimes shaded yellow, have thin petals and yellow stamens, and usually appear in clusters during a long flowering season. This 4 ft (1.2 m) shrub is thick and well branched, and has a compact, upright form. The dark green, thick foliage has a shading of bronze. **ZONES 5–10.**

BUATOIS, FRANCE, 1901

PARENTAGE UNKNOWN

L

**'Louis de Funès'** MEIrestif *(above)*
syn. 'Charleston 88'

MODERN, LARGE-FLOWERED/HYBRID TEA, ORANGE BLEND,
REPEAT-FLOWERING

This rose produces flowers of an intense apricot-orange with a cadmium yellow reverse. They are fairly double, with 15–25 petals, and open very quickly from long elegant buds. The foliage is medium, very dark, glossy and plentiful on a strong and upright bush. The buds open too quickly for the show bench or for indoor decoration. **ZONES 5–10.**

MEILLAND, FRANCE, 1987

('AMBASSADOR' × 'WHISKY MAC') × ('ARTHUR BELL' × 'KABUKI')

GENEVA GOLD MEDAL 1983, MONZA GOLD MEDAL 1983

L

### 'Louis XIV' *(above)*

OLD, CHINA, DARK RED, REPEAT-FLOWERING

Created during the high period of China Rose production in France, this royal namesake has been in the trade ever since it was introduced. It requires a warm climate and sun, which is fitting when one remembers that the king after whom the rose was named was known as The Sun King (1638–1715). The fragrant, dark crimson, double blooms with 25 petals are globular, medium sized and full. They nod in the hot sun, and turn a bright red shaded maroon. There is sparse foliage on the compact, bushy plant. **ZONES 5–10.**

GUILLOT, FRANCE, 1859

PERHAPS A SEEDLING OF 'GÉNÉRAL JACQUEMINOT'

## 'Louis Gimard'
*(above)*

OLD, MOSS, MEDIUM PINK

The flowers of this rose are arranged in tight clusters, and emerge from large mossy buds in mid-summer. They are very full and double and reach some 3 in (8 cm) across when fully open. The fragrant blooms are a rich cerise, brushed and highlighted magenta and pink. This is a sturdy shrub with stems that are well covered with purplish mossy stubble. The oval leaves are dark green. **ZONES 5–10.**

PERNET, FRANCE, 1877

PARENTAGE UNKNOWN

## 'Louise d'Arzens'
*(below)*

OLD, NOISETTE, WHITE, REPEAT-FLOWERING

Enjoying a revival in popularity in recent years, this modest climber has attractive cream and pink buds that open to double, creamy white flowers that are full and medium sized. There is some fragrance during its repeat-flowering. This robust shrub with glossy light green foliage can reach 10 ft (3 m) in a few years. François Lacharme of Lyon, France, produced a long series of popular roses that are still in the catalogues, including 'Saland' and 'Louis van Houtte'. **ZONES 5–10.**

LACHARME, FRANCE, 1861

PARENTAGE UNKNOWN

L

### 'Louise Odier' *(above)*
syn. 'Mme de Stella'

OLD, BOURBON, DEEP PINK, REPEAT-FLOWERING

A first-rate cut flower and a reliable repeat bloomer, this rose has long been popular. The round buds open to reveal large, very double, warm pink flowers. It is a perfect shape for a Bourbon—cupped at first, then becoming flat and round. The ragged center petals have a lavender tint. This is one of the most floriferous of the Old Garden Roses and the flowers are held on long stems. The arching canes are covered with soft, olive green leaves and maroon prickles. If left unpruned it can be used as a climber, although more often it is a valuable addition to the border. It tolerates some shade, and its rich fragrance makes it an excellent cut flower. It is the parent of many popular French roses. **ZONES 4–10.**

MARGOTTIN, FRANCE, 1851

SEEDLING OF 'EMILE COURTIER'

### 'Love' JACtwin

MODERN, LARGE-FLOWERED/HYBRID TEA, RED BLEND, REPEAT-FLOWERING

Three roses bred by William Warriner named 'Love', 'Honor' and 'Cherish' all won the All-America Rose Selection for 1980—a remarkable feat. 'Love' produces rather stumpy buds of a deep cerise color with a silvery white reverse. They are double with 40 or more tightly packed petals and open slowly to well-formed exhibition-type blooms that last for a long time. Flower production is fairly good. It is a disease-resistant plant with an upright, stocky habit, and many large thorns. Red and silver bicolors are not very common; this is one of the best of them. **ZONES 5–10.**

WARRINER, USA, 1980

SEEDLING × 'REDGOLD'

ALL-AMERICA ROSE SELECTION 1980, PORTLAND GOLD MEDAL 1980

**'Love Potion'** JACsedi *(above)*
syn. 'Purple Puff'

MODERN, CLUSTER-FLOWERED/FLORIBUNDA, MAUVE,
REPEAT-FLOWERING

'Love Potion' produces deep clear lavender
flowers in profusion. A low-spreading bush, it
has medium dark green and glossy foliage that
acts as a good foil to the large 30–40 petalled
blooms, which are produced in small clusters.
There are few prickles. It has a strong fragrance.
This variety is good for small beds and borders
and for inside decoration as it keeps well when
picked. **ZONES 5–10.**

CHRISTENSEN, USA, 1995

SEEDLING × 'DILLY DILLY'

**'Lovely Fairy'** SPEvu

MODERN, POLYANTHA, DEEP PINK, REPEAT-FLOWERING

'Lovely Fairy' is a deep pink sport of 'The Fairy',
with the same habit of growth and large clusters
of small, double flowers. It is ideal for planting
in warmer areas where the darker flowers keep
their color better. Because of its rambler blood,
it flowers later than most varieties but does so
continuously in summer and autumn, through to
early winter. The abundant foliage is glossy, mid-
green and disease free. This rose makes an ideal
standard and is also useful for low hedges and for
cascading over rocks and low walls. **ZONES 5–10.**

SPEK, THE NETHERLANDS, 1990

SPORT OF 'THE FAIRY'

## 'Lovely Lady' DICjubell *(above)*
### syn. 'Dickson's Jubilee'
**MODERN, LARGE-FLOWERED/HYBRID TEA, MEDIUM PINK, REPEAT-FLOWERING**

The double blooms of this rose develop slowly from large, oval buds into well-formed, fragrant flowers filled with about 35 petals. The color is a lively medium pink with a tint of coral-pink that is most attractive and lasts well. The blooms are good for cutting. 'Lovely Lady' makes a fine bedding variety and is also excellent as a standard rose. The glossy rich green foliage is particularly healthy; it makes a dense cover to ground level over a compact bush. **ZONES 5–10.**

DICKSON, UK, 1986

'SILVER JUBILEE' × ('EUROROSE' × 'ANABELL')

ROYAL NATIONAL ROSE SOCIETY CERTIFICATE OF MERIT 1983, BELFAST GOLD MEDAL 1988, ROYAL HORTICULTURAL SOCIETY AWARD OF GARDEN MERIT 1993, THE HAGUE SILVER MEDAL 1998

## 'Lovers' Meeting'
**MODERN, LARGE-FLOWERED/HYBRID TEA, ORANGE BLEND, REPEAT-FLOWERING**

The long, pointed buds of this rose open fairly quickly to double flowers with 25 petals that are a clear bright orange. The blooms, which are fragrant, are borne both singly and in clusters. The foliage is bronze in the young stages and growth is medium and upright. The plant has good disease resistance and the blooms hold their color well. This is an ideal rose for bedding where a bright color is required. **ZONES 5–10.**

GANDY, UK, 1980

SEEDLING × 'EGYPTIAN TREASURE'

ROYAL NATIONAL ROSE SOCIETY TRIAL GROUND CERTIFICATE 1982

L

### 'Loving Memory'

KORgund 81 *(above)*

syns 'Burgund 81',
'Red Cedar'

MODERN, LARGE-FLOWERED/
HYBRID TEA, MEDIUM RED,
REPEAT-FLOWERING

This rose is one of the best red garden and exhibition roses available. The tall plant produces long stems carrying large abundant, semi-glossy, rich green foliage. Well-formed buds open slowly to huge full blooms with 40 symmetrically arranged petals that are high centered with excellent exhibition form. There is a slight fragrance, and disease resistance is particularly good. The bush is rather too tall for bedding but is excellent for the back of a rose border; it can also be used as a very tall hedge. It is known as 'Red Cedar' in Australia, 'Loving Memory' in the UK and New Zealand, and 'Burgund 81' in Germany. **ZONES 5–10.**

KORDES, GERMANY, 1981

SEEDLING × SEEDLING OF
'RED PLANET'

### 'Loving Touch'

*(right)*

MODERN, MINIATURE,
APRICOT BLEND,
REPEAT-FLOWERING

The double, fragrant flowers of 'Loving Touch' have 25 petals and are a wonderful deep apricot in cool climates and a lighter apricot in hot climates. The large flowers are high centered and borne one to a stem or in small clusters of 3–5. It has attractive foliage on a well-rounded, healthy, disease-resistant bush. The bloom cycle is very fast on a vigorous and easy to maintain plant. **ZONES 5–11.**

JOLLY, USA, 1983

'RISE 'N' SHINE' × 'FIRST PRIZE'

AMERICAN ROSE SOCIETY
AWARD OF EXCELLENCE 1985

**'Lucetta'** AUSemi
*(above)*
syn. **'English Apricot'**
MODERN, MODERN SHRUB,
APRICOT BLEND,
REPEAT-FLOWERING

This elegant rose has arching growth and leaves that are large, polished and very healthy. The saucer-shaped flowers are 5 in (12 cm) across and open to flat, loose, semi-double blooms that keep their color extremely well. The clear pink buds open slowly and have a strong fragrance. Flower production is good and continuous. It is also classified as an English Rose. ZONES 4–10.

AUSTIN, UK, 1983

PARENTAGE UNKNOWN

**'Lutin'** *(right)*
MODERN, MINIATURE, DEEP
PINK, REPEAT-FLOWERING

This is a fine little Miniature Rose with 58 pointed petals making up a well-shaped bloom. Flowers are produced in small, well-filled clusters. This dwarf bushy plant grows to 12–15 in (30–38 cm) in height. Flower production is well above average and the repeat bloom is rapid. Disease resistance is good. 'Lutin' is an excellent rose for a very low border or for planting in a pot or container. ZONES 5–10.

BREEDER UNKNOWN, 1970

SPORT OF 'SCARLET GEM'

L

### 'Lyda Rose'  LETlyda  (above)

MODERN, MODERN SHRUB, WHITE BLEND

This rose was bred by Kleine Lettunich, the breeder of 'Mateos Pink Butterflies', and was named after her daughter and the song from 'Music Man'. 'Lyda Rose' has single, 2½ in (6 cm) wide flowers that are white, edged with delicate pink. They are borne in large clusters to give an apple blossom-like appearance. The fragrance is very strong. It is a disease-free and spreading plant with rich green foliage that will flower well even in the shade. It makes an excellent bushy, free-flowering hedge. **ZONES 5–10.**

LETTUNICH, USA, 1994

SEEDLING OF 'FRANCIS E. LESTER'

### 'Lydia'

MODERN, LARGE-FLOWERED/HYBRID TEA, DEEP YELLOW, REPEAT-FLOWERING

There are three roses named 'Lydia', one from 1933, another from 1973 and this variety from 1949, possibly the most durable of them. The long, pointed buds are an intense saffron yellow. They are high centered, very double and of medium size, and are produced prolifically. The foliage is dark green, leathery and glossy and growth is vigorous. After some 50 years in commerce, 'Lydia' is still remembered as a good rose for bedding; it has stood the test of time for a rose in the yellow range. **ZONES 5–10.**

ROBINSON, UK, 1949

'PHYLLIS GOLD' × SEEDLING

## 'Lykkefund' *(right)*
MODERN, RAMBLER, WHITE BLEND

This Danish Rambler follows its parent by producing huge fragrant trusses of semi-double blooms in one great flush in mid-summer. The medium-sized flowers are creamy yellow, darker at the center, and are tinged with pink; in the sun they fade to white. There are attractive orange-yellow stamens. This 'lucky find' is aptly named as it will cover a pergola or a fence with 18 ft (5 m) canes, or will arch over a pergola. The small, glossy, dark foliage has bronze edges.
**ZONES 5–10.**

OLESEN, DENMARK, 1930

SEEDLING OF *ROSA HELENAE* ×
'ZÉPHIRINE DROUHIN'

**L**

## 'Lyon Rose' *(above)*
syn. 'Lyon's Rose'

MODERN, LARGE-FLOWERED/
HYBRID TEA, ORANGE-PINK,
REPEAT-FLOWERING

'Lyon Rose' is of great importance historically as it is one of the Pernetiana strain of roses bred from *Rosa foetida persiana*—the rose that was the an-cestor of all the rich yellow, bright red and bicolor varieties of today. It has rather poor-textured flowers of pink, shaded coral-red, and yellow in the center. They are double with 44 petals, large and very fragrant. The bush is rather low and very spreading and the foliage is matt, pale green and not very abundant. This rose caused a sensation in the early part of the twentieth century because of its unique color. **ZONES 5–10.**

PERNET-DUCHER, FRANCE, 1907

'MME MÉLANIE SOUPERT' ×
SEEDLING OF 'SOLEIL D'OR'

BAGATELLE GOLD MEDAL 1909

M

### 'Ma Perkins' *(right)*

MODERN, CLUSTER-FLOWERED/
FLORIBUNDA, PINK BLEND,
REPEAT-FLOWERING

'Ma Perkins' gets its cupped flowers with central petals turning inwards from 'Red Radiance' and some of its shell pink color from 'Fashion'. The fragrant flowers are double, cupped and large to 3½ in (9 cm) across. When they are open, the lovely full blooms are a clear pink shaded with salmon. These last well both on the bush and when picked. The foliage is rich green and glossy on a tall and vigorous plant. David Austin saw the potential of the cupped, old world form flowers of this rose and used it in the breeding of 'Wife of Bath', which he has also used widely in the breeding of other varieties. ZONES 5–10.

BOERNER, USA, 1952

'RED RADIANCE' × 'FASHION'

NATIONAL ROSE SOCIETY
CERTIFICATE OF MERIT 1952,
ALL-AMERICA ROSE SELECTION
1953

### 'McGredy's Yellow' *(right)*

MODERN, LARGE-FLOWERED/
HYBRID TEA, MEDIUM YELLOW,
REPEAT-FLOWERING

This rose is one of the best available in the pale yellow range. The long, pointed buds open to large, slightly cupped double flowers containing 30 petals. The color is a clear soft yellow, which is rare in roses; the Modern Garden Rose 'Elina' is somewhat of the same shade. It has a slight fragrance. The foliage is glossy and bronze in the early stages, turning to mid-green on a vigorous, very free-flowering plant that continues to flower well into winter in warmer areas. Mildew can occur at times. **'Climbing McGredy's Yellow'** (Western Rose Co., USA, 1937) is a particularly strong climbing rose with lush, large green leaves and thick thorny canes. It produces an enormous crop of flowers

in spring, especially if the canes are tied down into a horizontal position at pruning. ZONES 5–10.

MCGREDY, UK, 1933

'MRS CHARLES LAMPLOUGH' ×
('THE QUEEN ALEXANDRA ROSE'
× 'J. B. CLARK')

NATIONAL ROSE SOCIETY GOLD
MEDAL 1930, PORTLAND GOLD
MEDAL 1956

M

### 'Madam President'
*(right)*

syn. 'Madame President'

MODERN, CLUSTER-FLOWERED/
FLORIBUNDA, PINK BLEND,
REPEAT-FLOWERING

'Madam President' has some of the most beautiful flowers of any rose. The buds are beautifully shaped and open slowly to very full blooms of camellia-like perfection that have 30 petals and are soft rose pink with a cream base. The flowers hold their form and color well and occur singly or in small clusters on a moderately sized bush. 'Madam President' is particularly quick to repeat-bloom. The foliage is smallish, dark green and profuse and disease resistance is good except for occasional black spot; it is an excellent rose for picking and lasts well indoors; it is also superb as a standard because of its bushy nature. This rose seems to be grown mainly in New Zealand and Australia where it is a recommended rose for general purposes. It has some fragrance. **ZONES 5–10.**

MCGREDY, NEW ZEALAND, 1975

SEEDLING × 'HANDEL'

### 'Mme Abel Chatenay' *(right)*

MODERN, LARGE-FLOWERED/
HYBRID TEA, PINK BLEND,
REPEAT-FLOWERING

'Mme Abel Chatenay' has had her 100th birthday and is still one of the most loved and popular of the very early Large-flowered Roses. With the Tea Rose 'Doctor Grill' as one parent and a Hybrid Perpetual as another, this could be just as easily classed as a Tea Rose. The pale pink buds are pointed, and open to full, double, pale pink blooms with a deeper center and strong carmine pink on the reverse. They are fragrant. The foliage is bronze when young, maturing to green. It is surprising that such a lovely rose received no awards, but in 1895 the only awards available were from the National Rose Society in England and that appeared to be for the quality of the flower, with no regard for the bush or habit of growth. **'Climbing Mme Abel Chatenay'** (Page, UK, 1917) is still one of the best and most repeat-flowering of all pink climbing roses. **ZONES 5–10.**

PERNET-DUCHER, FRANCE, 1895

'DOCTOR GRILL' × 'VICTOR VERDIER'

M

M

### 'Mme Alfred Carrière' *(right)*

OLD, NOISETTE, WHITE, REPEAT-FLOWERING

Known for its reliable health, this rampant climber produces a continuous display of pale, pinkish white blooms over a long period. There is yellow at the base below the curly central petals. The large, full, globular blooms have a Tea-like fragrance. The light, pale green foliage has well-serrated edges, and the flexible canes make it easy to train on a fence, wall, or pergola. It doesn't mind shade and can be propagated easily from cuttings. This popular rose was a creation of Joseph Schwartz, whose widow carried on his work—producing such famous plants as 'Mme Ernst Calvat' and 'Roger Lambelin'. In 1908 it was proclaimed 'the best white climber' with 62 out of 83 votes of the National Rose Society in England. ZONES 4–10.

SCHWARTZ, FRANCE, 1879

PARENTAGE UNKNOWN

ROYAL HORTICULTURAL SOCIETY AWARD OF GARDEN MERIT 1993

### 'Mme Alice Garnier' *(right)*
syn. 'Brownlow Hill Rambler'

MODERN, RAMBLER, PINK BLEND

The first part of the twentieth century found hybridizers in France creating a long list of *wichurana* climbers. This rampant Rambler bears many clusters of open, bright rose flowers with a center of yellow and light pink. The blooms are formed on long, slender branches. The flat rosettes of quilled and quartered petals have a strong fragrance

of apples. It reaches 15 ft (4.5 m) and is covered with abundant small, dark, glossy foliage when the young bronze shoots mature.

It does well in poor soil and tolerates shade. ZONES 5–10.

FAUQUE, FRANCE, 1906

*ROSA WICHURANA* × 'MME CHARLES'

M

## 'Mme Antoine Mari' *(above)*

OLD, TEA, PINK BLEND, REPEAT-FLOWERING

Antoine Mari of Nice, France, produced this
reliable Tea Rose during the period when Teas
and Chinas were very popular. The camellia-like
blooms are rosy flesh shaded lilac; sometimes
there are cream-white stripes. The quilled petals
create shapely, fragrant blooms that are double,
full and large. The buds are particularly beautiful
later in the season. This is a tidy plant suitable for
a container or for being trained on a warm wall.
It has plum-colored canes lined with light green
leaves; there are prickles. It does best in the sun
but in a protected spot. ZONES 6–11.

MARI, FRANCE, 1901

PARENTAGE UNKNOWN

## 'Mme Bérard'

OLD, CLIMBING TEA, ORANGE BLEND, REPEAT-FLOWERING

Looking very much like 'Gloire de Dijon', this
rose is salmon-yellow shaded salmon-rose. It is
double, large and cupped, and the petals unfold
in scrolls with muddled centers. In full sun the
flowers fade to pink and yellow. It will bloom
from late spring until the first frost, and critics
have claimed that this fragrant rose is one of the
best Climbing Teas. It reaches 10 ft (3 m) high
and wide, and is covered in dark green leaves.
Hardier than most Tea Roses, it likes a sunny
spot. Antoine Levet of Lyon, France, created
many well-known roses between 1866 and
1889, among them 'Paul Neyron' and 'Perle des
Jardins'. This one is sometimes listed with the
Noisettes. ZONES 5–10.

LEVET, FRANCE, 1872

'MME FALCOT' × 'GLOIRE DE DIJON'

## 'Mme Berkeley' *(left)*

OLD, TEA, PINK BLEND, REPEAT-FLOWERING

This rose is well known as an excellent cut flower. It is very double, well shaped and long in the bud. The petals are arranged very much like a Large-flowered Rose, and the centers of the blooms are salmon with a blowsy form. The lightly scented blooms appear all summer and into autumn. It is a compact, bushy plant that should be pruned regularly to keep its shape, and is a good candidate for the border or a container. It does best in the sun. ZONES 5–10.

BERNAIX, FRANCE, 1898

PARENTAGE UNKNOWN

M

## 'Mme Boll' *(above)*

OLD, PORTLAND/HYBRID PERPETUAL, DEEP PINK, REPEAT-FLOWERING

There is some dispute about the lineage of this rose, with one source giving a Hybrid Perpetual and 'Belle Fabert' as the parents and another classifying it as a Portland. It has been popular for nearly 150 years. The plump, carmine-rose blooms are large and open well. They are 4 in (10 cm) across, with large outer petals and many muddled inner ones. The very fragrant flowers appear late in spring and continue until the first frost. It has vigorous, stout canes that are covered with large leaves and dark gray prickles. The stems are short, bristly and glandular. ZONES 5–10.

BOLL AND BOYAU, FRANCE, 1859

PROBABLY 'BARONNE PRÉVOST' × 'PORTLANDICA'

'Climbing Mme Butterfly' *(above)*

## 'Mme Butterfly' *(above)*

MODERN, LARGE-FLOWERED/HYBRID TEA, LIGHT PINK,
REPEAT-FLOWERING

This rose is very similar to 'Ophelia', from which
it sported; in the 1920s and 1930s, exhibitors
were not allowed to show both varieties as the
judges could not tell them apart! The elegant
buds are long and pointed and open to fragrant,
double flowers with 28 petals. The foliage is
leathery, and the growth is moderate. **'Climbing
Mme Butterfly'** (Smith, UK, 1926) is one of the
best climbing roses, producing masses of lovely
buds in large clusters in spring. If spent blooms
are removed it flowers through summer and
into autumn, when the color is richer and the
blooms are larger and last longer. It is excellent
growing over an arch or on a wall. The flowers
can be damaged by thrips in spring. **ZONES 5–10.**

HILL & COMPANY, USA, 1918

SPORT OF 'OPHELIA'

M

M

### 'Mme Caroline Testout' *(above)*
syn. 'City of Portland'

MODERN, LARGE-FLOWERED/
HYBRID TEA, MEDIUM PINK,
REPEAT-FLOWERING

This rose was named after a Parisian couturière and, although well over a century old, it is still grown in gardens throughout the world. The buds are large and globular, and the large flowers are bright rose with a darker center tinted carmine. They are very double and very fragrant. The petals are inclined to turn inward at the center, giving a globular look. This rose was used by David Austin to produce 'Wife of Bath' and is in the pedigree of many of his Modern Shrub Roses (also classified as English Roses). It is a tough and hardy bush but the flowers are perhaps lacking a little in substance, a trifle papery in texture and they can ball in wet weather. 'Climbing Mme Caroline Testout' (Chauvry, France, 1901) is excellent on arches, pillars or pergolas, or the walls of houses, where its large, globular blooms and strong scent can be appreciated. It is disease free. ZONES 5–11.

PERNET-DUCHER, FRANCE, 1890

'MME DE TARTAS' ×
'LADY MARY FITZWILLIAM'

### 'Mme Charles' *(above)*

OLD, TEA, YELLOW BLEND/PINK BLEND, REPEAT-FLOWERING

This is one of the earlier French Teas. It has handsome buds that usually open to pink blooms, although some growers have reported it as having yellow blooms with a salmon center. They are full, semi-globular and appear in clusters. In the hot sun the color turns to sulfur. The shrub has no prickles, likes a warm position in the garden and will bloom throughout summer and into autumn. One early writer stated that it is an improved strain of 'Safrano'. ZONES 6–11.

DAMAIZIN, FRANCE, 1864

'MME DAMAIZIN' × SEEDLING

## 'Mme de la Rôche-Lambert'

OLD, MOSS, MAUVE,
REPEAT-FLOWERING

This rose flowers continuously throughout summer and autumn, the blooms emerging from shapely, feathery buds that are well covered with light green moss. The rich deep burgundy flowers are made up of many scrolled and fluted petals. These are highly scented and up to $3\frac{1}{2}$ in (8 cm) across. It is a broadly growing shrub to about 4 ft (1.2 m) high. The stems are heavily mossed with soft stubble and bear few thorns of consequence. The bright green leaves are round, soft and smooth. This is a classic among the Moss Roses, if a slight propensity to mildew can be overlooked. **ZONES 4–10.**

ROBERT, FRANCE, 1851

PARENTAGE UNKNOWN

ROYAL HORTICULTURAL SOCIETY
AWARD OF GARDEN MERIT 1993

M

## 'Mme de Sancy de Parabère' *(above)*
syns 'Mme Sancy de Parabère', 'Virginian Lass'

OLD, BOURSAULT, LIGHT PINK

This variety is one of four Boursaults cultivated today, a class of rose that originated in Paris. The clear, soft pink blooms are double, with the outer petals larger than the inside ones. The sweetly fragrant flowers are 5 in (12 cm) across, loose, circular and flat—they appear in large clusters. It blooms only once. This is the largest flowered form of its class, and can easily reach 15 ft (4.5 m) high. It does best in partial shade, is quite hardy and does well in poor soil and all kinds of weather. The autumn foliage is particularly attractive and there are no prickles. The experts cannot agree on its classification. **ZONES 4–10.**

BONNET, FRANCE, 1874

PARENTAGE UNKNOWN

### 'Mme de Tartas'
*(right)*

syn. 'Mme de Thartas'

OLD, TEA, LIGHT PINK,
REPEAT-FLOWERING

The large, cupped, blush pink blooms of this rose appear from early summer until the first frost. They are fully double, slightly fragrant, blowsy, and in the shade are an intense pink. It can be treated as a vigorous shrub or climber, or as a sprawling ground cover. The leathery, dark green foliage covers the large prickles. This is a most under-rated beautiful rose in mild climates that is an important ancestor of many Large-flowered Roses created during Victorian times. Jack Harkness believed it was the pollen parent for 'Mermaid'.
ZONES 6–11.

BERNÈDE, FRANCE, 1859

PARENTAGE UNKNOWN

### 'Mme de Watteville' *(right)*

OLD, TEA, YELLOW BLEND,
REPEAT-FLOWERING

The buds of 'Mme de Watteville' are held on long stalks and open to full, free, well-formed flowers. The large, very fragrant blooms are lemon, usually edged in pale pink; they resemble tulips on first opening and bloom throughout summer and into autumn.

Small, dark green, dense foliage covers the branching, low-growing shrub. It does best in full sun, which will help it avoid a tendency to mildew.

This modest rose is an ideal candidate for a container as it is more tender than other Tea Roses. ZONES 6–11.

GUILLOT, FRANCE, 1883

PARENTAGE UNKNOWN

## 'Mme Dieudonné' *(right)*
### syn. 'Mme L. Dieudonné'
MODERN, LARGE-FLOWERED/HYBRID TEA,
RED BLEND, REPEAT-FLOWERING

With four fiery red and orange
roses in its pedigree, it is no
surprise that this variety bears
luminous orange-red flowers
with gold undersides. The
long, pointed buds, which are
a beautiful rich bicolor, open
quickly to double blooms of
30 petals that are high centered,
large and fragrant. The full
blooms lose their intense color
rather quickly. The foliage is
dark and glossy on a medium-
sized, vigorous bush that can
suffer from mildew. **ZONES 5–10.**

MEILLAND, FRANCE, 1949

('MME JOSEPH PERRAUD' × 'BRAZIER') ×
('CHARLES P. KILHAM' × 'CAPUCINE
CHAMBARD')

NATIONAL ROSE SOCIETY CERTIFICATE
OF MERIT 1950

**M**

## 'Mme Driout' *(right)*
### syn. 'Mme Dreout'
OLD, CLIMBING TEA, PINK BLEND,
REPEAT-FLOWERING

Sometimes classed as a Climbing Large-flowered Rose, this
variety has shapely, beautiful
buds that open to flat, quartered
blooms of bright rose (deep red
in the shade) striped carmine;
the striping is more pronounced
in spring. The full, large flowers
are fragrant and repeat throughout spring and summer in
warmer climates. It is a vigorous
shrub that can be easily trained
on a small pergola or a wall with
full sun. The foliage is large and
dark. Those who have grown
this rose for some time say that
it is fussy and needs lots of
attention. It was discovered by
Bolut and Thirat on a visit to
Saint Dizier gardens, home of
Monsieur Driout, mayor of that
city. It is sometimes classified as
a Noisette Rose. **ZONES 5–10.**

THIRAT, FRANCE, 1902

POSSIBLE SPORT OF 'REINE MARIE HENRIETTE'

M

Mail Rose') was introduced in 1921 by the Ketten Brothers of Luxembourg; it is a good free-flowering climber producing an excellent crop in spring and flowering through to autumn. It is rather thorny but disease free. **ZONES 5–10.**

PERNET-DUCHER, FRANCE, 1913

'MME CAROLINE TESTOUT' × LARGE-FLOWERED ROSE

NATIONAL ROSE SOCIETY GOLD MEDAL 1913

### 'Mme Edouard Ory' *(bottom)*
OLD, MOSS, DEEP PINK, REPEAT-FLOWERING

The bright pink, fragrant flowers of this variety are full, globular and medium sized. As they age they fade to pale pink. There is a profuse blooming in late spring, with some further flowering later. It is an upright bush that is full of strong prickles. Moss Roses are actually Centifolia and Damask Roses that have developed a distinctive fragrant moss-like growth on the sepals, adding great elegance to the flower. They come in all colors, and some are repeat-flowering. **ZONES 4–10.**

ROBERT, FRANCE, 1854

PARENTAGE UNKNOWN

### 'Mme Edouard Herriot' *(top)*
syn. 'Daily Mail Rose'
MODERN, LARGE-FLOWERED/HYBRID TEA, ORANGE BLEND, REPEAT-FLOWERING

This rose caused a sensation when it was introduced because of its color. The pointed buds open to flowers that are coral-red, shaded yellow fading to pink, semi-double, large and fragrant. The full blooms are rather loose and quickly lose their color. The foliage is bronze in the early stages of growth and the bush has a spreading habit. Although bred in France and named after the wife of a French statesman, this variety won a competition in England run by the *Daily Mail* newspaper for a rose to be called the 'Daily Mail Rose', and in fact it is still known by that name in England.
**'Climbing Mme Edouard Herriot'**
(syn. 'Climbing Daily

**'Mme Ernst Calvat'** *(right)*
syns 'Mme Ernest Calvat',
'Pink Bourbon'
OLD, BOURBON, MEDIUM PINK,
REPEAT-FLOWERING

This rose has large, cabbage-like
blooms that are pink, shaded
darker pink. They are flat,
quartered, and become blowsy
as they open. There are many
yellow anthers. It does well in
the shade, especially where there
are hot summers, and makes an
excellent cut flower. It also does
well in poor soil, but it needs
to be established before it will
perform at its best; it is subject
to mildew. The arching canes
can reach 6 ft (1.8 m) and are
covered with dark green leaves
that are red underneath. Ernest
Calvat, who died in 1910, was
a glove manufacturer and
amateur horticulturist. This
rose was discovered by the
hybridizer's widow, Mme
Schwartz, who continued her
husband's work and also produced two famous roses: 'Roger
Lambelin' and 'La Tosca'.
**ZONES 4–10.**

SCHWARTZ, FRANCE, 1888

SPORT OF 'MME ISAAC PEREIRE'

**'Mme Fernandel'**  MEIsunaj
*(above)*
syn. 'Fernandel'
MODERN, CLUSTER-FLOWERED/FLORIBUNDA,
DEEP PINK, REPEAT-FLOWERING

Lyon Rose of the Century is an
award that is much sought after,
although it is not as prestigious
as it sounds, for five varieties
are so designated at Lyon every
year. 'Mme Fernandel' was
among them in 1989, and makes
a good item for the garden when
used in beds, borders or as a
hedge. The blooms are neatly
formed, urn shaped when
young, then becoming rounded
with tight centers and finally
cupped as their 30 or so petals
expand. They are deep pink,
verging on light red with a
shining quality, lightly scented,
and appear in small clusters on
firm stems through summer
and autumn. This plant grows
with an upright, bushy habit to
average height or slightly below,
and there is an ample covering
of crisp dark green foliage.
**ZONES 5–9.**

MEILLAND, FRANCE, 1989

PARENTAGE UNKNOWN

BAGATELLE GOLD MEDAL 1988, LYON ROSE
OF THE CENTURY 1989

M

### 'Mme Gabriel Luizet' *(below)*

OLD, HYBRID PERPETUAL,
LIGHT PINK, REPEAT-FLOWERING

Still a popular member of its class, this rose is bright silvery pink, paler at the edges. The pointed buds open to large, double flowers with 34 petals that are sometimes quartered. The plant blooms early and is quite fragrant and floriferous; there may also be later blooms. Stout, strong canes support the 6 ft

(1.8 m) shrub and the attractive foliage serves as a good background for the flowers. It does well in poor soil. This rose should be lightly pruned and shaped. Gabriel Luizet (1794–1872) was an arboriculturist who developed the practice of budding fruit trees for the first time.
**ZONES 5–10.**

LIABAUD, FRANCE, 1877

SEEDLING OF 'JULES MARGOTTIN'

### 'Mme Georges Bruant' *(below)*

MODERN, HYBRID RUGOSA,
WHITE, REPEAT-FLOWERING

There does not seem to be much of the lovely Tea Rose 'Sombreuil' in the make-up of 'Mme Georges Bruant' except for the color of the flowers and the delicacy of the petal texture. The buds are long and pointed, and the white flowers are semi-double, loose in form and are borne in clusters on a thorny, spreading, heavily foliaged shrub. They are fragrant and repeat very well. A few hips are produced but they are not as plentiful as on most other Rugosa roses. The plant makes a thick, impenetrable hedge with the advantage of blooms throughout spring, summer and into autumn. The foliage is healthy.
**ZONES 4–10.**

BRUANT, FRANCE, 1887

ROSA RUGOSA × 'SOMBREUIL'

## 'Mme Georges Delbard' DELadel

*(above)*

syns 'Mme Delbard', 'Mrs G. Delbard'

MODERN, LARGE-FLOWERED/
HYBRID TEA, DARK RED,
REPEAT-FLOWERING

This outstanding rose has dark red flowers with magnificent substance to the broad petals. The large buds open to very big, high-centered flowers with 40 petals. They are suitable for exhibition. There is no fragrance. The stems are very long, and blooms come mainly singly, opening very slowly to full blooms of great intensity of color and durability that keep particularly well when picked. The foliage is large, mid-green and semi-glossy, and the growth is tall and strong. ZONES 5–11.

DELBARD, FRANCE, 1982

('TROPICANA' × 'SAMOURAI') ×
('TROPICANA' × ['ROME GLORY'
× 'IMPECCABLE'])

## 'Mme Grégoire Staechelin' *(below)*

syn. 'Spanish Beauty'

MODERN, LARGE-FLOWERED CLIMBER, PINK BLEND

This is a great rose even though it flowers but once. The long, elegant buds open to soft delicate pink flowers, stained crimson mainly on the back of the petals. They are ruffled, come singly and in small clusters and are fragrant. If spent blooms are not removed, very large pear-shaped fruits are produced that change slowly from green to yellow-gold. It is an excellent pillar rose or can be used to cover an arch where its trusses of pale pink blooms show up well against its dark green foliage. ZONES 5–10.

DOT, SPAIN, 1927

'FRAU KARL DRUSCHKI' × 'CHÂTEAU DE CLOS VOUGEOT'

BAGATELLE GOLD MEDAL 1927, AMERICAN ROSE SOCIETY JOHN COOK
MEDAL 1929, ROYAL HORTICULTURAL SOCIETY AWARD OF GARDEN
MERIT 1993

M

M

### 'Mme Hardy' *(above)*

OLD, DAMASK, WHITE

This is certainly one of the most beautiful whites of the summer-flowering roses. The freely produced flowers appear in early summer and are arranged both in clusters and singly all over the plant for about 3 weeks. They are very fragrant and exquisitely formed, at first cupped and finally opening very flat. The blooms are consistently pure white and each has a central green pip. It is a tall, dense, prickly shrub with dark brownish wood and is generously endowed with soft, light green leaves. Sadly, in some weather conditions the foliage can sometimes be marred by brown blotches (probably scorch marks when hot sun follows rain), but this is by no means a serious fault. It is very easy to grow. **ZONES 4–11.**

HARDY, FRANCE, 1832

PARENTAGE UNKNOWN

ROYAL HORTICULTURAL SOCIETY AWARD OF GARDEN MERIT 1993

## 'Mme Henri Guillot' *(above)*

MODERN, LARGE-FLOWERED/
HYBRID TEA, RED BLEND,
REPEAT-FLOWERING

This early rose makes a good show in spring. The flowers are of a unique blend of orange, coral and red, are double with 25 petals and open very quickly to large, orange, flat flowers of good substance. There is a little fragrance and some rebloom after the spring flush. The rich green foliage is particularly large and extremely glossy. The bush form has lost its vigor, a fault that has occurred in many of the brightly colored roses of the early part of the twentieth century. 'Climbing Mme Henri Guillot' (Meilland, France, 1942) is a climbing form of 'Mme Henri Guillot'. ZONES 5–10.

MALLERIN, FRANCE, 1938

'ROCHEFORT' × SEEDLING OF
ROSA FOETIDA BICOLOR

BAGATELLE GOLD MEDAL 1936,
PORTLAND GOLD MEDAL 1938

## 'Mme Isaac Pereire' *(top right)*

syn. 'Le Bienheureaux de la Salle'

OLD, BOURBON, DEEP PINK,
REPEAT-FLOWERING

This famous rose has enjoyed almost universal praise. The huge, deep rose pink blooms are full and well formed upon opening, later becoming blowsy; a purple tint adds to the charm, especially in autumn. The very fragrant flowers are sometimes cupped and sometimes quartered, and they usually appear in clusters. It is a vigorous shrub to 7 ft (2.1 m) tall, and it is best pegged down or trained on a pillar, where it produces many laterals and more blooms. The long canes are covered with small prickles and deep green leaves. It does well in poor soil and in cool shade where summers are warm, but is subject to mildew. Mme Pereire was a member of a banking family during the reign of Napoleon III. ZONES 5–10.

GARÇON, FRANCE, 1881

PARENTAGE UNKNOWN

ROYAL HORTICULTURAL SOCIETY
AWARD OF GARDEN MERIT 1993

## 'Mme Joseph Schwartz'

syn. 'White Duchesse de Brabant'

OLD, TEA, WHITE,
REPEAT-FLOWERING

Still a popular rose after more than a century, this is one of the best white Teas still in commerce. The pure white blooms have pink overtones and are full, medium sized and cupped. The compact, fragrant, well-formed flowers, which have muddled centers, bloom throughout summer into autumn and are excellent cut flowers. The low-growing shrub has evergreen foliage, likes a cool, sunny position, and is good for container cultivation. It hates wet weather, when it is subject to black spot. ZONES 6–11.

SCHWARTZ, FRANCE, 1880

SPORT OF 'COMTESSE DE
LABARTHE'

M

M

### 'Mme Jules Bouché'
### *(left)*

MODERN, LARGE-FLOWERED/
HYBRID TEA, WHITE,
REPEAT-FLOWERING

This rose can always be
recognized by its zigzag
growth habit, produced
by the stems between
each node turning to
the left and then to the
right. The buds are
slender and dainty
and open to very large
double flowers, with
the centers of the
blooms shading to pale
blush. The strongly
fragrant flowers open
flat like a Tea Rose and
there are many over-
lapping petals, like a
camellia. Growth is tall
and flower production
is very high. There has
been no reduction in
vigor over the years.
ZONES 5–11.

CROIBIER, FRANCE, 1911
'PHARISÄER' × SEEDLING

### 'Mme Jules Gravereaux'   *(left)*

OLD, CLIMBING TEA, APRICOT BLEND, REPEAT-FLOWERING

As a cut flower this rose has no superior. The long
and pointed buds open to very large, very double,
very full flesh-peach blooms that are compact
and sometimes quartered. Yellow overtones are
apparent when the blooms have opened fully. It is
a bushy, lanky plant with lush, large, dark, glossy
foliage that can reach 12 ft (3.5 m) in height and
prefers dry, warm weather. It is subject to mildew.
This rose was named for the wife of an adminis-
trator of a large Paris department store.
ZONES 5–10.

SOUPERT & NOTTING, FRANCE, 1901
'RÊVE D'OR' × 'VISCOUNTESS FOLKESTONE'

## 'Mme Knorr'
*(right)*
syn. 'Mme de Knorr'
OLD, PORTLAND, MEDIUM PINK, REPEAT-FLOWERING

The large, full, flat blooms on this variety are light rose with white undersides and dark centers. They are medium sized and semi-double, rather loose in form and have a very sweet fragrance. There is some repeat-flowering after the summer flush. It does well in poor soil and is a good, small hedging plant because its strong fragrance will permeate the planting area. The healthy and abundant matt green foliage provides a strong background to the flowers.

Portlands are also known as Damask Perpetuals; there were 150 varieties at the height of their popularity between 1800 and 1850. **ZONES 5–11.**

VERDIER, FRANCE, 1855

PARENTAGE UNKNOWN

ROYAL HORTICULTURAL SOCIETY AWARD OF GARDEN MERIT 1993

## 'Mme Laurette Messimy' *(below)*
syn. 'Laurette Messimy'
OLD, CHINA, DEEP PINK, REPEAT-FLOWERING

This attractive rose has long, salmon-colored buds that turn into rose pink blooms with yellow centers. The loose, semi-double, fragrant flowers are large. It does well in cool summers, as the flowers fade in hot weather. It is a bushy, upright plant covered with many gray-green, glossy leaves. It is an excellent bedding plant, is suitable as a container plant, and is full of blooms from late spring to autumn. **ZONES 6–11.**

GUILLOT, FRANCE, 1887

'RIVAL DE PAESTUM' × 'MME FALCOT'

M

M

### 'Mme Lauriol de Barny' *(above)*

OLD, BOURBON, LIGHT PINK,
REPEAT-FLOWERING

As a cut flower, this
has to be the most
gorgeous garden variety.
Blooming earlier than
any of its clan, this rose
has silvery pink, full,
quartered blooms that
are large and very flat.
The heavy, drooping
sprays of sweetly
scented flowers on long
stems are frequently
the target of photog-
raphers. The arching
canes are covered with
smooth leaves and,
if pegged down, the
result is a bounty crop
of blooms. This is also
a good candidate for

a pillar as it easily
reaches 7 ft (2.1 m) in
two years. It does well
in the shade and in
poor soil. ZONES 5–10.

TROUILLARD, FRANCE, 1868

HYBRID OF *ROSA ARVENSIS*

### 'Mme Legras de St Germain' *(below left)*

OLD, ALBA, WHITE

The flowers of this rose
appear in clusters. Each
bloom is cup shaped at
first, opening to flat,
perfectly formed, very
double, cushion-like
rosettes that are about
2 in (5 cm) across.
There is a lovely scent.
The color is glowing
pure white with soft
lemony yellow centers.
'Mme Legras de St
Germain' can grow to
8 ft (2.5 m) tall in good
soil, and it is made up
of long, light to mid-
green, almost thornless
branches with plentiful
soft, light green foliage.
Clearly related to the
Damasks, this out-
standing rose is easy to
grow. Although like
many white, fully
double roses it dislikes
the rain, it is still
worthy of a place in
the garden as either a
free-standing shrub or
a climber. ZONES 4–10.

1846

PARENTAGE UNKNOWN

M

## 'Mme Léon Pain'
*(above)*

**MODERN, LARGE-FLOWERED/
HYBRID TEA, PINK BLEND,
REPEAT-FLOWERING**

This rose produces
pointed buds that open
to flowers of flesh pink
with an orange-yellow
center and salmon-pink
undersides to the petals.
The flowers are double
with 45 petals and are
fragrant. The full
blooms lose their color
rather quickly. 'Mme
Léon Pain' has a bushy
and vigorous growth
habit. **ZONES 5–11.**

GUILLOT, FRANCE, 1904

'MME CAROLINE TESTOUT' ×
'SOUVENIR DE CATHERINE
GUILLOT'

## 'Mme Lombard'
*(right)*
syns 'Mme Lambard',
'Mme Lambart'

**OLD, TEA, ORANGE-PINK,
REPEAT-FLOWERING**

This rose is often called
the 'cemetery rose'
because it is found in
cemeteries in great
numbers; it has an
amazing ability to stay
alive in desperate
situations. The long,
crimson buds open
to very double, large,
globular, rosy salmon
blooms with dark
centers. The cupped,
fragrant flowers vary
in color as they age,
deepening when fully
open and in the shade.

The blooming period
extends from late
spring until the first
frost in warm areas.
The flowers are best
in autumn when the
colors are richer. It
can be pruned to 5 ft
(1.5 m) or be allowed

to ramble to twice that
height. The leathery,
dark green leaves hide
numerous hooked
prickles, and in autumn
there is a large crop of
red hips. **ZONES 6–11.**

LACHARME, FRANCE, 1878

SEEDLING OF 'MME DE TARTAS'

### 'Mme Louis Laperrière' *(right)*

MODERN, LARGE-FLOWERED/
HYBRID TEA, MEDIUM RED,
REPEAT-FLOWERING

Still one of the best
dark red bedding roses,
this variety has very
well-formed flowers
of medium size that
have 40–50 petals and
are a rich dark crimson-
red. They have the
wonderful fragrance
of 'Crimson Glory'.
The abundant foliage
is dark green and disease
free on a bush that
grows to a moderate
size. There are many
flowers produced
continuously. Its bushy
habit lends itself to
use as a standard.
**ZONES 5–10.**

LAPERRIÈRE, FRANCE, 1951

'CRIMSON GLORY' × SEEDLING

BAGATELLE GOLD MEDAL 1950,
NATIONAL ROSE SOCIETY
CERTIFICATE OF MERIT 1952

### 'Mme Louis Lévêque' *(right)*

OLD, MOSS, MEDIUM PINK,
REPEAT-FLOWERING

The buds of this
rose are large, round
and sparsely mossed
and open to large,
consistently silvery
pink flowers of superb
quality, especially in
dry weather. The
blooms are packed
with crumpled petals;
some can attain a
diameter of 4 in
(10 cm). They are
richly endowed with
scent, and flowers

continue to appear
well into autumn. The
abundant foliage is
large, rich dark green
and smooth on an up-
right plant that grows

to some 4 ft (1.2 m)
high. The stems have
few thorns and little
or no moss. This
aristocratic rose is
unrivalled among the

paler colored Moss
Roses for charm and
general good behavior.
**ZONES 5–10.**

LÉVÊQUE, FRANCE, 1898

PARENTAGE UNKNOWN

## 'Mme Marie Curie'
*(right)*

syn. 'Québec'

MODERN, LARGE-FLOWERED/
HYBRID TEA, DEEP YELLOW,
REPEAT-FLOWERING

This was one of the earliest roses to be patented in the USA. The high-centered and well-formed flowers, which open from very attractive, long, pointed buds, are a rich yellow and contain 25 petals. They are of moderate size and have a slight fragrance and retain their color well. The foliage is dark green and healthy on a vigorous, compact bush that blooms profusely. There are no disease problems. This rose was named after Madame Curie, who was awarded the Nobel Prize for Physics, jointly with Pierre Curie and Antoine Henri Becquerel for the discovery of radio-activity, and later the Nobel Prize for Chemistry (1911) for the discovery of radium. ZONES 5–11.

GAUJARD, FRANCE, 1943

PARENTAGE UNKNOWN

ALL-AMERICA ROSE SELECTION
1944

## 'Mme Pierre Oger'
*(right)*

OLD, BOURBON, PINK BLEND,
REPEAT-FLOWERING

Its porcelain-like blooms have made this one of the most popular of the Old Garden Roses. The blush, creamy white blooms, with a lilac reverse, are cupped and loose and have dappled petals. The colors intensify in the sun. It has a long blooming season that extends from spring to the first frost. Narrow, upright branches support the heavy, delicately scented blooms. The abundant, light green leaves are oval and pointed, and dark prickles line the stalks. This is an ideal candidate for a container or for the back of a border. ZONES 4–10.

OGER, FRANCE, 1878

SPORT OF 'LA REINE VICTORIA'

### 'Mme Scipion Cochet' *(below left)*
OLD, TEA, PINK BLEND, REPEAT-FLOWERING

Too many hybridizers named a rose after this lady, and as a result the two Teas and one Hybrid Perpetual are often confused with one another. This fragrant rose has ovoid buds that open to pale pink blooms that turn white with a yellow center. They are full and tulip shaped and appear on erect stems. The center petals of the very double blooms are rather blowsy. It is one of the most floriferous Teas, blooming constantly in warm climates. A lanky shrub, it has thick, glossy leaves and many prickles and is a good container plant, as it rarely gets larger than 3 ft (1 m). It was named after the wife of a famous breeder in Grisy-Suisnes, France.
**ZONES 5–10.**

BERNAIX, FRANCE, 1872

'ANNA OLIVIER' × 'COMTESSE DE BRABANT'

### 'Mme Plantier'
*(above)*
OLD, ALBA, WHITE

The fragrant flowers of this rose are borne in large clusters. They are creamy at first, becoming mostly pure white with a little green pip in the center. It is a vigorous shrub or climber, sometimes classified as a Damask. As a climber it can attain a height of at least 20 ft (6 m), but it is more commonly seen as a relaxed shrub to about 10 ft (3 m) high. The gray-green stems are long, arching and almost thornless, and the grayish leaves are soft to touch. Unfortunately the individual blooms can easily shatter in the wind, but this is a minor fault.
**ZONES 4–10.**

PLANTIER, FRANCE, 1835

THOUGHT TO BE *ROSA ALBA* × *R. MOSCHATA*

## 'Mme Victor Verdier' *(top)*

OLD, HYBRID PERPETUAL, MEDIUM RED, REPEAT-FLOWERING

An outstanding cut flower, this rose is 3 in (8 cm) across when in full bloom. The clear crimson, double blooms are large, with 75 petals, flat and cupped. The outer petals are larger than the inner ones, and the blooms appear in clusters during summer and autumn. The second crop of blooms is considered more handsome. Attractive spring foliage fills the long canes, and there are some prickles. Disbudding of the shrub carefully in spring will increase the beauty of the bush and the flowers. ZONES 5–10.

VERDIER, FRANCE, 1863

'SENATEUR VAISE' × SEEDLING

## 'Mme Violet' *(below)*

MODERN, LARGE-FLOWERED/ HYBRID TEA, MAUVE, REPEAT-FLOWERING

The flowers of this rose are large, double and deep mauve. Flower production is average and the repeat cycle is rather slow. The blooms have a pleasant perfume. It has dark green, plentiful foliage and grows to medium height. 'Mme Violet' is not known in many countries but is a welcome addition to the mauve varieties. ZONES 5–11.

TERANISHI, JAPAN, 1981

(['LADY' × 'STERLING SILVER'] × ['LADY' × 'STERLING SILVER']) × SELF

M

### 'Mme Wagram, Comtesse de Turenne' *(right)*

OLD, TEA, PINK BLEND, REPEAT-FLOWERING

This popular Tea Rose has very large, ovoid buds that open to satiny pink blooms that turn a rosy red with a yellow base. The full, large flowers are 4–5 in (10–12 cm) across and have a red reverse on the petals. When open, the fragrant, long-lasting blooms have a rather blowsy form. It is a healthy, bushy plant with superb dark foliage and small prickles, that likes hot weather. It reaches 3 ft (1 m) at maturity, making an ideal candidate as a container plant, is strongly resistant to disease and will bloom from late spring until autumn. ZONES 6–10.

BERNAIX, FRANCE, 1894

PARENTAGE UNKNOWN

M

### 'Mme Zöetmans' *(right)*

OLD, DAMASK, WHITE

The lovely flowers of this rose are very full and fragrant. They are blush pink at first, paling to milky white, usually with a button of incurling petals in the center and finishing rather flat and cushion-like. Each flower is about 2½ in (6 cm) across and arranged as one of a small cluster, appearing in abundance in early summer for a relatively short season. It is a compact shrub that grows to about 4 ft (1.2 m) and has dark green, fairly thorny wood and copious bright mid-green foliage. It is probably closely related to the Gallicas. This is a first-class variety, not least for its tidy disposition as a shrub. ZONES 4–10.

MAREST, FRANCE, 1830

PARENTAGE UNKNOWN

## 'Madeleine Selzer'

syns 'Mme Selzer',
'Yellow Tausendschön'

OLD, RAMBLER, LIGHT YELLOW

Pale lemon blooms
that fade to white as
they age appear in
trusses on this rampant
Rambler. The flowers
are fully double and
fragrant and make a
strong impression
when cascading down
a trellis or tree during
their summer flower-
ing. It has bronze green
foliage in spring and
few prickles, and
reaches 10 ft (3 m)
in several years.
'Madeleine Selzer' is
a good Climber or
Rambler for a small
garden, but it does
need strong support
when mature. Ludwig
Walter of Severne in
Alsace, France, was an
amateur rose breeder.
ZONES 5–11.

WALTER, FRANCE, 1926

'TAUSENDSCHÖN' ×
'MRS AARON WARD'

## 'Mlle Franziska Krüger'

syn. 'Grand Duc
Heritier de
Luxembourg'

OLD, TEA, ORANGE-PINK,
REPEAT-FLOWERING

When Nabonnand
crossed two Tea Roses,
he produced this popu-
lar, floriferous rose that
blooms well in a warm
site. The copper-yellow
and pink fragrant
blooms open as cups
and then reflex into
half globes. The large
flowers have white
outer petals and a green
eye. If grown where the
blooms can be seen
from below, it is an
excellent climber that
can reach 7 ft (2.2 m)
on a wall. It also makes
a compact shrub if
pruned regularly. The
foliage is plentiful and
leathery with dark red
at the leaf edges. This
plant is highly disease
resistant, although the
blooms ball in wet
weather. ZONES 5–10.

NABONNAND, FRANCE, 1880

'CATHERINE MERMET' ×
'GÉNÉRAL SCHABLIKINE'

## 'Maestro'  MACkinju, MACinju  (above)

MODERN, LARGE-FLOWERED/HYBRID TEA, RED BLEND,
REPEAT-FLOWERING

This variety has oval buds that open to medium
red flowers with a painting of white washed
through the petals. The undersides of the petals
are a light silvery red. The double blooms have
28 petals and are borne singly and in small
clusters. There is a slight fragrance. The flowers
are very variable in color—in hot weather it is
almost pure red, but in cooler conditions the
hand painting is much more evident. The red
shade can be quite smoky, which adds greatly
to the effect. The foliage is matt olive green and
lush. This is a most interesting and unique rose.
ZONES 5–10.

MCGREDY, NEW ZEALAND, 1980

SEEDLING OF 'PICASSO' × SEEDLING

M

## 'Magali'

MODERN, LARGE-FLOWERED/HYBRID TEA, DEEP PINK,
REPEAT-FLOWERING

This rose carries deep carmine flowers: a color
that does not fade in the heat but is sometimes
considered rather harsh, which may be the cause
of its lack of popularity. The blooms are double
with 35–40 petals, of medium size and slightly
fragrant. There is good bloom production, and the
repeat-bloom is quick. The foliage is abundant,
mid-green and leathery on a vigorous and upright
plant. **ZONES 5–11.**

MALLERIN, FRANCE, 1952

'CHARLES P. KILHAM' × 'BRAZIER'

## 'Magenta'   *(below)*
syn. 'Kordes' Magenta'

MODERN, LARGE-FLOWERED/HYBRID TEA, MAUVE, REPEAT-FLOWERING

This spreading grower carries the most unusual
flowers of rosy lavender with overtones of brown.
Although they fade to a slate-mauve, they are
attractive at all times; some of the subtle color
of 'Lavender Pinocchio' can be seen in the open
flower. The full flowers occur in large clusters
on tall, arching growth and, like most mauve
roses, are very fragrant. The foliage is dark green,
leathery and profuse, and the growth is vigorous.
'Magenta' seems to prefer cool climates; the old
wood can burn in summer in hot climates if
exposed to the sun. **ZONES 4–11.**

KORDES, GERMANY, 1954

UNKNOWN YELLOW CLUSTER-FLOWERED ROSE ×
'LAVENDER PINOCCHIO'

M

M

## 'Maggie Barry'

MACoborn *(above)*

syn. 'Maggy Barry'

MODERN, LARGE-FLOWERED/
HYBRID TEA, PINK BLEND,
REPEAT-FLOWERING

This rose from Sam
McGredy is named
after a popular tele-
vision newsreader in
New Zealand. The bush
produces a continuous
supply of very shapely
buds in a distinct coral-
orange color. As they
open, they change to
coral-salmon and the
two colors combine
in the open blooms
to very good effect.
Growth is upright,
bushy and vigorous
and the plant is very
free flowering and
disease free. This is
an excellent rose for
bedding as the color is
bright but not harsh.
ZONES 5–10.

MCGREDY, NEW ZEALAND, 1993

'LOUISE GARDENER' ×
'WEST COAST'

## 'Magic Carpet'

JAClover *(top)*

MODERN, GROUND COVER,
MAUVE, REPEAT-FLOWERING

This rose has small,
semi-double lavender
flowers with a spicy
fragrance. It is a vig-
orous plant that grows
18–24 in (45–60 cm)
high and twice as
broad. The foliage
is dark green, glossy
and very resistant to
disease. This is an
attractive garden rose
because the repeat-
flowering is good and
the foliage is held well
into winter. It is ideal
for growing over rocks
or low walls, or for
mass planting in more
difficult positions
where other roses
would not prosper.
ZONES 5–10.

ZARY/WARRINER, USA, 1992

'IMMENSEE' × 'CLASS ACT'

ROSE OF THE YEAR 1996

### 'Magic Carrousel' MORrousel *(above)*

MODERN, MINIATURE, RED BLEND, REPEAT-FLOWERING

'Magic Carrousel' holds a treasured place in Miniature Rose history as the first of many varieties to attain Award of Excellence status. The double flowers are creamy white with a vivid red edge and a well-formed high center, a feature cloned from the Cluster-flowered parent. This striking color combination took the rose-buying public by storm when it was introduced and its popularity has not diminished. When the blooms are fully open the plant is at its best, displaying florets with bright golden stamens. Small, glossy green foliage covers this vigorous and bushy plant. ZONES 5–11.

MOORE, USA, 1972

'LITTLE DARLING' × 'WESTMONT'

AMERICAN ROSE SOCIETY AWARD OF EXCELLENCE 1975

### 'Magic Dragon' *(top right)*

MODERN, CLIMBING MINIATURE, DARK RED, REPEAT-FLOWERING

This is one of the few dark red Climbing Miniatures. The short, pointed buds open to dark red, double and decorative flowers. The foliage is small and leathery, and the plant is vigorous with an upright growth habit. The flowers tend to appear in small clusters with a loose form, but the plant is slow to repeat. The canes can be trained over either a fence, a wall or a trellis— good coverage might be slow to establish, but within a few years the canopy is dense and compact. It is a shame that this rose has been all but forgotten. ZONES 5–11.

MOORE, USA, 1969

([*ROSA WICHURANA* × 'FLORADORA'] × SEEDLING) × 'LITTLE BUCKAROO'

### 'Magic Meidiland' MEIbonrib
syn. 'Magic Meillandecor'

MODERN, GROUND COVER, MEDIUM PINK, REPEAT-FLOWERING

This is a Ground Cover Rose in a new color. The flowers, which are very double, small and deep magenta pink, are produced in clusters of 3–7 blooms. There is a spicy freesia-like fragrance according to Louise Coleman of Heirloom Roses in the USA. The very glossy foliage is bronze when young and growth is very spreading, to some 10 ft (3 m) across. It flowers for a very long period and is exceptionally disease free. ZONES 5–10.

MEILLAND, FRANCE, 1993

*ROSA SEMPERVIRENS* × ('MILROSE' × 'BONICA')

ANERKANNTE DEUTSCHE ROSE 1995

### 'Magna Charta'
syns 'Casper', 'Magna Carta'

OLD, HYBRID PERPETUAL, MEDIUM PINK, REPEAT-FLOWERING

This rose bears clusters of bright pink blooms with overtones of red. They are double, globular and quite large, and are held upright. Yielding a rich scent, the flowers cover the bush in summer with some autumn rebloom. Heavy, dark, glossy green leaves cover the vigorous bush, which usually reaches 10 ft (3 m) if left unpruned. There are fearsome prickles on an otherwise compact, erect, tidy shrub that does well in poor soil. Unfortunately, the blooms will ball in wet weather, and it is subject to mildew and black spot. 'Magna Charta' was named for one of the most important documents in English social and legal history. ZONES 5–11.

PAUL, UK, 1876

PARENTAGE UNKNOWN

M

### 'Magnifica'

syns *Rosa rugosa*
'Magnifica',
*R. eglanteria duplex*
'Weston', *R. rubiginosa*
*magnifica*

OLD, SWEET BRIAR, MAUVE

The cupped, purple-
red, semi-double
blooms of this variety
have white centers and
prominent stamens.
Both the flowers and
the foliage are fragrant,
although the leaves are
not as heavily scented
as expected of a Sweet
Briar. It is a hardy
shrub with dark, dense
foliage that will reach
6 ft (2 m) at maturity.
It does well in poor soil
and is a good choice for
a woodland garden or
for a hedge. Both the
flowers and bush do
well in the shade.
ZONES 4–11.

HESSE, GERMANY, 1916

SEEDLING OF 'LUCY ASHTON'

### 'Maiden's Blush'

syn. 'Small Maiden's
Blush'

OLD, ALBA, WHITE

This tall and upright
shrub bears soft,
double, globular,
medium-sized flowers
that are blush in color.
It does not repeat-
flower. It is a fine shrub
suitable for cottage
gardens. The French
called it 'Cuisse de
Nymphe'. There are
several variants of this
rose; for a deeper
colored one, the
French added the
qualification 'emué'.
They are all sweetly
scented. ZONES 4–11.

KEW GARDENS, UK, 1797

*ROSA ALBA* × *R. CENTIFOLIA*

### 'Maigold'  *(below)*

syn. 'Maygold'

MODERN, MODERN SHRUB,
DEEP YELLOW

This variety can be
used as a shrub or as
a climbing rose. The
flowers appear very
early, which is an
inheritance from
'Frühlingstag' or
'Frühlingsgold'. The
semi-double blooms
are a rich orange-
bronze, and have only
14 petals. They are
large, 4 in (10 cm)
across, cupped and
very fragrant. The
upright growth is
very thorny, and there
are next to no flowers
after the initial burst.
The glossy foliage can
be susceptible to black
spot. This rose holds
its color best in cool
climates; it is fleeting
but lovely in warm
areas and heralds
the rose season.
ZONES 4–11.

KORDES, GERMANY, 1953

'POULSEN'S PINK' ×
'FRÜHLINGSTAG' OR 'MCGREDY'S
WONDER' × 'FRÜHLINGSGOLD'

NATIONAL ROSE SOCIETY TRIAL
GROUND CERTIFICATE

M

### 'Majorette' MEIpiess *(right)*
### syn. 'Majorette 86'

MODERN, MINIATURE, MEDIUM RED, REPEAT-FLOWERING

Wonderful cardinal red flowers with yellowish white centers are borne on this rose in small clusters against a backdrop of glossy green, healthy foliage. The florets can be larger in cool climates, making the rose a candidate for classification as a Patio Rose. The clusters are supported by strong, straight stems. The repeat-bloom cycle time is fast (about 23 days) and the color is weather-proof in most climates. ZONES 5–11.

MEILLAND, FRANCE, 1986

'MAGIC CARROUSEL' × ('GRUMPY' × 'SCARLETTA')

GLASGOW SILVER MEDAL 1992

M

### 'Malaga' *(left)*

MODERN, LARGE-FLOWERED CLIMBER, DEEP PINK, REPEAT-FLOWERING

The blooms of this cultivar are reddish pink, with about 36 large petals that open from neat buds into flowers of somewhat ragged form. They are often carried in short-stemmed clusters, sometimes singly, and have a good fragrance. This makes a fine pillar rose—also very suitable for a wall or fence—repeatedly flowering through summer and autumn. 'Malaga' grows up to average extent with an upright, free-branching habit that is well furnished with glossy dark green foliage. ZONES 4–9.

MCGREDY, UK, 1971

('HAMBURGER PHOENIX' × 'DANSE DU FEU') × 'COPENHAGEN'

M

### 'Maman Cochet' *(above)*

OLD, TEA, PINK BLEND, REPEAT-FLOWERING

This popular rose has pointed buds that open to light pink blooms with a darker center and a yellow base. The double, high-centered flowers are large, to 4 in (10 cm) across, and cupped. The center petals form a rosette; in humid weather the thin petals ball. Some say it has a fresh Tea scent, while others say it is orris scented. 'Maman Cochet' does well in poor soil and is suitable as a container plant. Olive green, leathery leaves line the canes, which are covered with hooked prickles. If left unpruned it will reach 7 ft (2.1 m). It is an excellent cut flower. **'Climbing Maman Cochet'** (Upton, 1909) easily reaches 12 ft (3.5 m) in height. **ZONES 5–10.**

COCHET, FRANCE, 1893

'MARIE VAN HOUTTE' × 'MME LOMBARD'

## 'Mandarin'

**MODERN, CLUSTER-FLOWERED/FLORIBUNDA, MEDIUM RED, REPEAT-FLOWERING**

This is one of the many roses bred by Gene Boerner, who was affectionately known as 'Papa Floribunda' because of the number of first class Cluster-flowered Roses he bred. These were released by the firm Jackson and Perkins. The buds of 'Mandarin' are ovoid, and the semi-double flowers are a lively mandarin red. They have 18 petals, are high centered, occur in large clusters and are fragrant. The foliage is healthy and glossy on a vigorous and upright plant. The flower production is good. 'Mandarin' is an excellent rose for hedges and for borders but it is not seen much nowadays. **ZONES 5–10.**

BOERNER, USA, 1951

SPORT OF 'LILETTE MALLERIN' × SEEDLING OF A RED CLUSTER-FLOWERED ROSE

## 'Mandarin'   KORcelin   (below)

**MODERN, MINIATURE, ORANGE BLEND, REPEAT-FLOWERING**

The attractive orange-pink, double blooms of this rose give a classic cupped shape when they burst into flower. They become much flatter as they open and the outer petals gradually lose their orange tint, becoming much pinker. They are accentuated by the very dark green foliage. **ZONES 5–10.**

KORDES, GERMANY, 1987

PARENTAGE UNKNOWN

GLASGOW GOLD MEDAL 1994, DUBLIN CERTIFICATE OF MERIT

M

### 'Manettii' *(bottom)*

**syns** *Rosa manettii,*
*R. × noisettiana manettii*

OLD, NOISETTE, LIGHT PINK

This attractive shrub
was found at the famous
rose garden in Monza,
Italy, by the director
Signor Manetti. The
delicate pink flowers
with a purplish tinge
fill this vigorous shrub,
which is often found in
cemeteries. The leaves
are deeply scented and
appear on smooth, dark
brown, gracefully arch-
ing canes. 'Manettii'
is easy to propagate
from cuttings, and the
plant suckers; it is still
sometimes used for
grafting and it began
life as a rootstock for
other roses. It may be
a hybrid of 'Slater's
Crimson China' and
*Rosa moschata.*
**ZONES 4–11.**

MANETTI, ITALY, 1820s;
INTRODUCED BY RIVERS, UK, 1835

PARENTAGE UNKNOWN

### 'Mannheim' *(top)*

MODERN, MODERN SHRUB,
DARK RED, REPEAT-FLOWERING

This is one of Kordes'
many shrub roses of
the 1950s and 1960s
that he named after
German cities.
'Mannheim' produces
a continuous display of
double crimson flowers
in large clusters on an
upright bushy plant.

The repeat-flowering
is good. This rose,
which could equally be
classed as a Cluster-
flowered Rose, is
healthy and has leathery
dark green foliage.
It is a good rose for
hedges and for use
among perennials and
shrubs in a mixed
border. **ZONES 4–11.**

KORDES, GERMANY, 1958

'RUDOLPH TIMM' × 'FANAL'

M

## 'Manou Meilland'  MEItulimon  *(above)*

MODERN, LARGE-FLOWERED/HYBRID TEA, MAUVE/DEEP PINK, REPEAT-FLOWERING

This rose is like 'Baronne Edmond de Rothschild', with the same rich cyclamen pink flowers with silver undersides, but the growth is much shorter and more spreading. The large, double flowers have 50 petals, are fully cupped and appear in small clusters; they last very well without losing color. The abundant foliage is very dark green and glossy. 'Manou Meilland' makes an excellent border with 'Baronne de Rothschild', the only two roses of this color. Both are very popular. **ZONES 5–11.**

MEILLAND, FRANCE, 1980

('BARONNE EDMOND DE ROTHSCHILD' × 'BARONNE EDMOND DE ROTHSCHILD') × ('MA FILLE' × 'LOVE SONG')

PARIS GOLD MEDAL 1977, MADRID GOLD MEDAL 1978, NEW ZEALAND GOLD MEDAL 1980

## 'Manning's Blush'

OLD, SWEET BRIAR, WHITE, REPEAT-FLOWERING

The white blooms of this rose are flushed pink and open flat. The fragrant, double blooms have many petals, and the leaves are also fragrant. Like most Sweet Briar Roses, this one will bloom early in spring and have some repeat-bloom in autumn. It is a dense, stalwart shrub covered with small leaves that line the arching canes. It does well in poor soil, and reaches 5 ft (1.5 m) if left unpruned. This is a good candidate for the wild garden and is equally happy in the sun or shade. It is strongly disease resistant. **ZONES 4–11.**

PRE-1799

PARENTAGE UNKNOWN

## 'Many Happy Returns' HARwanted *(right)*
syn. 'Prima'

MODERN, MODERN SHRUB,
PINK BLEND/LIGHT PINK,
REPEAT-FLOWERING

This spreading and bushy rose bears large clusters of semi-double, soft pink flowers that last well. The mid-green foliage acts as a foil to the pale flowers. If the spent blooms are not removed, a large crop of roundish bright red hips are produced; these can look very effective with the autumn flowers. The flower production is very high, blooms being produced over a particularly long period. Its disease resistance is astonishing. This is a good rose for use with perennials and bulbs in a mixed border, where the flowers can show their unsophisticated charm.
ZONES 5–10.

HARKNESS, UK, 1991

'HERBSTFEUER' × 'PEARL DRIFT'

COURTRAI SILVER MEDAL 1987,
GENEVA GOLD MEDAL AND
PRIZE 1987, MONZA SILVER
MEDAL AND PRIZE 1987, ROYAL
NATIONAL ROSE SOCIETY TRIAL
GROUND CERTIFICATE 1988

### 'Marbrée' *(above)*

OLD, PORTLAND, RED BLEND,
REPEAT-FLOWERING

The marbled flowers of this rose come in sizeable clusters on longish stems. They are almost fully double and as much as 3 in (8 cm) across, with each large, purple-crimson petal smudged or speckled soft pink. When fully open, an array of yellow stamens show through to effect. After the first generous flush of flowers in mid-summer, this rose takes a little rest before blooming again in early autumn. The fragrance is of attar. It is tall for a Portland, and has ample, dark green, long, pointed foliage. It can be used in the border or as a hedge. It is a healthy and reliable landscaping plant.
ZONES 5–10.

MOREAU & ROBERT, FRANCE,
1858

PARENTAGE UNKNOWN

M

M

'Marcel Bourgouin' *(above)*
syn. 'Le Jacobin'

OLD, GALLICA, MAUVE

The rich red velvet blooms of this rose age to
gray-violet; the undersides of the petals are much
paler. The somewhat flat flowers, which appear in
early summer, are loosely double and blowsy, and
are at their best after fully opening. The fragrance
is very rich. The foliage is dark and velvety on an
erect shrub that will reach 5 ft (1.5 m) in height.
It likes a rich soil. Those who have grown this
rose say it is rather temperamental and needs
cosseting, but it is effective as a hedge and
tolerates some shade. **ZONES 4–10.**

CARBOEUF, FRANCE, 1899

SEEDLING OF 'BLANCHE MOREAU'

'Märchenland'
syn. 'Exception'

MODERN, CLUSTER-FLOWERED/FLORIBUNDA, ORANGE BLEND,
REPEAT-FLOWERING

This rose bears lovely rose-colored flowers tinted
with salmon. The semi-double blooms have
18 petals and come in large clusters of up to 40.
The large heads of fragrant flowers are quite eye-
catching in spring, and there is repeat-bloom in
summer and autumn. The foliage is dark green
and plentiful on a plant with a vigorous and
upright growth habit. 'Märchenland' makes an
excellent hedge or border and can be used to great
effect with perennial plants in mixed borders or
in shrubberies. **ZONES 5–10.**

TANTAU, GERMANY, 1951

'SWANTJE' × 'HAMBURG'

NATIONAL ROSE SOCIETY TRIAL GROUND CERTIFICATE 1952

M

### 'Marchesa Boccella' (above)

syns 'Jacques Cartier', 'Marquise Boccella', 'Marquise Boçella'

OLD, HYBRID PERPETUAL, LIGHT PINK, REPEAT-FLOWERING

The flowers of this rose develop from firm buds with feathery sepals and are borne in tight clusters; they open to fully double and quartered flowers, often with button eyes. They are up to 3 in (8 cm) across and are soft pink. The very fragrant blooms are produced in succession from mid-summer to late autumn. It is an upright, sturdy shrub to 4 ft (1.2 m) high, occasionally throwing up a taller shoot to 5 ft (1.5 m) or more. The stems are stout and strong and there are ample thorns. The foliage is light green when young, deepening to a blue-green with age; it is sometimes crinkly. This excellent rose makes both a good bedding variety and a fine hedge. In the USA it is sold as 'Jacques Cartier', but it must be exhibited at rose shows there as 'Marchesa Boccella'. Most authorities now believe 'Jacques Cartier' is the same rose as 'Marchesa Boccella'. **ZONES 4–9.**

DESPREZ, FRANCE, 1842

PARENTAGE UNKNOWN

### 'Marchioness of Londonderry'

OLD, HYBRID PERPETUAL, LIGHT PINK, REPEAT-FLOWERING

This rose is ivory white suffused with pink. The 50-petalled, cupped, full blooms are high centered, large, globular and fragrant. The flowers, which are carried on erect stalks, have large, thick, reflexed petals and look very much like Large-flowered Roses. This is a strong shrub covered with large, dull green leaves that will reach 6 ft (2 m) at maturity. The bush responds well to nourishment with good repeat-bloom. This rose makes a superb cut flower. **ZONES 5–10.**

DICKSON, UK, 1893

SEEDLING OF 'BARONNE ADOLPHE DE ROTHSCHILD'

### 'Maréchal Davoust'
*(right)*
syn. 'Maréchal Davout'

OLD, MOSS, MEDIUM PINK

The highly scented blooms of 'Maréchal Davoust' are crimson, deepening to almost purple. The flowers are packed with petals, each with a softer colored underside which, when reflexed, gives an overall mottled effect. It flowers freely during summer and is a disease-resistant shrub of sturdy, relatively tidy stature to some 5 ft (1.5 m) high in good soil. The stems are covered with brownish purple stubble, and the dark green foliage is a little coarse. It makes an effective hedge as it does well in poor soil, and it can also be pruned as a container plant. ZONES 4–11.

ROBERT, FRANCE, 1853

PARENTAGE UNKNOWN

**M**

### 'Maréchal Niel'
*(above)*

OLD, NOISETTE, MEDIUM YELLOW, REPEAT-FLOWERING

This popular rose has large, golden yellow blooms that appear in clusters on weak stems, so they are best grown where they can be seen from below. It does well on a trellis or pergola. The blooms are strongly Tea scented and make excellent cut flowers. It is used mostly as a climber and it has soft, dark green leaves, smooth bark and many dark red, hooked prickles. It does well in partial shade, but one must have patience with this beauty. Henri Pradel of Montauban, France, made customers buy 12 other plants before he would give them this rose, as it was in such demand. It was named for a French general, minister of war for Napoleon III. ZONES 6–11.

PRADEL, FRANCE, 1864

SEEDLING OF 'ISABELLA GRAY'

## 'Margaret' *(right)*

MODERN, LARGE-FLOWERED/
HYBRID TEA, PINK BLEND,
REPEAT-FLOWERING

'Margaret' is still a good garden rose even after over 40 years in commerce. The buds are large and well formed and open to well-shaped, long-lasting very double blooms. They are slightly globular, rose pink with silvery pink undersides and are very fragrant. The flower production is excellent and there are no disease problems. The plant, which is vigorous and has ample foliage, is a good bedding rose or it can be used as a hedge or border. ZONES 5–11.

DICKSON, UK, 1954

SEEDLING OF 'MAY WETTERN' ×
'SOUVENIR DE DENIER VAN
DER GON'

NATIONAL ROSE SOCIETY GOLD
MEDAL 1954

M

## 'Margaret Merril'

HARkuly *(above right)*

MODERN, CLUSTER-FLOWERED/
FLORIBUNDA, WHITE,
REPEAT-FLOWERING

This is a remarkable rose, as its many awards testify. The double, high-centered, white flowers have a faint blush tint in the center. There are 28 petals. It is large for a Cluster-flowered Rose, being up to 4 in (10 cm) across. The petals have very heavy substance and are very fragrant. The abundant foliage is big and glossy and the leaves come close to the bloom, giving a high-shouldered effect that shows the crisp flowers to perfection. 'Margaret Merril' is at its best in a cool climate but will tolerate a wide range of climates, and is a superb bedding rose with no disease problems. Flower production is exceptionally high on short to medium-length stems and repeat-bloom is quite remarkable. ZONES 5–11.

HARKNESS, UK, 1978

('RUDOLPH TIMM' ×
'DEDICATION') × 'PASCALI'

GENEVA GOLD MEDAL 1978, MONZA
GOLD MEDAL 1978, ROME GOLD
MEDAL 1978, ROYAL NATIONAL
ROSE SOCIETY EDLAND FRAGRANCE
AWARD 1978, NEW ZEALAND GOLD
MEDAL & FRAGRANCE AWARD
1982, RNRS JAMES MASON MEDAL
1990, AUCKLAND FRAGRANCE
AWARD 1992

### 'Margo Koster'
*(below)*
syn. 'Sunbeam'
MODERN, POLYANTHA, ORANGE
BLEND, REPEAT-FLOWERING

This rose is a sport of 'Dick Koster', which is in turn a sport of 'Annike Koster', which is a sport of 'Greta Kluis', which is a sport of 'Echo', which is a sport of the climbing rose 'Tausendschön'! The flowers of 'Margo Koster' are salmon-pink, small and cupped and are produced in small, tightly packed clusters. As with most Polyanthas, mildew can be a problem. The plant is short and vigorous, and it flowers well into autumn after a late start in the season. ZONES 4–11.

KOSTER, THE NETHERLANDS, 1931

SPORT OF 'DICK KOSTER'

### 'Marguerite Hilling' *(below left)*
syn. 'Pink Nevada'
MODERN, MODERN SHRUB,
MEDIUM PINK,
REPEAT-FLOWERING

This variety has all the attributes of 'Nevada', from which it sported at Hillings Nursery. It grows into a large spreading bush and produces enormous quantities of almost single, dark pink flowers along the arching canes. The wood is dark plum colored and the foliage is light green and abundant. It flowers freely through spring until autumn and is one of the best of all shrub roses. It needs little pruning except for an occasional removal of some old wood to encourage new growth. 'Nevada' was bred by Pedro Dot, who also introduced an amazing selection of very brightly colored modern roses.
ZONES 4–11.

HILLING, UK, 1959

SPORT OF 'NEVADA'

ROYAL HORTICULTURAL SOCIETY
AWARD OF GARDEN MERIT 1993

## 'Maria Lisa'

OLD, RAMBLER, PINK BLEND

This is a late member of the Rambler class, and has almost disappeared from public and even private gardens. Large clusters of small, single, fragrant blooms cover the vigorous plant. The flowers are clear rose pink with white centers. It has pliable canes that can easily be trained on pergolas or trellises. It has dark, leathery leaves with some prickles, blooms during early summer and is strongly disease resistant. ZONES 4–11.

LIEBAU, FRANCE, 1936

PARENTAGE UNKNOWN

## 'Mariandel' KORpeahn *(below)*
syns 'Carl Philip Kristian IV', 'The Times Rose'

MODERN, CLUSTER-FLOWERED/FLORIBUNDA, MEDIUM RED, REPEAT-FLOWERING

There are many good scarlet-crimson Cluster-flowered Roses, but 'Mariandel' is one of the very best. The semi-double flowers are produced in well-spaced clusters. The color is an intense bright red and the blooms hold their form and color well in both very hot and very cold conditions. The trusses of flowers also stand up to windy conditions very well. The abundant foliage is dark green, semi-glossy and red tinged in the early stages of growth. This rose is superb as a hedge or a bedding rose and is equally good in a border. It has become popular in many countries. ZONES 5–10.

KORDES, GERMANY, 1986

'TORNADO' × 'REDGOLD'

ROYAL NATIONAL ROSE SOCIETY PRESIDENT'S INTERNATIONAL TROPHY 1982, BELFAST CERTIFICATE OF MERIT 1986, GOLDEN ROSE OF THE HAGUE 1990, ROYAL HORTICULTURAL SOCIETY AWARD OF GARDEN MERIT 1993

M

### 'Marie de Blois'
*(right)*

OLD, MOSS, MEDIUM PINK

Reddish moss covers the buds of this rose before they open to reveal pink blooms with reflexed petals. The frilled blooms are globular, full and blowsy, and appear in random clusters, then repeat throughout the season. Bright green leaves cover the strongly disease-resistant bush, which does well in poor soil and is effective as a hedge if pruned to 5 ft (1.5 m). Moss Roses are mutations of the Centifolias; the moss covers the stem of the flower, the calyx, the sepals and even the leaflets. Robert created 'Sombreuil', another famous rose, at his nursery in Angers. ZONES 4–10.

ROBERT, FRANCE, 1852

PARENTAGE UNKNOWN

### 'Marie de Saint Jean' *(right)*
syn. 'Marie de St Jean'

OLD, PORTLAND, WHITE, REPEAT-FLOWERING

The exquisite white buds shaded dark pink on this variety open to pure white, full, plump blooms. The outside petals are larger than the rest, and the center of the bloom is muddled. Traces of dark pink edge the rose when it is fully open.

The strongly fragrant flowers measure 3 in (8 cm) across. It blooms for a long period in summer with some autumn rebloom, and has gray-green foliage on an upright, vigorous plant. The bark is light green and the thin canes hold lots of prickles. Portlands belong to a small class with strong character-istics—form, beauty, color and fragrance; they are also known for their short stems. ZONES 5–11.

DAMAIZIN, FRANCE, 1869

PARENTAGE UNKNOWN

## 'Marie Dermar'
*(right)*

OLD, NOISETTE, LIGHT YELLOW,
REPEAT-FLOWERING

The cream and flesh-colored blooms on 'Marie Dermar' have a yellowish tinge when fully open. The petals of the full, medium-sized, double blooms reflex, and there is a pleasant scent. The upright growth habit of this modest climber makes it a good choice for a small pillar or pergola. It has handsome foliage and a long summer-blooming period. This is a less famous creation of Geschwind (1829–1910), a genius at hybridizing who aimed to create winter-hardy roses that needed no protection. He produced two all-time popular roses—'Gruss an Teplitz' and 'Gipsy Boy'. ZONES 5–10.

GESCHWIND, HUNGARY, 1889
SEEDLING OF 'LOUISE D'ARZENS'

M

## 'Marie-Jeanne'
*(right)*

MODERN, POLYANTHA, WHITE,
REPEAT-FLOWERING

The flowers of 'Marie-Jeanne' are pale blush and occur in large clusters of up to 60. These well-formed blooms last well on the bush. The flowering is profuse in spring, fairly continuous through summer and is followed by a very good crop in autumn. There is a light scent. This is a tall grower for a Polyantha, and it is also very spreading. The foliage is glossy light green with bronze tints in the early stages of growth. It is a vigorous bush that can be left unpruned to form a small shrub, or it can be treated in the normal way. This is a good rose for a border or hedge, and it can be mixed among perennial plants of similar coloring. ZONES 4–11.

TURBAT, FRANCE, 1913
PARENTAGE UNKNOWN

## 'Marie Louise'

*(below)*

OLD, DAMASK, MEDIUM PINK

Thought by some to have originated in Empress Josephine's Malmaison garden around 1811 under a different name, this early flowering rose is pink with mauve overtones. The deliciously perfumed, double blooms are flat with a button eye. They are borne in fairly large clusters on the ends of the arching branches, which are often weighed to the ground by the size and number of the flowers, especially in rain. The blooms age to white. It is a lax shrub with dark greenish brown, moderately thorny branches and profuse foliage that does well in poor soil. Its 4 ft (1.2 m) height makes it an attractive container plant, and it has been known to survive years of neglect. Empress Josephine was the first wife of Napoleon and has become possibly the most famous woman in rose history. 'Marie Louise' is named after his second wife. **ZONES 5–10.**

PRE-1813

PARENTAGE UNKNOWN

## 'Marie Pavié' *(left)*
syn. 'Marie Pavic'

MODERN, POLYANTHA, WHITE, REPEAT-FLOWERING

The buds of this rose are small and very well formed. The flowers appear in small clusters above the foliage and are pale pink with a slightly deeper tint in the center. It is a particularly free-flowering plant and blooms over a very long period. The growth habit and shape of the flower clusters fit better in the China class than in the Polyantha class. It is bushy in growth with dark green foliage and very few thorns. This rose, which can be put to many uses in large or small gardens, is an excellent plant for low hedges, borders or small beds and is a wonderful addition to a mixed border. It is still popular after all these years. **ZONES 4–11.**

ALÉGATIÈRE, FRANCE, 1888

PARENTAGE UNKNOWN

M

## 'Marie van Houtte' *(right)*
syns 'Mlle Marie van Houtte', 'The Gem'

OLD, TEA, PINK BLEND, REPEAT-FLOWERING

With two excellent parents, a rose like this could hardly fail to win public approval. The waxy buds open to wonderful deep cream blooms suffused pink with a buff yellow base; in the sun the color deepens to a dark pink. The fragrant flowers are very double, high centered and large. They are long lasting and floriferous, and the strong stems on the sprawling plant hold the blooms well. The foliage is leathery dark green and there are many prickles. It loves the sun and hates rain, and its short growth makes it a good candidate for a container. This was once considered the most valuable white rose by professional gardeners. It is dedicated to Mademoiselle Marie van Houtte of Ghent, Belgium. 'Climbing Marie van Houtte' (Thomasville Nurseries Inc, USA, 1936) is the same as its parent in every way except that it will grow to 10 ft (3 m) in a short time. It is no longer in commerce. **ZONES 6–11.**

DUCHER, FRANCE, 1871

'MME DE TARTAS' × 'MME FALCOT'

M

### 'Marina' RinaKOR *(above)*
MODERN, CLUSTER-FLOWERED/FLORIBUNDA, ORANGE BLEND, REPEAT-FLOWERING

This is a charming garden rose that is also perfect for cutting. The shapely flower buds are a vivid pure orange with a yellow base to each petal. The double, medium-sized blooms, which have 30 petals and are fragrant, come in clusters of up to 15 blooms and hold their color very well. The foliage is glossy dark green on a bush that is of medium height and has an upright growth habit. Flower production is good and the plant is disease free. 'Marina' is suitable as a bedding plant, or for a border or hedge. **ZONES 5–10.**

KORDES, GERMANY, 1974

'COLOUR WONDER' × SEEDLING

ALL-AMERICA ROSE SELECTION 1981

### 'Marjorie Atherton'   *(left)*

MODERN, LARGE-FLOWERED/HYBRID TEA,
MEDIUM YELLOW, REPEAT-FLOWERING

This rose has the strong upright growth of 'Mount Shasta' and the plump buds and excellent foliage of 'Peace'. The color is soft maize yellow and keeps well. The large, oval buds open to long-lasting, double flowers with 25 petals and a beautiful rounded shape. The flower production is fairly good and there are no disease problems. The foliage is pale green. 'Marjorie Atherton' is one of the best Australian-raised roses. **ZONES 5–10.**

BELL, AUSTRALIA, 1977

'MOUNT SHASTA' × 'PEACE'

**M**

### 'Marjorie Fair'   HARhero   *(left)*
syns 'Red Ballerina', 'Red Yesterday'

MODERN, MODERN SHRUB, RED BLEND,
REPEAT-FLOWERING

This excellent crimson shrub rose has small, single flowers with 5 petals, each with a distinct white eye. They come in both small and very large clusters and blooming is continuous. The flowers, which hold well and do not fade, have a slight fragrance. The profuse foliage is light green and semi-glossy on a plant with a very dense and bushy habit; it grows to moderate height. It makes a good hedge and is also useful among perennials and shrubs in a mixed border; it can also be used as a large shrub if not pruned. It can suffer from mite attack in hot weather. **ZONES 4–10.**

HARKNESS, UK, 1977

'BALLERINA' × 'BABY FAURAX'

COPENHAGEN FIRST PRIZE 1977, NORDROSE GOLD MEDAL 1977, ROME GOLD MEDAL 1977, ROYAL NATIONAL ROSE SOCIETY TRIAL GROUND CERTIFICATE 1977, BADEN-BADEN GOLD MEDAL 1979, ANERKANNTE DEUTSCHE ROSE 1980, PARIS PAYSAGE PRIZE 1988

## 'Marjory Palmer' (right)

MODERN, POLYANTHA, MEDIUM
PINK, REPEAT-FLOWERING

This is one of the best low-growing roses bred by Australia's most famous hybridist. The plant is very spreading and has large, attractive, glossy green foliage and heads of rich pink, double flowers that open flat and quartered. Disease resistance is excellent and repeat-blooming usually quick. It has exceptional fragrance. It makes an excellent border rose and can be used as a low hedge, flowering over a very long period. A pale pink sport of this rose called 'Alister Clark' has recently been introduced.
**ZONES 4–11.**

CLARK, AUSTRALIA, 1936

'JERSEY BEAUTY' × SEEDLING

M

## 'Marlena' (above)

MODERN, CLUSTER-FLOWERED/
FLORIBUNDA, MEDIUM RED,
REPEAT-FLOWERING

This is one of the best low-growing Cluster-flowered Roses. The semi-double flowers have 18 petals and are crimson-scarlet. They are well formed in the bud, opening to flat full blooms of great substance that hold their color well. The blooms occur in small clusters of 5–15 flowers and completely cover the bush. 'Marlena' makes a superb low border or hedge, with the plants placed no further than 18 in (45 cm) apart for maximum effect where a ribbon of red is desired. The flowers look wonderful against the glossy, disease-resistant foliage.
**ZONES 5–10.**

KORDES, GERMANY, 1964

'GERTRUD WESTPHAL' ×
'LILLI MARLEEN'

BADEN-BADEN GOLD MEDAL
1962, BELFAST GOLD MEDAL
1966, ANERKANNTE DEUTSCHE
ROSE 1964

### 'Martha' (below)
syn. 'Marthe'
OLD, BOURBON, PINK BLEND, REPEAT-FLOWERING

From early summer into autumn this wonderful variety, one of the most popular of all garden roses, bears deep pink to mauve-pink, double, free-flowering blooms all over the long canes. These thornless stalks

can be easily trained on trellises or fences. The dark green, shiny foliage adds further to its charm; it does well in poor soil and tolerates some shade. It has strong fragrance, and the variety is both cold hardy and disease resistant. ZONES 5–10.

KNUDSEN, FRANCE, 1912
SPORT OF 'ZÉPHIRINE DROUHIN'

### 'Martin Frobisher' (below)
MODERN, HYBRID RUGOSA, LIGHT PINK, REPEAT-FLOWERING

This Canadian variety was bred using roses that were hardy in Arctic winters, and it is one of the best of all roses for cold climates; it also performs well in hot areas. The plant is tall and upright with distinctive gray-green foliage. The well-shaped buds open to fragrant, double flowers with 25 or so pale pink petals. The foliage and flowers look like an Alba Rose, and it would be interesting to find out if there is any Alba blood in the seedling parent. There are very few thorns. It makes an excellent hedge. ZONES 3–11.

SVEDJA, CANADA, 1968
'SCHNEEZWERG' × SEEDLING

M

### 'Mary Guthrie'
*(right)*

MODERN, POLYANTHA, MEDIUM
PINK, REPEAT-FLOWERING

This rose has single flowers with prominent stamens. The fragrant blooms come in small to large clusters and are cerise in color. They flower profusely and continuously, and the foliage is a rather dull green on a low, stocky plant. It is disease resistant. **ZONES 5–11.**

CLARK, AUSTRALIA, 1929
'JERSEY BEAUTY' × 'SCORCHER'

### 'Mary MacKillop'
*(bottom)*
syn. 'Mother Mary McKillop'

MODERN, LARGE-FLOWERED/
HYBRID TEA, PINK BLEND,
REPEAT FLOWERING

Mary MacKillop was the founder of the St Joseph's Order in Australia. The variety produces enormous quantities of well-formed, soft pink roses over a very long period. No sooner is one crop over than another is on the way, which makes this a superb rose for bedding and borders. The flowers are produced both singly and in small, well-spaced clusters on a disease-resistant plant that is dense and well foliaged. There is some fading in the older blooms. **ZONES 5–10.**

SWANE, AUSTRALIA, 1989
PARENTAGE UNKNOWN

M

### 'Mary Marshall'
*(right)*

MODERN, MINIATURE, ORANGE
BLEND, REPEAT-FLOWERING

The long, pointed buds of this rose open to beautifully shaped, orange-pink flowers with attractive yellow bases. These blooms are double, cupped and fragrant, and they have a good show quality. It is an excellent rose for beginners because it grows well with much basal activity and is completely disease resistant. The foliage is small and leathery in texture, and it covers the plant, which has a dwarf growth habit. The repeat-bloom cycle is fast. ZONES 5–11.

MOORE, USA, 1970

'LITTLE DARLING' × 'FAIRY
PRINCESS'

AMERICAN ROSE SOCIETY
AWARD OF EXCELLENCE 1975

### 'Mary Queen of Scots' *(right)*

OLD, SCOTS, MEDIUM PINK

This is one of the most popular survivors of the hundreds of Scots Roses that were produced during their heyday between 1790 and 1830. In recent years, these roses have grown in popularity because of their beauty and hardiness. 'Mary Queen of Scots' carries plum-tinted, gray-lilac buds that open to reveal contrasting light and dark, fragrant, pink petals crowned with prominent stamens. The small, exquisite blooms smother the foliage in late spring. It is a compact, round plant, reaching 3 ft (1 m) at maturity, and is covered with ferny, dense foliage of tiny leaves. There is a small number of awesome prickles. Round, dark maroon hips follow the flowers in autumn. According to legend, Mary Queen of Scots brought this rose from France and it was rediscovered by Lady Moore in Ireland. Jack Harkness, however, says this is not possible on historical grounds. Regardless of its origin, this frost-hardy rose is a perfect candidate for a small hedge or container, and is especially happy in seaside settings. ZONES 4–9.

PARENTAGE UNKNOWN

### 'Mary Rose' AUSmary
*(above)*

MODERN, MODERN SHRUB,
MEDIUM PINK,
REPEAT-FLOWERING

The slightly fragrant flowers of this popular rose, which are a strong rose pink with a touch of lavender, occur over a long period. The blooms open a little loose, and are borne at the end of long, arching shoots. It is a healthy bush that is as broad as it is tall and has produced two excellent sports—the almost white 'Winchester Cathedral' and the much softer pink 'Redouté'. Unfortunately the blooms shatter rather quickly after they have reached the full-blown stage. This self-shedding is good for garden display but means that this is not a good rose for picking. Also known as an English Rose, it was named after the flagship of Henry VIII which was raised from the Solent River 400 years after it sank.
ZONES 4–11.

AUSTIN, UK, 1983

PROBABLY 'WIFE OF BATH' ×
'THE MILLER'

### 'Mary Wallace'
*(above right)*

MODERN, LARGE-FLOWERED
CLIMBER, MEDIUM PINK,
REPEAT-FLOWERING

The pointed buds of this rose open to cupped, semi-double, fragrant flowers of a clear rose pink. They are large for a climbing rose. Blooming is most plentiful early in the season; there are few flowers in summer, but autumn blooming is more profuse. The flowers hold their color very well. This rose is a famous yard rose in the USA because of its tidy growth habit, to 10 ft (3 m) or so. The foliage is a rich green and glossy and there are no disease problems. It is suitable for a pillar or tripod or for growing into a small tree.
ZONES 4–11.

VAN FLEET, USA, 1924

*ROSA WICHURANA* × A PINK
LARGE-FLOWERED ROSE

M

M

### 'Mary Webb'
AUSwebb *(above)*

MODERN, MODERN SHRUB,
APRICOT BLEND,
REPEAT-FLOWERING

'Mary Webb' produces large, deeply cupped, many-petalled flowers of a pleasing soft apricot. There is a delicious fragrance. Flowering is continuous but there is rather a long period between flushes. The blooms are borne on a bushy plant with long stems and large, pale green leaves that are disease resistant. This rose, which is also known as an English Rose, was named after a Shropshire novelist who lived from 1881 to 1927. 'Mary Webb' is an excellent rose for picking as its soft color fits into most color schemes. It is also very versatile in the garden—both in soft color schemes or as a harmonizing agent for use between bright colors. ZONES 4–11.

AUSTIN, UK, 1985

SEEDLING × 'CHINATOWN'

### 'Mascotte'
*(above right)*

MODERN, LARGE-FLOWERED/
HYBRID TEA, MEDIUM PINK,
REPEAT-FLOWERING

The firm of Meilland has produced two roses with this name; this is the earlier introduction. The long, pointed buds are soft pink tinted with lilac, and open to blooms of great refinement. The large, extremely fragrant blooms have 35 petals and are borne on long stems. The open flowers are particularly attractive, as the lilac

tint is very pronounced at the edge of the petals. The foliage is dark, healthy and profuse, and the plant has good disease resistance. ZONES 5–11.

MEILLAND, FRANCE, 1951

'MICHÈLE MEILLAND' ×
'PRESIDENT HERBERT HOOVER'

## 'Masquerade'
*(below)*

MODERN, CLUSTER-FLOWERED/
FLORIBUNDA, RED BLEND,
REPEAT-FLOWERING

'Masquerade' was the first of the Cluster-flowered Roses that changed to a deeper color as the flowers matured, a feature inherited from the China Roses. The ovoid buds open to small, semi-double flowers, produced in huge clusters of up to 30 on strong stems. They are light yellow, changing to salmon-pink and finally to a muddy red, a striking effect. It is a strong-growing, disease-resistant rose with large, dark green, profuse foliage that makes a wonderful hedge, as it blooms over a long period. If spent blooms are not removed, a large crop of round red hips is produced, looking most attractive among the multicolored flowers. **'Climbing Masquerade'** (Dillan, UK, 1958) is a particularly vigorous climber that suits a tall pillar or fence. **ZONES 5–11.**

BOERNER, USA, 1949

'GOLDILOCKS' × 'HOLIDAY'

NATIONAL ROSE SOCIETY GOLD
MEDAL 1952

## 'Master Hugh'
*(right)*

MODERN, MODERN SHRUB,
DEEP PINK

The flowers of this delicate rose are rich rose pink and appear in clusters. Attractive orange-red, flagon-shaped hips follow, but in warm climates these are sparse. Its parent, *Rosa macrophylla*, comes from the Himalayas so it is not surprising that 'Master Hugh' suffers in hot, dry climates. The foliage is a little meager on a very tall, upright bush. This is an excellent rose in cold climates where it can be spectacular in full flower. **ZONES 4–10.**

MASON, UK, 1970

SEEDLING OF *ROSA
MACROPHYLLA*

ROYAL HORTICULTURAL SOCIETY
AWARD OF GARDEN MERIT 1993

**M**

### 'Matangi' MACman
*(above)*

MODERN, CLUSTER-FLOWERED/
FLORIBUNDA, RED BLEND,
REPEAT-FLOWERING

'Matangi' is one of
Sam McGredy's most
beautiful 'hand-painted'
roses. The oval buds
open to orange-red
blooms with a silvery
white eye and silver
undersides to the petals.
The color is more
intense in cooler
weather. The double
flowers with 30 petals
are large—up to 3½ in
(9 cm) across—and
are slightly fragrant.
The foliage is small but
profuse, and growth
is strong, upright and
bushy. Flower produc-
tion is excellent and
there are no disease
problems. Its unique
color makes this rose a
particularly lovely cut
flower. ZONES 5–10.

MCGREDY, NEW ZEALAND, 1974

SEEDLING × 'PICASSO'

ROME GOLD MEDAL 1974,
BELFAST GOLD MEDAL 1976,
PORTLAND GOLD MEDAL 1982,
ROYAL NATIONAL ROSE SOCIETY
PRESIDENT'S INTERNATIONAL
TROPHY 1974

### 'Matilda' MEIbeausai
*(above right)*
syns 'Charles
Aznavour', 'Pearl of
Bedfordview',
'Seduction'

MODERN, CLUSTER-FLOWERED/
FLORIBUNDA, WHITE,
REPEAT-FLOWERING

This rose, which is
excellent for climates
with coolish summers,
has well-formed buds
that open very quickly
to white blooms edged
with the softest rose

pink. These fade
extremely quickly to
white in hot weather.
The large, double
blooms have 15–20
petals and there is no
fragrance. The disease-
resistant foliage is
dark green and semi-
glossy on a short to
medium bushy plant.
Flower production is
remarkable, with an
extraordinarily quick
repeat cycle. 'Matilda'
is ideal for use as a
standard rose and is
lovely in the cool
weather of late autumn
and early winter, where
its delicate coloring
remains for a much
longer time. It is useful
for indoor decoration
where soft colors are
desired. ZONES 5–10.

MEILLAND, FRANCE, 1998

MEIGURAMI × 'NIRVANA'

BAGATELLE GOLD MEDAL 1987,
COURTRAI GOLD MEDAL 1987

## 'Matthias Meilland'
MEIfolio *(right)*

MODERN, CLUSTER-FLOWERED/
FLORIBUNDA, MEDIUM RED,
REPEAT-FLOWERING

The Meilland family always names good roses after members of the family, such as 'Papa Meilland', 'Michèle Meilland', 'Manou Meilland' and 'Mme Meilland' ('Peace'). 'Matthias Meilland' certainly lives up to expectations, being one of the very best bright red Cluster-flowered Roses. The unfading blooms, which have great substance, are double with 20–25 petals and occur in small and large well-spaced clusters. The extremely abundant foliage is medium sized, dark green, very glossy and disease resistant. Growth is strong and upright and flower production is excellent, which makes it one of the best roses for beds where a strong color is required. ZONES 5–10.

MEILLAND, FRANCE, 1985

('MME CHARLES SAUVAGE' ×
'FASHION') × ('POPPY FLASH' ×
'PARADOR')

FRANKFURT GOLD MEDAL 1989

### 'Mauve Melodée' *(above)*

MODERN, LARGE-FLOWERED/HYBRID TEA, MAUVE

The mauve-purple buds of this rose are long and pointed, and open to 20-petalled flowers that are 4–5 in (10–12 cm) across. They usually appear in small clusters and are very fragrant. The blooms are attractive at all stages and retain their color better than most varieties in this color range. It is a stronger grower than its parent 'Sterling Silver'. The foliage is dark and leathery on a vigorous, upright, disease-resistant plant. ZONES 5–11.

RAFFEL, USA, 1962

'STERLING SILVER' × SEEDLING

M

## 'Max Graf' *(left)*

syn. *Rosa rugosa* 'Max Graf'

MODERN, HYBRID RUGOSA, PINK BLEND

This is a very important rose as it is in the ancestry of most of the Modern Ground Cover Roses as well as many shrub roses. It was used by the great hybridist Kordes for breeding over a great many years. One of the earliest Ground Cover Roses, it has long, prostrate, trailing shoots with very attractive, disease-resistant wrinkled foliage. The shapely, single flowers are soft rose pink with golden stamens. It flowers only once in the season and, unlike most Hybrid Rugosas, does not set hips. It is an excellent rose for covering banks and difficult slopes, and is extremely hardy in cold climates. **ZONES 4–11.**

BOWDITCH, USA, 1919

PROBABLY *ROSA RUGOSA* × *R. WICHURANA*

M

## 'May Queen' *(left)*

MODERN, RAMBLER, MEDIUM PINK

This rose bears short-stemmed, rosy pink flowers with a hint of lilac, which appear in great profusion during the earlier part of summer. They are full petalled, of medium size, rounded in form and open quartered with an old-fashioned look. There is a modest fruity fragrance, and they give a beautiful show whatever the weather. Because the stems are flexible, the variety lends itself to many uses in the garden; it is especially suited to garlanding trellises, pergolas and pillars, to trail over low walls and fences or to grow in a place where it can naturalize itself as a hummocky ground-covering plant. 'May Queen' is a vigorous and arching plant that extends a little farther than is average for a climbing rose. The leaves are plentiful, glossy and dark, and create a handsome backcloth for the blooms. **ZONES 4–9.**

MANDA, USA, 1898

*ROSA WICHURANA* × 'CHAMPION OF THE WORLD'

### 'Mayor of Casterbridge'

AUSbrid *(right)*

MODERN, MODERN SHRUB, LIGHT PINK, REPEAT-FLOWERING

The flowers of this rose are medium sized, very full with 40 petals and a lovely light pink. The blooms have Old Garden Rose form, are borne in small clusters and are very fragrant. Flower production is extremely high. The foliage is medium sized, light green and leathery on a disease-resistant plant with an upright habit. The stems are moderately thorny. This rose, which is also known as an English Rose and makes a nice rounded shrub in the garden, was named after the 1886 novel by Thomas Hardy. **ZONES 5–10.**

AUSTIN, UK, 1996

PARENTAGE UNKNOWN

### 'Medallion' *(above)*

MODERN, LARGE-FLOWERED/ HYBRID TEA, APRICOT BLEND, REPEAT-FLOWERING

This rose, which was bred from two excellent garden roses, produces long, pointed buds of soft apricot that are double, large and full, like its parent 'South Seas'. The buds open slowly to well-shaped, full blooms that have a pleasant fragrance. The foliage is dark, leathery and abundant and growth is vigorous, upright and very healthy. 'Medallion' unfortunately does not seem to have been introduced into many countries outside the USA. **ZONES 5–10.**

WARRINER, USA, 1973

'SOUTH SEAS' × 'KING'S RANSOM'

PORTLAND GOLD MEDAL 1972, ALL-AMERICA ROSE SELECTION 1973

M

## 'Meg' *(below)*

MODERN, LARGE-FLOWERED
CLIMBER, APRICOT BLEND,
REPEAT-FLOWERING

This rose gets its climbing growth from 'Paul's Lemon Pillar' and some of its lovely soft salmon-apricot color and red stamens from 'Mme Butterfly'. The flowers have 10 petals that are very large for a single rose, up to 5½ in (13 cm) across. They occur in small and large clusters. The foliage is dark and glossy on a strong and upright plant. Repeat-flowering is fair in summer and slightly more profuse in autumn. It is a great rose for a pillar, a tripod or an arch and looks stunning against a brick house; it is popular in all climates. If spent blooms are not removed, a good crop of large round hips is produced in autumn. **ZONES 5–10.**

GOSSET, UK, 1954

'PAUL'S LEMON PILLAR' ×
'MME BUTTERFLY'

NATIONAL ROSE SOCIETY GOLD
MEDAL 1954

## 'Meg Merrilies'
*(bottom)*

OLD, SWEET BRIAR, DEEP PINK/
MEDIUM RED

This Old Garden Rose carries single flowers with dark pink or carmine petals that have a deep notch at the edges. They also have white bases that highlight the central boss of golden yellow stamens. The long, arching canes prefer part shade where the colors are shown to best effect during the summer flowering. It is a perfect candidate for the woodland garden or as hedging. The canes are covered with prickles, and in autumn a fine crop of hips appears. Both the flowers and foliage are fragrant and disease resistant. Named after a wild creature in Sir Walter Scott's novel *Guy Mannering*, Meg is the leader of the gypsies and nurse of Harry Pertram. **ZONES 4–9.**

PENZANCE, UK, 1894

*ROSA EGLANTERIA* × UNKNOWN
HYBRID PERPETUAL OR BOURBON
ROSE

### 'Meillandina'  MEIrov, MEIroy
*(right)*

MODERN, MINIATURE, MEDIUM RED,
REPEAT-FLOWERING

'Meillandina', from Marie-
Louisette Meilland, has scarlet
flowers with an attractive
contrasting yellow center. The
bright yellow eye in each bloom
is an eye-catching quality that
makes this rose quite spectacular in the garden setting. The
bush is vigorous and healthy.
The name has since been used
by the House of Meilland to
describe a range of Miniature
Roses of different colors, but
with the same growth habits;
a sort of series of clones with
differing colors. **ZONES 5–11.**

MEILLAND, FRANCE, 1975

'RUMBA' × ('DANY ROBIN' × 'FIRE KING')

### 'Melody Maker'  DICqueen
*(right)*

MODERN, CLUSTER-FLOWERED/FLORIBUNDA,
ORANGE-RED, REPEAT-FLOWERING

This excellent Cluster-flowered
Rose bears very full, brilliant
orange-red blooms that have
excellent color stability, and the
repeat-bloom is very rapid.
There is a light scent. The foliage is medium sized, dark
green and semi-glossy. It is an
excellent rose for bedding
schemes since it gives color
over a very long period, but it
can also be used as a low hedge
or border. An amazing number
of really good Cluster-flowered
Roses like this one, with disease-
free foliage and abundant
flower production, have been
produced by Pat and Colin
Dickson. **ZONES 5–10.**

DICKSON, UK, 1990

'ANISLEY DICKSON' × 'WISHING'

ROSE OF THE YEAR 1991, GLASGOW
CERTIFICATE OF MERIT 1996

M

### 'Memento' DICbar
*(right)*

MODERN, CLUSTER-FLOWERED/
FLORIBUNDA, RED BLEND,
REPEAT-FLOWERING

This good all-rounder from Pat Dickson has a profusion of large and globular buds that develop into strong salmon-red blooms. These cupped, double flowers have 20 petals, and are quite large for a Cluster-flowered Rose—up to 3 in (8 cm) across. They occur singly and in small to medium-sized clusters, and hold their color particularly well. The bushy plant is of medium height, and has an abundance of sage green, disease-resistant foliage. 'Memento', like most of Pat Dickson's Cluster-flowered Roses, makes an excellent bedder—especially among bright-colored bulbs and perennials— and is equally good as a hedge or border. There is a fine bed of it at Lady Dickson Park in Belfast, Northern Ireland, where it won a gold medal in 1980.
**ZONES 5–10.**

DICKSON, UK, 1978

'BANGOR' × 'ANABELL'

ROYAL NATIONAL ROSE SOCIETY
TRIAL GROUND CERTIFICATE
1977, BELFAST GOLD MEDAL
1980

### 'Memoriam' *(right)*

MODERN, LARGE-FLOWERED/
HYBRID TEA, LIGHT PINK,
REPEAT-FLOWERING

This terrific rose has long, pointed buds that open to clear pale pink double blooms filled with 55 petals that give a high center. These fragrant flowers are very large—up to 6 in (15 cm) across—and have superb exhibition form. In cool, wet weather the color becomes very pale. The foliage is dark and healthy, but a little subject to black spot. The plant is on the short side, although flower production is high and the repeat cycle is quick. The blooms lose their substance rather quickly when cut. **ZONES 5–10.**

VON ABRAMS, USA, 1961

('BLANCHE MALLERIN' × 'PEACE')
× ('PEACE' × 'FRAU KARL
DRUSCHKI')

PORTLAND GOLD MEDAL 1960,
ROYAL NATIONAL ROSE SOCIETY
CERTIFICATE OF MERIT 1961

M

### 'Memory Lane'

PEAvoodoo *(above)*

MODERN, CLUSTER-FLOWERED/
FLORIBUNDA, APRICOT BLEND,
REPEAT-FLOWERING

The long, pointed buds
of this rose open to fully
double flowers made
up of many light peach-
yellow petals. They
form a tight center,
and the outer petals
become reflexed as the
flower matures. The
color combines well
with the mid-green
foliage. **ZONES 5–10.**

PEARCE, UK, 1995

('GERALDINE' × SEEDLING) ×
SEEDLING

ROYAL NATIONAL ROSE SOCIETY
TRIAL GROUND CERTIFICATE 1993

### 'Menja' *(right)*

MODERN, MODERN SHRUB,
MEDIUM PINK,
REPEAT-FLOWERING

Not much is known
about the breeding of
'Menja'. It is a most
unusual and beautiful
rose with large trusses
of almost single, ex-
tremely cupped flowers
that stay cupped until
they fall. They are borne
in great panicles, and
from a distance resem-
ble 'Kalmia'. It is a
bushy grower with
plentiful light green,
disease-resistant foliage.
This is a rose that has
been overlooked and
should be much more
widely planted for
its unique beauty. It
repeats extremely well
and always attracts the
attention of rose lovers
when they see it for the
first time. It is excellent
as a hedge, or it can
be used to great
effect among bulbs,
perennials and other
shrubs. **ZONES 5–10.**

PETERSEN, DENMARK, 1960

'EVA' × *ROSA FILIPES*

### 'Mercedes' MerKOR (bottom)

MODERN, CLUSTER-FLOWERED/
FLORIBUNDA, ORANGE-RED,
REPEAT-FLOWERING

This variety was the first of the orange-red, medium-sized, durable roses for growing under glass. The buds are bright orange-red, and open to double flowers with 30–35 very high-centered petals. The flowers develop very dark edges to the petals in intense sunlight when grown outdoors; this is not a burning of the petals but a dark shading. The full blooms slowly fade in the garden to a dull, unattractive color.

'Mercedes' is quick to repeat and lasts a very long time when cut; the fragrance is only slight. The foliage is large and leathery and growth is moderate, and there is some tendency to black spot and mildew. There are newer varieties from Kordes that are better growers and are more disease resistant.
**ZONES 5–11.**

KORDES, GERMANY, 1974

'ANABELL' × SEEDLING

### 'Mermaid' (top)

OLD, MISCELLANEOUS, LIGHT
YELLOW, REPEAT-FLOWERING

The fragrant flowers of this rose are soft creamy yellow and are 5–6 in (12–15 cm) across. It comes into flower later than most varieties, but the display continues through summer and autumn and into winter. In warm areas it is gigantic—to 30 ft (9 m) or more across and 20 ft (6 m) high if given sufficient support. The dark foliage is glossy and the plant has large, red, hooked thorns. It needs no pruning but can be cut back when it gets out of control, which makes it a great rose for covering unsightly sheds and old trees. It should not be planted near paths because of the vicious thorns. The growth is much less vigorous in cold climates.
**ZONES 4–11.**

PAUL, UK, 1918

*ROSA BRACTEATA* ×
DOUBLE YELLOW TEA ROSE

NATIONAL ROSE SOCIETY
GOLD MEDAL 1917, ROYAL
HORTICULTURAL SOCIETY AWARD
OF GARDEN MERIT 1993

## 'Meteor' *(right)*

OLD, NOISETTE, DEEP PINK,
REPEAT-FLOWERING

This is one of the few
German-produced
Noisettes. It has large,
double, deep pink
blooms that are larger
than many others in
that class. The blowsy
flowers appear on long,
pliable canes with
Gallica-like foliage
and have a heavy, rich
fragrance and an ample
reblooming in autumn.
The shrub can reach
9 ft (2.7 m) in two
years, looking its best
in a woodland setting.
Geschwind was famous
in his time for his
winter-hardy roses.
ZONES 5–11.

GESCHWIND, HUNGARY, 1887
PARENTAGE UNKNOWN

M

## 'Mevrouw Nathalie Nypels' *(right)*
syn. 'Nathalie Nypels'

MODERN, POLYANTHA, MEDIUM
PINK, REPEAT-FLOWERING

One of the best of all
the Polyanthas, this
variety gives a constant
supply of pretty little
pink flowers borne in
small elegant clusters.
They are sweetly
scented. The flower
production is excellent
and the repeat-bloom
is rapid. It is quite low
growing, to about 2 ft
(60 cm) tall, and is
very spreading. The
unassuming clear pink
florets make it a useful
companion plant in
mixed borders, where
it never clashes or
looks out of place. It
can be used in a mixed
border, in a bed or as a
hedge. It is remarkable
that this pretty plant
with no special distinc-
tions is still grown.
ZONES 5–10.

LEENDERS, THE NETHERLANDS,
1919

'ORLÉANS ROSE' × ('COMTESSE
DU CAYLA' × *ROSA FOETIDA
BICOLOR*)

ROYAL HORTICULTURAL SOCIETY
AWARD OF GARDEN MERIT 1993

M

## 'Michelangelo'

**MACtemaik** *(above)*
**syn. 'The Painter'**

MODERN, CLUSTER-FLOWERED/
FLORIBUNDA, ORANGE BLEND,
REPEAT-FLOWERING

This variety has more subdued coloring than the other 'painted' roses from Sam McGredy; it is described as 'either a creamy lemon with bold orange stripes or blotches, or sometimes all orange with lemon striping and blotching'. The random pigments give an unusually realistic 'hand-painted' effect. The flowers are carried on firm stems in clusters, although their form is more like that of a Large-flowered Rose: high centered in the young blooms and becoming cupped as the many petals reflex. They are of good size, appear through summer and into autumn and have a light perfume. 'Michelangelo' is suitable for beds, borders and hedges, and the individual blooms look most attractive when cut for small indoor arrangements. It grows vigorously with an upright habit to above average height, and it is well clothed with dense, glossy dark green foliage, which is reddish when young.
**ZONES 5–9.**

MCGREDY, NEW ZEALAND, 1995

'LOIUSE GARDNER' ×
('AUCKLAND METRO' × SEEDLING
OF 'STARS 'N' STRIPES'

M

### 'Michèle Meilland' *(above)*

MODERN, LARGE-FLOWERED/HYBRID TEA, LIGHT PINK,
REPEAT-FLOWERING

The long and slender buds of this rose have a most refined shape. The color of the moderately sized blooms can vary from a soft salmon-pink, to rose pink, to a soft lilac, or they can be pale pink with a yellow base. Whatever the color, it is always beautiful, and is particularly free flowering. The bush is of medium size with rather plum-colored wood, and the abundant foliage is medium green and disease free. This is an excellent rose for bedding, and its bushy growth and freedom of flower make it a splendid rose for standards. **'Climbing Michèle Meilland'** (syn. 'Grimpant Michèle Meilland', 1951) is an excellent climbing rose that flowers from spring until autumn. It has moderately vigorous growth, which makes it ideal for a pillar or tripod. Its only fault is that some bushes are inclined to revert to the bush form when planted out. **ZONES 5–11.**

MEILLAND, FRANCE, 1945

'JOANNA HILL' × 'PEACE'

NATIONAL ROSE SOCIETY CERTIFICATE OF MERIT 1958

### 'Micrugosa' *(above)*
syn. *Rosa* × *micrugosa* 'Henkel'
MODERN, MODERN SHRUB, LIGHT PINK

This rose forms a large spreading shrub with excellent dense ferny leaves and single light pink flowers. These are produced on shortish shoots along the branches. The fruit is orange-red, round and most attractive; they ripen in late summer and do not persist very long on the plant. The rose produces good clear yellow autumn foliage in cold climates. It makes a good shrub rose for the shrubbery or can be planted in parks and woodland areas for its flowers, its fruit and its autumn foliage. The hips are covered with bristly hairs. ZONES 4–11.

PRE-1905

*ROSA ROXBURGHII* × *R. RUGOSA*

### 'Midas Touch'
JACtou *(above right)*
MODERN, LARGE-FLOWERED/ HYBRID TEA, DEEP YELLOW, REPEAT-FLOWERING

This well-named rose is a particularly bright yellow. The buds are moderately full, and open to large, fragrant blooms that hold their color very well. It is quick to repeat and flowers extremely freely over a long period. The foliage is large, abundant, matt mid-green, and there are small prickles on the peduncles. The growth is tallish, upright and bushy, and the disease resistance good. ZONES 5–11.

CHRISTENSEN, USA, 1992

'BRANDY' × 'FREISENSOHNE'

ALL-AMERICA ROSE SELECTION 1994

### 'Mignonette'
*(above)*
MODERN, POLYANTHA, LIGHT PINK, REPEAT-FLOWERING

This variety, one of the earliest Polyantha Roses, is still in most major rose collections after 120 years in commerce. The flowers, which are rosy blush in color, are 1 in (25 mm) across and come in small and large tightly packed clusters. The foliage is dark green on the upper surface of the leaf and reddish beneath, a characteristic inherited from China Roses. The leaves are small and glossy and there are red hooked prickles. It has a very dwarf and compact growth habit, but flower production is good. Bushes of 'Mignonette' should be planted very close together for maximum effect, which makes a useful low border. ZONES 4–11.

GUILLOT, FRANCE, 1880

PARENTAGE UNKNOWN

## 'Mikado'

syns 'Kohsai', 'Koh-sai'

MODERN, LARGE-FLOWERED/
HYBRID TEA, RED BLEND,
REPEAT-FLOWERING

This rose gets its brilliant
flame red color from
the Japanese-bred
Cluster-flowered Rose
'Kagayaki'. The double
flowers each have
25 petals with a yellow
base. These high-
centered blooms are
of exhibition form
and are usually borne
singly. The foliage is
glossy mid-green on
a tall and upright bush
with good disease
resistance. The flower
production is excellent.
'Mikado' is a lovely
bush rose for bedding
schemes where a bright
color is required, and
it can also be used
effectively when trained
as a standard.
ZONES 5–10.

SUZUKI, JAPAN, 1987

'FRAGRANT CLOUD' ×
'KAGAYAKI'

ALL-AMERICA ROSE SELECTION
1988

### 'Milkmaid' *(right)*

OLD, NOISETTE, WHITE

Known to be almost
exclusive to Australia
but deserving of a
far wider audience,
'Milkmaid' is one of
the happiest creations
of Alister Clark, who
became a famous
hybridizer during the
first half of the twentieth
century. The small,
semi-double blooms
range from creamy
yellow to white, with
a hint of yellowish
brown, and they appear
in clusters during the
late spring. The fragrant
blooms are comple-
mented by rich, dark
green foliage. A vigorous
climber, the variety
is an ideal subject for
pergolas, trellises, or
fences. Highly disease
resistant, this Noisette
Rose is fast growing
and is well suited to
a warm position.
ZONES 6–11.

CLARK, AUSTRALIA, 1925

'CRÉPUSCULE' × SEEDLING

### 'Millie Walters'

MORmilli *(top)*

MODERN, MINIATURE, ORANGE-
PINK, REPEAT-FLOWERING

On this variety, the
deep pink-coral,
double flowers with
45 petals are delicately
small and have a light
fragrance. The plant is
an upright, vigorous
and compact bush
sporting equally small,
mid-green, matt foli-
age. This rose has
consistently good
exhibition-type form
and the striking vivid
color holds well under
sun and high humidity.

The profusion of
blooms is indeed a
strength for this
highly-recommended
rose. It is considered
outstanding both for
the garden and as
an exhibition rose.
However, the plant
can be susceptible to
mildew if it is not
given the proper
protection. 'Millie
Walters' was named
after one of the great
first ladies of the
American Rose Society.
ZONES 5–11.

MOORE, USA, 1983

'LITTLE DARLING' × 'GALAXY'

M

### 'Milrose' DELbir

MODERN, CLUSTER-FLOWERED/
FLORIBUNDA, MEDIUM PINK,
REPEAT-FLOWERING

The medium-sized flowers of 'Milrose' are soft pink, semi-double and cupped and are borne in clusters of 5–15. There is a slight fragrance. This variety, which has light green glossy foliage and vigorous growth, is a good bedding rose as the flowers retain their color well; its bushy growth also makes it suitable for use as a standard. It is not well known outside France. **ZONES 5–10.**

DELBARD-CHABERT, FRANCE,
1965

'ORLÉANS ROSE' ×
('FRANCAIS' × 'LAFAYETTE')

BADEN-BADEN GOLD MEDAL
1964, GOLDEN ROSE OF THE
HAGUE 1978

### 'Minilights'

DICmoppet *(above right)*
syns 'Mini Lights',
'Goldfächer'

MODERN, MODERN SHRUB,
MEDIUM YELLOW,
REPEAT-FLOWERING

'Minilights' gets its bright color from 'Bright Smile' and its spreading growth and free-flowering from the excellent Cluster-flowered Rose 'White Spray'. The small, semi-double, medium yellow flowers have 5–15 petals. The blooms come in small clusters on most attractive small, glossy, dark green foliage. It is a plant with very quick repeat-bloom. A good border rose and excellent as a standard, 'Minilights' can also be used with bulbs and perennial plants in the mixed border. Its disease resistance is very good. **ZONES 5–10.**

DICKSON, UK, 1987

'WHITE SPRAY' × 'BRIGHT SMILE'

ROYAL NATIONAL ROSE SOCIETY
TRIAL GROUND CERTIFICATE 1985

### 'Minnehaha'

MODERN, RAMBLER, LIGHT PINK

The rose world has much to thank Dr Wichura of Germany for; he discovered the beautiful creeping white species that bears his name. Many superb Ramblers were raised from it in the early twentieth century and one, 'Dorothy Perkins', became a household name. 'Minnehaha' resembles it in many ways; the pink rosettes, however, are a little larger, and less stable in color, passing from rosy pink to blush white as they age. They are carried in clusters in great profusion. As the stems are lax, the variety makes a wonderful weeping standard, as well as being good for pillars, arches and anywhere that its trailing habit and cascading flowers can serve to cover unsightly objects. It does require a free circulation of air to lessen the risk of mildew, and there is not much scent. The plant makes many stems, and old spent ones can be cut out completely after flowering to allow space for new growth. The leaves are small, glossy, dark green and plentiful. This rose was named for the wife of Hiawatha, the main character in Longfellow's poem. **ZONES 4–9.**

WALSH, USA, 1905

*ROSA WICHURANA* ×
'PAUL NEYRON'

## 'Minnie Pearl'

SAVahowdy *(right)*

MODERN, MINIATURE, PINK
BLEND, REPEAT-FLOWERING

The long, elegant buds of this rose open to beautifully shaped, light pink flowers with much darker under-sides and the ideal high-centered form of their larger relatives, the Large-flowered Roses. The blooms are borne singly or in large clusters, always on strong, straight stems. This, together with the exquisite color combination, makes 'Minnie Pearl' the archetype of excellence in Miniature Roses. The foliage is semi-glossy and mid-green on this vigorous, upright plant that keeps its color and form better if it is given some relief from intense heat. This rose has never received any awards but is certainly a most worthy candidate. It was named for an American country and western entertainer, who was also a great comedienne.

ZONES 5–10.

SAVILLE, USA, 1982

('LITTLE DARLING' × 'TIKI') ×
'PARTY GIRL'

## 'Minnie Watson'

*(above)*

MODERN, LARGE-FLOWERED/
HYBRID TEA, LIGHT PINK,
REPEAT-FLOWERING

This variety, one of the best roses bred in Australia, was raised by an amateur and named after his mother. The large, well-shaped buds open to well-formed flowers of bright salmon-pink that are borne both singly and in small clusters. They are semi-double and retain their color well on the bush and there is some fragrance. The color is particularly luminous and the flowers look wonderful when arranged and used under artificial light. Flower production is amazing, with rapid regrowth and very small gaps between flushes. The foliage is rich green and extremely glossy and profuse, and the plant has excellent disease resistance. This is a great rose for use as a standard as its flowers completely cover the bush. ZONES 5–10.

WATSON, AUSTRALIA, 1965

'DICKSON'S FLAME' ×
'DICKSON'S FLAME'

M

## 'Miranda'

OLD, PORTLAND, MEDIUM PINK/LIGHT PINK, REPEAT-FLOWERING

Still a popular rose, 'Miranda' is often classified as a Damask Perpetual by some authorities. The medium, satiny pink, very double blooms are cupped, large and full. The thin petals are happiest in a warm site and dislike wet weather. The fragrant blooms appear in early summer with some repeat-flowering in early autumn. 'Miranda' is a compact shrub of medium size with light gray-green foliage that has serrated edges. It is an ideal plant for a small garden or as a hedge. The famous French hybridizer Cochet also named a popular Portland after Arthur de Sansal in 1855. **ZONES 4–9.**

DE SANSAL, FRANCE, 1869

PARENTAGE UNKNOWN

## 'Mirato'   *(below)*

MODERN, LARGE-FLOWERED/HYBRID TEA, MEDIUM PINK, REPEAT-FLOWERING

The ovoid buds of 'Mirato' open slowly to very well-formed flowers of a clear soft salmon-rose. The double blooms contain 30 petals and are very fragrant. The foliage is large and glossy on an upright and bushy plant with good disease resistance. This rose has not become popular as there are not enough flowers in each flush and too long an interval between flushes. It is, nevertheless, a good rose for picking and looks wonderful under artificial light. **ZONES 5–11.**

TANTAU, GERMANY, 1974

SEEDLING × SEEDLING

M

## 'Miriam Wilkins' *(left)*

OLD, HYBRID PERPETUAL, LIGHT PINK, REPEAT-FLOWERING

Named for the founder of the international heritage rose movement, this variety was discovered about ten years ago in a Santa Rosa cemetery in California, USA, growing on a wall. Unable to identify it, Philip Robinson decided to honor Miriam Wilkins. The deep pink, full flowers look a great deal like an Autumn Damask. Lacy sepals cover the buds. There is a strong fragrance, and the blooms appear throughout summer and into autumn. Quite healthy, the 4 ft (1.2 m) shrub has large, dark green leaves that are not subject to any disease. Miriam Wilkins is responsible for the enormous growth of Old Rose societies in the USA, Australia, New Zealand, England and France. **ZONES 5–10.**

ROBINSON, USA, 1981

SEEDLING

## 'Mischief' MACmi *(right)*

MODERN, LARGE-FLOWERED/HYBRID TEA, ORANGE-PINK, REPEAT-FLOWERING

'Mischief' is a lovely little rose that gets its freedom of flower and color from the great Cluster-flowered Rose 'Spartan'. The well-formed, medium-sized flowers are a strong silvery salmon-pink. They are double, with 28 petals, hold their color well and are fragrant. The flower production is amazing and the repeat cycle is extremely rapid. The foliage is light green and semi-glossy on a vigorous and upright plant of medium height. This rose, which is excellent for bedding and for use as a standard, has lost popularity over the last decade or so, which is a great pity as it is one of the best roses of the 1960s. **ZONES 5–11.**

MCGREDY, UK, 1961

'PEACE' × 'SPARTAN'

PORTLAND GOLD MEDAL 1965, NATIONAL ROSE SOCIETY PRESIDENT'S INTERNATIONAL TROPHY 1961

M

‘Miss All-American Beauty’ MEIdaud *(right)*
syn. ‘Maria Callas’

MODERN, LARGE-FLOWERED/
HYBRID TEA, DEEP PINK,
REPEAT-FLOWERING

‘Miss All-American Beauty’ is a great rose with deep rich pink flowers. The extremely fragrant blooms are double with 55 petals, large and cupped and hold their color well. The autumn blooms are magnificent, but growth is a little on the short side in summer heat. It gets its bushy habit and very healthy, disease-free foliage from its parent ‘Karl Herbst’. **‘Climbing Miss All-American Beauty’** (MEIudsur; syn. ‘Climbing Maria Callas’) was introduced by Meilland in 1969 and is one of the best deep pink climbing roses available. It has a copious supply of well-formed flowers in spring. ZONES 5–10.

MEILLAND, FRANCE, 1965

‘CHRYSLER IMPERIAL’ ×
‘KARL HERBST’

PORTLAND GOLD MEDAL 1966,
ALL-AMERICA ROSE SELECTION
1968

**M**

‘Miss Edith Cavell’
*(above right)*
syns ‘Edith Cavell’,
‘Nurse Cavell’

MODERN, POLYANTHA, DARK
RED, REPEAT-FLOWERING

To commemorate the 70th anniversary of Edith Cavell’s death, the vicar of Swardeston in Norfolk, England, asked Peter Beales to try to find the rose named after her. One gnarled old plant was found out of six that had been planted in 1934 in the garden of Mrs Doris Levine of Brundell near the Norfolk Broads. ‘Miss Edith Cavell’ is a lovely rose that produces small, globular flowers of rich crimson. There is little scent. The flowering is fairly continuous, but the plant can suffer from mildew. It makes a nice little border if bushes are planted close together. ZONES 4–11.

DE RUITER, THE NETHERLANDS,
1917

SPORT OF ‘ORLÉANS ROSE’

### 'Mission Bells' *(right)*

MODERN, LARGE-FLOWERED/HYBRID TEA,
PINK BLEND, REPEAT-FLOWERING

The buds of 'Mission Bells' are long and pointed and an unusual orange-pink. The double flowers have 40 high-centered petals and are large and fragrant. The foliage is dark and rather soft on a vigorous and very spreading bush. This is a rose of unusual color that is useful for bedding as it retains its color until petal fall. However, the stems are rather weak, which makes it unsuitable for picking. Flower production is extremely good and the repeat cycle is very rapid. **ZONES 5–10.**

MORRIS, USA, 1949

'MRS SAM MCGREDY' × 'MÄLAR-ROS'

ALL-AMERICA ROSE SELECTION 1950

M

### 'Mr Bluebird' *(right)*

MODERN, MINIATURE, MAUVE, REPEAT-FLOWERING

The oval buds of 'Mr Bluebird' open to charming, lavender-blue, semi-double flowers made up of 15 petals. Unfortunately, the form is loose and the blooms often shatter too quickly; the small florets are therefore at their best when the blooms first open. The foliage is dark and somewhat coarse, and the plant is free flowering, clean and easy to maintain. It is hard to understand how a Miniature could be created from the incestuous breeding of an Old Garden Rose. 'Old Blush' is believed to be 'The Last Rose of Summer' immortalized by Thomas Moore, the Irish poet. **ZONES 4–11.**

MOORE, USA, 1960

'OLD BLUSH' × 'OLD BLUSH'

M

'Climbing Mister Lincoln'  *(above)*

### 'Mister Lincoln'  *(top right)*

MODERN, LARGE-FLOWERED/HYBRID TEA, DARK RED,
REPEAT-FLOWERING

This splendid rose has urn-shaped buds that open
to dark red flowers with superb petal substance.
The buds can open rather quickly in summer.
The full blooms are at first cupped and then flat,
and there are 35 huge petals that are extremely
fragrant. The foliage is leathery, matt and dark.
Growth is extremely vigorous, making 'Mister
Lincoln' unsuitable for bedding but superb for
the back row of a rose bed. This is a very popular
rose in Mediterranean-type climates. **'Climbing
Mister Lincoln'** (Ram, India, 1974) is a magnificent Climber that flowers well through spring,
summer and autumn. It can be used on a pillar
or tripod but is too upright in growth and the
shoots are too strong to be trained horizontally.
**ZONES 5–11.**

SWIM & WEEKS, USA, 1964

'CHRYSLER IMPERIAL' × 'CHARLES MALLERIN'

ALL-AMERICA ROSE SELECTION 1965

### 'Mrs Aaron Ward'  *(above)*

MODERN, LARGE-FLOWERED/HYBRID TEA, YELLOW BLEND,
REPEAT-FLOWERING

This rose is a collector's item, as it is now difficult
to obtain. The buds are long, pointed and elegant
and open to flowers that are quite variable in
color, ranging from yellow to tones of salmon-
pink. They are double, high centered and fragrant.
The flowers are produced over a long period and
appear on a compact, dwarf bush. There can be a
long gap between flushes. **'Climbing Mrs Aaron
Ward'** (Dickson, UK, 1922) occurred 15 years
after the bush form was introduced. It has yellow
flowers that are washed with salmon-pink and is
a moderate and bushy grower suitable for pillars
or tripods. **ZONES 5–10.**

PERNET-DUCHER, FRANCE, 1907

PARENTAGE UNKNOWN

## 'Mrs Alston's Rose'
**(right)**

MODERN, POLYANTHA, RED
BLEND, REPEAT-FLOWERING

This is a particularly
good free-flowering
Polyantha, and it is one
of the few of this type
produced by Alister
Clark. The carmine-
red flowers appear in
small to medium-sized
clusters on a very
strong-growing plant.
The blooms hold their
color well. They are
not as prone to mildew
as most Polyanthas.
**ZONES 5–10.**

CLARK, AUSTRALIA, 1940

PARENTAGE UNKNOWN

## 'Mrs Anthony Waterer' *(bottom)*
syn. *Rosa rugosa*
'Mrs Anthony Waterer'

MODERN, HYBRID RUGOSA,
DARK RED, REPEAT-FLOWERING

'Mrs Anthony Waterer'
shows very little
influence of 'Général
Jacqueminot' except
in the foliage and the
color of the flowers.
The foliage is dark
green and plentiful
and in appearance is
halfway between a
Hybrid Perpetual and
a Rugosa. The flowers
are deep crimson,
semi-double with 20
petals and open flat.
They are very fragrant.
It is a vigorous, bushy
and cold-hardy plant
with some repeat-
bloom. It is excellent
for a medium-sized
hedge, and does not
set hips. **ZONES 4–11.**

WATERER & SONS, UK, 1898

*ROSA RUGOSA* × 'GÉNÉRAL
JACQUEMINOT'

M

### 'Mrs B. R. Cant'
*(above)*
OLD, TEA, MEDIUM PINK, REPEAT-FLOWERING

One parent of this rose is thought to be 'Red Safrano' (1867), a sport of the well-known 'Safrano', which this in no way resembles. This is a popular, reliable and successful Tea that has stood the test of time. The medium-sized, fully double flowers are rich red and silvery rose, tinged with blush at the bases of the petals. There is a pleasing Tea fragrance. 'Mrs B. R. Cant' forms a medium to high bush and repeats well throughout the season, as well as in winter in suitable climates. It is vigorous and easy to grow. 'Climbing Mrs B. R. Cant' (Hjort, USA, 1960) is a sport of the original. It is similar to the parent, but difficult to find these days.
ZONES 7–9.

CANT, UK, 1901
PARENTAGE UNKNOWN

### 'Mrs Doreen Pike'
AUSdor *(above right)*
MODERN, HYBRID RUGOSA, MEDIUM PINK, REPEAT-FLOWERING

This rose bred by David Austin has large, ruffled flowers that form rosettes of 40 petals. They are a warm rose pink and are very fragrant. Growth is low and bushy and there is plenty of small, pale green foliage. It makes an excellent border or low hedge and can also be used with bulbs and perennials in a mixed planting in the garden. Repeat-flowering is good and the plant is disease free.
ZONES 5–10.

AUSTIN, UK, 1993

'MARTIN FROBISHER' × 'ROSERAIE DE L'HAŸ'

## 'Mrs Dudley Cross' *(right)*

OLD, TEA, YELLOW BLEND, REPEAT-FLOWERING

This plant grows to a bush of medium size. The flowers are light yellow with some pink, which predominates as the blooms age. It is a good rose for cutting, and the flowers are long lasting. They are quite large and repeat well throughout the season. Mildew can be a problem in some areas.
**ZONES 7–9.**

PAUL, UK, 1907

PARENTAGE UNKNOWN

## 'Mrs F. W. Flight' *(above)*

MODERN, LARGE-FLOWERED CLIMBER, DEEP PINK

The flowers of this rose are rose pink and semi-double and are borne in small and large clusters. The foliage is large, rich green and rather soft and can occasionally suffer from mildew. It is a good rose for a short pillar or tripod as it rather exceeds 10 ft (3 m) in height. Flowering is very profuse early in the season but there is no repeat-bloom.
**ZONES 5–10.**

CUTBUSH, UK, 1905

'CRIMSON RAMBLER' × SEEDLING

### 'Mrs Foley Hobbs'
*(below)*

OLD, TEA, WHITE/PINK BLEND, REPEAT-FLOWERING

The flowers of this rose are perhaps better suited for exhibition than to the rigors of the garden. They are creamy white with variable pink at the tips of the petals. They are of considerable form and substance, perhaps

too much for the stems to bear. This is a conventional and reliable Tea Rose with a vigorous and robust growth habit. **ZONES 6–9.**

DICKSON, UK, 1910

PARENTAGE UNKNOWN

NATIONAL ROSE SOCIETY GOLD MEDAL 1910

### 'Mrs Fred Danks'
*(below)*

MODERN, LARGE-FLOWERED/ HYBRID TEA, MAUVE, REPEAT-FLOWERING

This variety, one of Alister Clark's best roses, has very long, slender buds that are an unusual deep rosy lilac. They open to large, semi-double flowers containing 20–25 petals, and there is a strong fragrance. Flower production is continuous and blooms are quite often available in the winter months. The foliage is large, leathery, extremely plentiful and disease free on a plant with a very tall and upright habit. It is so tall that it can be used as a pillar rose or as a tall hedge. It is not available outside Australia. **ZONES 5–10.**

CLARK, AUSTRALIA, 1951

PARENTAGE UNKNOWN

## 'Mrs Herbert Stevens' *(right)*

MODERN, LARGE-FLOWERED/
HYBRID TEA, WHITE,
REPEAT-FLOWERING

This rose has long, pointed, elegant buds that are pure white and open to full, high-centered, fragrant blooms. The foliage is very pale green and disease free. Its growth is very dense and bushy and flower production is extremely profuse. This rose is still very popular in the warmer countries of the world where it usually blooms well into winter. **'Climbing Mrs Herbert Stevens'** (syns 'Grimpant Mrs Herbert Stevens', 'Stevens'; Pernet-Ducher, France, 1922) has long pliable canes that are not as stiff as most climbing roses, which makes it ideal for use on arches and pergolas where the pure white flowers show up well against the backdrop of pale green foliage.
**ZONES 5–10.**

MCGREDY, UK, 1910

'FRAU KARL DRUSCHKI' ×
'NIPHETOS'

NATIONAL ROSE SOCIETY GOLD
MEDAL 1910

## 'Mrs John Laing' *(above)*

OLD, HYBRID PERPETUAL,
MEDIUM PINK,
REPEAT-FLOWERING

'François Michelon' is a seedling of the famous 'La Reine', one of the first Hybrid Perpetuals from Jean Laffay, who created the class. The flowerheads resemble cabbages; they are cupped, large, fully double and very fragrant, and the color is silvery lilac-pink. The stems are nearly thornless. 'Mrs John Laing' is a healthy plant with a vigorous growth habit and can grow in poor soils. It is free from mildew. Bennett is said to have received $45 000 for the US distribution rights of this rose. John Laing was a London horticulturalist who died in 1901.
**ZONES 5–9.**

BENNETT, UK, 1887

'FRANÇOIS MICHELON' ×
SEEDLING

NATIONAL ROSE SOCIETY GOLD
MEDAL 1885

M

M

### 'Mrs Mary Thomson' TOMone *(above)*

MODERN, MODERN SHRUB, PINK BLEND, REPEAT-FLOWERING

The semi-double flowers of this rose occur in large clusters. They are lilac pink with cream centers and prominent golden stamens. The form is informal and decorative and there is a distinctive fragrance. The plant has matt green foliage and is thornless. It has a bushy habit and is disease resistant. This rose was described by Australian rose breeder Ian Spriggs as 'the sort of rose we should all be trying to breed'. It was named in honor of the mother of the breeder, George Thomson of South Australia. ZONES 5–10.

THOMSON, AUSTRALIA, 1996

'DAPPLE DAWN' × 'OPHELIA'

### 'Mrs Norman Watson' *(above)*

MODERN, LARGE-FLOWERED CLIMBER, DEEP PINK, REPEAT-FLOWERING

The deep cherry pink flowers of this rose have no fragrance. The large florets have an informal form, and are borne in small clusters on a very vigorous bush that prefers to grow as a pillar rather than as a true climber. This old world rose is winter hardy with a long repeat-bloom cycle. It is disease resistant. Almost forgotten among the wide variety of more modern climbers, it retains the majesty of a bygone era. ZONES 5–10.

CLARK, AUSTRALIA, 1930

'RADIANCE' × 'GWEN NASH'

### 'Mrs Oakley Fisher' *(right)*

MODERN, LARGE-FLOWERED/
HYBRID TEA, DEEP YELLOW,
REPEAT-FLOWERING

This rose has buds of rich orange with random red flushes that open to buff copper flowers with golden stamens. The fragrant, single florets are borne in clusters on stems that often appear to have a weak appearance. It can be trained to resemble a lower-growing shrub rather than a tall Large-flowered Rose. 'Mrs Oakley Fisher' has endured for almost 75 years because of its charming flowers, which are set against a background of bronze, disease-resistant foliage. This classic rose has been described by various writers as a Large-flowered Rose, a Cluster-flowered Rose and a shrub rose. **ZONES 5–10.**

CANT, UK, 1921

PARENTAGE UNKNOWN

NATIONAL ROSE SOCIETY
CERTIFICATE OF MERIT 1921,
ROYAL HORTICULTURAL SOCIETY
AWARD OF GARDEN MERIT 1993

### 'Mrs Paul' *(below)*

OLD, BOURBON, LIGHT PINK,
REPEAT-FLOWERING

The flowers of 'Mrs Paul' are blush white, shaded rosy peach and resemble camellias. Its parent 'Mme Isaac Pereire' was one of the most famous Bourbons and has passed on its vigor and repeat-flowering qualities to its offspring. This is a slow grower to about 6 ft (1.8 m) under normal conditions. The Pauls, George and his uncle William, were considerable rose nurserymen and breeders in the nineteenth century. **ZONES 5–9.**

PAUL, UK, 1891

SEEDLING OF 'MME ISAAC
PEREIRE'

### 'Mistress Quickly'
AUSky

MODERN, MODERN SHRUB,
MEDIUM PINK,
REPEAT-FLOWERING

The small, medium
pink, very full flowers
of this variety, which
have 40 petals, are borne
in large clusters. There
is a slight fragrance.
The foliage is small,
mid-green and semi-
glossy, and there are a
few prickles. Growth is
bushy and medium.
'Mistress Quickly' will
form a nicely rounded
shrub and is useful in
the shrub or perennial
border or as a low
hedge. It is also classi-
fied as an English Rose.
ZONES 5–10.

AUSTIN, UK, 1995

'BLUSH NOISETTE' ×
'MARTIN FROBISHER'

### 'Mrs Reynolds Hole' *(top)*
OLD, TEA, PINK BLEND,
REPEAT-FLOWERING

This is a vigorous,
floriferous and fragrant
rose with long-stemmed
deep purplish pink
flowers that are good
for cutting. It was
named for the wife of
the celebrated Dean
Samuel Reynolds Hole,
the first President of
the (Royal) National
Rose Society from its
inception in 1876 until
his death in 1904.
ZONES 7–9.

NABONNAND, FRANCE, 1900

'ARCHIDUC JOSEPH' ×
'ANDRÉ SCHWARTZ'

### 'Mrs Richard Turnbull' *(above)*
MODERN, LARGE-FLOWERED
CLIMBER, WHITE BLEND

Handsome, creamy
white, single-petalled
flowers are the hall-
mark of this classic
example of a climber
from the middle of the
twentieth century. The
florets are large and
borne in small clusters.
It can be grown either
as a pillar or as a climber,
but bloom production
is best when it is trained
as a true climber. It is
an extremely vigorous
plant and will easily
grow to 30 ft (10 m).
ZONES 5–10.

CLARK, AUSTRALIA, 1945

HYBRID OF *ROSA GIGANTEA*

M

### 'Mrs Sam McGredy' *(above)*

MODERN, LARGE-FLOWERED/HYBRID TEA, ORANGE-PINK, REPEAT-FLOWERING

This rose has urn-shaped, pointed buds that open to large, scarlet-copper-orange flowers, with the undersides of the petals heavily flushed with red. The double florets have 40 petals and are very fragrant. The flower form begins as high centered, with the petals opening to show an inner lower center of symmetry. The plant is vigorous and tall and has beautiful reddish bronze foliage. Before World War II this rose was the talk of the town; it held its lofty position as a most popular rose until the appearance of 'Peace' in 1945 and has a prominent place in the history of roses. '**Climbing Mrs Sam McGredy**' (Guillaud, France, 1938; Royal Horticultural Society Award of Garden Merit 1993), which has tremendous vigor and bloom capacity, is a perfect climbing clone of its parent. It looks wonderful against a high wall or fence. **ZONES 5–10.**

MCGREDY, UK, 1929

('DONALD MACDONALD' × 'GOLDEN EMBLEM') × (SEEDLING × 'THE QUEEN ALEXANDRA ROSE')

NATIONAL ROSE SOCIETY GOLD MEDAL 1929, PORTLAND GOLD MEDAL 1956

### 'Mrs Wakefield Christie-Miller' *(above)*

MODERN, LARGE-FLOWERED/HYBRID TEA, PINK BLEND, REPEAT-FLOWERING

This rose has fragrant, double flowers that are a blush-shaded salmon with vermilion-rose undersides. The foliage is light green and leathery on a plant with a dwarf growth habit. In 1909, when this rose was introduced, the naming of roses reflected nineteenth-century Victorian formality. Its popularity was revived some years ago when it was wrongly identified as the long-lost 'Lady Mary Fitzwilliam'. However, it is delightful on its own merits. The large, fragrant, two-toned pink blooms look typically Edwardian. **ZONES 5–10.**

MCGREDY, UK, 1909

PARENTAGE UNKNOWN

M

### 'Mojave' *(above)*

MODERN, LARGE-FLOWERED/HYBRID TEA, ORANGE BLEND,
REPEAT-FLOWERING

This rose, bred from 'Charlotte Armstrong', has
the characteristic very long, pointed buds. They
are apricot-orange, tinted red and have prominent veining; the novel color makes this a popular
rose. The very fragrant, double flowers have 25
petals and are large—up to 4½ in (12 cm) across.
They open rather quickly in warm weather to
attractive blooms that slowly turn pink as they
age. The upright bush has profuse glossy foliage.
Each flush produces many flowers and the repeat-
bloom is rapid. **'Climbing Mojave'** (Trimper,
Australia, 1964) also has good repeat-bloom
through summer and autumn. **ZONES 5–10.**

SWIM, USA, 1954

'CHARLOTTE ARMSTRONG' × 'SIGNORA'

BAGATELLE GOLD MEDAL 1953, GENEVA GOLD MEDAL 1953,
ALL-AMERICA ROSE SELECTION 1954, NATIONAL ROSE SOCIETY
TRIAL GROUND CERTIFICATE 1955

### 'Moje Hammarberg' *(rose hip, top right)*
syn. *Rosa rugosa* 'Hammarberg'

MODERN, HYBRID RUGOSA, MAUVE, REPEAT-FLOWERING

This rose has double flowers of reddish violet that
are fragrant and occur on short weak stems. The
fruit is large, red and abundant—an uncommon
occurrence in very double Hybrid Rugosa roses.
Its health and vigor make it an ideal rose in cold
winter conditions. The hips are attractive in autumn
when they are interspersed with late flowers, and
the autumn foliage is an added bonus. **ZONES 3–9.**

HAMMARBERG, SWEDEN, 1931

PARENTAGE UNKNOWN

### 'Molineux' AUSmol *(above)*

MODERN, MODERN SHRUB, DEEP YELLOW, REPEAT-FLOWERING

The flowers of 'Molineux' are very rich yellow and
have a strong Tea scent. They open flat, hold their
color well, and are produced singly and in small
clusters. It flowers profusely on a short to medium-
sized, bushy plant with upright growth that has
no disease problems. This rose has an ideal bedding habit and is a good selection where a rich
yellow color is desired. It was the first of David
Austin's roses to win the President's Trophy of
the Royal National Rose Society for the best new
seedling rose of the year. It is useful to plant in
a position where David Austin's other two great
yellow roses, 'Graham Thomas' and 'Golden
Celebration', would be too tall. 'Molineux' is
also classified as an English Rose. **ZONES 5–11.**

AUSTIN, UK, 1994

'GRAHAM THOMAS' × 'GOLDEN SHOWERS'

ROYAL NATIONAL ROSE SOCIETY PRESIDENT'S INTERNATIONAL
TROPHY 1996, RNRS HENRY EDLAND MEDAL FOR FRAGRANCE 1996

### 'Molly Sharman-Crawford' *(above)*

OLD, TEA, WHITE, REPEAT-FLOWERING

This is a low-growing Tea Rose with large, full, high-centered, fragrant flowers. They are white, tinged with green. The plant has an upright and bushy growth habit. The rich green foliage is a little sparse. **ZONES 7–9.**

DICKSON, UK, 1908

PARENTAGE UNKNOWN

### 'Mon Cheri' AROcher *(top right)*

MODERN, LARGE-FLOWERED/HYBRID TEA, RED BLEND, REPEAT-FLOWERING

This distinctive rose has large, pointed buds that are a medium pink with a yellow base to each of the 38 petals. The double blooms are usually borne singly or in small clusters on very long stems and there is a light fragrance. On opening, the rose changes to dark red and the effect of the three colors (pink, yellow and red) on the bush together is very striking. The large, abundant foliage is semi-glossy and medium green on a medium to tall, upright plant. The influence of 'Double Delight' can be seen in the deepening of the color of the full blooms. **ZONES 5–10.**

CHRISTENSEN, USA, 1981

('WHITE SATIN' × 'BEWITCHED') × 'DOUBLE DELIGHT'

ALL-AMERICA ROSE SELECTION 1982

### 'Mondiale' KORozon *(bottom)*

MODERN, LARGE-FLOWERED/HYBRID TEA, PINK BLEND, REPEAT-FLOWERING

The buds of this rose are plump and pointed, which gives promise of the full-petalled blooms that follow. They are deep coral-pink in the center of the blooms, with yellow shading that flows from the base into each of the crisp petals. The outer petals fade to light pink as they age. There is little fragrance, and flowers are borne freely through summer and autumn. In warm climates and under glass, the growth becomes very tall; it is recommended for a hedge, the back of a border or to screen unsightly walls. It performs well as a cutting rose in all conditions. The habit is upright, with a dense cover of glossy leaves that are reddish when young. **ZONES 5–9.**

KORDES, GERMANY, 1993

PARENTAGE UNKNOWN

M

### 'Monika'   TANaknom
*(above)*

syn. 'Monica'

MODERN, LARGE-FLOWERED/
HYBRID TEA, PINK BLEND/
ORANGE BLEND,
REPEAT-FLOWERING

'Monika' has very long,
elegant buds that open
to well-formed flowers
of bright vermilion
with a golden base.
This rich color holds
well. The blooms are
usually produced singly
on long stems, making
this a good rose for
cutting, and they last
well when picked. The
bush grows tall and
has healthy, profuse,
dark green, glossy foli-
age with good disease
resistance. Flower
production is excellent.
It makes a superb
hedge and can be used
for continuous color at
the back of a rose bed.
ZONES 5–10.

TANTAU, GERMANY, 1985

PARENTAGE UNKNOWN

### 'Monsieur Tillier'
*(above right)*

OLD, TEA, ORANGE PINK/PINK
BLEND, REPEAT-FLOWERING

'Monsieur Tillier' has
deep rose to purple
flowers with orange
and russet shades, and
they open flattish. This
is a vigorous shrub of
medium height, but it
can grow to enormous
heights if planted in a
shrubbery. Like most
Tea Roses, it is too
tender to survive cold
winters. ZONES 7–9.

BERNAIX, FRANCE, 1891

PARENTAGE UNKNOWN

### 'Montezuma'
*(bottom)*

MODERN, LARGE-FLOWERED/
HYBRID TEA, ORANGE-PINK,
REPEAT-FLOWERING

This rose is variously
described as orange-
pink or salmon-red,
both being apt descrip-
tions. However, the
full blooms fade to
a rather dirty color,
a fault inherited from
'Floradora'. The
shapely buds open
slowly to double
flowers of 36 petals
with high centers. They
are about 4 in (10 cm)
across and there is
some fragrance. The
repeat-bloom is very
quick and flower
production is excellent.
The foliage is leathery
and semi-glossy on a
vigorous and compact
plant. This is still an
excellent garden rose,
although the color is
now considered a trifle
dull. ZONES 5–10.

SWIM, USA, 1955

'FANDANGO' × 'FLORADORA'

GENEVA GOLD MEDAL 1955,
NATIONAL ROSE SOCIETY GOLD
MEDAL 1956, PORTLAND GOLD
MEDAL 1957

### 'Moonbeam' AUSbeam *(top)*
MODERN, MODERN SHRUB, APRICOT BLEND, REPEAT-FLOWERING

'Moonbeam' is very free flowering. It covers itself with flowers at frequent intervals and has very long, pointed buds that are a soft apricot-pink, more pink than apricot. The color is particularly clear and fresh. The buds open to large, semi-double flowers containing 15–20 petals and a boss of golden stamens. The medium-sized bush has copious pale green foliage and no disease problems. This rose is excellent for a hedge or for bedding and also associates particularly well with bulbs and perennials. It is a lovely rose for picking, as the long buds hold well in the bud stage in cool weather. It is also known as an English Rose. **ZONES 4–11.**

AUSTIN, UK, 1983

PARENTAGE UNKNOWN

### 'Moonlight' *(center)*
MODERN, MODERN SHRUB, LIGHT YELLOW, REPEAT-FLOWERING

The fragrant flowers of 'Moonlight' are palest yellow fading to white, and have prominent yellow stamens. They are single and occur in small and large well-spaced clusters. The foliage is dark and glossy, acting as a good foil to the flowers. Growth is bushy and the repeat cycle is very good. The flowers are particularly attractive in autumn, when they keep their yellow color for a longer period. This variety makes an excellent hedge and is good with bulbs and perennials. There are no disease problems except for a touch of seasonal mildew. If the spent blooms are not removed, a copious supply of hips is produced that lasts for several months; these look very attractive among the late flowers. **ZONES 4–11.**

PEMBERTON, UK, 1913

'TRIER' × 'SULPHUREA'

NATIONAL ROSE SOCIETY GOLD MEDAL 1913

### 'Moonsprite' *(bottom)*
MODERN, CLUSTER-FLOWERED/FLORIBUNDA, LIGHT YELLOW, REPEAT-FLOWERING

This delightful little rose has never gained the popularity it deserves. The oval buds open to very full, fragrant flowers of creamy white, shading to amber yellow in the center. There are 80 petals, and blooms occur in small and large clusters. They are cupped at first and then open flat. The foliage is leathery and semi-glossy on a medium-sized, bushy plant with excellent flower production and quick repeat-bloom. It is still gaining popularity after over 40 years in commerce. **ZONES 5–10.**

SWIM, USA, 1956

'SUTTER'S GOLD' × 'ONDINE'

BADEN-BADEN GOLD MEDAL 1955, ROME GOLD MEDAL 1956

M

The foliage has 7 leaflets and is slightly glossy on a bushy shrub. The flowers always occur on new growth, and there is repeat-bloom. 'Modern Centennial' is able to withstand very cold winters without die-back of the canes. **ZONES 3–9.**

MARSHALL, CANADA, 1980

'PRAIRIE PRINCESS' × ('WHITE BOUQUET' × ['J. W. FARGO' × 'ASSINIBOINE'])

## 'Morden Fireglow'

MODERN, MODERN SHRUB, ORANGE-RED, REPEAT-FLOWERING

'Morden Fireglow' has bright orange-red flowers, a color that is rare in cold-hardy roses. The buds are pointed and open to loosely formed, fragrant blooms. The cupped, double flowers, which have 28 petals with red undersides, are borne in small clusters. It is a low, bushy plant with a good repeat-bloom cycle. Globular hips are produced if spent blooms are not removed. **ZONES 3–9.**

COLICUTT & MARSHALL, CANADA, 1989

SEEDLING × 'MORDEN CARDINETTE'

## 'Morden Blush'   *(above)*

MODERN, MODERN SHRUB, LIGHT PINK, REPEAT-FLOWERING

Bred by the Department of Agriculture in Canada for winter hardiness, 'Morden Blush' has flowers of light pink fading to ivory. The small, double blooms have 50 petals and open flat, and occur in sprays of 1–5. The foliage is medium green and matt on a low, bushy plant with repeat-bloom. This is an excellent small shrub where winter hardiness is an important factor, although it is not well known outside Canada and the colder areas of the USA. **ZONES 3–9.**

COLICUTT & MARSHALL, CANADA, 1988

('PRAIRIE PRINCESS' × 'MORDEN AMORETTE') × ('PRAIRIE PRINCESS' × ['WHITE BOUQUET' × {ROSA ARKANSANA × 'ASSINIBOINE'}])

## 'Morden Centennial'

MODERN, MODERN SHRUB, MEDIUM PINK, REPEAT-FLOWERING

This rose bred by the Department of Agriculture in Canada for severe winter conditions has double, medium pink flowers that occur in clusters of up to 15. Each bloom has 50 petals and there is a slight fragrance.

## 'Morden Ruby'
*(above left)*

MODERN, MODERN SHRUB, PINK
BLEND, REPEAT-FLOWERING

The buds of 'Morden Ruby' are oval, and open to very double, pink blend flowers. They are 3 in (8 cm) in diameter, and the early blooming is very heavy on a vigorous plant that repeats well. This rose is not well known outside the colder areas of Canada and northern USA. **ZONES 3–9.**

MARSHALL, CANADA, 1977

'FIRE KING' × ('J. W. FARGO' ×
'ASSINIBOINE')

## 'Morgengruss'
*(bottom)*
syn. 'Morning Greeting'

MODERN, MODERN SHRUB,
ORANGE-PINK,
REPEAT-FLOWERING

This extremely vigorous shrub rose grows to 9–10 ft (2.7–3 m) high and nearly as much across. The abundant foliage is glossy and light green. The ovoid buds open to very double blooms that occur in clusters and are pale pink tinted with orange-yellow. They are very fragrant. 'Morgengruss' is an excellent shrub for planting in parks for a colorful spring display; it needs a lot of room to develop its full potential. It is very good in cold climates. **ZONES 4–11.**

KORDES, GERMANY, 1962

PARENTAGE UNKNOWN

## 'Morletii'  *(top right)*
syns 'Inermis Morletii', 'Morlettii', *Rosa pendulina plena*

OLD, BOURSAULT, MAUVE

The Boursaults are thought, without great confidence, to be a cross between *Rosa pendulina* and *R. chinensis*. They have few if any thorns (*inermis* is Latin for 'unarmed'), and there are now only four Boursaults freely available; 'Morletii' was the last of them to be introduced. The plant grows in an arching way, normally to about 6 ft (1.8 m) tall and wide, and bears many clusters of smallish, double magenta flowers in early summer. It can be trained as a climber. The leaves and stems color well in spring and autumn, when they turn coppery orange. **ZONES 7–9.**

MORLET, FRANCE, 1883

PARENTAGE UNKNOWN

**'Morning Blush'**
*(above)*

OLD, ALBA, LIGHT YELLOW

Tall and upright in the
center, flowing out-
ward from the base like
a fountain, this shrub
needs plenty of room
to offer its best features.
The semi-double
blooms of light yellow,

edged with dark pink,
line the strong canes
for about a month
during early summer,
and the large, glossy
dark green leaves act as
a contrast to the velvet-
like petals. There is
some fragrance. Like
all Albas, this is a very
healthy rose not at all

afflicted with mildew
or black spot. As a
landscaping plant,
'Morning Blush' makes
a fine rose for the back
of a border or as a
hedge. Sievers is the
first modern breeder to
successfully create large
numbers of Albas; they
are all reasonably winter
hardy. ZONES 4–9.

SIEVERS, GERMANY, 1988

PARENTAGE UNKNOWN

**'Moth'** *(top)*
syn. 'The Moth'

MODERN, MODERN SHRUB,
MAUVE, REPEAT-FLOWERING

'Moth', which is also
known as an English
Rose, is a large, very
thorny shrub rose with
very thick canes. The
slim, elegant buds open
to semi-double, pale
pink blooms of 15 or
so petals with a central
boss of stamens. They
come on short laterals
on the last season's
growth and completely
cover the bush in

spring. The repeat
cycle is rather slow.
The bush has a rather
ungainly growth habit
with large thorny
wood and very angular
spreading growth.
In cool weather, the
flowers can be beautiful
but they open quickly
and do not hold well
in hot weather.
ZONES 5–10.

AUSTIN, UK, 1983

PARENTAGE UNKNOWN

**'Mothersday'**
syns 'Fête Des Mères',
'Morsdag', 'Mothers
Day', 'Muttertag'

MODERN, POLYANTHA, DARK
RED, REPEAT-FLOWERING

A great many
Polyantha Roses are
sports of 'Orléans
Rose' or 'Dick Koster';
'Mothersday' is a sport
of the latter. The small,
many-petalled flowers
are deep red and
globular and occur in
clusters of 5–20. The
foliage is small and
glossy on a plant with
a very dwarf habit.
Flower production
is good, but the repeat-
bloom is a little slow.
As is the case with most
Polyanthas, there can
be mildew problems.
This rose was grown in
large quantities in pots
in the past for forcing
into flower in time
for Mother's Day in
Europe. ZONES 4–11.

GROOTENDORST, GERMANY,
1949

SPORT OF 'DICK KOSTER'

## 'Mount Hood'

MACmouhoo *(right)*
syns 'Foster's
Melbourne Cup',
'Foster's Wellington
Cup'

MODERN, LARGE-FLOWERED/
HYBRID TEA, WHITE,
REPEAT-FLOWERING

The flowers of this rose
are ivory white with a
light fragrance. They
are very double, con-
taining 40–45 petals,
with good high sym-
metrical centers. The
blooms occur mainly
as clusters, giving the
bush a snow-capped
appearance. The foliage
is glossy deep green on
a full-branching, tall,
upright plant that has
excellent vigor and
disease resistance. It
has an amazing capacity
for bloom production,
but the flowers usually
require a little heat to
open fully. This rose
is a sister seedling of
another famous rose,
'Singin' in the Rain'.
It was named by the
hybridizer to recognize
the majestic snow-
capped Mount Hood,
which rises above the
Columbia Gorge on
the Oregon Trail in
northwestern USA.
ZONES 5–10.

MCGREDY, NEW ZEALAND, 1991

'SEXY REXY' × 'POT O' GOLD'

NEW ZEALAND GOLD MEDAL
1992, ALL-AMERICA ROSE
SELECTION 1996

## 'Mount Shasta'

*(below)*

MODERN, LARGE-FLOWERED/
HYBRID TEA, WHITE,
REPEAT-FLOWERING

'Mount Shasta' is still
one of the best white

roses available. The
buds are very large,
long and pointed and
most attractive. They
open to well-formed,
double flowers con-
taining 20–25 petals.

The fragrant, cupped
blooms are up to 5 in
(12 cm) across, and are
produced on very long
stems that are excellent
for picking at the bud
stage. The leathery
foliage is an unusual
gray-green color that
complements the
flowers well. Growth
is very vigorous and
upright. This rose is
whiter than 'Pascali'
and 'Tineke' and is
suitable for a wedding
bouquet. ZONES 5–10.

SWIM & WEEKS, USA, 1963

'QUEEN ELIZABETH' ×
'BLANCHE MALLERIN'

M

## 'Mountbatten'

**HARmantelle** *(bottom)*

MODERN, CLUSTER-FLOWERED/
FLORIBUNDA, MEDIUM YELLOW,
REPEAT-FLOWERING

This is a particularly
strong-growing,
healthy rose with
abundant foliage and
dense growth. The
clear soft yellow,
double flowers with
45 petals are cupped at
first, opening flat in the
full bloom stage. They
are borne singly and
several together on
long stems and are
fragrant. The foliage is
large, dark green and
glossy. The first flush
is very heavy and the
repeat cycle is good.
Although it has won
many awards, it has
not become as popular
as might have been
expected. **ZONES 5–10.**
HARKNESS, UK, 1982

'PEER GYNT' × (['ANNE
COCKER' × 'ARTHUR BELL'] ×
'SOUTHAMPTON')

ROYAL NATIONAL ROSE SOCIETY
CERTIFICATE OF MERIT 1979,
LYON ROSE OF THE CENTURY
1980, UK ROSE OF THE YEAR
1982, BELFAST GOLD MEDAL,
ORLÉANS GOLD MEDAL 1984,
COURTRAI GOLD MEDAL 1986,
GOLDEN ROSE OF THE HAGUE
1986, ROYAL HORTICULTURAL
SOCIETY AWARD OF GARDEN
MERIT 1993

## 'Mozart' *(top)*

MODERN, MODERN SHRUB, PINK
BLEND, REPEAT-FLOWERING

This excellent shrub
rose has fragrant, single
flowers that are deep
pink with a large white
eye. They are small and
occur in small to very
large clusters. There
is good repeat-bloom,
especially in autumn
when enormous
trusses of flowers are
produced; these last a
long time. The growth
is very vigorous and
spreading, and the
plant has excellent
resistance to disease.
It looks rather like
Harkness' 'Marjorie
Fair', and both are
excellent shrub roses.
**ZONES 4–11.**
LAMBERT, GERMANY, 1937

'ROBIN HOOD' ×
'ROTE PHARISÄER'

### 'München' *(above)*
**MODERN, MODERN SHRUB, DARK RED, REPEAT-FLOWERING**

This variety has long, pointed buds that open to semi-double, scarlet-crimson flowers with a light fragrance. The blooms are normally borne in small clusters on strong stems. The color of the blooms starts out as a very attractive cardinal red that acquires a lighter shading with exposure to full sun. The foliage is glossy dark green on a plant with a trailing growth habit. This is an extremely vigorous rose with a good repeat-bloom. **ZONES 4–10.**

KORDES, GERMANY, 1940

'EVA' × 'REVEIL DIJONNAIS'

### 'Mutabilis' *(top right)*
syns *Rosa chinensis mutabilis, R. × odorata* 'Mutabilis', 'Tipo Idéale'
**OLD, CHINA, YELLOW BLEND, REPEAT-FLOWERING**

This rose was probably first introduced to horticulture in 1934 by Swiss botanist Henri Correvon of Geneva, who obtained it from Prince Ghilberto Borromeo's garden at Isola Bella. It normally makes a large, spreading bush but can go up to the eaves on a house wall in time. The flowers are butterfly-like and are borne in masses. They open yellow, turn to pink and then crimson and have a long flowering period. 'Masquerade' seems to be derived from this rose. **ZONES 5–10.**

PROBABLY FROM CHINA AND INTRODUCED TO ITALY, PRE-1894

PARENTAGE UNKNOWN

ROYAL HORTICULTURAL SOCIETY AWARD OF GARDEN MERIT 1993

### 'My Choice' *(above)*
**MODERN, LARGE-FLOWERED/HYBRID TEA, PINK BLEND, REPEAT-FLOWERING**

The double flowers of this variety have 33 petals and are pink with a pale primrose yellow reverse. There is a very noticeable damask fragrance. The buds tend to be unattractive at the beginning but mature into wonderfully formed flowers with good substance and color. The blooms are exceptionally large, at 4–5 in (12–14 cm) across, while the foliage is a very attractive leathery green on a vigorous, tall-growing plant. It is not winter hardy and can suffer from powdery mildew and black spot if left unprotected during the growing season. This rose is best grown in warmer climates for peak performance. Curiously, it has been neglected by the rose-buying public in spite of its gold medals. **ZONES 5–11.**

LEGRICE, UK, 1958

'WELLWORTH' × 'ENA HARKNESS'

NATIONAL ROSE SOCIETY GOLD MEDAL 1958, NRS CLAY CUP FOR FRAGRANCE 1958, PORTLAND GOLD MEDAL 1961

M

### 'Nana Mouskouri' *(above)*
MODERN, CLUSTER-FLOWERED/FLORIBUNDA, WHITE,
REPEAT-FLOWERING

This rose has creamy white flowers with a pink
flush in the bud stage prior to opening. In warm
climates the flowers are almost pure white.
The double florets have about 30 petals and are
fragrant. The flower form is symmetrical with
the high centers making it a suitable variety for
exhibition purposes. The blooms, borne in small
to medium-sized clusters, cover the bush, making
for a beautiful garden display. The foliage is
medium dark green on an upright, compact bush.
It is a vigorous plant with good resistance to
mildew and black spot. It was named to honor
the celebrated Greek singer. ZONES 5–10.

DICKSON, UK, 1975

'REDGOLD' × 'ICED GINGER'

### 'Nancy Hayward' *(top right)*
MODERN, LARGE-FLOWERED CLIMBER, MEDIUM RED,
REPEAT-FLOWERING

The flowers of this variety are a bright cerise-red
fading to carmine-red. The large florets are single
petalled with a faint fragrance. The mid-green
foliage is very disease resistant. This vigorous
plant needs training to spread out over a fence
or high wall to maximize its bloom production
at each lateral. It lasts well as a cut flower for
indoors and needs little or no attention during
the season, except for removal of spent blooms.
'Nancy Hayward' has been successfully used on
balcony railings where it can bloom constantly,
providing color throughout the growing season.
ZONES 5–10.

CLARK, AUSTRALIA, 1937

'JESSIE CLARK' × SEEDLING

### 'Nancy Steen' *(above)*
MODERN, CLUSTER-FLOWERED/FLORIBUNDA, PINK BLEND,
REPEAT-FLOWERING

The large, fragrant, double flowers of this rose have
30 petals that are a blush pink with a pale cream
center. The blooms have a flat informal form
against a backdrop of dark green, glossy foliage.
It is a strong-growing plant bearing an abundance
of blooms that are always in clusters. While it has
been registered as a Cluster-flowered Rose, it resembles a Modern Shrub. The hybridizer named
this rose after one of New Zealand's most notable
rose growers who worked diligently to revive
interest in Old Garden Roses. ZONES 5–10.

SHERWOOD, NEW ZEALAND, 1976

'PINK PARFAIT' × ('OPHELIA' × 'PARKDIREKTOR RIGGERS')

### 'Narrow Water'
*(right)*

OLD, NOISETTE, LIGHT PINK,
REPEAT-FLOWERING

This rose is a medium
to tall Noisette with
delicate, small, rosette-
style lavender-pink
flowers that are borne
in sprays. It is reminis-
cent of 'Blush Noisette',
the original Noisette
rose. It is a desirable rose
to have in the garden.
Narrow Water Castle is
on a narrowing section
of the Carlingford
River between Newry
and Warrenpoint. This
river marks the bound-
ary between Eire and
Northern Ireland.
**ZONES 4–10.**

DAISY HILL NURSERY, IRELAND,
CIRCA 1883

SPORT OF 'NASTARANA'

### 'National Trust'
*(right)*
syn. 'Bad Nauheim'

MODERN, LARGE-FLOWERED/
HYBRID TEA, DARK RED,
REPEAT-FLOWERING

The bright red, weather-
proof flowers of this
variety have classic
Large-flowered form
and are supported
by strong stems. The
flowers are large—
with a 4 in (10 cm)
diameter—and very
double with 53 petals
but have no fragrance.
They are borne one to
a stem on a vigorous,
compact bush with a
short, neat habit. The
foliage is medium to
dark green and disease

resistant. This rose is
as near perfect as any
red Large-flowered
Rose could be, although
many agree with the
hybridizer that his
'Olympiad' introduced
in 1982 was a step
closer to that ideal of
perfection. It was named
for the 75th Anniversary
of the National Trust
in Great Britain.
**ZONES 4–11.**

MCGREDY, UK, 1970

'EVELYN FISON' ×
'KING OF HEARTS'

ROYAL NATIONAL SOCIETY
TRIAL GROUND CERTIFICATE
1969, BELFAST CERTIFICATE OF
MERIT 1972

### 'Nearly Wild'

MODERN, CLUSTER-FLOWERED/
FLORIBUNDA, MEDIUM PINK,
REPEAT-FLOWERING

Small pointed buds
open to rose pink,
single-petalled flowers.
They are borne in
clusters on long
straight stems and are

fragrant. The plant has
a bushy, compact growth
habit and reasonable
disease resistance.
Although this classic
rose is nearly extinct
and is no longer in
commerce, it can still
be observed growing
in many old museum
gardens and estates.
The seed parent,
'Dr W. Van Fleet', was
used extensively in rose

hybridizing but its
most famous contri-
bution came in 1997
when the World
Federation of Rose
Societies entered the
climbing sport 'New
Dawn' into the Rose
Hall of Fame as one of
the world's favorite
roses. **ZONES 4–10.**

BROWNELL, USA, 1941

'DR W. VAN FLEET' ×
'LEUCHTSTERN'

N

## 'Nestor'

OLD, GALLICA, MEDIUM RED

The flowers of 'Nestor' are very double, flat, cupped and quartered. The blooms are magenta with the outer petals a charming lilac-pink. This is a fine rose worthy of a spot in any garden. The foliage is light green on a plant of medium height. One can only speculate on the naming of the rose—it is probable that it was named after a Frenchman, and not the king of Pylos who accompanied the Greeks to the Trojan war. ZONES 4–9.

PRE-1848

PARENTAGE UNKNOWN

## 'Nevada' *(top)*

MODERN, MODERN SHRUB, WHITE, REPEAT-FLOWERING

'Nevada' has pink to apricot ovoid buds that open to large white flowers that are 4 in (10 cm) in diameter with a reverse that is sometimes splashed carmine. The weather-proof, single-petalled blooms are borne in clusters on short stems and cover the bush. The foliage is mid-green and usually disease resistant; in some wet climates black spot will develop if the plant is not pro-tected by spraying. It is a tall, vigorous plant growing to 7 ft (2 m) in most climates. Rarely without blooms, this rose has the grace and majesty of a Wild Rose combined with a Modern Shrub. As to its pollen parentage, there has been discus-sion that perhaps *Rosa moyesii fargesii*, a tetra-ploid form, was used. ZONES 4–10.

DOT, SPAIN, 1927

REPORTED TO BE 'LA GIRALDA' × HYBRID OF *ROSA MOYESII*

ROYAL HORTICULTURAL SOCIETY AWARD OF GARDEN MERIT 1993

## 'New Beginning'

SAVabeg *(bottom)*

MODERN, MINIATURE, ORANGE BLEND, REPEAT-FLOWERING

The bright orange-yellow, bicolored flowers of this variety have decorative form; they are double, made up of 40–50 petals, of medium size and are usually borne singly or in small sprays. It has no fragrance and the compact bush is covered with semi-glossy, mid-green foliage. This is best as a garden rose because it carries a constant production of blooms that do not fade too quickly in hot climates, although in cooler weather the color and form are much improved. The brilliant color makes it a suitable candidate for hanging baskets, borders and as a ground cover. This was the first Miniature Rose to be awarded the prestigious All-America Rose Selection award, which was previously reserved for large rose categories—a well-deserved honor for the hybridizer, Harm Saville. It is interesting to note that 'Zorina' was also the parent of many other prize-winning Cluster-flowered Roses. ZONES 5–11.

SAVILLE, USA, 1988

'ZORINA' × SEEDLING

ALL-AMERICA ROSE SELECTION 1989

## 'New Daily Mail' *(right)*

syn. 'Pussta'

**MODERN, CLUSTER-FLOWERED/FLORIBUNDA, DARK RED, REPEAT-FLOWERING**

This rose has globular buds that open to large, semi-double, dark red flowers with golden stamens. There is no fragrance. The foliage is a semi-glossy dark green on a vigorous, upright plant. This rose has two predecessors—the 1913 orange blend Large-flowered Rose, 'Daily Mail Rose', hybridized by Pernet-Ducher, and the crimson Large-flowered Rose, 'Daily Mail Scented Rose', bred by Archer in England in 1927. Furthermore, **'Climbing New Daily Mail'** was registered in 1989 by B. K. Patil of Bangalore, India. **ZONES 5–10.**

TANTAU, GERMANY, 1972

'LETKIS' × 'WALZERTRAUM'

## 'New Dawn' *(right)*

syns 'Everblooming Dr W. Van Fleet', 'The New Dawn'

**MODERN, LARGE-FLOWERED CLIMBER, LIGHT PINK, REPEAT-FLOWERING**

'New Dawn' has no faults and some great attributes that make it an all-time favorite of many rose growers. Large, double, fragrant, cameo pink flowers fading to a flesh-toned white are the hallmarks of this rose. The foliage is glossy, dark green and disease resistant on a bush that climbs to about 20 ft (6 m). It is winter hardy and blooms all year long with an exceptional crop of flowers, both in small clusters and one bloom per stem whatever the climate zone. The sweet scent of the blooms is another plus. The canes and stems are pliable enough to accommodate any garden design. After almost 67 years in existence, it was elected to the World Rose Hall of Fame in 1997 by the members of the World Federation of Rose Societies at their Triennial Convention in Benelux. **ZONES 4–10.**

DREER, USA, 1930

SPORT OF 'DR W. VAN FLEET'

ROYAL HORTICULTURAL SOCIETY AWARD OF GARDEN MERIT 1993, WORLD FEDERATION OF ROSE SOCIETIES WORLD'S FAVORITE ROSE 1997

## 'New Face' INTerclem

**MODERN, MODERN SHRUB, YELLOW BLEND, REPEAT-FLOWERING**

Peter Ilsink has produced a fascinating range of shrub roses, and this one is particularly suitable for gardens where there is ample space, for it is capable of growing to twice the extent of the average shrub rose. The single blooms are creamy yellow, with bright pink edging towards the petal rims. They are of small to medium size and appear in large sprays with excellent continuity through summer and autumn. For a big border or naturalized garden, this is a good rose, and the young flower sprays are suitable to cut for indoor flower arrangements. The plant grows upright with a dense, well-spread habit, and has prickly stems and medium-sized, semi-glossy leaves. **ZONES 4–9.**

ILSINK, THE NETHERLANDS, 1978

PARENTAGE UNKNOWN

BAGATELLE GOLD MEDAL 1981

N

suffer from powdery mildew if left unprotected. **ZONES 4–10.**

BOERNER, USA, 1947

'FLAMBEAU' × SEEDLING

NATIONAL ROSE SOCIETY CERTIFICATE OF MERIT 1950

### 'New Zealand'

MACgenev *(top right)*

syn. 'Aotearoa New Zealand'

MODERN, LARGE-FLOWERED/ HYBRID TEA, LIGHT PINK, REPEAT-FLOWERING

This rose has large, soft pink blooms with excellent shape and form that are borne singly on strong straight stems. The double florets have 30–35 petals with a strong honeysuckle fragrance. The foliage is glossy, dark green on a vigorous, upright bush with good overall shape and architecture. It prefers consistent temperatures on the warm side to show off its best characteristics. The real winner among its many attributes is the fragrance. The plant takes a year to establish in the garden and then it performs beautifully. It is a credit to Sam McGredy who attained the zenith of perfection in breeding Large-flowered Roses of exceptional character and quality. **ZONES 4–10.**

MCGREDY, NEW ZEALAND, 1991

'HARMONIE' × 'AUCKLAND METRO'

PORTLAND GOLD MEDAL AND FRAGRANCE AWARD 1996

### 'New Year' MACnewye

*(top left)*

syn. 'Arcadian'

MODERN, LARGE-FLOWERED/ HYBRID TEA, ORANGE BLEND, REPEAT-FLOWERING

The flowers of 'New Year' are a delightful blend of clear orange and golden yellow. The shapely florets have 20 petals and a light fragrance. They are borne in small clusters and sometimes one to a stem. In hot weather the blooms tend to open rather quickly but the prolific production compensates for this. The foliage is large and dark green on a tall, upright, vigorous bush that is also disease free. It is not winter hardy. Because of its dense bushy growth it is an ideal garden variety providing color throughout the growing season. In 1995 a climbing sport with 6–14 petals was discovered by Joe Burks of Texas, USA. **ZONES 5–10.**

MCGREDY, NEW ZEALAND, 1983

'MARY SUMNER' × SEEDLING

ALL-AMERICA ROSE SELECTION 1987

### 'New Yorker'

*(above)*

MODERN, LARGE-FLOWERED/ HYBRID TEA, MEDIUM RED, REPEAT-FLOWERING

The 35-petalled flowers are a velvety scarlet-red and show no evidence of fading in any climatic zones. The florets are large—almost 5 in (12 cm) in diameter. They have classical high centers with good symmetry and a fruity fragrance, and are grown one per stem with little or no clustering. It is a vigorous bush with many branches. It is winter hardy, but it can

## 'News' LEGnews
### (right)
MODERN, CLUSTER-FLOWERED/
FLORIBUNDA, MAUVE,
REPEAT-FLOWERING

The semi-double, fragrant flowers of this rose are a non-fading purple with golden yellow stamens. Borne in clusters against attractive glossy, olive green foliage, the large, weatherproof blooms have good staying power on the bush. It is a vigorous, medium-sized, upright bush with a tendency to spread, and has excellent repeat-cycle times. It is easy to maintain and disease resistant—characteristics acquired from its parents. After its introduction in 1970, a large bed was established in Queen Mary's Rose Garden in Regent's Park, London. It became the talk of the town and helped promote this rose, and rose growing, to the public. ZONES 4–10.

LEGRICE, UK, 1968

'LILAC CHARM' × 'SUPERB TUSCANY'

ROYAL NATIONAL ROSE SOCIETY GOLD MEDAL 1970, BELFAST CERTIFICATE OF MERIT 1970

## 'Niccolo Paganini'
MEIcairma  (top right)
syns 'Courage',
'Paganini'

MODERN, CLUSTER-FLOWERED/
FLORIBUNDA, MEDIUM RED,
REPEAT-FLOWERING

The buds of this variety are long with a graceful urn shape, and open into rounded blooms with neatly coiled centers that become quite large as the petals expand. They are a rich shade of red, with a shining, velvety look about them, but do not have more than a slight fragrance. The clusters appear with excellent continuity through summer and autumn, making this a popular choice for beds and borders or for a hedge. In warm climates it grows to average height with plentiful, crisp deep green foliage. ZONES 5–9.

MEILLAND, FRANCE, 1991

PARENTAGE UNKNOWN

GENEVA GOLD MEDAL 1989, ROSE OF THE CENTURY 1990, LYON PLUS BELLE ROSE DE FRANCE 1990

## 'Nice Day' CHEwsea
### (bottom)

MODERN, CLIMBING MINIATURE,
ORANGE-PINK,
REPEAT-FLOWERING

The small, fragrant, salmon-pink flowers

that adorn this rose each contain about 15–25 petals to form a neat rosette. They are borne in large and decorative clusters that are complemented by small, glossy bronze- to mid-green foliage. Its habit is decidedly climbing, but the plant can take several seasons to establish for maximum performance. Its color holds well in sunny climates, but it prefers cooler conditions where it can hold its color and bloom a lot longer. This is another major achievement by Chris Warner, who has developed a range of climbers in most color combinations. ZONES 5–10.

WARNER, UK, 1992

'SEASPRAY' × 'WARM WELCOME'

BRITISH ASSOCIATION OF ROSE BREEDERS SELECTION 1994

N

N

### 'Night Light'

POULlight *(right)*
syn. 'Night Life'

MODERN, LARGE-FLOWERED
CLIMBER, DEEP YELLOW,
REPEAT-FLOWERING

This rose has red-tinted pointed buds that open to reveal flowers of deep yellow, ageing to orange-yellow. The double florets have 27 petals and a light sweet scent. They are borne in sprays of 3–5 florets against large, glossy, dark green foliage on a tall, spreading bush that can grow to 8 ft (2.4 m) high in one season in warmer climates. The flowers can be up to 5 in (12 cm) in diameter. The form is more decorative than formal. ZONES 5–10.

POULSEN, DENMARK, 1982

'WESTERLAND' × 'PASTORALE'

### 'Nina Weibull'

MODERN, CLUSTER-FLOWERED/
FLORIBUNDA, DARK RED,
REPEAT-FLOWERING

The dark red flowers of 'Nina Weibull' do not fade easily. The florets are double and have an informal open form. They come in small clusters of 3–5 florets. The foliage is dark green on a compact bush with a short growth habit. It is generally prolific in bloom production, disease resistant and easy to grow. This rose is a great choice for a mass planting in the garden because of its consistent and uniform growth habit and constant color. ZONES 5–10.

POULSEN, DENMARK, 1962

'FANAL' × 'MASQUERADE'

### 'Niphetos' *(right)*

OLD, TEA, WHITE,
REPEAT-FLOWERING

This is a classic Tea Rose with very elongated, tapering buds that open to pure white blooms. They are quite remarkably delicate and are somewhat reminiscent of 'Maréchal Niel'. There is a pronounced tea fragrance. The foliage is pale green on a plant with a medium growth habit. In colder climates, this is a rose for the greenhouse. '**Climbing Niphetos**' sported from 'Niphetos' and was introduced by William Keynes and Co. in 1889. It is more vigorous than its parent and bears bigger flowers. ZONES 7–9.

BOUGÈRE, FRANCE, 1843

PARENTAGE UNKNOWN

## 'Nobilo's Chardonnay'

MACrelea *(right)*
syns 'Chardonnay',
'Chardony', 'Peachy'

MODERN, LARGE-FLOWERED/
HYBRID TEA, MEDIUM YELLOW,
REPEAT-FLOWERING

This rose has brilliant orange-yellow flowers. The large, double blooms have 35 petals, 4–5 in (10–12 cm) in diameter, high centered and symmetrical. The foliage is small and an attractive light green on a well-rounded, compact bush. The pollen parent is the result of crossing Kordes' 1974 orange-pink Large-flowered Rose 'Wienerwald' with Sam McGredy's 1979 yellow blend Large-flowered Rose 'Benson & Hedges Gold'. This cross succeeded in passing on the desirable characteristics of both these great roses. **ZONES 5–10.**

MCGREDY, NEW ZEALAND, 1984

'FREUDE' × ('WIENERWALD' ×
'BENSON & HEDGES GOLD')

## 'Noëlla Nabonnand' *(above)*

OLD, CLIMBING TEA, DARK RED

The large flowers of 'Noëlla Nabonnand' are semi-double with 21 petals and do not last long, either on the bush or as a cut flower. The sweetly scented blooms are a velvety crimson and the petals have a soft velvety texture. This vigorous, medium climber is well-foliated. There is a considerable early flush and lighter periodical flowering thereafter. In warmer climates, there can also be winter blooms. It was named for a member of the breeder's family. **ZONES 7–9.**

NABONNAND, FRANCE, 1901

'REINE MARIE HENRIETTE' ×
'BARDOU JOB'

## 'Norfolk' POUlfolk *(bottom right)*

MODERN, GROUND COVER,
MEDIUM YELLOW,
REPEAT-FLOWERING

These small, delicately scented flowers are a medium non-fading bright yellow. The double blooms come in weatherproof clusters. The foliage is glossy green on a compact, low-growing plant that grows to about 18–24 in (45–60 cm). Because it produces an abundance of color throughout the growing season and indeed flowers all year long, this rose is a welcome addition to the Ground Cover classification. It suits small spaces and containers. **ZONES 5–10.**

POULSEN, DENMARK, 1990

PARENTAGE UNKNOWN

N

### 'Norwich Castle'
*(bottom)*

MODERN, CLUSTER-FLOWERED/
FLORIBUNDA, ORANGE BLEND,
REPEAT-FLOWERING

Shapely buds on this variety open to rich copper-orange flowers that gradually change with age to a soft apricot. The double florets have 30 petals, a faint but detectable fruity fragrance, and are borne in small dense clusters. The blooms open from high centers to reveal a charming flat rosette. They are excellent cut flowers and there is a consistent supply of blooms throughout the growing season. The foliage is shiny mid-green on a vigorous, upright plant. It is winter hardy and can tolerate most soil types, including clay. In naming this rose, Peter Beales paid homage to the great Norman castle, now a museum, that dominates the East Anglian capital of Norwich, his home town. **ZONES 5–10.**

BEALES, UK, 1980

('WHISKY MAC' × 'ARTHUR
BELL') × 'BETTINA'

### 'Northern Lights'
*(above)*

MODERN, LARGE-FLOWERED/
HYBRID TEA, YELLOW BLEND,
REPEAT-FLOWERING

This variety has canary lemon flowers with a suffusion of rose pink on the outer petals. The large blooms are over 5 in (12 cm) across, have 50 petals and are very fragrant. They have perfect classical high centers with great symmetry. The blooms are borne one to a stem and later in the growing season in small clusters and trusses. They are ideal for exhibition at rose shows or cutting for indoors since, because of the large petal count, they are extremely long lasting. The foliage is deep green and glossy on a vigorous plant of medium height. The hybridizer lived in an area of Scotland where the Northern Lights could be seen.
**ZONES 4–10.**

COCKER, UK, 1969

'FRAGRANT CLOUD' × 'KINGCUP'

### 'Northamptonshire'   MATtdor  *(top left)*
MODERN, GROUND COVER, WHITE/LIGHT PINK, REPEAT-FLOWERING

The pearly pink flowers of this rose have a light sweet fragrance. The florets are 1–2 in (25–50 mm) in diameter; they have a cupped form and are borne in large clusters on strong stems. A carpet of attractive semi-glossy, mid-green foliage is produced in abundance. This rose blooms all year long, providing a long-lasting tapestry of color in the garden, and is ideal for a sunny bank or just cascading over a terrace. It was named by John Mattock for a wonderful county north of London. **ZONES 5–10.**

MATTOCK, UK, 1990

PARENTAGE UNKNOWN

ROYAL NATIONAL ROSE SOCIETY CERTIFICATE OF MERIT 1988

## 'Nova Zembla' *(above)*

MODERN, HYBRID RUGOSA, WHITE

The flowers of this flesh pink to nearly white rose are strongly fragrant. The double florets are large—4 in (10 cm) across—and are borne in large clusters on strong stems that need no additional support. The foliage is deep dark green on a vigorous plant that can grow to 9 ft (2.7 m) high, making it ideal as a pillar rose. Although it blooms only once at the very beginning of the season, the display of rosehips later in autumn provides a dramatic tapestry of orange-red for most of winter. **ZONES 4–10.**

MEES, UK, 1907

SPORT OF 'CONRAD FERDINAND MEYER'

## 'Nozomi' *(top right)*
### syn. 'Heideröslein Nozomi'

MODERN, CLIMBING MINIATURE, LIGHT PINK

The buds on this rose open to little, pale pink, single flowers that lighten to pearly pink. They are borne in trusses amid the small, glossy dark foliage, and have a light scent. The plant has a trailing habit and can be used as a climber or a ground cover. The blooms are produced on the previous year's wood, so only light pruning is recommended. 'Nozomi' means hope and was the name of the raiser's niece who died aged four. **ZONES 5–10.**

ONODERA, JAPAN, 1968

'FAIRY PRINCESS' (1955 VARIETY) × 'SWEET FAIRY'

ROYAL HORTICULTURAL SOCIETY AWARD OF GARDEN MERIT 1993

## 'Nuits de Young' *(above)*

OLD, MOSS, DARK RED

This is one of the darkest colored of all roses. The mossy buds open to small, roundly oval flowers that are borne in small clusters. The fragrant blooms are about $1\frac{1}{2}$ in (4 cm) across. They are deep blackcurrant purple with grayish overtones, and the whole effect of each fully open flower is that of velvet. When fully open they reveal a small group of golden yellow stamens. It is a slender growing, though dense shrub, relaxed in habit, to around 4 ft (1.2 m) high and wide. The stems are thornless but are densely covered with purplish brown, stubbly moss, and the leaves are rich dark green. This is a superb old variety that is most rewarding in spite of its relatively short flowering season in early summer. **ZONES 4–10.**

LAFFAY, FRANCE, 1845

PARENTAGE UNKNOWN

N

The foliage is large, glossy and dark green on a vigorous, upright bush growing 10 ft (3 m) tall or more. It is free flowering and easy to maintain and provides an abundance of blooms, as the repeat-flowering is good. When he named this rose, Wilhelm Kordes paid tribute to the palace and gardens of the city of Nymphenburg which is just outside Munich and has become a very popular tourist attraction. **ZONES 4–10.**

KORDES, GERMANY, 1954

'SANGERHAUSEN' × 'SUNMIST'

NATIONAL ROSE SOCIETY TRIAL GROUND CERTIFICATE 1954

### 'Nyveldt's White'
*(left)*
MODERN, HYBRID RUGOSA, WHITE, REPEAT-FLOWERING

These beautiful single-petalled snow-white flowers have golden yellow stamens. The large blooms have a very sweet fragrance. The foliage is dark green on a vigorous plant that reaches 7 ft (2.1 m) high. It flowers continuously but if left ungroomed a tremendous crop of orange-red hips will appear. This rose is winter hardy and shade tolerant. **ZONES 4–10.**

NYVELDT, THE NETHERLANDS, 1955

(ROSA RUGOSA RUBRA × R. CINNAMOMEA) × R. NITIDA

### 'Nur Mahal' *(top)*
MODERN, MODERN SHRUB, MEDIUM RED, REPEAT-FLOWERING

The bright crimson flowers have a strong musk scent. The semi-double florets are borne in clusters on strong straight stems. The small foliage is dark green on a vigorous bush with pillar-type growth to 8–10 ft (2.4–3 m). It is a very pleasing bush that with pruning can be trained to be a medium-sized plant that is disease free. Pemberton named this rose after the powerful wife of Emperor Jahangir of India, whom legend credits with the discovery of 'Attar of Roses'. **ZONES 5–10.**

PEMBERTON, UK, 1923

'CHÂTEAU DE CLOS VOUGEOT' × SEEDLING OF HYBRID MUSK

### 'Nymphenburg'
*(above left)*
MODERN, MODERN SHRUB, ORANGE-PINK, REPEAT-FLOWERING

Apricot-pink buds on this variety open to flowers that are a soft salmon-pink shaded orange towards the outer edges of the petals. The center is yellow. The blooms fade with age to a paler blended color. The fragrant florets are large, semi-double, and come in small and large clusters.

### 'Octavia Hill' HARzeal *(above)*

MODERN, CLUSTER-FLOWERED/FLORIBUNDA, MEDIUM PINK, REPEAT-FLOWERING

The clear medium pink flowers of this variety contain an astonishing 75 petals. They have a moderate Damask fragrance and occur in small sprays of neatly spaced blooms. The blooms are about 3 in (8 cm) in diameter and have a double quartered form. The foliage is a semi-glossy, dark green on a medium-sized compact bush. It is a fairly vigorous plant, but requires removal of spent blooms to initiate the next bloom cycle and promote new growth. The flowers are ideal for cutting as they last a long time. **ZONES 5–10.**

HARKNESS, UK, 1995

'ARMADA' × 'CORNELIA'

COURTRAI SILVER MEDAL 1995, THE HAGUE CERTIFICATE OF MERIT 1998

### 'Octavius Weld' *(top right)*

OLD, TEA, PINK BLEND, REPEAT-FLOWERING

'Octavius Weld' was found on a grave in Blakiston, South Australia, and given the name on the tombstone. In the late nineteenth century, South Australian gardeners imported bare-root roses from England and vied with one another over their collections of all kinds of plants. 'Octavius Weld' was probably imported in the 1890s. It grows quickly into a huge bush as wide as it is tall, with matt mid-green pointed leaflets. The flowers are very variable; in spring they can be rose pink, in summer soft pink tinged with cream, and in autumn and winter the color of clotted cream. They are produced continuously, both singly and in small clusters. Long buds develop into very flat blooms with short petaloids

in the center. The petal count varies from 25 to 40. The scent is typically Tea Rose. Repeat-bloom is rapid, even when spent blooms are not removed. In mild winters it may continue to flower. Mildew can be a slight problem in autumn. This is a lovely Tea Rose, but it is not grown outside Australia. **ZONES 5–9.**

PARENTAGE UNKNOWN

### 'Œillet Flamand' *(above)*

OLD, GALLICA, PINK BLEND

This rose resembles a pink carnation in shape. It is a conventional once-flowering Gallica. The flowers are pale pink, striped white and brighter pink. They are very double and very fragrant. The foliage is coarse and dark green on a plant with a vigorous, upright growth habit. Peter Beales has called it an 'interesting' rose. **ZONES 4–9.**

VIBERT, FRANCE, 1845

PARENTAGE UNKNOWN

O

### 'Œillet Parfait'

OLD, GALLICA, PINK BLEND

'Œillet Parfait' is a good if little-grown rose. The fragrant flowers are 1½–2 in (4–5 cm) across and are borne in small erect clusters. They are rich pink, paling to soft pink, and are fully double and cushion-like when fully open. This is a compact, tidy, fairly upright shrub to 3 ft (1 m) high, marginally taller in good soil. The thin, dark green shoots are well endowed with thorns and prickles, and the foliage is round, mid- to light green and quite small. It seems to prefer good soil and some mollycoddling to give of its best. **ZONES 4–10.**

FOULARD, FRANCE, 1841

PARENTAGE UNKNOWN

### 'Oklahoma' *(left)*

MODERN, LARGE-FLOWERED/
HYBRID TEA, DARK RED,
REPEAT-FLOWERING

This rose has long, pointed, ovoid buds that open to very dark red flowers with high centers and excellent symmetry. The florets are 5 in (12 cm) across, double with 45 petals and are very fragrant. They are borne one to a stem. The foliage is dark matt green on an extremely vigorous bush that grows as high as 7–8 ft (2.1–2.4 m) in one season. It does best in temperate climates: too much heat will scorch the dark red blooms and too much cold will turn them magenta. Its color and heavy scent have made this a very popular rose. Its name is derived from the state of Oklahoma in the USA; the translation is 'Red Man's Land'. There are two versions of 'Climbing Oklahoma'; in 1968 the original breeders produced the first climber, then in 1972 A. Ross & Son in Australia introduced the second. The vigor and performance of both climbers is excellent. **ZONES 5–10.**

SWIM AND WEEKS, USA, 1964

'CHRYSLER IMPERIAL' ×
'CHARLES MALLERIN'

JAPAN GOLD MEDAL 1963

### 'Old Blush'

*(bottom)*

syns 'Common Blush China', 'Common Monthly', 'Old Pink Daily ', 'Old Pink Monthly', 'Parsons' Pink China', *Rosa* × *odorata* 'Pallida'

OLD, CHINA, MEDIUM PINK,
REPEAT-FLOWERING

This variety is the most common of the China Roses that were brought to Europe from China, initiating the great revolution in rose breeding by introducing the repeat-flowering factor into once-flowering old European roses. The light pink, semi-double flowers are smallish and muddled and they have a slight fragrance that is reminiscent of sweet peas. It is a slow-growing, medium-sized, twiggy bush that is almost thornless. 'Old Blush' is said to be Thomas Moore's 'last rose of summer'. **'Climbing Old Blush'** is the same as its parent in all respects, except that it climbs very high and is suitable for pergolas and arches. **ZONES 6–9.**

MID-1700s

PARENTAGE UNKNOWN

O

### 'Old Master' MACesp
*(above)*

MODERN, CLUSTER-FLOWERED/
FLORIBUNDA, RED BLEND,
REPEAT-FLOWERING

The flowers of this variety are a striking combination of carmine with a silver eye and reverse. The florets have only 15 petals but what a color display—this is one of the first hand-painted creations from pioneer Sam McGredy. The fragrant blooms are large and reach about 4–5 in (10–12 cm) in diameter. They are borne in medium-sized sprays that add a bright color display to any garden. The foliage is semi-glossy, mid-green on a vigorous bushy plant with good disease-resistant characteristics. Winter hardy, it will tolerate most soil types and climates. With 'Old Master', Sam McGredy opened up a new avenue of breeding, bringing the rose world

yet another dimension in color to admire.
ZONES 4–10.
MCGREDY, NEW ZEALAND, 1974
'MAXI' × ('EVELYN FISON' × ['ORANGE SWEETHEART' × 'FRÜHLINGSMORGEN'])
ROYAL NATIONAL ROSE SOCIETY TRIAL GROUND CERTIFICATE 1973

### 'Old Port' MACkati
*(above right)*

MODERN, CLUSTER-FLOWERED/
FLORIBUNDA, MAUVE,
REPEAT-FLOWERING

The fragrant flowers of 'Old Port' are a wonderful blend of red and mauve, rather than purple. The double florets have 26–40 petals and an interesting flower form—old-fashioned quartered. In hot climates the color can fade to a grayish blend and most rose growers plant this in partial shade to help sustain the beautiful color. The foliage is matt mid-green on a bushy plant. In some cool climates vigor has been reported as poor; it does much better in temperate zones.

Spraying to protect the plant from black spot is recommended.
ZONES 5–10.
MCGREDY, NEW ZEALAND, 1990
(['ANYTIME' × 'EYEPAINT'] × 'PURPLE SPLENDOUR') × 'BIG PURPLE'

### 'Oldtimer' KORol
*(above)*

syns 'Coppertone', 'Old Time', 'Old Timer'
MODERN, LARGE-FLOWERED/
HYBRID TEA, ORANGE BLEND,
REPEAT-FLOWERING

The alternative name, 'Coppertone', is probably a better one, as the blooms often appear as copper-tan with orange highlights. Long pointed buds open to high-centered, old gold flowers with excellent symmetry. They are 5 in (12 cm) across and have a sweet fragrance. The foliage is glossy mid-green on a vigorous, well-rounded plant. Easy to grow and maintain, it prefers a warm spot in full sun in the garden. This rose is winter hardy and has excellent disease resistance. It has been popular with rose growers worldwide for more than 30 years.
ZONES 4–10.
KORDES, GERMANY, 1969
'CHANTRÉ' × 'BRONZE MASTERPIECE'

O

### 'Olé' *(above)*

MODERN, LARGE-FLOWERED/
HYBRID TEA, ORANGE-RED,
REPEAT-FLOWERING

'Olé' is also classified as a Grandiflora. The fragrant, ruffled flowers are a bright lipstick orange-red. The flowers are very double with more than 50 petals, and usually have classical high centers with good symmetry but can be cupped and informal in warm climates. They tend to grow as elegant clusters of 5–8 blooms on strong, straight, upright stems. The color can range from warm crimson, overlaid with orange to various luminous hues of red. The ruffled petals resemble carnations and the flowers are long lasting. The holly-like foliage is very disease resistant. **'Climbing Olé'** was discovered in 1982 by George Haight from San Jose, California. It grows to a height of 10–12 ft (3–3.5 m)

and can be trained to cover a fence, wall or railing. **ZONES 5–10.**

ARMSTRONG, USA, 1964

'ROUNDELAY' × 'EL CAPITAN'

### 'Olympic Torch' *(top right)*
syns 'Sei-ka', 'Seika'

MODERN, LARGE-FLOWERED/
HYBRID TEA, RED BLEND,
REPEAT-FLOWERING

The long pointed buds of this rose open to red and white flowers with a touch of gold at the center, becoming all red with age. The flower form is high centered with good symmetry, but the double flowers have no fragrance. The foliage is glossy bronze and leathery on a vigorous medium-sized, winter-hardy bush. In Japan 'Seika', the alternative name, means 'sacred fire'. This rose honored the holding of the 1966 Olympic Games in Tokyo in both languages. **ZONES 5–10.**

SUZUKI, JAPAN, 1966

'ROSE GAUJARD' ×
'CRIMSON GLORY'

NEW ZEALAND GOLD MEDAL 1971

### 'Omar Khayyám' *(above)*
OLD, DAMASK, LIGHT PINK

The double flowers of this rose emerge from feathery buds and are about 2 in (5 cm) across. The rather spiky petals are sometimes arranged to give a quartered effect. The fragrant flowers display a prominent button eye when fully open. Seldom achieving a height of 3 ft (1 m), this twiggy upright shrub has a somewhat erratic growth habit. Its gray-green shoots are viciously armed with variously sized thorns. The soft foliage is a grayish light green. It is excellent as a container plant, and looks great in mixed borders. Over 100 years ago, seeds from the rose on Omar Khayyám's grave in Nashipur in Iran were brought to England and planted on the grave of his translator, Edward Fitzgerald. **ZONES 4–10.**

1893

PARENTAGE UNKNOWN

### 'Onkaparinga' *(right)*

MODERN, MODERN SHRUB, APRICOT BLEND, REPEAT-FLOWERING

'Onkaparinga' produces clusters of large, well-formed, apricot-pink flowers that turn pink as they age. Flower production is good with pleasing continuity and fragrance. The plant has matt foliage, a tall and very spreading growth habit, and is disease resistant. ZONES 5–10.

THOMSON, AUSTRALIA, 1987

'CYMBALINE' × 'TROILUS'

### 'Opening Night' JAColber *(center)*

MODERN, LARGE-FLOWERED/HYBRID TEA, RED BLEND,
REPEAT-FLOWERING

The clear crimson buds of this rose unfold to reveal a lush display of velvety red petals that age to an attractive deep pink. The double florets have 25–30 petals and a light fragrance, and grow singly on strong straight stems. They are quite long lasting. The blooms are high centered and have a very symmetrical form, especially in cooler climates. The foliage is dark green and disease resistant and the plant has a vigorous, tall, upright habit. This is a great overall performer in the garden. Bred from two great red Large-flowered Roses, it has captured the attention of the rose-buying public in the USA. ZONES 5–10.

ZARY, USA, 1998

'OLYMPIAD' × 'INGRID BERGMAN'

ALL-AMERICA ROSE SELECTION 1998

O

### 'Ophelia' *(right)*

MODERN, LARGE-FLOWERED/HYBRID TEA, LIGHT PINK,
REPEAT-FLOWERING

'Ophelia' has elegant, double, marshmallow pink flowers with lemon centers. The fragrant blooms have 28 petals and are borne on long, straight, strong stems in clusters. The foliage is leathery on a vigorous, upright plant; the exact origin and parentage is a mystery. Whatever its source, it was extensively used to create even more great roses. It also has 35 sports to its credit. Named after Shakespeare's tragic heroine, this rose has achieved immortality. **'Climbing Ophelia'** (Dickson, UK, 1920) grows to 10–12 ft (3–3.5 m). ZONES 5–10.

WILLIAM, PAUL & SON, UK, 1912

POSSIBLY A CHANCE SEEDLING OF 'ANTOINE RIVOIRE'

### 'Orange Fire' *(above)*

MODERN, MINIATURE, ORANGE-PINK, REPEAT-FLOWERING

The short pointed buds develop into small flowers that are a mixture of orange and shades of pink to carmine. They are double, with 40 petals, and are produced in small, well-spaced clusters amid the glossy, leathery, dark foliage. The growth is bushy and upright, and flower production is adequate with a quick repeat-bloom. Unfortunately, the older flowers fade to a rather dirty color—a fault that was inherited from 'Floradora'. ZONES 5–9.

MOORE, USA, 1974

(*ROSA WICHURANA* × 'FLORADORA') × 'FIRE PRINCESS'

### 'Orange Honey' *(top right)*

MODERN, MINIATURE, ORANGE BLEND, REPEAT-FLOWERING

This rose carries pointed buds that open to reveal yellow-amber petals that unfurl to pure orange-yellow, double flowers of about 23 petals. They have a fruity fragrance and symmetrical high centers, but are usually more cupped. As the blooms age they develop a reddish color, which gives the rose an autumn effect. Flower production is prolific and the plant is covered in brilliant orange at most times. It has a spreading habit, which makes it an ideal choice for an eye-catching hanging basket. If grown in partial shade the bright orange color can be maintained for weeks. ZONES 5–11.

MOORE, USA, 1979

'RUMBA' × 'OVER THE RAINBOW'

### 'Orange Sensation' *(above)*

MODERN, CLUSTER-FLOWERED/FLORIBUNDA, ORANGE-RED, REPEAT-FLOWERING

These orange-vermilion-red flowers are flushed slightly darker at the edges. The double florets have 24 petals, are 3 in (8 cm) across and have a marked scent. The blooms occur in wonderfully shaped clusters that are long lasting and weather-proof. The foliage is light green on a very vigorous bush that grows to about 3 ft (1 m) high with some spreading. It is beautiful from bud to fully open bloom, easily making it a winner at most international rose trial grounds. It needs little maintenance and care. 'Climbing Orange Sensation', which can be trained onto walls or pillars, is very similar to its parent, although it may be less inclined to repeat-flower. ZONES 5–10.

DE RUITER, THE NETHERLANDS, 1961

'AMOR' × 'FASHION'

NATIONAL ROSE SOCIETY GOLD MEDAL 1961, GOLDEN ROSE OF THE HAGUE 1968

## 'Orange Sunblaze'

MEIjikatar *(right)*

syns 'Orange
Meillandina',
'Sunblaze'

MODERN, MINIATURE, ORANGE-
RED, REPEAT-FLOWERING

This rose has brilliant
orange flowers, un-
matched in the plant
world for vividness. The
double flowers of 35
petals have a decorative
cupped form that is
complemented by the
small, pointed, light
green foliage. The
blooms are normally
borne in small clusters
of 1–5 florets. 'Orange
Sunblaze' is an upright
and compact rose with
a fast repeat-bloom; it
is an excellent choice
for the garden and,
when grown in a con-
tainer, it can provide
a long succession of
small sprays of brilliant
color all year round.
**ZONES 5–10.**

MEILLAND, FRANCE, 1982

'PARADOR' × ('BABY BETTINA' ×
'DUCHESS OF WINDSOR')

## 'Orange Triumph'

*(right)*

MODERN, POLYANTHA, MEDIUM
RED, REPEAT-FLOWERING

These fragrant, deep
orange-red flowers are
borne in very large
clusters. The small
florets have a cupped
form and clusters are
provided in abundance
all year long. They last
remarkably well, and
are weather resistant.
The foliage is glossy
green on a compact,
vigorous, winter-hardy
plant that grows to
4–5 ft (1.2–1.5 m) tall.
This rose is considered
historically important
because its wonderful
characteristics have
been successfully
passed on to its many
progeny. **'Climbing
Orange Triumph'** was
introduced in 1945 by
Leenders of Holland. It
grows to some 10–12 ft
(3–3.5 m) and can be
easily trained to cover
a fence, wall or railing.
In 1953 Jacob Maarse
from the USA intro-
duced 'Orange Triumph

Superba', an orange
blend Polyantha. In
1960, F. Cant of
England introduced
an improved orange-
red non-climbing
Polyantha of 'Orange

Triumph' called
'Orange Triumph
Improved'. **ZONES 4–10.**

KORDES, GERMANY, 1937

'EVA' × 'SOLARIUM'

ROYAL NATIONAL ROSE SOCIETY
GOLD MEDAL 1937

O

### 'Oregold' TANolg *(left)*

syns 'Anneliesse Rothenberger', 'Miss Harp', 'Silhouette'

MODERN, LARGE-FLOWERED/ HYBRID TEA, DEEP YELLOW, REPEAT-FLOWERING

Deep golden yellow, double flowers with great substance and classic high centers with excellent symmetry are the hallmarks of this rose. The blooms have excellent holding capacity in cooler climates, lasting for weeks on the bush. The color is non-fading, but the blooms tend to open too quickly in warmer climates. It has a very light fragrance. The foliage is large, glossy and dark green on a tall, slightly spreading plant that is very disease resistant. While the bush may be slow in establishing itself, the rewards are worth waiting for—an abundance of blooms with fast repeat. The seed parent is a grand-daughter of 'Peace'. Still grown widely throughout the world, this rose has main-tained its popularity because of its color and vigor. **ZONES 5–10.**

TANTAU, GERMANY, 1975

'PICCADILLY' × 'COLOUR WONDER'

ALL-AMERICA ROSE SELECTION 1975

4–5 ft (1.2–1.5 m) tall in warmer climates, and is very tolerant of less than perfect growing conditions. **'Climbing Orangeade'** (Waterhouse Nursery, UK, 1964) is a climbing sport. **ZONES 5–10.**

MCGREDY, UK, 1959

'ORANGE SWEETHEART' × 'INDEPENDENCE'

NATIONAL ROSE SOCIETY GOLD MEDAL 1959, PORTLAND GOLD MEDAL 1965

### 'Orangeade' *(above)*

MODERN, CLUSTER-FLOWERED/ FLORIBUNDA, ORANGE-RED, REPEAT-FLOWERING

These flowers are such a bright orange-red that the color can sometimes overwhelm the eye. The semi-double flowers have a light fragrance and are borne in magnificent clusters. With age the blooms grow a little darker, bringing an even stronger color contrast with the golden yellow stamens at the open bloom stage. It is a vigorous upright bush that grows to about

## 'Oriental Charm'
*(right)*

MODERN, LARGE-FLOWERED/
HYBRID TEA, MEDIUM RED,
REPEAT-FLOWERING

Globular buds on this variety open to reveal bright orange-red flowers heavily veined with crimson, with golden yellow stamens providing the finishing artistic touch. The lightly fragrant florets are single, with 11 petals, and can be up to 3–4 in (8–10 cm) across. The flowers are quite different from any other single-petalled rose, as they resemble large oriental poppies. The color is fleeting and fades rather rapidly after the blooms open. The foliage is glossy dark green on a vigorous upright plant. The genealogy of 'Oriental Charm' is rich in rose history—'Mme Butterfly' is a sport of 'Ophelia'; 'Floradora' is the pollen parent of 'Queen Elizabeth'; and 'Charlotte Armstrong' is one of the great Large-flowered Roses of the twentieth century. **ZONES 5–10.**

DUEHRSEN, USA, 1960

('CHARLOTTE ARMSTRONG' ×
'GRUSS AN TEPLITZ') × ('MME
BUTTERFLY' × 'FLORADORA')

## 'Orpheline de Juillet' *(right)*
syn. 'July's Orphan'

OLD, GALLICA, MAUVE

The flowers of this rose are large and very double, and are crimson-purple, shading to bright red in the center. It has an upright, rather tall and moderately vigorous growth habit. This is not a conventional Gallica as it has some Damask characteristics. The reason for the name is unclear. William Paul mentions it in The Rose Garden (1848), but he was not the raiser as it was listed in Vibert's catalogue in 1836. **ZONES 4–9.**

PRE-1836

PARENTAGE UNKNOWN

O

**O**

### 'Oskar Scheerer'
*(below)*

MODERN, MODERN SHRUB, DARK RED, REPEAT-FLOWERING

The flowers on this variety are very dark garnet red with contrasting prominent yellow stamens. The florets are large and semi-double and occur in small clusters. There is no fragrance. The foliage is dark glossy green on a vigorous, upright-growing plant to about 6 ft (1.8 m) high with exceptional branching characteristics for increased bloom production. This rose is one of the first of the Modern Shrubs of medium vigor where the blooms are like Cluster-flowered Roses. It survives most weather conditions. ZONES 4–10.

KORDES, GERMANY, 1961

PARENTAGE UNKNOWN

ROYAL NATIONAL ROSE SOCIETY GOLD MEDAL 1961, ROYAL HORTICULTURAL SOCIETY AWARD OF MERIT 1962

### 'Osiria'   *(above)*

MODERN, LARGE-FLOWERED/HYBRID TEA, RED BLEND, REPEAT-FLOWERING

The long, pointed buds of 'Osiria' open to dark red flowers with a sparkling white reverse. In very warm climates, the dark red develops to a much blacker red tone. The large, very full, fragrant blooms contain more than 50 petals, and the flowers have classic Large-flowered form with high centers. The bloom size can be smaller in hot climates. The flowers generally come on short stems, which can be a serious handicap for the exhibitor. It is a vigorous, upright bush with good dark green foliage that has outstanding color and form but tends to be highly susceptible to powdery mildew. ZONES 5–11.

KORDES, GERMANY, 1978

'SNOWFIRE' × SEEDLING

## 'Othello'   *(above)*

MODERN, MODERN SHRUB, DARK RED, REPEAT-FLOWERING

'Othello' has large, showy flowers that are deep
blood red, gradually turning purple with age.
The blooms are well filled with petals and are
reminiscent of the Hybrid Perpetuals. They have
a very strong fragrance. This is a vigorous, upright
bush growing to about 5 ft (1.5 m) high in most
moderate climates, and it has an over-abundance
of thorns. Although it is hardy, it can suffer from
powdery mildew if left unprotected. Also known
as an English Rose, this variety was aptly named
for Shakespeare's Moor. ZONES 4–11.

AUSTIN, UK, 1987

'LILIAN AUSTIN' × 'THE SQUIRE'

## 'Our Molly'   DICreason   *(top right)*

MODERN, MODERN SHRUB, MEDIUM RED, REPEAT-FLOWERING

This charming, single-petalled rose bears flowers
that are the color of redcurrants with a silvery
white eye. The blooms are borne in massive clusters
which, unfortunately, have no fragrance. The foliage is mid-green on a plant with a tall, spreading
habit. One of the delightful characteristics of
this plant is the wonderful display of orange hips
in autumn. It was named for a charming and
prominent rosarian from Northern Ireland.
ZONES 4–10.

DICKSON, UK, 1994

PARENTAGE UNKNOWN

ROYAL NATIONAL ROSE SOCIETY TRIAL GROUND CERTIFICATE
1991, GLASGOW GOLD MEDAL 1996, THE PEOPLE'S CHOICE AWARD
IN GLASGOW 1996, DUBLIN PRIZE 1997, BELFAST PRIZE 1997

## 'Over the Rainbow'   *(above)*

MODERN, MINIATURE, RED BLEND, REPEAT-FLOWERING

The use of the exquisite Cluster-flowered Rose
'Little Darling' as seed parent has produced 'Over
the Rainbow', another prize-winning variety from
Moore's stable. The small, well-shaped, double
flowers are deep scarlet red with bright yellow
undersides. They have good high-centered form
and a light fragrance. Foliage is semi-glossy and
leathery in texture. This is a vigorous, upright
bush that can grow tall in warm climates, given the
chance, but it is subject to mildew if unprotected.
Valued as one of the best bicolored Miniatures,
the blooms can be quite large in cooler climates.
ZONES 5–11.

MOORE, USA, 1972

'LITTLE DARLING' × 'WESTMONT'

AMERICAN ROSE SOCIETY AWARD OF EXCELLENCE 1975

O

P

### 'Pacesetter'  SAVpace  *(above top)*

**MODERN, MINIATURE, WHITE, REPEAT-FLOWERING**

'Pacesetter' has long pointed buds that open
to pure white, fragrant flowers. The florets have
consistent Large-flowered form. Indeed the form
holds so well over days that this rose is an ideal
candidate for rose shows and is perfect for cut
flowers indoors. Bloom production is prolific
once the plant has established itself. The elegant
long stems add grace to charm. The foliage is dark
green with a matt texture finish on an upright,
compact bush. This rose was one of the first pure
white Miniature Roses and ruled the show tables
until the appearance of 'Snowbride'. It has maintained its popularity—many are still growing and
showing this classic rose. **ZONES 5–11.**

SCHWARTZ, USA, 1979

'MA PERKINS' × 'MAGIC CARROUSEL'

AMERICAN ROSE SOCIETY AWARD OF EXCELLENCE 1981

### 'Paddy McGredy'  MACpa  *(above)*

**MODERN, CLUSTER-FLOWERED/FLORIBUNDA, MEDIUM PINK,
REPEAT-FLOWERING**

The ovoid buds of this rose open to reveal large,
deep rose pink to carmine flowers containing
33 petals. The flowers have classic Large-flowered
form with high centers. They are occasionally
borne one to a stem and there is a good strong
fragrance. The foliage is leathery dark green, but it
can be susceptible to black spot. 'Paddy McGredy'
is a compact, vigorous bush that, when it was
introduced, attracted a great deal of attention for
its unique combination of Large-flowered and
Cluster-flowered characteristics, hailed as a major
breakthrough in rose breeding. Bloom production
is excellent, with large trusses covering the bush
so that the foliage is barely visible. It was named
for the breeder's sister. **ZONES 5–11.**

MCGREDY, UK, 1962

'SPARTAN' × 'TZIGANE'

NATIONAL ROSE SOCIETY GOLD MEDAL 1961

### 'Paddy Stephens'  MACclack  *(above)*

**MODERN, LARGE-FLOWERED/HYBRID TEA, ORANGE BLEND,
REPEAT-FLOWERING**

This variety has flowers that are a lovely salmon-
orange with good exhibition-type form in spring
but which tend to become smaller and flatter
later in the growing season. The blooms are best
at the fully open stage. The double florets, which
have 15–25 petals and a light fragrance, are borne
singly on stems that are usually straight and
strong. The foliage is large, dark green and disease
resistant on a compact bush. It looks its best in
cool climates; in warmer zones the color fades
rapidly. 'Paddy Stephens' was named for a rose
grower from New Zealand. **ZONES 5–10.**

MCGREDY, NEW ZEALAND, 1991

'SOLITAIRE' × {(['TOMBOLA' × ('ELIZABETH OF GLAMIS' × ('CIRCUS' ×
'GOLDEN FLEECE')] × 'MARY SUMNER') × SEEDLING}

## 'Painted Moon' DICpaint *(above)*

MODERN, LARGE-FLOWERED/HYBRID TEA, RED BLEND, REPEAT-FLOWERING

This lightly fragrant rose displays an extraordinary color change with ageing. The flowers start off yellow turning pink from the tips of the petals, then the pink deepens to a red until finally the petals are totally crimson. The blooms are large, double with 40 petals and cupped. They are carried in wide sprays, which allows a range of ageing to provide a startling color display on the bush. The foliage is semi-glossy and dark green on an upright bush with stocky growth characteristics. While it may have novelty appeal, it is also ideal for planting as a border or hedge. **ZONES 5–10.**

DICKSON, UK, 1989

'BONFIRE NIGHT' × 'SILVER JUBILEE'

ROYAL NATIONAL ROSE SOCIETY TRIAL GROUND CERTIFICATE 1989, BELFAST GOLD MEDAL 1993

## 'Palmengarten Frankfurt' KORsilan *(top right)* syns 'Beauce', 'Our Rosy Carpet'

MODERN, GROUND COVER, MEDIUM PINK, REPEAT-FLOWERING

This is an excellent Ground Cover Rose that grows to about 3 ft (1 m) in height and 4½ ft (1.3 m) in width. The plant is furnished with extremely healthy, semi-glossy, dark green foliage. The flowers are semi-double and are made up of 15–20 strong rose pink petals that hold their color well. These are produced in dense clusters. The blooms completely cover the bush through the season from spring to autumn and have a very quick repeat cycle. 'Palmengarten Frankfurt' makes a wonderful bedding plant. It has also been found to be particularly suitable for use in difficult positions such as on banks

and close to trees. It can also be trained as a tall or weeping standard. **ZONES 5–9.**

KORDES, GERMANY, 1988

PARENTAGE UNKNOWN

ANERKANNTE DEUTSCHE ROSE 1992

## 'Papa Gontier' *(above)*

OLD, TEA, PINK BLEND, REPEAT-FLOWERING

The fragrant flowers of this rose are bright coppery pink with a carmine-red reverse. They are semi-double and loose. It can be rather wiry and twiggy, but in suitable conditions can grow into a large shrub. This rose and 'Madame Hoste' are the parents of the well known 'Lady Hillingdon'. A climbing version of 'Papa Gontier' was introduced by Hosp in 1898. Many of the Tea Roses and the Large-flowered Roses mutate at some time from bush to climber, but the climbers tend to be less floriferous. Papa Gontier was a notable nurseryman in Montrouge in France. **ZONES 4–9.**

NABONNAND, FRANCE, 1883

SEEDLING OF 'DUCHESS OF EDINBURGH'

P

### 'Papa Hémeray'
*(left)*

**OLD, CHINA, RED BLEND, REPEAT-FLOWERING**

The flowers of this rose are an intense vermilion with white centers, and do not fade. The single blooms flower continuously through-out the season. It is a strong, low-growing shrub with an upright habit and few thorns. It is very suitable for bedding. **ZONES 7–9.**

HÉMERAY-AUBERT, FRANCE, 1912

'HIAWATHA' × 'PARSON'S PINK CHINA'

### 'Papa Meilland'

MEIsar, MEIcesar   *(center)*

**MODERN, LARGE-FLOWERED/ HYBRID TEA, DARK RED, REPEAT-FLOWERING**

The elegant, pointed buds of this rose open to reveal dark velvety crimson flowers of exquisite, classic Large-flowered form. The large, very fragrant blooms have about 35 petals. It always sends out one bloom per stem on strong, straight, long stems suitable for cutting for the home or for exhibition. The foliage is leathery, glossy and olive green on a vig-orous, upright, tall plant. Unfortunately it is quite susceptible to mildew and black spot, and it is not winter hardy, tending to die back in climates with even mild snowfall and frost. It was named by Alain Meilland as a tribute to his grand-father Antoine (1844–1971). **'Climbing Papa Meilland'** (Stratford, Australia, 1970) is in every respect a clone of its parent. As the canes gain height and air circulation is improved, the mildew and black spot problems are minimized. It takes about 2 to 3 years to establish itself. **ZONES 6–11.**

MEILLAND, FRANCE, 1963

'CHRYSLER IMPERIAL' × 'CHARLES MALLERIN'

BADEN-BADEN GOLD MEDAL 1962, JAMES ALEXANDER GAMBLE FRAGRANCE MEDAL 1974, WORLD FEDERATION OF ROSE SOCIETIES ROSE HALL OF FAME 1988

### 'Papillon'   *(bottom)*

**OLD, CLIMBING TEA, PINK BLEND, REPEAT-FLOWERING**

The flowers of this rose are coppery salmon-rose. They are medium-sized and semi-double and have been compared to a group of butterflies on a bush—hence the name ('papillon' is French for 'butterfly'). It is a free-flowering bush with copper leaves. It is best grown as a pillar rose as it is quite a slow climber, and has been known not to climb at all! It is sometimes classified as a Noisette. **ZONES 7–9.**

NABONNAND, FRANCE, 1881

TEA ROSE × NOISETTE ROSE

### 'Paprika' TANprik *(right)*
syn. 'Gavroche'

MODERN, CLUSTER-FLOWERED/
FLORIBUNDA, ORANGE-RED,
REPEAT-FLOWERING

When the long, pointed buds of this rose open, they reveal bright brick red or geranium red flowers with a very distinctive bluish zone at the base of the petals. The fragrant flowers are large and semi-double and are borne in large clusters or trusses against leathery, glossy, olive green foliage on a vigorous, upright bush that is 3 ft (1 m) high. The blooms are weatherproof, particularly against rain. In spite of competition in this color class of Cluster-flowered Roses, this variety has managed to remain popular even against the onslaught of recent introductions. It makes an ideal standard. **ZONES 5–10.**

TANTAU, GERMANY, 1958

'MÄRCHENLAND' × 'RED FAVORITE'

NATIONAL ROSE SOCIETY GOLD MEDAL 1959, GOLDEN ROSE OF THE HAGUE 1961

### 'Parade' *(bottom)*

MODERN, LARGE-FLOWERED CLIMBER, DEEP PINK, REPEAT-FLOWERING

'Parade' has ovoid buds that open to deep rose pink flowers often described as a rich cerise, close to crimson, that glows like fine silk. The large, cup-shaped blooms have 33 petals and are fragrant. They are borne in heavy clusters that often make the stems droop slightly. This is a hardy plant with glossy, dark green foliage that establishes itself rapidly and reaches a height of 10–12 ft (3–3.5 m). It prefers the pillar configuration to the spreading formation of classical climbers. It is a remarkably healthy free-blooming climber from the breeder perhaps best known for his Cluster-flowered Roses. **ZONES 4–10.**

BOERNER, USA, 1953

SEEDLING OF 'NEW DAWN' × 'CLIMBING WORLD'S FAIR'

ROYAL HORTICULTURAL SOCIETY AWARD OF GARDEN MERIT 1993

### 'Paradise' WEZeip *(top right)*
syn. 'Burning Sky'

MODERN, LARGE-FLOWERED/
HYBRID TEA, MAUVE,
REPEAT-FLOWERING

This rose has graceful, long, pointed buds that open to silvery

lavender blooms with distinctive shading to ruby red at the edge of the petals. The large, fragrant, classically shaped blooms have 28 petals. The foliage is glossy dark green on an upright, tall plant that prefers warmer climates to develop the full color chrome and hue. However, intense sunshine can cause the edges of the petals to burn and lose substance. In winter climates, die-back is common. For those who like this color class, this rose is a must, despite its faults. In moderate climates it performs well throughout the year. **ZONES 5–10.**

WEEKS, USA, 1978

'SWARTHMORE' × SEEDLING

ALL-AMERICA ROSE SELECTION 1979, PORTLAND GOLD MEDAL 1979

P

### 'Parks' Yellow Tea-scented China' *(left)*

syns 'Old Yellow Tea', *Rosa × odorata ochroleuca*, *R. indica ochroleuca*

OLD, TEA, MEDIUM YELLOW, REPEAT-FLOWERING

This is one of the four 'stud' China Roses from which the Teas and Noisettes were developed and which brought the repeat-flowering characteristic to modern roses. It was brought to England from China by J. D. Parks. It is considered to have been a hybrid between the wild China rose and *Rosa gigantea*, a Tea-scented wild climbing variety. It is a short climber bearing straw yellow, double, loose flowers with a faint Tea scent. It was from this rose that the light yellow was introduced into the later Teas and Noisettes. It was lost for some time, no doubt having been superseded by better developments, and possibly also the victim of cold winters. **ZONES 7–9.**

FROM CHINA, INTRODUCED BY PARKS, UK, 1824

PARENTAGE UNKNOWN

### 'Parkdirektor Riggers' *(left)*

MODERN, MODERN SHRUB, DARK RED, REPEAT-FLOWERING

The long, pointed buds of this rose open to reveal velvety crimson flowers with a small center of yellow stamens and a little white and purple at the base of the petals. The color is non-fading even in warm climates. The fragrant, semi-double blooms are borne in large clusters of up to 50 blooms on a plant that can reach up to 12 ft (3.5 m) high by 6 ft (1.8 m) wide. The foliage is glossy dark green on a vigorous, climbing, spreading plant that is disease resistant. This is one of the best Kordesii roses because of its freedom and abundance of flowers. When grown on a wall it may suffer from mildew and black spot if left unprotected. **ZONES 4–10.**

KORDES, GERMANY, 1957

*ROSA KORDESII* × 'OUR PRINCESS'

ANERKANNTE DEUTSCHE ROSE 1960

### 'Pariser Charme' *(top left)*

syn. 'Paris Charm'

MODERN, LARGE-FLOWERED/HYBRID TEA, MEDIUM PINK, REPEAT-FLOWERING

The ovoid buds of this rose open to salmon-pink flowers. The fragrant, well-formed blooms are double with 28 petals and often large, with a 5 in (12 cm) diameter. They come in large-sized clusters that can weigh down the stems, especially after rain. The foliage is glossy dark green on a vigorous, upright plant. It is one of more than 200 grandchildren bred from the Large-flowered Rose of the twentieth century, 'Peace'. **ZONES 5–10.**

TANTAU, GERMANY, 1965

'PRIMA BALLERINA' × 'MONTEZUMA'

ANERKANNTE DEUTSCHE ROSE 1966

## 'Parkzierde'

OLD, BOURBON, DARK RED

The name of this variety means 'Park Adornment' and it is certainly an apt name. This late Bourbon Rose produces scarlet-crimson double, open flowers on very long stems. They are suitable for cutting but the blooms fade rather quickly. The fragrant flowers are produced abundantly but briefly in early summer. 'Parkzierde' is a strong plant that grows to medium height. ZONES 5–9.

LAMBERT, GERMANY, 1911

PARENTAGE UNKNOWN

## 'Party Girl'  *(top)*

MODERN, MINIATURE, YELLOW BLEND, REPEAT-FLOWERING

'Party Girl' is perhaps the most famous of the Miniature Roses hybridized by the late Harm Saville of Rowley, Massachusetts, USA. This compact bush is adorned by apricot-yellow blooms with 23 petals of immaculate exhibition form. It prefers to send out large clusters of 10–18 florets that take several weeks to reach full maturity, adding grace and elegance to the garden all year long. In hot climates, the flowers appear to be almost white with a yellow base; in cooler and more moderate climates the blooms are characteristically yellow. This rose was named for Jan Shivers from Indiana who served as Chairman of the American Rose Society Prizes & Award Committee. ZONES 5–11.

SAVILLE, USA, 1979

'RISE 'N' SHINE' × 'SHERI ANNE'

AMERICAN ROSE SOCIETY AWARD OF EXCELLENCE 1982

## 'Parure d'Or'  DELmir

MODERN, LARGE-FLOWERED CLIMBER, YELLOW BLEND, REPEAT-FLOWERING

The golden yellow flowers of this variety are edged orange-red. The florets can be either single petalled or sometimes semi-double, and they are medium sized. The foliage is dark and glossy green on a vigorous, climbing, spreading plant. The repeat-bloom cycle times are excellent through-out the year. When naming this rose the breeders borrowed the French word 'parure', meaning a suite of matching jewelry such as the celebrated set of emeralds (necklace, earrings, tiara, etc.) that belonged to Empress Josephine. ZONES 5–11.

DELBARD-CHABERT, FRANCE 1968

('QUEEN ELIZABETH' × 'PROVENCE') × (SEEDLING OF 'SULTANE' × 'MME JOSEPH PERRAUD')

BAGATELLE GOLD MEDAL 1968

## 'Pascali'  LENip  *(above)*
syn. 'Blanche Pasca'

MODERN, LARGE-FLOWERED/HYBRID TEA, WHITE, REPEAT-FLOWERING

This variety has lightly fragrant, creamy clear white flowers that are double with 30 petals. They have classic exhibition-style form and are borne one to a stem, making them ideal for cutting or exhibition. They tend to be on the small side for a Large-flowered Rose. The foliage is dark green on a vigorous, compact bush. This rose is known for its disease resistance in all climates. Considering it was elevated to the Rose Hall of Fame by the Member Societies of the World Federation of Rose Societies, what other validation is needed that this rose is worth growing anywhere in the world? ZONES 5–11.

LENS, BELGIUM, 1963

'QUEEN ELIZABETH' × 'WHITE BUTTERFLY'

GOLDEN ROSE OF THE HAGUE 1963, NATIONAL ROSE SOCIETY CERTIFICATE OF MERIT 1963, PORTLAND GOLD MEDAL 1967, ALL-AMERICA ROSE SELECTION 1969, WORLD FEDERATION OF ROSE SOCIETIES ROSE HALL OF FAME 1991

P

### 'Passion' *(left)*
**MODERN, LARGE-FLOWERED/HYBRID TEA, MEDIUM RED, REPEAT-FLOWERING**

'Passion' has long, pointed buds that open to fragrant scarlet-cerise flowers. They are very large at 5 in (12 cm) across and are borne in small clusters on tall, upright, strong stems. The foliage is glossy dark green on a very vigorous bush. This rose is just one of the many offspring of the mighty 'Peace' from the House of Meilland in France. It is also known as a Grandiflora, as is 'Queen Elizabeth', which was introduced in the same year and was the very first variety of this classification. **ZONES 5–11.**

GAUJARD, FRANCE, 1954

'PEACE' × 'ALAIN'

### 'Pat Austin' AUSmum *(left)*
**MODERN, MODERN SHRUB, ORANGE-RED, REPEAT-FLOWERING**

The flowers on this variety are large and double, and display a bright and vivid combination of color, rich copper on the upperside of the petals and pale coppery yellow on the underside. The deeply cupped nature of the open flowers ensures that the two contrasting tones catch the eye as the large petals expand. It has a sharp fruity fragrance, and flowers continue to appear through summer and autumn. For a shrub border, especially where a splash of bright and unusual color is required, this is a useful rose. The plant grows vigorously to average size for a shrub rose with a bushy, spreading habit and large, semi-glossy, deep green leaves. The raiser David Austin named it in appreciation of his wife. It is also classified as an English Rose. **ZONES 4–9.**

AUSTIN, UK, 1995

PARENTAGE UNKNOWN

### 'Patio Charm' CHEwapri *(left)*
**MODERN, CLIMBING MINIATURE, APRICOT BLEND**

Set against the dark green foliage of this rose, the dark orange-apricot flowers are very bright and attractive. They develop from long and pointed buds to give well-shaped, double blooms. The outer petals reflex as they mature. 'Patio Charm' can be trained against a wall or small trellis, and is propagated by budding. **ZONES 5–10.**

WARNER, UK, 1994

'LAURA FORD' × 'ANNE HARKNESS'

### 'Patricia'

MODERN, LARGE-FLOWERED/
HYBRID TEA, MEDIUM RED,
REPEAT-FLOWERING

The flowers on this variety are a carmine flecked pink with an orange-yellow base to the petals. The florets are fragrant and have lovely color, particularly in autumn. The foliage is glossy dark green on a vigorous bush. This variety makes an ideal garden plant for the unending display of flowers throughout the year. **ZONES 5–11.**

CHAPLIN BROS LTD, UK, 1932

PARENTAGE UNKNOWN

### 'Patricia' KORpatri (below)

MODERN, CLUSTER-FLOWERED/
FLORIBUNDA, APRICOT BLEND,
REPEAT-FLOWERING

Although it is popular in Australia, this rose is only grown elsewhere as a cut-flower variety; 'Patricia' is at its best in warm climates. The flowers are a clear shade of salmon-pink, deeper on the petal rims and paler on the underside. They are of medium size with some 24 petals, and appear in clusters, becoming cupped to flat as they open out to make a bold show of color. The variety is excellent for cutting as the blooms last well, and it is also useful for beds and borders. It continues to produce flowers right through summer and autumn. There is a pleasing, if somewhat delicate fragrance. The plant grows tall and upright to average height, and it is furnished with rather broad, deep green leaves. Some authorities have questioned the parentage of this rose because it does not have the close resemblance in flower form and growth that is normally found in a sport. **ZONES 5–9.**

KORDES, GERMANY, 1972

SPORT OF 'ELIZABETH OF GLAMIS'

ORLÉANS GOLD MEDAL 1979

### 'Paul Cezanne'

JACdeli (below)

MODERN, LARGE-FLOWERED/
HYBRID TEA, YELLOW BLEND,
REPEAT-FLOWERING

The flowers of this variety are made up of petals that are basically yellow and deep coral, but each one has a different combination of stripes or dots, and some petals are divided half and half between the two shades. Like 'Picasso', 'Old Master' and other curiously colored roses with their names linked to painters, this is an interesting rose and will make a talking point in the garden. The medium-sized blooms are full-petalled and have a moderate fragrance. They appear singly or in clusters, on short stems, continuing through summer and autumn. It grows to average height with a bushy habit. Some growers consider 'Paul Cezanne' to be a Cluster-flowered Rose. **ZONES 4–9.**

JACKSON AND PERKINS, USA, 1992

PARENTAGE UNKNOWN

### 'Paul Crampel'

MODERN, POLYANTHA, ORANGE-RED, REPEAT-FLOWERING

The flowers of this variety are deep orange-scarlet, semi-double and appear freely in big clusters. They are of small to medium size, without much fragrance, and after the first great flush of bloom there is a pause before they come back into flower, continuing to show color through the rest of summer and autumn. This, with other Polyantha Roses, was exceedingly popular for bedding until the 1950s, when the Cluster-flowered Roses found favor by reason of their bigger flowers, brighter colors and better resistance to mildew. 'Paul Crampel' has the further disadvantage of having flowers that sometimes revert to the parent from which it sported, giving a discordant spray of crimson blooms alongside the orange-scarlet ones. The plants grow upright to the average height for a Polyantha Rose, with light green leaves. It is named after the nurseryman who is also remembered for the famous geranium he introduced. **ZONES 4–9.**

KERSBERGEN, THE NETHERLANDS, 1930

SPORT OF 'SUPERB'

### 'Paul Gauguin'  JACdebu  *(above left)*

MODERN, LARGE-FLOWERED/HYBRID TEA, RUSSET, REPEAT-FLOWERING

This rose is grown for its novelty value, derived from the most unusual color combinations in the flowers. They are made up of deep russet and light salmon, varying in their proportions from bloom to bloom, and marked with random patterns of dots, stripes and patches. The flowering continues through summer and autumn, and plants sited where they will catch the eye of visitors are sure to provide a talking point. One specialist provides it in standard form, presumably with this in mind. The variety grows neatly and compactly with mid-green foliage, to below average height. It is considered by some to be a Cluster-flowered Rose. **ZONES 4–9.**

PARENTAGE UNKNOWN

### 'Paul Lédé, Climbing'  *(above right)*

OLD, CLIMBING TEA, APRICOT BLEND, REPEAT-FLOWERING

This rose is a sport of the bush form, 'Paul Lédé', which was one of Pernet-Ducher's Large-flowered/Hybrid Teas derived from the 'Persian Yellow' (*Rosa foetida*). This was a breakthrough in the early twentieth century, and the roses were known for a while as Pernetianas. They brought in the intense yellow, and unfortunately black spot. This climbing form has flowers that have been variously described as soft peach-pink, yellow and apricot, carmine-pink and dawn yellow. They are fragrant and bloom freely and continuously. It has plentiful mid-green foliage. **ZONES 5–9.**

LOWE, UK, 1913

SPORT 'PAUL LEDÉ'

### 'Paul Neyron'

*(above)*

OLD, HYBRID PERPETUAL, MEDIUM PINK, REPEAT-FLOWERING

This is what many people think of as the 'cabbage rose', a name first given to the Centifolias by the English, who did not care for the alternative name of the roses of Provence. The fragrant flowers are very large, with as many as 50 petals; they are cupped and resemble peonies. It is a tall, upright, vigorous bush. ZONES 5–9.

LEVET, FRANCE, 1869

'VICTOR VERDIER' ×
'ANNA DE DIESBACH'

### 'Paul Noël'

MODERN, LARGE-FLOWERED CLIMBER, PINK BLEND, REPEAT-FLOWERING

The flowers of this rose are very double, and of medium to large size. They are a warm shade of rosy salmon-pink with a hint of yellow at the base and open wide to show a beautiful formation, with many ruffled petals jostling for space. The plant carries its blooms on short stems, singly or in small clusters, and they have a pleasing, delicate scent. The first flush is prolific. It is suitable for fences, arches and pergolas. The plant is vigorous, producing long, arching stems, and can grow farther than the average extent of a Climber Rose. 'Paul Noël' has shiny, dark green foliage. ZONES 4–9.

TANNE, FRANCE, 1913

*ROSA WICHURANA* ×
'MONSIEUR TILLIER'

### 'Paul Ricard'

MEInivoz

syns 'Moondance', 'Paul Richard', 'Spirit of Peace', 'Summer's Kiss'

MODERN, LARGE FLOWERED/ HYBRID TEA, YELLOW BLEND, REPEAT-FLOWERING

The flowers of this variety are large and very full, with about 40 broad petals; they open with high centers and maintain a wonderful symmetry of form. They are amber yellow, the color being richer in cool climates, and bleaching in warm ones to the extent that the outer petals become creamy buff with deeper amber tints in the heart of the bloom. The fragrance has been likened to spiced honey. It is good for cutting as the blooms are on stiff stems and last well, and is very suitable for beds, borders and as a hedge. It grows vigorously with a freely branching, bushy habit to above average height, and has large mid- to dark green foliage. ZONES 4–9.

MEILLAND, FRANCE, 1994

('HIDALGO' × 'MISCHIEF') ×
'AMBASSADOR'

ROME GOLD MEDAL 1991

### 'Paul Ricault'

*(above)*

OLD, CENTIFOLIA, MEDIUM PINK, REPEAT-FLOWERING

This rose has been variously classified as a Centifolia, a hybrid Bourbon and a Hybrid Perpetual. It bears very full, flat, quartered flowers which are a rosy carmine color. The petals are reflexed at the edges and recurved in the center. There is a pleasant scent. It is a strong, thorny shrub with long arching canes. Bourbons were China-Damask crosses and Hybrid Perpetuals were improved Bourbons, probably back-crossed, with Gallicas sometimes included. There was clearly a lot of breeding in this rose, but the official category of Centifolia seems unlikely, as it repeat-flowers. ZONES 4–9.

PORTEMER, FRANCE, 1845

PARENTAGE UNKNOWN

P

### 'Paul Shirville'

**HARqueterwife** *(below)*
syns 'Heart Throb',
'Saxo'

MODERN, LARGE-FLOWERED/
HYBRID TEA, ORANGE-PINK,
REPEAT-FLOWERING

The official color coding is misleading, for this variety is rosy salmon-pink, lighter in tone on the petal reverse. The flowers on the first blooming are especially good, being large, high centered and well formed. They are double, borne either singly or in threes, and have a sweet, enduring fragrance. Blooming continues through summer and autumn, but mid-season flowers are usually smaller. The variety makes a fine bed, hedge or standard rose. The semi-glossy leaves are large, purplish when young, maturing dark green, and are sometimes touched by seasonal mildew; they furnish a plant of vigorous, slightly spreading growth that reaches average height or less.
**ZONES 4–9.**

HARKNESS, UK, 1983

COMPASSION' × 'MISCHIEF'

ROYAL NATIONAL ROSE SOCIETY
EDLAND MEDAL FOR FRAGRANCE
AND CERTIFICATE OF MERIT
1982, NEW ZEALAND FRAGRANCE
PRIZE 1984, COURTRAI
GOLDEN ROSE 1989, ROYAL
HORTICULTURAL SOCIETY AWARD
OF GARDEN MERIT 1993

### 'Paul Transon'
*(bottom)*

MODERN, LARGE-FLOWERED
CLIMBER, ORANGE-PINK,
REPEAT-FLOWERING

'Paul Transon' has medium-sized double blooms that open flat to show a charming formation, with the center petals infolded in a random, confused fashion while the outer ones slowly reflex. They are bright coppery pink, paling as they age, and there is a pleasant apple scent. After a prolific first flush, a few flowers are likely to appear intermittently through summer and autumn, especially in warmer climates. This variety has the lax and arching stems of a Rambler, which means it lends itself to being trained up arches, tall pillars, pergolas and similar structures. In growth it will extend slightly beyond the average expected of a climbing rose. The shiny, dark green foliage is plentiful and attractive.
**ZONES 4–9.**

BARBIER, FRANCE, 1900

*ROSA WICHURANA* × 'L'IDEAL'

ROYAL HORTICULTURAL SOCIETY
AWARD OF GARDEN MERIT 1993

P

### 'Paulii' *(right)*
syns *Rosa rugosa* 'Paulii', *Rosa × paulii* 'Rehder', *R. rugosa repens alba* 'Paul'

MODERN, MODERN SHRUB, WHITE

The parentage of this variety is botanically interesting, and as an early Ground Cover Rose its novelty value was high at century's dawn. The clove-scented, medium-sized flowers are single and white, showing yellow stamens as they open. The folded petal tips give them a starry look, and they are borne in short-stemmed clusters on trailing shoots in summer. When grown from cuttings the growth is creeping and truly ground covering; budded plants tend to make mound-like, wide-spreading plants with arching, spiky stems. There are many vicious prickles. Though suitable for difficult sites where a tough utilitarian rose is required, and valued in cold climates for its hardiness, 'Paulii' has many more beautiful successors from which gardeners can choose. ZONES 3–9.

PAUL, UK, PRE-1903

BELIEVED TO BE
*ROSA ARVENSIS × R. RUGOSA*

### 'Paul's Early Blush'
*(above right)*
syn. 'Mrs Harkness'

OLD, HYBRID PERPETUAL, LIGHT PINK, REPEAT-FLOWERING

The flowers of this rose are silvery pink and appear a little earlier in the season than most roses. An unusual feature is that two different shades may appear in flowers in the same cluster and even in the same flower. They are large, very double and scented. It is a medium-sized, thorny bush with thick stems and dark green foliage. John Harkness first exhibited his sport in 1890, naming it for his mother Mary Ann (1826–81). The two sports appear identical and originated about the same time. ZONES 5–9.

PAUL, UK, 1893 AND HARKNESS, UK, 1893

SPORT OF
'HEINREICH SCHULTHEISS'

### 'Paul's Himalayan Musk Rambler' *(above)*

MODERN, RAMBLER, LIGHT PINK

This is an odd name. The true Himalayan Musk Rose or *Rosa moschata nepalensis* (syn. *R. brunonii*) has light green, narrow, long leaves and this rose is quite different, having duller and smaller foliage and a *R. multiflora* scent. This rose is considered to have been derived from *R. m. nepalensis* or from *R. filipes*, as it has the same thread-like flower stems. It is an enormous tree climber with long trailing stems. The small, lilac-pink, double flowers are produced in drooping clusters in summer. ZONES 4–9.

PAUL, UK, 1916

PARENTAGE UNKNOWN

ROYAL HORTICULTURAL SOCIETY AWARD OF GARDEN MERIT 1993

P

### 'Paul's Lemon Pillar' *(right)*

MODERN, LARGE-FLOWERED
CLIMBER, LIGHT YELLOW

The color coding has probably misled generations of gardeners, for the color of this variety is close to that of the pith of a lemon, not the outside of the fruit. The large, round buds show creamy yellow as the sepals part. When fully open, the sweetly scented flowers are like cabbages, very large and with broad overlapping petals. They hold their form for a long time; indeed this rose was for many years a favorite with exhibitors. The flowers appear only in summer and are vulnerable to rain, which causes petals to stick and fail to open. This rose is best firmly attached to a large wall, where the stiff thick branches can be spread out. The large, dark green leaves are rather sparse, and the plant can grow almost twice as big as the average climber. **ZONES 4–9.**

PAUL, UK, 1915

'FRAU KARL DRUSCHKI' ×
'MARÉCHAL NIEL'

NATIONAL ROSE SOCIETY GOLD
MEDAL 1915

### 'Paul's Scarlet Climber' *(above right)*

MODERN, LARGE-FLOWERED
CLIMBER, MEDIUM RED

Britain's Royal National Rose Society handbook *Roses To Enjoy* calls this a Cluster-flowered Climber, which correctly describes its appearance, for it produces many medium-sized blooms in large sprays. The flowers have about 30 petals in a bright but not brash shade of medium red; they open loosely cupped and have a very light honey scent. They are borne so prolifically that in summertime beneath the massed effect of color, the leaves are almost obscured from view. There is little or no repeat-flowering after this glorious show. 'Paul's Scarlet' is appropriate for use as a climber anywhere as the stems are pliable and plentiful. The only problem is its liability to mildew, which means that potentially

dry sites must be avoided. The plant grows vigorously to slightly more than average, with ample mid-green, semi-glossy foliage. **ZONES 4–9.**

PAUL, UK, 1915

SEEDLING OF 'PAUL'S CARMINE
PILLAR', PERHAPS CROSSED
WITH 'RÊVE D'OR'

NATIONAL ROSE SOCIETY GOLD
MEDAL 1915, BAGATELLE GOLD
MEDAL 1918

### 'Pax' *(above)*

MODERN, MODERN SHRUB,
WHITE, REPEAT-FLOWERING

'Commemorate peace by planting a bed of Pax' was the raiser's message to his customers in 1918. They would have needed considerable space to plant a whole bed, for one plant will comfortably exceed the average dimensions of a shrub rose, producing a succession of cupped, semi-double blooms through summer and autumn. They are borne in large trusses of up to 50 medium to large-sized flowers, which open white from creamy buds and show golden stamens and ruffled petals. There is a sweet fragrance, and the rose stands out well in a mixed border, the pale flowers contrasting beautifully with crisp dark foliage. **ZONES 4–9.**

PEMBERTON, UK, 1918

'TRIER' × 'SUNBURST'

NATIONAL ROSE SOCIETY
GOLD MEDAL 1918

**'Peace'** *(right)*
syns 'Mme Antoine
Meilland', 'Mme
A. Meilland', 'Béke',
'Fredsrosen', 'Gioia',
'Gloria Dei'

MODERN, LARGE-FLOWERED/
HYBRID TEA, YELLOW BLEND,
REPEAT-FLOWERING

This renowned rose set new standards of excellence for its vigor and beauty and also for its foliage, because it demonstrated that bush roses can attract the eye even when not in flower. The blooms are yellow flushed pink, full-petalled and rounded in form, with the ability to open slowly and look delightful at every stage. They have a pleasant scent, and maintain a good succession of bloom, seeming impervious to weather conditions and succeeding in a wide range of climates, though the yellow turns pale in hot conditions, while the pink flushes become more pronounced. This is a splendid variety for beds, borders, hedges and for cutting, and it is one of the best roses to grow in standard form. The vigorous, shrub-like plants grow larger than average for a bush rose, and have glossy, rich green leaves. The raiser dedicated what he rightly considered his masterpiece to the memory of his mother, Claudia, but commercial pressures dictated a string of alternative names in countries other than his own. **'Climbing Peace'** is offered for sale by several nurseries in the southern USA, South Africa, Australia and New Zealand but is rarely grown in cooler climates because for the plants to succeed, warm conditions are required. Where conditions suit, the variety can fulfil the catalogue's forecast of 'flower throughout the summer with peak levels reached in spring and fall'. It reaches a height of 15–20 feet (4.5–6 m). As a climbing sport of the bush form, it shares the same characteristics of flower and foliage but produces vigorous, long, clambering stems. The flowers are produced on side shoots off the wood that has been made in previous years, so an established plant will provide more bloom. **ZONES 4–9.**

MEILLAND, FRANCE, 1942

(['GEORGE DICKSON' ×
'SOUVENIR DE CLAUDIUS
PERNET'] × ['JOANNA HILL' ×
'CHARLES P. KILHAM']) ×
'MARGARET MCGREDY'

PORTLAND GOLD MEDAL 1944,
ALL-AMERICA ROSE SELECTION
1946, AMERICAN ROSE SOCIETY
GOLD MEDAL 1947, NATIONAL
ROSE SOCIETY GOLD MEDAL
1947, THE HAGUE GOLDEN ROSE
1965, WORLD FEDERATION OF
ROSE SOCIETIES HALL OF FAME
WORLD'S FAVORITE ROSE 1976,
ROYAL HORTICULTURAL SOCIETY
AWARD OF GARDEN MERIT 1993

**P**

## 'Peacekeeper'

HARbella *(above)*
syns 'The Peace
Keeper', 'United
Nations Rose'

MODERN, CLUSTER-FLOWERED/
FLORIBUNDA, PINK BLEND,
REPEAT-FLOWERING

Several light colors
blend together in this
rose, basically a mix
of coral-pink, salmon
and apricot tones on
a yellow background,
becoming light yellow
as the blooms age.
The flowers are fully
double, and are carried
in well-spaced clusters
of up to 10. They open
with neat centers,
maintaining a rounded
outline and good sym-
metry of form until
the petals fall. The first
flowering is prolific,
almost smothering
the bush, and a good
succession of bloom is
maintained throughout
summer and autumn.

The flowers have a
pleasant spicy scent,
and this is a suitable
garden rose for use
in bedding schemes,
to group in a border
or to plant as a hedge.
Individual blooms may
be cut for use in small
arrangements. The
plant grows to average
height with an upright,
bushy habit and a
good covering of light
green, glossy foliage.
'Peacekeeper' was
named to commemo-
rate the golden jubilee
of the United Nations
and initially sold in aid
of its work for children.
ZONES 4–9.

HARKNESS, UK, 1995

'DAME OF SARK' ×
'BRIGHT SMILE'

GENEVA GOLD MEDAL 1995,
THE HAGUE FIRST CLASS
CERTIFICATE 1995

## 'Peach Blossom'

AUSblossom *(bottom)*

MODERN, MODERN SHRUB,
LIGHT PINK, REPEAT-FLOWERING

The fragrant flowers of
this variety are large for
peach blossom, being
of medium size, but it
is well named, for the
blooms come in big
clusters on bowing
stems, are blush pink
with a light yellow
base, and have just
enough small petals
to make up 2 or 3
rows surrounding the
stamens, which show
up handsomely in the
depths of the flower.
When sunlight catches
the blooms it lends
them an almost trans-
parent quality. For a
shrub border, this
makes an unusual and
interesting item. It has
a shrubby, spreading
habit, grows to average
size, and has mid-
green glossy leaves.
ZONES 4–9.

AUSTIN, UK, 1990

'THE PRIORESS' × 'MARY ROSE'

P

### 'Peaches 'n' Cream'
*(above)*

MODERN, MINIATURE, PINK
BLEND, REPEAT-FLOWERING

Tapered buds open up
to light peach-pink,
fragrant flowers with
52 petals of good Large-
flowered exhibition
form. This rose was
certainly well named,
as the blooms are a
delicious blend of
peachy pink and
cream. This rose has
so many petals that it
may not open properly
in cold damp climates.
In warm climates it is
a good show rose for
exactly the opposite
reasons. The vigorous,
compact plant provides
an ample supply of
blooms throughout
the growing season.
It is interesting to
note that the parents
are a well-known pair
used previously by
Ralph Moore.
**ZONES 5–10.**

WOODCOCK, USA, 1976

'LITTLE DARLING' ×
'MAGIC WAND'

AMERICAN ROSE SOCIETY
AWARD OF EXCELLENCE 1977

### 'Pearl Drift'   LEGgab
*(right)*

MODERN, MODERN SHRUB,
WHITE, REPEAT-FLOWERING

Clusters of long,
pointed buds develop
into large, semi-double
pearly white flowers,
opening wide like big
saucers and showing
their golden stamens.
They are borne close
to the stems, have a
pleasing scent, and
appear with excellent
continuity through
summer and autumn.
This rose makes an ex-
cellent specimen plant,
or it can be planted in
a mixed border, or as a
single-species bed; it
will also make a good
low hedge. The growth
is vigorous and compact,
with a somewhat
spreading habit that is
shorter than average
for a shrub rose. The
leaves are large and
glossy, reddish when
young and ageing to
dark green. **ZONES 4–9.**

LEGRICE, UK, 1980

'MERMAID' × 'NEW DAWN'

ROYAL NATIONAL ROSE SOCIETY
CERTIFICATE OF MERIT 1979

### 'Peer Gynt'   KORol  *(top right)*

MODERN, LARGE-FLOWERED/HYBRID TEA, YELLOW BLEND,
REPEAT-FLOWERING

This is quite a solid rose, with 50 broad petals
composing each big rounded bloom. They are
yellow, edged reddish pink, and appear with freedom on their first flush and with good continuity
thereafter through summer and autumn, borne
sometimes singly and sometimes in open clusters.
They have a pleasing light scent, withstand bad
weather well and in the garden will make a very
satisfying bed, group or hedge or an effective
standard. This rose does better in cool climates
than in warm ones. It is well foliaged with large
olive green leaves, and grows sturdily with a
bushy, upright habit to average height or a little
below. **ZONES 4–9.**

KORDES, GERMANY, 1968

'COLOUR WONDER' × 'GOLDEN GIANT'

ROYAL NATIONAL ROSE SOCIETY CERTIFICATE OF MERIT 1967,
BELFAST GOLD MEDAL 1970

P

### 'Pélisson'
syn. 'Monsieur Pélisson'

OLD, MOSS, DARK RED

This short and tidy shrub to 4 ft (1.2 m) has stout, upright stems that are sparsely covered with dark green moss and few thorns. The leaves are small, dark green and coarsely serrated. For several weeks beginning in early summer, the small, round flower buds open to fragrant, fully double, medium-sized blooms with a distinct button center. They are purplish red, perhaps a little muddy and pale with age to pure pink. It is a healthy, yet little-known variety, which prefers a good, fertile soil. ZONES 5–9.

VIBERT, FRANCE, 1848

PARENTAGE UNKNOWN

### 'Penelope'    *(top)*
MODERN, MODERN SHRUB, LIGHT PINK, REPEAT-FLOWERING

This is a large, arching shrub with vigorous and disease-free growth. It flowers continuously through summer and into autumn and produces a lovely show of hips in winter. The trusses of double, medium-sized blooms are of a delicate light pink, fading to white with age. The blooms are sweetly scented. 'Penelope' makes an effective informal hedge, and is useful for growing over fences or walls. ZONES 3–11.

PEMBERTON, UK, 1924

'OPHELIA' × SEEDLING OR POSSIBLY 'WILLIAM ALLEN RICHARDSON' OR 'TRIER'

NATIONAL ROSE SOCIETY GOLD MEDAL 1925, ROYAL HORTICULTURAL SOCIETY AWARD OF GARDEN MERIT 1993

### 'Penny Lane'
*(bottom)*

MODERN, LARGE-FLOWERED CLIMBER, APRICOT BLEND, REPEAT-FLOWERING

This is the first Climber to be voted Rose of the Year in the UK. It is a significant addition to the range of repeat-blooming climbers, because of the old-fashioned nature of the flowers. They are filled with ruffled, informal petals, becoming larger and more beautiful as they expand. The color is pearly blush with light apricot in the depths of the fragrant flower. 'Penny Lane' blooms continuously through summer and autumn on long slender shoots, usually singly and sometimes in small clusters. The plant has flexible stems and grows vigorously to average height or more, making it ideal for pillars, pergolas, arches, walls and fences. The plentiful foliage is dark green and shiny. ZONES 5–10.

HARKNESS, UK, 1998

SEEDLING OF 'NEW DAWN'

UK ROSE OF THE YEAR 1998

P

## 'Pensioners' Voice'

FRYrelax *(above)*

MODERN, CLUSTER-FLOWERED/
FLORIBUNDA, APRICOT BLEND,
REPEAT-FLOWERING

'Pensioners' Voice' bears well-spaced clusters of long buds that open into neatly formed flowers, like small-scale Large-flowered Roses, with high centers and becoming cupped as the petals reflex. They are large for a Cluster-flowered Rose and are basically orange-apricot, with vermilion-red flushes towards the margins of the petals. It is a very colorful rose, although some blooms tend to be overgrown by younger shoots. It has a pleasant fragrance, and flowering is maintained through summer and autumn. It is best suited for planting as a group in a border with shorter plants in front, to disguise its rather willowy, uneven habit. The healthy plant grows to average height with ample mid-green foliage. ZONES 4–9.

FRYER, UK, 1989

'ALEXANDER' × 'SILVER JUBILEE'

NATIONAL ROSE SOCIETY TRIAL
GROUND CERTIFICATE 1989

## 'Peppermint Twist'

JACraw *(top right)*
syn. 'Red and White Delight'

MODERN, CLUSTER-FLOWERED/
FLORIBUNDA, RED BLEND
(STRIPED), REPEAT-FLOWERING

This rose was originally produced as 'Red and White Delight', but its name has since been changed to 'Peppermint Twist'. It is one of the parents of the award-winning Cluster-flowered Rose, 'Scentimental', the other parent being 'Playboy'. It is a fairly low-growing bush rose that produces white flowers with stripes of red and pink; the striping varies in its intensity. They develop from pointed buds that open fairly quickly to flat, perfumed blooms filled with 30 petals. These flowers appear in flushes that have quite a long period between them. This low and compact bush displays healthy, disease-resistant growth with mid-green, semi-glossy foliage. ZONES 5–9.

CHRISTENSEN, USA, 1992

'PINSTRIPE' × 'MAESTRO'

## 'Perdita' AUSperd

*(above)*

MODERN, MODERN SHRUB,
APRICOT BLEND,
REPEAT-FLOWERING

The medium to large-sized flowers of this rose are full-petalled and open cupped, becoming flat as the petals reflex. They are borne in close clusters, in a pretty shade of creamy blush with touches of apricot. After the initial blooming, more flowers are produced through summer and autumn, when the color tends to be pinker. It makes a welcome addition to the flower border, owing to its excellent scent. It is shorter than the average size for a shrub rose, with plentiful dark green foliage. Perdita, meaning 'the abandoned one', is the name of the heroine of Shakespeare's play, *A Winter's Tale*. ZONES 4–9.

AUSTIN, UK, 1983

'THE FRIAR' × (SEEDLING ×
'ICEBERG')

ROYAL NATIONAL ROSE SOCIETY
EDLAND MEDAL FOR FRAGRANCE
AND TRIAL GROUND CERTIFICATE
1984

## 'Perfect Moment'
KORwilma *(right)*
syn. 'Jack Dayson'

MODERN, LARGE-FLOWERED/
HYBRID TEA, RED BLEND,
REPEAT-FLOWERING

The flowers of this variety are rounded and full-petalled, of medium to large size, and are carried on stiff, upright stems. They are golden yellow on the lower part of the petals with a wide band of orange-red towards the margins, a dramatic combination. The brilliance of the color varies according to climate, needing sunshine but not too high a temperature, which is why this rose is particularly cherished in moderately warm countries. It has some fragrance, and flowers continue through summer and autumn. This plant is suitable for a bed, border and as a hedge, and, if they are cut at a young stage, the blooms are good for arrangements and to show. It grows vigorously to average height or more, with a bushy habit and glossy, dark green foliage.
ZONES 4–9.

KORDES, GERMANY, 1991

'NEW DAY' × SEEDLING

ALL-AMERICA ROSE SELECTION
1991

## 'Perfume Delight'
*(right)*

MODERN, LARGE-FLOWERED/
HYBRID TEA, MEDIUM PINK,
REPEAT-FLOWERING

'Perfume Delight' has long pointed buds that open into large, well-formed blooms, full of broad petals. They are a vivid deep pink with a light purplish tone, paling towards the petal tips and lighter on the petal reverse. The flowers lose their centers and become loosely cupped, showing serrated petal edges as they age. The sweet spicy fragrance can be excellent but can become elusive in hot dry conditions. Flowering continues through summer and autumn, and the variety is a good choice for beds, borders and as a hedge and also for cutting, as it has long flower stems; it also withstands the effects of rain. The plant grows vigorously with an upright, bushy habit to average height and has large, dark green, leathery leaves. There is some liability to fungus troubles, so it is not reliably winter hardy in cooler climates.
ZONES 5–9.

SWIM AND WEEKS, USA, 1973

'PEACE' × (['HAPPINESS' ×
'CHRYSLER IMPERIAL'] ×
'EL CAPITAN')

ALL-AMERICA ROSE SELECTION
1974

### 'Pergolèse' *(bottom)*

OLD, PORTLAND, MAUVE, REPEAT-FLOWERING

The flowers of this rose are smallish, flat and filled with petals that are quartered in the Old Rose style. They are very fragrant with a Damask scent. The color is a rich purple-crimson. It is a small to medium-sized, upright shrub with plenty of dark green foliage. The Portlands were produced by crossing the Chinas and the Damasks, and sometimes perhaps adding some Gallica, which was probably the case with this rose. If it is pruned in the summer, it will repeat-flower. **ZONES 5–10.**

ROBERT & MOREAU, FRANCE, 1860
PARENTAGE UNKNOWN

### 'Perla de Alcañada' *(top)*

syns 'Baby Crimson', 'Pearl of Canada', 'Perle de Alcañada', 'Wheatcroft's Baby Crimson'

MODERN, MINIATURE, DEEP PINK, REPEAT-FLOWERING

Well-formed buds open to bright pink double flowers which age to reddish carmine with a white base. Flower production is very good. The plant is a hardy, low growing bush that rarely grows above 10 in (25 cm) high. Developed in 1944, 'Perla de Alcañada' quickly

became a cornerstone in the development of modern Miniature Roses. The use of 'Rouletii' as the pollen parent brought into the useable genetic pool the earliest known Miniature Rose. Used by the House of Meilland as a basis for many of their Miniature introductions, this rose has earned its rightful place in rose history. 'Climbing Perla de Alcañada' was developed by Pedro Dot in 1950. **ZONES 5–10.**

DOT, SPAIN, 1944
'PERLE DES ROUGES' × 'ROULETII'

### 'Perla de Montserrat'

MODERN, MINIATURE, PINK BLEND, REPEAT-FLOWERING

The flowers of this rose are pink in the center, blending outwards to a paler pink on the edges

of the petals. The blooms have about 18 petals and are grown in small clusters. The foliage is also small and mid-green and the plant habit is compact and dwarf. Perhaps best known as the first Miniature Rose, 'Perla de Montserrat' quickly became popular because of its tiny size and its amazing vigor. It has all the charm of its pollen

parent in producing perfectly shaped tiny flowers. It is a great candidate for small containers or rockeries. Here again, the significance of this classic rose in the history of Miniature Roses has been overlooked as modern Miniatures developed a fuller range of color and form. **ZONES 5–10.**

DOT, SPAIN, 1945
'CÉCILE BRÜNNER' × 'ROULETII'

P

### 'Perle des Jardins'
*(above)*
OLD, TEA, LIGHT YELLOW, REPEAT-FLOWERING

This is an infuriating rose which is given to balling at the slightest hint of damp or humidity. It was a popular greenhouse rose in its day and well suited to that role. In a dry, sunny climate it can be superb. The large, fragrant flowers are straw yellow. They are full of petals which are pointed at first, opening flat in the Tea manner. It has a moderate growth habit, and the repeat-flowering depends on a dry spell. This rose is at its best in autumn. **'Climbing Perle des Jardins'** is similar to the bush, and is suitable for pergolas, arches and fences. ZONES 7–9.

LEVET, FRANCE, 1874

SEEDLING OF 'MADAME FALCOT'

### 'Perle d'Or'
*(above right)*
syn. 'Yellow Cécile Brünner'

MODERN, POLYANTHA, YELLOW BLEND, REPEAT-FLOWERING

This is sometimes called a China Rose, being the result of an early cross between strains of Multiflora and Tea Roses. Clusters of up to 30 very small, urn-shaped buds open into double, narrow-petalled blooms of honey pink, showing light apricot in their confused centers as they expand. The variety's name, which translates as 'golden pearl', reflects the raiser's aspiration to obtain a yellow Polyantha rose. The synonym suggests a relationship with 'Cécile Brünner'— there is no connection. The flowers appear throughout summer and autumn and are borne on a spindly, free-branching dwarf shrub of upright habit that can become a substantial plant in warm climates. The blooms emit a pleasing light fragrance, and for buttonholes and small floral arrangement this variety is a treasure. As a garden plant it has historic interest as well as intrinsic beauty, and is one to grow where it can be viewed. The leaflets are small, glossy and pointed and the whole plant, which looks quite frail, is surprisingly tough and long lived. The rose has long been credited to Dubreuil, but the *Journal des Roses* for 1900 states it was 'Developed by P. Rambaux in 1875 and released to commerce in 1883 by F. Dubreuil'. ZONES 4–9.

RAMBAUX, FRANCE, 1883

POSSIBLY A SEEDLING OF *ROSA MULTIFLORA* × 'MME FALCOT'

ROYAL HORTICULTURAL SOCIETY AWARD OF GARDEN MERIT 1993

### 'Perle Meillandécor'
MEIplatin
syns 'Pearl Meidiland'

MODERN, MODERN SHRUB/ GROUND COVER, LIGHT PINK

As one of the many beautiful roses in the series from Meilland for use as small bushes or ground covers, this spreading plant produces a multitude of blooms throughout the season. If the dead flowers are removed, it will bloom as long as the weather permits. The ovoid buds open to pale pink blooms that fade to white in the sun. They are double, flat, medium in size, and produce sprays of 3–15 flowers. The foliage is dark and glossy, and many prickles line the thin canes. In autumn there are many red, round hips. As it repeats so well and is robust, like all of its relatives it is used frequently in landscaping. ZONES 4–9.

MEILLAND, FRANCE, 1989

('SEA FOAM' × 'LUTIN') × 'SEA FOAM'

## 'Pernille Poulsen'
*(right)*

MODERN, CLUSTER-FLOWERED/
FLORIBUNDA, MEDIUM PINK,
REPEAT-FLOWERING

The blooms of this variety are in delicate shades of rose and coral pink, deepening towards the centers. They are fairly large for a Cluster-flowered Rose, are borne in clusters, with about 18 petals, and have a refreshing scent. After a free-flowering early flush, a good succession of bloom is maintained through summer and autumn. In the garden this is a good plant for bedding and borders, and it is useful for cutting. It has an upright, somewhat spreading habit, grows to average height or less, and is furnished with pointed, light to mid-green leaves. The name is that of the raiser's eldest daughter, herself now actively engaged with her husband, Mogens Olesen, in hybridizing roses.
ZONES 4–9.

POULSEN, DENMARK, 1965

'MA PERKINS' × 'COLUMBINE'

## 'Peter Frankenfeld'
*(bottom)*

MODERN, LARGE-FLOWERED/
HYBRID TEA, DEEP PINK,
REPEAT-FLOWERING

'The excellence of form is unique in a rose of such immensity', says Ludwig Taschner of South Africa, one of the world's most knowledgeable rosarians. The deep rose pink flowers have a carmine tinge, and are large and well formed with high centers and maintain a wonderful symmetry as the petals reflex. They have an agreeable fragrance. As an exhibition rose this is outstanding, because of the long-lasting nature of the flowers. They are also long stemmed, making them very suitable to grow for flower arrangement, and they can be used in beds and borders. Flowering continues through summer and autumn on a vigorous, upright, free-branching plant that grows to average height or above and is well furnished with healthy deep olive green leaves. The variety

is named after a comedian, a compatriot of the raiser. **'Climbing Peter Frankenfeld'** (Allen, Australia, 1975) shares the good flower and foliage qualities of its parent bush rose, but does not appear to have enjoyed the wide distribution that might have been expected as it is grown today only in Australia. It seems to do well there, providing cerise-pink pointed blooms prolifically on long, strong stems. Maybe the existence of many recent pink climbers that are not sports has turned growers away from those that are, in view of some past experiences where the repeat-flowering ability of sports has proved inferior. In a warm climate like that of Australia this is evidently not a problem with this variety.
ZONES 4–9.

KORDES, GERMANY, 1966

'BALLET' × 'FLOREX'

### 'Petite de Hollande' *(left)*
syns 'Petite Junon de Hollande', 'Pompon des Dames', *Rosa centifolia minor*
OLD, CENTIFOLIA, MEDIUM PINK

This short-growing and rather relaxed shrub to 4 ft (1.2 m) bears grayish green branches covered with reddish thorns and small, well-serrated, soft grayish green leaves. The small flowers are slightly cupped at first, then open flat to show a full set of layered petals, often with a button eye. There is a fine scent, but blooms appear only in early summer. It makes a useful shrub or low hedge and is excellent in tubs or urns. **ZONES 5–9.**
THE NETHERLANDS, PRE-1838
PARENTAGE UNKNOWN

### 'Petite Lisette' *(left)*
OLD, CENTIFOLIA, DEEP PINK

Similar to 'Petite de Hollande' in many ways, this rose is shorter in stature; it grows to no more than 3 ft (1 m) in height, and may be a little taller in very fertile soil. The soft leaves are gray-green, coarsely and heavily serrated and plentiful in number. They are a backdrop to the small flowers, which are full of deep rose pink petals when fully open. They are richly scented, mostly arranged in large clusters and appear only in early summer. 'Petite Lisette' is best planted in small groups, and also makes an excellent subject for growing in containers, or in smaller gardens. **ZONES 5–9.**
VIBERT, FRANCE, 1817
PARENTAGE UNKNOWN

### 'Petite Orléanaise' *(left)*
syn. 'Petite de Orléanaise'
OLD, CENTIFOLIA, MEDIUM PINK

This variety is clearly a Centifolia, but has some affinity to the Gallicas. The grayish green wood has many thorns and is covered with an abundance of small, grayish green foliage, which can be a little coarse. The shrub is quite tidy in overall habit, and grows to about 4 ft (1.2 m) high. The flowers, which appear in mid-summer, are pompon-like when fully open. They are arranged in small clusters and are rich clear pink and well scented. 'Petite Orléanaise' is suitable for the smaller garden or for growing in containers. **ZONES 5–9.**
CIRCA 1900
PARENTAGE UNKNOWN

P

## 'Pfälzer Gold'

TANalzergo *(bottom)*

syn. 'Moonlight Serenade'

MODERN, LARGE-FLOWERED/ HYBRID TEA, DEEP YELLOW, REPEAT-FLOWERING

There is a puzzle about this rose, for the official description in *Modern Roses 10* says it is deep yellow and has 20 petals, but flowers seen on plants in Australia are medium yellow in bud, then open quite pale, with blush tints on the outer petals as they reflex. Also, they are more fully petalled. Maybe the change of climate accounts for this, or the identity has been confused, as can happen in horticulture when distances of much less than 11,000 miles (17,700 km) are involved. In Japan the blooms accord with the official entry, being deep yellow with high centers and symmetrical form. The variety flowers through summer and autumn, but lacks fragrance. It grows upright to average height and has glossy leaves. **ZONES 4–9.**

TANTAU, GERMANY, 1981

PARENTAGE UNKNOWN

## 'Phantom' MACatsan,

MACcatsan *(above)*

syns 'Phantom of the Opera', 'The Phantom'

MODERN, MODERN SHRUB, MEDIUM RED, REPEAT-FLOWERING

This handsome shrub carries long, arching growths of large saucer-shaped scarlet-red flowers, which contrast well with the bright golden stamens. They consist of up to 12 petals, attractively waved and fluted, and have a light scent; blooming continues through summer and autumn. This variety can be used as an eye-catching plant for a border, as a specimen plant or as a weeping standard. Growing to average height with a wide spreading habit, it is furnished with large, mid-green, semi-glossy leaves. The parentage shown is from a New Zealand source; *Modern Roses 10* has it the other way round. **ZONES 4–9.**

MCGREDY, NEW ZEALAND, 1992

'EYEOPENER' × 'PANDEMONIUM'

NEW ZEALAND NOVELTY AWARD AND CERTIFICATE OF MERIT 1992

## 'Pharaoh' MEIfiga

*(top right)*

syns 'Farao', 'Pharaon'

MODERN, LARGE-FLOWERED/ HYBRID TEA, ORANGE-RED, REPEAT-FLOWERING

Despite the haul of gold medals, this rose has never become widely grown in Britain, and today it seems to be commercially available only in Israel and Australia. The reason is probably that although it holds its fiery scarlet color very well, however fierce the climate, it does not bloom with sufficient freedom. It has plump buds that open into large, high-centered flowers made up of stiff petals that are reluctant to reflex and have little or no fragrance. More blooms appear sporadically through summer and autumn. This variety can be useful in beds and borders, and it is good for cutting, as the stems are strong. The plant grows vigorously with an upright habit to average height and has dark, leathery, semi-glossy leaves. **ZONES 4–9.**

MEILLAND, FRANCE, 1967

('HAPPINESS' × 'INDEPENDENCE') × 'SUSPENSE'

GENEVA GOLD MEDAL 1967, MADRID GOLD MEDAL 1967, THE HAGUE GOLD MEDAL 1967, BELFAST GOLD MEDAL 1969

P

### 'Phyllis Bide'
*(bottom)*

MODERN, POLYANTHA, YELLOW
BLEND, REPEAT-FLOWERING

This climbing variety has some unusual features, notably its ability to produce blooms all through summer and autumn, an uncommon achievement for a climbing rose at the time it was introduced. The buds are like small cones and are carried in wide clusters on short stems. They open into fairly full rosette-shaped blooms of modest size, in a mixture of salmony pink and yellow shades. They are lightly scented, and their neat distribution within the cluster and overall on the plant is a pleasure to see. The plant grows vigorously with a branching habit and lax arching stems, making a splendid climber for fences, pillars and arches; it can also be used on a wall and as a weeping standard. It reaches average height and can be pruned to form a sizeable shrub for training on a tripod or against a supporting post. The leaflets are plentiful, narrow and shiny. **ZONES 4–9.**

BIDE, UK, 1923

'PERLE D'OR' × 'WILLIAM
ALLEN RICHARDSON' OR
'GLOIRE DE DIJON'

NATIONAL ROSE SOCIETY
GOLD MEDAL 1924, ROYAL
HORTICULTURAL SOCIETY AWARD
OF GARDEN MERIT 1993

### 'Picasso'   MACpic
*(top)*

MODERN, CLUSTER-FLOWERED/
FLORIBUNDA, PINK BLEND,
REPEAT-FLOWERING

The 'crayon' marks on the blush and carmine petals are the sensational feature of this variety, the first of Sam McGredy's 'hand-painted' roses. The blooms, quite large for a Cluster-flowered Rose, are borne in clusters on upright stems and are fairly double, having about 18 petals that open wide. There is a light scent, and flowers continue through summer and autumn. For a bed, in a border and as a talking point in the garden, this is an interesting rose. It is probably better in cool climates, as the crayon markings tend to disappear in hot weather. It grows to below average height with a spreading habit and dark green foliage. It can be affected by black spot. When the raiser desired to name this rose in Picasso's honor, he was rather taken aback by the artist's suggestion that McGredy pay him for the privilege! **ZONES 4–9.**

MCGREDY, UK, 1971

'MARLENA' × ('EVELYN FISON' ×
[ORANGE SWEETHEART' ×
'FRÜHLINGSMORGEN])

ROYAL NATIONAL ROSE SOCIETY
CERTIFICATE OF MERIT 1970,
BELFAST GOLD MEDAL 1973, NEW
ZEALAND GOLD MEDAL 1973

## 'Piccadilly' MACar
*(above)*

MODERN, LARGE-FLOWERED/
HYBRID TEA, RED BLEND,
REPEAT-FLOWERING

This rose is loved for its bright bicolored flowers which are scarlet on the inside and yellow on the outside of the petals. They open from pointed buds into large blooms with about 24 broad petals, which form high centers before reflexing to a cupped shape and then dropping cleanly. Because the flowers are not as full as many Large-flowered Roses, they are borne more freely, which adds to the variety's garden value, where it proves a marvellous bedding, border and hedge rose and also a fine standard. There is a light and pleasant scent, and flowering is well maintained through summer and autumn, bloom quality remaining high whatever the weather. The plant grows to average height with a well-spread bushy habit and a generous covering of handsome dark green glossy leaves, which are reddish when young. It was Reimer Kordes who, observing the 'bright lights' of this rose, suggested its name. **ZONES 4–9.**

MCGREDY, UK, 1959

'MCGREDY'S YELLOW' ×
'KARL HERBST'

NATIONAL ROSE SOCIETY
CERTIFICATE OF MERIT 1959,
MADRID GOLD MEDAL 1960,
ROME GOLD MEDAL 1960,
ROTTERDAM GOLD MEDAL,
NORD-ROSE AWARD

## 'Piccolo' TANolokip
*(below)*
syn. 'Piccola'

MODERN, CLUSTER-FLOWERED/
FLORIBUNDA, ORANGE-RED,
REPEAT-FLOWERING

Although this variety has the stature of a Patio Rose, the comparatively large size of the flowers means it fits better in the company of Cluster-flowered Roses wherever a low grower is required for a bed, in front of a border or to make a hedge. The faintly scented flowers are fairly double and neatly formed and open cupped, then become flat. They are borne prolifically on short upright stems, giving a lively display of vivid tomato red close to the foliage on the first flush of bloom and maintaining a good succession through summer and autumn, performing well regardless of weather conditions. The plant grows to well below average height and has a bushy, spreading habit. It is furnished with large, glossy, dark green leaves that are purplish when young. **ZONES 4–9.**

TANTAU, GERMANY, 1984

PARENTAGE UNKNOWN

P

## 'Picture' (above)

MODERN, LARGE-FLOWERED/HYBRID TEA, LIGHT PINK,
REPEAT-FLOWERING

In the 1930s, 'Picture' was a much sought after
treasure, wanted for its exquisitely formed rose
pink flowers. They have attractive camellia-like
whorled centers that retain their shape for a long
time while the outer petals gradually reflex. The
result is indeed as pretty as a picture for the eye,
though for the nose there is not much scent. To
make a group in a border, or to include in an
historic collection, this is a good rose to have, and
12 nurseries worldwide are still listing it, even
though over 60 years have elapsed since its introduction and its constitution is not as robust as it
was. Flowering continues sporadically through
summer and autumn on a plant that grows compactly to below average height and has a trim, upright habit and light green matt leaves. '**Climbing
Picture**' (Swim, USA, 1942) is a decorative Large-
flowered Rose of modest size, perfect for buttonholes and small flower arrangements. When this
climbing sport was introduced, with it came the
splendid opportunity of having quantities of these
flowers out at the same time. It grows somewhat
larger in extent than the average climbing rose,
and is best on a wall where it can spread out and
attach securely. In milder climates it is likely to
produce flowers following the summer display,
but elsewhere it is effectively a summer bloomer
only. The most suitable site is one that receives
sunshine and a reasonable amount of moisture,
because mildew will soon prove troublesome if
the roots are in dry soil. As with the bush form,
the flowers withstand bad weather well. ZONES 4–9.

MCGREDY, UK, 1932

PARENTAGE UNKNOWN

NATIONAL ROSE SOCIETY CERTIFICATE OF MERIT 1932

## 'Pierre de Ronsard' MEIviolin (above)
syns 'Eden', 'Eden Rose 88', 'Grimpant Pierre
de Ronsard'

MODERN, LARGE-FLOWERED CLIMBER, PINK BLEND,
REPEAT-FLOWERING

This variety is a vigorous climber with flowers like
an old-fashioned rose. They are large and full
with over 40 petals and are shaped like round
cabbages, opening to disclose a charming muddle
of infolded petals. The basic color is creamy
white, heavily suffused with lavender pink and
carmine. The blooms repeat-flower through
summer and autumn, and have a light fragrance.
'Pierre de Ronsard' will grow to the extent
expected of an average climber and is suitable
to grow on a wall or fence where the strong
branching shoots can spread out, or it can be
trained up a tall pillar, or grown with support
as a shrub. The leaves are large, bright green and
semi-glossy. Pierre de Ronsard (1524–85) was a
court poet in Scotland and France and was a very
keen gardener. ZONES 4–9.

MEILLAND, FRANCE, 1987

('DANSE DES SYLPHES' × 'HANDEL') × 'CLIMBING PINK WONDER'

P

### 'Pierre Notting'

OLD, HYBRID PERPETUAL, DARK
RED, REPEAT-FLOWERING

This rose has a very strong constitution, which perhaps explains its longevity in the catalogues. The flowers are blackish red shaded blue-violet. Provided the season is fair, they are large and globular and are disposed to ball badly in wet weather. The rose has an upright habit, and although repeat-flowering, it can be unreliable in the autumn. Pierre Notting was a famous rose grower from Luxembourg. **ZONES 5–9.**

PORTIMER, FRANCE, 1863

SEEDLING OF 'ALFRED COLOMB'

### 'Pigalle' MEIcloux
*(top)*
syns 'Chacock', 'Fakir', 'Jubilee 150', 'Pigalle 84'

MODERN, CLUSTER-FLOWERED/
FLORIBUNDA, ORANGE BLEND,
REPEAT-FLOWERING

Described by one of the few growers who supply it as 'a fun rose', 'Pigalle' bears creamy yellow flowers in which are blended shades of orange and orange-red. Shapely and full for a Cluster-flowered Rose, with some 40 petals, the blooms are carried in a huge candelabra on stems long and strong enough to provide an ample supply for cutting. There is no

appreciable scent. It is suitable for beds and borders and as a hedge. It grows vigorously with a tall, bushy habit to above average height and has tough, mid-green semi-glossy leaves. **ZONES 5–9.**

MEILLAND, FRANCE, 1984

'FRENZY' × (['ZAMBRA' ×
'SUSPENSE'] × 'KING'S RANSOM')

### 'Pink Bassino'
*(right)*
syn. 'Korbasren'

MODERN, MODERN SHRUB, PINK
BLEND, REPEAT-FLOWERING

It is difficult to know whether to call this a ground cover rose or a shrub rose, because although it spreads up to twice as wide as it is high it is not procum-bent. The 5-petalled flowers are light pink with a prominent white eye and are borne in clusters on firm, slim stems quite close to the foliage. They open like saucers to display

golden stamens and have an innocent air in their simplicity. There is a light fragrance and, after the prolific initial display, blooming continues throughout summer and autumn. 'Pink Bassino' is very suitable for borders, and in parks it is used for beds and landscap-ing. It grows vigorously

to below average height with a well-spread habit. The foliage is plentiful, bright green and shiny, reddish when young. **ZONES 4–9.**

KORDES, GERMANY, 1993

SEEDLING OF *ROSA WICHURANA*
× 'ROBIN REDBREAST'

ROYAL NATIONAL ROSE SOCIETY
TRIAL GROUND CERTIFICATE
1992, ANERKANNTE DEUTSCHE
ROSE 1993

P

with a bushy, rather spreading habit to below average height and has dark green glossy leaves. ZONES 5–9.

BOERNER, USA, 1956

'FASHION' × 'FANTASIA'

### 'Pink Cloud'
*(bottom)*

MODERN, LARGE-FLOWERED CLIMBER, MEDIUM PINK, REPEAT-FLOWERING

The genes of 'New Dawn' have contributed to scores of modern Climbers, through both parents in the case of 'Pink Cloud'. The large flowers are fairly full in an attractive shade of deep rose pink with a darker center, are borne in clusters, and open out into a cupped form. There is a Tea fragrance, and after a splendid first blooming the plant flowers intermittently through summer and autumn. The growth is about the average to be expected of a Climber, and the variety makes a very suitable choice for walls, fences, pillars and arches, or it can be kept pruned and made to form a substantial shrub. It is vigorous and has an upright, rather stiff branching habit and a good covering of robust glossy foliage. ZONES 4–9.

BOERNER, USA, 1952

'NEW DAWN' × A RED DWARF SEEDLING OF 'NEW DAWN'

### 'Pink Chiffon'
*(above)*

MODERN, CLUSTER-FLOWERED/ FLORIBUNDA, LIGHT PINK, REPEAT-FLOWERING

This Cluster-flowered Rose resembles the Old Garden Roses in the way its light pink blooms are crowded with petals. There are usually over 50 of them, folded against one another to create confused centers as the large flowers develop a cupped and finally a flat shape as they expand. The old flowers turn pale, especially in hot weather, but retain deeper pink tones in the depths of the blooms. They are produced in well-filled clusters and have a pleasing spicy scent. This is a pretty variety to group in a border, but it needs calm sunny conditions for best results as the blooms are easily spoiled by rain. It grows vigorously

### 'Pink Bells'    POUbells    *(top left)*

MODERN, GROUND COVER, DEEP PINK

These cheerful, bright rose pink flowers are even more beautiful when the blooms are fully open. The florets are double with 35 petals and have a light fragrance. The blooms are very weatherproof, with cycles lasting from late spring until early autumn. The foliage is small and midgreen with a semi-glossy look and the plant has a spreading habit, making it ideal for use as a ground cover. 'Pink Bells' is an innovation in the development of Miniature Roses. ZONES 5–10.

POULSEN, DENMARK, 1983

'MINI POUL' × 'TEMPLE BELLS'

### 'Pink Favorite' *(right)*
syn. 'Pink Favourite'
MODERN, LARGE-FLOWERED/HYBRID TEA, MEDIUM PINK,
REPEAT-FLOWERING

Those who recall 'Juno' remember a flower of heartstopping beauty—but the plant underneath never grew much. By crossing it with a vigorous strain the raiser hoped to recapture that beauty, 'Pink Favorite' being the creditable result. The flowers, borne singly, in threes or in candelabra fashion, are long, elegant and high centered, in a rather cold color, somewhere between bright rose and china pink. Although there are only about 24 petals, they are so contrived as to make the flowers look full and so firm that the variety has proved most successful for exhibitors, as well as a good garden rose for beds and borders. The fragrance is elusive, pleasant to some noses, negligible to others. It flowers freely through summer and autumn, stands bad weather well and does best in cooler climates. Its habit is free branching, somewhat splayed, and the leaves are beautiful, bright, long, smooth and polished. Though often praised for its good health, it shows recent signs of vulnerability to rust. **ZONES 4–9.**

VON ABRAMS, USA, 1956

'JUNO' × ('GEORGE ARENDS' × 'NEW DAWN')

PORTLAND GOLD MEDAL 1957

### 'Pink Grootendorst'
*(below)*
syn. *Rosa rugosa* 'Pink Grootendorst'
MODERN, HYBRID RUGOSA,
MEDIUM PINK,
REPEAT-FLOWERING

This variety carries clusters of many small frilly petalled rosettes, in appearance rather like a dianthus. They are fully double and a refreshing shade of rose pink, but have very little scent; they are charming for use in small flower arrangements, lasting many days. The dainty flowers are borne on a plant that entirely lacks their charm, being a gaunt and prickly shrub with small, rather pallid, coarse leaves. In a border it will provide color and interest throughout the growing season, for the plant is hardly ever out of flower through summer and autumn. It grows to average height and has an exemplary record of good health. **ZONES 4–9.**

GROOTENDORST,
THE NETHERLANDS, 1923

SPORT OF 'F. J. GROOTENDORST'

ROYAL HORTICULTURAL SOCIETY
AWARD OF GARDEN MERIT 1993

**P**

### 'Pink Iceberg'
*(above)*

MODERN, CLUSTER-FLOWERED/
FLORIBUNDA, PINK BLEND,
REPEAT-FLOWERING

This sport of 'Iceberg'
occurred in a garden in
Hobart, Tasmania.
It has all the good
qualities of its parent,
being disease resistant,
with light green foliage
and a light perfume.
Like 'Iceberg', it flowers
almost continuously
over a long period. Its
blooms are in varying
shades from pink to
white, often with a hand-
painted appearance.
They fade with age and
may be lighter in hot
weather. The stamens
are generally orange-
pink and the filaments
retain this color as the
flowers age. Some
flowers may be entirely
white with yellow
stamens, as in 'Iceberg'.
It is an attractive rose
and a perfect choice
for a standard or bush.
ZONES 5–10.

WEATHERLY, AUSTRALIA, 1997

SPORT OF 'ICEBERG'

### 'Pink La Sevillana'
MEIgeroka *(above right)*
syns 'Rosy La
Sevillana',
'Pink La Sevilliana',
'Pink Sevillana'

MODERN, CLUSTER-FLOWERED/
FLORIBUNDA, MEDIUM PINK,
REPEAT-FLOWERING

This sport resembles
its parent in all respects
save color, which is
deep pink in the young
flowers, lightening with
age. It bears clusters
of up to 5 small to
medium-sized, lightly
fragrant blooms on
long, flexible stems. They
are made up of 12 or so
petals, open with neat
centers, and become
cupped as they mature.
Flowers are generously
produced on the first
flush, and a succession
of color is well main-
tained through summer
and autumn. 'Pink
La Sevillana' makes a
useful plant for a
mixed border and is
particularly successful
as a hedge. The plant is
spreading and hedge-
like in habit, growing

to average height with
dense, dark green,
glossy foliage.
ZONES 4–9.

MEILLAND, FRANCE, 1985

SPORT OF 'LA SEVILLANA'

BADEN-BADEN GOLD MEDAL
1985, ANERKANNTE DEUTSCHE
ROSE 1986

### 'Pink Léda' *(above)*
syn. 'Painted Damask'
OLD, DAMASK, MEDIUM PINK

There are two forms of
'Léda', different only in
color—one is white and
the other pink. They
both have the intense
Damask fragrance and
although classed as
Summer Damasks,

there can be later
flowers. They are both
luxuriant shrubs. This
rose is thought to have
originated in France.
The blooms are clear
pink. The white form
originated in England.
It opens cream and
then becomes suffused
with blush, later turn-
ing crimson on the
edges of the petals. In
Greek mythology, Léda
was seduced by Zeus
who took the form
of a swan. She became
the mother of Helen of
Troy. ZONES 4–9.

PRE-1844

PARENTAGE UNKNOWN

P

### 'Pink Meidiland' MEIpoque
syns 'Rose Meillandécor', 'Schloß Heidegg'

MODERN, MODERN SHRUB, PINK BLEND, REPEAT-FLOWERING

This is one of several amenity shrubs produced by the Meilland firm, and is recommended as ideal for roadside planting and for green spaces in urban developments. It makes a vigorous, bushy plant with a dense covering of foliage, producing umbrella-like panicles with up to 20 lightly scented blooms. The pointed red buds open to medium-sized cupped blooms of deep pink, showing white eyes around the yellow stamens at the center. The color becomes paler as the flowers age, before dropping their petals cleanly. After the first prolific flush, more blooms follow on through summer and autumn. The height of the plant is less than average and the leaves are leathery and shiny, and reddish green, when young. **ZONES 4–9.**

MEILLAND, FRANCE, 1985

'ANNE DE BRETAGNE' × 'NIRVANA'

ANERKANNTE DEUTSCHE ROSE 1987

### 'Pink Meillandina' MEIjidiro (top left)
syn. 'Pink Sunblaze'

MODERN, MINIATURE, MEDIUM PINK, REPEAT-FLOWERING

These medium pink flowers have a distinctive gold center to the bloom and a rosette-type form. They are borne singly or in small clusters and there is no fragrance. The plant has small, pointed, mid-green foliage and a reliable succession of tiny flowers. It is mainly sold as small container-grown plants and can be grown indoors for a while before planting out in the garden. **ZONES 5–10.**

MEILLAND, FRANCE, 1982

PARENTAGE UNKNOWN

### 'Pink Panther' MEIcapinal (above)
syns 'Panthère Rose', 'Aachener Dom'

MODERN, LARGE-FLOWERED/HYBRID TEA, PINK BLEND, REPEAT-FLOWERING

In warm climates there is not so much difference in the colors within the flowers of this variety, apart from a deepening of the azalea pink tone near the petal margins, but cooler conditions show a marked contrast, the rims appearing as a definite rose red. The blooms at their best are beautiful, being large and high centered and having 40 or more petals. They can be borne singly, in clusters or in candelabra form. The flowers, which continue to appear through summer and autumn, have a light fruity scent and last well, coming to resemble peonies before the waved and fluted petals finally fall. This rose looks its best in a warm climate because rain can mark the blooms. A vigorous plant, it is useful for beds, borders and hedges, growing to average height with an upright, bushy habit and having bronzy, glossy leaves. **ZONES 5–9.**

MEILLAND, FRANCE, 1982

MEIGURAMI × MEINAREGI

THE HAGUE GOLD MEDAL 1981

### 'Pink Parfait'

*(above)*

MODERN, CLUSTER-FLOWERED/
FLORIBUNDA, PINK BLEND,
REPEAT-FLOWERING

For a supply of button-hole roses on a well-tempered plant, 'Pink Parfait' takes some beating. Clusters of 3 or more carmine buds open to light pink flowers of medium to large size, the shades of pink varying according to season and climate, sometimes with traces of peach-pink. Each loosely double bloom is neatly formed with a coiled center, the outer petals reflexing symmetrically. The initial display is prolific and the variety maintains an excellent succession of flowers through summer and autumn, though they tend to fly open and lose color quickly in hot weather. There is a light sweet scent and for the garden, this gives splendid value in a bed or border. It grows sturdily with an upright, bushy habit to slightly less than average height, and is well supplied with matt, mid-green foliage. ZONES 4–9.

SWIM, USA, 1960

'FIRST LOVE' × 'PINOCCHIO'

BADEN-BADEN GOLD MEDAL 1959, PORTLAND GOLD MEDAL 1959, ALL-AMERICA ROSE SELECTION 1961, NATIONAL ROSE SOCIETY GOLD MEDAL 1962

### 'Pink Peace'    MEIbil

*(above right)*

MODERN, LARGE-FLOWERED/
HYBRID TEA, MEDIUM PINK,
REPEAT-FLOWERING

The color of the flowers of this variety is an arresting, rather hard and dusty deep pink, and it shows up from a long way off, for the blooms, of some 60 broad petals, are among the largest produced in quantity on any rose. They are carried on stiff stems, have a sweet strong fragrance and last well when cut. On opening out they have a well-filled cupped form, and carry a very narrow but distinct line of blush white along their petal rims. 'Pink Peace' is suitable for a bed or border, but the strong color means it has to be sited so as not to clash with other garden items. Reflowering after the first flush continues through summer and autumn, with remarkable freedom, considering the size of the blooms. The plant is vigorous, growing upright to more than average height, and it has large, leathery, matt leaves. Whereas over 50 nurseries offer the bush form of 'Pink Peace', those supplying **'Climbing Pink Peace'** (MEIbilsar; Meilland, France, 1968) can probably be numbered on the fingers of one hand. Two reasons can be suggested for this. First, a number of good pink climbers that were not sports were already established at the time of its introduction, such as 'Aloha', 'Pink Cloud' and 'Pink Perpetue', and they could be relied on to give much more flower per square meter of growth. Second, the color of 'Pink Peace' is strident and not easy to mix with other roses, whether old or modern. Whatever the reason, and despite its vigor, the climbing form of 'Pink Peace' has never become widely grown. ZONES 4–9.

MEILLAND, FRANCE, 1959

('PEACE' × 'MONIQUE') × ('PEACE' × 'MRS JOHN LAING')

GENEVA GOLD MEDAL 1959, ROME GOLD MEDAL 1959

## 'Pink Pearl'  KORmasyl
### syn. 'Fee'
MODERN, LARGE-FLOWERED/HYBRID TEA,
LIGHT PINK, REPEAT-FLOWERING

This variety bears full-petalled
flowers of medium size that
open with neatly formed centers
and develop slowly as the outer
petals reflex to create a bloom
of elegance and symmetry. The
scented pearly blush blooms,
which appear through summer
and autumn, are borne on very
long stems, perfect for cutting,
and indeed this rose was named
to mark the 30th anniversary
of the National Association of
Flower Arrangement Societies
in the UK. 'Pink Pearl' needs a
sunny place and free circulation
of air, partly because shade will
draw the plant up and make it
lanky, and also because an open
site reduces the risk of mildew.
It grows well above average
height with a narrow, upright
habit and has rich dark green
foliage. ZONES 4–9.

MARTENS, GERMANY, 1989

SPORT OF 'CONGRATULATIONS'

## 'Pink Perpetue'
### (above right)
MODERN, CLUSTER-FLOWERED CLIMBER,
MEDIUM PINK, REPEAT-FLOWERING

This rose is a warm and pleasing
shade of rose pink. It has many
flowers, grows well and is easy
to train and generally healthy,
which explains why it has maintained its popularity for well
over 30 years. The blooms are
of medium size, rounded in
form, and with up to 36 petals
symmetrically arranged to form
a cup. They are spaced neatly
over the plant in short-stemmed
clusters, have a light and pleasing
scent, and continue to carry
their blooms through summer

and autumn so effectively that
it is unusual for there to be no
color on the plant during this
time. 'Pink Perpetue' can be
used on a wall, fence, pillar, arch
and even a pergola if the gardener is patient, for it extends
itself by steady rather than rapid
progress. It does not resent
being pruned. 'Pink Perpetue'
is a vigorous, stiff and free-
branching grower, well furnished
with dark leathery leaves.
The name requires no French
accents, as Walter Gregory
chose it simply for its pleasing
sound. ZONES 4–9.

GREGORY, UK, 1965

'DANSE DU FEU' × 'NEW DAWN'

NATIONAL ROSE SOCIETY CERTIFICATE
OF MERIT 1964

## 'Pink Prosperity'
MODERN, MODERN SHRUB, LIGHT PINK,
REPEAT-FLOWERING

This variety bears its dainty
small to medium-sized flowers
in big strong-stemmed clusters.
They have many small petals, of
which the outer ones are blush
pink and the remainder clear
pink with deeper shadings; the
petals lie back layer upon layer
as the blooms open like shallow
saucers. There is a musky
scent. It is useful in borders
and for hedging, growing very
vigorously with an upright habit
to average extent or more. It has
attractive dark green leaves.
ZONES 4–9.

BENTALL, UK, 1931

SEEDLING OF 'PROSPERITY'

## 'Pink Robusta' KORpinrob (top left)
syn. 'The Seckford Rose'

MODERN, MODERN SHRUB, MEDIUM PINK, REPEAT-FLOWERING

This rose owes much of its rugged character to 'Robusta', its pollen parent, which was raised from *Rosa rugosa*. The flowers are a warm shade of rose pink and appear in large, well-spaced clusters above the foliage on stiff upright stems. They are semi-double, loosely formed and quite big, so that when they open out in cupped form there is a telling display of color, which shows up from a distance. In a public park, or as a hedge or group in a garden border, this is a noticeable rose, giving excellent value as it flowers over a long period through summer and autumn, has a pleasing scent and makes sturdy vigorous growth to average height. It has a good health record and is well furnished with large, medium to dark green leaves. ZONES 4–9.

KORDES, GERMANY, 1986

('ZITRONENFALTER' × 'CLÄRE GRAMMERSTORF') × 'ROBUSTA'

ROYAL NATIONAL ROSE SOCIETY CERTIFICATE OF MERIT 1987

## 'Pink Rosette'
(above)

MODERN, CLUSTER-FLOWERED/ FLORIBUNDA, LIGHT PINK, REPEAT-FLOWERING

The plump buds on this variety look rather small, but they belie their appearance by opening into medium-sized blooms of some 50 petals that are borne in sprays. They are a warm shade of rose pink, deeper in the heart of the flower, and develop as the name promises into cupped flowers of rosette form, the petals so arrayed one row upon another that they look artificial, like roses on ladies' hats. There is a little fragrance, and a good succession of bloom is maintained through summer and autumn. 'Pink Rosette' is good for cutting, and in the garden makes a suitable item for a border, a bed, or a hedge; it performs best in a warm climate. The plant grows with a sprawling habit to below average height and has a covering of dark green, leathery leaves. ZONES 4–9.

KREBS, USA, 1948

PARENTAGE UNKNOWN

## 'Pink Silk' (bottom)

MODERN, LARGE-FLOWERED/ HYBRID TEA, MEDIUM PINK, REPEAT-FLOWERING

This English-bred rose is offered today only in Australia, where it is regarded as a useful variety for garden display and exhibition. The flowers are large and high centered, with about 40 broad petals, and open from pinky red buds to flowers of carmine rose, nearer to deep pink than the official medium pink color, and having a lustrous sheen. They have a pleasing light fragrance, and the plant continues to produce them through summer and autumn. It grows freely with a bushy habit to average height and has a covering of mid-green leaves. ZONES 4–9.

GREGORY, UK, 1972

'PINK PARFAIT' × SEEDLING

NEW ZEALAND GOLD MEDAL 1974

### 'Pink Symphony'

MEItonse *(right)*
syns 'Pink Symphonie',
'Pretty Polly',
'Sweet Sunblaze'

MODERN, MINIATURE, LIGHT
PINK, REPEAT-FLOWERING

Elegantly shaped buds
open to light, cardinal
pink flowers with a
light scent. The initial
high-centered form
disappears rapidly as
the blooms move
quickly to the fully
open stage. Bloom
production is excellent,
covering the bush with
flowers all year long.
The glossy, dark green
foliage is disease resistant. It is a medium-
sized, compact bush.
**ZONES 4–10.**

MEILLAND, FRANCE, 1987

'DARLING FLAME' ×
'AIR FRANCE'

GLASGOW GOLD MEDAL 1992

### 'Pink Wonder'

MEIhartfor *(right)*
syn. 'Kalinka'

MODERN, CLUSTER-FLOWERED/
FLORIBUNDA, LIGHT PINK,
REPEAT-FLOWERING

The 30 nurseries listing
this rose all grow it
as 'Kalinka'. It is par-
ticularly popular in
Australia, South Africa
and continental Europe,
but is not offered in
Britain and America.
Pointed salmon-pink
buds develop into semi-
double flowers of
charming informal
character. They are
borne sometimes singly,
sometimes in clusters,

have a light scent, and
after the main flush,
continue to show color
through summer and
autumn. As a border
rose or in a container,
this variety makes a
useful item to brighten
up the garden, and the
growth is sufficiently
dense for it to become
an effective hedge. The
plant grows with a
bushy, spreading habit
to average height and
is furnished with
glossy, deep green
leaves and stems that
have few thorns.
**'Climbing Pink Wonder'**
(MEIhartforsar;
Meilland, France,
1976) is sold, like the
bush, under its synonym.
It makes a vigorous
plant, growing in
extent to the average

height of a climber and
having an extended
period of bloom, con-
tinuing after the main
flush to show color
through summer and
autumn. Because the
growth is rather stiff, it
is easier to grow it on a
wall or fence where it
can be firmly attached,
but it can also be
trained on a tall pillar,

arch or pergola. The
comparative thornless-
ness of the bush form is
a particularly welcome
asset in the climber,
because it eases the
task of pruning.
**ZONES 4–9.**

MEILLAND, FRANCE, 1970

'ZAMBRA' × ('SARABANDE' ×
['GOLDILOCKS' × 'FASHION'])

MADRID GOLD MEDAL 1969,
BELFAST GOLD MEDAL 1972

P

## 'Pinkie' *(above)*

MODERN, POLYANTHA, MEDIUM
PINK, REPEAT-FLOWERING

'Pinkie' has been classed as both a Cluster-flowered Rose and a Miniature, but the Polyantha group fits this dainty item well. The small to medium-sized flowers, made up of 12 to 16 petals, are borne in large trusses. They are of that delicate rose pink color with a salmon touch termed neyron rose, are pleasantly scented and open cupped. In cool climates the plant stays very dwarf, but in milder conditions its proportions become like those of a small shrub. Flowering continues through summer and autumn, and there are many ways of using the variety in the garden, in a container, in any small space, or to edge the front of a border, or grow as a short-stemmed standard. The growth is low and bushy and the leaves, which normally have 7 leaflets, are semi-glossy, bright green and soft in texture. The film *Pinkie* inspired its name. Although it was introduced with less of a fanfare than the bush from which it sported, **'Climbing Pinkie'** (Dering, USA, 1952) is today more widely grown. The scented flowers are borne freely on stems that bow under the weight of so much bloom. The visual effect of the many nodding pink rosettes massed together is most appealing, and blooming continues with remarkable constancy through summer and autumn. This rose makes many shoots, growing with a dense habit to average height. It is easy to train and manage and is particularly useful for a pillar or arch, or to plant near a footpath, where its near thornlessness is a boon to all who pass by. This variety can also be trimmed and grown as a cascading shrub. ZONES 4–9.

SWIM, USA, 1947

'CHINA DOLL' × SEEDLING

ALL-AMERICA ROSE SELECTION 1948

## 'Playboy' *(above)*
### syn. 'Cheerio'

MODERN, CLUSTER-FLOWERED/
FLORIBUNDA, RED BLEND,
REPEAT-FLOWERING

Originating in northern Scotland, this rose has proved a real sun lover, for it is most popular in warm climates where the bright orange-yellow flowers with scarlet shading attain a size and intensity of color not so evident at home. The blooms are almost single, and open from clusters of pointed buds to display their flamboyant tones and reveal attractive golden stamens. The petals hold their color surprisingly well, and drop cleanly when the blooms are spent. There is only a light scent but in all other respects this rose is a model performer, quick to reflower as summer and autumn advance, excellent for beds, borders and hedges and serviceable as a cut flower. The plant is vigorous with a bushy, free-branching habit, growing a little below average height and with an ample covering of dark glossy foliage. The original name, 'Cheerio', was soon abandoned in favor of one that suits the ambience of the rose so well. ZONES 4–9.

COCKER, UK, 1976

'CITY OF LEEDS' × ('CHANELLE'
× 'PICCADILLY')

ROYAL NATIONAL ROSE SOCIETY
TRIAL GROUND CERTIFICATE
1975, PORTLAND GOLD MEDAL
1989

### 'Playgirl'   MORplag

MODERN, CLUSTER-FLOWERED/FLORIBUNDA,
MEDIUM PINK, REPEAT-FLOWERING

Ralph Moore used 'Playboy' in
his hybridizing, hoping that its
splendid foliage and freedom
of flower might be transmitted
to his own seedlings. With this
variety he achieved his aim, and
it makes such a perfect partner
that finding the right name for
it surely gave him little pause for
thought. The color of 'Playgirl'
is a ladylike if not demure shade
of pink, being a bright and
strong color that, as the simple
flowers open out like saucers,
serves to emphasize the contrast
with the yellow stamens.

They are freely borne through
summer and autumn, and serve
almost limitless purposes in
the garden, in beds, borders, as
hedges or for tubs and exhibition.
There is not much scent so it
must be the color that attracts
bees to the flowers so often.
The plant grows vigorously
with a dense and bushy habit to
average height, and has plentiful
semi-glossy foliage. **ZONES 4–9.**

MOORE, USA, 1986

'PLAYBOY' × 'ANGEL FACE'

### 'Pleasure'   JACpif *(top)*

MODERN, CLUSTER-FLOWERED/FLORIBUNDA,
MEDIUM PINK, REPEAT-FLOWERING

There is much warmth in
the rosy salmon-pink of this
rose, which bears large, lightly
fragrant flowers in rather close
sprays of up to 7 blooms. They
have over 30 petals and open
cupped, displaying to advantage
the pink tones, which are
intensified in the depths of the
flower. When fully developed
the flowers have an old-
fashioned look, with the petals
infolded at the center, and

ruffled at the margins. As a
garden plant it is an excellent
variety for beds and borders,
and after its initial prolific
blooming it continues to flower
right through summer and
autumn. The plant grows
compactly to average height
or less with a rounded, bushy
habit, and is furnished with
dark green leaves. **ZONES 4–9.**

WARRINER, USA, 1988

('MERCI' × 'FABERGÉ') × 'INTRIGUE'

ALL-AMERICA ROSE SELECTION 1990

### 'Pleine de Grâce'   LENgra
*(above)*

MODERN, MODERN SHRUB, WHITE

This variety covers itself with
large panicles, each composed
of up to 24 single flowers. They
are creamy white and single, with
the pervasive scent typical of
*Rosa filipes*, and make an amazing show for a short period in
summer. Space permitting, this
is well worth including in the
garden not only on account of
its beauty, but also because of
the rarity and innovative nature
of the cross. It is a fine specimen
plant and could be allowed to
romp in a wild garden. The plant
grows with a bushy, spreading
habit to above average height
and twice as wide as it is tall,
so it needs space. The leaves are
a yellowish green. The name,
meaning 'full of grace', is a
happy choice. **ZONES 4–9.**

LENS, BELGIUM, 1983

'BALLERINA' × *ROSA FILIPES*

P

### 'Poetry in Motion' HARelan *(right)*

MODERN, LARGE-FLOWERED/HYBRID TEA, YELLOW BLEND, REPEAT-FLOWERING

The flowers on this variety are large with over 30 big petals, opening with high centers, and usually borne individually on long stems. They become cupped and rounded in form, the petals reflexing slowly and maintaining an excellent symmetry within the bloom. The color is light yellow in the bud stage, becoming creamy primrose in the outer petals as the flower develops, the inner petals remaining yellow and showing golden highlights. The flowering period extends through summer and autumn and the late season blooms have particularly fine coloring. There is a strong, fruity scent, and for beds, borders and as a standard, this makes a very effective garden rose, one that gives flowers suitable for cutting, thanks to their lasting quality and long stems. The plant grows vigorously with a bushy, branching habit and is well endowed with large, leathery matt foliage. **ZONES 4–9.**

HARKNESS, UK, 1997

PARENTAGE UNKNOWN

COURTRAI SILVER MEDAL 1995, BRITISH ASSOCIATION OF ROSE BREEDERS BREEDERS' CHOICE 1997, ROYAL NATIONAL ROSE SOCIETY BRITISH ROSE AWARD 1998

### 'Polareis' syn. 'Polaris'

MODERN, LARGE-FLOWERED CLIMBER, WHITE

This little-known Rambler produces clusters of snow white, double blooms. They are fragrant. Glossy pale green foliage covers this vigorous plant. The spring bloom is profuse, but there is no repeat-flowering.

'Polareis' shows little influence from the Wild Rose parent, *Rosa foetida bicolor.* **ZONES 5–9.**

HORVARTH, USA, 1939

(ROSA WICHURANA × R. SETIGERA) × R. FOETIDA BICOLOR

### 'Polarstern' TANlarpost *(above)* syns 'Evita', 'Polar Star'

MODERN, LARGE-FLOWERED/HYBRID TEA, WHITE, REPEAT-FLOWERING

The creamy buds on this variety open to big, high-centered white flowers on tall, strong stems. This rose creates a commanding presence in the garden, partly because its color shows up so well, partly due to the freedom with which the flowers are borne, and partly because of its sturdy, vigorous growth. For a bed where a big plant is required it is a good choice, and it fits in well with other roses in mixed borders. There is not much scent, but it withstands wet weather better than most pale varieties and continues to bloom through summer and autumn. It has an upright, free-branching habit to above average height and has dark green matt leaves. **ZONES 4–9.**

TANTAU, GERMANY, 1982

PARENTAGE UNKNOWN

ROYAL NATIONAL ROSE SOCIETY CERTIFICATE OF MERIT 1985, UK ROSE OF THE YEAR 1985

### 'Polka' MEItosier *(above)*
syns 'Lord Byron', 'Polka 91', 'Scented Dawn',
'Twilight Glow'
MODERN, LARGE-FLOWERED CLIMBER, ORANGE BLEND,
REPEAT-FLOWERING

There is an old-fashioned air about this rose, due
to the way it opens wide and flat with the short
petals reflexing one layer upon another. The
blooms are double, of medium to large size, and
are carried singly or in small clusters on stiff
stems. They are coppery salmon, fading to salmon
pink as the petals expand but retaining copper
tones in the depths of the flower. There is only a
light scent, which is a pity in a flower of such warm
and welcoming appearance, but blooming continues through summer and autumn. 'Polka' is ideal
for pillars, walls and fences where a shorter than
average climber is required. The growth is vigorous
and rather shrubby, not rampant, and the plant
has a good coverage of glossy foliage. **ZONES 4–9.**
MEILLAND, FRANCE, 1992

'GOLDEN SHOWERS' × 'LICHTKÖNIGIN LUCIA'

### 'Pompon Blanc Parfait' *(above right)*
OLD, ALBA, WHITE

Not entirely typical of Alba Roses, 'Pompon Blanc
Parfait' is an upright-growing shrub to about 4 ft
(1.2 m) that makes many stiff, relatively thornless
stems. These bear closely-packed, smooth, semi-
glossy, light grayish green leaves, and in early
summer, flowers emerge from plump round buds.
These are arranged in tight bunches, with each
rosette-like, soft lilac-pink, fragrant flower opening flat. This rose continues to flower for a longer

season than most other Albas, and is suitable
for a herbaceous border or a shrubbery.
**ZONES 5–9.**
VERDIER, FRANCE, 1876

PARENTAGE UNKNOWN

### 'Pompon de Paris'
OLD, CHINA, MEDIUM PINK/DEEP PINK, REPEAT-FLOWERING

This rose bears clusters of fully double, upright
pink flowers. It was popular in Victorian times
when it was grown in containers. It is very dwarf
and is said to be identical to 'Rouletii', the original
Miniature Rose rediscovered by Major Roulet in
Switzerland in 1918, but there are differences in
cultivation. It is an almost evergreen bush that is
tiny and thorny. **'Climbing Pompon de Paris'** is
probably a sport of a Miniature Rose that grew in
France up to the late 1830s and then was lost. If
that is correct, how surprising it is that the sport
of a Miniature can prove so vigorous, for this variety, after a slowish start, can exceed the average
extent expected of a climber. The lightly scented
blooms, opening from well-filled clusters of
light red buds, are rich carmine-pink, fading to a
paler tone in strong sunshine. They make perfect
rosettes, with many small petals laid back row
upon row. The blooms come early, and there is
not usually any significant later bloom. A good
site for this rose is on a wall where the stems,
heavy with many leaves and flower clusters, can
be well anchored. The tiny leaves are mid-green
and very numerous. **ZONES 4–9.**
POSSIBLY FRANCE, CIRCA 1839

PARENTAGE UNKNOWN

P

### 'Popcorn' *(right)*
MODERN, MINIATURE, WHITE, REPEAT-FLOWERING

The ovoid buds of 'Popcorn' open to pure white flowers with golden yellow stamens and look just like freshly burst popcorn. The florets have only 13–15 petals and display an informal decorative form that is at its best when fully open. They have a scent that improves in warmer climates. The blooms are borne in clusters on a vigorous, completely disease-resistant plant that is furnished with fern-like foliage. It has an upright habit and is self-cleaning—there is no need to deadhead spent blooms as the blooms fall off and the next cycle starts immediately. Its sport, 'Gourmet Popcorn', is an even more vigorous plant with larger clusters and a better overall shape. **ZONES 4–11.**

MOREY, USA, 1973

'KATHARINA ZEIMET' × 'DIAMOND JEWEL'

### 'Poppy Flash'
MEIlena *(bottom)*
syn. 'Rusticana'
MODERN, CLUSTER-FLOWERED/FLORIBUNDA, ORANGE-RED, REPEAT-FLOWERING

The name 'Poppy Flash' indicates the bright red of this rose, which is lightened by a streak of golden yellow

on some of the petals. The color deepens from bright vermilion to pale scarlet as the loosely cupped blooms age. Medium-sized flowers are borne in close clusters, and there is a light fruity scent. The initial display of bloom is prolific and flowers appear through summer and autumn with good continuity. The plant grows vigorously with a bushy habit to average height and has semi-glossy, bronzy leaves. **'Climbing Poppy Flash'** (MEIlenasar; Paolino, France, 1975) is popular in warmer countries where it is sold commercially only under the synonym **'Climbing Rusticana'**.

It serves a similar purpose in the garden to that of the bush variety, in that it provides a hot color tone where required but at a higher level. Planting the climber behind a group of bushes of the same type would provide a hot spot indeed. 'Climbing Poppy Flash'

grows to average height, flowers freely on the first flush with sporadic later offerings and is comparatively thornless. **ZONES 4–9.**

MEILLAND, FRANCE, 1972

('DANY ROBIN' × 'FIRE KING') × ('ALAIN' × 'MUTABILIS')

GENEVA GOLD MEDAL 1970, ROYAL NATIONAL ROSE SOCIETY TRIAL GROUND CERTIFICATE 1970, ROME GOLD MEDAL 1972

P

## 'Porthos, Climbing'

LAPadsar *(right)*

MODERN, CLUSTER-FLOWERED
CLIMBER, ORANGE-RED,
REPEAT-FLOWERING

The bush form of this
climbing rose was in-
troduced in 1971 but
no date is officially
recorded for the
Climber, which appears
to be on sale today only
in France and Italy.
It bears well-filled
clusters of bright red
flowers on short stiff
stems in summertime,
with a sporadic bloom
late in summer and in
autumn. The blooms
are double, of small
to medium size and
open cupped and
rather flat. They last
well, but there is not
very much fragrance.
The plant is best suited
to walls, fences and
pillars, growing sturdily
to average height and
has shiny dark green
leaves. **ZONES 4–9.**

LAPERRIÈRE, FRANCE, POST-1971

PARENTAGE UNKNOWN

## 'Portrait' MEYpink
*(right)*
syn. 'Stéphanie de
Monaco'

MODERN, LARGE-FLOWERED/
HYBRID TEA, PINK BLEND,
REPEAT-FLOWERING

The double flowers
of this variety have
attractively muddled
centers as they open,
with many petals
folded against one
another in the heart
of the bloom. They
are large, and develop
showing rose pink in
the depths of the flower
and pale pink towards
the edges of the petals,
the two shades toning
in well together. As the
fragrant blooms are
carried on long stiff
stems, they are good
for cutting, and make a
prominent group in a
bed or border, providing
a good succession
of bloom through
summer and autumn.
It grows vigorously
and upright to average
height or more with a
free-branching, shapely
habit and has glossy
dark green leaves.
When 'Portrait' was
voted worthy of one of
the highest accolades in
the rose world it was
the first time the prize
had gone to an amateur
raiser. **ZONES 4–9.**

MEYER, USA, 1971

'PINK PARFAIT' × 'PINK PEACE'

ALL-AMERICA ROSE SELECTION
1972

P

### 'Pot o' Gold'

DICdivine  *(below)*

MODERN, LARGE-FLOWERED/
HYBRID TEA, MEDIUM YELLOW,
REPEAT-FLOWERING

This variety is well
named, for the yellow
flowers have a hint of
ochreous gold about
them. They are of
medium size with
about 30 petals, borne
sometimes singly but
quite often in an open
cluster of several
flowers and developing
from pointed buds into
cupped, rather flat,

neatly formed blooms.
These appear on the
plant through summer
and autumn, the early
and later flowers being
of particularly good
quality. There is a
delightful scent, and
for small arrangements
'Pot o' Gold' is a
treasure. It is also
suitable for beds and
borders, and makes
a fine standard. It
grows compactly and
vigorously with a
spreading habit to a little
below average height
and has ample mid-
green foliage. **ZONES 4–9.**

DICKSON, UK, 1980

'EUROROSE' × 'WHISKY MAC'

ROYAL NATIONAL ROSE SOCIETY
CERTIFICATE OF MERIT 1979,
BRITISH ASSOCIATION OF
ROSE BREEDERS, BREEDERS'
SELECTION 1980

### 'Potter & Moore'

AUSpot  *(below left)*

MODERN, MODERN SHRUB,
MEDIUM PINK,
REPEAT-FLOWERING

This variety is a kindly
shade of rose pink,
bearing full-petalled
blooms that open
cupped, diffusing a
pronounced fragrance.
They are freely pro-
duced on their first
flush and continue
to bloom through
summer and autumn.
In the garden they are
suitable for a border,
particularly in associa-
tion with Old Garden
Roses. The soft texture
of the petals means
that the blooms can
be affected by damp
weather and fail to
open properly. The
plant grows shorter
than the average shrub
rose, with a shrubby
habit. Potter & Moore
is a British company
specializing in toilet-
ries, and the variety's
launch coincided
with the release of their
new 'Rose' range.
**ZONES 4–9.**

AUSTIN, UK, 1988

'WIFE OF BATH' × SEEDLING

P

## 'Poulsen's Pearl' *(above)*

MODERN, CLUSTER-FLOWERED/FLORIBUNDA, LIGHT PINK,
REPEAT-FLOWERING

This is a rose of distinct character, producing a
wonderful show of saucer-shaped, single, pearl
pink flowers marked at the center with showy
reddish stamens. The flowers are well scented,
and appear in widely spaced clusters on strong,
wiry stems. After the first flush, more blooms
are produced through summer and autumn.
For gardeners who enjoy unusual roses, this is a
treasure, with an ethereal quality about it that
moved one devotee to describe it as 'the rose that
always lifts my soul'. The plant is healthy and
hardy, growing vigorously with a bushy, upright
habit to average height or less and with light to
mid-green, semi-glossy leaves. **ZONES 4–9.**

POULSEN, DENMARK, 1949

'ELSE POULSEN' × SEEDLING

## 'Prairie Dawn'

MODERN, MODERN SHRUB, MEDIUM PINK, REPEAT-FLOWERING

The Morden Experimental Farm in Manitoba has
sought to raise hardier roses, able to withstand
Canadian winters, and 'Prairie Dawn' is one of
the fruits of that work. The flowers are a warm
shade of luminous pink, of medium size and
full-petalled. On the current season's wood they
repeat their bloom after the main summer flush.
The plant grows vigorously with an upright habit,
to rather taller than average height and has dark
green glossy leaves. It is very hardy. **ZONES 3–9.**

MORDEN, CANADA, 1959

'PRAIRIE YOUTH' × ('ROSS RAMBLER' × ['DR W. VAN FLEET' ×
*ROSA PIMPINELLIFOLIA ALTAICA*])

## 'Président de Sèze' *(left)*

syn. 'Madame Hébert'

OLD, GALLICA, MAUVE

This beautiful Gallica bears two-toned flowers that are pale lilac-pink around the edges and crimson in the center. The color deepens with age. The cup-shaped blooms are double, tend to be convex and are borne in clusters. It is a loose, upright, medium to tall bush. **ZONES 4–9.**

MME HÉBERT, FRANCE, 1828

PARENTAGE UNKNOWN

ROYAL HORTICULTURAL SOCIETY AWARD OF GARDEN MERIT 1993

## 'President Herbert Hoover' *(left)*

syn. 'President Hoover'

MODERN, LARGE-FLOWERED/ HYBRID TEA, PINK BLEND, REPEAT-FLOWERING

'President Herbert Hoover' has long, pointed blooms that are colored orange, rose and gold and have a lighter reverse. They are borne on long stems and have a spicy fragrance. The leathery green foliage is sparse but healthy, and appears on an extremely vigorous variety that is good for cutting. **ZONES 4–9.**

CODDINGTON, USA, 1930

'SENSATION' × 'SOUVENIR DE CLAUDIUS PERNET'

NATIONAL ROSE SOCIETY GOLD MEDAL 1934, AMERICAN ROSE SOCIETY JOHN COOK MEDAL 1935

## 'Président Leopold Senghor' MElluminac *(above)*
syn. 'Président L. Senghor'

MODERN, LARGE-FLOWERED/ HYBRID TEA, DARK RED, REPEAT-FLOWERING

This dark red rose has cupped, double blooms with 25 petals that open from conical buds. They have a slight fragrance. It is a vigorous bushy plant with large glossy dark green foliage. **ZONES 4–9.**

MEILLAND, FRANCE, 1979

([{['SCARLET KNIGHT' × 'SAMOURAI'} × {'CRIMSON WAVE' × 'IMPERATOR'}] × ['PHARAOH' × 'PHAROAH']) × ('PHARAOH' × 'PHARAOH')

## 'Pretty Jessica'
AUSjess *(left)*

MODERN, MODERN SHRUB, DEEP PINK, REPEAT-FLOWERING

Also classified as an English Rose, 'Pretty Jessica' produces rosettes of medium-sized, pink flowers with 41 petals. They have a strong, Old Garden Rose scent. It is a bushy variety with a low-growing habit that is very suitable for a small garden. The foliage is mid-green and not overly disease resistant. **ZONES 4–9.**

AUSTIN, UK, 1983

'WIFE OF BATH' × SEEDLING

P

## 'Pride 'n' Joy' JACmo
*(below)*

MODERN, MINIATURE, ORANGE
BLEND, REPEAT-FLOWERING

This rose has ovoid buds that open to bright, medium orange flowers with an orange-cream reverse that fades to salmon-pink. The double (30–35 petals) florets have a fruity fragrance and can have high, well-formed centers that tend to open too quickly for exhibition. The foliage is dark green and disease resistant. This spreading, compact bush blooms profusely all year. It is a wonderful cut flower because of the contrast of the bright orange against the foliage. This is one of the few Miniature Roses recognized by the All-America Rose Society as worthy of the award. It was hybridized by the master of Cluster-flowered Roses, the late Bill Warriner of Jackson & Perkins. **ZONES 5–11.**

WARRINER, USA, 1991

'CHATTEM CENTENNIAL' ×
'PROMINENT'

ALL-AMERICA ROSE SELECTION
1992

## 'Prima Ballerina'
*(bottom)*

syns 'Première
Ballerine',
'Primaballerina'

MODERN, LARGE-FLOWERED/
HYBRID TEA, DEEP PINK,
REPEAT-FLOWERING

This rose produces heavily scented, semi-double, rose pink medium-sized blooms. The glossy foliage and vigorous, upright habit make it suitable for bedding. Although susceptible to mildew, it is still an important contributor to the culture of modern roses. **ZONES 4–9.**

TANTAU, GERMANY, 1957

SEEDLING × 'PEACE'

NATIONAL ROSE SOCIETY TRIAL
GROUND CERTIFICATE 1957

### 'Primevère' *(above)*
syn. 'Primrose'

OLD, LARGE-FLOWERED CLIMBER, YELLOW BLEND

This is a very vigorous non-repeating Climber and trailer, which grows in the *Rosa wichurana* manner. The large, primrose to canary yellow flowers are double and are borne in clusters of 4–5 blooms. They are slightly fragrant. The stems are long and the foliage is rich green and glossy. **ZONES 5–9.**

BARBIER, FRANCE, 1920

*ROSA WICHURANA* × 'CONSTANCE'

### 'Prince Camille de Rohan' *(right)*
syn. 'La Rosière, Climbing'

OLD, HYBRID PERPETUAL, DARK RED, REPEAT-FLOWERING

With such distinguished parentage, you would expect this rose to be a good one, and the blooms indeed merit great praise; they are fragrant, deep red, very double, with about 100 petals, large, imbricated and cupped. The growth habit can be sprawling, becoming more upright with age. However, there is a fault upon which all agree—the weak stems cannot fully support the weight of the flowers. It is sometimes repeat-flowering. **ZONES 5–9.**

VERDIER, FRANCE, 1861

POSSIBLY 'GÉNÉRAL JACQUEMINOT' × 'GÉANT DES BATAILLES'

### 'Prince Charles'  *(below)*

OLD, BOURBON, MAUVE

This medium to tall Bourbon is not unlike the
more well-known 'Bourbon Queen'. Large, deep
green leaves adorn almost thornless stems on
this vigorous bush. The well-scented, loose, semi-
double flowers are crimson or bright cherry.
There may also be some purple and some veining
in the flowers, leading to the American Rose
Society color attribution. There are few flowers
after mid-summer. ZONES 5–9.

HARDY, FRANCE, 1842

PARENTAGE UNKNOWN

### 'Prince Meillandina'

MEIrutral  *(above)*

syns 'Prince Sunblaze',
'Red Sunblaze'

MODERN, MINIATURE, DARK
RED, REPEAT-FLOWERING

This rose has dark
currant red flowers
that vary to bright
orange, depending on
the climate. The double
florets with 15–25 petals
have no fragrance,
and a large number
of clusters cover the
bush with color and
vibrancy. 'Prince
Meillandina' has very
dependable vigor and
bloom production. It
is a good garden variety
that is disease resistant
and easy to maintain.
ZONES 5–10.

MEILLAND, FRANCE, 1988

'PARADOR' × 'MOGRAL'

P

### 'Princeps' *(right)*

MODERN, LARGE-FLOWERED
CLIMBER, MEDIUM RED

This Climbing Rose
bears its very large red
flowers in summer.
They have only a slight
fragrance. It is most
suitable for growing on
pillars and low fences.
ZONES 4–9.

CLARK, AUSTRALIA, 1942

PARENTAGE UNKNOWN

### 'Princess Alice'

HARtanna *(right)*
syns 'Brite Lites',
'Zonta Rose'

MODERN, CLUSTER-FLOWERED/
FLORIBUNDA, MEDIUM YELLOW,
REPEAT-FLOWERING

'Princess Alice' is an
upright-growing bush
rose with rounded,
double yellow flowers
containing 22–28 petals.
Medium-sized and
slightly scented, the
blooms are borne in
many-flowered sprays
from spring to autumn.
The healthy foliage is
mid-green and semi-
glossy. It grows best
in cooler climates.
ZONES 4–9.

HARKNESS, UK, 1985

'JUDY GARLAND' ×
'ANNE HARKNESS'

DUBLIN GOLD MEDAL 1984,
ROYAL NATIONAL ROSE SOCIETY
TRIAL GROUND CERTIFICATE
1985, COURTRAI AND TOKYO
CERTIFICATES OF MERIT 1985,
ORLÉANS PRIZE 1987, THE
HAGUE SILVER MEDAL 1990

P

P

### 'Princess Margaret of England' MEllister, MEllisia *(above)*

syn. 'Princesse Margaret d'Angleterre'

MODERN, LARGE-FLOWERED/ HYBRID TEA, MEDIUM PINK, REPEAT-FLOWERING

'Princess Margaret of England' has large, high-centered, double, lightly scented flowers. Phlox-pink in color, they are borne singly or in clusters in spring; in autumn they appear singly and have a more intense tone. This is a vigorous, free-flowering upright bush with leathery, dark green foliage. **'Climbing Princess Margaret of England'** is suitable for walls and pillars. This is the second rose named for Princess Margaret. The first was from Benjamin Cant in 1932. **ZONES 4–9.**

MEILLAND, FRANCE, 1968

'QUEEN ELIZABETH' × ('PEACE' × 'MICHÈLE MEILLAND')

PORTLAND GOLD MEDAL 1977

## 'Princess Michael of Kent' HARlightly
*(right)*

MODERN, CLUSTER-FLOWERED/
FLORIBUNDA, MEDIUM YELLOW,
REPEAT-FLOWERING

The long, pointed buds on 'Princess Margaret of Kent' open into rounded, fully double, yellow, fragrant flowers that are borne singly or in clusters. With 38 petals each, they are long stemmed and appear from spring to autumn. This neat, compact bush has healthy, glossy green foliage and looks good in clumps in big borders. **ZONES 4–9.**

HARKNESS, UK, 1981

'MANX QUEEN' × 'ALEXANDER'

ROYAL NATIONAL ROSE SOCIETY
CERTIFICATE OF MERIT 1979,
BELFAST CERTIFICATE OF MERIT
1981, ORLÉANS PRIZE 1983

## 'Princesse Adélaide'
*(right)*

OLD, MOSS, LIGHT PINK

'Princesse Adélaide is a medium bush with dark green foliage, which is often variegated. The large, double flowers are soft pink, often variegated, with a pleasing scent. They are not very mossy. This rose is similar to the Gallicas, in which class it is sometimes placed. **ZONES 4–9.**

LAFFAY, FRANCE, 1845

PARENTAGE UNKNOWN

P

### 'Princesse de Monaco' MEImagarmic *(left)*

syns 'Grace Kelly', 'Preference', 'Princesse Grace', 'Princess of Monaco', 'Princesse Grace de Monaco'

MODERN, LARGE-FLOWERED/
HYBRID TEA, WHITE,
REPEAT-FLOWERING

The large high-centered blooms of 'Princesse de Monaco' are white edged with pink. They continue through summer and autumn, are very fragrant and are double, with 35 petals. The dark glossy foliage and upright growth make this a good garden rose; it is also popular on the exhibition table. ZONES 4–9.

MEILLAND, FRANCE, 1982

'AMBASSADOR' × 'PEACE'

### 'Princesse de Nassau' *(left)*
syn. 'Autumnalis'

OLD, NOISETTE, LIGHT YELLOW

This rose is more generally known as 'Autumnalis' and is a form of the Musk Rose related to 'Blush Noisette'. Graham Thomas has equated it with Laffay's 'Princesse de Nassau'. It is a medium Climber or Rambler, and bears sprays of small, creamy yellowish, double flowers, nicely scented in the musk way. There are few prickles and the stems grow in a zig-zag (similar to another Noisette 'Aimée Vibert'). It does not flower until late summer but continues to bloom for a while. The plant is a little tender. ZONES 7–9.

LAFFAY, FRANCE, 1835

PARENTAGE UNKNOWN

P

### 'Princesse de Sagan' *(above)*

OLD, CHINA, DARK RED, REPEAT-FLOWERING

This moderate shrub bears deep cherry red
maroon, double flowers, which are somewhat
cupped with sporadic extra petals. The solitary
flowers are well held on long stems at the ends of
thin branches. This rose would be hard to find
now, but could be 'discovered' in old locations.
**ZONES 7–9.**

DUBREUIL, FRANCE, 1887

PARENTAGE UNKNOWN

### 'Princesse Louise'

OLD, SEMPERVIRENS, WHITE

*Rosa sempervirens*, a tender wild Rambler from
southern Europe and northern Africa, has been
used to create a number of hybrids, notably
'Adélaïde d'Orleans' and 'Félicité-Perpétue', both
vigorous once-flowering Ramblers with small,
double white flowers. This rose is considered to
be intermediate between them. Its flowers are
creamy white, with the back petals shaded rose.
**ZONES 5–9.**

JACQUES, FRANCE, 1829

HYBRID OF *ROSA SEMPERVIRENS*

**'Prins Claus'** RUprins
syns 'Rosalynn Carter',
'Prince Klaus'

MODERN, CLUSTER-FLOWERED/
FLORIBUNDA, ORANGE-RED,
REPEAT-FLOWERING

A brilliant combination
of coral red and orange
creates a stunning
flower in this ever-
blooming rose. The
blooms are double,
high-centered like a
Hybrid Tea, and have
a spicy fragrance. The
flowers, with 28–32
petals, are borne singly
on long stems. The
straight prickles are
slightly curved around
mature canes. Dark,
glossy green foliage
covers the bushy, up-
right, tall, very strong
growth. ZONES 4–9.

DE RUITER, THE NETHERLANDS,
1978

SEEDLING × 'SCANIA'

**'Priscilla Burton'**
MACrat *(top)*

MODERN, CLUSTER-FLOWERED/
FLORIBUNDA, RED BLEND,
REPEAT-FLOWERING

From spring to autumn
this free-flowering bush
rose bears cupped,
semi-double bicolored
blooms in shades of
pale to deep pink, purple
and cerise. Produced
in clusters, they have
10 petals each and are
fragrant. It is vigorous
and upright in habit
with glossy dark green
foliage. ZONES 4–9.

MCGREDY, NZ, 1978

'OLD MASTER' × SEEDLING

ROYAL NATIONAL ROSE SOCIETY
PRESIDENT'S INTERNATIONAL
TROPHY 1976

**'Pristine'** JACpico
*(left)*

MODERN, LARGE-FLOWERED/
HYBRID TEA, WHITE,
REPEAT-FLOWERING

The long buds of this
rose open to huge high-
centered almost white
blooms shaded light
pink. The 25–30 petals
are overlapping and
there is a light scent.
The colors are unfading
under all climatic
conditions. This healthy
plant has deep green
leathery foliage and
strong upright stems.
It is ideal for bedding
and is suitable for
exhibition. ZONES 4–9.

WARRINER, USA, 1978

'WHITE MASTERPIECE' ×
'FIRST PRIZE'

PORTLAND GOLD MEDAL 1979,
ROYAL NATIONAL ROSE SOCIETY
EDLAND FRAGRANCE MEDAL
1979

## 'Prolifera de Redouté'

OLD, CENTIFOLIA, MEDIUM PINK

This medium to tall, lax shrub to about 6 ft (1.8 m) high has very dark green prickly stems covered in coarse, dark green foliage. At first, the deep rose pink, very double flowers are cabbage-like, then open flat and are very fragrant. 'Prolifera de Redouté' would be a most agreeable shrub were it not for its propensity for proliferation (another bud growing through the center of the flower). It is more suitable for a larger collection, rather than for general garden use. **ZONES 4–10.**

FRANCE, PRE-1824

PARENTAGE UNKNOWN

## 'Prominent' KORp *(above)*
syn. 'Korp'

MODERN, LARGE-FLOWERED, ORANGE-RED, REPEAT-FLOWERING

'Prominent' has large pointed buds that develop into bright orange-red blooms with 33 petals. Sometimes classified as Grandiflora, they have almost perfect form, are medium sized and are slightly fragrant. This free-flowering variety has an upright growth habit and matt green foliage. **ZONES 4–9.**

KORDES, GERMANY, 1971

'COLOUR WONDER' × 'ZORINA'

ROYAL NATIONAL ROSE SOCIETY CERTIFICATE OF MERIT 1970, PORTLAND GOLD MEDAL 1977, ALL-AMERICA ROSE SELECTION 1977

### 'Prosperity' *(left)*

**MODERN, MODERN SHRUB, WHITE, REPEAT-FLOWERING**

Large clusters of creamy white, fragrant blooms open from pale pink buds. Blooms are produced in profusion from early summer. The foliage is glossy green and the growth habit is medium and slightly lax. A good shrub or pillar rose, it requires feeding in mid-summer to encourage autumn color. **ZONES 4–9.**

PEMBERTON, UK, 1919

'MARIE-JEANNE' × 'PERLE DES JARDINS'

ROYAL HORTICULTURAL SOCIETY AWARD OF GARDEN MERIT 1994

### 'Prospero' AUSpero *(below)*

**MODERN, MODERN SHRUB, DARK RED, REPEAT-FLOWERING**

A bush rather than a shrub, 'Prospero' produces large, deep crimson, fragrant blooms that turn a deep purple. They have 40 small petals. Not very robust, this variety requires feeding and spraying to obtain a maximum return. It is also classified as an English Rose. **ZONES 4–9.**

AUSTIN, UK, 1982

'THE KNIGHT' × SEEDLING

## 'Proud Land'
*(right)*

MODERN, LARGE-FLOWERED/
HYBRID TEA, DARK RED,
REPEAT-FLOWERING

'Proud Land' has deep red flowers that are very double with 60 petals. They have a considerable scent and appear with good continuity through summer and autumn. It has an upright growing habit and leathery, dark green foliage that is reasonably healthy. **ZONES 4–9.**

MOREY, USA, 1969

'CHRYSLER IMPERIAL' ×
SEEDLING

## 'Proud Titania'

AUStania *(above)*

MODERN, MODERN SHRUB,
WHITE

An early variety in this family of roses from David Austin, 'Proud Titania' is also classified as an English Rose, and it can claim origins in the blend of Old and Modern Garden Roses. Although it is still listed by several growers, the raisers have discontinued it, possibly due to its susceptibility to disease. It produces large, double blooms with 35 petals that are flat, creamy white and fragrant. There is some doubt as to its repeat-flowering ability. The foliage is small and semi-glossy. **ZONES 4–9.**

AUSTIN, UK, 1982

SEEDLING × SEEDLING

P

### 'Puppy Love'
SAVapop *(right)*

MODERN, MINIATURE, ORANGE
BLEND, REPEAT-FLOWERING

Opening from elegantly
pointed buds, the small
flowers of this rose are
an attractive color
combination of pink,
coral and orange. The
double florets have a
light fragrance and
high well-formed
centers suitable for
exhibition. This is one
of the first roses to
bloom in the spring
and it has excellent
shape and color. With
only 23 petals, the
bloom matures very
slowly and so holds its
exhibition form. This
is a favorite with floral
arrangers because of its
lovely bud form and
eye-catching color, set
against lush, dark green
foliage. It has an up-
right, compact growth
habit and is clean and
easy to maintain.
'Puppy Love' is a good
choice for a border or a
container. ZONES 5–11.

SCHWARTZ, USA, 1978

'ZORINA' × SEEDLING

### 'Pure Bliss'  DICtator
*(above)*

MODERN, LARGE-FLOWERED/
HYBRID TEA, PINK BLEND,
REPEAT-FLOWERING

This aptly named var-
iety has large blooms
that are an extremely
pretty blend of soft
pink. Appearing
throughout summer
and autumn, they are
well formed and have
a slight scent. The
growth is moderate,
but very bushy and
healthy. 'Pure Bliss'
is a good bedding plant
that is also suitable for
growing as a standard.
ZONES 4–9.

DICKSON, UK, 1995

'ELINA' × ('SILVER JUBILEE' ×
['TYPHOON' × 'MAXI'])

BELFAST GOLD MEDAL 1997,
GENOA SILVER MEDAL 1994

### 'Purple Splendour'  *(right)*

MODERN, CLUSTER-FLOWERED/FLORIBUNDA, MAUVE,
REPEAT-FLOWERING

Small clusters of glowing purple, double, large
flowers with 26 petals are borne on 'Purple
Splendour' throughout summer and autumn.
They have a slight scent. It is suitable for beds.
**ZONES 4–9.**

LEGRICE, UK, 1976

'NEWS' × 'OVERTURE'

**P**

### 'Purple Tiger'

JACpurr  *(above)*

syn. 'Impressionist'

MODERN, CLUSTER-FLOWERED/
FLORIBUNDA, MAUVE,
REPEAT-FLOWERING

This innovative variety
has blooms with
remarkable coloring
that is deep purple and
then striped and
flecked with white and
mauve-pink. Produced
in small clusters from
summer to autumn,
they are open, with
26-40 petals, and have
some fragrance. The
foliage, which is glossy
green, grows on a short
bush that is almost
thornless. 'Purple
Tiger' is a good
bedding variety that
is unfortunately very
susceptible to black
spot. **ZONES 4–9.**

CHRISTENSEN, USA, 1991

'INTRIGUE' × 'PINSTRIPE'

## 'Quaker Star'

DICperhaps *(bottom)*

MODERN, LARGE-FLOWERED/
HYBRID TEA, ORANGE-PINK,
REPEAT-FLOWERING

'Quaker Star' has
very full flowers with
40 petals that are
orange with a silver
reverse, then age to
salmon with orange
edges to the petals.
They are borne mostly
singly throughout
summer and autumn;
unfortunately they
have little fragrance.
It is a bushy plant with
a short growth habit
and healthy, glossy,
mid-green foliage. It
is sometimes classified
as a Grandiflora.
ZONES 4–9.

DICKSON, UK, 1991

'ANISLEY DICKSON' × SEEDLING

ROYAL NATIONAL ROSE SOCIETY
CERTIFICATE OF MERIT 1989

## 'Quatre Saisons Blanc Mousseux'
*(left)*

syns 'Perpetual White
Moss', 'Rosier de
Thionville'

OLD, MOSS, WHITE,
REPEAT-FLOWERING

This Moss Rose of
distinction makes a
tidy and upright, yet
bushy shrub to some
5 ft (1.5 m) with stout
stems well clothed in
dark purplish green,
stubbly moss and
slightly mossy, mid-
green foliage. The
flower buds, which
are also well covered
with moss, are arranged
in small clusters on
short stalks and open
to white and fairly full,
medium-sized flowers.
They lose some of their
early promise as they
mature, but their lack
of significant beauty
is compensated for
by their profusion,
fragrance and constant
renewal through
summer and autumn.
ZONES 5–9.

LAFFAY, FRANCE, PRE-1837

SPORT OF 'QUATRE SAISONS'

**'Queen Elizabeth'** *(below)*
syns 'Queen of England',
'The Queen Elizabeth',
'The Queen Elizabeth Rose'
MODERN, CLUSTER-FLOWERED/FLORIBUNDA,
MEDIUM PINK, REPEAT-FLOWERING

Called a Grandiflora in some countries, this remarkable variety has maintained its popularity for over 40 years; it is a grower's dream as it produces a high percentage of saleable plants. It has large, pointed, medium pink blooms that have a high center. They appear throughout summer and autumn and are double, with 38 petals. A vigorous plant that, with light pruning, develops into an impressive shrub, it can be cut down hard in mid-winter about once every 6 years to rejuvenate it. Its large, glossy, dark green, leathery foliage is relatively resistant to disease, and it is an ideal variety for large borders, as a specimen plant or for hedging. The Queen Mother granted permission for her name to be associated with this rose on condition that it should be named in full—'The Queen Elizabeth Rose'. Any modification does not therefore carry the same validity.

**'Climbing Queen Elizabeth'** (syns 'Climbing The Queen Elizabeth Rose', 'Grimpant Queen Elizabeth'; Whisler, USA, 1957), the summer-flowering climbing variety, has somewhat suspect flower production. In all other respects it is similar to its parent. ZONES 4–9.

LAMMERTS, USA, 1954

'CHARLOTTE ARMSTRONG' × 'FLORADORA'

PORTLAND GOLD MEDAL 1954, NATIONAL ROSE SOCIETY PRESIDENT'S INTERNATIONAL TROPHY 1955, ALL-AMERICA ROSE SELECTION 1955, AMERICAN ROSE SOCIETY GOLD MEDAL 1957, GOLDEN ROSE OF THE HAGUE 1968, WORLD'S FAVORITE ROSE 1979

**'Queen Margrethe'** POUlskov,
POUskul *(bottom)*
syns 'Dronning Margrethe',
'Enchantment', 'Königin
Margrethe', 'Queen Margarethe'
MODERN, MODERN SHRUB, LIGHT PINK,
REPEAT-FLOWERING

'Queen Margrethe' is a relatively new shrub rose that bears light pink, double, medium-sized flowers with two dozen petals and an old-fashioned quartered form. They are carried in small clusters and resemble the English Roses of David Austin. There is a slight fragrance. The small, glossy mid-green foliage covers this shortish, bushy and compact rose. This neat, rounded shrub flowers repeatedly from spring to late autumn. Many breeders are now creating roses with an old-fashioned form. ZONES 5–10.

POULSEN, DENMARK, 1991

SEEDLING × 'EGESKOV'

NEW ZEALAND GOLD MEDAL 1993

Q

### 'Queen Mother'

KORquemu *(above)*

syn. 'Queen Mum'

MODERN, PATIO/DWARF
CLUSTER-FLOWERED, LIGHT PINK,
REPEAT-FLOWERING

This extremely free-flowering plant bears small clusters of loose, soft pink blooms throughout summer and autumn. They are slightly fragrant, 'Queen Mother' is a healthy plant with a slightly lax growth habit, that develops into a shrubby grower; it has glossy dark green foliage. **ZONES 4–9.**

KORDES, GERMANY, 1991

PARENTAGE UNKNOWN

ROYAL HORTICULTURAL SOCIETY
AWARD OF GARDEN MERIT 1994

### 'Queen of Bedders'
*(right)*

OLD, BOURBON, DEEP PINK,
REPEAT-FLOWERING

The fragrant flowers of this rose are a rich crimson and the plant flowers freely until autumn. It is a very compact Bourbon and so is very suitable at the front of borders. The stronger shoots should be shortened to encourage the bedding propensity. **ZONES 5–9.**

STANDISH & NOBEL, UK, 1871

SEEDLING OF 'SIR JOSEPH PAXTON'

## 'Queen of Bourbons' *(right)*

syns 'Bourbon Queen', 'Reine des Iles Bourbon', 'Souvenir de la Princesse de Lamballe'

OLD, BOURBON, PINK BLEND, REPEAT-FLOWERING

This rose is a well-known old favorite and is still grown widely. The rose pink flowers are semi-double, loose and cupped; they are well scented but do not repeat well. Although the plant can grow tall, it is best pruned to a bushy shrub. It has plenty of foliage and is very strong; it will survive even if it is neglected. This is most suitable for planting in a cottage garden. ZONES 5–9.

MAUGET, FRANCE, 1834

PARENTAGE UNKNOWN

## 'Queen of Hearts'

*(right)*

MODERN, LARGE-FLOWERED CLIMBER, MEDIUM PINK, REPEAT-FLOWERING

This vigorous summer-flowering Climber bears globular buds that develop into rich pink, double, fragrant flowers. It has dark foliage that contributes to a very vigorous climber, a good choice for growing on walls. ZONES 4–9.

CLARK, AUSTRALIA, 1920

'GUSTAVE GRÜNERWALD' × 'ROSY MORN'

## 'Queen of the Musks'

MODERN, MODERN SHRUB, PINK BLEND, REPEAT-FLOWERING

The open flowers of this variety are a deep blush and white. They appear with good continuity from summer to autumn and they have a very strong fragrance. 'Queen of the Musks' is a little-known shrub rose. It has dark ivy-green foliage and is a useful rose in borders and as a specimen plant. ZONES 4–9.

PAUL, UK, 1913

PARENTAGE UNKNOWN

Q

### 'Radiance' *(left)*
syn. 'Pink Radiance'

**MODERN, LARGE-FLOWERED/HYBRID TEA, LIGHT PINK, REPEAT-FLOWERING**

This vigorous grower has large, globular, cupped blooms of rose pink with a lighter reverse. The semi-double flowers have 23 petals and a considerable Damask fragrance. Suitable for bedding, this variety has a vigorous growth habit and large, leathery, very healthy foliage. **'Climbing Radiance'** was introduced in 1926 by Griffing in Florida. **ZONES 4–9.**

COOK, USA, 1908

'ENCHANTER' × 'CARDINAL'

### 'Radio Times' AUSsal *(left)*

**MODERN, MODERN SHRUB, MEDIUM PINK, REPEAT-FLOWERING**

This variety is one of David Austin's best recent introductions; it is also classified as an English Rose. The name was chosen to celebrate the 70th anniversary of the British magazine *Radio Times*. Throughout the warmer months, this shrub bears gentle rose pink, double blooms with a strong fragrance. They have many petals that give a formal rosette arrangement; the outer petals reflex as the flowers mature. **ZONES 5–10.**

AUSTIN, UK, 1994

PARENTAGE UNKNOWN

## 'Radox Bouquet'

HARmusky *(right)*

syn. 'Rosika'

MODERN, CLUSTER-FLOWERED/
FLORIBUNDA, MEDIUM PINK,
REPEAT-FLOWERING

The very fragrant
blooms of this variety
are produced in small
clusters, with 1–3
soft pink blooms per
cluster. The medium-
sized, cupped flowers
have 30 petals each.
The foliage is large,
glossy and mid-green
on an upright plant
that is useful for bed-
ding and for grouping
in borders. It is repeat-
flowering and has
large dark prickles.
ZONES 4–9.

HARKNESS, UK, 1981

('ALEC'S RED' × 'PICCADILLY') ×
('SOUTHAMPTON' ×
['CLÄRE GRAMMERSTORF' ×
'FRÜHLINGSMORGEN'])

GENEVA COUPE DE PARFUM
1980, BELFAST FRAGRANCE
PRIZE 1983, BELFAST CERTIFICATE
OF MERIT 1983, COURTRAI
CERTIFICATE OF MERIT 1983

## 'Radway Sunrise'

*(right)*

syn. 'Morning Colors'

MODERN, MODERN SHRUB,
ORANGE BLEND,
REPEAT-FLOWERING

This rose scored highly
for health and general
effect in the UK trials,
and was one of the
earliest successful
attempts to harness
the extraordinary color
genes of 'Masquerade'
in a shrub rose. The
young flowers, carried
in large trusses, are
yellow with cerise-pink
at the edges of the
petals and change to
deep cherry red as they
age. Composed of 7
large petals, they open
cupped to show reddish
gold stamens and have
a modest scent. In the
garden, this stalwart
plant makes a colorful
addition to shrub
borders, and continues
to bloom through
summer and autumn.
It grows with a vigorous,
free-branching, bushy
habit to above average
height for a shrub
rose, and is furnished
with dark green,
leathery leaves. It was
so named because the
Waterhouse nursery
was at Radway Green
in Cheshire, England.
ZONES 4–9.

WATERHOUSE NURSERY LTD, UK,
1962

'MASQUERADE' × SEEDLING

ROYAL NATIONAL ROSE SOCIETY
TRIAL GROUND CERTIFICATE 1962

R

### 'Rainbow's End'

SAValife *(right)*

**MODERN, MINIATURE, YELLOW BLEND, REPEAT-FLOWERING**

This rose is one of the most beautiful Miniature Roses ever created. The blooms are deep yellow with red edges, ageing to red all over. The blending of the yellow and red is truly eye-catching and usually draws murmurs of appreciation from everyone. The double florets with 35 petals have no fragrance. The foliage is small, dark green and glossy on an upright, compact, dense bush, covered with blooms at all stages. This compact rounded growth habit makes it ideal as a container-grown plant. This rose is still ranked as one of the most popular Miniature Roses. Recently, a climbing version was introduced. **ZONES 4–11.**

SAVILLE, USA, 1984

'RISE 'N' SHINE' × 'WATERCOLOR'

AMERICAN ROSE SOCIETY AWARD OF EXCELLENCE 1986

### 'Ralph's Creeper'

MORpapplay *(above)*

syns 'Creepy', 'Glowing Carpet', 'Highveld Sun'

**MODERN, MODERN SHRUB/ GROUND COVER, RED BLEND, REPEAT-FLOWERING**

This repeat-flowering ground cover has the potential to be used in a variety of situations in the garden. The flowers are deep orange-red with a bright yellow eye, with a reverse of bright yellow and white ageing to pinkish red. Loose and medium sized, the semi-double blooms, with 15 petals, are borne in sprays of 10–15. A moderate apple blossom scent and small, healthy, matt, dark green foliage is a bonus. If the blooms are not deadheaded, a crop of small round red fruit will be produced in autumn. This spreading plant is suitable for garden banks, window boxes, pots and hanging baskets. **ZONES 4–9.**

MOORE, USA, 1987

'PAPOOSE' × 'PLAYBOY'

## 'Rambling Rector'
*(right)*

MODERN, RAMBLER, WHITE

Although its origins are unknown, this rose is probably very old and must surely have started life in a vicarage garden. 'Rambling Rector' has an intense scent and semi-double, white flowers. Not suitable for a small garden, it will ramble extensively through trees, bearing masses of small clusters in summer. **ZONES 5–9.**

PRE-1912

POSSIBLY *ROSA MULTIFLORA* × *R. MOSCHATA*

ROYAL HORTICULTURAL SOCIETY AWARD OF GARDEN MERIT 1993

R

## 'Ramona' *(above)*
syn. 'Red Cherokee'

MODERN, MODERN SHRUB, MEDIUM RED, REPEAT-FLOWERING

'Ramona' is a vigorous, bushy, slightly lax plant with glossy foliage that is suitable for a border or as a specimen plant. It flowers early in summer with occasional bloom in autumn, and has large, single, fragrant blooms with 5 petals that are carmine-crimson. **ZONES 4–9.**

DIETRICH AND TURNER, USA, 1913

SPORT OF 'ANEMONE'

### 'Raubritter' *(left)*

MODERN, MODERN SHRUB,
LIGHT PINK

'Raubritter' bears
clusters of light pink,
double, globular
flowers. The foliage is
leathery and wrinkled.
Although occasionally
listed as a Climber,
this rose is more often
grown as a sprawling
shrub or ground
cover. Only summer
flowering, it is quite
spectacular. **ZONES 4–9.**

KORDES, GERMANY, 1936

'DAISY HILL' × 'SOLARIUM'

### 'Ray of Sunshine' COCclare *(left)*

MODERN, MODERN SHRUB,
MEDIUM YELLOW,
REPEAT-FLOWERING

The pointed buds of
this variety open into
clear bright unfading
yellow, small semi-
double blooms with
15 petals. Cupped and
fragrant, they are borne
in small sprays of 3–9.
The foliage is small,
dark green and glossy
on a low, bushy plant
that is suitable for
small borders, pots
and window boxes.
**ZONES 4–9.**

COCKER, UK, 1988

'SUNSPRITE' × ('CLÄRE
GRAMMERSTORF' ×
'FRÜHLINGSMORGEN')

R

## 'Raymond Chenault' *(right)*

MODERN, MODERN SHRUB,
MEDIUM RED,
REPEAT-FLOWERING

The large, bright red semi-double blooms of 'Raymond Chenault' have 16 petals and are borne in clusters. They have a slight scent and are repeat-flowering. The plant is vigorous and slightly lax, and has dark glossy foliage that is disease resistant. It is a good pillar rose that will also grow on pergolas or as a large shrub. **ZONES 4–9.**

KORDES, GERMANY, 1960

*ROSA KORDESII* × 'MONTEZUMA'

NATIONAL ROSE SOCIETY TRIAL
GROUND CERTIFICATE 1961

## 'Red Ace' AmRUda *(right)*
syn. 'Amanda'

MODERN, MINIATURE, DARK
RED, REPEAT-FLOWERING

The flowers of this variety are an attractive, dark, velvety crimson red and are borne in large clusters on strong, healthy, straight stems. The blooms are at their best when fully open, when they display their rich golden yellow stamens. This upright, compact bush is winter hardy and relatively disease free. The sprays are so beautiful that they are constant winners at the Royal National Rose Society shows in the UK, especially when displayed as groups of 5 and 12 sprays. **ZONES 4–10.**

DE RUITER, THE NETHERLANDS,
1982

'SCARLETTA' × SEEDLING

### 'Red Bells' POUlred
*(right)*

MODERN, MINIATURE/GROUND
COVER, MEDIUM RED

This vigorous ground-
cover variety has a
spreading growth habit
but, unfortunately, is
only summer flower-
ing. The small, double,
mid-red blooms have
35 petals, are produced
in large clusters and
have a slight fragrance.
The foliage is small,
mid-green, semi-glossy
and very healthy.
ZONES 4–9.

POULSEN, DENMARK, 1983

'MINI-POUL' × 'TEMPLE BELLS'

### 'Red Blanket'

INTercel, INTercell *(top)*

MODERN, MODERN SHRUB,
DEEP PINK, REPEAT-FLOWERING

'Red Blanket' is a bushy
ground cover with dull
deep pink, semi-double
small blooms. They
are borne in small
clusters, are slightly
fragrant, and occur on
the bush from summer
through to autumn.
This variety has small
dark green glossy
foliage and many
medium-sized thorns,
and is vigorous to
a height of 3–4 ft
(1–1.2 m). ZONES 4–9.

ILSINK, THE NETHERLANDS, 1979

'YESTERDAY' × SEEDLING

ROYAL HORTICULTURAL SOCIETY
AWARD OF GARDEN MERIT 1993

R

### 'Red Cascade' MOORcap

MODERN, CLIMBING MINIATURE, DARK RED,
REPEAT-FLOWERING

On this variety, pointed buds
open to an abundance of deep
red, cupped, fragrant flowers
containing about 40 petals.
The foliage is small and leathery
in texture. The plant habit is
prostrate or cascading, allowing
it to be used as a ground cover,
in a hanging basket or draped
over a wall. It is susceptible
to powdery mildew if left unprotected. This rose is a garden
favorite that provides a great
splash of brilliant color.
ZONES 5–11.

MOORE, USA, 1976

(*ROSA WICHURANA* × 'FLORADORA') ×
'MAGIC DRAGON'

AMERICAN ROSE SOCIETY AWARD OF
EXCELLENCE 1976

### 'Red Cross' MEIsoyris *(top)*

MODERN, LARGE-FLOWERED/HYBRID TEA,
MEDIUM RED, REPEAT-FLOWERING

This rose bears double blooms
with many attractively scalloped,
rich velvety red petals that
develop from long and pointed
buds. The flowers are produced
in great abundance and have a
quick repeat blooming. They are
good for cutting and there is
fragrance. The foliage is dark
green, plentiful and disease free.
Sales of this rose benefit the Red
Cross. ZONES 5–9.

MEILLAND, FRANCE, 1998
PARENTAGE UNKNOWN

### 'Red Devil' DICam *(bottom)*
syn. 'Coeur d'Amour'

MODERN, LARGE-FLOWERED/HYBRID TEA,
MEDIUM RED, REPEAT-FLOWERING

'Red Devil' has been described
as the most perfectly shaped big
Large-flowered Rose ever to
appear on the show bench. The
bright scarlet-crimson blooms
with a lighter reverse have
72 petals and high centers;
they also have a good scent.
The foliage is a glossy deep
green on a vigorous plant
that, although primarily
an exhibition variety, is also
strong enough to make a
spectacular bedding plant.
ZONES 4–9.

DICKSON, UK, 1970

'SILVER LINING' × 'PRIMA BALLERINA'

ROYAL NATIONAL ROSE SOCIETY CERTIFICATE
OF MERIT 1965, JAPAN GOLD MEDAL 1967,
BELFAST GOLD MEDAL 1969, PORTLAND
GOLD MEDAL 1970

R

### 'Red Favorite'  TANschweigru
*(below right)*
syns 'Holländerin', 'Red
Favourite', 'Salut à la Suisse',
'Schweizer Gruss'

MODERN, CLUSTER-FLOWERED/FLORIBUNDA,
MEDIUM RED, REPEAT-FLOWERING

'Red Favorite' has semi-double
flowers with 13 petals that are
medium in size and have a slight
fragrance. The blooms, which
are velvety ox-blood red, are
produced in medium-sized
clusters. The foliage is dark
green, leathery and glossy on a
vigorous, moderate-height
healthy plant that is suitable for
bedding. **ZONES 4–9.**

TANTAU, GERMANY, 1954

'KARL WEINHAUSEN' × 'CINNABAR'

ANERKANNTE DEUTSCHE ROSE 1950,
NATIONAL ROSE SOCIETY CERTIFICATE
OF MERIT 1952

### 'Red Masterpiece'  JACder
*(above)*

MODERN, LARGE-FLOWERED/HYBRID TEA,
DARK RED, REPEAT-FLOWERING

The deep red, double flowers
of this variety have high centers
and are very large and extremely
fragrant. 'Red Masterpiece' has
large, dark green, leathery foliage on a plant that is vigorous,
upright and repeat-flowering
and which is suitable for
bedding. **ZONES 4–9.**

WARRINER, USA, 1974

('SIREN' × 'CHRYSLER IMPERIAL') ×
('CARROUSEL' × 'CHRYSLER IMPERIAL')

### 'Red Meidiland' MEIneble *(above)*
syn. 'Rouge Meillandécor', 'Red Meillandécor'

MODERN, MODERN SHRUB, RED BLEND, REPEAT-FLOWERING

'Red Meidiland' is a vigorous, prostrate plant with single, medium-sized cupped flowers that are red with a white eye and have little fragrance. They are repeat-flowering and borne in clusters of 7–15. The disease-resistant, medium-sized foliage is glossy deep green and there are small, globular, red hips in autumn. A good plant for borders, banks, pots, window boxes and as a standard, this variety has been described by the raisers as being very hardy. ZONES 3–9.

MEILLAND, FRANCE, 1989

'SEA FOAM' × ('PICASSO' × 'EYEPAINT')

### 'Red Minimo' RUImired

MODERN, MINIATURE, DARK RED, REPEAT-FLOWERING

This micro-miniature boasts red semi-double flowers with 15–20 petals that are borne in clusters. They have no fragrance but a decorative form. The foliage is small, dark green and semi-glossy on a plant with a low and bushy habit. It produces quite a number of blooms for its size and so is frequently used in floral arrangements. This rose is the 'generic' red potted Miniature Rose to be found in most supermarkets— shoppers buy them, bring them home and then after blooming often throw them away. ZONES 5–11.

DE RUITER, THE NETHERLANDS, 1987

PARENTAGE UNKNOWN

R

## 'Red Nella' (right)

MODERN, LARGE-FLOWERED/
HYBRID TEA, MAUVE/LIGHT RED,
REPEAT-FLOWERING

The name of this rose was derived by reversing the breeder's name. It bears light sparkling red, slightly fragrant flowers that have a good form. They are double and occur singly or in small clusters on a tall, upright plant. There is a heavier display of blooms in spring than in the rest of the year. It is a good choice for overall garden display. **ZONES 5–10.**

ALLENDER, AUSTRALIA, 1991
PARENTAGE UNKNOWN

R

## 'Red Planet' (left)

MODERN, LARGE-FLOWERED/
HYBRID TEA, DARK RED,
REPEAT-FLOWERING

An extremely popular rose, 'Red Planet' has crimson, double flowers with 35 petals and considerable fragrance but lacks good form. The glossy foliage appears on a healthy plant that is repeat-flowering and is a reliable bedding variety. **ZONES 4–9.**

DICKSON, UK, 1970

'RED DEVIL' × SEEDLING

ROYAL NATIONAL ROSE SOCIETY
PRESIDENT'S INTERNATIONAL
TROPHY 1969

### 'Red Rascal' JACbed *(right)*

MODERN, MODERN SHRUB, MEDIUM RED,
REPEAT-FLOWERING

This pretty shrub has small, red, double flowers with 35 petals that are borne in sprays of 2–5. Repeat-flowering, they are cupped and have a slight fragrance. The mid-sized, red to brown thorns and the small, mid-green, semi-glossy foliage appear on a bushy grower that is suitable to plant in borders or to use as a specimen. ZONES 4–9.

WARRINER, USA, 1986

PARENTAGE UNKNOWN

### 'Red Ribbons'

KORtemma *(above)*

syns 'Mainaufeuer', 'Chilterns', 'Fiery Sunsation'

MODERN, MODERN SHRUB/
GROUND COVER, MEDIUM RED,
REPEAT-FLOWERING

This vigorous ground cover with its bright scarlet flowers has been well recognized in the principal rose-growing countries. The open, medium-sized flowers are semi-double with 10 petals, have a slight scent and are produced in small clusters from summer through to autumn. Bright green, healthy foliage and vigorous strong growth make this a very good new introduction that is ideal to cover banks, and is a good subject for pillars and as a standard. ZONES 4–9.

KORDES, GERMANY, 1990

PARENTAGE UNKNOWN

BADEN-BADEN GOLD MEDAL 1991

R

## 'Red Rosamini'

RUIredro *(right)*

MODERN, MINIATURE, DARK
RED, REPEAT-FLOWERING

The bright deep red
flowers of 'Red
Rosamini' are borne
in small clusters on an
attractive small plant.
The blooms have
decorative form but
tend to open rather
too quickly. However,
bloom production is
excellent all year long.
This rose is one of the
hardiest in the garden,
surviving the coldest of
winters. It is vigorous
and can be used as a
border or in a hanging
basket. **ZONES 4–11.**

DE RUITER, THE NETHERLANDS,
1987

PARENTAGE UNKNOWN

## 'Red Simplicity'

JACsimpl *(right)*
syn. 'Red Iceberg'

MODERN, MODERN SHRUB,
MEDIUM RED,
REPEAT-FLOWERING

This free-flowering
hedge rose has large,
bright red blooms that
blacken near the petal
edges and are borne in
small clusters. Repeat-
flowering, they are
semi-double with
15–25 petals and are
slightly fragrant. A vig-
orous, upright plant
that is slightly spread-
ing, 'Red Simplicity'
has medium-sized,
semi-glossy, mid-green
foliage. **ZONES 4–9.**

WARRINER, USA, 1991

SEEDLING × 'SUN FLARE'

R

## 'Redcoat'  AUScoat  *(right)*
syn. 'Red Coat'

MODERN, CLUSTER-FLOWERED/FLORIBUNDA, MEDIUM RED,
REPEAT-FLOWERING

The medium-sized, single flowers of 'Redcoat'
have 10 petals, and are borne in small clusters
of 1–5. Slightly fragrant, they are a moderate red.
It has hooked, brown thorns, dark green foliage
and a bushy growth habit. ZONES 4–9.

AUSTIN, UK, 1973

SEEDLING × 'GOLDEN SHOWERS'

R

## 'Redgold'  DICor  *(above)*
syns 'Rouge et Or', 'Alinka'

MODERN, CLUSTER-FLOWERED/FLORIBUNDA, YELLOW BLEND, REPEAT-FLOWERING

This repeat-flowering variety has gold flowers that are
edged with deep pink. The medium-sized blooms appear
in large clusters and have a slight fragrance. The foliage
is deep green on a vigorous, upright-growing plant that is
a very good bedding variety. ZONES 4–9.

DICKSON, UK, 1971

(['KARL HERBST' × 'MASQUERADE'] × 'FAUST') × 'PICCADILLY'

ROYAL NATIONAL ROSE SOCIETY CERTIFICATE OF MERIT 1966, PORTLAND GOLD
MEDAL 1969, ALL-AMERICA ROSE SELECTION 1971

## 'Redouté' AUSpale *(above)*
### syn. 'Margaret Roberts'

MODERN, MODERN SHRUB, LIGHT PINK, REPEAT-FLOWERING

Generally acclaimed as one of the most successful roses in this class, and also known as an English Rose, this repeat-flowering variety has soft pink, open, cupped blooms that are large but have little scent. It is a medium-sized shrub that is well furnished with disease-resistant, matt green foliage on very vigorous twiggy growth. 'Redouté' is a good subject for a specimen plant or to group in borders. **ZONES 4–9.**

AUSTIN, UK, 1992

SPORT OF 'MARY ROSE'

## 'Regatta' JACette

MODERN, LARGE-FLOWERED/HYBRID TEA, WHITE, REPEAT-FLOWERING

The large flowers of this variety are a weather-proof white with good exhibition form. The blooms are filled with almost 50 petals and are usually carried one to a stem. There is a strong fragrance and the plant is furnished with mid-green foliage. This 'Regatta' was bred for the cut-flower industry, and it should not be confused with the light pink Large-flowered Rose from Meilland that shares the same name. **ZONES 5–10.**

WARRINER, USA, 1986

'BERNADETTE' × 'COQUETTE'

## 'Regatta'  MEInimo  *(above)*
syns 'Penny Coelen', 'Prestige de Lyon',
'21 Again!'
MODERN, LARGE-FLOWERED/HYBRID TEA, LIGHT PINK,
REPEAT-FLOWERING

The flowers of this rose are a lovely clear light
pink. They are large and double, filled with
26–40 petals, and have a good fragrance. The
stems have very few prickles and the foliage tends
to be large and dark green with a matt finish.
'Regatta' produces an abundance of blooms
that continue throughout the year on a tall and
upright-growing bush that has very good disease
resistance. **ZONES 5–10.**

MEILLAND, FRANCE, 1992

MEIGURAMI × (MEINAREGI × MEIDRAGELAC)

GENEVA FRAGRANCE AWARD 1989

## 'Regensberg'  MACyoumis, MACyou  *(bottom)*
syns 'Buffalo Bill', 'Young Mistress'
MODERN, CLUSTER-FLOWERED/FLORIBUNDA, PINK BLEND,
REPEAT-FLOWERING

The large, semi-double flowers of this variety have
21 petals and are pink edged white with a white
center and a reverse of white. Cupped to flat and
having a fruity fragrance, they are 4 in (10 cm)
wide and have yellow stamens. A very short bushy
plant with luxuriant, mid-green foliage and one
of the most successful of the 'hand-painted'
varieties, 'Regensberg' is sometimes erroneously
classed as a Patio Rose although the large foliage
belies this description. A remarkable bedding
variety, it is also highly successful as a well-
rounded standard. **ZONES 4–9.**

MCGREDY, NEW ZEALAND, 1979

'GEOFF BOYCOTT' × 'OLD MASTER'

BRITISH ASSOCIATION OF ROSE BREEDERS 1979, BADEN-BADEN GOLD
MEDAL 1980, BELFAST CERTIFICATE OF MERIT 1981

## 'Reine des Centfeuilles' (right)

OLD, CENTIFOLIA, MEDIUM PINK

The scented flowers of this rose are some 2½ in (6 cm) across when fully open and are packed with rather fimbriated bright pink petals, creating a charming effect. It flowers in early mid-summer. The plant grows to a height of some 5 ft (1.5 m), and can be frustratingly disorderly in growth habit at times. It is amply endowed with mid-green grayish foliage and has a generous number of prickles. This little-known rose is especially useful for the wilder garden, owing to its sheer quantity of flowers. ZONES 4–9.

BELGIUM, 1824

PARENTAGE UNKNOWN

**R**

## 'Reine des Violettes' (right)

syn. 'Queen of the Violets'

OLD, HYBRID PERPETUAL, MAUVE, REPEAT-FLOWERING

This well-known and popular rose is oddly classed as a Hybrid Perpetual, although it looks like a Bourbon. It makes a medium to tall, full bush with Gallica-like purple flowers fading to violet, filled with 75 quilled and quartered petals,

each with a button eye. It flowers in summer, repeats in autumn and is nicely scented. The foliage is smooth green and is almost thornless. The vigor of this bush has enabled it

to survive successfully through the years, and it is one of the 'musts'. Its parent 'Pius IX' is no longer available. ZONES 5–9.

MILLET-MALLET, FRANCE, 1860

SEEDLING OF 'PIUS IX'

### 'Reine Marie Henriette' *(bottom)*

MODERN, LARGE-FLOWERED CLIMBER, MEDIUM RED, REPEAT-FLOWERING

Marie-Henriette was Queen of the Belgians, and her rose has worn well; it is still grown despite its considerable thorniness. The loose flowers, which are borne in clusters, are a pure cherry red color. There is some autumn repeat-flowering, although the main flush is produced in summer. It should be lightly pruned. 'Reine Marie Henriette' is notable as having been one of the parents of the beautiful 'Belle Portugaise', the other being *Rosa gigantea*.

**ZONES 7–9.**

LEVET, FRANCE, 1878

'MME BÉRARD' × 'GÉNÉRAL JACQUEMINOT'

### 'Reine Victoria' *(top)*

syn. 'La Reine Victoria'

OLD, BOURBON, MEDIUM PINK, REPEAT-FLOWERING

'Reine Victoria' displays rich pink blooms that have a tint of mauve. They are very double, with up to 40 silky textured petals, and cupped. The spring flush is profuse and from then on flowering is spasmodic. In autumn, the flowers are produced on very long stems. The growth is strong and upright with plentiful, close-jointed, matt pale green foliage. It produces long canes that are ideal for espalier work. Both this variety and its sport, 'Mme Pierrogers', suffer from black spot, although both are fragrant and good for cutting. This rose was named for Queen Victoria.

**ZONES 5–9.**

LABRUYÈRE, FRANCE, 1872

PARENTAGE UNKNOWN

R

flowers. The mid-green foliage is glossy, medium sized and abundant with good disease resistance. The leaves are often retained well into winter. This is a good rose for planting on banks, in large parks and on median strips. **ZONES 5–9.**

MEILLAND, FRANCE, 1993

PARENTAGE UNKNOWN

### 'Rembrandt' *(left)*

OLD, PORTLAND, ORANGE-RED, REPEAT-FLOWERING

This rose has vigorous growth in the Damask style and flowers over a long period. The large full flowers, which come on long stalks, are vermilion shaded carmine and are occasionally striped. It needs to be pruned only every few years, after the summer flowering, and it tends to flower more if the stems are allowed to lie flat. **ZONES 5–9.**

MOREAU & ROBERT, FRANCE, 1883

PARENTAGE UNKNOWN

### 'Relax Meillandecor' MEIdarwet *(top)*
syn. 'Relax Meidiland'

MODERN, GROUND COVER, PINK BLEND, REPEAT-FLOWERING

This variety, with a spread of 4–5 ft (1.2–1.5 m), carries medium-sized semi-double blooms with about 10 watermelon pink petals. They are produced in clusters of up to 12, and if not deadheaded, small red hips appear amid the late

## 'Remember Me'

COCdestin *(right & below)*

syn. 'Remember'

MODERN, LARGE-FLOWERED/
HYBRID TEA, ORANGE BLEND,
REPEAT-FLOWERING

This rose, which can justifiably be described as probably the deepest copper variety presently available, has in addition a subtle blend of yellow. It bears single or small clusters of double, large, cupped flowers with 20 petals and has little fragrance. The raisers are undecided as to its type, but Large-flowered is probably closer than Cluster-flowered. The foliage, which is dark and glossy, is small for the type, but the spreading plant is bushy and makes a good bedding variety and a marvelous standard. ZONES 4–9.

COCKER, UK, 1984

'ANN LETTS' × ('DAINTY MAID' × 'PINK FAVORITE')

BELFAST GOLD MEDAL 1986,
ROYAL NATIONAL ROSE SOCIETY
JAMES MASON GOLD MEDAL
1995, ROYAL HORTICULTURAL
SOCIETY AWARD OF GARDEN
MERIT 1993

## 'Remembrance'

HARxampton

MODERN, CLUSTER-FLOWERED/
FLORIBUNDA, MEDIUM RED,
REPEAT-FLOWERING

This variety bears large clusters of cupped, bright red medium-sized blooms with 32 petals. They have a slight scent. The foliage is dark green and glossy on a bushy plant that is truly repeat-flowering. 'Remembrance' is a healthy rose that is good in a bed or as a standard. ZONES 4–9.

HARKNESS, UK, 1992

'TRUMPETER' × 'SOUTHAMPTON'

GLASGOW GOLD MEDAL 1995

R

### 'Renae' *(left)*

MODERN, CLUSTER-FLOWERED
CLIMBER, MEDIUM PINK,
REPEAT-FLOWERING

This repeat-flowering
Climber or Rambler
has clusters of medium-
sized double flowers
with 43 petals. They are
mid-pink and have a
considerable scent.
The small, glossy
foliage is very healthy
on a vigorous plant. It
is a suitable subject for
pergolas and arches
and as a weeping
standard. ZONES 4–9.

MOORE, USA, 1954

'ÉTOILE LUISANTE' ×
'SIERRA SNOWSTORM'

### 'Renaissance' *(left)*

MODERN, LARGE-FLOWERED/
HYBRID TEA, ORANGE BLEND,
REPEAT-FLOWERING

The brilliant orange-
red flowers of this
variety are double and
develop from long,
pointed buds. There is
a moderate fragrance,
and the blooms are
followed by rounded
hips. The reasonably
prickly stems are
furnished with glossy
light green leaves.
'Renaissance' can be
propagated by budding.
ZONES 5–10.

GAUJARD, FRANCE, 1986

SEEDLING × 'PAMPA'

R

## 'Renaissance'  HARzart

MODERN, LARGE-FLOWERED/HYBRID TEA, WHITE, REPEAT-FLOWERING

A very highly scented variety, 'Renaissance' has pale blush pink flowers with a center of coral. The perfectly formed blooms are loose, giving a less formal appearance to a sophisticated color. This repeat-flowering, bushy plant performs well in beds, as a standard and as a cut flower. **ZONES 4–9.**

HARKNESS, UK, 1994

PARENTAGE UNKNOWN

BELFAST FRAGRANCE AWARD 1995, GLASGOW SILVER MEDAL 1996, GLASGOW FRAGRANCE AWARD 1996

## 'Rendez-vous'  LUCdod

MODERN, MODERN SHRUB, MEDIUM PINK

This medium-sized shrub has semi-double, medium blooms that are very fragrant. A bushy, healthy, free-flowering variety with matt green foliage, its repeat-blooming ability is doubtful. It is suitable for planting in large borders. **ZONES 4–9.**

LUCAS, UK, 1981

*ROSA WICHURANA* × 'ALAIN BLANCHARD'

## 'René André'  *(above)*

MODERN, RAMBLER, APRICOT BLEND

The first decade of the twentieth century saw a great surge in the breeding of the Ramblers from *Rosa wichurana* and *R. multiflora*. This rose is not common, but is freely available. Even more lax than others of its kind, it is suitable for hanging in trees, where it will grow to great heights. The stems will hang, carrying small flowers in a mixture of coppery pink and yellow, fading to soft pink. It will sometimes repeat a little. **ZONES 5–9.**

BARBIER, FRANCE, 1901

*ROSA WICHURANA* × 'L'IDÉAL'

R

### 'Réné d'Anjou'

OLD, MOSS, DEEP PINK

The buds of this rose are usually arranged in small clusters and are liberally clothed with bronzy brown moss. They appear in mid-summer and open to flowers of exquisite beauty. Each bloom is up to 3½ in (9 cm) across and is made up of many small crumpled petals that are randomly arranged to form flattish, fragrant cushions of a most lovely soft silvery pink. It has a bushy and upright habit and reaches 5 ft (1.5 m) high. The stems are covered in soft bronzy stubble and there are few thorns. The leaves are reddish when young, becoming dark green, serrated and leathery when older. This outstanding rose is worthy of more attention. It is extremely healthy and is also tolerant of most soils. ZONES 4–9.

ROBERT, FRANCE, 1853

PARENTAGE UNKNOWN

### 'Repandia' KORsami
syn. 'Kordes' Rose Repandia'

MODERN, MODERN SHRUB/ GROUND COVER, LIGHT PINK

A flat, spreading plant with light pink semi-double flowers, 'Repandia' is only summer flowering. The fragrant blooms are borne on a low-growing plant that will spread to 5 ft (1.5 m) and is one of the earliest of the modern Ground Cover Roses. It is furnished with small, glossy dark green foliage. ZONES 4–9.

KORDES, GERMANY, 1983

'THE FAIRY' × SEEDLING OF
ROSA WICHURANA

ANERKANNTE DEUTSCHE ROSE
1986

### 'Restless' *(above)*

MODERN, LARGE-FLOWERED/HYBRID TEA, MEDIUM RED, REPEAT-FLOWERING

This strongly fragrant variety was probably so named because it flowers continuously, nearly all year round in warm climates. The flat blooms are semi-double, with 10–15 dark crimson petals that open quickly from slim, long buds to full blooms that show the stamens. The habit is extremely tall and upright and the bush is covered with masses of matt mid-green foliage. 'Restless' is a superbly disease-resistant, vigorous bush rose that would make an excellent free-flowering tall hedge for a large estate. Attractive hips are produced if the spent blooms are not removed, although they do not seem to curtail the flowering very much. ZONES 5–9.

CLARK, AUSTRALIA, 1938

PARENTAGE UNKNOWN

R

## 'Rêve de Paris'
**MEIloïse** *(right)*

MODERN, LARGE-FLOWERED/
HYBRID TEA, ORANGE-PINK,
REPEAT-FLOWERING

This short and stocky
grower bears large,
semi-double flowers
that are glowing coral-
salmon. There is good
petal substance, and
the flowers are produced
in abundance with a
quick repeat blooming.
The foliage is mid-
green and semi-glossy,
and there are no
disease problems.
The blooms are ideal
for cutting, since the
color shows up well
under artificial light.
**ZONES 5–10.**

MEILLAND, FRANCE, 1985

PARENTAGE UNKNOWN

## 'Rêve d'Or' *(right)*
OLD, NOISETTE, MEDIUM
YELLOW, REPEAT-FLOWERING

The name of this rose
means 'golden dream'
or, more correctly,
'dream of gold'. The
large, semi-double
flowers are buff yellow,
fragrant, frilly and
quartered. The plant
climbs to great heights
and has strong branch-
ing stems, large hooked
red thorns and plenti-
ful foliage. It is a
handsome rose and in
1878 produced a well-
known sport, 'William
Allen Richardson',
which is more orange.
**ZONES 7–9.**

DUCHER, FRANCE, 1869

SEEDLING OF 'MME SCHULTZ'

R

## 'Réveil Dijonnais'

MODERN, LARGE-FLOWERED CLIMBER, RED BLEND,
REPEAT-FLOWERING

A remarkable rose that is equally happy as a climber or as a shrub, this variety has brilliant cerise-scarlet flowers with yellow centers and a yellowish reverse. Semi-double, cupped and having some scent, they are produced in abundance and in clusters on short stems from early to mid-summer with occasional blooms in autumn. 'Réveil Dijonnais' is a vigorous plant with thick, glossy bronze foliage. **ZONES 4–9.**

BUATOIS, FRANCE, 1931

'EUGÈNE FÜRST' × 'CONSTANCE'

PORTLAND GOLD MEDAL 1929

## 'Reverend H. d'Ombrain'  *(below)*

OLD, BOURBON, MEDIUM RED, REPEAT-FLOWERING

This rose is not easily available. The large, full, silvery carmine flowers are borne on a small to medium-sized bush. It can suffer from mildew, but this may depend on location and circumstance. It was named for the Reverend Henry Honeywood D'Ombrain, who was co-founder and first secretary of the (Royal) National Rose Society. **ZONES 5–9.**

MARGOTTIN, FRANCE, 1863

PARENTAGE UNKNOWN

R

## 'Rheinaupark'

KOReipark *(above)*

syn. *Rosa rugosa* 'Rheinaupark'

MODERN, MODERN SHRUB, MEDIUM RED, REPEAT-FLOWERING

This rose has wrinkled foliage and thorny stems on an upright, bushy, vigorous plant. It is excellent for hedging or as a specimen. The clusters of medium red, semi-double large blooms with 20 petals are slightly scented. 'Rheinaupark' requires little maintenance. **ZONES 3–9.**

KORDES, GERMANY, 1983

('GRUSS AN BAYERN' × SEEDLING) × SEEDLING OF *ROSA RUGOSA*

## 'Ringlet' *(above)*

MODERN, LARGE-FLOWERED CLIMBER, PINK BLEND, REPEAT-FLOWERING

This climbing variety is repeat-flowering. It produces clusters of single blooms that are white tipped pink and lilac. 'Ringlet' is a healthy plant with considerable vigor. **ZONES 4–9.**

CLARK, AUSTRALIA, 1922

'ERNEST MOREL' × 'BETTY BERKELEY'

R

### 'Rio Samba'   JACrite

**MODERN, LARGE-FLOWERED/HYBRID TEA, YELLOW BLEND,
REPEAT-FLOWERING**

'Rio Samba' has large blooms of yellow, fading
to peach pink, that are mostly borne singly. They
are double, with 15–25 petals, and have a slight
fragrance. This repeat-flowering variety has
medium-sized, dark green, matt foliage on an
upright, bushy plant that is suitable for bedding.
It has some thorns. **ZONES 4–9.**

WARRINER, USA, 1991

SEEDLING × 'SUNBRIGHT'

ALL-AMERICA ROSE SELECTION 1993

### 'Ripples'   *(top)*

**MODERN, CLUSTER-FLOWERED/FLORIBUNDA, MAUVE,
REPEAT-FLOWERING**

The semi-double flowers with 18 wavy petals on
'Ripples' are large and slightly fragrant. They are
a lovely lilac-lavender and appear in clusters,
adding novelty to the flower border. The foliage
is small and matt green, and is relatively disease
resistant. **ZONES 4–9.**

LEGRICE, UK, 1971

('TANTAU'S SURPRISE' × 'MARJORIE LEGRICE') × (SEEDLING ×
'AFRICA STAR')

### 'Rival de Paestum'   *(above)*

**OLD, TEA, WHITE, REPEAT-FLOWERING**

This Tea Rose is difficult to obtain. The small,
Tea-scented flowers are fully double, ivory white
tinted pink and tend to nod. It has plenty of dark
green foliage on a short, twiggy bush. Paestum,
a town in Italy, was credited by Virgil in his
Georgics with the twice-bearing roses, considered
to refer to the Autumn Damasks. **ZONES 7–9.**

BÉLUZE, FRANCE, 1841

PARENTAGE UNKNOWN

## 'Rob Roy' COrob *(right)*
MODERN, CLUSTER-FLOWERED/FLORIBUNDA, DARK RED,
REPEAT-FLOWERING

The dark red, medium-sized, double blooms
on 'Rob Roy' have 30 petals and a good classical
Cluster-flowered form. They are slightly fragrant
and are 4 in (10 cm) wide. The foliage is glossy
and healthy on an average-sized plant that is
suitable for bedding and also makes a good
standard. ZONES 4–9.

COCKER, UK, 1971

'EVELYN FISON' × 'WENDY CUSSONS'

ROYAL NATIONAL ROSE SOCIETY TRIAL GROUND CERTIFICATE 1969

## 'Robert le Diable'
*(right)*

OLD, GALLICA, MAUVE BLEND

This rose bears fragrant
flowers made up of
many petals. When
fully open, they reflex
around the edge of the
flowers to create a flat
cushion effect. If the
shape is unusual, the
color is even more so,
for it varies within each
bloom from deepest
purple to softest lilac,
mottled or splashed
with bright red. In very
dry weather the colors

intensify and deepen. It
is a sizeable, lax shrub,
growing as broad as it
is tall, which in good
soil can be up to 4 ft
(1.2 m) high. Arching

thorny stems are
covered with narrow,
dark green leaves. Few
roses have such in-
tensely colored blooms;
these, combined with

its semi-recumbent
stature, make this an
asset to any garden.
ZONES 4–9.

FRANCE, PRE-1837

PARENTAGE UNKNOWN

R

### 'Robert Léopold'
*(below)*

OLD, MOSS, PINK BLEND,
REPEAT-FLOWERING

The fragrant flowers of this rose have a background of orange-yellow and are flushed salmon and pink, but are not in any way gaudy. They can attain a size of up to 3 in (8 cm) in diameter. The blooms first appear in early summer and there is an occasional second crop in autumn. It is a shortish, tidy,

bushy shrub to 4 ft (1.2 m) high. The stems are unarmed, and are covered in gingery green, stubbly moss, as are the leaf stalks and flower buds. The leaves are bronzy when young, ageing to light green. This handsome shrub, one of only a few Moss Roses raised in the twentieth century, would not be out of place in any modern garden. **ZONES 5–9.**

BUATOIS, FRANCE, 1941
PARENTAGE UNKNOWN

### 'Robin Hood'
*(below)*
syn. 'Robin des Bois'

MODERN, MODERN SHRUB,
MEDIUM RED,
REPEAT-FLOWERING

With its pleasant shrub style, 'Robin Hood' is very free flowering and is also repeat-flowering. The simple, small, cherry red blooms are produced in large clusters and are slightly fragrant. A vigorous, dense, compact grower that does well in borders or as a specimen plant, this variety's chief claim to fame is that it was one of the parents of 'Iceberg'. **ZONES 4–9.**

PEMBERTON, UK, 1927

SEEDLING × 'MISS EDITH CAVELL'

R

### 'Robin Red Breast'
INTerrob  *(above)*
syn. 'Robin Redbreast'
MODERN, PATIO/DWARF
CLUSTER-FLOWERED, RED BLEND,
REPEAT-FLOWERING

The small, single blooms of this variety, which appear in clusters, are dark red with a white eye and a reverse of silver. They have no fragrance but they appear with good continuity from summer to autumn. It is a small, healthy, vigorous plant with bushy growth and lots of thorns that is suitable for pots and small borders and can also be used as a short standard. ZONES 4–9.

INTERPLANT, THE NETHERLANDS, 1983

SEEDLING × 'EYEPAINT'

### 'Robusta'  KORgosa
*(right)*
syns *Rosa rugosa* 'Robusta', 'Kordes' Rose Robusta'
MODERN, HYBRID RUGOSA,
MEDIUM RED,
REPEAT-FLOWERING

This extremely vigorous, repeat-flowering shrub carries all the characteristics of a Hybrid Rugosa, including a multitude of thorns. The large, crimson, single blooms with 5 petals are produced in small clusters and have a moderate fragrance. 'Robusta' is suited to large hedges if it is allowed to grow naturally, although in some countries it is cut down every winter to produce a medium-sized bush. Very healthy and with glossy dark green, leathery foliage, it is happier in cooler climates. ZONES 3–9.

KORDES, GERMANY, 1979

SEEDLING × *ROSA RUGOSA*

ANERKANNTE DEUTSCHE ROSE 1980, ROYAL NATIONAL ROSE SOCIETY CERTIFICATE OF MERIT 1980

## 'Rod Stillman'
*(left)*

**syn. 'Red Stillman'**

MODERN, LARGE-FLOWERED/
HYBRID TEA, LIGHT PINK,
REPEAT-FLOWERING

This variety has light pink flowers that are flushed with orange at the base. Extremely fragrant, they are large and have 35 petals. Vigorous in growth and with dark foliage and well-shaped blooms, 'Rod Stillman' is repeat-flowering and is suitable for bedding. **ZONES 4–9.**

HAMILTON, AUSTRALIA, 1948

'OPHELIA' × 'EDITOR MCFARLAND'

## 'Roger Lambelin'
*(left)*

OLD, HYBRID PERPETUAL, RED
BLEND, REPEAT-FLOWERING

The flowers of 'Roger Lambelin' are a bizarre crimson fading to maroon, with the 30 petals edged in white. It grows to a medium height, but needs good soil. Most authorities recommend 'Baron Girod de l'Ain' in preference to this rose; striped and picoteed sports are always apt to revert to the original, or vice versa. 'Fisher Holmes' lacks the white edge but has received glowing reports. **ZONES 5–9.**

SCHWARTZ, FRANCE, 1890

SPORT OF 'FISHER HOLMES'

R

## 'Roi de Siam'
*(right)*

OLD, CLIMBING TEA, MEDIUM
RED

This rose, although
an early introduction,
is still available from
specialist sources. The
large, semi-double,
rather muddled flowers
have rich pink tones. It
cannot be far removed
from the original 'stud'
roses, 'Parks' Yellow'
and 'Hume's Blush'.
The growth is tall and
not bushy and the
flowering is said to be
less than enthusiastic.
**ZONES 7–9.**

LAFFAY, FRANCE, 1825
PARENTAGE UNKNOWN

## 'Roller Coaster'
MACminmo  *(right)*
syn. 'Minnie Mouse'

MODERN, MINIATURE, RED
BLEND, REPEAT-FLOWERING

'Roller Coaster' has
striped red blend
flowers that are really
a beautiful random
mixture of red, creamy
yellow and white; no
two flowers are identical.
The florets are semi-
double with 6–14
petals, have a light scent
and tend to grow in
small clusters of 10–12
blooms. The bloom
cycle is fast with the
flowers fully open being
the most beautiful

stage, providing a
wonderful carpet of
bold color mixtures.
The foliage is small,
mid-green and glossy
on a tall, upright, vig-
orous plant. In semi-
tropical climates this
rose can grow like a
shrub and has a gangly
habit if left untended.
However, the spreading
habit makes it an ideal
choice for containers,
against a wall, or in a
raised bed where it can
spill over. This rose was
popular in Australia,
where it first appeared
as 'Minnie Mouse'.
**ZONES 5–10.**

MCGREDY, NEW ZEALAND, 1987

('ANYTIME' × 'EYEPAINT') ×
'STARS 'N' STRIPES'

R

## 'Romance' TANezamor
### (right)
syn. 'Romanze'
MODERN, MODERN SHRUB,
MEDIUM PINK,
REPEAT-FLOWERING

This bushy shrub has
medium pink, double
flowers with 20 petals.
They have a slight
fragrance and appear
continuously from
summer to autumn.
The foliage is medium,
dark green, semi-glossy
and healthy on a plant
that is most suited
to use in borders.
**ZONES 4–9.**

TANTAU, GERMANY, 1985

PARENTAGE UNKNOWN

BADEN-BADEN GOLD MEDAL
1985, ANERKANNTE DEUTSCHE
ROSE 1986, GOLDEN ROSE OF
THE HAGUE 1992

## 'Rosa Mundi'
### (right)
syns *Rosa gallica rosa
mundi* 'Weston',
*R. gallica variegata*
'Thory', *R. gallica
versicolor* 'Linnaeus',
*R. mundi*

OLD, GALLICA, PINK BLEND

The name of this
rose can mean either
'rose of the world'
or 'Rosamund's', a
woman said to have
been an unfortunate
mistress of Henry II.
It is a striped form of
the type and sometimes
reverts to it, and is pale
pink splashed with
crimson. It is sometimes
confused with the
Damask 'York and
Lancaster' (also called

'Versicolor'), which is
inferior. The branches
in these roses tend to
flop over under the
weight of the flowers,
and need support.
This can be solved by
pruning halfway in
early spring, giving a

better effect. 'Rosa
Mundi' can grow to a
medium to tall height
and is suitable for low
hedging. **ZONES 4–9.**

FIRST MENTIONED 1581

SPORT OF 'APOTHECARY'S ROSE'

ROYAL HORTICULTURAL SOCIETY
AWARD OF GARDEN MERIT 1993

## 'Rosabell' COCceleste
MODERN, CLUSTER-FLOWERED/
FLORIBUNDA, MEDIUM PINK,
REPEAT-FLOWERING

Incurved blooms give
this variety an old-
fashioned appearance.
Bright rose pink, the
medium-sized full
blooms are borne in
clusters on a free-
flowering, low-growing
plant. With its glossy
mid-green foliage it
is a good subject for
small beds, pots and
as a short standard.
**ZONES 4–9.**

COCKER, UK, 1986

SEEDLING × 'DARLING FLAME'

### 'Rosali' TANilasor
*(right)*
syn. 'Rosali 83'

MODERN, CLUSTER-FLOWERED/
FLORIBUNDA, MEDIUM PINK,
REPEAT-FLOWERING

The medium pink
blooms with 20 petals
on 'Rosali' are pro-
duced in small clusters;
they have no scent. The
average-sized foliage is
mid-green and glossy
on a repeat-flowering,
bushy plant that is
good for bedding.
ZONES 4–9.

TANTAU, GERMANY, 1983

PARENTAGE UNKNOWN

### 'Rosalie Coral'
CHEwallop *(bottom)*
syns 'Rocketear',
'Rosilia'

MODERN, CLIMBING
MINIATURE, ORANGE BLEND,
REPEAT-FLOWERING

On 'Rosalie Coral', clear
orange double flowers
with 15–25 petals open
to reveal a yellow 'eye'
that has some shading.
In cooler climates, the
deep orange has a
distinctive circle of
gold surrounding the
stamens. The blooms
have a light fragrance
and are borne in small
clusters amid glossy
mid-green foliage with
just a few prickles. This
plant grows 6 ft (1.8 m)
or more. ZONES 5–10.

WARNER, UK, 1992

('ELIZABETH OF GLAMIS' ×
['GALWAY BAY' × 'SUTTER'S
GOLD']) × 'ANNA FORD'

ROYAL NATIONAL ROSE SOCIETY
TRIAL GROUND CERTIFICATE 1990

R

R

## 'Rosamunde'

KORmunde *(above)*

MODERN, CLUSTER-FLOWERED/
FLORIBUNDA, MEDIUM PINK,
REPEAT-FLOWERING

A short-growing but
very free-flowering
variety, 'Rosamunde'
has deep pink and
salmon, medium-sized
blooms. The flowers
have a light scent and
are produced in small
clusters from summer
through to autumn.
This variety is most
suited to use in small
beds and pots.
**ZONES 4–9.**

KORDES, GERMANY, 1975
PARENTAGE UNKNOWN

## 'Rosarium Uetersen' KORtersen

*(right)*
syn. 'Uetersen'

MODERN, LARGE-FLOWERED
CLIMBER, DEEP PINK,
REPEAT-FLOWERING

When this rose is
enjoying its main flush,
the color impact is
powerful, thanks to the
enormous number of
deep rose pink flowers,
borne singly or in great
clusters. Well over 100
overlapping petals are
packed into medium
to large flowers that
open wide and almost
flat, admitting tints of
silvery pink as they age.
There is a light scent,
and after the main
glorious flush, some
blooms appear inter-
mittently in late summer
and autumn.
'Rosarium Uetersen'
grows well on a wall,
fence, pillar or arch. It
is hardy and withstands
bad weather well. The

growth is vigorous, and
the leaves are large,
glossy and plentiful.
**ZONES 3–9.**

KORDES, GERMANY, 1977
'KARLSRUHE' × SEEDLING

## 'Rose à Parfum de l'Haÿ' *(above)*

syns *Rosa rugosa* 'Rose à Parfum de l'Haÿ',
'Parfum de l'Haÿ'

**MODERN, HYBRID RUGOSA, MEDIUM RED, REPEAT-FLOWERING**

This very vigorous rose has flowers of cherry
carmine red that turn blue in heat. The blooms
are large and extremely fragrant and appear with
good continuity from summer to autumn. The
foliage, which is not particularly rugose, or
wrinkled, is matt green; in some gardens it is
susceptible to mildew. Occasionally this variety's
nomenclature can be confused with the famous
scented Hybrid Rugosa 'Roseraie de l'Haÿ'. It is a
subject for shrubberies or as a specimen plant.
**ZONES 3–9.**

GRAVEREAUX, FRANCE, 1901

('SUMMER DAMASK' × 'GÉNÉRAL JACQUEMINOT') × *ROSA RUGOSA*

## 'Rose d'Amour' *(bottom)*

syns *Rosa virginiana plena*, 'St Mark's Rose',
'The St Mark's Rose'

**OLD, MISCELLANEOUS, DEEP PINK, REPEAT-FLOWERING**

This large shrub, which grows very high and
wide, is probably a hybrid of the wild single type,
perhaps crossed with *Rosa carolina*. Almost

thornless, it bears numerous small, dainty pink
flowers over a long period from mid-summer.
A mature, free-standing bush of this rose is a
magnificent sight. It is very similar to 'Rose
d'Orsay', named for a Third Empire dandy who
wore it in his buttonhole. **ZONES 5–9.**

PRE-1759

THOUGHT TO BE A HYBRID OF *ROSA VIRGINIANA*

ROYAL HORTICULTURAL SOCIETY AWARD OF GARDEN MERIT 1993

R

## 'Rose de Meaux'
(right)

syns 'Pompon Rose',
*Rosa centifolia
pomponia* 'Lindley',
*R. dijoniensis,
R. pomponia* 'Roessig',
*R. pulchella* 'Willdenow'

OLD, CENTIFOLIA, MEDIUM PINK

In cultivation since it was first recorded in 1789, this summer-flowering rose bears small, double, pink flowers that have been compared with a dianthus, the petals being frilled rather than pompon-like. Erect and dwarf, it is suitable for small pot culture. In the Dark Ages, the Irish Saint Fiacre settled at Meaux and cultivated a garden. He became the patron saint of gardeners, and the Abbey at Meaux held his relics. There is also a white form of this rose. **ZONES 4–9.**

CULTIVATED 1789

PARENTAGE UNKNOWN

## R

## 'Rose de Rescht'
(right)

OLD, DAMASK, DEEP PINK,
REPEAT-FLOWERING

The flowers of 'Rose de Rescht' are arranged in tight clusters or bunches and are borne close to the foliage, each on short necks. The fully double, scented blooms are 1½ in (35 mm) across; they are cushion shaped when fully open and are freely produced from mid-summer to autumn. The color is rich fuchsia-red with hints of purple, sometimes paler in hot sun. It is a compact, dense shrub with dark green wood and a few stubby thorns, and grows up to 3 ft (1 m) high. The foliage is profuse, dark grayish green, rounded and durable. This is an outstanding rose that is quite easy to grow. **ZONES 5–9.**

FROM RASHT (IRAN) TO EUROPE
VIA LINDSAY, UK, 1940

PARENTAGE UNKNOWN

ROYAL HORTICULTURAL SOCIETY
AWARD OF GARDEN MERIT 1993

### 'Rose des Peintres'   *(right)*
syns 'Centfeuille des Peintres',
*Rosa × centifolia major*

OLD, CENTIFOLIA, MEDIUM PINK

This rather sprawling, tall plant is very
similar to *Rosa × centifolia* and has fully
double, clear pink, fragrant flowers that
show a center green button eye. The name
refers to the beautiful Dutch flower paintings of the eighteenth century, which made
considerable use of the Centifolias (Roses
of Provence), themselves a Dutch creation
according to rose lore. They were the
100-petalled roses that the English called
'cabbage roses'. **ZONES 4–9.**

PRE-1838

PARENTAGE UNKNOWN

### 'Rose du Roi'   *(right)*
syn. 'Lee's Crimson Perpetual'

OLD, PORTLAND, MEDIUM RED, REPEAT-FLOWERING

The fragrant flowers of this rose are
arranged in tight clusters and produced
continuously from mid-summer to
autumn. They are fully double, although
loosely formed, sometimes showing a few
yellow stamens when fully open. The soft
red color is mottled and smudged purple.
It is a sturdy shrub to 3 ft (1 m) high with
thorny dark green stems and plentiful
small, dark grayish green foliage. This was
one of the first Portlands to be introduced
and it has certainly stood the test of time
with distinction. It makes an excellent
container plant. **ZONES 5–9.**

ECOFFAY, FRANCE, 1819

PARENTAGE UNKNOWN

R

R

## 'Rose Gaujard'

GAUmo  *(above)*

MODERN, LARGE-FLOWERED/
HYBRID TEA, RED BLEND,
REPEAT-FLOWERING

The large flowers of 'Rose Gaujard' are cherry red with a pale pink and silvery white underside. Very double with 80 petals, the high-centered blooms are cupped, have a light scent and are produced from summer through to autumn. The foliage is large, leathery and glossy on a big, vigorous plant that has maintained its popularity for many years and appears to be capable of going on forever. The 'Peace' input is very evident in this respectable bedding rose.
**ZONES 4–9.**

GAUJARD, FRANCE, 1957

'PEACE' × SEEDLING OF 'OPERA'

ROYAL NATIONAL ROSE SOCIETY
GOLD MEDAL 1958

## 'Rose-Marie Viaud'
*(right)*

MODERN, RAMBLER, MAUVE

This rose is almost thornless and makes great arching shoots from which the large clusters of flowers hang down in mid-summer. This is similar to its parent, except that the small, semi-double flowers are a different shade, changing from cerise when opening to a bluer violet and gray. **ZONES 5–9.**

IGOULT, FRANCE, 1924

SEEDLING OF 'VEILCHENBLAU'

## 'Roselina' KORsaku
*(bottom)*
syns 'Playtime', 'Rosalina'

MODERN, HYBRID RUGOSA, PINK BLEND, REPEAT-FLOWERING

This Hybrid Rugosa has a semi-prostrate habit and is repeat-flowering. The single blooms are mid-pink and medium in size and are borne in small clusters. Described as being very tough and healthy and with typical rugose, or wrinkled, foliage, this is a good plant for landscaping in smaller gardens. **ZONES 4–9.**

KORDES, GERMANY, 1992

PARENTAGE UNKNOWN

BELFAST CRYSTAL PRIZE 1995

R

## 'Rosemary Harkness'

**HARrowbond** *(right)*

MODERN, LARGE-FLOWERED/
HYBRID TEA, ORANGE-PINK,
REPEAT-FLOWERING

The beautiful double blooms with 35 petals on 'Rosemary Harkness' have a good form and are orange-salmon with an orange-yellow reverse. They are fragrant and repeat their bloom from summer to autumn. A modern Large-flowered Rose that makes a good bedding variety, or is suitable for use as a standard, it has large, dark semi-glossy foliage on a bushy plant. **ZONES 4–9.**

HARKNESS, UK, 1985

'COMPASSION' × ('BASILDON BOND' × 'GRANDPA DICKSON')

BELFAST GOLD MEDAL 1987, BELFAST FRAGRANCE AWARD 1987, GLASGOW FRAGRANCE AWARD 1991, AUCKLAND FRAGRANCE AWARD 1995

## 'Rosemary Rose'
*(right)*

MODERN, CLUSTER-FLOWERED/
FLORIBUNDA, DEEP PINK,
REPEAT-FLOWERING

The large clusters of deep pink flowers on this variety are double, camellia shaped and of medium size. When first introduced it intrigued the rose world with its deep coppery foliage and, although maintaining its popularity in some nurseries, its tendency to mildew made this a variety that lost its appeal. 'Rosemary Rose' is a good bedding variety with a vigorous, bushy growth habit but is disappointing when used as a standard. **ZONES 4–9.**

DE RUITER, THE NETHERLANDS, 1954

'GRUSS AN TEPLITZ' × SEEDLING OF A CLUSTER-FLOWERED ROSE

ROYAL NATIONAL ROSE SOCIETY GOLD MEDAL 1954, ROME GOLD MEDAL 1954

R

## 'Rosendorf Sparrieshoop'

KORdibor *(above)*

MODERN, MODERN SHRUB,
LIGHT PINK, REPEAT-FLOWERING

This pretty, medium-sized shrub produces clusters of bright pale pink, semi-double blooms with 15 petals and with an apple scent. Repeat-flowering and very healthy, it is a bushy shrub that will grow equally happily in groups in a border or as a specimen plant.
**ZONES 4–9.**

KORDES, GERMANY, 1988
PARENTAGE UNKNOWN

## 'Rosenelfe' *(left)*
syn. 'Rose Elf'

MODERN, CLUSTER-FLOWERED/
FLORIBUNDA, MEDIUM PINK,
REPEAT-FLOWERING

This repeat-flowering variety, which is suitable for bedding, bears small to medium pink blooms that are double, with many petals, and scented. The large clusters of flowers appear on a medium-sized, thin bush with leathery, glossy foliage.
**ZONES 4–9.**

KORDES, GERMANY, 1939

'ELSE POULSEN' ×
'SIR BASIL MCFARLAND'

R

### 'Rosenfee' *(left)*

MODERN, CLUSTER-FLOWERED/FLORIBUNDA, LIGHT PINK,
REPEAT-FLOWERING

Big clusters of large open blooms that are rose
pink, then turn salmon with age, are borne on
this repeat-flowering variety. They have a slight
fragrance. 'Rosenfee' is a medium-sized bush with
good healthy foliage and suitable for bedding.
**ZONES 4–9.**

BOERNER, USA, 1967

PARENTAGE UNKNOWN

### 'Rosenresli' KORresli *(left)*
### syn. 'Love's Song'

MODERN, MODERN SHRUB, DEEP PINK, REPEAT-FLOWERING

The deep pink, fragrant flowers with salmon
tones on this rose are large, with 26–40 petals,
and are borne in medium-sized clusters. This
vigorous, repeat-flowering plant has dark green
glossy foliage and is suitable as a big shrub, on
pillars or on walls. **ZONES 4–9.**

KORDES, GERMANY, 1986

('NEW DAWN' × 'PRIMA BALLERINA') × SEEDLING

ANERKANNTE DEUTSCHE ROSE 1984

### 'Rosenstadt Zweibrücken' KORstatis *(left)*
### syns 'Morningrose', 'Rosenstadt'

MODERN, MODERN SHRUB, PINK BLEND, REPEAT-FLOWERING

This variety has large, open blooms with 20 petals
that are deep bright pink with a yellow base but
have little scent. A showy shrub that is remarkably
hardy, it has deep green healthy foliage and is a
good subject for borders and as a specimen plant.
**ZONES 3–9.**

KORDES, GERMANY, 1989

PARENTAGE UNKNOWN

R

### 'Roseraie de l'Haÿ'  *(right)*
syn. *Rosa rugosa* 'Roseraie de l'Haÿ'
MODERN, HYBRID RUGOSA, DARK RED, REPEAT-FLOWERING

Probably the most widely grown and certainly the most popular of all the Rugosa family, this rose is a typical Rugosa with vigorous, very thorny stems, that is very healthy and repeat-flowering. The big open flowers in small clusters are an intense crimson-purple with cream stamens and the scent is memorable, a rich concentration of cloves and honey. 'Roseraie de l'Haÿ' is probably the finest in its class and is useful in many situations, but it is most excellent as a hedge plant; a group of specimen plants in a wild garden will add color and scent. An unusual feature of this type of rose is that it does not have any hips. ZONES 4–9.

COCHET-COCHET, FRANCE, 1901

SAID TO BE A SPORT OF *ROSA RUGOSA RUBRA*

ROYAL HORTICULTURAL SOCIETY AWARD OF GARDEN MERIT 1993

### 'Roseromantic'  KORsommer  *(right)*
MODERN, CLUSTER-FLOWERED/FLORIBUNDA, WHITE, REPEAT-FLOWERING

'Roseromantic' bears large clusters of well-spaced palest pink single flowers that are 2 in (5 cm) across. They have a slight fragrance. The flowers completely cover the bush, which grows much taller than it does wide. The foliage is plentiful, small, dark and glossy on a very spreading bush. If spent flowers are not removed, a good crop of small, round hips is produced in clusters, these looking very attractive against the later flowers. This rose makes a very good low, spreading border or dwarf hedge that can also provide a light and airy effect when planted among bulbs and perennials of a similar color. ZONES 4–9.

KORDES, GERMANY, 1984

SEEDLING × 'TORNADO'

BADEN-BADEN GOLD MEDAL 1982

### 'Rosette Delizy'  *(right)*
OLD, TEA, YELLOW BLEND, REPEAT-FLOWERING

This colorful rose has flowers containing cadmium-yellow, apricot, brick red and carmine tones. The large, well-formed blooms may appear garish to some. It repeats well and the colors are more vibrant in cooler months. ZONES 7–9.

NABONNAND, FRANCE, 1922

'GENERAL GALLIÉNI' × 'COMTESSE BARDI'

R

### 'Rosina'

syns 'Josephine
Wheatcroft', 'Yellow
Sweetheart'

MODERN, MINIATURE, MEDIUM
YELLOW, REPEAT-FLOWERING

The double flowers of
this variety have 16
petals, are a pleasing
sunflower yellow and
are fragrant; the clear,
bright color is at its
best in cooler climates.
The foliage is glossy
light green on a
dwarf, compact plant
that grows 8–12 in
(20–30 cm) high. The
blooms appear in small
clusters. This rose
needs protection from
black spot, but it is
weatherproof and is a
popular Miniature for
borders and containers
in the UK. This classic
Miniature from the
hybridizing program
of early pioneer Pedro
Dot is still a favorite for
the garden. **ZONES 4–10.**

DOT, SPAIN, 1935

'EDUARDO TODA' × 'ROULETTI'

### 'Rosmarin '89'

KORfanto   *(top)*
syn. 'Rosmarin '90'

MODERN, MINIATURE, DEEP
PINK, REPEAT-FLOWERING

'Rosmarin '89' is a
very bushy, spreading
Miniature Rose
producing large, well-
shaped clusters of rich
pink, double blooms,
each containing 60–70
petals. The flowers are
produced very freely
and continuously and
are particularly long
lasting, and they are
excellent for cutting for
indoor use. If planted
very close together,
this rose makes a nice
little border. It should
not be confused with
the Kordes' variety
'Rosmarin', which was
introduced in 1965.
This can be difficult
as the older one is still
grown in many gardens
and is an excellent
rose. **ZONES 5–9.**

KORDES, GERMANY, 1990
PARENTAGE UNKNOWN

### 'Rosy Carpet'

INTercarp   *(left)*
syn. 'Matador'

MODERN, MODERN SHRUB,
DEEP PINK, REPEAT-FLOWERING

This is one of the first
introductions to
prove that the Modern
Garden Rose is a valuable
plant to enhance the
environment as a
subject for landscaping.
'Rosy Carpet' has open,
single, medium blooms
with 5 petals. Deep
pink, they are fragrant
and are produced in
clusters continuously
from summer through
to autumn. The dark
green glossy foliage
and a semi-spreading
growth habit make for
a plant that was and
still is used in big
planting schemes.
**ZONES 4–9.**

INTERPLANT, THE NETHERLANDS,
1984

'YESTERDAY' × SEEDLING

R

## 'Rosy Cheeks'

MODERN, LARGE-FLOWERED/
HYBRID TEA, RED BLEND,
REPEAT-FLOWERING

The large, fragrant blooms with 35 petals on 'Rosy Cheeks' are red with a reverse of yellow. The foliage is dark, glossy and disease resistant on a repeat-flowering bedding variety that has potential as an exhibition bloom. **ZONES 4–9.**

ANDERSON, UK, 1975

SEEDLING × 'IRISH GOLD'

## 'Rosy Cushion'

INTerall *(top)*

MODERN, MODERN SHRUB,
LIGHT PINK, REPEAT-FLOWERING

This repeat-flowering shrub has the potential to be a very prolific ground cover, and it has extremely good disease resistance. The small, light pink single blooms with 7–8 petals are borne in large clusters and have a slight fragrance. Dark green, glossy foliage and medium prickles appear on a good rose for environmental planting. **ZONES 4–9.**

ILSINK, THE NETHERLANDS, 1979

'YESTERDAY' × SEEDLING

GOLDEN ROSE OF THE HAGUE
1985, ROYAL HORTICULTURAL
SOCIETY AWARD OF GARDEN
MERIT 1993

## 'Rosy Mantle'

*(above)*

MODERN, LARGE-FLOWERED
CLIMBER, MEDIUM PINK,
REPEAT-FLOWERING

'Rosy Mantle' has large, fragrant, double blooms with a good Large-flowered shape. They are a warm, rosy pink and are produced with good succession from summer through to autumn. The dark foliage is a perfect foil for a variety that is equally at home growing on a wall or on a pillar. The flowers are good for cutting. **ZONES 4–9.**

COCKER, UK, 1968

'NEW DAWN' × 'PRIMA
BALLERINA'

ROYAL NATIONAL ROSE SOCIETY
TRIAL GROUND CERTIFICATE 1970

R

### 'Rote Max Graf'

KORmax *(right)*

syns *Rosa rugosa* 'Rote Max Graf', 'Red Max Graf'

MODERN, MODERN SHRUB, MEDIUM RED

Ovoid buds on this variety open to large, single, bright medium red flowers with 6 petals. Produced in clusters, they appear only in summer and are fragrant. An extremely vigorous, prostrate plant, it has dark leathery foliage that is almost wrinkled. 'Rote Max Graf' is a valuable variety in large plantings, with the bright scarlet blooms making a distinctive feature on a big plant. **ZONES 4–9.**

KORDES, GERMANY, 1980

*ROSA KORDESII* × SEEDLING

BADEN-BADEN GOLD MEDAL 1981

### 'Rotes Meer'

syns *Rosa rugosa* 'Rotes Meer', 'Exception', 'Purple Pavement'

MODERN, HYBRID RUGOSA, MEDIUM RED, REPEAT-FLOWERING

This rose bears fragrant, carmine-red, semi-double flowers, usually in clusters. The blooms continue through summer and autumn. Sizeable red hips appear late in the season. The shrub has a dense habit with prickly stems and small, semi-glossy leaves. **ZONES 4–9.**

BAUM, GERMANY, 1983

SEEDLING OF 'WHITE HEDGE'

### 'Rouge Meilland'

MEImalyna *(left)*

syns 'New Rouge Meilland', 'Rouge Meilland 84'

MODERN, LARGE-FLOWERED/ HYBRID TEA, MEDIUM RED, REPEAT-FLOWERING

'Rouge Meilland' has large, medium red flowers with 40 petals that have little scent. A vigorous, repeat-flowering variety, it has dark, semi-glossy foliage and an upright growth habit. **ZONES 4–9.**

MEILLAND, FRANCE, 1982

(['QUEEN ELIZABETH' × 'KARL HERBST'] × 'PHARAOH') × 'ANTONIA RIDGE'

R

## 'Rouletii' *(right)*
syn. *Rosa rouletii* 'Correvon'

OLD, CHINA, MEDIUM PINK, REPEAT-FLOWERING

This rose was found growing in a pot in a window
in Switzerland by M. Roulet and introduced by
M. Correvon of Geneva. A similar rose was grown
in England early in the nineteenth century and
was known as 'Miss Lawrance's Rose', Mary
Lawrance being an early flower illustrator. Many
varieties were grown up to mid-Victorian times,
but they died out with the introduction of the
Polyanthas. 'Rouletii' sparked new interest and
many, though not all, of the Miniatures of today
are descended from this rose. It is very tiny, a
'micro-miniature', with rose pink flowers half
a thumb width in diameter, and it is repeat-
flowering. There is disagreement as to whether
or not it is 'Pompon de Paris'. ZONES 7–9.

CORREVON, SWITZERLAND, 1922

CONSIDERED TO BE *ROSA CHINENSIS MINIMA*

## 'Royal Bassino' KORfungo *(below)*

MODERN, MODERN SHRUB, MEDIUM RED, REPEAT-FLOWERING

This improved form of the original repeat-
flowering ground cover has scarlet semi-double
blooms borne in moderate clusters that have a
light scent. It is a plant for the smaller garden;
it produces color throughout the season and has
a great resistance to disease. ZONES 4–9.

KORDES, GERMANY, 1990

PARENTAGE UNKNOWN

## 'Royal Bonica' MEIdomac, MEImodac
syn. 'Royal Bonnika'

MODERN, MODERN SHRUB, MEDIUM PINK, REPEAT-FLOWERING

This sport of 'Bonica' has blooms similar to its
parent. They are a deep shade of rose pink, and
the ageing flowers have less tendency to fade, but
there are rather more petals and the blooms
are larger. They appear through summer and
autumn. There is a slight scent. It is a fine variety
for beds and borders and forms a good hedge. It
grows vigorously, and has mid-green, semi-glossy
foliage. ZONES 5–9.

MEILLAND, FRANCE, 1994

SPORT OF 'BONICA'

BELFAST CERTIFICATE OF MERIT 1996

R

### 'Royal Gold' *(left)*

MODERN, LARGE-FLOWERED CLIMBER, MEDIUM YELLOW, REPEAT-FLOWERING

The very double golden yellow blooms with 35 petals on 'Royal Gold' are cupped and large. Borne singly or in small clusters and having a considerable fruity fragrance, they appear from summer to autumn. The foliage is glossy and very healthy and the growth habit vigorous on a climber that enjoys a warm low wall or pillar in a sheltered environment. **ZONES 4–9.**

MOREY, USA, 1957

'CLIMBING GOLDILOCKS' × 'LYDIA'

### 'Royal Highness' *(left)*

syns 'Königliche Hoheit', 'Königlicht Hoheit'

MODERN, LARGE-FLOWERED/HYBRID TEA, LIGHT PINK, REPEAT-FLOWERING

The large, very light soft pink double blooms with 43 petals on 'Royal Highness' have high centers and are very fragrant. A strong, upright, bushy grower, it is repeat-flowering and has dark, glossy, leathery foliage. It is a superb bedding variety. **ZONES 5–9.**

SWIM, USA, 1962

'VIRGO' × 'PEACE'

PORTLAND GOLD MEDAL 1960, MADRID GOLD MEDAL 1962, ALL-AMERICA ROSE SELECTION 1963, AARS DAVID FUERSTENBERG PRIZE 1964

### 'Royal Occasion' *(left)*

syn. 'Montana'

MODERN, CLUSTER-FLOWERED/FLORIBUNDA, ORANGE-RED, REPEAT-FLOWERING

The long, pointed buds of this rose open into semi-double, large, lightly fragrant flowers with 20 orange-scarlet petals. A healthy, repeat-flowering bedding rose, it has glossy deep green foliage and an upright habit. **ZONES 4–9.**

TANTAU, GERMANY, 1974

'WALZERTRAUM' × 'EUROPEANA'

ANERKANNTE DEUTSCHE ROSE 1974

R

## 'Royal Salute' MACros *(right)*
syn. 'Rose Baby'

MODERN, MINIATURE, MEDIUM RED, REPEAT-FLOWERING

The flowers of this rose are usually rose red, but in some climates such as England's they are a deep rose pink. The double florets have 30 petals and are borne in clusters. They tend to cover the compact, vigorous bush with dark green foliage, providing a dazzling display. The blooms are at their best when fully open, putting on an eye-catching performance in the garden. One of the first Miniatures introduced by the master hybridizer of Large-flowered and Cluster-flowered Roses, Sam McGredy, its popularity was limited to Great Britain where it was introduced to commemorate the Silver Jubilee of Queen Elizabeth II. **ZONES 5–10.**

MCGREDY, NEW ZEALAND, 1976

'NEW PENNY' × 'MARLENA'

ROYAL NATIONAL ROSE SOCIETY TRIAL GROUND CERTIFICATE 1972,
BRITISH ASSOCIATION OF ROSE BREEDERS, BREEDERS' SELECTION 1977

## 'Royal William' KORzaun *(above)*
syns 'Duftzauber '84', 'Fragrant Charm '84',
'Leonora Christine'

MODERN, LARGE-FLOWERED/HYBRID TEA, DARK RED,
REPEAT-FLOWERING

This exceptional variety has dark red, fragrant flowers with a velvety sheen. The large blooms have 35 petals and are repeat-flowering. The foliage is dark green, semi-glossy and disease resistant, and the growth habit is free and bushy. It is a good bedding variety. **ZONES 4–9.**

KORDES, GERMANY, 1984

'FEUERZAUBER' × SEEDLING

ROYAL NATIONAL ROSE SOCIETY TRIAL GROUND CERTIFICATE 1985,
ROSE OF THE YEAR 1987, ROYAL HORTICULTURAL SOCIETY AWARD
OF GARDEN MERIT 1993

R

### 'Rubens' *(above)*

OLD, TEA, WHITE,
REPEAT-FLOWERING

The flowers of this rose are creamy white, shaded with rose, and have pale gold centers. They are full, large and cup shaped, and occur quite early in the season. The plant is mildew free. If there is a fault, it is that the blooms are a little pendent. This rose is of conventional Tea style and growth. **ZONES 7–9.**

MOREAU & ROBERT, FRANCE, 1859

PARENTAGE UNKNOWN

### 'Ruby Anniversary'

HARbonny *(above)*

MODERN, CLUSTER-FLOWERED/
FLORIBUNDA, MEDIUM RED,
REPEAT-FLOWERING

This free-flowering, low-growing bushy variety produces ruby red, double, small flowers in medium-sized clusters from summer to autumn. They have some scent. A superb plant for pots, small borders and low hedges, it has small, shiny foliage. **ZONES 4–9.**

HARKNESS, UK, 1993

PARENTAGE UNKNOWN

BELFAST GOLD MEDAL 1995, ROYAL NATIONAL ROSE SOCIETY CERTIFICATE OF MERIT 1995

### 'Ruby Wedding'
*(left)*

MODERN, LARGE-FLOWERED/
HYBRID TEA, DARK RED,
REPEAT-FLOWERING

This respectable bedding variety bears large, deep red flowers with 44 petals. 'Ruby Wedding' repeats its bloom but the flowers have little scent. It is a bushy plant with a slightly spreading growth habit. **ZONES 4–9.**

GREGORY, UK, 1979

'MAYFLOWER' × SEEDLING

R

## 'Rugelda' KORruge
(above)

MODERN, HYBRID RUGOSA,
YELLOW BLEND,
REPEAT-FLOWERING

'Rugelda' has mid-green wrinkled foliage on a vigorous shrub that can be grown as a specimen plant or in groups in borders. The light yellow, double blooms are medium in size and have 25 petals. They have little scent. **ZONES 4–9.**

KORDES, GERMANY, 1992

PARENTAGE UNKNOWN

ANERKANNTE DEUTSCHE ROSE 1992

## 'Rugosa Magnifica'

MODERN, HYBRID RUGOSA,
MAUVE, REPEAT-FLOWERING

This fragrant variety produces reddish lavender flowers. They are double, but still show their golden stamens when fully open. Orange-red hips follow in autumn. The vigorous growth is spreading and very hardy. **ZONES 5–10.**

VAN FLEET, USA, 1905

PARENTAGE UNKNOWN

## 'Rumba' (above)
syn. 'Rhumba'

MODERN, CLUSTER-FLOWERED/
FLORIBUNDA, RED BLEND,
REPEAT-FLOWERING

An extremely free-flowering Cluster-flowered Rose, 'Rumba' bears large clusters of small to medium, cupped, reddish flowers with yellow centers. This medium-sized, repeat-flowering variety has a slight spicy fragrance. Disease resistant, it is a vigorous, bushy plant with glossy dark, leathery foliage. **ZONES 4–9.**

POULSEN, DENMARK, 1960

'MASQUERADE' × ('POULSEN'S BEDDER' × 'FLORADORA')

NATIONAL ROSE SOCIETY CERTIFICATE OF MERIT 1959

R

**'Ruskin'** *(above)*
syns *Rosa rugosa*
'Ruskin', 'John Ruskin'
MODERN, HYBRID RUGOSA,
DARK RED

This big Hybrid Rugosa
has deep crimson,
double flowers with
50 petals and a good
fragrance. They are
cupped and large, but
their repeat-flowering
ability is open to
doubt. The foliage is
large, rich green and
leathery on a strong,
bushy variety to 5 ft
(1.5 m) in height.
It can be planted in
groups, as a specimen
plant or as hedging
material. ZONES 4–9.

VAN FLEET, USA, 1928

'SOUVENIR DE PIERRE
LEPERDRIEUX' × 'VICTOR HUGO'

**'Rush'** LENmobri
*(above)*
MODERN, MODERN SHRUB,
PINK BLEND, REPEAT-FLOWERING

This bushy shrub bears
its single blooms with
5 petals in clusters of
3–32 from summer to
autumn. Pink with a
white eye, they have
a fruity fragrance. It is
upright-growing with
pale green foliage.
ZONES 4–9.

LENS, BELGIUM, 1983

('BALLERINA' × 'BRITANNIA') ×
*ROSA MULTIFLORA*

LYON ROSE OF THE CENTURY
1982, MONZA GOLD MEDAL
1982, ROME GOLD MEDAL 1982,
BAGATELLE GOLD MEDAL 1986,
THE HAGUE GOLD MEDAL 1988

## 'Russelliana' *(right)*
syns 'Old Spanish Rose', 'Russell's Cottage Rose', 'Scarlet Grevillea', 'Souvenir de la Bataille de Marengo'

OLD, MISCELLANEOUS, MAUVE

'Russelliana' bears magenta blooms that fade to mauve. They are fully double and flat and are borne in clusters. This strong-growing variety has rather coarse foliage and can grow to great heights. It is well worth a place in the garden. ZONES 5–9.

PRE-1837

POSSIBLY *ROSA MULTIFLORA* HYBRID × *ROSA SETIGERA*

## 'Rustica' MEIvilanic *(right)*
syns 'Stadt Basel', 'Ville de Bâle'

MODERN, CLUSTER-FLOWERED/ FLORIBUNDA, YELLOW BLEND, REPEAT-FLOWERING

The very long buds of 'Rustica' produce flowers of a yellow-peach blend with a buff yellow-orange reverse. They are cupped and double with 35 petals, are borne in clusters of 1–14 and have a slight fragrance. The dark, semi-matt foliage appears on a repeat-flowering plant that is semi-recumbent. It is a good bedding variety as well as a standard. ZONES 4–9.

MEILLAND, FRANCE, 1981

('QUEEN ELIZABETH' × SEEDLING) × 'SWEET PROMISE'

## 'Ruth Leuwerik'

MODERN, CLUSTER-FLOWERED/ FLORIBUNDA, MEDIUM RED, REPEAT-FLOWERING

The large, bright red double flowers with 30 petals on 'Ruth Leuwerik' are very fragrant. They appear in clusters on a rose that has maintained considerable popularity. The bronze foliage is healthy on a vigorous, bushy plant. Identical to its parent, the large, red, double blooms of **'Climbing Ruth Leuwerik'** are scattered over the long canes. The blooms are just as fragrant, and the bronze foliage is even more colorful. The vigorous canes are covered with red clusters all summer. ZONES 4–9.

DE RUITER, UK, 1961

'KÄTHE DUVIGNEAU' × 'ROSEMARY ROSE'

NATIONAL ROSE SOCIETY TRIAL GROUND CERTIFICATE 1960

R

### 'Sachsengruss' *(right)*
syns 'Saxon's Greeting', 'Tendresse'

OLD, HYBRID PERPETUAL, LIGHT PINK, REPEAT-FLOWERING

The well-formed flowers of this rose are a soft flesh pink. The blooms are very large. The growth habit and style of the plant is vigorous. ZONES 5–9.

NEUBERT, 1912

'FRAU KARL DRUSCHKI' × 'MME JULES GRAVEREAUX'

### 'Sadlers Wells' *(top)*

MODERN, MODERN SHRUB, PINK BLEND, REPEAT-FLOWERING

This free-flowering Modern Shrub still has its admirers. The semi-double flowers, which are produced in large clusters, are silvery pink laced with cherry red and are sweetly scented. The foliage is healthy and the bush has a moderate growth habit. The repeat cycle is good, making this a useful variety in borders. The flowers last a long time when cut. Sadlers Wells was the former name of England's Royal Ballet. ZONES 4–9.

BEALES, UK, 1983

'PENELOPE' × ' ROSE GAUJARD'

### 'Safrano' *(right)*

OLD, TEA, APRICOT BLEND,
REPEAT-FLOWERING

This is one of the early
Teas and is somewhat
remarkable, in that the
parentage is known.
This is because it was
the result of hand polli-
nation, an innovative
process at that time.
The large, fragrant,
semi-double flowers
are apricot-yellow
or saffron. The plant,
which is repeat-
flowering and resists
weather damage, used
to be very popular as a
buttonhole rose.
'Safrano' is best kept
out of full sun, as the
blooms can fade badly
to off-white. **ZONES 7–9.**

BEAUREGARD, FRANCE, 1839

'PARKS' YELLOW' ×
'MME DESPREZ'

S

### 'St Cecelia'   AUSmit
*(above)*

MODERN, MODERN SHRUB,
MEDIUM YELLOW,
REPEAT-FLOWERING

Plump buds open to
give this variety deeply
cupped flowers of
blush pink to light
apricot. They age
gracefully to cream and
have a strong myrrh
fragrance. Throughout
summer and autumn,
they are borne singly
or in small sprays of
3–12 amid the small,
matt mid-green foliage.
'St Cecelia' is free
blooming, but needs
protection from rust
and mildew. It is also
classified as an English
Rose. **ZONES 5–10.**

AUSTIN, UK, 1987

'WIFE OF BATH' × SEEDLING

### 'St Nicholas'
*(above)*

OLD, DAMASK, DEEP PINK

This upright-growing, sturdy shrub with green-gray wood and numerous sharp hooked thorns has mid- to dark green foliage, which is a little sparse on the lower branches. The pointed buds with feathery sepals unfold to semi-double flowers about 2½ in (6.5 cm) across, displaying a prominent array of golden yellow stamens. The blooms are fragrant and are silvery deep pink, remaining attractive as they pale to softer pink with age, and they are carried in well-filled clusters. Coming into flower in mid-summer, this rose should not be deadheaded because the autumn crop of red hips is very attractive.
**ZONES 5–10.**

JAMES, UK, 1950

POSSIBLY A DAMASK × GALLICA

### 'St Patrick'
WEKamanda *(bottom)*

MODERN, LARGE-FLOWERED/
HYBRID TEA, YELLOW BLEND,
REPEAT-FLOWERING

The golden yellow flowers of this rose are chartreuse green on the outer petals. The blooms are fully double, with 30–35 petals that give excellent, high-pointed centers suitable for exhibition, although summer heat is needed to bring out the best features of color and form. The foliage is mid-green and plenti-ful with good disease resistance. Born from two great exhibition varieties, 'St Patrick' is one of the few top award winners from an amateur breeder.
**ZONES 5–11.**

STRICKLAND, USA, 1995

'BRANDY' × 'GOLD MEDAL'

ALL-AMERICA ROSE SELECTION
1996

S

## 'St Swithun' AUSwith
*(right)*

MODERN, MODERN SHRUB,
LIGHT PINK, REPEAT-FLOWERING

The large, fragrant, pale pink flowers of 'St Swithun' are very full, with about 40 petals. They are borne in profusion in small clusters and the repeat-bloom is rapid, which makes this a welcome addition to any garden. The foliage is mid-green, semi-glossy and abundant on a bushy-growing plant that is also classified as an English Rose.
**ZONES 5–10.**

AUSTIN, UK, 1993

('MARY ROSE' × 'CHAUCER') ×
'C. F. MEYER'

## 'Salet' *(right)*

OLD, MOSS, MEDIUM PINK,
REPEAT-FLOWERING

This is an accommo-dating compact and sturdy shrub to about 3 ft (1 m) tall in most soils. Its stems are moderately thorny and sparsely covered with light-colored, reddish, mossy stubble. The buds are also mossy, but not excessively so, and develop into clear bright pink flowers that have a multitude of fluted, narrow petals to give an overall muddled effect, often with a central button. They are about 2½ in (6.5 cm) across, very fragrant and are pro-duced continuously either singly or in small clusters from mid-summer through to early winter. The leaves are small, bright green and soft to touch.
**ZONES 5–10.**

LACHARMÉ, FRANCE, 1854
PARENTAGE UNKNOWN

S

### 'Salita' KORmorlet

MODERN, LARGE-FLOWERED
CLIMBER, ORANGE BLEND,
REPEAT-FLOWERING

'Salita' bears clusters
of light orange-red,
medium-sized blooms
that are slightly
fragrant. A moderately
vigorous climber, it
looks very effective
growing on walls or
pillars. It also makes
an attractive shrub.
ZONES 4–9.

KORDES, GERMANY, 1987

PARENTAGE UNKNOWN

### 'Sally Holmes' *(top)*

MODERN, MODERN SHRUB,
WHITE, REPEAT-FLOWERING

This extremely popu-
lar, medium-sized
shrub rose has large,
open, creamy white
flowers with only
5 petals. There is a
lovely fragrance. It
has large, glossy, deep
green leaves on stiff
upright stems. If
pruned lightly, it will
develop into a well-
structured plant about
6 ft (1.8 m) high. 'Sally
Holmes' is ideal as a
specimen plant or in
groups in borders.
ZONES 4–9.

HOLMES, UK, 1976

'IVORY FASHION' × 'BALLERINA'

ROYAL NATIONAL ROSE SOCIETY
TRIAL GROUND CERTIFICATE
1975, BELFAST CERTIFICATE
OF MERIT 1979, BADEN-BADEN
GOLD MEDAL 1980, GLASGOW
FRAGRANCE AWARD 1993,
PORTLAND GOLD MEDAL 1993

### 'Samantha' JACanth, JACmantha *(above)*

MODERN, LARGE-FLOWERED/HYBRID TEA, MEDIUM RED,
REPEAT-FLOWERING

The medium-sized red flowers of this rose have
high centers and a good shape. There is some
scent. It is a vigorous, bushy variety with dark
green, leathery foliage and a good repeat cycle.
This is a bedding variety that can also be
displayed on the show table. ZONES 4–9.

WARRINER, USA, 1974

'BRIDAL PINK' × SEEDLING

## 'Sander's White Rambler' *(right)*

MODERN, RAMBLER, WHITE

This *wichurana*-type Rambler has small, white, rosette-style flowers that are borne in large clusters. The blooms have a fruity fragrance. The foliage is bright green and glossy. Although it is a little late in flowering, it is very reliable and is one of the better Ramblers. It can also be grown as an extended ground cover. Like the majority of the Ramblers, it flowers only once in the season. **ZONES 5–9.**

POSSIBLY FROM BELGIUM, INTRODUCED BY SANDER, UK, 1912

PARENTAGE UNKNOWN

ROYAL HORTICULTURAL SOCIETY AWARD OF GARDEN MERIT 1993

## 'Sandra' SandKOR *(right)*

MODERN, LARGE-FLOWERED/ HYBRID TEA, ORANGE-PINK, REPEAT-FLOWERING

The pure salmon blooms of 'Sandra' are high centered and contain 35 petals. There is a slight fragrance. It is an upright, bushy grower that has a good repeat cycle. It is a popular cut-flower variety. **ZONES 4–9.**

KORDES, GERMANY, 1981

'MERCEDES' × SEEDLING

S

### 'Sangerhausen'

**MODERN, MODERN SHRUB, DEEP PINK, REPEAT-FLOWERING**

The large, deep pink, semi-double blooms of this rose are slightly fragrant. It is a medium-sized shrub with large, leathery, wrinkled foliage that is a good specimen shrub. It also looks great planted in groups in borders. **ZONES 4–9.**

KORDES, GERMANY, 1938

'INGAR OLSSON' × 'EVA'

### 'Santa Catalina'   *(left)*

**MODERN, CLUSTER-FLOWERED CLIMBER, LIGHT PINK, REPEAT-FLOWERING**

This rose bears clusters of light pink, semi-double flowers containing 18 petals. Occasionally there is a deeper flush of pink in the flowers. The medium-sized blooms have a slight fragrance. **ZONES 4–9.**

MCGREDY, UK, 1970

'PADDY MCGREDY' × 'HEIDELBERG'

### 'Santana'   TANklesant   *(left)*

**MODERN, LARGE-FLOWERED CLIMBER, MEDIUM RED, REPEAT-FLOWERING**

'Santana' bears medium red, semi-double blooms containing 20 petals. The plant has a good repeat cycle, ensuring a steady supply of blooms, but unfortunately there is little scent. The foliage is medium green and glossy on a moderate-sized plant. This is a great rose for walls and pillars. **ZONES 4–9.**

TANTAU, GERMANY, 1985

PARENTAGE UNKNOWN

S

### 'Sarabande' MEIhand, MEIrabande *(right)*

MODERN, CLUSTER-FLOWERED/
FLORIBUNDA, ORANGE-RED,
REPEAT-FLOWERING

The flowers of this rose are bright orange-red. The slightly fragrant, semi-double blooms have 13 petals and are borne in large trusses on a low, bushy plant with semi-glossy foliage. It is an ideal bedding variety that makes a good standard. This is one of the great roses from the House of Meilland. **'Climbing Sarabande'** (MEIhandsar; Meilland, France, 1968; Japan Gold Medal 1968), is perfect for pillars and pergolas. **ZONES 4–9.**

MEILLAND, FRANCE, 1957

'COCORICO' × 'MOULIN ROUGE'

BAGATELLE GOLD MEDAL 1957, GENEVA GOLD MEDAL 1957, ROME GOLD MEDAL 1957, PORTLAND GOLD MEDAL 1958, ALL-AMERICA ROSE SELECTION 1960

### 'Sarah Arnot' *(bottom)*

MODERN, LARGE-FLOWERED/
HYBRID TEA, MEDIUM PINK,
REPEAT-FLOWERING

The flowers of 'Sarah Arnot' are warm rose pink. The double, high-centered blooms contain 25 petals and have a wonderful scent. The foliage is leathery on a vigorous, upright plant. This reliable bedding variety is also an excellent candidate for exhibition. **ZONES 4–9.**

CROLL, UK, 1957

'ENA HARKNESS' × 'PEACE'

NATIONAL ROSE SOCIETY GOLD MEDAL 1957

S

### 'Sarah van Fleet'  (right)

MODERN, HYBRID RUGOSA, MEDIUM PINK, REPEAT-FLOWERING

The lilac-pink, open, medium-sized flowers of this rose are produced in small clusters and look spectacular when in full flower. This is an extremely free-flowering and vigorous shrub, and it is very thorny. The upright habit makes it suitable for the back of the border or as a specimen plant. It is furnished with handsome, wrinkled, dull green foliage and can sometimes be subject to mildew and rust in autumn. It has virtually no fragrance and does not set hips, which is unusual for a Hybrid Rugosa. The plethora of large sharp thorns makes it a good hedge to discourage intruders. **ZONES 4–9.**

VAN FLEET, USA, 1926

REPORTED TO BE *ROSA RUGOSA* × 'MY MARYLAND'

### 'Saratoga'  (below)

MODERN, CLUSTER-FLOWERED/FLORIBUNDA, WHITE, REPEAT-FLOWERING

This popular rose has ovoid buds opening into large white blooms that are borne in small clusters. The double flowers are 4 in (10 cm) wide, have 33 petals and are reminiscent of gardenias. There is a lovely fragrance. It is a vigorous, bushy, short grower with glossy, leathery foliage that makes a good bedding rose or standard. **ZONES 4–9.**

BOERNER, USA, 1963

'WHITE BOUQUET' × 'PRINCESS WHITE'

ALL-AMERICA ROSE SELECTION 1964

S

### 'Satchmo' *(right)*

MODERN, CLUSTER-FLOWERED/
FLORIBUNDA, ORANGE-RED,
REPEAT-FLOWERING

The brilliant scarlet, double flowers of 'Satchmo' contain 25 petals, and are borne in small clusters. They have a slight fragrance. The foliage is dark and leathery on a plant with a bushy habit and a good repeat cycle. It is suitable as a bedding rose and also looks effective as a standard. It was named for the great jazz man Louis Armstrong, who died in 1971. **ZONES 4–9.**

MCGREDY, UK, 1970

'EVELYN FISON' × 'DIAMANT'

GOLDEN ROSE OF THE HAGUE 1975

### 'Savoy Hotel' HARvintage *(right)*
syns 'Integrity', 'Vercors', 'Violette Niestlé'

MODERN, LARGE-FLOWERED/HYBRID
TEA, LIGHT PINK, REPEAT-FLOWERING

The large, light pink flowers of 'Savoy Hotel' have deeper undersides. The high-centered blooms have a slight fragrance. This is a free-flowering rose with medium-sized, bushy growth and dark green, semi-glossy, healthy foliage. In temperate climates it is a first-class bedding rose, and a good choice for grouping in mixed borders. **ZONES 4–9.**

HARKNESS, UK, 1989

'SILVER JUBILEE' × 'AMBER QUEEN'

DUBLIN GOLD MEDAL 1988,
DORTMUND GOLD MEDAL 1991,
ROYAL HORTICULTURAL SOCIETY
AWARD OF GARDEN MERIT 1994,
PORTLAND GOLD MEDAL 1998

**S**

'Scabrosa' *(above)*
syns *Rosa rugosa scabrosa*, 'Rugosa Superba',
'Superba'

MODERN, HYBRID RUGOSA, MAUVE, REPEAT-FLOWERING

This rose was discovered by Harkness probably
before 1939. It has large, mauve-pink, single
flowers that contain only 5 petals. They are borne
in small clusters, and the plant is almost always
in bloom. The scent has been described as being
like that of a carnation. This free-growing shrub
is good as a hedge. The wrinkled foliage is light
green, and in autumn, large, round red hips
appear. **ZONES 4–9.**

INTRODUCED BY HARKNESS, UK, 1950

PARENTAGE UNKNOWN

ROYAL HORTICULTURAL SOCIETY AWARD OF GARDEN MERIT 1993

### 'Scarlet Gem' MEIdo *(right)*
syn. 'Scarlet Pimpernel'

MODERN, MINIATURE, ORANGE-RED, REPEAT-FLOWERING

This rose has ovoid buds that open to give orange-scarlet flowers with 58 petals. They have a lovely cupped form and a light fragrance, and because of the high petal count, the flowers are quite long lasting. The foliage is dark glossy green on a dwarf, compact bush that grows 12–15 in (30–38 cm) high. This is a vigorous little grower with attractive foliage and bloom color. It looks wonderful in a border or when planted in a container. ZONES 5–10.

MEILLAND, FRANCE, 1961

('MOULIN ROUGE' × 'FASHION') × ('PERLA DE MONTSERRAT' × 'PERLA DE ALCAÑADA')

### 'Scarlet Knight' MEIelec *(right)*
syn. 'Samourai'

MODERN, LARGE-FLOWERED/HYBRID TEA, MEDIUM RED, REPEAT-FLOWERING

The crimson-scarlet, double blooms of 'Scarlet Knight' are cupped and slightly fragrant. It has leathery, dark foliage on a vigorous plant with an upright, bushy habit that is a good bedding variety. 'Climbing Scarlet Knight' (syn. 'Climbing Samourai; Jack, Australia, 1972) is a vigorous rose that is very suitable for walls and pillars. ZONES 4–9.

MEILLAND, FRANCE, 1966

('HAPPINESS' × 'INDEPENDENCE') × 'SUTTER'S GOLD'

MADRID GOLD MEDAL 1966

### 'Scarlet Meidiland' MEIkrotal *(right)*
syn. 'Scarlet Meillandécor'

MODERN, MODERN SHRUB, MEDIUM RED, REPEAT-FLOWERING

The small, light cherry-red blooms of this rose have dark carmine-pink undersides. The blooms are semi-double with 20 petals and are borne in large clusters. There is very little fragrance. This is a prostrate, spreading plant with dark green, medium-sized foliage. It is suitable for landscaping, covering low walls and for hanging baskets. It also makes an effective ground cover. ZONES 4–9.

MEILLAND, FRANCE, 1987

MEITIRACA × 'CLAIR MATIN'

FRANKFURT GOLD MEDAL 1989

S

### 'Scarlet Queen Elizabeth' DICel
*(left)*

MODERN, CLUSTER-FLOWERED/
FLORIBUNDA, ORANGE-RED,
REPEAT-FLOWERING

---

'Scarlet Queen Elizabeth' bears clusters of medium-sized flowers of flame scarlet. There is a very delicate scent. The foliage is dark and extremely healthy. It is a useful bedding variety that has a good repeat cycle. **ZONES 4–9.**

DICKSON, UK, 1963

('KORONA' × SEEDLING) ×
'QUEEN ELIZABETH'

NATIONAL ROSE SOCIETY TRIAL
GROUND CERTIFICATE 1963,
GOLDEN ROSE OF THE HAGUE
1973

### 'Scented Air' *(left)*

MODERN, CLUSTER-FLOWERED/
FLORIBUNDA, ORANGE-PINK,
REPEAT-FLOWERING

---

This rose has a particu-larly lovely fragrance. The flowers are large, double and salmon-pink. They are borne in small clusters on a free-flowering, medium-sized bushy plant with handsome, large, healthy leaves. It is a very good bedding rose. **ZONES 4–9.**

DICKSON, UK, 1965

SEEDLING OF 'SPARTAN' ×
'QUEEN ELIZABETH'

ROYAL NATIONAL ROSE SOCIETY
CERTIFICATE OF MERIT 1965,
BELFAST GOLD MEDAL 1967,
GOLDEN ROSE OF THE HAGUE
1971

S

### 'Scentimental' WEKplapep *(above)*
MODERN, CLUSTER-FLOWERED/FLORIBUNDA, RED BLEND, REPEAT-FLOWERING

This is a striped Cluster-flowered Rose—the red and pink together create a startling visual impact. It is a bushy, free-flowering, vigorous plant with healthy, large, luxurious foliage. 'Scentimental' is a very modern-looking bedding rose that also makes a good standard. It has a fine fragrance. **ZONES 4–9.**

CARRUTH, USA, 1996

'PLAYBOY' × 'PEPPERMINT TWIST'

ALL-AMERICA ROSE SELECTION 1997

### 'Scepter'd Isle' AUSland *(above)*
MODERN, MODERN SHRUB, LIGHT PINK, REPEAT-FLOWERING

This rose is also classified as an English Rose. It bears large, light pink, double blooms that have a lovely scent. It is a shrubby plant with a good repeat cycle for large borders. **ZONES 4–9.**

AUSTIN, UK, 1996

PARENTAGE UNKNOWN

S

## 'Scharlachglut' *(above)*
syns 'Scarlet Fire', 'Scarlet Glow'

**MODERN, MODERN SHRUB, DARK RED**

The bright scarlet-crimson flowers of this variety
make a real splash of brilliant color in mid-summer.
The blooms are large, open and semi-double.
There is a crop of large, orange-red, round hips
in autumn, making it an attractive plant all year
round. It is a rampant, free-growing shrub with a
slightly lax habit. The ample foliage is dark green
and healthy. Although it flowers only once, it is a
good subject in large borders. **ZONES 4–9.**

KORDES, GERMANY, 1952

'POINSETTIA' × 'ALIKA'

ROYAL HORTICULTURAL SOCIETY AWARD OF GARDEN MERIT 1993

## 'Schneewalzer' TANrezlaw *(above right)*
syn. 'Snow Waltz'

**MODERN, LARGE-FLOWERED CLIMBER, WHITE**

The oval buds of this rose open to large, double
white flowers. They have a classic Large-flowered
form and the outer petals curl back when fully
open; there is some cream shading at the center
of the blooms. Borne singly or in small clusters,
the flowers appear on upright growth amid the
mid-green foliage. **ZONES 5–10.**

TANTAU, GERMANY, 1987

PARENTAGE UNKNOWN

## 'Schneezwerg'
*(right)*
syns 'Snow Dwarf',
'Snowdwarf'
MODERN, HYBRID RUGOSA,
WHITE, REPEAT-FLOWERING

Snow white flowers
with golden stamens
are the hallmark of
this semi-double rose.
The weatherproof
blooms are borne from
summer through to
autumn in small
clusters of 3–10 on
strong stems. The
foliage is typically
glossy, disease resistant
and rugosa-like on a
vigorous, medium-
sized bush growing
to a height of about 3 ft
(1 m). It has some
spreading characteris-
tics. If dead blooms are
not removed during
the growing season,
attractive orange hips
appear that make an
unusual display of
blooms and hips in
autumn. ZONES 4–10.

LAMBERT, GERMANY, 1912

POSSIBLY *ROSA RUGOSA* ×
HYBRID OF A POLYANTHA

ROYAL HORTICULTURAL SOCIETY
AWARD OF GARDEN MERIT 1993

## 'Schoener's Nutkana'   *(above)*
MODERN, MODERN SHRUB, MEDIUM PINK

The fragrant, single-petalled flowers of this
rose are a clear cerise-rose pink, 4 in (10 cm) in
diameter. The foliage is medium green and the
canes are almost thornless. Its growing habit is
dominated by arching canes on a vigorous bush
that reaches about 6 ft (1.8 m) high and 3 ft (1 m)
wide. This versatile rose can tolerate poor soil
conditions, shady areas in the garden and cold
winters. ZONES 4–10.

SCHOENER, USA, 1930

*ROSA NUTKANA* × 'PAUL NEYRON'

S

## 'Schoolgirl' *(left)*

MODERN, LARGE-FLOWERED
CLIMBER, APRICOT BLEND,
REPEAT-FLOWERING

The large flowers of this rose reach 4 in (10 cm) across. They have beautiful form and are apricot-orange, a rare color in climbers. The blooms are strongly fragrant and weatherproof. It has a stiff, vigorous growth habit and reaches a height of about 10 ft (3 m). The foliage is rather sparse and poorly covers the plant. 'Schoolgirl' can be successfully used either as a pillar or climber for a fence, wall or trellis, and it can be cultivated in a wide range of soils and climates. ZONES 5–10.

MCGREDY, UK, 1964

'CORAL DAWN' ×
'BELLE BLONDE'

## 'Schwarze Madonna'

KORschwama *(left)*
syns 'Barry Fearn',
'Black Madonna'

MODERN, LARGE-FLOWERED/
HYBRID TEA, DARK RED,
REPEAT-FLOWERING

This is a very dark crimson rose with a classic shape but little scent. The healthy foliage clothes a plant of moderate vigor. It is a good bedding variety and is also popular as a cut flower. ZONES 4–9.

KORDES, GERMANY, 1992

PARENTAGE UNKNOWN

S

### 'Scorcher' *(bottom)*

MODERN, LARGE-FLOWERED
CLIMBER, DARK RED

The lightly fragrant flowers of this rose can range from a brilliant scarlet-crimson to a deep strawberry or cherry red. The early season bloom is magnificent, but there are only a few later flushes. The florets are semi-double, and 4 in (10 cm) across. Large, wrinkled foliage adorns the vigorous bush which can be trained as a climber or pillar reaching about 10 ft (3 m) high. Hybridized by one of Australia's most distinguished breeders of the first half of the twentieth century, 'Scorcher' may well have an honored place in the hearts of many Australians despite fierce competition in this classification from later introductions such as 'Altissimo' or 'Danse du Feu'. 'Scorcher' is a cheerful addition to any garden.
**ZONES 5–10.**

CLARK, AUSTRALIA, 1922

'MME ABEL CHATENAY' ×
SEEDLING

### 'Sea Foam' *(top)*

MODERN, MODERN SHRUB,
WHITE, REPEAT-FLOWERING

The flowers of this rose are white to cream and are borne in small clusters. The double florets have a delicate fragrance. The foliage is small, glossy and dark green on a vigorous plant that tends to climb or trail, or is just semi-prostrate. It has been used extensively as a ground cover, as the canes are rarely longer than about 3 ft (1 m); this is not enough to be a true Climber, but it can be used as a weeping standard. The blooms cannot sustain bad weather conditions and this rose is more suitable for warmer climates with low rainfall. There is another 'Sea Foam', bred by William Paul in 1919, which is said to be a seedling of 'Mermaid'.
**ZONES 5–11.**

SCHWARTZ, USA, 1964

(['WHITE DAWN' × 'PINOCCHIO']
× ['WHITE DAWN' ×
'PINOCCHIO']) × ('WHITE DAWN'
× 'PINOCCHIO')

ROME GOLD MEDAL 1963,
AMERICAN ROSE SOCIETY DAVID
FUERSTENBERG PRIZE 1968

S

## 'Sea Pearl' *(right)*
### syn. 'Flower Girl'

MODERN, CLUSTER-FLOWERED/
FLORIBUNDA, PINK BLEND,
REPEAT-FLOWERING

The long, pointed buds of this rose open to soft pink flowers with a flushed pink and yellow reverse. They are 4–5 in (10–12 cm) across, semi-double with 24 petals, and well formed, and occur in clusters or trusses of 5 or more on strong straight stems. The blooms have a decided Large-flowered form in the early stages of opening, but they open wide with a change in color to a blend of orange and salmon-pink with a peach-pink reverse, fading with age. Eventually they become flecked with red. Although weather-proof, they are not sunproof and the delicate coral-pink and cream colors tend to bleach under the hot sun. The foliage is dark green on a tall, upright bush. ZONES 4–10.

DICKSON, UK, 1964

'KORDES' PERFECTA' ×
'MONTEZUMA'

ROYAL NATIONAL ROSE SOCIETY
CERTIFICATE OF MERIT 1964,
BELFAST FRIZZELL AWARD 1966

## 'Seagull'

MODERN, RAMBLER, WHITE

'Seagull' is a vigorous Rambler with pure white, semi-double flowers showing golden stamens. They are borne in clusters and have the characteristic Multiflora perfume. This rose and 'Thalia', descended from *Rosa multiflora* from 1895, were considered the best white Ramblers until they were challenged by those descended from *R. wichurana*, notably 'Sander's White', which were less susceptible to mildew. ZONES 4–10.

PRITCHARD, UK, 1907

*ROSA MULTIFLORA* × 'GÉNÉRAL JACQUEMINOT'

ROYAL HORTICULTURAL SOCIETY AWARD OF GARDEN MERIT 1993

## 'Sealing Wax'
*(right)*
syn. *Rosa moyesii*
'Sealing Wax'
MODERN, MODERN SHRUB,
MEDIUM PINK

'Sealing Wax' is one of the best of the *Rosa moyesii* hybrids as it produces a huge crop of bright red, flagon-shaped hips that persist for a long time. The flowers, however, are not as spectacular as those of *R. moyesii*, yet the growth is more manageable, which makes 'Sealing Wax' the better rose for a small garden. This variety likes a cool climate similar to its natural Himalayan habitat. The growth can burn in hot climates and it seems to need higher altitudes to fruit well. It is a spectacular plant in autumn and the hips are excellent for indoor displays. ZONES 5–10.
ROYAL HORTICULTURAL SOCIETY,
UK, 1938

HYBRID OF *ROSA MOYESII*

## 'Seashell' KORshel
*(right)*
MODERN, LARGE-FLOWERED/
HYBRID TEA, ORANGE-PINK,
REPEAT-FLOWERING

The short, pointed buds of 'Seashell' open to burnt orange, double flowers with 48 petals. In some climates the blooms can be a clear shade of coral-pink, sometimes deeper at the edges of the petals and seemingly lit with gold. They have a light fragrance. The bloom form has received praise for its beauty— the frilled petals overlap with the regularity of tiles on a roof. The foliage is mid-green and fairly disease resistant. It is an upright, healthy, vigorous bush, and is easy to grow. ZONES 4–10.
KORDES, GERMANY, 1976

SEEDLING × 'COLOUR WONDER'

ALL-AMERICA ROSE SELECTION
1976

S

## 'Seaspray' MACnew *(above)*

MODERN, MINIATURE, PINK BLEND, REPEAT-FLOWERING

'Seaspray' has pale pink semi-double flowers with a red flush towards the petal edges. They have a strong fragrance. The blooms tend to occur in clusters on a low, spreading plant covered with bright green foliage. The flowers are plentiful, the plant is easy to maintain and is always clean and healthy. In some climates the color can be exquisite—a unique combination of palest pink flushed darker pink on the edges of the petals. It can be used as a ground cover as it is profuse in bloom on strong, lateral canes. ZONES 5–10.

MCGREDY, NEW ZEALAND, 1982

'ANYTIME' × 'MOANA'

## 'Secret' HILaroma

MODERN, LARGE-FLOWERED/HYBRID TEA, PINK BLEND, REPEAT-FLOWERING

The seductively fragrant, light pink flowers of this rose are edged with deep pink. The large, double blooms contain 26–40 petals and are borne singly on strong, straight stems. They have classic Large-flowered form with high symmetrical centers, and are suitable for cutting or exhibition. The blooms are attractive at all stages. The foliage is mid-green and semi-glossy on a tall bush. The plant, which derives its vigor from the award-winning seed parent 'Pristine', has an excellent fragrance that never fails to attract visitors to the garden. It prefers cooler climates. ZONES 4–10.

TRACY, USA, 1992

'PRISTINE' × 'FRIENDSHIP'

ALL-AMERICA ROSE SELECTION 1994

## 'Senateur Amic' *(above)*

MODERN, LARGE-FLOWERED CLIMBER, MEDIUM RED

The brilliant scarlet buds begin as if they were Hybrid Teas but soon open to flat, semi-double, blowsy blooms. The rich color has a yellow base, and most blooms are single with a few semi-double ones. With a lovely fragrance, the rose is an early visitor to the garden, especially in warm climates. The dark, glossy leaves are long and add to the charm of this vigorous climber. It is similar to its relative, 'Belle of Portugal', and the two go well together, especially if trained up a tree. It is tender but will survive in colder climates with some protection. ZONES 5–10.

NABONNAND, FRANCE, 1924

'GIGANTEA' HYBRID

### 'Sequoia Gold'
MORsegold *(right)*

MODERN, MINIATURE, MEDIUM
YELLOW, REPEAT-FLOWERING

The flowers of this rose are a bright medium yellow, fading with age to a lighter yellow. The florets are double with 30 petals and have a fruity fragrance. They have typical high-pointed centers suitable for exhibition and occur in small clusters of 3–7 flowers. The foliage is glossy mid-green on a plant with a low-growing, spreading habit. Because the bloom cycle is fast, the plant is covered with blooms all season long. In the heat of summer, the color can fade rapidly. This rose was named to celebrate the 50th anniversary of the establishment of the Sequoia Nursery in Visalia, California.

**ZONES 5–11.**

MOORE, USA, 1986

('LITTLE DARLING' × 'LEMON
DELIGHT') × 'GOLD BADGE'

AMERICAN ROSE SOCIETY
AWARD OF EXCELLENCE 1987

### 'Serratipetala'
*(above)*

syns **'Fimbriata à Pétales Frangés'**, *Rosa chinensis serratipetala,* **'Rose Oeillet de Saint Arquey Vilfray'**

OLD, CHINA, PINK BLEND,
REPEAT-FLOWERING

This is an unusual rose, as it has the sparse China growth but is considerably taller and bushier. The flowers are carnation-like with fringed and serrated petals. They repeat throughout the season, but the blooms are fewer and smaller in the later months. The flowers can vary from deep red to pink in cool weather. Attributed to Jacques but 'rediscovered' in France in 1912, this rose was promoted with great *eclat*. It is generally described as a curiosity, but it is well worth a place in the garden. However, the Grootendorst range of Hybrid Rugosas, with similar carnation-type flowers, are better.

**ZONES 7–9.**

JACQUES, FRANCE, 1831

PARENTAGE UNKNOWN

S

## 'Seven Sisters' *(below)*

OLD, MISCELLANEOUS, PINK BLEND

This is a form of *Rosa multiflora* with similar growth, larger leaves and bigger double flowers. The trusses can bear up to 7 flowers ranging from deep cerise-purple to pale mauve, or even off-white; each flower is a different shade and changes as it ages. The growth is very vigorous and it can cover a large area. It is perhaps better on a wall in cooler areas, as it needs some protection from frost. **ZONES 5–9.**

JAPAN, 1817

PARENTAGE UNKNOWN

## 'Sevilliana'

MODERN, MODERN SHRUB, PINK BLEND, REPEAT-FLOWERING

The pointed, ovoid buds of this rose open to light claret-rose flowers with a yellow base. The fragrant, semi-double blooms, which contain 15–20 petals, are slightly cupped and are borne in large solid trusses. The foliage is tinted copper on an upright shrub-type bush that reaches about 4 ft (1.2 m) high. The plant is in constant bloom and is winter hardy. If it is left to set fruit, it produces masses of bright red hips. The late Griffith Buck is well known in America for his pioneering work in creating a line of winter-hardy shrubs. **ZONES 4–10.**

BUCK, USA, 1976

('VERA DALTON' × 'DORNRÖSCHEN') × (['WORLD'S FAIR' × 'FLORADORA'] × 'APPLEJACK')

## 'Sexy Rexy' MACrexy *(below)*

syn. 'Heckenzauber'

MODERN, CLUSTER-FLOWERED/FLORIBUNDA, MEDIUM PINK, REPEAT-FLOWERING

'Sexy Rexy' has medium to light pink flowers that are borne on strong straight stems in large clusters. The fragrant, double blooms have 40 petals, and the flower form is more like that of a camellia, opening flat with a nice colorful finish. The trusses last for weeks and the repeat cycle is fast, although for continuous blooming the plant requires some deadheading. The foliage is small and mid-green on a compact, healthy, disease-resistant bush. This rose is a great contribution to the development of colorfast, productive and easily maintained Cluster-flowered Roses. **ZONES 5–11.**

MCGREDY, NEW ZEALAND, 1984

'SEASPRAY' × 'DREAMING'

NEW ZEALAND GOLD MEDAL 1984, ROYAL NATIONAL ROSE SOCIETY CERTIFICATE OF MERIT 1985, GLASGOW GOLD MEDAL 1989, AUCKLAND GOLD MEDAL 1990, PORTLAND GOLD MEDAL 1990, ROYAL HORTICULTURAL SOCIETY AWARD OF GARDEN MERIT 1993, RNRS JAMES MASON GOLD MEDAL 1996

## 'Sharifa Asma'
AUSreef  *(right)*
syn. 'Sharifa'
MODERN, MODERN SHRUB,
LIGHT PINK, REPEAT-FLOWERING

The flowers of this rose
are a nearly translucent
blush pink with just a
touch of gold at the
base. They are shallow
cupped with a petal
count somewhere in
the range of 50–100,
and show a perfect
rosette-like form at the
fully open stage. It has
a honey-like fragrance.
The petals can quickly
dehydrate under hot,
sunny conditions. The
foliage is mid-green on
a short, upright plant
reaching a height of 4 ft
(1.2 m). It was named
for a member of the
Omani royal family.
**ZONES 4–10.**

AUSTIN, UK, 1989

'MARY ROSE' × 'ADMIRED
MIRANDA'

## 'Sheer Bliss'  JACtro
*(right)*
MODERN, LARGE-FLOWERED/
HYBRID TEA, WHITE BLEND,
REPEAT-FLOWERING

This variety has urn-
shaped flowers that are
white with just a hint
of pink. In cool climates,
however, there is a
deeper shade of pink
in the centers. The
double florets contain
35 petals and are large,
to 4–5 in (10–12 cm)
across. They have a
detectable spicy scent.
The exhibition-type
blooms are naturally
borne singly on strong
straight stems. The
foliage is long, thin
and matt on an upright
plant with a spreading
habit that is a vigorous
grower, sending up
many stems. Its show-
winning perfection
has made this rose
popular with florists
for use in wedding
bouquets. 'Sheer Bliss'
is one of the many
prize-winning roses
hybridized by the late
Bill Warriner of
Jackson & Perkins.
**ZONES 5–10.**

WARRINER, USA, 1985

'WHITE MASTERPIECE' ×
'GRAND MASTERPIECE'

JAPAN GOLD MEDAL 1984, ALL-
AMERICA ROSE SELECTION 1987

S

## 'Sheer Elegance' TWObe

MODERN, LARGE-FLOWERED/HYBRID TEA, ORANGE-PINK,
REPEAT-FLOWERING

'Sheer Elegance' has pointed buds that open to soft pink flowers with dark pink edges to the petals. The large, cupped, double florets contain 43 petals, and are borne singly on strong straight stems. There is a strong musk fragrance. In cooler climates the flower form is classical, with the petals reflexing to give a symmetrical shape to the blooms; in warm climates the form is not as good, but this is compensated for by an improvement in the color of the blooms. The foliage is large, dark green and glossy on a tall, upright, disease-resistant plant. An easy rose to grow, it is one of many All-America Rose Selection Large-flowered Roses hybridized by Jerry Twomey from San Diego, California. **ZONES 5–10.**

TWOMEY, USA, 1989

'PRISTINE' × 'FORTUNA'

ALL-AMERICA ROSE SELECTION 1991, PORTLAND GOLD MEDAL 1994

## 'Sheila's Perfume' HARsherry *(above)*

MODERN, CLUSTER-FLOWERED/FLORIBUNDA, YELLOW BLEND,
REPEAT-FLOWERING

'Sheila's Perfume' has yellow flowers edged red, with a flower form and size that could pass for a Large-flowered Rose. The weatherproof, semi-double blooms with 20 petals are fragrant. They are borne singly and in clusters on strong, short stems. The foliage is dark, semi-glossy green, often too plentiful and certainly disease resistant. This medium-sized compact bush tends to spread in warm climates, and it is one of the finest roses ever raised by the breeder. It was named to honor his wife. **ZONES 4–11.**

SHERIDAN, UK, 1985

'PEER GYNT' × ('DAILY SKETCH' × ['PADDY MCGREDY' × 'PRIMA BALLERINA'])

EDLAND FRAGRANCE AWARD 1981, ROYAL NATIONAL ROSE SOCIETY TORRIDGE AWARD 1991, GLASGOW SILVER MEDAL 1989, GLASGOW FRAGRANCE AWARD 1989

## 'Sheri Anne'

MORsheri *(right)*

MODERN, MINIATURE, ORANGE-
RED, REPEAT-FLOWERING

'Sheri Anne' has long, pointed buds that reveal beautifully shaped orange-red flowers with a yellow base to the petals. The florets are semi-double containing 17 petals and are fragrant. The foliage is glossy green and leathery on a vigorous, upright bush. This rose has been used extensively by breeders all over the world as it has proved to be an extremely good parent. Described as one of the pillars of modern rose breeding from Moore, this decorative little rose has a delicate touch of yellow on the reverse of its petals and will make an enthusiastic follower of all who grow it because it does well even without attention. The repeat cycle is good, but it can get black spot if left unprotected. 'Sheri Anne' is a major achievement for Moore, in that its parents and grandparents have successfully transmitted their desirable qualities to all of their offspring.
ZONES 5–10.

MOORE, USA, 1973

'LITTLE DARLING' ×
'NEW PENNY'

AMERICAN ROSE SOCIETY
AWARD OF EXCELLENCE 1975

## 'Shining Hour'

JACyef *(right)*

MODERN, LARGE-FLOWERED/
HYBRID TEA, DEEP YELLOW,
REPEAT-FLOWERING

The attractive ovoid buds on 'Shining Hour' open to reveal deep bright yellow, double flowers containing 33 petals. The cupped blooms have high symmetrical centers and a moderate fruity fragrance, and are borne both one to a stem and in small sprays of 3–5 flowers. The foliage is large, dark green and semi-glossy on an upright bush. Bill Warriner crossed two of his creations to produce this wonderful rose, which is known as a Grandiflora in America. It has retained the colorfast yellow of the Cluster-flowered 'Sun Flare' and the tall habit of the seed parent, the Large-flowered 'Sunbright'.
ZONES 5–11.

WARRINER, USA, 1989

'SUNBRIGHT' × 'SUN FLARE'

ALL-AMERICA ROSE SELECTION
1991

S

## 'Shocking Blue'

KORblue *(above)*

MODERN, CLUSTER-FLOWERED/
FLORIBUNDA, MAUVE,
REPEAT-FLOWERING

'Shocking Blue' has heavily scented flowers that are a rich lilac-mauve. The double blooms have classic Large-flowered exhibition form, that is, high centers with symmetrical outlines. They are borne in wide sprays against the backdrop of large, glossy foliage. It is a very vigorous grower, reaching 3–4 ft (1–1.2 m) tall. This variety has a number of advantages that somehow contradict themselves: the color is not as good for effective contrast against the dark green foliage, and although it is free flowering, spent blooms need to be removed to encourage the next bloom cycle to begin, otherwise the repeat cycle can be slow. This rose has been used extensively by other breeders to attempt to transmit its superior color qualities and growth habit to their seedlings. **ZONES 4–10.**

KORDES, GERMANY, 1974

SEEDLING × 'SILVER STAR'

## 'Shot Silk' *(below)*

MODERN, LARGE-FLOWERED/
HYBRID TEA, PINK BLEND,
REPEAT-FLOWERING

The cherry-cerise flowers on 'Shot Silk' shade to golden yellow at the bases. The fragrant double blooms have 27 petals with classic high centers. This old favorite of rose growers in the early part of the twentieth century has a truly inspired name for there is something silky about the texture of the petals. This vigorous, upright plant has slightly curled, glossy dark green foliage. In the 1920s, during its greatest popularity, this rose was planted because of the healthy glossy leaves and the novel bloom color. Today's choice of Large-flowered Roses, particularly since the advent of 'Peace' in 1945, has meant that 'Shot Silk' has lost some of its appeal. Nevertheless, it is still grown in some parts of the world. **'Climbing Shot Silk'** (Knight, Australia, 1931; Royal Horticultural Society Award of Garden Merit 1993) can reach 10 ft (3 m) high. Few climbers in this unique color range have both fragrance and healthy foliage. **ZONES 5–10.**

DICKSON, UK, 1924

SEEDLING OF 'HUGH DICKSON' ×
'SUNSTAR'

NATIONAL ROSE SOCIETY GOLD
MEDAL 1923

## 'Showbiz' TANweieke
*(right)*

syns 'Bernhard Däneke Rose', 'Ingrid Weibull'

MODERN, CLUSTER-FLOWERED/
FLORIBUNDA, MEDIUM RED,
REPEAT-FLOWERING

'Showbiz' has bright and bold medium red flowers that are pro-duced in fairly large clusters of 10–30 blooms on very strong basal canes. The semi-double florets with 20 petals have no fragrance. The clusters can last several weeks on the bush before they need to be removed in order to encourage the next cycle. The foliage is dark, glossy green and disease free on a plant with a low, compact habit that reaches 2–4 ft (60 cm–120 cm) in height. This rose is one of the best choices from the menu for a low-growing red Cluster-flowered Rose with grace, color and poise. ZONES 4–10.

TANTAU, GERMANY, 1981

PARENTAGE UNKNOWN

ALL-AMERICA ROSE SELECTION
1985

## 'Shreveport' KORpesh
*(right)*

MODERN, LARGE-FLOWERED/
HYBRID TEA, ORANGE BLEND,
REPEAT-FLOWERING

The ovoid buds of this rose open to reveal blended orange and salmon-pink flowers with 50 petals. The blooms have good symmetrical form with high centers and are generally borne on strong, straight stems in small clusters of 3–5 flowers. There is a light Tea scent. The foliage is large and mid-green and has small prickles that are hooked down-ward. The plant, which is known as a Grandiflora in America, is tall and upright. It was named to honor the city of Shreveport, which is home to the American Rose Society and its extensive rose gardens. ZONES 5–11.

KORDES, GERMANY, 1981

'ZORINA' × 'UWE SEELER'

ALL-AMERICA ROSE SELECTION
1982

S

## 'Shropshire Lass'

*(above)*

MODERN, MODERN SHRUB,
LIGHT PINK

'Shropshire Lass' has fragrant, single-petalled blooms that are blush pink. They are large, to 5 in (12 cm) across. This rose grows like a large shrub or climber but is more compact in habit, and has lush, mid-green foliage. It is tough and winter hardy. In earlier times it would have been classified as an Alba; however, the breeder has chosen to classify it along with his English Roses, although it is not re-peat-flowering. With this 1968 creation, David Austin honors the English countryside where he has lived all his life. ZONES 4–10.

AUSTIN, UK, 1968

'MME BUTTERFLY' × 'MME LEGRAS ST GERMAIN'

## 'Signature'   JACnor

*(below)*

MODERN, LARGE-FLOWERED/
HYBRID TEA, DEEP PINK,
REPEAT-FLOWERING

The sharply pointed, wine red buds on this variety slowly unfurl into deep pink blooms with impeccable high centers. This is a splendid symmetrical, three-dimensional rose, worthy of competing with all the best show winners. The petal sheen bounces the color outward in a dazzling display of color chrome and hue. The large florets are 5 in (12 cm) in diameter, double with 50 petals and have a fruity fragrance. The foliage is large, dark green, and susceptible to mildew and black spot if left unprotected, on a vigorous, medium-sized, compact bush. In cool wet climates the foliage can drop off if it becomes diseased. Praised for its qualities of color, size and form, 'Signature' can proudly take its place with 'Peace' in the evolutionary develop-ment of high-quality Large-flowered Roses. ZONES 5–11.

WARRINER, USA, 1996

'HONOR' × 'FIRST FEDERAL RENAISSANCE'

## 'Silk Hat' AROsilha, AROsilma *(right)*

MODERN, LARGE-FLOWERED/
HYBRID TEA, MAUVE,
REPEAT-FLOWERING

The red-purple flowers of 'Silk Hat' have cream undersides, creating almost a fuchsia petal front look. The double blooms have 45 petals and are symmetrically formed with high centers. The large petal count means the blooms have good staying power, lasting weeks in moderate climates. They are borne singly on strong straight stems and are weather-proof. There is a light fragrance. The foliage is large and matt mid-green on a medium-sized, compact bush. The plant is slow to establish but, once settled, the flower production is good to excellent. ZONES 5–10.

CHRISTENSEN, USA, 1986

'IVORY TOWER' × ('NIGHT 'N'
DAY' × 'PLAIN TALK')

## 'Silver Anniversary' JAClav
syn. 'Heather'

MODERN, LARGE-FLOWERED/HYBRID TEA, MAUVE, REPEAT-FLOWERING

This variety has medium lavender flowers with a hint of yellow at the bases. The double, urn-shaped, exhibition-type blooms have 25–30 petals and a heavy damask fragrance. They are borne singly on long, straight, sturdy stems. The foliage is large and dark green on a tall, upright plant that is susceptible to mildew if left unprotected. There is another rose by the same name from Olesen of Denmark introduced in 1994; it is a lovely white Large-flowered Rose with 41 petals and the blooms tend to occur in small clusters. ZONES 5–10.

CHRISTENSEN, USA, 1990

'CRYSTALLINE' × 'SHOCKING BLUE'

S

## 'Silver Jubilee'
**(right)**

MODERN, LARGE-FLOWERED/
HYBRID TEA, PINK BLEND,
REPEAT-FLOWERING

The fragrant flowers on this famous rose are silvery pink with darker undersides. The double blooms with 33 petals have perfect form and high centers that unfurl gracefully to reveal a portrait in absolute symmetry. They are large, to about 5 in (12 cm) in diameter in cool climates. The foliage is glossy dark green on a vigorous, medium-sized bush with very good bloom production. This rose has received praise worldwide for its beauty in color, form and vigor. It was named to mark the 25th anniversary of the reign of Queen Elizabeth II. There is no doubt that this was Alex Cocker's greatest masterpiece. **ZONES 5–10.**

COCKER, UK, 1978

(['HIGHLIGHT' × 'COLOUR WONDER'] × ['PARKDIREKTOR RIGGERS' × 'PICCADILLY']) × 'MISCHIEF'

ROYAL NATIONAL ROSE SOCIETY PRESIDENT'S INTERNATIONAL TROPHY 1977, BELFAST GOLD MEDAL 1980, PORTLAND GOLD MEDAL 1981, JAMES MASON GOLD MEDAL 1985, ROYAL HORTICULTURAL SOCIETY AWARD OF GARDEN MERIT 1993

## 'Silver Lining'
**(right)**

MODERN, LARGE-FLOWERED/
HYBRID TEA, PINK BLEND,
REPEAT-FLOWERING

The variations in color of the silvery pink flowers on 'Silver Lining' are caused by the climate. The color can range from brighter colors to bicolors of pink and silver, most people finding the color very attractive. The double blooms contain 30 petals and are quite large, at 5 in (12 cm) across. They are fragrant and have classic Large-flowered form with good symmetry and good overall shape. The foliage is dark green and polished on a vigorous, medium-sized bush. **ZONES 5–10.**

DICKSON, UK, 1958

'KARL HERBST' × SEEDLING OF 'EDEN ROSE'

NATIONAL ROSE SOCIETY GOLD MEDAL 1958, PORTLAND GOLD MEDAL 1964

### 'Silver Moon'

*(above)*

MODERN, LARGE-FLOWERED
CLIMBER, WHITE

The long, pointed buds of this rose open to creamy white flowers with an amber base and darker stamens. The blooms are semi-double with 20 petals, large to 5 in (12 cm) across and have a light fragrance. The foliage is large, leathery and glossy green on a vigorous plant that easily grows to 20 ft (6 m) high. In spite of providing only one bloom cycle, it is worth the space for the magnificent early season flowers. **ZONES 4–10.**

VAN FLEET, USA, 1910

(*ROSA WICHURANA* ×
'DEVONIENSIS') × *R. LAEVIGATA*

### 'Silver Wedding'

MODERN, LARGE-FLOWERED/
HYBRID TEA, MAUVE,
REPEAT-FLOWERING

This variety has delicately fragrant flowers that are lavender-lilac fading with age to soft lilac. The large blooms are 4 in (10 cm) across and cupped and are borne mainly in small clusters. The foliage is semi-glossy and mid-green on an upright, vigorous bush. There are two other roses with the same name. The first is a 1921 sport of 'Ophelia' that was introduced by the

Amling Company in the USA. The other **'Silver Wedding'** (shown above) is a lovely Large-flowered Rose with creamy white blooms and

matt mid-green leaves. It was introduced by Gregory in the UK in 1976. **ZONES 5–10.**

LEENDERS, THE NETHERLANDS,
1965

'STERLING SILVER' × SEEDLING

S

### 'Simplicity'  JACink
*(right)*

MODERN, CLUSTER-FLOWERED/
FLORIBUNDA, MEDIUM PINK,
REPEAT-FLOWERING

The long, pointed buds of this rose open to reveal clear medium pink flowers. The semi-double blooms contain 18 petals and have a decorative form. They can be quite large in certain climates, reaching 4 in (10 cm) across. They always come in medium-sized clusters and have a light fragrance. The foliage is mid-green, and is resistant to pests and diseases. 'Simplicity' is healthy and easy to grow and

maintain; growers in the USA have taken to growing it as a hedge-row for an attractive landscape design.
**ZONES 5–11.**

WARRINER, USA, 1978

'ICEBERG' × SEEDLING

NEW ZEALAND GOLD MEDAL 1976

### 'Singin' in the Rain'
MACivy  *(below)*
syns 'Love's Spring',
'Spek's Centennial'

MODERN, CLUSTER-FLOWERED/
FLORIBUNDA, APRICOT BLEND,
REPEAT-FLOWERING

The flowers of this rose are an apricot-copper that lights up any garden. The moderately full florets have 25–30 petals and a light scent, and are borne in large clusters. The foliage is glossy dark green on a medium, upright, free-branching plant that is always in bloom, providing a colorful display all year. It is easy to grow, and resistant to mildew and black spot. Both floral arrangers and exhibitors admire this rose for its vibrant color and wonderful inflorescence.
**ZONES 5–11.**

MCGREDY, NEW ZEALAND, 1991

'SEXY REXY' × 'POT O' GOLD'

ROYAL NATIONAL ROSE SOCIETY
GOLD MEDAL 1991, ALL-
AMERICA ROSE SELECTION 1995

### 'Sir Edward Elgar' AUSprima *(above)*

MODERN, MODERN SHRUB, MEDIUM RED/LIGHT RED, REPEAT-FLOWERING

'Sir Edward Elgar' has crimson-cerise flowers that contain 40–50 petals and are borne one to a stem. The flower form is cupped at first, with the large blooms finally becoming a wonderful flat masterpiece. The foliage is mid-green and semi-glossy on an upright bush reaching 3–4 ft (1–1.2 m) high. This rose was bred from two of David Austin's previous successes in this classification and was named to honor the famous English composer noted for his compositions for royal occasions. **ZONES 5–10.**

AUSTIN, UK, 1992

'MARY ROSE' × 'THE SQUIRE'

### 'Sir Cedric Morris'

MODERN, LARGE-FLOWERED CLIMBER, WHITE

'Sir Cedric Morris' has small buds that open to reveal globular, single-petalled, white flowers with prominent golden anthers. They are borne in large clusters containing as many as 20–40 blooms and have a sweet and pervading fragrance. In the summer bloom cycle the huge clusters are evenly spaced in mass profusion. The foliage is elongated and finely toothed with the stems armed with many thorns. The large prickles are derived from the seed parent. It is a very vigorous grower that blooms only in summer; however, the masses of blooms in the one lavish crop are well worth the wait. It sets hips, which provide a spectacular autumn display of bright orange fruit. **ZONES 4–10.**

MORRIS, UK, 1980

*ROSA GLAUCA* × SEEDLING

S

### 'Sir Thomas Lipton'

MODERN, HYBRID RUGOSA, WHITE, REPEAT-FLOWERING

This rose bears pure white flowers on a plant that is best described as a small rambler reaching 6–8 ft (1.8–2.4 m) tall. It has a vigorous, spreading habit and dark, leathery foliage. The strongly fragrant blooms are double and have a good cupped form, and appear with good continuity from summer to autumn. **ZONES 4–10.**

VAN FLEET, USA, 1900

*ROSA RUGOSA ALBA* × 'CLOTILDE SOUPERT'

### 'Sir Walter Raleigh'

AUSspry *(bottom)*

MODERN, MODERN SHRUB, MEDIUM PINK, REPEAT-FLOWERING

'Sir Walter Raleigh' has rich creamy pink flowers with a form that has been likened to a peony. The florets have over 40 petals, have a cupped form and sport golden stamens in the center. The large blooms are borne singly and are very fragrant. The foliage is dark green and semi-glossy on an upright, vigorous plant that blooms throughout the year. It is extremely hardy and can withstand harsh winter conditions. This rose can be used for a border, low fence and even as a trained pillar, spilling out its heavy fragrance in most climates. It was named by David Austin to commemorate the founding of the first English-speaking colony in America. **ZONES 4–10.**

AUSTIN, UK, 1985

'LILIAN AUSTIN' × 'CHAUCER'

### 'Slater's Crimson China' *(top)*

syns 'Belfield', 'Chinese Monthly Rose', 'Old Crimson China', *Rosa chinensis semperflorens*

OLD, CHINA, MEDIUM RED, REPEAT-FLOWERING

This is one of several roses brought to Europe from the Orient, which were then crossed with the once-flowering old European roses. Many hybrids were raised, giving rise in due course to the current wide range of repeat-blooming varieties. Its small, open, semi-double crimson blooms are of a shade not previously known in Europe and are borne constantly on a low-growing, open, twiggy bush with small, red-tinted leaves. Long believed extinct, it was rediscovered by rosarian Richard Thomson at Belfield in Bermuda in 1956. **ZONES 7–9.**

CIRCA 1790

PARENTAGE UNKNOWN

S

## 'Smarty' INTersmart

MODERN, MODERN SHRUB, LIGHT PINK, REPEAT-FLOWERING

This remarkable rose bears small, almost single flowers with 7–10 light pink petals. They are borne mainly in medium-sized clusters amid the matt, bright green foliage. Repeat-bloom is fast, and there is no need to remove spent blooms to promote the next bloom cycle. 'Smarty' is a low-growing, wide-spreading, hardy and vigorous bush that is easy to grow; it makes an ideal ground cover. There are many small prickles. **ZONES 5–11.**

ILSINK, THE NETHERLANDS, 1979

'YESTERDAY' × SEEDLING

## 'Smooth Melody'

HADmelody  *(left)*

MODERN, CLUSTER-FLOWERED/ FLORIBUNDA, RED BLEND, REPEAT-FLOWERING

'Smooth Melody' carries oval buds that open to give reddish flowers with white centers, white under-sides and red edges, ageing darker. The blooms are double, with about two dozen petals, loosely urn shaped, and have a heavy fruity fragrance. They are produced in small sprays of 3 or 4 amid the semi-glossy, dark green and disease-resistant foliage. **ZONES 5–11.**

DAVIDSON, USA, 1990

'ROYAL FLUSH' × 'SMOOTH LADY'

## 'Smooth Prince'

HADprince  *(below left)*

MODERN, LARGE-FLOWERED/ HYBRID TEA, MEDIUM RED, REPEAT-FLOWERING

This thornless variety is the product of a cross between two other thornless roses from the same series bred by Harvey Davidson. The oval buds open to reveal deep pink-red flowers with a great fruity fragrance. They are double with 27 petals that give an exceptional exhibition form, and are borne singly amid the semi-glossy, mid-green foliage. 'Smooth Prince' has a superior resistance to disease, and is considered a great garden variety with no problems or major faults. Oblong hips are produced in autumn, although they do not set seed. **ZONES 5–11.**

DAVIDSON, USA, 1990

'SMOOTH SAILING' × 'OLD SMOOTHIE'

S

### 'Snow Ballet'

CLAysnow

syn. 'Snowballet'

MODERN, MODERN SHRUB, WHITE, REPEAT-FLOWERING

This interesting shrub produces very large, pure white blooms with 45 petals and a light fragrance. They are produced throughout the warmer months in small and large clusters amid the small and glossy dark green foliage. This disease-resistant plant does not grow tall but prefers to spread outward to create a ground-cover effect. 'Snow Ballet' is a prize-winning variety but is gradually losing its popularity owing to keen competition from some of the white-flowered ground covers from Europe. **ZONES 4–10.**

CLAYWORTH, NEW ZEALAND, 1977

'SEA FOAM' × 'ICEBERG'

BADEN-BADEN GOLD MEDAL 1980

### 'Snow Bride'

*(below)*

syn. 'Snowbride'

MODERN, MINIATURE, WHITE, REPEAT-FLOWERING

Lovely creamy white flowers with excellent Large-flowered form make this rose suitable for exhibition. The florets occur one to a stem or in large clusters. As the petals reflex in a classical manner, the

form is maintained for days. This rose has won many prizes at shows throughout the USA and in the UK. The foliage is small, dark green and glossy on a compact, vigorous plant. This outstanding white Miniature has been popular for more than 16 years because of its ability to consistently produce beautiful

weatherproof blooms on a healthy plant. In some climates it may need some protection from powdery mildew. **ZONES 4–10.**

JOLLY, USA, 1982

'AVENDEL' × 'ZINGER'

AMERICAN ROSE SOCIETY AWARD OF EXCELLENCE 1983

### 'Snow Carpet'

MACcarpe *(bottom)*

syn. 'Blanche Neige'

MODERN, MINIATURE, WHITE, REPEAT-FLOWERING

The small, pompon-style, snow white flowers on this variety have just a hint of cream in cooler climates. The blooms have 55 petals and a light fragrance. This rose was a major breakthrough in the development of Miniature ground covers with a sprawling, vigorous habit and dainty foliage. It generally forms giant mounds of informal flowers against a background of small, mid-green foliage. When it is first transplanted it may sulk for a while, but it will establish itself within months. It has also been used as a weeping tree rose. **ZONES 5–10.**

MCGREDY, NEW ZEALAND, 1980

'NEW PENNY' × 'TEMPLE BELLS'

ROYAL NATIONAL ROSE SOCIETY TRIAL GROUND CERTIFICATE 1978, BADEN-BADEN GOLD MEDAL 1982, ROYAL HORTICULTURAL SOCIETY AWARD OF GARDEN MERIT 1993

S

## 'Snow Meillandina'

MEIgovin *(right)*
syn. 'Snow Sunblaze'
MODERN, MINIATURE, WHITE,
REPEAT-FLOWERING

This dwarf and very
spreading rose is ideal
for hanging baskets.
The very double
flowers with 40–50
petals are pure white
with a touch of yellow
at the bases. They
open slowly from oval
buds to flat, full blooms
that are abundant, long
lasting and have a
quick repeat bloom.
There is good disease
resistance, and the
stems are covered with
many small thorns.

'Snow Meillandina'
is inclined to produce
very full flowers in
spring that have coarse,
vegetative centers,
which is the reason
why it is being replaced
for pot culture by
a newer Meilland
variety called 'Bridal
Meillandina'.
ZONES 5–10.

MEILLAND, FRANCE, 1991
SPORT OF 'LADY SUNBLAZE'

## 'Snowflake' *(top)*

MODERN, RAMBLER, WHITE

This vigorous Rambler
produces clusters of
double white blooms.
It is a conventional lax
*Rosa wichurana* hybrid

with dark glossy
foliage. As it has been
superseded by better
types, it is now only
available from a few
outlets. There are three
other roses with the
name 'Snowflake': a
Tea Rose from 1890, a

Large-flowered Rose
from Kordes in 1970
and a Miniature from
1977. ZONES 5–9.

CANT, UK, 1922

PARENTAGE UNKNOWN

NATIONAL ROSE SOCIETY GOLD
MEDAL 1921

S

### 'Snowline' *(right)*
syn. 'Edelweiß'

MODERN, CLUSTER-FLOWERED/
FLORIBUNDA, WHITE,
REPEAT-FLOWERING

This classic rose from
the 1960s gives medium-
sized, pure white or
creamy blooms that
have a light fragrance.
Double, with 31 petals,
they are produced
freely in large trusses
on this low-growing
plant with glossy dark
foliage. As it grows to
about 3 ft (1 m) high,
it is an ideal bedding
or border selection.
**ZONES 5–10.**

POULSEN, DENMARK, 1970

PARENTAGE UNKNOWN

ROYAL NATIONAL ROSE SOCIETY
TRIAL GROUND CERTIFICATE 1970

### 'Softee'  MORfree
*(right)*

MODERN, MINIATURE, WHITE,
REPEAT-FLOWERING

This novel Miniature
Rose has creamy white
decorative flowers with
about 35 petals that
tend to open quickly
to the fully open stage.
The florets have a light
fragrance. The stems
have very few thorns
and no prickles, and
the foliage is small and
medium green on a
spreading, compact
bush. White pompon-
like flowers borne in
clusters cover the bush, making it an attractive
garden plant. There is
a climbing sport of
this rose that can be
successfully trained on a veranda or over
a handrail to stunning
effect. **ZONES 5–10.**

MOORE, USA, 1983

PARENTAGE UNKNOWN

## 'Softly Softly'

HARkotur *(right)*

MODERN, CLUSTER-FLOWERED/
FLORIBUNDA, PINK BLEND,
REPEAT-FLOWERING

The flowers of this rose are pink to creamy pink depending on the climate in which it is grown. The blooms are double, with 35 petals, large and have a light fragrance. The foliage is an attractive olive green. 'Softly Softly' is considered by some to be a Large-flowered Rose. The variety was named after a very popular television series in the UK during the 1980s. ZONES 5–10.

HARKNESS, UK, 1977

'WHITE COCKADE' ×
(['HIGHLIGHT' × 'COLOUR
WONDER'] × ['PARKDIREKTOR
RIGGERS' × 'PICCADILLY'])

## 'Soleil d'Or' *(right)*

MODERN, LARGE-FLOWERED/
HYBRID TEA, YELLOW BLEND,
REPEAT-FLOWERING

This rose is remarkable because it was the first of the class of Pernetianas now incorporated into the Large-flowered Roses. A breakthrough was made in introducing the deep yellow and range of orange shades of its wild parent to the Modern Garden Roses. The foliage is rich green, with ferny leaves similar to *Rosa foetida*. The deep orange-yellow to tawny gold-shaded red flowers are very large, double, cupped and flattish, with muddled centers. Unfortunately, a susceptibility to black spot was transmitted to many of its class; this has now been almost bred out and the new colors are part of the heritage of Modern Large- and Cluster-flowered Roses. ZONES 5–9.

PERNET-DUCHER, FRANCE, 1900

(SEEDLING OF 'ANTOINE DUCHER'
× *ROSA FOETIDA PERSIANA*) ×
LARGE-FLOWERED ROSE

S

### 'Solfaterre' *(left)*
syn. 'Solfatare'

OLD, NOISETTE, MEDIUM
YELLOW, REPEAT-FLOWERING

'Solfaterre' is a vigor-
ous Noisette climber
that, like its parent, will
ascend into a tree. The
fragrant, light sulfur-
yellow flowers are
large, double and flat-
tish and are produced
freely. Too much sun
will bleach them and
this should be borne in
mind when siting the
plant. ZONES 7–9.

BOYAU, FRANCE, 1843

SEEDLING OF 'LAMARQUE'

### 'Solitaire' MACyefre
*(above)*

MODERN, LARGE-FLOWERED/
HYBRID TEA, YELLOW BLEND,
REPEAT-FLOWERING

The large blooms are
similar to the famous
'Peace', especially in
shape and color. This
vigorous, tall grower
reaches 6–8 ft (2–2.5 m)
high by 3–4 ft (1–1.2 m)
wide. The fragrant
blooms are weather-
proof. ZONES 5–10.

MCGREDY, NEW ZEALAND, 1987

'FREUDE' × 'BENSON & HEDGES
GOLD'

ROYAL NATIONAL ROSE SOCIETY
PRESIDENT'S INTERNATIONAL
TROPHY 1985

### 'Sombreuil'

*(bottom)*

syn. 'Colonial White'

OLD, CLIMBING TEA, WHITE, REPEAT-FLOWERING

The flowers of this rose typify the Old Rose style. They are white, with an occasional touch of rose and yellow. The flat, quilled, quartered and very double blooms can probably best be described as refined. They are well scented. The plant climbs to a moderate height. Mlle de Sombreuil was a heroine of the French Revolution who is reputed to have drunk a glass of the blood of an aristocrat to prove her father's non-aristocratic status. This rose is among the hardier of the Teas. ZONES 7–9.

ROBERT, FRANCE, 1850
SEEDLING OF 'GIGANTESQUE'

### 'Sommermärchen'

KORpinka *(top)*

syns 'Berkshire', 'Pink Sensation', 'Summer Fairy Tales', 'Xenia'

MODERN, MODERN SHRUB, DEEP PINK, REPEAT-FLOWERING

This vigorous grower can also be considered a Ground Cover Rose as it makes a shallow pyramid of itself, spreading twice as far as its modest height. It is suitable for the front of a large bed, or grouped by itself.

The medium-sized, semi-double flowers are carried freely in clusters through summer and autumn on long, arching stems. They are deep cherry pink, with gold stamens, and have a pleasing scent. The dark glossy leaves make this an attractive plant. ZONES 4–9.

KORDES, GERMANY, 1991
'WEISSE IMMENSEE' × SEEDLING
ROYAL NATIONAL ROSE SOCIETY TRIAL GROUND CERTIFICATE 1992, BADEN-BADEN, GENEVA AND GLASGOW GOLD MEDALS 1996

S

### 'Sonia' MEIhelvet *(below)*
### syns 'Sonia Meilland', 'Sweet Promise'
MODERN, LARGE-FLOWERED/HYBRID TEA, PINK BLEND,
REPEAT-FLOWERING

This is probably the most popular greenhouse rose in the world. It bears salmon-pink flowers that are suffused with coral to yellow as they emerge from the elegant, long buds. The blooms are large, with a strong fruity fragrance, but the color can fade in hot climates. It has thick, attractive, dark green foliage. It may also need protection from fungal diseases. 'Sonia' was one of the top money earners for the House of Meilland. It prefers full sun and rich well-drained soil. **ZONES 5–11.**

MEILLAND, FRANCE, 1974

'ZAMBRA' × ('BACCARÀ' × 'WHITE KNIGHT')

### 'Sonnenschirn' TANmirsch *(below)*
### syn. 'Broadlands'
MODERN, MODERN SHRUB, LIGHT YELLOW, REPEAT-FLOWERING

The pale creamy yellow flowers of this rose are borne profusely in big clusters that have a sweet fresh scent. The blooms are double and cupped. 'Sonnenschirn' blooms throughout the year in warm climates, and the plant is a dense and spreading, vigorous bush that is suitable as a ground cover since it grows to no more than 2 ft (60 cm) high. **ZONES 4–10.**

TANTAU, GERMANY, 1993

PARENTAGE UNKNOWN

ROYAL NATIONAL ROSE SOCIETY PRESIDENT'S INTERNATIONAL
TROPHY 1995, BRITISH ASSOCIATION OF ROSE BREEDERS,
BREEDERS' SELECTION 1996

S

### 'Sophie's Perpetual' *(right)*
syns 'Bengal Centifolia', 'Dresden China', 'Paul's Dresden China'

OLD, CHINA, PINK BLEND, REPEAT-FLOWERING

This 'discovered' rose was re-introduced in 1960, having been found and named for Countess Beckendorf by rosarian Humphrey Brooke. The flowers, which are globular and somewhat cupped, are a pale blush pink over-laid with cerise-crimson, particularly on the outer petals. The scent is good and the bush repeats continually. It can be grown as a shrub or moderate climber and is almost thornless. The foliage is dark green. **ZONES 7–9.**

PRE-1928

PARENTAGE UNKNOWN

### 'Soupert et Notting' *(right)*

OLD, MOSS, DEEP PINK, REPEAT-FLOWERING

'Soupert et Notting' deserves attention owing to its repeat-flowering and short stature, never attaining heights of over 3 ft (1 m), even in good soil. The shrub is formed by numerous thin and upright shoots, which are sparsely adorned with brownish green moss. The foliage is small and bright grayish-green, and the flower buds are moderately mossy and arranged in small clusters. Relatively small for a Moss Rose, the flowers are $1\frac{1}{2}$–2 in (4–5 cm) across, initially cupped, then flat, very full but tidily formatted and fragrant. **ZONES 5–10.**

PERNET PÈRE, FRANCE, 1874

PARENTAGE UNKNOWN

### 'South Seas' *(right)*
syn. 'Mers du Sud'

MODERN, LARGE-FLOWERED/HYBRID TEA, ORANGE-PINK, REPEAT-FLOWERING

There are two opinions about this upright variety: some people rave about the very large, coral-pink blooms, while others find them loose and informal. They are double, with up to 48 petals, cupped to flat in shape and fragrant. The color tends to fade to silvery white with age. The blooms are borne on long, straight stems, and while the plant is vigorous, flowering is somewhat shy. **ZONES 5–11.**

MOREY, USA, 1962

'RAPTURE' × SEEDLING OF A LARGE-FLOWERED CLIMBER

S

### 'Southampton'
syn. 'Susan Ann'

MODERN, CLUSTER-FLOWERED/
FLORIBUNDA, APRICOT BLEND,
REPEAT-FLOWERING

This variety was selected by the Civic Authority in Southampton, England to bear the name of the port. Its flowers have about 28 apricot petals, which form a pleasing shape, and are carried in moderate-sized clusters on a tall and spreading bush. 'Southampton' is well regarded in the UK for its color and vigor, and it even does well in hot climates as the flowers do not fade with age. The foliage is glossy green and disease resistant. ZONES 5–11.

HARKNESS, UK, 1971

('ANN ELIZABETH' × 'ALL GOLD')
× 'YELLOW CUSHION'

ROYAL NATIONAL ROSE SOCIETY
TRIAL GROUND CERTIFICATE
1971, BADEN-BADEN SILVER
MEDAL 1973, BELFAST
GOLD MEDAL 1974, ROYAL
HORTICULTURAL SOCIETY AWARD
OF GARDEN MERIT 1993

### 'Souvenir d'Alphonse Lavallée'  *(above)*
OLD, HYBRID PERPETUAL, DARK RED, REPEAT-FLOWERING

This floriferous rose bears dark velvety crimson to maroon flowers that are susceptible to burning in hot sun. They have a rich scent. A rather sprawling shrub, it makes a tall plant if tethered, or it can be grown as a short climber. It is somewhat similar to 'Souvenir du Docteur Jamain'. Alphonse Lavallée was an amateur dendrologist and one-time President of the French National Horticultural Society. He died in 1884. ZONES 5–9.

VERDIER, FRANCE, 1884

PARENTAGE UNKNOWN

### 'Souvenir de Christophe Cochet'
*(rose hips, left)*

MODERN, HYBRID RUGOSA, MEDIUM PINK, REPEAT-FLOWERING

Soft pink, semi-double flowers with pale yellow anthers and brisk sepals adorn this rose throughout summer. They are large with a lovely scent and in autumn, large red hips are formed. 'Souvenir de Christophe Cochet' is a vigorous grower with typical, wrinkled, Rugosa-looking leaves. It is winter hardy. ZONES 4–10.

COCHET-COCHET, FRANCE, 1894

PARENTAGE UNKNOWN

## 'Souvenir de Claudius Denoyel'

MODERN, LARGE-FLOWERED
CLIMBER, DARK RED,
REPEAT-FLOWERING

The long, pointed buds of this rose open to rich crimson-red flowers tinted with scarlet. They are very large, cupped and fragrant. This is a fairly vigorous Climber, although the blooming is not particularly profuse, especially after the initial spring flush. It can be used on a pillar, pergola or on a wall. **ZONES 5–10.**

CHAMBARD, FRANCE, 1920

'CHÂTEAU DE CLOS VOUGEOT' ×
'COMMANDEUR JULES
GRAVEREAUX'

ROYAL HORTICULTURAL SOCIETY
AWARD OF GARDEN MERIT 1993

## 'Souvenir de la Malmaison' *(above)*
syn. 'Queen of Beauty'

OLD, BOURBON, LIGHT PINK, REPEAT-FLOWERING

This, the most famous and possibly the most beautiful of the Bourbon Roses, was named for Empress Josephine's famous home in Paris. The fragrant flowers are large, quartered and very double. They are pale flesh pink, becoming paler with age. The blooms ball in wet weather, a general complaint about the Old Garden Roses and one from which the Modern Roses are a good deal freer. The repeat-flowering plant is low growing and bushy. This rose caused such a stir that it is said that Mme Béluze used to hide at the window at night to watch for thieves who might try to steal cuttings. **'Climbing Souvenir de la Malmaison'** (Bennett, UK, 1938) grows to about 6 ft (1.8 m) high. It should be kept out of the rain, or it will produce a great crop of balled, unopened blooms. **ZONES 5–9.**

BÉLUZE, FRANCE, 1843

'MME DESPREZ' × TEA ROSE

## 'Souvenir de Mme Auguste Charles'

OLD, BOURBON, MEDIUM PINK,
REPEAT-FLOWERING

The flowers of this rose are small and compact. They are full of petals and somewhat resemble a camellia. The color is between flesh and rosy pink. It is a tall, lax plant in the Bourbon manner and has rather coarse leaves. It is most suitable for a column or perhaps for tying down. **ZONES 5–9.**

MOREAU & ROBERT, FRANCE,
1866

PARENTAGE UNKNOWN

S

### 'Souvenir de Mme Boullet' *(right)*

MODERN, LARGE-FLOWERED/
HYBRID TEA, DEEP YELLOW,
REPEAT-FLOWERING

Long and pointed buds reveal deep yellow flowers that cover this rose in summer. They are large, well formed and full, and come mostly one per stem. The color tends to fade in hot climates. 'Souvenir de Mme Boullet' is vigorous with a tendency to spread rather than grow tall. It is not hardy. **'Climbing Souvenir de Madame Boullet'** is a sport discovered by the Californian rose breeders Howard and Smith in 1930. It retains all the desirable characteristics of the parent, except that it can be trained onto walls and pillars. **ZONES 7–11.**

PERNET-DUCHER, FRANCE, 1921

'SUNBURST' × SEEDLING

### 'Souvenir de Mme Léonie Viennot' *(above)*

OLD, CLIMBING TEA, YELLOW
BLEND, REPEAT-FLOWERING

This rose is a Tea climber par excellence that will go high into trees and is very long lived. The large, loosely shaped flowers are light rose pink with yellow and coppery orange tints and perhaps a little gold. Some find the color just a little harsh and reminiscent of 'Lorraine Lee'. It flowers early with a long period and an occasional later repeat. It flowers on old wood, so the less pruning the better, but there will always be plenty of very old wood to cut out. This rose is highly recommended. **ZONES 7–9.**

BERNAIX, FRANCE, 1898

'GLOIRE DE DIJON' × SEEDLING

### 'Souvenir de Philemon Cochet' *(right)*

MODERN, HYBRID RUGOSA, WHITE, REPEAT-FLOWERING

The flowers of this sport resemble the parent in every way, except that they have a greatly increased complement of petals and are not as prolific. The white blooms with a rose center are so double that they resemble perfect spheres when fully open. The variety is not as prolific as the parent. Philemon Cochet was the brother of the breeder. **ZONES 4–10.**

COCHET-COCHET, FRANCE, 1899

SPORT OF 'BLANC DOUBLE DE COUBERT'

### 'Souvenir de St Anne's' *(right)*

OLD, BOURBON, LIGHT PINK, REPEAT-FLOWERING

This sport was discovered in the garden of St Anne's, a property of Lady Ardilaun near Dublin. Graham Thomas recounts that it was preserved for many years by Lady Moore of Rathfarnham in Dublin. This rose has fewer petals than its parent and stands up better to rain, but it is less spectacular. However, it is more fragrant, the scent residing, according to Thomas, in the many stamens. It makes a very bushy, quite tall shrub. **ZONES 5–9.**

HILLING, UK, 1950

SPORT OF 'SOUVENIR DE LA MALMAISON'

ROYAL HORTICULTURAL SOCIETY AWARD OF GARDEN MERIT 1993

**S**

### 'Souvenir de Thérèse Lovet' *(above)*

OLD, TEA, DEEP RED, REPEAT-FLOWERING

The deep, rather dull, crimson color of this
variety's flowers is not all that usual in the Teas,
and a comparison with 'Francis Dubreuil' springs
to mind. The plant enjoys vigorous growth and
has dark green foliage and big hooked thorns.
This rose needs a hot climate. It is very popular
in Australia. **ZONES 7–9.**

LEVET, FRANCE, 1886

'ADAM' × 'SAFRANO À FLEURS ROUGES'

### 'Souvenir d'Elise Vardon' *(bottom)*

OLD, TEA, WHITE BLEND, REPEAT-FLOWERING

This is a moderately
strong-growing Tea
Rose with somewhat
delicate, tender flowers.
The medium-sized
flowers are very double
and fragrant. The color
is not really white,
though it can fade
to white; it has been
variously described
as chamois, bronzish
cream, bronzish pink
and creamy fawn.
**ZONES 7–9.**

MAREST, FRANCE, 1855

PARENTAGE UNKNOWN

### 'Souvenir du Docteur Jamain' *(top right)*

OLD, HYBRID PERPETUAL, DARK RED, REPEAT-FLOWERING

The fragrant blooms of
this rose are dark wine
colored with purple
shades. The petals have
good substance and
verge on black. It is a
tall-growing shrub that
can be grown against
a wall, but should be
located to avoid strong
sunlight, which is apt
to burn the flowers.
This rose needs plenty
of nourishment to
ensure good growth
and reliable repeat-
flowering. **ZONES 5–9.**

LACHARME, FRANCE, 1865

SEEDLING OF 'CHARLES LEFÉBVRE'

S

## 'Souvenir d'un Ami' *(right)*

OLD, TEA, LIGHT PINK, REPEAT-FLOWERING

The cupped, double and intensely fragrant flowers of 'Souvenir d'un Ami' are pale rose, tinted with salmon. The bush is vigorous and tall. This was one of the best-loved roses of Victorian England, because of its hardiness and ease of cultivation. The name means 'in remembrance of a friend', which sounds romantic, but it has been said that the friend was only the person who negotiated the deal between the amateur raiser and the distributor. ZONES 7–9.

BELOT-DEFOUGÈRE, FRANCE, 1846

PARENTAGE UNKNOWN

## 'Sparkling Scarlet'

MEIhaiti, MEIhati *(right)*
syn. 'Iskra'

MODERN, CLUSTER-FLOWERED CLIMBER, MEDIUM RED, REPEAT-FLOWERING

The bright scarlet-red flowers of 'Sparkling Scarlet' have a strong fruity scent. They also have 13 petals per bloom and are of medium size. This variety makes a wonderful display with its large clusters on strong stems that seem to last a long time. It grows to about 10 ft (3.5 m) high by about 5 ft (1.5 m) wide. ZONES 4–11.

MEILLAND, FRANCE, 1970

'DANSE DES SYLPHES' × 'ZAMBRA'

PARIS GOLD MEDAL 1969

## 'Sparrieshoop'
(*right*)

MODERN, MODERN SHRUB,
LIGHT PINK, REPEAT-FLOWERING

Named for the village where Kordes' have their now famous nursery, 'Sparrieshoop' has long, pointed buds that open to almost single, sweetly scented flowers that are borne in large trusses of apple blossom pink. They are large and sweetly fragrant with many golden yellow stamens. The bush tends to cover itself with flowers throughout the season. The vigorous growth habit permits the long canes, which are bronze when young, to be trained as either a short climber or a big spreading shrub; it seems to have inherited its rampant growth from its Sweet Briar parent, 'Magnifica'. The glossy dark foliage is subject to mildew if not protected. 'Sparrieshoop' has enjoyed well over 40 years of popularity worldwide. ZONES 4–11.

KORDES, GERMANY, 1953

('BABY CHÂTEAU' × 'ELSE POULSEN') × 'MAGNIFICA'

PORTLAND GOLD MEDAL 1971

## 'Spartan'  (*right*)
syn. 'Aparte'

MODERN, CLUSTER-FLOWERED/
FLORIBUNDA, ORANGE-RED,
REPEAT-FLOWERING

The pointed buds of this cultivar open to give vibrant orange-red to reddish coral flowers that have good symmetry and shape. These large blooms are produced either singly or in small clusters, and they have a strong fragrance. They provide a stunning display amid the glossy dark green leaves that adorn this vigorous bush. In spite of all the awards gained by this variety, it failed to win the prestigious All-America Rose Selection; the introducers therefore gave 'Spartan' extra publicity, which included colored pages in both *Time Magazine* and *The Saturday Evening Post.* In the years that followed its introduction, it has been used extensively as a breeding parent with much success. ZONES 5–11.

BOERNER, USA, 1955

'GERANIUM RED' × 'FASHION'

NATIONAL ROSE SOCIETY PRESIDENT'S INTERNATIONAL TROPHY 1954, PORTLAND GOLD MEDAL 1955, AMERICAN ROSE SOCIETY DAVID FUERSTENBERG PRIZE 1957, ARS NATIONAL GOLD CERTIFICATE 1961

### 'Spectacular' *(right)*

syns 'Danse du Feu', 'Mada'

**MODERN, LARGE-FLOWERED CLIMBER, ORANGE-RED, REPEAT-FLOWERING**

The oval buds of this rose open to scarlet-red, fragrant flowers with 33 petals that have a cupped to flat shape. They occur mainly in clusters against glossy bronze foliage. 'Spectacular' is free flowering and maintains a colorful display throughout the season. It is very hardy, even tolerating shade, but is susceptible to black spot if left unprotected. It will climb to about 8–10 ft (2.5–3.5 m) high. **ZONES 4–10.**

MALLERIN, FRANCE, 1953

'PAUL'S SCARLET CLIMBER' × SEEDLING OF *ROSA MULTIFLORA*

### 'Spencer' *(right)*

**OLD, HYBRID PERPETUAL, LIGHT PINK, REPEAT-FLOWERING**

'Spencer' bears satin pink flowers with outer petals reflexed with white. They are cupped, flat and very double, befitting the Hybrid Perpetual class. They are so full, however, that they open badly in rain. It is a medium-sized shrub in the style of its progenitor 'Merveille de Lyon' and is presumably liable to sport back to it. **ZONES 5–9.**

PAUL, UK, 1892

SPORT OF 'MERVEILLE DE LYON'

S

### 'Spice Drop' SAVswet *(below)*

MODERN, MINIATURE, ORANGE-PINK, REPEAT-FLOWERING

Small salmon-pink buds on this variety open to salmon-pink flowers with 35 petals. The double florets have good-quality exhibition-type form and are carried one to a stem. The attractive, well-formed flowers literally cover the tiny bush with color and are borne throughout the flowering season. The dwarf, compact plant is well furnished with foliage that is small, semi-glossy and dark green. This rose is one of those preferred by floral artists for their Miniature Rose designs. It is best grown in a container, where it will be easy to keep clean. 'Spice Drop' is a winner in every respect and its popularity is guaranteed. **ZONES 5–10.**

SAVILLE, USA, 1982

('SHERI ANNE' × 'GLENFIDDICH') × (SEEDLING OF A MOSS ROSE × ['SARABANDE' × 'LITTLE CHIEF'])

### 'Spiced Coffee'

MACjuliat *(bottom)* syns 'Old Spice', 'Vidal Sassoon'

MODERN, LARGE-FLOWERED/HYBRID TEA, RUSSET, REPEAT-FLOWERING

This variety is a real novelty rose that can attract attention on account of its unusual color. In cool climates, the color is more pink and lavender; in hot climates, the color is at its best—a real putty tone. The very fragrant blooms have only 15–25 petals and are borne amid the matt green leaves. The variety is mainly of interest to floral arrangers because of the color. Unfortunately it lacks sufficient vigor and diseases such as mildew and black spot can be a major problem. 'Spiced Coffee' seems to have inherited some of its elegance from its award-winning seed parent 'Harmonie'. **ZONES 5–11.**

MCGREDY, NEW ZEALAND, 1990

'HARMONIE' × 'BIG PURPLE'

BRITISH ASSOCIATION OF ROSE BREEDERS, BREEDERS' SELECTION 1994

## 'Splendens'
syns 'Ayrshire
Splendens', *Rosa
arvensis splendens*
OLD, AYRSHIRE, WHITE

*Rosa arvensis*, the rose
of the field, is native to
southern England and
considered by some to
have been Shakespeare's
Musk Rose. This rose
is one of a number of
scramblers and ramblers
that were developed
from it in the early
nineteenth century.
The synonym 'Ayrshire
Splendens' comes from
the Earl of Loudon
in Ayrshire, who was
involved in its develop-
ment. This rambling
variety is possibly the
best of the hybrids,
with loose white flowers
with hints of pink. Like
its parent, it tolerates
shade. Perhaps its most
interesting feature is
its scent, which has
been likened to myrrh,
a scent that is also
found in the Albas
'Belle Amour' and
'Belle Isis' and in some
of the modern David
Austin roses, notably
'Constance Spry'.
'Splendens' flowers
only once and has very
lax growth. **ZONES 5–9.**

PRE-1837

HYBRID OF *ROSA ARVENSIS*

## 'Splendens' *(top)*
syns 'Frankfurt', *Rosa
gallica splendens*
OLD, GALLICA, MEDIUM RED

This Old Garden
Rose has semi-double,

crimson blooms with
purplish overtones.
They have an excellent
contrasting mass of
golden yellow stamens
at the centers. In the
garden, this is a
colorful rose near
the back of any mixed
border. **ZONES 5–10.**

PRE-1583

PARENTAGE UNKNOWN

## 'Spong' *(right)*
OLD, CENTIFOLIA, MEDIUM PINK

A dwarfish type
Centifolia, this variety
has little pink flowers
that are fragrant and
rather more open
than pompons with
randomly arranged
centers. These are
borne in sizeable
clusters and flower
only once in early
summer. A notable
fault of the blooms is
that they do not drop

after fading; instead,
they remain on the
plant, which necessi-
tates deadheading if
the plant is to remain
tidy. It makes a good
and healthy bush for
the front of a border
or among herbaceous
plants. It is also good in
tubs or urns, and the
grayish green, prickly
stems are covered by

similar-colored,
medium-sized, serrated
leaves. The rather
ordinary name is said
to be that of a gardener
who took it up. 'Rose
de Meaux' and 'Petite
de Hollande' are better
medium pink
Centifolia Roses.
**ZONES 4–9.**

FRANCE, CIRCA 1805

PARENTAGE UNKNOWN

S

### 'Squatters Dream' *(right)*

MODERN, MODERN SHRUB, MEDIUM YELLOW, REPEAT-FLOWERING

The bright medium yellow flowers on this
variety become much lighter with age. Single and
moderately fragrant, they look attractive against
the dark bronze-green leaves. This bush has a
dwarf growth habit. ZONES 7–10.

CLARK, AUSTRALIA, 1923

*ROSA GIGANTEA* SEEDLING × *ROSA GIGANTEA* SEEDLING

### 'Stacey Sue' *(below)*

MODERN, MINIATURE, LIGHT PINK, REPEAT-FLOWERING

'Stacey Sue' has short, pointed buds that open
to soft pink flowers with almost 60 petals. The
florets have a light fragrance and a rosette-type
form. They are produced in clusters on strong
stems that cover the bushy plant. This healthy
plant has small, glossy green foliage and repeats
quickly, but has a tendency to spread if not
groomed. It can create a beautiful mound of
sprays with lovely light pink flowers, but it is not
widely known outside the UK. ZONES 5–11.

MOORE, USA, 1976

'ELLEN POULSEN' × 'FAIRY PRINCESS'

ROYAL HORTICULTURAL SOCIETY AWARD OF GARDEN MERIT 1993

### 'Stainless Steel'

WEIkblusi

MODERN, LARGE-FLOWERED/
HYBRID TEA, MAUVE,
REPEAT-FLOWERING

This rose is well
named, as it produces
clear silvery gray-
lavender flowers. Each
large, well-formed
bloom has 35–40 petals
and is borne mostly
singly, but there are a
few clusters. They are
very fragrant, which is
the case with most roses
of this color, and last
well, so are good for
picking. The foliage is
large and abundant,
mid-green and semi-
glossy, and its habit is
tall and vigorous. The
flower production is
good and it is quick
to repeat. The color is
unlike that of any other
rose, and it combines
well with most roses
with mauve shades.
ZONES 5–11.

CARRUTH, USA, 1991

'BLUE NILE' × 'SILVERADO'

S

## 'Stanwell Perpetual'  *(right)*

OLD, SCOTS, WHITE, REPEAT-FLOWERING

This rose was found as a seedling in a garden in
Stanwell, and what an extraordinary find it was.
It has the habit and leaves of the Scots Roses and
very much more of the repeat-flowering features
of the Autumn Damasks. It bears pale blush pink
flowers that are double, flat and quilled, and have
quartered petals. It flowers repeatedly, if not
really perpetually, and has a delicious fragrance.
This is a lax, thorny bush of medium to tall
height. The foliage is small, ferny and burnet-like
with 9 leaflets; the stems are very prickly. Old
wood should be cut from the base each season
to stimulate new growth. ZONES 4–9.

LEE, UK, 1838

POSSIBLY A REPEAT-FLOWERING
DAMASK × SCOTS

## 'Starina'  MEIgabi,

MEIgali  *(above)*

MODERN, MINIATURE, ORANGE-
RED, REPEAT-FLOWERING

The blooms on
'Starina' are orange-
scarlet-vermilion and
are borne singly or in
small clusters. They
are beautifully formed
exhibition-type, double
florets, complemented
by small, glossy green
foliage. It has a dwarf
habit and is a classical
Miniature Rose of the
twentieth century,
defining the standard
for what is expected
of Miniature Roses.
Its popularity has
spread worldwide and
it is regarded as the
'Peace' of Miniature
Roses. ZONES 5–10.

MEILLAND, FRANCE, 1965

('DANY ROBIN' × 'FIRE KING') ×
'PERLA DE MONTSERRAT'

JAPAN GOLD MEDAL 1968,
ANERKANNTE DEUTSCHE ROSE
1971

S

## 'Stars 'n' Stripes'
*(right)*

**MODERN, MINIATURE, RED BLEND, REPEAT-FLOWERING**

This rose has long, pointed buds that open to reveal flowers that are an evenly striped carmine red and white. The florets have 21 petals, a sweet fragrance and are borne in clusters. The foliage is light to mid-green on a tall, upright bush, making it ideal for a hedge. With this rose, Moore achieved his wish to introduce striping into the Miniature breeding line. He began by crossing the Cluster-flowered 'Little Darling' with the Hybrid Perpetual 'Ferdinand Pichard', to produce a key seedling he named Striped #14. Using 'Little Chief' as a seed parent and Striped #14 as the pollen parent, Moore produced the first step in evolving striped Miniatures. That rose was destined to become 'Stars 'n' Stripes' and was introduced in time to help celebrate the bicentennial of the United States in 1976. Needless to say, it has played an important role in the development of other striped varieties. **ZONES 5–10.**

MOORE, USA, 1975

'LITTLE CHIEF' × ('LITTLE DARLING' × 'FERDINAND PICHARD')

## 'Steffi Graf' HELgraf *(above)*

**MODERN, LARGE-FLOWERED/HYBRID TEA, MEDIUM PINK, REPEAT-FLOWERING**

The plump buds of this bush rose open to perfectly formed, tight-centered, urn-shaped blooms on upright stems. They are mostly borne singly. The color is light pink, although there are touches of deep pink, especially around the petal edges. The foliage is dark green. **ZONES 5–10.**

HETZEL, GERMANY, 1993

PARENTAGE UNKNOWN

## 'Stephens' Big Purple' STEbigpu
*(right)*

syns 'Big Purple', 'Nuit d'Orient'

MODERN, LARGE-FLOWERED/ HYBRID TEA, MAUVE BLEND, REPEAT-FLOWERING

This rose was bred by the late Pat Stephens of Te Awamatu, New Zealand. Both Paddy and his wife were leading rose exhibitors for a great many years. 'Stephens' Big Purple' is the deepest purple of all Large-flowered Roses; the large and oval buds open slowly to reveal double flowers with 35 petals. They are very fragrant and are produced on long stems on a tall, upright bush with large, matt mid-green, healthy foliage. This is a good producer but it is a little slow to repeat bloom. It can be up to exhibition standard in cool weather and is a good rose for cutting, where its unique color and strong perfume can be appreciated indoors. **ZONES 5–10.**

STEPHENS, NEW ZEALAND, 1985

SEEDLING × 'PURPLE SPLENDOUR'

## 'Sterling Silver'
*(right)*

MODERN, LARGE-FLOWERED/ HYBRID TEA, MAUVE BLEND, REPEAT-FLOWERING

This variety was one of the first of the silvery mauve roses. The color is very beautiful, quite different from all other varieties, and the petals unfold from long, pointed buds to form double flowers with good substance. They are high centered, cupped and strongly scented at the full bloom stage, and usually appear in small clusters. Sadly, the flower production is not high and the repeat blooming is rather slow. The foliage is glossy, large and disease free on this rather short and upright plant, although it is still worth growing for its unique color, which is much more blue than most mauve roses. The blooms are good for cutting, looking best in silver and pewter containers. **ZONES 5–11.**

FISHER, USA, 1957

SEEDLING × 'PEACE'

S

## 'Strawberry Swirl'
*(right)*

MODERN, MINIATURE, RED
BLEND, REPEAT-FLOWERING

The oval buds on this rose open to blooms with 48 petals that are red mixed with white and are reminiscent of the Gallica 'Rosa Mundi', although the form is like a Large-flowered Rose. The florets are double and display their Moss character with many fine prickles on the stems. It is a spreading bush that puts out long and arching canes, along which the flowers grow. This rose is ideal for planting on a bank or in a hanging basket. The unique color combination delighted many rosarians with the random swirling effect across the petals. **ZONES 5–10.**

MOORE, USA, 1978

'LITTLE DARLING' × SEEDLING
OF A MINIATURE ROSE

## 'Stretch Johnson'
MACfirwal *(right)*
syns 'Rock 'n' Roll', 'Tango'

MODERN, MODERN SHRUB,
RED BLEND, REPEAT-FLOWERING

This is one of Sam McGredy's best hand-painted roses: the flowers are brilliant orange-scarlet with yellow centers and an attractive suffusion of orange through the petals. The undersides of the 15 petals are silvery orange. The blooms are borne in small and large clusters on a tall, almost climbing bush. The foliage is mid-green, semi-glossy, close jointed and very profuse. In autumn, large shoots appear from the base bearing large heads of colorful blooms. Like all the hand-painted roses, it produces its best flowers in autumn or during cool weather. It is excellent as an eye-catching pillar rose. **ZONES 4–11.**

MCGREDY, NEW ZEALAND, 1988

'SEXY REXY' × 'MAESTRO'

ROYAL NATIONAL ROSE SOCIETY
GOLD MEDAL 1988, GLASGOW
SILVER MEDAL 1992, GOLDEN
ROSE OF THE HAGUE 1993,
ROYAL HORTICULTURAL SOCIETY
AWARD OF GARDEN MERIT 1993

## 'Sue Lawley'

MACspash, MACsplash

(*right*)

syn. 'Spanish Shawl'

MODERN, CLUSTER-FLOWERED/
FLORIBUNDA, RED BLEND,
REPEAT-FLOWERING

This rose has medium red flowers with light pink edges and silvery pink undersides, which add to the hand-painted effect. There are 20 petals and the clusters of 3–7 blooms are lightly scented. The matt foliage is red when young, ageing to bright green, on a tall and very bushy plant. There are many small prickles. The flowering is profuse, with very rapid repeat blooming and its disease resistance is very good. The color contrast is at its best in cool weather. **ZONES 5–10.**

MCGREDY, NEW ZEALAND, 1980

(['LITTLE DARLING' ×
'GOLDILOCKS']) × [('EVELYN
FISON' × ('CORYANA' ×
'TANTAU'S TRIUMPH')} ×
('JOHN CHURCH' × 'ELIZABETH
OF GLAMIS')]) × ('EVELYN FISON'
× ['ORANGE SWEETHEART' ×
'FRÜHLINGSMORGEN'])

ROYAL NATIONAL ROSE SOCIETY
CERTIFICATE OF MERIT 1977,
NEW ZEALAND GOLD MEDAL
1981

## 'Suma'   HARsuma

(*right*)

MODERN, GROUND COVER,
MEDIUM RED,
REPEAT-FLOWERING

This sister seedling of 'Nozomi' has many petalled, rose red blooms that pale with age. The spring crop is particularly lovely and covers the entire bush, followed by a lesser summer bloom and spasmodic bloom in the autumn. The canes are very prostrate on the ground and hug the soil, yet there is a dense covering of small foli-age, which makes it an excellent rose for cascading over rocks or walls. The thin canes are very pliable and easy to manipulate, so the rose can also be trained upward as a little climber on a pole. 'Suma' will never exceed 12 in (30 cm) in height, but it can grow 4 ft (1.2 m) wide, so it should be given enough space. **ZONES 5–10.**

ONODERA, JAPAN, 1989

PARENTAGE UNKNOWN

ROYAL HORTICULTURAL SOCIETY
AWARD OF GARDEN MERIT 1993

S

### 'Summer Blush'

SIEsummer *(above)*

OLD, ALBA, DEEP PINK

Rolf Sievers has crossed forms of *Rosa alba* with those of *R. kordesii* to produce a number of Alba Roses. The summer flowers of this variety are medium red, which is interesting since all other Alba Roses are white or shades of pink. The blooms open to show centers of incurved petals; there are 30–40 petals altogether. 'Summer Blush' is disease resistant, and tough, healthy foliage covers this gracefully arching plant. There is a very strong fragrance. Winter hardiness is extremely good, which makes it suitable for Canada, the northern USA and northern Europe. **ZONES 4–9.**

SIEVERS, GERMANY, 1988

PARENTAGE UNKNOWN

### 'Summer Dream'

JACshe *(right)*

MODERN, LARGE-FLOWERED/ HYBRID TEA, APRICOT BLEND, REPEAT-FLOWERING

The double, apricot-pink flowers of this rose have 30 petals to form medium-sized blooms with high centers and good

exhibition form. They are usually borne singly on long stems, so are good for cutting, and there is also a slight fruity fragrance. 'Summer Dream' has matt mid-green foliage on a plant with an upright growth habit. The repeat cycle is good and the plant has excellent resistance to disease. **ZONES 5–10.**

WARRINER, USA, 1987

'SUNSHINE' × SEEDLING

### 'Summer Fashion'

JACale *(top)*

syn. 'Arc de Triomphe'

MODERN, CLUSTER-FLOWERED/
FLORIBUNDA, YELLOW BLEND,
REPEAT-FLOWERING

The color of this rose is really quite beautiful; the 20 or so petals are light yellow and edged with soft salmon-pink, and as the flower ages, the pink spreads over the yellow. The fragrant, double flowers are large for a Cluster-flowered Rose and are borne both singly and in small, well-shaped clusters. The foliage is large, mid-green, abundant and semi-glossy, and covers a bush that is a little on the small side. The repeat-flowering is a little slow, but 'Summer Fashion' always attracts attention because of its unusual, attractive color. It makes a good standard rose and is suitable as a low border. ZONES 5–10.

WARRINER, USA, 1986

'PRECILLA' × 'BRIDAL PINK'

### 'Summer Holiday'

*(right)*

MODERN, LARGE-FLOWERED/
HYBRID TEA, ORANGE-RED,
REPEAT-FLOWERING

This is a much better rose than its parent 'Superstar'. The long, pointed buds open to flowers that are an intense orange-scarlet, and the clear color holds well on the bush without fading. The fragrant, double blooms have about 50 high-centered petals, and are produced on very long stems. It is a vigorous, bushy plant with abundant, semi-glossy, dark green foliage. The flower production is profuse and continuous and there are no disease problems. This rose makes an excellent hedge. ZONES 5–11.

GREGORY, UK, 1967

'SUPERSTAR' × SEEDLING

ROYAL NATIONAL ROSE SOCIETY
TRIAL GROUND CERTIFICATE 1968

### 'Summer Lady'   TANyoal

MODERN, LARGE-FLOWERED/HYBRID TEA, PINK BLEND,
REPEAT-FLOWERING

The slender, velvety cream-pink buds of this plant open to give deeper pink blooms overlaid with a salmon tint deep into the center of the bloom. They have an excellent, high-centered form, but lack enough petals to hold perfection for long. The lush green foliage is plentiful, and there is a nice fragrance. ZONES 5–10.

TANTAU, GERMANY, 1993

PARENTAGE UNKNOWN

### 'Summer Snow'
*(above)*

MODERN, CLUSTER-FLOWERED/
FLORIBUNDA, WHITE,
REPEAT-FLOWERING

It is unusual for a bush rose to have sported from a climbing rose, but this is the case with 'Summer Snow', which sported two years after the climber was introduced. The white, slightly scented flowers are large for a Cluster-flowered Rose, reaching 3 in (8 cm) across, and are borne in large, well-spaced clusters. The abundant foliage is very pale green on a plant with a low and very bushy growth habit. Mildew can be a problem in damp weather. This rose makes a nice bushy border or low hedge, and is also useful in groups among bulbs and perennials. ZONES 5–10.

PERKINS, USA, 1938

SPORT OF 'CLIMBING SUMMER SNOW'

### 'Summer Sunshine'
*(bottom)*
syn. 'Soleil d'Eté'

MODERN, LARGE-FLOWERED/
HYBRID TEA, DEEP YELLOW,
REPEAT-FLOWERING

The oval buds of 'Summer Sunshine' open to lightly fragrant flowers that are brilliant yellow. They are double, with 24 petals, high centered to cupped, and up to 5 in (12 cm) across. It is usually the first rose to bloom each spring and one of the last to finish in early winter. It also opens very quickly in summer heat and reaches its peak production and performance in the cool autumn months where the red tints in the outer petals are much more pronounced. The foliage is leathery, very dark green and semi-glossy, and growth is upright and bushy. There is only a little mildew in the autumn. 'Summer Sunshine' is one of the best yellow roses for bedding and for borders. ZONES 5–11.

SWIM, USA, 1962

'BUCCANEER' ×
'LEMON CHIFFON'

### 'Summer Wine'

KORizont   *(top)*

MODERN, LARGE FLOWERED
CLIMBER, DEEP PINK/MEDIUM
PINK, REPEAT-FLOWERING

This climbing rose has
charming flowers of
coral-pink with
prominent red stamens.
The semi-double, very
fragrant blooms are
produced in clusters
and they hold well if
picked in the bud stage;
they show up well
against the dark green
foliage. It is a vigorous,
tall and upright plant
and is excellent for
pillars, tripods,
pergolas or arches
where its unsophisticated
flowers can act as a
contrast to double
varieties. ZONES 5–10.

KORDES, GERMANY, 1984

PARENTAGE UNKNOWN

ROYAL NATIONAL ROSE SOCIETY
TRIAL GROUND CERTIFICATE
1982, ROYAL HORTICULTURAL
SOCIETY AWARD OF GARDEN
MERIT 1993

### 'Sun Flare'   JACjem
*(right)*
syn. 'Sunflare'

MODERN, CLUSTER-FLOWERED/
FLORIBUNDA, MEDIUM YELLOW,
REPEAT-FLOWERING

The long, pointed buds
of 'Sun Flare' open to
flat, medium yellow,
double flowers with
20–30 petals, showing
attractive stamens.
They are borne in
small to medium-sized,
well-spaced clusters
of 3–15 blooms with a
slight fragrance. The
foliage is small, glossy
and disease free. This
is a superb rose for a
low hedge or for
bedding and makes
an ideal standard. If
spent blooms are not
removed, a large crop
of round red hips are
produced. The awards
prove that it is a good
rose for exhibition.
**'Climbing Sun Flare'**,
introduced in 1987,
is a welcome addition
to the small list of
yellow climbers. With
its glossy foliage and
ample flowers, it makes
an excellent rose for
pergolas, tripods or
poles. ZONES 5–10.

WARRINER, USA, 1981

'SUNSPRITE' × SEEDLING

JAPAN GOLD MEDAL 1981,
ALL-AMERICA ROSE SELECTION
1983, PORTLAND GOLD MEDAL
1985

S

### 'Sunblest' *(right)*
syn. 'Landora'

MODERN, LARGE-FLOWERED/
HYBRID TEA, DEEP YELLOW,
REPEAT-FLOWERING

This is one of the best yellow roses; it bears copious supplies of mid- to deep yellow, well-shaped flowers that contain 38 pointed petals. The slightly fragrant, double blooms are up to 5 in (12 cm) across and the color is very attractive at all times. The stems are of medium length, which makes this good for cutting. The blooms last well on this strong, tall and healthy bush with pale green, glossy foliage. Disease resistance is good for a yellow rose, but there can be some black spot. 'Climbing Sunblest' is an excellent sport with lush pale green foliage and excellent flower production. It is a strong plant that is suitable on pillars, tripods or fences.
ZONES 5–10.

TANTAU, GERMANY, 1970
SEEDLING × 'KING'S RANSOM'
JAPAN GOLD MEDAL 1971,
ROYAL NATIONAL ROSE SOCIETY
TRIAL GROUND CERTIFICATE
1972, NEW ZEALAND GOLD
MEDAL 1973

### 'Sundowner'   MACche, MACcheup *(right)*

MODERN, LARGE-FLOWERED/
HYBRID TEA, APRICOT BLEND,
REPEAT-FLOWERING

'Sundowner' is an enormous grower and produces very long-stemmed flowers that are apricot-orange with yellow bases to the petals. The fragrant, double blooms have 35 petals of excellent form, and are borne amid the healthy, mid-green foliage on this very upright-growing bush. The plant is a little susceptible to mildew during autumn.

Its long stems and bright color make 'Sundowner' an excellent rose for cutting for indoor display. It is also a wonderful rose to use with fruit and berries for autumn interior decoration.
ZONES 5–10.

MCGREDY, NEW ZEALAND, 1978
'BOND STREET' × 'PEER GYNT'
ALL-AMERICA ROSE SELECTION
1979

S

### 'Sunlit' *(right)*

MODERN, LARGE-FLOWERED/
HYBRID TEA, APRICOT BLEND,
REPEAT-FLOWERING

One of Alister Clark's best roses, 'Sunlit' bears the richest apricot flowers, which are double, globular and are borne in profusion for a great length of time. This rose even flowers well into winter in mild climates. It has a low to medium growth habit with a abundance of mid-green foliage. There are no disease problems. In 1937, there were very few apricot roses as rich in color as 'Sunlit', and because of its color and freedom of bloom, it is still a popular rose. **ZONES 5–10.**

CLARK, AUSTRALIA, 1937

PARENTAGE UNKNOWN

### 'Sunmaid' *(center)*

MODERN, MINIATURE, YELLOW
BLEND, REPEAT-FLOWERING

The flowers of this rose are a bright combination of yellow and orange looking spectacular against dark glossy foliage. The yellow deepens in full sun. The florets occur mainly in clusters of 4–10 blooms. This low, compact grower is a good choice for a border or in a mass planting. It has a tendency to mildew and rust if left unprotected. It is often regarded by many rosarians as the best multicolored Miniature Rose. **ZONES 5–10.**

SPEK, THE NETHERLANDS, 1972

PARENTAGE UNKNOWN

### 'Sunny June'
*(bottom)*

MODERN, MODERN SHRUB, DEEP
YELLOW, REPEAT-FLOWERING

This first-class shrub rose has many pointed buds that open quickly to single, medium-sized flowers of deep canary yellow with amber stamens. They are produced in small to large clusters with a slight spicy fragrance. The flowering is continuous from spring to late autumn, and if the buds are picked when tight, they last well indoors. The growth is strong and upright. 'Sunny June' can be used as a large shrub or trained on a pillar; the deep yellow flowers show up very well against the profuse, glossy green foliage. It is one of the best repeat-flowering, yellow shrub roses available. **ZONES 5–10.**

LAMMERTS, USA, 1952

'CRIMSON GLORY' ×
'CAPTAIN THOMAS'

S

S

### 'Sunseeker' DICracer *(left)*
### syns 'Duchess of York', 'Sarah Duchess of York'

MODERN, CLUSTER-FLOWERED/FLORIBUNDA, ORANGE-RED, REPEAT-FLOWERING

This recent introduction has bright orange-red flowers suffused with sulfur yellow. They are small, yet filled with about 25–40 petals, and borne in small clusters on a very low bush amid mid-green, semi-glossy foliage. It has a light scent. This is a lovely little rose for pots or window boxes, and also makes a free-flowering border that provides bright color over a long period. There are no disease problems. ZONES 5–10.

DICKSON, UK, 1994

'LITTLE PRINCE' × 'GENTLE TOUCH'

ROYAL NATIONAL ROSE SOCIETY TRIAL GROUND CERTIFICATE 1991, BELFAST GOLD MEDAL 1994, GLASGOW SILVER MEDAL 1994

### 'Sunset Boulevard'
### HARbabble *(bottom)*

MODERN, CLUSTER-FLOWERED/FLORIBUNDA, ORANGE-PINK, REPEAT-FLOWERING

Launched as the 'Rose of the Year' at the Hampton Court Flower Show in 1997, 'Sunset Boulevard' has very well-shaped buds that open to glowing apricot-orange flowers, which are borne in small clusters. The rose has only a moderate fragrance, but the substance is excellent. It is a low, compact, free-flowering bush with a rapid repeat. There are no disease problems. It makes an excellent bedding rose and is also suitable for the front of the border. ZONES 5–11.

HARKNESS, UK, 1997

'HAROLD MACMILLAN' × 'FELLOWSHIP'

ROYAL NATIONAL ROSE SOCIETY TRIAL GROUND CERTIFICATE 1996, UK ROSE OF THE YEAR 1997

## 'Sunset Celebration' FRYxotic (*right*)

syns 'Chantoli', 'Exotic', 'Warm Wishes'

MODERN, LARGE-FLOWERED/
HYBRID TEA, ORANGE-PINK,
REPEAT-FLOWERING

The peachy salmon blooms of this cultivar are of medium to large size with neatly formed high centers. Although the petals number fewer than 30, they are wide and substantial, opening slowly to create a long-lasting and shapely flower. They are usually carried singly, sometimes in a wide cluster, and are fragrant and good for cutting. In the garden, this is a good subject for a bed of one variety and to group in a border. It continues to produce flowers through summer and autumn, and seems unaffected by wind and rain. The plants grow vigorously with a bushy habit to average height or more, with ample dark foliage. ZONES 4–9.

FRYER, UK, 1994

'POT O' GOLD' × (SEEDLING ×
'CHESHIRE LIFE')

ROYAL NATIONAL ROSE SOCIETY
TRIAL GROUND CERTIFICATE
1993, BELFAST GOLD MEDAL
1996, GOLDEN ROSE OF THE
HAGUE 1997, ALL-AMERICA ROSE
SELECTION 1998

## 'Sunset Song' COCasun (*right*)

MODERN, LARGE-FLOWERED/
HYBRID TEA, APRICOT BLEND/
ORANGE BLEND,
REPEAT-FLOWERING

This tall and upright grower produces large heads of flowers on long stems. The pointed buds open to double flowers with 45 petals of good form. The blooms are produced both singly and several to a cluster; they are apricot-orange, and last well. There is some fragrance. The abundant foliage is glossy and light olive green. In autumn, large candelabra-like growth appears with side shoots long enough for cutting. ZONES 5–10.

COCKER, UK, 1981

('SABINE' × 'CIRCUS') ×
'SUNBLEST'

ROYAL NATIONAL ROSE SOCIETY
TRIAL GROUND CERTIFICATE 1979

S

## 'Sunsprite' KORresia
*(right)*

syns 'Friesia',
'Korresia'

MODERN, CLUSTER-FLOWERED/
FLORIBUNDA, DEEP YELLOW,
REPEAT-FLOWERING

This rose is one of the best deep yellow Cluster-flowered Roses. The attractive, oval buds open to flat, double flowers with 28 symmetrically arranged petals. These large blooms are rich yellow, extremely fragrant and are produced in great quantities; the repeat-blooming is very fast. The foliage is abundant, dark green and very glossy on a plant with a short to medium, stocky habit. The open blooms shatter rather quickly, which makes them unsuitable for cutting, although deadheading keeps the bush neat and tidy. This is one of the best of all bedding roses, and makes a very colorful low hedge, as well as a standard.
**ZONES 5–11.**

KORDES, GERMANY, 1977

'FRIEDRICH WÖRLEIN' ×
'SPANISH SUN'

BADEN-BADEN GOLD MEDAL
1972, JAMES ALEXANDER
GAMBLE FRAGRANCE AWARD
1979, JAMES MASON MEMORIAL
MEDAL 1989

## 'Super Dorothy'
HELdoro

MODERN, RAMBLER, MEDIUM
PINK, REPEAT-FLOWERING

This rose causes a sensation whenever it is seen; the blooms are similar to those of 'Dorothy Perkins' but it continues to bloom through summer and autumn, which makes 'Super Dorothy' a wonderful weeping rose. The pink flowers are borne in small clusters and last well on the bush. It is not quite as vigorous as 'Dorothy Perkins', but this does not matter because of the freedom of flowering. 'Super Dorothy' has become popular in Europe since its introduction, and has now been introduced into the USA and Australia. It is suitable for pillars, tripods and arbors as its repeat-flowering provides color for much longer than any other rambling rose.
**ZONES 5–10.**

HETZEL, GERMANY, 1986

'DOROTHY PERKINS' × UNIDENTI-
FIED REPEAT-FLOWERING ROSE

## 'Super Excelsa'
HELexa

MODERN, RAMBLER, DARK RED,
REPEAT-FLOWERING

This rose has all the good qualities of 'Excelsa', with the added bonus of repeat-flowering through summer and autumn. The crimson-red flowers appear in small clusters and its vigorous and pliable growth makes it perfect for training over arches and pergolas. Unfortunately there is some mildew at times. 'Super Excelsa' is also suitable for pillars, and is excellent when grafted onto a weeping rose. **ZONES 5–10.**

HETZEL, GERMANY, 1986

'EXCELSA' × UNIDENTIFIED
REPEAT-FLOWERING ROSE

ANERKANNTE DEUTSCHE ROSE
1992

### 'Super Fairy'  HELSvfair  *(right)*

MODERN, RAMBLER, LIGHT PINK, REPEAT-FLOWERING

The flowers of 'Super Fairy' are light pink,
double with 15–25 petals, and are borne in
large clusters. The fragrant blooms are
$1\frac{1}{2}$ in (35 mm) across. The foliage is mid-
green and glossy on a strong plant that
grows to 3 ft (1 m) high and has long pliable
canes. Flowering is continuous, which is
very rare in a rambling rose. This is one of
the repeat-flowering Ramblers raised by
Karl Hetzel; others include 'Super Dorothy'
and 'Super Excelsa'. ZONES 4–11.

HETZEL, GERMANY, 1992

PARENTAGE UNKNOWN

### 'Superb Tuscan'  *(right)*
syn. 'Tuscany Superb'

OLD, GALLICA, MAUVE

This very old rose has larger
leaves and flowers than its
parent. The semi-double,
maroon-purple flowers have
pronounced yellow stamens.
It is a medium-sized, upright
plant with small dark green
leaves. It will sucker freely
unless grafted with the union
above the ground. The origin
of this beautiful old rose is lost
in antiquity. ZONES 4–9.

RIVERS, UK, PRE-1837

SPORT OF 'TUSCANY'

ROYAL HORTICULTURAL SOCIETY AWARD
OF GARDEN MERIT 1993

S

## 'Surpasse Tout' *(left)*
syn. 'Cérisette la Jolie'

OLD, GALLICA, MEDIUM RED

Many Gallicas were selected in the early nineteenth century before the later Bourbons and Hybrid Perpetuals with repeat-flowering characteristics ended the fashion. This one has deep cerise-maroon flowers and is fragrant. The flowers are full with a button eye. It is said to be rather sparse and leggy and grows to medium height. **ZONES 4–9.**

THE NETHERLANDS, PRE-1832

PARENTAGE UNKNOWN

## 'Surrey' KORlanum *(bottom)*
syns 'Sommerwind', 'Vent d'Eté'

MODERN, GROUND COVER, LIGHT PINK, REPEAT-FLOWERING

This excellent Ground Cover Rose grows much wider than it does tall: up to 3 ft (1 m) tall and 4 ft (1.2 m) wide. The plant smothers itself with great clusters of soft pink, double blooms that deepen to rose pink in the heart of the flower. They show up well against the small, dark green, disease-resistant foliage. 'Surrey' is very popular in the UK where it is used with pleasing results when planted in large drifts in front of taller-growing varieties. Most of the varieties named after English counties are bred in Denmark or Germany. **ZONES 5–10.**

KORDES, GERMANY, 1988

'THE FAIRY' × SEEDLING

ROYAL NATIONAL ROSE SOCIETY GOLD MEDAL 1987, ROYAL HORTICULTURAL SOCIETY AWARD OF GARDEN MERIT 1993

S

## 'Susan Hampshire'  MEInatac
### *(right)*

MODERN, LARGE-FLOWERED/HYBRID TEA,
LIGHT PINK, REPEAT-FLOWERING

This is a very good garden rose
with vigorous, upright growth
and ample foliage. The very
fragrant, rich pink, double
flowers, with 40 petals, are large
and globular. It makes an ideal
bedding rose because the plants
are well foliaged to ground
level and the rich rose pink
color holds well in all weather
conditions. The strong scent is
also a great asset. It was named
for a prominent television star
in the UK. **ZONES 5–11.**

PAOLINO, FRANCE, 1972

('MONIQUE' × 'SYMPHONIE') ×
'MARIA CALLAS'

## 'Susan Louise'
### *(right)*

MODERN, MODERN SHRUB,
LIGHT PINK, REPEAT-FLOWERING

'Susan Louise' is a
repeat-flowering form
of 'Belle Portugaise',
and is credited to
Charles Adams of San
Jose, California. The
large floppy blooms
are a light flesh pink.
It flowers spectacularly,
but only briefly in
summer. 'Susan
Louise' is rather tender
and is suitable only
for warm climates.
It seems to have caught
on only in Australia,
where it is readily
available. **ZONES 7–9.**

ADAMS, USA, 1929

SEEDLING OF 'BELLE
PORTUGAISE'

S

## 'Sussex' POUlave
*(right)*

syn. 'Apricot Cottage Rose'

MODERN, GROUND COVER, APRICOT BLEND, REPEAT-FLOWERING

This is one of the series of roses named after English counties introduced by Mattocks of Oxford from various continental breeders. The flowers of 'Sussex' are attractive apricot buff, double, with about two dozen petals, small and cupped. They are borne in both small and large clusters, and are produced over a very long period on this low and spreading bush. The foliage is small, mid-green and plentiful. 'Sussex' is suitable for use as a low border and for forming mounds where a soft color is required. **ZONES 5–10.**

POULSEN, DENMARK, 1991

PARENTAGE UNKNOWN

## 'Sutter's Gold'
*(right)*

MODERN, LARGE-FLOWERED/ HYBRID TEA, ORANGE BLEND, REPEAT-FLOWERING

This is one of the great roses of the 1950s. Bred from 'Charlotte Armstrong', which is noted for its very long elegant buds, 'Sutter's Gold' has inherited the slim bud and flower form of that parent. The color is gold and orange overlaid with Indian red. It opens to a rather loose full bloom of 30 petals that form a high-centered, large and very fragrant flower. They open quickly in summer heat. The copious foliage is dark green and leathery on an upright and vigorous plant. Its many awards are testimony to its great qualities, and it is still grown in most countries of the world after 50 years in commerce. **'Climbing Sutter's Gold'** is a first class climbing rose with magnificent rich dark green, leathery foliage. **ZONES 5–10.**

SWIM, USA, 1950

'CHARLOTTE ARMSTRONG' × 'SIGNORA'

PORTLAND GOLD MEDAL 1946, BAGATELLE GOLD MEDAL 1948, ALL-AMERICA ROSE SELECTION 1950, NATIONAL ROSE SOCIETY CERTIFICATE OF MERIT 1951, JAMES ALEXANDER GAMBLE FRAGRANCE MEDAL 1966

## 'Swan' AUSwhite
### (right)

MODERN, MODERN SHRUB,
WHITE BLEND,
REPEAT-FLOWERING

The lightly fragrant blooms of 'Swan' are extra large and contain at least 60 petals. The color is cream in the bud stage, then the bloom opens to show soft primrose yellow at the center with cream shading on the outer petals; the whole flower becomes cream as it ages. It is at its best in warm, dry weather because the petals spot in the rain or after heavy dews. The bush is extremely strong and healthy and has large, glossy pale green foliage. 'Swan' is a magnificent rose for large arrangements as it holds its color and form when cut. In cold areas, the bush is much smaller with a re-duction in the number of flowers. The variety can be easily recognized by the quilled petals. In warm climates, it can be grown effectively on a pillar or tripod; it can also look good trained horizontally along a wall or fence where flower produc-tion is even greater. 'Swan' is also classified as an English Rose.
**ZONES 5–10.**

AUSTIN, UK, 1987

('CHARLES AUSTIN' × SEEDLING)
× 'ICEBERG'

## 'Swan Lake' (right)
syn. 'Schwanensee'

MODERN, LARGE-FLOWERED
CLIMBER, WHITE BLEND,
REPEAT-FLOWERING

The well-shaped buds of this rose open slowly to double, well-formed, fragrant blooms with 50 pale pink petals. They are produced on long stems and are suitable for exhibition. Flowering is continuous, although the most shapely and long-lasting blooms are seen in autumn. The plant has a moderately vigorous growth habit and the foliage is mid-green, abundant and disease free. It is ideal for pillars, tripods and fences. **ZONES 4–11.**

MCGREDY, UK, 1968

'MEMORIAM' × 'HEIDELBERG'

S

### 'Swany' MEIburenac
### (right)

MODERN, GROUND COVER,
WHITE, REPEAT-FLOWERING

The oval buds on this
variety open to pure
white, cup-shaped
flowers with an
astonishing 95 petals.
The blooms come in
clusters that can cover
the entire bush. The
foliage is glossy bronze
on a very vigorous,
spreading plant.
'Swany' was probably
the forerunner of the
shrub 'Bonica' from
the same breeder. It
makes an ideal ground
cover, even on a steep
bank where the canes
can tumble downward.
It derives its spreading
habit from the
species seed parent.
**ZONES 4–11.**

MEILLAND, FRANCE, 1978

*ROSA SEMPERVIRENS* ×
'MLLE MARTHE CARRON'

ROYAL HORTICULTURAL SOCIETY
AWARD OF GARDEN MERIT 1994

### 'Swarthmore'
MEItaras  *(right)*

MODERN, LARGE-FLOWERED/
HYBRID TEA, PINK BLEND,
REPEAT-FLOWERING

The flowers of
'Swarthmore' are a
subtle blend of several
shades of pink and
light red with a wash
of mauve-pink. They
are large and double
with 50 petals that
form a high center
and a good exhibition
shape. There is some
fragrance. The blooms
are produced on long
stems and last well
when cut, but flower
production is average
with long gaps between
flushes. The foliage is
dark green, leathery
and abundant, and
covers a tall, vigorous
bush. The stems are
very dark. **ZONES 5–10.**

MEILLAND, FRANCE, 1963

('INDEPENDENCE' × 'ROUGE
MEILLAND') × 'PEACE'

## 'Sweet Chariot'  MORchari
### (right)
### syn. 'Insolite'
MODERN, MINIATURE, MAUVE,
REPEAT-FLOWERING

'Sweet Chariot' has lavender to
purple blend flowers that age to
a superb mixture of lavender hues.
The florets have 40 petals, and
come in large clusters that take
several weeks to bloom out. One
distinguishing feature of this rose
is its overpowering fragrance;
no matter where it is planted in
the garden, the heavy Damask
scent can be detected. The foliage is small and mid-green on
an upright, vigorous, spreading
plant. It is excellent in a hanging
basket, as the canes arch downward to cover the container and
the clusters hang out, spreading
their fragrance in the surrounding air. **ZONES 5–10.**

MOORE, USA, 1984

'LITTLE CHIEF' × 'VIOLETTE'

## 'Sweet Dream'  FRYminicot
### (right)
### syn. 'Sweet Dreams'
MODERN, CLUSTER-FLOWERED/FLORIBUNDA,
APRICOT BLEND, REPEAT-FLOWERING

This variety has well-formed
blooms of soft peachy apricot
that are borne both singly and
in large clusters; they have a
strong, sweet scent. It is a small,
cushion-like bush with very
dense, glossy, healthy foliage.
'Sweet Dream' is a grand rose for
low edging, borders or for tubs
and containers. Disease resistance is good and the flowers
hold their color well. **ZONES 5–10.**

FRYER, UK, 1988

SEEDLING × (['ANYTIME' × 'LIVERPOOL
ECHO'] × ['NEW PENNY' × SEEDLING])

BRITISH ASSOCIATION OF ROSE BREEDERS ROSE
OF THE YEAR 1988, BELFAST CERTIFICATE OF
MERIT 1990, ROYAL HORTICULTURAL SOCIETY
AWARD OF GARDEN MERIT 1993

S

## 'Sweet Inspiration'

JACsim *(above)*

MODERN, CLUSTER-FLOWERED/
FLORIBUNDA, MEDIUM PINK,
REPEAT-FLOWERING

This well-named rose produces large quantities of very clear medium pink flowers with 25 petals that are cream at the bases. They are large—to 4 in (10 cm) across—with cream at the base of each petal. They have good substance and are borne in small and large clusters that last well on the bush with very little fading. The foliage is mid-green and matt, and there are very few thorns. 'Sweet Inspiration' is a bushy, strong and upright plant that is excellent for both bedding and borders, since flower production is prolific and continuous. **ZONES 5–10.**

WARRINER, USA, 1993

'SUNFLARE' × 'SIMPLICITY'

ALL-AMERICA ROSE SELECTION 1993

## 'Sweet Juliet'  AUSleap
*(right)*

MODERN, MODERN SHRUB,
APRICOT BLEND,
REPEAT-FLOWERING

This rose has small buds that open to large, very cupped flowers that form many-petalled rosettes with a distinct button eye. They are soft, delicate apricot, fading to almost white at the petal edges, and have a strong Tea-like fragrance. The foliage

has very pointed, pale green leaflets with a brownish tinge, and covers a very upright and strong shrub, which produces a thicket of canes in autumn. It is a great pity that many of these late growths do not flower since the spring flush is most prolific; if it flowered as well in autumn as in spring, this would be one of the best David Austin varieties. It is also classified as an English Rose. **ZONES 5–10.**

AUSTIN, UK, 1989

'GRAHAM THOMAS' ×
'ADMIRED MIRANDA'

BELFAST FRAGRANCE AWARD 1992

S

## 'Sweet Magic'

DICmagic *(right)*

MODERN, PATIO/DWARF
CLUSTER-FLOWERED, ORANGE
BLEND, REPEAT-FLOWERING

This variety has orange-gold pointed buds that open to reveal bright orange flowers with golden highlights. The florets are semi-double with 15–25 petals, have no fragrance and open quickly to flat flowers displaying prominent stamens. The medium-sized flowers are produced in wonderful clusters on a neat, well-rounded bush with dark green shiny foliage that is a perfect complement to the bright florets. This plant is easy to grow, healthy and weather-proof. It does well in containers, borders and patios. The centerpiece of the Royal National Rose Society Rose Festival in 1986 was a massive display of 'Sweet Magic' that captured the audience because of its intensity of color and grace. **ZONES 5–10.**

DICKSON, UK, 1986

'PEEK A BOO' × 'BRIGHT SMILE'

ROYAL NATIONAL ROSE SOCIETY
TRIAL GROUND CERTIFICATE
1986, RNRS ROSE OF THE YEAR
1987, ROYAL HORTICULTURAL
SOCIETY AWARD OF GARDEN
MERIT 1993

## 'Sweet Memories' WHAmemo

MODERN, PATIO/DWARF CLUSTER-FLOWERED, LIGHT YELLOW,
REPEAT-FLOWERING

The flowers of this rose are produced in large clusters of soft lemon with a distinctive, old-fashioned and quartered look. The bloom production is prolific and free, and there is a light scent. Light green, disease-resistant foliage covers the plant, which grows to about 1–2 ft (30–60 cm) high in moderate climates. It is suitable for a container or for planting in a border. **ZONES 5–11.**

SPORT OF 'SWEET DREAM'

S

## 'Sweet Surrender'

MODERN, LARGE-FLOWERED/HYBRID TEA, MEDIUM PINK,
REPEAT-FLOWERING

The double flowers of 'Sweet Surrender' are clear
silvery pink. They are 5 in (12 cm) across, and
have 40 petals to form the shape of a cup; there
is a strong Tea Rose fragrance. The foliage is
dark, leathery and disease free on a plant with
a strong growth habit and above-average flower
production with a quick repeat-bloom. Its parent,
'Tiffany', also received an All-America Rose
Selection award. Both roses have a strong
perfume, long stems and beautifully shaped
flowers of a good strong color. **ZONES 5–11.**

WEEKS, USA, 1983

SEEDLING × 'TIFFANY'

ALL-AMERICA ROSE SELECTION 1983

## 'Sydonie' *(below)*
syn. 'Sidonie'

OLD, HYBRID PERPETUAL, MEDIUM PINK, REPEAT-FLOWERING

This rose has brilliant soft pink flowers that are
flat and quartered and are borne in clusters.
They have muddled centers and frilled petals.
It is a small to medium bush and in some ways
looks more like a Portland. It has the characteristic
Damask fragrance and is said to be susceptible to
black spot. **ZONES 5–9.**

DORISY, FRANCE, 1846

SEEDLING OF 'BELLE DE TRIANON'

## 'Sympathie' *(right)*

syn. 'Sympathy'

MODERN, LARGE-FLOWERED
CLIMBER, MEDIUM RED,
REPEAT-FLOWERING

This variety bears clusters of lightly scented, blood red flowers, each with 20 or more petals that develop to a fairly large size and open cupped. The intensely deep, yet bright color stands out beautifully against the background of rich green shiny foliage. The first flush of bloom is prolific, but the later repeats in summer are rather sporadic; repeat-flowering improves later in the season to give a good autumn display. 'Sympathie' descends from the raiser's Kordesii line and is a vigorous, fast-growing and adaptable plant; it produces long, arching stems and is very well suited to fences, walls and pergolas. ZONES 4–9.

KORDES, GERMANY, 1964

'WILHELM HANSMANN' ×
'DON JUAN'

ANERKANNTE DEUTSCHE ROSE
1966

## 'Symphony' AUSlett *(right)*

syns 'Allux Symphony', 'Symphonie'

MODERN, MODERN SHRUB,
LIGHT YELLOW,
REPEAT-FLOWERING

This variety produces medium-sized flowers composed of over 40 small petals, usually in close clusters. They open to a medium shade of yellow, paler towards the petal edges, then become rosette shaped as the petals expand and finally age to pink. They have a very pleasing fragrance and continue to appear through summer and autumn, being happiest in warmer weather. 'Symphony' is a suitable rose for a cheerful group near the front of a shrub border or for a bed. It grows upright with a fairly compact, bushy habit to below average height and has plentiful shiny foliage. It was named for the Allux commercial enterprise in connection with the Breast Cancer Fund for Wales. The variety is also classified as an English Rose. ZONES 4–9.

AUSTIN, UK, 1986

'THE KNIGHT' ×
'YELLOW CUSHION'

S

T

'Taboo' TANelorak *(above)*
syns 'Barkarole', 'Grand Château'
MODERN, LARGE-FLOWERED/HYBRID TEA, DARK RED,
REPEAT-FLOWERING

The flowers of this variety are long and slender
and are made up of broad petals that form high
centers in classic Large-flowered style. They
are among the darkest red roses to be found,
and as they are carried on long stems they
provide plenty of blooms for cutting; they have
a moderate scent. The succession of bloom
is well maintained through summer and
autumn and, with all these points in its favor,
'Taboo' should be a most desirable variety.
Unfortunately, it has a poor growth habit,
the plant appearing splayed and lopsided,
which greatly reduces its value as a rose for
beds and borders. It is best grown in a cutting
garden where the flowers can be taken but the
plant does not continually confront the eye.
It grows vigorously and unevenly to above
average height and has large, dark glossy leaves.
ZONES 4–9.

EVERS, GERMANY, 1988

PARENTAGE UNKNOWN

'Talisman' *(above)*
MODERN, LARGE-FLOWERED/HYBRID TEA, YELLOW BLEND,
REPEAT-FLOWERING

This variety was one of the few pre-1939 Large-
flowered Roses to retain its popularity for many
years after the war. In its favor is the wonderful
freedom of flower, the ability to bloom again
quickly, a neat bedding habit and a pretty combination of colors—for in its 30 petals can be
found scarlet, pink, copper and gold shades mixed
together. The flowers show beautifully coiled
centers as the petals begin to part, then they
open out like saucers to reveal the stamens. In
the young stage, the blooms make wonderful
buttonholes; they were formerly cultivated as cut-
flower roses, their straight, springy stems making
them admirably suited for that purpose. They
have a sweet fruity scent. This is a good rose to
grow for both horticultural and historical reasons.
The plant is moderately vigorous and has an
upright, narrow habit, growing to average height
or less, with light green, leathery, semi-glossy
leaves. **'Climbing Talisman'** (Western, USA,
1930) gives a splendid first flush of bloom,
followed by occasional flowers later in the season.
It produces long, arching stems and grows to
slightly more than the extent normally expected
of a climber, with flowers and leaves identical to
those of the bush form. **ZONES 4–9.**

MONTGOMERY, USA, 1929

'OPHÉLIA' × 'SOUVENIR DE CLAUDIUS PERNET'

AMERICAN ROSE SOCIETY GOLD MEDAL 1929, ARS JOHN COOK GOLD
MEDAL 1932

## 'Tall Story' DICkooky

MODERN, CLUSTER-FLOWERED/
FLORIBUNDA, MEDIUM YELLOW,
REPEAT-FLOWERING

This variety is often listed as a Ground Cover Rose, but it grows rather like a shallow pyramid. The medium-sized blooms have a cool look, resembling butter fresh from the dairy. They are semi-double, borne in neatly spaced sprays on graceful arching stems and appear on the plant at various levels, giving a wonderfully airy effect. There is a pleasing scent, and flowers are produced with good succession through summer and autumn. 'Tall Story' is a lovely rose to use where a specimen plant is needed for a small space. It can also be grouped in a border or bed. By the nature of its growth, the bush will be amply adorned with bright green glossy leaves to the ground. It has a spreading habit. **ZONES 4–9.**

DICKSON, UK, 1984

'SUNSPRITE' × 'YESTERDAY'

ROYAL HORTICULTURAL SOCIETY
AWARD OF GARDEN MERIT 1993

## 'Tamora' AUStamora
*(top)*

MODERN, MODERN SHRUB,
APRICOT BLEND,
REPEAT-FLOWERING

Reddish orange buds on this variety open into fairly large flowers of apricot-yellow, deeper in their hearts and paling towards the margins. They are made up of over 40 silky textured petals that are arranged layer upon layer in an old-fashioned style; the petals part to form a deep cup in the center of the blooms. There is a sharp fragrance, and flowers continue through summer and autumn. 'Tamora' is suitable for a group in a shrub border and is recommended for warm climates. It is vigorous, rather spreading in habit and grows to below the average height of a shrub rose. The foliage is small, dark and semi-glossy. 'Tamora' is also classified as an English Rose. **ZONES 4–9.**

AUSTIN, UK, 1983

'CHAUCER' ×
'CONRAD FERDINAND MEYER'

## 'Tapis Jaune' RUgul
*(below)*

**syns 'Golden Penny', 'Goldpenny', 'Guletta'**

MODERN, MINIATURE, MEDIUM
YELLOW, REPEAT-FLOWERING

Often known as 'Guletta', 'Tapis Jaune' carries double flowers of about 20 yellow petals. These blooms are small and produced both singly and in clusters of 3–5 amid the glossy dark green leaves. The growth is low and compact. 'Tapis Jaune' flowers profusely, there is a quick repeat flowering, and good disease resistance. The clear yellow does not fade, and the blooms have good substance with a thick petal texture. It is a wonderful rose for pots, small beds and low borders. **ZONES 5–10.**

DE RUITER, THE NETHERLANDS,
1973

'ROSY JEWEL' × 'ALLGOLD'

T

## 'Tapis Volant'

LENplat *(above)*

MODERN, MODERN SHRUB, PINK
BLEND, REPEAT-FLOWERING

This is an example of
innovative breeding on
the part of Louis Lens,
here uniting the genes
of *Rosa wichurana* and
*R. multiflora* with other
strains. The resultant
shrub is a low, wide
plant bearing masses
of small, pinky white
blooms. They are
produced in clusters of
7–36, and some sprays
continue to appear
later in summer when
the initial generous
flush is over. There is
a fruity fragrance. This
is an interesting rose
to have for its botanical
value, and an attractive
plant for the garden
in its own right. It
grows vigorously with
a spreading, trailing
habit and is well
furnished with plentiful
reddish green foliage
and red-brown
prickles. The name
means 'flying carpet'.
ZONES 4–9.

LENS, BELGIUM, 1982

(ROSA LUCIAE × SEEDLING) ×
(R. MULTIFLORA ADENOCHEATA
× 'BALLERINA')

KORTRIJK GOLD MEDAL 1987

## 'Tarrawarra'

MODERN, POLYANTHA, PINK
BLEND, REPEAT-FLOWERING

This variety started out
as a seedling at the
Nieuwesteeg nursery
in Victoria, Australia.
The flowers are
produced in great
abundance in small
to large clusters of
10–40 blooms. They
are small, only 1 in
(2.5 cm) or so across,
and contain 28 pale
salmon-pink petals that
open fully to cream,
with just a trace of
salmon at the edges.
At the center is a boss
of golden stamens—a
very refreshing effect.
'Tarrawarra' forms a
small, rounded plant
with dense, dark green,
rough-textured foliage.
It makes an excellent
border or low hedge
and flowers continu-
ously from spring until
late autumn. For maxi-
mum effect, the bush
needs to be planted in
groups, close together.
ZONES 5–10.

NIEUWESTEEG, AUSTRALIA, 1992

PARENTAGE UNKNOWN

## 'Tatjana' KORtat
### (right)
syn. 'Rosenthal'

**MODERN, LARGE-FLOWERED/
HYBRID TEA, DARK RED,
REPEAT-FLOWERING**

Like many other dark red roses, the petals of this rose reflect the sunlight to give a shimmer of velvet. The blooms are rounded in form, made up of rather short petals and are most neatly formed, opening cupped and yielding a rich scent. They may be carried singly or in candelabra fashion, usually with long stems. They are well suited for borders, continuing in bloom through summer and autumn. The plant grows vigorously with a bushy, upright and dense habit to above average height, and has large, dark green, semi-glossy leaves.
**ZONES 4–9.**

KORDES, GERMANY, 1970

'LIEBESZAUBER' × 'PRÄSIDENT
DR H. C. SCHRODER'

## 'Tausendschön'
### (above)
syn. 'Thousand
Beauties'

**MODERN, RAMBLER, PINK BLEND**

This Rambler bears loose clusters of large, double, pink flowers with white centers. The stems are nearly thornless. Its ancestry includes the red Hybrid Perpetual 'Général Jacqueminot' and 'Pâquerette', the first dwarf Polyantha. It sported a dwarf form, **'Baby Tausendschön'** (syn. 'Echo') in 1914, which is the parent of many useful Polyantha pot roses. Both forms flower only once.
**ZONES 5–9.**

SCHMIDT, GERMANY, 1906

'DANIEL LACOMBE' ×
'WEISER HERUMSTREICHER'

T

## 'Tchin-Tchin' MEIkinosi
### (right)
### syn. 'Parador'

**MODERN, LARGE-FLOWERED/HYBRID TEA,
YELLOW BLEND, REPEAT-FLOWERING**

The flowers of this variety are golden yellow and quite large, so as their 30 petals expand into a symmetrical cupped form they display a bold expanse of color. The blooms do not have much fragrance but they stand bad weather well and repeat their bloom satisfactorily through summer and autumn. 'Tchin-Tchin', which is useful for beds and borders and has flowers that last well when cut for arrangements, grows to average height and has dark green, leathery leaves. The raisers brought out two roses known as 'Tchin-Tchin' with the synonym 'Parador' in the same year, which has confused many growers and gardening writers. One is an orange-red Cluster-flowered Rose, and the other yellow—described here. **ZONES 5–10.**

PAOLINO, FRANCE, 1978

(['ZAMBRA' × 'SUSPENSE'] × 'KING'S RANSOM')
× ('KABUKI' × 'DR A. J. VERHAGE')

## 'Tea Rambler' (above)

**MODERN, RAMBLER, ORANGE-PINK**

One of the early hybrids from the famous 'Engineer's Rose', this variety has quite large, semi-double, pink flowers with shades of orange. They are borne in profusion in early summer and are fragrant, befitting the Tea strain. It is a vigorous climbing rose that is less prone to mildew than might be expected. This is a very worthwhile rose to plant, but it must be given enough space. **ZONES 5–9.**

PAUL, UK, 1904

'CRIMSON RAMBLER' × TEA ROSE

### 'Tear Drop'

MODERN, MINIATURE, WHITE,
REPEAT-FLOWERING

The single to semi-
double flowers of this
rose have 6–14 white
petals and prominent
yellow stamens. The
florets are flat and
the same size as those
seen on a Patio Rose.
The blooms have a
light fragrance and
look like a white cloud
over the ground. The
foliage is small and
glossy mid-green on
a low, hardy plant that
flowers all season long,
and is shaped like a
dinner plate. The
weatherproof blooms
seem to have an air of
innocence about them,
and are admired for
their rather simple
form and beauty. 'Tear
Drop' is ideal for tiny
beds, at the front of a
border, or even in a
small container for the
patio. **ZONES 4–11.**

DICKSON, UK, 1988

'PINK SPRAY' × 'BRIGHT SMILE'

### 'Teddy Bear'

SAVabear *(above)*

MODERN, MINIATURE, RUSSET,
REPEAT-FLOWERING

The oval buds of
this variety open to
terracotta-colored
flowers with lighter
undersides, ageing
to mauve-pink. The
florets are double with
28 petals, urn shaped
with Large-flowered
form, and have a light
fragrance. These blooms
are borne either singly
or in small sprays of
3–5 amid the dark
green and semi-glossy
foliage on an upright
and vigorous plant.
This rose represented
a major breakthrough
in color, particularly as
the open bloom shows
its brown petals with
deep golden stamens
in the center; the color
is certainly unique and
people seem to either
instantly like it or hate
it! The blooms are long
lasting when cut for
the home or left on
the bush. It has a nice
rounded growth habit,
but the plant can suffer
from mildew if left un-
protected. **ZONES 4–11.**

SAVILLE, USA, 1989

'SACHET' × 'RAINBOW'S END'

### 'Temple Bells'

MODERN, CLIMBING MINIATURE,
WHITE, REPEAT-FLOWERING

Large, white single
flowers with beautiful
yellow stamens are the
hallmark of this rose.
The florets are borne
in trusses and have just
a hint of fragrance.
It is a vigorous and
spreading plant,
but needs about two
seasons to become
well-established before
it really performs. In
some climates it has
been used as a ground
cover rather than as a
climber, and with good
results. The use of
*Rosa wichurana* as a
seed parent has given
'Temple Bells' the
ability to ramble, climb
and crawl along the
ground. **ZONES 5–10.**

MOREY, USA, 1971

*ROSA WICHURANA* ×
'BLUSHING JEWEL'

T

## 'Tender Blush'
*(right)*

OLD, ALBA, LIGHT PINK

With rounded, double blooms that emerge from plump buds, 'Tender Blush' is a pretty light pink rose with a creamy shade to the petals when fully open. The foliage is dark green. Like most Albas, this variety is easy to grow, even in semi-shade. **ZONES 5–10.**

SIEVERS, GERMANY, 1988

PARENTAGE UNKNOWN

## 'Tender Night'
MEIlaur  *(below right)*
syns 'Florian',
'Sankt Florian'

MODERN, CLUSTER-FLOWERED/
FLORIBUNDA, MEDIUM RED,
REPEAT-FLOWERING

This variety creates a bold show, bearing its currant red flowers in large, showy trusses. They are of medium to large size, are made up of about 24 petals and carry a slight fruity fragrance. The hard petal texture enables the blooms to with-stand hot sun better than many reds. This is a well-behaved rose for a bed, low hedge, or to plant near the front of a border. It grows with a compact, up-right habit to average height or less, and has leathery, medium-sized, semi-glossy foli-age. **'Climbing Tender Night'** (MEIlaursar; syn. 'Climbing Florian'; 1976) resembles the parent rose in all respects, except that it gives only a limited amount of flower after the main flush. In growth, it is strong and arching to slightly more than the average extent expected of a Cluster-flowered Climber. **ZONES 4–9.**

MEILLAND, FRANCE, 1971

'TAMANGO' × ('FIRE KING' × 'BANZAI')

ROME GOLD MEDAL 1971

### 'Tequila' MEIgavesol
(*right*)

MODERN, CLUSTER-FLOWERED/
FLORIBUNDA, ORANGE BLEND,
REPEAT-FLOWERING

The flowers of this
rose are colorful Indian
red on the uppersides
and golden orange
shading to yellow on
the undersides, which
gives them a lively,
vibrant tone. They are
of medium size, neatly
formed with about 18
petals and are carried
in small, even clusters
that are produced
freely during the initial
flush. They continue
to appear through
summer and autumn
and there is only a
slight scent. 'Tequila'
is especially good
for hedges and for
containers. It is also
suitable for beds and
borders. It grows vig-
orously to average
height and has plentiful
dark green foliage.
**ZONES 4–9.**

MEILLAND, FRANCE, 1982

'POPPY FLASH' × ('RUMBA' ×
[MEIKIM × 'FIRE KING'])

### 'Tequila Sunrise'
DICobey (*right*)
syn. 'Beaulieu'

MODERN, LARGE-FLOWERED/
HYBRID TEA, RED BLEND,
REPEAT-FLOWERING

An asset of this variety
is its ability to keep on
flowering, for it is rare
during summer and
autumn not to find
several of its bright
yellow and red blooms
cheering up the garden.
The flowers are of
medium size, rounded
in form, and are made
up of broad, bright
yellow petals that are
randomly tipped and
margined with red. They
are carried sometimes
singly and quite often
in wide, candelabra-
type sprays, which
afford plenty of blooms
for flower arranging.
They open slowly, taking
on a cupped form; they

should be deadheaded
because the old petals
discolor. For beds,
borders and hedges,
this is a popular rose.
It grows vigorously with
a bushy, free-branching
habit to average
height, and is furnished
with glossy dark green
leaves. **ZONES 4–9.**

DICKSON, UK, 1989

'BONFIRE NIGHT' × 'FREEDOM'

ROYAL NATIONAL ROSE SOCIETY
GOLD MEDAL 1988, BELFAST
GOLD MEDAL 1991, GLASGOW
SILVER MEDAL 1991, ROYAL
HORTICULTURAL SOCIETY AWARD
OF GARDEN MERIT 1993

T

### 'Texas' POUltex *(right)*
syn. 'Golden Piccolo'

MODERN, MINIATURE, MEDIUM YELLOW,
REPEAT-FLOWERING

The bright medium yellow
blooms of this rose are
unfading, even in strong
sunlight. They are double with
good high centers suitable for
exhibition and can have a light
fragrance. The foliage is small,
matt mid-green on a very
upright, tall plant. This vigorous
bush gives a high yield of
blooms, borne one to a stem
throughout the season. 'Texas',
one of the best colorfast yellows
on the Miniature Rose scene,
is generally disease resistant and
hardy. ZONES 5–10.

POULSEN, DENMARK, 1984
PARENTAGE UNKNOWN

### 'Texas Centennial' *(right)*

MODERN, LARGE-FLOWERED/HYBRID TEA,
RED BLEND, REPEAT-FLOWERING

It was a lucky Texan who noticed these distinctive, vibrantly
colored flowers growing on
'President Herbert Hoover'.
This proved to be a marketable,
and valuable, mutation. The
color is deep strawberry red
with some gold shading, lighter
in the center of the blooms and
becoming a gentler blend of
pink, red and orange as the
petals age. The flowers resemble
those of the parent in form,
being of medium size, prettily
coiled as the buds open loosely
with reflexing petals. They are
held upright on long, straight
stems and have a sweet spicy
fragrance, which makes them
excellent subjects for buttonholes and for cutting, though
they need to be taken young or
they will fly open quickly. 'Texas
Centennial' makes a wonderful
hedge, screening or border
plant. In growth, it is similar to
the parent rose, though it is not
as tall, growing vigorously and
upright to above average height
and having large, leathery
leaves. ZONES 4–9.

WATKINS, USA, 1935
SPORT OF 'PRESIDENT HERBERT HOOVER'
PORTLAND GOLD MEDAL 1935

### 'Thalia' *(right)*

MODERN, RAMBLER, WHITE

'Thalia' was also known as the 'White Rambler' and was well regarded until it was replaced by the better 'Sander's White', so it is not seen much today. The flowers are small, double and well scented, and are borne in clusters. In Greek mythology, Thalia was the Muse of comedy and pastoral poetry. **ZONES 4–10.**

SCHMITT, FRANCE, 1895

ROSA MULTIFLORA × 'PÂQUERETTE'

### 'The Alexandra Rose' AUSday
### syn. 'Alexandra Rose'

MODERN, MODERN SHRUB, PINK BLEND, REPEAT-FLOWERING

This variety has simple 5-petalled flowers of beautiful coloring, yellow towards the center of the flowers and rose red towards the petal rims, fading to rose pink as the blooms age. They are of medium size, borne in large clusters and are slightly fragrant, and there is continual production throughout summer and autumn. This is a useful addition to the mixed shrub border, where its gentle colors and guileless flower character will harmonize readily with other plants. It grows vigorously and with reasonable compactness to average height and is well endowed with mid-green, semi-glossy foliage. **ZONES 4–9.**

AUSTIN, UK, 1993

('SHROPSHIRE LASS' × 'SHROPSHIRE LASS') × 'HERITAGE'

### 'The Bishop' *(right)*
### syn. 'Le Rosier Évêque'

OLD, CENTIFOLIA, MAUVE

Although sometimes grouped with Gallica Roses, this ancient rose has many features that are characteristic of Centifolias. In growth habit, it is fairly upright and dense with thorny stems and dark green foliage. The flowers are flat when fully open and are composed of many evenly layered, bluish purple and magenta petals that have hints of lilac and gray: a most unusual combination that gives an almost violet effect when viewed from a distance. The individual blooms can be as much as 3 in (8 cm) across; they appear in mid-summer and are arranged in small, fragrant clusters fairly close to the foliage. **ZONES 4–9.**

LISTED BY FRANÇOIS, FRANCE, 1790

PARENTAGE UNKNOWN

T

### 'The Countryman' AUSman *(left)*
syn. 'Countryman'
MODERN, MODERN SHRUB, MEDIUM PINK, REPEAT-FLOWERING

This distinctive rose from David Austin, which is also classified as an English Rose, brings a reinfusion of Portland genes into Modern Garden Roses. Its medium-sized flowers are deceptive, for to the eye it does not at first appear that they can hold as many as 40 petals. They are peony-like when young in a warm shade of deep pink, and open like large loose rosettes, with a good fragrance. Normally there are two distinct flushes of bloom, in summer and in autumn, and additional intermittent blooms can be encouraged if old flowers are removed. 'The Countryman' is suitable for a border, but owing to its undisciplined and tangled growth, some flowers become half-hidden in the foliage. It is remarkably healthy and grows vigorously to below average height, having a covering of medium green matt leaves that are soft to the touch. **ZONES 4–9.**
AUSTIN, UK, 1987

'LILIAN AUSTIN' × 'COMTE DE CHAMBORD'

### 'The Bride' *(above)*
OLD, TEA, WHITE, REPEAT-FLOWERING

'Catherine Mermet' has flesh pink blooms and has produced several sports. This one is said to be an improvement on the parent, with better shaped flowers and a more floriferous habit. It has a hint of pale lilac-pink in it, particularly on the petal edges. **ZONES 7–9.**
MAY, USA, 1885

SPORT OF 'CATHERINE MERMET'

### 'The Dark Lady'
AUSbloom *(right)*
syn. 'Dark Lady'
MODERN, MODERN SHRUB, DARK RED, REPEAT-FLOWERING

The flowers of this variety are dark red; they are very full, with over 40 petals to make up a fairly large bloom. When the petals part, the blooms show some resemblance to tree peonies in form, becoming purplish as they age. A few flowers are usually borne together in a small cluster, and their combined weight may cause the stems to bow. There is a sharp fragrance. This is an interesting rose to grow in a border, though it may require special care to thrive; if it is planted in a raised bed, the flowers can be better appreciated. It is from David Austin and is also classified as an English Rose. It grows upright with a bushy habit to less than average height and has dark green, semi-glossy leaves. ZONES 4–9.

AUSTIN, UK, 1991

'MARY ROSE' × 'PROSPERO'

### 'The Doctor'   *(right)*
MODERN, LARGE-FLOWERED/ HYBRID TEA, MEDIUM PINK, REPEAT-FLOWERING

In its heyday this rose's huge satiny pink blooms were one of the most familiar sights in the garden, standing out because of their size and also because the color is so confident and cheering. It is surprising that fewer than 30 petals, albeit very big ones, make up these flowers, because their rounded, blowsy heads give such an impression of fullness. The scent is strong and sweet and likened to verbena. The plant is not so impressive; because it fails to make new wood freely; there is only limited summer bloom after the first flush, though there is

usually a good display in autumn. It grows to below average height and has attractive but rather sparse shiny foliage. 'The Doctor' deserves a place in the garden for reasons of history, scent and sentiment, for in its name is preserved the memory of the great rosarian Dr J. H. Nicolas, French by birth, who became an American citizen and was honored by the growers of America. ZONES 4–9.

HOWARD, USA, 1936

'MRS J. D. EISELE' × 'LOS ANGELES'

NATIONAL ROSE SOCIETY GOLD MEDAL 1938

T

### 'The Fairy' *(right)*
syns 'Fairy', 'Féerie'
MODERN, POLYANTHA, LIGHT
PINK, REPEAT-FLOWERING

Although this rose comes into bloom later than almost any other, once it starts it provides a prolific show for weeks on end. The rosette-shaped flowers are made up of scores of tiny petals, and are carried in dainty sprays all over the bush in an even tone of light rose pink. Even during rare intervals through summer and autumn when not in flower, the plant remains attractive, forming hummocks of small, bright, pointed leaves. 'The Fairy' has all manner of uses: as a low hedge, to front a border, trail over a low wall, occupy a small space or to be planted in a container. Its only failing is a lack of fragrance. If kept pruned it will stay quite dwarf, or it can achieve the stature of a small shrub by being allowed to grow unchecked; it is also excellent as a weeping standard. 'Climbing The Fairy' has all the characteristics of the bush form except that it produces long, arching stems and is capable of extending nearly half as far again as an average climber. It is not a rapid grower, and the continuity of bloom is not maintained as successfully as in the bush form. **ZONES 4–9.**

BENTALL, UK, 1932

'PAUL CRAMPEL' × 'LADY GAY'

ROYAL HORTICULTURAL SOCIETY
AWARD OF GARDEN MERIT 1993

### 'The Friar' *(right)*
MODERN, MODERN SHRUB,
LIGHT PINK, REPEAT-FLOWERING

The flowers of this variety are blush edged white, and open from plump pointed buds to reveal small petals enfolded one against another in an old-fashioned style without any particular pattern or symmetry in their arrangement. They are scented and continue appearing throughout summer and autumn on an upright, dark-leafed shrub that grows with moderate vigor to

less than average height. Although less successful in cooler climates, 'The Friar' clearly improves its performance in sunshine, and is popular as a rose for the shrub border in Australia, New Zealand and parts of the USA. It takes its name, as do several others in these pages prefaced by the definite article, from a character in Chaucer's *The Canterbury Tales*. 'The Friar' is from David Austin and is also classified as an English Rose. **ZONES 4–9.**

AUSTIN, UK, 1969

'IVORY FASHION' × SEEDLING

## 'The Garland'
### syn. 'Wood's Garland'
**OLD, MISCELLANEOUS, WHITE**

A characteristic of this rose is the way it carries many clusters of tiny buds upright on bowing shoots. They appear for a glorious burst of bloom in high summer, covering the plant with a wealth of small, semi-double blooms that open flat to display a mixture of shades—blush pink, very pale yellow and white. The flowers have a light scent. The plant makes vigorous growth, producing many shoots, and is suitable for pergolas, covering unsightly objects and in places where it can romp un-hindered. The leaflets are small and dark.

WELLS, UK, 1835

*ROSA MOSCHATA ×
R. MULTIFLORA*

ROYAL HORTICULTURAL SOCIETY
AWARD OF GARDEN MERIT 1993

## 'The Herbalist' AUSsemi *(above)*
### syn. 'Herbalist'
**MODERN, MODERN SHRUB, DEEP PINK, REPEAT-FLOWERING**

The flowers of this variety are of medium to large size, with about 12 petals, in that shade of deep pink that borders on light red. They are carried in small clusters and open saucer shaped, showing attractive golden stamens, and blooms continue to appear through summer and autumn, making this a very desirable plant for the garden border. It grows sturdily with a neat, bushy, rather spreading habit to a little less than average height and is furnished with semi-glossy foliage. The raiser, David Austin, chose the name on account of the rose's likeness to 'Officinalis', the 'Apothecary's' Rose', but it unfortunately lacks the powerful fragrance of that variety. It is also classified as an English Rose. **ZONES 4–9.**

AUSTIN, UK, 1991

SEEDLING × 'LOUISE ODIER'

### 'The Lady' FRYjingo
(*below*)

MODERN, LARGE-FLOWERED/
HYBRID TEA, YELLOW BLEND,
REPEAT-FLOWERING

Having hybridized a pair of Cluster-flowered Roses, the raiser must have been pleasantly surprised to find this Large-flowered Rose among the resultant seedlings, with its high center and exhibition quality. The blooms are honey yellow with some salmon shading on the petals, and are carried sometimes singly, sometimes in wide-spaced clusters, but always on long stems, so they are very good for flower arrangement. There is a light scent and the production of quality blooms through summer and autumn is remarkably good, the big flowers seeming impervious to the effects of wind and rain. In the garden this is a useful border rose. The habit is rather uneven, which detracts from its value for bedding. 'The Lady' grows vigorously to average height and has a covering of mid-green, semi-glossy leaves. The name is that of a British magazine, and this rose was named to mark its centenary.
**ZONES 4–9.**

FRYER, UK, 1985

'PINK PARFAIT' × 'REDGOLD'

ROYAL NATIONAL ROSE SOCIETY
TRIAL GROUND CERTIFICATE 1982,
BADEN-BADEN GOLD MEDAL 1987,
ROYAL HORTICULTURAL SOCIETY
AWARD OF GARDEN MERIT 1993

### 'The McCartney Rose' MEIzeli
syns 'McCartney Rose', 'Paul McCartney', 'Sweet Lady', 'The MacCartney Rose'

MODERN, LARGE-FLOWERED/
HYBRID TEA, MEDIUM PINK,
REPEAT-FLOWERING

The color of the flowers of this variety is a rich deep pink, and a most satisfying heavy fragrance comes from them. The blooms have up to 40 petals, forming a high center in the young flowers, which become cupped as they develop. There is a good continuity of bloom through summer and autumn, and in the garden this is a neat grower for a bed or border. The growth of the plant is vigorous and upright, to about average height, though the mid-green, semi-glossy leaves are likely to be susceptible to black spot in a bad year. It was named for the celebrated ex-Beatle.
**ZONES 4–9.**

MEILLAND, FRANCE, 1991

('NIRVANA' × 'PAPA MEILLAND')
× 'FIRST PRIZE'

BAGATELLE FRAGRANCE PRIZE
1988, GENEVA GOLD MEDAL
1988, LE ROEUIX GOLD MEDAL
AND FRAGRANCE PRIZE 1988,
MADRID FRAGRANCE PRIZE 1988,
MONZA GOLD MEDAL AND
FRAGRANCE PRIZE 1988, PARIS
GOLD MEDAL 1988, BELFAST
FRAGRANCE PRIZE 1993,
DURBANVILLE FRAGRANCE PRIZE
1993, PARIS FRAGRANCE PRIZE
1993

T

## 'The Nun' AUSnun
*(right)*
syn. 'Candida'
MODERN, MODERN SHRUB,
WHITE, REPEAT-FLOWERING

The lightly fragrant flowers of this rose at their best have a beautiful and unusual form, like that of a tulip, with the stamens seen peeping up from the depths of the cup. They are almost pure white and are held on slim stems well apart in open sprays, 'giving', says the raiser, 'an effect of dainty purity', though he goes on to mention that owing to the fragile nature of the construction, the petals do not always remain in place. It is therefore in spells of warm, settled weather that this variety is at its best. The plant continues to show color through summer and autumn and makes an interesting addition to the rose border, where it will grow to the size of an average shrub rose. **ZONES 4–9.**

AUSTIN, UK, 1987

SEEDLING OF 'THE PRIORESS'

## 'The Pilgrim'
AUSwalker *(bottom)*
syns 'Gartenarchitekt Günther Schulze', 'Pilgrim'
MODERN, MODERN SHRUB,
MEDIUM YELLOW,
REPEAT-FLOWERING

The softly textured blooms are beautifully formed, made up of scores of small infolded petals that form an intricately constructed flat flower with rich hints of yellow in their young centers, paling to creamy buff. They are carried in clusters on strong stems, have a pleasing scent and continue to appear through summer and autumn. 'The Pilgrim' is from David Austin and is also classified as an English Rose. It is an excellent rose to plant in a border, either as a specimen plant or in a group, where it will prove useful for cutting for small arrangements. It grows vigorously with a compact and graceful habit to average height and is amply furnished with polished-looking mid-green foliage. **ZONES 4–9.**

AUSTIN, UK, 1991

'GRAHAM THOMAS' × 'YELLOW BUTTON'

T

cation of a connoisseur. The plant grows to about half the height of an average shrub rose and has a skimpy provision of dark leaves. It is from David Austin and is also classified as an English Rose. **ZONES 4–9.**

AUSTIN, UK, 1990

'LILIAN AUSTIN' × 'THE SQUIRE'

## 'The Prioress'
### (bottom)
MODERN, MODERN SHRUB, LIGHT PINK, REPEAT-FLOWERING

This rose bears clusters of medium-sized flowers that are made up of about 24 petals, the globular form of the young blooms resembling that of the Bourbon Rose recorded in the parentage. The flowers are pearly pink and become cupped on opening, revealing prominent and attractive stamens. There is a light fragrance, and good continuity of bloom is maintained through summer and autumn. 'The Prioress' is from David Austin and is also classified as an English Rose. It is suitable for a mixed bed or border, where it will make a vigorous bush with an upright habit to about average height. The leaves are fairly large and mid- to dark green. **ZONES 4–9.**

AUSTIN, UK, 1969

'REINE VICTORIA' × SEEDLING

## 'The Prince'
AUSvelvet   **(top)**
MODERN, MODERN SHRUB, DARK RED, REPEAT-FLOWERING

The flower is everything in this variety. The inky buds are hard and round and open into rich deep crimson blooms of intricate construction like wide, shallow rosettes, full of petals folded against their neighbors as they strive to open out. The crimson tones soon change to royal purple, and there is an Old Garden Rose scent. 'The Prince' is best sited where the unusual character of the blooms can be enjoyed, but where the plant is not readily in view, for the weak flower stems and poor constitution are serious visual drawbacks in its overall performance. Given a warm climate and good cultivation, it can thrive, but it needs the dedi-

## 'The Reeve' AUSreeve (right)
MODERN, MODERN SHRUB, DEEP PINK, REPEAT-FLOWERING

The flowers of this rose are intensely dark pink. They are very full, with almost 60 petals, and are borne sometimes singly, sometimes in small clusters. In the bud and young flower stages they are globe shaped with incurving petals, and open cupped like blowsy peonies. They have a good fragrance and blooming continues through summer and autumn. Because it has a lax, trailing character, the plant is suitable to grow where it can be allowed to form a tangled group in a mixed border, or allowed to run over a low retaining wall. It grows to about half the height of an average shrub rose with an untidy, spreading habit, and has prickly stems and a provision of small, rough-textured dark foliage that is reddish when young. It is from David Austin and is also classified as an English Rose.

**ZONES 4–9.**

AUSTIN, UK, 1979

'LILIAN AUSTIN' × 'CHAUCER'

## 'The Squire' AUSire, AUSquire (right)
syn. 'Country Squire'
MODERN, MODERN SHRUB, DARK RED, REPEAT-FLOWERING

Judged by the flowers alone, this could be considered one of the world's loveliest red roses. It is from David Austin and is also classified as an English Rose. The deeply cupped blooms look sumptuous, with over 100 petals perfectly arranged to create a quartered-rosette effect as they expand. There is also a good fragrance, but it is sad to record that the plant is unworthy of so fine a flower. It makes a somewhat leggy bush, stingy with its blooms and sparse with its foliage, and not proof against fungus troubles

on the leaves it has. Siting the variety in the garden is therefore a problem; one answer is to grow it in a move-able container so that it can be given extra feeding, and when good flowers come, they can be made a focal point and enjoyed. 'The Squire' is an open, bushy shrub of less than average height with dark rough-textured foliage.

**ZONES 4–9.**

AUSTIN, UK, 1977

'THE KNIGHT' × 'CHÂTEAU DE CLOS VOUGEOT'

T

### 'The Temptations' WEKaq
*(top)*

MODERN, LARGE-FLOWERED/HYBRID TEA,
PINK BLEND, REPEAT-FLOWERING

This variety's flowers have the classic symmetry of form of the best Large-flowered Roses, and though they are not extra large, being composed of up to 30 broad petals, they make the best of what they have. The color is an appealing blend of orchid pink tones, paler in the center of the petals. There is a light fruity scent and, once the main flush is over, flowers continue to appear in summer and autumn, the late blooms being finer in quality and color. 'The Temptations' is useful for exhibition and cutting, blooms usually being produced one to a stem, and is suitable in the garden as a hedge and for beds and borders. It grows with moderate vigor and an upright habit to average height or more and has dark green, semi-glossy leaves. The singing group for which it was named has been responsible for many hits. ZONES 5–9.

WINCHEL, USA, 1993

'PARADISE' × 'ADMIRAL RODNEY'

AMERICAN ROSE CENTER GOLD MEDAL 1989

### 'The Wife of Bath' AUSbath
*(bottom)*
syn. 'Wife of Bath'

MODERN, MODERN SHRUB, PINK BLEND,
REPEAT-FLOWERING

This variety is from David Austin and is also classified as an English Rose. It bears medium-sized flowers of old-fashioned character that are deep rose pink on the upper-sides of the petals and blush pink on the undersides. They open with the petals tightly folded to show their deeper tones, and as the blooms expand they become looser in form and lighter in color. There is a strong myrrh scent, and the continuity of flower through summer and autumn is well maintained. 'The Wife of Bath' can be used in a bed or border, yet it will suit a container as it is a comparatively short grower that forms a bushy, twiggy plant to below average height. It has small, mid-green leaves. ZONES 4–9.

AUSTIN, UK, 1969

'MME CAROLINE TESTOUT' ×
('MA PERKINS' × 'CONSTANCE SPRY')

T

## 'The Yeoman'

AUSyeo *(bottom)*

MODERN, MODERN SHRUB,
ORANGE-PINK,
REPEAT-FLOWERING

The flowers of this variety have a touch of pale apricot in the heart of their rosy pink petals, which gives them a pleasing translucent quality. They are full petalled and become cupped as they open, giving off a strong fragrance of myrrh. There is a prolific first flush of bloom, after which sporadic flowers may appear until autumn brings another respectable display. This is not a very strong-growing rose, but it will reward good cultivation, and in fertile soil can make a handsome addition to the shrub border. It may be expected to grow lower than average height with a compact habit and large mid-green leaves. It is from David Austin and is also classified as an English Rose. ZONES 4–9.

AUSTIN, UK, 1969

'IVORY FASHION' × ('CONSTANCE SPRY' × 'MONIQUE')

## 'Thérèse Bugnet'

*(top)*
syn. 'Teresa Bugnet'

MODERN, HYBRID RUGOSA,
MEDIUM PINK,
REPEAT-FLOWERING

This is a vigorous, hardy plant whose complicated breeding line includes some of the wild roses best able to withstand Canadian winters. The flowers are quite large, being made up of some 36 wavy, folded, soft-textured petals. They are reddish pink, paling as they age, open out like shallow saucers and have an excellent sweet fragrance. Like most Rugosa hybrids, this one continues in bloom all through summer and autumn. The flowers are good to cut, while the near absence of prickles on the flower stalks is an added benefit. 'Thérèse Bugnet' grows easily and vigorously, and for a shrub border where

minimal attention can be given and substantial growth is required, it is an excellent choice. It reaches above average height and has long, rather smooth leaves not characteristic of a Rugosa. The raiser named it for a close member of the family. ZONES 3–9.

BUGNET, CANADA, 1950

([ROSA ACICULARIS × R. RUGOSA KAMTCHATICA] × [R. AMBLYOTIS × R. RUGOSA PLENA]) × 'BETTY BLAND'

T

### 'Thisbe' *(bottom)*

MODERN, MODERN SHRUB,
LIGHT YELLOW,
REPEAT-FLOWERING

This is one of the loveliest of the shrub roses. The flowers are borne close together in the cluster, so in full bloom the effect is that of a fluffy cloud of chamois yellow. They open like rosettes with many small petals, showing amber stamens and imparting a light sweet fragrance. After a generous first flush of bloom, more flowers are produced at intervals through summer and autumn, and in the garden this is a lovely shrub for a border, preferably by a path so that its unostentatious beauty can be enjoyed. The plant grows vigorously with a bushy, upright habit to average height and is well furnished with semi-glossy, olive green leaves. **ZONES 4–9.**

PEMBERTON, UK, 1918

SPORT OF 'DAPHNE'

**T**

### 'Thérèse de Lisieux'

ORAblan *(top)*
syn. 'St Thérèse de Lisieux'

MODERN, LARGE-FLOWERED/
HYBRID TEA, WHITE,
REPEAT-FLOWERING

Theresa Martin was made a saint many years after her death in 1896; she was famous for helping the poor. To commemorate the centenary of her death, this rose was introduced by the Carmelite Monastery in Victoria, Australia. 'Thérèse de Lisieux' produces double white flowers with over 24 petals with a blush of soft shell pink at the edges. The blooms are carried in profusion, both singly and in small clusters, and there is a quick repeat. This upright bush is covered with glossy deep green, disease-resistant foliage. **ZONES 5–10.**

ORARD, FRANCE, 1992

PARENTAGE UNKNOWN

## 'Tiffany' *(right)*

MODERN, LARGE-FLOWERED/HYBRID TEA, PINK BLEND,
REPEAT-FLOWERING

The flowers of this variety are large and full
petalled and formed in the classical Large-
flowered style, with high centers and maintaining
wonderful symmetry of form as the petals reflex.
They combine rose pink and rosy salmon shades,
with hints of gold at the petal base, and are
carried on long firm stems, sometimes singly and
sometimes in clusters. They have good fragrance
and are excellent for cutting, though they may
spoil in rain. 'Tiffany' is an excellent choice for
beds and borders or to form a hedge, and blooms
with commendable freedom through summer and
autumn. The plant grows vigorously and upright
to above average height and has plentiful deep
green glossy foliage. 'Climbing Tiffany' (Lindquist,
USA, 1958) has the same lovely fragrant flowers
as found on the bush form, although it is less
popular. It produces vigorous, arching stems,
ideal for training over a support. ZONES 4–9.

LINDQUIST, USA, 1954

'CHARLOTTE ARMSTRONG' × 'GIRONA'

PORTLAND GOLD MEDAL 1954, ALL-AMERICA ROSE SELECTION 1955,
GAMBLE FRAGRANCE MEDAL 1962

## 'Tiki' *(below)*

MODERN, CLUSTER-FLOWERED/
FLORIBUNDA, PINK BLEND,
REPEAT-FLOWERING

The fragrant flowers
of this variety are quite
large and their 30 petals
give them the shape of
Large-flowered Roses,
high centered at first,
becoming cupped as
they age. They are a
blend of light shell pink
and pearly cream and
are produced freely,
usually in clusters but
sometimes singly.
Flowering continues
through summer and
autumn, some of the
finest roses being pro-
duced in cooler spells.
This rose is a good
choice for planting in
beds, borders and as a
hedge, where the pale
coloring of the blooms
contrasts beautifully
with its dark foliage.
It grows vigorously
with an upright, bushy
habit to average height.
In Maori mythology,
Tiki was the creator
of the first man; Sam
McGredy named the
rose after a visit to New
Zealand. ZONES 4–9.

MCGREDY, UK, 1964

'MME LÉON CUNY' × 'SPARTAN'

### 'Till Uhlenspiegel'
*(below)*

OLD, SWEET BRIAR, RED BLEND

Although it is classed with the Sweet Briars, this variety has little in common with them, for in both flower and foliage it takes after its Cluster-flowered seed parent. It bears, in enormous clusters, saucer-like blooms of bright carmine with white eyes that flower profusely in early summer. They do not repeat-bloom and the scent is slight. It grows larger than average

with a vigorous, free-branching habit and has dark green glossy leaves. ZONES 4–9.

KORDES, GERMANY, 1950

'HOLSTEIN' × 'MAGNIFICA'

### 'Timeless'    JACecond
*(bottom)*

MODERN, LARGE-FLOWERED/ HYBRID TEA, DEEP PINK/LIGHT RED, REPEAT-FLOWERING

As the blooms of this variety unfold, the colors vary between deep pink and medium red, the inside surface of the petal being deeper than the outside. It is a warm mixture, and the sizeable flowers display much of it as they open to reveal perfectly formed high centers on upright, strong stems. They open slowly, keeping their symmetrical shape, thanks to the firm texture of the 30 or so petals, but the fragrance is only slight. The blooms continue through summer and autumn and this is a dependable rose for a bed, border or hedge. It grows sturdily with an upright habit to average height and has dark, semi-glossy foliage. ZONES 4–9.

ZARY, USA, 1996

SEEDLING × 'KARDINAL'

ALL-AMERICA ROSE SELECTION 1997

T

### 'Tineke' *(right)*

MODERN, LARGE-FLOWERED/
HYBRID TEA, WHITE,
REPEAT-FLOWERING

This rose is widely grown for the florists' market. It carries plump pointed buds with a greenish tint that develop into large flowers of almost pure creamy white, made up of about 50 broad petals. They are high centered, open slowly to a cupped form and are borne on strong straight stems, ideal for cutting. 'Tineke' needs a warm climate because the blooms are blemished by cold wind and rain. It produces new flower stems readily, giving excellent continuity of bloom through summer and autumn. The plant is vigorous, growing to average height or more with a cover of large, semi-glossy, dark green leaves. **ZONES 4–9.**

SELECT ROSES BV,
THE NETHERLANDS, 1989

PARENTAGE UNKNOWN

### 'Tinkerbell' SUNtink *(above)*

MODERN, MINIATURE, LIGHT
PINK, REPEAT-FLOWERING

The petals of these soft pink flowers reflex gracefully to form an almost porcelain-like rose. The florets have outstanding Large-flowered form and are borne one to a stem as well as in clusters on long, straight stems. It has a strong fragrance. The foliage is glossy green on a tall, upright bush. Gardeners are recommended to remove the central bud on the clusters so that all flowers come into bloom at the same time: this gives a colorful umbrella effect. **ZONES 5–10.**

SCHUURMAN, NEW ZEALAND,
1992

'WHITE DREAM' × 'EVELIEN'

### 'Tino Rossi' MEIcelna

MODERN, LARGE-FLOWERED/
HYBRID TEA, MEDIUM PINK,
REPEAT-FLOWERING

The flowers of this variety are of medium to large size, rounded in form, and well filled with over 50 petals. In color they are a rather cool shade of light salmony pink, with pretty rose pink veining. There is an excellent fragrance, and good continuity of flowering is maintained through summer and autumn. This rose is very suitable for use in beds and borders, to grow as a hedge and as a source of cut flowers. It grows vigorously with a bushy, upright habit to average height and has an ample coverage of semi-glossy, mid-green foliage. The variety was named as a tribute to the celebrated singer. ZONES 4–9.

MEILLAND, FRANCE, 1990

'PINK PANTHER' × ('DREAM' ×
'JARDINS DE BAGATELLE')

BAGATELLE FRAGRANCE AWARD
1989

### 'Tintinara' DICuptight
*(below)*

MODERN, LARGE-FLOWERED/
HYBRID TEA, LIGHT RED,
REPEAT-FLOWERING

This variety has big flowers borne on well-spaced clusters, of the type that in the USA are termed Grandifloras. They have about 24 petals and open with a high-centered form, becoming cupped. The color is unusual, being poppy red with the inner petals a lighter porcelain rose, and there is a light fragrance. 'Tintinara' gives a prolific first flowering, followed by further cycles of growth and bloom through summer and autumn, making it a good performer as a bedding and border rose or to form a hedge. It makes a strong, upright plant to above average height and is densely clothed in large glossy leaves. On being asked why he named this after an obscure township in South Australia, the raiser said he had never heard of the place and had chosen to call it 'Tintinara' simply because it sounded good. ZONES 4–9.

DICKSON, UK, 1995

'MELODY MAKER' ×
(SEEDLING × 'BRIGHT SMILE')

THE HAGUE GOLD MEDAL 1994

### 'Tip Top' TANope

MODERN, CLUSTER-FLOWERED/
FLORIBUNDA, ORANGE-PINK,
REPEAT-FLOWERING

In stature this rose belongs with the Patio Roses, but the flowers and leaves are proportionately too large for it to sit happily with the other members of this recent group and it is better regarded as a truncated Cluster-flowered Rose. As such it is a convenient rose to edge a border or to put in a small bed by itself, or to use as a dwarf hedge. The medium-sized flowers are semi-double and open saucer shaped, showing their stamens. The fresh-looking, rosy salmon blooms are carried close to the plant in short-stemmed clusters. There is a slight scent, and good continuity of bloom through summer and autumn. The plant has a low, spreading habit and has deep green leaves that provide ample cover at the start of the season, but often suffer loss through black spot. ZONES 4–9.

TANTAU, GERMANY, 1963

PARENTAGE UNKNOWN

## 'Titian' *(right)*

MODERN, CLUSTER-FLOWERED/
FLORIBUNDA, DEEP PINK,
REPEAT-FLOWERING

This variety has well-formed flowers of deep carmine pink, though their brilliance is such that they have the remarkable property of appearing scarlet when caught by the sun and viewed from a distance. They open out rather flat, and the color tone intensifies as the large, full-petalled blooms age. Flowers continue to appear through the growing season, the autumn bloom being especially fine, and there is a light scent. Although classified as a Cluster-flowered Rose the plant takes on the dimensions of a shrub or pillar in warm areas, growing vigorously with an upright, arching habit to above average height; it is easy to grow in a border, with or without support. The foliage is rounded and mid-green. **ZONES 4–9.**

RIETHMULLER, AUSTRALIA, 1950
PARENTAGE UNKNOWN

## 'Tivoli' POUlduce
*(right)*
syn. 'Tivoli Gardens'

MODERN, LARGE-FLOWERED/
HYBRID TEA, MEDIUM YELLOW,
REPEAT-FLOWERING

These flowers are of medium to large size and consist of up to 40 petals. The blooms are rounded in form and are borne sometimes singly, sometimes in small clusters. The color is clear yellow, a positive but gentle shade. There is a light fragrance, and blooms are produced with good continuity through summer and autumn. 'Tivoli' is a dependable variety for a bed or border, or to plant as a hedge.

It grows vigorously with a compact, free-branching habit up to average height and has large, dark green semi-glossy foliage. This Danish-raised variety is named after one of Copenhagen's main attractions. **ZONES 4–9.**

POULSEN, DENMARK, 1996
PARENTAGE UNKNOWN

T

### 'Toby Tristam'
*(top)*

**MODERN, RAMBLER, WHITE**

Scores of pointed buds appear close together in big trusses on this variety, and when they open their 5-petalled flowers wide, the overall effect is like seeing many golden-hearted, tiny saucers. The blooms are creamy white; their great profusion lasts for only a short period in summer, but where space is available this is a horticultural delight, suitable for growing up a tree or in a wild garden. It grows with arching, clambering stems and mid-green foliage up to three times the extent of an average climbing rose. In autumn, there are small orange hips. This rose is perhaps a *Rosa multiflora* seedling, but little seems to be known about the parentage. **ZONES 4–9.**

HILLIER, UK, CIRCA 1970

PARENTAGE UNKNOWN

### 'Tom Tom' *(bottom)*

**MODERN, CLUSTER-FLOWERED/ FLORIBUNDA, DEEP PINK, REPEAT-FLOWERING**

This variety bears clusters of red-pink flowers composed of about 24 petals. They are large by comparison with the size of the plant, and open with high centers like small-scale Large-flowered Roses before becoming flat. They have a light spicy scent and after the main flush, they continue to appear through summer and autumn, the late season flowering being especially good. The plant grows with a compact habit and is excellent for bedding where a short grower is required, or to edge a border. The growth is vigorous and the habit upright and bushy, to below average height. It is well furnished with deep green matt foliage. **ZONES 4–9.**

LINDQUIST, USA, 1957

'IMPROVED LAFAYETTE' × 'FLORADORA'

T

### 'Tom Wood'

OLD, HYBRID PERPETUAL, MEDIUM RED, REPEAT-FLOWERING

This rose bears large, rather dull cherry red, double flowers. It is a reasonably short-growing bush with a good constitution, that is apparently free of mildew. The plant repeat-flowers well in autumn, but seems to be available only in Europe. **ZONES 5–10.**

DICKSON, UK, 1896

PARENTAGE UNKNOWN

### 'Top Marks' FRYministar *(above)*

MODERN, MINIATURE, MEDIUM RED, REPEAT-FLOWERING

What a perfect name for this rose! It has flowers that are a sparkling vibrant vermilion, and hold their color well in sunny climates. Although the florets have an informal look, they cover the bush with an attractive mass of color. The plant is very hardy but it can suffer from black spot if left unprotected. 'Top Marks' has been a consistent winner at rose trials in Europe where it has captured the attention of the rose-growing public. **ZONES 4–10.**

FRYER, UK, 1992

PARENTAGE UNKNOWN

GENEVA CERTIFICATE OF MERIT 1990, ROYAL NATIONAL ROSE SOCIETY GOLD MEDAL AND ROSE OF THE YEAR 1992, BADEN-BADEN GOLD MEDAL

### 'Topaz Jewel' MORyelrug
syns 'Rustica 91', 'Gelbe Dagmar Hastrup',
'Yellow Dagmar Hastrup',
'Yellow Fru Dagmar Hartopp'

MODERN, HYBRID RUGOSA, MEDIUM YELLOW, REPEAT-FLOWERING

Though not the first yellow Hybrid Rugosa
as sometimes claimed, this variety is the most
suitable one for the average garden. It grows
lower than the average shrub rose with a spreading, free-branching habit and carries primrose
yellow flowers that open to display creamy gold
stamens. They consist of some 24 attractively
curled petals and develop into wide, loosely
cupped blooms with a pleasing fruity fragrance.
'Topaz Jewel', which makes a valuable addition
to the shrub border as a specimen plant or group,
has somewhat uneven and untidy growth and a
tendency for some blooms to be hidden in new
foliage, so it is less effective in a bed by itself. The
foliage is matt, rugged and rich green, but not
as proof against disease as most Hybrid Rugosas,
nor does the plant produce the typical Hybrid
Rugosa hips. ZONES 4–9.

MOORE, USA, 1987

'GOLDEN ANGEL' × 'BELLE POITEVINE'

### 'Toprose' COCgold *(above)*
syn. 'Dania'

MODERN, CLUSTER-FLOWERED/FLORIBUNDA, DEEP YELLOW,
REPEAT-FLOWERING

The distinction between the Cluster-flowered and
Large-flowered Roses seems to disappear when
'Toprose' is on view, for it carries fairly large, full-
petalled blooms of classic Large-flowered form at
the top of long stems and, though sometimes
borne singly, they often appear in a close group
of 3. The color is a bright, shining and even
shade of yellow. There is a light scent, and the
continuity of bloom through summer and autumn
is well maintained. This variety is best suited for a
group in a border or as a hedge. The plant grows
vigorously to average height and has handsome
bright green leaves. ZONES 4–9.

COCKER, UK, 1991

(['CHINATOWN' × 'GOLDEN MASTERPIECE'] × 'ADOLF HORSTMANN') ×
'YELLOW PAGES'

BADEN-BADEN GOLD MEDAL 1987, BELFAST AND GLASGOW
CERTIFICATES OF MERIT 1993

## 'Topsi'

MODERN, CLUSTER-FLOWERED/FLORIBUNDA, ORANGE-RED,
REPEAT-FLOWERING

Only a handful of nurseries now offer this
beautiful rose which, when new, caused a
sensation by reason of its color, a luminous
orange-scarlet of startling brightness. The semi-
double blooms appear in short-stemmed clusters
and look large against this low-growing plant.
They are freely produced and open like saucers.
The plant puts much of its energy into making
new flowering shoots; however, this led to its
decline, insufficient ripened wood being made to
prevent die-back in hard winters. 'Topsi' is best
enjoyed in a small bed or container where it can
be given good treatment, including preventive
spraying against rust and black spot. It has a
very short, spreading growth habit and large,
mid-green leaves. **ZONES 4–9.**

TANTAU, GERMANY, 1972

'FRAGRANT CLOUD' × 'FIRE SIGNAL'

ROYAL NATIONAL ROSE SOCIETY PRESIDENT'S INTERNATIONAL
TROPHY 1972

## 'Tornado'  KORtor  (*above*)

MODERN, CLUSTER-FLOWERED/FLORIBUNDA, ORANGE-RED,
REPEAT-FLOWERING

This dependable, bright, free-flowering rose
grows vigorously with an upright, bushy habit
and carries its semi-double blooms in showy
clusters close to the plant on short, rigid stems.
The flowers are orange-red, dark and bright and
open cupped, giving a glimpse of bright golden
stamens within the center petals. Little scent can
be detected, but in other respects—continuity of
bloom through summer and autumn, ability to
shrug off bad weather, and the way the spent
flowers drop their petals cleanly—this is a well-
behaved garden item for use in beds, borders,
as a low hedge and in containers, growing to
average height and having shiny dark green
foliage. **ZONES 4–9.**

KORDES, GERMANY, 1973

'EUROPEANA' × 'MARLENA'

ANERKANNTE DEUTSCHE ROSE 1972

T

## 'Torvill & Dean'

LANtor *(right)*

MODERN, LARGE-FLOWERED/
HYBRID TEA, PINK BLEND,
REPEAT-FLOWERING

It was a public relations coup on the raiser's part to secure news headlines about this rose within hours of the Olympic medal success of Jayne Torvill and Christopher Dean. It is aptly named for, as one writer puts it, 'pink and gold dance together across the petals'. The flowers are large and rounded, composed of 36 pale yellow petals on which appear flushes of the palest salmony pink. There is a light scent and flowers appear through summer and autumn, looking their best in cool climates. It is suitable for beds, borders or to form a hedge. It grows vigorously with an upright habit to average height and has deep green, semi-glossy foliage. ZONES 4–9.

SEALAND, UK, 1984

'GRANDPA DICKSON' ×
'ALEXANDER'

## 'Touch of Class'

KRIcarlo *(right)*
syns 'Marachal Le Clerc',
'Maréchal le Clerc'

MODERN, LARGE-FLOWERED/
HYBRID TEA, ORANGE-PINK,
REPEAT-FLOWERING

The flowers of this variety are large and beautifully formed, with high centers surrounded by many petals in a neat and symmetrical arrangement. The color is an attractive combination of pale creamy pink, suffused with coral pink. As the blooms slowly open they hold their centers for a long time, yielding a light Tea fragrance, and because they are produced on long stems, they are excellent to cut. The flowers continue blooming satisfactorily through summer and autumn, achieving their best quality in cooler temperatures. This is a good garden rose to use in a bed, border or as a hedge, growing vigorously and upright to above average height and being well furnished with large dark green leaves that are reddish when young and sometimes touched by seasonal mildew. ZONES 4–9.

KRILOFF, FRANCE, 1984

'MICÄELA' × ('QUEEN
ELIZABETH' × 'ROMANTICA')

ALL-AMERICA ROSE SELECTION
1986, PORTLAND GOLD MEDAL
1988

## 'Toulouse-Lautrec' MEIrevolt (right)

MODERN, LARGE-FLOWERED/HYBRID TEA,
MEDIUM YELLOW, REPEAT-FLOWERING

The flowers of this rose are
large and very full, with over
40 petals. They are formed in
old-fashioned style with a
random arrangement of the
petals, which gives them a soft
outline and a rather fluffy effect,
and have a pleasing scent.
Usually the blooms are borne
one to a stem and they continue
to appear through summer and
autumn. 'Toulouse-Lautrec'
is suitable for a mixed bed or
border or to make a hedge. It
grows strongly to average height
with a bushy habit and has
medium to dark green glossy
foliage. It was named for the
French artist. ZONES 4–9.

MEILLAND, FRANCE, 1993

'AMBASSADOR' ×
('KING'S RANSOM' × 'SUNBLEST')

MONZA FRAGRANCE PRIZE 1993

## 'Tour de Malakoff' (right)

OLD, CENTIFOLIA, MAUVE

A tall, lax-growing shrub
attaining a height of 6 ft (1.8 m)
or more in rich soil, 'Tour de
Malakoff' has grayish green,
moderately thorny stems that
are covered with a profusion
of medium-sized, mid- to
dark green leaves. The fragrant
flowers are fully double, quite
large—up to 4 in (10 cm) in
diameter—and flat when fully
open. Their color is most
unusual, especially on the outer
petal edges: magenta flushed
purple with lilac and grayish

highlights. The outer petals
reflex as the flower matures,
and when fully open, golden
stamens show through to add to
the overall luminosity. It can be
used as a wall plant or pillar rose
or can be grown on a tripod.
ZONES 4–10.

SOUPERT AND NOTTING, LUXEMBOURG, 1856

POSSIBLY A BOURBON × A GALLICA

T

rose was launched to mark its centenary. **ZONES 4–9.**

WARRINER, USA, 1988

'IMPATIENT' × SEEDLING

ALL-AMERICA ROSE SELECTION 1989

### 'Tradescant' AUSdir (*bottom*)

MODERN, MODERN SHRUB, DARK RED, REPEAT-FLOWERING

The flowers of 'Tradescant' are medium in size, open out almost flat and are carried in small clusters. They are deep wine crimson to purple with a handsome bloom on their petals, which number upwards of 40 and are folded tightly against one another, giving a quartered effect. There is a good fragrance, and blooms continue through summer and autumn. This rose is suitable near the front of a shrub border where, given good cultivation, it will grow to about half the size of an average shrub rose with a low, arching, spreading habit and a complement of dark green, semi-glossy leaves. In warm climates the stems grow long enough to be trained on pillars. From David Austin, it is also classi-fied as an English Rose. **ZONES 4–9.**

AUSTIN, UK, 1993

'PROSPERO' × ('CHARLES AUSTIN' × 'GLOIRE DE DUCHER')

### 'Tournament of Roses' JACient (*above*) syns 'Berkeley', 'Poesie'

MODERN, LARGE-FLOWERED/ HYBRID TEA, MEDIUM PINK, REPEAT-FLOWERING

In America, where this variety is widely grown, it is called a Grandiflora, an appro-priate name for such a stalwart grower whose big clusters of sizeable flowers carried on firm stems are noticeable in the rose garden. The blooms have a neat symmetry and show contrasting tones of pink as the petals unfold, deep pink on their outer surfaces and creamy pink within. There is a light spicy scent, and an excellent continuity of bloom is maintained through summer and autumn, the color

being particularly fine in warmer weather. It is a good variety for a hedge, group or bed, being vigorous and growing upright to above average height with glossy green leaves. The name refers to the annual rose parade held in Pasadena, and this

## 'Träumerei' KORrei, ReiKOR *(right)*
syns 'Dreaming', 'Reverie'

MODERN, CLUSTER-FLOWERED/ FLORIBUNDA, ORANGE BLEND, REPEAT-FLOWERING

The color of this well-behaved rose is a pure coral-orange, and the flowers develop from long slender buds into rounded, low-centered blooms with neatly formed hearts, holding their form but dropping off the plant quickly and cleanly when they are spent. They are carried sometimes singly, sometimes in a cluster, have good fragrance, continue in bloom through summer and autumn and tolerate bad weather. This variety is suitable for bedding and borders or to make a hedge, as it grows vigorously with a bushy, free-branching habit to average height. There is a dense covering of reddish young leaves that become dark green with age. The synonyms are translations of the German name, which is the title of a piano work by Robert Schumann. ZONES 5–10.

KORDES, GERMANY, 1974
'COLOUR WONDER' × SEEDLING

## 'Travemünde'
KORrantu *(right)*

MODERN, CLUSTER-FLOWERED/ FLORIBUNDA, MEDIUM RED, REPEAT-FLOWERING

The flowers of this very deep red rose are carried in crowded clusters, giving a rich and colorful effect. They are full petalled, of middling size and are carried on strong stems, but there is little fragrance. During summer and autumn the continuity of bloom is well maintained, and the flowers resist bad weather well. Because the variety is so dark, it merits a site where it can be viewed from a distance and where it will be lit up by the sun. The bush grows strongly with an upright, bushy habit to average height and has dark green leaves that are reddish when young. The rose was named for a town in North Germany. ZONES 4–9.

KORDES, GERMANY, 1968
'LILLI MARLEEN' × 'AMA'
ANERKANNTE DEUTSCHE ROSE 1966

T

### 'Traviata' *(top)*

MODERN, LARGE-FLOWERED/
HYBRID TEA, RED BLEND,
REPEAT-FLOWERING

This is a strikingly
pretty rose, made up
of some 30 wavy petals
that are bright red
over much of their
petal area, save for
prominent white
patches towards the
base. The blooms,
which are quite large,
open with high centers
before developing a
loosely cupped shape.
They have a satisfying
fragrance, and con-
tinue in production
through summer
and autumn, the late
season blooms being
particularly fine. This
variety is very suitable
for beds and borders.
It grows vigorously
with a bushy habit to
average height, making
plenty of basal shoots,
and is furnished with
bronze-green, leathery
leaves. **ZONES 4–9.**

MEILLAND, FRANCE, 1962

'BACCARÀ' × ('INDEPENDENCE' ×
'GRAND'MÈRE JENNY')

### 'Treasure Trove'
*(right)*

MODERN, RAMBLER, APRICOT
BLEND

'Kiftsgate' is a form
of *Rosa filipes* that
grows to enormous
proportions; it was
found and grown
at Kiftsgate Court
in Gloucestershire in
England. 'Treasure
Trove' is a chance

seedling of it found by
John Treasure in his
garden in Staffordshire.
The felicitous name
was suggested by
Graham Thomas. It is
an enormous climber
that bears large trusses
of medium-sized,
cupped, semi-double
flowers with 23 petals.
The blooms are apricot,
mauve, pink and cream,

and are strongly
scented. **ZONES 7–9.**

TREASURE, UK, 1977

'KIFTSGATE' × CHINA ROSE
(POSSIBLY 'OLD BLUSH')

### 'Trevor Griffiths'
AUSold

MODERN, MODERN SHRUB,
MEDIUM PINK,
REPEAT-FLOWERING

These flowers are quite
large and well filled
with petals that are
somewhat randomly
and informally arranged,
giving the effect of an
old-fashioned rose.
They are a warm and
deepish shade of rose
pink, have a pleasing
scent and appear
through summer and
autumn. The plant has
a spreading habit,
growing to average
height, with rough-
textured, dark green
leaves. 'Trevor Griffiths'
is a good rose for a
border. It was named
for the celebrated New
Zealand rosarian whose
enthusiasm, writing
and photography have
brought numerous
under-appreciated
varieties to notice.
It is also classified
as an English Rose.
**ZONES 4–9.**

AUSTIN, UK, 1994

'WIFE OF BATH' × 'HERO'

### 'Tricolore de Flandre' *(top)*
OLD, GALLICA, PINK BLEND

This Gallica resembles the better known 'Camaieux'. The double flowers are pale pink, heavily striped with purple and have a pleasing fragrance. The plant is upright but not very tall and has been recommended for growing in a pot. It can revert to monochrome, and flowers only once. **ZONES 4–9.**

VAN HOUTTE, BELGIUM, PRE-1846

PARENTAGE UNKNOWN

### 'Trier' *(bottom)*
MODERN, RAMBLER, WHITE, REPEAT-FLOWERING

This rose is an upright bush or short climber

with small leaves and small, creamy yellow flowers with a rosy flush. They are almost single. There are much better short climbing roses, but this rose is of considerable historical interest for rosarians. In England, the Reverend Joseph Pemberton crossed 'Trier' with a series of other roses to create a group of Modern Shrubs called the Hybrid Musks. They became, and remain, successful and popular. **ZONES 5–9.**

LAMBERT, GERMANY, 1904

PROBABLY A SELF-SEEDLING OF 'AGLAIA'

### 'Triolet' ORAdon
syn. 'Tanned Beauty'
MODERN, LARGE-FLOWERED/ HYBRID TEA, APRICOT BLEND, REPEAT-FLOWERING

Of all the Modern Garden Roses, this one probably displays the most impressive color combinations: the tan-colored buds open to blooms of perfect Large-flowered shape with tight centers of cream; the undersides of the outer petals are tan. These outer petals curl back as the bloom matures. The vigorous shrub produces flowers that are suitable for exhibition or indoor display. They appear through summer, and in autumn the color seems more intense due to the hips and leaves. Another plus for this rose is its very good fragrance. **ZONES 5–11.**

ORARD, FRANCE, 1995

PARENTAGE UNKNOWN

T

### 'Troilus' AUSoil
*(below)*

MODERN, MODERN SHRUB,
APRICOT BLEND,
REPEAT-FLOWERING

This variety bears large flowers made up of 40 or more petals that lie back row upon row, showing a dainty array of petal tips. They are often borne in large, heavy clusters. The blooms are cream and honey with a hint of apricot. They have a pleasing scent. 'Troilus' is suitable for a shrub border, faring best in warm climates where the honey-apricot color is enriched; in cooler regions it is recommended for the greenhouse. The plant grows sturdily with an upright habit to average height and has large, dark green, semi-glossy leaves. It is also classified as an English Rose. **ZONES 4–9.**

AUSTIN, UK, 1983

('DUCHESSE DE MONTEBELLO' ×
'CHAUCER') × 'CHARLES AUSTIN'

### 'Triomphe du Luxembourg' *(top)*

OLD, TEA, PINK BLEND,
REPEAT-FLOWERING

This strong Tea Rose bears very double, salmon-pink flowers that change to buff pink with age. It was one of the more celebrated roses of its time and was very expensive, retailing at 35 francs in 1836. Its full name would have been 'Triomphe of the Luxembourg Gardens', which are in Paris and where Alexandre Hardy was the chief horticulturist. Some writers erroneously substitute 'de' for 'du' in the name. **ZONES 7–9.**

HARDY, FRANCE, CIRCA 1835
PARENTAGE UNKNOWN

## 'Tropicana' TANorstar
### *(top)*
### syn. 'Super Star'
MODERN, LARGE-FLOWERED/
HYBRID TEA, ORANGE-RED,
REPEAT-FLOWERING

This rose was significant at its time of introduction because of its pure rosy vermilion color, which had a luminous quality superior to anything found before in a Large-flowered Rose. The flowers are substantial and well formed, borne either singly or in wide-spaced candelabra heads. There is a light scent. As a cut flower and for exhibition, it is useful and continues to produce flowers very satisfactorily through summer and autumn, the mid-season ones often appearing with ragged edges to the petals. 'Tropicana' is used in beds and borders, though its growth habit tends to be uneven and it is liable to mildew readily where the circulation of air is limited. The plant grows vigorously with a lanky habit to average height or above, and has rather small matt leaves. **'Climbing Tropicana'** (TANgosar, TANgostar; syn. 'Climbing Super Star'; Boerner, USA, 1971) has never become popular, though in a position where there is plenty of air circulating through the plant, such as a pergola or open fence, it can make strong arching growth, being capable of extending somewhat farther than the average climbing rose.
**ZONES 4–9.**

TANTAU, GERMANY, 1960
(SEEDLING × 'PEACE') ×
(SEEDLING × 'ALPINE GLOW')
NATIONAL ROSE SOCIETY
PRESIDENT'S INTERNATIONAL
TROPHY 1960, PORTLAND GOLD
MEDAL 1961, ALL-AMERICA ROSE
SELECTION 1963, AMERICAN ROSE
SOCIETY GOLD MEDAL 1967

## 'Trumpeter' MACtrum
### *(bottom)*
MODERN, CLUSTER-FLOWERED/
FLORIBUNDA, ORANGE-RED,
REPEAT-FLOWERING

The admirable qualities that have justly earned many awards for 'Trumpeter' include the freedom with which it produces its showy clusters of bright red flowers throughout the season, and the manner in which it displays them on a neat, clean-foliaged plant. The blooms are of medium size, full petalled and open loosely cupped, standing up to all kinds of weather, and falling cleanly when spent. Their only drawback is that the scent is light. It is excellent in beds, borders, as a low hedge and in standard form. It grows vigorously, making plenty of new shoots, with an up-right, bushy habit to below average height and with a plentiful covering of deep green leaves. The name is a reference to Louis Armstrong in whose honor the seed parent 'Satchmo' was named.
**ZONES 4–9.**

MCGREDY, NEW ZEALAND, 1977
'SATCHMO' × SEEDLING
NEW ZEALAND STAR OF THE
SOUTH PACIFIC 1977, PORTLAND
GOLD MEDAL 1981, ROYAL
NATIONAL ROSE SOCIETY JAMES
MASON GOLD MEDAL 1991,
ROYAL HORTICULTURAL SOCIETY
AWARD OF GARDEN MERIT

### 'Tumbling Waters'   POUltumb  *(bottom)*
**MODERN, CLUSTER-FLOWERED/FLORIBUNDA, WHITE,
REPEAT-FLOWERING**

The raiser seems unsure whether to call this variety
a bush or a shrub rose. It produces cascades of
neatly formed white blooms with remarkable
continuity throughout summer and autumn.

They are of medium size, semi-double and open
cupped, showing yellow stamens and yielding
a light sweet fragrance. 'Tumbling Waters' makes
a hummocky, spreading plant after the manner of
a ground-cover rose except that it is not procum-
bent enough to be truly so described. It is ideal for
mixed borders, performs well in containers, and
makes a graceful umbrella standard. The white
flowers show up effectively against the rich green
foliage. **ZONES 4–9.**
POULSEN, DENMARK, 1997
PARENTAGE UNKNOWN

### 'Tuscany'   *(left)*
### syn. 'The Old Velvet Rose'
**OLD, GALLICA, MAUVE**

'Tuscany' is a very old rose that bears semi-double,
maroon-purple flowers on a medium-sized,
upright bush. One of the plant's most attractive
features is the show of yellow stamens. It is
probable that this is the 'Velvet Rose' described
by herbalist John Gerard in 1596. **ZONES 4–10.**
POSSIBLY OF ITALIAN ORIGIN, PRE-1596
PARENTAGE UNKNOWN

T

## 'Tutu Mauve'
*(right)*

MODERN, CLUSTER-FLOWERED/
FLORIBUNDA, MAUVE,
REPEAT-FLOWERING

The flowers of this
variety are fairly large
for a Cluster-flowered
Rose and consist of
30 petals. They open
from small clusters
of plump buds into
rounded blooms that
become cupped and
display a range of
unconventional color,
with mauve and rose
shading on a magenta
base. The flowers
are produced over a
long period through
summer and autumn
and have a light scent.
It is suitable for
planting in mixed beds
and borders, being
best in warm climates,
because the texture of
the petals is such that
they do not enjoy cold
or wet conditions.
The bush grows with
moderate vigor and
a bushy habit to below
average height.
**ZONES 4–9.**

DELBARD-CHABERT, FRANCE,
1963

PARENTAGE UNKNOWN

MADRID GOLD MEDAL 1962

## 'Tzigane'  *(right)*
syn. 'Tiz'

MODERN, LARGE-FLOWERED/
HYBRID TEA, RED BLEND,
REPEAT-FLOWERING

The strikingly beautiful
blooms are large and
well formed, with
broad petals, and open
with high centers,
becoming cupped.
The petals are bright
scarlet red inside and
chrome yellow outside,
as startling a bicolor
as may be imagined.
There is some fragrance.
'Tzigane' is perhaps
grown more for
sentiment and historic
interest today, but it
can still surprise the
onlooker with its
beauty. As a plant it is
a moderate performer,
not free with its new
wood, and is apt to die
back in hard winters. It
grows with an upright
habit to below average
height and has glossy
foliage that resembles
the color of a copper
beech. A tzigane is a
Hungarian gypsy
dance. **ZONES 4–9.**

MEILLAND, FRANCE, 1951

'PEACE' × 'J. B. MEILLAND'

T

UV

### 'Ulrich Brunner Fils' *(right)*
syn. 'Ulrich Brunner'

OLD, HYBRID PERPETUAL, DEEP
PINK, REPEAT-FLOWERING

'Paul Neyron' is the quintessential giant-flowered, big Hybrid Perpetual of the nineteenth century and still flaunts its 'neyron' pink flowers. This rose, its offspring, has bright cerise-red, large, cupped, fragrant flowers of the same style. The bush is upright and vigorous. Ulrich Brunner, the son, was a rosarian of Lausanne. **ZONES 5–9.**

LEVET, FRANCE, 1881

SEEDLING OF 'PAUL NEYRON'

### 'Uncle Joe' *(right)*
syns 'El Toro', 'Toro'

MODERN, LARGE-FLOWERED/
HYBRID TEA, DARK RED,
REPEAT-FLOWERING

The flowers of this dark red variety are extremely large and full, with high centers and symmetrical Large-flowered form. They are so long lasting that this becomes a fault, because the old petals hang on and become unsightly. Flowers continue to appear through summer and autumn, and some noses are able to detect a little fragrance. 'Uncle Joe' is vigorous and performs best in sunny climates, for the broad petals are likely to stick together and fail to open in cool or wet conditions. It lasts for ages as a cut flower; the rose 'Goliath', a mainstay of the export flower trade in India, is reputed to be this rose under another name. The plant grows vigorously with an upright habit to above average height and has large, dark leathery leaves. **ZONES 4–9.**

KERN, USA, 1972

(['MIRANDY' × 'CHARLES
MALLERIN'] × SEEDLING)

U

### 'Uncle Merc' *(right)*

MODERN, CLUSTER-FLOWERED/FLORIBUNDA, MEDIUM PINK,
REPEAT-FLOWERING

'Uncle Merc' is a Cluster-flowered form with flowers that are a blend of pinks. They are produced singly and in clusters on a bushy, medium-sized plant with matt mid-green foliage. Disease resistance is good. Buds are shapely, and open to medium-sized blooms of 20 petals. There is a slight fragrance and repeat-blooming is rather slow. **ZONES 5–10.**

PARENTAGE UNKNOWN

### 'Uncle Walter' MACon *(center)*

MODERN, LARGE-FLOWERED/HYBRID TEA, MEDIUM RED,
REPEAT-FLOWERING

The flowers of this variety are crimson scarlet, high centered and fairly large, with about 30 wide petals, and open rather loosely on very tall stems. They are often carried in open clusters, and the overall effect is more like a big shrub than a Large-flowered bush. Disbudding produces better quality flowers. There is a light fragrance, and continuity of bloom is maintained through summer and autumn. 'Uncle Walter' needs careful placement or it will dominate its neighbors; towards the back of a border is a suitable place, or it could be treated as a climber and grown on a support. It grows very vigorously with a tall, free-branching habit to well above average height. The leaves are large, crimson when young, then maturing to bronze-green, and plentiful. Raiser Sam McGredy named the rose for his uncle, Walter Johnston, who looked after the nursery during his infancy. **ZONES 4–9.**

MCGREDY, UK, 1963

'DETROITER' × 'HEIDELBERG'

NATIONAL ROSE SOCIETY CERTIFICATE OF MERIT 1963,
SCANDINAVIA NORD-ROSE AWARD

### 'UNICEF' COCjojo *(bottom)*
syn. 'The Audrey Hepburn Rose'

MODERN, CLUSTER-FLOWERED/FLORIBUNDA, ORANGE BLEND,
REPEAT-FLOWERING

These flowers are carried in upright sprays and contain quite an assortment of orange, peach and apricot-yellow shades, with deep rose red flushes along the margins of the petals as they mature. They are of medium size, full petalled with neat tight centers, and open loosely cupped. There is a slight scent. This is a suitable rose for a hedge, bed or border, growing with an upright habit to average height or less and having ample rich green foliage. It was named for the United Nations' Children's Fund. **ZONES 4–9.**

COCKER, UK, 1993

'ANNE COCKER' × 'REMEMBER ME'

GLASGOW CERTIFICATE OF MERIT 1995

U

### 'Uwe Seeler' KORsee
*(left)*

syns 'Gitta Grummer',
'Orange Vilmorin',
'Rainer Maria Rilke'

OLD, CLUSTER-FLOWERED/
FLORIBUNDA, ORANGE BLEND,
REPEAT-FLOWERING

The color of this rose is a luminous salmon-orange. The fairly full flowers are formed with high centers like Large-flowered Roses; they are borne singly or in small clusters and fulfil the requirements of a modern Cluster-flowered Rose by blooming freely and dropping their spent petals cleanly. They have a pleasant scent and appear with good continuity through summer and autumn. 'Uwe Seeler' is useful for bedding, grouping in a border or as a hedge. It grows vigorously with an upright, bushy habit to average height and has dense semi-glossy foliage that is reddish when young.
**ZONES 4–9.**

KORDES, GERMANY, 1970

'QUEEN ELIZABETH' ×
'COLOR WONDER'

### 'Unique Blanche'
*(above)*
syns 'Blanche Unique',
*Rosa centifolia alba*,
'Unica Alba',
'Vièrge de Clery',
'White Provence'

OLD, CENTIFOLIA, WHITE

'Unique Blanche' is a typical Centifolia—a lax shrub to about 4 ft (1.2 m)—it has darkish wood with plentiful thorns and dark green, deeply serrated foliage. The flowers are creamy white to pure white and are made up of many rather narrowly fluted petals, giving a distinctly ragged appearance when fully open. Sometimes these petals are folded inward within the center to form a button in the middle of the flower; at other times they open up to show off a few yellow stamens. Each fragrant bloom is usually about 3 in (8 cm) across and they appear on the bush rather later than most other once-flowering roses. This plant is well named; it is the only pure white Centifolia now commonly used in landscaping.
**ZONES 5–10.**

UK, 1775

POSSIBLY A SPORT OF
'CABBAGE ROSE'

U

### 'Valencia' KOReklia *(right)*
syns 'New Valencia', 'Valeccia', 'Valencia 89'
MODERN, LARGE-FLOWERED/HYBRID TEA, APRICOT BLEND, REPEAT-FLOWERING

The light copper-yellow blooms of this variety are among the purest in this color in the rose garden. They are fairly large, full of petals, usually borne singly on long stems and open with high centers in classic Large-flowered Rose form, becoming cupped before the petals fall. They have a sweet enduring fragrance, and there is a good continuity of bloom through summer and autumn. A fine rose for the border and for cutting, 'Valencia' has a some-what splayed and uneven growth habit which makes it less appropriate for a bed or hedge. It grows vigorously with a rather open aspect to average height and is adorned with rich green, leathery leaves. **ZONES 4–9.**

KORDES, GERMANY, 1989

PARENTAGE UNKNOWN

DURBANVILLE GOLD MEDAL 1988, ROYAL NATIONAL ROSE SOCIETY EDLAND FRAGRANCE MEDAL 1989, RNHS CERTIFICATE OF MERIT 1989

### 'Valentine Heart' DICogle *(right)*
syns 'St Andrew's', 'Tinon'
MODERN, CLUSTER-FLOWERED/FLORIBUNDA, MEDIUM PINK/PINK BLEND, REPEAT-FLOWERING

There are only 20 or so petals in the flowers of this variety, but their tight centers encompass a wide range of subtle colors to charming effect. The buds are the palest of scarlet, opening with blush pink on the insides of the petals and then taking on variable hues of rosy lilac and pink, giving a wonderful depth to the flowers. The fragrant

blooms are produced with good continuity throughout summer and autumn. 'Valentine Heart' is a good rose for a bed or the front of a border, where its fresh and cheerful appearance can be readily enjoyed, and can be drawn on for buttonholes and small flower arrangements.

The plant grows bushily with a slightly spreading habit to below average height and has dark foliage. **ZONES 4–9.**

DICKSON, UK, 1990

'SHONA' × 'POT O' GOLD'

GENEVA GOLD MEDAL 1988, ROYAL NATIONAL ROSE SOCIETY CERTIFICATE OF MERIT 1988, BELFAST CERTIFICATE OF MERIT 1992

V

### 'Vanguard' *(below)*

MODERN, HYBRID RUGOSA,
ORANGE-PINK,
REPEAT-FLOWERING

This is an untypical
Rugosa cross that bears
very large, pale orange-
apricot to salmon
flowers that open with
a confused arrange-
ment of petals. They
have an excellent
fragrance, and bloom
through summer and
autumn. 'Vanguard'
requires careful placing
in the garden because it
can grow twice the
height of the average
shrub rose; the back
of a shrub border is a
suitable position, or it
can be used to make a
dense high hedge. It is
tolerant of poorer soil
and grows vigorously
with an upright habit,
with plentiful light
glossy foliage that
is burnished and
wrinkled. ZONES 3–9.

STEVENS, USA, 1932
(ROSA WICHURANA ×
R. RUGOSA ALBA) × 'ELDORADO'
AMERICAN ROSE SOCIETY
DR W. VAN FLEET MEDAL 1933,
AMERICAN ROSE SOCIETY DAVID
FÜRSTENBERG PRIZE 1934

### 'Vanilla' KORplasina
*(below left)*
syn. 'Our Vanilla'

MODERN, CLUSTER-FLOWERED/
FLORIBUNDA, WHITE (SHADED
GREEN), REPEAT-FLOWERING

This greenhouse rose
has attracted notice by
reason of its unusual
coloring: the flowers
are creamy white with
a distinct green patina.
They are fairly small
and are made up of
firm petals that unfold
very slowly, meanwhile
holding the blooms
in an attractive shape
for a very long time.
As is usual with hard-
petalled florists' roses,
no fragrance is detect-
able. 'Vanilla' can
be cultivated under
glass for the benefit of
having the flowers to
cut and as a talking
point for visitors, but
it is not recommended
for the garden except
in warm climates. It
continues to bear
blooms through summer
and autumn and grows
to average height or
more, with leathery
leaves. ZONES 5–9.

KORDES, GERMANY, 1994
PARENTAGE UNKNOWN

### 'Vanity' *(above)*

MODERN, MODERN SHRUB,
DEEP PINK, REPEAT-FLOWERING

This is a plant that seems unsure of its identity; classified as a shrub, the trailing character of the stems makes it easier to treat as a short climber. The medium-sized blooms are deep pink, with only a few rather untidily arranged petals, and open to show yellow stamens. The lightly scented flowers are borne in wide clusters on long, arching stems, and repeat-bloom through summer and autumn. It can be included in a shrub border, where it will spread and eventually become a large undisciplined thicket, or it can be trained against a wall, fence or pillar, making an effective climbing plant. The foliage is semi-glossy and rather sparse. ZONES 4–9.

PEMBERTON, UK, 1920

'CHÂTEAU DE CLOS VOUGEOT' ×
SEEDLING

### 'Variegata di Bologna' *(right)*

OLD, BOURBON, RED BLEND,
REPEAT-FLOWERING

These fragrant flowers are white, striped purplish red; they are double and globular and are borne in clusters. There are few repeat flowers after the main summer flush. The plant is tall and lax and needs good cultivation, without which it is susceptible to black spot. It will occasionally sport back to the parent. The foliage is somewhat coarse and sparse. It can be grown as a short climber, or pruned to a bush. ZONES 5–9.

BONFIGLIOLI & SON, ITALY, 1909

SPORT OF 'VICTOR EMMANUEL'

V

Viaud' and 'Violette'.
It flowers early in the
season. ZONES 5–9.

SCHMIDT, GERMANY, 1909

'CRIMSON RAMBLER' ×
'ERINNERUNG AN BROD'

ROYAL HORTICULTURAL SOCIETY
AWARD OF GARDEN MERIT 1993

### 'Velvet Fragrance'
FRYperdee  *(left)*
syn. 'Velours Parfumé'
MODERN, LARGE-FLOWERED/
HYBRID TEA, DARK RED,
REPEAT-FLOWERING

These flowers are
among the deepest reds
grown today, their
velvety petal texture
being apparent when
sun lights the blooms.
They are large and high
centered, with over
40 long petals, and are
often borne singly or
sometimes several
together in a wide spray,
in either case on stems
long enough to cut for
indoor decoration.
There is good continu-
ity of bloom through
summer and autumn
and, as the name and
awards testify, the
flowers carry a satisfy-
ing fragrance. 'Velvet
Fragrance' looks well
planted as a group. It
grows strongly with an
upright, rather lanky
habit to above average
height and has large,
dark green, semi-glossy
leaves. ZONES 4–9.

FRYER, UK, 1988

SEEDLING × SEEDLING

ROYAL NATIONAL ROSE SOCIETY
EDLAND FRAGRANCE AWARD
1988, RNRS TRIAL GROUND
CERTIFICATE 1988, BADEN-BADEN
FRAGRANCE AWARD 1990

### 'Veilchenblau'
*(above)*
syns 'Blue Rambler',
'Blue Rosalie',
'Violet Blue'

MODERN, RAMBLER, MAUVE

This popular Rambler
in the *Rosa multiflora*
style is vigorous, semi-
rigid and almost thorn-
less; it has fresh green
leaves. The fragrant
flowers, taking after the
'male' parent, are violet
streaked with white,
fading to gray. They are
small, semi-double and
incurved, and show
prominent yellow
stamens. This is the
best known of the three
similar violet-purple
Ramblers, the others
being 'Rose-Marie

V

### 'Velvet Hour'  (above)

MODERN, LARGE-FLOWERED/HYBRID TEA, DARK RED,
REPEAT-FLOWERING

The blooms of this variety are a rich dark blood
red and are carried firmly on strong tall stems.
They are of modest size for a Large-flowered Rose
and neatly formed in the young blooms. As they
open, the edges of the reflexing petals furl into
points, giving a spiky effect. There is a sweet
scent, and the continuity of bloom through
summer and autumn is satisfactorily maintained.
'Velvet Hour' can be used for beds and borders
and as a hedge, and is certainly an asset for
cutting, as the blooms last well. It grows with an
upright habit to above average height and has a
respectable covering of dark green, semi-glossy
foliage. ZONES 4–9.

LEGRICE, UK, 1978

PARENTAGE UNKNOWN

### 'Venusta Pendula'

OLD, AYRSHIRE, WHITE

The origin of this rose is unknown, but it was
reintroduced by Kordes in Germany in 1928.
For a short account of the Ayrshire Roses, see
'Splendens'. This is a moderately rampant
Climber or Rambler that bears clusters of small,
white flushed pink, double flowers that practically
smother the plant in its short flowering season.
There is practically no scent. If grown through
a tree, for which it is eminently suitable, the
effect is in fact pendulous and *venusta* (Latin for
beautiful). ZONES 4–9.

PARENTAGE UNKNOWN

V

### 'Versailles' DELset
### *(bottom)*
### syn. 'Castel'

**MODERN, LARGE-FLOWERED/
HYBRID TEA, LIGHT PINK,
REPEAT-FLOWERING**

This variety has light pink, double blooms that develop from ovoid buds. It is an average-sized bush with an upright growth habit and dark green, glossy, leathery leaves. The soft, cupped, slightly fragrant blooms are formed freely and are found in typical Large-flowered formations. 'Versailles' suffers from mildew and black spot late in the season, so it is best to conduct a sound eradication program from the beginning of the season. At its release it was a winner of many awards, although it has been overlooked greatly by professional growers; it is not now widely grown, and as it was not released in all countries, it will be difficult to find plants in many nurseries. **ZONES 5–11.**

DELBARD-CHABERT, FRANCE, 1967

('QUEEN ELIZABETH' × 'PROVENCE') × ('MICHÈLE MEILLAND' × 'BAYADÈRE')

BADEN-BADEN GOLD MEDAL 1965, BAGATELLE GOLD MEDAL 1966, GENEVA GOLD MEDAL 1966

### 'Verdi' *(top)*

**MODERN, MODERN SHRUB,
MAUVE BLEND,
REPEAT-FLOWERING**

Only very few nurseries list this rose, which is a Modern Shrub with a strong scent similar to that of *Rosa moschata*, the Musk Rose. The pinkish mauve flowers are borne in massed sprays, covering the shiny green foliage on an upright plant. 'Verdi' needs to be well cared for if it is to flower well. **ZONES 5–10.**

LENS, BELGIUM, 1984

'MR BLUEBIRD' × 'VIOLET HOOD'

V

### 'Verschuren' *(right)*

MODERN, LARGE-FLOWERED/HYBRID TEA,
LIGHT PINK, REPEAT-FLOWERING

This Large-flowered Rose produces classically formed blooms that are medium pink in the urn-shaped stage, then mellow out to a gentle light pink as they open more fully. The variegated mid-green leaves are splashed with pale yellow— a rare and highly valued characteristic. **ZONES 5–10.**

VERSCHUREN, THE NETHERLANDS, 1904

PARENTAGE UNKNOWN

### 'Vesper' *(below right)*

MODERN, CLUSTER-FLOWERED/FLORIBUNDA,
ORANGE BLEND, REPEAT-FLOWERING

Another of the unusually colored Cluster-flowered Roses bred by the late Edward LeGrice, 'Vesper' produces striking apricot-brown flowers. They develop from well-shaped buds to give small to large, very well-spaced clusters. Each bloom is semi-double and has 20 petals. There is a slight fragrance. Green and leathery foliage covers this short and stocky bush. The spring and autumn flushes are most appealing, although the flowers fade rather quickly in summer. The small leaves are blue-gray, and disease resistance is average, with some susceptibility to black spot and mildew early in the season. Pruning should be carefully done to achieve a good, well-rounded bush that will bring pleasure in spring. 'Vesper' is a good rose for cutting. **ZONES 5–10.**

LEGRICE, UK, 1966

PARENTAGE UNKNOWN

ROYAL NATIONAL ROSE SOCIETY TRIAL
GROUND CERTIFICATE 1967

V

### 'Vestey's Pink Tea' *(right)*

OLD, TEA, MEDIUM PINK,
REPEAT-FLOWERING

This rose was redis-covered in Lady Vestey's garden, although the original name is not known. 'Vestey's Pink Tea' forms a medium-sized, spreading bush with rather large, curved thorns and mid-green, semi-glossy foliage that is very free of disease. The flowers are deep rose pink with a cream base to each petal; a suffusion of cream runs through the pink. There are 30–40 petals, forming a full flower that is attractively cupped. The buds are well shaped and the blooms keep their color well. This variety will flower continuously in mild climates, with the best flowers usually seen in autumn and winter. There is a typical Tea Rose scent. **ZONES 5–10.**

PARENTAGE UNKNOWN

### 'Vestey's Yellow Tea' *(right)*

OLD, TEA, LIGHT YELLOW,
REPEAT-FLOWERING

This Tea Rose was reintroduced into commerce from Lady Vestey's garden. The original name has been lost. 'Vestey's Yellow Tea' is an unusual rose, since it produces masses of loose, semi-double flowers of 10–15 petals, and there are a few petals in the center of the flower. The blooms are medium to large, and are pro-duced in small clusters. In warm weather, the blooms are cream and fade to white, but in cool weather they are a most attractive soft yellow, the same color as 'McGredy's Yellow'. The bush is tall and very spreading with an abundance of mid-green, semi-glossy foliage. There is a slight perfume. 'Vestey's Yellow Tea' covers itself with flowers from ground level upward; it is an excellent rose to plant in groups for continuous color. **ZONES 5–10.**

PARENTAGE UNKNOWN

## 'Vi's Violet' MORvi
**MODERN, MINIATURE, MAUVE, REPEAT-FLOWERING**

These soft lavender flowers fade very quickly—before the bloom even opens fully. The blooms are double and have a light fragrance, appearing amid the matt mid-green foliage that is subject to mildew and other fungi. This plant is a compact, upright bush, which has no resistance whatsoever to disease. Frequent spraying is absolutely essential to maintain a healthy plant. **ZONES 5–10.**

MOORE, USA, 1991

SEEDLING × 'ANGEL FACE'

## 'Vick's Caprice' *(above)*
**OLD, HYBRID PERPETUAL, PINK BLEND, REPEAT-FLOWERING**

The large, fragrant flowers of this rose contain 25 petals. They are lilac rose, often striped white and carmine, and are cupped. The blooms are inclined to ball in wet weather. The plant has a bushy, compact habit and can revert to the original, as is the way with such sports. It is noticeably shorter in growth than the parent, which is a 'La Reine' type of Hybrid Perpetual. The Hybrid Perpetuals were extremely varied because of their complex hybridity, and the experts used to divide them into 12 distinct groups. **ZONES 5–9.**

VICK, USA, 1891

SPORT OF 'ARCHIDUCHESSE ELISABETH D'AÛTRICHE'

V

## 'Vicomtesse Pierre du Fou'

MODERN, LARGE-FLOWERED CLIMBER, ORANGE-PINK,
REPEAT-FLOWERING

This rampant Climber needs ample space and
sunlight to produce its best blooms, which have a
very fragrant, unfading scent. The large, double
flowers are red and age to a deeper orange-pink.
The strongly wooded plant is easy to prune
because of its wealth of growth, although the
framework will have to be carefully planned,
and priority must be given to carefully training
lateral canes at pruning to produce the best early
blooms. It will repeat-flower in good conditions,
which is unusual for a Climber of this period.
Growth is vigorous, and the foliage is large, glossy
and bronze. This variety is not widely grown, and
is found only in specialist catalogues. **ZONES 6–11.**

SAUVAGEOT, FRANCE, 1923

'L'IDEAL' × 'JOSEPH HILL'

## 'Victor Borge' POUlvue *(below)*
syn. 'Michael Crawford'

MODERN, LARGE-FLOWERED/HYBRID TEA, ORANGE BLEND,
REPEAT-FLOWERING

This rose was named after two very talented
people and is better known in some countries
as 'Michael Crawford'. The bush is healthy and
vigorous and is a medium to tall grower with a
good coverage of leaves, and resistance to mildew
in warm areas. The well-shaped buds open to
large salmon-orange flowers with a brushing of
light peach. They are fully double and are carried
singly or in small clusters, and there is some scent
but it can be washed out in damp weather. If
the bush is well fed it is disease free. The repeat-
flowering is spontaneous, which allows the plant
to produce large splashes of color in the garden,
provided it is planted in full sun. **ZONES 5–10.**

POULSEN, DENMARK, 1995

PARENTAGE UNKNOWN

COURTRAI CERTIFICATE OF MERIT 1990, BELFAST CERTIFICATE
OF MERIT 1992

## 'Victor Emmanuel'
*(right)*

OLD, BOURBON, DEEP RED,
REPEAT-FLOWERING

This moderately vigorous bush bears large, double, richly colored velvety black blooms. It would be very hard to find these days, and is more celebrated as a parent of 'Variegata di Bologna'. Victor Emmanuel II (1820–78, King of Sardinia) was also the first king of unified Italy. Some rosarians say this rose is a Hybrid Perpetual.
**ZONES 5–9.**

GUILLOT PÈRE, FRANCE, 1859

PARENTAGE UNKNOWN

## 'Victor Hugo'

OLD, HYBRID PERPETUAL, DEEP
RED, REPEAT-FLOWERING

The flowers of 'Victor Hugo' are double and contain 30 petals. They are carmine-red shaded purple, globular and of medium size. It is said to require very good cultivation, and is available from only a few specialist growers. There are also a Bourbon and a Meilland Large-flowered Rose with the same name. Victor Hugo was a famous French writer (1802–85). This was the breeder's last rose.
**ZONES 5–10.**

SCHWARTZ, FRANCE, 1884

'CHARLES LEFÈBVRE' × SEEDLING

## 'Victoriana' *(right)*

MODERN, CLUSTER-FLOWERED/
FLORIBUNDA, ORANGE BLEND,
REPEAT-FLOWERING

This unusual rose has its best flowers in cooler regions and tends to lose its individuality in the heat of summer. The very dark burnt orange blooms have a brown appearance, with the centers of the flowers a lighter shade—it is certainly evocative of that timeless era. The plant itself grows into a vigorous low bush and is an ideal choice for a patio or small standard rose, as well as being ideal for a low border or mass planting in an area that is to be kept short. Its health is good and with some preventive measures it can remain free of disease all season. Many rose nurseries do not grow this bush as it is hard to find growth that will be suitable for propagation. 'Victoriana' is slightly fragrant and has a good repeat-flowering. **ZONES 5–10.**

LEGRICE, UK, 1977

PARENTAGE UNKNOWN

V

### 'Ville de Londres'

OLD, GALLICA, DEEP PINK

This rose seems to be available only in Europe. It bears double, medium-sized flowers that are a lovely cerise-pink. They are fragrant. The plant has a compact growth habit. François Joyaux believes the rose sold by this name may be 'La Gloire des Jardins' (Descemet, France, pre-1815). **ZONES 4–9.**

POSSIBLY VIBERT, FRANCE, PRE-1850

PARENTAGE UNKNOWN

### 'Vino Delicado'  *(above)*

MODERN, LARGE-FLOWERED/HYBRID TEA, MAUVE, REPEAT-FLOWERING

This classically formed Large-flowered Rose has mauve flowers that are tinged on the outside with tones of darker purple. The color is a novelty and is difficult to match in the garden bed. The well-formed buds open quickly to full blown flowers that exude a slight rose fragrance. It is an upright-growing bush with large, leathery foliage. 'Vino Delicado' is one of a number of rose plants developed to widen the spectrum of the *Rosa* color range towards blue. It had its part to play but other roses, such as 'Paradise' and 'Blue Moon', grow and perform in a better way. **ZONES 5–10.**

RAFFEL, USA, 1972

SEEDLING × 'MAUVE MELODEE'

### 'Violacée'

OLD, MOSS, MAUVE

This is now a very rare rose, and should not be confused with 'Violacea' (syn. 'La Belle Sultane'), a very desirable Gallica. The flowers are purple, shaded violet to grayish pink. They are full and large. **ZONES 4–9.**

SOUPERT AND NOTTING, LUXEMBOURG, 1876

SHOWS STRONG AFFINITY TO *ROSA GALLICA*

V

## 'Violet Carson'

MACio *(right)*

MODERN, CLUSTER-FLOWERED/
FLORIBUNDA, ORANGE-PINK/
PINK BLEND, REPEAT-FLOWERING

'Violet Carson' produces masses of blooms throughout the season. The light-petalled, strong salmon-pink blooms open from classically styled buds and are produced in clusters in large heads. It is a vigorous, low-growing bush that is quick to repeat-flower. Pruning in winter is an easy task on the short stout growth. It is an ideal plant for hedging and border plantings, providing a mass of color that will endure and be very rewarding, with little input and maximum joy. 'Violet Carson' has dark green, glossy foliage and is suited to most climates, especially hotter regions; it is grown worldwide. ZONES 5–10.

MCGREDY, NEW ZEALAND, 1964

'MME LÉON CUNY' × 'SPARTAN'

ROYAL NATIONAL ROSE SOCIETY
CERTIFICATE OF MERIT 1963

## 'Violette' *(right)*

MODERN, RAMBLER, MAUVE

This is a wonderfully free-growing climber. The flowers have two rows of deep violet petals that are quite showy. The flowers appear abundantly in the first flush of bloom and it does not flower again, as it concentrates

on its growth for the next year. It is a healthy, vigorous grower that suffers only a little mildew late in the season on new shoots.

At pruning, the long canes should be trained horizontally for the best quality blooms and most pleasing effect. A great climber

for walls and trellis work, 'Violette' has few thorns and light green shiny leaves. ZONES 4–11.

TURBAT, FRANCE, 1921

PARENTAGE UNKNOWN

V

## 'Violette Parfumée'  DORient
*(left)*

syn. 'Melodie Parfumée'

**MODERN, LARGE-FLOWERED/HYBRID TEA, MAUVE BLEND, REPEAT-FLOWERING**

The bluish green foliage of this upright bush rose combines well with the mauve-pink flowers. These are double and urn-shaped with tight centers, opening out flat as the flowers mature to show golden yellow stamens. **ZONES 5–10.**

DORIEUX, FRANCE, 1995

PARENTAGE UNKNOWN

BADEN-BADEN FRAGRANCE AWARD 1995, BAGATELLE GOLD MEDAL 1995, BAGATELLE FRAGRANCE AWARD 1995

## 'Violinista Costa'
*(below left)*

**MODERN, LARGE-FLOWERED/HYBRID TEA, RED BLEND, REPEAT-FLOWERING**

The red to darker red flowers of 'Violinista Costa' have an open Cluster-flowered style and a loose form. The small-growing bush has many thorns on the stems. Disease resistance is fair but it will need attention to keep it from developing mildew on its young shoots in cooler weather. Despite this it is a very reliable rose that suits a range of situations and growing habits; it can be used as a standard as well as a bush, providing a spectacle when in full flower. A remarkable characteristic of this rose is that after dead-heading or pruning, one's hands smell delightfully of rose water. **ZONES 5–10.**

CAMPRUBI, SPAIN, 1936

'SENSATION' × 'SHOT SILK'

V

## 'Virgo'  *(bottom)*

syn. 'Virgo Liberationem'

MODERN, LARGE-FLOWERED/
HYBRID TEA, WHITE,
REPEAT-FLOWERING

'Virgo' produces some of the finest classic white Large-flowered Roses available and is a plant that is well worth growing. The tall, high-pointed buds open out to fully double white flowers of great purity and perfection. The upright bush is tall and has thick, light green leaves with a susceptibility to mildew, which should be prevented by spraying a fungicide early in the growing season. The freedom and repeat-flowering frequency of this bush is similar to the older Large-flowered varieties, although it has been outshone in recent years by other roses that bloom in a shorter time and with less fungus disease. However 'Virgo' is worth growing and is freely available in all rose nurseries. ZONES 5–10.

MALLERIN, FRANCE, 1947

'BLANCHE MALLERIN' ×
'NEIGE PARFUM'

NATIONAL ROSE SOCIETY GOLD
MEDAL 1949

## 'Vivid'  *(right)*

OLD, BOURBON, MAUVE/
LIGHT RED

'Vivid' bears very bright, fully double flowers that are magenta to magenta-pink. They are fragrant. This is a tall, upright, rather prickly shrub that is very vigorous. It has been recommended as being suitable for a pillar or trellis, as is the case for many Bourbons. It repeats only occasionally. ZONES 5–9.

PAUL, UK, 1853

PARENTAGE UNKNOWN

V

fragrance, and flowering is well maintained through summer, and particularly good again in autumn. In a shrub border, or as a specimen plant, or in a bed, this is an attractive garden rose, complemented by plentiful light green shiny foliage. It is a vigorous, robust shrub of average height and spreading habit. The mouthful of a name was too much for an Australian grower, who, realizing it referred to an aviary, considered 'Kookaburra' more acceptable. **ZONES 4–9.**

KORDES, GERMANY, 1991

PARENTAGE UNKNOWN

ANERKANNTE DEUTSCHE ROSE 1989

### 'Vogue' *(bottom)*

**MODERN, CLUSTER-FLOWERED/FLORIBUNDA, PINK BLEND, REPEAT-FLOWERING**

'Vogue' has a sweet scent that endures and so is irresistible to many growers. The loose, semi-double, cherry pink flowers appear in clusters; when fully open the blooms are flat. The color fades over the flower's life and can tend to be washed out. The bush is vigorous, with minimal care needed to keep it healthy throughout the year. This variety has good repeat-flowering on a medium-sized, vigorous, upright plant with glossy foliage. It is available through some specialist rose nurseries now but has been surpassed, as many newer varieties offer much more. **ZONES 5–10.**

BOERNER, USA, 1951

'PINOCCHIO' × 'CRIMSON GLORY'

PORTLAND GOLD MEDAL 1950, GENEVA GOLD MEDAL 1950, NATIONAL ROSE SOCIETY CERTIFICATE OF MERIT 1951, ALL-AMERICA ROSE SELECTION 1952

V

### 'Vogelpark Walsrode'

**KORlomet** *(top)*
syn. 'Kookaburra'

**MODERN, MODERN SHRUB, LIGHT PINK, REPEAT-FLOWERING**

The color is a delicate shade of light pink, fading to a pale blush as the blooms open wide, showing golden stamens. They are fairly full, of medium to large size, and borne very freely in clusters at different levels on the plant, creating a delightful effect. There is a sweet light

## 'Vol de Nuit' DELrio
*(right)*
**syn. 'Night Flight'**

MODERN, LARGE-FLOWERED/
HYBRID TEA, MAUVE,
REPEAT-FLOWERING

The lovely mauve tones of 'Vol de Nuit' have pleased many rose growers since its introduction in 1970; the flower color is strong, with some paler toning towards the outer edges of the petals as the blooms age. The fully double blooms repeat well and are found in ones and twos with good long stems for picking. The vigorous, upright bush has good disease resistance that is easy to maintain, forming a strong framework for good production of flowers. Care must be taken to protect the flowers from the harsher early season weather, as the blooms' delicate nature can sometimes be spoilt by adverse weather. **ZONES 5–11.**

DELBARD, FRANCE, 1970

('HOLSTEIN' × ['BAYADÈRE' ×
'PRÉLUDE']) × 'SAINT-EXUPERY'

ROME GOLD MEDAL 1970

## 'Voodoo' AROmiclea
*(right)*

MODERN, LARGE-FLOWERED/
HYBRID TEA, ORANGE BLEND,
REPEAT-FLOWERING

'Voodoo' has vibrant salmon-red, orange and yellow-orange flowers that are crisp and clear and of exhibition form. They are fully double with 35 petals and have little or no scent. The bush grows to medium height, is upright and quick to reshoot after flowering. The glossy leaves are thick and hard with good resistance to disease, and the abundant thorns protect the stocky, tough plant. Black spot needs to be watched for late in the season when the best blooms are being produced. It is an ideal plant for a massed individual planting as the color can be difficult to blend. It is available widely from rose nurseries that have comprehensive lists. **ZONES 5–11.**

CHRISTENSEN, USA, 1984

(['CAMELOT' × 'FIRST PRIZE'] ×
'TYPHOO TEA') × 'LOLITA'

ALL-AMERICA ROSE SELECTION
1986

**V**

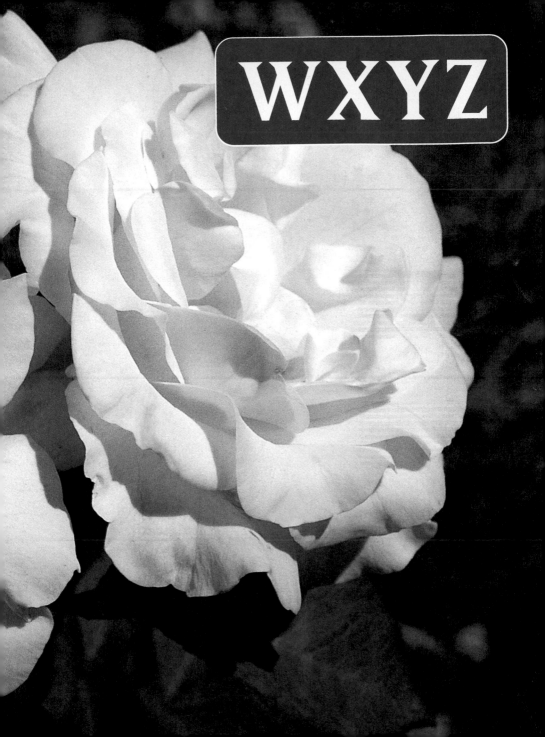

WXYZ

### 'Waiheke' MACwaihe
### (right)
### syn. 'Waikiki'

MODERN, LARGE-FLOWERED/
HYBRID TEA, ORANGE-PINK,
REPEAT-FLOWERING

This rose produces a lovely spectacle of medium orange and pinkish blooms on good stems. The blooms, which are easily picked for display, are usually solitary but can sometimes be found in small clusters of 5–9 and carry a lovely spicy fragrance. The outside petals on the double flowers reflex well, and in cooler weather are darker pink on the edges. The health of 'Waiheke' is good and only normal rose maintenance is needed to keep its leaves and flowers in first-class order. Glossy leaves and quick repeat-flowering make this variety a good addition to any garden. **ZONES 5–10.**

MCGREDY, NEW ZEALAND, 1987

'TONY JACKLIN' ×
'YOUNG QUINN'

### 'Waldfee' (above)

OLD, HYBRID PERPETUAL,
MEDIUM RED,
REPEAT-FLOWERING

It is extraordinary that a Hybrid Perpetual Rose should be produced at this late date. It has not really caught on, however, and is available from only a few outlets. The flowers are large and are borne in small clusters. They are fragrant, camellia-shaped and blood red. The foliage is glossy on a plant with a vigorous growth habit. It can reach almost the height of a short climber. A waldfee is a wood fairy. **ZONES 5–9.**

KORDES, GERMANY, 1960

'INDEPENDENCE' ×
'MRS JOHN LAING'

W

### 'Wandering Minstrel' HARquince
### syn. 'Daniel Gélin'

MODERN, CLUSTER-FLOWERED/FLORIBUNDA, ORANGE-PINK,
REPEAT-FLOWERING

A large-flowering Cluster-flowered Rose that
changes color according to the temperature,
'Wandering Minstrel' bears orange-pink blooms
that intensify with yellow as cooler weather slows
the flower formation and growth of the bush.
Although only a small grower, it is fine in borders
and is ideal for banks or rockeries. Small clusters
of double blooms with 28 petals cover the bush
all season; it is a good repeat-bloomer and has a
moderate scent. Disease will need to be watched
for as the small growth encourages this, and some
preventive measures should be taken early and
late in the season to ensure that bush growth
and bloom quality is kept at its best. **ZONES 5–10.**

HARKNESS, UK, 1986

'DAME OF SARK' × 'SILVER JUBILEE'

COURTRAI SILVER MEDAL 1989, GLASGOW CERTIFICATE OF
MERIT 1989

### 'Wapiti' MEInagre *(above)*
### syns 'Dazzla', 'Dazzler', 'Laurence Olivier', 'Striking'

MODERN, CLUSTER-FLOWERED/FLORIBUNDA, RED BLEND,
REPEAT-FLOWERING

This rose was released under several different
names that suited the different markets to which
it was introduced. The loose flowers, with two or
so rows of petals that give a ruffled effect, open
flat in large clusters of color. The bright red
flowers give a good show and cover the bush well
when in full bloom. Their perfume is slight and
they are not ideal for cutting; 'Wapiti' is better
suited to mass plantings in the garden. Disease
resistance is good, but the bush will need attention
to keep it healthy throughout the season. It is also
an ideal plant for a border or area that is in need
of brightening up, but it is not widely grown and
could prove difficult to find. **ZONES 5–10.**

MEILLAND, FRANCE, 1988

PARENTAGE UNKNOWN

GENEVA GOLD MEDAL 1987, MONZA GOLD MEDAL 1987, ROME GOLD
MEDAL 1987

**W**

### 'Warm Welcome'
CHEwizz **(right)**

MODERN, CLIMBING
MINIATURE, ORANGE-RED,
REPEAT-FLOWERING

'Warm Welcome' bears fragrant, single to semi-double, orange-vermilion flowers with yellow bases. They are borne in clusters at all levels on the plant, so it is covered from head to toe. The foliage is dark green and semi-glossy and adorns this relatively tall, upright plant that should be trained as a climber. It is disease free and reliable, and can be used as a pillar or to brighten up a fence. This rose was a break-through in hybridizing because it is a free-blooming, low-maintenance Climbing Miniature with small flowers and foliage. **ZONES 5–10.**

WARNER, UK, 1992

'ELIZABETH OF GLAMIS' ×
(['GALWAY BAY' × 'SUTTER'S
GOLD'] × 'ANNA FORD')

ROYAL NATIONAL ROSE SOCIETY
PRESIDENT'S INTERNATIONAL
TROPHY 1988, ROYAL
HORTICULTURAL SOCIETY
AWARD OF GARDEN MERIT 1993

### 'Warrior' **(bottom)**
MODERN, CLUSTER-FLOWERED/
FLORIBUNDA, ORANGE-RED,
REPEAT-FLOWERING

This fully double variety has lovely flowers that shine out from the garden bed. The scarlet-red blooms are found on short stems in small clusters, opening to give a slight glimpse of the stamens. The prolifically produced, quality blooms are good for cutting and repeat well if the bush is pruned and deadheaded when necessary. The light green foliage is healthy and robust, with a good tolerance to disease and other seasonal problems. **ZONES 5–10.**

LEGRICE, UK, 1977

'CITY OF BELFAST' ×
'RONDE ENDIABLEE'

ROYAL NATIONAL ROSE SOCIETY
TRIAL GROUND CERTIFICATE 1977

W

## 'Warwick Castle'
AUSlian  *(right)*

MODERN, MODERN SHRUB,
DEEP PINK, REPEAT-FLOWERING

The beautiful, fully double flowers of this variety have the true appeal and charm of the Old Garden Roses it was bred to complement. The rich pink, scented blooms open flat without showing stamens and have a perfection that is a delight to display in the house. Also classified as an English Rose, the medium-sized shrub has an upright habit and forms a solid bush that is both resistant to disease and easy to prune. The flowers are found from spring onward and it is quick to repeat all season. 'Warwick Castle' has been replaced by many newer releases that offer more disease resistance and improved flowering habits. However, it is worth growing and will always be rewarding. **ZONES 5–10.**

AUSTIN, UK, 1986

'THE REEVE' × 'LILIAN AUSTIN'

## 'Warwickshire'
KORkandel

MODERN, MODERN SHRUB,
PINK BLEND, REPEAT-FLOWERING

The 5-petalled flowers of this rose are small, borne very freely in short-stemmed clusters and make a noticeable impact because of their shape and coloring.

They open like saucers to display creamy blush centers fringed with deep reddish pink. The effect is strange; the shrub seems to watch you with its many white eyes. There is little scent, and flowering continues through summer and autumn. Rain can dim the brilliance of the blooms, making them look tired and jaded. In the garden, this variety can be used where a low, spreading shrub is required, because it grows well below average height; it could almost be considered a Ground Cover Rose, because it is nearly twice as wide as it is high. There is a good complement of deep green foliage.
**ZONES 5–9.**

KORDES, GERMANY, 1991

PARENTAGE UNKNOWN

## 'Water Music'  *(above)*

MODERN, LARGE-FLOWERED CLIMBER, DEEP PINK

Bred by Australian Ron Bell, 'Water Music' is a large climbing rose that produces deep pink, double flowers with 20 petals early in the season. The flowers are darker on the petal edges, fading as they age, and are slightly fragrant. This variety grows well in the warm climate of Australia, but is largely unknown in the rest of the world. Disease resistance is good on a spreading plant with medium-sized, glossy dark green foliage. It is an example of a rose that has been released by an Australian breeder into his local market without a large distribution network. **ZONES 5–10.**

BELL, AUSTRALIA, 1982

'HANDEL' × SEEDLING

W

### 'Watercolor'

*(above)*

syn. 'Watercolour'

MODERN, MINIATURE, MEDIUM PINK, REPEAT-FLOWERING

The long, pointed buds of this rose open to reveal flowers that are a beautiful blend of light and deep pink. The blooms are double, with about two dozen petals, and have a light fragrance. The flower form is a typical exhibition style and tends to hold well even on sunny days, usually in sprays of 3–5 flowers, but one bloom per stem can occur in warm climates. The foliage is large and glossy dark green on a vigorous, upright plant that is healthy and easy to maintain. **ZONES 5–10.**

MOORE, USA, 1975

'RUMBA' × ('LITTLE DARLING' × 'RED GERMAIN')

### 'Wedding Day'

*(right)*

syn. 'English Wedding Day'

MODERN, RAMBLER, WHITE

*Rosa sinowilsonii* was discovered in China in 1904; it is a single, white, vigorous rose.

'Wedding Day' is an improved version with rampant growth and clear green foliage. The white flowers are larger and have pronounced orange stamens. They are borne in big trusses and have a citrus scent. **ZONES 7–9.**

STERN, UK, 1950

*ROSA SINOWILSONII* × SEEDLING

W

## 'Weisse Immensee'

KORweirim *(right)*
syns 'Partridge',
'Kordes' Rose Weiss
Immensee', 'Lac Blanc'
MODERN, MODERN SHRUB,
WHITE

This is a wonderful
ground-covering rose
to grow on a bank or
in a terraced garden
where it can be seen
at its best. The single,
5-petalled flowers start
out a light shade of
pink, but quickly fade
to white as they age
and cover the bush
well. They are very
fragrant and appear on
a spreading plant with
a mass of healthy, glossy
dark green foliage.
Long canes run along
the ground and can
easily become entwined
among other garden
plants. This bush is
very hardy and will
need little attention
to keep it clean and
disease free. Flowering
is early and it will not
repeat. ZONES 5–10.

KORDES, GERMANY, 1982

'THE FAIRY' × SEEDLING OF
*ROSA WICHURANA*

ROYAL NATIONAL ROSE SOCIETY
CERTIFICATE OF MERIT 1984

## 'Wendy Cussons'

*(bottom)*
MODERN, LARGE-FLOWERED/
HYBRID TEA, MEDIUM RED,
REPEAT-FLOWERING

'Wendy Cussons' bears
fully double, medium
red flowers which are
evenly distributed over
the plant and have a
strong fragrance. They
are high centered and
large, with 30 petals,
and the foliage is glossy
and dark on a well-
branched plant. Health
and vigor are strong
points of the bush, and
in warm climates it can
become difficult to
control, with rampant
growth and little bloom.
It is an ideal plant for
cool areas with climates
that hinder vigorous
growth and promote
the full intensity of the
beautiful flowers.
'Climbing Wendy
Cussons' (Gregory and
Follen, UK, 1967) was
released in Germany.
ZONES 5–10.

GREGORY & SON LTD, UK, 1963

PROBABLY 'INDEPENDENCE' ×
'EDEN ROSE'

NATIONAL ROSE SOCIETY
PRESIDENT'S INTERNATIONAL
TROPHY 1959, GOLDEN ROSE
OF THE HAGUE 1964, PORTLAND
GOLD MEDAL 1964

W

### 'Wenlock' AUSwen

*(below)*

MODERN, MODERN SHRUB, MEDIUM RED, REPEAT-FLOWERING

This cultivar has a wonderful scent that is fitting for a crimson-red rose. The fully double flowers are found on short stems and the bush is an ideal choice for a border or low hedge as it does not become obtrusive in the garden. The flowers turn cerise with age. The repeat-flowering is quick and it produces a mass of blooms to start the flowering season in spring. 'Wenlock' is upright with a good shape, pruning easily into a small shrub. Care is needed to keep it disease free and healthy all season as the large leaves can become infected in cool regions. Also classified as an English Rose, it is freely available at most rose nurseries. **ZONES 5–10.**

AUSTIN, UK, 1984

'THE KNIGHT' × 'GLASTONBURY'

### 'West Coast'

MACnauru

syns 'Metropolitan', 'Penthouse'

MODERN, LARGE-FLOWERED/ HYBRID TEA, MEDIUM PINK, REPEAT-FLOWERING

This variety is a Large-flowered Rose bred by Sam McGredy in New Zealand. The slightly scented, medium pink flowers are double and are found singly or in small clusters on a strong bush. The repeat-flowering is good and the plant is reasonably disease resistant, although it will need attention in areas where disease is common. 'West Coast' is a bushy grower with matt light green foliage. It is not widely grown and is available from only a few North American nurseries. **ZONES 5–10.**

MCGREDY, NEW ZEALAND, 1987

(['YELLOW PAGES' × 'KABUKI'] × 'GOLDEN GATE') × (POULSEN SEEDLING × 'PICASSO')

### 'Westerland'

KORlawe, KORwest

*(below left)*

MODERN, CLUSTER-FLOWERED/ FLORIBUNDA, APRICOT BLEND, REPEAT-FLOWERING

The bright apricot-orange flowers of 'Westerland' are a colorful addition to any garden. The double blooms have a ruffled look, the petals having slightly serrated edges, and there is a pleasant scent. Clusters of the flowers appear regularly on the bush, with a short time between repeat-flowering. This vigorous, upright bush grows to medium height and has large, soft, dark green foliage that can suffer from disease. It is widely grown and is freely available in those countries where it has been released. **ZONES 5–10.**

KORDES, GERMANY, 1969

'FRIEDRICH WORLEIN' × 'CIRCUS'

ANERKANNTE DEUTSCHE ROSE 1974, ROYAL HORTICULTURAL SOCIETY AWARD OF GARDEN MERIT 1993

W

### 'Western Sun' *(top)*

MODERN, LARGE-FLOWERED/
HYBRID TEA, DEEP YELLOW,
REPEAT-FLOWERING

This rose produces
deep yellow flowers
on a strong bush with
dark foliage. The fully
double flowers are
large, with a purity of
color that is a joy to
behold. The small bush
is susceptible to disease
early and late in the
season. The finest
examples of the flower
are in late summer
and autumn when
the color and form
develop and mature
slowly. They are
ideal to cut if short
stems are required.
**ZONES 5–10.**

POULSEN, DENMARK, 1965

SEEDLING OF 'GOLDEN SCEPTER'
× 'GOLDEN SUN'

### 'Westfalenpark'

KORplavi *(bottom)*
syns 'Chevreuse',
'Kordes' Rose
Westfalenpark'

MODERN, MODERN SHRUB,
APRICOT BLEND,
REPEAT-FLOWERING

This shrub rose is
suitable for mass
planting and gives a
spectacle in vast areas
like public parks or
roadside plantings.
'Westfalenpark' has
large, double, apricot
flowers that are
scented. The bush has
big, glossy dark green
foliage and a spreading
habit that will require
some attention if it is
to be planted into a
confined space. Rarely
grown, it is available
from only a few
specialist nurseries.
**ZONES 5–10.**

KORDES, GERMANY, 1987

SEEDLING × 'LAS VEGAS'

### 'Whisky Mac' TANky
*(right)*

syn. 'Whisky'

MODERN, LARGE-FLOWERED/
HYBRID TEA, YELLOW BLEND,
REPEAT-FLOWERING

This delightful rose produces wonderful, rich apricot-yellow blooms. The fully double flowers are found singly or in small groups all through the flowering season. 'Whisky Mac' has an open style of growth with a slightly spreading nature; it makes a stout bush that has a good covering of thorns. The disease resistance is only fair, however, and the bush needs attention during the cooler months to prevent fungal disease spoiling the leaves. By far the best blooms are produced in cool climates where the color is intensified by the slowness of the developing flowers. **'Climbing Whisky Mac'** (ANDmac; syn. 'Climbing Whisky'; Anderson's Rose Nurseries, UK, 1985) has bronze-yellow flowers, vigorous growth and good disease resistance. **ZONES 5–10.**

TANTAU, GERMANY, 1967

PARENTAGE UNKNOWN

### 'White Angel'
*(right)*

MODERN, MINIATURE, WHITE,
REPEAT-FLOWERING

The dainty buds of this rose open to reveal attractive, small white flowers with pointed petals. There is a light fragrance and the foliage is a complementary light green. The vigorous dwarf bush is a true example of what a Miniature plant should look like: very petite in every characteristic. 'White Angel' is short in stature but very branched, which adds to its ability to produce many more blooms than normal. This rose has lost much of its popularity now that more attractive white Miniature Roses have been introduced. The parentage is an award-winning cross of a Rambler with a Cluster-flowered Rose. **ZONES 5–10.**

MOORE, USA, 1971

(*ROSA WICHURANA* ×
'FLORADORA') × ('LITTLE
DARLING' × SEEDLING OF A RED
MINIATURE ROSE)

AMERICAN ROSE SOCIETY
AWARD OF EXCELLENCE 1975

### 'White Bath'  *(right)*
syns 'Shailer's White Moss', 'Clifton Moss',
*Rosa centifolia albo-muscosa, R. muscosa alba*
OLD, MOSS, WHITE

The common Moss is pink; this variety is a white
sport that can revert in part or in whole on the
bush. 'White Bath' has very bright flowers that
are fully double, fragrant and arranged in small,
tight clusters. A distinguishing feature is a purple
smudge or two showing through from under the
surface of the leaves. It is a shrub of medium size
and vigor, generously clothed on the stems and
buds with ginger-colored, stubbly moss—the
main reason for growing it. The rounded foliage
is grayish dark green and soft to the touch. This
lovely rose shows a clear affinity to the Damasks.
ZONES 4–9.

SHAILER, UK, 1788

SPORT OF *ROSA CENTIFOLIA MUSCOSA*

ROYAL HORTICULTURAL SOCIETY AWARD OF GARDEN MERIT 1993

### 'White Bella Rosa'  *(right)*
syn. 'Bella Weisse'
MODERN, CLUSTER-FLOWERED/FLORIBUNDA, WHITE,
REPEAT-FLOWERING

This small-growing rose has all the features of its
parent, the only difference being the color of its
flowers. These are semi-double and white with a
tinge of pink in cool weather. They open flat and
show stamens clearly. Known as a good parent for
breeding, neither 'Bella Rosa' nor its progeny are
widely grown. Disease resistance is good and it
needs only minimal care during the season. Better
varieties exist and should be sought instead.
ZONES 5–10.

KORDES, GERMANY, 1990

SPORT OF 'BELLA ROSA'

### 'White Bells'  POUlwhite  *(right)*
MODERN, MINIATURE, WHITE

This rose is a counterpart clone to 'Pink Bells'
and 'Red Bells', both with the same parentage and
growth habit. It has white flowers with creamy
lemon centers that fade with age. The lightly
fragrant blooms have 35 petals, and these are set
against the small, very glossy green foliage on a
spreading plant. 'White Bells' tends to grow larger
than its sister seedlings, as it sends out long,
disease-resistant canes with many flowers. It needs
a season to establish and then it performs in an
exceptional manner. Flowers appear freely over
an extended period in late spring and summer.
The plant has been used successfully as both a
weeping standard and a ground cover. Winter die-
back is minimal in warm climates. ZONES 5–10.

POULSEN, DENMARK, 1983

'MINI-POUL' × 'TEMPLE BELLS'

W

### 'White Cécile Brünner' *(top)*

MODERN, POLYANTHA, WHITE,
REPEAT-FLOWERING

This sweet little bush produces some of the best posy flowers possible. A small-growing plant, it is a delight for those who persist in growing it. The small, creamy white blooms are double and have a slight scent, and are found on short stems among delicate leaves. Sometimes the bush will not perform well, while in other situations it will grow extremely easily and produce flowers all season. The growth needs some attention to disease during cool weather as the tight growth tends to encourage health problems. **ZONES 5–10.**

FRAQUE, 1909

SPORT OF 'CÉCILE BRÜNNER'

### 'White Christmas' *(bottom)*

MODERN, LARGE-FLOWERED/
HYBRID TEA, WHITE,
REPEAT-FLOWERING

Bred in 1953, this Large-flowered Rose is still popular. The fully double, high-centered flowers have around 50 petals in each bloom but suffer badly from botrytis in rain and damp weather. The compact, upright bush is vigorous and produces its fragrant blooms throughout the season. The light green foliage is leathery. **ZONES 5–10.**

HOWARD AND SMITH, USA, 1953

'SLEIGH BELLS' × SEEDLING

## 'White Cockade' *(below)*

MODERN, LARGE-FLOWERED CLIMBER, WHITE, REPEAT-FLOWERING

'White Cockade' is a robust climber that produces a mass of white, double blooms in the first flush of the season; they have a sweet subtle scent. The growth is vigorous and healthy and requires minimal attention for disease and other problems. Flowering is almost entirely at the beginning of the season, and it produces only a limited show during the remainder of the year. The strong growth is easy to prune and can be very effective for covering walls and fences that will hold its weight. The legacy of 'New Dawn' is evident in this offspring with its glossy leaves and classic flowers. **ZONES 5–9.**

COCKER, UK, 1969

'NEW DAWN' × 'CIRCUS'

ROYAL HORTICULTURAL SOCIETY AWARD OF GARDEN MERIT 1993

## 'White Dawn'

MODERN, LARGE-FLOWERED CLIMBER, WHITE

'White Dawn' has many similarities to 'New Dawn'. The low, climbing growth is vigorous and is covered generously with thorns to deter the unwelcome. The glossy leaves are small and cover the growth well; they are resistant to disease and need little attention to keep them producing worthwhile growth for the next year. The white blooms are found early in the season, so it is best to prepare some good lateral canes while pruning in winter. The double, gardenia-shaped, fragrant flowers with 35 petals are produced in clusters. It is available only from specialist rose growers. **ZONES 5–9.**

LONGLEY, USA, 1949

'NEW DAWN' × 'LILY PONS'

### 'White Dorothy'
*(left)*
syn. 'White Dorothy Perkins'

MODERN, RAMBLER, WHITE

The parent of this variety, with its sprays of pink flowers, is perhaps the best known of the very lax Ramblers; it was created by Jackson and Perkins in the USA in 1901, the seed parent being 'Mme Gabriel Luizet'. However, both the parent and the sport are subject to mildew. ZONES 5–9.

CANT, UK, 1908

SPORT OF 'DOROTHY PERKINS'

### 'White Dream'
LENblank, LENvir *(bottom)*
syn. 'Sentinel'

MODERN, MINIATURE, WHITE, REPEAT-FLOWERING

The white flowers of this rose contain 35 petals and have high centers, which show Large-flowered form. They have a light scent and occur mainly in small clusters. Although the blooms can be larger than expected for a Miniature Rose, they have good shape from bud to bloom. 'White Dream' is a vigorous low grower with a tendency to sprawl. Commonly grown in England and New Zealand, the bloom form is almost as good as that of 'Pacesetter' and 'Starglo'. ZONES 5–10.

LENS, BELGIUM, 1982

PARENTAGE UNKNOWN

W

### 'White Flower Carpet' NOAschnee *(above)*
syns 'Emera Blanc', 'Opalia', 'Schneeflocke'
MODERN, CLUSTER-FLOWERED/FLORIBUNDA, WHITE,
REPEAT-FLOWERING

'White Flower Carpet' has small, double blooms that provide good cover on the bush. The plant is low growing. Disease resistance is reasonably good and it needs little attention if it is to remain healthy all season. This variety is good for mass planting on a bank or bed where low height is a consideration. 'White Flower Carpet' is freely available and is commonly grown from cuttings instead of from a grafted plant. ZONES 5–10.

NOACK, GERMANY, 1991

'IMMENSEE' × 'MARGARET MERRILL'

ANERKANNTE DEUTSCHE ROSE 1991, ROYAL NATIONAL ROSE SOCIETY GOLD MEDAL 1991, GOLDEN ROSE OF THE HAGUE 1995, GLASGOW CERTIFICATE OF MERIT 1996

### 'White Gem' MEIturusa
MODERN, MINIATURE, WHITE, REPEAT-FLOWERING

The long and pointed buds of this rose open to soft ivory flowers that are shaded with pale tan and are filled with an overwhelming 90 petals. The petals reflex beautifully to give that perfect exhibition form so admired at rose shows. Both blooms and foliage can be larger in cool climates; the flowers have a light fragrance and are borne singly or in clusters at all times. The leaves are large and glossy dark green, and adorn this upright, vigorous bush that reaches an average height. 'White Gem' has not been received well in the USA; there are many other superior whites, so it has been relegated to a common garden variety. ZONES 5–10.

MEILLAND, FRANCE, 1976

'DARLING FLAME' × 'JACK FROST'

### 'White Grootendorst'
MODERN, HYBRID RUGOSA, WHITE, REPEAT-FLOWERING

This Hybrid Rugosa forms a medium garden shrub and provides a pleasant change in the way the rose bed looks. The growth is branching and upright, forming a good framework for the flowers, which are found all over the bush and repeat throughout the season. The semi-double flowers are white; the petals have a frilled edge that is quite charming. Disease resistance is good and will remain so all season with little attention. The best blooms appear early in the season and at the end just before the onset of winter. 'White Grootendorst' is one of a group of plants that have sported from one parent; they are all good and it is well worth growing them together. This plant is best suited to cool climates as it does not do well in very hot conditions. ZONES 5–10.

EDDY, USA, 1962

SPORT OF 'PINK GROOTENDORST'

**W**

### 'White Lightnin'
**AROwhif** *(right)*

MODERN, LARGE-FLOWERED/
HYBRID TEA, WHITE,
REPEAT-FLOWERING

This rose produces large, double blooms with 30 petals on a strong, vigorous, upright-growing bush. The flowers are pure white and open in classic Large-flowered style. The scent is strong, lasting the entire life of the flowers. Picking is easy and the blooms look wonderful in a vase. The bush is healthy and able to resist most diseases with minimal attention through the season. Repeat-flowering is quick and it is a good addition to any garden. **ZONES 5–10.**

SWIM, USA, 1980

'ANGEL FACE' × 'MISTY'

ALL-AMERICA ROSE SELECTION
1981

### 'White Maman Cochet' *(above)*

OLD, TEA, WHITE,
REPEAT-FLOWERING

Both the parent and the sport are vigorous and strong plants that can grow into large shrubs. This one has white flowers—but not entirely so, as pink flushing is common. The buds are long and big, and the blooms have been described as blowsy. They ball badly in wet weather.

**'Climbing White Maman Cochet'** (Knight, Australia, 1907) is a vigorous climbing version of the bush that bears flowers inclined towards yellow. It is suitable only for a warm climate and is quite popular in Australia. **ZONES 7–9.**

COOK, USA, 1896

SPORT OF 'MAMAN COCHET'

W

## 'White Masterpiece'

JACmas *(above)*

MODERN, LARGE-FLOWERED/
HYBRID TEA, WHITE,
REPEAT-FLOWERING

This variety produces large, high-pointed flowers that are borne singly atop a moderate bush. The blooms are not freely produced and mark in bad weather. Slightly fragrant and of double form, they have a greenish tinge that is lost in warm climates, although it can carry through in the fully open bloom in cooler climates. Disease control should be carried out all season as the bush will not produce its best blooms unless it is maintained. Exquisite flowers are produced on this plant. **ZONES 5–10.**

BOERNER, USA, 1969

PARENTAGE UNKNOWN

## 'White Meidiland'

MEIcoublan *(right)*

syns 'Blanc Meillandécor', 'Alba Meidiland'

MODERN, MODERN SHRUB, WHITE, REPEAT-FLOWERING

Originally released as a Ground Cover Rose, this unusual plant is one of a series introduced by Meilland of France for landscaping. It is largely disease free and for that reason is ideally suited for roadways and gardens that receive little care. The flowers are very full, with 40 petals, appearing in flushes each year to cover the bush in a mass of white. Pruning is not normally practised in the usual way, but a general reduction of plant size can be applied each winter. It has a spreading growth habit and is clothed with medium-sized, glossy dark green foliage. **ZONES 5–10.**

MEILLAND, FRANCE, 1986

'TEMPLE BELLS' × MEIGURAMI

**W**

it gives a profusion of color all year long. **ZONES 5–10.**

MEILLAND, FRANCE, 1984

'KATHARINA ZEIMET' ×
'WHITE GEM'

AMERICAN ROSE SOCIETY
TOP GARDEN ROSE IN PROOF OF
THE PUDDING SURVEY 1991

### 'White Pet' *(bottom)*
syn. 'Little White Pet'
MODERN, POLYANTHA, WHITE,
REPEAT-FLOWERING

'White Pet' is sometimes classified as a Dwarf Sempervirens, and makes a compact shrub, bearing flowers all through the season. The fully double flowers are white with a pink tinge on the buds that sometimes continues during cool weather. When fully open, the flowers have a pompon look and are easily cut for display. The strong, vigorous growth is complemented by glossy leaves, and there is good disease resistance. The bush is great for borders and also does well as a standard or patio rose. Widely propagated by Old Garden Rose nurseries, it is easily grown and is an asset to any garden.

### 'Climbing White Pet'
(Corboeuf, France, 1894) is also available. **ZONES 5–10.**

HENDERSON, USA, 1879

SPORT OF 'FÉLICITÉ-PERPÉTUE'

ROYAL HORTICULTURAL SOCIETY
AWARD OF GARDEN MERIT 1993

### 'White Meillandina' MEIblam
*(top)*
syn. 'Yorkshire Sunblaze'
MODERN, MINIATURE, WHITE,
REPEAT-FLOWERING

The white, semi-double, medium-sized flowers of this rose have no fragrance, but they combine well with the small and light green foliage on the compact bush. 'White Meillandina' is a prolific bloomer that is very disease resistant, so it is an ideal choice for growing in a container. As one of the popular 'Sunblaze' series introduced by the House of Meilland in France, this variety is an attractive addition to any garden because

### 'White Queen Elizabeth' *(above)*
syn. 'Blanc Queen Elizabeth'

MODERN, CLUSTER-FLOWERED/ FLORIBUNDA, WHITE, REPEAT-FLOWERING

'White Queen Elizabeth' is a bud sport from the well-known Large-flowered Rose 'Queen Elizabeth'. It inherits all the characteristics of its parent: strong, disease-resistant growth, vigor, and free flower production. This fragrant rose also has the same flower formation, rather informal and open, but differs in color, which is white with the faintest tinge of cream. This makes it interesting but not striking as it lacks the brightness usually found in a white rose. It is a tall grower and is best planted at the back of a rose bed. **ZONES 5–10.**

BANNER, UK, 1965

SPORT OF 'QUEEN ELIZABETH'

### 'White Simplicity'
JACsnow *(right)*

MODERN, CLUSTER-FLOWERED/ FLORIBUNDA, WHITE, REPEAT-FLOWERING

This free-flowering bush is disease resistant and healthy in most conditions, suffering only in weather that is ideal for disease. The large, double white flowers open flat to show the stamens clearly. Repeat-flowering is quick and the plant's growth habit makes it an outstanding specimen for a border or hedge. Widely grown, 'White Simplicity' is readily available from rose nurseries. **ZONES 5–10.**

WARRINER, USA, 1991

PARENTAGE UNKNOWN

W

### 'White Sparrieshoop'

*(top)*

syn. 'Weisse aus Sparrieshoop'

MODERN, MODERN SHRUB, WHITE, REPEAT-FLOWERING

This rose shares the characteristics of its parent in all respects except for the color, which is a clear white. The saucer-shaped blooms are quite large with a few waved petals, and reveal golden stamens. They have a pleasing fragrance and continue to give a good display through summer and autumn. As a free-flowering shrub rose of average height and width, 'White Sparrieshoop' makes a handsome border or specimen plant. It grows vigorously with an upright, bushy habit and is furnished with leathery, glossy foliage that is reddish when young. ZONES 4–9.

KORDES, GERMANY, 1962

SPORT OF 'SPARRIESHOOP'

### 'White Spray'

*(bottom)*

MODERN, CLUSTER-FLOWERED/ FLORIBUNDA, WHITE, REPEAT-FLOWERING

'White Spray' is a free-flowering bush that is not dissimilar to its parent, 'Iceberg'. The flowers are borne in clusters all over the bush and have a stem length that is useful for cutting. Its health is good, and it only requires disease control early in the season. The well-formed, white flowers are double and have a slight fragrance. Released in 1968, this rose has been over-shadowed by its parent. ZONES 5–10.

LEGRICE, UK, 1968

SEEDLING × 'ICEBERG'

## 'White Wings' *(top)*

MODERN, LARGE-FLOWERED/
HYBRID TEA, WHITE,
REPEAT-FLOWERING

The flowers of 'White Wings', which are borne in clusters, look like white wings, as they turn and angle from each other when fully open. The 5-petalled flowers open flat to show chocolate-colored anthers, and have a sweet scent. The foliage is leathery on a moderately vigorous, upright, medium-sized plant that is easy to cultivate. The American Rose Society rated it as 7.7 when it was released, which helped make it popular at that time. Rarely grown now, it is still available from specialist rose nurseries. **ZONES 5–10.**

KREBS, USA, 1947

'DAINTY BESS' × SEEDLING

## 'Wichmoss'
*(bottom)*

MODERN, RAMBLER, LIGHT PINK

The result of an attempt to produce a Rambler with mossed buds, 'Wichmoss' rambles well in the lax manner usual for *Rosa wichurana*, and has fragrant flowers. The moss is said to be susceptible to mildew. The flowers are pale pink and semi-double, fading to creamy white. There do not appear to have been other similar attempts, though Ralph Moore in California has produced many mossed Miniatures. This is an interesting rose for the garden. **ZONES 5–9.**

BARBIER, FRANCE, 1911

*ROSA WICHURANA* × 'SALET'

W

### 'Wickwar'

MODERN, MODERN SHRUB, LIGHT PINK

*Rosa soulieana* is an unusual Wild Rose introduced to Europe from western China in 1896. It bears clusters of large, single, white flowers that are followed by a crop of yellow-orange hips. The blooms are very fragrant. This seedling has pink flowers and is not as big, but it retains the other interesting qualities of the parent. It makes a large bush with grayish green leaflets and many prickles, and appears to be available only in England and France from specialist growers. ZONES 7–9.

STEADMAN, UK, 1960

SEEDLING OF *ROSA SOULIEANA*

### 'Will Scarlet' *(top)*

MODERN, MODERN SHRUB, MEDIUM RED, REPEAT-FLOWERING

This variety has bright red, semi-double flowers that open flat to clearly show stamens. The color fades to cerise as they age. The continuous flowering of these attractive blooms makes it a colorful sight in the garden. This vigorous, upright-growing shrub is disease resistant, but like many roses it can succumb when bad conditions prevail. 'Will Scarlet' is widely grown, although its richness of tone is best suited to cool climates. ZONES 5–9.

HILLING, UK, 1948

SPORT OF 'SKYROCKET'

NATIONAL ROSE SOCIETY TRIAL GROUND CERTIFICATE 1957

### 'William Allen Richardson' *(bottom)*

OLD, NOISETTE, YELLOW BLEND, REPEAT-FLOWERING

The growth of this rose is less vigorous than that of the parent but the flowers are much deeper in color, being deep orange-yellow. Medium in size and borne freely, they are neat and quartered in shape. Although it lacks fragrance, this rose has retained considerable popularity and is widely grown. ZONES 7–9.

DUCHER, FRANCE, 1878

SEEDLING OF 'RÊVE D'OR'

### 'William and Mary'  *(right)*

MODERN, MODERN SHRUB, PINK BLEND

This variety was bred by Peter Beales and was one
of the first three shrub roses that he introduced.
An interesting rose, it has inherited the vigorous
growth of 'Constance Spry'. The flowers are
strongly scented, large and fully double, with the
loose, informal blooms decorating the bush in
true old-fashioned style. The deep silvery pink
petals are highlighted with carmine and are produced both singly and in clusters. A lovely show
of bloom appears in early summer. The growth is
strong and upright and it can be used as a small
climber. The matt green foliage blends well with
herbaceous plants, and its informal growth also
mixes well in a shrub border. It flowers poorly in
warm climates. ZONES 5–10.

BEALES, UK, 1988

SEEDLING OF 'CONSTANCE SPRY'

### 'William Baffin'

MODERN, MODERN SHRUB, DEEP PINK, REPEAT-FLOWERING

This is a tough and hardy rose suitable for those
colder areas where most roses cannot thrive.
The beautiful loose blooms are semi-double and
strawberry pink, with a touch of white towards
the centers which are lit up by golden stamens,
and appear in clusters of up to 30 from summer
to autumn. There is little fragrance. 'William
Baffin' can be grown as a specimen shrub, planted
to form an impenetrable hedge or trained on a
support as a climber. The plant is very vigorous,
with upright, slightly arching stems embellished
with robust, glossy and healthy foliage. The name
commemorates the famous explorer who sought
the Northwest Passage. ZONES 3–9.

SVEJDA, CANADA, 1983

*ROSA KORDESII* × SEEDLING

### 'William Grant'  *(above)*

OLD, GALLICA, DEEP PINK, REPEAT-FLOWERING

When this gorgeous Gallica is in full bloom
during summer it gives an abundance of rich
pink, single to semi-double, cupped flowers.
They are carried in small clusters and open flat to
show a central boss of golden yellow stamens.
The rose has a climbing habit and a wonderful
fragrance. It was found by William Grant—one
of the contributors to this book—growing on a
fence by an abandoned petrol station in Oregon,
USA. The nursery that propagated it named it
after its finder. ZONES 5–10.

PARENTAGE UNKNOWN

W

### 'William Lobb'
*(top)*
syns 'Duchesse
d'Istrie', 'Old Velvet
Moss'
OLD, MOSS, MAUVE

Deservedly one of the
most popular Moss
Roses, 'William Lobb'
grows vigorously to 8 ft
(2.5 m). Its long, firm
stems, covered in
grayish brown moss,
have many stout thorns
and are overlaid with
dark gray-green,
medium-sized and
coarse, well-serrated
foliage. The buds have
much soft, mid- to
dark green moss. The
semi-double flowers
are almost ragged in
structure but neverthe-

less charming,
especially when fully
open and displaying
the centers of golden
yellow stamens that
contrast so beautifully
with the purplish
petals, which have a

lavender-pink reverse.
Deep down near the
base, each petal is
flecked with white.
There is a strong scent
and the flowers appear
in mid-summer in
great profusion. It is

useful as both a tall
shrub or small climber
on walls, trellises and
arches. It will need
support. ZONES 5–10.
LAFFAY, FRANCE, 1855
PARENTAGE UNKNOWN

### 'William
Shakespeare'
AUSroyal *(bottom)*
MODERN, MODERN SHRUB,
DARK RED, REPEAT-FLOWERING

Also classified as an
English Rose, 'William
Shakespeare' produces
attractive, rich crimson
flowers and was created
by David Austin to
develop the red strain
in this series. It is not,
however, one of the
better varieties in the
line as it is susceptible
to rust and black
spot, which is hard to
control. The rosette-
formed flowers have a
rich, Damask scent and
are borne in sprays of
3–7. This tall, upright
plant has large, semi-
glossy, dark green
foliage and red thorns.
ZONES 5–10.
AUSTIN, UK, 1987
'THE SQUIRE' × 'MARY ROSE'

## 'William III' *(right)*

OLD, SCOTS, MAUVE

The Scots Roses were in vogue in the early nineteenth century, but most are now lost; this is one of the few survivors. It is a dwarf bush that suckers strongly, making a vigorous and prickly thicket. The small, spicy scented flowers with 15 petals are magenta-crimson, fading to lilac-pink with age. There are black hips in autumn and plenty of seeds. **ZONES 4–9.**

PARENTAGE UNKNOWN

## 'Wiltshire' KORmuse *(bottom)*

MODERN, MODERN SHRUB, MEDIUM PINK,
REPEAT-FLOWERING

The flowers of this variety are bright pink, of medium size, fairly full of petals, borne in clusters and have an open cupped shape. Because they appear on a plant with a low, untidy habit, they are easily overgrown by younger shoots, so their full beauty is not always easy to appreciate. There is a light fragrance, and flowering is well maintained through summer and autumn. In the garden, 'Wiltshire' can be used as a ground-cover plant towards the front of a border, to trail over a wall or to use in a substantial container. The habit is low, and the plant spreads about twice as far as its height. The foliage is plentiful and shiny. **ZONES 4–9.**

KORDES, GERMANY, 1993

'PARTRIDGE' × SEEDLING

ROYAL NATIONAL ROSE SOCIETY CERTIFICATE
OF MERIT 1991, BRITISH ASSOCIATION OF
ROSE BREEDERS, BREEDERS' CHOICE 1993,
GLASGOW CERTIFICATE OF COMMENDATION
1994

W

### 'Wimi' TANrowisa
*(left)*
syn. 'Willy Millowitch Rose'

**MODERN, LARGE-FLOWERED/ HYBRID TEA, PINK BLEND, REPEAT-FLOWERING**

The flowers of this lovely rose are pink, blended with soft creamy white at the centers and medium pink at the outer edges of the petals. The effect these colors give is quite striking. 'Wimi' is a vigorous bush that reaches a medium size, and it has a fair resistance to disease. 'Wimi' has not been introduced worldwide, so it may prove a difficult plant to obtain. **ZONES 5–9.**

TANTAU, GERMANY, 1982
PARENTAGE UNKNOWN

### 'Winchester Cathedral' AUScat
*(below left)*
syn. 'Winchester'
**MODERN, MODERN SHRUB, WHITE, REPEAT-FLOWERING**

This variety is identical to its parent in every way except color. The white blooms are bright and free, but sometimes revert on the bush to pink, like its parent, or both pink and white. This is either an endearing habit or a nuisance, depending on the individual taste of the grower. The frequency of flowering and the wonderful loose blooms make this plant ideal for any garden; it is untroubled by disease right through the year. 'Winchester Cathedral' has a habit like that of an Old Garden Rose, which makes it easy to prune and grow. It is also classified as an English Rose. **ZONES 5–9.**

AUSTIN, UK, 1988
SPORT OF 'MARY ROSE'

W

## 'Windrush' AUSrush
### (right)
MODERN, MODERN SHRUB,
LIGHT YELLOW,
REPEAT-FLOWERING

This is a large shrub that bears lovely soft yellow, semi-double blooms. Although they fade a little when fully open, the stamens are clearly visible at this stage and their dark color is a striking contrast to the light-colored petals. It repeats quickly, and because the shrub is vigorous, there are few times in the summer when it is without flowers. 'Windrush' must be deadheaded regularly to achieve a continuous bloom, but if this process is relaxed near the start of autumn, the plant will produce an abundant crop of rosehips. It is a strong plant with good disease resistance. The variety is also classified as an English Rose.
**ZONES 5–9.**

AUSTIN, UK, 1984

SEEDLING × ('CANTERBURY' ×
'GOLDEN WINGS')

## 'Winnipeg Parks'
### (right)
MODERN, MODERN SHRUB,
DEEP PINK, REPEAT-FLOWERING

The pointed buds of this rose open into cupped, deep pink-red flowers of medium size. The blooms have a velvety texture and are neatly formed with about 20 petals that show yellow stamens. They are borne singly or in small sprays and have a slight fragrance. Although the blooms do not last long, they give a good succession of flowers through summer and autumn. Because it is very frost hardy, 'Winnipeg Parks' is a useful, medium-sized rose to grow in cold climates. This shrubby plant is well covered with matt mid-green leaves, which have a reddish tinge when young.
**ZONES 3–9.**

COLLICUT, CANADA, 1990

('PRAIRIE PRINCESS' × 'CUTHBERT
GRANT') × (SEEDLING ×
'MORDEN CARDINETTE')

**W**

can be larger in cool climates where a darker shading effect on the petals makes the rose even more attractive. When fully open, the quality of the flowers is further enhanced by the bright golden yellow stamens. It is an extremely vigorous plant and also self-cleaning: spent blooms fall off by themselves before the next bloom cycle begins. This award-winning rose has a previous American Rose Society award winner as its seed parent. **ZONES 5–10.**

SAVILLE, USA, 1884

'PARTY GIRL' × 'SHOCKING BLUE'

AMERICAN ROSE SOCIETY AWARD OF EXCELLENCE 1985

### 'Wise Portia' AUSport
*(center)*

MODERN, MODERN SHRUB, MAUVE, REPEAT-FLOWERING

Introduced in 1982, 'Wise Portia' is one of the earliest in David Austin's English Rose group. The flowers open to pinky mauve but have a large variation of tone over the season; the best blooms are produced in cool weather. The bush is a poor grower and there is a great need to keep disease under control, as it is susceptible to all the common fungus problems. It needs treatment and nurturing throughout the season to make it

perform well and produce its best blooms. The rewards for the gardener are wonderful; when cut, the long-lasting blooms fill a room with their strong fragrance. It was named for the heroine of Shakespeare's *The Merchant of Venice.* **ZONES 5–9.**

AUSTIN, UK, 1982

'THE KNIGHT' × 'GLASTONBURY'

### 'Wishing' DICkerfuffle
*(bottom)*
syn. 'Georgie Girl'

MODERN, CLUSTER-FLOWERED/ FLORIBUNDA, MEDIUM PINK/ ORANGE-PINK, REPEAT-FLOWERING

'Wishing' bears flowers that are a mixture of apricot and pink, although pink is dominant. The medium-sized, lightly scented blooms are borne in clusters. They are double but not too full, and cover this low-growing bush repeatedly through the warmer months. It is not susceptible to disease, but it is always wise to take preventive measures. **ZONES 5–9.**

DICKSON, UK, 1985

'SILVER JUBILEE' × 'BRIGHT SMILE'

ROYAL NATIONAL ROSE SOCIETY CERTIFICATE OF MERIT 1984, BELFAST CERTIFICATE OF MERIT 1986, GLASGOW CERTIFICATE OF MERIT 1988

### 'Winsome' SAVawin
*(top)*

MODERN, MINIATURE, MAUVE, REPEAT-FLOWERING

The purple-red flowers of 'Winsome' have over 40 petals. They have no scent, nor do they fade, and are borne singly on this upright bush with semi-glossy, mid-green foliage. The blooms

## 'Woburn Abbey' *(right)*
MODERN, CLUSTER-FLOWERED/FLORIBUNDA,
ORANGE BLEND, REPEAT-FLOWERING

The orange flowers of this
cultivar have an intense yellow
glow in cool weather. They are
fully double and form freely on
short stems all over the small-
growing plant. They are good
for cutting, and the repeat cycle
is good. Leathery, glossy mid-
green foliage covers this tough,
disease-resistant plant. 'Woburn
Abbey' takes its name from the
stately home of the Dukes of
Bedford. **ZONES 5–9.**

SIDEY AND COBLEY, UK, 1962

'MASQUERADE' × 'FASHION'

NATIONAL ROSE SOCIETY TRIAL GROUND
CERTIFICATE 1961

## 'Work of Art' MORart *(below)*
MODERN, CLIMBING MINIATURE, ORANGE
BLEND, REPEAT-FLOWERING

The short buds of this variety
open to orange, urn-shaped
blooms with undersides that are
blended with yellow. They are
double, with about 35 petals, are
borne in small clusters and can
be larger with high centers in
cool climates. The flowers hold
their form for a long time. It is a
very vigorous climber, reaching
6 ft (1.8 m) high, and has long
canes that can be fanned out to
achieve a larger area of color.
This is a great plant in the
garden; the color is truly a work
of art! **ZONES 6–10.**

MOORE, USA, 1989

SEEDLING OF A YELLOW CLIMBING
MINIATURE × 'GOLD BADGE'

W

### 'Xavier Olibo' *(above)*

OLD, HYBRID PERPETUAL, DEEP RED, REPEAT-FLOWERING

'Xavier Olibo' is almost an exact version of the parent, but the flowers are a much darker red. They are spectacular, but the plant must be well grown and requires some care. **ZONES 5–9.**

LACHARMÉ, FRANCE, 1865

SPORT OF 'GÉNÉRAL JACQUEMINOT'

X

## 'Yakimour' MEIpsilon
### (top)
MODERN, LARGE-FLOWERED/
HYBRID TEA, RED BLEND,
REPEAT-FLOWERING

This rose is not available to most gardeners. It bears double, medium red flowers with a full complement of petals that are slightly paler on the undersides, showing just a hint of gold. The foliage is glossy bright green and covers a vigorous, tidy bush with a fast repeat bloom. Unfortunately it is susceptible to black spot and mildew. **ZONES 5–9.**

MEILLAND, FRANCE, 1980

PARENTAGE UNKNOWN

BADEN-BADEN GOLD MEDAL
1985

## 'Yankee Doodle'
YanKOR

MODERN, LARGE-FLOWERED/
HYBRID TEA, YELLOW BLEND,
REPEAT-FLOWERING

This German-bred rose has all the appeal of an Old Garden Rose with the added advantage of repeat-flowering. The large buds open to full, rich yellow and peachy pink flowers; the outer petals turn and hold the center of the blooms in place. They are borne either singly or in small clusters and have no scent, and can be ruined in wet weather. The glossy leaves are slightly susceptible to disease, particularly in cooler weather when there can be a problem with black spot. This lovely rose was an award winner in 1976, and still retains its popularity after more than three decades. **ZONES 5–9.**

KORDES, GERMANY, 1965

'COLOUR WONDER' ×
'KING'S RANSOM'

ALL-AMERICA ROSE SELECTION
1976

## 'Yellow Bantam'
### (bottom)
MODERN, MINIATURE, LIGHT
YELLOW, REPEAT-FLOWERING

The tiny pointed lemon buds of this rose open to small yellow to white flowers. They are so small that this rose qualifies as a micro-miniature. The blooms are double with 25 petals and have a light fragrance. The bloom form is decorative.

It is a dwarf bush growing no higher than 10 in (25 cm) and is recommended as a container-grown plant where it enjoys being pot bound, just as orchids do. Unfortunately 'Yellow Bantam' has become obscure in the USA due to the ready availability of more modern roses in this color class. **ZONES 5–10.**

MOORE, USA, 1960

(ROSA WICHURANA ×
'FLORADORA') ×
'FAIRY PRINCESS'

Y

### 'Yellow Button'

AUSlow *(top)*

MODERN, MODERN SHRUB,
YELLOW BLEND,
REPEAT-FLOWERING

'Yellow Button' was
an early introduction
from David Austin,
and it showed the
world his objective
in his rose breeding
program. It produces
yellow, rosette-shaped
blooms, and these open
to a wonderful flower
that is excellent for
cutting. The form
holds well, so it is ideal
for posies and hand-
held arrangements.
However, the low bush
is not strong and
succumbs to disease
easily, so it needs much
work to keep it healthy.
For this reason it has
been removed from
many rose growers' lists
and is not now widely
available. ZONES 5–9.

AUSTIN, UK, 1975

'WIFE OF BATH' × 'CHINATOWN'

### 'Yellow Charles Austin' AUSyel

*(bottom)*

MODERN, MODERN SHRUB,
LIGHT YELLOW,
REPEAT-FLOWERING

This rose is identical to
its parent in every way
except for the color
of the flowers, which
are fully double, clear
yellow and have a full
rosette shape. There is
a good fragrance and
the blooms keep well,
provided they are cut
when it is cool. The
bush is healthy but

needs to be maintained
when conditions are
cool and damp, usually
early and late in the
season. The growth
habit is strong, and in
warm climates the
plant can grow quite
large; summer pruning
reduces growth and
encourages more
flowers. It is not widely
available. 'Yellow
Charles Austin' is also
classified as an English
Rose. ZONES 5–9.

AUSTIN, UK, 1981

SPORT OF 'CHARLES AUSTIN'

### 'Yellow Fairy'

POUlfair

MODERN, MODERN SHRUB,
MEDIUM YELLOW,
REPEAT-FLOWERING

'Texas' is a yellow
Miniature Rose, and
the concept of breeding
it with 'The Fairy',
aiming to create a
dainty yellow shrublet,
was a good one.
The result is slightly
disappointing because
'Yellow Fairy' lacks
much of the grace and
charm of its pollen
parent. The flowers
are small, made up of
a dozen or so small
petals, formed like
rosettes, and are borne
very freely in sprays.
They are a pleasing
shade of medium
yellow when the
blooms are young, but
they turn brown with
age and may fail to
open altogether in wet
weather. The growth is
uneven, and although
many arching stems are
produced, the overall
effect appears wispy
due to insufficient leaf
cover. As an example
of an interesting cross,
a place in the rose
garden for this rose
can be justified; it
grows below average
height with small, light
green, semi-glossy
leaves. ZONES 5–9.

OLESEN, DENMARK, 1988

'TEXAS' × 'THE FAIRY'

MADRID GOLD MEDAL 1988

Y

## 'Yesterday' *(top)*
### syn. 'Tapis d'Orient'
MODERN, POLYANTHA, MEDIUM
PINK, REPEAT-FLOWERING

This rose has won many awards and is well recommended for the garden; its semi-double flowers are borne in clusters that make a beautiful spectacle when in full bloom. They are mid-to violet-pink and the buds are a darker shade against the open flowers. The blooms last well when cut. This medium-sized shrub with thin and vigorous, disease-free growth forms an attractive round bush. Rows of 'Yesterday' look very effective in the garden. **ZONES 5–9.**

HARKNESS, UK, 1974

('PHYLLIS BIDE' × 'SHEPHERD'S DELIGHT') × 'BALLERINA'

ROYAL NATIONAL ROSE SOCIETY CERTIFICATE OF MERIT 1972, MONZA GOLD MEDAL 1974, BADEN-BADEN GOLD MEDAL 1976, ANERKANNTE DEUTSCHE ROSE 1978, ROYAL HORTICULTURAL SOCIETY AWARD OF GARDEN MERIT 1993

## 'Yolande d'Aragon'
### *(right)*
OLD, HYBRID PERPETUAL,
MAUVE, REPEAT-FLOWERING

The very full and large flowers of 'Yolande d'Aragon' are bright purple-pink. They are produced in big clusters and are very fragrant. There is a good autumn repeat, provided deadheading, summer pruning and feeding are practised. The bush is of moderate height with upright growth and light green foliage. Yolande was the wife of Louis II of Anjou and the Two Sicilies. Considering its antiquity, it is in remarkably plentiful supply, being available from many outlets. Some authorities classify it as a Perpetual Damask (Portland). The first Hybrid Perpetuals were developed from the Portlands. **ZONES 5–9.**

VIBERT, FRANCE, 1843

PARENTAGE UNKNOWN

Y

## 'York and Lancaster' *(top)*

syns *Rosa damascena versicolor*, 'Versicolor', 'York et Lancastre'

OLD, DAMASK, PINK BLEND

A lanky, lax-growing shrub of branching habit, 'York and Lancaster' has grayish green wood armed with hooked, sharp thorns. The many leaves are also grayish green and have a soft texture. The blooms are carried on long stalks in nodding, loose clusters, each raggedly semi-double and about 2½ in (6.5 cm) across. Their color is variable, some consisting of soft mid-pink and others consistently white; both shades may even be present in the same flower. The variety is very fragrant, but a little shy in its yield of blooms. Historically it is interesting, but it is not a rose to greatly enhance the average garden. ZONES 5–10.

PRE-1629

PARENTAGE UNKNOWN

## 'Yorkshire Bank'

RUtrulo *(center)*

syn. 'True Love'

MODERN, LARGE-FLOWERED/ HYBRID TEA, NEAR WHITE, REPEAT-FLOWERING

The double flowers of 'Yorkshire Bank' are a rich creamy pale yellow, paling to white. They display attractive stamens when fully open. The glossy leaves have some disease resistance, but the plant will need some care through the season to help it produce a bountiful supply of lovely blooms. The parentage should have resulted in a hugely successful cross, but this has not been the case. It is not widely grown, but is available in most countries. ZONES 5–9.

DE RUITER, THE NETHERLANDS, 1979

'PASCALI' × 'PEER GYNT'

GENEVA GOLD MEDAL 1979, NEW ZEALAND GOLD MEDAL 1979

## 'Youki San'    MEIdona *(bottom)*

syn. 'Mme Neige'

MODERN, LARGE-FLOWERED/ HYBRID TEA, WHITE, REPEAT-FLOWERING

This rose bears large and unusual, semi-double flowers that open flat to reveal pure white petals and striking gold and red stamens. It is a low-growing plant that is best suited to warm, dry climates where mildew and black spot are easily controlled. At the time of intro-duction, 'Youki San' was widely used in floral decoration. It is well worth growing. ZONES 5–9.

MEILLAND, FRANCE, 1965

'LADY SYLVIA' × 'WHITE KNIGHT'

BADEN-BADEN GOLD MEDAL 1964

Y

## 'Young at Heart'
*(right)*

MODERN, LARGE-FLOWERED/
HYBRID TEA, APRICOT BLEND,
REPEAT-FLOWERING

The shapely, fully
double flowers of this
rose are a long-lasting
soft apricot-pink, and
have a strong fragrance.
The plant has an
upright growth habit
with glossy, dark green
foliage. It needs to be
monitored in cool,
damp weather when
disease resistance is
poorest. 'Young at
Heart' produces vig-
orous canes from basal
growth, so pruning is
easy. It was introduced
as Australian Rose
of the Year in 1989.
It is becoming more
difficult to obtain.
**ZONES 5–9.**

ARMSTRONG, USA, 1988
PARENTAGE UNKNOWN

## 'Young Quinn'
MACbern *(above)*
syn. 'Yellow Wonder'

MODERN, LARGE-FLOWERED/
HYBRID TEA, MEDIUM YELLOW,
REPEAT-FLOWERING

The oval buds of
'Young Quinn' open to
double blooms of about
30 large petals that are
of good substance. The
full blooms are borne
singly on tall stems
amid the huge, glossy
rich green, attractive
leaves. The profuse
flowers are edged with
pink as they age, and
keep very well when
cut. 'Young Quinn' is a
good, disease-resistant
rose for a tall hedge or
for the back of a rose
bed. **ZONES 5–10.**

MCGREDY, NEW ZEALAND, 1975
'PEER GYNT' × 'KISKADEE'
BELFAST GOLD MEDAL 1978

Y

### 'Yves Piaget'   MElvildo
*(left)*
syns 'Queen Adelaide',
'The Royal Brompton
Rose'
MODERN, LARGE-FLOWERED/
HYBRID TEA, DEEP PINK,
REPEAT-FLOWERING

This rose was released
under the name 'Queen
Adelaide' in some
countries. The fully
double, pink flowers
are very sweetly scented
and have an old rose
charm about them.
'Yves Piaget' is a
medium-sized shrub
with stout growth and
produces blooms all
season. The resistance
to disease is good in
warm, dry climates, but
it is susceptible to black
spot in cool, damp
weather. This unusual
plant is well worth
growing for its scent
alone. ZONES 5–9.

MEILLAND, FRANCE, 1985

(['PHARAOH' × 'PEACE'] ×
['CHRYSLER IMPERIAL' ×
'CHARLES MALLERIN']) ×
'TAMANGO'

GENEVA GOLD MEDAL AND
FRAGRANCE AWARD 1982,
LE ROEULX GOLD MEDAL AND
FRAGRANCE AWARD 1982,
BELFAST FRAGRANCE AWARD
1986, BAGATELLE FRAGRANCE
AWARD 1992

### 'Yvonne Rabier'
*(below left)*
MODERN, POLYANTHA, WHITE,
REPEAT-FLOWERING

This cultivar produces
some of the best
white flowers of the
Polyantha Roses. They
are double and are
borne in clusters that
cover the bush when in
full bloom. The leaves
are disease resistant,
although some control
may be needed in areas
that are constantly
damp; it grows well
in warmer climates.
'Yvonne Rabier' makes
an ideal patio standard
and, as it is quite low,
it is also wonderful for
edging a rose bed.
ZONES 5–9.

TURBAT, FRANCE, 1910

*ROSA WICHURANA* ×
UNIDENTIFIED POLYANTHA ROSE

ROYAL HORTICULTURAL SOCIETY
AWARD OF GARDEN MERIT 1993

Y

## 'Zambra' MEIalfi
### *(right)*

MODERN, CLUSTER-FLOWERED/
FLORIBUNDA, ORANGE BLEND,
REPEAT-FLOWERING

The bright orange
flowers of 'Zambra'
open flat; the blooms
have only a few petals
that make up almost
two rows and show the
stamens off well. There
is a slight scent. The
bush is susceptible to
mildew and black spot
and growers who are
not careful will soon
have a plant that is bare
of leaves and in a poor
state. Better varieties
are available. In its
heyday it created a
great sensation because
the color was so
bright and unusual.
**'Climbing Zambra'**
(MEIalfisar; 1969) is
not too rampant, and
can easily be managed
if grown on a wall or
fence. **ZONES 5–9.**

MEILLAND, FRANCE, 1961

('GOLDILOCKS' × 'FASHION') ×
('GOLDILOCKS' × 'FASHION')

BAGATELLE GOLD MEDAL 1961,
NATIONAL ROSE SOCIETY
CERTIFICATE OF MERIT 1961,
ROME GOLD MEDAL 1961

## 'Zéphirine Drouhin' *(right)*

syns 'Belle Dijonnaise',
'Charles Bonnet',
'Ingegnoli Prediletta',
'Mme Gustave Bonnet'

OLD, BOURBON, MEDIUM PINK,
REPEAT-FLOWERING

This thornless rose can
be grown as a pillar
rose, over an arch,
or as a moderate to
large, open shrub. The
fragrant, medium-sized
flowers are semi-double
and loose petalled.
They are cerise-pink
with a white base. This
vigorous plant is easy
to cultivate. 'Kathleen
Harrop' is a pink sport
of this rose. Both make
good hedge roses but
should be kept away
from walls for fear of
black spot. **ZONES 5–10.**

BIZOT, FRANCE, 1868

PARENTAGE UNKNOWN

ROYAL HORTICULTURAL SOCIETY
AWARD OF GARDEN MERIT 1993

**Z**

### 'Zinger' *(top)*

MODERN, MINIATURE, MEDIUM
RED, REPEAT-FLOWERING

'Zinger' has long, pointed, elegant buds that open to medium bright red flowers with contrasting golden stamens. The florets have 11 petals and are fragrant. The blooms are borne one to a stem but more often in small clusters and do not burn even in hot climates. The bloom cycle is fast on a prolific plant. Its vigorous, spreading habit can be used to advantage, especially in rock gardens. 'Zorina', the Cluster-flowered seed parent, is commonly used in the hybridization of large roses, and here it has been used with great success, as 'Zinger' won the prestigious American Rose Society Award of Excellence.
**ZONES 5–10.**

SCHWARTZ, USA, 1978

'ZORINA' × 'MAGIC CARROUSEL'

AMERICAN ROSE SOCIETY
AWARD OF EXCELLENCE 1979

### 'Zoé'

syn. **'Moussue Partout'**

OLD, MOSS, MEDIUM PINK

The flowers of 'Zoé' are rose pink, globular and well mossed on a conventional plant. It is generally available.
**ZONES 4–9.**

PRADEL, FRANCE, 1861

PARENTAGE UNKNOWN

### 'Zweibrücken'

*(below)*

MODERN, MODERN SHRUB, DARK
RED, REPEAT-FLOWERING

This rose was introduced in 1955 following an outstanding performance at the German Rose Trials. It has a vigorous climbing habit and is covered with deep crimson, fully double flowers. The blooms last well in the garden, but do not have a long life when picked and taken indoors. **ZONES 5–9.**

KORDES, GERMANY, 1955

*ROSA KORDESII* × 'INDEPENDENCE'

BADEN-BADEN BRONZE MEDAL
1956

### 'Zwergkönig 78'  KORkönig  *(above)*
### syn. 'Dwarf King'

MODERN, MINIATURE, DARK RED, REPEAT-FLOWERING

'Zwergkönig 78' has fragrant, cupped, carmine
flowers with 25 petals. The foliage is glossy green
on a vigorous, compact, hardy bush, only 8–10 in
(20–25 cm) high. The original 'Zwergkönig'
was the darkest of the Miniatures with its ruffled
flowers almost black-red. This new rose has the
reputation of being stronger and easier to grow
and with a much brighter color tone. **ZONES 5–10.**

KORDES, GERMANY, 1978

PARENTAGE UNKNOWN

### 'Zwergkönigin 82'  KORwerk
### syn. 'Dwarf Queen 82'

MODERN, MINIATURE, MEDIUM PINK, REPEAT-FLOWERING

Apart from the color difference, 'Zwergkönigin
82' is similar in every way to 'Zwergkönig 78'.
It grows taller than most Miniatures, and is a
wonderful tidy bush that produces long stems
with beautifully shaped medium pink blooms.
**ZONES 5–10.**

KORDES, GERMANY, 1982

KORKÖNIG × 'SUNDAY TIMES'

Z

# REFERENCE TABLE

This table presents a simple listing of the roses in this book to help you select one that suits your tastes.
The group to which the rose belongs is given in the individual text entries.
The colors listed in the table reflect the general color classification in the headings to the text entries.
A short description can be found in the individual entries.

| NAME | Bloom Color | Fragrance Amount | Flowering Habit | Flowering Incidence |
|---|---|---|---|---|
| **WILD ROSES** | | | | |
| Rosa acicularis nipponensis | deep pink | moderate | small clusters | once |
| Rosa arkansana | medium pink | slight | corymb | once |
| Rosa arvensis | white | slight | small clusters | once |
| Rosa banksiae normalis | white | moderate | corymb | once |
| Rosa blanda | medium pink | slight | small clusters | once |
| Rosa bracteata | white | none | singly | repeat |
| Rosa brunonii | white | moderate | corymb | once |
| Rosa californica | light pink | none | corymb | once |
| Rosa canina | light pink | moderate | small clusters | once |
| Rosa carolina | medium pink | none | singly | once |
| Rosa chinensis | medium pink/dark red | none | singly | repeat |
| Rosa cinnamomea | mauve | moderate | singly | once |
| Rosa davidii | light pink | none | corymb | once |
| Rosa ecae | deep yellow | none | singly | once |
| Rosa eglanteria | light pink | moderate | small clusters | once |
| Rosa elegantula 'Persetosa' | medium pink | slight | small clusters | once |
| Rosa fedtschenkoana | white | moderate | small clusters | once |
| Rosa filipes | white | moderate | corymb | once |
| Rosa foetida | medium yellow | moderate | singly | once |
| Rosa foliolosa | medium pink | slight | singly | once |
| Rosa forrestiana | deep pink | none | small clusters | once |
| Rosa gallica | deep pink | strong | small clusters | once |
| Rosa gentiliana | white | none | large clusters | once |
| Rosa gigantea | white | strong | small clusters | once |
| Rosa giraldii | medium pink | none | small clusters | once |
| Rosa glauca | medium pink | slight | small clusters | once |
| Rosa helenae | white | moderate | corymb | once |
| Rosa holodonta | light pink | slight | small clusters | once |
| Rosa hugonis | medium yellow | slight | singly | once |
| Rosa laevigata | white | slight | singly | once |
| Rosa longicuspis | white | slight | corymb | once |
| Rosa · macrantha 'Macrantha' | light pink/white | moderate | small clusters | once |

| NAME | Bloom Color | Fragrance Amount | Flowering Habit | Flowering Incidence |
|---|---|---|---|---|
| Rosa moschata | white | strong | corymb | once |
| Rosa moyesii | medium red | none | singly | once |
| Rosa mulliganii | white | moderate | corymb | once |
| Rosa multiflora | white | slight | corymb | once |
| Rosa nitida | medium pink | moderate | small clusters | once |
| Rosa nutkana | medium pink | slight | singly | once |
| Rosa pendulina | deep pink/mauve | none | small clusters | once |
| Rosa pimpinellifolia | white | none | singly | once |
| Rosa pisocarpa | medium pink | none | small clusters | once |
| Rosa pomifera | medium pink | slight | small clusters | once |
| Rosa primula | light yellow | strong | singly | once |
| Rosa roxburghii | medium pink | slight | singly | repeat |
| Rosa rugosa | mauve | strong | small clusters | repeat |
| Rosa sempervirens | white | slight | corymb | once |
| Rosa sericea pteracantha | white | none | singly | once |
| Rosa setipoda | light pink | moderate | corymb | once |
| Rosa soulieana | white | moderate | corymb | once |
| Rosa stellata mirifica | mauve | slight | singly | once |
| Rosa sweginzowii | medium pink | slight | small clusters | once |
| Rosa tomentosa | light pink | strong | small clusters | once |
| Rosa virginiana | medium pink | slight | small clusters | open |
| Rosa webbiana | medium pink | moderate | singly | once |
| Rosa wichurana | white | slight | corymb | once |
| Rosa willmottiae | mauve | slight | singly | once |
| Rosa woodsii | medium pink | none | small clusters | once |
| Rosa xanthina | medium yellow | slight | small clusters | once |
| **CULTIVARS** | | | | |
| Aalsmeer Gold | deep yellow | slight | small clusters | repeat |
| Abbaye de Cluny | apricot blend | slight | singly | repeat |
| Abbeyfield Rose | deep pink | slight | small clusters | repeat |
| Abbotswood | medium pink | slight | small clusters | once |
| Abraham Darby | orange-pink | strong | small clusters | repeat |

| NAME | Bloom Color | Fragrance Amount | Flowering Habit | Flowering Incidence |
|---|---|---|---|---|
| Acapulco | red blend | slight | small clusters | repeat |
| Acey Deucy | medium red | slight | small clusters | repeat |
| Adair Roche | pink blend | slight | small clusters | repeat |
| Adam | medium pink | slight | singly | repeat |
| Adam Messerich | medium red | moderate | small clusters | repeat |
| Adelaïde d'Orléans | white | moderate | small clusters | once |
| Admiral Rodney | pink blend | strong | small clusters | repeat |
| Adolf Horstmann | yellow blend | slight | singly | repeat |
| Agatha Christie | pink | moderate | small clusters | repeat |
| Agathe Incarnata | medium pink | strong | small clusters | once |
| Aglaia | light yellow | slight | large clusters | once |
| Agnes | light yellow | moderate | singly | repeat |
| Agnes Bernauer | light pink | strong | singly | repeat |
| Aicha | deep yellow | strong | small clusters | once |
| Aimable Rouge | deep pink | moderate | singly | repeat |
| Aimée Vibert | white | strong | umbel | repeat |
| Alain | medium red | slight | large clusters | repeat |
| Alain Blanchard | mauve | moderate | small clusters | once |
| Alba Maxima | white | slight | small clusters | once |
| Alba Meidiland | white | none | small clusters | repeat |
| Alba Semi-plena | white | slight | large clusters | once |
| Alba Suaveolens | white | strong | large clusters | once |
| Albéric Barbier | white | moderate | small clusters | once |
| Albertine | orange-pink | moderate | small clusters | once |
| Alchymist | apricot blend | moderate | small clusters | once |
| Alec's Red | medium red | moderate | singly | repeat |
| Alexander | orange-red | none | small clusters | repeat |
| Alexandre Girault | pink blend | moderate | small clusters | once |
| Alfred Colomb | pink blend | strong | small clusters | repeat |
| Alfred de Dalmas | light pink | slight | small clusters | repeat |
| Alida Lovett | light pink | slight | small clusters | once |
| Alister Clark | light pink | moderate | small clusters | repeat |
| Alister Stella Gray | light yellow | moderate | small clusters | repeat |
| Alleluia | red blend | none | singly | repeat |
| Allen Chandler | medium red | slight | singly | repeat |
| Allgold | medium yellow | slight | large clusters | repeat |
| Allotria | orange-red | none | large clusters | repeat |
| Aloha | medium pink | moderate | singly | repeat |
| Alpine Sunset | apricot blend | moderate | singly | repeat |
| Altissimo | medium red | none | small clusters | once |
| Amadis | dark red | none | small clusters | once |
| Amalia | dark red/light red | none | small clusters | repeat |
| Amatsu-Otome | yellow blend | slight | small clusters | repeat |

| NAME | Bloom Color | Fragrance Amount | Flowering Habit | Flowering Incidence |
|---|---|---|---|---|
| Ambassador | orange blend | none | small clusters | repeat |
| Amber Queen | apricot blend | slight | small clusters | repeat |
| Amelia | medium pink | strong | small clusters | once |
| America | orange-pink | strong | small clusters | repeat |
| American Beauty | deep pink | strong | singly | repeat |
| American Heritage | yellow blend | none | singly | repeat |
| American Home | dark red | strong | singly | repeat |
| American Pillar | pink blend | none | large clusters | once |
| Améthyste | mauve | none | large clusters | once |
| Amy Johnson | medium pink | slight | small clusters | repeat |
| Amy Robsart | deep pink | moderate | singly | once |
| Anabell | orange blend | moderate | small clusters | repeat |
| Anaïs Ségalas | pink blend | moderate | small clusters | once |
| Anastasia | white | none | singly | repeat |
| Andalusien | medium red | none | small clusters | repeat |
| Anemone | light pink | none | singly | repeat |
| Angel Darling | mauve | slight | small clusters | repeat |
| Angel Face | mauve | strong | small clusters | repeat |
| Angela | deep pink | none | small clusters | repeat |
| Angela Rippon | medium pink | slight | small clusters | repeat |
| Ann Endt | dark red | moderate | small clusters | repeat |
| Anna de Diesbach | deep pink | strong | singly | repeat |
| Anna Ford | orange blend | slight | large clusters | repeat |
| Anna Livia | orange-pink | slight | small clusters | repeat |
| Anna Olivier | pink blend | moderate | small clusters | repeat |
| Anna Pavlova | light pink | strong | small clusters | repeat |
| Anne Cocker | orange-pink | none | small clusters | repeat |
| Anne de Bretagne | deep pink | none | small clusters | repeat |
| Anne Diamond | apricot blend | none | small clusters | repeat |
| Anne Harkness | apricot blend | none | truss | repeat |
| Anne-Marie de Montravel | white | slight | large clusters | repeat |
| Annie Vibert | white blend | moderate | large clusters | repeat |
| Another Chance | white | slight | singly | repeat |
| Anthony Meilland | medium yellow | slight | small clusters | repeat |
| Antike 89 | pink blend | slight | small clusters | repeat |
| Antique Rose | medium pink | slight | singly | repeat |
| Antique Silk | white | none | small clusters | repeat |
| Antoine Rivoire | light pink | slight | singly | repeat |
| Antonia Ridge | medium red | slight | singly | repeat |
| Anusheh | red blend | slight | small clusters | repeat |
| Apart | mauve blend | moderate | small clusters | repeat |
| Apollo | medium yellow | slight | singly | repeat |
| Apothecary's Rose | deep pink | strong | small clusters | once |

| NAME | Bloom Color | Fragrance Amount | Flowering Habit | Flowering Incidence |
| --- | --- | --- | --- | --- |
| Apple Blossom | light pink | slight | truss | once |
| Apricot Gem | apricot blend | none | small clusters | repeat |
| Apricot Nectar | apricot blend | moderate | small clusters | repeat |
| Apricot Silk | apricot blend | slight | small clusters | repeat |
| April Hamer | pink blend | slight | singly | repeat |
| Aquarius | pink blend | slight | small clusters | repeat |
| Archduke Charles | red blend | moderate | small clusters | repeat |
| Archiduc Joseph | pink blend | moderate | small clusters | repeat |
| Archiduchesse Elizabeth d'Autriche | medium pink | slight | small clusters | repeat |
| Ardoisée de Lyon | mauve | strong | singly | repeat |
| Ards Rover | dark red | strong | singly | once |
| Arethusa | yellow blend | none | small clusters | repeat |
| Arianna | pink blend | slight | singly | repeat |
| Arielle Dombasle | orange blend | slight | small clusters | repeat |
| Arizona | orange blend | moderate | small clusters | repeat |
| Armada | medium pink | moderate | small clusters | repeat |
| Arthur Bell | medium yellow | moderate | small clusters | repeat |
| Arthur de Sansal | mauve | strong | small clusters | repeat |
| Arthur Hillier | deep pink | none | small clusters | once |
| Artistry | orange blend | slight | small clusters | repeat |
| Aspen | medium yellow | none | small clusters | repeat |
| Assemblage des Beautés | dark red | strong | small clusters | once |
| Asso di Cuori | dark red | none | singly | repeat |
| Asta von Parpart | mauve | slight | large clusters | once |
| Astrée | pink blend | strong | singly | repeat |
| Athena | white blend | none | singly | repeat |
| Auckland Metro | white blend | moderate | small clusters | repeat |
| Auguste Gervais | apricot blend | moderate | small clusters | once |
| Auguste Renoir | medium pink | strong | singly | repeat |
| Augustine Guinoisseau | white blend | strong | small clusters | repeat |
| Australia Felix | pink blend | moderate | small clusters | repeat |
| Australia's Olympic Gold Rose | deep yellow | moderate | clusters | repeat |
| Autumn Damask | medium pink | strong | small clusters | repeat |
| Autumn Delight | white | moderate | large clusters | repeat |
| Autumn Sunlight | orange-red | moderate | small clusters | repeat |
| Autumn Sunset | apricot blend | strong | large clusters | repeat |
| Ave Maria | orange-pink | moderate | small clusters | repeat |
| Avon | dark red | strong | small clusters | repeat |
| Awakening | light pink | moderate | small clusters | repeat |
| Baby Alberic | light yellow | none | small clusters | repeat |
| Baby Bio | deep yellow | none | small clusters | repeat |
| Baby Darling | apricot blend | none | small clusters | repeat |
| Baby Faurax | mauve | slight | large clusters | repeat |

| NAME | Bloom Color | Fragrance Amount | Flowering Habit | Flowering Incidence |
| --- | --- | --- | --- | --- |
| Baby Gold Star | deep yellow | slight | small clusters | repeat |
| Baby Katie | pink blend | none | small clusters | repeat |
| Baby Love | deep yellow | slight | small clusters | repeat |
| Baby Masquerade | red blend | none | small clusters | repeat |
| Baccará | orange-red | none | small clusters | repeat |
| Ballerina | medium pink | moderate | large clusters | repeat |
| Bantry Bay | medium pink | slight | small clusters | repeat |
| Banzai '83 | yellow blend | slight | small clusters | repeat |
| Baron de Bonstetten | dark red | strong | singly | repeat |
| Baron de Wassenaer | medium deep pink | strong | small clusters | once |
| Baron Girod de l'Ain | red blend | moderate | small clusters | repeat |
| Baron J. B. Gonella | pink blend | moderate | small clusters | repeat |
| Baronne Adolphe de Rothschild | light pink | none | singly | repeat |
| Baronne Edmond de Rothschild | red blend | strong | small clusters | repeat |
| Baronne Henriette de Snoy | pink blend | moderate | small clusters | repeat |
| Baronne Prévost | medium pink | moderate | singly | repeat |
| Bassino | medium red | none | small clusters | repeat |
| Beauté | apricot blend | moderate | small clusters | repeat |
| Beautiful Britain | orange-red | none | small clusters | repeat |
| Beauty of Rosemawr | pink blend | slight | small clusters | repeat |
| Beauty Secret | medium red | slight | small clusters | repeat |
| Bel Ange | medium pink | moderate | small clusters | repeat |
| Bella Rosa | medium pink | slight | small clusters | repeat |
| Belle Amour | light pink | strong | small clusters | once |
| Belle Blonde | medium yellow | moderate | singly | repeat |
| Belle de Crécy | mauve | moderate | small clusters | once |
| Belle des Jardins | mauve blend | moderate | small clusters | once |
| Belle Epoque | orange blend | moderate | small clusters | repeat |
| Belle Isis | light pink | strong | small clusters | once |
| Belle Poitevine | medium pink | moderate | small clusters | repeat |
| Belle Portugaise | light pink | moderate | small clusters | once |
| Belle sans Flatterie | mauve blend | moderate | small clusters | once |
| Belle Story | light pink | moderate | small clusters | repeat |
| Bengale Rouge | medium red | moderate | small clusters | repeat |
| Bengali | orange-red | none | small clusters | repeat |
| Bennett's Seedling | deep yellow | slight | small clusters | once |
| Benita | white | slight | small clusters | repeat |
| Benson and Hedges Gold | yellow blend | slight | small clusters | repeat |
| Benvenuto | medium red | slight | small clusters | repeat |
| Berlin | orange blend | slight | large clusters | repeat |
| Bernstein-Rose | deep yellow | slight | small clusters | repeat |
| Berries 'n' Cream | pink blend | slight | small clusters | repeat |
| Betty Harkness | orange blend | moderate | large clusters | repeat |

| NAME | Bloom Color | Fragrance Amount | Flowering Habit | Flowering Incidence |
|---|---|---|---|---|
| Betty Prior | medium pink | none | small clusters | repeat |
| Betty Uprichard | apricot blend | strong | small clusters | repeat |
| Bewitched | medium pink | moderate | singly | repeat |
| Bing Crosby | orange blend | slight | singly | repeat |
| Bishofsstadt Paderborn | orange-red | moderate | small clusters | repeat |
| Bishop Darlington | apricot blend | moderate | small clusters | repeat |
| Bit o' Sunshine | deep yellow | slight | small clusters | repeat |
| Black Beauty | dark red | none | small clusters | repeat |
| Black Boy | dark red | moderate | small clusters | once |
| Black Ice | dark red | none | small clusters | repeat |
| Black Jade | dark red | none | small clusters | repeat |
| Black Velvet | dark red | moderate | singly | repeat |
| Blairii No. 2 | light pink | strong | small clusters | once |
| Blanc de Vibert | white | strong | small clusters | repeat |
| Blanc Double de Coubert | white | strong | small clusters | repeat |
| Blanche Moreau | white | strong | small clusters | repeat |
| Blanchefleur | white | strong | small clusters | once |
| Blaze | medium red | slight | large clusters | once |
| Blessings | orange-pink | slight | small clusters | repeat |
| Bleu Magenta | mauve | slight | small clusters | once |
| Bloomfield Abundance | light pink | slight | small clusters | repeat |
| Bloomfield Courage | red blend | none | large clusters | once |
| Bloomfield Dainty | medium yellow | moderate | small clusters | repeat |
| Blossomtime | medium pink | moderate | small clusters | repeat |
| Blue Bajou | mauve blend | slight | large clusters | repeat |
| Blue Moon | mauve | strong | small clusters | repeat |
| Blue Nile | mauve | strong | large clusters | repeat |
| Blue Parfum | mauve | strong | small clusters | repeat |
| Blue Peter | mauve blend | slight | small clusters | repeat |
| Blue River | mauve blend | strong | small clusters | repeat |
| Blueberry Hill | mauve | moderate | small clusters | once |
| Blush Damask | light pink | strong | small clusters | once |
| Blush Hip | light pink | strong | small clusters | once |
| Blush Noisette | white | moderate | large clusters | repeat |
| Blush Rambler | light pink | slight | large clusters | once |
| Bobbie James | white | strong | large clusters | once |
| Bobby Charlton | pink blend | strong | singly | repeat |
| Bon Silene | deep pink | moderate | small clusters | repeat |
| Bonfire Night | red blend | none | small clusters | repeat |
| Bonica | medium pink | none | small clusters | repeat |
| Bonn | orange-red | moderate | large clusters | repeat |
| Borderer | pink blend | none | small clusters | repeat |
| Botanica | light pink | strong | large clusters | repeat |

| NAME | Bloom Color | Fragrance Amount | Flowering Habit | Flowering Incidence |
|---|---|---|---|---|
| Botzaris | white | strong | small clusters | once |
| Bougainville | pink blend | slight | small clusters | repeat |
| Boule de Neige | white | strong | small clusters | once |
| Bouquet d'Or | yellow blend | moderate | small clusters | repeat |
| Bourgogne | medium red | moderate | small clusters | once |
| Bow Bells | deep pink | slight | small clusters | repeat |
| Boys' Brigade | medium red | none | large clusters | repeat |
| Brandy | apricot blend | slight | singly | repeat |
| Brass Ring | orange blend | none | large clusters | repeat |
| Breath of Life | apricot blend | slight | small clusters | repeat |
| Breathless | deep pink | slight | singly | repeat |
| Bredon | apricot blend | moderate | small clusters | repeat |
| Breeze Hill | apricot blend | moderate | small clusters | once |
| Brenda | light pink | slight | small clusters | once |
| Brennus | dark red | slight | small clusters | once |
| Bridal Pink | medium pink | slight | small clusters | repeat |
| Bride's Dream | light pink | slight | singly | repeat |
| Brigadoon | pink blend | moderate | small clusters | repeat |
| Bright Smile | medium yellow | slight | small clusters | repeat |
| Broadway | yellow blend | moderate | singly | repeat |
| Bronze Masterpiece | apricot blend | moderate | singly | repeat |
| Brother Cadfael | medium pink | strong | small clusters | repeat |
| Brown Velvet | russet | slight | small clusters | repeat |
| Brownie | russet | slight | small clusters | repeat |
| Buccaneer | medium yellow | moderate | small clusters | repeat |
| Buff Beauty | apricot blend | moderate | small clusters | repeat |
| Bullata | medium pink | moderate | small clusters | once |
| Bulls Red | medium red | none | small clusters | repeat |
| Burgundian Rose | pink blend | slight | small clusters | once |
| Burnaby | light yellow | slight | small clusters | repeat |
| Buttons 'n' Bows | deep pink | slight | small clusters | repeat |
| By Appointment | apricot blend | slight | small clusters | repeat |
| Cabbage Rose | medium pink | strong | small clusters | once |
| Café | russet | slight | small clusters | repeat |
| Calocarpa | medium pink | strong | small clusters | repeat |
| Camaieux | mauve | strong | small clusters | once |
| Camaieux Fimbriata | mauve | moderate | small clusters | once |
| Cambridgeshire | red blend | none | large clusters | repeat |
| Camélia Rose | light pink | none | small clusters | repeat |
| Camelot | apricot blend | moderate | small clusters | repeat |
| Cameo | orange-pink | none | large clusters | repeat |
| Canary Bird | deep yellow | none | singly | once |
| Candelabra | orange blend | slight | small clusters | repeat |

| NAME | Bloom Color | Fragrance Amount | Flowering Habit | Flowering Incidence |
|---|---|---|---|---|
| Candella | red blend | none | singly | repeat |
| Candy Rose | red blend | slight | large clusters | repeat |
| Candy Stripe | pink blend | slight | small clusters | repeat |
| Cannes Festival | yellow blend | slight | singly | repeat |
| Cantabrigiensis | light yellow | slight | singly | once |
| Canterbury | medium pink | moderate | small clusters | repeat |
| Capitaine Basroger | red blend | strong | small clusters | once |
| Capitaine John Ingram | mauve | strong | small clusters | once |
| Cappa Magna | medium red | none | large clusters | once |
| Captain Christy | light pink | slight | small clusters | once |
| Cardinal de Richelieu | mauve | strong | small clusters | once |
| Cardinal Hume | mauve blend | slight | large clusters | repeat |
| Cardinal Song | medium red | slight | singly | repeat |
| Carefree Beauty | medium pink | slight | small clusters | repeat |
| Carefree Wonder | pink blend | none | small clusters | repeat |
| Carina | medium pink | moderate | singly | repeat |
| Carla | orange-pink | slight | singly | repeat |
| Carmen | medium red | strong | small clusters | repeat |
| Carmenetta | light pink | slight | singly | once |
| Carol | pink blend | slight | singly | repeat |
| Caroline de Monaco | creamy white | none | singly | repeat |
| Carrot Top | orange blend | none | small clusters | repeat |
| Carrousel | medium red | moderate | small clusters | repeat |
| Casino | light yellow | slight | singly | repeat |
| Cassandre | medium red | slight | small clusters | repeat |
| Caterpillar | light pink | none | truss | repeat |
| Cathedral | apricot blend | slight | small clusters | repeat |
| Catherine Deneuve | orange-pink | strong | singly | repeat |
| Catherine Guillot | deep pink | strong | small clusters | repeat |
| Cécile Brunner | light pink | moderate | large clusters | repeat |
| Celeste | light pink | strong | small clusters | once |
| Céline Delbard | orange blend | none | small clusters | repeat |
| Céline Forestier | light yellow | strong | small clusters | repeat |
| Celsiana | light pink | moderate | small clusters | once |
| Centenaire de Lourdes | medium pink | none | large clusters | repeat |
| Centifolia | medium pink | strong | small clusters | once |
| Centifolia Muscosa | medium pink | moderate | small clusters | once |
| Century Two | medium pink | moderate | singly | repeat |
| Cerise Bouquet | deep pink | moderate | large clusters | repeat |
| Champagne | yellow blend | slight | singly | repeat |
| Champagne Cocktail | yellow blend | moderate | small clusters | repeat |
| Champion | yellow blend | moderate | singly | repeat |
| Champion of the World | medium pink | strong | singly | repeat |

| NAME | Bloom Color | Fragrance Amount | Flowering Habit | Flowering Incidence |
|---|---|---|---|---|
| Champlain | dark red | slight | large clusters | repeat |
| Champneys' Pink Cluster | light pink | strong | large clusters | repeat |
| Champs-Elysées | dark red | slight | singly | repeat |
| Chanelle | orange-pink | slight | small clusters | repeat |
| Charles Albanel | medium red | moderate | small clusters | repeat |
| Charles Austin | apricot blend | moderate | small clusters | repeat |
| Charles de Gaulle | mauve blend | strong | small clusters | repeat |
| Charles de Mills | mauve | strong | small clusters | once |
| Charles Lawson | deep pink | moderate | small clusters | repeat |
| Charles Lefèbvre | dark red | moderate | singly | repeat |
| Charles Mallerin | dark red | strong | singly | repeat |
| Charles Rennie Mackintosh | pink blend | strong | small clusters | repeat |
| Charlotte (Austin) | light yellow | moderate | small clusters | repeat |
| Charlotte Armstrong | deep pink | moderate | small clusters | repeat |
| Charlotte Rampling | medium red | strong | small clusters | repeat |
| Charmian | medium pink | strong | small clusters | repeat |
| Château de Clos Vougeot | dark red | strong | small clusters | repeat |
| Chaucer | medium pink | strong | small clusters | repeat |
| Cherish | orange-pink | slight | small clusters | repeat |
| Cherry Brandy '85 | orange blend | moderate | singly | repeat |
| Cherry Meillandecor | red blend | none | small clusters | repeat |
| Cheshire Life | orange-red | slight | singly | repeat |
| Chianti | mauve blend | strong | small clusters | once |
| Chicago Peace | pink blend | slight | small clusters | repeat |
| China Doll | medium pink | slight | truss | repeat |
| Chinatown | deep yellow | strong | small clusters | repeat |
| Chivalry | red blend | none | singly | repeat |
| Chloris | light pink | strong | small clusters | once |
| Chorus | orange-red | slight | small clusters | repeat |
| Christian Dior | medium red | slight | small clusters | repeat |
| Christopher Columbus (Meilland) | orange blend | slight | singly | repeat |
| Chrysler Imperial | dark red | strong | small clusters | repeat |
| Cider Cup | orange blend | slight | small clusters | repeat |
| Cinderella | white | moderate | small clusters | repeat |
| Circus | yellow blend | moderate | small clusters | repeat |
| City of Auckland | orange blend | strong | singly | repeat |
| City of Belfast | orange-red | none | truss | repeat |
| City of Leeds | orange-pink | slight | small clusters | repeat |
| City of London | light pink | strong | small clusters | repeat |
| City of York | white | moderate | large clusters | repeat |
| Clair Matin | medium pink | moderate | large clusters | repeat |
| Claire Jacquier | light yellow | moderate | large clusters | once |
| Claire Rose | medium pink | strong | small clusters | repeat |

| NAME | Bloom Color | Fragrance Amount | Flowering Habit | Flowering Incidence |
|---|---|---|---|---|
| Clarita | orange-red | slight | singly | repeat |
| Class Act | white | slight | small clusters | repeat |
| Classic Sunblaze | medium pink | slight | small clusters | repeat |
| Cleopatra | red blend | slight | singly | once |
| Clio | light pink | moderate | singly | repeat |
| Clos Fleuri Blanc | white | slight | small clusters | repeat |
| Clos Vougeot | medium red | none | small clusters | once |
| Clytemnestra | orange-pink | moderate | large clusters | repeat |
| Cocktail | red blend | slight | small clusters | repeat |
| Cocorico | orange-red | none | small clusters | repeat |
| Colette | light pink | strong | small clusters | repeat |
| Colibri | orange blend | slight | small clusters | repeat |
| Colorama | red blend | moderate | small clusters | repeat |
| Colour Wonder | orange blend | slight | small clusters | repeat |
| Commandant Beaurepaire | pink blend | moderate | small clusters | once |
| Compassion | orange-pink | moderate | small clusters | repeat |
| Complicata | pink blend | strong | small clusters | once |
| Comte Boula de Nanteuil | mauve | strong | small clusters | once |
| Comte de Chambord | pink blend | strong | small clusters | repeat |
| Comtesse Cécile de Chabrillant | pink blend | moderate | singly | repeat |
| Comtesse de Murinais | white | strong | small clusters | once |
| Comtesse du Cayla | orange blend | slight | small clusters | repeat |
| Concerto | medium red | slight | small clusters | repeat |
| Conditorum | dark red | strong | small clusters | once |
| Confidence | pink blend | moderate | singly | repeat |
| Congratulations | orange-pink | slight | small clusters | repeat |
| Conrad Ferdinand Meyer | light pink | strong | small clusters | repeat |
| Coppélia | orange blend | none | large clusters | repeat |
| Coral Cluster | pink blend | none | small clusters | repeat |
| Coral Satin | orange-pink | moderate | small clusters | once |
| Coralin | orange-red | none | small clusters | repeat |
| Cordula | orange-red | slight | small clusters | repeat |
| Cornelia | pink blend | strong | large clusters | repeat |
| Coronado | red blend | moderate | singly | repeat |
| Corso | orange blend | slight | singly | repeat |
| Cottage Rose | medium pink | slight | small clusters | repeat |
| Country Dancer | deep pink | moderate | small clusters | repeat |
| Country Lady | orange blend | slight | singly | repeat |
| Country Living | light pink | moderate | small clusters | repeat |

| NAME | Bloom Color | Fragrance Amount | Flowering Habit | Flowering Incidence |
|---|---|---|---|---|
| Coupe d'Hébé | deep pink | strong | small clusters | repeat |
| Courtoisie | orange blend | moderate | small clusters | repeat |
| Courvoisier | deep yellow | moderate | small clusters | repeat |
| Cramoisi Picoté | red blend | moderate | small clusters | once |
| Crépuscule | apricot blend | slight | small clusters | repeat |
| Cressida | apricot blend | strong | small clusters | repeat |
| Crested Moss | medium pink | strong | small clusters | once |
| Cricket | orange blend | slight | small clusters | repeat |
| Crimson Globe | dark red | strong | small clusters | once |
| Crimson Glory | dark red | strong | singly | repeat |
| Crimson Shower | medium red | slight | large clusters | repeat |
| Criterion | pink blend | moderate | singly | repeat |
| Crystal Palace | apricot blend | moderate | small clusters | repeat |
| Crystalline | white | moderate | small clusters | repeat |
| Cuddles | orange-pink | slight | small clusters | repeat |
| Cuisse de Nymphe Emué | medium pink | strong | small clusters | once |
| Cupcake | medium pink | none | small clusters | repeat |
| Cupid | light pink | none | large clusters | once |
| Cuthbert Grant | dark red | slight | small clusters | repeat |
| Cymbaline | light pink | strong | small clusters | repeat |
| D'Aguesseau | medium red | moderate | small clusters | once |
| Daily Mail Scented Rose | red blend | strong | small clusters | repeat |
| Dainty Bess | light pink | moderate | small clusters | repeat |
| Dairy Maid | light yellow | none | large clusters | repeat |
| Dame de Coeur | medium red | moderate | singly | repeat |
| Dame Edith Helen | medium pink | strong | small clusters | repeat |
| Dame Prudence | light pink | strong | small clusters | repeat |
| Dame Wendy | medium pink | slight | small clusters | repeat |
| Danaë | light yellow | slight | large clusters | repeat |
| Danse des Sylphes | orange-red | none | small clusters | repeat |
| Dapple Dawn | light pink | none | large clusters | repeat |
| Darling Flame | orange-red | slight | small clusters | repeat |
| Dawn Chorus | orange blend | none | small clusters | repeat |
| Day Light | apricot blend | none | small clusters | repeat |
| Daybreak | medium yellow | strong | small clusters | repeat |
| Daydream | red blend | slight | small clusters | repeat |
| De la Maître-Ecole | mauve | strong | small clusters | once |
| De Meaux | medium pink | moderate | small clusters | once |
| Dearest | pink blend | slight | small clusters | repeat |
| Deb's Delight | pink blend | moderate | small clusters | repeat |
| Debutante | light pink | moderate | small clusters | once |
| Deep Secret | dark red | strong | singly | repeat |
| Delambre | deep pink | strong | small clusters | repeat |

| NAME | Bloom Color | Fragrance Amount | Flowering Habit | Flowering Incidence |
|---|---|---|---|---|
| Delicata | light pink | moderate | small clusters | repeat |
| Demokracie | dark red | slight | large clusters | repeat |
| Denise Grey | light pink | slight | large clusters | repeat |
| Dentelle de Bruxelles | light pink | moderate | small clusters | repeat |
| Dentelle de Malines | medium pink | slight | small clusters | once |
| Desprez à Fleur Jaune | yellow blend | moderate | small clusters | repeat |
| Deuil de Paul Fontaine | mauve | moderate | small clusters | repeat |
| Devoniensis | white | slight | small clusters | repeat |
| Diabolotin | medium red | slight | small clusters | repeat |
| Diadem | medium pink | none | small clusters | repeat |
| Diamond Jubilee | light yellow | moderate | singly | repeat |
| Dick Koster | deep pink | none | small clusters | repeat |
| Dicky | orange-pink | slight | small clusters | repeat |
| Die Welt | orange blend | slight | singly | repeat |
| Diorama | yellow blend | moderate | singly | repeat |
| Dirigent | medium red | slight | large clusters | repeat |
| Disco Dancer | orange-red | slight | small clusters | repeat |
| Dr A. J. Verhage | deep yellow | moderate | singly | repeat |
| Dr Eckener | pink blend | moderate | small clusters | repeat |
| Dr Huey | dark red | slight | small clusters | repeat |
| Dr Jackson | medium red | none | singly | repeat |
| Dr W. Van Fleet | light pink | moderate | small clusters | once |
| Dolly Parton | orange-red | strong | singly | repeat |
| Don Juan | dark red | strong | small clusters | repeat |
| Donau | mauve | slight | small clusters | once |
| Doris Tysterman | orange blend | slight | small clusters | repeat |
| Dornröschen | pink blend | moderate | small clusters | repeat |
| Dorola | deep yellow | moderate | small clusters | repeat |
| Dorothy Perkins | light pink | moderate | large clusters | once |
| Dortmund | medium red | slight | small clusters | repeat |
| Double Delight | red blend | strong | small clusters | repeat |
| Douceur Normande | medium pink | none | small clusters | repeat |
| Dove | light pink | slight | small clusters | repeat |
| Dream | light pink | none | small clusters | repeat |
| Dream Time | medium pink | moderate | small clusters | repeat |
| Dreaming Spires | deep yellow | strong | small clusters | repeat |
| Dresden Doll | light pink | slight | small clusters | repeat |
| Drummer Boy | dark pink | slight | small clusters | repeat |
| Dublin Bay | medium red | moderate | small clusters | repeat |
| Duc de Cambridge | mauve | moderate | small clusters | once |
| Duc de Fitzjames | dark red/deep pink | strong | small clusters | once |
| Duc de Guiche | mauve | strong | small clusters | once |
| Duchess of Portland | medium red | moderate | small clusters | repeat |

| NAME | Bloom Color | Fragrance Amount | Flowering Habit | Flowering Incidence |
|---|---|---|---|---|
| Duchesse d'Angoulême | light pink | strong | small clusters | once |
| Duchesse d'Auerstädt | yellow | slight | small clusters | repeat |
| Duchesse de Brabant | light pink | moderate | small clusters | repeat |
| Duchesse de Buccleugh | red blend | moderate | small clusters | once |
| Duchesse de Montebello | pink | strong | small clusters | once |
| Duet | medium pink | none | small clusters | repeat |
| Duftrausch | medium pink | strong | singly | repeat |
| Duke of Edinburgh | dark red | strong | singly | repeat |
| Duke of Windsor | orange blend | strong | singly | repeat |
| Dundee Rambler | white | slight | large clusters | once |
| Dunwich Rose | white | none | singly | once |
| Duplex | medium pink | slight | small clusters | once |
| Dupontii | white | strong | truss | once |
| Dupuy Jamain | medium red | moderate | singly | repeat |
| Düsterlohe | deep pink | slight | small clusters | once |
| Dutch Gold | medium yellow | moderate | small clusters | repeat |
| Earthquake | red blend | none | small clusters | repeat |
| Easlea's Golden Rambler | yellow blend | moderate | small clusters | once |
| Easter Morning | white | slight | small clusters | repeat |
| Echo | pink blend | none | truss | repeat |
| Éclair | dark red | moderate | small clusters | repeat |
| Eclipse | light yellow | moderate | singly | once |
| Eddie's Jewel | medium red | none | large clusters | once |
| Eden Rose | deep pink | strong | singly | repeat |
| Edith Clark | medium red | slight | small clusters | repeat |
| Edith Holden | russet | slight | large clusters | repeat |
| Editor Stewart | medium red | none | small clusters | repeat |
| Eglantyne | light pink | strong | small clusters | repeat |
| Eiffel Tower | medium pink | moderate | singly | repeat |
| Elegance (Brownell) | medium yellow | moderate | small clusters | repeat |
| Elegance (Buyl) | pink blend | moderate | small clusters | repeat |
| Elegant Beauty | light yellow | none | singly | repeat |
| Elina | light yellow | slight | small clusters | repeat |
| Elizabeth Harkness | light yellow | moderate | singly | repeat |
| Elizabeth of Glamis | orange-pink | slight | small clusters | repeat |
| Ellen | apricot blend | strong | small clusters | repeat |
| Ellen Poulsen | medium pink | slight | large clusters | repeat |
| Ellen Willmott | yellow blend | none | small clusters | repeat |
| Elmshorn | deep pink | slight | large clusters | repeat |
| Elveshörn | medium pink | slight | small clusters | repeat |
| Elysium | medium pink | moderate | small clusters | repeat |
| Emanuel | apricot blend | strong | small clusters | repeat |
| Emily | light pink | moderate | singly | repeat |

| NAME | Bloom Color | Fragrance Amount | Flowering Habit | Flowering Incidence |
|---|---|---|---|---|
| Emily Gray | deep yellow | moderate | small clusters | once |
| Éminence | mauve | strong | small clusters | repeat |
| Empereur du Maroc | red | strong | small clusters | once |
| Empress Joséphine | medium pink | moderate | small clusters | once |
| Empress Michiko | light pink | strong | small clusters | repeat |
| Ena Harkness | medium red | strong | small clusters | repeat |
| Enfant de France | light pink | strong | singly | repeat |
| English Elegance | pink blend | slight | small clusters | repeat |
| English Garden | apricot blend | slight | small clusters | repeat |
| English Miss | light pink | moderate | small clusters | repeat |
| Eos | red blend | none | small clusters | once |
| Erfurt | pink blend | strong | small clusters | repeat |
| Erinnerung an Brod | red blend | moderate | small clusters | repeat |
| Ernest H. Morse | medium red | strong | singly | repeat |
| Erotika | dark red | strong | singly | repeat |
| Escapade | mauve | slight | large clusters | repeat |
| Especially For You | medium yellow | strong | small clusters | repeat |
| Essex | medium pink | none | small clusters | repeat |
| Etain | orange-pink | slight | large clusters | repeat |
| Ethel | light pink | none | small clusters | once |
| Étoile de Hollande | medium red | strong | small clusters | repeat |
| Étoile de Lyon | medium yellow | moderate | singly | repeat |
| Eugène Fürst | deep red | moderate | singly | repeat |
| Eugénie Guinoiseau | medium red | moderate | small clusters | once |
| Euphrates | pink blend | none | small clusters | once |
| Euphrosyne | medium pink | strong | large clusters | once |
| Europeana | red | slight | small clusters | repeat |
| Eurostar | medium yellow | moderate | small clusters | repeat |
| Eutin | dark red | slight | large clusters | repeat |
| Eva | red blend | slight | truss | repeat |
| Evangeline | pink blend | moderate | small clusters | once |
| Evelyn | apricot blend | strong | small clusters | repeat |
| Evening Star | white | slight | small clusters | repeat |
| Everest Double Fragrance | light pink | moderate | small clusters | repeat |
| Excellenz von Schubert | deep pink | none | large clusters | repeat |
| Excelsa | medium red | none | small clusters | once |
| Exciting | medium red | none | singly | repeat |
| Exploit | deep pink/medium red | none | small clusters | repeat |
| Eyeopener | medium red | none | small clusters | repeat |
| Eyepaint | red blend | slight | large clusters | repeat |
| F. J. Grootendorst | medium red | slight | large clusters | repeat |
| Fair Bianca | white | moderate | small clusters | repeat |
| Fair Play | mauve | slight | large clusters | repeat |

| NAME | Bloom Color | Fragrance Amount | Flowering Habit | Flowering Incidence |
|---|---|---|---|---|
| Fairy Damsel | dark red | none | small clusters | repeat |
| Fairy Dancers | apricot blend | moderate | small clusters | repeat |
| Fairyland | light pink | moderate | small clusters | repeat |
| Falkland | white | slight | small clusters | once |
| Fame! | deep pink | slight | small clusters | repeat |
| Fandango | orange-red | moderate | small clusters | repeat |
| Fantin-Latour | light pink | strong | small clusters | once |
| Fascination | orange-pink | none | singly | repeat |
| Fashion | pink blend | moderate | small clusters | repeat |
| Felicia | pink blend | strong | large clusters | repeat |
| Félicité Parmentier | light pink | strong | small clusters | once |
| Félicité-Perpétue | white | moderate | large clusters | once |
| Fellenberg | medium red | slight | small clusters | repeat |
| Ferdinand Pichard | red blend | moderate | small clusters | repeat |
| Ferdy | deep pink | none | small clusters | once |
| Festival | red blend | none | small clusters | repeat |
| Feuerwerk | orange blend | none | small clusters | repeat |
| Feuerzauber | orange-red | none | singly | repeat |
| Fidélio | orange-red | slight | small clusters | repeat |
| Figurine | white | slight | small clusters | repeat |
| Fimbriata | light pink | strong | small clusters | repeat |
| Finale | orange blend | none | small clusters | repeat |
| Financial Times Centenary | deep pink | strong | small clusters | repeat |
| Fiona | dark red | slight | small clusters | repeat |
| First Edition | orange-pink | slight | small clusters | repeat |
| First Lady | deep pink | slight | singly | repeat |
| First Light | light pink | moderate | large clusters | repeat |
| First Love | light pink | slight | small clusters | repeat |
| First Prize | pink blend | slight | singly | repeat |
| Fisher and Holmes | dark red | moderate | small clusters | repeat |
| Fisherman's Friend | dark red | moderate | small clusters | repeat |
| Flaming Peace | red blend | moderate | singly | once |
| Flamingo | light pink | slight | singly | once |
| Flammentanz | medium red | moderate | small clusters | repeat |
| Flower Carpet | deep pink | none | small clusters | repeat |
| Flower Power | orange-red | moderate | small clusters | repeat |
| Flutterbye | yellow blend | moderate | small clusters | repeat |
| Folklore | orange blend | moderate | small clusters | repeat |
| Fortune's Double Yellow | yellow blend | moderate | small clusters | once |
| Fortuniana | white | moderate | singly | once |
| Fountain | medium red | strong | small clusters | repeat |
| Fourth of July | red blend | moderate | large clusters | repeat |
| Fragrant Cloud | orange-red | strong | singly | repeat |

| NAME | Bloom Color | Fragrance Amount | Flowering Habit | Flowering Incidence |
|---|---|---|---|---|
| Fragrant Delight | orange-pink | strong | small clusters | repeat |
| Fragrant Dream | apricot blend | strong | small clusters | repeat |
| Fragrant Hour | orange-pink | strong | small clusters | repeat |
| Fragrant Plum | mauve | strong | large clusters | repeat |
| Frances Phoebe | white | none | singly | repeat |
| Francesca | apricot blend | slight | small clusters | repeat |
| Francine Austin | white | slight | large clusters | repeat |
| Francis Dubreuil | dark red | strong | small clusters | repeat |
| Francis E. Lester | white | moderate | large clusters | once |
| François Juranville | orange-pink | moderate | small clusters | once |
| Frau Astrid Spath | deep pink | slight | large clusters | repeat |
| Frau Karl Druschki | white | none | singly | repeat |
| Fred Loads | orange-red | moderate | small clusters | repeat |
| Frederic Mistral | light pink | strong | small clusters | repeat |
| Freedom | deep yellow | moderate | singly | repeat |
| Freisinger Morgenröte | orange blend | moderate | small clusters | repeat |
| French Lace | white | slight | small clusters | repeat |
| Frensham | dark red | slight | truss | repeat |
| Frenzy | red blend | moderate | small clusters | repeat |
| Fresh Pink | light pink | slight | large clusters | repeat |
| Freude | orange-red | moderate | singly | repeat |
| Friendship | deep pink | strong | singly | repeat |
| Fritz Nobis | pink blend | strong | truss | once |
| Fru Dagmar Hastrup | medium pink | slight | small clusters | repeat |
| Frühlingsanfang | white | moderate | small clusters | once |
| Frühlingsduft | pink blend | strong | small clusters | once |
| Frühlingsgold | medium yellow | moderate | small clusters | once |
| Frühlingsmorgen | pink blend | none | small clusters | once |
| Frühlingszauber | medium pink | slight | small clusters | once |
| Fruité | orange blend | moderate | small clusters | repeat |
| Fuchsia Meidiland | deep pink | none | small clusters | repeat |
| Fulgurante | medium red | none | singly | repeat |
| Fulton MacKay | yellow blend | moderate | small clusters | repeat |
| Gabriel Noyelle | apricot blend | moderate | small clusters | repeat |
| Gabriella | medium red | none | small clusters | repeat |
| Galaxy | dark red | none | small clusters | repeat |
| Galway Bay | orange-pink | slight | small clusters | repeat |
| Garden Party | white | slight | small clusters | repeat |
| Gardenia | white | slight | small clusters | once |
| Garnette | dark red | none | small clusters | repeat |
| Gärtendirektor Otto Linne | deep pink | none | large clusters | repeat |
| Gavno | orange blend | none | small clusters | repeat |
| Géant des Batailles | medium red | strong | small clusters | repeat |

| NAME | Bloom Color | Fragrance Amount | Flowering Habit | Flowering Incidence |
|---|---|---|---|---|
| Geisha | medium pink | none | small clusters | repeat |
| Gene Boerner | medium pink | none | small clusters | repeat |
| Général Gallieni | red blend | moderate | small clusters | repeat |
| Général Jacqueminot | red blend | strong | small clusters | repeat |
| Général Kléber | medium pink | strong | small clusters | once |
| Général Schablikine | orange-pink | moderate | small clusters | repeat |
| Gentle Touch | light pink | slight | small clusters | repeat |
| Georg Arends | medium pink | strong | small clusters | repeat |
| George Dickson | medium red | moderate | singly | repeat |
| Georges Vibert | red blend | strong | small clusters | once |
| Geraldine | orange blend | slight | small clusters | repeat |
| Geranium | medium red | none | small clusters | once |
| Gerbe Rose | light pink | slight | small clusters | once |
| Gertrude Jekyll | medium pink | moderate | small clusters | repeat |
| Ghislaine de Féligonde | light yellow | slight | large clusters | repeat |
| Gilbert Bécaud | yellow blend | slight | singly | repeat |
| Gilda (Geschwind) | dark red/mauve | none | small clusters | once |
| Gina Lollobrigida | deep yellow | slight | singly | repeat |
| Gingernut | russet | moderate | small clusters | repeat |
| Gingersnap | orange blend | slight | small clusters | repeat |
| Gipsy | orange-red | slight | large clusters | repeat |
| Gipsy Boy | dark red | slight | small clusters | repeat |
| Gitte | apricot blend | strong | singly | repeat |
| Givenchy | red blend | moderate | small clusters | repeat |
| Glad Tidings | dark red | none | large clusters | repeat |
| Gladsome | medium pink | slight | large clusters | once |
| Glamis Castle | white | strong | small clusters | repeat |
| Glastonbury | red blend | moderate | small clusters | repeat |
| Glenfiddich | deep yellow | slight | small clusters | repeat |
| Gloire de Chédane-Guinoisseau | medium red | moderate | singly | repeat |
| Gloire de Dijon | orange-pink | moderate | small clusters | repeat |
| Gloire de Ducher | dark red | moderate | singly | repeat |
| Gloire de France | light pink | strong | small clusters | repeat |
| Gloire de Guilan | light pink | strong | small clusters | once |
| Gloire des Mousseux | medium pink | strong | small clusters | once |
| Gloire des Rosomanes | medium red | moderate | large clusters | once |
| Gloire Lyonnaise | white | moderate | small clusters | once |
| Gloria Mundi | orange-red | none | large clusters | repeat |
| Gloriana 97 | mauve | slight | small clusters | repeat |
| Glory of Edsell | light pink | none | singly | once |
| Goethe | mauve blend | slight | small clusters | once |
| Gold Badge | medium yellow | slight | small clusters | repeat |
| Gold Glow | deep yellow | slight | singly | repeat |

| NAME | Bloom Color | Fragrance Amount | Flowering Habit | Flowering Incidence |
|---|---|---|---|---|
| Guy de Maupassant | medium pink | strong | small clusters | repeat |
| Gwen Nash | pink blend | slight | small clusters | once |
| Gypsy Moth | orange-pink | none | small clusters | repeat |
| Hakuun | white | slight | small clusters | repeat |
| Hamburg | dark red | slight | large clusters | repeat |
| Hamburger Phoenix | medium red | none | small clusters | repeat |
| Hampshire | medium red | none | small clusters | repeat |
| Handel | red blend | none | small clusters | repeat |
| Hansa | medium red | strong | small clusters | repeat |
| Hansa-Park | mauve | slight | small clusters | repeat |
| Happy | medium red | none | truss | repeat |
| Happy Child | medium yellow | strong | small clusters | repeat |
| Happy Wanderer | medium red | slight | small clusters | repeat |
| Harison's Yellow | dark yellow | moderate | small clusters | once |
| Harlekin | pink blend | moderate | small clusters | repeat |
| Harmonie | orange-pink | strong | small clusters | repeat |
| Harry Wheatcroft | yellow blend | slight | singly | repeat |
| Harvest Fayre | orange blend | slight | small clusters | repeat |
| Hawkeye Belle | white | strong | small clusters | repeat |
| Headliner | pink blend | slight | singly | repeat |
| Heart of Gold | yellow blend/deep yellow | strong | small clusters | repeat |
| Hebe's Lip | white | moderate | small clusters | once |
| Heidekönigin | light pink | slight | small clusters | repeat |
| Heidelberg | medium red | slight | small clusters | repeat |
| Heideröslein | yellow blend | moderate | large clusters | repeat |
| Heideschnee | white | none | large clusters | repeat |
| Heidesommer | white | moderate | large clusters | repeat |
| Heidi | medium pink | none | large clusters | repeat |
| Heinrich Münch | medium pink | moderate | singly | once |
| Helen Traubel | pink blend | moderate | singly | repeat |
| Helmut Schmidt | medium yellow | slight | singly | repeat |
| Henri Martin | medium red | strong | large clusters | once |
| Henry Hudson | white | strong | small clusters | repeat |
| Henry Kelsey | medium red | moderate | large clusters | repeat |
| Henry Nevard | dark red | strong | singly | repeat |
| Heritage | light pink | strong | small clusters | repeat |
| Hermosa | light pink | slight | small clusters | repeat |
| Hertfordshire | deep pink | none | large clusters | repeat |
| Hiawatha | red blend | none | large clusters | once |
| Hidalgo | medium red | strong | singly | repeat |
| High Hopes | medium pink | slight | small clusters | repeat |
| Highdownensis | medium red | none | small clusters | once |

| NAME | Bloom Color | Fragrance Amount | Flowering Habit | Flowering Incidence |
|---|---|---|---|---|
| Gold Medal | medium yellow | slight | small clusters | repeat |
| Goldbusch | medium yellow | slight | small clusters | repeat |
| Golden Celebration | deep yellow | moderate | small clusters | repeat |
| Golden Chersonese | medium yellow | slight | small clusters | once |
| Golden Delight | medium yellow | moderate | small clusters | repeat |
| Golden Holstein | deep yellow | slight | small clusters | repeat |
| Golden Jubilee | medium yellow | moderate | small clusters | repeat |
| Golden Masterpiece | medium yellow | slight | small clusters | repeat |
| Golden Scepter | deep yellow | slight | small clusters | repeat |
| Golden Showers | medium yellow | moderate | small clusters | repeat |
| Golden Wedding | deep yellow | none | small clusters | repeat |
| Golden Wings | light yellow | slight | small clusters | repeat |
| Golden Years | medium yellow | slight | small clusters | repeat |
| Goldener Olymp | deep yellow | slight | small clusters | repeat |
| Goldfinch | light yellow | slight | large clusters | once |
| Goldilocks | medium yellow | slight | small clusters | repeat |
| Goldstern | medium yellow | none | small clusters | repeat |
| Goldtopas | medium yellow | slight | small clusters | repeat |
| Good As Gold | deep yellow | moderate | small clusters | repeat |
| Gourmet Pheasant | medium red | none | large clusters | repeat |
| Gourmet Popcorn | white | slight | truss | repeat |
| Grace Darling | white | slight | small clusters | repeat |
| Grace de Monaco | light pink | strong | singly | repeat |
| Graham Thomas | deep yellow | slight | small clusters | repeat |
| Granada | red blend | moderate | small clusters | repeat |
| Grand Hotel | medium red | none | small clusters | repeat |
| Grand Nord | white | slight | singly | repeat |
| Grand Siècle | pink blend | slight | small clusters | repeat |
| Grand'mère Jenny | yellow blend | moderate | singly | repeat |
| Great Maiden's Blush | light pink | strong | small clusters | once |
| Great News | mauve | strong | singly | repeat |
| Great Western | mauve | moderate | large clusters | once |
| Green Ice | white | none | small clusters | repeat |
| Green Rose | green | none | small clusters | repeat |
| Griseldis | medium pink | none | large clusters | once |
| Grootendorst Supreme | dark red | slight | small clusters | repeat |
| Gros Choux d'Hollande | light pink | strong | small clusters | once |
| Gros Provins Panaché | mauve | strong | small clusters | once |
| Gruss an Aachen | light pink | slight | small clusters | repeat |
| Gruss an Teplitz | medium red | strong | small clusters | repeat |
| Gruss an Zabern | white | moderate | small clusters | once |
| Guinée | dark red | strong | small clusters | repeat |
| Guitare | orange blend | strong | small clusters | repeat |

| NAME | Bloom Color | Fragrance Amount | Flowering Habit | Flowering Incidence |
|---|---|---|---|---|
| Hilda Murrell | medium pink | moderate | small clusters | repeat |
| Himmelsauge | mauve | strong | small clusters | once |
| Hippolyte | mauve | strong | small clusters | once |
| Holy Toledo | apricot blend | none | small clusters | repeat |
| Homère | pink blend | moderate | small clusters | repeat |
| Honeyflow | pink blend | moderate | truss | repeat |
| Honor | white | slight | singly | repeat |
| Honorable Lady Lindsay | pink blend | none | small clusters | repeat |
| Honoré de Balzac | pink blend | moderate | singly | repeat |
| Honorine de Brabant | pink blend | moderate | small clusters | repeat |
| Hot Chocolate | russet | none | small clusters | repeat |
| Hot Tamale | yellow blend | slight | small clusters | repeat |
| Hugh Dickson | medium red | strong | small clusters | repeat |
| Hula Girl | orange blend | moderate | small clusters | repeat |
| Hume's Blush Tea-scented China | light pink | strong | small clusters | repeat |
| Hunter | medium red | moderate | small clusters | repeat |
| Hurdy Gurdy | red blend | none | small clusters | repeat |
| Iceberg | white | slight | large clusters | repeat |
| Iced Ginger | orange blend | slight | small clusters | repeat |
| Iced Parfait | light pink | slight | small clusters | repeat |
| Ilse Krohn Superior | white | strong | small clusters | repeat |
| Immensee | light pink | moderate | small clusters | repeat |
| Impératrice Farah | white | none | small clusters | repeat |
| Improved Cécile Brünner | orange-pink | slight | small clusters | repeat |
| Ingrid Bergman | dark red | slight | singly | repeat |
| Inner Wheel | pink blend | none | small clusters | repeat |
| International Herald Tribune | mauve blend | slight | truss | repeat |
| Intervilles | medium red | moderate | small clusters | repeat |
| Intrigue | mauve | strong | small clusters | repeat |
| Invincible | dark red | slight | small clusters | repeat |
| Ipsilanté | mauve | strong | small clusters | once |
| Irene of Denmark | white | moderate | small clusters | repeat |
| Irene Watts | white | moderate | small clusters | repeat |
| Irish Elegance | orange blend | none | small clusters | repeat |
| Irish Gold | medium yellow | moderate | small clusters | repeat |
| Irish Rich Marbled | red blend | slight | singly | once |
| Ispahan | medium pink | strong | small clusters | once |
| Ivory Fashion | white | slight | small clusters | repeat |
| Jacaranda | medium pink | slight | singly | repeat |
| Jack Frost | white | moderate | small clusters | repeat |
| Jackie | light yellow | slight | small clusters | repeat |
| Jacqueline Nebout | medium pink | moderate | small clusters | repeat |
| James Mason | medium red | strong | small clusters | once |

| NAME | Bloom Color | Fragrance Amount | Flowering Habit | Flowering Incidence |
|---|---|---|---|---|
| James Mitchell | deep pink | moderate | small clusters | once |
| James Veitch | mauve | moderate | singly | repeat |
| Janet Morrison | deep pink | moderate | small clusters | repeat |
| Janina | orange blend | none | small clusters | repeat |
| Jaquenetta | apricot blend | slight | small clusters | repeat |
| Jardins de Bagatelle | white | moderate | singly | repeat |
| Jazz | orange blend | slight | small clusters | repeat |
| Jean Bach Sisley | pink blend | slight | small clusters | repeat |
| Jean Ducher | orange-pink | slight | small clusters | repeat |
| Jean Giono | yellow blend | none | small clusters | repeat |
| Jean Kenneally | apricot blend | slight | small clusters | repeat |
| Jean Mermoz | medium pink | slight | large clusters | repeat |
| Jeanne D'Arc | white | moderate | small clusters | once |
| Jeanne de Montfort | medium pink | moderate | small clusters | once |
| Jeanne Lajoie | medium pink | none | small clusters | repeat |
| Jennifer | pink blend | moderate | small clusters | repeat |
| Jenny Duval | mauve | strong | small clusters | once |
| Jens Munk | medium pink | moderate | small clusters | repeat |
| Jersey Beauty | light yellow | strong | small clusters | once |
| Joanna Hill | light yellow | strong | small clusters | repeat |
| Joasine Hanet | mauve | strong | small clusters | repeat |
| Johann Strauss | pink blend | slight | small clusters | repeat |
| John Cabot | medium red | none | small clusters | repeat |
| John Clare | deep pink | slight | small clusters | repeat |
| John Davis | medium pink | strong | small clusters | repeat |
| John F. Kennedy | white | slight | small clusters | repeat |
| John Hopper | pink blend | moderate | singly | repeat |
| John S. Armstrong | dark red | slight | small clusters | repeat |
| John Waterer | dark red | slight | small clusters | repeat |
| Joie de Vivre | pink blend | moderate | small clusters | repeat |
| Josephine Baker | dark red | slight | small clusters | repeat |
| Josephine Bruce | medium red | moderate | small clusters | repeat |
| Joseph's Coat | red blend | slight | small clusters | repeat |
| Joy of Health | medium pink | none | small clusters | repeat |
| Judy Fischer | medium pink | none | small clusters | repeat |
| Jules Margottin | medium pink | slight | singly | repeat |
| Julia Mannering | light pink | moderate | small clusters | repeat |
| Julia's Rose | russet | none | small clusters | once |
| Julie de Mersan | medium pink | moderate | small clusters | once |
| Juliischka | medium red | none | small clusters | repeat |
| Juno | light pink | strong | small clusters | once |
| Just Joey | orange blend | moderate | small clusters | repeat |
| Kabuki | deep yellow | slight | singly | repeat |

| NAME | Bloom Color | Fragrance Amount | Flowering Habit | Flowering Incidence |
|---|---|---|---|---|
| Kaikoura | orange blend | none | small clusters | repeat |
| Kardinal | medium red | none | singly | repeat |
| Karen Julie | orange-red | none | singly | repeat |
| Karl Herbst | medium red | slight | singly | repeat |
| Karlsruhe | deep pink | slight | small clusters | repeat |
| Kassel | orange-red | slight | small clusters | repeat |
| Katharina Zeimet | white | slight | truss | repeat |
| Kathleen | light pink | slight | large clusters | repeat |
| Kathleen Ferrier | orange-pink | slight | small clusters | repeat |
| Kathleen Harrop | light pink | moderate | small clusters | repeat |
| Kathryn Morley | light pink | slight | small clusters | repeat |
| Kazanlik | deep pink | strong | small clusters | once |
| Keepsake | pink blend | slight | small clusters | repeat |
| Kent | white | slight | large clusters | repeat |
| Kerryman | pink blend | slight | small clusters | repeat |
| Kew Rambler | medium pink | slight | truss | once |
| Kiese | medium red | slight | small clusters | once |
| Kiftsgate | white | moderate | truss | once |
| Kimono | pink blend | moderate | small clusters | repeat |
| King's Ransom | deep yellow | slight | small clusters | repeat |
| Kiss | orange-pink | none | small clusters | repeat |
| Kitty Kininmonth | deep pink | slight | small clusters | repeat |
| Königin von Dänemark | medium pink | strong | small clusters | once |
| Konrad Adenauer | dark red | strong | small clusters | repeat |
| Konrad Henkel | medium red | slight | small clusters | repeat |
| Kordes' Brillant | orange blend | none | large clusters | repeat |
| Korona | orange-red | none | small clusters | repeat |
| Ko's Yellow | yellow blend | none | small clusters | repeat |
| Kristin | red blend | none | small clusters | repeat |
| Kronprincessin Viktoria | white | moderate | small clusters | repeat |
| L. D. Braithwaite | dark red | moderate | small clusters | once |
| La Belle Distinguée | medium red | slight | small clusters | once |
| La Belle Sultane | dark red | slight | small clusters | once |
| La France | light pink | strong | small clusters | repeat |
| La Marne | pink blend | none | large clusters | repeat |
| La Marseillaise | dark red | moderate | singly | repeat |
| La Mortola | white | strong | truss | once |
| La Noblesse | light pink | strong | small clusters | once |
| La Paloma 85 | white | slight | small clusters | repeat |
| La Reine | medium pink | moderate | small clusters | repeat |
| La Sévillana | orange-red | none | large clusters | repeat |
| La Ville de Bruxelles | deep pink | strong | small clusters | once |
| L'Abondance | white | slight | small clusters | once |

| NAME | Bloom Color | Fragrance Amount | Flowering Habit | Flowering Incidence |
|---|---|---|---|---|
| Lady Curzon | medium pink | moderate | small clusters | repeat |
| Lady Diana | light pink | slight | small clusters | repeat |
| Lady Hillingdon | yellow blend | moderate | singly | repeat |
| Lady Huntingfield | medium yellow | slight | small clusters | repeat |
| Lady Like | pink blend | slight | singly | repeat |
| Lady Mary Fitzwilliam | light pink | slight | small clusters | repeat |
| Lady Meilland | orange-pink | none | singly | repeat |
| Lady of the Dawn | light pink | slight | small clusters | repeat |
| Lady Penzance | orange-pink | strong | small clusters | once |
| Lady Roberts | apricot blend | moderate | singly | repeat |
| Lady Rose | orange-pink | moderate | singly | repeat |
| Lady Sunblaze | light pink | none | small clusters | repeat |
| Lady Sylvia | light pink | strong | singly | repeat |
| Lady Waterlow | pink blend | moderate | small clusters | repeat |
| Lady X | mauve | none | singly | repeat |
| Lafayette | deep pink | slight | small clusters | repeat |
| Lagerfeld | mauve | strong | small clusters | repeat |
| L'Aimant | mauve | strong | small clusters | repeat |
| Lamarque | white | strong | small clusters | repeat |
| Lancôme | deep pink | none | singly | repeat |
| Las Vegas | orange blend | slight | small clusters | repeat |
| Laughter Lines | pink blend | slight | small clusters | repeat |
| Laura | orange blend | slight | singly | repeat |
| Laura Ashley | mauve | slight | large clusters | repeat |
| Laura Ford | medium yellow | slight | small clusters | repeat |
| Lauré Davoust | light pink | slight | truss | once |
| Lavaglut | dark red | slight | small clusters | repeat |
| Lavender Dream | mauve | none | small clusters | repeat |
| Lavender Jewel | mauve | slight | small clusters | repeat |
| Lavender Lace | mauve | slight | small clusters | repeat |
| Lavender Lassie | mauve | strong | small clusters | repeat |
| Lavender Pinocchio | mauve | slight | small clusters | repeat |
| Lawinia | medium pink | slight | small clusters | repeat |
| Lawrence Johnston | medium yellow | moderate | small clusters | repeat |
| Le Havre | medium red | strong | singly | repeat |
| Le Rêve | light yellow | slight | small clusters | once |
| Le Rouge et Le Noir | dark red | none | small clusters | repeat |
| Le Vésuve | pink blend | none | small clusters | repeat |
| Leander | apricot blend | moderate | small clusters | repeat |
| Leaping Salmon | orange-pink | strong | small clusters | repeat |
| Léda | white | moderate | small clusters | once |
| Legend | medium red | slight | singly | repeat |
| Lemon Blush | light yellow | moderate | small clusters | once |

| NAME | Bloom Color | Fragrance Amount | Flowering Habit | Flowering Incidence |
|---|---|---|---|---|
| Lemon Delight | medium yellow | none | small clusters | repeat |
| Lemon Sherbet | light yellow | slight | singly | repeat |
| Lemon Spice | light yellow | strong | small clusters | repeat |
| Léonardo de Vinci | light pink | none | small clusters | repeat |
| Léonie Lamesch | orange blend | none | large clusters | repeat |
| Léontine Gervais | apricot blend | moderate | small clusters | once |
| Les Amoureux de Peynet | deep pink | slight | large clusters | repeat |
| Leverkusen | light yellow | slight | small clusters | once |
| Leveson Gower | orange-pink | slight | small clusters | repeat |
| Lichtkönigin Lucia | medium yellow | moderate | small clusters | repeat |
| Liebeszauber | medium red | none | small clusters | repeat |
| Lilac Charm | mauve | slight | small clusters | repeat |
| Lilac Rose | pink blend | moderate | small clusters | repeat |
| Lilian Austin | orange-pink | moderate | small clusters | repeat |
| Lilli Marleen | medium red | slight | small clusters | repeat |
| Limelight | light yellow | slight | small clusters | repeat |
| Lincoln Cathedral | orange blend | slight | singly | repeat |
| Linda Campbell | medium red | none | large clusters | repeat |
| Little Artist | red blend | none | small clusters | repeat |
| Little Darling | yellow blend | moderate | small clusters | repeat |
| Little Flirt | red blend | slight | small clusters | repeat |
| Little Gem | deep pink | strong | small clusters | repeat |
| Little Girl | orange-pink | none | small clusters | repeat |
| Little Jackie | orange blend | moderate | small clusters | repeat |
| Little Opal | light pink | slight | singly | repeat |
| Liverpool Echo | orange-pink | slight | small clusters | repeat |
| Liverpool Remembers | orange-red | moderate | singly | repeat |
| Living Fire | orange blend | slight | small clusters | repeat |
| Lolita | apricot blend | slight | small clusters | repeat |
| Long John Silver | white | moderate | small clusters | once |
| Lord Gold | deep yellow | none | small clusters | repeat |
| Lord Penzance | yellow blend | moderate | small clusters | once |
| Lordly Oberon | light pink | strong | small clusters | repeat |
| L'Oréal Trophy | orange blend | none | singly | repeat |
| Lorraine Lee | pink blend | moderate | small clusters | repeat |
| L'Ouche | pink blend | slight | small clusters | repeat |
| Louis de Funès | orange blend | none | small clusters | repeat |
| Louis XIV | dark red | slight | small clusters | repeat |
| Louise Gimard | medium pink | moderate | small clusters | repeat |
| Louise d'Arzens | white | slight | small clusters | once |
| Louise Odier | deep pink | moderate | small clusters | repeat |
| Love | red blend | none | small clusters | repeat |
| Love Potion | mauve | moderate | small clusters | repeat |

| NAME | Bloom Color | Fragrance Amount | Flowering Habit | Flowering Incidence |
|---|---|---|---|---|
| Lovely Fairy | deep pink | slight | truss | repeat |
| Lovely Lady | medium pink | slight | singly | repeat |
| Lovers' Meeting | orange blend | slight | small clusters | repeat |
| Loving Memory | medium red | none | small clusters | repeat |
| Loving Touch | apricot blend | none | singly | repeat |
| Lucetta | apricot blend | slight | small clusters | repeat |
| Lutin | pink blend | none | large clusters | repeat |
| Lyda Rose | white | none | small clusters | repeat |
| Lydia | deep yellow | slight | small clusters | repeat |
| Lykkefund | white | slight | large clusters | once |
| Lyon Rose | orange-pink | strong | singly | repeat |
| Ma Perkins | pink blend | moderate | small clusters | repeat |
| McGredy's Yellow | medium yellow | slight | small clusters | repeat |
| Madam President | pink blend | none | small clusters | repeat |
| Mme Abel Chatenay | pink blend | slight | singly | repeat |
| Mme Alfred Carrière | white | strong | small clusters | repeat |
| Mme Alice Garnier | pink blend | moderate | large clusters | once |
| Mme Antoine Mari | pink blend | slight | small clusters | repeat |
| Mme Bérard | orange blend | slight | small clusters | repeat |
| Mme Berkeley | pink blend | slight | small clusters | repeat |
| Mme Boll | deep pink | moderate | singly | repeat |
| Mme Butterfly | light pink | strong | small clusters | repeat |
| Mme Caroline Testout | medium pink | slight | singly | repeat |
| Mme Charles | yellow blend | slight | small clusters | repeat |
| Mme de la Rôche-Lambert | mauve | strong | small clusters | once |
| Mme de Sancy de Parabère | light pink | none | small clusters | once |
| Mme de Tartas | light pink | slight | small clusters | repeat |
| Mme de Watteville | yellow blend | strong | small clusters | repeat |
| Mme Dieudonné | red blend | moderate | singly | repeat |
| Mme Driout | pink blend | moderate | small clusters | repeat |
| Mme Edouard Herriot | orange blend | slight | small clusters | repeat |
| Mme Edouard Ory | deep pink | moderate | small clusters | once |
| Mme Ernst Calvat | medium pink | strong | small clusters | repeat |
| Mme Fernandel | deep pink | none | small clusters | repeat |
| Mme Gabriel Luizet | light pink | moderate | singly | repeat |
| Mme Georges Bruant | white | slight | small clusters | repeat |
| Mme Georges Delbard | dark red | none | singly | repeat |
| Mme Grégoire Staechelin | pink blend | moderate | small clusters | once |
| Mme Hardy | white | strong | small clusters | once |
| Mme Henri Guillot | red blend | slight | small clusters | repeat |
| Mme Isaac Pereire | deep pink | strong | small clusters | repeat |
| Mme Joseph Schwartz | white | moderate | small clusters | repeat |
| Mme Jules Bouché | white | slight | singly | repeat |

| NAME | Bloom Color | Fragrance Amount | Flowering Habit | Flowering Incidence |
|---|---|---|---|---|
| Mme Jules Gravereaux | apricot blend | moderate | small clusters | repeat |
| Mme Knorr | medium pink | strong | small clusters | repeat |
| Mme Laurette Messimy | deep pink | none | small clusters | repeat |
| Mme Lauriol de Barny | light pink | strong | small clusters | once |
| Mme Legras de St Germain | white | strong | small clusters | once |
| Mme Léon Pain | pink blend | moderate | small clusters | repeat |
| Mme Lombard | orange-pink | slight | small clusters | repeat |
| Mme Louis Laperrière | medium red | strong | small clusters | repeat |
| Mme Louis Lévêque | medium pink | strong | small clusters | once |
| Mme Marie Curie | deep yellow | slight | small clusters | repeat |
| Mme Pierre Oger | pink blend | slight | small clusters | repeat |
| Mme Plantier | white | strong | small clusters | once |
| Mme Scipion Cochet (Bernaix) | pink blend | moderate | singly | repeat |
| Mme Victor Verdier | medium red | strong | singly | once |
| Mme Violet | mauve | none | small clusters | repeat |
| Mme Wagram, Comtesse de Turenne | pink blend | moderate | small clusters | repeat |
| Mme Zöetmans | white | moderate | small clusters | once |
| Madeleine Selzer | light yellow | strong | truss | once |
| Mlle Franziska Krüger | orange-pink | slight | small clusters | repeat |
| Maestro | red blend | slight | small clusters | repeat |
| Magali | deep pink | slight | small clusters | repeat |
| Magenta | mauve | strong | large clusters | repeat |
| Maggie Barry | pink blend | slight | singly | repeat |
| Magic Carpet | mauve | none | large clusters | repeat |
| Magic Carrousel | red blend | slight | small clusters | repeat |
| Magic Dragon | dark red | none | small clusters | repeat |
| Magic Meidiland | medium pink | none | small clusters | repeat |
| Magna Charta | medium pink | moderate | singly | repeat |
| Magnifica | mauve | moderate | small clusters | repeat |
| Maiden's Blush | white | strong | small clusters | once |
| Maigold | deep yellow | moderate | small clusters | once |
| Majorette | medium red | none | small clusters | repeat |
| Malaga | deep pink | strong | singly | repeat |
| Maman Cochet | pink blend | moderate | singly | repeat |
| Mandarin (Boerner) | medium red | moderate | large clusters | repeat |
| Mandarin (Kordes) | orange-red | slight | small clusters | repeat |
| Manetti | light pink | none | small clusters | once |
| Mannheim | dark red | none | small clusters | repeat |
| Manning's Blush | white | moderate | small clusters | once |
| Manou Meilland | mauve | moderate | small clusters | repeat |
| Many Happy Returns | pink blend | slight | small clusters | repeat |
| Marbrée | red blend | slight | small clusters | repeat |
| Marcel Bourgoin | mauve | moderate | small clusters | once |

| NAME | Bloom Color | Fragrance Amount | Flowering Habit | Flowering Incidence |
|---|---|---|---|---|
| Märchenland | orange blend | slight | large clusters | repeat |
| Marchesa Boccella | light pink | moderate | small clusters | repeat |
| Marchioness of Londonderry | light pink | strong | singly | repeat |
| Maréchal Davoust | medium pink | moderate | small clusters | once |
| Maréchal Niel | medium yellow | moderate | small clusters | repeat |
| Margaret | pink blend | slight | small clusters | repeat |
| Margaret Merril | white | strong | small clusters | repeat |
| Margo Koster | orange blend | none | large clusters | repeat |
| Marguerite Hilling | medium pink | slight | small clusters | repeat |
| Maria Lisa | pink blend | none | large clusters | once |
| Mariandel | medium red | slight | small clusters | repeat |
| Marie de Blois | medium pink | moderate | small clusters | once |
| Marie de Saint Jean | white | moderate | small clusters | repeat |
| Marie Dermar | light yellow | slight | small clusters | repeat |
| Marie-Jeanne | white | slight | large clusters | repeat |
| Marie Louise | medium pink | strong | singly | once |
| Marie Pavié | white | none | small clusters | repeat |
| Marie van Houtte | pink blend | moderate | singly | repeat |
| Marina | orange blend | moderate | large clusters | repeat |
| Marjorie Atherton | medium yellow | slight | singly | repeat |
| Marjorie Fair | red blend | slight | truss | repeat |
| Marjory Palmer | medium pink | slight | small clusters | repeat |
| Marlena | medium red | none | large clusters | repeat |
| Martha | pink blend | slight | small clusters | repeat |
| Martin Frobisher | light pink | moderate | small clusters | repeat |
| Mary Guthrie | medium pink | moderate | large clusters | repeat |
| Mary MacKillop | pink blend | none | small clusters | repeat |
| Mary Marshall | orange blend | slight | small clusters | repeat |
| Mary Queen of Scots | white | slight | singly | once |
| Mary Rose | medium pink | strong | small clusters | repeat |
| Mary Wallace | medium pink | moderate | small clusters | once |
| Mary Webb | apricot blend | strong | small clusters | repeat |
| Mascotte | medium pink | moderate | singly | repeat |
| Masquerade | red blend | slight | small clusters | repeat |
| Master Hugh | deep pink | slight | small clusters | once |
| Matangi | red blend | slight | small clusters | repeat |
| Matilda | white | none | small clusters | repeat |
| Matthias Meilland | medium red | none | small clusters | repeat |
| Mauve Melodée | mauve | moderate | small clusters | repeat |
| Max Graf | pink blend | slight | small clusters | once |
| May Queen | medium pink | strong | small clusters | once |
| Mayor of Casterbridge | light pink | strong | small clusters | repeat |
| Medallion | apricot blend | moderate | small clusters | repeat |

| NAME | Bloom Color | Fragrance Amount | Flowering Habit | Flowering Incidence |
|---|---|---|---|---|
| Meg | apricot blend | moderate | small clusters | repeat |
| Meg Merrilies | deep pink medium red | moderate | small clusters | once |
| Meillandina | medium red | none | small clusters | repeat |
| Melody Maker | orange-red | none | small clusters | repeat |
| Memento | red blend | none | small clusters | repeat |
| Memoriam | light pink | moderate | singly | repeat |
| Memory Lane (Pearce) | apricot blend | slight | large clusters | repeat |
| Menja | medium pink | slight | large clusters | repeat |
| Mercedes | orange-red | slight | small clusters | repeat |
| Mermaid | light yellow | moderate | small clusters | repeat |
| Meteor (Geschwind) | deep pink | strong | small clusters | repeat |
| Mevrouw Nathalie Nypels | medium pink | moderate | small clusters | repeat |
| Michelangelo | orange blend | none | small clusters | repeat |
| Michele Meilland | light pink | slight | small clusters | repeat |
| Micrugosa | light pink | slight | singly | repeat |
| Midas Touch | deep yellow | slight | small clusters | repeat |
| Mignonette | light pink | none | large clusters | repeat |
| Mikado | red blend | slight | singly | repeat |
| Milkmaid | white | moderate | large clusters | repeat |
| Millie Walters | orange-pink | slight | small clusters | repeat |
| Milrose | medium pink | slight | small clusters | repeat |
| Minilights | medium yellow | none | small clusters | repeat |
| Minnehaha | light pink | slight | large clusters | once |
| Minnie Pearl | pink blend | slight | small clusters | repeat |
| Minnie Watson | light pink | slight | small clusters | repeat |
| Miranda | medium pink/ light pink | moderate | small clusters | repeat |
| Mirato | medium pink | none | large clusters | repeat |
| Miriam Wilkins | light pink | moderate | singly | repeat |
| Mischief | orange-pink | moderate | singly | repeat |
| Miss All-American Beauty | deep pink | moderate | singly | repeat |
| Miss Edith Cavell | dark red | none | small clusters | repeat |
| Mission Bells | pink blend | moderate | singly | repeat |
| Mr Bluebird | mauve | none | large clusters | repeat |
| Mister Lincoln | dark red | strong | small clusters | repeat |
| Mrs Aaron Ward | yellow blend | moderate | singly | repeat |
| Mrs Alston's Rose | red blend | none | large clusters | repeat |
| Mrs Anthony Waterer | dark red | strong | small clusters | repeat |
| Mrs B. R. Cant | medium pink | moderate | singly | repeat |
| Mrs Doreen Pike | medium pink | moderate | large clusters | repeat |
| Mrs Dudley Cross | yellow blend | slight | small clusters | repeat |
| Mrs F. W. Flight | deep pink | none | small clusters | once |
| Mrs Foley Hobbs | pink blend | slight | small clusters | repeat |

| NAME | Bloom Color | Fragrance Amount | Flowering Habit | Flowering Incidence |
|---|---|---|---|---|
| Mrs Fred Danks | mauve | moderate | small clusters | repeat |
| Mrs Herbert Stevens | white | moderate | singly | repeat |
| Mrs John Laing | medium pink | strong | small clusters | repeat |
| Mrs Mary Thomson | pink blend | strong | large clusters | repeat |
| Mrs Norman Watson | deep pink | slight | small clusters | repeat |
| Mrs Oakley Fisher | deep yellow | slight | small clusters | repeat |
| Mrs Paul | light pink | slight | small clusters | once |
| Mistress Quickly | medium pink | slight | large clusters | repeat |
| Mrs Reynolds Hole | pink blend | moderate | small clusters | repeat |
| Mrs Richard Turnbull | white blend | none | small clusters | once |
| Mrs Sam McGredy | orange-pink | slight | singly | repeat |
| Mrs Wakefield Christie-Miller | pink blend | slight | small clusters | repeat |
| Mojave | orange blend | moderate | singly | repeat |
| Moje Hammarberg | mauve | strong | small clusters | repeat |
| Molineux | deep yellow | strong | small clusters | repeat |
| Molly Sharman-Crawford | white | moderate | small clusters | repeat |
| Mon Cheri | red blend | slight | small clusters | repeat |
| Mondiale | pink blend | slight | small clusters | repeat |
| Monika | pink blend | slight | singly | repeat |
| Monsieur Tillier | orange-pink/ pink blend | slight | small clusters | repeat |
| Montezuma | orange-pink | slight | small clusters | repeat |
| Moonbeam | apricot blend | moderate | small clusters | repeat |
| Moonlight | light yellow | moderate | small clusters | repeat |
| Moonsprite | light yellow | strong | small clusters | repeat |
| Morden Blush | light pink | none | small clusters | repeat |
| Morden Centennial | medium pink | slight | large clusters | repeat |
| Morden Fireglow | orange-red | slight | small clusters | repeat |
| Morden Ruby | pink blend | none | small clusters | repeat |
| Morgengruss | orange-pink | strong | small clusters | repeat |
| Morletii | mauve | none | small clusters | once |
| Morning Blush | light yellow | moderate | small clusters | repeat |
| Moth | mauve | slight | small clusters | repeat |
| Mothersday | dark red | none | large clusters | repeat |
| Mount Hood | white | slight | small clusters | repeat |
| Mount Shasta | white | slight | small clusters | repeat |
| Mountbatten | medium yellow | slight | small clusters | repeat |
| Mozart | pink blend | slight | large clusters | repeat |
| München | dark red | slight | small clusters | repeat |
| Mutabilis | yellow blend | none | small clusters | repeat |
| My Choice | pink blend | moderate | singly | repeat |
| Nana Mouskouri | white | slight | small clusters | repeat |
| Nancy Hayward | medium red | none | small clusters | repeat |

| NAME | Bloom Color | Fragrance Amount | Flowering Habit | Flowering Incidence |
|---|---|---|---|---|
| Nancy Steen | pink blend | moderate | small clusters | repeat |
| Narrow Water | light pink | moderate | large clusters | repeat |
| National Trust | dark red | none | singly | repeat |
| Nearly Wild | medium pink | slight | small clusters | repeat |
| Nestor | medium red | slight | small clusters | once |
| Nevada | white | moderate | small clusters | repeat |
| New Beginning | orange blend | none | small clusters | repeat |
| New Daily Mail | dark red | none | small clusters | repeat |
| New Dawn | light pink | moderate | small clusters | repeat |
| New Face | yellow blend | slight | large clusters | repeat |
| New Year | orange blend | slight | singly | repeat |
| New Yorker | medium red | moderate | singly | repeat |
| New Zealand | light pink | moderate | small clusters | repeat |
| News | mauve | slight | truss | repeat |
| Niccolo Paganini | medium red | none | small clusters | repeat |
| Nice Day | orange-pink | slight | large clusters | repeat |
| Night Light | deep yellow | moderate | small clusters | repeat |
| Nina Weibull | dark red | none | small clusters | repeat |
| Niphetos | white | moderate | small clusters | repeat |
| Nobilo's Chardonnay | medium yellow | slight | small clusters | repeat |
| Noella Nabonnand | dark red | moderate | small clusters | once |
| Norfolk | medium yellow | none | small clusters | repeat |
| Northamptonshire | white | none | small clusters | repeat |
| Northern Lights | yellow blend | strong | small clusters | repeat |
| Norwich Castle | orange blend | slight | small clusters | repeat |
| Nova Zembla | white | strong | small clusters | repeat |
| Nozomi | light pink | none | large clusters | once |
| Nuits de Young | dark red | strong | small clusters | once |
| Nur Mahal | medium red | strong | large clusters | repeat |
| Nymphenburg | orange-pink | moderate | large clusters | repeat |
| Nyveldt's White | white | strong | small clusters | repeat |
| Octavia Hill | medium pink | moderate | small clusters | repeat |
| Octavius Weld | pink blend | moderate | small clusters | repeat |
| Œillet Flamand | pink blend | strong | small clusters | once |
| Œillet Parfait | pink blend | moderate | small clusters | once |
| Oklahoma | dark red | strong | singly | repeat |
| Old Blush | medium pink | slight | small clusters | repeat |
| Old Master | red blend | slight | small clusters | repeat |
| Old Port | mauve | moderate | small clusters | repeat |
| Oldtimer | orange blend | slight | small clusters | repeat |
| Olé | orange-red | moderate | small clusters | repeat |
| Olympic Torch | red blend | none | small clusters | repeat |
| Omar Khayyám | light pink | strong | small clusters | once |

| NAME | Bloom Color | Fragrance Amount | Flowering Habit | Flowering Incidence |
|---|---|---|---|---|
| Onkaparinga | apricot blend | strong | small clusters | repeat |
| Opening Night | red blend | slight | singly | repeat |
| Ophelia | light pink | strong | small clusters | repeat |
| Orange Fire | orange-pink | none | small clusters | repeat |
| Orange Honey | orange blend | moderate | small clusters | repeat |
| Orange Sensation | orange-red | moderate | small clusters | repeat |
| Orange Sunblaze | orange-red | slight | small clusters | repeat |
| Orange Triumph | medium red | slight | large clusters | repeat |
| Orangeade | orange-red | slight | small clusters | repeat |
| Oregold | deep yellow | slight | singly | repeat |
| Oriental Charm | medium red | slight | small clusters | repeat |
| Orpheline de Juillet | mauve | moderate | small clusters | once |
| Osiria | red blend | moderate | singly | repeat |
| Oskar Scheerer | dark red | strong | large clusters | repeat |
| Othello | dark red | strong | small clusters | repeat |
| Our Molly | medium red | none | large clusters | repeat |
| Over the Rainbow | red blend | slight | small clusters | repeat |
| Pacesetter | white | moderate | small clusters | repeat |
| Paddy McGredy | medium pink | moderate | small clusters | repeat |
| Paddy Stephens | orange blend | slight | singly | repeat |
| Painted Moon | red blend | slight | small clusters | repeat |
| Palmengarten Frankfurt | medium pink | none | small clusters | repeat |
| Papa Gontier | pink blend | slight | small clusters | repeat |
| Papa Hémeray | red blend | none | large clusters | repeat |
| Papa Meilland | dark red | strong | small clusters | repeat |
| Papillon (Nabonnand) | pink blend | slight | small clusters | repeat |
| Paprika | orange-red | slight | large clusters | repeat |
| Parade | deep pink | moderate | small clusters | repeat |
| Paradise | mauve | slight | small clusters | repeat |
| Pariser Charme | medium pink | strong | small clusters | repeat |
| Parkdirektor Riggers | dark red | slight | large clusters | repeat |
| Parks' Yellow Tea-scented China | medium yellow | moderate | small clusters | once |
| Parkzierde | dark red | moderate | small clusters | once |
| Party Girl | yellow blend | slight | small clusters | repeat |
| Parure d'Or | yellow blend | none | small clusters | repeat |
| Pascali | white | none | small clusters | repeat |
| Passion | medium red | moderate | small clusters | repeat |
| Pat Austin | orange-red | strong | small clusters | repeat |
| Patio Charm | apricot blend | slight | small clusters | repeat |
| Patricia (Chaplin Bros Ltd) | medium red | moderate | small clusters | repeat |
| Patricia (Kordes) | apricot blend | slight | small clusters | repeat |
| Paul Cezanne | yellow blend | none | small clusters | repeat |
| Paul Crampel | orange-red | none | large clusters | repeat |

| NAME | Bloom Color | Fragrance Amount | Flowering Habit | Flowering Incidence |
|---|---|---|---|---|
| Paul Gauguin | russet | none | small clusters | repeat |
| Paul Ledé, Climbing | apricot blend | moderate | singly | repeat |
| Paul Neyron | medium pink | strong | singly | repeat |
| Paul Noël | pink blend | none | small clusters | once |
| Paul Ricard | yellow blend | moderate | small clusters | repeat |
| Paul Ricault | medium pink | strong | singly | repeat |
| Paul Shirville | orange-pink | strong | small clusters | repeat |
| Paul Transon | orange-pink | moderate | small clusters | repeat |
| Paulii | white | moderate | small clusters | repeat |
| Paul's Early Blush | light pink | strong | singly | repeat |
| Paul's Himalayan Musk Rambler | light pink | slight | large clusters | once |
| Paul's Lemon Pillar | light yellow | strong | singly | once |
| Paul's Scarlet Climber | medium red | slight | large clusters | once |
| Pax | white | moderate | large clusters | repeat |
| Peace | yellow blend | slight | small clusters | repeat |
| Peacekeeper | pink blend | moderate | small clusters | repeat |
| Peach Blossom | light pink | slight | large clusters | repeat |
| Peaches 'n' Cream | pink blend | slight | small clusters | repeat |
| Pearl Drift | white | slight | small clusters | repeat |
| Peer Gynt | yellow blend | slight | singly | repeat |
| Pélisson | dark red | moderate | small clusters | once |
| Penelope (Pemberton) | light pink | moderate | truss | repeat |
| Penny Lane (Harkness) | apricot blend | moderate | small clusters | repeat |
| Pensioners' Voice | apricot blend | moderate | small clusters | repeat |
| Peppermint Twist | red blend | slight | small clusters | repeat |
| Perdita | apricot blend | moderate | small clusters | repeat |
| Perfect Moment | red blend | slight | singly | repeat |
| Perfume Delight | medium pink | strong | small clusters | repeat |
| Pergolese | mauve | moderate | small clusters | repeat |
| Perla de Alcañada | deep pink | none | small clusters | repeat |
| Perla de Montserrat | deep pink | none | small clusters | repeat |
| Perle des Jardins | light yellow | moderate | small clusters | once |
| Perle d'Or | yellow blend | slight | large clusters | repeat |
| Perle Meillandecor | light pink | none | large clusters | repeat |
| Pernille Poulsen | medium pink | slight | small clusters | repeat |
| Peter Frankenfeld | deep pink | none | small clusters | repeat |
| Petite de Hollande | medium pink | moderate | small clusters | once |
| Petite Lisette | deep pink | strong | small clusters | once |
| Petite Orléanaise | medium pink | strong | small clusters | once |
| Pfälzer Gold | deep yellow | none | small clusters | repeat |
| Phantom | medium red | slight | large clusters | repeat |
| Pharaoh | orange-red | moderate | singly | repeat |
| Phyllis Bide | yellow blend | none | large clusters | repeat |

| NAME | Bloom Color | Fragrance Amount | Flowering Habit | Flowering Incidence |
|---|---|---|---|---|
| Picasso | pink blend | none | small clusters | repeat |
| Piccadilly | red blend | moderate | small clusters | repeat |
| Piccolo | orange-red | none | small clusters | repeat |
| Picture | light pink | slight | small clusters | repeat |
| Pierre de Ronsard | pink blend | slight | small clusters | repeat |
| Pierre Notting | dark red | moderate | singly | once |
| Pigalle | orange blend | moderate | small clusters | repeat |
| Pink Bassino | pink blend | none | truss | repeat |
| Pink Bells | deep pink | slight | small clusters | repeat |
| Pink Chiffon | light pink | moderate | large clusters | repeat |
| Pink Cloud | medium pink | moderate | large clusters | repeat |
| Pink Favorite | medium pink | slight | large clusters | repeat |
| Pink Grootendorst | medium pink | slight | large clusters | repeat |
| Pink Iceberg | pink blend | slight | large clusters | repeat |
| Pink La Sevillana | medium pink | none | small clusters | repeat |
| Pink Léda | medium pink | moderate | small clusters | once |
| Pink Meidiland | pink blend | none | small clusters | repeat |
| Pink Meillandina | medium pink | none | small clusters | repeat |
| Pink Panther | pink blend | slight | small clusters | repeat |
| Pink Parfait | pink blend | slight | small clusters | repeat |
| Pink Peace | medium pink | strong | singly | repeat |
| Pink Pearl | light pink | slight | singly | repeat |
| Pink Perpetue | medium pink | slight | small clusters | repeat |
| Pink Prosperity | light pink | moderate | truss | repeat |
| Pink Robusta | medium pink | slight | small clusters | repeat |
| Pink Rosette | light pink | slight | small clusters | repeat |
| Pink Silk | medium pink | none | singly | repeat |
| Pink Symphony | light pink | slight | small clusters | repeat |
| Pink Wonder | light pink | slight | small clusters | repeat |
| Pinkie | medium pink | moderate | large clusters | repeat |
| Playboy | red blend | none | small clusters | repeat |
| Playgirl | medium pink | none | small clusters | repeat |
| Pleasure | medium pink | none | small clusters | repeat |
| Pleine de Grâce | white | strong | large clusters | repeat |
| Poetry in Motion | yellow blend | moderate | small clusters | repeat |
| Polareis | white | slight | small clusters | repeat |
| Polarstern | white | none | small clusters | repeat |
| Polka | orange blend | moderate | small clusters | repeat |
| Pompon Blanc Parfait | white | strong | small clusters | once |
| Pompon de Paris | medium pink/deep pink | none | small clusters | repeat |
| Popcorn | white | moderate | small clusters | repeat |
| Poppy Flash | orange-red | moderate | small clusters | repeat |

| NAME | Bloom Color | Fragrance Amount | Flowering Habit | Flowering Incidence |
|---|---|---|---|---|
| Porthos, Climbing | orange-red | none | small clusters | repeat |
| Portrait | pink blend | moderate | small clusters | repeat |
| Pot o' Gold | medium yellow | strong | small clusters | repeat |
| Potter & Moore | medium pink | moderate | small clusters | repeat |
| Poulsen's Pearl | light pink | none | truss | repeat |
| Prairie Dawn | medium pink | none | small clusters | repeat |
| Président de Sèze | mauve | strong | small clusters | once |
| President Herbert Hoover | pink blend | moderate | small clusters | repeat |
| President Leopold Senghor | dark red | none | small clusters | repeat |
| Pretty Jessica | deep pink | strong | small clusters | repeat |
| Pride 'n' Joy | orange blend | moderate | small clusters | repeat |
| Prima Ballerina | deep pink | moderate | singly | repeat |
| Primevere | yellow blend | slight | small clusters | once |
| Prince Camille de Rohan | dark red | strong | small clusters | once |
| Prince Charles | mauve | slight | small clusters | once |
| Prince Meillandina | dark red | none | small clusters | repeat |
| Princeps | medium red | slight | small clusters | once |
| Princess Alice | medium yellow | slight | large clusters | repeat |
| Princess Margaret of England | medium pink | slight | singly | repeat |
| Princess Michael of Kent | medium yellow | slight | small clusters | repeat |
| Princesse Adélaïde | light pink | moderate | small clusters | repeat |
| Princesse de Monaco | white | slight | small clusters | repeat |
| Princesse de Nassau | light yellow | moderate | large clusters | repeat |
| Princesse de Sagan | dark red | none | small clusters | repeat |
| Princesse Louise | white | none | large clusters | once |
| Prins Claus | orange-red | moderate | singly | repeat |
| Priscilla Burton | red blend | moderate | small clusters | repeat |
| Pristine | white | moderate | small clusters | repeat |
| Prolifera de Redouté | medium pink | strong | small clusters | once |
| Prominent | orange-red | slight | small clusters | repeat |
| Prosperity | white | moderate | large clusters | repeat |
| Prospero | dark red | strong | small clusters | repeat |
| Proud Land | dark red | moderate | singly | repeat |
| Proud Titania | white | strong | small clusters | repeat |
| Puppy Love | orange blend | slight | small clusters | repeat |
| Pure Bliss | pink blend | moderate | small clusters | repeat |
| Purple Splendour | mauve | slight | small clusters | repeat |
| Purple Tiger | mauve | slight | small clusters | repeat |
| Quaker Star | orange-pink | none | large clusters | repeat |
| Quatre Saisons Blanc Mousseux | white | moderate | small clusters | repeat |
| Queen Elizabeth | medium pink | moderate | small clusters | repeat |
| Queen Margrethe | light pink | slight | small clusters | repeat |
| Queen Mother | light pink | slight | small clusters | repeat |

| NAME | Bloom Color | Fragrance Amount | Flowering Habit | Flowering Incidence |
|---|---|---|---|---|
| Queen of Bedders | deep pink | moderate | small clusters | repeat |
| Queen of Bourbons | pink blend | strong | small clusters | repeat |
| Queen of Hearts | medium pink | moderate | small clusters | repeat |
| Queen of the Musks | pink blend | strong | large clusters | repeat |
| Radiance | light pink | strong | small clusters | repeat |
| Radio Times | medium pink | strong | small clusters | repeat |
| Radox Bouquet | medium pink | moderate | small clusters | repeat |
| Radway Sunrise | orange blend | slight | truss | repeat |
| Rainbow's End | yellow blend | none | small clusters | repeat |
| Ralph's Creeper | red blend | moderate | large clusters | repeat |
| Rambling Rector | white | strong | large clusters | once |
| Ramona | medium red | slight | small clusters | repeat |
| Raubritter | light pink | moderate | truss | once |
| Ray of Sunshine | medium yellow | slight | small clusters | repeat |
| Raymond Chenault | medium red | moderate | small clusters | repeat |
| Red Ace | dark red | slight | small clusters | repeat |
| Red Bells | medium red | slight | large clusters | repeat |
| Red Blanket | deep pink | slight | small clusters | repeat |
| Red Cascade | dark red | none | small clusters | repeat |
| Red Cross | medium red | moderate | small clusters | repeat |
| Red Devil | medium red | moderate | singly | repeat |
| Red Favorite | medium red | slight | truss | repeat |
| Red Masterpiece | dark red | strong | small clusters | repeat |
| Red Meidiland | red blend | none | small clusters | repeat |
| Red Minimo | dark red | none | small clusters | repeat |
| Red Nella | light red | none | small clusters | repeat |
| Red Planet | dark red | strong | singly | repeat |
| Red Rascal | medium red | slight | small clusters | repeat |
| Red Ribbons | medium red | none | large clusters | repeat |
| Red Rosamini | dark red | none | small clusters | repeat |
| Red Simplicity | medium red | slight | small clusters | repeat |
| Redcoat | medium red | slight | small clusters | repeat |
| Redgold | yellow blend | slight | large clusters | repeat |
| Redouté | light pink | slight | small clusters | repeat |
| Regatta (Warriner) | white | strong | singly | repeat |
| Regatta (Meilland) | light pink | moderate | singly | repeat |
| Regensberg | pink blend | slight | large clusters | repeat |
| Reine des Centfeuilles | medium pink | strong | small clusters | once |
| Reine des Violettes | mauve | strong | small clusters | repeat |
| Reine Marie Henriette | medium red | moderate | small clusters | repeat |
| Reine Victoria | medium pink | strong | small clusters | repeat |
| Relax Meillandecor | pink blend | none | large clusters | repeat |
| Rembrandt | orange-red | moderate | small clusters | repeat |

| NAME | Bloom Color | Fragrance Amount | Flowering Habit | Flowering Incidence |
|---|---|---|---|---|
| Rose-Marie Viaud | mauve | moderate | large clusters | once |
| Roselina | pink blend | slight | small clusters | repeat |
| Rosemary Harkness | orange-pink | strong | small clusters | repeat |
| Rosemary Rose | deep pink | moderate | truss | repeat |
| Rosendorf Sparrieshoop | light pink | none | small clusters | repeat |
| Rosenelfe | medium pink | moderate | small clusters | repeat |
| Rosenfee | light pink | slight | small clusters | repeat |
| Rosenresli | deep pink | strong | small clusters | repeat |
| Rosenstadt Zweibrücken | pink blend | none | small clusters | repeat |
| Roseraie de l'Haÿ | dark red | strong | small clusters | repeat |
| Roseromantic | white | slight | small clusters | repeat |
| Rosette Delizy | yellow blend | moderate | small clusters | repeat |
| Rosina | medium yellow | none | small clusters | repeat |
| Rosmarin '89 | deep pink | slight | small clusters | repeat |
| Rosy Carpet | deep pink | slight | large clusters | repeat |
| Rosy Cheeks | red blend | strong | small clusters | repeat |
| Rosy Cushion | light pink | slight | large clusters | repeat |
| Rosy Mantle | medium pink | moderate | small clusters | repeat |
| Rote Max Graf | medium red | moderate | small clusters | repeat |
| Rotes Meer | medium red | none | small clusters | repeat |
| Rouge Meilland | medium red | none | small clusters | repeat |
| Rouletii | medium pink | none | small clusters | repeat |
| Royal Bassino | medium red | none | large clusters | repeat |
| Royal Bonica | medium pink | slight | small clusters | repeat |
| Royal Gold | medium yellow | moderate | small clusters | repeat |
| Royal Highness | light pink | moderate | singly | repeat |
| Royal Occasion | orange-red | slight | small clusters | repeat |
| Royal Salute | medium red | none | small clusters | repeat |
| Royal William | dark red | moderate | singly | repeat |
| Rubens | white | moderate | singly | repeat |
| Ruby Anniversary | medium red | none | small clusters | repeat |
| Ruby Wedding | dark red | none | small clusters | repeat |
| Rugelda | yellow blend | none | small clusters | repeat |
| Rugosa Magnifica | mauve | moderate | small clusters | repeat |
| Rumba | red blend | slight | small clusters | repeat |
| Rush | pink blend | moderate | large clusters | repeat |
| Ruskin | dark red | strong | small clusters | repeat |
| Russelliana | mauve | strong | large clusters | once |
| Rustica | yellow blend | slight | small clusters | repeat |
| Ruth Leuwerik | medium red | moderate | small clusters | repeat |
| Sachsengruss | light pink | moderate | small clusters | repeat |
| Sadlers Wells | pink blend | slight | small clusters | repeat |
| Safrano | apricot blend | moderate | small clusters | repeat |

| NAME | Bloom Color | Fragrance Amount | Flowering Habit | Flowering Incidence |
|---|---|---|---|---|
| Remember Me | orange blend | slight | small clusters | repeat |
| Remembrance | medium red | slight | small clusters | repeat |
| Renae | medium pink | moderate | large clusters | repeat |
| Renaissance (Gaujard) | orange blend | moderate | small clusters | repeat |
| Renaissance (Harkness) | white | strong | small clusters | repeat |
| Rendez-vous | medium pink | moderate | small clusters | repeat |
| René André | apricot blend | moderate | small clusters | once |
| René d'Anjou | deep pink | strong | small clusters | once |
| Repandia | light pink | moderate | large clusters | repeat |
| Restless | medium red | moderate | small clusters | repeat |
| Rêve de Paris | orange-pink | slight | small clusters | repeat |
| Rêve d'Or | medium yellow | moderate | small clusters | repeat |
| Réveil Dijonnais | red blend | moderate | small clusters | repeat |
| Reverend H. d'Ombrain | medium red | moderate | small clusters | repeat |
| Rheinaupark | medium red | slight | small clusters | repeat |
| Ringlet | pink blend | slight | large clusters | repeat |
| Rio Samba | yellow blend | slight | small clusters | repeat |
| Ripples | mauve | slight | small clusters | repeat |
| Rival de Paestum | white | moderate | singly | repeat |
| Rob Roy | dark red | slight | small clusters | repeat |
| Robert le Diable | mauve blend | strong | small clusters | once |
| Robert Léopold | pink blend | moderate | small clusters | repeat |
| Robin Hood | medium red | slight | large clusters | repeat |
| Robin Red Breast | red blend | none | small clusters | repeat |
| Robusta (Kordes) | medium red | moderate | small clusters | repeat |
| Rod Stillman | light pink | moderate | singly | repeat |
| Roger Lambelin | red blend | slight | small clusters | repeat |
| Roi de Siam | medium red | slight | small clusters | repeat |
| Roller Coaster | red blend | none | small clusters | repeat |
| Romance | medium pink | slight | small clusters | repeat |
| Rosa Mundi | pink blend | none | singly | once |
| Rosabell | medium pink | slight | small clusters | repeat |
| Rosali | medium pink | none | small clusters | repeat |
| Rosalie Coral | orange blend | slight | small clusters | repeat |
| Rosamunde | medium pink | slight | small clusters | repeat |
| Rosarium Uetersen | deep pink | moderate | small clusters | repeat |
| Rose à Parfum de l'Haÿ | medium red | strong | small clusters | repeat |
| Rose d'Amour | deep pink | slight | small clusters | once |
| Rose de Meaux | medium pink | moderate | small clusters | once |
| Rose de Rescht | deep pink | strong | small clusters | repeat |
| Rose des Peintres | medium pink | strong | small clusters | once |
| Rose du Roi | medium red | strong | small clusters | repeat |
| Rose Gaujard | red blend | slight | small clusters | repeat |

| NAME | Bloom Color | Fragrance Amount | Flowering Habit | Flowering Incidence |
|---|---|---|---|---|
| St Cecelia | medium yellow | moderate | small clusters | repeat |
| St Nicholas | deep pink | strong | small clusters | repeat |
| St Patrick | yellow blend | slight | small clusters | repeat |
| St Swithun | light pink | strong | small clusters | repeat |
| Salet | medium pink | strong | small clusters | repeat |
| Salita | orange blend | none | small clusters | repeat |
| Sally Holmes | white | slight | large clusters | repeat |
| Samantha | medium red | none | small clusters | repeat |
| Sander's White Rambler | white | moderate | large clusters | once |
| Sandra | orange-pink | none | singly | repeat |
| Sangerhausen | deep pink | moderate | large clusters | repeat |
| Santa Catalina | light pink | slight | small clusters | repeat |
| Santana | medium red | none | small clusters | repeat |
| Sarabande | orange-red | slight | small clusters | repeat |
| Sarah Arnot | medium pink | moderate | small clusters | repeat |
| Sarah van Fleet | medium pink | strong | small clusters | repeat |
| Saratoga | white | moderate | small clusters | repeat |
| Satchmo | orange-red | slight | small clusters | repeat |
| Savoy Hotel | light pink | slight | singly | repeat |
| Scabrosa | mauve | moderate | small clusters | repeat |
| Scarlet Gem | orange-red | slight | small clusters | repeat |
| Scarlet Knight | medium red | slight | small clusters | repeat |
| Scarlet Meidiland | medium red | none | large clusters | repeat |
| Scarlet Queen Elizabeth | orange-red | slight | small clusters | repeat |
| Scented Air | orange-pink | strong | small clusters | repeat |
| Scentimental | red blend | strong | small clusters | repeat |
| Scepter'd Isle | light pink | strong | small clusters | repeat |
| Scharlachglut | dark red | none | small clusters | repeat |
| Schneewalzer | white | none | small clusters | repeat |
| Schneezwerg | white | none | small clusters | repeat |
| Schoener's Nutkana | medium pink | moderate | small clusters | once |
| Schoolgirl | apricot blend | strong | small clusters | repeat |
| Schwarze Madonna | dark red | none | small clusters | repeat |
| Scorcher | dark red | slight | small clusters | once |
| Sea Foam | white | slight | large clusters | repeat |
| Sea Pearl | pink blend | none | small clusters | repeat |
| Seagull | white | moderate | corymb | once |
| Sealing Wax | medium pink | none | small clusters | once |
| Seashell | orange-pink | slight | singly | repeat |
| Seaspray | pink blend | moderate | small clusters | repeat |
| Secret | pink blend | strong | small clusters | repeat |
| Senateur Amic | medium red | moderate | singly | once |
| Sequoia Gold | medium yellow | moderate | small clusters | repeat |

| NAME | Bloom Color | Fragrance Amount | Flowering Habit | Flowering Incidence |
|---|---|---|---|---|
| Serratipetala | pink blend | none | small clusters | repeat |
| Seven Sisters | pink blend | moderate | truss | once |
| Sevilliana | pink blend | moderate | small clusters | repeat |
| Sexy Rexy | medium pink | slight | large clusters | repeat |
| Sharifa Asma | light pink | strong | small clusters | repeat |
| Sheer Bliss | white | moderate | singly | repeat |
| Sheer Elegance | orange-pink | moderate | singly | repeat |
| Sheila's Perfume | yellow blend | strong | singly | repeat |
| Sheri Anne | orange-red | slight | small clusters | repeat |
| Shining Hour | deep yellow | moderate | singly | repeat |
| Shocking Blue | mauve | moderate | small clusters | repeat |
| Shot Silk | pink blend | moderate | small clusters | repeat |
| Showbiz | medium red | none | small clusters | repeat |
| Shreveport | orange blend | slight | small clusters | repeat |
| Shropshire Lass | light pink | slight | small clusters | repeat |
| Signature | deep pink | slight | singly | repeat |
| Silk Hat | mauve | slight | singly | repeat |
| Silver Anniversary | mauve | slight | small clusters | repeat |
| Silver Jubilee | pink blend | slight | small clusters | repeat |
| Silver Lining | pink blend | moderate | singly | repeat |
| Silver Moon | white | slight | small clusters | once |
| Silver Wedding | mauve | slight | singly | repeat |
| Simplicity | medium pink | slight | small clusters | repeat |
| Singin' in the Rain | apricot blend | moderate | small clusters | repeat |
| Sir Cedric Morris | white | strong | large clusters | once |
| Sir Edward Elgar | medium red | slight | small clusters | repeat |
| Sir Thomas Lipton | white | moderate | small clusters | repeat |
| Sir Walter Raleigh | medium pink | strong | small clusters | repeat |
| Slater's Crimson China | medium red | none | singly | repeat |
| Smarty | light pink | none | large clusters | repeat |
| Smooth Melody | red blend | strong | small clusters | repeat |
| Smooth Prince | medium red | strong | singly | repeat |
| Snow Ballet | white | slight | small clusters | repeat |
| Snow Bride | white | slight | small clusters | repeat |
| Snow Carpet | white | none | small clusters | repeat |
| Snow Meillandina | white | none | small clusters | repeat |
| Snowflake | white | strong | small clusters | once |
| Snowline | white | none | small clusters | repeat |
| Softee | white | slight | small clusters | repeat |
| Softly Softly | pink blend | slight | small clusters | repeat |
| Soleil d'Or | yellow blend | moderate | small clusters | repeat |
| Solfaterre | medium yellow | slight | small clusters | repeat |
| Solitaire (McGredy) | yellow blend | moderate | singly | repeat |

| NAME | Bloom Color | Fragrance Amount | Flowering Habit | Flowering Incidence |
|---|---|---|---|---|
| Sombreuil | white | strong | small clusters | repeat |
| Sommermärchen | deep pink | slight | large clusters | repeat |
| Sonia | pink blend | moderate | small clusters | repeat |
| Sonnenschirn | light yellow | none | large clusters | repeat |
| Sophie's Perpetual | pink blend | moderate | small clusters | repeat |
| Soupert et Notting | deep pink | strong | small clusters | repeat |
| South Seas | orange-pink | slight | singly | repeat |
| Southampton | apricot blend | slight | small clusters | repeat |
| Souvenir d'Alphonse Lavallée | dark red | strong | small clusters | repeat |
| Souvenir de Christophe Cochet | medium pink | moderate | small clusters | repeat |
| Souvenir de Claudius Denoyel | dark red | moderate | small clusters | repeat |
| Souvenir de la Malmaison | light pink | strong | small clusters | repeat |
| Souvenir de Mme Auguste Charles | medium pink | slight | small clusters | repeat |
| Souvenir de Mme Boullet | deep yellow | slight | small clusters | repeat |
| Souvenir de Mme Léonie Viennot | yellow blend | moderate | small clusters | repeat |
| Souvenir de Philemon Cochet | white | strong | small clusters | repeat |
| Souvenir de St Anne's | light pink | moderate | small clusters | repeat |
| Souvenir de Thérèse Lovet | deep red | none | small clusters | repeat |
| Souvenir d'Elise Vardon | white | slight | small clusters | repeat |
| Souvenir du Docteur Jamain | dark red | moderate | small clusters | repeat |
| Souvenir d'un Ami | light pink | moderate | small clusters | repeat |
| Sparkling Scarlet | medium red | moderate | small clusters | repeat |
| Sparrieshoop | light pink | moderate | large clusters | repeat |
| Spartan | orange-red | moderate | small clusters | repeat |
| Spectacular | orange-red | slight | large clusters | repeat |
| Spencer | light pink | slight | singly | repeat |
| Spice Drop | orange-pink | slight | small clusters | repeat |
| Spiced Coffee | russet | moderate | small clusters | repeat |
| Splendens (Pre-1583) | medium red | strong | large clusters | once |
| Spong | medium pink | strong | small clusters | once |
| Squatters Dream | medium yellow | moderate | small clusters | repeat |
| Stacey Sue | light pink | none | small clusters | repeat |
| Stainless Steel | mauve | strong | small clusters | repeat |
| Stanwell Perpetual | white | slight | small clusters | repeat |
| Starina | orange-red | none | small clusters | repeat |
| Stars 'n' Stripes | red blend | moderate | small clusters | repeat |
| Steffi Graf | medium pink | none | singly | repeat |
| Stephens' Big Purple | mauve blend | strong | singly | repeat |
| Sterling Silver | mauve blend | strong | small clusters | repeat |
| Strawberry Swirl | red blend | none | small clusters | repeat |
| Stretch Johnson | red blend | slight | small clusters | repeat |
| Sue Lawley | red blend | slight | small clusters | repeat |
| Suma | medium red | none | large clusters | repeat |

| NAME | Bloom Color | Fragrance Amount | Flowering Habit | Flowering Incidence |
|---|---|---|---|---|
| Summer Blush | deep pink | slight | small clusters | once |
| Summer Dream | apricot blend | slight | small clusters | repeat |
| Summer Fashion | yellow blend | moderate | small clusters | repeat |
| Summer Holiday | orange-red | moderate | singly | repeat |
| Summer Lady | pink blend | strong | singly | repeat |
| Summer Snow | white | slight | large clusters | repeat |
| Summer Sunshine | deep yellow | slight | small clusters | repeat |
| Summer Wine | medium pink | moderate | small clusters | repeat |
| Sun Flare | medium yellow | slight | small clusters | repeat |
| Sunblest | deep yellow | slight | small clusters | repeat |
| Sundowner | apricot blend | strong | small clusters | repeat |
| Sunlit | apricot blend | slight | small clusters | repeat |
| Sunmaid | yellow blend | none | small clusters | repeat |
| Sunny June | deep yellow | slight | large clusters | repeat |
| Sunseeker | orange-red | slight | small clusters | repeat |
| Sunset Boulevard | orange-pink | slight | small clusters | repeat |
| Sunset Celebration | orange-pink | moderate | singly | repeat |
| Sunset Song | apricot blend/orange blend | slight | small clusters | repeat |
| Sunsprite | deep pink | strong | small clusters | repeat |
| Super Dorothy | medium pink | moderate | large clusters | repeat |
| Super Excelsa | dark red | moderate | large clusters | repeat |
| Super Fairy | light pink | moderate | large clusters | repeat |
| Superb Tuscan | mauve | strong | small clusters | once |
| Surpasse Tout | medium red | strong | small clusters | once |
| Surrey | light pink | none | large clusters | repeat |
| Susan Hampshire | light pink | strong | singly | repeat |
| Susan Louise | light pink | slight | small clusters | repeat |
| Sussex | apricot blend | none | truss | repeat |
| Sutter's Gold | orange blend | strong | singly | repeat |
| Swan | white blend | slight | small clusters | repeat |
| Swan Lake | white blend | slight | small clusters | repeat |
| Swany | white | none | small clusters | repeat |
| Swarthmore | pink blend | slight | singly | repeat |
| Sweet Chariot | mauve | strong | large clusters | repeat |
| Sweet Dream | apricot blend | moderate | large clusters | repeat |
| Sweet Inspiration | medium pink | none | large clusters | repeat |
| Sweet Juliet | apricot blend | moderate | small clusters | repeat |
| Sweet Magic | orange blend | none | small clusters | repeat |
| Sweet Memories | light yellow | moderate | large clusters | repeat |
| Sweet Surrender | medium pink | strong | singly | repeat |
| Sydonie | medium pink | strong | small clusters | repeat |
| Sympathie | medium red | strong | small clusters | repeat |

| NAME | Bloom Color | Fragrance Amount | Flowering Habit | Flowering Incidence |
|---|---|---|---|---|
| Thérèse Bugnet | medium pink | moderate | small clusters | repeat |
| Thérèse de Lisieux | white | slight | small clusters | repeat |
| Thisbe | light yellow | strong | large clusters | repeat |
| Tiffany | pink blend | strong | small clusters | repeat |
| Tiki | pink blend | none | small clusters | repeat |
| Till Uhlenspiegel | red blend | none | small clusters | once |
| Timeless | deep pink | none | small clusters | repeat |
| Tineke | white | none | singly | repeat |
| Tinkerbell | light pink | none | small clusters | repeat |
| Tino Rossi | medium pink | moderate | small clusters | repeat |
| Tintinara | light red | moderate | small clusters | repeat |
| Tip Top | orange-pink | slight | small clusters | repeat |
| Titian | deep pink | slight | small clusters | repeat |
| Tivoli | medium yellow | slight | small clusters | repeat |
| Toby Tristam | white | moderate | truss | once |
| Tom Tom | deep pink | slight | small clusters | repeat |
| Tom Wood | medium red | moderate | small clusters | repeat |
| Top Marks | medium red | slight | small clusters | repeat |
| Topaz Jewel | medium yellow | moderate | small clusters | repeat |
| Toprose | deep yellow | slight | large clusters | repeat |
| Topsi | orange-red | slight | small clusters | repeat |
| Tornado | orange-red | slight | small clusters | once |
| Torvill & Dean | pink blend | slight | small clusters | repeat |
| Touch of Class | orange-pink | slight | small clusters | repeat |
| Toulouse-Lautrec | medium yellow | moderate | singly | repeat |
| Tour de Malakoff | mauve | strong | small clusters | once |
| Tournament of Roses | medium pink | none | small clusters | repeat |
| Tradescant | dark red | moderate | small clusters | repeat |
| Traumerei | orange blend | strong | small clusters | repeat |
| Travemünde | medium red | none | large clusters | repeat |
| Traviata | red blend | moderate | small clusters | repeat |
| Treasure Trove | apricot blend | strong | truss | once |
| Trevor Griffiths | medium pink | strong | small clusters | repeat |
| Tricolore de Flandre | pink blend | moderate | small clusters | once |
| Trier | white | moderate | large clusters | repeat |
| Triolet | apricot blend | strong | small clusters | repeat |
| Triomphe du Luxembourg | pink blend | moderate | small clusters | repeat |
| Troilus | apricot blend | strong | small clusters | repeat |
| Tropicana | orange-red | moderate | small clusters | repeat |
| Trumpeter | orange-red | slight | small clusters | repeat |
| Tumbling Waters | white | slight | large clusters | repeat |
| Tuscany | mauve | moderate | small clusters | once |
| Tutu Mauve | mauve | slight | small clusters | repeat |

| NAME | Bloom Color | Fragrance Amount | Flowering Habit | Flowering Incidence |
|---|---|---|---|---|
| Symphony | light yellow | strong | small clusters | repeat |
| Taboo | dark red | moderate | singly | repeat |
| Talisman | yellow blend | moderate | small clusters | repeat |
| Tall Story | medium yellow | slight | small clusters | repeat |
| Tamora | apricot blend | none | small clusters | repeat |
| Tapis Jaune | medium yellow | none | small clusters | repeat |
| Tapis Volant | pink blend | moderate | large clusters | repeat |
| Tarrawarra | pink blend | slight | large clusters | once |
| Tatjana | dark red | strong | small clusters | repeat |
| Tausendschön | pink blend | slight | large clusters | once |
| Tchin-Tchin | yellow blend | none | small clusters | repeat |
| Tea Rambler | orange-pink | moderate | small clusters | once |
| Tear Drop | white | slight | small clusters | repeat |
| Teddy Bear | russet | slight | small clusters | repeat |
| Temple Bells | white | slight | small clusters | repeat |
| Tender Blush | light pink | moderate | small clusters | once |
| Tender Night | medium red | moderate | small clusters | repeat |
| Tequila | orange blend | slight | small clusters | repeat |
| Tequila Sunrise | red blend | slight | small clusters | repeat |
| Texas (Poulsen) | medium yellow | slight | small clusters | repeat |
| Texas Centennial | red blend | moderate | small clusters | repeat |
| Thalia | white | moderate | large clusters | once |
| The Alexandra Rose | pink blend | slight | large clusters | repeat |
| The Bishop | mauve | moderate | small clusters | once |
| The Bride | white | moderate | small clusters | repeat |
| The Countryman | medium pink | strong | small clusters | repeat |
| The Dark Lady | dark red | moderate | small clusters | repeat |
| The Doctor | medium pink | strong | small clusters | repeat |
| The Fairy | light pink | none | large clusters | repeat |
| The Friar | light pink | strong | small clusters | repeat |
| The Garland | white | slight | small clusters | once |
| The Herbalist | deep pink | slight | small clusters | repeat |
| The Lady | yellow blend | slight | small clusters | repeat |
| The McCartney Rose | medium pink | strong | small clusters | repeat |
| The Nun | white | slight | small clusters | repeat |
| The Pilgrim | medium yellow | moderate | small clusters | repeat |
| The Prince | dark red | strong | small clusters | repeat |
| The Prioress | light pink | moderate | small clusters | repeat |
| The Reeve | deep pink | strong | small clusters | repeat |
| The Squire | dark red | strong | small clusters | repeat |
| The Temptations | pink blend | moderate | small clusters | repeat |
| The Wife of Bath | pink blend | slight | small clusters | repeat |
| The Yeoman | orange-pink | strong | small clusters | repeat |

| NAME | Bloom Color | Fragrance Amount | Flowering Habit | Flowering Incidence |
|---|---|---|---|---|
| Tzigane | red blend | moderate | small clusters | repeat |
| Ulrich Brunner Fils | deep pink | strong | small clusters | repeat |
| Uncle Joe | dark red | none | singly | repeat |
| Uncle Merc | medium pink | slight | singly | repeat |
| Uncle Walter | medium red | slight | singly | repeat |
| UNICEF | orange blend | slight | small clusters | repeat |
| Unique Blanche | white | strong | small clusters | once |
| Uwe Seeler | orange blend | moderate | small clusters | repeat |
| Valencia | apricot blend | moderate | singly | repeat |
| Valentine Heart | medium pink/pink blend | strong | small clusters | repeat |
| Vanguard | orange-blend | moderate | small clusters | repeat |
| Vanilla | white (shaded green) | none | small clusters | repeat |
| Vanity | deep pink | strong | large clusters | repeat |
| Variegata di Bologna | red blend | moderate | small clusters | once |
| Veilchenblau | mauve | moderate | large clusters | once |
| Velvet Fragrance | dark red | strong | small clusters | repeat |
| Velvet Hour | dark red | moderate | small clusters | repeat |
| Venusta Pendula | white | slight | large clusters | once |
| Verdi | mauve blend | moderate | large clusters | repeat |
| Versailles | light pink | slight | small clusters | repeat |
| Verschuren | light pink | slight | small clusters | repeat |
| Vesper | orange blend | slight | small clusters | repeat |
| Vestey's Pink Tea | medium pink | slight | small clusters | repeat |
| Vestey's Yellow Tea | light yellow | moderate | small clusters | repeat |
| Vi's Violet | mauve | moderate | small clusters | repeat |
| Vick's Caprice | pink blend | moderate | small clusters | repeat |
| Vicomtesse Pierre du Fou | orange-pink | strong | small clusters | repeat |
| Victor Borge | orange blend | slight | small clusters | repeat |
| Victor Emmanuel | deep red | moderate | small clusters | once |
| Victor Hugo | deep red | strong | singly | repeat |
| Victoriana | orange blend | slight | small clusters | repeat |
| Ville de Londres | deep pink | moderate | small clusters | once |
| Vino Delicado | mauve | slight | singly | repeat |
| Violacée | mauve | strong | small clusters | once |
| Violet Carson | orange-pink/pink blend | slight | large clusters | repeat |
| Violette | mauve | moderate | large clusters | once |
| Violette Parfumée | mauve blend | strong | singly | repeat |
| Violinista Costa | red blend | moderate | singly | repeat |
| Virgo | white | slight | singly | repeat |
| Vivid | mauve | moderate | small clusters | repeat |
| Vogelpark Walsrode | light pink | slight | small clusters | repeat |

| NAME | Bloom Color | Fragrance Amount | Flowering Habit | Flowering Incidence |
|---|---|---|---|---|
| Vogue | pink blend | slight | small clusters | repeat |
| Vol de Nuit | mauve | strong | small clusters | repeat |
| Voodoo | orange blend | moderate | singly | repeat |
| Waiheke | orange-pink | slight | small clusters | repeat |
| Waldfee | medium red | slight | small clusters | repeat |
| Wandering Minstrel | orange-pink | slight | small clusters | repeat |
| Wapiti | red blend | none | large clusters | repeat |
| Warm Welcome | orange-red | moderate | large clusters | repeat |
| Warrior | orange-red | slight | truss | repeat |
| Warwick Castle | deep pink | strong | small clusters | repeat |
| Warwickshire | pink blend | none | large clusters | repeat |
| Water Music | deep pink | slight | small clusters | repeat |
| Watercolor | medium pink | slight | small clusters | repeat |
| Wedding Day | white | strong | truss | once |
| Weisse Immensee | white | moderate | large clusters | repeat |
| Wendy Cussons | medium red | strong | small clusters | repeat |
| Wenlock | medium red | strong | small clusters | repeat |
| West Coast | medium pink | slight | small clusters | repeat |
| Westerland | apricot blend | strong | small clusters | repeat |
| Western Sun | deep yellow | none | singly | repeat |
| Westfalenpark | apricot blend | moderate | small clusters | repeat |
| Whisky Mac | yellow blend | moderate | small clusters | repeat |
| White Angel | white | slight | small clusters | repeat |
| White Bath | white | strong | small clusters | once |
| White Bella Rosa | white | slight | large clusters | repeat |
| White Bells | white | slight | small clusters | repeat |
| White Cécile Brünner | white | slight | large clusters | repeat |
| White Christmas | white | moderate | small clusters | repeat |
| White Cockade | white | moderate | small clusters | repeat |
| White Dawn | white | moderate | small clusters | repeat |
| White Dorothy | white | slight | large clusters | once |
| White Dream | white | slight | small clusters | repeat |
| White Flower Carpet | white | slight | small clusters | repeat |
| White Gem | white | slight | small clusters | repeat |
| White Grootendorst | white | slight | small clusters | repeat |
| White Lightnin | white | moderate | small clusters | repeat |
| White Maman Cochet | white | slight | small clusters | repeat |
| White Masterpiece | white | slight | singly | repeat |
| White Meidiland | white | none | small clusters | repeat |
| White Meillandina | white | none | small clusters | repeat |
| White Pet | white | none | large clusters | repeat |
| White Queen Elizabeth | white | slight | small clusters | repeat |
| White Simplicity | white | none | small clusters | repeat |

| NAME | Bloom Color | Fragrance Amount | Flowering Habit | Flowering Incidence |
| --- | --- | --- | --- | --- |
| White Sparrieshoop | white | slight | large clusters | repeat |
| White Spray | white | moderate | large clusters | repeat |
| White Wings | white | slight | large clusters | repeat |
| Wichmoss | light pink | slight | large clusters | once |
| Wickwar | light pink | strong | small clusters | once |
| Will Scarlet | medium red | slight | large clusters | repeat |
| William Allen Richardson | yellow blend | moderate | small clusters | repeat |
| William and Mary | pink blend | strong | small clusters | once |
| William Baffin | deep pink | none | small clusters | once |
| William Grant | deep pink | slight | small clusters | repeat |
| William Lobb | mauve | strong | small clusters | once |
| William Shakespeare | dark red | strong | small clusters | repeat |
| William III | mauve | moderate | small clusters | once |
| Wiltshire | medium pink | none | large clusters | repeat |
| Wimi | pink blend | strong | small clusters | repeat |
| Winchester Cathedral | white | moderate | small clusters | repeat |
| Windrush | light yellow | strong | small clusters | repeat |
| Winnipeg Parks | deep pink | slight | small clusters | repeat |
| Winsome | mauve | none | small clusters | repeat |
| Wise Portia | mauve | strong | small clusters | repeat |
| Wishing | medium pink | slight | small clusters | repeat |
| Woburn Abbey | orange blend | moderate | large clusters | repeat |
| Work of Art | orange blend | slight | small clusters | repeat |

| NAME | Bloom Color | Fragrance Amount | Flowering Habit | Flowering Incidence |
| --- | --- | --- | --- | --- |
| Xavier Olibo | deep red | strong | small clusters | repeat |
| Yakimour | red blend | slight | small clusters | repeat |
| Yankee Doodle | yellow blend | slight | small clusters | repeat |
| Yellow Bantam | light yellow | none | small clusters | repeat |
| Yellow Button | yellow blend | slight | large clusters | repeat |
| Yellow Charles Austin | light yellow | slight | small clusters | repeat |
| Yellow Fairy | medium yellow | slight | large clusters | repeat |
| Yesterday | medium pink | slight | truss | repeat |
| Yolande d'Aragon | mauve | strong | small clusters | repeat |
| York and Lancaster | pink blend | moderate | small clusters | once |
| Yorkshire Bank | white | moderate | small clusters | repeat |
| Youki San | white | strong | small clusters | repeat |
| Young at Heart | apricot blend | moderate | small clusters | repeat |
| Young Quinn | medium yellow | slight | singly | repeat |
| Yves Piaget | deep pink | strong | singly | repeat |
| Yvonne Rabier | white | none | large clusters | repeat |
| Zambra | orange blend | slight | small clusters | repeat |
| Zéphirine Drouhin | medium pink | strong | small clusters | repeat |
| Zinger | medium red | moderate | small clusters | repeat |
| Zoe | medium pink | strong | small clusters | once |
| Zweibrücken | dark red | slight | large clusters | repeat |
| Zwergkönig 78 | dark red | none | small clusters | repeat |
| Zwergkönigin 82 | medium pink | none | small clusters | repeat |

# Index